THE
SIMON & SCHUSTER
ENCYCLOPEDIA
OF ANIMALS

THE SIMON & SCHUSTER ENCYCLOPEDIA OF ANIMALS

A Visual Who's Who of the World's Creatures

CONSULTANT EDITOR DR. PHILIP WHITFIELD

SIMON & SCHUSTER EDITIONS

Simon & Schuster Editions
Rockefeller Center
1230 Avenue of the Americas
New York, NY 10020

First published in Great Britain by Marshall Publishing

SIMON & SCHUSTER EDITIONS and colophon are trademarks of Simon & Schuster Inc.

Consultant Editor: **Dr. Philip Whitfield**
Biology Department, King's College, University of London
This edition updated by: **Richard Walker**
Consultants:
Mammals: **Professor D. M. Stoddart,**
Zoology Department, University of Tasmania, Hobart, Australia
Birds: **I.C.J. Galbraith,**
Ornithology Department, British Museum (Natural History), Tring, Hertfordshire
Reptiles and Amphibians: **Professor Barry Cox,**
Biology Department, King's College, University of London
Fishes: **Alwyne Wheeler,**
British Museum (Natural History), London

Artists:
Mammals: **Graham Allen**
Dick Twinney
Birds: **Michael Woods**
Malcolm Ellis
Keith Brewer
Reptiles and Amphibians: **Alan Male**
Fishes: **Colin Newman**

This edition designed and updated by **Axis Design**
Senior Editor: **Jo Wells**
Senior Designer: **Siân Keogh**
Assistant Technician: **Christos Chrysanthou**

1 3 5 7 9 10 8 6 4 2

Manufactured in Germany

Library of Congress Cataloging-in-Publication Data is available.

ISBN 0-684-85237-3

CONTENTS

FOREWORD

The value of a natural history such as this, so concise and beautifully illustrated, can hardly be overestimated, both as a reference work for identification and as a teaching tool. I sometimes think that we in the West are somewhat complacent about magnificent books like this – we tend to take them for granted. We should not. When I was in Madagascar, probably one of the most interesting areas, biologically speaking, in the world, I was horrified to find that the only means of identification of some of their unique fauna available to the ordinary Malagasy was a series of blurred and not very well-drawn pictures of lemurs on the backs of matchboxes.

It is a sobering thought that within the next 80 to 100 years, many of the fascinating creatures so beautifully described here will vanish unless world governments start thinking in terms of conservation and not desecration. It is the appearance of books like this that, hopefully, will help stem the tide of extermination now sweeping the world.

With its fine illustrations and its careful and unusual layout, this is an excellent encyclopedia. It really is a sort of who's who of the animal world showing who is related to whom. It is so deftly written and arranged that it will be of immense value to both the professional and amateur naturalist, and certainly every school should have a copy.

I am delighted to recommend it to all who have an interest in and who value the fascinating planet we live on.

This foreword was written for the first edition of The Animal Encyclopedia by the late Gerald Durrell, world-famous naturalist and founder of The Jersey Wildlife Preservation Trust.

INTRODUCTION

HUMAN BEINGS ARE VERTEBRATE ANIMALS, AS ARE ALL OUR ESSENTIAL DOMESTICATED CREATURES AND MOST OF THE DOMINANT LARGE ANIMALS IN EVERY EARTHLY ECOSYSTEM. THE FEW SUCCESSFUL, LARGE, INVERTEBRATE ANIMALS THAT DO EXIST, GIANT SQUID FOR EXAMPLE, SERVE TO EMPHASIZE BY THEIR VERY RARITY THE PRE-EMINENT POSITION OF VERTEBRATES. BETWEEN THEM, THE MAMMALS, BIRDS, REPTILES, AMPHIBIANS AND FISHES RULE THE SEA AND THE LAND. IN RIVERS, LAKES, SWAMPS AND EVEN IN THE AIR, IT IS VERTEBRATE ANIMALS THAT PROVIDE THE OBVIOUS ANIMAL SEGMENT OF LIVING COMMUNITIES.

One particular feature links creatures as diverse as lampreys, sharks, salmon, frogs, alligators, eagles and chimpanzees and makes them a natural grouping – an organic and interrelated assemblage. All vertebrates have vertebrae, that is, a longitudinal series of skeletal elements along their main nerve tract, the spinal cord. Not all, however, have a back-bone exactly like ours, consisting of distinct, bony blocks, although all the higher, most recently developed types do. These latter animals include the bony fishes, amphibians, reptiles, birds and mammals. The cartilaginous fishes – sharks, rays and skates, for example – have vertebrae, but these consist of cartilage rather than bone; and the even more primitive lampreys have only simple rudiments of vertebral structures, close to the spinal cord.

When compared with invertebrate groups, such as corals, flatworms, worms, mollusks, crustaceans, spiders and insects, there is little doubt that the vertebrate type of body organization provides the potential for the most intricate and sophisticated animals. Animals have been called the most exquisite and complicated machines in the known universe, and, if this is so, the higher vertebrates are the most complex and subtle of these already remarkable entities. In the light of this perspective, zoology, which might sometimes appear to be an esoteric speciality, becomes one of the most demanding and vital disciplines – the attempt to understand these extraordinary machines.

This book sets out to provide a comprehensive catalog of the staggering range of animal types within the vertebrate group.

From the 45,000 or so species of living vertebrates, a selection has had to be made to represent their diversity to best effect. It is clearly impossible to be comprehensive at the species level, so we have looked at a higher level in the classification hierarchy and organized the book at family level, at which it is possible to be comprehensive.

The classification of animals into groups often seems a mystifying or intimidating exercise, as does the scientific naming of animals that goes with it. But both are merely an attempt to organize the creatures into recognizable groups which show their relationships. The Latin- or Greek-based names are enormously useful because of their stability: the scientific name of a creature remains the same all over the world, but it may have dozens of common names. An animal species is a group of animals that can, at least potentially, successfully breed with one another. This is a natural grouping based on the intrinsic attributes and activities of the animals themselves. Each species is given a unique, two-part name in which the second component is specific to that species. The tiger, for example, is called *Panthera tigris*. *Panthera* is its generic name – the genus *Panthera* contains 5 different species of big cat – while *tigris* is its specific name, which refers only to the tiger. The generic and specific names are always printed in italic.

The species names are only the first two rungs of a taxonomical ladder of hierarchy. Many more rungs are required in order to encompass the patterns of similarity which exist. In ascending order, the most commonly used levels are species, genus, family, order, class and phylum; ultimately all animals are grouped together in the Kingdom (classification began in pre-republican days) Animalia.

To return to the tiger, this animal and all other cats belong to the cat family, Felidae, and all have certain physical and behavioral characteristics in common. This family is grouped with other families of related animals, such as dogs, viverrids and mustelids, in the Order Carnivora, and this and all other orders of mammals belong to the Class Mammalia. It is at the vital, family level that this book is comprehensive. A résumé of the major characteristics of each family is accompanied by a number of representative examples of the family, so that although each species cannot be shown, a close relative of it will be. Each order is also mentioned. Some of the larger families, such as the Rodent Family Muridae, which includes old world rats and mice, are split up into many subfamilies, since this facilitates the description of the various groups and avoids gross generalization.

Only in the Fish section has this level of comprehensiveness had to be changed. Here, because of the enormous number of families – many of them little known – it has not been possible to deal with fish diversity in terms of a comprehensive analysis of all fish families. Instead, every order of fish is described, and, where relevant, important families are considered separately.

In something so complex as taxonomy, there is bound to be argument, and there are many areas of disagreement in the ordering and grouping of particular species and families; in this book the consultants have followed what they believe to be the best guidelines. Where there is particular controversy over the placing of a particular species, this is mentioned in the text.

The tiger is a species of cat, and everyone knows – or thinks they know – what a tiger looks like. However, species do not consist of identical individuals. Enormous genetic diversity exists within a species, as a cursory examination of our own species, *Homo sapiens*, reveals. In many animal species it is possible to identify groupings, known as subspecies or races. These often represent geographically localized forms of a species that show characteristic differences from one another. This accounts, for example, in the birds for the sometimes quite striking differences in plumage between individuals of the same species. The tiger, too, has half a dozen geographically distinct subspecies, which vary in size and in fur coloration and patterning. Subspecies of a species can still interbreed. All subspecies, however, are human-defined and they are essentially arbitrary, unlike the species themselves, which correspond more or less precisely to actual interbreeding groups of animals.

This book is a catalog and, as with any catalog, part of its organization emphasizes similarities. Similar animals are grouped into their family assemblages and this format enables the shared habits and structures of related animals to be easily grasped. Ultimately though, there is another way of responding to the patterns of animal organization delineated here. Instead of emphasizing the shared characteristics, one can marvel at the almost infinite inventiveness of the life-styles and physical structure of vertebrate animals that is a joy in itself. There is space and opportunity enough in this book to savor the amazing diversity of mammals, birds, reptiles, amphibians and fishes and to find fascination in the contrasts, even between members of the same family.

Philip Whitfield

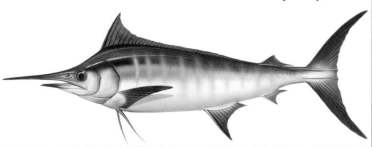

CLASSIFICATION AND EVOLUTION

Classification enables biologists to make sense of the diversity of vertebrate animals and other groups of living organisms. We have already seen how species, such as the tiger, are identified and named and then collected together in progressively larger groups with other species that share similar characteristics. This hierarchy of groupings – or taxa – ranges from the smallest, at species level, through genus, family, order, class and phylum, to the largest taxon at the level of the kingdom. This system has its roots in the work of the Swedish naturalist Carolus Linnaeus (1707–78). When Linnaeus drew up his classification scheme, species were regarded as unchanging. His system was essentially a static one that pigeonholed species and organized them, much as a librarian would place books in a library.

The widespread acceptance of Charles Darwin's theory of evolution in the latter part of the nineteenth century brought a new significance to classification. Evolution means that species change over time, with some species dying out and others appearing. A classification system based on similarities between species may, in addition to providing an organizational framework, also indicate natural patterns within the living world – how species are related through descent from a common ancestor, an ancient extinct organism from which they inherited shared characteristics. Once the theory of evolution was accepted, a dynamic classification system that indicates phylogeny or evolutionary history could be created.

What characteristics do biologists use when classifying animals? Traditionally, taxonomists – the biologists who specialize in classification – have used information based on anatomy, physiology and embryology. More recently, taxonomists have been able to use biochemical data including the similarities of genetic material. This includes using analysis of genetic material – DNA and RNA – and of proteins as a means to determine the relatedness of species: the more similar the structure of these chemicals, the more closely related the species. However, certain pitfalls are placed in the taxonomist's way. For example, common characteristics shared by different species may not indicate a relation but instead be caused by convergent evolution. This is the evolution of similar characteristics in unrelated organisms that have independently evolved the same adaptations to similar ways of life. An extreme example of this is the "fishlike" body shape shared by both sharks and whales, two completely unrelated species. Characteristics used in classification should be homologous; that is, have the same evolutionary origin.

The problem for the taxonomist is to determine which characteristics are most important in relatedness. The "weight" that is attached to different characteristics underpins the differences between systems of classification.

There are two major methods of classification, or systematics, in use today. Traditional systematics groups organisms using both ancestral and derived characteristics in order to show their phylogenetic relationships. It produces the traditional classification found in many textbooks. It may include groups called clades that

are monophyletic – a group of living things that have a single common ancestor – as well as groups called grades – a group of related species that do not share a single common ancestor. Phylogenetic systematics, or cladistics, is a method used by many modern taxonomists which is thought to be the most natural means of classification. The only groups recognized in cladistics are clades, the members of which share unique derived characteristics. Clades are arranged in a branching diagram, or cladogram, that shows which clades are more closely related than others, thereby indicating their phylogeny. Only clades can be given names. This contrasts with traditional systematics where, for example, groups with different ancestry are "lumped" together in a grade called "reptiles".

While the grouping of vertebrates in the Animal Encyclopedia is based on more traditional systematics in order to make the book easier to use, the sequence of groups within the book reflects the phylogeny of vertebrates indicated by cladistics.

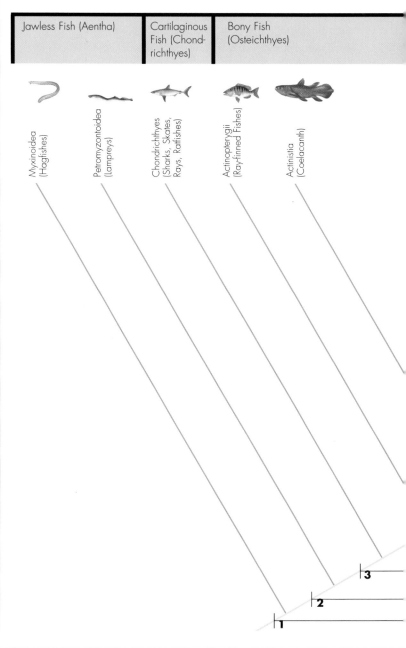

Jawless Fish (Aentha)	Cartilaginous Fish (Chondrichthyes)	Bony Fish (Osteichthyes)

Myxinoidea (Hagfishes)

Petromyzontoidea (Lampreys)

Chondrichthyes (Sharks, Skates, Rays, Ratfishes)

Actinopterygii (Ray-finned Fishes)

Actinistia (Coelacanth)

3

2

1

Cladogram showing possible phylogenetic relationships among living vertebrates. The cladogram shows how the major vertebrate groups are related. All the vertebrates found above a certain branch point on the cladogram are related by shared derived characters. The process of producing a cladogram generates groups within groups, an arrangement known as a nested structure.

On the left of the cladogram is the most inclusive group, while on the right is the least inclusive. For example, the name Tetrapoda includes all vertebrates with four limbs: that is, every group to the right of number 7. By contrast, the name Mammalia, at the right of the diagram, includes only those vertebrates with hair and mammary glands. The numbers below the cladogram identify some of the derived characteristics that distinguish groups. The traditional classification at the top of the cladogram is included by way of comparison.

KEY TO CLADISTICS

1 Distinct head region; brain consisting of three regions
2 Vertebrae
3 Jaws; paired fins
4 Swim bladder or lung derived from gut
5 Fins with supporting skeleton
6 Connection between nasal and oral cavities
7 Paired front and rear limbs
8 Eggs with protective internal membranes
9 Shell encloses body trunk
10 Skull with two openings: one in cheek and one in roof
11 Opening in skull in front of eye
12 Feathers, endothermy (warm-bloodedness)
13 Hair, mammary glands, endothermy (evolved independently from birds)

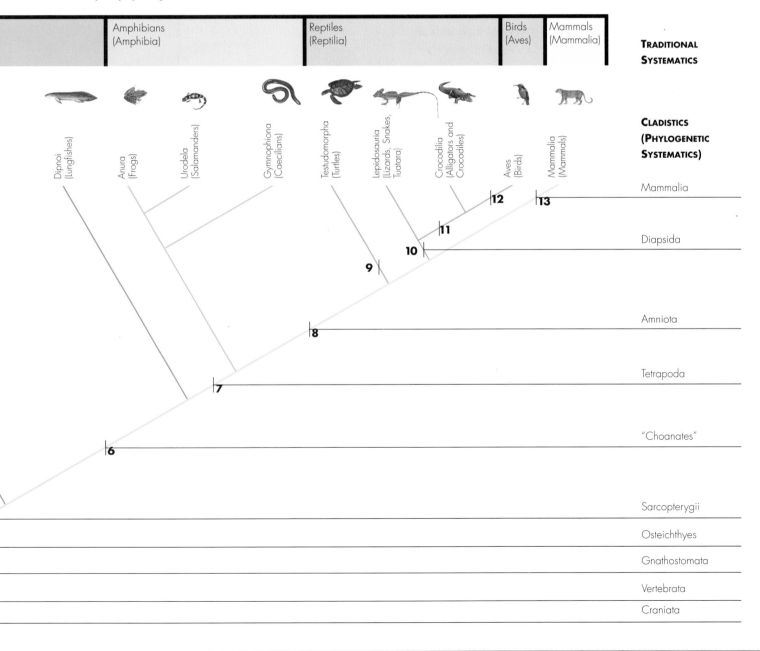

ANIMALS UNDER THREAT

The living world is a dynamic entity. In all habitats, from the Arctic to the Sahara Desert, and from tropical rainforests to coral reefs, there is constant competition for resources both within and between species. The struggle to survive in these competitive conditions favors some individuals more than others. Such selection is the force behind evolution, the gradual change of species over time as they adapt to changing requirements and conditions. The process of evolution has ensured that, as the millennia pass, some species become extinct, while new species emerge.

In recent centuries, however, the rate of extinctions has accelerated far beyond that which should be occurring naturally. Many of the world's animal species are in danger of extinction or are becoming rare. And the number of animals becoming extinct or threatened with extinction is increasing year by year. The World Conservation Union (IUCN) estimates that, as far as vertebrates are concerned, the following are threatened with extinction:

- 25 per cent of mammal species
- 11 per cent of bird species

And of those species that have been evaluated in these groups:

- 20 per cent of reptile species
- 25 per cent of amphibian species
- 34 per cent of fish species (mainly freshwater fish)

More often than not, the main threat to animal species is posed by human pressures. Human population numbers have risen exponentially in recent centuries. Increasing demands for living space, agricultural land, water, and raw materials, have led to extensive habitat loss, including the destruction of vast tracts of forest. Deforestation still continues, most notably in the felling of the tropical rainforests that are the most species-rich of all habitats, and within which species are becoming extinct

before they can be identified. The diversity of the unique endemic fauna found on oceanic islands is being depleted by human population pressure and the introduction of alien species such as cats, dogs, and rats. Pollution, road building and urban sprawl are also taking their toll worldwide.

Extinction of a species does not simply mean removing a name from a long list. Life forms are interdependent, and interact with each other in complex ways often too subtle for human comprehension. Any significant decrease in species numbers, or the loss of a species, has a knock-on effect on other species in its ecosystem.

It is important to maintain biodiversity because it underpins the dynamism and success of ecosystems, and ultimately of the entire biosphere.

The work of IUCN and other organizations in listing threatened animals is vital in order to pinpoint the habitats and species most at risk, and to provide the hard information necessary for both governments and non-governmental bodies to devise workable conservation strategies, and to make governments aware of the effects of their policies on the future of the world's biological resources. Conservation strategies have removed some vertebrates that were listed as threatened in the first edition of the Animal Encyclopedia from the at-risk list; unfortunately, this second edition also sees a greater number of other vertebrate species attaining threatened status.

HOW TO USE THIS BOOK

NAMES

Common and scientific names are given for each species. Common names tend to vary greatly, but the most generally accepted version is used. In some instances, where there are two names of equal importance, both are given thus: Common/Brown Noddy.

RANGE AND HABITAT

The normal range of a species is explained as fully as possible, given the limitations of space. The animal's particular habitat helps to clarify its precise occurrence within a large range. In some instances, where a species has been introduced outside its native range by man, accidentally or deliberately, this is added.

SIZE

Sizes are given as approximate total lengths unless otherwise stated; in birds this is the length from bill tip to tail tip; in turtles and tortoises the length of the shell is given. Exceptions are made where individual circumstances demand: for example, where a bird has an exceptionally long tail, this measurement may be given separately. In the Mammals section, two separate measurements are given: head and body length, and tail length. The vast range of sizes of the animals has meant that the drawings cannot be to a single scale.

Purple Honeycreeper *Cyanerpes caeruleus*

RANGE Trinidad; N. South America to Bolivia, Paraguay, Brazil

HABITAT Rainforest, forest edge, mangroves, plantations

SIZE 4 in (10 cm)

Groups of purple honeycreepers frequent flowering trees in many different types of wooded areas. Fruit, especially bananas, and insects are important foods, but these birds also perch by flowers and suck nectar from them with their long, curved bills. Male and female differ in plumage; the male is largely bluish-purple and black, with yellow legs, while the female is rich green, with buff and blue patches on the head and breast.

The female builds a cup-shaped nest in the fork of a tree or bush and lays 2 eggs, which she incubates for 12 to 14 days. The young leave the nest about 14 days after hatching.

CONSERVATION STATUS

Many of the world's vertebrate animals are monitored by the World Conservation Union (IUCN) and associated organizations to determine whether individual species are at risk or are becoming rare. Species that are threatened are listed in the Red List of Threatened Animals that is produced by the IUCN.

Whether a species is at risk is determined using quantitative criteria that include its present and projected population size, its distribution, and the viability of its population if small and shrinking. The Red List uses specific categories to describe the degree of threat, and these are the categories used in this book. The meaning of the symbols and the categories of threat are given below.

Threatened Species

Species in these three categories are collectively termed "threatened".

CRITICALLY ENDANGERED (CR)

Species faces an extremely high risk of extinction in the wild.

ENDANGERED (EN)

Species faces a very high risk of extinction in the wild in the near future.

VULNERABLE (VU)

Species faces a high risk of extinction in the wild in the medium-term future.

Lower Risk Species

These are species that are at risk but do not fit into the "threatened" categories. The Lower Risk (LR) category is divided into three subcategories.

LOWER RISK: conservation dependent (LR:cd)

Species which is the focus of a conservation program. If this program stopped, the species would qualify for one of the threatened categories within five years.

LOWER RISK: near threatened (LR:nt)

Species which are not the subject of a conservation program and are close to qualifying for VULNERABLE status.

LOWER RISK: least concerned (LR:lc)

Species which appeared in earlier Red Lists but have been removed.

Extinct or Near-Extinct Species

EXTINCT IN THE WILD (EW)

Species that has been wiped out in its natural habitat.

EXTINCT (EX)

According to available evidence, the last individual of that species has died.

DATA DEFICIENT (DD)

Used when too little is known about an animal to assess its population numbers or conservation status.

MAMMALS

The peak of vertebrate adaptability.

THERE ARE ABOUT 4,000 SPECIES OF MAMMAL, WHICH ARE THE MOST ADAPTABLE AND DIVERSE GROUP OF VERTEBRATES ON OUR PLANET TODAY. WHALES, DOLPHINS AND SEALS ARE IMPORTANT MEMBERS OF THE ANIMAL COMMUNITY IN THE SEAS, WHILE FORMS SUCH AS OTTERS AND BEAVERS ARE SUCCESSFUL IN FRESHWATER HABITATS. ON DRY LAND, A HUGE DIVERSITY OF MAMMAL TYPES PROSPERS UNDERGROUND, ON THE LAND SURFACE AND IN TREES AND OTHER VEGETATION. MAMMALS HAVE EVEN TAKEN TO THE AIR IN THE FORM OF BATS, THE NIGHT-FLYING INSECTIVORES. IN ALL THESE NICHE TYPES, MAMMALS REVEAL A STARTLING VARIABILITY IN FEEDING STRATEGIES: SOME FEED ONLY ON PLANT MATERIAL, OTHERS ON SMALL INVERTEBRATES. MANY KILL AND EAT OTHER VERTEBRATES, INCLUDING MAMMALS, WHILE SOME EAT ALMOST ANYTHING. TO BEGIN TO UNDERSTAND THE REASONS FOR THE ADAPTABILITY AND SUCCESS OF MAMMALIAN LINES OF EVOLUTION, IT IS NECESSARY TO LOOK AT WHAT A MAMMAL IS, HOW IT IS CONSTRUCTED, HOW IT OPERATES PHYSICALLY AND BEHAVIORALLY AND WHAT ITS ANCESTORS WERE LIKE.

Tree Anteater

A mammal is an endothermic (warm-blooded), four-limbed, hairy vertebrate (an animal with a backbone). Male mammals inseminate females internally, using a penis, and females, typically, retain their developing fetuses within the uterus, where the bloodstreams of mother and offspring come close together (but do not fuse) in a placenta. The time spent in the womb by the developing fetus is known as the gestation period and varies from group to group. Some mammals, such as rabbits, rodents and many carnivores, are born naked, blind and helpless; while others, such as cattle and deer, are small, but fully formed and capable, versions of the adult. Mothers produce milk for their young from skin-derived mammary glands.

The vast majority of mammals possess these characteristics, but a few exceptions, real and apparent, must be taken into account. Whales and their relatives and manatees have only forelimbs. There is no doubt, however, from their skeletal structure, that these highly modified aquatic

Indri

animals are derived from four-legged ancestors. However, the monotremes – the platypus and echidnas – are highly uncharacteristic mammals. They have retained the egg-laying habits of their reptilian ancestor and do not form placentas. The pouched mammals, or marsupials, also have a method of reproduction that differs from that of the placenta-forming mammals. Kangaroos, wallabies and their relatives retain a thin shell around the developing young inside the mother's body, but it breaks down before the offspring emerges to crawl into the pouch and attach itself to a milk-delivering nipple. Some species do have a primitive placenta. The marsupial young is born in a far less advanced state than most mammals and finishes its development in the pouch.

Knowledge of the ancestry of mammals is based largely on the study of fossil remains of parts of skeletons. Mammals evolved from reptiles about 220 million years

Golden Lion Tamarind

•ago. During the "age of dinosaurs" between 230 and 65 million years ago, mammals remained small and were shrewlike in appearance and lifestyle. When the dinosaurs became extinct 65 million years ago, the mammals adapted to the wide range of habitats and niches vacated by the extinct reptiles. The mammals have continued their explosive expansion into different types of life and environment to become the dominant group of land-dwelling vertebrates and an important part of aquatic life.

Apart from reproductive sophistication, mammals are remarkable in a number of ways. They have large, complex brains, and acute and well-integrated sensory systems. They employ a range of vocal, visual and olfactory means of communication with other species and with members of their own species – communication with the latter is important in the organization of family and social groupings. The keratinous hairs that grow out of mammalian skin insulate the body and are part of a complex of temperature-regulation mechanisms with which mammals maintain a constant, high body temperature, irrespective of external climatic conditions. Metabolic heat, especially that produced by brown fat in the body, can be used to offset heat losses and can be transferred around the body via the circulatory system, which is powered by the four-chambered heart. The body can be cooled by the evaporation of sweat secretions at the body surface. All this temperature-control "machinery" is under the control of the hypothalamus in the brain. When temperature control becomes energetically impossible, for example in low temperatures, some mammals are able to hibernate.

During the hibernatory sleep, the animal's body temperature drops to close to that of the surroundings, and its heart and respiration slow dramatically so that it uses the minimum of energy. Thus it is able to survive for as long as several months on stored fat.

The astonishing diversity of present day mammals is illustrated in the following pages, which review each living family and describe representative examples. Briefly, the range of types is as follows. The primitive monotremes and the marsupials – the majority of which are found in Australia – have already been mentioned. Australia separated from the southern continents before it could receive any eutherian mammals. Thus the marsupial mammal fauna was able to radiate into a diverse range of forms which mirrors the types of placental mammals found in the rest of the world. There are burrowing, tree-dwelling, ant-eating, herbivorous and predatory marsupials, and marsupial analogues exist or have existed for almost all placental mammals except bats, whales and seals.

The placental mammals form a diverse and successful group that includes the insectivores such as shrews, hedgehogs and moles, bats, sloths, anteaters,

Gorilla

armadillos, pangolins, primates (to which humans belong), rodents, rabbits, whales, dolphins and porpoises, carnivores (cats, dogs, mustelids and bears), seals, aardvark, elephants, hyraxes, manatees and the dugong, uneven-toed hoofed mammals such as tapirs, horses and rhinoceroses, and the even-toed (cloven-hoofed) hoofed mammals such as pigs, peccaries, camels, deer, cattle, sheep and goats.

The evolutionary success of the mammals is hard to

Lion

1 Duck-billed platypus

2 Red kangaroo

3 Giant anteater

4 Tree pangolin

5 Black-tailed jackrabbit

6 Thirteen-lined ground squirrel

7 Elephant shrew

8 European hedgehog

9 Mountain tree shrew

10 Ring-tailed lemur

Cladogram showing possible phylogenetic relationships of the mammals. Three major groups are discernible, separated on the basis of their reproductive biology. The monotremes lay eggs which are incubated and hatch outside the body. The other two groups – the marsupials and the eutherian mammals – are closely related but have followed separate evolutionary paths for 200 million years. Marsupials, which include kangaroos, opossums, and bandicoots, give birth to underdeveloped young which continue their development inside a pouch. The eutherian mammals – those whose young are nurtured via a placenta in the uterus – make up the bulk of the mammals, and include all those mammalian groups shown to the right of the marsupials on this cladogram.

evalutate. As measured by the dominance of a particular group or its species diversity, success must be the result of an amalgam of intrinsic biological merit and chance. But no other major class of vertebrates has ever conquered such a variety of habitats so completely. The advent of modern humans has probably increased the rate of mammalian

Capybara

extinctions in some groups, but others, such as the rodents, are evolving into new ecological niches created by man's activities. At the present time, the mammals are an overwhelmingly successful group, and it may be true that its most dominant species – man – holds the future of the planet in his hands.

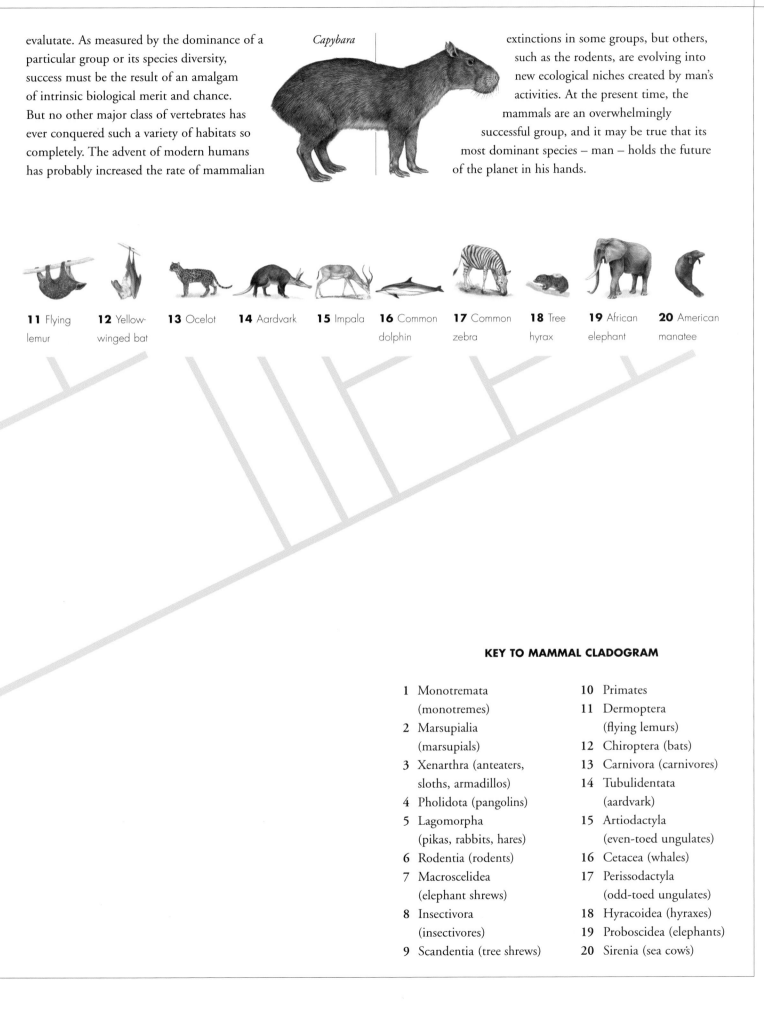

11 Flying lemur

12 Yellow-winged bat

13 Ocelot

14 Aardvark

15 Impala

16 Common dolphin

17 Common zebra

18 Tree hyrax

19 African elephant

20 American manatee

KEY TO MAMMAL CLADOGRAM

1 Monotremata (monotremes)
2 Marsupialia (marsupials)
3 Xenarthra (anteaters, sloths, armadillos)
4 Pholidota (pangolins)
5 Lagomorpha (pikas, rabbits, hares)
6 Rodentia (rodents)
7 Macroscelidea (elephant shrews)
8 Insectivora (insectivores)
9 Scandentia (tree shrews)

10 Primates
11 Dermoptera (flying lemurs)
12 Chiroptera (bats)
13 Carnivora (carnivores)
14 Tubulidentata (aardvark)
15 Artiodactyla (even-toed ungulates)
16 Cetacea (whales)
17 Perissodactyla (odd-toed ungulates)
18 Hyracoidea (hyraxes)
19 Proboscidea (elephants)
20 Sirenia (sea cows)

ECHIDNAS AND PLATYPUS

ORDER MONOTREMATA

Two families with a combined total of only 3 living species make up this order. Although well-adapted for their environments, monotremes are considered primitive mammals in that they retain some reptilian characteristics of body structure and they lay eggs. However, they also possess the essential mammalian characteristics of body hair and mammary glands. Monotremes are probably a parallel development, rather than a stage in the evolution of mammals. A problem in understanding the origins of this order is that no fossil monotremes have been found.

TACHYGLOSSIDAE: ECHIDNA FAMILY

There are 2 species of echidna, previously known as spiny anteater. Both are covered with coarse hairs, and their backs are set with spines. They have elongated, slender snouts and strong limbs and are powerful diggers. Echidnas, like other anteating species have no teeth and very weak jaws. Termites, ants and other small arthropods are swept into the mouth by a long, sticky tongue, which can reach well beyond the tip of the snout. The insects are then crushed between the tongue and the roof of the mouth.

Long-beaked Echidna *Zaglossus bruiini*

RANGE	New Guinea
HABITAT	Forest
SIZE	Body: 17–30 in (45–77 cm) Tail: vestigial

The long-beaked echidna is larger than the short-beaked and has fewer, shorter spines scattered among its coarse hairs. The snout is two-thirds of the head length and curves slightly downward. There are five digits on both hind and forefeet, but on the former, only the three middle toes are equipped with claws. Males have a spur on each of the hind legs. This echidna is primarily a nocturnal animal that forages for its insect food on the forest floor.

The breeding female has a temporary abdominal brood patch, in which her egg is incubated and in which the new born young remains in safety, feeding and developing. Little is known about the life of this rarely seen animal, but it is believed to have similar habits to those of the short-beaked echidna.

There were once thought to be 3 species in this genus, but now all are believed to be races of this one species. The population of echidnas in New Guinea is declining because of forest clearance and overhunting, and the animal is much in need of protection.

Short-beaked Echidna *Tachyglossus aculeatus*

RANGE	Australia, Tasmania, S.E. New Guinea
HABITAT	Grassland, forest
SIZE	Body: 13¾–19¾ in (35–50 cm) Tail: 3½ in (9 cm)

The short-beaked echidna has a compact, round body, closely set with spines. At the end of its naked snout is a small, slitlike mouth, through which its long tongue is extended 6 to 7 in (15 to 18 cm) beyond the snout. The tongue is coated with sticky saliva, so that any insect it touches is trapped. Echidnas have no teeth but break up their food between horny ridges in the mouth. Termites, ants and other small invertebrates form their main diet.

Echidnas have five digits, all equipped with strong claws, on both hind and forefeet. Males also have spurs on each hind leg which may be used in defense. They are excellent diggers and, if in danger, they will rapidly dig themselves into the ground. However, they do not live in burrows, but in hollow logs or among roots and rocks. The echidnas' capacity for temperature regulation is poor, and in cool weather they hibernate.

On her abdomen, the breeding female has a temporary patch, or groove, which develops at the start of the breeding season. When she has laid her leathery-shelled egg, she transfers it to the patch, where it incubates for between 7 and 10 days. The egg is coated with sticky mucus which helps it to stay in the groove. When the young echidna hatches, it is only ½ in (1.25 cm) long and helpless, so it must remain on the mother's abdomen while it develops.

The female produces plenty of milk from mammary glands but she has no nipples, so the baby feeds by sucking on specially adapted areas of abdominal skin through which the milk flows. Once the spines develop, at about 3 weeks, the young is no longer carried by its mother.

ORNITHORHYNCIDAE: PLATYPUS FAMILY

The single species of this family is an extraordinary animal in appearance, due to the strange combination of a beak, fur and webbed feet, but it is perfectly adapted for its way of life.

The platypus was discovered 200 years ago, and when the first specimen arrived at London's Natural History Museum, scientists were so puzzled by it that they believed the specimen to be a fake.

Platypuses are now protected by law and are quite common in some areas.

Platypus *Ornithorhynchus anatinus*

RANGE Australia, Tasmania

HABITAT Lakes, rivers

SIZE Body: 18 in (46 cm)
Tail: 7 in (18 cm)

The platypus is a semi-aquatic animal, and many of its physical characteristics are adaptations for its life as a freshwater predator.

Its legs are short but powerful, and the feet are webbed, though the digits retain large claws, which are useful for burrowing. On the forefeet the webs extend beyond the claws and make efficient paddles. On land, however, the webbing can be folded back in order to free the claws for digging.

On each ankle the male platypus has a spur which is connected to poison glands in the thighs. These spurs are used against an attacker or against a competing platypus, but they are never used against prey. The poison is not fatal to man, but does cause intense pain.

The platypus's eye and ear openings lie in furrows, which are closed off by folds of skin when the animal is submerged. Thus, when hunting under water, the platypus relies on the sensitivity of its leathery bill – which is sensitive to both touch and electric currents produced by prey – to find its prey. The nostrils are toward the end of the upper bill but can only function when the platypus's head is in air. Young platypuses have teeth, but adults have horny, ridged plates on both sides of the jaws which are used for crushing prey.

The platypus feeds mainly at the bottom of the water, making dives lasting for a minute or more in order to probe the mud with its bill for crustaceans, aquatic insects and larvae. It also feeds on frogs and other small animals and on some plants. Platypuses have huge appetites, consuming up to 2¼ lb (1 kg) of food each night.

Short burrows, dug in the river bank above the water level, are used by the platypus for refuge or during periods of cool weather. In the breeding season, however, the female digs a burrow 40 ft (12 m) or more in length, at the end of which she lays her clutch of 2 or 3 eggs on a nest of dry grass and leaves; the rubbery eggs are cemented together in a raft. She plugs the entrance to the burrow with moist plant matter, and this prevents the eggs from drying out during the 7- to 14-day incubation period.

When the young hatch, they are only about 1 in (2.5 cm) long and helpless. Until they are about 5 months old, they feed on milk, which issues from slits in the mother's abdominal wall. Unlike echidnas, they do not draw up tucks of skin into pseudonipples, but simply lap and suck the milk off their mother's abdominal fur.

OPOSSUMS AND COLOCOLO

INFRACLASS METATHERIA

MARSUPIAL MAMMALS

There are 260 species of marsupial mammals in North and South America and in Australasia east of Wallace's line (an imaginary line drawn between Borneo and Sulawesi, and Bali and Lombok). Marsupials evolved at about the same time as the true (placental) mammals, but were replaced by them over much of their range. Australia has only marsupial mammals because it separated from the ancient southern continents of Gondwanaland after it had been populated by early marsupials, but before placental mammals arrived. In Australia marsupials have realized their true potential and have adapted to a variety of ecological niches and have exploited all available habitats.

The principal characteristic of marsupial mammals is their reproduction. Instead of retaining young inside the uterus until they are well developed, as in placental mammals, the gestation period is extremely short – as brief as 11 days – and the young finish their development inside a pouch on the mother's belly.

ORDER DIDELPHIMORPHA

DIDELIPHIDAE: OPOSSUM FAMILY

This order contains the opossum family only. There are more than 70 species of opossum and they are found from the southern tip of South America northward to southeast Canada. Opossums are all basically rat-shaped animals, with scaly almost hairless tails and rather unkempt fur. Some species possess a proper pouch, while others carry their young between two flaps of skin on the belly.

Most opossums are forest dwellers, although one exceptional species has taken to an aquatic way of life. They feed on leaves, shoots, buds and seeds, and insects may also be eaten.

Pale-Bellied Mouse Opossum *Marmosa robinsoni*
RANGE Belize to N.W. South America; Trinidad, Tobago, Grenada
HABITAT Forest, dense scrubland
SIZE Body: 6½–7¼ in (16.5–18.5 cm) Tail: 10¼–11 in (26–28 cm)

The mouse opossum has a long, pointed nose and huge eyes, which indicate its nocturnal way of life. This opossum is more shrewlike than mouselike in appearance. It makes no permanent home, but constructs temporary daytime nests in tree holes or old birds' nests.

An agile climber, the mouse opossum uses its long, prehensile tail as a fifth limb.

Mouse opossums breed two or three times a year, and litters of up to 10 young are born after a gestation period of 17 days. The young must cling to the mother's fur as she moves around, since mouse opossums do not have proper pouches.

Virginia Opossum *Didelphis virginiana*
RANGE S.E. Canada through USA to Central America: Nicaragua
HABITAT Forest, scrubland
SIZE Body: 12¾–19¾ in (32.5–50 cm) Tail: 10–21 in (25.5–53.5 cm)

The only marsupial found north of Mexico and the largest of the opossum family, the Virginia opossum may weigh up to 12 lb (5.5 kg). It is a successful creature, which has adapted to modern life, scavenging in refuse tips and bins. Should this creature be threatened, by a dog, bobcat, eagle or mink for example, it may react by feigning death. This habit of "playing possum" may result in the predator losing interest or give the opossum vital seconds to make its escape.

In Canada, opossums breed once a year, in spring, but in the south of the range, two or even three litters of 8 to 18 young may be produced in a year. Usually only about 7 of a litter survive pouch life. In the southern USA, opossums are trapped by man for their fur and flesh.

Water Opossum/Yapok *Chironectes minimus* **LR:nt**
RANGE Mexico, south through Central and South America to Argentina
HABITAT Freshwater lakes and streams
SIZE Body: 10½–12¾ in (27–32.5 cm) Tail: 14¼–15¾ in (36–40 cm)

The water opossum, or yapok, is the only marsupial to have adapted to aquatic life. It lives in bankside burrows, emerging after dusk to swim and search for fish, crustaceans and other invertebrates, which it carries to the riverbank to eat. The opossum's long tail helps to control its movement through water.

It uses its broadly webbed hind feet to propel itself through the water. Its fur is oily and water repellant.

In December, water opossums mate, and produce a litter of about 5 young, born some 2 weeks later. The fur-lined pouch is closed by a strong ring of muscle and fatty secretions create a water-tight seal so that the young inside remain quite dry, even when the mother is totally immersed in water. It is not known how the young obtain sufficient oxygen in their hermetically sealed environment.

Short-tailed Opossum *Monodelphis brevicaudata*

RANGE Venezuela and The Guianas to N. Argentina

HABITAT Forest

SIZE Body: 4–5 in (11–14 cm) Tail: 1¼–2½ in (4.5–6.5 cm)

Although the short-tailed opossum lives in forested country, it is a poor climber and tends to stay on the forest floor. During the day it shelters in a leafy nest, which it builds in a hollow log or tree trunk. It emerges at night to feed on seeds, shoots and fruit, as well as on insects, carrion and some small rodents, which it kills with a powerful bite to the back of the head.

Litters of up to 14 young are born at any time of year and cling to their mother's nipples and the surrounding fur, since she has no pouch. When they are older, they ride on her back.

ORDER PAUCITUBERCULATA

CAENOLESTIDAE: SHREW OPOSSUM FAMILY

There are only 7 known species of shrew opossum, which belong to the only family in this order. All live in inaccessible forest and grassland regions of the High Andes. None is common, and the family is poorly known. Shrew opossums are small, shrewlike animals, with thin limbs, a long, pointed snout and slender, hairy tail. Their eyes are small, and they seem to spend much of their lives in underground burrows and on surface runways. It is likely that there are more species yet to be discovered.

Shrew Opossum *Caenolestes obscurus*

RANGE Colombia, Venezuela

HABITAT Montane forest

SIZE Body: 3½–5in (9–13 cm) Tail: 3½–4¾ in (9–12 cm)

The shrew opossum lives on the forest floor and shelters in hollow logs or underground chambers during the day. At dusk, it emerges to forage around in the surface litter for small invertebrate animals and fruit.

Shrew opossums may be far more common than is generally thought, but their inhospitable habitat makes studying them difficult. Nothing is known of their reproductive habits.

ORDER MICROBIOTHERA

MICROBIOTHERIIDAE: COLOCOLO FAMILY

There is a single family in this order, and a single species in this family, which appears to be closely related to the opossums.

Colocolo *Dromiciops gliroides* **VU**

RANGE Chile, W. Argentina

HABITAT Forest

SIZE Body: 4¼–5 in (11–12.5 cm) Tail: 3½–4 in (9–10 cm)

The colocolo occurs in high-altitude and lowland forest, especially in areas where Chilean Bamboo grows. It feeds mainly on insects and other invertebrates, but may also eat vegetation. It makes nests using bamboo leaves. In the colder parts of the range, colocolos hibernate in winter, but in more temperate regions, they remain active all year round.

Colocolos breed in spring. Litters contain up to 5 young which cling to the mother's fur, because there is no true pouch.

DASYURID MARSUPIALS

ORDER DASYUROMORPHA

This order includes two families of carnivorous and insectivorous marsupials that are found in Australia, Tasmania, and New Guinea.

DASYURIDAE: DASYURID MARSUPIAL FAMILY

This family of approximately 58 species contains a wide variety of marsupials, from tiny mouse-sized creatures, which live on the forest floor, to large, aggressive predators. Many zoologists regard it as the least advanced family of Australian marsupials because all members have fully separated digits – fused digits are a characteristic of advanced families of marsupials. Yet its success is undoubted, for representatives are found in all habitats, from desert to tropical rain forest.

Most of the dasyurids have poorly developed pouches and resort to carrying their small, underdeveloped young about underneath them, either clinging to the mother's fur or dangling from her teats like bunches of grapes. Unlike the American opossums, which carry older young on their backs, the dasyurids deposit their offspring in nests when they become too large to carry around with them.

Pygmy Planigale *Planigale maculata*

RANGE N. and E. Australia

HABITAT Arid bush and scrub

SIZE Body: 2–2½ in (5–5.5 cm) Tail: 2¼ in (5.5 cm)

The pygmy planigale shelters in a burrow during the day and emerges at night to search for food. Although it is smaller than a white mouse, it feeds on large insects, such as grasshoppers (which it kills by biting off the head) and small birds. In one night, a pygmy planigale may eat its own weight in food.

Little is known of the reproduction and social organization of these animals. They appear to be solitary and to give birth to up to 12 young between December and March.

Brown Antechinus *Antechinus stuartii*

RANGE E. seaboard of Australia

HABITAT Forest

SIZE Body: 3¾–4¼ in (10–12 cm) Tail: 4–4¾ in (10–12 cm)

The brown antechinus is a secretive, nocturnal animal, that is common in the forests surrounding Australia's major cities. It climbs well and probably searches for insect food in Eucalyptus and Acacia trees.

Mating, which is a violent procedure in this species that can last about 5 hours, occurs in August. A litter of 6 or 7 young is born after a gestation period of 30 to 33 days. The babies cling to the nipples on the mother's belly until they become so large that they impede her movements. They are then left in an underground nest while the mother hunts for food. The offspring reach sexual maturity and breed almost a year after birth. As a result of a hormone imbalance, the males of the species can mate only once before they die.

Mulgara *Dasycercus cristicauda* **Vu**

RANGE C. Australia

HABITAT Desert, spinifex bush

SIZE Body: 5–8½ in (12.5–22 cm) Tail: 2¼–5 in (7–13 cm)

The mulgara is perfectly adapted for life in one of the world's most inhospitable, hot, dry environments. It protects itself from the extreme heat of the desert by remaining in its burrow until the heat of the day has passed. Even when it leaves its underground home it tends to stay in places that have been in shadow.

The staple diet of the mulgara consists mainly of insects, but lizards, newborn snakes and mice are also eaten. This creature never drinks. It derives all of its liquid requirements from its prey and in order to preserve water its kidneys are highly developed to excrete extremely concentrated urine.

Mulgaras breed from June to September and the usual litter contains 6 or 7 young. The pouch is little more than two lateral folds of skin.

Kowari *Dasyuroides byrnei*

RANGE C. Australia

HABITAT Desert, grassland

SIZE Body: 6½–7 in (16.5–18 cm)
Tail: 5–5½ in (13–14 cm)

The kowari lives, either singly
or in small groups, in underground burrows. At night, it
emerges to search among the grass tussocks for insects, lizards
and various small birds.

Kowaris breed in winter, from May to October, and produce
litters of 5 or 6 young after a gestation period of 32 days.

Fat-tailed Dunnart *Sminthopsis crassicaudata*

RANGE W. Australia, E. to W. Queensland, W. New South Wales and
W. Victoria

HABITAT Woodland, heath, grassland

SIZE Body: 3–3½ in (8–9 cm) Tail: 2¼–3½ in (5.5–8.5 cm)

The fat-tailed dunnart stores fat in special cells at the base of its
tail. In the wet season, when the food supply of insects and spiders
is abundant, the dunnart builds up its fat reserves. During the dry
season it lives off these reserves and its tail gradually slims. If the
drought persists longer than usual, the dunnart's body temperature
falls and it enters a state of torpor so that its fat reserve lasts longer.

Dunnarts start to breed when they are about 4 months old
and produce litters about every 12 weeks. Courtship is aggressive
and males indulge in vicious fights for females on heat.

Quoll *Dasyurus viverrinus* **LR:nt**

RANGE S.E. Australia and Tasmania

HABITAT Forest

SIZE Body: 13¾–17¾ in
(35–45 cm) Tail: 8¼–11¾ in
(21–30 cm)

The quoll is one of 6 species of
cat-sized predatory dasyurid,
specialized for life as carnivores. At
one time quolls were ruthlessly destroyed
by poultry keepers, but they are now known to do as

much good as harm, by killing rodents, rabbits and invertebrate
pests and helping to maintain the ecological balance. Quolls make
their homes in rock piles or in hollow logs and emerge only at
night in order to search for food.

The breeding season lasts from May to August. The
quoll is one of the few marsupials known in which
the litter size at birth is far higher than the
number that can be supported by the mother – a
phenomenon known as superfetation. Up to
18 young are born after a gestation period of about
20 days, but within 48 hours of birth 10 or more of the babies
will die. The young quolls spend the early weeks of their lives in
the mother's well-developed pouch and later emerge to clamber
all over her, clinging to her fur as she feeds. They are weaned at
4½ months.

Tasmanian Devil *Sarcophilus harrisii*

RANGE Tasmania

HABITAT Dry forest

SIZE Body: 20½–31½ in (52.5–80 cm) Tail: 9–11¾ in (23–30 cm)

This powerfully built marsupial has the reputation of being a
vicious killer of sheep and as a result great numbers were once
hunted by farmers. Numbers have now recovered. In fact, the
Tasmanian devil is more of a scavenger of dead sheep than a
killer of live ones. Its massive head and enormous jaws,
resembling those of the hyena, allow it to smash through bones.
Before the Tasmanian wolf became extinct, Tasmanian devils
lived almost exclusively on the carcasses discarded by the wolf.

Tasmanian devils live in dens in rock piles and under tree
stumps and are normally nocturnal. Sometimes, however, they
emerge during the day to bask in the sun. Tasmanian devils
can live for up to 8 years. They breed in the second
year, producing a litter of about 4 young in early
winter (May or June). The babies remain
inside the mother's well-developed
pouch for 15 weeks. They
are weaned at about
20 weeks old.

NUMBAT, MARSUPIAL MOLE, BANDICOOTS AND WOMBATS

MYRMECOBIIDAE: NUMBAT FAMILY

The single species in this Australian family is a small marsupial, which is adapted to the ecological niche that is filled by anteaters in other parts of the world. It was formerly called the banded anteater and feeds in a similar manner to anteaters.

Numbat *Myrmecobius fasciatus* **VU**

RANGE S.W. Australia

HABITAT Forest

SIZE Body: 6¾–10¾ in (17.5–27.5 cm) Tail: 5–6¾ in (13–17cm)

The numbat is active during the day. It feeds mainly on termites, although ants and some other small invertebrates are also eaten. Its sticky tongue, which is about 4 in (10 cm) long, is used to sweep insects into its mouth, where they are crushed by the numbat's poorly developed teeth. A captive numbat was observed to eat 10 to 20 thousand termites daily.

Between January and May, the female numbat produces a litter of 4 young. The mother has no pouch. The young cling to her nipples and she drags them around as she searches for food.

ORDER PERAMELEMORPHA

This order includes about 21 species of omnivorous marsupials which are found in Australia and New Guinea. There are two families in the order – the bandicoots and bilby; and the New Guinean bandicoots.

PERAMELIDAE: BANDICOOT FAMILY

There are about 12 species of bandicoot, widely distributed over Australia in a range of habitats, from desert to rain forest. The family includes the Bilby or Rabbit Bandicoot. Most of the bandicoots use their strong, clawed front feet to dig for insects larvae and plant roots and tubers.

Eastern Barred Bandicoot

Perameles gunnii **VU**

RANGE Australia, S. Victoria; Tasmania

HABITAT Woodland, heathland

SIZE Body: 9¾–15¾ in (25–40 cm)
Tail: 3–7 in (7.5–18 cm)

Like most bandicoots, the eastern barred bandicoot is a very aggressive, belligerent creature, which lives alone. The males occupy large territories and consort with females for only as long as is necessary for mating.

Primarily a nocturnal animal, it emerges from its nest at dusk to forage for earthworms and other small invertebrates. Probing deep into the soil with its long nose, the bandicoot digs eagerly when food is located.

Although the female bandicoot has 8 nipples, she seldom produces more than 4 or 5 young. The gestation period of 11 days is one of the shortest of any mammal and is followed by 8 weeks in the pouch.

Brown Bandicoot *Isoodon obesulus*

RANGE S. Australia, Queensland; Tasmania

HABITAT Scrub, forest

SIZE Body: 11¾–13¾ in (30–33 cm) Tail: 3–7 in (7.5–18 cm)

The brown bandicoot occurs in areas of dense ground cover and can survive in quite dry places, as long as it has somewhere to hide from eagles and foxes. It appears to locate prey, such as earthworms and beetle larvae, by scent and leaves small conical marks with its long nose as it forages about. Ant larvae and subterranean fungi are also eaten, as well as scorpions, which it nips the tails off before consuming them.

Reproduction is closely linked to the local rainfall pattern, and many brown bandicoots breed all year round. A litter of up to 5 young is born after an 11-day gestation and is weaned at 2 months.

Rabbit-bandicoot

Macrotis lagotis **EN**

RANGE C. and N.W. Australia

HABITAT Woodland, arid scrub

SIZE Body: 7¾–21½ in
(20–55 cm)
Tail: 4½–10¾ in (11.5–27.5 cm)

The rabbit-bandicoot lives alone in a burrow system, which it digs with its powerful forepaws. The burrow descends 2m (6ft) or more, and the bandicoot is thus protected from the heat of the day. After dark, when the air is cool, the rabbit-bandicoot emerges to feed on termites and beetle larvae, which it digs from the roots of wattle trees. It may also eat some of the fungi that grow around the roots.

Courtship is brief and aggressive, as with most bandicoots. The litter of 3 young is born between March and May and the young spend 8 weeks in the mother's pouch.

ORDER NOTORYCTEMORPHA

NOTORYCTIDAE: MARSUPIAL MOLE FAMILY

The two species in this Australian marsupial family have a clear resemblance to the placental moles and lead a similar existence.

Southern Marsupial Mole *Notoryctes typhlops* **EN**

RANGE S.W. Australia

HABITAT Desert

SIZE Body: 3½–7 in (9–18 cm) Tail: ½–1 in (1.25–2.5 cm)

The marsupial mole is superbly adapted to a burrowing way of life. It has large, shovellike forepaws, no eyes and silky fur, which helps it move easily through the sandy soil.

Marsupial moles do not dig permanent burrows for as they travel through the soft sand the tunnel falls in immediately behind them. They feed on earthworms and other underground invertebrates, such as beetle larvae, and come to the surface quite frequently, although they move awkwardly on land.

Nothing is known of the reproductive habits of the marsupial mole, but since the female's pouch contains only two nipples, presumably only 2 young are born at a time.

The testes of the male never descend into a scrotum, but remain in the body, close to the kidneys.

ORDER DIPROTODONTA

More than half of the Australian marsupials, including the koala, kangaroos, and possums, belong to this order. Most diprotodonts are primarily plant eaters, but many also eat insects. Some species feed on nectar or other plant secretions.

VOMBATIDAE: WOMBAT FAMILY

The 3 species of wombat all live in Australia, 1 in Tasmania also. They are strong, powerfully built marsupials, which superficially resemble badgers. With their long, bearlike claws, they excavate vast burrow systems and tear up underground roots and tubers for food. They are strictly vegetarian and often raid cultivated fields to feed on the soft, developing ears of corn.

Common Wombat *Vombatus ursinus*

RANGE E. Australia, Tasmania

HABITAT Forest, scrub

SIZE Body: 27½ in–4 ft (70cm–1.2 m) Tail: vestigial

This wombat is a common forest animal along Australia's eastern seaboard and is often found at high altitudes in the Snowy Mountains.

It digs burrows that may stretch for more than 42 ft (13 m) from the entrance and go down more than 6 ft (2 m). It is not known whether wombats are gregarious below ground, but the number of burrows occurring together suggests that they may be. Above ground, the wombat follows regularly used pathways through the forest.

The female gives birth in late autumn, usually to a single young, which remains in the pouch, where there are two nipples, for about 3 months. Once out of the pouch, it forages with its mother for several months before living independently. It is not unusual for wombats to live for more than 20 years.

KOALA, HONEY POSSUM, PHALANGERS, GLIDING POSSUMS AND RINGTAILS

PHASCOLARCTIDAE: KOALA FAMILY

The single species in this family is one of Australia's best-known marsupials and also the species most specialized and adapted for life in the trees.

During the first three decades of this century, koalas were hunted for their skins, and in 1924 alone, over 2 million were exported. Today the koala is no longer threatened, and following strict conservation measures, populations are increasing throughout its range.

Koala *Phascolarctos cinereus* **LR:nt**

RANGE	E. Australia
HABITAT	Dry forest
SIZE	Body: 23½–33½ in (60–85 cm) Tail: vestigial

The arboreal koala rarely leaves the safety of the trees. It comes down to the ground only in order to pass from one tree to another. Its diet is limited, consisting of the leaves and shoots of a few species of Eucalyptus. An adult will consume just over 20 lb (1 kg) of leaves a day.

Koalas live singly or in small groups, consisting of a single male with a harem of females. They breed in summer, and each female produces a single young after a gestation of about a month. The tiny koala enters the pouch, which opens backward, and remains there for 5 or 6 months. After this period of pouch life it rides on its mother's back. After weaning, the mother feeds her young on semidigested leaves.

Many koalas suffer from the infectious fungal disease cryptococcosis, which causes lesions or abscesses in the lungs, joints and brain. The disease can be transferred to man, often with fatal results. It is thought that the source of the fungal infection is soil, which koalas regularly eat, apparently as an aid to digestion.

TARSIPEDIDAE: HONEY POSSUM FAMILY

The only member of its family, the honey possum is a zoological enigma because it has no obvious close relatives. In general appearance it resembles the other small possums, but its feet are quite different. The second and third digits on each hind foot are totally fused with two tiny claws at the tip of the fused digit.

Honey Possum *Tarsipes rostratus*

RANGE	S.W. Australia
HABITAT	Heathland with bushes and trees
SIZE	Body: 2¾–3¼ in (7–8.5 cm) Tail: 3½–4 in (9–10 cm)

Occasionally the honey possum will eat small insects, but it mainly feeds on the pollen and nectar of the flowers of the Banksia, a flowering shrub. The honey possum's tongue, with its bristly tip, resembles that of a hummingbird or nectar-feeding bat and can be extended about 1 in (2.5 cm) beyond the tip of the nose. The teeth are poorly developed. Tough ridges on the palate are used to scrape nectar and pollen off the tongue.

The honey possum often hangs upside down while feeding, using its prehensile tail as a fifth limb. In midwinter, the honey possums mate, and females give birth to 2 young after a gestation of about 4 weeks. The young remain in the pouch until they are about 4 months old.

PHALANGERIDAE: PHALANGER FAMILY

The 18 species in this family occur in Australia, New Guinea and Sulawesi. The totally Australian species are known as possums, those from the islands are known as phalangers. All are nocturnal and arboreal and use their prehensile tails as a fifth limb when climbing. Leaves, gum from wattle trees and insects are the main foods, but small birds and lizards may also be eaten.

Brush-tailed Possum

Trichosurus vulpecula

Range Australia, Tasmania; introduced into New Zealand

Habitat Forest, woodland

Size Body: 12½–22¾ in (32–58 cm)
Tail: 9½–13¾ in (24–35 cm)

The brush-tailed possum is the only native marsupial to have benefited from man's encroachment on virgin land, for it has become adapted to living on man's buildings and to feeding on refuse. In natural conditions, it eats young shoots, flowers, leaves and fruit, with some insects and young birds.

Breeding occurs once or twice a year, normally with 1 young in each litter. The gestation period is 17 days, and the young possum then stays in the pouch for about 5 months.

ACROBATIDAE: PYGMY GLIDING POSSUM FAMILY

There are 7 species of these tiny, mouse-sized possums in Australia and New Guinea. All are arboreal.

Pygmy Glider *Acrobates pygmaeus*

Range E. and S.E. Australia

Habitat Dry forest

Size Body: 2¼–3¼ in (6–8.5 cm)
Tail: 2¼–3¼ in (6.5–8.5 cm)

The pygmy glider lives at the top of tall forest trees. Its flight membrane – flaps of skin between wrists and heels – enables it to glide from tree to tree. The tail gives directional stability. The tips of its digits are broad and deeply furrowed, to help it grip when landing. The pygmy glider eats insects, gum, nectar and pollen. A litter of 2 to 4 young is born in July or August.

PETAURIDAE: STRIPED AND LESSER GLIDING POSSUM FAMILY

There are about 9 species in this family found in Australia and New Guinea. All species are tree-dwellers and some glide from branch to branch.

Sugar Glider *Petaurus breviceps*

Range E. and N. Australia; New Guinea

Habitat Woodland

Size Body: 4¼–6 in (11–15 cm)
Tail: 4¾–7 in (12–18 cm)

The sugar glider feeds on the sugary sap that oozes from wounds on the bark of wattle and gum trees, returning to the same tree for several days. Sugar gliders live in groups of up to 20, in holes in trees. They use their gliding membranes to leap up to 180 ft (55 m) between trees.

A litter of 2 or 3 is born after a 21-day gestation. The young leave the mother's pouch at 3 or 4 months old.

PSEUDOCHEIRIDAE: RING-TAILED AND GREATER GLIDING POSSUM family

This family includes 14 tree-living species. Their prehensile tails are used to grip while climbing.

Greater Glider *Petauroides volans*

Range E. Australia

Habitat Forest

Size Body: 11¾–18¾ in (30–48 cm) Tail: 17¾–21½ in (45–55 cm)

The greater glider is the largest of Australia's gliding marsupials, weighing up to 3 lb (1.4 kg). It lives in holes, high in the trees, and feeds on leaves and shoots. This animal can glide 330 ft (100 m) or more, from tree to tree, using its long tail to steer.

In midwinter, the female gives birth to 1 young, which spends 4 months in the pouch.

KANGAROOS

MACROPODIDAE: KANGAROO FAMILY

There are about 46 species of kangaroo, and the family is regarded by most authorities as the most advanced of all the 18 surviving families of marsupials, because both the teeth and feet are greatly modified. The hind feet are extremely large – the origin of the family's scientific name – and the thumb is totally absent. Digits 2 and 3 are slender and bound together by skin; digit 4 is massive and armed with a long, tough claw, and digit 5 is only a little smaller. Males and females generally look alike, except for the pouch structure of the female. In some of the larger species of kangaroo, the male is slightly larger than his mate.

A kangaroo has fewer teeth than other marsupials, and these are high-crowned and deeply folded. They are similar to those of the placental mammals of the family Bovidae (sheep and cattle). Kangaroos eat only plant matter. Some are browsers, while others are grazers.

The main characteristic of kangaroos is their method of moving on two legs. They make a series of great bounds, during which the long hind legs propel the body forward with considerable force. A long, powerful tail acts as a counterbalance, providing stability on landing. Although hopping may seem an awkward form of locomotion, at speeds of more than 12 mph (20 km/h) it is more efficient in terms of energy use than quadrupedal running. Kangaroos often have to travel long distances to find food, so speed and efficiency are important, and selective pressures for fast movement are great.

Members of the kangaroo family occur in Australia and New Guinea and also in Tasmania and the Bismarck Islands. Some are forest-dwellers, but others live in hot, arid areas and during the worst of the day's heat they seek the shade of a rocky outcrop and regularly salivate over their upper arms to cool themselves. If intense drought continues for so long that the females can no longer make milk for their young, the sucklings are expelled from the pouch and perish. When the rains arrive and food supplies return, a reserve embryo, which has been held in a suspended state of development, is implanted in the uterus and a new pregnancy begins without the female having to mate again. In this way, kangaroos cope successfully with their harsh environment. Most kangaroos produce only 1 young at a time.

Red-legged Pademelon
Thylogale stigmatica

RANGE Australia: E. Queensland, E. New South Wales

HABITAT Wet forest

SIZE Body: 20¾–24½ in (53–62 cm) Tail: 12½–17¾ in (32–45 cm)

The red-legged pademelon is one of 4 pademelon species, all of which are solidly built forest-dwellers, slightly heavier in the hindquarters than the graceful kangaroos of the open plains. Pademelons are adaptable creatures that can occupy a variety of habitats, provided that there is plenty of cover. They sometimes occur in herds, but there are also solitary individuals. At dusk, pademelons emerge to forage for leaves, buds, shoots and fruit.

Usually a single young is produced, although twins do occur.

Spectacled Hare-wallaby *Lagorchestes conspicillatus* **LR:nt**

RANGE N. and C. Australia

HABITAT Desert grassland

SIZE Body: 15¾–19¾ in (40–50 cm) Tail: 13¾–17¾ in (35–45 cm)

There are 4 species of small hare-wallaby inhabiting the arid and desert grasslands of Australia. They build themselves rough, grassy nests among the tough spinifex vegetation. If disturbed, the hare-wallaby behaves much like a hare – leaping off in a zigzag manner.

Spectacled hare-wallabies lead solitary lives, only coming together with each other for mating. This isolation is necessary because of the extreme difficulty of eking out an existence in the inhospitable desert environment.

The young are produced singly at any time of year and become sexually mature at about a year old.

Yellow-footed Rock Wallaby *Petrogale xanthopus* **LR:nt**

RANGE C. and E. Australia

HABITAT Rocky outcrops, boulder piles

SIZE Body: 19¾–31½ in (50–80 cm) Tail: 15¾–27½ in (40–70 cm)

The yellow-footed, or ring-tailed rock wallaby is the most handsomely marked of the rock wallabies. It has long been exploited for its high-quality fur and is now found in a few isolated areas only.

All rock wallabies live in the most inhospitable regions of the outback. They are remarkably agile and their feet are adapted for scrambling around on rocks, with broad, soft pads and strong claws. Unlike true kangaroos the rock wallaby's long tail does not have a thickened base and is not used for support.

Rock wallabies feed on whatever plant material they can find. Breeding takes place throughout the year, but if drought conditions persist too long, the rock wallabies sacrifice any young in their pouches.

Quokka *Setonix brachyurus* **Vu**

RANGE S.W. Australia

HABITAT Dense vegetation

SIZE Body: 18¾–23½ in (47.5–60 cm) Tail: 9¾–13¾ in (25–35 cm)

The quokka was once widespread over the southwest of Australia, but shooting for sport quickly reduced the population to a low level. Today the quokka occurs in only a few swampy valleys in the Darling Range, near Perth, but it is abundant on Rottnest and

Bald Islands, just off the coast. Quokkas have a good nose for fresh water, and on Rottnest Island travel as far as 1½ miles (2.5 km) to find it. They have learned to scavenge on refuse dumps for food in times of drought and sparse plant supply, and are also able to supplement their protein intake by utilizing urea, a urinary waste product. In this respect, they resemble desert mammals.

The female quokka gives birth to 1 tadpole-sized young after a gestation period of 17 days and mates again the following day. The embryo resulting from this second mating is held free in the uterus and will implant and start development only after the earlier offspring has left the pouch. Quokkas first breed when they reach about 2 years old.

It is to be hoped that the development of Rottnest Island as an important recreational site for the people of Perth can be achieved without destroying the habitat of this intelligent little wallaby.

Lumholtz's Tree Kangaroo
Dendrolagus lumholtzi **LR:nt**

RANGE Australia: N.E. Queensland

HABITAT Rain forest

SIZE Body: 20½–31½ in (52–80 cm) Tail: 16½–36½ in (42–93 cm)

Only 7 species of kangaroo, 2 of which occur in Australia and 5 in New Guinea, have taken to life in the trees. Unlike most arboreal mammals, they have few adaptations for this specialized way of life; their hind feet are singularly undeveloped for climbing, but their front feet are better adapted for grasping than those of other kangaroos. They are, however, remarkably agile in trees, and their long tails, although not prehensile, give considerable stability. Grass, leaves and fruit are their main foods, and they frequently climb backward down trees to the ground to graze.

Small groups live together and sleep in the same tree. Little is known of their breeding habits other than that they produce 1 young at any time of year. Tree kangaroos are not rare, but their secretive way of life and the denseness of their forest habitat make them hard to observe.

KANGAROOS CONTINUED

Red Kangaroo *Macropus rufus*

RANGE C. Australia

HABITAT Grassy arid plains

SIZE Body: 3¼–5¼ ft (1–1.6 m) Tail: 3–3½ ft (90 cm–1.1 m)

The red kangaroo is the largest living marsupial. An old male can attain a weight of about 154 lb (70 kg). The male has a deep russet-red coat, the female has a bluish-gray coat and is often referred to as the "blue flier".

Red kangaroos live on the arid grassland of the desert in small herds, which consist of an adult male and several females. During the heat of the day, they shelter by rocky outcrops or in the shade of trees and emerge in the evening to feed and drink. Weight for weight, kangaroos eat as much as sheep, but they convert their food more efficiently.

Breeding occurs throughout the year, and the gestation lasts 30 to 40 days. A few hours before the birth, the mother starts to clean and nuzzle at her pouch. Sitting back, with her tail bent forward between her hind legs, and holding the pouch open with her forelimbs, she licks it inside and out, often continuing until the moment of birth.

The newborn offspring weighs only 1/40 oz (0.75 g) and is 1/30,000 of its mother's weight. The tiny baby has well-developed front claws, which it uses to clamber up into the pouch. Once safely inside, it takes a nipple into its mouth. The nipple grows with the baby to reach 4 in (10 cm) long at the time of weaning. The mother's milk changes as the baby grows, becoming richer and more fatty during the later phase of lactation.

The young kangaroo spends about 240 days in the mother's pouch and then accompanies her for a further 120 days. During this period the young "joey" will occasionally put its head into the pouch to suckle, even though the pouch may already contain a younger sibling.

During intense drought conditions, most pouch young die, but the loss will be made up from a stock of "reserve" embryos carried in the mother's uterus.

Until recently, red kangaroos were hunted on a massive scale, but this practise is now subject to strict government controls.

New Guinea Forest Wallaby *Dorcopsis veterum*

RANGE New Guinea

HABITAT Lowland rain forest

SIZE Body: 19¼–31¼ in (49–80 cm) Tail: 11¾–21½ in (30–55 cm)

In most respects, the New Guinea forest wallaby appears to resemble the Australian pademelons, but very little is known of this retiring species. The tip of the forest wallaby's tail is armed with a few broad, tough scales, the function of which remains a mystery. Whenever possible, forest wallabies feed on grass, but they also eat a variety of other plant foods. They are seldom observed by day and may lie up in leafy nests until dusk. Little is known of their breeding habits, except that only 1 young is carried at a time.

Bridled Nail-tailed Wallaby *Onychogalea fraenata* **EN**

RANGE Australia: C. Queensland

HABITAT Thick scrub

SIZE Body: 17¾–26¼ in (45–67 cm) Tail: 13–26 in (33–66 cm)

The 2 species of nail-tailed wallaby derive their name from a scale, like a small fingernail, hidden in the thick hair at the tip of the long, thin tail. Its function is unknown. In the middle of the nineteenth century, the bridled nail-tailed wallaby was abundant over much of eastern and southeastern Australia, but in this century, it was unrecorded for several decades until a population was discovered in central Queensland, in 1974. Competition by rabbits for food, predation by red foxes and hunting are major causes of its decline. Conservation measures are in hand and will need to be applied for many years if this species is to survive in the wild.

Thick scrub is used for food and cover by nail-tailed wallabies. Nothing is known of their breeding habits except that they usually produce 1 young at a time.

Swamp Wallaby *Wallabia bicolor*

RANGE E. and S.E. Australia

HABITAT Dense thickets, rocky gullies

SIZE Body: 25½–35½ in (65–90 cm) Tail: 25¼–33¾ in (64–86 cm)

Swamp wallabies occur in small herds but are often hard to see because of their habit of lying down when danger threatens. Only when the danger is imminent do the wallabies break cover and scatter in different directions with explosive speed. Their diet is varied, and they readily switch from one plant species to another. This flexibility means that they can become pests of agricultural crops, and some measure of control is often necessary locally.

Breeding takes place throughout the year, and the female produces 1 young, which stays in her pouch for about 300 days. It continues to feed for 60 days after leaving the mother's pouch.

POTOROIDAE RAT-KANGAROO FAMILY

There are 10 species of rat kangaroo found in Australia. They are smaller than their close relatives the kangaroos. They have long tails and elongated hind feet which, in most species, are used for bipedal hopping movement. As well as feeding on vegetation, some rat-kangaroos also eat insects and other invertebrates.

Musky Rat-kangaroo *Hypsiprymnodon moschatus*

RANGE Australia: N.E. Queensland

HABITAT Rain forest

SIZE Body: 9¼–13¼ in (23.5–33.5 cm) Tail: 5–6¾ in (13–17 cm)

The musky rat-kangaroo is unique in two ways. It has a well-formed first digit, or thumb, on each hind foot and it is the only kangaroo to regularly give birth to twins. The young are usually born in the rainy season (February to May), but this can vary.

The musky rat-kangaroo is also unusual in that it often moves around on four legs in the manner of a rabbit. Little is known of the social habits of this species, but they seem to move singly or in pairs. Both the male and female produce a pungent musky odor, but the reason for this is not known.

Their diet includes a wide range of plant matter, from palm berries to root tubers, and they also eat insects and earthworms.

Potoroo *Potorous tridactylus*

RANGE E. Australia, S.W. corner of W. Australia; Tasmania

HABITAT Low, thick, damp scrub

SIZE Body: 11¾–15¾ in (30–40 cm) Tail: 6–9½ in (15–24 cm)

Despite its small size and rabbitlike appearance, the potoroo has all the characteristics of reproduction of the larger kangaroos and moves with a similar gait. Although it may occasionally move on all fours, it usually bounds along on its strong hind legs, covering 12 to 18 in (30 to 45 cm) with each hop. It is nocturnal, emerging at dusk to forage for plants, roots, fungi and insects.

Potoroos breed at any time of year, and the single young spends 17 weeks in the pouch.

Rufous Rat-kangaroo *Aepyprymnus rufescens*

RANGE E. Australia: Queensland to C. New South Wales

HABITAT Grassland, woodland

SIZE Body: 15–20½ in (38–52 cm) Tail: 13¾–15¾ in (35–40 cm)

The largest of the rat-kangaroos, the rufous rat-kangaroo builds a grassy nest in which it shelters from the heat of the day. It has little fear of humans and will enter foresters' camps and even feed from the hand. This lack of fear makes the animals vulnerable to attack by dogs and red foxes, and while their populations are in no immediate danger, the future survival of these little kangaroos is a cause for concern.

They breed slowly – a maximum of 2 young a year – but nothing more is known of their breeding habits.

ANTEATERS AND SLOTHS

ORDER XENARTHRA

T his order includes 4 families of mammals all of which have gone along the evolutionary track of tooth reduction or loss in connection with their specialized diet of insects, such as ants and termites. The families are the anteaters, the three-toed sloths, the two-toed sloths, and the armadillos.

MYRMECOPHAGIDAE: AMERICAN ANTEATER FAMILY

There are 4 species of American anteater found in Mexico and Central and South America as far south as northern Argentina. They normally inhabit tropical forests, but also occur in grassland. All forms have extremely elongate snouts and no teeth. Their tongues are long and covered with a sticky salivary secretion, which enables them to trap insects easily. The anteaters break into ant or termite nests by means of their powerful clawed forefeet, each of which has an enlarged third digit. The largest species, the giant anteater, is ground-dwelling, while the other, smaller species are essentially arboreal.

Giant Anteater *Myrmecophaga tridactyla* **VU**

RANGE	Central America, South America to N. Argentina
HABITAT	Forest, savanna
SIZE	Body: 3¼–4 ft (1–1.2 m) Tail: 25½–35¼ in (65–90 cm)

The remarkable giant anteater is the largest of its family. It has a long snout, a distinctive black stripe across its body and a bushy, long-haired tail. Using its powerful foreclaws, the anteater breaks open ant or termite mounds and feeds on huge quantities of the insects and their eggs and larvae. Its long tongue can be extended as much as 24 in (61 cm) and is covered

with sticky saliva, that traps insects. As it wanders in search of food supplies, the anteater walks on its knuckles, thus protecting its sharp foreclaws. Unlike other anteaters, this species does not climb trees, although it readily enters water and can swim. Except for females with young, giant anteaters usually live alone. In areas far from human habitation, the giant anteater is active in the daytime, but near people it is only active at night.

The female produces 1 young after a gestation period of about 190 days. The offspring is carried on the mother's back and stays with her until her next pregnancy is well advanced.

Northern Tamandua *Tamandua mexicana*

RANGE	S. Mexico, through Central and South America, N.W. Venezuela and N.W. Peru
HABITAT	Forest
SIZE	Body: 21¼–22¾ in (54–58 cm) Tail: 21½–21¾ in (54.5–55.5 cm)

This anteater is a tree dweller. It is smaller than its giant relative and has a prehensile tail, which it uses as a fifth limb. The underside of the tail is naked to improve its grip. On the ground, the northern tamandua moves slowly and clumsily.

It is active mainly at night, when it breaks open the nests of tree-living ants and termites and feeds on the insects. Like all anteaters, it has a long, protrusible tongue, which is covered with sticky saliva, enabling it to trap its prey.

If attacked, the northern tamandua strikes out at its adversary with its powerful foreclaws. The female gives birth to 1 young. The length of the gestation is unknown. The youngster is carried on its mother's back but may be set down on a branch while she feeds.

Silky Anteater *Cyclopes didactylus*

RANGE S. Mexico, Central and South America to Bolivia and Brazil

HABITAT Forest

SIZE Body: 6–7 in (15–18 cm) Tail: 7–7¾ in (18–20 cm)

The silky anteater is an arboreal animal that climbs with agility. It has a prehensile tail and long feet with special joints, which enable the claws to be turned back under the foot when grasping branches so that they do not become blunted. This anteater rarely comes down to the ground, but sleeps in a hollow tree or on a branch during the day and is active at night, searching for ants and termites. Like its relatives, it uses its sharp, powerful foreclaws to break into ant and termite nests and its long, sticky tongue for gobbling up the insects. Silky anteaters are often attacked by large birds of prey.

Little is known about the silky anteater's breeding habits. The female produces 1 young, which both parents feed on regurgitated insects.

BRADYPODIDAE: THREE-TOED SLOTH FAMILY

There are five species, and two families, of sloth that all live in the tropical forests of Central and South America. These highly adapted mammals are so specialized for life in the trees that they are unable to walk normally on the ground. Most of their life is spent among the branches, where they hang upside-down by means of their curved, hooklike claws. They feed on leaves and other plant material. The three species of three-toed sloths have three digits on both their front and hind feet.

Three-toed Sloth *Bradypus tridactylus*

RANGE S. Venezuela, The Guianas, N. Brazil

HABITAT Forest

SIZE Body: 19¾–23½ in (50–60 cm) Tail: 2½–2¾ in (6.5–7 cm)

The three-toed sloth is so well adapted to living upside down, hanging from branches by its hook-like claws, that its hair grows in the opposite direction from that of other mammals and points downward when the sloth is hanging in its normal position. Each of the outer hairs is grooved, and green algae grow in these grooves giving the sloth a greenish tinge, which helps to camouflage it amid the foliage of its habitat.

This sloth's head is short and broad. It has two more neck vertebrae than is normal for mammals, giving a greater range of head movement. It climbs slowly, moving one limb at a time, and swims quite well. On the ground it drags its body forward with its hooked limbs. The three-toed sloth descends about once a week to defecate in a hole that it digs with its tail.

Leaves and tender buds, particularly those of Cecropia trees, are the three-toed sloth's main food. The sloth's sight and hearing are poor, and it depends on smell and touch to find food.

The female produces 1 young after a gestation of 120 to 180 days. She even gives birth hanging in the trees. The offspring is suckled for about a month and then fed on regurgitated food.

MEGALONYCHIDAE: TWO-TOED SLOTH FAMILY

The two species of sloth in this family have two clawed digits on their front feet and three on their hind feet.

Two-toed Sloth *Choloepus didactylus* **DD**

RANGE Venezuela, N. Brazil, Guyana, Suriname, French Guiana

HABITAT Forest

SIZE Body: 23½–25¼ in (60–64 cm) Tail: absent or vestigial

The two-toed sloth eats, sleeps and gives birth while hanging upside down in the trees. Each forefoot has two digits, closely bound together with skin, each of which bears a large, curved claw. Although all its movements are extremely slow, the two-toed sloth can strike out quickly to defend itself and inflict a serious wound with its claws. On the ground, it can only drag itself along, but it swims easily. The two-toed sloth sleeps during the day, keeping still to avoid detection by enemies and to conserve energy. It becomes active at night when it feeds on leaves, twigs and fruit.

The female gives birth to a single baby after a gestation of at least 263 days. The young sloth clings to its mother while she hangs in the trees.

ARMADILLOS AND PANGOLINS

DASYPODIDAE: Armadillo Family

The 20 species of armadillo all occur in the New World, from the southern states of the USA through Central and South America to Chile and Argentina.

Armadillos are digging animals, that are usually active at night. They have short, powerful limbs with strong, curved claws. They can dig burrows rapidly and some species do this as a means of escaping predators. When they are not active, armadillos rest underground in their burrows. Their skin is dramatically modified to form extremely tough, articulated plates – made of bone covered by horn – which cover the top of the tail, the back, sides, ears and front of the head. This provides the animal with excellent protection. Two armadillo species can curl themselves up into a ball so that their limbs and vulnerable underparts are protected by the armor.

Giant Armadillo *Priodontes maximus* **En**

RANGE Venezuela to N. Argentina

HABITAT Forest

SIZE Body: 29½ in–3¼ ft (75 cm–1 m) Tail: 19¾ in (50 cm)

The largest of its family, the giant armadillo may weigh up to 132 lb (60 kg). Its body is armored with movable horny plates, and there are only a few hairs on the skin between the plates. It may have as many as 100 small teeth, but these are gradually shed with age. The claws on its forefeet are particularly long – those on the third digits measuring up to 7¾ in (20 cm). A fairly agile animal, the giant armadillo can support itself on its hind legs and tail, while digging or smashing a termite mound with its powerful forelimbs. It feeds on ants, termites, other insects and also on worms, spiders, snakes and carrion. If attacked, it can only partially roll itself up and is more likely to flee.

The breeding habits of this armadillo are little known. The female produces 1 or 2 young.

Nine-banded Armadillo *Dasypus novemcinctus*

RANGE S. USA, through Central and South America to Peru and N. Argentina

HABITAT Arid grassland, semidesert

SIZE Body: 17¾–19¾ in (45–50 cm) Tail: 9¾–15¾ in (25–40 cm)

This is the most common and widespread armadillo species. It usually has 9 bands of horny plates across its body, though this can range from 8 to 11. It has powerful, clawed forefeet.

The nine-banded armadillo spends the daylight hours in a burrow, which may house several individuals, and emerges at night to root about in search of food, investigating holes and crevices with its tapering snout for insects, spiders, small reptiles, amphibians and eggs.

The female nearly always gives birth to a litter of 4 identical young of the same sex, which she suckles for about 2 months.

Pink Fairy Armadillo *Chlamyphorus truncatus* **En**

RANGE C. W. Argentina

HABITAT Dry sandy plains

SIZE Body: 5–6 in (12.5–15 cm) Tail: 1 in (2.5 cm)

This tiny armadillo, with its pale pink armor, emerges from its burrow at dusk to feed on ants in particular, but also on worms, snails and plant material. It digs with its forefeet and supports its rear on its rigid tail, thus freeing its hind limbs for kicking away earth. It has five claws on each foot.

This species has proved difficult to keep in captivity, and its breeding habits remain unknown.

ORDER PHOLIDOTA

MANIDAE: PANGOLIN FAMILY

The pangolin family is the only one in its order. The family contains 7 species of nocturnal ant-eating and termite-eating mammals, found in Africa and south and Southeast Asia. The typical pangolin has the same general body shape as that of the American giant anteater, but is covered with enormous overlapping scales, like the bracts of a pinecone. The scales are movable and sharp edged and are probably developed from modified hairs (like the horn of a rhinoceros). The pangolin has no teeth in its elongate head but it does have an extremely long, protrusible tongue, which it uses to catch its prey.

Giant Pangolin *Manis gigantea*

RANGE Africa: Senegal, east to Uganda, south to Angola

HABITAT Forest, savanna

SIZE Body: 29½–31½ in (75–80 cm) Tail: 19¾–25½ in (50–65 cm)

The giant pangolin is the largest of the family. The female is smaller than the male. This species sleeps by day in a burrow and is active mainly between midnight and dawn, when it searches for ants and termites. Its powerful foreclaws can break into nests above or below ground.

Though the pangolin's movements are slow and deliberate, it can walk on its hind limbs – using its tail for balance – as well as on all fours. It can also swim.

When threatened, this species rolls into a ball, which protects it from most enemies. It may also lash out with its sharp-scaled tail and spray urine and anal gland secretions.

The single baby is born in an underground nest after a gestation period of about 5 months. The newborn pangolin's soft scales harden in about 2 days. After a month or so, the youngster accompanies its mother on feeding trips sitting on the base of her tail. It is weaned at about 3 months.

Tree Pangolin *Manis tricuspis*

RANGE Africa: Senegal to W. Kenya, south to Angola

HABITAT Rain forest

SIZE Body: 13¾–17¾ in (35–45 cm) Tail: 19¼–23½ in (49–60 cm)

The tree pangolin has distinctive scales on its back. Each scale has three pronounced points on its free edge. In older animals the points of the scales become worn. An adept climber, the tree pangolin has a very long prehensile tail, with a naked pad on the underside of the tip that helps it to grip.

During the day, it sleeps on the branch of a tree or in a hole, which it digs in the ground, and emerges at night to feed on tree-dwelling ants and termites, which it detects by smell. It tears open arboreal nests with its powerful forelimbs and sweeps up the insects with deft movements of its long tongue. Like all pangolins, it shows a strong preference for particular species of ant and termite and will reject others. The food is ground down in the pangolin's muscular, horny-surfaced stomach.

The female gives birth to a single young after a gestation period of 4 to 5 months. Its scales harden after a couple of days, and at 2 weeks of age, it starts to go on feeding trips with its mother.

PIKAS, RABBITS AND HARES

ORDER LAGOMORPHA

There are 2 families and about 68 species in this order: the pikas, and the rabbits and hares. For many years, these herbivores were regarded as a subgroup of the rodents, but a detailed examination of their structure, dentition and chewing mechanisms suggests that the two groups are distinct but related.

OCHOTONIDAE: PIKA FAMILY

There are about 21 species of pika, all in the same genus. They live in north and central Asia and 2 species also occur in North America. Pikas are smaller than rabbits and have short, rounded ears and no visible tail.

Northern Pika *Ochotona alpina*

RANGE Siberia, Mongolia, N.E. China, Japan: Hokkaido

HABITAT Rocky mountain slopes, forest

SIZE Body: 7¾–9¾ in (20–25 cm)

A small, short-legged animal, this pika cannot run fast like a rabbit, but moves in small jumps, rarely venturing far. It lives in family groups and takes shelter in a den, made among rocks or tree roots. Grass and slender plant stems are its main food, and, like all pikas, it gathers extra food in late summer and piles it in heaps like little haystacks to use in the winter. If they run short of food in winter, pikas tunnel through the snow to reach their stores.

There may be up to three litters a year, depending on the region. Each litter contains 2 to 5 young, born after a gestation period of 30 or 31 days.

LEPORIDAE: RABBIT AND HARE FAMILY

Found in forest, shrubby vegetation, grassland, tundra and on mountain slopes in the Americas, Europe, Asia and Africa, the rabbits and hares are an extremely successful family of small herbivorous mammals. The common rabbit has been introduced in Australia and New Zealand, where it has proved itself to be remarkably adaptable. Compared with pikas, the 47 or so species of rabbit and hare have become highly adapted for swift running, with disproportionately well-developed hind limbs. They also have long, narrow ears and small tails. Their teeth are adapted for gnawing vegetation – they have chisel-shaped upper incisors (which grow throughout life) for biting and large cheek teeth for chewing.

Brown Hare

Lepus europaeus

RANGE Europe (not Iceland or northern Scandinavia), N. Iran, N.E. China; introduced in North and South America, Australia and New Zealand

HABITAT Open country, farmland, woodland

SIZE Body: 17¼–30 in (44–76 cm)
Tail: 2¾–4¼ in (7–11 cm)

A fast-running hare, with long hind limbs, the brown, or European hare is mainly active at dusk and at night. During the day it remains in a shallow depression in the ground, known as a form, which is concealed among vegetation. It feeds on leaves, buds, roots, berries, fruit, fungi, bark and twigs. It is usually a solitary animal.

The female may have several litters a year, each of between 1 and 6 young, which are born in the form, fully furred and active, with their eyes open. They are suckled for about 3 weeks and leave their mother about a month after birth.

Black-tailed Jack Rabbit *Lepus californicus*

RANGE USA: Oregon, east to South Dakota and Missouri, south to N. Mexico; introduced in some eastern states of USA

HABITAT Prairie, cultivated land, arid scrub

SIZE Body: 18¼–24¾ in (46.5–63 cm) Tail: 2–4½ in (5–11.5 cm)

Identified by its long ears and large black-striped tail, this jack rabbit has powerful, elongate hind limbs and moves with a fast, bounding gait. For short periods, it may attain speeds of up to 35 mph (56 km/h) and tends to run rather than to take cover if

threatened. In summer it eats green plants and grass, and more woody vegetation in winter. This rabbit, like all lagomorphs, eats its feces. It is thought to obtain additional nutrients when the material passes through its digestive system a second time.

Several litters of 1 to 6 young may be born each year. The gestation period is 43 days on average. The young are born fully furred, with their eyes open, in a shallow depression on the ground.

Snowshoe Hare *Lepus americanus*

Range Alaska, Canada, N. USA

Habitat Forest, swamps, thickets

Size Body: 14¼–20½ in (36–52 cm) Tail: 1–2¼ in (2.5–5.5 cm)

Also known as the varying hare, this animal has a dark-brown coat in summer that turns white in winter, except for a black edging on the ear tips. This coat is of undoubted camouflage value, although in fact it is a yellowish-buff, with only the visible tips of the hairs pure white. Usually active at night and in the early morning, the snowshoe hare feeds on juicy green plants and grass in summer and twigs, shoots and buds in winter. The population of these hares fluctuates tremendously on a roughly 10-year cycle, due to food availability and predator interactions. Breeding begins in March, and there may be two or three litters, each of 1 to 7, young, which are born well furred, with open eyes.

Greater Red Rockhare *Pronolagus crassicaudatus*

Range Africa: E. South Africa

Habitat Stony country with scattered vegetation, forest edge

Size Body: 16½–19¾ in (42–50 cm) Tail: 2¼–5½ in (6–14 cm)

The greater red rockhare lives alone in a small territory and is usually active at dusk and at night, feeding on grass and green-leaved plants. During the day, it rests in a shallow depression, or

form, near cover of grass or rocks, and if alarmed, it darts into a rock crevice or hole. Like all hares, its hearing is acute and its sight and sense of smell are also good.

The female gives birth to 1 or 2 fully haired young after a gestation period of about a month.

Volcano Rabbit *Romerolagus diazi* **EN**

Range Mexico: S.E. of Mexico City

Habitat Slopes of volcanoes

Size Body: 11¼–12¼ in (28.5–31 cm) Tail: vestigial

This unusual rabbit, with its extremely restricted distribution, is now rare and strictly protected. It has short, rounded ears and trots, rather than hops, on its short legs as it moves along the runways it makes in the grass. Mainly active at night and at dusk, it feeds on grass and young shoots. Volcano rabbits live in colonies and dig burrows for shelter.

The wild population of this species may be as low as 1,300, but a captive colony exists in the zoo on Jersey in the Channel Islands.

Hispid Hare *Caprolagus hispidus* **EN**

Range Bangladesh, India, Nepal

Habitat Forest, grassy bamboo thickets

Size Body: about 18½ in (47 cm) Tail: 1 in (2.5 cm)

Also known as the bristly or Assam rabbit, the hispid hare has an unusual coat of coarse, bristly fur; its ears are short and broad and its legs stout. It lives alone or in pairs and digs a burrow for shelter. Grass shoots, roots and bark are its main foods.

RABBITS AND HARES CONTINUED

Swamp Rabbit

Sylvilagus aquaticus

RANGE S. C. USA: Georgia to Texas

HABITAT Marshland, swamps, wet woodland

SIZE Body: 17¾–21½ in (45–55 cm) Tail: 2¼ in (6 cm)

The robust, large-headed swamp rabbit takes to water readily and is an expert swimmer and diver. It swims to avoid danger when pursued and also to reach islets or other new feeding areas. With its large, splayed toes, it also moves easily on damp, muddy land.

Mainly nocturnal, the swamp rabbit emerges from its shelter beneath a log or in a ground hollow at any time of the day after heavy rain and feeds on grass, herbs and aquatic vegetation. It may also forage in grain fields, where these are near swamps. Although usually docile, rival males will attack each other in ferocious, face-to-face fights, sometimes inflicting serious wounds.

A litter of 1 to 6 young, usually 2 or 3, is born, after a gestation period of about 40 days, in a shallow depression in the ground lined with grass and fur. The young are born furred, and their eyes open a few days after birth. There are thought to be two litters a year.

Brush Rabbit *Sylvilagus bachmani*

RANGE W. coast of N. America: British Columbia to Baja California

HABITAT Chaparral, thick brush or scrub

SIZE Body: 10½–13 in (27–33 cm) Tail: ¾–1½ in (2–4 cm)

The small, brown brush rabbit has a tiny tail and rounded ears. The rabbits living in hot inland regions to the south of the range tend to have longer ears than those living on the cooler, humid northern coast.

Presumably this is because sound does not travel as well in hot, dry air as in moist, cool air and so they need the larger ears to pick up sounds more effectively. This shy elusive rabbit stays hidden in cover of dense undergrowth for much of the time, venturing out for only short distances to feed on a wide variety of green plants and taking almost anything within reach. It moves along well-trodden runways through the vegetation, but does not make a burrow.

There are three or four litters a year, between January and June. Each litter contains 3 to 5 young, born after a gestation of about 27 days in a shallow hollow in the ground, which is lined with grass and fur. The young are born blind, but with a covering of fine fur.

Desert Cottontail *Sylvilagus audubonii*

RANGE USA: California to Montana, south to Arizona and Texas; N. Mexico

HABITAT Open plains with scattered vegetation, wooded valleys, sagebrush

SIZE Body: 11¾–15 in (30–38 cm) Tail: 2–3 in (5–7.5 cm)

The desert cottontail is distinguished from the brush rabbit, with which it overlaps in the south of its range, by its larger size and ears and by its grayish coat.

Often abroad at any time of day, it is, however, most active in the late afternoon and at night, when it feeds on grass, leaves of various plants including cultivated plants, and fruit. It can do much damage to gardens and crops. Never far from some form of cover, it darts for safety if alarmed, the white underside of its tail momentarily revealed as it is flicked up. A burrow or a shallow depression in the ground is used for shelter.

Breeding takes place in spring or throughout the year, depending on the area. A litter of between 1 and 5 blind, helpless young is born after a gestation period of between 26 and 30 days.

Pygmy Rabbit *Brachylagus idahoensis* **LR:nt**

RANGE N.W. USA: Oregon, Idaho, Montana, Utah, Nevada, N. California

HABITAT Arid areas with sagebrush

SIZE Body: 9–11½ in (23–29 cm) Tail: ¾–1¼ in (2–3 cm)

The only member of its genus, this small rabbit has thick, soft fur and short hind legs. It lives in a burrow that it excavates itself and does not often venture far from its home. During much of the day, it rests up in the burrow, emerging at dusk to feed on sagebrush and any other available plant matter. Its main enemies are coyotes and owls, and if alarmed, the pygmy rabbit takes refuge in its burrow, which usually has 2 or 3 entrances.

Litters of 5 to 8 young are born between May and August.

European Rabbit

Oryctolagus cuniculus

RANGE Europe (except far north and east), N.W. Africa; introduced in many countries including New Zealand, Australia, Chile

HABITAT Grassland, cultivated land, woodland, grassy coastal cliffs

SIZE Body: 13¾–17¾ in (35–45 cm) Tail: 1½–2¾ in (4–7 cm)

The ancestor of the domestic rabbit, this species has been introduced into many areas outside its native range and has been so successful as to become a major pest in some places. Smaller than a hare, with shorter legs and ears, the common rabbit is brownish on the upperparts, with buffy-white underneath. The feet are equipped with large, straight claws.

Gregarious animals, these rabbits live in burrows, which they dig near to one another, and there may be a couple of hundred rabbits in a colony, or warren. They are most active at dusk and during the night, but may emerge in the daytime in areas where they are undisturbed. Grass and leafy plants are their main foods, but rabbits also eat vegetable and grain crops and can damage young trees. In winter, they eat bulbs, twigs and bark if more succulent foods are unavailable. As a warning of approaching danger, a rabbit may thump the ground with its hind foot.

There may be several litters a year, born in the spring and summer in Europe. There are 3 to 9 young in a litter, and the gestation period is 28 to 33 days. Young are born naked, blind and helpless in a specially constructed burrow, lined with vegetation and fur, which the mother plucks from her belly. They do not emerge from the burrow until about 3 weeks old. The female is on heat again 12 hours after the birth, but not all pregnancies last the term, and many embryos are resorbed. Only about 40 per cent of litters conceived are born. On average a female will produce 11 live young in a year.

Sumatran Short-eared Rabbit *Nesolagus netscheri* **CR**

RANGE S.W. Sumatra

HABITAT Forested mountain slopes at 2,000–4,600 ft (600–1,400 m)

SIZE Body: 14¼–15¾ in (36–40 cm) Tail: ½ in (1.5 cm)

The only member of its family to have a definitely striped coat, the Sumatran rabbit has buffy-gray upperparts with brown stripes and a line down the middle of its back, from nose to tail. The tiny tail and the rump are reddish, while the limbs are grayish-brown.

This unusual rabbit is now extremely rare, even in areas where it was once abundant, because of large-scale clearance of its forest habitat for cultivation.

Primarily nocturnal, the Sumatran rabbit spends the day in a burrow, but it is believed to take over an existing hole, rather than to dig its own. It feeds on leaves and stalks of plants in the forest undergrowth.

SQUIRRELS

ORDER RODENTIA

The largest of the mammalian orders, Rodentia contains at least 1800 species in 28 families.

SCIURIDAE: SQUIRREL FAMILY

There are about 260 species of squirrel and generally they are alert, short-faced animals. Some have taken to burrowing and live in vast subterranean townships (prairie dogs); others run and hop about over logs and stones (chipmunks); and many have taken to life in the trees (tree and flying squirrels). Most forms are active by day and are among the most brightly-colored of all mammals. Their eyes are large and vision, including color vision, good. The few nocturnal species, such as the flying squirrels, are more drab in appearance. Males and females generally look alike.

Squirrels have a wide distribution, occurring in all parts of the world except for southern South America, Australia, New Zealand, Madagascar and the deserts of the Middle East. In temperate climates they undergo periods of dormancy in cold weather. Dormancy differs from true hibernation in that the creature wakes every few days for food. True hibernation occurs in a limited number of squirrel species. Squirrels are social animals and have evolved a complex system of signaling with their bushy tails. They are also quite vocal, and most can make a variety of sounds.

European Red Squirrel *Sciurus vulgaris* **LR:nt**

RANGE Europe, east to China, Korea and Japan: Hokkaido.

HABITAT Evergreen forest

SIZE Body: 7¾–9½ in (20–24 cm) Tail: 6–7¾ in (15–20 cm)

Until the arrival of the North American gray squirrel in Britain at the beginning of this century, the only European species was the red squirrel. Populations are now declining in Britain, but red squirrels are still abundant in Europe and Asia. Conifer cones are their main food, although in summer they also eat fungi and fruit. The length of the breeding season is dictated by local climate. In a good year

a female may produce two litters of about 3 young each. The young are born in a tree nest, called a drey, which also doubles as winter quarters.

Gray Squirrel *Sciurus carolinensis*

RANGE S.E. Canada, E. USA; introduced in Britain and South Africa

HABITAT Hardwood forest

SIZE Body: 9–11¾ in (23–30 cm) Tail: 8¼–9 in (21–23 cm)

The gray squirrel's natural home is the oak, hickory and walnut forests of eastern North America, where its numbers are controlled by owls, foxes and bobcats. It feeds on seeds and nuts. An adult squirrel takes about 2¾ oz (80g) shelled nuts each day. It will also eat eggs, young birds and insects. Occasionally gray squirrels strip the bark from young trees to gain access to the nutritious sap beneath.

Two litters are produced each year, in early spring and summer. There are up to 7 young in a litter, but usually only 3 or 4 survive. Males are excluded from the nest and take no part in rearing the young. In Great Britain, the introduced gray squirrel is ousting the native red squirrel.

African Giant Squirrel *Protoxerus stangeri*

RANGE W. Africa, east to Kenya; Angola

HABITAT Palm forest

SIZE Body: 8½–13 in (22–33 cm) Tail: 9¾–15 in (25–38 cm)

Sometimes called the oil-palm squirrel, this species feeds primarily on nuts from the oil palm. In regions where calcium is scarce, it has been observed to gnaw bones and ivory. The African giant squirrel is a secretive creature, and its presence is usually only detected by a booming call, which it utters when disturbed. Little is known of its breeding habits, but it probably breeds throughout the year.

Indian Striped Palm Squirrel *Funambulus palmarum*

RANGE C. and S. India, Sri Lanka

HABITAT Palm forest

SIZE Body: 4½–7 in (11.5–18 cm)
Tail: 4½–7 in (11.5–18 cm)

With their distinctive stripes, these little squirrels superficially resemble chipmunks. They are highly active animals, foraging by day for palm nuts, flowers and buds. They may damage cotton trees by eating the buds, but when they feed on the nectar of the silky oak flowers, they do good by pollinating the flowers that they investigate.

Males are aggressive and fight for females, but once mating has taken place, they show no further interest in females or young. About three litters, each containing about 3 young, are born during the year. The gestation period is 40 to 45 days. Young females are sexually mature at 6 to 8 months old.

Black Giant Squirrel *Ratufa bicolor*

RANGE Myanmar to Indonesia

HABITAT Dense forest

SIZE Body: 11¾–17¾ in (30–45 cm) Tail: 11¾–19¾ in (30–50 cm)

The 4 species of giant squirrel are, as their name implies, very large, and they can weigh up to 6½ lb (3 kg). Black giant squirrels are extremely agile, despite their size, and can leap 20 ft (6 m) or more through the trees; as they do so, their tails trail down like rudders. They feed on fruit, nuts, bark and a variety of small invertebrate animals. Singly or in pairs, they shelter in nests in tree holes. In the breeding season a huge nest is made in which the female produces 1, sometimes 2, young after a gestation of about 4 weeks.

African Palm Squirrel

Epixerus ebii **LR:nt**

RANGE Ghana, Sierra Leone

HABITAT Dense forest; near swamps

SIZE Body: 9¾–11¾ in (25–30 cm)
Tail: 11–11¾ in (28–30 cm)

The African palm squirrel is one of the rarest rodents on record. Forest clearance and swamp-draining activities present an intolerable disturbance to this species, from which it may not recover. However, the inaccessibility of its habitats affords it a measure of protection in some parts of its range. It is believed to feed largely on the nuts of the *Raphia* swamp palm, but it probably eats other foods as well. Nothing is known of its breeding habits nor the reasons for its rarity.

Prevost's Squirrel *Callosciurus prevostii*

RANGE S.E. Asia

HABITAT Forest

SIZE Body: 7¾–11 in (20–28 cm) Tail: 6–9¾ in (15–25 cm)

The sharp contrast of colors in the coat of Prevost's squirrel makes it one of the most distinctive members of the family (the generic name means "beautiful squirrel").

These squirrels forage by day for seeds, nuts, buds, shoots and, occasionally birds' eggs and insects. They live singly or in pairs. Shortly before giving birth, the female leaves her normal nest in a hollow tree and builds a nest of sticks and leaves high up in the branches. Here, safe from the attentions of ground-living predators, she gives birth to a litter of 3 or 4 young. It is not known how many litters each female produces in a year, but in some parts of the range there may be as many as four.

SQUIRRELS CONTINUED

African Ground Squirrel
Xerus erythropus

RANGE Africa: Morocco to Kenya

HABITAT Forest, scrub, savanna

SIZE Body: 8½–11¾ in (22–30 cm) Tail: 7–10½ in (18–27 cm)

Rather like that of its North American counterpart, the fur of the African ground squirrel is harsh and smooth, with practically no underfur. It lives in extensive underground burrow systems, which it digs with its strong forepaws. Very tolerant of humans, it carries out its routine of searching for seeds, berries and green shoots by day. These squirrels are a social species and greet one another with a brief "kiss" and a flamboyant flick of the tail.

Mating occurs in March or April and litters of 3 or 4 young are born after a gestation of about 4 weeks. In some areas, African ground squirrels are thought to inflict a poisonous bite; the basis for this mistaken belief is that their salivary glands contain streptobacilli, which cause septicaemia.

Thirteen-lined Ground Squirrel
Spermophilus tridecemlineatus

RANGE S.C. Canada, C. USA

HABITAT Short, arid grassland

SIZE Body: 6¾–11½ in (17–29 cm) Tail: 2¼–5½ in (6–14 cm)

These strikingly marked little rodents are active during the day and are often seen in considerable numbers, although their social groups are far looser than those of prairie dogs.

Like other ground squirrels, they have keen eyesight and frequently rear up on their haunches to survey the scene, searching for predators such as hawks, bobcats and foxes. If danger threatens, the squirrels disappear into their burrows. Although some squirrels live among piles of boulders, most dig burrows which vary in size and complexity. Large squirrels may dig tunnels, which are 200 ft (60 m) or more in length, with side chambers. Younger individuals make smaller, shallower burrows. Seeds, nuts, fruit, roots and bulbs form the main bulk of the diet of these squirrels, but they sometimes eat insects, birds' eggs and even mice. In winter, they hibernate, having gained layers of body fat to sustain them through the winter. Their body temperature falls to about 35.6°F (2°C) and their hearts beat only about 5 times a minute, compared to 200 to 500 times in active animals.

After hibernation the squirrels mate; the gestation period is about 4 weeks, and a litter of up to 13 blind, helpless young is born in early summer. The eyes of the young open at about 4 weeks. They are independent of the mother at about 6 weeks.

Black-tailed Prairie Dog *Cynomys ludovicianus*

RANGE C. USA

HABITAT Grassland (prairie)

SIZE Body: 11–12½ in (28–32 cm) Tail: 3¼–3¾ in (8.5–9.5 cm)

The prairie dog derives its common name from its stocky, terrierlike appearance and from its sharp, doglike bark, which it utters to herald danger. One of the most social rodent species, prairie dogs live in burrows called townships, containing several thousands of individuals. They emerge by day to graze on grass and other vegetation and can damage cattle ranges. Feeding is interspersed by socializing, accompanied by chattering.

Females give birth to litters of up to 10 young from March to May, after a 4-week gestation period. After being weaned at 7 weeks, the young disperse to the edge of the township. Prairie dogs are most commonly preyed on by eagles, foxes and coyotes.

Eastern Chipmunk *Tamias striatus*

RANGE S.E. Canada, E. USA

HABITAT Forest

SIZE Body: 5¼–7½ in (13.5–19 cm) Tail: 3–4½ in (7.5–11.5 cm)

The chipmunk is one of the best-known small mammals in North America, for its lack of fear of man and its natural curiosity make it a frequent sight at camping and

picnic
sites. Chipmunks
dig burrows under logs
and boulders, emerging in the
early morning to forage for acorns, cherry
stones, nuts, berries and seeds. Occasionally they are sufficiently
numerous to cause damage to crops.

During the autumn chipmunks store food supplies for use
during the winter; they do not truly hibernate, but just become
somewhat lethargic during winter.

A single litter of up to 8 young is born each spring.
Although weaned at 5 weeks, the young stay with their mother
for some months. They have a lifespan of about 5 years.

Woodchuck *Marmota monax*

RANGE Alaska, Canada,
S. to E. USA
HABITAT Forest
SIZE Body: 17¾–24 in (45–61 cm)
Tail: 7–9¾ in (18–25 cm)

The woodchuck, or ground hog
as it is called in some regions,
is a heavily built, rather
belligerent rodent. Woodchucks
feed in groups, and, ever fearful of
the stealthy approach of a mountain
lion or coyote, one member of the
group keeps watch while the others
search for edible roots, bulbs,
tubers and seeds.

The young – 4 or 5 in a
litter – are born in late spring and grow very quickly. By autumn
they have achieved adult size and are forced away from the
parental nest by the aggression of the male. Woodchucks may
live for as long as 15 years.

Red Giant Flying Squirrel *Petaurista petaurista*

RANGE Asia: Kashmir to S. China; Sri Lanka, Java, Borneo
HABITAT Dense forest
SIZE Body: 15¾–22¾ in (40–58 cm) Tail: 17–25 in (43–63 cm)

The broad membrane that joins the ankles to the
wrists of this handsome creature does not allow
true flight, but the squirrel can glide up to
1,500 ft (450 m). Gliding enables the squirrel to
move from one tall tree to another without

having to descend to the ground each
time. By day, these squirrels rest in
hollow trees, coming out at dusk to
search for nuts, fruit, tender twigs,
young leaves and flower buds to eat. They live singly, in pairs or
in family groups.

Little is known of the reproductive habits of these squirrels,
but they appear to have just 1 or 2 young in each of 2 or 3
litters a year. Because the young are not seen to ride on the
mother's back, it is assumed that they are deposited in a safe
refuge while the mother feeds. These substantial rodents are
hunted by local tribespeople for their flesh.

Northern Flying Squirrel *Glaucomys sabrinus*

RANGE Alaska, Canada, N. and W. USA, Appalachian mountains
HABITAT Forest
SIZE Body: 9¼–10½ in (23.5–27 cm) Tail: 4¼–7 in (11–18 cm)

By stretching out all four limbs when it jumps, the flying
squirrel opens its flight membrane, which extends from wrists to
ankles, and is able to glide from one tree to another. Speeds of as
much as 360 ft/min (110 m/min) may be achieved.

Normally the squirrels forage about in the treetops for nuts,
living bark, lichens, fungi, fruit and berries, only taking to the
air should an owl or other predator appear. In autumn, stocks of
nuts and dried berries are laid up in hollow trees, for the flying
squirrels do not hibernate in winter.

At any time from April onward, young are born in a softly
lined nest in a hollow tree. There are normally between 2 and 6
young in a litter, and they suckle for about 10 weeks, an
unusually long period for small rodents. It is thought that this is
because an advanced level of development is necessary before
gliding can be attempted.

The northern flying squirrel is threatened in the
southernmost parts of its range.

POCKET GOPHERS AND POCKET MICE

GEOMYIDAE: POCKET GOPHER FAMILY

There are some 32 species of pocket gopher distributed throughout North America, from 54° North to Panama and from coast to coast. They spend most of their lives underground, in complex and wide-ranging burrow systems which they dig with their chisellike incisor teeth and strong, broad paws. Gophers occur wherever the soil is soft and supports rich vegetation – roots and tubers form the main diet.

The burrowing activities of these animals tend to be detrimental to grassland and great efforts are made to exterminate pocket gophers, which reproduce at a prodigious rate.

Plains Pocket Gopher *Geomys bursarius*

RANGE C. USA: Canadian border to S.C. USA

HABITAT Sandy soil in sparsely wooded areas

SIZE Body: 7–9½ in (18–24 cm) Tail: 4–5 in (10–12.5 cm)

Pocket gophers get their common name from the two deep, fur-lined cheek pouches, which can be crammed full of food to transport back to the nest. They lead solitary lives, the male leaving its burrow only to find a female during the breeding season. After mating, he returns to his burrow. A litter of 2 or 3 young is born after a gestation of 18 or 19 days. The young are weaned at 28 days but stay in their mother's burrow until they are about 2 months old. They are sexually mature at 3 months.

Although ranchers consider pocket gophers pests, their burrowing does aerate the soil and thus, in the long term, improves the productivity of the pastureland.

Northern Pocket Gopher *Thomomys talpoides*

RANGE S.W. Canada to Colorado, USA

HABITAT Grassland and open forest to altitudes of 13,000 ft (4,000 m)

SIZE Body: 9¾–11¾ in (25–30 cm) Tail: 2¼–3¾ in (6–9.5 cm)

The northern pocket gopher often lives in areas which experience intense winter weather, but it does not hibernate. It builds up huge piles of roots and bulbs in underground larders and survives during the winter on these stores. Pairs mate in early spring. Litters of up to 10 young are born after a gestation of 18 days. Females may mate again almost immediately, giving birth a few days after the first litter is weaned.

HETEROMYIDAE: POCKET MOUSE FAMILY

There are about 60 species of pocket mouse and kangaroo rat, with considerable variations in external appearance. Some are mouselike and live in dense forest, others have long hind legs, bound along like kangaroos and live in deserts and arid plains. They eat seeds, as well as insects and other invertebrates, and have deep, fur-lined cheek pouches in which food can be transported. They are fertile animals, some species producing three or four litters a year. The family occurs in North, Central and South America.

Silky Pocket Mouse *Perognathus flavus*

RANGE USA: Wyoming, south to Texas; Mexico

HABITAT Low arid plains

SIZE Body: 2¾–3½ in (6–9 cm) Tail: 2–4 in (5–10 cm)

The silky pocket mouse has dense, soft fur which it keeps in immaculate condition. Although nocturnal, when it emerges from its burrows the sand is still hot, and to prevent the soles of its feet from burning they are covered by thick pads of soft fur, which also act like snowshoes, spreading the body weight more evenly. It moves on all fours or on its hind legs only.

Breeding seasons are from April to June and August to September, and there are normally 4 young in a litter. They are born deep in the burrow system and first emerge to forage for seeds at about 3 weeks old.

Californian Pocket Mouse *Chaetodipus californicus*

RANGE USA: California; south to Mexico: Baja California

HABITAT Arid sandy plains

SIZE Body: 3–5 in (8–12.5 cm) Tail: 4–5¾ in (10–14.5 cm)

Californian pocket mice dig extensive burrow systems in the sandy soil of their habitat. The entrance is usually sited underneath a small shrub or bush to provide some shade and protection from predators. The mice feed largely on seeds, transporting them back to the burrow in their cheek pouches. They also eat green plants on occasion. Their bodies are adapted to survive without drinking. The breeding season lasts from April to September, but there is a marked decline in activity during the hottest part of the summer. Up to 7 young are born in each litter, after a gestation of about 25 days.

Pale Kangaroo-mouse *Microdipodops pallidus*

RANGE USA: W. C. Nevada

HABITAT Wind-swept sand-dunes

SIZE Body: 2½–3¼ in (6.5–8 cm) Tail: 2½–4 in (6.5–10 cm)

This rodent covers great distances in order to find food in its barren habitat. It has powerful hind legs for bounding, with broad flat feet, fringed with stiff hairs. As the mouse hops, its long tail is used as a counterbalance and gives it the appearance of a small kangaroo.

Kangaroo-mice are long-lived and breed more slowly than other members of their family. In particularly hot, dry summers, they do not breed at all.

Desert Kangaroo-rat *Dipodomys deserti*

RANGE USA: Nevada, south to Mexico

HABITAT Arid brush and grassland

SIZE Body: 12–15 in (10–20 cm)
Tail: 7–8½ in (18–21.5 cm)

Desert kangaroo-rats dig their burrows in well-drained, easily

dug soils. They are nocturnal and travel great distances in search of food. Since their kidneys are four times more efficient than a human's, they can live their whole lives without ever drinking.

Breeding occurs in any month of the year. Litters of up to 5 young are born after a gestation period of about 30 days.

Mexican Spiny Pocket Mouse *Liomys irroratus*

RANGE USA: S.W. tip of Texas; Mexico

HABITAT Arid woodland

SIZE Body: 4–5¼ in (10–13.5 cm) Tail: 3¾–6¾ in (9.5–17 cm)

The coat of the Mexican spiny pocket mouse bears stiff, grooved hairs, which form a protective shield around the body, helping to deter some of its predators.

This mouse prefers lush, succulent vegetation to eat, but it also forages for seeds and roots, which it carries back to its burrow in its cheek pouches.

Breeding takes place at any time of year, and litters usually contain about 4 young.

Forest Spiny Pocket Mouse

Heteromys anomalus

RANGE Colombia, Venezuela; Trinidad

HABITAT Tropical rain forest

SIZE Body: 5–6¼ in (12.5–16 cm)
Tail: 5–7¾ in (13–20 cm)

This shy, nocturnal rodent lives in burrows on the forest floor. It collects seeds, buds, fruit, leaves and shoots and carries them back to its burrows for eating.

Litters of about 4 young are born at any time of the year, but mostly in spring and early summer.

MOUNTAIN BEAVER, BEAVERS, SPRINGHARE, AND SCALY-TAILED SQUIRRELS

APLODONTIDAE: MOUNTAIN BEAVER FAMILY

This rodent family contains a single species, the mountain beaver. Its common name is particularly inappropriate because this heavy-bodied, burrowing animal is neither a beaver nor associated with high country. Indeed, its ancestry and evolution are poorly understood despite the fact that the fossil record suggests that the family is an ancient one.

Mountain Beaver/Aplodontia *Aplodontia rufa*

RANGE N.W. USA

HABITAT Moist forest

SIZE Body: 11¾–17 in (30–43 cm) Tail: 1 in (2.5 cm)

The mountain beaver is a solitary creature, and each adult digs its own burrow system of underground nest and tunnels. Although it climbs poorly, rarely going up trees, almost any plant material, including bark and twigs, is eaten by the mountain beaver, and it makes stores of food to keep it going through the winter months.

In spring, beavers produce a litter of 2 or 3 young, which are born in a nest lined with dry vegetation.

CASTORIDAE: BEAVER FAMILY

The 2 species of beaver both lead semiaquatic lives and are excellent swimmers. Their hind feet are webbed and they have broad, flat, hairless tails. Males and females look alike, but males tend to have larger anal scent glands. These glands produce a musky-smelling secretion, which is probably used for marking territory boundaries.

Beavers are always found near waterways surrounded by dense growths of trees, such as willow, poplar, alder and birch.

They feed on the bark, twigs, roots and leaves of these trees and use their enormous incisor teeth to fell trees for use in the construction of their complex dams and lodges.

Beavers make dams to create their desired living conditions. A pair starts by damming a stream with branches and mud to create a lake, deep enough not to freeze to the bottom in winter, in which to hoard a winter food supply of branches. A shelter with sleeping quarters is made of branches, by the dam or on an island or bank, or a burrow is dug in the river bank. When beavers have felled all the available trees in their territory, they dig canals into the woods to float back trees from farther afield. Most of the beavers' activity takes place at night.

American Beaver *Castor canadensis*

RANGE N. America: Alaska to Texas

HABITAT Rivers, lakes, with wooded banks

SIZE Body: 28¾ in–4¼ ft (73 cm–1.3 m) Tail: 8¼–11¾ in (21–30 cm)

One of the largest rodents, the American beaver weighs up to 60 lb (27 kg) or more. It is well adapted for its aquatic habits: the dense fur provides both waterproofing and insulation and its ears and nostrils can be closed off by special muscles when it is under water allowing it to stay submerged for up to 15 minutes.

A beaver colony normally consists of an adult pair and their young of the present and previous years. Two-year-old young are driven out to form their own colonies. Autumn is a busy time for the beavers, when they must make repairs to the lodge and dam and stockpile food for the winter. They mate in midwinter and the young, usually 2 to 4, are born in the spring. The young are well developed at birth and are able to swim and feed themselves after about a month.

Eurasian Beaver *Castor fiber* **LR:nt**

RANGE Now only in parts of Europe, Russia and China

HABITAT Rivers, lakes, with wooded banks

SIZE Body: 28¾ in–4¼ ft (73 cm–1.3 m) Tail: 8¼–11¾ in (21–30 cm)

The largest European rodent, this beaver has the same habits and much the same appearance as the American beaver, and they are considered by some experts to be one species. Like its American counterpart, this beaver builds complex dams and lodges but, where conditions are right, may simply dig a burrow in the river bank which it enters under water. It feeds on bark and twigs in the winter and on all kinds of vegetation in summer.

Females are thought to mate for life, but the male in a pair may mate with other females. Litters of up to 8 (usually 2 to 4) young are born in spring.

PEDETIDAE: SPRINGHARE FAMILY

This African rodent family contains a single species, the springhare. Its forelegs are short but the hind legs are relatively long and powerful, and it leaps along in hops of at least 10 ft (3 m). The long bushy tail acts as a counterbalance.

Springhare *Pedetes capensis* **VU**

RANGE Kenya to South Africa

HABITAT Dry open country

SIZE 13¾–17 in (35–43 cm) Tail: 14½–18½ in (37–47 cm)

When alarmed or traveling distances, springhares bound along like kangaroos, but when feeding, they move on all fours. A nocturnal animal as a rule, the springhare spends the day in its burrow. It feeds on bulbs, roots, grain and sometimes insects. Several burrows occur together, some occupied by individuals, others by families. There is probably only one litter a year of 1 or 2 young.

ANOMALURIDAE: SCALY-TAILED SQUIRREL FAMILY

The 7 species of scaly-tailed squirrel are all tree-dwelling rodents found in the forests of west and central Africa. Apart from a single "non-flying" species, they all have broad membranes at the sides of the body which can be stretched out to allow the animal to glide through the air. Scaly-tailed squirrels are not closely related to true squirrels (*Sciuridae*).

Beecroft's Flying Squirrel
Anomalurus beecrofti

RANGE W. and C. Africa

HABITAT Forest

SIZE Body: 11¾–16 in (30–40.5 cm)
Tail: 9–17 in (23–43 cm)

Beecroft's flying squirrel travels from tree to tree, rarely descending to the ground. With flight membranes extended, it leaps off one branch and glides up to 300 ft (90 m), to land on another tree. It finds all its food up in the trees and feeds on berries, seeds and fruit, as well as on some green plant material. Most of its activity takes place at night. These rodents generally live singly or in pairs and make dens in tree holes. They produce two litters a year of 2 or 3 young each.

Zenker's Flying Squirrel *Idiurus zenkeri* **LR:nt**

RANGE Cameroon, Zaire

HABITAT Forest

SIZE Body: 2¼–4 in (6–10 cm) Tail: 3–5 in (7.5–13 cm)

This small flying squirrel has an unusual tail with long hairs projecting from each side, giving it a feathery appearance. Like its relatives, Zenker's squirrel is mainly nocturnal and feeds on berries, seeds and fruit. A gregarious species, it lives in holes in trees in groups of up to a dozen.

NEW WORLD RATS AND MICE

SIGMODONTINAE: NEW WORLD RATS AND MICE SUBFAMILY

This is one of the 17 subfamilies of the huge rodent family Muridae which contains rats, mice, voles, gerbils, hamsters and others. There are about 400 species in this subfamily. Members occur in all habitats, from deserts to humid forests. These undistinguished but abundant little rodents are of immense importance as the primary consumers in their range and occupy a basic position in a number of food chains.

Baja California Rice Rat *Oryzomys peninsulae*

RANGE Mexico: tip of Baja California

HABITAT Damp land in dense cover

SIZE Body: 9–13 in (22.5–33 cm) Tail: 4¼–7 in (11–18 cm)

There are about 50 species of rice rat, all looking much like the Baja California species and leading similar lives. They feed mostly on green vegetation, such as reeds and sedges, but also eat fish and invertebrates. They can become serious pests in rice fields and can cause severe damage to the plants. They weave grassy nests on reed platforms above water level or, in drier habitats, excavate burrows in which they breed throughout the year, producing up to 7 young in each litter.

Spiny Rice Rat *Neacomys guianae*

RANGE Colombia, east to Guyana

HABITAT Dense humid forest

SIZE Body: 2¾–4 in (7–10 cm)
Tail: 2¾–4 in (7–10 cm)

This species is distinguished by the spiny coat, which grows thickly on the rat's back, but sparsely on its flanks. Little is known of these rodents, which live on the floors of the most impenetrable forests, but it is believed that they probably breed the year round, producing litters of 2 to 4 young.

American Climbing Mouse *Rhipidomys venezuelae*

RANGE W. Venezuela

HABITAT Dense forest

SIZE Body: 3¼–6 in (8–15 cm) Tail: 7–9¾ in (18–25 cm)

This secretive, nocturnal mouse lives in the deepest forest. Although it makes its nest in a burrow beneath the roots of a tree, it spends much of its life high in the treetops, feeding on lichens, small invertebrates and plants such as bromeliads. Equipped with strong, broad feet and long, sharp claws, it is an agile climber, and its long tail acts as a counterbalance when it jumps from one branch to the next. Climbing mice breed throughout the year, and the usual litter is 2 to 5 young.

Western Harvest Mouse *Reithrodontomys megalotis*

RANGE USA: Oregon, south to Panama

HABITAT Grassland

SIZE Body: 2–5½ in (5–14 cm) Tail: 2¼–3½ in (6–9 cm)

Harvest mice tend to prefer overgrown pastures to cultivated farmland. In summer, they weave globular nests, up to 7 in (17.5 cm) in diameter, attached to stalks of vegetation.

Litters of about 4 young are born in these nests after a gestation period of about 23 days.

Deer Mouse *Peromyscus maniculatus*

RANGE Canada to Mexico

HABITAT Forest, grassland, scrub

SIZE Body: 4¾–8½ in (12–22 cm) Tail: 3¼–7 in (8–18 cm)

Deer mice are agile, running and hopping with ease through dense bush. They construct underground nests of dry vegetation and may move house several times a year. They have a catholic diet, consisting almost equally of plant and animal matter. Young deer mice start to breed at 7 weeks, and litters of up to 9 young are born after a gestation of between 3 and 4 weeks.

Golden Mouse
Ochrotomys nuttalli

RANGE S.E. USA

HABITAT Brushy and thicketed scrub

SIZE Body: 3¼–3¾ in (8–9.5 cm) Tail: 2¾–3¾ in (7–9.5 cm)

The golden mouse spends most of its life among the vines of wild honeysuckle and greenbrier. It weaves a nest, which may hold a family or a single mouse. It also builds rough feeding platforms, where it sits to eat seeds and nuts. Golden mice breed from spring to early autumn. The gestation period is about 4 weeks, and there are usually 2 or 3 young in a litter.

Northern Grasshopper Mouse *Onychomys leucogaster*

RANGE S. Canada to N. Mexico

HABITAT Semiarid scrub and desert

SIZE Body: 3½–5 in (9–13 cm) Tail: 1¼–2¼ in (3–6 cm)

This mouse is largely carnivorous. Grasshoppers and scorpions are its main prey, but it may even eat its own kind. These mice nest in burrows, which they dig themselves or find abandoned, and breed in spring and summer, producing litters of 2 to 6 young after a 33-day gestation.

South American Field Mouse *Akodon reinhardti*

RANGE Brazil

HABITAT Woodland, cultivated land

SIZE Body: 4½–5¾ in (11.5–14.5 cm) Tail: 2–4 in (5–10 cm)

There are about 43 species of South American field mice. They are active day and night, although most above-ground activity takes place at night. They feed on a wide range of plant matter. Usually two litters are produced each year, in November and March, with up to 7 young in each. The pregnant and nursing females use special breeding chambers situated in the burrows.

Arizona Cotton Rat *Sigmodon arizonae* **EN**

RANGE USA: S.E. California, Arizona, south to Mexico

HABITAT Dry grassland

SIZE 5–7¾ in (12.5–20 cm) Tail: 3–5 in (7.5–12.5 cm)

Cotton rats are so abundant that they are sometimes declared a plague. They normally feed on plants and small insects, but when populations are high they take the eggs and chicks of bobwhite quail as well as crayfish and fiddler crabs. The female produces her first litter of up to 12 young when just 10 weeks old. This species is now endangered because of the destruction of its habitat.

White-throated Woodrat *Neotoma albigula*

RANGE USA: California to Texas, south to Mexico

HABITAT Scrub, lightly forested land

SIZE Body: 11–15¾ in (28–40 cm) Tail: 3–7¼ in (7.5–18.5 cm)

A group of up to 100 of these rats will build a nest up to 6½ ft (2 m) across from any readily available material, usually in a pile of rocks or at the base of a tree. The rats forage for shoots, fruit and other plant food. Litters contain between 1 and 4 young.

Fish-eating Rat *Ichthyomys stolzmanni*

RANGE E. Ecuador, Peru

HABITAT Near rivers and lakes

SIZE Body: 5¾–8¼ in (14.5–21 cm) Tail: 5¾–7½ in (14.5–19 cm)

Fish-eating rats have partially webbed feet and swim strongly. The upper incisor teeth are simple, spikelike structures, used to spear fish, which is then dragged ashore for consumption. The rats produce one or two litters of young each year.

HAMSTERS AND MOLE-RATS

CRICETINAE: HAMSTER SUBFAMILY

The true hamsters are small burrowing rodents, found in the Old World from Europe eastward through the Middle East and central Asia. There are 18 species known, all of which are characterized by a body shape similar to that of a thickset rat with a short tail.

All species have capacious cheek pouches, which are used for carrying food back to the burrow. When full, the cheek pouches may extend back beyond the level of the shoulder blades.

Common Hamster *Cricetus cricetus*

RANGE	W. Europe to C. Russia
HABITAT	Grassland, cultivated land
SIZE	Body: 8½–11¾ in (22–30 cm) Tail: 1¼–2¼ in (3–6 cm)

The common hamster occupies a burrow system with separate chambers for sleeping and food storage. It feeds on seeds, grain, roots, potatoes, green plants and insect larvae. In late summer it collects food for its winter stores. Grain is a particularly favoured food source, and up to 22 lb (10 kg) may be hoarded. From October to March or April, the hamster hibernates, waking periodically in order to feed on its stores.

During the summer, females usually produce two litters, each of 6 to 12 young, which themselves bear young when they are just 2 months old.

Golden Hamster *Mesocricetus auratus* **EN**

RANGE	N.W. Syria
HABITAT	Steppe
SIZE	Body: 6¾–7 in (17–18 cm) Tail: ½ in (1.25 cm)

Golden hamsters are primarily nocturnal creatures, but they may be active at times during the day. Adults live alone in burrow systems which they dig for themselves. They are omnivorous, feeding on

vegetation seeds, fruit and even small animals. Their cheek pouches are large and, when filled are double the width of the animal's head and shoulders.

Golden hamsters are highly aggressive and solitary creatures, and females must advertise clearly when they are sexually receptive. They do this by applying a specific vaginal secretion to rocks and sticks in their territories, and cease to mark as soon as the receptive phase of the estrous cycle is over. The usual litter contains 6 or 7 young, and there may be several litters a year.

The domesticated strain of the species makes a popular pet.

Dwarf Hamster *Phodopus sungorus*

RANGE	Kazakstan, Mongolia, N. China
HABITAT	Arid plains, sand dunes
SIZE	Body: 2–4 in (5–10 cm) Tail: absent

This small, yet robust, hamster is active at night and at dawn and dusk. Little is known about it, but its habits seem to be similar to those of other hamsters. It feeds on seeds and plant material and fills its cheek pouches with food supplies to carry back to its burrow.

Dwarf hamsters are more sociable than their golden cousins and may occur in quite large colonies. They are so well adapted to their cool habitat that they do not breed well at room temperature. Litters usually contain 2 to 6 young, which are weaned at 21 days. Females mate again immediately after giving birth, so they can produce litters at three-weekly intervals.

SPALACINAE: BLIND MOLE-RAT SUBFAMILY

This small subfamily of highly specialized burrowing rodents probably contains only the 8 species found in the eastern Mediterranean area, the Middle East, Ukraine and northern Africa. They are heavy-bodied rodents, with short legs, small feet and a remarkable absence of external projections – there is no tail, external ears are not apparent, and there are no external openings for the tiny eyes that lie buried under the skin.

Lesser Mole-rat *Spalax leucodon* **VU**

RANGE	S.E. Europe; Ukraine, Turkey
HABITAT	Grassland and cultivated land
SIZE	Body: 6–12 in (15–30.5 cm) Tail: absent

Mole-rats live in complex burrow systems, with many chambers and connecting tunnels, which they dig with their teeth and heads, rather than with their feet. They feed underground on roots, bulbs and tubers but may occasionally venture above ground at night to feed on grasses, seeds and even insects.

One litter of 2 to 4 young is born in early spring, after a gestation of about 4 weeks.

MYOSPALACINAE: EASTERN ASIATIC MOLE-RAT SUBFAMILY

There are 6 species in this subfamily, found in Russia and China. These mole-rats are stocky, burrowing rodents, well equipped with heavily clawed limbs for digging. They do not have external ears, but their tiny eyes are apparent, and there is a short, tapering tail.

Common Chinese Zokor *Myospalax fontanierii* **VU**

RANGE	China: Szechuan to Hopei Provinces
HABITAT	Grassland, steppe
SIZE	Body: 6–10½ in (15–27 cm) Tail: 1¼–2¾ in (3–7 cm)

The zokor lives in long burrows, which it digs with amazing speed among the roots of trees and bushes, using its long, sharp claws. As it goes, it leaves behind a trail of "mole hills" on the surface. Grain, roots and other underground parts of plants form the main part of its diet.

The zokor ventures above ground only occasionally at night, because it runs the risk of being caught by an owl.

RHYZOMYINAE: MOLE AND BAMBOO RAT SUBFAMILY

There are 6 species in this subfamily, which fall into two closely related groups – 2 species of East African mole-rats and 4 species of Southeast Asian bamboo rats. All species are plant-eating, burrowing rodents.

Giant Mole-rat *Tachyoryctes macrocephalus*

RANGE	Africa: Ethiopia
HABITAT	Montane grassland
SIZE	Body: 7–10 in (18–25.5 cm) Tail: 2–3 in (5–8 cm)

The giant mole-rat has a stout, molelike body and small, yet functional eyes. It is a powerful burrower, equipped with short, strong limbs and claws. When a pile of soil has built up behind it, the animal turns and pushes the soil to the surface with the side of its head and one forefoot.

It is active both during the day and at night and feeds on plant material both above and below ground. Surprisingly for such a common species, nothing is known of the breeding habits of this mole-rat.

Bamboo Rat *Rhizomys sumatrensis*

RANGE	Indo-China, Malaysia, Sumatra, Thailand, Myanmar
HABITAT	Bamboo forest
SIZE	Body: 13¾–18¾ in (35–48 cm) Tail: 4–6 in (10–15 cm)

The bamboo rat has a heavy body, short legs and a short, almost hairless tail. Its incisor teeth are large and strong, and it uses these and its claws for digging. It burrows underground near clumps of bamboo, the roots of which are its staple diet. It also leaves its burrow to feed on bamboo, plants, seeds and fruit. The usual litter is believed to contain between 3 and 5 young, and there may be more than one litter a year.

CRESTED RAT, SPINY DORMICE AND RELATIVES

LOPHIOMYINAE: CRESTED RAT SUBFAMILY

A single species is known in this group – the crested or maned rat is found in dense mountain forests in East Africa. The animal's general appearance is not at all ratlike, for it is about the size of a guinea pig and has long, soft fur and a thick, bushy tail. The female is generally larger than the male.

Crested Rat *Lophiomys imhausi*

RANGE E. Africa

HABITAT Forest

SIZE Body: 10–14¼ in (25.5–36 cm)
Tail: 5½–7 in (14–18 cm)

Crested rats are skilled climbers, leaving their daytime burrows at night to collect leaves, buds and shoots among the trees.

Along the neck, back and part of the tail is a prominent mane of coarse hairs which can be erected when the animal is excited or alarmed. The raised crest exposes a long scent gland running down the back, which produces a stifling odor to deter predators. The hairs lining the gland have a unique, wicklike structure to help broadcast the odor.

Another curious feature of these rodents is the reinforced skull, the significance of which is not known.

NESOMYINAE: MADAGASCAN RAT SUBFAMILY

This subfamily includes 11 species, of which 10 are found only in Madagascar and 1 occurs in South Africa. It is a varied group, and the species seem to have become adapted to fill different ecological niches, although they share some common features.

It has been suggested of this subfamily, however, that they are not all of common ancestry and that a considerable amount of evolutionary convergence has occurred.

Madagascan Rat *Nesomys rufus*

RANGE Madagascar

HABITAT Forest

SIZE Body: 7½–9 in (19–23 cm) Tail: 6¼–7½ in (16–19 cm)

This species of Madagascan rat is mouselike in appearance, with long, soft fur and a light-colored belly. Its hind feet are long and powerful, and the middle three toes are elongated. It seems likely that the Madagascan rat is an adept climber, using its sharp claws to grip smooth bark.

Although little is known of this creature's habits, it is probable that its diet is made up of small invertebrates, buds, fruit and seeds. Nothing is known of its breeding cycle.

White-tailed Rat *Mystomys albicaudatus*

RANGE South Africa

HABITAT Grassland, arid plains

SIZE Body: 5½–7 in (14–18 cm) Tail: 2–3 in (5–8 cm)

The white-tailed rat is the only member of its group to occur outside Madagascar. It is a nocturnal creature and spends the day in an underground hole, emerging at dusk to feed on seeds and other plant material. It is said that the strong smell of these rodents repels mammalian predators, such as suricates and mongooses, but they are caught by barn, eagle and grass owls.

White-tailed rats appear to breed throughout the year, producing litters of 4 or 5 young. A curious feature of the early development of these rats is that the young become firmly attached to the female's nipples and are carried about by her. They only detach themselves when about 3 weeks old.

PLATACANTHOMYINAE: SPINY DORMOUSE SUBFAMILY

There are 2 species in this subfamily. Their common name originates from the flat, pointed spines that are intermixed with the fur, particularly on the back.

Spiny dormice are well adapted for tree-climbing, for their feet are equipped with sharp claws and padded soles, and the digits spread widely.

Malabar Spiny Dormouse *Platacanthomys lasiurus*

RANGE S. India

HABITAT Forest, rocks

SIZE Body: 5–8¼ in (13–21 cm) Tail: 3–4 in (7.5–10 cm)

The Malabar spiny dormouse lives in trees and feeds on seeds, grain and fruit. The long tail, with its dense, bushy tip, is used as a balancing aid when the animal is moving in trees. A nest of leaves and moss is made for shelter in a hole in a tree or among rocks.

This rodent sometimes becomes an agricultural pest because of its diet, and it has been known to destroy quantities of crops such as ripe peppers.

Although spiny dormice are not uncommon, nothing is known of the breeding habits of these secretive rodents. The other species of the subfamily, the Chinese pygmy dormouse, *Typhlomys cinereus*, lives in forest in southeast China.

OTOMYINAE: AFRICAN SWAMP RAT SUBFAMILY

There are about 11 species in this group, all found in Africa, south of the Sahara to Cape Province. They inhabit a wide variety of habitats and climatic zones, including mountains, arid regions and swampy areas. All members of the subfamily are competent swimmers.

A characteristic of the group is that the members have only two pairs of mammary glands, situated in the lower abdomen.

Swamp Rat *Otomys irroratus*

RANGE Zimbabwe to South Africa

HABITAT Damp grassland, swamps

SIZE 5–7¾ in (13–20 cm) Tail: 2–6¾ in (5–17 cm)

A plump-bodied rodent, the African swamp rat has a rounded, volelike head and small ears. Characteristic features are the grooves on each side of the incisor teeth.

Active day and night, this rat feeds on seeds, berries, shoots and grasses. It will enter water readily and even dive to escape danger. Its nest is usually above ground and is made of plant material, although in some areas swamp rats make use of burrows discarded by other species.

Young females reach sexual maturity at 10 weeks of age, males about 3 weeks later. Although swamp rats seldom damage man's crops, their parasites do transmit tick-bite fever and possibly bubonic plague. Swamp rats are an important food source for many larger predators.

Karroo Rat *Parotomys brantsii*

RANGE South Africa: Cape Province

HABITAT Sandy plains

SIZE Body: 5¼–6¾ in (13.5–17 cm) Tail: 3–4¾ in (7.5–12 cm)

Karroo rats are gregarious animals which live in colonies. They dig burrows and sometimes also build nests of sticks and grass above the burrows. They are nervous, wary animals and stay near their shelters most of the time.

Leaves of the saltbush tree provide the bulk of their diet, and they generally feed during the day. Every 3 or 4 years, their population increases dramatically, and they feed on agricultural crops, causing considerable damage.

Karroo rats are believed to breed about four times a year, producing litters of 2 to 4 young.

VOLES AND LEMMINGS

ARVICOLINAE: VOLE AND LEMMING SUBFAMILY

There are about 120 species in this group of rodents, found in North America, northern Europe and Asia; lemmings tend to be confined to the more northerly regions. All species are largely herbivorous and they usually live in groups or colonies. Many dig shallow tunnels, close to the ground surface, and clear paths through the grass within their range. Others are partly aquatic and some species climb among low bushes.

Local populations of voles and lemmings are subject to cyclical variation in density, with boom years of greatly increased population occurring every few years.

Norway Lemming

Lemmus lemmus

RANGE	Scandinavia
HABITAT	Tundra, grassland
SIZE	Body: 5–6 in (13–15 cm) Tail: ¾ in (2 cm)

The boldly patterned Norway lemming is active day and night, alternating periods of activity with short spells of rest. Grasses, shrubs and particularly mosses make up its diet; in winter it clears runways under the snow on the ground surface in its search for food. These lemmings start to breed in spring, under the snow, and may produce as many as eight litters of 6 young each throughout the summer.

Dramatic population explosions occur every three or four years or so. It is not known what causes these, but a fine, warm spring following two or three years of low population usually triggers an explosion that year or the next. As populations swell, lemmings are forced into surrounding areas. More and more are driven out. Many are eaten by predators, and more lose their lives crossing rivers and lakes, but they do not "commit suicide".

Southern Bog Lemming *Synaptomys cooperi*

RANGE	N.E. USA; S.E. Canada
HABITAT	Bogs, meadows
SIZE	Body: 3¼–4¼ in (8.5–11 cm) Tail: ¾ in (2 cm)

Sociable animals, southern bog lemmings live in colonies of up to about 30 or so. They make burrows just under the ground surface and also clear a network of paths, or runways, on the

surface, where they keep the grass cut and trimmed; little piles of cuttings punctuate these runways. Bog lemmings are active day and night. They have powerful jaws and teeth and feed largely on plant material.

Breeding continues throughout the spring and summer, and females produce two or three litters a year of 1 to 4 young each.

Sagebrush Vole *Lemmiscus curtatus*

RANGE	W. USA
HABITAT	Arid plains
SIZE	Body: 3¾–4¼ in (9.5–11 cm) Tail: ½–1¼ in (1.5–3 cm)

As its common name suggests, this pale-colored vole is particularly common in some areas of arid plains where the sagebrush is abundant. It makes shallow burrows near the ground surface and is active at any time of the day and night. This vole feeds on the sagebrush, after which it was named, and on other green vegetation and produces several litters a year of 4 to 6 young each.

Southern Mole-vole *Ellobius fuscocapillus*

RANGE	C. Asia
HABITAT	Grassy plains
SIZE	Body: 4–6 in (10–15 cm) Tail: ¼–¾ in (0.5–2 cm)

The mole-vole is a more habitual burrower than other voles and lemmings and is more specifically adapted for underground life. Its snout is blunt, its eyes and ears small to minimize damage from the soil, and it has short, strong legs. It probably uses its teeth to loosen the soil when burrowing, for while its incisors are stronger than is usual in

endangered in Mongolia

voles, its claws, although adequate, are n[...]
other burrowing rodents.

Mole-voles feed on roots and other underground parts of
plants. Like moles, they make shallow tunnels in which to search
for food and deeper, more permanent
tunnels for nesting. They breed
at any time of year (the timing
is probably dictated by the availability of food) and produce 3 or
4 young in each litter.

Bank Vole *Clethrionomys glareolus*

RANGE Europe (not extreme north or south), east to C. Asia

HABITAT Woodland

SIZE Body: 3¼–4¼ in (8–11 cm) Tail: 1¼–2½ in (3–6.5 cm)

The bank vole feeds on
softer plant material
than most voles. It
will climb on
bushes to find its
food, eating buds, leaves
and fruit, as well as some
insects. It is active night and day,
with several rest periods, and, like other voles, it clears well-
defined runways in the grass and makes shallow tunnels. Nests
are usually made under logs or among treeroots, and in summer
females produce several litters of 3 to 5 young each.

Meadow Vole *Microtus pennsylvanicus*

RANGE Canada, N. and W. USA, N. Mexico

HABITAT Grassland, woodland, often near water

SIZE Body: 3½–5 in (9–12.5 cm) Tail: 1¼–2½ in (3.5–6.5 cm)

The meadow vole is a highly adaptable
species. It is found in a
wide range of
habitats. It is a social
animal, but each
adult has its own
territory. The voles move
along runways which they clear in the grass and keep trimmed.
They feed on plant material, such as grass, seeds, roots and bark.
A nest of grass is made in the ground or in a shallow burrow
under the runways.

The female is a prolific breeder, producing at least three and
often as many as twelve or thirteen litters a year of up to 10
young each. The gestation period is 3 weeks, and females start to
breed at only 3 weeks old.

Muskrat *Ondatra zibethicus*

RANGE Canada, USA; introduced in Europe

HABITAT Marshes, freshwater banks

SIZE Body: 9¾–14¼ in (25–36 cm) Tail: 7¾–11 in (20–28 cm)

The muskrat is an excellent swimmer and in fact this large
rodent spends much of its life in water. It has webbed hind feet
and a long, naked, vertically flattened tail which it uses as a
rudder. It feeds on aquatic and land vegetation and occasionally
on some mussels, frogs and fish. It usually digs a burrow in the
bank of a river, but where conditions permit, it builds a lodge
from plant debris in shallow water and inside it constructs a dry
sleeping platform above water level. The lodge may
shelter as many as 10 animals.

At the onset of the breeding season, the muskrats' groin
glands enlarge and produce a musky secretion, believed to
attract male and female to one another. They breed from April
to August in the north, and throughout the winter in the south
of their range. Two or three litters of 3 or 4 young are born after
a gestation of 29 or 30 days.

European Water Vole *Arvicola terrestris*

RANGE Europe, east to E. Siberia and Mongolia

HABITAT Freshwater banks, grassland

SIZE Body: 5½–7½ in (14–19 cm) Tail: 1½–4 in (4–10 cm)

Although competent in water, the European water vole is less
agile than the more specialized muskrats and beavers. It makes a
burrow in the bank of a river or stream or burrows into the
ground, if far from water. Grasses and other plant material are
its main food. Water voles breed in summer, producing several
litters of 4 to 6 young.

GERBILS

GERBILLINAE: GERBIL SUBFAMILY

There are some 87 or so members of this subfamily of rodents, all of which come from central and western Asia and Africa. They are all well adapted for arid conditions and many occur only in apparently inhospitable deserts. Chief among their adaptations is a wonderfully efficient kidney, which produces urine several times more concentrated than in most rodents, thus conserving moisture. Water loss from the lungs is a major problem for desert-dwelling animals, and all gerbils have specialized nose bones which act to condense water vapour from the air before it is expired. This essential water is then reabsorbed into the system.

To keep their bodies as far as possible from the burning sand, gerbils have long hind legs and feet, the soles of which are insulated with dense pads of fur. Their bellies are pure white in order to reflect radiated heat. Finally, gerbils adapt to desert life by being strictly nocturnal, never emerging from their burrows until the heat of the day has passed.

Gerbils are all seed-eaters and make large stores of food during the brief periods when the desert blooms. Gerbils never occur in great densities, although they are abundant enough to be an important source of food for predators such as fennec foxes and snakes.

Large North African Gerbil *Gerbillus campestris*

RANGE   Africa: Morocco to Somalia

HABITAT   Sandy desert

SIZE   Body: 4–5½ in (10–14 cm)
Tail: 4¼–4¾ in (11–12 cm)

There are about 35 species in the genus *Gerbillus*, all found from Morocco eastward to Pakistan. All occupy the driest deserts and eke out their existence in the most inhospitable environments. The large North African gerbil occurs in groups of 12 or more, living in simple, poorly made burrows, dug in the sand. The gerbils remain hidden by day, emerging at dusk to search for insects, seeds and windblown vegetation. They never drink, but derive all the water they need from the fats contained in seeds. This gerbil breeds throughout the year, producing litters of up to 7 young after a gestation of 20 or 21 days.

South African Pygmy Gerbil *Gerbillurus paeba*

RANGE   S. Africa: S.W. Angola to Cape Province

HABITAT   Desert

SIZE   Body: 3½–4¾ in (9–12 cm) Tail: 3¾–6 in (9.5–15 cm)

Of the 4 species of pygmy gerbil which are found in the southwestern corner of Africa, *Gerbillurus paeba* appears to be the most widespread.

It constructs simple burrows in sandy or gravelly soil, usually with one entrance higher than the other to improve ventilation. Pygmy gerbils feed on whatever plant and animal food is available. When the desert plants bloom, the gerbils lay in stores of seeds and fruit in underground larders.

They usually breed about twice a year, but in times of abundant food supplies may breed up to four times in a year. The young are fed by their mother for up to a month.

Greater Short-tailed Gerbil *Dipodillus maghrebi*

RANGE   Africa: N. Morocco

HABITAT   Upland, arid semidesert

SIZE   Body: 3½–5 in (9–12.5 cm)
Tail: 2½–2¾ in (6.5–7 cm)

Among the many gerbil species in North Africa, the greater short-tailed gerbil occupies a specific and specialized ecological niche. It inhabits the foothills and mid-regions of the Atlas mountains and lives among boulder fields and rock scree. Like all gerbils, it is an active animal, emerging at night to forage among the sparse vegetation for seeds, buds and insects. It may have to travel considerable distances each night to find food.

The female gives birth to a litter of about 6 young in undeground brood chambers.

Great Gerbil *Rhombomys opimus*

RANGE Iran, east to Mongolia and China

HABITAT Arid scrubland

SIZE Body: 6¼–7¾ in (16–20 cm)
Tail: 5–6¼ in (13–16 cm)

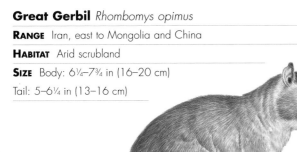

The great gerbil occupies a wide range of habitats, from the cold central Asiatic mountains to the Gobi desert, with its high summer temperatures. It is an adaptable animal, which changes its behavior to suit its environment. In winter, its activity is in inverse proportion to the depth of snow, and in some colonies the gerbils come to the surface only rarely. Large colonies can do much damage to crops and irrigation channels and great gerbils are considered pests in parts of central Asia.

They are herbivorous animals and build up stores of 130 lb (60 kg) or more of plant material in their burrows on which to live in winter. During the winter, huge numbers of these gerbils are preyed on by owls, stoats, mink and foxes. In spring, however, their rapid breeding soon replenishes the colonies.

Indian Gerbil *Tatera indica*

RANGE W. India, Sri Lanka

HABITAT Plains, savanna, arid woodland

SIZE Body: 6–7½ in (15–19 cm) Tail: 7¾–9¾ in (20–25 cm)

The Indian gerbil is a sociable animal, living communally in deep burrow systems with many entrances. Often these entrances are loosely blocked with soil to discourage the entry of predatory snakes and mongooses. Sometimes the populations of this species increase to such an extent that the animals leave their normal habitat and invade fields and gardens in search of bulbs, roots, green vegetation, insects and even eggs and young birds.

Indian gerbils breed throughout the year, producing litters of up to 8 young. It is thought that these animals are a reservoir of bubonic plague.

Fat-tailed Gerbil *Pachyuromys duprasi*

RANGE Africa: Algerian Sahara to S.W. Egypt

HABITAT Sandy desert

SIZE Body: 4¼–5¼ in (10.5–14 cm) Tail: 1¾–2¼ in (4.5–6 cm)

This little gerbil derives its name from its habit of storing fat in its stubby tail. During periods when food is abundant, the tail enlarges in size and may even become too fat to be carried. In lean times, the fat is used up and the tail decreases again. These gerbils spend their days in underground burrows, emerging at night to search for whatever seeds and grubs they can find in the scant vegetation. They have enormous ear bones and very acute hearing, which may help them to locate underground insects. Litters of about 6 young are produced throughout the year and the gestation period is 19 to 22 days. The young gerbils are independent at about 5 weeks old.

Fat Sand Rat *Psammomys obesus*

RANGE Libya, east to Saudi Arabia

HABITAT Sandy desert

SIZE Body: 5½–7¼ in (14–18.5 cm) Tail: 4¾–6 in (12–15 cm)

The fat sand rat overcomes the problem of the unpredictability of desert food supplies by laying down a thick layer of fat all over its body when food is abundant. It then lives off this fat when food is short.

Active day and night, this gerbil darts about collecting seeds and other vegetation which it carries back to its burrow. In early spring, a brood chamber is made and lined with finely shredded vegetation, and the first litter of the year is born in March.

There are usually 3 to 5 young in a litter and the breeding season continues until late summer.

CLIMBING MICE AND POUCHED RATS

DENDROMURINAE: AFRICAN CLIMBING MOUSE SUBFAMILY

There are about 21 species of climbing mice, all of which occur in Africa, south of the Sahara. They are linked by certain skull and tooth characteristics, but otherwise they are quite a varied group. Most are agile climbers and have an affinity for tall vegetation, but some species are ground-living. Many forms have extremely long tails which they wrap around stems and twigs for extra stability. Although abundant, these rodents do not occur in the large groups characteristic of mice and voles. Many species live in extremely dense forest.

One climbing mouse, *Dendroprionomys rousseloti*, is known only from four specimens caught in Zaire, but this may indicate the degree of research effort rather than rarity.

African Climbing Mouse *Dendromus mesomelas*

RANGE Cameroon to Ethiopia, south to South Africa

HABITAT Swamps

SIZE Body: 2¼–4 in (6–10 cm) Tail: 2¾–4¾ in (7–12 cm)

The most striking feature of this little rodent is its prehensile tail, which acts as a fifth limb when the mouse climbs the stems of plants. Climbing mice are strictly nocturnal and are always on the alert for owls, mongooses and other predators. They feed on berries, fruits and seeds, and occasionally search for lizards and the eggs and young of small birds. Sometimes they manage to climb into the suspended nests of weaver finches, and there are records of them establishing their own nests in these secure hammocks, although they usually build nests of stripped grass at the base of grass stems.

Climbing mice breed throughout the year, producing litters of 3 to 5 young.

Fat Mouse *Steatomys krebsii*

RANGE Angola, Zambia, south to South Africa

HABITAT Dry, open, sandy plains

SIZE Body: 2¾–4 in (7–10 cm) Tail: 1½–1¾ in (4–4.5 cm)

Fat mice are adapted for life in the seasonal parts of southern Africa. In the rainy season, when seeds, bulbs and insects are abundant, the mice gorge, becoming quite fat. In the dry season, when plant growth stops, they live off their stores of fat. They live singly or in pairs in underground burrows, breeding in the wet season and produce litters of 4 to 6 young.

CRICETOMYINAE: AFRICAN POUCHED RAT SUBFAMILY

There are about 6 species of African pouched rat, all with deep cheek pouches for the transportation of food. They occur south of the Sahara and occupy a range of habitats, from sandy plains to the densest forests. One species has taken to living close to human refuse dumps, scavenging for a living.

Normally African pouched rats live alone in underground burrows, which they construct or take over from other species. The burrows include separate chambers for sleeping, excreting and, if the rat is female, breeding. Larder chambers are used as food stores for the dry season. Pouched rats move every few weeks to a new burrow.

Giant Pouched Rat *Cricetomys emini*

RANGE Sierra Leone to Malawi

HABITAT Dense forest

SIZE Body: 9¾–17¾ in (25–45 cm)
Tail: 14¾–18 in (36–46 cm)

As its name implies, the giant pouched rat is a substantial rodent, weighing up to about

2½ lb (1 kg). It lives in dark forests or areas of dense scrub. It emerges from its burrow at night in order to forage for roots, tubers, fruit and seeds. Some of the food is eaten where it is found, but much is taken back to the burrow in the rat's capacious cheek pouches.

Giant rats live singly, associating only briefly with others for mating, which occurs at all times of the year. Litters contain 2 or 3 young, born after a gestation period of about 6 weeks.

Long-tailed Pouched Rat *Beamys hindei* **VU**

RANGE Kenya, Tanzania

HABITAT Forest

SIZE Body: 5–7½ in (13–19 cm) Tail: 4–6 in (10–15.5 cm)

The long-tailed pouched rat occurs in a restricted part of central Africa, although the related *Beamys major* extends as far south as northern Zimbabwe.

This rat seems to spend much of its life underground in a complex burrow system which it constructs. It feeds mainly on the underground storage organs of plants – tubers and bulbs – although the presence of seeds in its food stores suggests that it spends some time above ground searching for food.

Groups of up to two dozen rats live together, breeding at all times of the year. Litters contain 1 to 5 young, which are mature at about 5½ months.

MURINAE: OLD WORLD RATS AND MICE SUBFAMILY

This subfamily of almost 500 species of rodents contains some of the world's most successful mammals. They are highly adaptable and extremely tolerant of hostile conditions.

Many of this subfamily are pests, wreaking havoc on stored grain and root crops, while others act as reservoirs for diseases. Rats and mice occur throughout the world and have followed man across the world, even to the remote polar regions and to the tops of mountain ranges.

Australian Water Rat *Hydromys chrysogaster*

RANGE Tasmania, Australia, New Guinea; Aru, Kai and Bruni Islands

HABITAT Swamps, streams, marshes

SIZE Body: 7¾–13¾ in (20–35 cm) Tail: 7¾–13¾ in (20–35 cm)

There are about 17 species of water rats, most of which inhabit rivers and swamps in Australia, New Guinea and its associated islands, and the Philippines.

This imposing rodent has a sleek, streamlined appearance, and is well suited to its aquatic habits. Its partially webbed hind feet enable it to perform complex maneuvers in the water. It feeds on small fish, frogs, crustaceans and water birds which it pursues and captures. Catches are often taken to a special food store for later consumption.

In the south of their range, water rats breed in early spring, producing a litter of 4 or 5 young; farther north they may breed all year round.

Eastern Shrew Mouse *Pseudohydromys murinus* **CR**

RANGE N.E. New Guinea

HABITAT Montane forest

SIZE Body: 3¼–4 in (8.5–10 cm) Tail: 3½–3¾ in (9–9.5 cm)

The Eastern shrew mouse, or false water rat, is known from a few specimens taken at between 6,900 and 9,000 ft (2,100 and 2,700 m) in dense forest. Little is known about the natural history of this animal, but since it does not have webbed feet, it probably does not have an aquatic lifestyle. Its long, strong tail may aid in climbing, and it probably spends much of its time seeking food in the shrub layer of the rain forest.

OLD WORLD RATS AND MICE

Harvest Mouse
Micromys minutus **LR:nt**

RANGE Europe, E. Russia, Korea, S. China, N. India

HABITAT Hedgerows, reedbeds

SIZE Body: 2¼–3 in (5.5–7.5 cm) Tail: 2–3 in (5–7.5 cm)

These mice are among the smallest rodents. A fully grown male weighs about ½ oz (7 g). Harvest mice build tennis-ball-sized nests of finely stripped grass among reed stems or grass heads where the litter of up to 12 young is born and reared. Adults feed on seeds and small insects. They are the only Old World mammals to have truly prehensile tails.

Wood Mouse *Apodemus sylvaticus*

RANGE Ireland, east to C. Asia

HABITAT Forest edge

SIZE Body: 3¼–5¼ in (8–13 cm) Tail: 2¾–3¾ in (7–9.5 cm)

The wood mouse is one of the most common European small rodents. Wood mice emerge from their nests under the roots of trees in the evening and often forage in pairs for seeds, insects and seasonal berries. They usually breed between April and November, but may continue through the winter, if food supplies are abundant.

Rough-tailed Giant Rat *Hyomys goliath*

RANGE New Guinea

HABITAT Forest

SIZE Body: 11½–15¼ in (29–39 cm) Tail: 9¾–15 in (25–38 cm)

This rat derives its common name from the thick overlapping scales covering the underside of its tail. The scales are often worn down, and it is thought that they prevent the tail from slipping when it is used as a brace for climbing. This shy, secretive species is poorly studied, but it appears to feed on epiphytic plants on the branches of trees and on insects.

African Grass Rat *Arvicanthis abyssinicus*

RANGE W. Africa to Somalia and Zambia

HABITAT Savanna, scrub, forest

SIZE Body: 4¾–7½ in (12–19 cm) Tail: 3½–6¼ in (9–16 cm)

The grass rat is a highly social rodent, living in colonies which sometimes number up to a thousand. The rats dig burrows in the earth or, alternatively, may establish themselves in a pile of rocks. Their staple food is probably grass seeds, but they also eat sweet potatoes and cassava. They breed throughout the year.

Four-striped Grass Mouse *Rhabdomys pumilio* **DD**

RANGE C. Africa, south to the Cape of Good Hope

HABITAT Grass, scrub

SIZE Body: 33½–5¼ in (9–13 cm) Tail: 3¼–5 in (8–12.5 cm)

This common rodent lives in a burrow that opens into thick vegetation. It feeds on a wide variety of plant and animal food. In central Africa, these mice breed  through the year, producing up to six litters annually, with 4 to 12 young per litter. In the south, the breeding season is limited to September through to May, and four litters are born.

Black Rat/House Rat *Rattus rattus*

RANGE Worldwide (originally native to Asia)

HABITAT Associated with humans

SIZE Body: 7¼–10¼ in (20–26 cm) Tail: 7¾–9½ in (20–24 cm)

The house, or ship, rat, carrying with it such diseases as bubonic plague, typhus and rabies is sometimes said to have altered human destiny more than any man or woman. Wherever man has gone, and in all his activities, the rat has been his persistent, but unwanted companion.

The success of this species is due to its

extremely wide-ranging diet and its rapid rate of reproduction. Litters of up to 10 young are born every 6 weeks or so.

Brown Rat/Norway Rat *Rattus norvegicus*

RANGE Worldwide (originally native to E. Asia and Japan)

HABITAT Associated with humans

SIZE Body: 9¾–11¾ in (25–30 cm) Tail: 9¾–11¾ in (25–32 cm)

The brown rat is a serious pest, living alongside man wherever he lives and feeding on a wide range of food. Brown rats carry *Salmonella* and the bacterial disease tularaemia, but rarely the plague. They breed throughout the year, and the gestation period is 21 days.

Stick-nest Rat *Leporillus conditor* **VU**

RANGE S. C. Australia; Franklin Island, South Australia

HABITAT Arid grassland

SIZE Body: 5½–7¾ in (14–20 cm)
Tail: 5¼–7 in (13–18 cm)

Stick-nest rats build huge nests of sticks and debris, each inhabited by a pair or by a small colony of rats. The rats are vegetarian but may occasionally eat insects. They breed during the wet season, producing litters of 4 to 6 young.

Mosaic-tailed Mouse *Melomys cervinipes*

RANGE N. E. Australia

HABITAT Forest, usually near water

SIZE Body: 3½–6¾ in (9–17 cm) Tail: 4¼–6¾ in (11–17 cm)

The scales on the tails of most rats and mice are arranged in rings, but in this species they resemble a mosaic. These mice breed during the

rainy season – November to April – and produce litters of up to 4 young. They are active climbers and often rest up in pandanus trees in nests made of finely shredded grass and leaves.

House Mouse *Mus musculus*

RANGE Worldwide

HABITAT Fields; associated with man

SIZE Body 2½–3¾ in (6.5–9.5 cm) Tail: 2¼–4¼ in (6–10.5 cm)

Mice eat relatively little, but they spoil vast quantities of stored food such as grain. Wild mice are nocturnal and feed on grass seeds and plant stems and, occasionally, on insects.

Hopping Mouse *Notomys alexis*

RANGE C. Australia

HABITAT Dry grassland, spinifex scrub

SIZE Body: 3½–7 in (9–18 cm)
Tail: 4¾–9 in (12–23 cm)

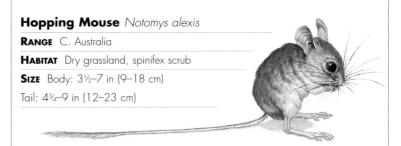

The Australian counterpart of the kangaroo rats of North Africa and North America, this rodent emerges from its cool, humid burrows only at night. It feeds on seeds, roots and any green vegetation. Hopping mice breed during the winter months, producing litters of 2 to 5 young.

Greater Bandicoot Rat *Bandicota indica*

RANGE India to S. China; Taiwan, Sumatra, Java

HABITAT Forest, scrub; often near man

SIZE Body: 6¼–14¼ in (16–36 cm) Tail: 6¼–10¼ in (16–26 cm)

These rodents are serious pests in agricultural areas because they not only spoil grain but also steal quantities of food for their own underground larders. They breed throughout the year and bear litters of 10 to 12 young.

DORMICE, JUMPING MICE AND JERBOAS

MYOXIDAE: DORMOUSE FAMILY

There are about 21 species of dormouse found in Africa, Europe, northern Asia and Japan. These nocturnal rodents resemble short, fat squirrels and most have bushy tails. In late summer and autumn, most dormice build up their body fat reserves and then hibernate during the winter. They wake periodically to feed on the fruit and nuts that they store for winter consumption.

Fat Dormouse/Edible Dormouse *Glis glis*

RANGE Europe, Asia

HABITAT Forest

SIZE Body: 6–7 in (15–18 cm)
Tail: 5¼–6¼ in (13–16 cm)

The largest of its family, the fat dormouse has a long bushy tail and rough pads on its paws which help to facilitate climbing. It feeds on nuts, seeds, berries and fruit and occasionally catches insects and small birds. In summer, it makes a nest of plant fiber and moss up in a tree, but its winter hibernation nest is usually made nearer the ground in a hollow tree or in an abandoned rabbit burrow. The female produces a litter of 2 to 6 young in early summer.

Japanese Dormouse *Glirurus japonicus*

RANGE Japan (except Hokkaido)

HABITAT Montane forest

SIZE Body: 2½–3¼ in (6.5–8 cm) Tail: 1½–2 in (4–5 cm)

A tree-dwelling, nocturnal rodent, the Japanese dormouse spends its days in a tree hollow or in a nest built in the branches. It feeds at night on fruit, seeds, insects and birds' eggs. In winter it hibernates in a hollow tree or even in a man-made shelter, such as an attic or nesting box. After hibernation, the dormice mate, and the female gives birth to 3 to 5 young in June or July. Occasionally a second litter is produced in the month of October.

African Dormouse *Graphiurus murinus*

RANGE Africa, south of the Sahara

HABITAT Varied, forest, woodland

SIZE Body: 3¼–6½ in (8–16.5 cm)
Tail: 3¼–5¼ in (8–13 cm)

African dormice are agile creatures which move swiftly over bushes and vegetation in search of seeds, nuts, fruit and insects. They shelter in trees or rock crevices and, although primarily nocturnal, may be active by day in dense dark forests. Up to three litters of 2 to 5 young are born in summer.

Desert Dormouse *Selevinia betpakdalaensis* **EN**

RANGE S.E. Kazakhstan

HABITAT Desert

SIZE Body: 2¾–3¼ in (7–8.5 cm) Tail: 2¾–3¾ in (7–9.5 cm)

This species was discovered in 1938. The desert dormouse digs a burrow for shelter in which it is believed also to hibernate. It feeds largely on insects, but also eats plants and makes winter food stores of plant material in its burrow. It moves with short jumps on its hind legs.
In late spring, the mice mate and produce litters of up to 8 young.

DIPODIDAE: JUMPING MOUSE AND JERBOA FAMILY

The 49 species in this family are small mouse-shaped rodents, with long hind limbs used for jumping. Some species can leap up to 6½ ft (2 m). Jumping mice live in open and forested land and swamps, throughout eastern Europe, Asia and North America. Jerboas live in deserts, semi-arid zones and steppe country in North Africa and Asia, where they construct complex burrow systems.

Meadow Jumping Mouse *Zapus hudsonius*

Range Canada, N.E. and N.C. USA

Habitat Open meadows, woodland

Size Body: 2¾–3¼ in (7–8 cm)
Tail: 4–6 in (10–15 cm)

Meadow jumping mice feed on seeds, fruit and insects for which they forage on the ground, bounding along in a series of short jumps. They are primarily nocturnal, but in wooded areas may be active day and night under cover of the vegetation. In summer they make nests of grass and leaves on the ground, in grass or under logs; but in winter, they dig burrows or make small nests just above ground in which to hibernate.

They do not store food but, prior to hibernation, gain a substantial layer of body fat that sustains them. From October to April, the jumping mouse lies in its quarters in a tight ball, its temperature only just above freezing, and its respiration and heart rates greatly reduced to conserve energy.

Meadow jumping mice produce two or three litters a year. Most mate for the first time shortly after emerging from hibernation. The 4 or 5 young are born after about 18 days.

Northern Birch Mouse *Sicista betulina*

Range N. and C. Europe, E. Siberia

Habitat Woodland

Size Body: 2–2¾ in (5–7 cm) Tail: 3¼–4 in (8–10 cm)

This rodent is easily distinguished by the dark stripe down its back and by its tail, which is about one and a half times the length of its body. It spends the day in its burrow, emerging at night to search for insects and small invertebrates to eat. It also feeds on seeds and fruit. It hibernates from October to April. Females produce a litter of 3 to 5 young in May or June, after a gestation of 4 or 5 weeks.

Northern Three-toed Jerboa *Dipus sagitta*

Range C. Asia: Caucasus to N. China

Habitat Sand dunes, steppe, pine forest

Size Body: 4–5¼ in (10–13 cm)
Tail: 6–7½ in (15–19 cm)

The northern three-toed jerboa feeds on plants, seeds and insects. It needs very little water and is able to survive on the water contained in its food. In summer, it spends its days in a shallow burrow and emerges in the evening to travel to its feeding grounds, leaping along on its powerful hind limbs.

In autumn, it digs a deeper burrow and hibernates from November to March. Jerboas mate soon after awakening and may have two litters of 2 to 5 young in a season.

Great Jerboa *Allactaga major*

Range Ukraine, east to China

Habitat Steppe, semidesert

Size Body: 3½–6 in (9–15 cm) Tail: 6¼–8½ in (16–22 cm)

The great jerboa and 10 of the 11 other species in the genus *Allactaga* have five toes on each hind foot. Great jerboas feed on seeds and insects, which they find by combing through the sand with the long slender claws on their front feet. They are nocturnal, spending the day in burrows; they also hibernate in burrows. One or two litters are produced each year.

CTENODACTYLIDAE: GUNDI FAMILY

The 5 species of gundi are found in Africa. They are extremely agile and can climb almost vertical rock faces. All members of the family are highly vocal and can utter a range of birdlike trills and twitters.

Gundi *Ctenodactylus gundi*

Range Africa: Sahara

Habitat Rocky outcrops

Size Body: 6¼–7¾ in (16–20 cm) Tail: ½–¾ in (1–2 cm)

Shy animals, gundis feed only at night on a range of plant material which they usually take back to the safety of a rock crevice to consume. The gestation period of gundis is about 40 days, and the usual litter size is 1 or 2 young, which are able to run about immediately after birth.

PORCUPINES

HYSTRICIDAE: OLD WORLD PORCUPINE FAMILY

The 11 species in this family are all large rodents, unmistakable in their appearance, with long spines, derived from hairs, covering back, sides and parts of the tail. Porcupines live in desert, forest and savanna regions of Africa, parts of Asia and Indonesia, and the Philippines. Most are primarily ground living creatures; they move in a clumsy, shuffling manner which rattles their spines. They are generally nocturnal animals and live in burrows, which they dig, or in holes or crevices. They feed on plant material, such as roots, bulbs, tubers, fruit and bark, and on some carrion. Males and females look alike.

Indonesian Porcupine *Thecurus sumatrae*

RANGE Sumatra

HABITAT Forest

SIZE Body: 21¼ in (54 cm) Tail: 4 in (10 cm)

The Indonesian porcupine's body is covered with flattened spines, interspersed with short hairs. The spines are longest on the back and sides, becoming smaller on the tail; on the underside of the body, the spines are rather more flexible than those elsewhere. The specialized "rattling" quills on the tail expand near the tips; these expanded portions are hollow so that the quills rattle when they are vibrated together as a warning to potential enemies.

Crested Porcupine *Hystrix africaeaustralis*

RANGE Africa: Senegal to Cape Province

HABITAT Forest, savanna

SIZE Body: 28–33 in (71–84 cm) Tail: up to 1 in (2.5 cm)

The crested porcupine is a stout-bodied rodent, with sharp spines up to 12 in (30 cm) long on its back. Specialized hollow quills on the tail can be rattled in warning when the tail is vibrated. If, despite its warnings, a porcupine is still threatened,

it will charge backward and drive the sharp, backward-curving spines into its enemy. The spines detach easily from the porcupine but cannot actually be "shot" as was once believed. Crested porcupines are slow-moving animals that rarely climb trees. They dig burrows in which they spend the day, emerging at night to feed. They are thought to produce two litters a year of 2 to 4 young each. The young are born with soft spines and remain in the nest until their spines harden, when they are about 2 weeks old.

Asian Brush-tailed Porcupine *Atherurus macrourus*

RANGE S.E. Asia: Assam to the Malay Peninsula

HABITAT Forest, often near water

SIZE Body: 15¾–21½ in (40–55 cm) Tail: 6–9¾ in (15–25 cm)

The slender, ratlike brush-tailed porcupine, has a distinctive long tail, tipped with a tuft of bristles. The spines of this species are flattened and grooved and most are short.

During the day, the brush-tailed porcupine shelters in a burrow, among rocks or even in a termite mound and emerges at night to hunt for food, mostly plants, roots, bark and insects. An agile creature, it will climb trees and runs well. It has partially webbed feet and is able to swim. Groups of up to 8 individuals shelter and forage together.

There are 3 other species of brush-tailed porcupine in this genus, all with similar appearance and habits.

Long-tailed Porcupine *Trichys fasciculata*

RANGE S.E. Asia: the Malay Peninsula, Sumatra, Borneo

HABITAT Forest

SIZE Body: 11–18½ in
(28–47 cm)
Tail: 6¾–9 in (17–23 cm)

The spines of the long-tailed porcupine are flattened and flexible, but shorter and less well developed than those of other species. The long tail breaks off easily, and many adults are found in this condition.

These porcupines are good climbers and have broad paws, with strong digits and claws for holding on to branches.

ERITHIZONTIDAE: NEW WORLD PORCUPINE FAMILY

The 10 species of New World porcupine are generally similar in appearance to the Old World species and have the same coarse hair and specialized spines. Unlike the Old World porcupines, they are largely tree-living, and the feet are adapted for climbing, with wide soles and strong digits and claws. Six of the species have prehensile tails – a prehensile tail is one equipped with muscles which allow it to be used as a fifth limb, for curling around and grasping branches. Males and females look alike.

New World porcupines are generally, but not exclusively, nocturnal and spend their days in hollows in trees or in crevices in the ground. Both males and females mark their home range with urine. The family occurs throughout North, Central and South America.

North American Porcupine

Erithizon dorsatum

RANGE Canada; USA: Alaska, W. states, south to New Mexico, some N.E.states.

HABITAT Forest

SIZE Body: 18–22 in (46–56 cm)
Tail: 7–9 in (18–23 cm)

A thickset animal, this porcupine has spines on its neck, back and tail and some longer spines, armed with minute barbs at their tips. It is slow and clumsy, but climbs trees readily in order to feed on buds, twigs and bark. In summer, it also feeds on roots and stems of flowering plants and even on some crops. It does not hibernate.

The porcupines mate at the beginning of winter, and the courting male often sprays the female with urine before mating, perhaps to prevent other males attempting to court her. After a gestation period of 7 months, the young, usually only 1, is born in the late spring. It is well developed at birth, with fur, open eyes and soft quills which harden within an hour. A few hours after birth, the young porcupine can climb trees and feed on solid food.

Tree Porcupine

Coendou prehensilis

RANGE Bolivia, Brazil, Venezuela

HABITAT Forest

SIZE Body: 11¾–24 in
(30–61 cm)
Tail: 13–17¾ in (33–45 cm)

The body of the tree porcupine is covered with short, thick spines. Its major adaptation to arboreal life is its prehensile tail, which it uses to grasp branches when it is feeding. The tail lacks spines and the upper part of its tip is naked, with a callused pad to give it extra grip. The hands and feet, too, are highly specialized for climbing, with long curved claws on each digit.

Tree porcupines are mainly nocturnal, and slow but sure climbers. They feed on leaves, stems and some fruits. Females seem to produce only 1 young a year.

Upper Amazon Porcupine *Echinoprocta rufescens*

RANGE Colombia

HABITAT Forest

SIZE Body: 18 in (46 cm) Tail: 4 in (10 cm)

The Upper Amazon porcupine has a short, hairy tail that is not prehensile. Its back and sides are covered with spines which become thicker and stronger toward the rump. It is an arboreal animal and generally inhabits mountainous areas over 2,600 ft (800 m). Little has been discovered about the breeding habits and biology of this species of porcupine.

GUINEA PIGS, CAPYBARA, PACARANAS, PACAS AND AGOUTIS

CAVIIDAE: GUINEA PIG/CAVY FAMILY

There are about 14 species in this interesting and entirely South American family of ground-living rodents. Within the group are forms known as guinea pigs or cavies, mocos or rock cavies, and the Patagonian "hares", locally called "maras". Cavies and rock cavies have the well-known chunky body shape of domestic guinea pigs, with short ears and limbs, a large head and a tail which is not externally visible. Maras have a more harelike shape, with long legs and upstanding ears.

Cavies feed on plant material, and their cheek teeth continue to grow throughout life to counteract the heavy wear caused by chewing such food. Most live in small social groups of up to 15 or so individuals; sometimes they join in larger groups of as many as 40. They do not hibernate, even in areas which experience low temperatures.

Cavy/Guinea pig *Cavia tschudii*

RANGE Peru to N. Argentina

HABITAT Grassland, rocky regions

SIZE Body: 7¾–15¾ in (20–40 cm) Tail: no visible tail

These nocturnal rodents usually live in small family groups of up to 10 individuals, but may form larger colonies in particularly suitable areas. Although their sharp claws are well suited for digging burrows, they often use burrows made by other species or shelter in rock crevices. They feed at dawn and dusk, largely on grass and leaves.

Cavies breed in summer, or throughout the year in mild areas, producing litters of 1 to 4 young after a gestation of 60 to 70 days. The young are well developed at birth and can survive alone at 5 days old. This species is the probable ancestor of the domestic guinea pig, which is kept as a pet and also widely used in scientific research laboratories. Cavies are still kept by upland Indians as a source of fine, delicate meat.

Rock Cavy

Kerodon rupestris

RANGE N.E. Brazil

HABITAT Arid rocky areas

SIZE Body: 7¾–15¾ in (20–40 cm) Tail: no visible tail

Similar in build to the cavy, the rock cavy has a longer, blunter snout and longer legs. It shelters under rocks or among stones and emerges in the afternoon or evening to search for leaves to eat. It will climb trees to find food. The female rock cavy is believed to produce two litters a year, each of 1 or 2 young.

Mara *Dolichotis patagonum* **LR:nt**

RANGE Argentina

HABITAT Open arid land

SIZE Body: 27¼–29½ in (69–75 cm)

Tail: 1¾ in (4.5 cm)

The mara has long, slender legs and feet, well adapted for running and bounding along at speeds as great as 181 mph (30 km/h) in the manner of a hare or jack rabbit. Indeed, the mara fills the niche of the hare in an area where this group is absent.

On each hind foot there are three digits, each with a hoof-like claw; each forefoot bears four digits, armed with sharp claws. Maras are active in the daytime and feed on any available plant material. They dig burrows or take existing ones over from other animals, and the litter of 2 to 5 young is born in a nest made in the burrow.

HYDROCHAERIDAE: CAPYBARA FAMILY

This family contains only 1 species, the capybara, which is the largest living rodent. It resembles a huge guinea pig, with a large head and square muzzle, and lives in dense vegetation near lakes, rivers or marshes.

Capybara *Hydrochaeris hydrochaeris*

RANGE Panama to E. Argentina

HABITAT Forest, near water

SIZE Body: 3¼–4¼ ft (1–1.3 m) Tail: vestigial

The capybara spends much time in water and is an excellent swimmer and diver, it has partial webs between the digits of both its hind and forefeet. When swimming, only its eyes, ears and nostrils show above the water. Capybaras feed on plant material, including aquatic plants, and their cheek teeth grow throughout life to counteract the wear and tear of chewing. They live in family groups and are active at dawn and dusk. In areas where they are disturbed, capybaras may be nocturnal.

Males and females look alike, but the scent gland on the nose is larger in the male. They mate in spring, and 2 well-developed young are born after a gestation of 15 to 18 weeks.

DINOMYIDAE: PACARANA FAMILY

This South American family contains 1 apparently rare species, the false paca, or pacarana, so called because its striking markings are similar to those of the paca.

Pacarana *Dinomys branickii* **En**

RANGE Colombia to Bolivia

HABITAT Forest

SIZE Body: 28¾ –31 in (73–79 cm) Tail: 7¾ in (20 cm)

The pacarana is slow-moving and docile with short, strong limbs and powerful claws. It feeds on leaves, stems and fruit, and sits on its haunches to examine and eat its food. Its cheek teeth grow continuously. It is probably nocturnal. Little is known of its breeding habits but 2 young normally seem to be born in a litter.

AGOUTIDAE: PACA FAMILY

The two species in this family are found in Central and South America. Pacas are large, nocturnal, ground-dwelling rodents that have limbs well-adapted to running.

Paca *Agouti paca*

RANGE S. Mexico to Suriname, south to Paraguay

HABITAT Forest, near water

SIZE Body: 23½–31 in (60–79 cm)
Tail: 1 in (2.5 cm)

The nocturnal paca is usually a solitary animal. It spends its day in a burrow, which it digs in a riverbank, among tree roots or under rocks, emerging after dark to feed. It swims readily. It is believed to produce two litters a year of 1, rarely 2, young.

DASYPROCTIDAE: AGOUTI FAMILY

The 13 species in this family are medium to large ground-living rodents found in Central and South America. They split naturally into two groups: the daytime-active agoutis, and the acouchis, about which less is known. The members of this family have legs adapted for walking, running, or galloping. Most species have been hunted. They eat leaves, fruit, roots, and stems, all of which may be hoarded in underground stores.

Agouti *Dasyprocta leporina*

RANGE Venezuela, E. Brazil; Lesser Antilles

HABITAT Forest, savanna

SIZE Body: 16–24½ in (41–62 cm) Tail: ½–1¼ in (1–3 cm)

Agoutis are social animals and are active in the daytime. They are good runners and can jump up to 6½ ft (2 m) vertically, from standing. Agoutis dig burrows in riverbanks or under trees or stones, and tread well-defined paths from burrows to feeding grounds. They mate twice a year and bear litters of 2 to 4 young.

CHINCHILLAS AND RELATIVES

CHINCHILLIDAE: VISCACHA AND CHINCHILLA FAMILY

There are about 6 species in this family which is found only in South America. All species have dense, beautiful fur and the importance of the chinchillas, in particular to the fur trade has led to their becoming relatively endangered as a wild species.

The hind limbs of the Chinchillidae are longer than their forelimbs and they are good at running and leaping; they are also good climbers. They feed on plants, including roots and tubers, and their cheek teeth grow throughout life. Social animals, they live in small family groups which are part of larger colonies. Where the ground is suitable, they dig burrows, but otherwise they shelter under rocks.

Plains Viscacha

Lagostomus maximus

RANGE	Argentina
HABITAT	Grassland
SIZE	Body: 18½–26 in (47–66 cm)
	Tail: 6–7¾ in (15–20 cm)

The plains viscacha is a robust rodent with a large head and blunt snout. Males are larger than females. Colonies of plains viscachas live in complex burrows, with networks of tunnels and entrances. They are expert burrowers, digging mainly with their forefeet and pushing the soil with their noses – their nostrils close off to prevent soil from entering them.

Females breed once a year or sometimes twice in mild climates. There are usually 2 young, born after a gestation period of 5 months.

Chinchilla *Chinchilla laniger* **VU**

RANGE	N. Chile
HABITAT	Rocky, mountainous areas
SIZE	Body: 8¾–15 in (22.5–38 cm)
	Tail: 3–6 in (7.5–15 cm)

Chinchillas are attractive animals, with long ears, large eyes and bushy tails. They live in colonies of 100 or more, sheltering in holes and crevices in rocks. They feed on any available vegetation, sitting up on their rear haunches to eat and holding their food in their front paws.

Female chinchillas are larger than males and are aggressive toward one another. They breed in winter, usually producing two litters of 1 to 6 young. The gestation period is 111 days, and the young are suckled for 6 to 8 weeks.

The chinchilla's exceedingly soft, dense coat is the cause of its present extreme rarity in the wild, although it is now farmed all over the world for its valuable fur.

CAPROMYIDAE: HUTIA FAMILY

There are now about 12 living species in this family – several other species have become extinct relatively recently. All the surviving species are found on West Indian islands.

Hutia *Geocapromys ingrahami* **VU**

RANGE	Bahamas
HABITAT	Forest
SIZE	Body: 11¾–19¾ in (30–50 cm) Tail: 6–11¾ in (15–30 cm) **E**

The hutia feeds mostly on fruit and leaves, but it occasionally eats small invertebrates and reptiles. It is a good climber and seeks some of its food in the trees. Active in the daytime, it shelters in a burrow or rock crevice at night. It is believed to breed all year round, provided that the temperature stays above 60°F (15°C), and produces litters of 2 to 9 young.

Hutias have been unable to cope with man's introduction of mongooses and dogs to the West Indies, and as a result many species may be heading for imminent extinction.

MYOCASTORIDAE: COYPU FAMILY

The single species in this family – the coypu or nutria – is a semi-aquatic rodent that is a native of South America.

Coypu/Nutria *Myocastor coypus*

RANGE Bolivia and S. Brazil to Chile and Argentina; introduced in North America, Europe and Asia

HABITAT Near marshes, lakes, streams

SIZE Body: 17–24¾ in (43–63 cm)

Tail: 9¾–16½ in (25–42 cm)

The semiaquatic coypu is a skilled swimmer and diver and looks like a beaver with a rat's tail. Its hind feet are webbed and it has dense fur. Coypus feed on aquatic vegetation and possibly on mollusks. They dig burrows in river banks, clear trails in their territory and are extremely destructive to plants and crops. By escaping from the farms where they are bred for their fur, these animals have colonized new areas all over the world, and are sometimes considered pests because of the damage that they are capable of doing.

Two to three litters of up to 10 young are produced during the year, and the gestation period is 132 days. Young coypus can swim only a few hours after birth.

OCTODONTIDAE: OCTODONT RODENT FAMILY

The 9 species of octodont rodent all occur in South America. Most resemble rats with round noses and long furry tails. They are all good burrowers and feed on plant material.

Degu *Octodon degus*

RANGE W. Peru, Chile

HABITAT Mountains, coastal regions

SIZE Body: 5–7½ in (12.5–19.5 cm) Tail: 4–6¼ in (10–16 cm)

The degu is a stout, short-legged rodent with a large head for its size. Active during the day, it feeds on plants, bulbs and tubers. It is thought to breed all year round and may produce several litters a year of 2 young each.

CTENOMYIDAE: TUCO-TUCO FAMILY

This family of 38 species, all found in South America, is believed by some authorities to be a group of relatives of the octodont rodents which has become highly specialized for an underground existence.

Tuco-tuco *Ctenomys talarum*

RANGE E. Argentina

HABITAT Grassland

SIZE Body: 6¾–9¾ in (17–25 cm)

Tail: 2¼–4¼ in (6–11 cm)

Tuco-tucos look very much like North American pocket gophers (*Geomyidae*) and lead similar lives in complex burrow systems. Their front teeth are enormous relative to body size and are used, when burrowing, to loosen the soil. Tuco-tucos spend nearly all their lives underground and feed on roots, tubers and stems.

In winter and spring, the tuco-tucos mate, and a single litter of 2 to 5 young is born after a gestation of about 15 weeks.

ABROCOMIDAE: CHINCHILLA-RAT FAMILY

There are 2 species only of chinchilla-rat, both native to South America. As their common name suggests, their fur resembles that of the chinchilla, although it is of poorer quality, and they have a ratlike body shape.

Chinchilla-rat *Abrocoma bennetti*

RANGE Chile

HABITAT High coastal plains

SIZE Body: 7½–9¾ in (19–25 cm)

Tail: 5¼–7 in (13–18 cm)

A resident of cold, bleak mountain regions, the chinchilla-rat is a little-known creature. It feeds on plant food and its cheek teeth grow throughout life. Mainly a ground-dweller, it can also climb trees in search of food. Chinchilla-rats live in burrows or rock crevices.

SPINY RATS, CANE RATS AND RELATIVES

ECHIMYIDAE: AMERICAN SPINY RAT FAMILY

The 63 or so species of American spiny rat are found from Nicaragua in the north to central Brazil in the south. Most are robust, ratlike creatures with a more or less spiny coat of sharp hairs. They are herbivorous, feeding on a variety of plant material. Most prefer to live close to rivers and streams.

Like many South American rodents, spiny rats have a long gestation and give birth to well-developed young which can run around when only a few hours old.

Gliding Spiny Rat *Diplomys labilis*

RANGE Panama

HABITAT Forest

SIZE Body: 9¾–19 in (25–48 cm) Tail: 7¾–11 in (20–28 cm)

Well adapted for arboreal life, the gliding spiny rat has long, strong toes and sharp, curved claws with which it can grip the smoothest of bark. Its common name derives from its habit of leaping from branch to branch, spreading its limbs to utilize its gliding membrane as it does so.

Gliding spiny rats make their nests in hollows in trees near water. They breed throughout the year, producing litters of 2 young after a gestation period of about 60 days. The young are able to clamber around among the branches only a few hours after they are born.

Armored Rat *Hoplomys gymnurus*

RANGE Nicaragua, south to Colombia and Ecuador

HABITAT Rain forest, grassy clearings

SIZE Body: 8¾–12½ in (22–32 cm) Tail: 6–9¾ in (15–25 cm)

The most spiny of all the spiny rats, the armored rat has a thick coat of needle-sharp hairs along its back and flanks. These

rodents live in short, simple burrows in the banks of streams and emerge at night to forage for food. They breed throughout the year, producing litters of 1 to 3 young.

THRYONOMYIDAE: CANE RAT FAMILY

The 2 species of cane rat are found throughout Africa, south of the Sahara. They are substantial rodents, weighing up to 15½ lb (7 kg), and they are the principal source of animal protein for some tribes. In the cane fields they cause serious damage to the crop, stripping the cane of its outer bark to expose the soft central pith on which they feed.

Cane Rat *Thryonomys swinderianus*

RANGE Africa, south of the Sahara

HABITAT Grassy plains, sugarcane plantations

SIZE Body: 13¾–24 in (35–61 cm) Tail: 2¾–9¾ in (7–25 cm)

Cane rats do not normally live in burrows, preferring instead to construct a sleeping platform from chopped-up vegetation when needed. Occasionally, though, they do take over disused aardvark or porcupine burrows or seek refuge among a pile of

boulders. In southern Africa, cane rats are known to mate from April to June and to give birth to litters of 2 to 4 young after a gestation period of 2 months. The young cane rats are well-developed at birth – their eyes are open and they are able to run around soon after they are born.

PETROMURIDAE: DASSIE RAT FAMILY

The single species in this family is an unusual rodent that looks more like a squirrel than a rat. Its common name links it in habit with the dassie, or rock hyrax, for both creatures share a love of the sun and spend much time basking on rocks, moving from place to place to catch the strongest rays. While the others bask, one member of the colony keeps a lookout for predators, such as mongooses, eagles or leopards, uttering a shrill warning call if danger threatens.

Dassie Rat *Petromus typicus*

RANGE Africa: Angola, Namibia, N.W. South Africa

HABITAT Rocky, arid hills

SIZE Body: 5½–7¾ in (14–20 cm) Tail: 5¼–7 in (13–18 cm)

Dassie rats live in large colonies and are active in the daytime. They feed on fruit, seeds and berries. They mate in early summer (October) and give birth in late December to a litter of 1 or 2 young.

BATHYERGIDAE: MOLE-RAT FAMILY

There are 8 species of mole-rat, all found in Africa, south of the Sahara. They are highly specialized for a subterranean life, for they are virtually blind and have powerful incisor teeth and claws for digging. Their skulls also are heavy and strong, and they use their heads as battering rams. The underground storage organs of plants – tubers and bulbs – are their main food, and worms and insect larvae may be eaten occasionally. Most have thick velvety coats which resemble that of the mole, but the naked mole-rat is quite hairless.

Cape Dune Mole-rat *Bathyergus suillus*

RANGE South Africa to Cape of Good Hope

HABITAT Sand dunes, sandy plains

SIZE Body: 6¾–13 in (17.5–33 cm) Tail: 1½–2¾ in (4–7 cm)

This is the largest member of the mole-rat family. The Cape dune mole-rat may weigh up to 3 lb (1.5 kg). It has relatively huge incisor teeth (each one measuring ¹⁄₁₂ in (2 mm) across) and a fearsome bite.

It builds extensive burrow systems, usually close to the surface, which can be a serious menace to root crops. Between November and December females give birth to between 3 and 5 well-developed young.

Naked Mole-rat *Heterocephalus glaber*

RANGE Somalia, Ethiopia, N. Kenya

HABITAT Arid steppe, light sandy soil

SIZE Body: 3¼–3½ in (8–9 cm) Tail: 1½ in (3.5–4 cm)

This species, the smallest of its family, is one of the most curious mammals known, with a unique social structure more similar to some insects than to any other mammal. Each colony of naked mole-rats numbers about 100 individuals and is ruled by a single queen, who alone breeds. The queen is tended by a few non-workers of both sexes, which are fatter and more sluggish than the other colony members – the workers. It is the workers that dig the burrows and gather the roots and tubers for the whole colony to eat.

The queen appears to be able to inhibit the sexual maturation of all the other females in the colony, but how this is achieved is not known. The queen breeds throughout the year and may produce up to 20 young in each litter. If she dies or is removed, then one of the non-worker female becomes the new queen and begins to breed.

ELEPHANT SHREWS AND TENRECS

ORDER MACROSCELIDEA

MACROSCELIDIDAE:
ELEPHANT SHREW FAMILY

The 15 species of African elephant shrews have extraordinary trunklike noses. Although once assigned to the insectivores, elephant shrews are now classified in their own order.

Short-eared Elephant Shrew
Macroscelides proboscideus **VU**

RANGE Africa: Namibia, South Africa: Cape Province

HABITAT Plains, rocky outcrops

SIZE Body: 3¾–5 in (9.5–12.5 cm)
Tail: 3¾–5½ in (9.5–14 cm)

Elephant shrews are active day and night. They eat termites (sometimes burrowing into termite mounds), seeds, fruit and berries. The elephant shrews hop and jump from twig to branch on their powerful hind legs, using their tails as counterbalances.

A litter of 1 or 2 well-developed young is born during the rainy season. The young can walk and jump almost as soon as they are born and appear to suckle for only a few days.

ORDER INSECTIVORA

This order includes about 384 species found all over the world, except in Australia and the southern half of South America. Most are ground-dwelling or burrowing animals which feed on insects and invertebrates.

TENRECIDAE: TENREC FAMILY

This family includes the 24 species, all restricted to Madagascar and the Comoro Islands, and the 3 West African otter shrews. Tenrecs have adapted to a number of different lifestyles. *Tenrec* resembles the North American opossum. *Setifer* resembles hedgehogs. *Microgale* resembles shrews, and *Oryzorictes* has molelike characteristics.

All tenrecs retain some reptilian features, regarded as primitive in mammals, such as the cloaca, where the urogenital and anal canals open into a common pouch.

Tailless Tenrec *Tenrec ecaudatus*

RANGE Madagascar, Comoro Islands

HABITAT Brushland, dry forest clearings, highland plateaux

SIZE Body: 10½–15¼ in (27–39 cm)
Tail: ½–¾ in (10–16 mm)

The tailless tenrec bears a resemblance to a hedgehog with a sparse coat, set with stiff hairs and spines. It is active at night, searching for insects, worms and roots and fruit.

In the dry season, tailless tenrecs hibernate in deep burrows which they plug with soil. Before hibernation, the tenrec builds up its fat reserves to sustain it through its 6-month sleep. In early October, immediately after hibernating, tenrecs mate. Up to 25 young are born in November and about 16 survive.

Greater Hedgehog Tenrec *Setifer setosus*

RANGE Madagascar

HABITAT Dry forest, highland plateaux

SIZE Body: 6–7½ in (15–19 cm) Tail: ½–¾ in (10–16 mm)

The greater hedgehog tenrec has short, sharp spines, which cover its back like a dense, prickly mantle. If disturbed, it rolls itself into a ball and emits a series of squeaks and grunts. The female produces a litter of up to 6 young in January. The young have soft spines at birth, which harden in 2 weeks.

Streaked Tenrec

Hemicentetes semispinosus

RANGE	Madagascar
HABITAT	Scrub, forest edge
SIZE	Body: 6¼–7½ in (16–19 cm) Tail: vestigial

Although it is less densely spined than the hedgehog tenrec, the streaked species can still protect itself by partially curling up. When the creature is alarmed, a small patch of heavy spines in the middle of the back vibrate rapidly, making a clicking noise. The mother is believed to communicate with her young in this way.

Streaked tenrecs do not hibernate, but they do remain inactive during spells of cool weather. Like other tenrecs, they feed on insects and other invertebrates.

Females are sexually mature at 8 weeks, and produce a litter of 7 to 11 young between December and March after a gestation of at least 50 days.

Rice Tenrec *Oryzorictes hova*

RANGE	Madagascar
HABITAT	Marshy areas
SIZE	Body: 3–5 in (8–13 cm) Tail: 1¼–2 in (3–5 cm)

Rice tenrecs, so called because they occupy the banks beside rice fields, spend most of their lives underground; their forelimbs are well adapted for digging. They feed on invertebrates, but there is some evidence that they also eat mollusks and crustaceans.

Although rice tenrecs are seen above ground only at night, they may be active underground at all hours. Nothing is known of their breeding habits, but they are sufficiently abundant to achieve pest status in the rice growing areas of Madagascar.

Giant Otter Shrew *Potomogale velox*

RANGE	W. and C. equatorial Africa
HABITAT	Streams: sea level to 6,000 ft (1,800 m)
SIZE	Body: 11½–14 in (29–35 cm) Tail: 9½–11½ in (24–29 cm)

Although they are geographically separated from the other tenrecs, the 3 otter shrews are believed to be a subfamily of the *Tenrecidae*. The giant otter shrew is, overall, the largest living insectivore and does bear a strong superficial resemblance to the otter, with its flattened head and heavy tail. Its coat is dense with a glossy overlayer of guardhairs.

Giant otter shrews live in burrows with entrances below water level. They emerge at dusk to hunt for crabs, fish and frogs, which they pursue through the water with great agility. They live solitary lives, but consort in pairs shortly before mating. Litters of 2 to 3 young are born throughout the year.

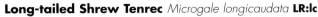

Long-tailed Shrew Tenrec *Microgale longicaudata* **LR:lc**

RANGE	Madagascar
HABITAT	Forest: sea level to montane
SIZE	Body: 2–6 in (5–15 cm) Tail: 3–6½ in (7.5–17 cm)

The shrew tenrec, as its name implies, occupies the ecological niche filled by shrews in other parts of the world. The coat is short, but dense, and quite lacking in the spines that are so common in other members of this family.

Although it climbs well and the distal third of its tail is prehensile, the shrew tenrec seems to feed mostly on grubs, worms and insects on the forest floor.

This species is active at all hours of the day and night, but each individual maintains its own pattern of rest and activity. They do not appear to hibernate. Little is known of the breeding habits, but they are believed to produce litters of 2 to 4.

GOLDEN MOLES AND HEDGEHOGS

CHRYSOCHLORIDAE: GOLDEN MOLE FAMILY

The 18 species of golden moles bear a close resemblance to the true moles, but are, in fact, only distantly related. They have cylindrical bodies, short powerful limbs and no visible tail. Their fur is thick and dense and the metallic lustre it imparts gives the group its name. Golden moles are blind, their eyes being reduced to mere vestiges covered by fused hairy eyelids. The shovellike paws on their forelimbs are used for digging, and the enlarged flattened claws on the "index" and middle digits are employed as cutting edges.

Golden moles are found only in Africa, south of a line linking Cameroon with Tanzania. They occur in all habitats from rugged mountainous zones to sandy plains.

Cape Golden Mole *Chrysochloris asiatica*

RANGE South Africa: W. Cape Province

HABITAT Workable soil up to 9,000 ft (2,800 m)

SIZE Body: 3½–5½ in (9–14 cm)

Tail: absent

The Cape golden mole is a frequent visitor to gardens and farmland in much of southern Africa. It reveals its presence by raised tunnel tracks radiating out from a bush or shed. At night the moles may travel on the surface, and in damp weather they root about for beetles, worms and grubs.

Once a year, in the rainy season, females produce litters of 2 to 4 young. Shortly before the birth the mother makes a round grass-lined nest in a special breeding chamber. The young suckle for almost 3 months until their teeth erupt.

Hottentot Golden Mole *Amblysomus hottentotus*

RANGE South Africa

HABITAT Sand or peat plains

SIZE Body: 3¼–5 in (8.5–13 cm) Tail: absent

The Hottentot golden mole differs from other species in that it has only two claws on each forepaw. When these animals occur in orchards and young plantations, their burrowing may seriously disturb roots and kill the trees, but generally they do more good than harm by eating insects, beetle larvae and other invertebrate pests.

Pairs breed between November and February when rainfall is high. They produce a litter of 2 young.

Giant Golden Mole *Chrysospalax trevelyani* **EN**

RANGE South Africa: E. Cape Province

HABITAT Forest

SIZE Body: 8–9½ in (20–24 cm) Tail: absent

As its name implies, the giant golden mole is the largest of its family and weighs up to 3 lb (1.5 kg). It is a rare species and is now on the brink of extinction.

Giant golden moles hunt above ground for beetles, small lizards, slugs and giant earthworms. When disturbed they dart unerringly toward their burrow entrance and safety, but how they are able to locate it is not known.

During the winter rainy season they are believed to produce a litter of 2 young.

ERINACEIDAE: HEDGEHOG FAMILY

This family contains 20 species of two superficially quite distinct types of animal: the hedgehogs, and the gymnures, or moonrats. Members of the hedgehog subfamily occur extensively across Europe and Asia to western China, and in Africa as far south as Angola. Moonrats live in Indo-China, Malaysia, Borneo, the Philippines and northern Burma. All feed on a varied diet of worms, insects and mollusks, as well as some berries, frogs, lizards and birds.

In the northern part of their range, hedgehogs hibernate during the winter months, but in warmer areas this is not necessary.

Western European Hedgehog *Erinaceus europaeus*

RANGE Britain, east to Scandinavia and Romania; introduced in New Zealand

HABITAT Scrub, forest, cultivated land

SIZE Body: 5½–10½ in (13.5–27 cm) Tail: ½–2 in (1–5 cm)

One of the most familiar small mammals in Europe, the hedgehog gets its name from its piglike habit of rooting around for its invertebrate prey in the hedgerows. It is quite vocal and makes a range of grunting, snuffling noises. The upper part of the head and the back are covered in short, banded spines. If threatened, the hedgehog rolls itself up, and a longitudinal muscle band, running around the edge of the prickly cloak, acts as a drawstring to enclose the creature within its spiked armor. The chest and belly are covered with coarse springy hairs.

Hedgehogs produce 1, sometimes 2, litters of about 5 young each year. The young are weaned at about 5 weeks. In the north of their range, hedgehogs hibernate throughout the winter.

Desert Hedgehog *Paraechinus aethiopicus*

RANGE N. Africa, Middle East to Iraq

HABITAT Arid scrub, desert

SIZE Body: 5½–9 in (14–23 cm) Tail: ½–1½ in (1–4 cm)

The desert hedgehog resembles its slightly larger European cousin, but its coloration is more variable. Generally the spines are sandy-buff with darker tips, but dark and white forms are not uncommon. Desert hedgehogs dig short, simple burrows in which they pass the day. At night, when the air is cool, they emerge to search for invertebrates and the eggs of ground-nesting birds. Scorpions are a preferred food; the hedgehogs nip

off the stings before eating them. In common with most desert mammals, these hedgehogs probably have highly adapted kidneys, enabling them to exist for long periods without water.

In July or August desert hedgehogs breed, producing a litter of about 5 young.

Moonrat *Echinosorex gymnurus*

RANGE Cambodia, east to Burma

HABITAT Forest, mangrove swamps

SIZE Body: 10–17¼ in (26–44 cm) Tail: 8–8¼ in (20–21 cm)

One of the largest insectivores, the moonrat has a long snout, an unkempt appearance and an almost naked, scaly tail. It can defend itself by producing a foul, fetid odor from a pair of anal glands, which repels all but the most persistent predators.

Moonrats live in crevices between tree roots, or in hollow logs. They emerge around dusk to forage for mollusks, insects and worms. Some fruit, and fish and crabs too, may be eaten. Little is known of the moonrats' breeding habits, but they seem to breed throughout the year, producing 2 young at a time.

Mindanao Moonrat *Podogymnura truei* **EN**

RANGE Philippines: Mindanao

HABITAT Upland forest and forest edge, from 5,250 to 7,500 ft (1,600–2,300 m)

SIZE Body: 5–6 in (13–15 cm) Tail: 1½–2¾ in (4–7 cm)

This curious creature is restricted to a small natural range and has never been common. Now, because of logging operations and slash-and-burn agriculture, much of its habitat is being destroyed and its survival is seriously threatened. It has long soft fur and a tail with more hairs than that of *Echinosorex*. It feeds on insects, worms and even carrion, which it finds in grasses and among stands of moss. Nothing is known of the breeding habits of the Mindanao moonrats.

SHREWS

SORICIDAE: SHREW FAMILY

There are more than 280 species of shrew, distributed throughout most of the world, except Australia and New Zealand, the West Indies and most of South America. Shrews are insectivores and most lead inoffensive lives among the debris of the forest floor or on pastureland, consuming many types of invertebrate. Water shrews are known to overpower frogs and small fish, which they kill with venomous bites – the saliva of many shrews contains strong toxins. Carrion may also be included in the shrew's diet.

Shrews are active creatures with high metabolisms. Their hearts may beat more than 1,200 times every minute and, relative to their body size, they have enormous appetites. Even in cold northern regions, they do not hibernate in winter; it would be impossible for them to build up sufficient fat reserves. Although shrews are heavily preyed upon by owls and hawks, acrid-smelling secretions from well-developed flank glands seem to deter most mammalian predators.

Some species of shrew are reported to eat their own feces and perhaps those of other creatures. By doing so, they boost their intake of vitamins B and K and some other nutrients. This habit may be related to the shrews' hyperactive life and enhanced metabolism. Shrews rely heavily on their senses of smell and hearing when hunting – their eyes are tiny and probably of little use.

Masked Shrew *Sorex cinereus*

RANGE N. North America to New Mexico

HABITAT Moist forest

SIZE Body: 1¾–3¾ in (4.5–9.5 cm) Tail: 1–3 in (2.5–8 cm)

The masked shrew is a common species throughout North America, though less abundant in the arid regions to the south. It inhabits the surface layer of forest, living in and around burrows made by itself and other woodland animals. It is active day and night with about seven periods of feeding activity in each 24 hours. Earthworms and snails are preferred foods, but masked shrews eat a wide range of invertebrate prey.

Generally solitary animals, male and female pair only for mating. Several litters of up to 10 young are born during the late spring and summer. The young are weaned after about a month, but the family may remain together for another month – the only time during which these shrews are sociable.

Short-tailed Shrew *Blarina brevicauda*

RANGE E. USA

HABITAT Almost all terrestrial habitats

SIZE Body: 3–4 in (7.5–10.5 cm) Tail: ½–1¼ in (1.5–3 cm)

This abundant and widespread species is unusual in two ways. First, it seems to be partly gregarious since in captivity it seeks out the company of other shrews. Second, it often climbs trees for food – most shrews climb only rarely. In much of the USA, the short-tailed shrew is an important controlling influence on larch sawflies and other destructive forest pests on which it feeds. It builds a grassy nest under a stump or log and produces three or four litters a year of up to 9 young each. The gestation period is 17 to 21 days.

Giant Mexican Shrew *Megasorex gigas*

RANGE W. coastal strip of Mexico

HABITAT Rocky or semidesert, dry forest

SIZE Body: 3–3½ in (8–9 cm) Tail: 1½–2 in (4–5 cm)

The giant Mexican shrew has large prominent ears. In common with most desert mammals, it is active only at night, when it emerges from crevices between boulders or under rocks to search for insects and worms. Although it eats up to three-quarters of its own weight every 24 hours, it seems only to feed at night, unlike other shrews which feed throughout the day. Its breeding habits are not known.

Sri Lankan Long-tailed Shrew *Crocidura miya* **EN**

RANGE Sri Lanka

HABITAT Damp and dry forest, savanna

SIZE Body: 2–2½ in (5–6.5 cm) Tail: 1½–1¾ in (4–4.5 cm)

This shrew, with its long, lightly haired tail, spends much of its life among the debris of the forest floor where damp, cool conditions encourage a rich invertebrate population on which it feeds. It also eats small lizards and young birds on occasion. Strong-smelling scent glands seem to protect the shrew itself from much predation.

The breeding season of the long-tailed shrew lasts from March until November. The female produces about five litters in this time, each of about 6 young. After 8 days, the young leave the nest for the first time, each gripping the tail of the one in front in its mouth as the caravan, led by the mother, goes in search of food. This habit seems to be restricted to this particular genus of shrew.

Pygmy White-toothed Shrew *Suncus etruscus*

RANGE S. Europe, S. Asia, Africa

HABITAT Semiarid grassland, scrub, rocky hillsides

SIZE Body: 1¼–2 in (3.5–5 cm) Tail: 1–1¼ in (2.5–3 cm)

Usually regarded as the world's smallest terrestrial mammal, a fully grown pygmy shrew weighs about ¹⁄₁₄ oz (2 g). How such a tiny mammal can survive is not fully understood, but it must have a constant and reliable source of food, and that is one reason why it is restricted to the warmer parts of the Old World. Its coat is dense to prevent undue heat loss from its tiny body.

Pygmy shrews eat spiders and insects almost as large as themselves, including grasshoppers and cockroaches.

Nothing is known of the breeding habits of pygmy white-toothed shrews, but they remain quite abundant, and it may be that their small size protects them from heavy predation, since they share their habitat with larger, more tempting species.

Mouse Shrew *Myosorex varius*

RANGE South Africa, north to the Limpopo

HABITAT Moist areas, forest, scrub, river banks

SIZE Body: 2¼–4¼ in (6–11 cm) Tail: 1¼–2¼ in (3–5.5 cm)

The mouse shrew is perhaps the most primitive of existing shrews. It has two more teeth in its lower jaw than is normal among other members of the shrew family and thus resembles the extinct early mammals. In other respects, however, it is like most other shrews.

The mouse shrew does not appear to make or use burrows, but instead seeks out holes and hollows for daytime shelter. It makes small nests out of shredded grass for sleeping and for use as nurseries for its young.

Females produce up to 6 litters a year, each of 2 to 4 young.

Armored Shrew *Scutisorex somereni*

RANGE Africa: Uganda, near Kampala

HABITAT Forest

SIZE Body: 4¾–6 in (12–15 cm) Tail: 2¾–3¾ in (7–9.5 cm)

This is one of the most unusual members of the shrew family. The armored shrew has a spine which is fortified and strengthened by a mesh of interlocking bony flanges and rods. Despite this unique skeletal structure, the armored shrew moves much like other shrews, although its predatory behavior is characterized by rather ponderous and apparently well thought-out movements.

There are reports that an armored shrew is able to support the weight of a grown man without being crushed.

Armored shrews appear to eat plant food as well as invertebrates. They are believed to breed throughout the year.

SOLENODONS, MOLES AND FLYING LEMURS

SOLENODONTIDAE: SOLENODON FAMILY

There are 2 species only of solenodons alive today – *Solenodon cubanus* on Cuba and *Solenodon paradoxus* on the neighbouring islands of Haiti and the Dominican Republic. They are rather ungainly, uncoordinated creatures and, although they are about the size of rats, they look more like shrews with their probing snouts. Their eyes are small and rheumy and they are far more nocturnal than the wide-eyed rats.

Solenodons grow and breed slowly and this, combined with the predatory attacks of dogs and cats, means that their survival is now threatened. Conservation areas are being established for these animals, but their future is far from secure.

Cuban Solenodon *Solenodon cubanus* EN

RANGE Cuba

HABITAT Montane forest

SIZE Body: 11–12½ in (28–32 cm) Tail: 6½–10 in (17–25 cm)

Solenodons have a varied diet. At night they search the forest floor litter for insects and other invertebrates, fungi and roots. They climb well and feed on fruits, berries and buds, but have more predatory habits too. With venom from modified salivary glands in the lower jaw, the solenodon can kill lizards, frogs, small birds or even rodents. Solenodons seem not to be immune to the venom of their own kind, and there are records of cage mates dying after fights. They produce litters of 1 to 3 young.

TALPIDAE: MOLE FAMILY

The majority of the 29 species of mole lead an underground life, but 2 species of desman and the star-nosed mole are adapted for an aquatic life. Moles are widespread throughout Europe and Asia, south to the Himalayas, and from southern Canada to northern Mexico. They need habitats with soft soil so that they are able to dig their extensive burrow systems.

All moles have highly modified hands and forearms, which act as pickax and shovel combined. Moles seldom come above ground and their eyes are tiny and covered with hairy skin. Their tactile sense is highly developed, however, and their facial bristles respond to the tiniest vibrations. Moles can move backwards or forwards with equal ease – when reversing, the stumpy tail is held erect and the sensory hairs on it provide warning of any approaching danger.

Pacific Mole *Scapanus orarius*

RANGE North America: British Columbia to Baja California

HABITAT Well-drained deciduous forest

SIZE Body: 4½–7¼ in (11–18.5 cm) Tail: ¾–2¼ in (2–5.5 cm)

The Pacific, or coast, mole and its close relatives, the broad-footed mole and Townsend's mole, all have nostrils which open upward. Their eyes are much more visible than those of other species, but this does not necessarily mean that their sight is better. Like other moles, they live underground and rarely venture up to the surface.

Coast moles feed on earthworms and soil-dwelling larvae and do much good by devouring the larvae of insect pests. Between 2 and 5 young are born in early spring after a 4-week gestation period.

European Mole *Talpa europaea*

RANGE Europe, E. Asia

HABITAT Pasture, forest, scrub

SIZE Body: 3½–6½ in (9–16.5 cm) Tail: 1¼–1½ in (3–4 cm)

The extensive burrow systems in which European moles live are excavated rapidly. A single individual can dig up to 66 ft (20 m) in one day. The moles feed primarily on earthworms, but also eat a wide range of other invertebrates, as well as snakes, lizards, mice and small birds.

In early summer the female produces a litter of up to 7 young, born in a leaf-lined underground nest and weaned at about 3 weeks. Occasionally there is a second litter.

Hairy-tailed Mole *Parascalops breweri*

RANGE S.E. Canada, N.E. USA

HABITAT Well-drained soil in forest or open land

SIZE Body: 4½–5½ in (11.5–14 cm) Tail: ¾–1½ in (2–3.5 cm)

As its name implies, this species is characterized by its almost bushy tail. Otherwise it is similar to other moles in habits and appearance. Hairy-tailed moles dig extensive tunnels at two levels: an upper level just beneath the surface, used in warm weather, and a lower tunnel, used as a winter retreat. The moles mate in early April and litters of 4 or 5 young are born in mid-May. The eastern mole, *Scalopus aquaticus* also a North American species, closely resembles the hairy-tailed, but has a nearly naked tail.

Star-nosed Mole *Condylura cristata*

RANGE S.E. Canada, N.E. USA

HABITAT Any area with damp soil

SIZE Body: 4–5 in (10–12.5 cm) Tail: 2¼–3¼ in (5.5–8 cm)

This species of mole has a fringe of 22 fingerlike tentacles, surrounding the nostrils, which it uses to search for food on the bottoms of ponds and streams. Although star-nosed moles dig and use tunnel systems, they seldom feed within them. They are excellent swimmers and divers and feed largely on aquatic crustaceans, small fish, water insects and other pond life. Their fur is heavy and quite waterproof. The female gives birth to a litter of 2 to 7 young in spring. The young are born with well-developed nostril tentacles.

Russian Desman *Desmana moschata* **VU**

RANGE E. Europe to C. W. Asia

HABITAT Pools and streams in densely vegetated areas

SIZE Body: 7–8½ in (18–21.5 cm) Tail: 6¾–8½ in (17–21.5 cm)

The largest member of the mole family, the desman has forsaken the underground for the aquatic life, although it does excavate short burrows as bank side residences. When swimming, the desman's flattened tail acts as a rudder and propellor. Its webbed feet, with their fringing hairs, make effective paddles. Desmans feed on a variety of aquatic life from fish and amphibians to insects, crustaceans and mollusks. Now much reduced in numbers, the desman is the subject of intensive conservation measures and there are projects to reintroduce the species in parts of its former range.

ORDER DERMOPTERA

CYNOCEPHALIDAE: FLYING LEMUR FAMILY

There are only 2 species of flying lemur or colugo. They were once classified as insectivores but are now given their own order.

Philippine Flying Lemur/Colugo *Cynocephalus volans* **VU**

RANGE Philippines

HABITAT Forest

SIZE Body: 15–16½ in (38–42 cm) Tail: 8¾–10½ in (22–27 cm)

This lemur "flies" with the aid of a gliding membrane (patagium) which stretches from the neck to the wrists and ankles and to the tip of the tail. It can glide through the trees for up to 450 ft (135 m). Almost helpless on the ground, it is an agile climber. It feeds on shoots, buds, fruit and flowers from a range of forest trees. Its main predator is the Philippine eagle. Flying lemurs mate in February, and after 2 months the female gives birth to a single young which she carries with her until it grows too heavy.

TREE SHREWS

ORDER SCANDENTIA

TUPAIIDAE Tree Shrew Family

There is a single family in the order Scandentia, containing approximately 16 species of tree shrew, which live in the forests of eastern Asia, including Borneo and the Philippines. These biologically interesting, but visually undistinguished, mammals have affinities with the order Insectivora, because of their shrewlike appearance, and with the order Primates because of their complex, convoluted brains. They have been included in both of these orders. Most modern zoologists agree, however, that tree shrews should be placed in a distinct order so that their uniqueness is emphasized, rather than hidden in a large, diverse order. Until much more is known of their biology, tree shrews will remain an enigma.

Tree shrews resemble slim, long-nosed squirrels in general appearance, and their ears are squirrellike in shape and relative size. Their feet are modified for an arboreal existence, having naked soles equipped with knobbly pads, which provide tree shrews with a superb ability to cling to branches. This ability is enhanced by the presence of long flexible digits, with sharp, curved claws. The 16 species range from 4 to 8½ in (10 to 22 cm) in body length, with tails of 3½ to 8¾ in (9 to 22.5 cm). They run rapidly through the forest canopy, and most are active in the daytime, searching for insects and fruit to consume. They drink frequently and are also fond of bathing.

Despite the name, tree shrews are not exclusively arboreal, and many species spend a good deal of time on the ground. Their senses of smell, sight and hearing are good. Tree shrews usually live in pairs, and males, particularly, are aggressive toward one another. The borders of a pair's territory are marked with urine and glandular secretions.

There are between 1 and 4 young in a litter, but most usually only 1 or 2. The babies are born in a separate nest separate from the adults' normal sleeping quarters. The female visits her young only once a day or even every other day. The young are able to take sufficient milk in a short period to sustain them during her absences. Males and females look similar, but males are usually larger.

Tree shrews bear a close resemblance to fossils of the earliest mammals, so it may be assumed that the first true mammals looked, and possibly behaved, like these animals.

Common Tree Shrew *Tupaia glis*

RANGE S. and S.E. Asia: India to Vietnam and Malaysia, S. China, Indonesia

HABITAT Rain forest, woodland, bamboo scrub

SIZE Body: 5½–9 in (14–23 cm) Tail: 4¾–8¼ in (12–21 cm)

The common tree shrew is a squirrellike creature, with a long, bushy tail. It is active and lively and climbs with great agility in the trees, though it also spends a great proportion of its time on the ground feeding. Its diet is varied and includes insects (particularly ants), spiders, seeds, buds and probably also small birds and mice. This shrew normally lives alone or with a mate.

Breeding seems to occur at any time of year, and a rough nest is made in a hole in a fallen tree or among tree roots. In Malaysia, where breeding of this species has been most closely observed, females produce litters of 1 to 3 young after a gestation of 46 to 50 days. The newborn young are naked, with closed eyes, but are ready to leave the nest about 33 days after birth.

Mountain Tree Shrew *Tupaia montana* **VU**

RANGE Borneo

HABITAT Montane forest

SIZE Body: 4¼–6 in (11–15 cm) Tail: 4–6 in (10–15 cm)

The mountain tree shrew has a long, bushy tail and a slender, pointed snout. Although it is agile in trees, it spends much of its time on the ground, searching for food. Insects, fruit, seeds and leaves are all included in its diet, and it will sit back on its

haunches to eat, holding the food in both its forepaws. This species is thought to be slightly more social than other shrews and may live in small groups.

Breeding takes place at any time during the year. Litters, normally of 2 young, are born after a gestation period of between 49 and 51 days.

Philippine Tree Shrew *Urogale everetti* **VU**

RANGE Philippines: Mindanao

HABITAT Rain forest, montane forest

SIZE Body: 6¾–7¾ in (17–20 cm) Tail: 4¼–6¾ in (11–17 cm)

A particularly elongate snout and a rounded, even-haired tail characterize the Philippine tree shrew. Its fur is brownish, but with orange or yellow underparts. This shrew is mainly active during the day. It climbs well and runs fast on the ground.

Its diet is varied and includes insects, lizards, young birds and birds' eggs and fruit.

In the wild Philippine tree shrews are thought to nest on the ground or on cliffs. Their breeding habits have been observed in captivity, where females have produced 1 or 2 young after a gestation period of 54 to 56 days.

Madras Tree Shrew *Anathana elliotti* **VU**

RANGE C. and S. India

HABITAT Rain forest, thorny woodland

SIZE Body: 6¼–7 in (16–18 cm)

Tail: 6¼–7½ in (16–19 cm)

The Madras tree shrew is a squirrellike creature, which is similar in most aspects to the tree shrews of the *Tupaia* genus. It is identified, however, by its larger ears, heavier snout and the pale stripe on each shoulder.

The Madras tree shrew is active during the day, moving in trees and on the ground, searching for insects and probably fruit to eat. Little is known about its breeding habits, but they are probably similar to those of the *Tupaia* tree shrews.

Feather-tailed Tree Shrew *Ptilocercus lowi*

RANGE Malaysia, Sumatra, Borneo

HABITAT Rain forest

SIZE Body: 4¾–5½ in (12–14 cm) Tail: 6¼–7 in (16–18 cm)

This tree shrew is easily identified by its unusual tail, which is naked for much of its length, but has tufts of hair on each side of the terminal portion, making it resemble a feather. Its ears, which are large and membranous, stand away from the head. Its hands and feet are larger, relative to body size, than those of other tree shrews. The feather-tailed tree shrew is thought to be nocturnal. It spends much of its life in trees and is a good climber, using its tail for balance and support and spreading its toes and fingers wide for grip. Insects, fruit and some lizards are its main foods.

Bornean Smooth–tailed Tree Shrew *Dendrogale melanura* **VU**

RANGE Borneo

HABITAT Montane forest above 3,000 ft (900 m)

SIZE Body: 4¼–6 in (11–15 cm)

Tail: 3½–5½ in (9–14 cm)

Feather-tailed tree shrews nest in holes in trees or branches, well off the ground, but their breeding habits are not known. They generally live in pairs.

This species is the smallest of the tree shrews. It is distinguished by its smooth, short-haired tail, which ends in a point. Its body fur, too, is short and close with a dark reddish-brown on the back and lighter orange-buff on the underparts. More arboreal than the other members of its family, it finds much of its insect food on the lower branches of trees. Its breeding habits are not known.

MOUSE–LEMURS, LEMURS AND AYE-AYE

ORDER PRIMATES

There are about 233 species of primate divided into two main groups. The Strepsirhini includes more primitive primates, such as lemurs, the aye-aye, and lorises and tarsiers. The Haplorhini includes the tarsiers, monkeys, and apes.

CHEIROGALEIDAE: Mouse-lemur Family

The 7 species of mouse-lemur and dwarf-lemur occur in forest areas throughout the island of Madagascar and are among the smallest species of the primate order.

Russet Mouse-lemur *Microcebus rufus*

RANGE	E. Madagascar
HABITAT	Forest
SIZE	Body: 5–6 in (12.5–15 cm)
	Tail: 5–6 in (12.5–15 cm)

Mainly nocturnal in its habits, this tiny primate moves swiftly and nimbly on fine branches amid dense foliage. It uses its long tail for balance and will leap across gaps between trees. It also comes down to the ground to forage in leaf litter for beetles. Insects and small vertebrates are its main foods, supplemented by fruit and buds. Though they normally move and hunt alone, russet mouse-lemurs often sleep in small groups in nests made in hollow trees or constructed from leaves.

LEMURIDAE: Lemur Family

There are about 10 species of lemur, all found in Madagascar and the nearby Comoro Islands. Most live in wooded areas and are agile tree-climbers.

Ring-tailed Lemur *Lemur catta* **VU**

RANGE	S. Madagascar
HABITAT	Dry, rocky country with some trees
SIZE	Body: 17¾ in (45 cm) Tail: 21½ in (55 cm)

The ring-tailed lemur has a pointed muzzle, large eyes and triangular ears. Its fur is thick and soft, and its

bushy, distinctively ringed tail accounts for more than half its total length. Both sexes have special scent glands on the lower forelimbs. Males have larger glands than females, with a horny spur near each and scent glands on the upper arms, under the chin and by the penis. Females have scent glands in the genital region. The lemurs use the secretions in these glands to mark territory boundaries, but will also mark when excited or disturbed. Troops of between 20 and 40 lemurs occupy a territory. Females and young form the core. Females are dominant. Males move between troops.

Ring-tailed lemurs are active during the day, sometimes climbing up trees, but also spending much time on the ground on all fours, with tail erect. They feed on fruit, leaves, bark, grass and resin, which they chisel from the trees with their lower incisors.

After a gestation of about 136 days females usually produce 1 young, though sometimes there are litters of 2 or 3. Babies are born well haired with open eyes and are independent at 6 months.

Ruffed Lemur

Varecia variegata **EN**

RANGE	N.E. and E. Madagascar
HABITAT	Rain forest
SIZE	Body: 23½ in (60 cm)
	Tail: 23½ in (60 cm)

Distinguished by its long ruff, this lemur has white and black, brown or rufous fur. The ruffed lemur is a nimble climber. It is most active at dusk and during the first part of the night when it forages in the trees for fruit, leaves and bark. It rarely descends to the ground.

In November, after a gestation period of between 99 and 102 days the female ruffed lemur produces between 1 and 3 young. She gives birth in a nest in a hole in a tree or on a forked branch, which she lines with her own fur.

INDRIDAE: INDRI, AVAHI AND SIFAKA FAMILY

The 5 species in this family occur in the scrub country and forests of Madagascar. In all of these lemurs the snout is shortened and bare of fur giving them a resemblance to monkeys.

Verreaux's Sifaka

Propithecus verreauxi **VU**

RANGE W. and S. Madagascar

HABITAT Dry and rain forest

SIZE Body: 17¾ in (45 cm)
Tail: 21½ in (55 cm)

This large, long-limbed sifaka has a naked black face, large eyes, and ears that are nearly concealed by its fur. Coloration is highly variable, ranging from yellowish-white to black or a reddish-brown.

Troops of up to 10 animals occupy a well-defined territory, the boundaries of which are marked with urine or with secretions from the male's throat gland. They feed in the morning and afternoon on leaves, buds and fruit and are relaxed in their movements, spending much of the day resting and sun-bathing. Sifakas are primarily arboreal but sometimes come down to the ground.

Young are born from the end of June to August after a gestation of about 130 days. Females usually produce 1 young, which is suckled for about 6 months.

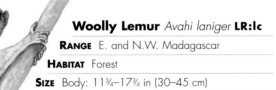

Woolly Lemur *Avahi laniger* **LR:lc**

RANGE E. and N.W. Madagascar

HABITAT Forest

SIZE Body: 11¾–17¾ in (30–45 cm)
Tail: 13–15¾ in (33–40 cm)

A nocturnal animal, the long-limbed woolly lemur sleeps up in the trees by day. It is active at night, when it searches for fruit, leaves and buds to eat. It is an agile climber and only occasionally descends to the ground, where it moves in an upright position.

The young are usually born in late August or September after a gestation period of about 150 days. The female normally produces a single young, which she suckles for about 6 months.

Indri *Indri indri* **EN**

RANGE N.E. Madagascar

HABITAT Forest up to 6,000 ft (1,800 m)

SIZE Body: 24–28 in (61–71 cm)
Tail: 1¼–2¼ in (3–6 cm)

The largest of the lemurs, the indri is easily identified by its stumpy tail. It has a longer muzzle than the sifakas and a naked black face. Indris live in family groups and are active during the day at all levels of the forest, looking for leaves, shoots and fruit.

Mating takes place in January or February, and the females give birth to 1 young after a gestation period of between 4½ and 5½ months.

DAUBENTONIIDAE: AYE-AYE FAMILY

The single species of aye-aye is a nocturnal, arboreal animal, found in the dense forests of Madagascar.

Aye-aye *Daubentonia madagascariensis* **EN**

RANGE Formerly N.E. Madagascar, now only in nature reserves

HABITAT Rain forest

SIZE Body: 14½–17½ in (36–44 cm) Tail: 19¾–23½ in (50–60 cm)

Well adapted for life in the trees, the extraordinary aye-aye has specialized ears, teeth and hands. It emerges from its nest at night to search for food, mainly insect larvae, plant shoots, fruit and eggs. All of its digits are long and slender, but the third is particularly elongate. The aye-aye uses this finger to tap on tree trunks to locate wood-boring insects. It listens for movement with its large, sensitive ears, and probes with its finger to winkle out the prey. Sometimes it tears open the wood with its powerful teeth. It also uses its teeth to open eggs or coconuts.

Every 2 or 3 years, females produce a single young, which is suckled for over a year.

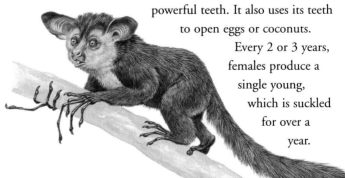

LORISES, GALAGOS AND TARSIERS

LORIDAE: LORIS FAMILY

The 5 species in this primate family are found in Africa, India, Southeast Asia. It includes the lorises, potto and angwantibo, which have short tails or no tails at all and are slow and deliberate in their movements.

Slender Loris *Loris tardigradus* **VU**

RANGE Sri Lanka, S. India

HABITAT Rain forest, open woodland, swamp forest

SIZE Body 7–10¼ in (18–26 cm)

Tail: absent or vestigial

The slender loris spends most of its life in trees, where it moves slowly and deliberately on its long, thin limbs. It has a strong grip with its efficient grasping hands, and its thumbs and great toes are opposable. A nocturnal animal, it spends the day sleeping up in the trees, its body rolled up in a ball. Toward evening, it becomes active and hunts for insects – particularly grasshoppers – lizards, small birds and their eggs, as well as some shoots and leaves. It approaches prey stealthily, with its usual deliberate movements, and then quickly grabs it with both hands.

In India, the slender loris is known to breed twice a year, births occurring most often in May and December. Usually 1 young (but sometimes 2) is born, which makes its own way to the mother's teats, clinging to her fur.

Slow Loris *Nycticebus coucang*

RANGE S. and S.E. Asia E. India to Malaysia; Sumatra, Java, Borneo, Philippines

HABITAT Dense rain forest

SIZE Body: 10¼–15 in (26–38 cm) Tail: vestigial

A plumper, shorter-limbed animal than its relative the slender loris, the slow loris is, however, similar in its habits. It spends the day sleeping up in a tree, its body rolled into a tight ball. At night, it feeds in the trees on insects, birds' eggs, small birds and shoots and fruit. It seldom comes down to the ground. A slow but accomplished climber, its hands and feet are strong and capable of grasping so tightly that it can hang by its feet alone. The thumb and great toe are opposable to the digits.

Breeding takes place at any time of year, and 1 young (sometimes 2) is born after a gestation period of 193 days. Slow lorises are thought to live in family groups.

Potto *Perodicticus potto*

RANGE W., C. and E. Africa

HABITAT Forest, forest edge

SIZE Body: 11¾–15¾ in (30–40 cm)

Tail: 2–4 in (5–10 cm)

A thickset animal with dense fur, the potto has strong limbs and grasping feet and hands; the great toe and thumb are opposable. At the back of its neck are four horny spines, projections of the vertebrae that pierce the thin skin. The potto can quickly seize insect prey with its hands; snails, fruit and leaves are also eaten.

The female gives birth to 1 young a year, after a gestation of 6 to 6½ months. Although weaned at 2 or 3 months, the young may stay with its mother for up to a year.

Angwantibo

Arctocebus calabarensis **LR:nt**

RANGE W. Africa Nigeria, Cameroon, south to Congo River

HABITAT Dense rain forest

SIZE Body: 9¾–15¾ in (25–40 cm)

Tail: about ½ in (1.25 cm)

Also known as the golden potto because of the sheen to its fur, the arboreal angwantibo has strong hands and feet, adapted for grasping branches. Its first finger is a mere stump, and the second toe is much reduced. A skilled, but slow, climber, the angwantibo is active at night, when it feeds mostly on insects, especially caterpillars, and also on snails, lizards and fruit. Outside the breeding season, it is usually solitary.

Females give birth to 1 young after a gestation of 131 to 136 days. Offspring are weaned at 4 months and fully grown at 7.

GALAGONIDAE: GALAGO FAMILY.

The 9 species of galagos, or bushbabies are found only in Africa. All species are arboreal. They have long limbs and tails and are excellent leapers.

Greater Bushbaby
Otolemur crassicaudatus

RANGE Africa: Kenya, south to South Africa: Natal

HABITAT Forest, wooded savanna, bushveld, plantations

SIZE Body: 10½–18½ in (27–47 cm)
Tail: 13–20½ in (33–52 cm)

The greater bushbaby is a strongly built animal, with a pointed muzzle and large eyes. Its hands and feet are adapted for grasping, with opposable thumbs and great toes. Much of the bushbaby's life is spent in the trees, where it is active at night and feeds on insects, reptiles, birds and birds' eggs and plant material. It makes a rapid pounce to seize prey and kills it with a bite. It has a call like the cry of a child (hence the name bushbaby) made most frequently in the breeding season.

The female is territorial. She gives birth to a litter of 1 to 3 young between May and October, after a gestation of 126 to 136 days. Males leave the mother's territory following puberty, but young females maintain their social relationship with the mother.

Lesser Bushbaby
Galago senegalensis

RANGE Africa: Senegal to Somalia and Tanzania

HABITAT Savanna, bush, woodland

SIZE Body: 5½–8¼ in (14–21 cm)
Tail: 7¾–11¾ in (20–30 cm)

More active and lively than its relative the greater bushbaby, this species moves with great agility in the trees and hops and leaps with ease. Like all its family, it sleeps up in the trees during the day and hunts for food at night. Spiders, scorpions, insects, young birds, lizards, fruit, seeds and nectar are all included in its diet.

The lesser bushbaby lives in a family group, the members of which sleep together but disperse on waking.

Breeding habits vary slightly in different areas of the range. In regions where there are two rainy seasons, females have two litters a year, each usually of only 1 offspring. In areas where there is only one rainy season, females produce one litter, often, but not always, of twins. The gestation period varies between 128 and 146 days, and the young are fully developed at approximately 4 months.

TARSIIDAE: TARSIER FAMILY

The 4 species in this family occur in the Philippines and Indonesia. These little prosimian primates are primarily nocturnal and arboreal and climb and jump with great agility. They are better adapted to leaping than any other primates, with their elongate hind legs and feet (which are as long as the head and body combined) and grasping fingers. Their long tails are naked. The tarsiers' large, forward pointing eyes equip it well for night time hunting.

Western Tarsier
Tarsius bancanus

RANGE Sumatra, Borneo

HABITAT Secondary forest, scrub

SIZE Body: 3¼–6¼ in (8.5–16 cm)
Tail: 5¼–10½ in (13.5–27 cm)

The western tarsier, like its two relatives, is identified by its long, naked tail and extremely large, round eyes. Its forelimbs are short and its hind limbs are long because of the adaptation of the tarsus, or ankle bones. This enables the tarsier to leap. The specialized tarsus is of course, the origin of both the common and scientific names.

A nocturnal, mainly arboreal animal, the tarsier sleeps during the day, clinging to a branch with its tail. At dusk, it wakes to prey on insects, its main food, which it catches by making a swift pounce and seizing the insect in its hands.

Courtship is highly active, involving much chasing and jumping in the trees. Breeding occurs at any time of year, and females give birth to 1 young after a gestation of about 6 months. The young tarsier is born well furred, with its eyes open, and is capable of climbing and hopping almost immediately. It becomes sexually mature at about 1 year. Pairs tend to occupy a territory with their one offspring and mark the boundary of their territory with urine.

MARMOSETS AND TAMARINS

CALLITRICHIDAE: MARMOSET AND TAMARIN FAMILY

Marmosets and tamarins make up 1 of the 2 families of primates that occur in the New World. Together with the monkeys, family Cebidae, they are known as the flat-nosed, or platyrrhine, monkeys. There are about 20 species of marmoset and tamarin, but more may sometimes be listed, depending on whether some variations are regarded as subspecies or species in their own right. Apart from the mouse-lemurs, marmosets are the smallest primates, varying from mouse-size to squirrel-size. Their fur is soft, often silky, and many have tufts or ruffs of fur on their heads. Their tails are furry and are not prehensile.

Active in the daytime, marmosets and tamarins are primarily tree-dwelling but do not have grasping hands or opposable thumbs like most primates. Neither do they swing from branch to branch, but they are rapid and agile in their movements and bound swiftly through the trees in a similar manner to squirrels. Their diet is varied, including both plant and animal material.

At night, marmosets sleep curled up in holes in trees. They are social animals and live in small family groups. The usual number of young is 2, and the male assists his mate by carrying one of the twins on his back. Often extremely vocal, marmosets make a variety of high-pitched cries.

Goeldi's Marmoset
Callimico goeldii **VU**

RANGE Upper Amazon basin
HABITAT Scrub, forest
SIZE Body: 7–8½ in (18–21.5 cm) Tail: 9¾–12½ in (25–32 cm)

Few Goeldi's marmosets have been seen or captured, and details of their habits are not well known. This marmoset is identified by the long mane around its head and shoulders and by the long hairs on its rump. It forages at all levels of the trees and bushes, searching for plant matter, such as berries, and for insects and small vertebrates. An agile animal, it walks and runs well and leaps expertly from branch to branch. It often goes down to the ground and will seek refuge on the ground when alarmed by a predator such as a bird of prey.

Strong, long-lasting pair bonds exist between males and females, and Goeldi's marmosets usually live in family groups of parents and offspring. The female bears a single young as a rule, after a gestation of 150 days. These marmosets are highly vocal and communicate with a variety of trills and whistles.

The exact state of the population of this species of marmoset is uncertain, but it is known to be rare and to have a patchy, localized distribution. In recent years it has suffered badly from the destruction of large areas of forest and from illegal trapping. More information is needed on these marmosets in order to set up suitable reserves and to ensure the survival of the species.

Pygmy Marmoset *Cebuella pygmaea*

RANGE Upper Amazon basin
HABITAT Tropical forest
SIZE Body: 5½–6¼ in (14–16 cm) Tail: 6–7¾ in (15–20 cm)

This is the smallest marmoset and one of the smallest primates. The pygmy marmoset is active in the daytime, but may rest at noon. It is particularly vulnerable to attack by large birds of prey because of its size, so it tries to keep out of sight and to avoid danger. It moves either extremely slowly or in short dashes, punctuated by moments of frozen immobility. Its cryptic coloration also helps it to hide from predators.

The pygmy marmoset is primarily a tree-dweller and sleeps in holes in trees. However, it does come down to the ground occasionally in order to feed or to move from one tree to another. It mainly eats fruit, insects, small birds and birds' eggs. It is also thought to feed on sap from trees, which it obtains by gnawing a hole in the bark.

Pygmy marmosets live in troops of 5 to 10 individuals in which the females are dominant.

Silvery Marmoset
Callithrix argentata

RANGE Brazil, Bolivia

HABITAT Forest, tall grass

SIZE Body: 6–11¾ in (15–30 cm)
Tail: 7–15¾ in (18–40 cm)

This marmoset can be recognized by its silky, silvery white body fur. It has no hair on its face and ears, which are reddish in color. There is often some gray on its back, and its tail is black.

With quick, jerky movements, the silvery marmoset runs and hops through the trees and bushes in its habitat, looking for food such as fruit, leaves, tree exudates, insects, spiders, small birds and birds' eggs. It usually moves in groups of 2 to 5.

Like most marmosets, it has a range of expressions, including facial grimaces and raising of the eyebrows, which are used to threaten rivals or enemies.

The female gives birth to 1 or 2 young, occasionally 3, after a gestation of 140 to 150 days. The male assists at the birth and is largely responsible for the care of the young.

Golden Lion Tamarin
Leontopithecus rosalia **CR**

RANGE S.E. Brazil

HABITAT Coastal forest

SIZE Body: 7½–8½ in (19–22 cm)
Tail: 10¼–13¼ in (26–34 cm)

A beautiful animal, this tamarin has a silky golden mane covering its head and shoulders and concealing its ears.

In common with the other members of its family, it leaps from branch to branch with great agility as it searches for fruit, insects, lizards, small birds and birds' eggs to eat. It lives in small groups and is highly vocal.

The female gives birth to 1 or 2 young, rarely 3, after a gestation of 132 to 134 days. The father assists in the care of the young, giving them to the mother at feeding time and by later preparing their first solid food by squashing and softening it in his fingers.

Habitat destruction has severely threatened this species.

Emperor Tamarin *Saguinus imperator*

RANGE W. Brazil, E. Peru, N. Bolivia

HABITAT Lowland forest

SIZE Body: 7–8¼ in (18–21 cm)
Tail: 9¾–12½ in (25–32 cm)

Easily identified by its flowing white mustache, the emperor tamarin is one of 12 species included in this genus. It is an active, agile animal, moving with quick, jerky movements in the shrubs and trees as it searches for fruit, tender vegetation insects, spiders, small vertebrate animals and birds' eggs. It lives in small groups and makes a great variety of shrill sounds.

The female produces twin offspring after a gestation of about 5 months. The father assists at the birth and cleans the newly born young. Like many other marmosets, he also helps at feeding time by handing the baby to the mother.

Black and Red Tamarin
Saguinus nigricollis

RANGE S. Colombia to adjacent areas of Ecuador and Brazil

HABITAT Primary and secondary forest

SIZE Body: 6–11 in (15–28 cm) Tail: 10½–16½ in (27–42 cm)

This tamarin is typical of its genus, with its unspecialized, short, broad hands, equipped with claws, and a small body. The hairs around its mouth are white, but the skin under the mustache is pigmented, as are the genitalia.

Family groups, consisting of a male, a female and 1 or 2 young, live in a defined territory – the female marks branches on the boundaries of the territory with secretions of her anal glands and urine. Insects, leaves and fruit are the main foods of these tamarins.

The female gives birth to 2 young after a gestation of 140 to 150 days.

NEW WORLD MONKEYS

CEBIDAE: NEW WORLD MONKEYS

Most of the New World monkeys of the family Cebidae are much larger in size than any of the marmosets and tamarins – the other group of flat-nosed (platyrrhine) American monkeys. There are about 43 species, including capuchins, howler monkeys, woolly monkeys, sakis and uakaris. Typically these monkeys have long, hairy tails, which in some species are prehensile and of great importance in arboreal locomotion.

With a few exceptions, cebid monkeys conform to the flat-nosed appearance so characteristic of New World monkeys. The nostrils are wide apart and open to the sides; they are a major distinguishing feature between New and Old World monkeys which have nostrils placed close together and opening forward. The long, thin fingers of the hands are useful manipulative organs and bear strong nails, but the thumbs are not opposable. The big toe, however, is large and can be opposed against the other toes for gripping branches. Thus equipped, cebid monkeys are excellent runners and leapers in wooded habitats in Central and South America, from Mexico in the north to Argentina in the south. They are gregarious and live in family-based groups with much vocal and visual communication. Diet is largely vegetarian.

Douroucouli/Night Monkey

Aotus trivirgatus

RANGE Panama to Paraguay (patchy distribution)

HABITAT Forest

SIZE Body: 9½–14½ in (24–37 cm)
Tail: 12¼–15¾ in (31–40 cm)

The douroucouli has a heavily furred body and tail and is characterized by its large eyes and round head. It is usually grayish in colour, with dark markings on the head, and has an inflatable sac under the chin that amplifies its calls. A nocturnal monkey, it can see very well at night and moves with agility in the trees, leaping and jumping with ease. It rarely descends to the ground.

Fruit, leaves, insects and spiders are its main foods, but it also takes some small mammals and birds. Douroucoulis usually live in pairs, accompanied by their offspring. Several families may group together during the day to sleep in a hollow tree or in a nest among foliage. The female gives birth to a single young, which clings to its mother for the first few weeks of life before it starts to climb alone.

Monk Saki *Pithecia monachus*

RANGE Upper Amazon basin

HABITAT Forest

SIZE Body: 13¾–18¾ in (35–48 cm) Tail: 12¼–20 in (31–51 cm)

The monk saki has long, shaggy hair framing its face and on its neck, and a thick, bushy tail. A shy wary animal, it is totally arboreal, living high in the trees and sometimes descending to lower levels, but not to the ground. It generally moves on all fours, but may sometimes walk upright on a large branch and will leap across gaps. During the day, it moves in pairs or small family groups, feeding on fruit, berries, honey, some leaves, small mammals, such as mice and bats, and birds.

The female gives birth to 1 young.

Black-bearded Saki

Chiropotes satanas

RANGE N. South America to Brazil

HABITAT Forest

SIZE Body: 14¼–20½ in (36–52 cm) Tail: 14¼–19¾ in (36–50 cm)

The black-bearded saki is identified by its prominent beard and the long black hair on its head, the rest of the coat is reddish chestnut or blackish-brown. The tail is thick and heavily furred. Little is known of the habits of this monkey in the wild other than that it lives in large trees and feeds mainly on fruit. It requires many square kilometres of undisturbed habitat for successful breeding, however, and the widespread felling of primary forest poses a threat to its long-term survival.

White-fronted Capuchin *Cebus albifrons*

RANGE Parts of Colombia, Venezuela, upper Amazon area; Trinidad

HABITAT Forest

SIZE Body: 11¾–15 in (30–38 cm) Tail: 15–19¾ in (38–50 cm)

A lively, intelligent monkey like all the capuchins, this species is slender and long-limbed, with a partially prehensile tail. There is considerable variation in color over the range, but these capuchins are usually different shades of brown. Alert and fast-moving, they are inquiring by nature, have great manual dexterity and investigate all sorts of plants and fruit in the hope that they may be edible. Shoots, fruit, insects, young birds and birds' eggs are all part of their diet. Primarily arboreal, these capuchins do sometimes descend to the ground and may venture across open country. They are gregarious and live in territories in groups of 20 or 30. The female usually gives birth to 1 young, although twins have been known. The offspring is suckled for several months and is carried around by both parents.

Dusky Titi *Callicebus moloch*

RANGE Colombia to Bolivia

HABITAT Forest, thickets

SIZE Body: 11–15¼ in (28–39 cm) Tail: 13–19¼ in (33–49 cm)

An inhabitant of densely vegetated areas, the dusky titi often occurs in damp, waterlogged forest. It can move quite fast if necessary, but rarely does so. It generally stays within a fairly small area, feeding on fruit, insects, spiders, small birds and birds' eggs. Active in the daytime, it moves in pairs or family groups, which communicate by means of a wide repertoire of sounds. Dusky titis have rounded heads and thick, soft coats

and frequently adopt a characteristic posture, with the body hunched, limbs close together and tail hanging down.

The female gives birth to 1 young.

Squirrel Monkey *Saimiri sciureus*

RANGE Colombia to Amazon basin

HABITAT Forest, cultivated land

SIZE Body: 10¼–14¼ in (26–36 cm) Tail: 13¾–16½ in (35–42 cm)

The squirrel monkey is slender, with a long, mobile tail. It has a short, brightly coloured coat. It is highly active and lively, feeding during the day on fruit, nuts, insects, spiders, young birds and eggs, and it occasionally comes to the ground to feed. Squirrel monkeys sometimes raid fruit plantations. They are social and live in bands of 12 to 30 or more.

The female gives birth to 1 young after a gestation of 24 to 26 weeks. The newborn infant is able to climb soon after birth and receives little attention from its parents.

Bald Uakari *Cacajao calvus* **VU**

RANGE W. Brazil

HABITAT Forest

SIZE Body: 20–22½ in (51–57 cm) Tail: 6–6¼ in (15–16 cm)

The distinctive bald uakari has a naked face, long, shaggy hair and a beard. It is normally white but looks reddish in the sunlight. Its tail is fairly short – the 3 species of uakari are the only New World monkeys to have short tails. Extremely agile on all fours, this uakari rarely leaps, since it does not have a long, counterbalancing tail. It frequents the tree-tops, feeding largely on fruit, but also on leaves, insects, small mammals and birds. It seldom descends to the ground. Bald uakaris live in small troops of several adult males, females and young of different ages. They are active in the daytime.

NEW WORLD MONKEYS CONTINUED

three. This arrangement does, however, make delicate manipulation of food items difficult. Red howlers leap well and use their prehensile tails for support. They sometimes go down to the ground and will even cross open land and they are good swimmers. Leaves and some fruit are the red howlers' staple diet. At night, these monkeys sleep in the trees on branches.

Breeding appears to occur at any time of year, and the female gives birth to 1 young after an average gestation of 20 weeks. The young howler clings to its mother's fur at first and later rides on her back. It is suckled for 18 months to 2 years.

Red Howler

Alouatta seniculus

RANGE Colombia to mouth of Amazon River, south to Bolivia

HABITAT Forest, mangroves

SIZE Body: 31½–35½ in (80–90 cm) Tail: 31½–35½ in (80–90 cm)

One of the largest New World monkeys, the red howler has reddish-brown fur and a sturdy body and legs. Its tail is prehensile, with an extremely sensitive naked area on the underside near the tip. All male howlers are renowned for the incredibly loud calls produced by their specialized larynxes, and this apparatus is most developed in the red howler. The chief adaptation of the larynx is the greatly expanded hyoid bone surrounding it that makes a resonating chamber for the sound. The jaw is expanded and deepened to accommodate the bulbous larynx and sports a thick beard. The male red howler occupies a territory and leads a troop of, usually, 6 to 8 animals. In order to defend his territory, he shouts for long periods at rival groups to signal his possession. Most shouting is done in the early morning and late afternoon, but red howlers may be heard at any time of day – from over 1¾ miles (3 km) away.

Red howlers live and move adeptly in the trees, although they frequent large branches because of their sturdy build. Their digits are adapted to facilitate grasping branches. The first two fingers are separated and opposable to the other

Black Howler

Alouatta caraya

RANGE S. Brazil to N. Argentina

HABITAT Forest

SIZE Body: 31½–35½ in (80–90 cm) Tail: 31½–35½ in (80–90 cm)

Only male black howlers are black; females are brown. They live in troops, probably containing more than 1 male, and occupy territories, which they defend by their powerful shouts. The bulbous larynx, concealed under the beard, amplifies the shouts. Black howlers tend to be quieter and have smaller territories than red howlers.

This strongly built monkey has powerful limbs and a prehensile tail. It lives in the trees and eats leaves and fruit. The female gives birth to 1 young after a gestation of about 20 weeks. The offspring stays with her for up to 2 years.

Black Spider Monkey

Ateles paniscus **LR:lc**

RANGE N. South America to Brazil and Bolivia

HABITAT Forest

SIZE Body: 15¾–23½ in (40–60 cm) Tail: 23½–31½ in (60–80 cm)

Only surpassed by the gibbons for grace and agility in the trees, the black spider monkey, with its extremely long limbs and tail, is the most adept and acrobatic of all New World monkeys. This species is light in build, with a small head. The spider monkey has the most highly developed prehensile tail of all mammals and uses it as a fifth limb to grasp branches or food items as it moves through the trees. The monkey's whole weight can be supported by the tail, and when hanging by the tail with the long arms outstretched it has an amazing reach. Part of the underside of the tail nearest the tip is naked and patterned with fine grooves, resembling human fingerprint patterns. These increase friction and thus aid grip.

Spider monkeys frequently swing through the trees, using their hands like hooks to hang on to the branches. The hands are accordingly modified, with long, curved digits and only vestigial thumbs. While this structure makes the hands ideal for swinging in trees, it impedes delicate manipulation of food, but the monkey often uses its highly sensitive tail in order to gather food and to hold items, such as fruit, while it takes off the skin with its teeth.

Black spider monkeys rarely come to the ground. They feed in the trees, mainly on fruit and some nuts. They live in groups of 15 to 30 animals in a home range, but a group may split into smaller parties while foraging during the day. Most feeding is done in the early morning and the afternoon.

The female gives birth to 1 young after an average gestation of about 20 weeks. The young is dependent on its mother for 10 months or so.

Woolly Spider Monkey
Brachyteles arachnoides **EN**

RANGE S.E. Brazil

HABITAT Coastal forest

SIZE Body: about 24 in (61 cm)
Tail: about 26¼ in (67 cm)

The woolly spider monkey usually has a yellowish-gray to brown or reddish coat, and the naked facial skin is often red, especially when the animal becomes excited.

Its body is powerful and its limbs are long and slender. Like the spider monkeys, it has a highly efficient prehensile tail, which it uses as a fifth limb to help it move through the trees. The underside of the tail near the tip is naked and extremely sensitive. Woolly spider monkeys often move by swinging from branch to branch, although their thumbs are vestigial and of little use for such locomotion.

Wooly spider monkeys are active in the daytime when they feed in trees, mainly on fruit. They are gregarious animals, but little more is known of their social habits in the wild.

Common Woolly Monkey
Lagothrix lagotricha **LR:lc**

RANGE Upper Amazon basin

HABITAT Forest up to 6,600 ft (2,000 m)

SIZE Body: 19¾–26¾ in (50–68 cm)
Tail: 23½–28¼ in (60–72 cm)

Heavier in build than the spider monkeys, the common woolly monkey has short, thick hair. Its head is rounded, its body robust, and it has a prominent belly.

Fast and agile in the trees, it moves on all fours and by swinging hand over hand, but it is less graceful than the spider monkeys. Its thumbs and toes are well developed for grasping branches, and it has a strong, prehensile tail with a sensitive naked area near the tip.

Woolly monkeys are highly gregarious and live in troops of up to 50 animals. They forage in the daytime for plant material, mostly fruit, but are less active than many other New World monkeys. Primarily tree-dwelling, they do, nevertheless, often come down to the ground, where they walk upright, using their long tails as counterbalances.

The female gives birth to 1 offspring after a gestation period of 18 to 20 weeks. The young monkey holds on to the fur of its mother's belly or back at first and is carried around, but after a few weeks it is able to clamber about the branches unaided. The female suckles her young for 12 months or more. Common woolly monkeys become sexually mature at about 4 years old.

OLD WORLD MONKEYS

CERCOPITHECIDAE: OLD WORLD MONKEY FAMILY

The monkeys and apes of the Old World are usually grouped together as the catarrhine primates – those with closely spaced nostrils that face forward or downward. The Old World monkeys themselves are the largest group of catarrhines, with about 80 species known, in Africa, Asia and Indonesia. There are a few general differences between Old and New World monkeys. The Old World species are generally larger and often have bare buttock pads, which may be brightly colored, and their tails, although they are often long, are seldom, if ever, fully prehensile.

The family includes the macaques, baboons, mandrills, mangabeys, guenons, langurs, colobus and leaf monkeys and many other forms. Almost all are daytime-active animals, with excellent vision, hearing and sense of smell. Most are arboreal, but baboons are ground-feeding specialists, and the macaques are found both in the trees and on the ground. Generally Old World monkeys live in family or larger groups and communicate by a variety of visual and vocal signals. Males are often considerably larger than females.

Barbary Ape *Macaca sylvanus* **VU**

RANGE Gibraltar; Africa: Morocco, N. Algeria

HABITAT Rocky areas, forest clearings on mountains

SIZE Body: 21½–29½ in (55–75 cm) Tail: absent

The barbary ape is a robust, tailless monkey, with a rounded head and short muzzle. Males are larger than females and have longer hair on the crown. Formerly found elsewhere in southwest Europe, barbary apes now occur outside Africa only on Gibraltar, where the population is reinforced with animals from North Africa.

Barbary apes live in troops of 10 to 30 males, females and young in a defined territory. They sleep in trees or among rocks and feed in the early morning and afternoon, taking a rest at midday. They climb well and forage in trees and on the ground for grass, leaves, berries, fruit, roots, insects and spiders, and will plunder gardens and crops.

Females give birth to a single young, rarely twins, after a gestation of about 7 months. Births occur at any time of year, but peak from May to September. Males help females look after and carry young in the first few days. The offspring suckles for about 3 months and stays with the mother for up to 6 months.

Stump-tailed Macaque *Macaca arctoides* **VU**

RANGE Myanmar, S. China to Malaysia

HABITAT Forest, cultivated land

SIZE Body: 19¾–27½ in (50–70 cm) Tail: 1½–4 in (4–10 cm)

Distinguished by its pink-tinged face, shaggy hair and short tail, the stump-tailed macaque is an aggressive, fearless monkey that often invades gardens and cultivated fields. It spends much of its time on the ground but also climbs up into trees to sleep or to find food or a safe refuge, although it is not a particularly agile animal. Leaves, fruit, roots and crops, such as potatoes, are its main foods, and it usually picks up the items with its hands. Two cheek pouches are used for storing food, which is later removed and chewed at leisure. Stump-tailed macaques are active in the daytime and live in groups of 25 to 30, led by a dominant individual. Members of the group continually chatter and squeal to each other, and they also communicate by means of a wide range of facial expressions. Males are larger than females.

Little is known about reproduction in the wild, but females are thought to produce an infant every other year.

Japanese Macaque *Macaca fuscata* **EN**

RANGE Japan

HABITAT High-altitude forest

SIZE Body: 19¾–29½ in (50–75 cm)
Tail: 9¾–11¾ in (25–30 cm)

The only monkey found in Japan, the Japanese macaque is the sole primate other than man able to withstand a cold, snowy winter and near-freezing temperatures. In some parts of its

range, it spends long periods immersed up to the neck in thermal pools. It is medium sized and well-built, with dense fur and long whiskers and beard. Active both on the ground and in trees, it feeds mainly on nuts, berries, buds, leaves and bark.

Social groups of up to 40 individuals live together, led by an older male. The relationship between females and their mothers is extremely important; as long as their mother lives, females remain in association with her, even when they have their own young, and such female groups are the core of a troop. Males stay with their mothers and kin until adolescence, when they may join a peripheral group of males that drifts between troops. After a period in such a group, or alone, the male joins a troop, usually not that of his birth.

Females give birth to 1 young after a gestation period of between 6 and 7 months.

Bonnet Macaque *Macaca radiata*

RANGE S. India

HABITAT Forest, scrub, cultivated and suburban areas

SIZE Body: 13¾–23½ in (35–60 cm) Tail: 18¾–25½ in (48–65 cm)

The common name of this macaque is derived from its unruly cap of dark hairs on its crown. Its face is normally pale pink, but the faces of lactating females are dark red. Males are much larger than females. The bonnet macaque is agile and active and spends most of its time in the trees. It moves easily on the ground and swims well. It feeds on leaves, fruit, nuts, seeds, insects, eggs and sometimes lizards.

The female gives birth to 1 young, sometimes twins, after a gestation period of about 150 days.

White-cheeked Mangabey *Cercocebus albigena*

RANGE Africa: Cameroon to Uganda, Kenya, Tanzania

HABITAT Forest

SIZE Body: 18–27½ in (45–70 cm) Tail: 27 in–3¼ ft (70 cm–1 m)

A slender, elegant monkey, the white cheeked mangabey is distinguished by its conspicuous eyebrow tufts and the mane of long hairs running down its neck and shoulders. Its semi-

prehensile tail is immensely long and mobile and covered with rather shaggy hairs. Males of the species are larger than females and have longer tails.

These mangabeys sleep and spend nearly all their time in trees; they feed during the day on fruit, nuts, leaves, bark and insects. Troops of 10 to 30 animals live together and are extremely noisy, constantly chattering and shrieking to one another across the tree tops.

The female gives birth to 1 young after a gestation of 174 to 180 days. The young is suckled for up to 10 months.

Agile Mangabey *Cercocebus galeritus* **LR:nt**

RANGE Africa: S.E. Nigeria, Zaire to E. Kenya

HABITAT Rain and swamp forest

SIZE Body: 17¾–25½ in (45–65 cm) Tail: 17¾–29½ in (45–75 cm)

This is a slender, but strongly built monkey. The agile mangabey has long legs and tail and a fringe of hairs on its forehead. There are several races, which vary slightly in coloration, one has no fringe on the forehead.

The details of this mangabey's daily habits are poorly known, but it is thought to be active on the ground and in trees and to feed on leaves, fruit, crops and insects.

It lives in troops of 12 to 20 animals, consisting of several old males, mature females and their young.

OLD WORLD MONKEYS CONTINUED

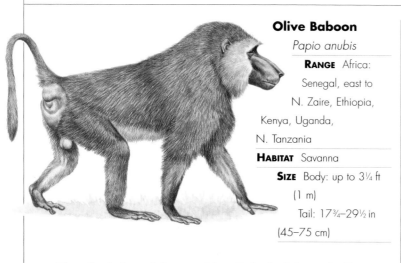

Olive Baboon
Papio anubis

RANGE Africa: Senegal, east to N. Zaire, Ethiopia, Kenya, Uganda, N. Tanzania

HABITAT Savanna

SIZE Body: up to 3¼ ft (1 m) Tail: 17¾–29½ in (45–75 cm)

The olive baboon is large and heavily built. It has a doglike muzzle and powerful teeth. Males have a mane around neck and shoulders and are larger than females. The tail has a tuft at its end, and the buttock area is naked, with broad callosities.

Olive baboons live in troops of 20 to 150 animals, organized in a strict hierarchy. They are mainly ground-living, but sleep at night in trees or rocks and travel to feeding grounds in the morning. Older juveniles lead, followed by females and young juveniles; then older males, mothers and infants. Young males bring up the rear. Baboons eat grass, seeds, roots, leaves, fruit, bark, insects, invertebrates, eggs, lizards and young mammals.

The female gives birth to 1 young, rarely 2, after a gestation of about 187 days. The baby clings to its mother's belly, but at 4 or 5 weeks rides on her back. It takes its first solid food at 5 or 6 months and is weaned and independent at 8 months. It is guarded by the mother until it is about 2 years old.

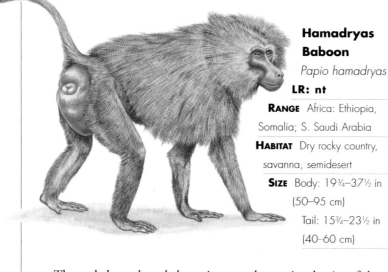

Hamadryas Baboon
Papio hamadryas
LR: nt

RANGE Africa: Ethiopia, Somalia; S. Saudi Arabia

HABITAT Dry rocky country, savanna, semidesert

SIZE Body: 19¾–37½ in (50–95 cm) Tail: 15¾–23½ in (40–60 cm)

The male hamadryas baboon is as much as twice the size of the female and has a heavy mane around its neck and shoulders. Females and younger males lack the mane and have brownish hair. Like all baboons, this species has a doglike muzzle and a sloping back. Family troops of an old male and several females and their young live together, sleeping in trees or among rocks at night and wandering in search of food during the day. They eat almost any plants, insects and small animals.

The peak breeding season is May to July, and the female produces 1, rarely 2, young after a gestation period of between 170 and 175 days.

Chacma Baboon *Papio ursinus*

RANGE Africa: Angola, Zambia to South Africa

HABITAT Savanna, rocky areas

SIZE Body: up to 3¼ ft (1 m) Tail: 15¾–29½ in (40–75 cm)

A large, yet slender baboon, with a prominent muzzle and a sloping back, the chacma baboon carries its tail in a characteristic posture as if "broken" near the base. It lives in troops of about 30 to 100 individuals, sleeping among rocks or in trees at night and searching for food during the day. These baboons feed early and late in the day and rest up at midday. Almost any plant and animal matter, such as leaves, fruit, insects, small invertebrates, lizards, birds and young mammals, is included in their varied diet, but they are predominantly vegetarian.

When on heat, the bare skin around the female's genital region swells, and at the peak of her fertile period only high-ranking males may mate with her. This is common to all savanna baboons.

The female gives birth to a single young, very rarely twins, after a gestation of 175 to 193 days, and suckles her offspring for about 8 months.

Drill *Mandrillus leucophaeus* **EN**

RANGE Africa: S.E. Nigeria, Cameroon

HABITAT Forest

SIZE Body: 17¾–35½ in (45–90 cm) Tail: 2¼–4¾ in (6–12 cm)

A powerfully built forest baboon, with a large head and a short, stumpy tail, the drill has a long muzzle, a ridged face and large nostrils. Males are much larger than females, sometimes twice the size, and have heavy manes on neck and shoulders. The skin of the buttock pads and the area around them is brightly colored, and the hue becomes more pronounced when the animal is excited. Although it climbs well and sleeps in low branches, the drill is essentially a ground-dwelling animal and moves about easily on all fours.

It lives in family troops of 20 or more individuals, which may join with other troops to form bands of as many as 200. The baboons communicate with each other using a variety of deep grunts and sharp cries, as well as with up and down movements of the head with mouth closed, to express threat, or side to side movements with teeth exposed, to express friendship. Old males dominate the troop and guard its safety; they are formidable animals, well equipped for fighting, with their sharp teeth and strong limbs.

Drills feed on plant matter, insects and small invertebrate and vertebrate animals.

Young are born at all times of year. The female produces 1 baby after a gestation of about 7 months.

Mandrill *Mandrillus sphinx* **LR:nt**

RANGE Africa: Cameroon, Gabon, Congo

HABITAT Forest

SIZE Body: 21½–37½ in (55–95 cm) Tail: 2¾–4 in (7–10 cm)

Male mandrills are large and heavily built with an long snout marked with deep, often colorful ridges. Adult females are much smaller and have less pronounced facial ridges and coloration. Mandrills sleep in trees, but live and feed on the ground in troops of about 20 to 50 animals, led by 1 or more old males. They eat fruit, nuts, leaves, insects and small invertebrates and vertebrates.

Births occur at any time of year, peaking from December to February. A single young is born after a gestation of about 7½ months.

Gelada *Theropithecus gelada* **LR:nt**

RANGE Africa: Ethiopia

HABITAT Mountains: rocky ravines, alpine meadows

SIZE Body: 19¾–29½ in (50–75 cm) Tail: 17¾–21½ in (45–55 cm)

The impressive gelada has a distinctive head, with a somewhat upturned muzzle marked with ridges, and the nostrils are located well back, not at the end of the muzzle as in other baboon species. The gelada's long sidewhiskers project backward and upward, and there is a heavy mane over the neck and shoulders, which can sometimes reach almost to the ground in the older males.

On the chest and throat there are three areas of bare red skin, which the male expands and brings into full view in his aggressive, threat posture. Females are about half the size of males and have much lighter manes.

The gelada is a ground-dweller and it even sleeps on rocky ledges and cliffs. It lives in family groups which comprise several females and their young, led by a large mature male. These family groups may sometimes gather into large troops of several hundred animals. Young and unattached males may form their own social units.

In the morning, the geladas leave the cliffs where they have slept and move off to alpine meadows, where they feed largely on plant material, such as grasses, seeds and fruit, and on insects and other small animals. They do not have a specific territory, and the male keeps his family together by means of a variety of calls and facial gestures. Geladas have excellent vision, hearing and sense of smell.

Most young are born between February and April. The female produces a single offspring, rarely twins, after a gestation period of between 147 and 192 days. The mother suckles the young gelada for up to 2 years and after giving birth, she will not have a period of heat for another 12 to 18 months.

OLD WORLD MONKEYS CONTINUED

Vervet Monkey *Cercopithecus aethiops*

RANGE Africa: Senegal to Somalia, south to South Africa

HABITAT Savanna, woodland edge

SIZE Body: 15¾–31½ in (40–80 cm) Tail: 19¾–27½ in (50–70 cm)

There are many races of this medium-to-large monkey, which vary in their facial markings and whiskers. Generally, however, they have black faces, white whiskers and grayish or yellowish-olive hair. Although they sleep and take refuge in trees, these adaptable monkeys forage in open country and will run some distance on the ground. They also climb, jump and swim well. Family troops of an old male and several females and young live together and may join with other troops during the day. Generally rather quiet monkeys, males utter a harsh cry, and others may scream when frightened. Mainly vegetarian animals, they feed on leaves, shoots, fruit, flowers, seeds and bark, but also eat some insects, spiders, lizards, birds' eggs and young birds.

Breeding occurs at any time of year. The female gives birth to a single young after a gestation of 175 to 203 days and suckles it for about 6 months. For the first few weeks, the baby clings to its mother's belly, but starts to leave her at 3 weeks and to climb at 4 weeks old. When males become sexually mature, their scrotums adopt a blue-green hue.

De Brazza's Monkey *Cercopithecus neglectus*

RANGE Africa: Cameroon, south to Angola, east to Uganda

HABITAT Rain and swamp forest, dry mountain forest near water

SIZE Body: 15¾–23½ in (40–60 cm)
Tail: 20¾–33½ in (53–85 cm)

The robust, heavily built De Brazza's monkey has a conspicuous reddish-brown band, bordered with black, on its forehead, and a well-developed white beard. Its back slopes upward to the tail so that the rump is higher than the shoulders. Females look similar to males, but are smaller. Active during the day, this monkey is a good climber and swimmer and also moves with speed and agility on the ground, where it spends a good deal of its feeding time. Leaves, shoots, fruit, berries, insects and lizards are its main foods, and it will also raid crops. It lives in small family groups comprising an old male and several females with young. Sometimes there are larger troops of 30 or more animals.

The female gives birth to 1 young after a gestation of 177 to 187 days. After a week, the baby first starts to leave the safety of its mother body, and by 3 weeks, it is starting to climb and run.

Red-bellied Guenon *Cercopithecus erythrogaster* **VU**

RANGE Africa: Nigeria

HABITAT Forest

SIZE Body: about 18 in (45 cm) Tail: about 23½ in (60 cm)

This apparently rare monkey has a dark face with a pinkish muzzle, fringed with white side-whiskers. The breast and belly are usually reddish-brown, hence the common name, but can be gray in some individuals. Females look similar to males but have grayish underparts, arms and legs. Few specimens of this monkey have been found, and its habits are not known.

Diana Monkey *Cercopithecus diana* **VU**

RANGE Africa: Sierra Leone to Ghana

HABITAT Rain forest

SIZE Body: 15¾–22½ in (40–57 cm)
Tail: 19¾–29½ in (50–75 cm)

A slender, elegant monkey, the diana monkey has most striking coloration with its black and white face, white beard and chest and distinctive patches

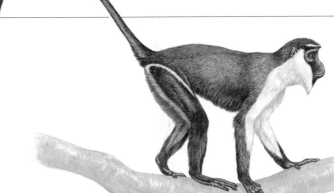

of bright
chestnut on its back
and hind limbs. There are also conspicuous
white stripes on the otherwise dark hair of each thigh. Females
are smaller than males, but in other respects look similar.

An excellent climber, the diana monkey spends virtually all
its life in the middle and upper layers of the forest and is noisy
and inquisitive. Troops of up to 30 animals live together, led by
an old male. They are most active in the early morning and late
afternoon, when they feed on leaves, fruit, buds and other plant
matter, and also on some insects and birds' eggs and young.

The female bears a single young after a gestation period of
about 7 months and suckles it for 6 months.

Talapoin *Miopithecus talapoin*

RANGE Africa: Gabon to W. Angola

HABITAT Rain forest, mangroves, always
near water

SIZE Body: 9¾–15¾ in (25–40 cm)
Tail: 14¼–20½ in (36–52 cm)

One of the smallest African
monkeys, the talapoin has a slender body, a round
head, which is large relative to body size, and prominent
ears. Its legs are longer than its arms, and its tail exceeds
its head and body length.

Talapoins live in family troops of 12 to 20 or so
individuals, and each troop has its own territory,
although several troops may sometimes unite into a
larger group. These monkeys sleep in bushes and
mangroves and are active in the day time, particularly in
the early morning and late afternoon. Good climbers and
runners, they enter water readily and swim and dive well.
Leaves, seeds, fruit, water plants, insects, eggs and small animals
are all included in their diet, and they will raid plantation crops.

Most births occur between November and March. After a
gestation of about 6½ months, the female produces a single
young, which is born well haired and with its eyes open. The
young talapoin develops quickly and takes its first solid food at
3 weeks; it is largely independent at 3 months, although it
continues to suckle until it is 4 or 5 months old.

Patas Monkey *Erythrocebus patas*

RANGE Africa: Senegal, east to Ethiopia, south to Tanzania

HABITAT Grassland, dry savanna, forest edge, rocky plateaux

SIZE Body: 19¾–29½ in (50–75 cm) Tail: 19¾–29½ in (50–75 cm)

The slender,
long-legged
patas monkey is
among the fastest
moving of all primates on
the ground. It can attain
speeds of up to 31 mph
(50 km/h). The male may be as
much as twice the size of the female, and
the lower parts of his limbs are pure white; the limbs of females
are fawn or yellowish-white. Patas monkeys live in troops,
comprising an old male and up to 12 females and their young,
and occupy a large territory. They sleep in trees, usually at the
edge of forest, but spend virtually all of their day on the ground,
searching for fruit, seeds, leaves, roots, insects, lizards and birds'
eggs. While the troop feeds, the male leader keeps a look-out for
danger and warns his harem of the approach of any enemies.

Most births occur from December to February, and females
produce 1 young after a gestation of 170 days. The baby takes
its first solid food at about 3 months old.

Allen's Swamp Monkey *Allenopithecus nigroviridis* **LR:nt**

RANGE Africa: E. congo, Zaire

HABITAT Swampy forest

SIZE Body: 15¾–19½ in (40–50 cm) Tail: 17¾–21½ in (45–55 cm)

Allen's swamp monkey is sturdily built with relatively short
limbs and tail. Its head is rounded, with ruffs of whiskers from
the ears to the mouth. Males are slightly larger than females, but
otherwise look similar. Little is known about the habits of these
monkeys. They live in troops and feed on leaves, fruit and nuts
and also snails, crabs, fish and insects. They climb and jump
well and
enter water
readily.

The
female produces a
single young, which
clings to her belly and
suckles for 2 or
3 months.

OLD WORLD MONKEYS CONTINUED

Angolan Black and White Colobus *Colobus angolensis*

RANGE Africa: Angola to Kenya

HABITAT Forest

SIZE Body: 19¾–26¼ in (50–67 cm)
Tail: 24¾–35½ in (63–90 cm)

Colobus monkeys have long limbs and tails and robust bodies. They have only four fingers on each hand, their thumbs being vestigial or absent. The Angolan colobus is one of several black and white species and, with its sturdy body and rounded head, is typical of its genus. It is identified by the characteristic long white hairs on its shoulders, but the many races of this species differ slightly in the extent of the white on shoulders and tail.

These monkeys live in family troops of several females and their young, led and guarded by an old male. As young males mature, they either go off alone or found their own troops. Each troop has its own territory, with feeding areas and sleeping trees, but may sometimes join with other troops to form a group of 50 or so. The animals are active in the daytime, with a period of rest or grooming at midday. Much of their food, such as leaves, fruit, bark and insects, is found in the trees, where they run and leap with astonishing agility, so they rarely need to descend to the ground.

Breeding takes place all year round. The females give birth to 1 young after a gestation of 147 to 178 days. The baby starts to climb at 3 weeks, but suckles and stays with its mother for well over a year. Females will suckle young other than their own.

Red Colobus *Procolobus badius* **LR:nt**

RANGE Africa: Senegal to Ghana, Cameroon, Zaire, Uganda, Tanzania

HABITAT Rain, swamp and secondary forest, usually near water

SIZE Body: 18–27½ in (46–70 cm)
Tail: 16½–31½ in (42–80 cm)

There are many races of this slender, long-tailed colobus, with coloration ranging from orange-red to reddish-brown, often with black on the back and shoulders. The underparts are reddish-yellow to gray or white. Females are smaller than males, but otherwise look similar.

The red colobus lives in a troop of 50 to 100 animals made up of many small family groups, each comprising a male and several females and their young. The colobus troops are active during the day, when they feed among the branches on flowers, shoots, fruit and leaves, leaping acrobatically from tree to tree.

The female produces 1 young after a gestation period of between 4 and 5½ months. She nurses the infant until it is ready to be weaned at between 9 and 12 months.

Olive Colobus

Procolobus verus **LR:nt**

RANGE Africa: Sierra Leone to Ghana

HABITAT Rain, swamp and secondary forest

SIZE Body: 17–19¾ in (43–50 cm)
Tail: 22½–25¼ in (57–64 cm)

This species is the smallest of the colobus monkeys. The olive colobus has a little, rounded head, a short muzzle and rather subdued coloration. Male and female are about the same size, but the female lacks the crest of upright hairs that the male sports on his crown. This colobus lives in a family troop comprising an old male and several females and their young, usually 6 to 10 in all. Sometimes the group may be bigger, containing up to 20 individuals, with several adult males.

The monkeys sleep and take refuge in the middle layers of the forest, but feed on the lowest branches. These monkeys do not climb into the treetops and only rarely come down to the ground. Leaves and some flowers are their staple diet. They are rather quiet monkeys and make few sounds.

Reproductive details are not known for this species except that the mother carries her baby in her mouth for the first few weeks after birth – a habit shared only with other species of colobus.

of their remote, mountainous range, few snub-nosed monkeys have yet been observed or caught. They are said to live in troops of 100 or more and to feed on fruit, buds, leaves and bamboo shoots.

Hanuman Langur *Semnopithecus entellus*

RANGE India, Sri Lanka

HABITAT Forest, scrub, arid rocky areas

SIZE Body: 20 in–3¼ ft (51 cm–1 m)
Tail: 28 in–3¼ ft (72 cm–1 m)

Proboscis Monkey *Nasalis larvatus* **VU**

RANGE Borneo

HABITAT Mangroves, river banks

SIZE Body: 20¾–30 in (53–76 cm)
Tail: 21½–30 in (55–76 cm)

The sturdily built proboscis monkey lives in the tree-tops of mangrove swamp jungles, where the trees are strong and rigid and do not attain enormous heights. It is an agile animal and runs and leaps in the branches, using its long tail as a counterbalance; its long fingers and toes aid grip. The male is considerably larger than the female, perhaps twice her weight, and has an extraordinarily long, bulbous nose. When he makes his loud, honking call, the nose straightens out. The female has a much smaller nose and a quieter cry.

Proboscis monkeys live in small groups of 1 or 2 adult males and several females and their young. They are most active in the morning, when they feed on leaves and shoots of mangrove and pedada trees, as well as on the fruit and flowers of other trees. Much of the rest of the day is spent basking in the tree tops, where they also sleep at night.

Mating takes place at any time of year, and the female produces a single young after a gestation of about 166 days. These monkeys are difficult to keep in captivity and are becoming increasingly rare in the wild.

This large, long-limbed monkey has a black face and prominent eyebrows. It adapts well to many different habitats and will live near human habitation and raid shops and houses for food. In the Himalayas, the langur is believed to make regular migrations, moving up the mountains in summer and down again in winter.

Although it is an agile climber, the langur spends more than half of its time on the ground, where it finds much of its food. It is almost entirely vegetarian, feeding on leaves, shoots, buds, fruit and seeds. Very rarely it will eat insects.

Langurs live in groups of 1 or more adult males with females and juveniles, usually about 15 to 35 individuals in all, although in some areas groups of 80 or 90 have been observed. There are also, however, smaller all-male groups containing 4 to 15 animals. In groups with only one male, he is in sole charge of the movements and daily routine, and life is peaceful; in larger groups, the males contest and squabble, even though there is a dominant male.

Breeding takes place at any time of year except in areas with marked seasonal changes, where births are concentrated into the 2 or 3 most climatically favorable months. The female gives birth to 1, occasionally 2, young after a gestation period of between 6 and 7 months. Other females in the troop will often show a great interest in the newborn infant, and the mother allows them to touch it shortly after its birth. For the first few weeks of its life the baby clings tightly to its mother, but at 4 weeks it starts to move short distances independently and, at 3 months, it is allowed to play with other infants and to take some solid food. The infant continues to suckle for between 10 and 15 months, but nevertheless undergoes much stress during the weaning period.

Snub-nosed Langur *Rhinopithecus roxellana*

RANGE S.W. and S. China, Tibet

HABITAT Mountain forest; winters in lower valleys

SIZE Body: 19¾–32½ in (50–83 cm) Tail: 20 in–3¼ ft (51 cm–1 m)

This large, long-tailed monkey has a distinctive upturned nose, hence its common name, and golden hairs on its forehead, throat and cheeks. Because

GIBBONS

HYLOBATIDAE: GIBBON FAMILY

The 9 species of gibbons are found in Southeast Asia, Sumatra, Java and Borneo. Like the apes, gibbons lack an external tail and have a protruding jaw. The gibbons are agile, slender primates weighing between 11 and 28 lb (5 and 13 kg).

The gibbons are specialized arboreal forms very different externally from the great apes. They probably have the most remarkable adaptations of all mammals for rapid locomotion through trees. Gibbons use their extremely long hands to swing through the forest canopy and are spectacularly skilful climbers. All gibbons have long, slender hands, with the thumb deeply divided from the index finger. This gives additional flexibility. When standing upright the gibbon's long arms touch the ground, so they are often carried above the head. Gibbons are primarily vegetarian, but will also eat a diet of insects, young birds and eggs. The male and female of the gibbon species are generally similar in size.

Black Gibbon

Hylobates concolor **EN**

RANGE Indo-China, Hainan

HABITAT Rain forest

SIZE Body: 17¾–24¾ in (45–63 cm) Tail: absent

There are several subspecies of black, or crested, gibbons, occurring in various parts of Indo-China. The subspecies differ in details of fur coloration. The male black gibbon is slightly larger than the female and has a tuft of hair on the crown. The female is buff colored, sometimes with black patches.

Gibbons communicate with complex calls which help to maintain their pair bonds. The male has a throat sac, which acts as a resonating chamber to amplify his voice.

Black gibbons feed on a variety of foods, mostly ripe fruit, buds, leaves and insects, although occasionally small vertebrates may also be eaten.

Siamang

Hylobates syndactylus **LR:nt**

RANGE Malaysia, Sumatra

HABITAT Mountain forest

SIZE Body: 29½–35½ in (75–90 cm) Tail: absent

The largest of the gibbons, the siamang has entirely black fur. It is also distinguished by the web that unites the second and third toes of each foot. Siamangs are tree-dwelling and extremely agile, despite their size. They swing between branches and may walk upright on stronger tree boughs. At night, they sleep on high, strong branches. Fruit, especially figs, is a staple food, and they also eat flowers, leaves and shoots, some insects and even birds' eggs.

Adult siamang pairs live together in a territory with their offspring of different ages, but unmated adults live alone. Families communicate by short barks and a distinctive whooping call, which is amplified by the inflatable throat sac. The female siamang gives birth to a single young after a gestation of 230 to 235 days. The newborn baby is almost hairless and clings to its mother for safety and warmth.

Kloss's Gibbon *Hylobates klossii* **VU**

RANGE Mentawi Islands west of Sumatra

HABITAT Hill and lowland rain forest

SIZE Body: 25½–27½ in (65–70 cm) Tail: absent

Kloss's gibbon looks like a small version of the siamang and is very similar in its habits. It is the smallest of the gibbons. It is thought to represent the form and structure of ancestral gibbons. Strictly tree-dwelling, it leaps and swings in the trees with great dexterity and feeds on fruit, leaves, shoots and, perhaps, insects.

Family groups, each consisting of an adult pair and up to 3 offspring, occupy a territory and sleep and feed together. Females give birth to a single young.

Lar Gibbon

Hylobates lar **LR:nt**

RANGE S. Burma, Malaysia, Thailand, Kampuchea, Sumatra

HABITAT Rain forest, dry forest

SIZE Body: 16½–22½ in (42–58 cm)
Tail: absent

The lar gibbon may be black or pale buff, but the hands, feet, brow band and sides of the face are always pale. Like all gibbons, it is tree-dwelling and rarely descends to the ground. It moves in the trees by swinging from branch to branch by means of its long arms or by running upright along large branches.

Largely vegetarian, the lar gibbon feeds on fruit, leaves, shoots, buds and flowers and occasionally on insects.

Lar gibbons live in family groups of 2 to 6 individuals: an adult male and female and their young of different ages. The pair call to each other daily in a complex duet which is thought to reinforce their bond.

Females give birth to 1 young at intervals of between 2 and 4 years. The gestation period is between 7 and 7½ months. Young gibbons remain with their mothers for at least 2 years and are suckled by her throughout this period.

Pileated Gibbon *Hylobates pileatus* **VU**

RANGE S.E. Thailand

HABITAT Forest

SIZE Body: 17–23½ in (43–60 cm)
Tail: absent

The pileated, or capped, gibbons derive their common names from the black cap on the heads of both sexes. Like all gibbons, they are born white and the adult pigmentation gradually spreads over the body down from the head. By the time they reach sexual maturity male pileated gibbons are completely black, while the females are buff colored with a black cap.

Pileated gibbons are strongly territorial and males scream and shout abuse to one another across their territory boundaries, although they seldom fight. The males give startling, loud solo calls at or before dawn.

This species feeds on a mixed diet of leaves, buds, tree resin and insects.

Hoolock Gibbon

Hylobates hoolock **DD**

RANGE Bangladesh, E. India, S. China, Myanmar

HABITAT Hill forest

SIZE Body: 18–24¾ in (46–63 cm)
Tail: absent

The hoolock has the long limbs and the shaggy fur that is characteristic of gibbons. Males and females are thought to be about the same size. The adult males are blackish-brown in color and the females are yellow-brown. Newborn hoolock gibbons are grayish-white and gradually darken as they age to become black at a few months old. The female's color fades at puberty, which occurs at about 6 or 7 years of age.

The hoolock gibbon is almost entirely tree-dwelling. It sleeps in the trees and in the daytime it swings itself quickly and easily from branch to branch and tree to tree, searching for food. Fruit, leaves and shoots make up the majority of its diet, but it will also sometimes supplement this with spiders, insects, larvae and birds' eggs.

Family groups, which comprise of a mated pair and their young, live together. Normally each family group feeds in its own territory, but several families may occasionally gather in the same feeding area.

The hoolock's loud calls are an important form of communication both within its own group and between groups. Mating occurs at the start of the rainy season, and females each bear a single young, some time between November and March.

APES

HOMINIDAE: APE FAMILY

The family Hominidae includes great apes – the orangutan, gorilla, and chimpanzees – and human beings. Great apeas are larger and more robust than their relatives the gibbons. An adult male gorilla can weigh as much as 595 lb (270 kg) while chimpanzees can weigh between 106 and 176 lb (48 and 80 kg).

All apes are able to walk on their hind legs, if briefly, although most – apart from humans – normally travel on all fours. Gorillas and chimpanzees are largely terrestrial, but the orangutan spends much of its time in the trees, where it swings from branch to branch with surprising agility. While gorillas are vegetarian animals, the chimpanzees and orangutans are more omnivorous in their eating habits.

Apes are generally gregarious and live in family-based groups which forage together during the day, and build sleeping nests at night. Male great apes are considerably larger than females and may have other special characteristics.

Orangutan

Pongo pygmaeus **VU**

RANGE Sumatra, Borneo
HABITAT Rain forest
SIZE Height: 4–5 ft (1.2–1.5 m) Tail: absent

The orangutan, with its reddish-brown, shaggy hair, has a strong, heavily built body and is the second-largest primate. The arms are long and powerful and reach to the ankles when the animal stands erect; there is a small thumb on each broad hand that is opposable to the first digit. The orangutan's legs are relatively short and are weaker than the arms. Males are much larger and heavier than the females and are also identified by the cheek flaps that surround the face of the mature adult. All adults have fatty throat pouches.

Orangutans live alone, in pairs or in small family groups and are active in the daytime at all levels of the trees. They walk along large branches on all fours or erect and sometimes swing by their hands from branch to branch. On the ground, they walk on all fours or stand erect. Fruit is their staple diet, but

they also feed on leaves, seeds, young birds and eggs. The orangutan sleeps in the trees in a platform nest made of sticks. It may make a new nest every night.

After a gestation period of more than 9 months, the female gives birth to a single young. She cares for her offspring for some time (one captive young was suckled for 6 years) and the baby clings to the mother's fur as she moves around in the trees.

Gorilla *Gorilla gorilla* **EN**

RANGE Africa: S.E. Nigeria to W. Zaire; E. Zaire into adjacent countries
HABITAT Rain forest up to 3,000 m) 10,000 ft)
SIZE Male height: 5½–6 ft (1.7–1.8 m) Female height: 4½–5 ft (1.4–1.5 m) Tail: absent

The largest and most robust of the primates, the gorilla is also a gentle, intelligent and sociable animal, which lives a peaceful, quiet existence if undisturbed. Its body, covered with coarse black hair, is massive with a short broad trunk and wide chest and shoulders. The head is large, with a short muzzle, and the eyes and ears small; old males have high crowns. The muscular arms are longer than the short, thick legs, and the broad hands are equipped with short fingers and thumbs. Males are bigger and heavier than females, and those over 10 years old have silvery-gray hair on their backs – hence the name silverback, given to old males. There are two races: the lowland and the mountain gorilla, also referred to as the eastern and western races.

On the ground, gorillas normally move in a stooped posture, with the knuckles of the hands resting on the ground, but they do stand erect on occasion. Females and juveniles climb trees, but males rarely do so because of their great bulk. Gorillas live in a closeknit group of a dominant male, 1 or 2 other males, several females and young; some groups may contain only the dominant male, 2 or 3 females and young. The group wanders in a home range of 4 to 15½ sq miles (10 to 40 km²), which is not defended or marked at the boundaries. There may be some conflict with neighboring groups, but encounters are generally avoided by communications such as drumming on the ground from a distance. Old males will threaten rivals by standing erect and beating the chest, while roaring and barking, and sometimes by tearing up and throwing plants. When the leader of a troop dies, younger males contest for dominance.

Gorillas are active in the daytime. The troop rises between 6 am and 8 am. It feeds for a while on plant material, such as leaves, buds, stalks, berries, bark and ferns, and then has a period of rest and relaxation. Gorillas do not appear to drink, but get the water they need from their juicy diet. They feed again in the afternoon and then retire for the night in nests made of twigs and leaves. Young gorillas under 3 years old sleep with their mothers, but all others have their own nests.

Breeding appears to take place at any time of year. The female gives birth to a single young after a gestation of more than 9 months. The young is completely dependent and clings to its mother's fur at first, but it is able to sit up at 3 months and to walk and climb at 5 months. It suckles for 12 to 18 months and remains with its mother for about 3 years.

Pygmy Chimpanzee/Bonobo *Pan paniscus* **EN**

RANGE Africa: Zaire

HABITAT Rain forest

SIZE Body: 21½–23½ in (55–60 cm) Height: up to 3¼ ft (1 m) Tail: absent

Similar to the chimpanzee, this species (sometimes regarded as only a sub-species), has longer, thinner legs, a more slender body and a narrow face. Its hair and facial skin are black. It moves in the trees and on the ground, feeding mainly on fruit, but also on leaves and shoots. A gregarious animal, the pygmy chimpanzee lives in a family group, and several families may gather in a good feeding area. Otherwise its habits are much the same as those of the chimpanzee.

The female bears 1 young, after a gestation of 227 to 232 days, which stays with her for up to 3 years.

Chimpanzee *Pan troglodytes* **EN**

RANGE Africa: Guinea to Zaire, Uganda and Tanzania

HABITAT Rain forest, savanna with woodland

SIZE Body: 26–37 in (68–94 cm) Height: 4–5 ft (1.2–1.7 m) Tail: absent;

The intelligent, social chimpanzee has a wide range of sounds and gestures for communication and is probably one of the most expressive of all animals. Thickset and robust, but more lightly built than the gorilla, the chimpanzee has a strong body and long limbs. The powerful arms are longer than the legs. Its hands and feet are narrow and long, with opposable thumbs on the hands. Males are slightly larger than females. There is great variability in the color of hair and facial skin, but the hair is generally blackish and the face light, darkening in older individuals. The rounded head bears broad, prominent ears, and the lips are mobile and protrusible.

Chimpanzees climb well but spend most of the time on the ground, where they generally walk on all fours, even though they stand erect on occasion, as when their hands are full of food.

Their social structure is more variable than that of the gorilla. Rain forest animals live in troops of males; of females with young; of males and females with young, or of adults of both sexes without young. The composition of the troop often changes. Savanna chimpanzees generally live in more stable troops of 1 or more males, several females and their young. They occupy a home range, the size of which depends on the size of the troop and on the food supply. Neighboring troops meet with much noise and communication, but there is usually little aggression involved.

Active in the daytime, chimpanzees rise at dawn and feed mainly on plant material, such as fruit, nuts, leaves, shoots and bark, and on eggs and insects. They will use stems or twigs as tools, to winkle termites or ants from their hiding places. Savanna chimpanzees will kill young animals for food by holding them by the hind limbs and striking their heads on the ground. At night, chimpanzees usually sleep in the trees, each making its own nest with interwoven, broken and bent branches. Young under 3 years old sleep with their mothers.

Females have regular periods of heat with swelling of the genital region, and may be mated by all the males in the troop.

Usually 1 young is born, sometimes twins, after a gestation of 227 to 232 days. The young animal lives closely with its mother for 2 to 3 years.

FRUIT BATS

ORDER CHIROPTERA

One species in every four mammals is a bat, yet remarkably little is known of this order. Bats are the only mammals capable of sustained flight, as opposed to gliding, which they achieve by means of their well-designed wings. The four elongated fingers of each hand support the flight membrane, which is also attached to the ankles and sometimes also incorporates the tail.

PTEROPODIDAE: FRUIT BAT FAMILY

There are about 166 species of these large, fruit-eating bats, sometimes known as flying foxes, found in the tropical and subtropical regions of the Old World. Their eyes are large, their ears simple in structure like those of rodents, and they have a keen sense of smell. Males and females look alike.

On each hand there is a sturdy thumb, equipped with a robust claw. Some species have an extra claw at the tip of the second digit where it protrudes from the wing membrane.

Using their claws and their hind feet, fruit bats make their way along the branches of their feeding trees in search of fruit. Some also feed on pollen and nectar.

Greater Fruit Bat *Pteropus giganteus*

RANGE S. and S.E. Asia

HABITAT Forest, scrub

SIZE Body: 13¾–15¾ in (35–40 cm) Wingspan: 5 ft (1.5 m) Tail: absent

The wingspan of the greater fruit bat is the largest of any bat. It is a highly sociable creature and roosts by day in large trees in flocks of several thousand. At dusk the flocks take to the air and disperse in search of food.

The greater fruit bat crushes fruit between its peglike teeth to obtain the juice and spits out the seeds and flesh. Soft flesh, such as banana, is swallowed.

There is no general breeding season for this species, but in each part of its huge range births are more or less synchronized. One young is born after a gestation period of about 6 months and is carried about by its mother until it is 8 weeks old.

Hammerheaded Bat *Hypsignathus monstrosus*

RANGE Africa: Gambia to Uganda and Angola

HABITAT Mangrove and other swamps

SIZE Body: 10–12 in (25–30 cm) Wingspan: 27–37 in (70–95 cm) Tail: absent

The hammerheaded bat derives its name from a curious nasal swelling which develops in the male. The function of the male's strangely shaped nose remains a mystery, though it may be used to enhance the volume of his mating call. The hammerhead is one of the noisiest bats. Males gather in special trees and display to the females by chorusing for hours. The females visit this "lek" in order to pick out their mates.

Hammerheaded bats roost in small numbers. They feed on the juices of mangoes and soursops and may also have carnivorous tendencies. Females produce a single young after a gestation of 5½ months.

Egyptian Rousette Bat *Rousettus aegyptiacus*

RANGE Africa, east to India and Malaysia

HABITAT Forest; caves, tombs, temples

SIZE Body 4¼–5 in (11–13 cm)
Wingspan: 12–18 in (30–45 cm)
Tail: ½ in (1.5 cm)

Egyptian rousette bats roost deep in caves or tombs in large colonies, sometimes numbering millions of bats.

This species seems to rely on echolocation for flight navigation in the dark places that it inhabits. They are the only fruit bats to use this method of guidance, which is so important to the insectivorous bat species. The Egyptain rousette bat feeds on fruit juices, flower nectar and pollen and plays a useful ecological role as a pollinator. The bats must travel great distances each night in order to find enough food to survive.

The breeding season is from December to March. Females produce 1 young after a gestation of 15 weeks. The young bat clings to its mother and is transported everywhere until it can fly. It begins to feed on fruit at the age of 3 months.

Franquet's Fruit Bat

Epomops franqueti

RANGE Africa: Nigeria to Angola, east to Zimbabwe and Tanzania

HABITAT Forest, open country

SIZE Body: 5–7 in (13.5–18 cm) Wingspan: 9–10 in (23–25 cm) Tail: absent

Franquet's fruit bat is also known as the epauleted bat on account of the distinct patches of white fur on each shoulder. Rather than crushing fruit to release the juice, this bat sucks it out. It encircles the fruit with its lips, pierces the flesh with its teeth and, while pushing the tongue up against the fruit, it sucks, using the action of its pharyngeal pump. Franquet's bats breed throughout the year, producing a single young at a time after a gestation of 3½ months.

Harpy Fruit Bat

Harpyionycteris whiteheadi

RANGE Philippines

HABITAT Forest, up to 5,575 ft (1,700 m)

SIZE Body: 5½–6 in (14–15 cm) Wingspan: 9–12 in (23–30 cm) Tail: absent

The prominent incisor teeth of the harpy fruit bat appear to operate almost like the blades of a pair of scissors, and the bat seems to use them to snip off figs and other fruit from the trees.

Tube-nosed Fruit Bat

Nyctimene major

RANGE Sulawesi to Timor, New Guinea, N. Australia, Solomon Islands

HABITAT Forest

SIZE Body: 3–4¾ in (7–12 cm) Wingspan: 8–11 in (20–28 cm) Tail: ½–1 in (1.5–2.5 cm)

This bat has a pair of nasal scrolls which stand out on each side of the head like snorkel tubes. Their exact function is not clear, but they may help the bat to locate ripe fruit by bestowing a "stereo" effect on the nose. Guavas, figs and even the pulp of young coconuts make up the diet of the tube-nosed bat. Pieces of fruit are torn out with the teeth and then chewed and kneaded against the chest and belly. Only the juice is consumed, the rest is dropped to the ground.

Tube-nosed bats seem less social than other fruit bats and usually roost alone. They cling to the trunks of trees and are afforded some camouflage by their spotted wings. They breed in September and October and produce 1 young.

Long-tongued Fruit Bat

Macroglossus minimus

RANGE Myanmar, east to Malaysia and Bali

HABITAT Forest, plantations

SIZE Body: 2¼–2¾ in (6–7 cm) Wingspan: 5½–6¾ in (14–17 cm) Tail: vestigial

The long-tongued fruit bat is one of the smallest fruit bats. It has adopted a solitary way of life, possibly in order to make itself less obvious to predators. By day it roosts in rolled-up banana or hemp leaves, emerging at dusk to feed on pollen and nectar from plants. It will also eat fruit, and is considered a plantation pest in some parts of its range.

These bats are quite vocal and make a shrieking noise at night. They breed between August and September, producing a single young after a gestation period of between 12 and 15 weeks.

Queensland Blossom Bat

Syconycteris australis

RANGE S. New Guinea, south to Australia: New South Wales

HABITAT Wet and dry forest

SIZE Body: 2–2½ in (5–6 cm) Wingspan: 4¾–6 in (12–15 cm) Tail: vestigial

The Queensland blossom bat is the smallest fruit bat. It inhabits eucalyptus and acacia forests and seems to feed almost exclusively on the pollen and nectar of the many species of these trees. The bat feeds by inserting its long brushlike tongue deep into the long-necked blooms. As it travels from tree to tree it pollinates the flowers on which it feeds.

Females give birth to a tiny infant in the summer – in November or December.

MOUSE-TAILED BATS AND SHEATH-TAILED BATS

RHINOPOMATIDAE: MOUSE-TAILED BAT FAMILY

Mouse-tailed bats derive their name from their long, naked tails which equal the head and body in length. Their tails are not joined to the body with a membrane as they are in other families. There are 3 species, found from the Middle East through India to Thailand and Sumatra. These bats have occupied certain pyramids in Egypt for 3 millennia or more.

Greater Mouse-tailed Bat
Rhinopoma microphyllum

RANGE West Africa, North Africa, Middle East, India, Sumatra

HABITAT Treeless arid land

SIZE Body: 2¼–3 in (6–8 cm)
Wingspan: 6¾–10 in (17–25 cm)
Tail: 2¼–3 in (6–8 cm)

Colonies of thousands of mouse-tailed bats occupy roosts in large ruined buildings, often palaces and temples.

They feed exclusively on insects and, in those areas where a cool season temporarily depletes the food supply, the bats may enter a deep sleep resembling torpor. Before they enter this state they lay down thick layers of fat on their bodies, which may weigh as much as the bats themselves, and with this they can survive for many weeks with neither food nor water. As they sleep, the accumulated fat is used up and by the time the cold season is passed, nothing of it remains.

Mouse-tailed bats mate at the beginning of spring and the female produces a single offspring after a gestation period of about 4 months. The young bat is weaned at 8 weeks, but does not attain sexual maturity until its second year.

EMBALLONURIDAE: SHEATH-TAILED BAT FAMILY

There are 47 species of bat in this family and all have a characteristic membrane which spans the hind legs, the tail originates beneath the membrane and penetrates it through a small hole. The advantages of this arrangement are not clear, but the bat is able to adjust this versatile "tailplane" during flight by movements of its legs only, and it is possible that it may improve its aerial abilities.

Sheath-tailed bats range over tropical and subtropical regions of the world in a variety of habitats, but never far from trees. They are primarily insect-eaters, but may supplement their diet with additional fruit.

Scent-producing glandular sacs on the wings, in the crooks of the elbows, are another characteristic of these bats. The thick, pungent secretions of these glands are more profuse in males than females and may assist females in their search for mates.

Proboscis Bat *Rhynchonycteris naso*
RANGE S. Mexico to C. Brazil
HABITAT Forest, scrub; near water
SIZE Body: 1¼–1¾ in (3.5–4.5 cm) Wingspan: 4¾–6¼ in (12–16 cm)
Tail: ½–¾ in (1–2 cm)

Characteristic features of the proboscis bat are its long snout and the tufts of gray hair on its forearms.

Proboscis bats fly relatively slowly and are therefore ill-suited for hunting up in the tree-tops where they would make easy prey for birds. Instead they have developed the habit of feeding on insects, which they catch on the wing just above the surfaces of ponds, lakes and rivers.

Proboscis bats sometimes roost in rocky crevices, but often just cling to rocks or to concrete, where their color pattern gives them a resemblance to patches of lichen. Individuals roost a considerable distance from one another, perhaps to enhance the effect of the camouflage.

Between April and July, females each give birth to 1 young. Until the young bat is about 2 months old and able to fend for itself, its mother chooses a dark safe roost inside a log, or deep within a pile of stones, in which to leave it.

Two-lined Bat

Saccopteryx leptura

RANGE Mexico to Bolivia and Brazil

HABITAT Lowland forest

SIZE Body: 1½–2 in (4–5 cm) Wingspan: 7–8¾ in (18–22 cm)
Tail: ½ in (1 cm)

The two-lined bat is one of the most strikingly marked of all
bats. Its common name is derived from the pair of wavy white
lines running down its back from the nape of the neck to the
rump. The lines serve to break up the body shape of the bat and
may also provide some camouflage.

The male has a pair of well-developed saclike glands in the
wing membrane, just above the crooks of the arms. The purpose
of the sacs is not known, but it is thought that they may be used
to attract females.

In Mexico, two-lined bats have been observed roosting under
concrete bridges and on the walls of buildings. Each individual
seems faithful to its roosting place, returning each morning to
the precise spot that it left the evening before. Females give birth
to young in the rainy season when their food supply – beetles
and moths – is most plentiful. The young are weaned before
they are 2 months old.

Old World Sheath-tailed Bat

Emballonura monticola

RANGE Thailand to Malaysia, Java,
Sumatra, Borneo and Sulawesi

HABITAT Rain forest

SIZE Body: 1½–2¼ in (4–6 cm)
Wingspan: 6¼–7 in
(16–18 cm)
Tail: ½ in (1 cm)

Old World sheath-tailed bats generally roost in rock fissures or
caves in the forest in groups of a dozen or so. At dusk they
depart simultaneously to feed and then return together at dawn.
They appear to feed in the top layer of the tallest trees and to
supplement their insect diet with fruit and occasionally flowers.

Although little is known of the breeding habits of the Old
World sheath-tailed bats, they are likely to breed throughout the
year, producing 1 young at a time.

Tomb Bat *Taphozous longimanus*

RANGE India, Sri Lanka to east to S. E. Asia

HABITAT Coconut groves, scrub, ruined tombs
and palaces

SIZE Body: 2¾–3½ in (7–9 cm)
Wingspan: 9¾–13 in (25–33 cm)
Tail: ¾–1½ in (2–3.5 cm)

This bat's common name is
derived from its habit of
roosting inside manmade
structures, such as tombs.
Tomb bats appear in Chinese paintings of 2,000 years
ago – almost the oldest recorded artistic impression of a
bat. They are neat little creatures with short shiny coats.

Tomb bats leave their roosts in the evening and fly up as
high as 330 ft (100 m) at dusk in search of their insect prey. As
the night progresses, they gradually descend. While hunting,
tomb bats emit loud cries which are easily heard by human ears.

White Bat *Diclidurus virgo*

RANGE S. Mexico, Central America

HABITAT Forest, open land

SIZE Body: 2–3¼ in (5–8 cm) Wingspan: 7–11¾ in (18–30 cm)
Tail: ½–1 in (1.5–2.5 cm)

The white bat, with its white fur and wing membrane, is a
truly spectral creature. Since almost all other bats are dark, it
is a mystery why this species should be white. However, it is
just as successful at hunting insect prey as its dark relatives,
which suggests that there is no evolutionary disadvantage in the
light coloration. Another curious feature is the presence of
saclike glands in the tail membrane. There are no wing glands.

It roosts in caves or crevices, usually alone, but occasionally
in pairs. It appears to breed throughout the year.

HOG-NOSED BAT, SLIT-FACED BATS AND FALSE VAMPIRES

CRASEONYCTERIDAE: HOG-NOSED BAT FAMILY

The single species in this family was first discovered in 1973 in the karst region of western Thailand. It is the smallest bat yet recorded and may be the world's smallest mammal.

Hog-nosed Bat
Craseonycteris thonglongyai **EN**
RANGE Thailand
HABITAT Limestone caves, bamboo forests and teak plantations
SIZE Body: 1¼ in (3 cm)
Wingspan: 4¼–5 in (11–12.5 cm)
Tail: absent

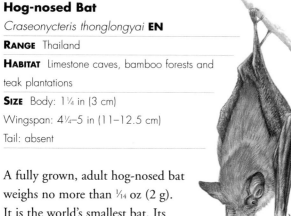

A fully grown, adult hog-nosed bat weighs no more than ¹⁄₁₄ oz (2 g). It is the world's smallest bat. Its upperparts are brown to reddish or gray. The fur on the underside is slightly paler than that on the rest of the body, and the wings darker.

Its piglike nose is thought to be an adaptation for gleaning small insects and other invertebrates off the surface of leaves. At dusk, hog-nosed bats emerge from the caves, where they roost in small colonies, and forage around the tops of bamboo clumps and in the dense foliage of teak trees, which their tiny bodies can easily penetrate. Nothing is known of their breeding habits.

NYCTERIDAE: SLIT-FACED BAT FAMILY

There are 12 species in this family. All are distinguished by a distinctive pair of slits in the sides of the face which extend laterally from the nostrils to just above the eyes. Like most complex facial features in bats, these slits are thought to play a part in beaming ultrasonic signals, which the bat uses in conjunction with its well developed ears in order to find its way in the dark and to locate its prey. This family is generally insectivorous, though spiders and scorpions will also be eaten.

Another unusual feature of the slit-faced bat is the tail, which extends to the end of the tail membrane and then terminates in a "T" shaped bone, unique among mammals.

Female slit-faced bats give birth twice a year.

Egyptian Slit-faced Bat *Nycteris thebaica*
RANGE Middle East, Africa, south of the Sahara; Madagascar
HABITAT Dry plains, forest
SIZE Body: 1¾–3 in (4.5–7.5 cm) Wingspan: 6¼–11 in (16–28 cm) Tail: 1½–3 in (4–7.5 cm)

Egyptian slit-faced bats feed on a variety of invertebrate animals which they catch in trees or even on the ground. Scorpions seem to be a particularly favored food. The bats generally give birth to a single offspring in January or February and are thought to produce a second later in the year.

MEGADERMATIDAE: FALSE VAMPIRE FAMILY

In the struggle for survival among the many bat species, one family has evolved as specialist predators on other bats. The false vampire swoops silently down on a smaller bat and seems to chew it for a while before devouring the meat – a habit that led to the belief that these bats sucked blood. This is now known not to be the case and, in fact, not all false vampires are even carnivorous; those that are use their predatory skills only to supplement an insectivorous diet. There are 5 species of false vampire, all with long ears and fluted nose leaves.

Greater False Vampire
Megaderma lyra
RANGE India to Myanmar, S. China, Malaysia
HABITAT Forest, open land
SIZE Body: 2½–3¼ in (6.5–8.5 cm)
Wingspan: 9–11¾ in (23–30 cm) Tail: absent

The greater false vampire regularly supplements its diet of insects, spiders and other invertebrates with prey, such as bats, rodents, frogs and even fish. Groups of 3 to 50 false vampires roost together and are usually the sole inhabitants of their caves. Presumably their predatory tendencies deter other bats from sharing their abode.

False vampires mate in November, and 1 young is born after a gestation of 20 weeks. Shortly before females are due to give birth, males leave the roost and return 3 or 4 months later, to resume communal roosting.

Heart-nosed Bat *Cardioderma cor*

RANGE E. C. Africa: Ethiopia to Tanzania

HABITAT Forest, scrub

SIZE Body: 2¾–3½ in (7–9 cm) Wingspan: 10–13½ in (26–35 cm) Tail: absent

The heart-nosed bat closely resembles the greater false vampire in appearance and way of life, but has a wider, heartshaped nose leaf.

Like its relatives, it feeds on vertebrate animals as well as insects. Before the heat of the day has passed, the heart-nosed bat emerges from its roost and swoops to catch lizards – it will even enter houses in pursuit of rodents or wall lizards.

It is a strong flier and can take off from the ground carrying a load as big as itself. Heart-nosed bats attack smaller bats in flight, "boxing" them with their powerful wings to upset their directional stability.

Australian False Vampire bat *Macroderma gigas* **VU**

RANGE N. and W. tropical Australia

HABITAT Forest with rock caves

SIZE Body: 4½–5½ in (11.5–14 cm) Wingspan: 18–23½ in (46–60 cm) Tail: absent

On account of its pale coloration, the Australian false vampire is popularly known as the ghost bat. It is one of the most carnivorous of bats and feeds almost exclusively on mice, birds, geckos and other bats. Its method of attack is to flop down on the unsuspecting prey and

enmesh it in its strong wings, then to deliver a single killing bite to the back of the prey's neck. It then takes off from the ground carrying a dead rodent and flies to a feeding perch in cave or tree.

Like all false vampires, this species has long ears which are joined by a membrane extending about halfway up their length.

Males forsake the communal roost in September or October, just before the young bats are due to be born. By January the young bats are as large as their mothers and accompany them on nighttime hunting trips. The males move back into the roosts by April.

This handsome species is now rare and active conservation measures are urgently required in order to ensure its survival.

Yellow-winged Bat
Lavia frons

RANGE Africa: Senegal to Kenya

HABITAT Swamps, lakes in forest and open country

SIZE Body: 2½–3 in (6.5–8 cm) Wingspan: 9½–11¾ in (24–30 cm) Tail: absent

The yellow-winged bat is a strikingly colored species. The body fur color is variable, ranging through blue-gray or brown to whitish. However, the ears and wings are always yellowish-red. This species has large ears and eyes. Its nose leaf – the fleshy growth around the nostrils and mouth, which is believed to be used to help with echolocation – is the most prominent feature of the false vampire family.

The yellow-winged bat roosts in trees and bushes, where only the flickering of its long ears gives away its presence. These bats often fly in the daytime, but seem to feed only during the night hours.

In contrast to the other false vampires, yellow-winged bats appear to restrict themselves to insect food. Their method of hunting is rather like that of the flycatcher birds. The bat hides on its favorite perch in a tree, quiet and still and obscured by the foliage. When an insect flies nearby the bat swoops down from the branch to snap it up, then returns to its hunting perch to lie in wait again.

Yellow-winged bats breed throughout the year; males do not leave the communal roost for the birth season.

HORSESHOE BATS

RHINOLOPHIDAE: HORSESHOE BAT FAMILY

The shape of the fleshy structure surrounding the nose distinguishes the horseshoe bat from other insectivorous bats. While most small bats emit their ultrasonic cries through open mouths, horseshoe bats "shout" through their nostrils. The nose leaf acts as an adjustable megaphone, enabling the bat to direct its "radar" beam wherever it wishes. Two other structures on the face, the lancet above the nostrils and the sella, which partially separates them, are immensely muscular and can vibrate at the same frequency as the sound pulse. Horseshoe bats wrap their wings around their bodies when roosting.

There are 132 species of horseshoe bat found in temperate and tropical parts of the Old World as far east as Japan and Australia. This order also includes about 63 species that were formerly classified in an order of their own – the Old World Leaf-nosed bats. Males and females generally look alike. Many of these bats are extremely numerous and of great benefit to man since they feed entirely on insects and destroy many insect pests.

Lesser Horseshoe Bat *Rhinolophus hipposideros* **VU**

RANGE   Europe, Asia, N. Africa

HABITAT   Open country with caves

SIZE   Body: 2¾–4 in (7–10 cm) Wingspan: 9–10 in (22.5–25 cm) Tail: ½–1 in (1.5–2.5 cm)

The lesser horseshoe bat is similar to the greater, and equally fluttering in flight, but it is more maneuvrable and hunts far more in the air. In summer it roosts in trees, hollow logs and houses, making incessant chattering noises. In winter the bats make short migrations to winter hibernation quarters in caves, which are frost-free but not necessarily dry.

Philippine Horseshoe Bat *Rhinolophus philippinensis* **LR:nt**

RANGE   Philippine Islands

HABITAT   Primary forest, broken land

SIZE   Body: 2¾–3½ in (7–9 cm) Wingspan: 9–10¼ in (23–26 cm) Tail: ½–1 in (1.5–2.5 cm)

Within the rich bat fauna of its native islands, the Philippine horseshoe bat occupies its own special niche. It feeds on large slow-flying insects and on heavily armored ground beetles and using its sharp teeth, can slice through the thick wing cases and wings before devouring the insects.

Hibernation is not necessary in the Philippine climate and the bats remain active throughout the year. Breeding also occurs throughout the year. Young mature in their second year, and males are smaller than females.

Greater Horseshoe Bat *Rhinolophus ferrumequinum* **LR: cd**

RANGE   Europe, Asia, N. Africa

HABITAT   Forest; open and cultivated land

SIZE   Body: 4½–5 in (11–12.5 cm) Wingspan: 13–14 in (33–35 cm) Tail: 1–1½ in (2.5–4 cm)

The greater horseshoe bat is rather slow and fluttering in flight and not adept at catching insects in the air. It feeds largely on the ground, swooping down on beetles with unerring accuracy. These bats hibernate from October to March and often choose winter quarters deep within caves, crevices or potholes. Thousands hibernate together and make long migrations to reach these quarters. The female gives birth to 1 young in April and carries it about until it is 3 months old.

Persian Trident Bat *Triaenops persicus*

RANGE Egypt, east to Iran, south to the Gulf of Eilat

HABITAT Arid land, semi-desert

SIZE Body: 1½–2¼ in (3.5–5.5 cm)
Wingspan: 6–7½ in (15–19 cm) Tail: ½ in (1.5 cm)

The Persian trident bat and the other 2 species in its genus are distinguished from the rest of their family by the structures above the nose disc. These bats roost in underground cracks and tunnels and emerge while it is still light to fly fast and low over the ground to their feeding areas where, high in the foliage, small insects are hunted down.

Trident bats breed between December and May. The births coincide with the rains. A single young is born and is left in the roost while its mother hunts.

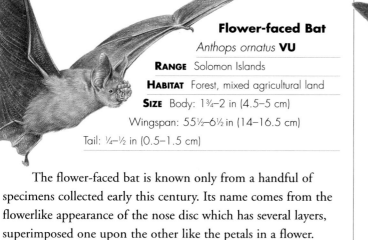

Flower-faced Bat

Anthops ornatus **VU**

RANGE Solomon Islands

HABITAT Forest, mixed agricultural land

SIZE Body: 1¾–2 in (4.5–5 cm)
Wingspan: 5½–6½ in (14–16.5 cm)

Tail: ¼–½ in (0.5–1.5 cm)

The flower-faced bat is known only from a handful of specimens collected early this century. Its name comes from the flowerlike appearance of the nose disc which has several layers, superimposed one upon the other like the petals in a flower. Why such a bizarre device is required is not known.

Trident Leaf-nosed Bat *Asellia tridens*

RANGE N. Africa, east to India

HABITAT Arid scrub

SIZE Body: 2–2¼ in (5–6 cm)

Tail: ¾–1 in (2–2.5 cm)

The common name of this species comes from its three-pronged nasal lancet. Hundreds of these bats roost together in underground tunnels and cracks. They emerge in early evening to skim over the surface of the land toward palm groves where, in the shade and moisture, insects abound. Beetles and moths are favored foods.

Large Malay Leaf-nosed Bat

Hipposideros diadema

RANGE S.E. Asia, New Guinea, Solomon Islands, N.E. Queensland

HABITAT Forest, often near human habitation

SIZE Body: 2¾–4 in (7–10 cm)
Wingspan: 9–10 in (22.5–25 cm)
Tail: 1–1¼ in (2.5–3 cm)

This sociable bat roosts in groups of many hundreds in caves or abandoned old buildings. At dusk the bats depart from their roost in order to hunt for food. They forage around flowers, snapping up insects, and occasionally they will tear open figs in order to dig out insect larvae hidden inside, at the same time consuming the fig pulp and seeds.

The single young bat is usually born some time between November and December.

Tail-less Leaf-nosed Bat *Coelops frithi*

RANGE Bangladesh through Indo-China to Java

HABITAT Forest

SIZE Body: 1–1¾ in (3–4.5 cm) Wingspan: 4¼–5¼ in (11–13 cm)

Tail: absent

The tailless leaf-nosed bat has a much less complex nose disc than its relatives. Its ears are shorter and more rounded than is usual in this family. Its broad wings make it extremely maneuverable in the air (although its poorly developed hind legs mean that it can not move easily on land) and it feeds on insects which it chases on the wing.

Small groups of a dozen or more tailless leaf nosed bats shelter together during the day in hollow trees or in human dwellings.

In Java, it has been observed that births occur towards the end of February.

FISHERMAN, MUSTACHED, NEW WORLD LEAF-NOSED AND FREE-TAILED BATS

NOCTILIONIDAE: FISHERMAN BAT FAMILY

There are 2 species in this family, also known as Bulldog Bats, both found in Central America and northern South America. They inhabit swampy forests and mangroves and, as their name implies, feed on fish.

Fisherman Bat

Noctilio leporinus

RANGE Mexico, south to Argentina; Antilles, Trinidad

HABITAT Forest, mangrove swamps

SIZE Body: 4–5¼ in (10–13 cm) Wingspan: 11–12 in (28–30 cm) Tail: ½–1 in (1–2.5 cm)

With powerful, stiff-winged flight, the fisherman bat swoops to within an inch of the water, dipping briefly to impale a small fish with its long sharp claws and scoop it into its mouth. Fisherman bats also use their feet to catch insects, both in the water and the air, and these make up a substantial part of their diet in some regions. Just how they locate their prey is unknown, but, since they emit floods of ultrasound while hunting, it is thought that they can detect tiny ripples made by a surfacing fish.

In November or December fisherman bats mate, and a single young is born after a gestation of about 16 weeks.

MORMOOPIDAE: MUSTACHED BAT FAMILY

There are 8 species in this family, also known as Naked-backed bats which ranges from southern Arizona to Brazil. The bats derive their name from the fringe of hairs surrounding the mouth. Some species have wing membranes that meet and fuse in the middle of the back. These membranes give the back a naked appearance.

Mustached Bat

Pteronotus parnielli

RANGE N. Mexico to Brazil; West Indies

HABITAT Lowland tropical forest

SIZE Body: 1½–3 in (4–7.5 cm)
Wingspan: 8–13 in (20–33 cm)
Tail: ½–1¼ in (1.5–3 cm)

In addition to the fringe of hairs around its mouth, this bat has a platelike growth on its lower lip and small fleshy papillae projecting down from the upper lip. This structure helps the bat to collect its insect food.

Mustached bats are gregarious and roost in large groups in caves. They lie horizontally and do not hang in the usual manner of bats. Young are usually born in May when the bats' food supply is most abundant. Most females have just 1 young a year.

Leaf-chinned Bat *Mormoops megalophylla*

RANGE Arizona to N. South America; Trinidad

HABITAT Forest, scrub, near water

SIZE Body: 2–2½ in (6–6.5 cm) Wingspan: 10–11 in (25–28 cm) Tail: 1 in (2.5 cm)

A pair of fleshy flaps on the chin, and peglike projections on the lower jaw distinguish this species. Leaf-chinned bats shelter in caves, tunnels and rock fissures. They hunt somewhat later than most bats, emerging after dark to look for insects. They fly close to the ground and often feed near pools and swamps.

MOLOSSIDAE: FREE-TAILED BAT FAMILY

The 80 species of free-tailed bat occur in the warmer parts of the Old and New World. The typical free-tailed bat has a rodentlike tail, which extends well beyond the free edge of the tail membrane, and rather narrow wings, which beat more rapidly than those of other insectivorous bats. Free-tailed bats feed entirely on insects, favoring hard-shelled species. They roost in vast hordes, and their droppings create guano which is used in the fertilizer industry.

Egyptian Free-tailed Bat *Tadarida aegyptiaca*

RANGE N. Africa, Middle East

HABITAT Arid scrub land

SIZE Body: 2¼–2¾ in (5.5–7 cm) Wingspan: 6¾–7½ in (17–19 cm) Tail: 1¼–2 in (3–5 cm)

One of the most common mammals in the Middle East, the Egyptian free-tailed bat roosts in groups of many thousands. Almost any sizeable crevice suffices, even if it is already occupied by another animal. The bats mate in late winter and the female gives birth to a single young after a gestation of 77 to 84 days. A second pregnancy may follow immediately.

Velvety Free-tailed Bat

Molossus ater

RANGE S. Mexico, Central America, Trinidad

HABITAT Scrub, savanna, forest

SIZE Body: 2½–3½ in (6–9 cm) Wingspan: 10–11 in (26–28 cm) Tail: 1¼–1½ in (3–4 cm)

This species has dense, short, velvety fur. It hunts insects and catches several at a time, cramming them into its cheek pouches. On returning to its roost, the bat devours its catch. This behavior may have evolved to reduce the time the bats are out and at risk of predation. One or two litters are born in summer.

Mastiff Bat *Eumops perotis*

RANGE S.W. USA, Mexico, N. South America

HABITAT Forest, near human habitation

SIZE Body: 2¾–4 in (7–10 cm) Wingspan: 11–12 in (28–30 cm) Tail: 1½–2¼ in (4–6 cm)

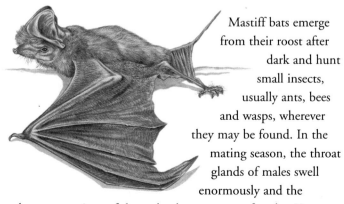

Mastiff bats emerge from their roost after dark and hunt small insects, usually ants, bees and wasps, wherever they may be found. In the mating season, the throat glands of males swell enormously and the odorous secretions of these glands may attract females. Young are born in late summer, and twins are not uncommon.

Wroughton's Free-tailed Bat

Otomops wroughtoni **CR**

RANGE S. India, Sri Lanka

HABITAT Open, partially forested land

SIZE Body: 3¾–4¼ in (9.5–11 cm) Wingspan: 11–12 in (28–30 cm) Tail: 1¼–2 in (3–5 cm)

This species roosts in small groups or alone; few specimens have been collected. Females give birth to a single young in December.

PHYLLOSTOMATIDAE: NEW WORLD LEAF-NOSED BAT FAMILY

As night descends over the Central and South American jungles, leaf-nosed bats emerge from their roosts to feed on the pollen and nectar of flowers. About 140 species of leaf-nosed bat have evolved to exploit this particular way of life. Generally they are small, but the American false vampire has a wingspan which may exceed 3¼ ft (1 m), making it the largest New World bat.

Leaf-nosed bats may be tailless or have tiny tails in the tail membrane. Most members of the family have a nose leaf – a flap of tissue above the nostrils, but it is usually a simple flap of skin.

These abundant bats transfer pollen between flowers and a number of plants have become adapted to pollination by bats – flowering at night and producing heavy, musky odors.

This order includes the three species of vampire bat which are totally adapted to a diet of blood. These are the only mammals to qualify as parasites.

Short-tailed Leaf-nosed Bat

Carollia perspicillata

RANGE S. Mexico to S. Brazil

HABITAT Forest, plantations

SIZE Body: 2–2½ in (5–6.5 cm) Wingspan: 8¼–9¾ in (21–25 cm) Tail: ¼–½ in (0.5–1.5 cm)

This bat feeds almost entirely on ripe fruit, such as bananas, figs, guavas and plantains, which it locates by smell. There is no defined breeding season for this species, and females produce their single youngster at any time of the year.

NEW WORLD LEAF-NOSED BATS

Long-tongued Bat

Glossophaga soricina

RANGE N. Mexico to Brazil, Paraguay and Argentina; West Indies

HABITAT Woodland, often arid

SIZE Body: 2–2½ in (5–6.5 cm) Wingspan: 7¾–9½ in (20–24 cm) Tail: ¼ in (0.5 cm)

The long-tongued bat is the mammalian equivalent of the hummingbird. This bat hovers in front of flowers and scoops up pollen and nectar from deep within them with the aid of its long tongue. Tiny bristles on its surface help the pollen to stick fast.

Female bats form maternity colonies in summer, rejoining their original roosts when the young are born. Twins do occur, but a single young is more common.

American False Vampire

Vampyrum spectrum **LR:nt**

RANGE S. Mexico to Peru and Brazil; Trinidad

HABITAT Forest, often near human habitation

SIZE Body: 5–5¼ in (12.5–13.5 cm)

Wingspan: 31½ in–3¼ ft (80 cm–1 m) Tail: absent

This species, formerly believed to be a blood–sucker, is now known to kill and eat rodents, birds and other bats. It is surprisingly agile on all fours and stalks mice stealthily; it then kills by an accurate pounce, which breaks the prey's neck or shatters its skull.

The bats breed in June and the females are most solicitous parents, licking their young incessantly and feeding them pieces of chewed mouse flesh as they approach weaning.

Tent–building Bat *Uroderma bilobatum*

RANGE S. Mexico to Peru and Brazil; Trinidad

HABITAT Forest, plantations

SIZE Body: 2¼–3 in (5.5–7.5 cm)

Wingspan: 7¾–9½ in (20–24 cm) Tail: absent

The tent–building bat is alert and active by day and has developed a simple way of creating a shady refuge. Fan-shaped palm leaves are partially bitten through in a semicircular line, a third of the way along a frond. The end of the frond then collapses, making a tent–shaped refuge, from which the bats fly out in search of ripe fruit. A colony of 20 or 30 bats may share a tent.

Pregnant females establish maternity tents and young are born between February and April. The young remain in the maternity tent until they are able to fly. Males live alone or in small groups during the breeding season, returning to the females when the young are weaned.

Spear-nosed Bat *Phyllostomus hastatus*

RANGE Belize to Peru, Bolivia and Brazil; Trinidad

HABITAT Forest, broken country

SIZE Body: 4–5¼ in (10–13 cm) Wingspan: 17¼–18½ in (44–47 cm) Tail: 1 in (2.5 cm)

One of the larger American bats, the spear-nosed has virtually abandoned an insectivorous diet in favor of a carnivorous one. It feeds on mice, birds and small bats and occasionally also on insects and fruit.

Huge flocks of these bats shelter in caves and abandoned buildings and at dusk they depart together for their feeding grounds.

Young are born between May and June in the communal roost.

Yellow-shouldered Bat *Sturnira lilium*

RANGE N. Mexico to Paraguay and Argentina; Jamaica

HABITAT Lowland forest

SIZE Body: 2¼–2¾ in (6–7 cm) Wingspan: 9½–10½ in (24–27 cm)
Tail: absent

The yellow-shouldered bat feeds on ripe fruit and roosts alone or
in small groups in old buildings, hollow trees or high up in the
crowns of palm trees.

In the north of their range, these bats breed throughout the
year, but in the south the young are born between May and July.
Females generally produce 1 infant at a time.

Little Big-eared Bat *Micronycteris megalotis*

RANGE S.W. USA to Peru, Brazil; Trinidad,
Tobago and Grenada

HABITAT Dry scrub to tropical rain forest

SIZE Body: 1½–2½ in (4–6.5 cm) Wingspan: 6¼–7¾ in
(16–20 cm) Tail: ¼–½ in (0.5–1 cm)

Little big-eared bats roost in small groups in a great
variety of shelter holes. They emerge as dusk is
falling and swoop around fruit trees, chasing heavy,
slow-flying insects, such as cockchafers, or plucking
cockroaches from the ground. They appear to supplement this
diet with the pulp of fruit, such as guava and bananas. Young
are born between April and June, most females give birth to a
single offspring.

Jamaican Fruit-eating Bat *Artibeus jamaicensis*

RANGE N. Mexico to Brazil and N. Argentina; West Indies

HABITAT Scrub, forest

SIZE Body: 3–3½ in (7.5–9 cm)
Wingspan: 9–10¼ in (23–26 cm)
Tail: absent

This bat is one of the most efficient
mammalian food processors: it
feeds on fruit, which passes

through its gut in as little as 15 minutes. There is no time for
bacterial action to destroy material, so the bat is an important
distributor of seeds.

The breeding season lasts from February to
July, and females give birth to 1, sometimes
2, young.

Cuban Flower Bat *Phyllonycteris poeyi* **LR:nt**

RANGE Cuba

HABITAT Primary forest, cultivated land

SIZE Body: 3–3¼ in (7.5–8 cm) Wingspan: 8¼–9 in (21–23 cm)
Tail: ½ in (1–1.5 cm)

The Cuban flower bat has little or no nose leaf. It is a gregarious
bat and roosts in thousands in caves and rock fissures. It uses its
long, slender tongue to suck and lap up nectar and pollen from
many types of flowers, and it also feeds on fruit.

These bats breed throughout the year; young are left in the
roost until they are able to fly.

Vampire Bat *Desmodus rotundus*

RANGE N. Mexico to C. Chile,
Argentina and Uruguay

HABITAT Forest

SIZE Body: 3–3½ in (7.5–9 cm)
Wingspan: 6¼–7 in (16–18 cm) Tail: absent

The vampire, like most bats, hunts at night. It has the most
specialized diet of all bats, existing only on blood. It approaches
its victim by alighting quietly on the ground a few feet away
then walking over on all fours. With its four razor-sharp canine
teeth, the vampire then makes a small, painless incision on a
hairless or featherless part of the animal, such as the snout. The
edges of the bat's long, protruded tongue are bent downward
and form a tube, through which saliva is pumped out to prevent
the blood from clotting while the bat sucks it in.

About half an hour's feeding each night is
sufficient for a vampire bat, and
although the host loses only a small
amount of blood, the bite of the bat may
transmit various diseases between animals
through its saliva, including rabies.

EVENING BATS

VESPERTILIONIDAE: EVENING BAT FAMILY

There are some 318 species in this family, found around the world from the tropics to as far as about 68° North. Many species hibernate for 5 or 6 months to survive the winter in harsh northern latitudes.

Most have quite simple muzzles, though a few species have a nose-leaf and some have tubular nostrils. Ear sizes vary enormously and the color is generally quite dull.

Nearly all species are insectivorous, although one or two feed on fish which they scoop from the water. Insects are usually caught in the air, the bat tossing the insect into its tail membrane with its wing. All these bats make use of echolocation for finding prey and for plotting their flight course.

Evening bats are extremely numerous in the cool, northern parts of the world. Without their massive consumption of blackflies, midges and mosquitoes, life for humans during the short northern summers would be distinctly more uncomfortable.

Little Brown Bat *Myotis lucifugus*

RANGE N. America: from 62°N, south to Mexico

HABITAT Forest, built-up areas

SIZE Body: 1½ in (4 cm) Wingspan: 5½–7 in (14–18 cm)
Tail: 1 in (2.5 cm)

A common species in North America, the little brown bat adapts equally well to cold and hot climates. In the warmer parts of their range little brown bats do not hibernate, but northern populations may migrate hundreds of miles to hibernation sites. It feeds on whatever insects are abundant locally.

In summer, the females segregate themselves and roost in maternity sites. A single young, sometimes twins, is born in May or June after a gestation period of between 50 and 60 days. The young are mature at 1 year.

Fish-eating Bat *Pizonyx vivesi*

RANGE Coasts of Baja California and
W. Mexico

HABITAT Caves, coastal rock piles

SIZE Body: 2¾–3¼ in (7–8.5 cm)
Wingspan: 9¾–12½ in (25–32 cm)
Tail: 2–2½ in (5–6.5cm)

This species is specialized for feeding on fish. It has feet with long rakelike toes, ending in razor-sharp claws. Late in the evening, the bat flies low over the sea and takes small fish and crustaceans from the surface by impaling them on its claws. It is not known how it locates its prey, but its "radar" system might be capable of noting irregularities in the water caused by a fish moving close to the surface.

The female bat bears a single young in May or June and carries her infant with her until it is half-grown. It is then left in a secure roost with other young, while the mother hunts.

Common Long-eared Bat *Plecotus auritus*

RANGE N. Europe, east to N.E. China and Japan

HABITAT Sheltered, lightly wooded areas

SIZE Body: 1½–2 in (4–5 cm) Wingspan: 9–11 in (23–28 cm)
Tail: 1¼–1¾ in (3–4.5 cm)

The distinguishing feature of the common long-eared bat is its large ears, which are three-quarters the length of its head and body combined. The ears are an essential part of the bat's hunting equipment. They are extremely sensitive and are used to listen for the movements and calls of insect prey as well as to pick up the echoes of the bat's echolocation pulses which bounce back off solid objects, such as obstacles in the bat's path or prey.

In summer these bats roost in buildings and trees and hunt primarily for the night-flying noctuid moths. They also feed on midges, mosquitoes and other flies, often picking them off vegetation in dive-bombing, swooping flights.

The female gives birth to a single young in June, and females and young form nursery roosts. Long-eared bats are mature at about a year old.

Common Pipistrelle *Pipistrellus pipistrellus*

RANGE Europe, east to Kashmir

HABITAT Open land

SIZE Body: 1¼–1¾ in (3–4.5 cm)
Wingspan: 7½–9¾ in (19–25 cm) Tail: 1–1¼ in (2.5–3 cm)

Perhaps the commonest European bats, pipistrelles roost in groups of up to a thousand or more in lofts, church spires, farm buildings and the like. In winter, these bats migrate to a suitable dry cave to hibernate in colonies of 100,000 or more. They feed on insects, eating small prey in flight but taking larger catches to a perch to eat. Births occur in mid-June and twins have been recorded. The bats actually mate in September, prior to hibernation, and the sperm is stored in the female for 7 or 8 months before fertilization occurs and gestation starts.

Big Brown Bat *Eptesicus fuscus*

RANGE N. America: Alaska to Central America; West Indies

HABITAT Varied, often close to human habitation

SIZE Body: 2–3 in (5–7.5 cm)
Wingspan: 10¼–14½ in (26–37 cm)
Tail: 1¾–2¼ in (4.5–5.5 cm)

Big brown bats eat almost all insects except, it seems, moths, and also manage to catch water beetles. They have been recorded flying at a speed of 15½ mph (25 km/h). They will enter houses to hibernate, although huge numbers migrate to caves in Missouri and other southern states for this purpose. Young are born from April to July; a single young is the rule west of the Rockies, but twins are common in the east.

Red Bat *Lasiurus borealis*

RANGE N. America

HABITAT Forested land with open space

SIZE Body: 2¼–3¼ in (6–8 cm) Wingspan: 14¼–16½ in (36–42 cm) Tail: 1¾–2 in (4.5–5 cm)

The red bat's fur varies in shade from brick–red to rust, suffused with white. Males are more brightly colored than females. The species is unique among bats in the size of its litters, regularly giving birth to 3 or 4 young in June or early July. The female carries her young with her at first, even though their combined weights may exceed her own body weight. North American red bats migrate southward in autumn and north again in spring.

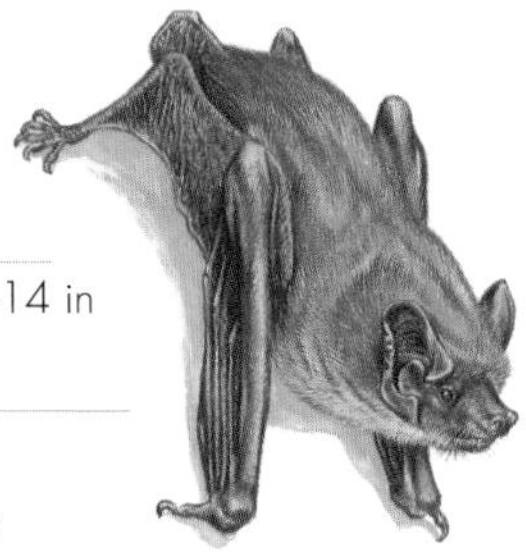

Noctule *Nyctalus noctula*

RANGE Europe, east to Japan

HABITAT Forest, open land

SIZE Body: 2¾–3¼ in (7–8 cm) Wingspan: 12½–14 in (32–35.5 cm) Tail: 1¼–2¼ in (3–5.5 cm)

One of the largest evening bats, the noctule feeds mainly on maybugs, crickets and dorbeetles, and there are reports of its killing house mice. In winter, noctules hibernate in trees or lofts, usually in small groups, but roosts of a few hundred do occur. They breed in June, producing 1, or sometimes 2 or even 3, young.

Barbastelle
Barbastella barbastellus **VU**

RANGE Europe, Morocco, Canary Islands

HABITAT Open land, often near water

SIZE Body: 1½–2 in (4–5 cm)
Wingspan: 9½–11 in (24.5–28 cm)
Tail: 1½–1¾ in (4–4.5 cm)

In early evening, often before sunset, barbastelles emerge to hunt for insects flying low over water or bushes. Males and females segregate for the summer and females form maternity colonies. From late September, barbastelles congregate in limestone regions to hibernate in deep, dry caves.

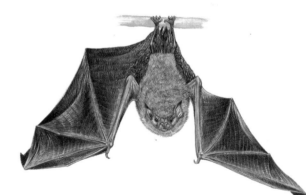

Painted Bat *Kerivoula argentata*

RANGE Africa: S. Kenya, Namibia, Natal

HABITAT Arid woodland

SIZE Body: 1¼–2¼ in (3–5.5 cm) Wingspan: 7–11¾ in (18–30 cm) Tail: 1¼–2¼ in (3–5.5 cm)

Small groups of painted bats are often found in the most unlikely roosts, such as in the suspended nests of weaver finches and sunbirds, or under the eaves of African huts. Doubtless the bright and broken coloration of these bats is a form of camouflage to protect them while they roost in vulnerable sites. Nothing is known of their breeding biology.

FUNNEL-EARED, SMOKY, DISC-WINGED, SUCKER-FOOTED AND SHORT-TAILED BATS

NATALIDAE: FUNNEL-EARED BAT FAMILY

The 5 species of funnel-eared bat occur in cavernous country in tropical South America. The family name comes from the large funnel-shaped ears, the outer surfaces of which bear glandular projections. Males and females look alike, except that on their muzzles males have thick glandular, or sensory projections, the function of which is not known.

Mexican Funnel-eared Bat *Natalus stramineus*

RANGE N. Mexico to Brazil; Lesser Antilles

HABITAT Tropical lowlands

SIZE Body: 1¼–2¼ in (3–5.5 cm) Wingspan: 7–9½ in (18–24 cm)
Tail: 2–2¼ in (5–6 cm)

Funnel-eared bats roost in caves and mines, sometimes in huge numbers, but more often in groups of about a dozen. The bats emerge at dusk to search for slow-flying insects, and they themselves fly with fluttering, rather mothlike movements. Breeding takes place at any time of the year, and the sexes segregate just before the young are born.

FURIPTERIDAE: SMOKY BAT FAMILY

There are 2 species in this family, both characterized by their smoky coloration, by being thumbless and by having extremely long tail membranes. The family occurs in tropical South America and in Trinidad.

Smoky Bat *Furipterus horrens*

RANGE Costa Rica, northern South America: E. Peru, Guianas, Brazil; Trinidad

HABITAT Forest

SIZE Body: 1½–2¼ in (4–6 cm) Wingspan: 8½–11¾ in (22–30 cm)
Tail: 1½–2¼ in (4–6 cm)

Unlike other bats, the smoky bat has no clawed thumbs, so that when it alights on the wall of its cave or tunnel roost, it must perform an aerial somersault in order to grasp the surface with its hind feet. Another curious feature of this bat and its fellow species is the high forehead – the snout and the brow join almost at right angles.

Practically nothing is known of the biology of either species of smoky bat. They certainly feed on insects, but how they avoid competing with the many other species of insect-eating bat within their range is not understood.

THYROPTERIDAE: DISC-WINGED BAT FAMILY

The 2 species in this family occur in Central America and in tropical South America, as far as Peru and southern Brazil. They derive their common name from suction pads at the base of each thumb and on the ankles. These discs are attached to the bat by short stalks and enable it to climb rapidly up smooth leaves and bare tree trunks. A curious characteristic of disc-winged bats is that they usually hang head upward when roosting – a feat made possible by the powerful suction discs.

Honduran Disc–winged Bat *Thyroptera discifera*

RANGE Belize, south to Ecuador and Peru

HABITAT Forest

SIZE Body: 1¼–2 in (3–5 cm) Wingspan: 7–9¾ in (18–25 cm)
Tail: 1–1¼ in (2.5–3 cm)

This small insect–eating bat has a similar high forehead to that
of the smoky bat, but again the reasons for this are not known.
It can climb up smooth surfaces, even glass, by means of its
sucker discs, the suction pressure from a single disc is quite
sufficient to support the entire weight of the bat. Suction is
applied or released by specialized muscles in the forearms.

Disc–winged bats have unusual roosting habits: they roost in the
young, curled leaves of plants such as bananas. These leaves, before
they unfurl, form long tubes, and several bats may roost in a single
leaf, anchored by their suckers to the smooth surface. The bats must
find a new leaf practically every day as the previous roost unfurls.

Breeding takes place throughout the year, and the sexes do
not appear to segregate before the females give birth. A single
young is the normal litter and the mother carries it about with
her until it weighs more than half her body weight. Her flying
ability is not impaired by this extra load. Subsequently the
young bat is left in the roost while she hunts.

MYZOPODIDAE: OLD WORLD SUCKER-FOOTED BAT FAMILY

The single species of sucker-footed bat is restricted to the island
continent of Madagascar. The Myzopodidae is the only family
of bats found solely on that island and represents a relict species,
cut off from Africa when Madagascar
broke free from that land mass.

Sucker–footed Bat
Myzopoda aurita **VU**

RANGE Madagascar

HABITAT Forest

SIZE Body: 2–2¼ in (5–6 cm)
Wingspan: 8½–11 in (22–28 cm) Tail: 1¾–2 in (4.5–5 cm)

Superficially the sucker-footed bat resembles the disc-winged

bats of the New World, for there are large suction discs at the
base of each thumb and on each ankle. But the discs of this bat
are quite immobile, in sharp contrast to those of the disc-winged
bat, which are connected to the body by mobile stalks, and they
appear to be less efficient.

The bat roosts inside curled leaves or hollow plant stems,
and sometimes the smooth trunk of a tree may also serve it as a
temporary nest.

Nothing is known of the breeding or feeding habits of these
bats and they seem to be rather rare. Logging and the
destruction of large areas of their forest habitat may be posing a
threat to their survival.

MYSTACINIDAE: NEW ZEALAND SHORT-TAILED BAT FAMILY

The sole member of its family, the short–tailed bat is one of
New Zealand's two native species of mammal (the other is a
Vespertilionid bat called *Chalinolobus tuberculatus*).

New Zealand Short–tailed Bat *Mystacina tuberculata* **VU**

RANGE New Zealand

HABITAT Forest

SIZE Body: 2–2¼ in (5–6 cm) Wingspan: 8½–11 in (22–28 cm)
Tail: ½–¾ in (1.5–2 cm)

The short-tailed bat has a thick mustache fringing its small
mouth. Each bristle of the mustache has a
spoon-shaped tip. Its thumbs bear not
only the usual heavy claws, but also
have tiny secondary talons at their
base and the hind feet have sharp claws.

Beetles and other ground-dwelling insects seem to
form the bulk of the diet of the short-tailed bat. As an
adaptation to hunting on the ground it is agile on all fours and
can run rapidly, even up steeply sloping objects. The wing
membranes are furled in such a way that the forearms can be
used as walking limbs.

The short-tailed bat does not hibernate (the other New
Zealand bat does). It roosts in small groups in hollow trees. A
single young is born in October.

DOGS

ORDER CARNIVORA

There are 11 families in this order – dogs and foxes, bears, raccoons, mustelids, civets, mongooses, hyenas, cats, sea lions, walrus and true seals. Typically these animals are flesh-eating predators, but not all are totally carnivorous, and a specialized few feed only on plant matter. The last three families are adapted to life in water, their limbs have become flippers although they are still able to move, albeit awkwardly, on land, where they all spend part of their lives.

CANIDAE: DOG FAMILY

Dogs and their close relatives – the jackals, wolves, coyotes and foxes – represent one of the most familiar groups of carnivorous mammals. This familiarity is partly due to the fact that dogs were the first animals to be fully domesticated by man.

The family contains about 34 recognized species and is distributed almost worldwide. Domesticated versions aside, dogs are absent only from New Zealand, New Guinea, Madagascar and some other islands. The dingo was introduced into Australia by aboriginal man.

All dogs have the well-known, muscular, long-legged body, generally with a bushy tail. The ears are usually large, triangular in outline and erect, and the muzzle is long.

Canids are excellent runners, able to sustain a high speed for considerable distances, and long pursuits are an important part of the hunting technique of many species. Some canids hunt down large prey animals in packs, while others, such as foxes, are typically solitary hunters. Males and females generally look alike, although males are often slightly larger than females.

Coyote
Canis latrans
RANGE Alaska, Canada, USA (formerly absent from S.E. but now spreading there); Mexico, Central America
HABITAT Prairies, open woodland
SIZE Body: 33½–37½ in (85–95 cm) Tail: 11¾–15 in (30–38 cm)

A highly adaptable animal, the coyote has managed to thrive, even to increase its population, despite being trapped and poisoned for many years. Although the coyote probably does kill some sheep, young cattle and poultry, its diet consists mainly of rodents and rabbits and in this way it is of service to the farmer. It also eats snakes, insects, carrion, fruit, berries and grasses and will enter water to catch fish, frogs and crustaceans.

Coyote pairs mate in late winter, and a litter of 5 to 10 young is born after a gestation of 63 to 65 days. The male brings all the food for the female and young at first, but later both parents hunt for food. The young leave when about 6 or 7 months old to find their own home range.

The coyote is the North American equivalent of the jackals, which occur in Asia and Africa. Together with wolves, jackals are the ancestors of domestic dogs.

Gray Wolf *Canis lupus* **LR: lc**
RANGE E. Europe (isolated populations in Spain and Italy), east to India, Russia; Canada, USA: now only N. Michigan and Wisconsin; Mexico
HABITAT Tundra, steppe, open woodland and forest
SIZE Body: 3¼–4½ ft (1–1.4 m) Tail: 11¾–18¾ in (30–48 cm)

One of the ancestors of the domestic dog, the gray wolf is a powerful muscular animal, with a thick, bushy tail. Wolves vary in color from almost white in the Arctic to yellowish-brown or nearly black farther south. Intelligent, social animals, wolves live in family groups or in packs that sometimes include more than one family or other individuals besides the family.

The pack members hunt together, cooperating to run down prey such as deer, caribou and wild horses, and they also eat small animals such as mice, fish and crabs. Social hierarchy in the pack is well-organized and is maintained by ritualized gestures and postures; the leading male signals his rank by carrying his tail higher than the others do. Pairs remain together for life.

The female gives birth to 3 to 8 pups after a gestation of about 63 days. Born blind and hairless, the pups venture outside the den at 3 weeks, and the whole pack then helps to care for and play with them.

Dingo *Canis dingo*

RANGE Australia

HABITAT Sandy desert to wet and dry sclerophyll forest

SIZE Body: about 5 ft (1.5 m)
Tail: about 14 in (35 cm)

The dingoes are descended from domesticated dogs which were introduced by the aboriginal human inhabitants of Australia many thousands of years ago. In anatomy and behavior dingoes are indistinguishable from domestic dogs, but the two have interbred for so long that there are now few pure dingoes. They live in family groups, but may gather into bigger packs to hunt large prey. Originally they fed on kangaroos, but when white settlers started to kill off the kangaroos, dingoes took to feeding on introduced sheep and rabbits.

A litter of 4 or 5 young is born in a burrow or rock crevice after a gestation period of about 9 weeks. The young are suckled by the mother for a period of 2 months and stay with their parents for at least a year.

Arctic Fox

Alopex lagopus

RANGE Arctic regions of Europe, Asia and N. America

HABITAT Tundra, open woodland

SIZE Body: 18–26¾ in (46–68 cm) Tail: up to 13¾ in (35 cm)

One of the few truly arctic mammals, the arctic fox has well-furred feet and small, rounded ears. It feeds on ground-dwelling birds, lemmings and other small rodents and also eats the leftovers from polar bear kills and carrion, such as stranded marine animals.

Burrows, usually in the side of a hill or cliff, provide shelter. Despite the harsh environment in which they live arctic foxes do not hibernate and are able to withstand temperatures as low as –58°F (–50°C).

Each pair produces a litter of 4 to 11 young between May and June after a gestation period of 51 to 57 days. The offspring are cared for by both parents.

Red Fox

Vulpes vulpes

RANGE Canada, USA (not Florida or Rockies); Europe (except Iceland); Asia to Japan and Indo-China; introduced in Australia

HABITAT Woodland, open country; recently increasing in urban areas

SIZE Body: 18–33¾ in (46–86 cm) Tail: 12–21¾ in (30.5–55.5 cm)

The versatile, intelligent red fox adapts well to different conditions and has excellent senses and powers of endurance. Although sometimes it moves about at all hours, it is most typically active at night, resting during the day in a burrow abandoned by another animal or dug by itself. It lives alone outside the breeding season and is a skilful hunter, preying largely on rodents but also on rabbits, hares, birds, insects and invertebrates. Fruit and berries are also eaten in autumn, and the red fox has also taken to scavenging on refuse in urban areas.

A litter of 4 young is born after a gestation of between 51 and 63 days. The male hunts for food for his family until the female is able to leave the cubs alone to hunt herself or else to take them out foraging.

Fennec Fox *Vulpes zerda*

RANGE N. Africa: Morocco to Egypt, south to N. Niger, Sudan; east to Sinai Peninsula and Kuwait

HABITAT Desert, semidesert

SIZE Body: 14½–16 in (37–41 cm) Tail: 7½–8¼ in (19–21 cm)

The smallest of the foxes, the fennec fox is identified by its relatively huge ears. It shelters in burrows, which it digs in the sand, and is generally active at night, when it preys on small rodents, birds, insects and lizards.

Fennec foxes are sociable animals which mate for life. Each pair or family has its own territory. A litter of 2 to 5 young is born in spring after a gestation period of 50 to 51 days.

DOGS CONTINUED

Dhole *Cuon alpinus* **VU**

RANGE C. and E. Asia, south to Sumatra and Java

HABITAT Forest, woodland; open country in north of range

SIZE Body: 30 in–3¼ ft (76 cm–1 m) Tail: 11–18¾ in (28–48 cm)

Dholes, or Asiatic wild dogs, are gregarious animals, which live in family groups or in packs of up to 30 that contain several families. Most of their hunting is done in the daytime, and although they are not particularly fast runners, dholes pursue their prey in a steady relentless chase, finally exhausting the victim. Both smell and sight are important to them when tracking their prey. Because they hunt in packs, dholes are able to kill animals much larger than themselves, such as deer, wild cattle sheep and pigs, water buffalo and the banteng.

A litter of 2 to 6 young is born after a gestation of about 9 weeks, in a sheltered spot among rocks or a hole in a bank. Several females may breed near each other. Dholes are now becoming rare after years of persecution by man, and they are also affected by the greatly reduced populations of many of their prey animals. They are protected in some parts of the range.

Bush Dog *Speothos venaticus* **VU**

RANGE Central and South America: Panama to Peru, Brazil and Paraguay

HABITAT Forest, savanna

SIZE Body: 22½–29½ in (57.5–75 cm) Tail: 5–6 in (12.5–15 cm)

Stocky and terrierlike, the bush dog has short legs and tail. It is now rare throughout its range, and little is known of its habits in the wild. A nocturnal dog, it is believed to hunt in packs, preying mainly on rodents, such as pacas and agoutis. Bush dogs swim well and readily pursue prey into water.

During the day, they take refuge in a hole or crevice, often the abandoned burrow of an armadillo. They mark the edges of their territory with urine and secretions from anal glands.

Litter are thought to contain 4 or 5 young, which are tended by both parents.

Maned Wolf

Chrysocyon brachyurus

LR: nt

RANGE South America: Brazil, Bolivia, Paraguay, Uruguay, N. Argentina

HABITAT Grassland, swamp edge

SIZE Body: 4 ft (1.2 m) Tail: about 12 in (30 cm)

Similar to a red fox in appearance, with its long legs and muzzle, the maned wolf has a yellowish-red coat of fairly long hair, with an erectile mane on the neck and shoulders. The tail may be white or white-tipped. A wary, solitary animal, the maned wolf lives in remote areas and is active mainly at night. It runs fast with a loping gallop. It has less stamina than many canids and does not usually run down its prey. Large rodents, such as pacas and agoutis, birds, reptiles and frogs are all caught, and it also feeds on insects, snails and some fruit.

Up to 5 young are born after a gestation of about 2 months. At first, they have short legs and muzzles.

Crab-eating Fox *Cerdocyon thous*

RANGE South America: Colombia to N. Argentina

HABITAT Open woodland, grassland

SIZE Body: 23½–27½ in (60–70 cm) Tail: 11¾ in (30 cm)

The first specimen of this fox ever examined had a crab in its mouth hence the common name, but in fact crabs are only one item in a wide-ranging diet. This fox is also known as the common zorro. Mainly nocturnal and solitary, the crab-eating fox spends the day in a shelter, often a burrow abandoned by another animal.

It hunts small rodents, such as mice and rats, lizards, frogs and crabs and also feeds on insects and fruit, and digs for turtle eggs. Poultry also figures in the diet of the crab-eating fox.

The female gives birth to a litter of 2 to 6 young.

Raccoon-dog *Nyctereutes procyonoides*

RANGE E. Siberia, N.E. China, Japan, N. Indo-China; introduced in E. and C. Europe

HABITAT Forest and rocky banks near rivers and lakes

SIZE Body: 19¾–21½ in (50–55 cm) Tail: 5–7 in (13–18 cm)

Foxlike in build, but with shorter legs and tail, the raccoon-dog has a dark patch on each side of its face, reminiscent of the raccoon's black mask. It lives alone or in family groups of 5 or 6 and is primarily nocturnal. During the day, it shelters in a den among rocks or bushes, in a hollow tree or in a burrow abandoned by another animal. A raccoon-dog may sometimes dig its own burrow.

Usually found near water, the raccoon-dog is an excellent swimmer and frogs and fish are major food items. It also eats rodents, acorns, fruit and berries and scavenges on carrion and refuse around human habitation.

A litter of 6 to 8 young is born after a gestation of about 2 months. The pups are independent at about 6 months old.

Hunting Dog *Lycaon pictus* **EN**

RANGE Africa, south of the Sahara to South Africa: Transvaal; (not in rain forest areas of W. and C. Africa)

HABITAT Savanna, plains, semidesert, mountains up to 10,000 ft (3,000 m)

SIZE Body: 31½ in–3½ ft (80 cm–1.1 m)
Tail: 11¾–15¾ in (30–40 cm)

Recognized by its dark-brown, black or yellowish coat, well mottled with light patches, the hunting dog has long legs and a short, extremely powerful muzzle. Hunting dogs live in packs of 6 to 30 or more, sometimes up to 90 individuals with a high degree of social cooperation and interaction between individuals in the pack. They communicate by means of gestures and body postures and a few calls. Nomadic animals, hunting dogs roam over a wide area looking for their prey and only remain in one place for more than a few days when the young are too small to travel.

During much of the day, the dogs rest and groom themselves in the shade. Most hunting is done in the early morning and evening or on bright, moonlit nights. After a mass greeting ceremony between pack members, the dogs move off to search for prey, such as gazelle, impala and zebra. Once the prey has been located by sight, the dogs follow it slowly for a while before starting the final chase. They may concentrate on one victim or follow several members of a herd before all switching to one particular animal. When close enough, the dogs start to bite the prey wherever they can, often seizing its legs and tail and causing it to fall. They disembowel it and immediately start tearing it to pieces and feeding. The pack shares the kill without aggression, allowing young animals to feed first and disgorging meat to latecomers. Some pack members return to the den and disgorge meat for the adults guarding the young. By expert cooperation, by taking turns in the chase and by combined attack, packs of hunting dogs can successfully bring down prey much bigger than themselves, even large wildebeest.

The female gives birth to 2 to 16 young (usually 7) after a gestation period of 69 to 72 days. The litter is born in a burrow, such as an abandoned aardvark or warthog hole, and more than one female may share the den. The young are blind at birth, but their eyes open at about 2 weeks, and they soon begin to venture out of the den. They are suckled for about 3 months and then fed on regurgitated food by pack members from the age of 2 weeks. The whole pack takes an interest in the young and will feed any motherless pups. At 6 months the young begin to learn to hunt and accompany the pack.

BEARS

URSIDAE: BEAR FAMILY

The 9 species of bear are an evolutionary offshoot of doglike ancestors. The family also includes the two species of panda which have previously been placed in their own family, or with the raccoon family.

Dogs and their relatives consume a certain amount of plant material in their largely carnivorous diet, and this omnivorous tendency is increased in the bears, which are adaptable consumers of a wide range of foods, including insects, small vertebrates, grass, leaves, fruit and nuts. Bears' teeth reflect their diet and they lack the shearing blades of cats and dogs which are necessary for tearing meat.

Bears are large, sturdily built animals, with big heads, short limbs and exceptionally short tails. They have flat, five toed feet with long, curving claws. Male and female look alike.

Only the polar bear inhabits Arctic regions; the others all occur in temperate and tropical areas of the northern hemisphere, and 1 species lives in northern South America. In cold, winter weather, many bears undergo a period of torpor. This winter sleep is not true hibernation, since temperature and respiration rate do not fall drastically, as they do in true hibernators.

Spectacled Bear

Tremarctos ornatus **VU**

RANGE South America: Venezuela, Colombia, Ecuador, Peru, W. Bolivia

HABITAT Forest, savanna, mountainous areas up to 10,000 ft (3,000 m)

SIZE Body: 5–6 ft (1.5–1.8 m) Tail: 2¾ in (7 cm)

The spectacled bear is the only South American bear species. It is generally black or dark brown in color, with white markings around the eyes, which are the origin of its common name, and sometimes on the neck. Mainly a forest dweller, although it also ranges into open country, this bear feeds largely on leaves, fruit and roots. It is also thought to prey on animals such as deer and vicuna. It is a good climber and sleeps in a tree in a large nest that it makes from sticks. The spectacled bear lives alone or in a family group. The female produces a litter of up to 3 young after a gestation period of 8 to 9 months.

Big Brown Bear/Grizzly Bear *Ursus arctos*

RANGE Europe: Scandinavia to Balkans, scattered populations in France, Italy and Spain; Russia; Asia, north of Himalayas; Alaska, W. Canada, mountainous areas of W. USA

HABITAT Forest, tundra

SIZE Body: 5–8¼ ft (1.5–2.5 m) Tail: absent

Many subspecies are covered by the scientific name *U. arctos*, including the Kodiak bear and the grizzly bears. At least 2 races of grizzly are rare or endangered. The races vary in color from pale yellowish-fawn to dark brown or nearly black. All are large, immensely strong bears, and they are among the biggest carnivores. The bears live alone or in family groups and are active night or day, although in areas where bears have been persecuted, they are nocturnal.

The diet varies greatly from area to area but may include plant material, such as fruit, nuts, roots and seaweed, as well as insects, fish, small vertebrates and carrion. Alaskan brown bears feed heavily on migrating salmon. Most individuals are too slow to catch wild, hoofed mammals, although they have been known to kill bison. Many are too heavy to climb trees. In late summer and autumn, the bears fatten up on vast quantities of fruit and berries in preparation for the winter sleep – a period of torpor, not true hibernation.

Females breed every 2 or 3 years and produce litters of 1 to 4 young after a gestation of 6 to 8 months. The new born young are blind and tiny, usually weighing only about 10½ to 25 oz (300 to 700 g). They remain with the mother for a year, sometimes longer.

American Black Bear
Ursus americanus

RANGE Alaska, Canada, USA: patchy distribution in New England, through Pennsylvania to Tennessee, Florida, S. Georgia, Mississippi, Louisiana, mountainous areas of the west; N. Mexico

HABITAT Wooded areas, swamps, national parks

SIZE Body: 5–6 ft (1.5–1.8 m) Tail: 4¾ in (12 cm)

American black bears vary in color from glossy black to dark brown reddish–brown or almost white. There is often a small white patch on the chest. This bear was once found throughout much of the USA, but it now lives only in the wilder, uninhabited areas and in national parks, where it is thriving. Black bears are usually active at night, when they roam for long distances in search of food, such as fruit, berries, nuts, roots and honey. They also eat insects, small mammals, fish and even carrion and refuse. Their sense of smell is good, but their hearing and eye sight are only fair. In autumn, black bears gorge on fruit to fatten themselves for their long winter sleep.

Except for females with cubs, black bears are usually solitary. A litter of 1 to 4 young is born in January or February after a gestation of about 7 months.

Asiatic Black Bear *Ursus thibetanus* **VU**

RANGE Afghanistan to China, Siberia, Japan, Korea, Taiwan, Hainan, S.E. Asia

HABITAT Forest and brush up to 11,800 ft (3,600 m)

SIZE Body: 4¼–5¼ ft (1.3–1.6 m) Tail: 2¾–4 in (7–10 cm)

Asiatic black bears are usually black, with some white markings on the snout and chest, some may be reddish or dark brown.

They mainly eat plant matter and may raid crops or climb trees to obtain fruit and nuts. As well as eating insect larvae and ants, they can be aggressive predators and may kill cattle, sheep and goats. The female has a litter of 2 cubs, which are blind and extremely small at birth. The cubs stay with their mother until they are almost fully grown.

Polar Bear
Ursus maritimus **LR: cd**

RANGE Arctic Ocean to southern limits of ice floes

HABITAT Coasts, ice floes

SIZE Body: 7¼–8¼ ft (2.2–2.5 m) Tail: 3–5 in (7.5–12.5 cm)

A huge bear, with an unmistakable creamy-white coat, the polar bear is surprisingly fast and can easily outrun a caribou over a short distance. It wanders over a larger area than any other bear and, of course, swims well. Seals, fish, seabirds, arctic hares, caribou and musk-oxen are the polar bear's main prey, and in the summer it also eats berries and leaves of tundra plants.

Normally solitary animals outside the breeding season, polar bears mate in midsummer. A litter of 1 to 4 young is born after a gestation of about 9 months, and the young bears remain with their mother for about a year. Thus females breed only every other year.

Sun Bear *Helarctos malayanus* **DD**

RANGE S.E. Asia, Sumatra, Borneo

HABITAT Mountain and lowland forest

SIZE Body: 3½–4½ ft (1.1–1.4 m) Tail: absent

The sun bear is the smallest bear species. It nevertheless has a strong, stocky body and powerful paws, with long, curved claws that help it climb trees. It spends the day in a nest in a tree, sleeping and sunbathing, and searches for food at night.

Using its strong claws, the sun bear tears at tree bark in order to expose insects, larvae and the nests of bees and termites; it also preys on junglefowl and small rodents. Fruit and coconut palm, too, are part of its diet.

There are usually 2 young, born after a gestation period of about 96 days. The young are cared for by both parents.

RACCOONS AND PANDAS

Giant Panda *Ailuropoda melanoleuca* **EN**

RANGE Mountains of C. China

HABITAT Bamboo forest

SIZE Body: 4–5 ft (1.2–1.5 m) Tail: 5 in (12.5 cm)

One of the most popular, newsworthy mammals, the giant panda is a rare, elusive creature and surprisingly little is known of its life in the wild. It is large and heavily built, with a massive head, stout legs and a thick, woolly black and white coat, often with a brownish tinge to the black.

The panda's forepaw is specialized for grasping bamboo stems, its main food. It has an elongated wrist bone that effectively provides a sixth digit, against which the first and second digits can be flexed. The panda consumes huge amounts of bamboo in order to obtain sufficient nourishment and thus spends 50 to 75 per cent of its day feeding. It is also thought to eat some other plants and, occasionally, small animals.

Normally solitary, unless breeding or caring for young, pandas are primarily ground-dwelling, but regularly climb trees for shelter or refuge. The male leaves his territory to find a mate and courts her by uttering whines and barks. He will drive off any rival males before mating. The female gives birth to 1 blind, helpless young, which weighs only about 5 oz (140 g). It is tiny in comparison to its mother, which may weigh as much as 255 lb (115 kg). The cub grows rapidly, however, and by the time it reaches 8 weeks old it is more than 20 times its birth weight.

Lesser/Red Panda *Ailurus fulgens* **EN**

RANGE Nepal to Myanmar, S.W. China

HABITAT Bamboo forest

SIZE Body: 20–25 in (51–63.5 cm) Tail: 11–19 in (28–48.5 cm)

The lesser or red panda, with its beautiful rusty-red coat and long, bushy tail, resembles a raccoon more than it dos its giant relative. This creature is primarily nocturnal and spends the day sleeping, curled up on a branch with its tail over its head or its head tucked on to its chest. It feeds at night on the ground, on bamboo shoots, grass, roots, fruit and acorns and may also occasionally eat mice, birds and birds' eggs. The red panda is a quiet creature unless provoked, when it rears up on its hind legs and hisses.

It lives in pairs or family groups. In the spring the female gives birth to 1 to 4 young, usually only 1 or 2, after a gestation period of 90 to 150 days. The longer gestations recorded are thought to include a period of delayed implantation, during which the fertilized egg lies dormant in the womb, only starting to develop at the time that will ensure birth at the optimum season for the young's survival. The young stay with their mother for up to a year.

PROCYONIDAE: RACCOON FAMILY

There are about 18 species in this family, all of which inhabit temperate and tropical areas of the Americas. They are all long-bodied, active animals, thought to be closely linked to the dog-bear line of carnivore evolution. The raccoons are good climbers and spend much of their life in trees.

Males are usually longer and heavier than females, but otherwise the sexes look alike.

Raccoon

Procyon lotor

RANGE USA, south to Panama, S.Canada,

HABITAT Wooded areas, near water, swamps

SIZE Body: 16–23½ in (41–60 cm) Tail: 7¾–15¾ in (20–40 cm)

Raccoons have coped well with the twentieth century and today are even spotted in cities, scavenging for food. The raccoon is stocky but agile, with thick, grayish fur and a bushy tail ringed with black bands. Its pointed face has a characteristic "bandit" mask across the eyes. On the forepaws are long, sensitive digits, with which the raccoon dexterously handles food. Mainly active at night, the raccoon is a good climber and can swim if necessary. Its wide-ranging diet includes aquatic animals, such as frogs and fish, small land animals, birds, turtle eggs, nuts, seeds, fruit and corn.

A litter of 3 to 6 young is born in spring after a gestation period of about 65 days. The young raccoons' eyes are open at about 3 weeks. They young start to go out with their mother at about 2 months old, remaining with her until autumn.

Olingo *Bassaricyon gabbii* **LR:nt**

RANGE Central America, south to Venezuela, Colombia and Ecuador

HABITAT Forest

SIZE Body: 13¾–18¾ in (35–47.5 cm) Tail: 15¾–18¾ in (40–48 cm)

An expert climber, the olingo spends much of its life in trees and rarely descends to the ground. Using its long tail to help it balance, it leaps from tree to tree and runs along the branches. It is primarily nocturnal, and although it lives alone or in pairs, joins in groups with other olingos and with kinkajous to search for food. Fruit is its staple diet, but it also eats insects, small mammals and birds.

Breeding takes place at any time of year, and there is usually only 1 young in a litter, born after a gestation of 73 or 74 days. The female chases her mate away shortly before the birth and rears her offspring alone.

Coati *Nasua nasua*

RANGE Arizona south to Argentina

HABITAT Woodland, lowland forest

SIZE Body: 17–26¼ in (43–67 cm) Tail: 17–26¾ in (43–68 cm)

The coati is a muscular, short-legged animal, with a long, banded tail and a pointed, mobile snout. It lives in groups of up to 40 individuals, which hunt together day and night, resting in the heat of the day. With its mobile snout, the coati probes holes and cracks in the ground, rocks or trees, searching for the insects, spiders and other small ground-dwelling invertebrates that are its staple diet. Fruit and larger animals, such as lizards, are also eaten.

After mating, the group splits up and females go off alone to give birth. A litter of 2 to 7 young is born after a gestation of about 77 days, usually in a cave or a nest in a tree. Once the young are about 2 months old, the females and their offspring regroup with yearlings of both sexes. Males over 2 years old only accompany the group for the mating period. Even then they are subordinate to females.

Kinkajou *Potos flavus*

RANGE E. Mexico, through Central and South America to Brazil

HABITAT Forest

SIZE Body: 16–22½ in (41–57 cm) Tail: 15¾–22 in (40–56 cm)

The tree-dwelling kinkajou is an agile climber. It uses its prehensile tail as a fifth limb, leaving its hands free to pick food. During the day, the kinkajou rests, usually in a hole in a tree. It forages at night, mainly feeding on fruit and insects and sometimes small vertebrates. Its long tongue is used to extract soft flesh from fruit, such as mangoes, and for licking up nectar, insects and honey.

The female gives birth to 1 young, rarely 2, after a gestation of 112 to 118 days. The young kinkajou takes its first solid food at about 7 weeks and is independent at about 4 months old. It is able to hang by its prehensile tail after about 8 weeks.

MUSTELIDS, WEASELS AND MARTENS

MUSTELIDAE: MUSTELID FAMILY

The mustelid family of carnivores is a successful and diverse group of small to medium-sized mammals. There are about 65 species in 23 genera from all regions of the world except Australia and Madagascar and 2 species have been introduced into New Zealand to control rodents. Although there is a moderate range of physique, most mustelids conform to the pattern of long, supple body, short legs and long tails. Males are almost invariably larger than females.

Mustelids have adapted to various ecological niches. There are burrowers, climbers and swimmers. One species, the sea otter, is almost entirely marine.

Secretions from anal scent glands are used to mark territory boundaries. Some species, notably polecats and skunks, have particularly foul-smelling secretions which they spray in defence.

Stoat *Mustela erminea*
RANGE Europe, Asia, N. USA, Greenland; introduced in New Zealand
HABITAT Forest, tundra
SIZE Body: 9½–11½ in (24–29 cm) Tail: 3–4¾ in (8–12 cm)

The stoat is a highly skilled predator. It kills by delivering a powerful and accurate bite to the back of the prey's neck. Rodents and rabbits are the stoat's main diet, but it will also kill and eat other mammals – including some bigger than itself – as well as birds, eggs, fish and insects. At the beginning of winter, in the northern part of its range, the stoat loses its dark fur and grows a pure white coat, only the black tail-tip remaining. This white winter pelt is the ermine prized by the fur trade.

Stoats produce a litter of 3 to 7 young in April or May. The male assists in caring for and feeding the young, which are helpless at birth. Their eyes do not open until they are about 3 weeks old, but at 7 weeks old young males are already larger than their mother.

There are 15 species of *Mustela*, including the minks which are now farmed for their dense fur.

Black-footed Ferret *Mustela nigripes* **EW**
RANGE N. America: formerly Alberta to N. Texas
HABITAT Prairie
SIZE Body: 15–17¾ in (38–45 cm) Tail: 5–6 in (12.5–15 cm)

The black-footed ferret feeds mainly on prairie dogs, which are considered farm pests and large numbers are poisoned. The destruction of the ferret's prey has caused a drastic decline in their numbers and they are now protected by law. There is still a danger of extinction, however, and its survival depends on ongoing conservation. The black-footed ferret is generally nocturnal. In June the female produces a litter of 3 to 5 young.

Least Weasel *Mustela nivalis*
RANGE Europe, N. Africa, Asia, N. America; introduced in New Zealand
HABITAT Farmland, woodland
SIZE Body: 7–9 in (18–23 cm) Tail: 2–2¾ in (5–7 cm)

This weasel is the smallest carnivore. In the northern part of its range its coat changes color in winter. The least weasel preys mostly on mice which it pursues in their burrows. It is most active by night, but will hunt in the daytime. One or two litters a year, of 4 or 5 young are born.

Western Polecat *Mustela putorius*
RANGE Europe
HABITAT Forest
SIZE Body: 15–18 in (38–46 cm) Tail: 5–7½ in (13–19 cm)

This solitary and nocturnal animal hunts rodents, birds, reptiles and insects, mostly on the ground. The offensive secretions from the polecat's anal scent glands are used for defence and to mark territory. It breeds once or twice a year, bearing litters of 5 to 8 young.

American Marten *Martes americana*

Range Canada, N. USA

Habitat Forest, woodland

Size Body: 14–17 in (35.5–43 cm) Tail: 7–9 in (18–23 cm)

The American marten is agile and acrobatic with a bushy tail. It spends much of its time in the trees, where it preys on squirrels. It also hunts on the ground and eats small animals and insects, fruit and nuts.

Martens make dens in hollow trees and produce yearly litters of 2 to 4 blind, helpless young, usually in April. Their eyes open at 6 weeks and they attain adult weight at about 3 months.

Sable *Martes zibellina*

Range Siberia; Japan: Hokkaido

Habitat Forest

Size Body: 15–18 in (38–45 cm) Tail: 5–7½ in (12–19 cm)

The sable is one of 7 species of marten. It is a ground dweller and eats small mammals, as well as fish, insects, honey, nuts and berries. A yearly litter of 2 or 3 young is born in a burrow.

The sable has long been hunted for its fur. Conservation is now underway in Russia to save the decreasing wild population.

Grison *Galictis vittata*

Range S. Mexico to Peru and Brazil

Habitat Forest, open land

Size Body: 18½–21½ in (47–55 cm) Tail: 6 in (16 cm)

The grison is an agile animal, good at climbing and swimming. It feeds on frogs and worms as well as other ground-living creatures. The abandoned burrow of another animal or a rock or tree-root crevice serves it as a den. A litter of 2 to 4 young is produced in the burrow in October.

There are 3 species of grison, all of which live in Central and South America. The local population uses grisons in the same way as ferrets, for flushing out chinchillas.

Tayra *Eira barbara*

Range S. Mexico to Argentina; Trinidad

Habitat Forest

Size Body: 24–27 in (60–68 cm)
Tail: 15–18½ in (38–47 cm)

The single species of tayra runs, climbs and swims well. It preys on small mammals, such as tree squirrels and rodents, and also feeds on fruit and honey.

Tayras move in pairs or small family groups and are active at night and in the early morning. They are believed to produce a yearly litter of 2 to 4 young.

Zorilla *Ictonyx striatus*

Range Aftica: Senegal and Nigeria to South Africa

Habitat Savanna, open country

Size Body: 11–15 in (28.5–38.5 cm) Tail: 8–12 in (20.5–30 cm)

Also known as the striped polecat, the single species of zorilla ejects a nauseating secretion from its anal glands when alarmed. It is primarily nocturnal and feeds on rodents, reptiles, insects and birds' eggs. By day it rests in a burrow, or a crevice in rocks. There is a litter of 2 or 3 young.

MUSTELIDS CONTINUED

Wolverine *Gulo gulo* **VU**

RANGE Scandinavia, Siberia, Alaska, Canada, W. USA

HABITAT Coniferous forest, tundra

SIZE Body: 25½–34¼ in (65–87 cm) Tail: 6½–10 in (17–26 cm)

The single species of wolverine is a heavily built animal, immensely strong for its size and capable of killing animals larger than itself. Although they are largely carnivorous, wolverines also feed on berries. They are solitary animals and are mainly ground-dwelling, but they can climb trees.

Each male holds a large territory with 2 or 3 females, and mates in the summer. The female wolverine bears 2 or 3 young in the following spring, usually after a period of delayed implantation. Delayed implantation is an interesting phenomenon allowing animals to mate at the ideal time and bear young at the ideal time, even though the intervening period is longer than their actual gestation. The fertilized egg remains in a suspended state in the womb and development starts only after the required period of dormancy. The young suckle for about 2 months and remain with their mother for up to 2 years, at which time they are driven out of her territory. They become sexually mature at about 4 years of age.

Ratel *Mellivora capensis*

RANGE Africa; Middle East to N. India

HABITAT Steppe, savanna

SIZE Body: 23½–27½ in (60–70 cm) Tail: 7¾ –11¾ in (20–30 cm)

The stocky ratel is also known as the honey badger because of its fondness for honey. In Africa a honey–eating association has developed between the ratel and a small bird, the honey guide. Calling and flying just ahead, the bird leads the ratel to a wild bees' nest. With its powerful foreclaws, the ratel then breaks open the nest, and both partners share the spoils. The unusually tough hide of the ratel protects it from bee stings and is also a good defence in another way: the skin is so loose on the body that the animal can twist about in its skin and even bite an attacker which has a hold on the back of its neck. In addition to honey and bee larvae, the ratel eats small animals, insects, roots, bulbs and fruit and will occasionally attack large animals such as sheep and antelope.

Although sometimes active in the daytime, ratels are generally nocturnal animals. They live singly or in pairs and produce a litter of 2 young in an underground burrow or a nest among rocks. The gestation period is between 6 and 7 months.

Eurasian Badger *Meles meles*

RANGE Europe to Japan and S. China

HABITAT Forest, grassland

SIZE Body: 22–32 in (56–81 cm) Tail: 4–7¾ in (11–20 cm)

The gregarious Eurasian badger lives in family groups in huge burrows with networks of underground passages and chambers and several entrances. A burrow system, or sett, may be used by successive generations of badgers, each making additions and alterations. Bedding material of grass, hay and leaves is gathered into the sleeping chambers and occasionally dragged out to air in the early morning. Around the sett are play areas, and the boundaries of the group's territory are marked by latrine holes.

Badgers are generally nocturnal and emerge from the sett around dusk. They are playful creatures, and at this time the young and adults will indulge in boisterous romping. Such play helps the badgers to strengthen their social bonds, crucial to group-living animals.

Badgers feed on large quantities of earthworms as well as on small animals, bulbs, fruit and nuts. They mate in the summer when social acitivity is at its height, but gestation of the fertilized eggs does not start until such a time as to ensure that the 2 to 4 young are not born until the following spring.

American Badger *Taxidea taxus*

RANGE S.W. Canada to C. Mexico

HABITAT Open grassland, arid land

SIZE Body: 16½–22 in (42–56 cm) Tail: 4–6 in (10–15 cm)

The single species of *Taxidea* is the only New World badger. It has a rather flattened body shape, but is otherwise similar to other badgers.

The American badger is a solitary creature. It is generally active at night, although it will come out of its burrow during the day. It is an excellent digger and burrows rapidly after disappearing rodents – its main food. Birds, eggs and reptiles make up the rest of its diet. It will sometimes bury a large food item for storage.

The badgers mate in late summer, but the 6-week gestation period does not begin until February, so the litter is born only the following spring. The 1 to 5 young, usually 2, are born on a grassy bed in the burrow and are covered with silky fur. Their eyes open at 6 weeks and they suckle for several months.

In northern parts of its range and at high altitudes, the American badger sleeps for much of the winter, surviving on its stored fat. However, it does not truly hibernate and becomes active in mild spells.

Hog Badger *Arctonyx collaris*

RANGE N. China, N.E. India, Sumatra

HABITAT Wooded regions in uplands and lowlands

SIZE Body: 21½–27½ in (55–70 cm) Tail: 5–6½ in (12–17 cm)

Similar in shape and size to the Eurasian badger, the hog badger is distinguished by its white throat and mostly white tail. The common name refers to the badger's mobile, piglike snout, used for rooting for plant and animal food. It is a nocturnal animal and spends its day in a rock crevice or deep burrow. Its habits are much the same

as those of the Eurasian badger. Like all badgers, the hog badger has anal scent glands with potent secretions, and its black and white markings constitute a warning to enemies that it is a formidable opponent.

The breeding habits of the hog badger are not well known, but in one observation a female gave birth to 4 young in April.

Stink Badger *Mydaus javanensis*

RANGE Sumatra, Java, Borneo

HABITAT Dense forest

SIZE Body: 15–20 in (37.5–51 cm)
Tail: 2–3 in (5–7.5 cm)

The 2 species of stink badger have particularly powerful anal gland secretions. The stink badger's scent is said to be as evil-smelling as those of skunks. When threatened or alarmed, the stink badger raises its tail and ejects a stream of the fluid. However, like musk, although foul in concentration, the secretion can be sweet-smelling in dilution and was formerly used in the making of perfume. This nocturnal creature lives in a burrow and feeds on worms, insects and small animals. The second species, the Palawan badger, *M. marchei*, inhabits the Philippine and Calamian islands.

Chinese Ferret Badger *Melogale moschata*

RANGE N.E. India, S. China, IndoChina, Java, Borneo

HABITAT Grassland, open forest

SIZE Body: 13–17 in (33–43 cm)
Tail: 6–9 in (15–23 cm)

Distinctive masklike face markings distinguish the Chinese ferret badger from other oriental mustelids. This badger lives in burrows or crevices and is active at dusk and at night. It is a good climber and feeds on fruit, insects, small animals and worms. Ferret badgers are savage when alarmed and their anal secretions are foul-smelling.

The female gives birth to a litter of up to 3 young in May or June. There are 2 other species of ferret badger, both are found in Southeast Asia.

MUSTELIDS CONTINUED

Striped Skunk *Mephitis mephitis*

RANGE S. Canada to N. Mexico

HABITAT Semiopen country, woods, grassland

SIZE Body: 11–15 in (28–38 cm)

Tail: 7–10 in (18–25 cm)

Notorious for its pungent anal gland secretions, the striped skunk is one of the most familiar mustelids. It does not use its foul-smelling secretions against rival skunks, only against enemies. The fluid is an effective weapon because the smell temporarily stops the victim's breathing.

The striped skunk is a nocturnal animal, spending the day in a burrow or in a den beneath old buildings, wood or rock piles. It feeds on mice, eggs, insects, berries and carrion.

A litter of 5 or 6 young is born in early May in a den lined with vegetation. The hooded skunk, *M. macroura,* is a similar and closely related species; the black and white markings of both skunks are highly variable and constitute a warning display.

Hog-nosed Skunk *Conepatus mesoleucus*

RANGE S. USA to Nicaragua

HABITAT Wooded and open land

SIZE Body: 13¾–19 in (35–48 cm) Tail: 6½–12 in (17–31 cm)

There are 7 species of hog-nosed skunk, all found in the southern USA and South America.

This nocturnal, solitary, slow-moving animal has the coarsest fur of all skunks. The common name derives from the animal's long piglike snout, which it uses to root in the soil for insects and grubs. It will also eat snakes, small mammals and fruit.

The hog-nosed skunk makes its dens in rocky places or abandoned burrows. The female produces a litter of 2 to 5 young each year.

Western Spotted Skunk *Spilogale gracialis*

RANGE W. USA to C. Mexico

HABITAT Wasteland, brush and wooded areas

SIZE Body: 9–13½ in (23–34.5 cm)

Tail: 4¼–8½ in (11–22 cm)

The white stripes and spots of the western spotted skunk are infinitely variable – no two animals have quite the same markings. A nocturnal, mainly terrestrial animal, this skunk usually makes its dens underground, but it is a good climber and sometimes shelters in trees. Rodents, birds, eggs, insects and fruit are the main items in its diet.

In the south of the spotted skunk's range, young are born at any time of year, but farther north the 4 or 5 young are produced in spring. The gestation period is about 4 months.

Eurasian Otter *Lutra lutra*

RANGE Europe, N. Africa, Asia

HABITAT Rivers, lakes, sheltered coasts

SIZE Body: 21½–31½ in (55–80 cm)

Tail: 12–19½ in (30–50 cm)

Although agile on land, otters have become well adapted for an aquatic life. The Eurasian otter has a slim body, but its tail is thick, fleshy and muscular to propel it in water. Its feet are webbed and its nostrils and ears can be closed when it is in water. Its fur is short and dense and keeps the skin dry by trapping a layer of air around the body. It eats fish, frogs, water birds, voles and other water creatures.

Otters are solitary, elusive creatures, now rare in much of their range. They den in a river bank in a burrow called a holt and are most active at night. Even adult otters are playful. A litter of 2 or 3 young is born in the spring – or at any time of year in the south of the otter's range. There are 8 species of *Lutra,* all with more or less similar habits and adaptations.

Giant Otter

Pteronura brasiliensis **VU**

RANGE Venezuela to Argentina

HABITAT Rivers, slow streams

SIZE Body: 1¼–5 ft (1–1.5 m) Tail: 27½ in (70 cm)

The giant otter is similar in appearance to *Lutra* species, but is larger and has a flattened tail with crests on each edge. It generally travels in a group and is active during the day.

Giant otters feed on fish eggs, aquatic mammals and birds. They den in holes in a river bank or under tree roots and produce yearly litters of 1 or 2 young.

Now endangered, the giant otter is protected in some countries, but enforcement of the law in the vast, remote areas of its range is difficult and numbers are still decreasing.

African Clawless Otter *Aonyx capensis*

RANGE Africa: Senegal, Ethiopia, South Africa

HABITAT Slow streams and pools; coastal waters, estuaries

SIZE Body: 37–39 in (95–100 cm) Tail: 21½ in (55 cm)

The African clawless otter swims and dives as well as other otters, although its feet have only small connecting webs. As its name suggests, this otter has no claws other than tiny nails on the third and fourth toes of the hind feet. It has less dense fur than most otters so has not been hunted as extensively.

Crabs are the most important item of the clawless otter's diet, and it is equipped with large, strong cheek teeth for crushing the hard shells, it also feeds on mollusks, fish, reptiles, frogs, birds and small mammals. Like most otters, it comes ashore to eat and feeds from its hands. Clawless otters seem to be particularly skilful with their hands.

Clawless otters do not dig burrows, but live in crevices or under rocks in family groups, in pairs or alone. The litter of 2 to 5 young stays with the parents for at least a year.

Sea Otter *Enhydra lutra*

RANGE Bering Sea; USA: California coast

HABITAT Rocky coasts

SIZE Body: 1¼–4 ft (1–1.2 m) Tail: 10–14½ in (25–37 cm)

This species is the most highly adapted of all of the otter family for an aquatic existence. The sea otter spends almost all of its life at sea, always in water less than 66 ft (20 m) deep. Its body is streamlined and its legs and tail are short. The hind feet are webbed and flipperlike, and the forefeet are small.

Unlike most other marine mammals, the sea otter does not have an insulating layer of fat under its skin, but instead relies on a layer of air trapped in its dense fur for protection against the cold water. This otter spends a lot of time and effort on grooming its dense, glossy fur because the fur's insulating and waterproof qualities are lessened if it becomes unkempt.

Sea otters feed on clams, sea urchins, mussels, abalone and other mollusks which they collect from the sea bed and eat while lying in the water. In order to cope with the hard shells of much of its food, the sea otter has discovered how to use rocks as tools. When diving for food, the sea otter also brings up a rock from the sea bed. Placing the stone on its chest as it lies on its back in the water, the otter bangs the prey against the stone until the shell breaks, revealing the soft animal inside.

At dusk, the sea otter swims into the huge kelp beds which are found in its range and entangles itself in the weed so that it does not drift during the night while it sleeps.

Sea otters breed every two years or so and give birth to 1 pup after a gestation period of between 8 and 9 months. The pup is born in an unusually well-developed state, with its eyes open and a full set of milk teeth. The mother carries and nurses the pup on her chest as she swims on her back.

At one time sea otters were hunted for their beautiful fur and became rare, but they have been protected by law for some years.

CIVETS

VIVERRIDAE: CIVET FAMILY

The 34 or so species in this family include civets, palm civets, and Malagasy civets. They are found in south-west Europe, Africa, Madagascar, and Asia.

The civet family closely resembles the ancestors of the carnivores and they are believed to have remained more or less unchanged for millions of years, although between species within the family there is great variation in build. Most have large, pointed ears on the top of the head, five toes with claws and at least partial webbing. The coat is usually spotted or striped in some way.

Most civets are nocturnal, solitary tree-dwellers and they are generally omnivorous, though the palm civet will eat only fruit.

Many species emit a strong-smelling oily secretion from anal scent glands (civet glands) which is used to advertise the presence of the animal in a territory and probably to attract a mate. The active ingredient of these secretions – musk – has been used by man in the manufacture of perfume for several centuries and for some African and oriental countries it remains an important export, despite the introduction of synthetic musk.

African Linsang *Poiana richardsoni*
RANGE Africa: Sierra Leone to Zaire
HABITAT Forest
SIZE Body: 13 in (33 cm) Tail: 15 in (38 cm)

A nocturnal animal, the African linsang is a good climber and spends more time in the trees than on the ground. During the day it sleeps in a nest, built of green vegetation in a tree, and then emerges at night to hunt for insects and young birds. It also feeds on fruit, nuts and plant material. Elongate and slender, this linsang is brownish-yellow to gray, with dark spots on the body and dark bands ringing the long tail.

Little is known of the African linsang's breeding habits. It is thought that each female has 2 or 3 young once or twice a year.

Banded Linsang
Prionodon linsang
RANGE Thailand, Malaysia, Sumatra, Borneo
HABITAT Forest
SIZE Body: 14¾–17 in (37.5–43 cm)
Tail: 12–14 in (30.5–35.5 cm)

The slender, graceful banded linsang varies from whitish-gray to brownish-gray in color, with four or five dark bands across its back and dark spots on its sides and legs. It is nocturnal and spends much of its life in trees, where it climbs and jumps skilfully, but it is just as agile on the ground. Birds, small mammals, insects, lizards and frogs are all preyed on, and this linsang also eats birds' eggs.

The breeding habits of this species are not well known, but it is believed to bear two litters a year of 2 or 3 young each. Young are born in a nest in a hollow tree or in a burrow.

Masked Palm Civet *Paguma larvata*
RANGE Himalayas to China, Hainan, Taiwan, S.E. Asia, Sumatra, Borneo
HABITAT Forest, brush
SIZE Body: 19¾–30 in (50–76 cm) Tail: 20–25¼ in (51–64 cm)

The masked palm civet has a plain gray or brownish-red body, with no stripes or spots, but with distinctive, white masklike markings on the face. It is nocturnal and hunts in the trees and on the ground for rodents and other small animals, as well as for insects, fruit and plant roots. The secretions of its anal glands are extremely strong-smelling and can be sprayed considerable distances to discourage any attacker.

A litter of 3 or 4 young is born in a hole in a tree. The young are grayer than adults and do not have conspicuous face masks at first, but gradually develop them with age.

African Palm Civet *Nandinia binotata*

RANGE Africa: Guinea, east to S. Sudan, south to Mozambique

HABITAT Forest, savanna, woodland

SIZE Body: 17¼–23½ in (44–60 cm) Tail: 18¾–24½ in (48–62 cm)

Active at night, the African palm civet is a skilful climber and spends much of its life in trees. Its diet is varied, ranging from insects, lizards, small mammals and birds to many kinds of fruit (which may sometimes be its sole food), leaves, grass and some carrion. It is a solitary animal and it spends the day resting in the shelter of the trees.

The male tends to be larger and heavier than the female and both have short legs and long, thick tails. The short muzzle is adorned with long whiskers. Usually grayish-brown to dark reddish-brown in color, this civet has a pale, creamy spot on each shoulder. This is the origin of its other common name – the two-spotted palm civet.

The male occupies a home range and he uses his scent gland to mark its boundaries. Mating takes place in June and the female gives birth to a litter of 2 or 3 young after a gestation period of about 64 days.

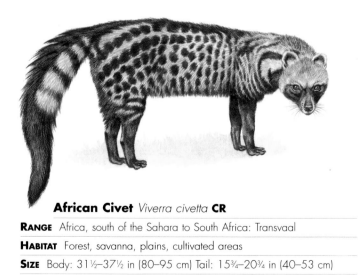

African Civet *Viverra civetta* **CR**

RANGE Africa, south of the Sahara to South Africa: Transvaal

HABITAT Forest, savanna, plains, cultivated areas

SIZE Body: 31½–37½ in (80–95 cm) Tail: 15¾–20¾ in (40–53 cm)

Large and doglike, the African civet has a broad head, strong neck and long legs. The hind legs are longer than the forelegs.

Its coat is generally gray, with darker legs, chin and throat, and the back and flanks are patterned with dark stripes and patches. The size and spacing of these dark markings is highly variable.

By day, the African civet sleeps in a burrow or in cover of vegetation or rocks. It rarely climbs trees except to escape from an enemy, but it swims well. It emerges from its sleeping place at night to forage on the ground in its territory, which it marks with heaps of dung and by leaving marks from its scent gland on trees, shrubs, rocks and grass. Mammals (up to the size of young antelope), birds (including poultry and their eggs), reptiles, frogs, toads and insects are all hunted, and this civet will also take some carrion, as well as eating fruit and berries.

The female becomes sexually mature at about 1 year old and gives birth to 1 to 4 young in each litter, usually 2, after a gestation period of between 63 and 68 days. The young take their first solid food at about 3 weeks, and often kill insects for themselves at an early age. They are weaned at about 3 months. The mother calls her young to her when she wants to share food with them with a distinctive chuckling call. The female may produce as many as three litters a year.

Congo Water Civet *Osbornictis piscivora*

RANGE Africa: N.E. Zaire

HABITAT Rain forest near streams

SIZE Body: 17¾–19¾ in (45–50 cm)
Tail: 13¾–16½ in (35–42 cm)

The Congo water civet, which is also known as the aquatic genet and the fishing genet, is an elusive animal that has been seen only rarely. It is thought to be nocturnal and to lead a semi-aquatic life. It is believed to feed largely on fish, and possibly also on crustaceans and other aquatic creatures, which it probably finds by touch with its naked palms under rocks, then grabbing with its semi-retractile claws and delivering a quick, sharp killing bite.

The Congo water civet has a slender body and a small head with a pointed snout. It has short legs and the hind legs are longer than the forelegs. The tail is long, thick and bushy. The civet's coat is reddish, chestnut-brown, with darker hair on the backs of the ears and the middle of the back and tail, and a white chin and throat.

CIVETS CONTINUED

Small-spotted
Genet *Genetta genetta*

RANGE S.W. Europe: S.W. France, Spain and Portugal; Africa, Middle East

HABITAT Semidesert, scrub, savanna

SIZE Body: 19¾–23½ in (50–60 cm)
Tail: 15¾–18¾ in (40–48 cm)

The small-spotted genet is a slender, short-legged animal. It is marked with dark spots, which may form lines down its whitish to brownish-gray body. Its head is small and its muzzle is pointed. The genet's long, impressive tail is encircled down its length with black bands.

An agile, graceful animal, the small-spotted genet moves on land with its tail held straight out behind and climbs well in trees and bushes.

It spends the day sleeping in an abandoned burrow of another animal, in a rock crevice or on the branch of a tree and starts to hunt at dusk.

Sight, hearing and sense of smell are good, and the genet stalks its prey, crouching almost flat before pouncing. Most prey, such as rodents, reptiles and insects, is taken on the ground, but the genet will climb trees to take roosting or nesting birds; it also kills poultry.

The small-spotted genet normally lives alone or in pairs. A litter of 2 or 3 young is born in a hole in the ground, in a tree, or among rocks after a gestation period of between 68 and 77 days. The young genets are born blind, and their eyes open after between 5 and 12 days. They are suckled for up to 3 months and become fully independent by about 9 months.

Binturong *Arctictis binturong*

RANGE S.E. Asia, Palawan, Sumatra, Java, Borneo

HABITAT Forest

SIZE Body: 24–38 in (61–96.5 cm) Tail: 22–35 in (56–89 cm)

A large viverrid with long, coarse fur, the binturong has distinctive ear tufts and a prehensile tail, which it uses as a fifth limb when climbing. It is the only carnivore other than the kinkajou, a member of the raccoon family, to possess such a tail.

During the day, it sleeps up in the trees and emerges at night to climb slowly, but skilfully, among the branches, searching for fruit and other plant matter, as well as insects, small vertebrates and carrion.

After a gestation of 90 to 92 days, the female produces a litter of 1 or 2 young. Both parents care for the young, which are born blind and helpless.

Fanalouc *Eupleres goudotii* **EN**

RANGE N. Madagascar

HABITAT Rain forest, swamps

SIZE Body: 18–19¾ in (46–50 cm) Tail: 8½–9½ in (22–24 cm)

The fanalouc, also known as the small toothed mongoose, with its long, slender body, pointed muzzle and short legs, does resemble a mongoose. The hind legs are longer than the forelegs. The tail is thick and bushy. Active at dusk and during the night, the fanalouc does not climb or jump well, but slowly hops along the ground, searching for earthworms (its main food), insects, water snails, frogs and sometimes even small mammals and birds. It readily wades into water in pursuit of prey. When food is abundant, the fanalouc stores fat near the base of its tail and lives on it during the dry season.

Fanaloucs pair for life. Each pair lives in a territory, the boundaries of which are marked with secretions from the scent glands. The female bears 1 young, after a gestation of about 12 weeks, which is born with a full covering of hair and with its eyes open; it is weaned at 9 weeks.

These civets are becoming rare outside nature reserves due to the destruction of forests, competition from introduced civets, and overhunting.

Otter-civet *Cynogale bennettii* **EN**

RANGE Indo-China, Malaysia, Borneo, Sumatra

HABITAT Swamps, near rivers

SIZE Body: 22½–26¼ in (57–67 cm) Tail: 5–7¾ in (13–20 cm)

The otter-civet spends much of its life in water and has several adaptations for its aquatic habits. Like many aquatic mammals, it has short, dense underfur, which is waterproof, covered by a layer of longer, coarse guard hairs. Its nostrils open upward and can be closed off by flaps, and the ears can also be closed. The otter-civet's feet are supple and have broad webs; these webs are only partial and do not extend to the tips of the digits, so the animal is able to move as well on land as in water.

With only the tip of its nose above the water, the otter-civet is almost invisible as it swims and so is able to ambush creatures that come to the water's edge to drink, as well as taking prey in water. Fish, small mammals, birds and crustaceans are all included in the otter-civet's diet, and it also eats fruit. It has long, sharp teeth for seizing prey and broad, flat molars, which it uses to crush hard-shelled items such as crustaceans. On land, it climbs well and may take refuge in a tree if attacked, rather than making for water.

A litter of 2 or 3 young is born in a burrow or hollow tree. They become independent at about 6 months old.

Fossa *Cryptoprocta ferox* **VU**

RANGE Madagascar

HABITAT Forest

SIZE Body: 23½–29½ in (60–75 cm) Tail: 21½–27½ in (55–70 cm)

The largest Madagascan carnivore, the fossa resembles a cat as much as a viverrid and has a rounded, catlike head, but with a longer muzzle. Its body is slender and elongate and its hind legs are longer than its forelegs, which raises the animal's rear. The tail is long and the coat reddish-brown. Its catlike physique in fact resulted in it once being classified as part of the felid order.

The fossa is mainly active at dusk and at night. It is an excellent climber and is equally agile in trees and on the ground. It lives alone and hunts for mammals up to the size of lemurs, as well as for birds, lizards, snakes and insects. It will also kill domestic poultry.

Fossas mate between September and October and the female bears 2 or 3 young in a burrow, a hole in a tree or a den among rocks after a gestation period of about 3 months. She cares for them alone. The young are born with their eyes closed and they open at between 16 and 25 days. They are weaned at 4 months and are fully grown and independent at 2 years, although they do not reach sexual maturity for another 2 years.

Banded Palm Civet *Hemigalus derbyanus*

RANGE Malaysia, Sumatra, Borneo

HABITAT Forest

SIZE Body: 16–20 in (41–51 cm) Tail: 9¾–15 in (25–38 cm)

The banded palm civet has a slender, elongate body and a tapering, pointed snout. It is usually whitish to orange buff in color, with broad, dark stripes on the head and neck, behind the shoulders and at the base of the tail.

The banded palm civet is a nocturnal animal and rests during the day in holes in tree trunks. It is an excellent climber, with strong feet well adapted to life in the trees, and it forages for its prey in trees, on the forest floor and beside streams. Worms and locusts are its main foods, but it also eats rats, lizards, ants, spiders, crustaceans, land and aquatic snails and frogs. Little is known of its breeding habits, though between 1 and 3 young are born in each litter and the offspring begin to eat solid food at about 10 weeks old.

MONGOOSES

HERPESTIDAE MONGOOSE FAMILY

The 37 species of mongooses are found in Africa, Madagascar, and Asia. They are small, fast-moving, ground-dwellers with long, cylindrical bodies well-adapted to chasing prey, such as insects, scorpions, and small vertebrates, down burrows.

Bushy-tailed Mongoose *Bdeogale crassicauda*

RANGE E. Africa: Kenya to Zimbabwe and Mozambique

HABITAT Coastal forest, savanna

SIZE Body: 15¾–19¾ in (40–50 cm) Tail: 7¾–11¾ in (20–30 cm)

This robust mongoose has a broad muzzle, sturdy legs and a broad, heavily furred tail. It is an elusive, nocturnal animal, which rests by day in a burrow, often one taken over from another animal, or in a hole in a tree. At night it hunts for insects and lizards, snakes, rodents and other small creatures.

Indian Mongoose
Herpestes auropunctatus

RANGE Iraq to India, south to Malaysia; introduced in West Indies, Hawaii and Fiji

HABITAT Desert, open scrub, thin forest, dense forest

SIZE Body: 13¾ in (35 cm) Tail: 9¾ in (25 cm)

This widespread mongoose varies in appearance according to its environment, though generally the soft, silky fur is olive-brown and the tail is shorter than the head and body length.

At night, the Indian mongoose rests in a burrow, which it digs itself. During the day it hunts for food, treading the same paths repeatedly under the cover of vegetation. It eats almost anything it can catch, such as rats, mice, snakes, scorpions, wasps and other insects. It is useful to man because it keeps pest species, such as rats, at bay and it has been introduced into areas outside its native range for this purpose.

Females may produce two litters of 2 to 4 young a year, after a gestation of about 7 weeks. The newborn are blind and hairless, and their mother carries them in her mouth.

Marsh Mongoose *Atilax paludinosus*

RANGE Africa, south of the Sahara

HABITAT Marshland, tidal estuaries, swamps

SIZE Body: 17¾–23½ in (45–60 cm) Tail: 11¾–15¾ in (30–40 cm)

The large, sturdily built marsh mongoose is an expert swimmer and diver and is probably the most aquatic of all mongooses. Its feet are not webbed, but have short, strong claws. This nocturnal mongoose swims or roams stream banks or marshes in search of crabs, insects, fish, frogs and snakes. It crushes hard-shelled animals, such as crabs, by dashing them against a rock or tree.

This species has complex scent marking behavior – standing on its forepaws, with its tail over its back, to mark the underside of branches with scent from its anal glands.

Marsh mongooses live alone or in pairs or small family groups. The female gives birth to 1 to 3 young in a burrow or in a nest amid a pile of vegetation.

Banded Mongoose *Mungos mungo*

RANGE Africa, south of the Sahara

HABITAT Savanna, often near water

SIZE Body: 11¾–17¾ in (30–45 cm) Tail: 7¾–11¾ in (20–30 cm)

The banded mongoose has a stout body and a rather short snout and tail. Its color varies from olive-brown to reddish-gray, and light and dark bands alternate across its back from shoulders to tail. It is active in the day – in hot weather in the morning and evening only – and also sometimes emerges on moonlit nights. It is a good climber and swimmer. The banded mongoose often digs and forages in the ground and in leaf litter for food such as insects, spiders, scorpions, lizards, snakes, small mammals and birds. It also eats fruit, plant shoots and eggs.

Family troops of up to 30 animals live together, sheltering in hollow trees, rock crevices or burrows. If attacked, they defend themselves vigorously.

A litter of 2 to 6 young is born in a burrow after a gestation of about 8 weeks. The infants' eyes open at 10 days.

Cusimanse *Crossarchus obscurus*

Range Africa: Sierra Leone to Ghana

Habitat Rain forest

Size Body: 11¾–15¾ in (30–40 cm) Tail: 6–9¾ in (15–25 cm)

The cusimanse has a long, narrow head and snout. The nose protrudes beyond the lower lip. It lives in family groups of up to 12 animals, which keep in touch with chattering calls as they search for food. They dig for worms, woodlice, spiders, snails and insects and also eat crabs, frogs, reptiles, small mammals and birds and their eggs. To break eggs and hard-shelled prey, cusimanse throw them against a tree or stone. At night, they sleep in burrows, which they often dig in old termite mounds. They only climb to escape enemies.

The female bears several litters a year, each of 2 to 4 young. The gestation period is about 70 days.

White-tailed Mongoose *Ichneumia albicauda*

Range Africa, south of the Sahara

Habitat Savanna, dense bush, forest edge, often near water

Size Body: 18½–27 in (47–69 cm) Tail: 14¼–19¾ in (36–50 cm)

This mongoose has a bushy tail, which is usually gray at its base, becoming white or off-white at the tip. It lives alone or in pairs and is normally nocturnal, though in secluded areas it may emerge in late afternoon. It is a poor climber and can swim, though it rarely does so. It hunts mainly on the ground and eats insects, frogs, reptiles, rodents, ground-living birds, snails, crabs, eggs, berries and fruit.

The female gives birth to a litter of 2 or 3 young.

Meerkat *Suricata suricatta*

Range Africa: Angola to South Africa

Habitat Open country, savanna, bush

Size Body: 9¾–12¼ in (25–31 cm) Tail: 7½–9½ in (19–24 cm)

The meerkat, also known as the suricate, has the long body and short legs typical of many mongooses. Its coat is mainly grayish-brown to light gray in color, marked with dark bands

across the body, but it has dark ears and nose and a light-colored head and throat. The belly fur is thin and helps the meerkat to regulate its body temperature. It sits up sunning itself or lies on warm ground to increase its temperature and reduces it by lying belly-down in a cool, dark burrow.

Meerkats are gregarious and live in family units. Sometimes several families live together in a group of 30 or so. The colony occupies a home range, which contains shelters, such as burrows or rock crevices, and feeding sites. The animals move to a different area several times a year when food supplies dwindle. Meerkats are good diggers. They make burrows with several tunnels and chambers.

Active in the daytime, they forage in pairs or small groups, often sitting up on their hindlegs to watch for prey or danger. They eat insects, spiders, scorpions, centipedes, small mammals, lizards, snakes, birds and their eggs, snails, roots, fruit and other plant material. Meerkats have good hearing and sense of smell and excellent eyesight. They are constantly alert for birds of prey, their main enemies, and dive for cover if alarmed. They cover short distances quickly, but do not climb or jump well.

Breeding takes place mainly between October and April. The female gives birth to 2 to 5 young, usually 2 or 3, in a grass-lined underground chamber after a gestation of about 77 days. The young are born blind, but their eyes open 12 to 14 days after birth, and they take their first solid food at 3 or 4 weeks.

Salano *Salanoia concolor* **VU**

Range N.E. Madagascar

Habitat Rain forest

Size Body: 13¾–15 in (35–38 cm) Tail: 7–7¾ in (18–20 cm)

Salanos are gregarious. They pair for life and live in family groups in a territory, marking the boundaries with secretions from their anal glands. At night, salanos rest in a burrow that they dig or take over from other animals, or in hollow trees. During the day, they search for insects (their main food), reptiles, amphibians, and occasionally small mammals and birds. It eats eggs, which it cracks by hurling them against a stone or tree with its hind legs.

The female gives birth to 1 young.

HYENAS

HYAENIDAE: HYENA FAMILY

The hyenas of Africa and southwest Asia and the aardwolf of southern Africa together constitute a small family of land-dwelling carnivores that is related to viverrids and cats, although all hyenas have an extremely doglike body form.

The 3 species of hyena, particularly, resemble dogs, but are more heavily built in the forequarters than their hindquarters. They have massive heads. Indeed the jaws of the spotted hyena, the largest member of the group, are the most powerful of any mammal. All hyenas are able to crush the biggest bones of their prey in order to extract the marrow.

Hyenas specialize in feeding on carrion, often the kills of lions and other large carnivores in their range, and are able to drive smaller predators, such as cheetah, away from their own kills. They are, however, also predators in their own right, particularly spotted hyenas. By hunting in packs they can kill animals as large as zebras. Near villages and towns, hyenas are useful scavengers and feed on any refuse that is left out at night.

The aardwolf is a highly adapted offshoot of the hyena stock. It is more lightly built, has a narrow, pointed head, large ears and tiny teeth. It feeds mostly on termites.

Males and females look alike in all members of the family, but males may be larger.

group with young, the aardwolf lives alone in a territory centred on a den, which may be the abandoned burrow of an aardvark or a hole it digs itself. The boundaries of the territory are marked by anal gland secretions. Active at night, the aardwolf has extremely acute hearing and can detect the movements of termites, its main food. These are lapped from the ground or grass by means of the aardwolf's long tongue, which is covered with sticky saliva, making the task easier. It also eats other insects, birds' eggs, small mammals and reptiles.

A litter of 2 to 4 young is born in a burrow. After weaning, both parents feed the young on regurgitated termites.

Striped Hyena *Hyaena hyaena*

RANGE Africa: Senegal to Tanzania; Middle East to India

HABITAT Dry savanna, bush country, semidesert, desert

SIZE Body: 3¼–4 ft (1–1.2 m) Tail: 9¾–13¾ in (25–35 cm)

The striped hyena is identified by the dark stripes on its gray or yellowish-gray body and by the erectile mane around its neck and shoulders that extends down the middle of its back. Males are usually larger than females and both have the heavy head and sloping back typical of the hyenas.

Although they live in pairs in the breeding season, striped hyenas are generally solitary animals. Each has a home range, which must contain some thick cover. The territorial boundaries are marked by anal-gland secretions rubbed on to grass stems.

The striped hyena is active at night. It feeds on carrion, such as the remains of the kills of big cats, and preys on young sheep and goats, small mammals, birds, lizards, snakes and insects; it will also eat fruit. Striped hyenas stay well away from the larger spotted hyenas.

After a gestation of about 3 months, a litter of 2 to 4 young is born in a hole in the ground or among rocks. Both parents help to care for the young, which are blind at birth and are suckled for up to a year.

Aardwolf *Proteles cristatus*

RANGE Africa: Sudan, south to South Africa, Angola

HABITAT Open dry plains, savanna

SIZE Body: 25½–31½ in (65–80 cm) Tail: 7¾–11¾ in (20–30 cm)

A smaller and more lightly built version of the hyena, the aardwolf has a pointed muzzle, slender legs and an erectile mane on the neck and along the back. There are dark stripes on its yellowish to reddish-brown body and legs. Unless in a family

Brown Hyena *Hyaena brunnea* **LR:lc**

RANGE Africa: Angola to Mozambique, south to N. South Africa

HABITAT Dry savanna, plains, semidesert

SIZE Body: 3½–4 ft (1.1–1.2 m) Tail: 9¾–11¾ in (25–30 cm)

This hyena has an appearance that is typical of its family, with a bulky head and a back which slopes toward the rear. The brown hyena has long, rough hair over much of its body, with a mane of even longer hair on the neck and shoulders. Its coat is usually dark brown to brownish-black in color, with a lighter brown mane and legs.

Unless in a family group, the brown hyena tends to be a solitary animal, although it does sometimes gather with others at a big carcass or to form a hunting pack. It lives in a large territory, which it marks with secretions from its anal scent glands and with piles of dung.

During the day the brown hyena sleeps in a burrow, often one which has been abandoned by another animal, such as an aardvark. Alternatively it will rest among rocks or tall grass. It emerges at night and may travel long distances in search of carrion or to hunt prey, such as rodents, birds (including domestic poultry), reptiles or wounded large animals. It is primarily a scavenger and the bulk of its diet consists of insects, small vertebrates as well as eggs and fruit and vegetables. Near the coast, brown hyenas will also feed on dead fish, mussels and the stranded corpses of seals and whales on the shore. When this species discovers a large source of food it will remove and hide parts of its find in small caches and return to them later.

The mother gives birth to a litter of 2 to 4 blind, helpless young in the safety of a burrow after a gestation period of between 92 and 98 days. The young are suckled by the mother for about 3 months, but remain with their parents for up to 18 months, during which time the male supplies them with solid food in the den.

Although this species is protected in game reserves, brown hyenas are considered as pests by local people because of their habit of attacking livestock. As a consequence large numbers have been killed by farmers.

Spotted Hyena *Crocuta crocuta* **LR:cd**

RANGE Africa, south of the Sahara

HABITAT Semidesert to moist savanna

SIZE Body: 4–6 ft (1.2–1.8 m) Tail: 9¾–11¾ in (25–30 cm)

The spotted hyena is the largest member of the hyena family. It has a big, powerful head, slender legs and a sloping back. Its tail is short and bushy, and a short mane covers its neck and shoulders. The head and feet are always a lighter brown than the rest of the body, and irregular dark spots are scattered over the whole body. The spots vary greatly in their color and arrangement between individuals.

The spotted hyena is an inhabitant of open country and does not enter forest. It lives in packs of 10 to 30 or so animals (sometimes as many as 100), each pack occupying its own territory. The boundaries of the territory are marked with urine, droppings and anal-gland secretions and are carefully guarded to keep out rival packs. Males are dominant in the pack.

Hyenas sleep in burrows, which they dig themselves. Alternatively, they rest among tall grass or rocks. They emerge at dusk and are normally active at night only, although they may hunt during the day in some areas. As well as feeding on carrion, spotted hyenas cooperate to hunt large mammals, such as antelope, zebra and domestic livestock. The victim is often brought down by a bite in the leg and then torn to pieces by the pack while it is still alive. Spotted hyenas are extremely noisy animals, making a variety of howling screams when getting ready for the hunt, as well as eerie sounds like laughter when they kill and when mating.

When courting, spotted hyenas eject strong-smelling anal-gland secretions, and the male prances around the female and rolls her on the ground. The gestation period is between 99 and 130 days, and the 1 or 2 young are born in a burrow. Their eyes are open and some teeth are already through at birth. The young are suckled for between a year and 18 months, by which time they are able to join the hunting pack.

CATS

FELIDAE CAT FAMILY

There are approximately 36 species in the cat family as classified here, but numbers differ according to source, and there is considerable disagreement as to the organization of the family. Of all predators, cats are probably the most efficient killers. Coloring, size and fur patterning vary within the family, but all species from the smallest to the largest are basically similar in appearance and proportions to the domestic cat – an ideal predatory body form.

Cat bodies are muscular and flexible, and the head is typically shortened and rounded, with large forward-directed eyes. Limbs can be proportionately short or long, but in all species except the cheetah, there are long, sharp, completely retractile claws on the feet for the grasping of prey. The overpowering of prey animals, however, practically always involves a bite from the powerful jaws, which are armed with well-developed, daggerlike canines. Shearing cheek teeth, carnassials, are used for slicing through flesh.

This successful family is distributed almost worldwide, being absent only from Antarctica, Australasia, the West Indies and some other islands, and from Madagascar, which is inhabited by the catlike viverrids, the fossas. Male and female look alike in most species, but males are often slightly larger.

Sadly, the fine fur of the cats has long been coveted by man, and many species have been hunted until they are rare and in danger of extinction.

African Golden Cat *Profelis aurata* **LR:lc**

RANGE Africa: Senegal to Zaire (not Nigeria), Kenya

HABITAT Forest, forest edge

SIZE Body: 28¼–36½ in (72–93 cm) Tail: 13¾–17¾ in (35–45 cm)

A robust, medium-sized cat, the golden cat has rather short, sturdy legs and small, rounded ears. Coloration varies enormously from brownish-red to slate-gray on the upper parts; some golden cats have distinct spots all over the body, some only on the underside.

An inhabitant of dense forest, this cat spends much of its life in trees

and is mainly active at night. During the day it sleeps up in a tree. It is a solitary, elusive creature and little is known of its habits. It preys on mammals up to the size of small antelope and on birds up to the size of guineafowl.

Leopard Cat *Prionailurus bengalensis*

RANGE S.E. Asia, Sumatra, Borneo, Java, Philippines

HABITAT Forest

SIZE Body: about 23½ in (60 cm) Tail: about 14 in (35 cm)

A nocturnal, rarely seen creature, the leopard cat rests during the day in a hole in a tree. It is an agile climber and preys on small birds and on mammals up to the size of squirrels and hares; it may occasionally kill a small deer. The coloration and pattern of the leopard cat are variable, but it is usually yellowish, gray or reddish-brown on the upper parts of the body, with a whitish belly, and is dotted overall with dark spots. These spots are in regular lines and may merge to form bands.

The breeding habits of this cat are not well known, but the female is thought to produce litters of 3 or 4 young in a cave or a den under fallen rocks.

Pampas Cat *Oncifelis colocolo* **LR:lc**

RANGE South America: Ecuador, Peru, Brazil to S. Argentina

HABITAT Open grassland, forest

SIZE Body: 23½–27½ in (60–70 cm) Tail: 11½–12½ in (29–32 cm)

A small, but sturdily built animal, the pampas cat has a small head and thick, bushy tail. Its long fur is variable in color, ranging from yellowish-white to brown or silvery-gray. In the north of its range, it lives in forest and, although primarily ground-dwelling, will take refuge in trees. Farther south, it inhabits the vast grasslands, where it takes cover among the tall pampas grass. Active at

night, it hunts small mammals, such as cavies, and ground-dwelling birds, such as tinamous.

The female gives birth to litters of 1 to 3 young after a gestation thought to be about 10 weeks.

Caracal *Caracal caracal*

RANGE Africa (except rain forest belt); Middle East to N.W. India

HABITAT Savanna, open plains, semidesert, sand desert

SIZE Body: 25½–35½ in (65–90 cm) Tail: 7¾–11¾ in (20–30 cm)

The caracal has long, slender legs, a rather flattened head and long, tufted ears. A solitary animal, it occupies a home range, which it patrols in search of prey. It is most active at dusk and at night, but may also emerge in the daytime. It eats a variety of mammals, from mice to reedbuck, and it also feeds on birds, reptiles, and domestic sheep, goats and poultry.

The male caracal courts his mate with yowls similar to those of the domestic cat. In a well-concealed den in a rock crevice, tree hole or abandoned burrow, the female bears a litter of 2 or 3 young after a gestation of 69 or 70 days. The young suckle for 6 months and are not independent until 9 to 12 months old.

Mountain Lion *Puma concolor*

RANGE S.W. Canada, W. USA, Mexico, Central and South America

HABITAT Mountainsides, forest, swamps, grassland

SIZE Body: 3¼–5¼ ft (1–1.6 m) Tail: 23½–33½ in (60–85 cm)

The widespread mountain lion, also known as the cougar or puma, is now becoming increasingly rare and some subspecies are in danger of extinction.

It varies greatly in color and size over its range, but tawny and grayish-brown are predominant. A solitary creature, the mountain lion occupies a defined territory. A male's home range may overlap with the territories of one or more females, but not with the territory of another male.

Normally active in the early morning and evening, the mountain lion may emerge at any time. Its main prey are mule deer and other deer, but it also eats rodents, hares and occasionally, domestic cattle. Having stalked its prey, the mountain lion pounces and kills with a swift bite to the nape of the neck.

Young are born in the summer in the temperate north and south of the range, or at any time of year in the tropics. Male and female pair for the season, maybe longer, and during his mate's period of sexual receptivity, or heat, the male fights off any rivals. The litter of 2 to 4 young is born after a gestation of 92 to 96 days in a den, among rocks or in thick vegetation, which the female may use for some years. At 6 or 7 weeks old the young start to take solid food, brought to them by their mother, and remain with her for 1 or even 2 years.

Lynx *Lynx lynx*

RANGE Europe: Scandinavia, east through Asia to Siberia

HABITAT Coniferous forest, scrub

SIZE Body: 31½ in–4¼ ft (80 cm–1.3 m) Tail: 1½–3 in (4–8 cm)

The lynx is recognized by its short tail and its tufted ears and cheeks. Its coat varies in coloration over its wide range, particularly in the degree of spotting, which may be either faint or conspicuous. Although strictly protected in most countries, lynx are becoming scarce, and some races are in danger of extinction. A solitary, nocturnal animal, the lynx stalks its prey on the ground or lies in wait for it in low vegetation. Hares, rodents, young deer and ground-living birds, such as grouse, are its main prey.

Breeding normally starts in the spring, and a litter of 2 or 3 young is born in a den among rocks or in a hollow tree, after a gestation of about 63 days. The cubs remain with their mother throughout their first winter.

CATS CONTINUED

Ocelot *Leopardus pardalis*

RANGE USA: Arizona, Texas; Mexico, Central and South America to N. Argentina

HABITAT Humid forest, thick bush, marshy areas

SIZE Body: 37½ in–4¼ ft (95 cm–1.3 m)
Tail: 10½–15¾ in (27–40 cm)

The characteristic dark markings that pattern the ocelot's coat are so variable that no two animals are quite alike. Generally nocturnal, the ocelot sleeps on a branch or in cover of vegetation during the day and emerges at night to hunt for small mammals, such as young deer and peccaries, agoutis, pacas and other rodents, as well as birds and snakes. It is an extremely secretive animal and rarely shows itself in open country. Males and females live in pairs in a territory, but do not hunt together.

Ocelots mate at night, and courting males make loud, screeching calls, similar to those of domestic cats. A litter of 2 young, sometimes 4, is born after a gestation of about 70 days, in a safe den in a hollow tree or in thick vegetation.

These beautiful cats have become rare, both because of the destruction of their forest habitat and because they have long been hunted for their fur. It is now illegal in many countries to trade ocelot skins, but such laws are hard to enforce, when the demand continues, and the black market price is high.

Bobcat *Lynx rufus*

RANGE S. Canada, USA (mostly western states), Mexico

HABITAT Chaparral, brush, swamp, forest

SIZE Body: 25½ in–3¼ ft (65 cm–1 m) Tail: 4¼–7½ in (11–19 cm)

The bobcat is short-tailed, like the lynx, but is generally smaller than the latter and has less conspicuous ear tufts. It varies considerably in size, the largest individuals occurring in the north of the range, and the smallest in Mexico. Adaptable to a variety of habitats, the bobcat is ground-dwelling, but does climb trees and will take refuge in a tree when chased. It is solitary and nocturnal for the most part, but may hunt in the daytime in winter. Small mammals, such as rabbits, mice, rats and squirrels, are its main prey, and it also catches ground-dwelling birds such as grouse. It hunts by stealth, slowly stalking its victim until near enough to pounce.

The female bobcat gives birth to a litter of 1 to 6 young, usually 3, after a gestation of about 50 days. The young first leave the den at about 5 weeks and start to accompany their mother on hunting trips at between 3 and 5 months old.

Pallas's Cat *Otocolobus manul* **LR:lc**

RANGE C. Asia: Iran to W. China

HABITAT Steppe, desert, rocky mountainsides

SIZE Body: 19¾–25½ in (50–65 cm) Tail: 8¼–12¼ in (21–31 cm)

Pallas's cat has a robust body and short, stout legs. Its head is broad, and its ears low and wide apart, protruding only slightly from the fur. The fur varies in color from pale gray to yellowish-buff or reddish-brown and is longer and more dense than that of any other wild cat. An elusive, solitary creature, this cat lives in a cave or rock crevice or a burrow taken over from another mammal, such as a marmot, usually emerging only at night to hunt. It preys on small mammals, such as mice and hares, and on birds.

Mating occurs in spring, and females give birth to litters of 5 or 6 young in summer.

Serval *Leptailurus serval*

RANGE Africa, south of the Sahara to South Africa: S. Transvaal

HABITAT Savanna, open plains, woodland

SIZE Body: 25½–35½ in (65–90 cm) Tail: 9¾–15 in (25–35 cm)

A slender, long-legged cat, with a small head and broad ears, the serval has a graceful, sprightly air. Coloration varies from yellowish-brown to dark olive-brown; lighter-colored animals tend to have rows of large black spots on their fur, while darker individuals are dotted with many fine spots. Servals have excellent sight and hearing. It is usually active in the daytime and lives in a small territory, the boundaries of which are marked with urine. It is generally solitary, but a female may enter a male's territory. Mammals, from the size of rodents up to small antelope, are its main prey. It also eats birds, poultry, lizards, insects and fruit. A litter of 1 to 4, usually 2 or 3, young is born in a safe den among rocks or vegetation or in a burrow taken over from another mammal. The gestation period is 67 to 77 days.

Wild Cat *Felis silvestris*

RANGE Scotland, S. Europe; Africa (not Sahara), Middle East to India

HABITAT Forest, scrub, savanna, open plains, semidesert

SIZE Body: 19¾–25½ in (50–65 cm) Tail: 9¾–15 in (25–38 cm)

One of the ancestors of the domestic cat, the wild cat is similar in form but slightly larger, and has a shorter, thicker tail, which is encircled with black rings. Coloration varies according to habitat, cats in dry sandy areas being lighter than forest-dwelling cats. Largely solitary and nocturnal, the wild cat lives in a well-defined territory. Although it is an agile climber, it stalks most of its prey on the ground, catching small rodents and ground-dwelling birds.

Rival courting males howl and screech as they vie for the attention of a female, and it is she who eventually makes the selection. She bears 2 or 3 young after a gestation of 63 to 69 days. The young first emerge from the den, in a cave, hollow tree or fox hole, when they are 4 or 5 weeks old and leave their mother after about 5 months.

Cheetah *Acinonyx jubatus* **VU**

RANGE Africa, east to Asia: E. Iran

HABITAT Open country: desert, savanna

SIZE Body: 3½–4½ ft (1.1–1.4 m) Tail: 25½–31½ in (65–80 cm)

The cheetah is the fastest of the big cats, able to attain speeds of 69½ mph (112 km/h). Its body is long and supple, with high muscular shoulders, and its legs are long and slender. The tail aids balance during the cheetah's high-speed sprints.

Cheetahs live in territories in open country, alone, in pairs or in family groups. They are active in the daytime, and sight is the most important sense in hunting. Having selected its prey when in hiding, the cheetah stalks its victim and then attacks with a short, rapid chase, knocking over the prey and killing it with a bite to the throat. Hares, jackals, small antelope, the young of larger antelope, and birds, such as guineafowl, francolins, bustards and young ostriches, are the cheetah's main prey. Several adults may, however, cooperate to chase and exhaust larger animals such as zebra.

Rival males compete in bloodless struggles for the attention of a female. She bears a litter of 2 to 4 young after a gestation of 91 to 95 days and brings them up alone. The young stay with the mother for up to 2 years.

Clouded Leopard *Neofilis nebulosa* **VU**

RANGE Nepal to S. China, Taiwan, Sumatra, Borneo

HABITAT Forest

SIZE Body: 24½–41¾ in (62–106 cm) Tail: 24–35¾ in (61–91 cm)

The rare, elusive clouded leopard has a long, powerful body, relatively short legs and a long tail. It is a good climber and hunts by pouncing from trees, as well as by stalking prey on the ground. Birds, pigs, small deer and cattle are the clouded leopard's main victims, and it kills with a single bite from its exceptionally long canine teeth.

A litter of 1 to 5 cubs is born after a gestation period of between 86 and 92 days.

CATS CONTINUED

Lion *Panthera leo* **VU**

RANGE Africa, south of the Sahara; N.W. India;
formerly more widespread in Asia

HABITAT Open savanna

SIZE Body: 4½–6½ ft (1.4–2 m)
Tail: 26¼ in–3¼ ft (67 cm–1 m)

The lion is powerfully built with a broad head, thick, strong legs and a long tail, tipped with a tuft of hair that conceals a claw-like spine. The male is larger than the female and has a heavy mane on the neck and shoulders which may be light yellow to black. Body color varies from tawny-yellow to reddish-brown.

Lions spend 20 or more hours a day resting and normally hunt during the day, but in areas where they are persecuted they are active only at night. They live in groups (prides) consisting of up to 3 adult males and up to 15 females and their young, in a territory that is defended against intruders. A small group of young males may live together.

Lions prey on mammals, such as gazelle, antelope and zebra, and may cooperate to kill larger animals, such as buffalo. Smaller animals and birds, even crocodiles, may also be eaten. Lionesses do most of the hunting, often in groups. Lions stalk their prey and approach it as closely as possible then make a short, rapid chase and pounce. They kill with a bite to the neck or throat.

Breeding occurs at any time of year. A litter of 1 to 6 young, usually 2 or 3, is born after a gestation of 102 to 113 days. The cubs are suckled for about 6 months, but from 3 months an increasing proportion of their food is meat. The cubs are left behind with one or two adults while the rest of the pride goes off to hunt, but if a kill is made, a lioness will return and lead them to it. Once they are over 4 months old, the cubs accompany their mothers everywhere. They become sexually mature at about 18 months old; young males are driven from the pride at about this age, but females remain with their family.

Jaguar *Panthera onca* **LR:nt**

RANGE S.W. USA, N. Mexico, Central and
South America to N. Argentina

HABITAT Forest, savanna

SIZE Body: 5–6 ft (1.5–1.8 m) Tail: 27½–35¾ in (70–91 cm)

The jaguar is the largest South American cat. This powerful creature has a deep chest and massive, strong limbs. Its coloration varies from light yellow to reddish-brown, with characteristic dark spots on the coat.

Although not quite as graceful and agile as the leopard, the jaguar climbs trees, often to lie in wait for prey. It is also an excellent swimmer. Like lions, jaguars cannot sustain high speeds and depend on getting close to prey in order to make successful kills. Peccaries and capybaras are often prey, and jaguars also kill mountain sheep, deer, otters, rodents, ground-living birds, turtles, caimans and fish.

Normally solitary animals, male and female jaguars stay together for a few weeks when breeding. A litter of 1 to 4 young is born, after a gestation period of between 93 and 105 days, in a secure den in vegetation, among rocks or in a hole in a river bank. The female is aggressive in her protection of the young from any intruder, including even the father.

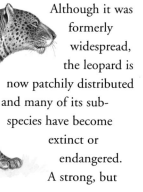

Leopard *Panthera pardus*

RANGE Asia: Siberia to Korea, Sri Lanka and Java; Middle East; Africa

HABITAT Desert to forest, lowland plains to mountains

SIZE Body: 4¼–6¼ ft (1.3–1.9 m) Tail: 3½–4½ ft (1.1–1.4 m)

Although it was formerly widespread, the leopard is now patchily distributed and many of its sub-species have become extinct or endangered. A strong, but elegant, cat, it has a long body and relatively short legs. Most leopards are buff or tawny, with characteristic rosette-shaped black spots, but some are entirely black and are known as panthers. Panthers and leopards are otherwise identical.

Leopards are solitary and normally hunt day or night, but in areas where they are persecuted, they are nocturnal. They swim and climb well and often lie basking in the sun on a branch. Their sight and sense of smell are good, and their hearing is exceptionally acute.

Prey includes mammals such as large antelope, young apes (particularly baboons and monkeys), birds, snakes, fish and domestic livestock. Large items may be dragged up into a tree for safety while the leopard feeds; it will also feed on carrion.

Females have regular fertile periods, and males may fight over sexually receptive females. The litter of 1 to 6, but usually 2 or 3, young is born in a den in a rock crevice or hole in a tree after a gestation period of about 90 to 112 days. The young are suckled for 3 months and become independent at between 18 months and 2 years. The mother hunts alone and if she makes a kill, she hides it while she goes to fetch her cubs to share her food. Older cubs may catch some small prey, such as insects for themselves.

Tiger *Panthera tigris* **EN**

RANGE Siberia to Java and Bali

HABITAT Forest

SIZE Body: 6–9¼ ft (1.8–2.8 m) Tail: about 3ft (91 cm)

The largest of the big cats, the tiger has a massive, muscular body and powerful limbs. Males and females look similar, but males have longer, more prominent, cheek whiskers. Coloration varies from reddish-orange to reddish-ochre, and the pattern of the tiger's distinctive dark, vertical stripes is extremely variable between individuals. Tigers of the northern subspecies tend to be larger and paler than tropical subspecies.

Tigers are generally shy, nocturnal creatures and usually live alone, although they are not unsociable and are on amicable

terms with their neighbors. They climb well, move gracefully on land, and are capable of galloping at speed when chasing prey. Wild pigs, deer, and cattle, such as gaur and buffalo, are the tiger's main prey, and it also kills other mammals, such as the sloth bear.

Male and female associate for only a few days in order to mate. The female gives birth to a litter of, usually 2 or 3 young after a gestation period of 103 to 105 days. The young may stay with their mother for several years.

Most races of these magnificent animals are now rare and the Bali and Java tigers are now extinct because of indiscriminate killing earlier this century and the destruction of forest habitats.

Snow Leopard *Uncia uncia* **EN**

RANGE Pakistan, Afghanistan, Himalayas, east to China

HABITAT Mountain slopes, forest

SIZE Body: 4–5 ft (1.2–1.5 m) Tail: about 3ft (91 cm)

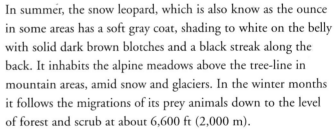

In summer, the snow leopard, which is also know as the ounce in some areas has a soft gray coat, shading to white on the belly with solid dark brown blotches and a black streak along the back. It inhabits the alpine meadows above the tree-line in mountain areas, amid snow and glaciers. In the winter months it follows the migrations of its prey animals down to the level of forest and scrub at about 6,600 ft (2,000 m).

This powerful, agile animal is capable of making huge leaps over ravines. The snow leopard stalks its prey, such as ibex, markhor, wild sheep and goats, boar and ground-dwelling birds, such as pheasants, partridges and snowcocks. In winter this leopard will also sometimes take domestic livestock.

Females may sometimes be accompanied by young, but otherwise snow leopards are solitary animals, constantly roaming around their enormous territories. They are active mainly in the early morning and late afternoon. The female gives birth to 2 or 3 cubs (but there may occasionally be 4 or 5), after a gestation period of between 98 and 103 days. The young start to accompany their mother on hunting trips when they are about 2 months old.

FUR SEALS, SEA LIONS AND WALRUS

OTARIIDAE: SEA LION FAMILY

There are approximately 14 species of fur seal and sea lion. The main features that distinguish these animals from the seals, family Phocidae, are the presence of external ears and their ability to tuck the hind flippers forward to facilitate locomotion on land. Sea lions occur in the southern Atlantic and Indian oceans and in the North and South Pacific, and come to land, or haul out, on coasts and islands.

Generally gregarious, these animals haul out in large numbers at traditional breeding sites, called rookeries, where males compete for the best territories. Males are considerably larger than females, and have big, bulbous heads.

Females give birth to the young conceived the previous year and mate again some days later. Mating and giving birth are synchronized in this convenient manner as a result of the phenomenon of delayed implantation. The embryo lies dormant for a period before development starts, thus ensuring the correct timing of the birth without producing young of undue size.

South American Fur Seal

Arctocephalus australis

RANGE South Pacific and Atlantic Oceans, from Brazil around to Peru

HABITAT Breeds on coasts and islands

SIZE 4½–6 ft (1.4–1.8 m)

The South American fur seal usually has deep reddish-brown underfur, the male has a coarse mane. It feeds on marine invertebrates, fish, squid and penguins and prefers to haul out on rocky coasts.

These fur seals are extremely territorial in the breeding season. Males take up their territories in November, competing for the prime spots and rigorously enforcing boundaries, since those with the best and largest sites mate with the most females. Males are joined 2 weeks later by the females, who give birth to their young within a few days. The female remains with her pup for up to 12 days, during which period she mates with the male whose territory she is in, then goes to sea to feed, returning at intervals to suckle the pup. The males rarely leave their territories until all the mating is over.

Northern Fur Seal *Callorhinus ursinus* **VU**

RANGE Bering Sea, Okhotsk Sea

HABITAT Breeds on islands in range such as Aleutian and Pribilof Islands

SIZE 5–6 ft (1.5–1.8 m)

Northern fur seals have larger rear flippers than other otariids, and both male and female have a pale patch on the neck. The male may be four times the female's weight. Usually alone or in pairs at sea, these fur seals feed on fish and squid and rarely come to land outside the breeding season.

Males establish territories on the breeding beaches before females arrive to give birth to their young. The female stays with her single offspring for 7 days before going off on brief feeding trips, returning to suckle it at intervals.

California Sea Lion *Zalophus californianus*

RANGE Pacific coasts: British Columbia to Mexico; Galápagos Islands

HABITAT Breeds on coasts and islands in south of range

SIZE 5½–7¼ ft (1.7–2.2 m)

This attractive sea lion takes well to training and is the most commonly seen species in circuses and marine shows. Females and juveniles are tan-colored when dry, while the larger males are brown; males are also distinguished by the horny crest on their heads. Social animals, these sea lions occur in groups and often come on to land outside the breeding season. They feed mainly on fish, octopus and squid.

Males gather at a breeding site, but only establish territories when the females arrive and start to give birth; territories are ill-defined and somewhat unstable. The female produces 1 young, and mates again a few days later.

Australian Sea Lion *Neophoca cinerea* **LR:lc**

RANGE Off S. and S.W. Australia

HABITAT Coasts and islands

SIZE Up to 7¾ ft (2.4 m)

A nonmigratory species, this sea lion does not travel far from the beach where it was born and often comes out on to land throughout the year. It moves quite easily on land despite its bulk and may travel several kilometers. Fish, squid and penguins are its main foods.

This is a gregarious species, and is usually found in small groups. The males establish well-defined territories, which they defend vigorously, and usually manage to prevent females on their sites from leaving. The female produces 1 young and remains with it for 14 days, during which time she mates. She then goes to sea, returning at 2-day intervals in order to suckle the pup, which she feeds for up to 2 years.

Steller Sea Lion *Eumetopias jubatus* **EN**

RANGE N. Pacific Ocean

HABITAT Breeds on Pribilof and Aleutian Islands, Kurile Islands, islands in Okhotsk Sea, coasts of N. America to San Miguel Island off S. California

SIZE 7¾–9¼ ft (2.4–2.8 m)

The largest otariid, the steller sea lion overlaps in its range with the California sea lion, but is distinguished by its size and lighter color. It feeds on fish, squid and octopus. Examination of stomach contents have revealed that the steller sea lion dives to 600 ft (180 m) or more to find food.

Males establish well-defined territories at breeding grounds and maintain the boundaries with ritual threat displays. They remain there throughout the breeding period, mating with the females in their area, and do not feed for about 2 months. Shortly after arriving, the female gives birth to 1 young. She remains with the pup constantly for the first 5 to 13 days before going briefly to sea to feed, leaving her pup in the company of other young.

ODOBENIDAE: WALRUS FAMILY

The single species of walrus resembles the sea lions in that its hind flippers can be brought forward in order to help it move on land. However, it cannot move as fast or adeptly as sea lions, and will often just drag itself forward.

Walrus *Odobenus rosmarus*

RANGE Arctic Ocean; occasionally N. Atlantic Ocean

HABITAT Pack ice, rocky islands

SIZE Male: 8¾–11½ ft (2.7–3.5 m) Female: 7¼–9½ ft (2.2–2.9 m)

The largest, heaviest pinniped, the male walrus is a huge animal. The male has large, heavy tusks, which have evolved from the upper canine teeth, which extend downward. Females also have tusks, but they are shorter and thinner. Walruses have thick skin, which acts as a protection against injury. The adult males tend to have less hair than females and young males.

Walruses swim quite slowly and use mainly their hind quarters for propulsion. They are good divers and feed on bottom living invertebrates, particularly mollusks, of which they consume only the soft muscular foot or siphon. How they extract these is still a mystery, but it is thought to be through some form of suction. They also feed on crustaceans, starfish, fish and even mammals.

Walruses are gregarious throughout the year. During the mating season, they congregate in traditional areas, where males compete for space near potential mates and display. After mating implantation is delayed by 4 or 5 months. Gestation is 11 months, so females can breed every other year at most. Usually 1 young is born (rarely 2) and the calf may be suckled for up to 2 years.

SEALS

PHOCIDAE: SEAL FAMILY

Often known as earless seals because they lack external ears, the 19 species in this family have made the most complete transition from terrestrial to aquatic way of life of all the pinnipeds. Their hind flippers cannot be turned forward like those of other pinnipeds. They move on land by dragging themselves forward with the foreflippers. They are skilful swimmers and divers, moving with undulatory movements of the hind portion of the body and the hind flippers. Seals have sophisticated mechanisms to enable them to dive deeply for food and to stay underwater for long periods. During a dive, the heart rate may drop from 120 to about 4 beats a minute, but without any drop in blood pressure. This is achieved by the restriction of the blood supply to the muscles of the heart and to the brain, thus reserving the blood oxygen for only the most vital organs.

The body of a seal is typically torpedo shaped, thick layers of fatty blubber under the skin accounting for much of its weight. The flippers as well as the body are furred, and the seals undergo an annual molt.

In some species, males are much bigger and heavier than females, but in others, females are the larger sex. Some are monogamous, but others, such as the elephant seals, are gregarious and polygamous. In most species there is a delay between fertilization and the actual start of gestation – delayed implantation. This ensures that birth and mating can be accomplished within the short period while the seals are on land.

Gray Seal *Halichoerus grypus*
RANGE N. Atlantic Ocean
HABITAT Breeds on rocky coasts of Scandinavia and Britain; Iceland and Faroe Islands; Labrador, Gulf of St. Lawrence, Newfoundland
SIZE 5¼–7½ ft (1.6–2.3 m)

The largest of the seals, excepting the elephant seals, a male gray seal may weigh up to 660 lb (300 kg) and be more than twice as heavy as a female. The male is also identified by his massive shoulders, covered with thick skin which forms heavy folds and wrinkles and by the elongated snout, rounded forehead and wide, heavy muzzle. The female has a flatter profile and a daintier, more slender muzzle.

Gray seals travel far from breeding sites, but stay mostly in coastal waters, feeding on fish and also on some crustaceans, squid and octopus.

The timing of breeding differs in the three areas of the gray seal's range, but females always arrive at breeding grounds first and give birth before the males appear. The males take up positions on the beach. The older, experienced individuals get the best places, but there is little fighting, and males may move sites from day to day. Having suckled her pup for about 3 weeks, the female mates and then leaves the area.

Harp Seal *Pagophilus groenlandica*
RANGE N. Atlantic and Arctic Oceans: N. Russia to Scandinavia and Greenland; Labrador, Newfoundland
HABITAT Subarctic and arctic waters
SIZE 5¼–6¼ ft (1.6–1.9 m)

The harp seal is identified by its black head and the dark band along its flanks and over its back; the rest of the body is usually pale gray, but this is highly variable. It is an expert, fast swimmer, and spends much of the year at sea making regular north-south migrations. It can also move fast over ice if necessary. Fish and crustaceans are the harp seal's main foods, and it is renowned for its ability to dive deeply and stay underwater for long periods in search of food.

It is generally a gregarious species, and only old males live alone. Females form whelping groups on the ice and give birth to their young in late February and early March. The pups are suckled for 2 to 4 weeks, growing rapidly on the nourishing milk, which is rich in fat. They are then left by the mothers, who go off to feed for a few weeks before migrating north to summer feeding grounds. Courting males fight rivals with their teeth and flippers and probably mate with females 2 or 3 weeks after they have given birth.

Common Seal/Harbor Seal *Phoca vitulina*

RANGE N. Atlantic and N. Pacific Oceans

HABITAT Temperate and subarctic coastal waters

SIZE 4½–6 ft (1.4–1.8 m)

The common seal has a proportionately large head and short body and flippers. Although often gray with dark blotches, these seals vary considerably in coloration and spots may be light gray to dark brown or black. Males are larger than females.

Generally non-migratory, the common seal often hauls out on protected tidal rocks and even travels up rivers and into lakes. It feeds mostly during the day on fish, squid and crustaceans and has been known to make dives lasting 30 minutes, although they normally last only 4 or 5 minutes.

Courtship and mating take place underwater. The single pup is closely guarded by its mother and suckles for 2 to 6 weeks. Born in an advanced state of development, the pup can swim from birth and dive for 2 minutes when 2 or 3 days old. After weaning, the pup is left, and the mother mates again.

Crabeater Seal *Lobodon carcinophagus*

RANGE Antarctic

HABITAT Edge of pack ice

SIZE 6½–7¾ ft (2–2.4 m)

Crabeater seals may well be the most abundant of all pinnipeds, and in their remote habitat they have few enemies other than killer whales. Capable of rapid movement over the ice, the crabeater seal thrusts with alternate forelimbs and the pelvis, and it is thought to achieve speeds of as much as 15½ mph (25 km/h). Krill, small shrimplike crustaceans, are its main food, which are strained from the water by means of the seal's trident-shaped teeth.

Births and mating probably occur from October to the end of December. The pup is well developed at birth and suckles for about 5 weeks.

Bearded Seal *Erignathus barbatus*

RANGE Arctic Ocean

HABITAT Shallow waters; breeds on ice floes

SIZE 6¾–7¾ ft (2.1–2.4 m)

Numerous long bristles on the snout are the identifying feature of the bearded seal and the source of its common name. It is a robust, heavily built species, in which females are slightly longer than males. Bottom-dwelling invertebrates, such as crustaceans and mollusks, and fish are its main foods.

During the breeding season the males call underwater. The female gives birth to 1 pup each year from the age of about 6 years. The pup, which can swim immediately, suckles for between 12 and 18 days, during which time the female usually mates again.

SEALS CONTINUED

Leopard Seal *Hydrurga leptonyx*

RANGE Southern Ocean

HABITAT Pack ice, coasts, islands

SIZE 9¾–11½ ft (3–3.5 m)

An unusually slender seal, the leopard seal is built for speed and has a large mouth, well suited to grasping the penguins, and sometimes other seals, that are its main prey. It catches penguins under water or as they move off the ice and, using its teeth, tears away the skin with great efficiency before eating them. Squid, fish and crustaceans are also caught.

Mating is thought to take place from January until March, but there is little information available.

Northern Elephant Seal *Mirounga angustirostris*

RANGE Pacific coast of N. America: Vancouver Island to C. Baja California

HABITAT Breeds on offshore islands

SIZE Male: up to 19¾ ft (6 m) Female: up to 9¾ ft (3 m)

The largest seal in the northern hemisphere, the male elephant seal may weigh a massive 6,000 lb (2,700 kg), much of it accounted for by the thick layer of blubber. Females rarely weigh more than 2,000 lb (900 kg). Because of its size, this species was a major target for commercial sealers, and by the end of the nineteenth century the population was dangerously low. Only one of the breeding islands appeared to be used, and that by only a hundred or so seals. With strict protection, numbers have increased since then, and between 1957 and 1976, the population tripled to over 47,000 – a remarkable recovery.

Northern elephant seals feed on fish and squid and make long, deep dives. Adult males haul out for breeding in late November and fight for dominance in the social hierarchy – high-ranking males mate with most females. With the aid of the greatly enlarged nasal chamber, which creates the elephantine snout, males utter loud, vocal threats against rivals. Females arrive a couple of weeks after males and each gives birth to a single pup, which is suckled for about a month. The bond between mother and young is close, and the female defends the pup from other adults and rarely leaves the breeding colony, existing on her blubber until the pup is weaned. She then mates again and leaves the breeding ground. Weaned pups gather in a group on the beach, where they remain for another month, living on fat reserves built up while suckling.

longest duration 73 minutes. Dives to 1,000 and 1,300 ft (300 and 400 m) are common, and antarctic cod, which are abundant at these depths, are one of the Weddell seal's main food species. This seal is able to reach such depths because, when diving, its heart rate slows down to 25 per cent of the predive rate.

Weddell seals are normally solitary outside the breeding season, but young animals may form groups. In the breeding season, males seem to set up underwater territories, which females can enter freely. The female gives birth on land to 1 pup, with which she stays constantly for about 12 days. She then spends about half of her time in water until the pup is weaned at about 6 weeks. When only 7 weeks old, the pup is able to dive to 295 ft (90 m). Females mate once their pups are weaned.

Mediterranean Monk Seal *Monachus monachus* **CR**

RANGE W. Atlantic Ocean: Canary Islands to Mediterranean Sea; Turkish coast of Black Sea

HABITAT Breeds on rocky islets and cliffs

SIZE 7½–8¾ ft (2.3 m–2.7 m)

The Mediterranean monk seal is becoming rare now that its previously remote hauling-out spots on islets and cliffs are becoming more accessible to humans with motor boats and scuba diving equipment. These seals often become entangled in fishing nets. They are extremely upset by any disturbance, and mothers and pregnant females in particular are nervous of any approach, and when the females are in danger or under stress pregnancies may be spontaneously aborted.

Births occur between May and November, with a peak in September and October. The pups are suckled for about the first 6 weeks of their lives.

Weddell Seal *Leptonychotes weddelli*

RANGE Antarctic

HABITAT Edge of pack ice

SIZE Up to 9½ ft (2.9 m)

The Weddell seal is one of the larger seals in the family. It has a small head in proportion to its body and an appealing, short-muzzled face. The female is longer than the male.

It makes deeper, longer dives than any other seal, the maximum recorded depth being 2,000 ft (600 m), and the

Hooded Seal *Cystophora cristata*

RANGE N. Atlantic Ocean: arctic and subarctic waters

HABITAT Edge of pack ice

SIZE 6½–8½ ft (2–2.6 m)

Hooded seals spend much of their lives in open seas, diving deeply in search of fish and squid, which are their main food source.

Hooded seals make regular migrations to areas of pack ice in the Denmark Strait and east of Greenland. On the pack ice the adults gather to haul out and molt. After molting, the seals disperse again to reassemble at breeding grounds in different areas the following spring.

Pups are born in March on ice floes and are suckled for between 7 and 12 days. During this period, the female is courted by a male, who stays in the water near to her and her pup, chasing away any rivals. If necessary, the male hauls out and displays or fights, making threat calls that are amplified by his enormous inflatable nasal sac. The female then mates with her successful suitor about 2 weeks after giving birth.

AARDVARK AND PIGS

ORDER TUBULIDENTATA

ORYCTEROPODIDAE AARDVARK FAMILY

There is one family in this order, containing a single species that lives in Africa. Its relationship to other mammal groups is obscure. The aardvark's teeth are unique: they have no enamel and consist of dentine columns, interspersed with tubes of pulp.

Aardvark *Orycteropus afer*

RANGE Africa, south of the Sahara

HABITAT All regions with termites, from rain forest to dry savanna

SIZE Body: 3¼–5¼ ft (1–1.6 m) Tail: 17½–23½ in (44.5–60 cm)

The aardvark is a solitary, nocturnal, insect-eating animal. Its sight is poor, but its other senses are excellent, it has large ears, which are normally held upright but can be folded and closed, and highly specialized nostrils for sniffing out its prey. Dense hair surrounds the nostrils and seals them off when the aardvark digs. It uses its powerful forelimbs to excavate burrows for shelter and to smash the nests of the ants and termites that are its main food. It sweeps up the prey with its long, sticky tongue.

The female gives birth to a single young after a gestation of 7 months. The offspring is suckled for 4 months.

ORDER ARTIODACTYLA

This, the largest and most diverse order of hoofed herbivorous mammals. Artiodactyls have an even number of toes. Weight is carried on digits 3 and 4, which are typically encased in hoofs. The first digit is absent, and digits 2 and 5 are reduced. Artiodactyls can run rapidly and have specialized teeth for eating vegetation, which is digested in a four-chambered stomach with the aid of enzymes and symbiotic micro-organisms.

SUIDAE: PIG FAMILY

Pigs are more omnivorous than other artiodactyls. There are about 9 species, found in Europe, Asia and Africa, usually in forested or brush areas. Pigs are stocky, with long heads and mobile, flattened snouts used to root for food. The upper canine teeth usually form tusks. Each foot has four toes, but only the third and fourth reach the ground and form hooves.

Bush Pig *Potamochoerus porcus*

RANGE Africa, south of the Sahara; Madagascar

HABITAT Forest, bush, swamps, thickets in savanna

SIZE Body: 3¼–5 ft (1–1.5 m) Tail: 11¾–17¾ in (30–45 cm)

This pig has an elongate snout and long, tufted ears. Its bristly coat varies from reddish to grayish-brown, with a white dorsal mane and whiskers. Bush pigs live in groups of up to 12 or so, led by an old male. They eat almost anything, including grass, roots, fruit, small mammals, birds and carrion. Normally active in the day, they are nocturnal in areas where they are hunted.

Breeding occurs throughout the year, particularly when food is abundant. The female gives birth to 3 to 6 young after a gestation of 120 to 130 days.

Warthog *Phacochoerus aethiopicus*

RANGE Africa: Ghana to Somalia, south to South Africa: Natal

HABITAT Savanna, treeless open plains

SIZE Body: 3½–4½ ft (1.1–1.4 m) Tail: 13¾–19¾ in (35–50 cm)

The warthog has long legs, a large head and a broad muzzle with tusks. The big head bears two wartlike protuberances (the origin of the common name). Its bristly coat is sparse and a mane of bristles runs to the middle of the back. There are whiskers on the lower jaw. The female is smaller than the male.

Warthogs live in family groups in a territory that may be

shared by several families. They prefer to have water for drinking and wallowing in their range and shelter, such as holes among rocks, where they rest. Warthogs eat short grass, fruit, bulbs, tubers, roots and occasionally small mammals and carrion.

The breeding season tends to be associated with local rainy seasons. The female gives birth to 2 to 4 young after a gestation of 170 to 175 days. The young suckle for up to 4 months, but after a week, leave the burrow to feed on grass.

Wild Boar *Sus scrofa*

RANGE S. and C. Europe, N.W. Africa; Asia to Siberia, south to Sri Lanka, Taiwan and S.E. Asia

HABITAT Forest, woodland

SIZE Body: 3½–4¼ ft (1.1–1.3 m) Tail: 6–7¾ in (15–20 cm)

This ancestor of the domestic pig has a heavy body covered with dense, bristly hair, thin legs and a long snout. The male has prominent tusk. Wild boars live alone or in small groups of up to 20. Males stay separate from, but close to, the females. Active at night and in the morning, they forage over a wide area, digging for bulbs and tubers and also eating nuts and other plant material, as well as insect larvae and, occasionally, carrion. This agile, fast-moving animal, is aggressive if alarmed.

Breeding seasons vary with regional climate. In Europe, wild boars mate in winter and give birth to up to 10 young in spring or early summer, after a gestation of about 115 days.

Bearded Pig *Sus barbatus*

RANGE Malaysia, Sumatra, Borneo

HABITAT Rain forest, scrub, mangroves

SIZE Body: 5¼–6 ft (1.6–1.8 m) Tail: 7¾–11¾ in (20–30 cm)

The bearded pig has an elongate head, a narrow body, abundant whiskers on its chin and a bristly wartlike protuberance beneath each eye. These warts are more conspicuous in males than in females. Fallen fruit, roots, shoots and insect larvae are this pig's staple foods.

After a gestation of about 4 months, the female gives birth to 2 or 3 young.

Giant Forest Hog *Hylochoerus meinertzhageni*

RANGE Africa: Liberia, Cameroon, east to S. Ethiopia, Tanzania, Kenya

HABITAT Forest, thickets

SIZE Body: 5–6 ft (1.5–1.8 m) Tail: 9¾–13¾ in (25–35 cm)

The largest of the African pigs, the giant forest hog has a huge elongate head, a heavy body and rather long legs for its family. Its muzzle is broad, and there are glandular swellings in the skin under its eyes and across its cheeks. Males are bigger and heavier than females.

These pigs live in family groups of up to 12, and pairs remain together for life. They wander over a large, but undefined range, feeding on grass, plants, leaves, buds, roots, berries and fruit. Mostly active at night and in the morning, they rest during the heat of the day in dense vegetation.

The female gives birth to 1 to 4 young, sometimes up to 8, after a gestation period of 4 to 4½ months.

Babirusa *Babyrousa babyrussa* **VU**

RANGE Sulawesi, Sula Islands

HABITAT Moist forest, lake shores and river banks

SIZE Body: 34¼–42 in (87–107 cm) Tail: 10½–12½ in (27–32 cm)

The babirusa has unusual upper tusks, which grow upward through the muzzle and curve back toward the eyes. Only males have prominent lower tusks, and these are thought to be a sexual characteristic used to attract females. Elusive animals, babirusas prefer to forage in dense cover near water. They are fast runners and good swimmers, even in the sea. They move in small groups, the male doing most of the rooting and unearthing of food, while females and young trail behind, feeding on items such as roots, berries, tubers and leaves.

The female gives birth to 2 young after a gestation period of between 125 and 150 days.

PECCARIES AND HIPPOPOTAMUSES

TAYASSUIDAE: PECCARY FAMILY

The 3 species of peccary occur only in the New World, from the southwestern USA to central Argentina. The New World equivalent of pigs in their habits, peccaries resemble pigs, but are smaller and differ from them in a number of ways. First, they have only three toes on each hind foot (pigs have four); second, peccaries have a prominent musk gland on the back about 74 in (20 cm) in front of the tail; and third, their tusks are directed downward, not upward like those of pigs.

Chaco Peccary *Catagonus wagneri* **EN**

RANGE Bolivia, Argentina, Paraguay

HABITAT Semiarid thorn scrub, grassland

SIZE Body: about 3¼ ft (1 m) Tail: 34¼ in (87 cm)

Once thought to be extinct, the chaco peccary is now believed to be reasonably abundant in areas where it is left undisturbed, although the species as a whole is vulnerable. The animals have suffered from excessive hunting and from the loss of much of their thorn scrub habitat, which has been cleared for cattle ranching.

A long tailed, long-legged animal, this species is active during the day and has better vision than other peccaries. It moves in small groups of up to 6 animals, among which there are strong social bonds, and feeds largely on cacti and the seeds of leguminous plants.

White-lipped Peccary *Tayassu pecari*

RANGE Mexico, Central and South America to Paraguay

HABITAT Forest

SIZE Body: 37½ in–3¼ ft (95 cm–1 m) Tail: 1–2¼ in (2.5–5.5 cm)

The white-lipped peccary has a heavy body, slender legs and a long, mobile snout. A gregarious animal, it gathers in groups of 50 to 100 individuals of both sexes and all ages. Active in the

cooler hours of the day, these peccaries are fast, agile runners, even over rugged ground. Using their sensitive snouts, they dig on the forest floor searching for plant material, such as bulbs and roots, and for small animals. Although their sight is poor and hearing only fair, these peccaries have an acute sense of smell and can find bulbs underground by scent alone.

The female gives birth to a litter of 2 young after a gestation period of about 158 days.

Collared Peccary *Tayassu tajacu*

RANGE S.W. USA, Mexico, Central and South America to Patagonia

HABITAT Semidesert, arid woodland, forest

SIZE Body: 29½–35½ in (75–90 cm) Tail: ½–1¼ in (1.5–3 cm)

Collared peccaries are robust, active animals, able to run fast and swim well. They live in groups of 5 to 15 individuals, and the musky secretions of the gland on each animal's back seem to play a part in maintaining the social bonds of the herd, as well as being used for marking territory. With their sensitive snouts, collared peccaries search the ground for roots, herbs, grass and fruit; they also eat insect larvae, worms and small vertebrates. In summer, they feed only in the morning and evening, but in winter they are active all day, treading well-worn, regular paths through their home range. Hearing is the most acute of this peccary's senses.

Several males in a herd may mate with a female on heat, and there is rarely fighting or rivalry. After a gestation of 142 to 149 days, the female leaves the herd and gives birth to 2 or 3 young. The young are soon active and the family rejoins the herd after a couple of days.

HIPPOPOTAMIDAE: HIPPOPOTAMUS FAMILY

There are 2 species of hippopotamus both found only in Africa, although fossil evidence shows that the family was once more widely distributed in the southern parts of the Old World. Both species are amphibious, spending much of their lives in water, and they have various adaptations for this mode of life, including nostrils that can be closed and specialized skin glands that secrete an oily, pink substance, which protects their virtually hairless bodies from external damage.

Hippopotamus *Hippopotamus amphibius*

RANGE Africa, south of the Sahara to Namibia
and South Africa: Transvaal

HABITAT Rivers or lakes in grassland

SIZE Body: Male 10½–13¾ ft (3.2–4.2 m) Female 9¼–12 ft (2.8–3.7 m)
Tail: 13¾–19¾ in (35–50 cm)

One of the giants of Africa, the hippopotamus has a bulky body and a massive head and mouth equipped with an impressive set of teeth; the canine teeth form tusks. Its legs are short and thick, and there are four webbed toes on each foot.

When the hippopotamus is in water, it lies with much of its vast body submerged; often only the bulging eyes, ears and nostrils are visible. It swims and dives well and can walk along the river or lake bottom. Daytime hours are spent mainly resting in water or on the shore, then, in the evening, the hippopotamus emerges to graze on land, taking short grass and other plants and fallen fruit.

Hippopotamuses play a vital role in the ecology of inland waters, both by keeping down bankside vegetation and by excreting tons of fertilizing manure into the water, which encourages the growth of plankton and invertebrates and thus sustains the whole ecosystem.

Hippopotamuses are gregarious animals and live in groups of up to 15 or so, sometimes more, led by an old male. Males are aggressive and will fight for prime positions on the river bank or for dominance of the group. To threaten or challenge a rival, the male opens his mouth in a huge, yawning gape and bellows. All adults are fierce in defence of their young.

Mating takes place in water at any time of year, but is generally timed so that births coincide with the rains and thus, the luxuriant growth of grass. A single young is born on land or in shallow water after a gestation period of 233 to 240 days. The young is suckled for about a year, and females usually give birth every 18 months to 2 years.

Pygmy Hippopotamus

Hexaprotodon liberiensis **VU**

RANGE Guinea to Nigeria

HABITAT Rain forest, swamps and thickets near water

SIZE Body: 5½–6¼ ft (1.7–1.9 m)
Tail: 6–8¼ in (15–21 cm)

The pygmy hippopotamus is much less aquatic than its giant relative and has a proportionately smaller head and longer legs; only the front toes are webbed. It lives near water, but stays on land for much of the time, feeding at night on leaves, swamp vegetation and fallen fruit and also on roots and tubers which it digs up. Usually alone, except for breeding pairs or females with young, it occupies a territory, which it defends against rivals. When alarmed, the pigmy hippopotamus seeks refuge in dense cover or in water.

The female gives birth to a single young after a gestation of 180 to 210 days. The young stays with its mother for up to 3 years. Rare over almost all its range, the pygmy hippopotamus may have become extinct in some places. The population has suffered from excessive hunting, combined with the destruction of large areas of its forest habitat.

CAMELS

CAMELIDAE: CAMEL FAMILY

The 4 surviving species in this formerly more diverse family are the most primitive of the ruminants, or cud-chewing animals. Of the 4, dromedaries and most of the bactrian camels are wholly domesticated. There are still wild bactrians in the Gobi Desert, and guanacos and vicuñas maintain wild populations in parts of South America.

Camels and their relatives have highly specialized feet. They have evolved to the point of having only two toes on each foot, but the foot bones are expanded sideways to produce the support for two broad, flat pads on each foot, with a nail on the upper surface of each toe. This foot structure is particularly well developed in the camel species and it enables them to walk on soft, sandy soil, where conventional hoofs would sink in deeply.

The head of a camelid is relatively small, with an elongate snout terminating in a cleft upper lip. Vegetation is cropped by using long, forward-pointing lower incisors that work against tough upper gums. Camelids have complex three-chambered stomachs and ruminate, or chew the cud.

The humps of the 2 species of camel are fat stores, which provide food reserves – vital in the unpredictable conditions of the camel's desert habitat.

Guanaco

Lama guanicoe

RANGE South America: Peru to Patagonia

HABITAT Semidesert to about 16,500 ft (5,000 m)

SIZE Body: 4–5½ ft (1.2–1.7 m) Tail: 9¾ in (25 cm)

The guanaco is a slender, long-limbed animal, which is capable of fast movement over rugged terrain and is able to leap nimbly up mountain trails. It is adaptable to heat or cold and lives in open country and feeds on grass.

Males are polygamous and lead harems of 4 to 10 females with their young, which they defend, fighting off any rivals or intruders that try to steal one of their females. Young males and males without harems also form herds.

The female gives birth every other year, producing a single young after a gestation period of between 10 and 11 months. The young guanaco is active soon after birth and is able to run with speed and grace.

Llamas and alpacas are domesticated forms of the guanaco and they are bred as draft animals and fleece producers respectively. They interbreed readily with one another and with wild guanacos.

Vicuña *Vicugna vicugna* **LR:cd**

RANGE South America: Peru to N. Chile

HABITAT Semi-arid grassland at altitudes over 13,000 ft (4,000 m)

SIZE Body: 4½–5¼ ft (1.4–1.6 m) Tail: 6 in (15 cm)

The vicuña's tawny-brown coat is thick and woolly and longest on the sides. It enables the animal to tolerate the cold, snow and ice of its mountain habitat. Gregarious animals, vicuñas live in groups of up to 15 females led by a male, or in all-male herds. The harem band lives in a territory which is fiercely guarded by the adult male; at the first sign of any danger he alerts the females so that they can escape. Male troops consist mainly of young animals and do not have a specific territory but wander nomadically. Since most of the best grazing is appropriated by the territorial family males, these nomads are continually trespassing and being driven away. Rival males have a characteristic habit of spitting at each other as they fight.

Vicuñas are fast, graceful animals, capable of maintaining speeds of 29 mph (47 km/h) over long distances, even at high altitudes. They feed on grass and small plants. Eyesight is their most acute sense while hearing is fair and smell poor.

The female gives birth to 1 young after a gestation period of between 10 and 11 months. The young can stand and walk soon after birth and suckles for about 10 months. Vicuñas have long been hunted by man for their fine wool and meat, but despite this, a few years ago the vulnerable population was said to be on the increase again.

Bactrian Camel *Camelus bactrianus* **EN**

RANGE C. Asia: China, Mongolia

HABITAT Desert, steppe

SIZE Body: about 9¾ ft (3 m) Tail: about 21 in (53 cm)

The bactrian (two-humped) camel has been domesticated, but has not spread outside its native range to the same extent as the dromedary. Only a small number of bactrian camels live wild in the Gobi Desert, and even these may be part domestic stock. It is thought that Mongolian stocks may be slowly increasing.

Apart from its two humps, the main characteristic of the bactrian camel is its long, shaggy hair, which keeps it warm in winter, but is shed in summer, leaving the body almost naked. Docile, slow moving animals, these camels move with a rolling gait which is the result of their ability to raise both legs on one side at the same time. They feed on virtually any vegetation, such as grass, the foliage of trees and bushes, and small plants.

After a gestation of 370 to 440 days, the female gives birth to 1 young, which is active within only 24 hours. It is suckled for about a year and fully grown when about 5 years old.

Dromedary *Camelus dromedarius*

RANGE N. Africa, Middle East; introduced in Australia

HABITAT Semiarid and arid grassland, desert, plains

SIZE Body: 7¼–11 ft (2.2–3.4 m) Tail: 19¾ in (50 cm)

The dromedary, or one-humped camel now exists only as a domesticated animal, which it has been, so it is thought, since 4000 B.C. Before then it probably lived in North Africa and Arabia. Today there are two main types: a heavily built,

slow-moving animal used as a beast of burden, and a light graceful, fast-running racer, used for riding. Both have short, coarse hair, longest on the crown, neck, throat and hump.

Dromedaries feed on grass and any other plants and can survive in areas of sparse, tough vegetation

Certain adaptations fit the dromedary for life in hot, dry climates; the most significant is its ability to go for long periods without drinking, linked with its ability to conserve water in the body. Its hump is an important specialization. It gives protection from the sun by absorbing heat and carries fat stores, which are metabolized to provide energy and water. The camel does not store water in the hump, but can do so in the stomach lining. The kidneys are able to concentrate urine to avoid water loss, and moisture can be absorbed from fecal material. The body temperature of the camel drops at night and rises so slowly during the day that the animal does not need to sweat to cool itself for a long time. During an extended period without water, the camel is able to lose up to 27 per cent of its body weight without detrimental effect. This loss can be recovered in 10 minutes by drinking. In one experiment, a thirsty camel drank 104 litres (27 gal) in a few minutes.

Females breed every other year. After a gestation of 365 to 440 days, the female moves away from the herd to give birth to a single calf. When it is able to walk, after a day or so, they rejoin the herd. The calf is suckled for almost a year, but starts to nibble plants as soon as it is born, and by 2 months old is regularly eating vegetation.

CHEVROTAINS, MUSK DEER AND DEER

TRAGULIDAE: CHEVROTAIN FAMILY

There are 4 species of chevrotain, or mouse deer, found in tropical forest and mangrove swamps in Africa and Asia. They are tiny, delicate creatures, which look like minute deer with mouselike heads, but are probably related to camels and pigs. They stand only 7¾ to 13¾ in (20 to 35 cm) high at the shoulder and weigh only 5 to 10¼ lb (2.3 to 4.6 kg). Active at night, they feed largely on plants and fruit.

Water Chevrotain *Hyemoschus aquaticus* **LR:nt**

RANGE Africa: Guinea to cameroon, Zaire, Gabon, Central African Republic

HABITAT Forest, near water

SIZE Body: 29½–33½ in (75–85 cm) Tail: 4–6 in (10–15 cm)

About the size of a hare, with a hunched back, small head and short, slender legs, the water chevrotain has a variable pattern of white spots on its back and up to three white stripes along its flanks. It rests during the day in thick undergrowth or in a hole in a river bank and emerges at night to forage for grass, leaves and fruit, as well as some insects crabs, fish, worms and small mammals. Water chevrotains are solitary except in the breeding season, each individual occupying its own territory. Chevrotains always live near water and are good swimmers; if danger threatens, they often escape by diving deeply.

At breeding time, the male simply finds the female by scent, and they mate without aggression. The female gives birth to a single young after a gestation period of about 4 months. The young is suckled for 8 months but begins to take some solid food at 2 weeks old.

Lesser Malay Chevrotain

Tragulus javanicus

RANGE S.E. Asia, Indonesia

HABITAT Lowland forest, usually near water

SIZE Body: 15¾–18½ in (40–47 cm)

Tail: 2–3¼ in (5–8 cm)

The tiny, deerlike Malay chevrotain has a robust body on extremely slender legs. It has no horns, but in males, the canine teeth in the upper jaw are enlarged into tusks. A nocturnal creature, it lives in the dense undergrowth, making little tunnel-like trails; it feeds on grass, leaves, fallen fruit and berries. It lives alone except when breeding. The female gives birth to 1 young after a gestation of about 5 months.

MOSCHIDAE: MUSK DEER FAMILY

The 4 species of musk deer, all in the genus *Moschus*, occur in central and northeastern Asia. Sometimes classified with the chevrotains or with the true deer, musk deer are in several respects intermediate between these two groups. They stand about 19¾ to 23½ in (50 to 60 cm) high at the shoulder and have no horns, but they do possess large tusks, formed from the upper canine teeth. The name musk deer comes from the waxy secretions produced by a gland on the abdomen of the male.

Forest Musk Deer

Moschus chrysogaster **LR:nt**

RANGE Himalayas to C. China

HABITAT Forest, brushland at 8,500–11,800 ft (2,600–3,600 m)

SIZE Body: about 3¼ ft (1 m)

Tail: 1½–2 in (4–5 cm)

Long, thick, bristly hairs cover the body of the forest musk deer and help to protect the animal from the often harsh weather conditions of its habitat. Male and female look more or less alike, but the male has larger tusks, developed from the upper canine teeth, and a gland on the abdomen, which secretes musk during the breeding season. Only mature males have these glands.

Usually solitary, musk deer may occasionally gather in groups of up to 3. They are active in the morning and evening, feeding on grass, moss and shoots in summer and lichens, twigs and buds in winter.

At the onset of the breeding season, males fight to establish dominance and access to the females. They wrestle with their necks, trying to push one another to the ground, and may inflict deep wounds with their tusks. The female gives birth to 1 young after a gestation of about 160 days.

CERVIDAE: DEER FAMILY

There are about 40 species of true deer, distributed over North and South America, Europe, northwest Africa and Asia. Found in habitats ranging from the Arctic to the tropics, deer are slim long-legged, elegant herbivores. Their most obvious characteristic is the pair of antlers, possessed by males of all species except the Chinese water deer. Most deer shed and regrow their antlers in an annual cycle, shedding them in late winter or early spring and growing them in summer, before the autumn rutting contests for dominance.

Chinese Water Deer *Hydropotes inermis* **LR:nt**

RANGE	China, Korea; introduced in England
HABITAT	River banks with reedbeds and rushes, grassland, fields
SIZE	Body: 30½ in–3¼ ft (77.5 cm–1 m) Tail: 2¼–3 in (6–7.5 cm)

The only true deer to lack antlers, the Chinese water deer has tusks, formed from enlarged upper canine teeth; these are larger in males than in females. Both male and female have small scent glands on each side of the groin and are the only deer to possess such glands. A nocturnal animal, this deer usually lives alone or in pairs and rarely gathers in herds. It feeds on reeds, coarse grass and other vegetation.

Males contest in fierce fights for dominance in the rutting season before breeding. After a gestation period of about 6 months, the female gives birth to 4 young – this is the largest litter produced by any deer.

Chinese Muntjac *Muntiacus reevesi*

RANGE	S.E. China, Taiwan; introduced in England and France
HABITAT	Dense vegetation, hillsides; parkland in introduced range
SIZE	Body: 31½ in–3¼ ft (80 cm–1 m) Tail: 4¼–7 in (11–18 cm)

The antlers of the male Chinese muntjac are small, rarely exceeding 6 in (15 cm) in length, but this deer also has tusks, formed from the upper canine teeth; females have smaller tusks than males. The Chinese muntjac lives in a territory, which it rarely leaves, and it prefers to stay hidden in the cover of vegetation. It lives alone or in pairs and seldom forms herds. Primarily nocturnal, it may be active in the morning in quiet, undisturbed areas. It feeds on grass, low-growing leaves and shoots.

In dominance contests during the rutting season, males fight with their tusks, rather than their antlers, and make doglike barking noises. The female usually gives birth to 1 young after a gestation period of about 6 months.

Tufted Deer *Elaphodus cephalophus* **DD**

RANGE	S. China, N. Myanmar
HABITAT	Dense undergrowth, near water
SIZE	Body: about 5¼ ft (1.6 m) Tail: 2¾–4¾ in (7–12 cm)

The male tufted deer is characterized by the tuft of hair on the forehead at the base of the antlers. The antlers themselves are short and are often almost hidden by the tuft. This species is a nocturnal, normally solitary deer. It feeds on grass and other plant material.

The female gives birth to a single young after a gestation of about 6 months.

DEER CONTINUED

Père David's Deer
Elaphurus davidianus

RANGE Originally China; now in wildlife parks and reintroduced in China

HABITAT Wildlife parks

SIZE Body: 6½ ft (2 m) Tail: 14 in (35 cm)

This interesting deer became extinct in the wild in the late 19th century. However, at the beginning of this century, some of the few remaining specimens left in China were brought to England to live in the grounds of Woburn Abbey, in Bedfordshire, where they have thrived. Populations of Père David's deer can now be found in zoos and parks around the world and they have been reintroduced in China.

Père David's deer has a mane of thick hair around its neck and throat and a longer tail than most deer. One tine of each antler usually points backward, while the other points upward and forks. Although they feed mainly on grass, the deer supplement their diet with water plants. For most of the year they live in herds led by a dominant male, but the male lives alone for 2 months before and 2 months after the rutting season.

In the rutting season, the males fight to gain dominance over a harem. Females give birth to 1 or 2 young after a gestation of about 288 days.

White-tailed deer
Odocoileus virginianus

RANGE S. Canada, USA, Central and South America to Peru and Brazil

HABITAT Forest, swamps, open brushland

SIZE Body: 5–6½ ft (1.5–2 m) Tail: up to 11 in (28 cm)

One of the most adaptable animals in the world, the white-tailed deer is found from near-Arctic regions to the tropics. Its adaptability is reflected in its feeding habits: it browses and grazes on many kinds of grasses, weeds, shrubs, twigs, fungi, nuts and lichens. A slender, sprightly creature, the white-tailed deer has a long tail, white on its underside a white band across its nose and a white patch on the throat.

White-tailed deer are shy, elusive animals and they do not usually congregate in large herds. In severe winter weather, however, they may congregate in a group in a sheltered spot, out of the cold wind.

It is not certain whether or not males are polygamous, but in the breeding season, they engage in savage battles over mates. The gestation period is between 6½ and 7 months. Young females usually produce only a single offspring, but older females may produce litters of 2 or even 3. The infants are able to walk and run right away and stay close to their mother. They are suckled for about 4 months.

Moose *Alces alces*

RANGE N. Europe and Asia: Scandinavia to Siberia; Alaska, Canada, N. USA; introduced in New Zealand

HABITAT Coniferous forest, often near lakes and rivers

SIZE Body: 8¼–9¼ ft (2.5–3 m) Tail: 2–4¾ in (5–12 cm)

The largest of the deer, the moose is identified by its size, its broad, overhanging muzzle and the flap of skin, known as the bell, hanging from its throat. The massive antlers of the male are flattened and palmate, with numerous small branches.

The moose is less gregarious than other deer and is usually alone outside the breeding season. In winter, it feeds on woody plants, but in summer water plants are also eaten. It wades into water to feed and swims well.

Bellowing males display to attract females, and they engage in fierce contests with rivals. Following an 8-month gestation, the female gives birth to a single calf, occasionally to twins. The calf is suckled for about 6 months, but stays with its mother for about 12 months.

Caribou/Reindeer *Rangifer tarandus*

RANGE N. Europe and Asia: Scandinavia to Siberia; Alaska, Canada, Greenland

HABITAT Tundra

SIZE Body: 4–7½ ft (1.2–2.2 m)
Tail: 4¾ in (10–21 cm)

Once divided into several species, all caribou and reindeer, including the domesticated reindeer, are now considered races of a single species. The races vary in coloration from almost black to brown, gray and almost white. The caribou is the only deer in which both sexes have antlers. The antlers are unique in that the lowest, forward pointing tine is itself branched.

Females are gregarious and gather in herds with their young, but adult males are often solitary. Some populations migrate hundreds of miles between their breeding grounds on the tundra and winter feeding grounds farther south. Grass and other tundra plants are their main food in summer, but in winter caribou feed mainly on lichens, scraping away the snow with their hooves to expose the plants.

In autumn, males fight for harems. The female produces 1 (occasionally 2) young after a gestation of about 240 days. Calves can run with the herd within a few hours of birth.

Wapiti/Red Deer *Cervus elaphus*
(conspecific with *C. canadensis*)

RANGE W. Europe, N.W. Africa, Asia to W. China, N.W. America; introduced in New Zealand

HABITAT Open deciduous woodland, mountains, plains, moorland

SIZE Body: 5¼–8¼ ft (1.6–2.5 m)
Tail: 4¾–10 in (12–25 cm)

Known as the wapiti, or elk, in North America and the red deer in Britain, this deer is reddish-brown in summer but grayish-brown in winter. Most older males have antlers with two forward-pointing tines near the base, while young males usually have one tine. In autumn and winter, the male has a mane of longer hair on the neck.

A gregarious species, red deer live in herds and are active in the morning and late afternoon or evening, feeding on grass, heather, leaves and buds.

In the autumn, males take part in fierce, antler-clashing fights in order to obtain territories and to gather harems of females to mate with. The males defend their females throughout the breeding season and then return to all male herds in the winter. Females give birth to 1 calf, rarely 2, after a gestation period of about 8 months. The young deer is able to walk a few minutes after birth.

Roe Deer *Capreolus capreolus*

RANGE Europe and Asia: Britain to S.E. Siberia, S. China

HABITAT Woodland

SIZE Body: 37½ in–4½ ft (95 cm–1.3 m) Tail: ¼–1½ in (2–4 cm)

The smallest of the native European deer, the roe deer is unique in having almost no tail. It has a pale rump, and the rest of its coat is reddish-brown in summer and grayish-brown in winter. Fawns have a spotted coat. The antlers of the male never have more than three points apiece.

These shy, graceful deer are generally solitary, except during the breeding season, but they may gather in small groups in the winter. The roe deer are active at night and they browse on shrubs and broadleafed trees.

In the breeding season, the male takes a territory and marks its boundaries by rubbing the trunks of trees with his antlers until the bark is frayed and the wood exposed. He has only 1 mate and defends her and his territory against rivals.

The period between mating and birth is 9 or 10 months, which is much longer than that of most deer and includes a period of delayed implantation. Once the egg is fertilized, it lies dormant in the uterus for about 4 months before it implants in the womb and true gestation begins. This mechanism ensures that both mating and birth can take place at the optimum time of year.

Before giving birth to her 1 or 2 young, the female roe deer chases away her offspring from the previous year.

DEER, GIRAFFES AND PRONGHORNS

Pampas Deer *Ozotoceros bezoartieus* **LR:nt**

RANGE South America: Brazil, Paraguay, Uruguay, N. Argentina

HABITAT Grassland, open plains

SIZE Body: 3½–4¼ ft (1.1–1.3 m) Tail: 4–6 in (10–15 cm)

Pampas deer once lived only in pampas grass, but now much of this land is used for agriculture and the deer may frequent woodland. The male has antlers and glands in the feet which give off a garlicky smell, noticeable over ½ mile (1 km) away. In winter, the deer live alone or in pairs. In spring they may form larger groups. They rest in cover during the day and emerge in the evening to feed on grass. Some races are now rare, due to hunting and loss of habitat. The male stays with the female after her 1 offspring is born and helps her to guard it.

Northern Pudu *Pudu mephistophiles* **LR:nt**

RANGE South America: Colombia to N. Peru

HABITAT Forest, swampy savanna at 6,600–13,000 ft (2,000–4,000 m)

SIZE Body: 25½ in (65 cm) Tail: 1–1¼ in (2.5–3.5 cm)

The smallest New World deer, the northern pudu has a rounded back and small, simple antlers. Its dark-brown hair is thick and dense. Little is known of its habits, but it is thought to live in small groups or alone and to eat leaves, shoots and fruit. Females produce a single young, sometimes twins, usually between November and January.

GIRAFFIDAE: GIRAFFE FAMILY

The giraffe family is a specialized offshoot of the deer family. It probably originated in the Old World and is now reduced to only 2 species: the giraffe and the okapi, both found in Africa. Both animals have unique, skin-covered, blunt horns, which are not shed. The giraffe is the tallest terrestrial animal.

Giraffe *Giraffa camelopardalis* **LR:cd**

RANGE Africa, south of the Sahara

HABITAT Savanna

SIZE Body: 9¾–13 ft (3–4 m) Tail: 3–3½ ft (90 cm–1.1 m)

The giraffe, with its long legs and its amazingly long neck, when erect stands up to 11 ft (3.3 m) at the shoulder and nearly 19½ ft (6 m) at the crown. Its characteristic coloration of a light body and irregular dark spots is very variable, both geographically and between individuals, some animals may be almost white or black, or even unspotted. Both male and female have skin-covered horns, one pair on the forehead and sometimes a smaller pair farther back, on the crown and

some animals have another small horn, or bump, in between. The tail ends in a tuft of long hairs.

Gregarious animals, giraffes usually live in troops of up to 6, sometimes 12, and may occasionally gather in larger herds. A troop consists of females and their offspring, led by a male. Males fight over females, wrestling with their heads and necks. The troop ambles around its territory, feeding mostly in the early morning and afternoon on the foliage, buds and fruits on the top of acacia and thorn trees. They may also eat grass, plants and grain crops. At midday, giraffes rest in shade and at night lie down for a couple of hours or rest standing.

Females give birth to a single offspring, rarely twins, after a gestation of between 400 and 468 days. Births invariably occur at first light. The young is suckled for 6 to 12 months and continues to grow for 10 years.

Okapi *Okapia johnstoni* **LR:nt**

RANGE Zaire

HABITAT Rain forest

SIZE Body: 4–6½ ft (1.2–2 m) Tail: 11¾–16½ in (30–42 cm)

An inhabitant of dense forest, the okapi, though long hunted by the local pygmy tribes, was only made known to the outside world in 1901, when it was discovered by the then Governor of Uganda. He thought it was related to the zebra because of its stripes, but, in fact, it bears a remarkable resemblance to primitive ancestors of the giraffe. The okapi has a compact body, which slopes down toward the hindquarters, and stripes on its legs. Only males possess short, skin-covered horns, similar to those of the giraffe. The tongue is so long that the okapi can use it to clean its own eyes and eyelids.

Okapis live alone, each in its own home range, and meet only in the breeding season.

They eat leaves, buds and shoots of trees (which they reach with their long tongues), grass, ferns, fruit, fungi and manioc.

Pairing usually takes place between May and June or November and December, but may occur at any time. The female gives birth to 1 young after a gestation of 421 to 457 days. The young okapi suckles for up to 10 months and is not fully developed until 4 or 5 years of age.

ANTILOCAPRIDAE: PRONGHORN FAMILY

The North American pronghorn, found in Canada, USA and northern Mexico is the sole living representative of a New World group of antelopelike ruminants. There is also, however, a body of opinion that suggests this animal should be included in the cattle family Bovidae, but it is kept apart on account of its curious horn structure.

Pronghorn

Antilocapra americana

RANGE C. Canada, W. USA, Mexico

HABITAT Open prairie, desert

SIZE Body: 3¼–5 ft (1–1.5 m) Tail: 3–4 in (7.5–10 cm)

Male and female pronghorns have true, bony horns, although those of females are small. The horns are covered with sheaths of specialized, fused hairs, which are shed annually. The small, forward-pointing branch on each horn, is part of the sheath.

One of the fastest mammals in North America, the pronghorn can achieve speeds of up to 40 mph (65 km/h). It is also a good swimmer. In summer, it moves in small, scattered groups but congregates in larger herds of up to 100 animals in winter. Pronghorns are active during the day, feeding mostly in the morning and evening on grasses, weeds and shrubs. White hairs on the pronghorn's rump become erect if the animal is alarmed and act as a warning signal.

Some males collect harems, fighting rivals. The female gives birth to her young after a gestation of 230 to 240 days. There is usually only 1 in a female's first litter, older females produce 2 or 3 young. Only 4 days after birth, pronghorns can run.

Pronghorns are now rare, due to overhunting, competition from domestic livestock and the destruction of their habitat.

BOVIDS

BOVIDAE: BOVID FAMILY

This biologically and economically important family of herbivorous ungulates contains about 137 species, of which domesticated cattle, sheep and goats must be the best known members. The family probably originated in Eurasia and moved only recently to North America; it is absent from South America and most diverse in Africa.

Over their wide range, bovids utilize almost all types of habitat, from grassland, desert and tundra to dense forest. Coupled with this diversity of habitat is great diversity of body form and size, and bovids range between buffaloes and tiny antelope. There are, however, common features within the group. Fore and hind toes are reduced to split, or artiodactyl (even-toed), hoofs, based on digits 3 and 4. There is a complex four-chambered stomach in which vegetable food is degraded by microorganism symbiosis. Linked with this digestive system, bovids chew the cud, bringing up food from the first stomach and re-chewing it. Normally both male and female have defensive hollow horns, which are larger in the male.

Greater Kudu *Tragelaphus strepsiceros* **LR:cd**
RANGE Africa: Lake Chad to Eritrea, Tanzania; Zambia to Angola and South Africa; introduced in N. Mexico
HABITAT Thick acacia bush; rocky, hilly country; dry river beds, near water.
SIZE Body: 6–8 ft (1.8–2.45 m) Tail: 13¾–21½ in (35–55 cm)

The large, slender male kudu has long horns, which spread widely in two to three open spirals; the female occasionally has small horns. When running, the bull lays his horns flat along his back.

Over the kudu's wide range, there are variations in coloration and the number of stripes on the sides. Kudu are browsers feeding early and late on leaves, shoots and seeds and, in dry areas, wild melons. They also make night raids on cultivated fields and can jump over a 6½ ft (2 m) fence. Their senses of hearing and smell are good, although their sight seems poor.

Kudu live mostly in herds of 6 to 12 females with young, sometimes with 1 or 2 older bulls. Otherwise males are solitary or form bachelor herds. After a gestation of about 7 months, the female produces 1 calf, which suckles for about 6 months.

Eland *Ttagelaphus oryx* **LR:cd**
RANGE Africa: Ethiopia, E. Africa to Angola and South Africa; mostly in game parks in Namibia, N. Cape Province, Natal, Mozambique
HABITAT Open plains, savanna, mopane bush, montane forest to 14,750 ft (4,500 m), semidesert
SIZE Body: 6¾–11½ ft (2.1–3.5 m)
Tail: 19¾–35½ in (50–90 cm)

The eland is the largest of the antelopes. A fully grown bull may weigh 2,000 lb (900 kg). Cows are smaller and more slight, with lighter horns and no mat of hair on the forehead. Eland live in troops of 6 to 24 animals and are always on the move, looking for food and water. In times of drought, they wander widely and form large herds. Old solitary bulls are common; young bulls form male troops. Eland are browsers, feeding in the morning, at dusk, and even on moonlit nights, on leaves, shoots, melons, tubers, and bulbs. They have a good sense of smell and sight.

There is usually 1 calf, born after a gestation of 8½ to 9 months; it lies hidden for a week, then follows the female, who suckles it for about 6 months.

Bongo
Tragelaphus eurycerus **LR:nt**

RANGE Africa: Sierra Leone to Sudan (not Nigeria), Kenya, Tanzania

HABITAT Forest, bush, bamboo jungle

SIZE Body: 5½–8¼ ft (1.7–2.5 m) Tail: 17¾–25½ in (45–65 cm)

The adult male bongo is the largest of the forest-dwelling antelopes and may weigh up to 500 lb (227 kg); the chestnut coloured coat darkens with age in the male. Both sexes have narrow, lyre-shaped horns, which they lay along their slightly humped backs when running, to prevent them catching branches. Shy animals, bongos rest in dense cover during the day, browsing at dawn and dusk on leaves, shoots, bark, rotten wood and fruit, they also dig for roots with their horns. At night they venture into clearings and plantations to feed on grass.

They live in pairs or small groups of females and young with a single male. Old males are solitary. One young is born after a gestation of 9½ months.

Nyala
Tragelaphus angasii **LR:cd**

RANGE Africa: Malawi to South Africa: Natal

HABITAT Dense lowland forest, thickets in savanna, near water

SIZE Body: 4½–6½ ft (1.35–2 m) Tail: 15¾–21½ in (40–55 cm)

Nyala live in dense cover, emerging only at dusk and dawn. Males are large and slender, with big ears and shaggy coats. Females and juveniles are reddish-brown and lack the long fringe of hair underneath the body, horns and the white facial chevron that distinguish the males. Females are much smaller than males. Nyala live in groups of 8 to 16 cows and young, sometimes with one or more bulls. Solitary bulls and herds of bulls also occur.

Near the end of the dry season, herds of up to 50 animals may form. They browse on leaves, shoots, bark and fruit, (standing on their hind legs to reach the leaves) and new grass.

A single young is born after a gestation of 8½ months, females mate a week after the birth.

Nilgai
Boselaphus tragocamelus **LR:cd**

RANGE Peninsular India (not Sri Lanka)

HABITAT Forest, low jungle

SIZE Body: 6½–6¾ ft (2–2.1 m) Tail: 18–21¼ in (46–54 cm)

The nilgai is the only member of its genus and is the largest antelope native to India. It has slightly longer front legs than hind ones and a long, pointed head. The male has short horns and a tuft of hair on the throat; both sexes have short, wiry coats, reddish-brown in the male and lighter in the female. Females and calves live in herds. Males are usually solitary or form small parties. Nilgai are browsers but also like fruit and sugarcane and can do considerable damage to the crop.

Females commonly produce 2 calves after a gestation of about 9 months. Bulls fight each other on their knees for available females, which mate again immediately after calving.

Four-horned Antelope
Tetracerus quadricornis **VU**

RANGE Peninsular India (not Sri Lanka)

HABITAT Open forest

SIZE Body: 30 ft (1 m) Tail: 5 in (12.5 cm)

This little antelope is the only one in its genus. The male is unique among Bovidae in having two pairs of short, unringed, conical horns: the back pair 3¼ to 4 in (8 to 10 cm) long, the front pair 1 to 1½ in (2.5 to 4 cm) long; these maybe merely black, hairless skin. These are not gregarious antelope – normally only two are found together, or a female with her young. They graze on grasses and plants and drink often, running for cover at the least hint of danger with a peculiar, jerky motion.

Four-horned antelope mate during the rainy season and usually produce between 1 and 3 young after a gestation period of about 6 months.

BOVIDS

Gaur *Bos frontalis* **VU**

RANGE India, S.E. Asia

HABITAT Hill forest

SIZE Body: 6½–8¼ ft (2–2.5 m)
Tail: 23½–31½ in (60–80 cm)

Once common in hilly, forested areas throughout their range, gaur now only occur in scattered herds in remote areas and in parks and reserves. Gaur are legally protected, but this is hard to enforce except in reserves, and the population is still threatened.

The gaur is a strong, heavily built animal, with a massive head, thick horns and a prominent muscular ridge on its shoulders that slopes down to the middle of its back. Females are smaller than males and have shorter, lighter horns. Gaur range in colour from reddish to dark brown or almost black, with white hair on the lower half of the legs. In small herds of up to 12 animals, they take shelter in the shade and seclusion of forest in the heat of the day and at night, but they venture out into the open to feed in the early morning and late afternoon, when they graze and also sometimes browse on the leaves and bark of available trees.

During the breeding season, the timing of which varies from area to area, bulls roam through the forest searching for females on heat. When a male finds a mate, he defends her from other males. The female moves slightly away from the herd to give birth to her offspring in a safe, secluded spot; they rejoin the herd a few days later.

Banteng *Bos javanicus* **EN**

RANGE Bali, Myanmar to Java, Borneo

HABITAT Forested, hilly country to 6,600 ft (2,000 m)

SIZE Body: 6½ ft (2 m) Tail: 33½ in (85 cm)

The banteng is blue-black, with white stockings and rump, and is quite cowlike in its appearance; females and young are a bright reddish-brown. Bulls may reach 5 ft (1.5 m) at the shoulder, and they have a hairless shield on the crown between the horns. Wary and shy, bantengs are found in thickly forested areas, where there are glades and clearings in which they can graze during the night. In the monsoon season, they move up the mountains and browse on bamboo shoots.

Gregarious animals, bantengs live in herds of 10 to 30 animals, although occasionally large bulls may become solitary. They mate during the dry season, and females produce 1 or 2 calves after a gestation of 9½ to 10 months. Small populations of two subspecies are found: *B. j. biarmicus* in Burma, Thailand and parts of Indo-China; *B. j. lowi* in Borneo.

Asian Water Buffalo *Bubalus arnee* **EN**

RANGE India, S.E. Asia; introduced in Europe, Africa, Philippines, Japan, Hawaii, Central and South America, Australia

HABITAT Dense growth, reed grass in wet areas

SIZE Body: 8¼–9¾ ft (2.5–3 m)
Tail: 23½ in–3¼ ft (60 cm–1 m)

A large, thickset, clumsy creature, with huge splayed hoofs, the water buffalo stands 5 to 6 ft (1.5 to 1.8 m) at the shoulder. It has a long, narrow face, and the span of its flattened, crescent-shaped horns is the largest of all bovids – they can measure as much as 4 ft (1.2 m) along the outer edge. Its bulky body is sparsely covered in quite long, coarse, blackish hair, and there is a tuft of coarse hair in the middle of the forehead. Water buffaloes feed early and late in the day and at night on the lush grass and vegetation that grows near and in lakes and rivers. When not feeding, they spend much of their time submerged, with only their muzzles showing above water, or wallowing in mud, which, when dried and caked, gives them some protection from the insects that plague them. Water buffaloes are gregarious and live in herds of various sizes. In the breeding season, males detach a few cows from the main herd and form their own harems. Each cow produces 1 or 2 calves after a gestation of 10 months, which it suckles for almost a year. Water buffaloes live for about 18 years.

Tame and docile, these animals have been domesticated and used as beasts of burden in India and Southeast Asia since about 3000 B.C. They also yield milk of good quality and their hides make excellent leather. It is estimated that the domestic population in India and Southeast Asia alone is now at least 75 million and water buffaloes have been widely introduced in countries where conditions are suitable. Some of these introduced populations have become feral, as in Australia. Truly wild stocks number no more than 2,000.

Lowland Anoa *Bubalus depressicornis* **EN**

RANGE Sulawesi

HABITAT Lowland forest

SIZE Body: 5¼–5½ ft (1.6–1.7 m) Tail: 7–12½ in (18–31 cm)

The anoa is the smallest of the buffaloes, an adult male standing only 27 to 42 in (69 to 106 cm) at the shoulder. However, it is stockily built, with a thick neck and short, heavy horns, which are at most 15 in (38 cm) long. Although wary, the anoa is aggressive when cornered. Juveniles have thick, woolly, yellow-brown hair, which becomes dark brown or blackish, blotched with white, in adults; old animals may have almost bare skins. Perhaps because of this, anoas appear to enjoy bathing and wallowing in mud. They feed alone during the morning, mainly on water plants and young cane shoots, then spend the rest of the day lying in the shade, generally in pairs. They only form herds just before the females are due to calve. Usually 1 young is born after a gestation of 9½ to 10 months.

When unmolested, anoas have a life span of 20 to 25 years, but destruction of their normal habitat has driven them into inaccessible, swampy forest, and their survival is further threatened by unrelenting hunting for their horns, meat and thick hides.

Wild Yak *Bos grunniens* **VU**

RANGE W. China, Tibetan plateau, N. India, Kashmir

HABITAT Desolate mountain country to 20,000 ft (6,100 m)

SIZE Body: Male up to 10½ ft (3.25 m) Tail: 19¾–31½ in (50–80 cm)

Originally these massive animals were found throughout their range, but centuries of hunting and persecution have forced them to retreat into remote and inaccessible areas of mountain tundra and ice desert, and now they cannot live in warm, lowland areas. Sturdy and sure-footed and covered in long, blackish-brown hairs which form a fringe reaching almost to the ground, they are, however, well equipped to cope with the rigours of the rough terrain and extremely harsh climate within their habitat.

Male Yaks may stand up to 6½ ft (2 m) at the shoulder, females are smaller and weigh only about one-third as much as males. Both males and females have heavy, forward-curving horns, which they use for defence. When a group is threatened, they form a phalanx, facing outward with horns lowered, with the calves encircled for protection.

Yaks feed morning and evening on whatever vegetation they can find, spending the rest of the time relaxing and chewing the cud. They are usually found in large groups consisting of females and young with a single bull; bachelor bulls roam in groups of 2 or 3. The female produces 1 calf in the autumn, after a gestation period of between 9½ and 10 months.

Although wild yaks are an endangered species, they have been domesticated for centuries in Tibet, where, as well as being used as pack animals and to pull carts, they also provide milk, meat, hides and hair and wool, which the local population weave into warm cloth. Domestic yaks are usually about half the size of wild ones and are often without horns. The coat of the domestic yak is redder than that of the wild yak, mottled with brown, black and sometimes white.

BOVIDS

American Bison *Bison bison*
LR:cd

RANGE N. America

HABITAT Prairie, open woodland

SIZE Body: 6¾–11½ ft (2.1–3.5 m) Tail: 19¾–23½ in (50–60 cm)

Although there were once millions of bison roaming the North American grasslands, wholesale slaughter by the early European settlers brought this species almost to extinction by the beginning of the twentieth century. Since then, due to a great extent to the efforts of the American Bison Society, herds have steadily been built up in reserves, where they exist in a semiwild state, and it is estimated that there are now about 20,000 American bison.

The male may be as much as 9½ ft (2.9 m) at the shoulders, which are humped and covered in the shaggy, brownish-black fur that also grows thickly on the head, neck and forelegs. The female looks similar to the male but is smaller; young are more reddish brown. Both sexes have short, sharp horns.

Primarily grazers, bison live in herds that vary from a family group to several thousand; huge numbers formerly made seasonal migrations in search of better pasture. They feed morning and evening, and during the day rest up, chewing the cud or wallowing in mud or dust baths in order to rid themselves of parasites.

During the mating season, bulls fight amongst themselves for cows. The cows give birth to a single calf, away from the herd, after a gestation period of 9 months. Within an hour or two of the birth both the mother and calf rejoin the herd. The calf is suckled for about 12 months and it remains with its mother until it reaches sexual maturity at about 3 years old.

European Bison *Bison bonasus* **EN**

RANGE E. Europe

HABITAT Open woodland, forest

SIZE Body: 6¾–11½ ft (2.1–3.5 m) Tail: 19¾–23½ in (50–60 cm)

Like its American counterpart, the European bison, which was formerly found throughout Europe, has been reduced to semiwild herds in reserves: three in Poland and eleven in what was the USSR, with the largest in the Bialowieza Forest on the border between them. The drop in numbers has been caused by the almost total eradication of forests, for these bison are browsers, living mainly on leaves, ferns, twigs, bark and, in autumn, almost exclusively on acorns.

The European bison closely resembles the American, but is less heavily built, with longer hind legs. It has more scanty, shorter hair on the front of the body and head, and the horns, too, are lighter and much longer, reaching as much as 20 in (51 cm) in the male. The female produces a single calf after a gestation period of 9 months and it remains with her for 2 to 3 years.

African Buffalo *Synceros caffer* **LR:cd**

RANGE Africa, south of the Sahara

HABITAT Varied, always near water

SIZE Body: 6¾–9¾ ft (2.1–3 m) Tail: 29½ in–3½ ft (75 cm–1.1 m)

The powerfully built African buffalo is the only member of its genus, although 2 types exist, the smaller, reddish forest-dwelling buffalo, *S. c. nanus*, and *S. c. caffer*, described here, which lives in savanna and open country. It has a huge head with a broad, moist muzzle, large drooping ears and heavy horns, the bases of which may meet across the forehead. An aggressive animal and a formidable fighter, it is extremely dangerous to hunt, since it may charge without provocation or, if wounded, wait in thick bush and attack a pursuing hunter. Apart from man, its enemies are the lion and occasionally the crocodile, both of which usually succeed in killing only young or sick animals.

African buffaloes have adapted to live in a variety of conditions, from forest to semidesert, wherever there is adequate grazing and plenty of water, for they drink morning and evening and enjoy lying in water and wallowing in mud. They feed mainly at night, on grass, bushes and leaves, resting up in dense cover during the day. Although their eyesight and hearing are poor, they have a strongly developed sense of smell.

Buffaloes are gregarious, living in herds which range from a dozen or so to several hundred animals, often led by an old female, but dominated by a mature bull. Old bulls are ousted from the herd and live alone in groups of 2 to 5.

Although normally silent, buffaloes bellow and grunt during the mating season which varies throughout the range and appears to be related to climate. A single calf is born after a gestation period of 11 months; it is covered in long, blackish-brown hair, most of which is lost as it matures. African buffaloes live for about 16 years.

Bay Duiker *Cephalophus dorsalis* **LR:nt**

RANGE Africa: Sierra Leone to E. Zaire and N. Angola

HABITAT Thick forest and jungle

SIZE Body: 27½ in–3¼ ft (70 cm–1 m) Tail: 3–6 in (8–15 cm)

The subfamily Cephalophinae contains two groups: the forest duikers, of which the bay duiker is one, and the bush duikers. The bay duiker is typical of its group, with rather slender legs, a slightly hunched back and a smooth, glossy coat. Both male and female have small backward-pointing horns, which are sometimes obscured by the crest of hairs on the forehead. Duikers are timid and when disturbed dash for thick cover – the name duiker means "diving" buck. They are mainly active at night when they feed on grass, leaves and fruit, even scrambling up into bushes or on logs to reach them.

Bay duikers live singly or in pairs and produce 1 young after a gestation period of 7 to 8 months. The young is independent at about 3 months old.

Yellow Duiker

Cephalophus silvicultor **LR:nt**

RANGE Africa: Senegal to Kenya, Zambia, N. Angola

HABITAT Moist highland forest

SIZE Body: 3¾–4¾ ft (1.15–1.45 m)
Tail: 4¼–8 in (11–20.5 cm)

Another forest duiker and the largest of its subfamily, the yellow duiker is remarkable for the well-developed crest of hairs on its forehead and for the yellowish-orange patch of coarse, erectile hairs that grow in a wedge shape on its back. Both sexes have long, thin sharp-pointed horns. The young loses its dark coloration at about 8 months.

Yellow duikers live in pairs or alone, keeping to thick cover. They are active at night. Their varied diet includes leaves, grass, herbs, berries, termites, snakes, eggs and carrion. They are hunted by man for meat and have many other enemies, including leopards, jackals, pythons and large birds of prey.

Common/Gray Duiker *Sylvicapra grimmia*

RANGE Africa, south of the Sahara

HABITAT All types except desert and rain forest, up to 15,000 ft (4,600 m)

SIZE Body: 31½ in–3¾ ft (80 cm–1.15 m) Tail: 4–8½ in (10–22 cm)

The common bush duiker has a straighter back and thicker, grizzled coat than the forest duiker. The crest is quite well developed. The male has sharp horns, which the female does not always have. Common duikers can survive in almost any habitat from scrub country to open grassland. The male establishes a fiercely defended territory. At night they browse on leaves and twigs, (standing on their hind legs to reach them) and also eat fruit, berries, termites, snakes, eggs and guineafowl chicks.

Usually found alone or in pairs, they may form small groups in the breeding season, which varies throughout the range and appears to be linked to the rains. The female produces 1 young after a gestation of 4 to 4½ months; normally 2 young are born each year.

BOVIDS

Lechwe

Kobus leche **LR:cd**

RANGE Africa: Zaire, Zambia, Angola, Botswana, South Africa

HABITAT Flood plains, swamps, lakes

SIZE Body: 4¼–5½ ft (1.3–1.7 m) Tail: 11¾–17¾ in (30–45 cm)

There are 3 races of lechwe, whose coloration varies from bright chestnut to grayish-brown. In all races, the male has thin, lyre-shaped horns, up to 3 ft (91 cm) long, which form a double curve; they are particularly fine in *K. l. kafuensis*. With their long, pointed, widespreading hoofs, lechwe are perfectly adapted to an aquatic way of life and cannot move quickly on dry ground. They come out of the water only to rest and calve, spending most of their time wading in water up to about 20 in (50 cm) deep, where they feed on grasses and water plants. They swim well and will even submerge, with only the nostrils showing, if threatened. Apart from man, they are preyed on mainly by lion, cheetah, hyena and hunting dogs.

Lechwe are sociable and form herds of several hundred during the breeding season, when males fight fiercely, even though they are not territorial. At other times, young males form large, single-sex herds. After a gestation period of 7 to 8 months, the female produces a single calf, which she suckles for 3 to 4 months.

Uganda Kob *Kobus kob thomasi* **LR:cd**

RANGE Africa: Uganda to south of Lake Victoria

HABITAT Open grassy plains, lightly wooded savanna, near permanent water

SIZE Body: 4–6 ft (1.2–1.8 m) Tail: 7–15¾ in (18–40 cm)

A graceful, sturdily built, medium-sized antelope, the Uganda kob is a subspecies of the nominate race, which it closely resembles except that the white on the face completely encircles the eyes. Male and female look alike, but only the male has horns, which are lyre shaped, with an S-curve when seen from the side. Kob usually live in single sex herds of 20 to 40, sometimes up to 100. They are grazers, feeding usually in the morning and at dusk, although during the day they will go into the water and eat water plants. They are preyed on mainly by lion, leopard, spotted hyena and hunting dogs. These solitary animals often lie flat and hide when threatened.

In the breeding season, each rutting male has an area 30 to 50 ft (9 to 15 m) in diameter, which he defends against other males. Females move freely through these rutting areas, mating with several males. One young is born after a gestation period of 8½ to 9 months, and, since the female mates again almost at once, two births are possible in a year.

Common/Defassa Waterbuck

Kobus ellipsiprymnus **LR:cd**

RANGE Africa, south of the Sahara to the Zambezi, east to Ethiopia

HABITAT Savanna, woodland, stony hills, near water

SIZE Body: 6–7¼ ft (1.8–2.2 m) Tail: 8¼–17¾ in (22–45 cm)

The many races of this waterbuck vary in coloration from yellowish-brown or reddish-brown to gray and grayish-black; some have a white ring or patch on the rump. It has large, hairy ears, which are white inside and tipped with black, and the male has heavy, much-ringed horns, which sweep back in a crescent shape. A large animal, standing 4 to 4½ ft (1.2 to 1.4 m) at the shoulder, it weighs 350 to 500 lb (159 to 227 kg). Glands in the skin exude a musky-smelling oily secretion, and the meat is easily tainted when the animal is skinned, so it is not much hunted. The chief predators are lion, leopard and hunting dogs. True to their name, waterbuck spend much time near water and drink often, they take refuge in reedbeds when threatened. They are grazers feeding on tender young grass shoots.

Common waterbuck move in small herds of up to 25, usually females and young with a master bull; young bulls form bachelor herds. The female produces 1 young after a gestation of about 9 months.

Southern Reedbuck
Redunca arundinum **LR:cd**

RANGE Africa: Zaire, Tanzania, south to South Africa

HABITAT Open plains, hilly country with light cover, near water

SIZE Body: 4–4½ ft (1.2–1.4 m) Tail: 7–11¾ in (18–30 cm)

A medium-sized antelope, about 3 ft (91 cm) at the shoulder, the common reedbuck is a graceful animal, with distinctive movements. It runs with a rocking motion, flicking its thick, hairy tail, and the male marks and defends his territory by displaying his white throat patch and making bouncing leaps with his head raised. Reedbuck also make a characteristic clicking sound when running and whistle through their noses when alarmed. The female resembles the male but is smaller and lacks his ridged, curved horns; juveniles are a grayish-brown. Reedbuck are always found near water, although not in it, and they spend much time lying up in reedbeds or tall grass. They graze on grass and shoots and will raid crops.

Reedbuck are usually found alone, in pairs or in small family groups. A single young is born after a gestation period of 7¾ months and reaches maturity, acquiring adult coloration, at about a year old.

Roan Antelope *Hippotragus equinus* **LR:cd**

RANGE Africa, south of the Sahara

HABITAT Open woodland, dry bush, savanna, near water

SIZE Body: 8–8½ ft (2.4–2.6 m) Tail: 23½–27½ in (60–70 cm)

There are approximately 6 races of roan antelope, which vary in coloration from gray to reddish-brown. The roan is a large antelope, the largest in Africa after the eland and kudu, and as the name suggests, it superficially resembles a horse, with its long face and stiff, well-developed mane. The male's backward-curving horns are short but strong; the female's are lighter. Roan antelope usually live in herds of up to 20 females and young, led by a master bull, often alongside oryx, impala, wildebeest, buffalo, zebra and ostriches. Young males

form bachelor herds. The roan antelope is preyed on mainly by lion, leopard, hunting dogs and hyena. At least 90 per cent of the roan's food intake is grass, and they rarely eat leaves or fruit, so they need to drink often.

Roan antelope are aggressive, and males will fight on their knees with vicious, backward sweeps of their horns. In the breeding season, the bull detaches a cow from the herd and they live alone for a while. The female produces 1 calf after a gestation of 8½ to 9 months; it attains sexual maturity at 2½ to 3 years old.

Rhebok *Pelea capreolus* **LR:cd**

RANGE South Africa

HABITAT Grassy hills and plateaux with low bush and scattered trees

SIZE Body: 3–3¼ ft (1–1.2 m) Tail: 4–7¾ in (10–20 cm)

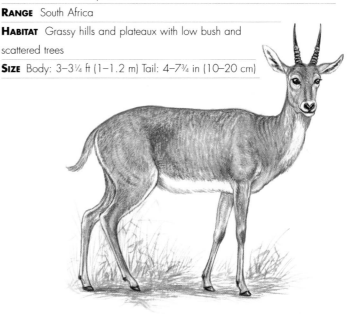

A small, graceful antelope, weighing 50 lb (22.5 kg) at most, the rhebok is covered in soft, woolly hair. The male has upright, almost straight horns, 6 to 10½ in (15 to 27 cm) long. Rhebok feed on grass and the leaves of shrubs and are very wary, bouncing off the moment they are disturbed, with a run that jerks up their hindquarters. They are found in family parties, consisting of a master ram with a dozen or more females and young; immature males are normally solitary. The male is highly territorial and marks out his fairly extensive range by tongue clicking, display and urination. Despite his small size, the ram is extremely pugnacious and is known to attack and even kill sheep, goats and mountain reedbuck; he will also attack smaller predators.

In the breeding season, males stage fierce mock battles without actually doing any harm, and they will also chase each other. One, sometimes 2, young are born after a 9½-month gestation.

BOVIDS

Arabian Oryx

Oryx leucoryx **EN**

RANGE S.E. Saudi Arabia: Rub' al Khali area

HABITAT Desert

SIZE Body: 5¼ ft (1.6 m) Tail: 17¾ in (45 cm)

This is the smallest and rarest of the oryx and the only one found outside Africa. It lives in extreme desert conditions, feeding on grass and shrubs and travelling widely in order to find food. It is well adapted to its arid habitat, for it can live without drinking, obtaining the moisture it needs from its food, it also uses its hoofs and horns to scrape out a hollow under a bush or alongside a dune in which to shelter from the sun.

Although generally sociable, male oryx fight among themselves in the breeding season, and if cornered, will attack. One young is born after an 8-month gestation.

The present endangered status of the Arabian oryx is the result of overhunting, for its slender horns, its hide and meat are all prized. This led to its extinction in the wild although captive breeding programs have now resulted in its re-introduction.

Blue Wildebeest *Connochaetes taurinus* **LR:cd**

RANGE Africa: S. Kenya to N. South Africa

HABITAT Open grassland, bush savanna

SIZE Body 5½–8 ft (1.7–2.4 m) Tail: 23½ in–3¼ ft (60 cm–1 m)

The clumsy appearance of the blue wildebeest, the lugubrious expression given by its black face and tufty beard, its rocking-horse gait and its constant snorts and grunts have earned it a reputation as a "clown". Nevertheless, it is a most successful species.

Wildebeest are extremely gregarious, and herds numbering tens of thousands may be seen in East Africa during the dry season, when they make migrations of as much as 1,000 miles (1,600 km) in search of water and grazing. Breeding herds usually consist of up to 150 females and young, with 1 to 3 males. The bulls patrol the outside of their herd, keeping it closely grouped and defending a zone around it, even when migrating. Wildebeest feed almost exclusively on grass and need to drink often. They are frequently seen in association with zebra and ostrich; perhaps the wariness of the former offers them some protection against their common predators: lion, cheetah, hunting dog and hyena.

The female looks like the male but is smaller. After a gestation period of 8½ months, she produces 1 calf, which can stand within 3 to 5 minutes of birth.

Addax *Addax nasomaculatus* **EN**

RANGE Africa: E. Mauritania, W. Mali; patchy distribution in Algeria, Chad, Niger and Sudan

HABITAT Sandy and stony desert

SIZE Body: 4¼ ft (1.3 m) Tail: 9¾–13¾ in (25–35 cm)

With its heavy head and shoulders and slender hindquarters, the addax is a clumsy-looking animal. Coloration varies widely between individuals, but there is always a mat of dark-brown hair on the forehead, and both sexes have thin, spiral horns.

Addax are typical desert dwellers, with their large, widespreading hoofs, which are well-adapted to walking on soft sand. They never drink, instead obtaining all the moisture they need from their food, which includes succulents. Their nomadic habits are closely linked to the sporadic rains, for addax appear to have a special ability to find the patches of desert vegetation that suddenly sprout after a downpour. They are normally found in herds of between 20 and 200.

The female produces 1 young after a gestation period of 8½ months.

Haartebeest *Alcelaphus buselaphus* **LR:cd**

RANGE Africa, south of the Sahara

HABITAT Grassy plains

SIZE Body: 5½–8 ft (1.7–2.4 m) Tail: 17¾–27½ in (45–70 cm)

The nominate race, the bubal haartebeest, is extinct, but there are 12 subspecies, a further 2 of which (*A. b. swayne and A. b. tora*) are endangered, due to disease, hunting and destruction of their natural habitat.

Haartebeest are strange-looking animals, with backs that slope down slightly from high shoulders and long heads, with a pedicle on top from which spring the horns. Both male and female have horns, which show great intraspecific variation in both size and shape. Coloration also varies from deep chocolate to sandy fawn; females are paler than males.

These sociable antelope are found in herds of from 4 to 30, consisting of females and young with a master bull. He watches over his herd, often from a vantage point, usually on top of a termite mound.

Although haartebeest can go for long periods without water, they drink when they can and enjoy wallowing; they also use salt licks with avidity. They are partial to the young grass that grows after burning and often graze with zebra, wildebeest and gazelle and, like these, are preyed on largely by lion.

A single calf is born after a gestation period of 8 months. It remains with its mother for about 3 years, at which time young males form a troop of their own.

Bontebok *Damaliscus dorcas* **LR:cd**

RANGE South Africa: W. Cape Province

HABITAT Open grassland

SIZE Body: 4½–5¼ ft (1.4–1.6 m) Tail: 11¾–17¾ in (30–45 cm)

The strikingly marked bontebok was at one time almost extinct but is now fully protected and out of danger, and the population in game reserves numbers several thousand. The very similar blesbok,

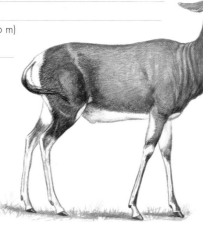

D. d. phillipsi (= *albifrons*), was also endangered, but it too is now flourishing, since it has been established in many reserves.

The sexes look alike, but females and juveniles are paler. Bontebok are grazers, active morning and evening. When disturbed, they move off swiftly upwind in single file. They are remarkably agile and can scale fences or wriggle under or through them.

The female produces a single calf after a 7½-month gestation period, and young remain with their mothers until they are about 2 years old, when young males form bachelor herds. Outside the breeding season, bontebok live in mixed herds of from 20 to 500 animals.

Sassaby/Tsessebi *Damaliscus lunatus* **LR:cd**

RANGE Africa, south of the Sahara, east to Ethiopia, Somalia

HABITAT Open plains, flood plains, grassland with scattered bush

SIZE Body: 5–6½ ft (1.5–2 m) Tail: 15¾–23½ in (40–60 cm)

The nominate race of sassaby is found from Zambia to northern South Africa. It is probably conspecific with *D. korrigum*, known as the tiang or topi, which is found elsewhere in its range. Together, sassabys and topis are the most numerous of all antelope in Africa. In shape they are similar to the true haartebeests, but neither the slope of the back nor the length of the head are so exaggerated. Coloration and horns vary from race to race and between sexes. Females are usually paler than males. Sassabys are active early and late in the day, when they feed on grass and herbage and also drink. They are able, however, to go without water for as long as 30 days.

Sassabys are not as gregarious as the haartebeests and generally move in small parties of 8 to 10 individuals, which may join up to form herds of up to 200 animals in the dry season. The mature male is highly territorial and marks his central stamping ground with dung and with scent, by rubbing his face and neck on bushes, grass stems and the ground. He watches over his territory and his harem and defends them from rivals and predators.

The female produces a single calf after a gestation period of 7½ to 8 months.

BOVIDS

Klipspringer *Oreotragus oreotragus* **LR:cd**

RANGE Africa: N. Nigeria, east to Somalia, south to South Africa

HABITAT Rocky outcrops, hills, mountains to 13,000 ft (4,000 m)

SIZE Body: 29½ in–3¾ ft (75 cm–1.15 m)
Tail: 2¾–9 in (7–23 cm)

The klipspringer occurs where there are rocky outcrops interspersed with grassy patches and clumps of bush. It is fairly small, with strong legs and blunt-tipped hoofs the consistency of hard rubber. It fills a niche similar to that of the chamois. As it leaps about among the rocks, it is cushioned from bumps by its long thick, bristly coat. The female is slightly heavier than the male and except in 1 race, *O. o. schilllngsi,* does not have horns.

Klipspringers are sometimes found in small parties, more often in pairs, in a territory marked out by glandular secretions and defended against interlopers. They feed morning and evening and on moonlit nights, and will stand on their hind legs to reach the leaves, flowers and fruit that form the bulk of their diet. They also eat succulents, moss and some grass and drink when water is available.

Klipspringers probably mate for life. The female produces 1 young after a gestation of about 7 months, and there may be 2 young born in a year.

Beira Antelope

Dorcatragus megalotis **VU**

RANGE Africa: Somalia

HABITAT Dry, bush-clad mountains, stony hills

SIZE Body: 31½–35½ in (80–90 cm)
Tail: 2¼–3 in (6–7.5 cm)

A rare antelope, the beira is often mistaken for the klipspringer, although it has a slightly longer head, much bigger ears and longer, slimmer legs. The hind legs, especially, are long, with the result that the rump is higher than the shoulders. There is no crest, and only the male has horns; the female is larger than the male.

Beiras live in pairs or small family parties on extremely stony hillsides close to a grassy plain. Their highly specialized hoofs have elastic pads underneath which give a good grip on the stones. Beiras feed in the early morning and late afternoon on leaves of bushes, particularly mimosa, grass and herbage and do not need to drink.

Little is known of their habits or biology, for not only are they rare but their coloration blends so well with the background that they are impossible to spot unless they move. The female gives birth to a single young.

Oribi *Ourebia ourebi* **LR:cd**

RANGE Africa: Sierra Leone to Ethiopia, Tanzania, Zambia, South Africa

HABITAT Wide, grassy plains with low bush, near water

SIZE Body: 3–3½ ft (92 cm–1.1 m) Tail: 2¼–4¼ in (6–10.5 cm)

The oribi is small and graceful, with a long neck and slender legs, longer behind than in front. The silky coat has a sleek, rippled look, and the black-tipped tail is conspicuous when the animal runs. Below each large, oval ear there is a patch of bare skin that appears as a black spot. The female has no horns and is larger than the male.

Pairs or small parties of up to 5 animals live together in a territory, which the dominant male marks out by rubbing glandular secretions on twigs and grass stems. Here the oribis have regular runs, resting and defecating places.

They are active early and later in the day and on moonlit nights, when they feed on grass, plants and leaves. During the day and when danger threatens, they lie quietly in long grass or by a bush or rock.

The female gives birth to 1 young after a gestation period of between 6½ and 7 months.

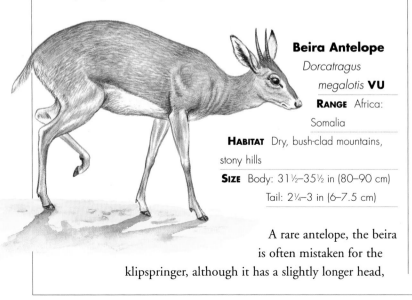

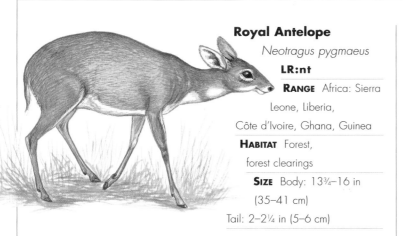

Royal Antelope
Neotragus pygmaeus

LR:nt

RANGE Africa: Sierra Leone, Liberia, Côte d'Ivoire, Ghana, Guinea

HABITAT Forest, forest clearings

SIZE Body: 13¾–16 in (35–41 cm) Tail: 2–2¼ in (5–6 cm)

This dainty, compact little animal, the smallest African antelope, weighs 7 to 10 lb (3 to 4.5 kg) – not much more than a rabbit. Indeed, it is called "king of the hares" by local tribespeople and so "royal" antelope by Europeans. It has a rounded back and a short tail, which it holds tightly against its rump. The male has tiny, sharp horns, which the female lacks; young are darker in colour than adults.

Royal antelopes live in pairs or alone in a small territory, which they usually mark out with dung heaps. They are timid and secretive and are mainly active at night, when quite large numbers may feed together on leaves, buds, shoots, fungi, fallen fruit, grass and weeds. They sometimes venture into vegetable plots and cocoa and peanut plantations. Although they are preyed on by a wide range of mammals, birds and even large snakes, their small size often enables them to slip away unseen from danger, with their bellies almost on the ground. Their vulnerability is also compensated for by their astounding ability to leap, like springboks, as much as 10 ft (3 m) up into the air.

Royal antelopes probably pair for life. The female produces a single young at a time.

Kirk's Dik-dik *Madoqua kirki*

RANGE Africa: Somalia to Tanzania; S.W. Angola, Namibia

HABITAT Bush country with thick undergrowth and scattered trees

SIZE Body: 21½–22½ in (55–57 cm) Tail: 1½–2¼ in (4–6 cm)

There are 7 races of this small, dainty antelope, which occur in two widely separated regions.

Coloration of the soft coat varies from pale gray-brown in dry habitats to a much darker shade in wet habitats. The nose is slightly elongated and the legs long and thin, with the hind legs always bent, so the hindquarters slope downward. Males have tiny horns, with a crest of long hair between them. The slightly larger female does not have horns.

Dik-diks are found alone or in pairs often with their 2 most recent young. Males scent-mark and fiercely defend the boundaries of a clearly defined territory, within which there are regularly used paths and places for resting and defecating. Shy, secretive animals, dik-diks browse at sunset and at night on leaves, shoots, buds and flowers, especially those of the Acacia. They also eat fallen fruit, and dig up roots and tubers with their horns and hoofs and frequent salt licks. They do not need to drink. Their many enemies include leopard, caracal, serval, wild cats, eagles and man.

Dik-diks pair for life and produce 1 young after a gestation period of 6 months; there are two litters a year.

Cape Grysbok
Raphicerus melanotis

LR:cd

RANGE Africa: South Africa

HABITAT Grassy plains, bush savanna at the foot of hills

SIZE Body: 23½–29½ in (60–75 cm) Tail: 2–3 in (5–8 cm)

This rough-coated, stocky little antelope has relatively short legs, slightly longer behind, which give it a sloping back. Males have short, sharply pointed horns and generally darker coloration than females. The grysbok is solitary outside the breeding season, and each establishes a fairly small territory, which is marked out by means of scent and dropping sites. This antelope feeds in the morning and late in the afternoon on the foliage of trees and bushes and it is particularly fond of grapevine leaves.

During the day, the grysbok rests up in the shade of a bush or rock or in areas of long grass. Its main predators are leopards, caracals and crowned eagles, and when threatened, the antelope lies flat, darting away with a zigzag gallop when the enemy approaches, only to dive suddenly for cover and disappear again.

The breeding biology of the grysbok is not very well known, but it is believed to be similar to that of the steenbok, which produces a single young after a gestation period of about 5½ months.

BOVIDS

Impala *Aepyceros melampus* **LR:cd**

RANGE Africa: Kenya, Uganda, south to N. South Africa

HABITAT Light mopane woodland, acacia savanna

SIZE Body: 4–5¼ ft (1.2–1.6 m) Tail: 11¾–17¾ in (30–45 cm)

A graceful, medium-sized antelope, with a glossy coat, the impala is identified by the unique bushy tuft of dark hairs above the hind "heels", the vertical dark stripes on white on the back of the thighs and tail and, in the male, the long, elegant, lyre-shaped horns. The impala is remarkable also for its fleetness and for the amazing leaps it makes – as far as 33 ft (10 m) and as high as 10 ft (3 m) – seemingly for enjoyment, as well as to escape from predators.

Impalas are extremely gregarious, and in the dry season troops may join to form herds of 200 or so. They are active day and night and eat quantities of grass and leaves, flowers and fruit. In the breeding season, the ram establishes a territory and a harem of 15 to 20 females which he defends fiercely; immature males form separate troops. After a gestation period of 6½ to 7 months, the female produces 1 young, which is born at midday, when many predators are somnolent, and remains hidden until it is strong enough to join the herd.

Blackbuck

Antilope cervicapra **VU**

RANGE India, Nepal, Pakistan

HABITAT Open grassy plains

SIZE Body: 4 ft (1.2 m) Tail: 7 in (18 cm)

The only species in its genus, the blackbuck is one of the few antelope in which the coloration of male and female is dissimilar. The dominant male in the herd is dark, almost black on back and sides and has long, spirally twisted horns; the female is yellowish-fawn and lacks horns. Subordinate males have smaller horns and retain female coloration. They only darken and develop large horns if they assume the dominant position in a herd, following the death of the leading male.

Blackbucks feed largely on grass and are active morning and evening, resting in the heat of the day. The female is unusually alert, and it is she who first gives warning of danger. When alarmed blackbucks flee with leaps and bounds that soon settle into a swift gallop.

Blackbucks are normally found in herds of 15 to 50 – smaller groups consisting of a dominant male with females and young; as males mature, they are driven out and form their own small parties. The breeding male sets up a territory and defends it and his harem against rivals. One young, sometimes 2, is born after a gestation period of 6 months.

Springbok

Antidorcas marsupialis

LR:cd

RANGE Africa: Angola, South Africa, Botswana (Kalahari Desert)

HABITAT Treeless grassland (veld)

SIZE Body: 4–4½ ft (1.2–1.4 m) Tail: 7½–10½ in (19–27 cm)

The brightly coloured, strikingly marked springbok has a most unusual glandular pouch in its skin that stretches from the middle of the back to the base of the tail. When the animal is excited or alarmed, the pouch opens and reveals a crest of long, stiff, white hairs. Male and female look alike, both with ridged strong horns. The springbok's name is derived from its ability to bound as high as 11½ ft (3.5 m) into the air, half a dozen times in succession, either in alarm or play, with back curved, legs stiff and crest displayed.

Springboks eat the leaves of shrubs and bushes and grass and are independent of water. They were once exceedingly numerous, and in times of drought, herds of up to a million would make long migrations in search of fresh grazing, devastating the pasture and farmland that lay in their path. As a result, thousands were slaughtered, but they have now been reintroduced throughout their range and are again thriving. In the breeding season, the male may establish a territory and a harem of 10 to 30, but large mixed herds are the norm. The female produces 1 young after a gestation period of about 6 months.

Dibatag
Ammodorcas clarkei **VU**

RANGE Africa: Somalia,
E. Ethiopia

HABITAT Sandy or grassy plains
with scattered bushes

SIZE Body: 5–5¼ ft (1.5–1.6 m)
Tail: 11¾–14¼ in (30–36 cm)

Although superficially it resembles the gerenuk, the dibatag is much grayer, and the male has shorter and quite different horns. The long, thin, black-tufted tail is generally held upright when the animal is running and gives it its name, which derives from the Somali words dabu (tail) and tag (erect). These animals live in pairs or family parties, consisting of an adult male and 3 to 5 females with young, in a seasonal territory, moving with the rains wherever food supplies are plentiful. They are active morning and evening, browsing on leaves and young shoots of bushes, which, like the gerenuk, they stand on their hind legs to reach. They also eat flowers, berries and new grass; they do not need to drink.

As a rule, 1 calf is born in the rainy season after a gestation of 6 to 7 months but it is possible for a female to produce 2 young in a year.

Gerenuk *Litocranius walleri* **LR:cd**

RANGE Africa: Somalia, Ethiopia to Kenya, Tanzania

HABITAT Dry thornbush country, desert

SIZE Body 4½–5¼ ft (1.4–1.6 m)
Tail: 9–13¾ in (23–35 cm)

This large, graceful-looking gazelle is remarkable chiefly for its long neck (gerenuk means giraffe-necked in Somali) and for its long legs. It has a small, narrow head, large eyes and mobile lips, there are tufts of hair on the knees, and the short, almost naked tail is held close against the body except in flight, when it is curled up over the animal's back. The male has horns and is larger than the female.

Gerenuks are usually found in pairs or family parties consisting of a male and 2 to 5 females with young. They are browsers, living almost entirely on leaves and young shoots of thorny bushes and trees, which they reach by standing against the trunk on their hind legs, using a foreleg to pull down the branches, and stretching their necks. They feed morning and evening, standing still in the shade at midday. They are quite independent of water. Their main predators are cheetah, leopard, lion, hyena and hunting dog.

A single young is born, usually in the rainy season, after a gestation of about 6½ months.

Thomson's Gazelle
Gazella thomsonii **LR:cd**

RANGE Africa: Sudan,
Kenya, N. Tanzania

HABITAT Open plains with
short grass

SIZE Body: 31½ in–3½ ft (80 cm–1.1 m)
Tail: 7½–10½ in (19–27 cm)

This graceful, small gazelle has a distinctive broad, dark stripe along its sides in marked contrast to the white underparts. The male is larger than the female and has much stronger horns. There are about 15 races of Thompson's gazelle which show only minor variations of colouring or horn size. They feed morning and evening, mainly on short grass and a small amount of foliage. They need to drink only when grazing is dry. Their chief predators are cheetah, lion, leopard, hyena and hunting dog.

These gazelles live in loosely structured groups, which may vary between 1 old ram with 5 to 65 females; herds of 5 to 500 young males; and groups of pregnant and recently calved females. When grazing is good, mature male may establish a territory which he marks by urination and droppings and by scraping and smearing of ground and bushes with horns and glandular secretions. Females calve at any time of year after a 6-month gestation and may produce 2 calves a year.

BOVIDS

Saiga *Saiga tatarica* VU

RANGE River Volga to C. Asia

HABITAT Treeless plains

SIZE Body: 4–5½ ft (1.2–1.7 m)
Tail: 3–4 in (7.5–10 cm)

The saiga is migratory and well-adapted to its cold, windswept habitat. It has a heavy fawnish-cinnamon coat, with a fringe of long hairs from chin to chest. In the winter it changes to a uniformly creamy-white and becomes thick and woolly. It is thought that the saiga's enlarged nose, with downward-pointing nostrils, may be an adaptation for warming and moisturizing air. The nasal passages are lined with hairs, glands and mucous tracts. In each nostril there is a sac, lined with mucous membranes that appears in no other mammal but the whale. The male's horns are thought to have medicinal value by the Chinese; this led to overhunting. Saigas have been protected since 1920, and there are now over a million of them.

Saigas feed on low-growing shrubs and grass, and in autumn large herds gather and move off southward to warmer, lusher pastures. When spring comes, groups of 2 to 6 males begin to return northward, followed by the females. In May, after a gestation of about 5 months, the female gives birth to 1 to 3 young, which are suckled until the autumn.

Serow *Capricornis sumatraensis* VU

RANGE N. India to central and S. China;
S.E. Asia to Sumatra

HABITAT Bush and forest at
2,000–9,000 ft (600–2,700 m)

SIZE Body: 4½–5 ft (1.4–1.5 m)
Tail: 3–8¼ in (8–21 cm)

The slow, but sure-footed serow, with its short, solid hoofs, is found on rocky slopes and ridges of thickly vegetated mountains. It is active early and late in the day, feeding on grass and leaves; it lies up in the shelter of an overhanging rock for the rest of the time. The hairs on its back and sides are light at the base and black at the tip, giving the coat an overall dark appearance, there is a completely black stripe along the center of the back, and the mane varies from white to black on different individuals. Both male and female have horns, which they use to defend themselves, particularly against the dogs with which they are hunted by the Chinese, who believe that different parts of the serow have great healing properties.

Little is known of their breeding habits but 1, or more often 2, young are born after a gestation of about 8 months.

Common Goral *Nemorhaedus goral* LR:nt

RANGE Bhutan, India, Nepal, Pakistan

HABITAT Mountains at 3,300–6,600 ft (1,000–2,000 m)

SIZE Body: 3–4¼ ft (90 cm–1.3 m)
Tail: 3–7¾ in (7.5–20 cm)

These animals are mountain-dwellers, found where there are grassy hills and rocky outcrops near forests. They have long, sturdy legs and their long coats, of guardhairs overlaying a short, woolly undercoat, give them a shaggy appearance. Male and female look alike, both possessing horns. The male has a short, semi-erect mane.

Apart from old bucks, which live alone for most of the year, gorals normally live in family groups of 4 to 8. They feed on grass in the early morning and late afternoon, resting on a rocky ledge in the middle of the day. The female gives birth to 1, rarely 2, young after a gestation of about 6 months.

Mountain Goat *Oreamnos americanus*

RANGE N. America: Rocky Mountains from Alaska to
Montana, Idaho, Oregon; introduced in South Dakota

HABITAT Rocky mountains above the tree line

SIZE Body: 4¼–5¼ ft (1.3–1.6 m)
Tail: 6–7¾ in (15–20 cm)

This splendid-looking animal is not a true goat, but a goat-antelope, and is the only one in its genus. It is found among boulders and rocky screes above the tree line and is well adapted to its cold, harsh habitat. It has thick, woolly underfur and a long, hairy, white coat, which is particularly thick and stiff on the neck and shoulders, forming a ridge, or hump. The hooves have a hard, sharp rim, enclosing a soft, spongy inner pad, which gives the mountain goat a good grip for clambering on on rocks and ice. Both sexes have beards and black, conical horns.

Mountain goats are slow-moving, but sure-footed, climbing to great heights and seemingly inaccessible ledges in their search for grass, sedges and lichens to eat. They also browse on the leaves and shoots of trees and will travel considerable distances to search out salt licks. In winter they come down to areas where the snow is not too deep. In really severe weather, they may take refuge under overhanging rocks or in caves.

These goats are probably monogamous, and the female produces 1 or 2 kids in the spring after a gestation of about 7 months. The young kids are remarkably active and within half an hour of birth are able to jump about among the rocks.

Chamois *Rupicapra rupicapra*

RANGE Europe to Middle East

HABITAT Mountains

SIZE Body: 35½ in–4¼ ft (90 cm–1.3 m) Tail: 1¼–1½ in (3–4 cm)

For nimbleness, audacity and endurance, the chamois is unparalleled among mountaindwellers. It thrives in wild and inhospitable surroundings, where weather conditions may be savage, and has been known to survive as long as 2 weeks without food. It is the only species in its genus. It is slimly built, with distinctive horns that rise almost vertically, then sweep sharply backward to form a hook. The legs are sturdy, and the hoofs have a resilient, spongy pad underneath, which gives the chamois a good grip. The coat is stiff and coarse, with a thick, woolly underfleece.

Chamois graze on the tops of mountains in summer, on herbs and flowers; in winter, they come farther down the slopes and browse on young pine shoots, lichens and mosses. They are wary animals and a sentinel is always posted to warn of danger. Females and young live together in herds of 15 to 30. Old males are solitary except in the rutting season in the autumn. Fighting is common among males, with older rams locking horns. The female usually has 1 kid, but 2 or 3 are fairly common.

Ibex *Capra ibex*

RANGE European Alps, Middle East

HABITAT Alps to 10,000 ft (3,000 m)

SIZE Body: 5 ft (1.5 m) Tail: 4¾–6 in (12–15 cm)

From Roman times, different parts of these animals have been regarded as possessing healing powers, and ibex were hunted to the point of extinction. Today, however, a few small, protected herds survive in reserves. The male ibex has long, backward-sweeping horns; the female has shorter horns. The coat is a brownish-gray. Longer hair on the back of the neck forms a mane in old males. The male has a small beard.

The ibex live above the tree line, only descending to the upper limits of forest in the harshest winter conditions. In summer, they climb up into alpine meadows, where they graze on grass and flowers. At this time, females are found with young and subadults, and males form their own groups, within which token fights often take place to establish an order of rank. Only in the winter rutting season do males rejoin female herds. The female gives birth to 1 young after a gestation period of between 5 and 6 months.

BOVIDS

Musk Ox *Ovibos moschatus*

RANGE N. Canada, Greenland

HABITAT Tundra

SIZE Body: 6¼–7½ ft (1.9–2.3 m) Tail: 3½–4 in (9–10 cm)

In prehistoric times, the musk ox occurred throughout northern Europe, Siberia and North America. It was largely exterminated, surviving only in northern Canada and Greenland; however, it has now been successfully reintroduced in Norway and Alaska. It is the only species in its genus.

The musk ox is superbly equipped for life in harsh, arctic conditions, for it has a dense undercoat, which neither cold nor water can penetrate and an outer coat of long, coarse hair that reaches almost to the ground and protects it from snow and rain. The broad hooves prevent it from sinking in soft snow. Both sexes have heavy horns that almost meet at the base, forming a broad, tough frontal plate. Facial scent glands in the bull emit a strong, musky odour in the rutting season, hence the animal's name.

Musk oxen are gregarious, living in herds of as many as 100. In the mating season, young bulls are driven out by old master bulls and form small bachelor groups or remain solitary. The female produces 1 young after a gestation period of 8 months.

When threatened, musk oxen form a circle, facing outward with horns lowered, with the young in the middle; this is an effective defence against wolves, their natural enemies, but not against men with guns. Musk oxen feed mainly on grass, but they also eat mosses, lichens and leaves and will dig through the snow in order to find food.

Himalayan Tahr *Hemitragus jemlahicus* **VU**

RANGE India: Kashmir (Pir Pamjal Mountains), Punjab; Nepal, Sikkim

HABITAT Tree-covered mountain slopes

SIZE Body: 3½ ft (1.1 m) Tail: 3½ in (9 cm)

Although the tahr appears much like a goat, with its heavy, shaggy coat that forms a mane around the shoulders, it differs from true goats in having a naked muzzle and no beard. The horns are long and not twisted, and there are glands on the feet.

Tahrs are goatlike in their habits – they live on precipitous mountainsides, where they climb and leap with supreme ease. They are gregarious, living in herds of 30 to 40 on almost any vegetation they can reach. Wary animals, they always post a sentinel to watch for danger.

The breeding season peaks in the winter, when the female gives birth to 1 or 2 young after a 6 to 8-month gestation.

Takin *Budorcas taxicolor* **VU**

RANGE Asia: Myanmar; China: Szechuan and Shensi Provinces

HABITAT Dense thickets in mountain forest, 7,900–14,000 ft (2,400–4,250 m)

SIZE Body: 4 ft (1.2 m) Tail: 4 in (10 cm)

The takin lives in dense bamboo and rhododendron thickets near the upper limits of the tree line in some of the most rugged country in the world. It is a clumsy-looking, solidly built animal, with thick legs and large hoofs with dew claws. The coat ranges from yellowish-white to blackish-brown, always with a dark stripe along the back. Both males and females have horns.

Old bulls are generally solitary, but in summer they join large herds. They graze in the evening on grass and herbage near the tops of mountains; in winter takin move down to the valleys, where they live in smaller groups, eating grass, bamboo and willow shoots. They are shy, and spend most of their time under cover following regularly used paths through the thickets to their grazing grounds and salt licks.

The female produces 1 young after a gestation of about 8 months; it is able to follow its mother after about 3 days.

Barbary Sheep

Ammotragus lervia **VU**

RANGE N. Africa: Atlantic coast to Red Sea, south to N. Mali and Sudan; introduced in S.W. USA

HABITAT Dry, rocky, barren regions

SIZE Body: 4¼–6¼ ft (1.3–1.9 m) Tail: 9¾ in (25 cm)

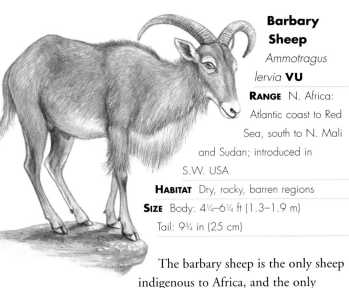

The barbary sheep is the only sheep indigenous to Africa, and the only species in the genus. The mane of long, soft, thick hairs on its throat, chest and upper forelegs differentiates it from other wild sheep, but, like them, both sexes have horns, those of the female being almost as heavy as the male's.

Small family parties, consisting of a breeding pair and their offspring of various litters, wander about in search of food: grass, herbaceous plants, and leaves and twigs of low-growing bushes. They obtain all the water they need from this diet and by licking up dew. Barbary sheep, having no cover in which to hide when danger threatens, rely on the camouflage effect of their sandy coloured coats and remain perfectly still. They are killed by man for their flesh, hides, hair and sinews.

In captivity, barbary sheep produce one litter a year of 1 or 2 young. They have been successfully crossed with domestic goats, and the offspring with chamois.

American Bighorn *Ovis canadensis* **LR:cd**

RANGE N.W. America

HABITAT Upland and mountainous areas

SIZE Body: 4–6 ft (1.2–1.8 m) Tail: 6 in (15 cm)

The American bighorn is found on high mountain pastures in summer, when groups of males or females with young graze independently on grass and herbage. In winter, they form mixed herds and move to lower pastures.

The high-ranking male bighorn sheep is a most impressive animal, with massive spiral horns up to 3¾ ft (1.15 m) long. Horn size is of great significance in establishing rank order among males; smaller-horned

and, therefore, lower-ranking males are treated as females by dominant males, which perhaps prevents them being driven out of the herd. In the rutting season, high-ranking males of comparable horn size have fierce battles rushing at each other and crashing their horns together. The fighting may proceed for hours, and occasionally an animal is killed. Females have exceptionally short horns.

Ewes produce 1 or 2 lambs, born after a gestation period of about 6 months, and are assiduous in care of the young.

Mouflon *Ovis orientalis* **VU**

RANGE Sardinia, Corsica; C. and S. Asia, introduced in Germany, Hungary, Austria and Czechoslovakia

HABITAT Rugged mountains

SIZE Body: 4 ft (1.2 m) Tail: 2¾ in (7 cm)

The mouflon, the wild sheep of Europe, is now found only in reserves in Sardinia and Corsica, but even there is inadequately protected. The male has long, spiral horns, often with the tips curving inward; those of the female are short. It has a woolly underfleece, covered in winter by a coarse, blackish-brown top coat, with a distinctive white saddle patch in the male. In the summer this patch disappears. The female and young are gray or darker brown, with no patch.

Mouflon are active early and late in the day and do not wander far, even when food is scarce. They appear to be able to eat every type of vegetation – grass, flowers, buds and shoots of bushes and trees, even poisonous plants such as deadly nightshade, and so manage to survive.

They live in separate groups composed of females with young or males on their own in the summer. In the rutting season, a mature ram will detach a female from the herd and mate with her. Fierce fighting may take place if an old ram is challenged, but there are seldom casualties.

The ewe produces 1 lamb after a gestation period of 5 months.

RIVER DOLPHIN AND PORPOISES

ORDER CETACEA

There are 77 species of whale, dolphin and porpoise. They are the only aquatic mammals to spend their entire lives in water. All are streamlined animals with strong, horizontally set tail flukes. Their front limbs are modified into flippers and there are no visible hind limbs. As a general rule, whales produce only one young at a time, although twins are known.

There are two groups within the order. First, the toothed whales, with 67 species of small whale, dolphin and porpoise, all of which prey on fish and squid. To help locate their prey, they use a form of ultrasonic sonar: they emit high-frequency clicking sounds which bounce off objects, the echoes informing the whale with astonishing accuracy of the size, distance and speed of travel of the object. All of these whales have teeth, some a pair, some as many as 200.

In the second group are the 10 largest whales, known as the baleen whales. These marine giants feed on tiny planktonic animals, which they extract from the sea by filtering water through plates of fringed horny material hanging from their upper jaws. These baleen plates, as they are called, act as sieves to trap the plankton. There are 3 families of baleen whale: rorquals, gray and right whales.

PLATANISTIDAE: RIVER DOLPHIN FAMILY

The 5 species in this family all inhabit rivers in South America and Asia. They look alike and are grouped as a family, but the resemblance may be more to do with evolutionary pressures of similar habitat than close relationship. All the river dolphins are small for cetaceans, with long slender beaks and prominent rounded foreheads. The rivers these dolphins inhabit are muddy and full of sediment, and visibility is poor; as a result they rely heavily on echolocation to find food and avoid obstacles, and their eyes have become much reduced.

Boutu *Inia geoffrensis* **VU**

RANGE	Amazon basin
HABITAT	Rivers, streams
SIZE	6–9 ft (1.8–2.7 m)

The boutu has a strong beak, studded with short bristles, and a mobile, flexible head and neck. Most boutus have a total of 100 or more teeth. Their eyes, although small, seem to be more functional than those of other river dolphins. Boutus feed mainly on small fish and some crustaceans, using echolocation clicks to find their prey. Boutus live in pairs and seem to produce young between July and September.

Ganges Dolphin *Platanista gangetica* **EN**

RANGE	India: Ganges and Brahmaputra river systems
HABITAT	Rivers, streams
SIZE	5–8 ft (1.5–2.4 m)

The Ganges dolphin has a beak, which can be as long as 18 in (46 cm), and has up to 120 teeth. Its forehead curves up steeply from the beak. An agile animal, it generally swims on its side and returns to the normal upright position to breathe. It can dive for a maximum of 3 minutes at a time, but usually remains underwater for about 45 seconds.

The Ganges dolphin is blind – its eyes have no lenses – but it finds its food by skilful use of echolocation signals. It feeds mainly on fish and some shrimps and hunts in the evening and at night. The dolphins are usually seen in pairs and may gather in groups of 6 or so to feed. They mate in autumn, and the calves are born the following summer after a gestation period of about 9 months.

Whitefin Dolphin/Baiji *Lipotes vexillifer* **CR**

RANGE	China: Yangzte River; formerly Lake Tungting
HABITAT	Muddy-bottomed rivers
SIZE	6½–8 ft (2–2.4 m)

Since 1975 this species has been protected by law in China, but although the total numbers are not known, population still seems to be low. The whitefin dolphin has a slender beak, which

turns up slightly at the tip, and a total
of 130 to 140 teeth. With little or no
vision, it relies on sonar for hunting prey, mainly fish, but may
also probe in the mud with its beak for shrimps.

Groups of 2 to 6 dolphins move together, sometimes
gathering into larger groups for feeding. In the rainy summer
season, they migrate up small swollen streams to breed, but no
further details are known of their reproductive behavior.

PHOCOENIDAE: PORPOISE FAMILY

Although the name porpoise is sometimes erroneously applied to
members of other families, strictly speaking, only the 6 members
of this family are porpoises. They are small, beakless whales,
rarely exceeding 7 ft (2.1 m) in length, and usually with
prominent dorsal fins. They have 60 to 80 spatular teeth and
feed mainly on fish and squid.

Porpoises live in coastal waters throughout the northern
hemisphere, often ascending the estuaries of large rivers. One
species, the spectacled porpoise, *Phocoena dioptrica*, occurs off
the coasts of South America.

Common Porpoise/Harbor Porpoise

Phocoena phocoena **VU**

RANGE N. Atlantic, N. Pacific Oceans; Black and Mediterranean Seas

HABITAT Shallow water, estuaries

SIZE 4½–6 ft (1.4–1.8 m)

Gregarious, highly vocal animals,
porpoises live in small groups of up to 15 individuals. There is
much communication within the group, and porpoises will
always come to the aid of a group member in distress. Porpoises
feed on fish, such as herring and mackerel, and can dive for up
to 6 minutes to pursue prey, which are pin-pointed by the use
of echolocation clicks.

Breeding pairs mate in July and August and perform
prolonged courtship rituals, caressing one another as they
swim side by side. The gestation period is between 10 and 11

months, and calves are suckled for about 8 months.
While her calf feeds the mother lies on her side at the
surface so that it can breathe easily.

Dall's Porpoise *Phocoenides dalli* **LR:cd**

RANGE Temperate N. Pacific Ocean

HABITAT Inshore and oceanic deeper waters

SIZE 6–7½ ft (1.8–2.3 m)

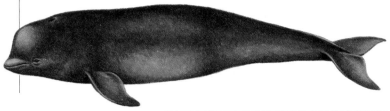

Dall's porpoise is larger and heavier than most porpoises. Its
head is small, and the lower jaw projects slightly beyond the
upper. It lives in groups of up to 15, which may gather in
schools of 100 or more to migrate north in summer and south
in winter. It feeds on squid and fish, such as hake, and most
probably uses echolocation when hunting.

Pairs mate at any time of the year, and the young are suckled
for as long as 2 years.

Finless Porpoise *Neophocaena phocaenoides*

RANGE E. and S.E. Asia: Pakistan to Borneo and Korea; Yangtze River,
E. China Sea

HABITAT Coasts, estuaries, rivers

SIZE 4½–6 ft (1.4–1.8 m)

The finless porpoise is different from other porpoises in that it
has a prominent rounded forehead, which gives the appearance
of a slight beak, and a ridge of small rounded projections just
behind where the dorsal fin should be. Finless porpoises dive for
less than a minute in search of prey and are quick and agile in
the water. They feed largely on crustaceans, squid and fish and
are skilful echolocators. Although finless porpoises generally
move in pairs, groups of up to 10 are sometimes seen. Little is
known of their breeding behavior, but young calves travel
clinging to the projections on their mothers' backs.

DOLPHINS

DELPHINIDAE: DOLPHIN FAMILY

There are 32 species in this, the largest, most diverse cetacean family, which is found in all oceans and some tropical rivers. Most have beaked snouts and slender streamlined bodies and they are among the smallest whales. Typically, the dolphin has a bulging forehead, housing the melon, a lens-shaped pad of fat thought to help focus the sonar beams. A few species, notably the killer whale, are much larger and do not have beaks. Male dolphins are usually larger than females, and in some species the sexes differ in the shape of their flippers and dorsal fins. Dolphins swim fast and feed by making shallow dives and surfacing several times a minute. They are extremely gregarious and establish hierarchies within their social groups.

Indo-Pacific Humpbacked Dolphin *Sousa chinensis* **DD**
RANGE Indian Ocean, S.W. Pacific Ocean, Yangtze River
HABITAT Coasts, estuaries, swamps
SIZE 6½–10 ft (2–3 m)

The young of this species all have the normal streamlined body shape, but adults have humps of fatty tissue on the back. The beak is long, and there is a total of at least 120 teeth. These dolphins feed in shallow water on fish, mollusks and crustaceans and use echolocation when searching for prey. They are gregarious creatures, living in groups of up to 20 individuals.

Striped Dolphin *Stenella coeruleoalba* **LR:cd**
RANGE Atlantic and Pacific Oceans, temperate and tropical areas
HABITAT Deep offshore waters
SIZE 8–10 ft (2.4–3 m)

Color is variable in this species, but there is always a dark stripe running along the side and usually a dark band curving from the dorsal

fin toward the eye. Striped dolphins have between 90 and 100 teeth and feed on small fish, squid and shrimps. They move in large schools of several hundred, even several thousand individuals, which are organized into age-segregated groups. Females breed about every 3 years. The gestation period is 12 months, and calves are nursed for between 9 and 18 months.

Common Dolphin *Delphinus delphis* **LR:lc**
RANGE Worldwide, temperate and tropical oceans
HABITAT Coastal and oceanic waters
SIZE 7–8½ ft (2.1–2.6 m)

The classic dolphin depicted by artists for centuries, the common dolphin is a beautifully marked animal with a long beak and pointed flippers. The markings are the most complex of any whale and are extremely variable. There are a number of geographically recognizable forms of this widespread species.

Dolphins live in hierarchical groups of 20 to 100 or more; groups sometimes join together, forming huge schools. There are many reports of these highly intelligent social animals coming to the aid of injured companions. Active animals, they roll and leap in the water and often swim at the bows of ships. Although they normally breathe several times a minute, they can dive for as long as 5 minutes to depths of 920 ft (280 m) to feed on fish and squid and certainly make good use of echolocation when hunting. Young are born in the summer, after a gestation period of 10 or 11 months.

Bottle-nose Dolphin *Tursiops truncatus* **DD**
TRUNCATUS RANGE Worldwide, temperate and tropical oceans
HABITAT Coastal waters
SIZE 10–14 ft (3–4.2 m)

Now the familiar performing dolphin in zoos and on screen, this dolphin is a highly intelligent animal which is, tragically, still hunted and killed by man in some areas. It is a sturdy creature with a broad, high fin and a short, wide beak. Its lower jaw projects beyond the upper and this, combined with the curving line of the mouth, gives it its characteristic smiling expression.

Bottle-nose dolphins live in groups of up to 15 individuals, sometimes gathering into larger schools, and there is much cooperation and communication between the group members. They feed mainly on bottom-dwelling fish in inshore waters, but also take crustaceans and large surface-swimming fish. They are highly skilful echolocators, producing a range of click sounds in different frequencies to analyze any object at a distance with great precision. Up to 1,000 clicks a second are emitted.

Breeding pairs perform gentle courtship movements, caressing one another before copulation. Gestation lasts 12 months, and two adult females assist the mother at the birth and take the calf, which is normally born tail first, to the surface for its first breath. The mother feeds her calf for about a year, so there must be at least a 2-year interval between calves. Like all whales, the bottle-nose dolphin produces extremely rich milk with a fat content of over 40 per cent to satisfy the high energy demands of her fast-growing youngster.

Killer Whale *Orcinus orca* **LR:cd**

RANGE Worldwide, particularly cooler seas

HABITAT Coastal waters

SIZE 23–32 ft (7–9.7 m)

The largest of the dolphin family, the killer whale is a robust yet streamlined animal, with a rounded head and no beak. The characteristic dorsal fin of an adult male is almost 6½ ft (2 m) high; and while the fins of females and juveniles are much smaller and curved, they are still larger than those of most other cetaceans. Adults have a total of 40 to 50 teeth.

Killer whales are avid predators and feed on fish, squid, sea lions, birds and even other whales. Their echolocation sounds are unlike those of other dolphins and are probably used to find food in turbid water.

Extended family groups of killer whales live together and cooperate in hunting. They have no regular migratory habits, but do travel in search of food.

Long-finned Pilot Whale *Globicephala melaena* **LR:lc**

RANGE N. Atlantic Ocean; temperate southern oceans

HABITAT Coastal waters

SIZE 16–28 ft (4.8–8.5 m)

The long-finned pilot whale has an unusual square-shaped head and long, rather narrow flippers. Pilot whales have a vast repertoire of sounds, some of which are used for echolocation purposes. Squid is their main food, but they also feed on fish, such as cod and turbot. Social groups are made up of 6 or more whales and they have particularly strong bonds. Groups may join into larger schools. Gestation lasts about 16 months and the mother feeds her young for well over a year.

The range of this species is unusual in that it occurs in two widely separated areas.

Risso's Dolphin *Grampus griseus* **DD**

RANGE Worldwide, temperate and tropical oceans

HABITAT Deep water

SIZE 10–13 ft (3–4 m)

Most adult Risso's dolphins are badly marked with scars, apparently caused by members of their own species, since the marks correspond to their own tooth pattern. The body of this dolphin is broad in front of the fin and tapers off behind it. It has no beak, but there is a characteristic crease down the centre of the forehead to the lip. There are no teeth in the upper jaw and only three or four in each side in the lower jaw. Squid seems to be its main food.

SPERMWHALES AND WHITE WHALES

PHYSETERIDAE: SPERM WHALE FAMILY

There are 3 species of sperm whale, 1 of which is the largest of all toothed whales, while the other 2 are among the smallest whales. Their characteristic feature is the spermaceti organ, located in the space above the toothless upper jaw; this contains a liquid, waxy substance which may be involved in controlling buoyancy when the whale makes deep dives. All sperm whales have underslung lower jaws but have little else in common.

Pygmy Sperm Whale *Kogia breviceps* **LR:lc**

RANGE All oceans

HABITAT Tropical, warm temperate seas

SIZE 10–11 ft (3–3.4 m)

Its underslung lower jaw gives the pygmy sperm whale an almost sharklike appearance, belied by its blunt, square head. The pygmy sperm whale's head accounts for only about 15 per cent of its total length. There are 12 or more pairs of teeth in the lower jaw. Short, broad flippers are located far forward, near the head. The body tapers off markedly behind the small dorsal fin.

Pygmy sperm whales are thought to be shy, slow-moving animals. They feed on squid, fish and crabs from deep and shallow water. These whales have often been sighted alone, but they are thought to form social units of 3 to 5 individuals.

Little is known of the reproductive habits of pygmy sperm whales. Gestation is believed to last about 9 months; calves are born in the spring and fed by the mother for about a year.

Dwarf Sperm Whale *Kogia simus* **LR:lc**

RANGE All oceans

HABITAT Tropical and subtropical seas

SIZE 8–9 ft (2.4–2.7 m)

Superficially similar to the pygmy sperm whale, the dwarf sperm whale tends to have a more rounded head than its relative, though there is considerable individual variation in shape. The whale's lower jaw is set back, and it contains up to 11 pairs of teeth.

Little is known of the biology and habits of this whale, but fish and squid are believed to be its main items of diet. Species found in the stomachs of dwarf sperm whales are all known to live at depths of more than 250 m) 800 ft), so there seems little doubt that these whales make prolonged dives for food.

Sperm Whale *Physeter catodon* **VU**

RANGE All oceans

HABITAT Temperate and tropical waters

SIZE 36–66 ft (11–20 m)

The largest of the toothed whales, the sperm whale has a huge head, as great as one-third of its total body length, and a disproportionately small lower jaw, set well back from the snout. On its back is a fleshy hump and behind this are several smaller humps. Its flippers are short, but the tail is large and powerful and useful for acceleration. Surrounding the nasal passages in the huge snout is a mass of the waxy substance known as

spermaceti. When the whale dives, it allows these passages to fill with water and by controlling the amount and temperature of the water taken in at different depths, it can alter the density of the wax and thus the buoyancy of its whole body. This enables the whale to make its deep dives and to remain at neutral buoyancy, while searching for prey. Sperm whales are known to dive to 3,300 ft (1,000 m) and may dive to more than twice this depth. They feed mainly on large, deepwater squid, as well as on some fish, lobsters and other marine creatures. Their sonar system is vital for finding prey in the black depths of the ocean.

All sperm whales migrate toward the poles in spring and back to the Equator in autumn, but females and young do not stray farther than temperate waters. Adult males, however, travel right to the ice caps in high latitudes. They return to the tropics in winter and contest with each other in order to gather harem groups consisting of 20 to 30 breeding females and young. Males under about 25 years old do not generally hold harems, but gather in bachelor groups.

The gestation period for sperm whales is about 14 to 16 months. When a female gives birth, she is surrounded by attendant adult females, waiting to assist her and to help the newborn to take its first breath at the surface. As with most whales, usually only 1 young is produced at a time, but twins have been known. Mothers suckle their young for up to 2 years.

MONODONTIDAE: WHITE WHALE FAMILY

There are 2 species in this family, both of which live in Arctic waters. They are distinctive whales with many features in common. Both have more flexible necks than is usual for whales, and their tails, too, are highly maneuvrable. They do not have dorsal fins. In both species males are larger than females.

White Whale *Delphinapterus leucas* **VU**

RANGE	Arctic Ocean and subarctic waters
HABITAT	Shallow seas, estuaries, rivers
SIZE	13–20 ft (4–6.1 m)

The white whale is often known as the beluga. It has a rounded, plump body and just a hint of a beak. There is a short raised ridge along its back where the dorsal fin would normally be. At birth, these whales are a dark brownish-red colour, but they then turn a deep blue-gray and gradually become paler until, at about 6 years of age, they are a creamy-white colour. They have about 32 teeth.

White whales feed on the bottom in shallow water, mainly on crustaceans and some fish. They actually swim underneath pack ice and can break their way up through the ice floes in order to breathe.

Sexual maturity is attained when the whales are between 5 and 8 years old. The whales mate in spring and calves are born in the summer after a gestation period of about 14 months. Since the young are suckled for at least a year, white whales are able to breed only every 3 years or so.

All white whales are highly vocal and make a variety of sounds for communication, as well as clicks used for echolocation. Their intricate songs caused them to be known as sea canaries by the nineteenth century whalers. White whales congregate in herds of hundreds of individuals in order to migrate south in winter and then return to rich northern feeding grounds in summer.

Narwhal *Monodon monoceros* **DD**

RANGE	High Arctic Ocean (patchy distribution)
HABITAT	Open sea
SIZE	13–20 ft (4–6.1 m)

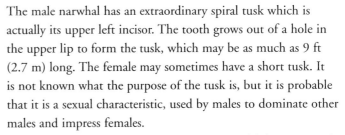

The male narwhal has an extraordinary spiral tusk which is actually its upper left incisor. The tooth grows out of a hole in the upper lip to form the tusk, which may be as much as 9 ft (2.7 m) long. The female may sometimes have a short tusk. It is not known what the purpose of the tusk is, but it is probable that it is a sexual characteristic, used by males to dominate other males and impress females.

Narwhals feed on squid, crabs, shrimps and fish. Groups of 6 to 10 whales form social units and may gather into larger herds when migrating. They do make click sounds, as well as other vocal communications, but it is not certain whether or not these are used for echolocation.

Narwhals mate in early spring, and gestation lasts 15 months. Mothers feed their calves for up to 2 years. At birth, calves are a dark blue-gray but as they mature this changes to the mottled brown of adults.

BEAKED WHALES

ZIPHIIDAE: BEAKED WHALE FAMILY

There are 18 species of beaked whale, found in all oceans. Most are medium-sized whales with slender bodies and long narrow snouts, some species have bulging, rounded foreheads. A particular characteristic of the family is the pair of grooves on the throat. Although Shepherd's beaked whale has more than 50 teeth, all other beaked whales have only one or two pairs, and the arrangement and shape of these are a useful means of defining identification.

Beaked whales feed largely on squid. They are deep divers and are believed to dive deeper and to remain submerged for longer periods than any other marine mammals. They generally move in small groups, but adult males are often solitary.

Although the second-largest family of whales (the dolphin family is the largest with 32 species), beaked whales are a little-known group. Some species are known to exist only from a few skulls and bones. The 12 species in the genus *Mesoplodon* are particularly unresearched but interesting. Only males have functional teeth, with a single pair protruding from the lower jaw. The shape and length of these differ from species to species, culminating in *M. Iayardi*, in which the backward-pointing teeth grow upward out of the mouth like tusks.

Northern Bottle-nose Whale *Hyperoodon ampullatus* **LR:cd**

RANGE	Arctic, N. Atlantic Oceans
HABITAT	Deep offshore waters
SIZE	24–33 ft (7.3–10 m)

A sturdy, round-bodied whale, the northern bottle-nose has a prominent bulbous forehead that is particularly pronounced in older males. Males are generally larger than females. The adult male has only two teeth, which are in the lower jaw, but these are often so deeply embedded in the gums that they cannot be seen. Adult females also have only two teeth, and these are always embedded in the gum. Some individuals have further vestigial, unusable teeth in the gums.

Squid, some fish, such as herring and sometimes starfish, make up the main diet of the northern bottle-nose whale. A member of a deep-diving family, the bottle-nose is believed to dive to greater depths than any other whale and certainly remains under water for longer.

These are gregarious whales, and they collect in social units of 4 to 10 individuals, a group usually consisting of a male and several females with young. Pairs mate in spring and summer, and gestation lasts about 12 months. The whales are sexually mature at between 9 and 12 years of age.

Since commercial whaling of this species began in 1887, populations have been seriously depleted.

Cuvier's Beaked Whale *Ziphius cavirostris* **DD**

RANGE	All oceans, temperate and tropical areas
HABITAT	Deep waters
SIZE	21–23 ft (6.4–7 m)

Cuvier's beaked whale has the typical tapering body of its family and a distinct beak. Adult males are easily distinguished by the two teeth which protrude from the lower jaw. In females, however, these teeth remain embedded in the gums. The colouring of this species is highly variable – Indo-Pacific whales are generally various shades of brown, many individuals have darker backs or almost white heads, while in the Atlantic, Cuvier's whales tend to be a gray or gray-blue colour. All races of beaked whales, however, are marked with scars and with discolored oval patches that are caused by the feeding action of parasitic lampreys.

Squid and deep-water fish are the main food of Cuvier's whales, and they make deep dives, lasting up to 30 minutes, in order to find their prey.

There is no definite breeding season, and calves are born at any time of the year. Groups of up to 15 individuals live and travel together.

Sowerby's Beaked Whale

Mesoplodon bidens **DD**

RANGE	N. Atlantic Ocean
HABITAT	Deep, cool coastal waters
SIZE	16½–20 ft (5–6 m)

There are 12 closely related species of beaked whale in the genus *Mesoplodon*. Most species tend to live in deep water, staying clear of ships, so they are rarely seen and their habits are little known or documented.

All have fairly well-rounded bodies, with small flippers in proportion to body size. Males are larger than females. Mature whales are generally marked with many scars; some of these are caused by parasites and others are, perhaps the result of fights between individuals of the same species.

Sowerby's beaked whale was the first beaked whale to be recognized officially and described as a species, in 1804. The male has a pointed tooth at each side of the lower jaw. Females have smaller teeth in this position or no visible teeth at all. Squid and small fish are the main food of Sowerby's whale.

Its breeding habits are not known, but it is thought to migrate south in winter and to give birth in its wintering area.

Shepherd's Beaked Whale *Tasmacetus shepherdi* **DD**

RANGE	New Zealand seas; off coasts of Argentina and Chile
HABITAT	Coasts, open ocean
SIZE	20–22 ft (6–6.6 m)

Shepherd's beaked whale was not discovered until 1933, and very few individuals have since been found or sighted. Until recently, the species was believed to occur only around New Zealand, but in the 1970s identical specimens were found off Argentina and Chile. This species is unique in its family for its tooth pattern. Shepherd's beaked whale has a pair of large teeth at the tip of its lower jaw, with 12 or more pairs behind them, and about 10 pairs in the upper jaw. It resembles the rest of the family in habits and appearance. Squid and fish are believed to be its main food.

Baird's Beaked Whale *Berardius bairdi* **LR:cd**

RANGE	Temperate N. Pacific Ocean
HABITAT	Deep water over 3,300 ft (1,000 m)
SIZE	33–39 ft (10–12 m)

The largest of the beaked whales, Baird's beaked whale has a distinctive beak, with the lower jaw extending beyond the upper. A pair of large teeth protrudes at the tip of the lower jaw, and behind these is a pair of smaller teeth.

Female Baird's whales are generally larger than males and lighter in color, but they have smaller teeth. Adult males are usually marked with scars, caused by their own species, suggesting that there is much rivalry and competition for leadership of groups of breeding females.

The normal social unit is a group of 6 to 30, led by a dominant male. The whales mate in midsummer and gestation lasts for 10 months, sometimes longer.

The migration pattern of this species is the exact opposite of the normal migration habits of whales. They spend the summer in warm waters to the south of their range off California and Japan, then move northwards in winter to the cooler waters of the Bering Sea and similar areas. These movements are most probably connected with the local abundance of food supplies. Baird's whales are deep divers and feed on squid, fish, octopus, lobster, crabs and other marine invertebrates.

Arnoux's beaked whale, *B. arnouxii*, which occurs in the temperate South Pacific and South Atlantic, is the closely related southern counterpart of Baird's whale. Although rarely seen, it is believed to be similar in both appearance and habits.

GRAY WHALE, RORQUALS AND RIGHT WHALES

ESCHRICHTIIDAE: GRAY WHALE FAMILY

There is a single species in this family, which is in some ways intermediate between the rorqual and right whales, the other 2 baleen whale families. The gray whale differs from both of these in that it has two or sometimes four throat grooves instead of the 100 or more in the other baleen whales.

Gray Whale *Eschrichtius robustus* **LR:cd**

RANGE N.E. and N.W. Pacific Ocean

HABITAT Coastal waters

SIZE 40–50 ft (12.2–15.3 m)

The gray whale has no dorsal fin, but there is a line of bumps along the middle of its lower back. Its jaw is only slightly arched and the snout is pointed. Males are larger than females. Like all baleen whales, it feeds on small planktonic animals by filtering water through rows of fringed horny plates, suspended from the upper jaw. Any creatures in the water are caught on the baleen plates and the water is expelled at the sides of the mouth. Using its tongue, the whale takes the food from the baleen to the back of its mouth to be swallowed. The gray whale feeds at the bottom of the sea, unlike other baleen whales, stirring up the sediment with its pointed snout then sieving the turbulent water.

Gray whales perform migrations of some 12,500 miles (20,000 km) between feeding grounds in the north and breeding grounds in the south. They spend the summer months in the food-rich waters of the Arctic, when they do most of their feeding for the year. At the breeding grounds, they gather to perform courtship rituals, and breeding animals pair off with an extra male in attendance. They lie in shallow water and, as the pair mate, the second male lies behind the female, apparently supporting her. The gestation period is 12 months, so the calf is born at the breeding grounds a year after mating has taken place and travels north with its mother when it is about 2 months old.

BALAENOPTERIDAE: RORQUAL FAMILY

There are 6 species of rorqual whale. All except the humpback whale are similar in appearance, but they differ in size and color. Most have about 300 baleen plates on each side of the jaws and there are a large number of grooves on the throat.

Minke Whale, *Balaenoptera acutorostrata* **LR:nt**

RANGE All oceans, temperate and polar areas

HABITAT Shallow water, estuaries, rivers, inland seas

SIZE 26–33 ft (8–10 m)

The smallest of the rorqual family, the minke whale has a distinctive, narrow pointed snout and 60 to 70 throat grooves. In polar areas, minke whales feed largely on planktonic crustaceans, but temperate populations eat fish and squid more often than any other baleen whale. Out of the breeding season, these whales tend to occur alone or in pairs, but they may congregate in rich feeding areas. Gestation lasts 10 or 11 months and calves are suckled for 6 months.

Sei Whale *Balaenoptera borealis* **EN**

RANGE All oceans (not polar regions)

HABITAT Open ocean

SIZE 49–65½ ft (15–20 m)

The sei whale is streamlined and flat-headed and can achieve speeds of 26 mph (50 km/h). It eats almost any kind of plankton, as well as fish and squid, usually feeding near the surface. Family groups of 5 or 6 whales occur and pair bonds are strong and may last for years. The gestation period is 12 months, and the calf is fed by its mother for 6 months.

Blue Whale *Balaenoptera musculus* **EN**

RANGE All oceans

HABITAT Open ocean

SIZE 82–105 ft (25–32 m)

The largest mammal that has ever existed, the blue whale may weigh more than 161 US t (146 te). Its body is streamlined and, despite its enormous bulk, it is graceful in the water. It has 64 to 94 grooves on its throat. These gigantic whales feed entirely on small planktonic crustaceans and, unlike many baleen whales, are highly selective, taking only a few species. They feed during the summer months, which they spend in nutrient-rich polar waters, and over this period take up to 4.4 US t (4.1 te) of small shrimps apiece each day.

In autumn, when ice starts to cover their feeding grounds, the blue whales migrate toward the Equator but eat virtually nothing while in the warmer water. They mate during this period and, after a gestation of 11 or 12 months, the calves are born in warm waters the following year.

Even though blue whales have been protected since 1967, populations of this extraordinary animal are still low, and it is in danger of extinction.

Humpback Whale

Megaptera novaeangliae **VU**

RANGE All oceans

HABITAT Oceanic, coastal waters

SIZE 48–62 ft (14.6–19 m)

The humpback has a distinctly curved lower jaw and an average of 22 throat grooves. Its most characteristic features are the many knobs on the body and the flippers, which are about 16 ft (5 m) long and scalloped at the front edges. Humpback whales are more gregarious than blue whales and are usually seen in family groups of 3 or 4, although they may communicate with many other groups.

In the southern hemisphere, humpbacks feed on planktonic crustaceans, but in the northern hemisphere they eat small fish. Populations in both hemispheres feed in polar regions in summer and then migrate to tropical breeding areas for the winter. The gestation period is 11 or 12 months, and a mother feeds her calf for almost a year.

Humpbacks perform the most extraordinary, complex songs of any animal. The songs may be repeated for hours on end and are specific to populations and areas. They may change from year to year.

BALAENIDAE: RIGHT WHALE FAMILY

It is in the 3 species of right whale that the baleen apparatus is most extremely developed. Right whales have enormous heads, measuring more than a third of their total body length, and highly arched upper jaws to carry the long baleen plates. They have no throat grooves.

Regarded by whalers as the "right" whales to exploit, they have been killed in such numbers by commercial whalers over the last century that they are rare today.

Bowhead Whale/Greenland Right Whale

Balaena mysticetus **LR:cd**

RANGE Arctic Ocean

HABITAT Coastal waters

SIZE 49–65½ ft (15–20 m)

The bowhead has a massive head and a body that tapers sharply toward the tail. Its jaws are strongly curved to accommodate the 15 ft (4.5 m) long baleen plates, the longest of any of the filter-feeding whales.

Bowheads feed on the smallest planktonic crustaceans, which they catch on the fine fringes of their baleen. They mate in early spring, the gestation period is 10 to 12 months, and the calf is fed for almost a year. Occasionally twins are produced.

HORSES AND TAPIRS

ORDER PERISSODACTYLA

There are only 3 surviving families of perissodactyl – or odd-toed, hoofed mammals: horses, tapirs and rhinoceroses. Nine other families, now extinct, are known from fossils.

EQUIDAE: HORSE FAMILY

Horses, asses and zebras make up a family of about 8 species of hoofed mammals, highly adapted for fast, graceful running. In this group the foot has evolved to a single hoof on an elongate third digit. The family has a natural distribution in Asia and Africa, but the domesticated horse has spread to other areas.

In the wild, all equids live in herds, migrate regularly and feed mainly on grass. Their teeth are adapted for grass-cropping and grinding, with chisel-shaped incisors and large premolars and molars, with convoluted surfaces. The skull is elongate to accommodate the large cheek teeth.

Common Zebra *Equus burchelli*

RANGE	E. and S. Africa
HABITAT	Grassy plains, lightly wooded savanna, hills
SIZE	Body: 6¼–7¾ ft (1.9–2.4 m) Tail: 17–22½ in (43–57 cm)

Great variation in pattern occurs in these zebras, both between individuals and the subspecies. Toward the south of the range, stripes on the hind parts of the body generally become lighter. The body is rounded, and the legs slender. A small erect mane runs down the back of the neck. The body varies from white to yellowish with light to dark brown or black stripes.

Common zebras leave their resting place at dawn and move to grazing grounds to feed on grass and sometimes leaves and bark. They must drink regularly.

Zebras live in families of up to 6 females and their young, each family led by an old male. When the male is 16 to 18 years old, he is peacefully replaced by a younger male of 6 to 8 years and then lives alone. Several families may form large herds, but they can still recognize each other by sight, sound and scent.

The female gives birth to a single young, rarely twins, after a gestation of about a

year. Until the foal learns to recognize its mother – in 3 or 4 days – she drives other animals away. It suckles for about 6 months and is independent at about a year.

Grevy's Zebra

Equus grevyi **EN**

RANGE	E. Africa: Kenya, Ethiopia
HABITAT	Savanna, semidesert
SIZE	Body: 8½ ft (2.6 m) Tail: 27½–29½ in (70–75 cm)

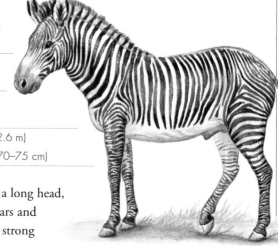

Grevy's zebra has a long head, broad, rounded ears and a relatively short, strong neck. An erect mane runs from its crown down the back of its neck. Its body is white with black stripes, both narrower and more numerous than those of the common zebra. Grevy's zebra grazes during the day, and rests in shade in the noon heat. It likes to drink daily. Mature males live alone, each in his own territory. Males without a territory form troops. Females and young live in separate troops of a dozen or more. In the dry season, male and female troops migrate. Lone males stay on unless there is a severe drought.

The female gives birth to a single young after a gestation of about a year. A foal can recognize its mother after a few days. It suckles for 6 months and stays with its mother for up to 2 years.

African Ass *Equus africanus* **CR**

RANGE	N.E. Africa
HABITAT	Open grassy plains, rugged rocky country, semidesert, mountains
SIZE	Shoulder height: 4 ft (1.2 m)

This ancestor of the domestic ass is rare in the wild due to hunting and competition from domestic stock. The remaining animals are probably cross-bred with domestic stock. Of the 4 subspecies, 1 is extinct and 2 nearly so.

The African ass has a

large head with long, narrow ears, and short, smooth hair, which varies from yellowish-brown to bluish-gray in color. It is a good climber and is adept at moving over rugged country. It feeds on grass, herbage and sometimes foliage, and needs to drink regularly. Most active at dusk and night-time and in the early morning, it spends much of the day resting in shade. Females live in loose-knit troops with their young or in mixed troops of young animals. Older males live alone or in male troops.

The female gives birth to 1 young after a gestation period of between 330 and 365 days.

Przewalski's Wild Horse *Equus przewalskii* **EW**

RANGE Mongolia, W. China

HABITAT Plains, semidesert

SIZE Body: 6–6½ ft (1.8–2 m) Tail: 35½ in (90 cm)

This ancestor of the domestic horse has an erect mane and no forelock. Populations have declined drastically because of hunting, cold winters and competition and interbreeding with domestic animals. True wild horses are now extinct, but they are bred in captivity as part of a breeding program including many zoos. They live in small herds, each led by a dominant male. Young are born in April or May.

Onager/Asiatic wild ass *Equus hemionus* **VU**

RANGE Iran, Afghanistan, Russia

HABITAT Steppe, gorges, river margins

SIZE Body: about 6½ ft (2 m) Tail: 16¾ in (42.5 cm)

The onager has declined due to human settlement, competition for grazing from domestic livestock, and hunting. In summer, the onager lives in high grassland areas, feeding on many types of grass. It needs a good supply of fresh water to survive. Onagers live in troops of up to 12 females and their young, each led by a dominant male. Females give birth to a single young after a gestation period of about a year.

TAPIRIDAE: TAPIR FAMILY

The 4 living species of tapir are thought to resemble the ancestors of the perissodactyls. These stocky, short-legged animals, have four toes on the forefeet and three on the hind feet. Short, bristly hair covers the body giving it a smooth appearance. The snout and upper lip are elongated into a short, mobile trunk. Tapirs are mainly nocturnal forest-dwellers and feed on vegetation. Of the 4 species, 3 occur in Central and South America and 1 in Southeast Asia.

Malayan Tapir *Tapirus indicus* **VU**

RANGE S.E. Asia: Myanmar to Malaysia, Sumatra

HABITAT Humid, swampy forest

SIZE Body: 8¼ ft (2.5 m) Tail: 2–4 in (5–10 cm)

The Malayan tapir has a unique grayish-black and white coloration. Its trunk is longer and stronger than those of the tapirs from South America. A shy, solitary animal, it is active only at night. It eats aquatic vegetation and the leaves, buds and fruit of some land plants. It swims well and, if alarmed, heads for water.

The female gives birth to a single young after a gestation of about 395 days. The young tapir is camouflaged with stripes and spots, which disappear at about 6 to 8 months. Malayan tapirs have been badly affected by the destruction of large areas of forest and are now extremely rare.

Brazilian Tapir *Tapirus terrestris* **LR:nt**

RANGE South America: Colombia, Venezuela, south to Brazil and Paraguay

HABITAT Rain forest, near water or swamps

SIZE Body: 6½ ft (2 m) Tail: 2–3 in (5–8 cm)

The Brazilian tapir is nearly always found near water. It moves quickly even over rugged land and is a good swimmer. It is dark brown and its low erect mane runs from the crown to the back of the neck. Its mobile snout is used to feed on leaves, buds, shoots, small branches, fruit, grass, and water plants.

The female gives birth to a single spotted and striped young after a gestation period of 390 to 400 days.

RHINOCEROSES AND HYRAXES

RHINOCEROTIDAE: RHINOCEROS FAMILY

There are 5 species of rhinoceros, found in Africa and Southeast Asia, and all have huge heads with one or two horns and a prehensile upper lip, which helps them to browse on tough plant material. The legs are short and thick, with three hoofed toes on each foot, and the skin is extremely tough, with only a few hairs. Male and female look similar. Females have smaller horns.

Indian Rhinoceros

Rhinoceros unicornis **EN**

RANGE Nepal, N.E. India

HABITAT Grassland in swampy areas

SIZE Body: 13¾ ft (4.2 m) Tail: 29½ in (75 cm)

The Indian rhinoceros is the largest of the Asian species. It has a thick, dark-gray hide, studded with many small protuberances. The skin falls into deep folds at the joints.

Both sexes have a single horn on the head, but the female's horn is smaller. Generally a solitary animal, the Indian rhinoceros feeds in the morning and evening on grass, weeds and twigs and rests during the rest of the day.

Females give birth to 1 young after a gestation of about 16 months. Calves suckle for about 2 years.

Sumatran Rhinoceros *Dicerorhinus sumatrensis* **CR**

RANGE Indonesia, Malaysia, Myanmar, Thailand, Vietnam

HABITAT Dense forest, near streams

SIZE 8¼–9¼ ft (2.5–2.8 m) Tail: about 23½ in (60 cm)

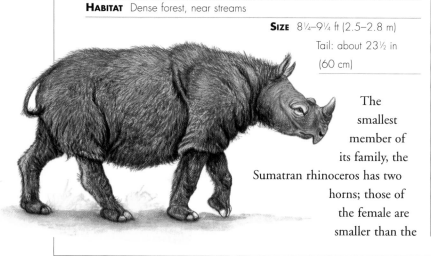

The smallest member of its family, the Sumatran rhinoceros has two horns; those of the female are smaller than the

male's. Bristlelike hairs are scattered over the thick skin and fringe the edges of the ears. Sumatran rhinoceroses are usually solitary, although a male and female pair may live together. They feed mostly in the early morning and evening on leaves, twigs, fruit and bamboo shoots and may trample small trees in order to browse on their foliage. Like other rhinoceroses, this species has good hearing and sense of smell, but its sight is poor.

The female bears a single young after a gestation period of between 7 and 8 months.

Square-lipped/White Rhinoceros

Ceratotherium simum **LR:cd**

RANGE Africa: N.W. Uganda and adjacent regions; Zimbabwe to N. South Africa

HABITAT Savanna

SIZE Body: 11¾–16½ ft (3.6–5 m) Tail: 3–3¼ ft (90 cm–1 m)

The largest living land animal after the elephant, the square-lipped rhinoceros has a hump on its neck and a long head, which it carries low. Its muzzle is broad, with a squared upper lip. This rhinoceros is generally grayish in color but takes on the color of the mud in which it has been wallowing.

The square-lipped rhinoceros is a placid animal and tends to flee from trouble rather than attack. Each old male occupies his own territory, which may be shared by younger males, but the female is sociable and is usually accompanied by her own young and another female with young. They feed only on grass, grazing and resting from time to time throughout the day and night.

The female gives birth to 1 calf after a gestation of about 16 months. The calf suckles for at least a year and stays with its mother for 2 or 3 years, leaving only when the next calf is born.

Black Rhinoceros *Diceros bicornis* **CR**

RANGE Africa: S. Chad and Sudan to South Africa

HABITAT Bush country, grassland, woodland

SIZE Body: 9¾–11¾ ft (3–3.6 m) Tail: 23½–27½ in (60–70 cm)

The black rhinoceros is actually gray, but its color varies depending on the mud in which it wallows. It has a large head which bears two and sometimes three horns, but no hump. The upper lip is pointed and mobile and helps it to browse on the leaves, buds and shoots of small trees and bushes. Black rhinoceroses live alone, except for mothers and young. Adults live in overlapping ranges, with boundaries marked by dung heaps. Male and female remain together for only a few days when mating. The female gives birth to 1 calf after a gestation of about 15 months. The calf suckles for about a year and stays with its mother for 2 or 3 years, until her next calf is born.

ORDER HYRACOIDEA

PROCAVIIDAE: HYRAX FAMILY

Small herbivores found in Africa and the Middle East, the hyraxes, conies or dassies generally look like rabbits with short, rounded ears. There are about 6 species, and the family is the only one in its order. Some hyraxes are agile climbers in trees, while others inhabit rocky koppies, or small hills. The feet have flattened nails, resembling hoofs, and a central moist cup that works as an adhesive pad when the hyrax climbs.

Tree Hyrax *Dendrohyrax arboreus*

RANGE Africa: Kenya to South Africa: Cape Province

HABITAT Forest

SIZE Body: 15¾–23½ in (40–60 cm)
Tail: absent

The tree hyrax is an excellent climber and lives in a tree hole or rock crevice where it rests during the day. It emerges in the afternoon or evening to feed in the trees and on the ground on leaves, grass, ferns, fruit and other plant material. Insects, lizards and birds' eggs are also eaten on occasion.

Tree hyraxes normally live in pairs and are extremely noisy animals, uttering a wide range of loud screams, squeals and grunts. A litter of 1 or 2 young is born after a gestation period of about 8 months.

Small-toothed Rock Hyrax *Heterohyrax brucei*

RANGE Africa: Egypt to South Africa: Transvaal; Botswana and Angola

HABITAT Open country, plains to mountains, forest, savanna

SIZE Body: 15¾–22½ in (40–57 cm)
Tail: absent

Despite its name, this hyrax lives among trees as well as rocks. Depending on its habitat, it finds shelter in crevices or holes. Rock hyraxes are sociable animals and they form colonies of up to 30 animals, each colony generally consists of several old males, many breeding females and their young. The rock hyraxes feed during the day, mainly on leaves of trees, but also on small plants and grass.

The female gives birth to 1 or 2 young, rarely 3, after a gestation period of between 7½ and 8 months.

Large-toothed Rock Hyrax *Procavia capensis*

RANGE Arabian Peninsula; Africa: N.E. Senegal to Somalia and N. Tanzania, S. Malawi, S. Angola to South Africa: Cape Province

HABITAT Rocky hillsides, rock piles

SIZE Body: 17–18½ in (43–47 cm)
Tail: absent

This hyrax lives among rocky outcrops and it is an agile climber. It feeds mostly on the ground on leaves, grass, small plants and berries, but readily climbs to feed on fruits, such as figs. In winter bark is eaten. The hyraxes spend much of the rest of the day lying in the sun or shade in order to maintain their body temperature, and at night they huddle together in order to minimize loss of body heat. These hyraxes are sociable and live in colonies of 50 or more individuals.

Males are aggressive at mating time and reassert their dominance over rivals and younger males. The female gives birth to 1 to 6 young, usually 2 or 3, after a gestation period of between 7 and 8 months.

ELEPHANTS, DUGONG AND MANATEES

ORDER PROBOSCIDEA

The elephants are the only surviving representatives of this once diverse and widespread group, which formerly contained many species of huge herbivorous mammal.

ELEPHANTIDAE: ELEPHANT FAMILY

The two species of elephant are by far the largest terrestrial mammals; they may stand up to 13 ft (4 m) at the shoulder and weigh as much as 13,000 lb (5,900 kg). One species lives in Africa, the other in India and Southeast Asia. Elephants have thick, pillarlike legs, and their feet are flattened, expanded pads. On the head are huge ears, which are fanned to and fro to help dissipate excess body heat. The elephant's most remarkable of adaptations, the trunk, is an elongated nose and upper lip, which is extremely flexible and has a manipulative tip. This sensitive organ is used for gathering food, drinking, smelling and fighting.

Both species of elephant have suffered badly from destruction of forest and vegetation in their range, and large numbers have been killed for their ivory tusks. Although hunting is now strictly controlled, poaching continues.

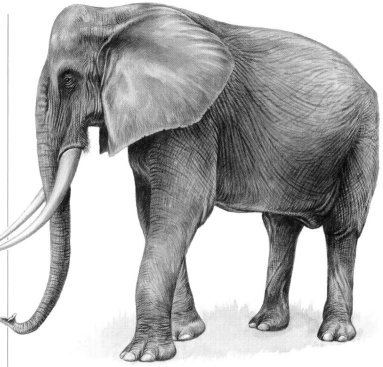

African Elephant *Loxodonta africana* **EN**

RANGE	Africa, south of the Sahara
HABITAT	Forest, savanna
SIZE	Body: 19¾–24½ ft (6–7.5 m) Tail: 3¾–4¼ ft (1–1.3 m)

The African elephant has larger ears and tusks than the Asian species and two finger-like extensions at the end of its trunk. Females are smaller than males and have shorter tusks. Elephants rest in the midday heat and have one or two periods of rest at night, but are otherwise active at any time, roaming in search of food. Depending on its size, an elephant may consume up to 440 lb (200 kg) of plant material a day, all of which is grasped with the trunk and placed in the mouth. The diet includes leaves, shoots, twigs, roots and fruit from many plants, as well as cultivated crops on occasion.

Elephants are social animals, particularly females. A troop centers around several females and their young of various ages. As they mature, young males form separate all-male troops. Old males may be shunned by the herd when they are displaced by younger males.

Breeding occurs at any time of year, and a female on heat may mate with more than one male. The gestation period is about 22 months, and usually only 1 young is born. The female clears a secluded spot for the birth and is assisted by other females. The calf is suckled for at least 2 years and remains with its mother even longer. She may have several calves of different ages under her protection and gives birth every 2 to 4 years.

Asian Elephant *Elephas maximus* **EN**

RANGE	India, Sri Lanka, S.E. Asia, Sumatra
HABITAT	Forest, grassy plains
SIZE	Body: 18–21¼ ft (5.5–6.5 m) Tail: 4–5 ft (1.2–1.5 m)

Although an equally impressive animal, the Asian elephant has smaller ears than its African counterpart, a more humped back and only one fingerlike extension at the end of its mobile trunk. The female is smaller than the male and has only rudimentary tusks.

The main social unit is a herd led by an old female and including several females, their young and an old male, usually all related. Other males may live alone but near to a herd, and will sometimes feed or mate with members of the herd. The herd rests in the heat of the day, but spends much of the rest of the time feeding on grass, leaves, shoots, and fruit, all of which

they search out and grasp with their trunks. Their hearing and sense of smell are excellent, and eyesight poor.

The male's heat period, called musth, may be accompanied by a secretion from a gland on the side of the head, and animals can become excited and unpredictable. The female usually gives birth to a single young after a gestation of about 21 months.

ORDER SIRENIA

Sirenians are the only completely aquatic herbivorous mammals. The 2 families – dugongs and manatees – contain 4 species. All have streamlined bodies and flipperlike forelimbs. The hind limbs have been lost in the formation of a tail.

DUGONGIDAE: DUGONG FAMILY

There is now only 1 species in this family, the other member, Steller's sea cow, having been exterminated in the 18th century by excessive hunting, only 25 years after its discovery.

Dugong *Dugong dugon* **VU**

RANGE Coast of E. Africa, Indian Ocean, Red Sea to N. Australia

HABITAT Coastal waters

SIZE Up to 9¾ ft (3 m)

The dugong is a
large, but
streamlined, animal,
identified by its tail, which has a crescent-shaped, horizontal fluke. Its head is heavy, with a fleshy, partially divided snout. The male has two tusks formed from the incisor teeth, but these are usually barely visible under the fleshy lips. Its nostrils are placed on the upper surface of the muzzle, so the dugong can breathe, while remaining almost submerged. Seaweed and sea grass are its main food.

The dugong is a shy, solitary animal, and it leads a quiet, sedentary life, lying on the sea bed for much of the time and only rising to the surface every couple of minutes in order to breathe.

Little is known of the dugong's reproductive habits, but the gestation period is thought to be about a year. The single young is born in the water and is helped to the surface by its mother.

TRICHECHIDAE: MANATEE FAMILY

There are 3 species of manatee; 2 of which live in fresh water in West Africa and the Amazon, and the third in coastal waters of the tropical Atlantic Ocean.

American Manatee

Trichecus manatus **VU**

RANGE Atlantic Ocean:
Florida to Guyana

HABITAT Coastal waters

SIZE Up to 9¾ ft (3 m)

The manatee has a heavier body than the dugong and is also distinguished by its oval, horizontal tail fluke. There are three nails in each of its flippers, which the manatee uses to gather food. It feeds at night, foraging by touch and smell. Its diet is quite varied, since it will eat any sort of vegetation and also often also takes in small invertebrate animals with the plants.

For much of the day, the manatee lies on the sea bed, rising every couple of minutes in order to breathe at the surface.

Manatees are social animals and live in family groups, which sometimes gather together in larger herds.

The gestation period is about a year. One young is born in water and is helped by its mother to the surface to breathe.

BIRDS

Feathered conquerors of the air.

DISTRIBUTED OVER THE SURFACE OF THE EARTH AND INHABITING ALMOST EVERY POSSIBLE AREA OTHER THAN THE DEEP OCEAN ARE OVER 9,000 SPECIES OF BIRD. RANGING IN SIZE FROM TINY HUMMINGBIRDS, WEIGHING ONLY A FEW GRAMS, TO THE OSTRICHES THAT STAND TALLER THAN THE AVERAGE HUMAN BEING, BIRDS HAVE A SPECIAL PLACE IN HUMAN CONSCIOUSNESS. BIRDS ARE OFTEN BOLDLY MARKED OR COLORED, HAVE COMPLEX FAMILY AND GROUP BEHAVIOR, ARE EASILY OBSERVED AND, ABOVE ALL, HAVE THE POWER OF FLIGHT. CONSEQUENTLY THEY HAVE ALWAYS STIMULATED MUCH INTEREST, PLEASURE, WONDERMENT, EVEN ENVY, IN HUMAN BEINGS.

Reed Cormorant

Birds are warm-blooded, air-breathing vertebrates with four limbs, the front pair of which are modified to provide muscle -powered wings that, in the vast majority of living birds, give the potential for active flight. Birds can be unambiguously identified as such by their feathers – a feature which all birds, without exception, possess, and which no other member of the animal kingdom shares.

Much of the unique nature of a bird's body structure is linked to its need for a low take-off weight and a good power-to-weight ratio. Like mammals, birds are descended from reptilian ancestors. They have taken, evolutionarily speaking, the heavy-boned, scaly, elongate body of a reptile and turned it into a light, compact flying machine with a feather-covered outer surface. The bones have become slim, thin-walled and filled with air sacs, deriving from the walls of the lungs. All skeletal structures are pared down to produce maximum strength with minimum weight, and the heavy reptilian skull has changed to a light, almost spherical cranium, terminating in a toothless beak covered with horny plates.

Like reptilian scales and mammalian hairs, feathers are constructed largely from the tough protein keratin. They exist in a vast range of shapes, sizes and colors and have a variety of functions: first, they provide a light, flexible, thermally insulating protective layer over the bird's surface, crucial for maintaining the bird's high constant body temperature, which can reach (42°C) 107.6°F. Second, the colors and patterns of

feathers are the prime means of visual communication between birds; third, and perhaps most importantly, the large aero-foiled shaped feathers of the wings and those of the tail provide the bird's flight surfaces. The wing feathers are attached to the highly modified bones of the forelimbs and provide the main lift and thrust for flight, while the tail feathers help the bird steer during flight. The tail feathers are attached to a stumpy remnant of a tail, quite unlike that of the birds' reptilian ancestors.

The earliest fossil bird, *Archaeopteryx*, dating from the upper Jurassic period 160 million years ago, demonstrates an intriguing intermediate stage in the progressive loss of reptilian characteristics as birds evolved. *Archaeopteryx* had feathers and wings, but it also had teeth in its jaws and a typically reptilian set of tail vertebrae – it was, effectively, a feathered, winged reptile.

Although air offers relatively little resistance to motion, take off and active flight require a massive output of power from the bird. The relatively huge breast muscles of a bird,

Northern Goshawk

Black Capped Lory

attached to a deep keel on the breastbone, deliver this power to the basal bone of the wing, the humerus. For these muscles to operate at the necessary high power output, good blood circulation is required and an exceptionally efficient respiratory system, to supply oxygen at the required rate. Birds have four-chambered hearts, similar to those of mammals, but independently evolved, which can operate extremely rapidly: a sparrow's heart beats 500 times a minute, a hummingbird's up to 1,000 times a minute in flight.

Equally a bird's respiratory system seems to take the air-breathing lung to the limits of its capability. Paired lungs, with throughflow, are only one part of the bird's extensive and efficient respiratory system, which also includes many air sacs.

The ability to extract oxygen from the air much more rapidly and efficiently than a mammal is able to do helps to explain the astoundingly fast wing-beats of a hummingbird, the lightning flight of some swifts and the capacity of some birds to fly at altitudes where the atmosphere contains little oxygen.

In some bird families it is usual for males and females to have similar plumage; in others the sexes differ in appearance. Although there are some interesting exceptions (for example, the females of many species of birds of prey are larger than the males), when the sexes differ, the male bird is the larger and more colorfully feathered, and the female has duller plumage, which may help to conceal her on the nest. For most, but not all birds, there is a single breeding season in any year. Typically in this period, cock birds find and protect nesting territories and may sing or display to intimidate rival males and attract mates. Fertilization is internal, but apart from a few species, the male bird does not possess a penis but only a small erectile protuberance at the base of his cloaca (the reproductive opening) through which sperm passes into the female's cloaca.

Birds lay eggs containing large yolks, the food reserves for the developing embryo, surrounded by a tough, mineralized shell. The egg is formed as the ovum passes from the ovary down the oviduct to the outside world, successive layers of white, inner and outer shell membranes, being added on the way. Most birds lay their eggs in some form of nest, where they are incubated, or kept warm, by one or both parents while the embryo develops. The young of some birds, such as ducks and pheasants, hatch covered with downy feathers and are able to walk immediately, while the young of others, such as blackbirds and most other songbirds are born naked and helpless and need a period of feeding and care from the parents.

Among the 23 orders of living birds, a remarkable variety of modifications has taken place to the basic avian body, with the most crucial adaptations being to feet, legs, beaks and wings. There are large long-legged walking birds, such as ostriches, rheas, emus and cassowaries, that have completely lost the power of flight. There are other flightless birds, such as the penguins, that have wings adapted as underwater paddles. At the opposite extreme are the insectivorous swifts, birds so aerial that it is possible that their only contact with the ground throughout life may be at the nest. There are highly specialized predators of the night (owls, nightjars) and of the daylight hours (eagles, hawks, falcons), with strong beaks and killing talons. Almost any type of small animal or vegetable food is the diet of some bird species – a shrike pouncing on a grasshopper, a hummingbird extracting nectar and a parrot feeding on a jungle fruit, all testify to the breathtaking diversity of the bird kingdom.

Laminated Toucan

Cladogram showing possible phylogenetic relationships of birds.
Traditionally, birds have been placed in 27 or 28 orders. This
classification has been in place since the 1930s and was based
originally on evidence from fossil birds with more recent
modifications. As with any classification it can be difficult to tell the
difference between true phylogenetic relationships and the
similarities found between completely unrelated species that are the
result of convergence, the independent evolution of similar
characteristics and life-styles. Unrelated species have in the past been
"lumped" together in groups such as the "flycatchers" simply because
of similarities that have arisen independently. Attempts to take a
more objective view of bird classification have included the use of

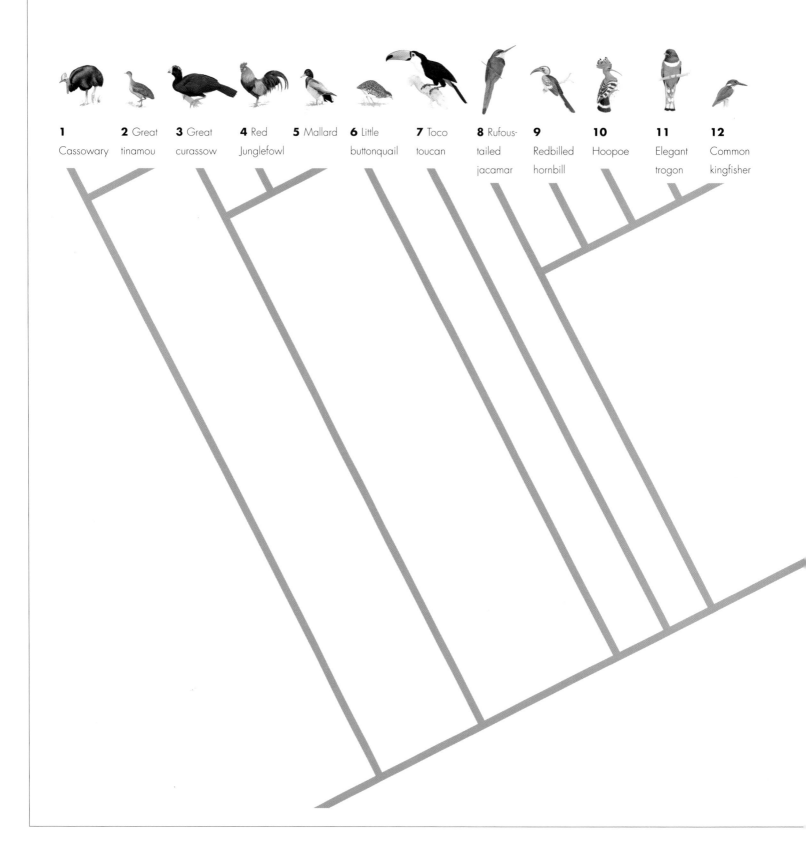

1
Cassowary

2 Great
tinamou

3 Great
curassow

4 Red
Junglefowl

5 Mallard

6 Little
buttonquail

7 Toco
toucan

8 Rufous-
tailed
jacamar

9
Redbilled
hornbill

10
Hoopoe

11
Elegant
trogon

12
Common
kingfisher

DNA analysis to determine affinities between birds. DNA (deoxyribonucleic acid) is the genetic material found in all body cells that determines an organism's characteristics. The more closely related two species are, the more similar the chemical composition of their respective DNA molecules. A new classification based on DNA analysis recognizes 23 orders, and is the one shown on this cladogram and the one used throughout this book. Although this provides a new framework for bird classification, it is still very much under review and will undoubtedly change in the future as new evidence appears and new criteria are employed to determine relationships between birds.

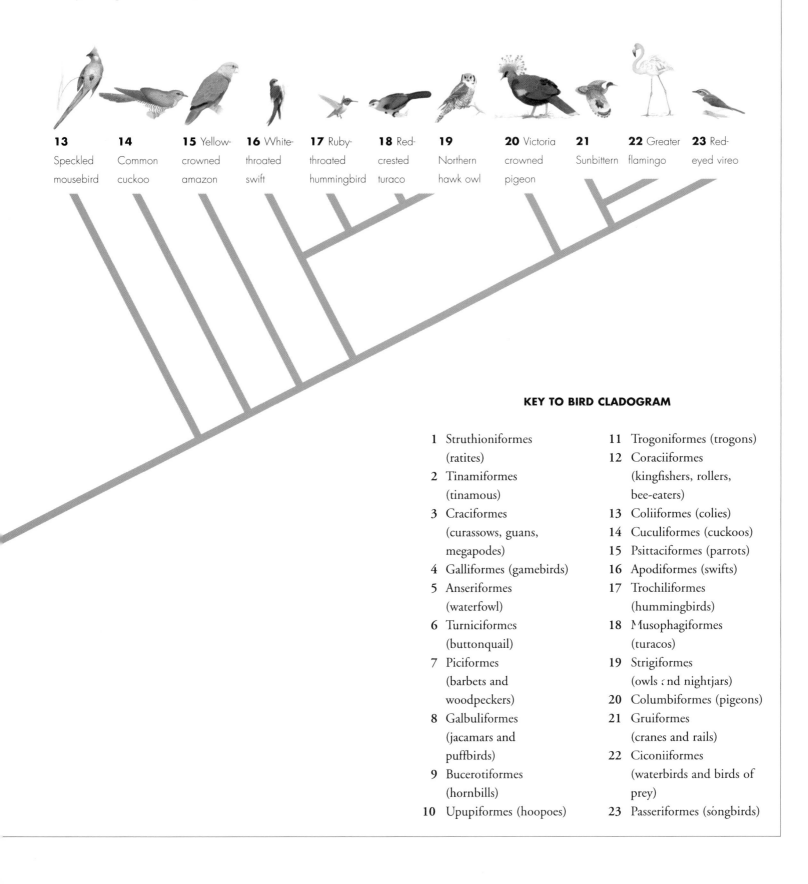

13 Speckled mousebird

14 Common cuckoo

15 Yellow-crowned amazon

16 White-throated swift

17 Ruby-throated hummingbird

18 Red-crested turaco

19 Northern hawk owl

20 Victoria crowned pigeon

21 Sunbittern

22 Greater flamingo

23 Red-eyed vireo

KEY TO BIRD CLADOGRAM

1 Struthioniformes (ratites)
2 Tinamiformes (tinamous)
3 Craciformes (curassows, guans, megapodes)
4 Galliformes (gamebirds)
5 Anseriformes (waterfowl)
6 Turniciformes (buttonquail)
7 Piciformes (barbets and woodpeckers)
8 Galbuliformes (jacamars and puffbirds)
9 Bucerotiformes (hornbills)
10 Upupiformes (hoopoes)

11 Trogoniformes (trogons)
12 Coraciiformes (kingfishers, rollers, bee-eaters)
13 Coliiformes (colies)
14 Cuculiformes (cuckoos)
15 Psittaciformes (parrots)
16 Apodiformes (swifts)
17 Trochiliformes (hummingbirds)
18 Musophagiformes (turacos)
19 Strigiformes (owls and nightjars)
20 Columbiformes (pigeons)
21 Gruiformes (cranes and rails)
22 Ciconiiformes (waterbirds and birds of prey)
23 Passeriformes (songbirds)

RATITES

ORDER STRUTHIONIFORMES

Ratites is the informal name given to a mixed group of running birds with some dramatic morphological differences from all other birds that belong to the order Struthioniformes. Apart from the fowl-sized kiwis of New Zealand, ratites are all extremely large ground-living birds, with massive, muscular legs for powerful running. Their wings are much reduced in size and are not functional. The ratite breastbone is flat and small and has no central keel – in other birds this keel serves for the attachment of the flight muscles. The word "ratite" means "raft-like" as opposed to carinate, applicable to all other birds and meaning "keeled".

There are four living ratite families – ostrich, emu and cassowaries, rheas, and kiwi.

STRUTHIONIDAE: OSTRICH FAMILY

Ostriches are the largest living birds. There is now only a single species, living in Africa, but formerly the family's range extended from southern Europe to Mongolia as well as throughout Africa.

Ostrich *Struthio camelus*

RANGE Africa

HABITAT Grasslands, arid land

SIZE 6–9 ft (1.75–2.75 m) tall

The ostrich is too big to fly but has become so perfectly adapted to high-speed running that it is the fastest creature on two legs. At speeds of up to 44 mph (70 km/h), it can easily outstrip

most enemies. Powerful legs, flexible knees and supple two-toed feet are its adaptations for speed. The ostrich has lost its strong wing feathers, but the male has soft, curling plumes which were once much in demand for fashionable hats and boas. Female birds are slightly smaller than males and have brownish plumage and off-white wings and tails. Juveniles are grayish-brown.

Ostriches eat mostly plant food, but occasionally feed on small reptiles. They are nomadic, wandering in small groups in search of food. At breeding time, the male collects a harem of 2 to 5 females. One female scrapes a shallow pit in the ground in which to lay her eggs and the rest of the harem probably use the same nest. The eggs are the largest laid by any bird – the equivalent in volume of about 40 hen's eggs. The male bird takes over the incubation of the eggs at night and shares in the task of nurturing the young.

RHEIDAE: RHEA FAMILY

Rheas are the South American equivalents of the ostrich and are the heaviest of the New World birds. Although they have larger wings than other ratites, they are still unable to fly, but they are good swimmers and fast runners. There are two species.

Greater Rhea *Rhea americana* **LR:nt**

RANGE South America, east of the Andes

HABITAT Open country

SIZE 5 ft (1.5 m) tall

Greater rheas live in flocks of between 20 and 30 birds. Male and female birds look much alike. They feed on plants, seeds, insects and some small animals. At breeding time, the male bird displays, and gathers together a harem of females. He then leads his mated females to a shallow nest which he has prepared, and they all lay their eggs in this one nest making a clutch of up to 18 eggs in total which the male rhea then incubates.

CASUARIIDAE: CASSOWARY FAMILY

This family contains the one surviving species of emu – the second largest living bird – and three species of cassowaries. Emus live in the open country of Australia and can run fast. Cassowaries are found in the tropical forests of Australasia, including some islands. They are large, powerful birds, well adapted for forest life. Because of the isolating effects of island habitats, many races have evolved with minor differences.

Emu *Dromaius novaehollandiae*

RANGE Australia

HABITAT Arid plains, woodland, desert

SIZE 6½ ft (2 m) tall

Emus have remained common in Australia despite having been destroyed as serious pests on farmland. They can run at speeds of up to 30 mph (48 km/h) and also swim well. Fruit, berries and insects make up the bulk of their diet. The female lays between 7 and 10 dark-green eggs, with a characteristic pimply texture, in a hollow in the ground. The male incubates the eggs for about 60 days.

Southern Cassowary *Casuarius casuarius* **VU**

RANGE N. Australia, New Guinea

HABITAT Rain forest

SIZE 5 ft (1.5 m) tall

The southern cassowary is an impressive bird with long, hairlike quills which protect it from the forest undergrowth. Its wings are vestigial, but its legs are extremely powerful and armed with sharp-toed feet, capable of inflicting severe wounds. The bald but brightly colored head and neck bear brilliant wattles and a horny casque. As the cassowary moves through the dense forest in search of seeds, fruits and berries, it holds this prominent casque well forward to help break a path. Male and female look alike, but the female is larger. The female lays 3 to 6 green eggs in a shallow, leaf-lined nest on the ground.

APTERYGIDAE: KIWI FAMILY

Kiwis are flightless forest birds. There are 3 species, all of which are found in New Zealand only.

Brown Kiwi *Apteryx australis* **VU**

RANGE New Zealand

HABITAT Forest

SIZE 27½ in (70 cm)

The brown kiwi, which is the national emblem of New Zealand, is a rarely seen, nocturnal creature. It has rudimentary wings concealed under coarse, hairlike body feathers. Its legs are short and stout with powerful claws, which it uses for scratching around the forest floor in search of the insects, worms and berries which make up its diet. The nostrils are at the tip of the bird's pointed bill and it seems to have a good sense of smell – rare among birds.

Females are larger than males, but the sexes otherwise look similar. The female lays 1 or 2 eggs in a burrow where they are incubated by the male. Each egg weighs about 1 lb (450 g) and is exceptionally large in proportion to the adult bird's body.

TINAMOUS, MEGAPODES AND CURASSOWS

ORDER TINAMIFORMES

TINAMIDAE: TINAMOU FAMILY

Tinamous are fowllike ground birds, found in a variety of habitats from Mexico to Argentina. They can fly, but are weak and clumsy and, although built for running, their best defence is to remain still, relying on their protective coloring. They feed on seeds, berries and insects. There are 47 species of tinamou.

Great Tinamou *Tinamus major*

RANGE S. Mexico to Bolivia and Brazil

HABITAT Rain forest, cloud forest

SIZE 18 in (46 cm)

The great tinamou, like all members of its family, is polygamous and females lay up to 12 eggs, often in different nests. With their vivid, clear colors – blue, green and pink – and highly glazed surface, these eggs are among the most beautiful of all birds' eggs.

ORDER CRACIFORMES

This order of moderate to large gamebirds includes two families – megapodes are ground-dwellers with a unique nesting technique; curassows, guans and chachalacas live in forests and are predominantly arboreal although curassows spend some time on the ground.

MEGAPODIIDAE: MEGAPODE FAMILY

The 19 species in this family all occur from the Philippines to Australia and central Polynesia. Males and females look more or less alike, and all have large, strong legs and feet. They feed on insects, small vertebrate animals, seeds and fruit.

Megapodes do not brood their eggs in the normal way, but lay them in mounds of decaying vegetation or sand, and allow them to be incubated by natural heat.

Malleefowl *Leipoa ocellata* **VU**

RANGE S. Australia

HABITAT Mallee (arid eucalyptus woodland)

SIZE 21½–24 in (55–61 cm)

Despite its arid habitat, the male malleefowl manages to create an efficient incubator mound, which he is engaged in tending for much of the year. In winter, he digs a pit and fills it with plant material. Once this has been moistened by the winter rains, he covers it with sand, and the sealed-off vegetation starts to rot and to build up heat. The malleefowl keeps a constant check on the temperature by probing the mound with his beak and keeps it to about 91°F (33°C). He controls any temperature fluctuations by opening the mound in order to cool it, or by piling on more sand.

The laying season lasts some time, since the female lays her 15 to 35 eggs one at a time, at intervals of several days in holes made in the mound by the male. The chicks hatch about 7 weeks after laying and struggle out unaided. They are wholly independent and can fly within a day.

Common Scrubfowl *Megapodius freycinet*

RANGE E. Indonesia to Melanesia; N. and N.E. Australia

HABITAT Rain forest and drier areas

SIZE 17¾ in (45 cm)

An active, noisy bird, the scrubfowl seldom flies, but seeks refuge in trees if disturbed. In some areas these birds make simple incubation mounds in sand, which are then warmed by the sun or, on some islands, by volcanic activity. In rain forest, they make huge mounds, up to 16 ft (5 m) high, containing decomposing plant material. The eggs are laid in tunnels dug into the mound.

CRACIDAE: CURASSOW FAMILY

There are about 50 species in this family, found in the neotropical zone from south Texas to northern Argentina. All are nonmigratory forest birds, often adapted for a tree-dwelling life. Many species have crests or casques on their heads.

Great Curassow *Crax rubra*

RANGE Mexico to Ecuador
HABITAT Tropical rain forest
SIZE 37 in (94 cm)

Great curassows roost and nest in trees, but also spend a good deal of time on the ground. They feed on fruit, leaves and berries. The males have a loud, booming ventriloquial call that seems to be amplified by the elongated trachea. This call is used in courtship display and to threaten other males.

Curassows make an untidy nest of twigs and leaves in a bush or tree and lay 2 eggs. Both parents feed and care for the chicks.

Nocturnal Curassow *Nothocrax urumutum*

RANGE South America: upper Amazon basin
HABITAT Tropical rain forest
SIZE 26 in (66 cm)

The nocturnal curassow is, in fact, active during the day, searching for its plant food. It sings only at night, however, making a booming call. In males, the voice is amplified by means of an extended trachea. The sexes look alike, with bare, brightly colored faces, ample crests and brown and rufous plumage.

Crested Guan *Penelope purpurascens*

RANGE Mexico, south to Venezuela, Ecuador
HABITAT Lowland rain forest and drier areas
SIZE 35 in (89 cm)

Primarily tree-living birds, crested guans forage in small groups up in the treetops, walking slowly along the branches and leaping across gaps. They will, however, come down to the ground to collect fallen fruit and seeds and to find drinking water. Male and female birds look alike.

In the breeding season, guans perform a wing-drumming display. While in flight, the bird begins to beat its wings at twice the normal speed, producing a whirring sound that is maintained for several seconds. A bulky nest, sited in a tree, is made from twigs and lined with leaves. The usual clutch is 2 or 3 eggs, and the female guan does most of the incubation.

Plain Chachalaca *Ortalis vetula*

RANGE USA: extreme S. Texas; Mexico, Central America
HABITAT Brush, thickets in rain forest; drier areas
SIZE 20–24 in (51–61 cm)

The plain chachalaca's common name is derived from its three syllable call, "cha-cha-lak", and like the curassow's, its voice is amplified by its elongated trachea. Groups of birds set up a deafening chorus, morning and evening. Primarily a tree-dwelling bird, the plain chachalaca feeds on berries, fruit, leaves and shoots and some insects. It also comes down to the ground to search for some of its food. A small frail nest is made of twigs, up in a tree or bush, and the female incubates the clutch of 3 or 4 eggs. Male and female chachalacas look alike.

PHEASANTS, GROUSE AND TURKEYS

ORDER GALLIFORMES

Galliformes are typical gamebirds. There are three families in the order – pheasants and their relatives; guineafowl; and New World quails.

PHASIANIDAE: PHEASANT, GROUSE, AND TURKEY FAMILY

This large and complex family of small to large gamebirds includes quails, partridges, pheasants, Old World quails, grouse, and turkeys. The 177 species in the family are found in open to forest habitats from arctic tundra to tropical forests in all continents apart from South America and Antarctica. Most are plump, rounded birds which usually feed and nest on the ground, but often roost for the night in the trees. Their wings are short and powerful and capable of strong, but not sustained, low-level flight. Most are seed-eating birds which scratch around for food with their stout, unfeathered legs and strong claws, but many also eat insects and other small invertebrates as well as fruits and berries.

Males and females have different plumage coloration in many species, particularly the larger pheasants. Some of the smaller, plainer birds are monogamous, while in the more ornate species, the males tend to be polygamous. The nest is usually simple, often a scrape on the ground; chicks are born fully covered with down and can leave the nest soon after hatching.

Many members of this family have been successfully introduced outside their native range. Some are well known as gamebirds, hunted for sport and eaten by humans.

Common Quail *Coturnix coturnix*

RANGE Europe, Asia, east to Lake Baikal; N. India, Africa; winters Mediterranean coast, Africa, Asia to S. India, Thailand

HABITAT Grassland, farmland

SIZE 7 in (18 cm)

One of the smallest birds in the pheasant family, the quail is a neat, rounded bird with a weak bill and legs. The female resembles the male in build, but has an unmarked buff throat and a closely spotted breast. A rarely seen bird, the quail forages in the undergrowth and although it can fly it tends to run through vegetation in order to escape danger, rather than flying. It flies considerable distances when migrating. It feeds mainly on seeds, but eats some small invertebrates, particularly in the summer.

Breeding takes place in early summer, and the female lays one clutch of 9 to 15 eggs in a plant-lined scrape on the ground. She incubates her eggs for 16 to 21 days.

Painted Quail *Coturnix chinensis*

RANGE India to S.E. China, Malaysia, Indonesia, Australia

HABITAT Swamp, grassland

SIZE 6 in (15 cm)

This tiny bird is typical of the eastern quails, which tend to be more boldly patterned than the European birds. The female painted quail has duller plumage than the male, being mainly buff-colored with a barred breast. Painted quails forage in vegetation and feed on seeds and insects.

The female lays 4 to 8 eggs in a shallow scrape on the ground. She incubates the clutch for about 16 days.

Himalayan Snowcock *Tetraogallus himalayensis*

RANGE W. Himalayas

HABITAT Mountain slopes

SIZE 22 in (56 cm)

The Himalayan snowcock is one of 7 species of snowcock, all of which are found at high altitudes in Asia. Typical of its group, it is a large bird with coloration which blends well with its environment. In the early morning, pairs or groups of up to 5 snowcocks fly down the hillsides from their roosts to find water to drink. The rest of the day is spent slowly coming back up, feeding on the way on roots, tubers, green plants, berries and seeds.

Breeding takes place between April and June. Courting males are especially noisy at this time, making loud five-note whistles. The female lays 5 to 7 eggs in a hollow scrape in the ground among stones. She incubates the clutch for 27 or 28 days.

Red-legged Partridge *Alectoris rufa*

RANGE S.W. Europe to S.E. France, N. Italy, Corsica; introduced in Britain, Azores, Madeira and Canary Islands

HABITAT Scrub, moorland, farmland

SIZE 12½–13¼ in (32–34 cm)

A typical partridge, with a larger bill, stronger legs and longer tail than the quails, the red-legged partridge is distinguished by the white stripe above each eye, the black-bordered white throat and the red bill and legs. Males and females look alike, but juveniles are less vividly colored. These birds roost in trees and bushes but feed on the ground, mainly on plants, although they occasionally eat insects and frogs. They are reluctant to fly, and prefer to escape danger by running. Breeding begins in April or May. Red-legged partridges are monogamous and make long-lasting pair bonds. The female lays 10 to 16 eggs in a shallow scrape which the male makes on the ground and lines with leaves. The clutch is incubated by both parents for about 23 or 24 days.

Red-necked Francolin *Francolinus afer*

RANGE Africa, south of the Equator, except S.W.

HABITAT Bush, cultivated land, savanna

SIZE 16 in (41 cm)

The francolins are large gamebirds, with strong bills and characteristic patches of bare skin on the head or neck. Over 30 species occur in Africa, but a few francolins live in Asia. The red-necked francolin has red skin around its eyes and on its neck. It is typical of the group. Its breast is covered with broad dark streaks which help to camouflage it. Males and females look alike.

In small family groups, francolins forage for plant food and insects. They fly well and take refuge in trees if disturbed. They nest on the ground and females lay 5 to 9 eggs.

Red Spurfowl *Galloperdix spadicea*

RANGE India

HABITAT Brush, scrub, bamboo, jungle, woodland

SIZE 14¼ in (36 cm)

A type of partridge, the male red spurfowl has distinctive scalloped plumage and naked red skin around each eye. The female's grayish plumage is barred and spotted with black.

Pairs or groups of up to 5 spurfowl forage together, scratching in the undergrowth for seeds, tubers and berries, as well as slugs, snails and termites.

The timing of the breeding season varies from area to area, according to conditions; although this is usually between January and June, it can be at any time of year. The nest is a shallow scrape on the ground dug among bamboo or scrub, and scantily lined with a few leaves or blades of grass. The female lays 3 to 5 eggs which she incubates alone. The male helps to care for the young.

Crested Partridge/Roulroul *Rollulus rouloul*

RANGE Myanmar to Sumatra and Borneo

HABITAT Floor of dense forest on lowland or hills

SIZE 10 in (25.5 cm)

The crested partridge is the most attractive and unusual of the wood partridges. The male is instantly recognizable by his red brushlike crest; he also has red skin around the eyes and a red patch on his bill.

The female bird has a few long feathers on her head but lacks the crest.

These partridges move in mixed groups of up to 12, occasionally more, feeding on seeds, fruit, insects and snails. They lay 5 or 6 eggs in a domed nest, which is atypical for the family. The young return to the nest at night.

PHEASANTS CONTINUED

Temminck's Tragopan *Tragopan temminckii* **LR:nt**

RANGE Mountains of W. China, N. Myanmar and S.E. Tibet

HABITAT Forest

SIZE 25¼ in (64 cm)

Like all the 5 species of tragopan, the male Temminck's tragopan is a striking bird, with beautiful, elaborate plumage. The female is much plainer, with rufous to grayish-brown plumage on the upperparts and a buff or white throat and light-brown underparts.

This tragopan is even more unsocial and more arboreal in its habits than other tragopans and prefers cool, damp forest. It feeds on seeds, buds, leaves, berries and insects.

At the start of the breeding season, the male courts his mate by displaying his brilliant plumage. The nest is made in a tree, and the female lays 3 to 6 eggs.

Red Junglefowl *Gallus gallus*

RANGE Himalayas to S. China, S.E. Asia, Sumatra, Java; introduced in Sulawesi, Lesser Sunda Islands

HABITAT Forest, scrub, cultivated land

SIZE 17–30 in (43–76 cm) including tail: 11 in (28 cm) in male

The ancestor of the domestic fowl, the red junglefowl is a colorful bird. The female is much smaller and duller than the male. She has mainly brown plumage and some chestnut on the head and neck. Several races of red junglefowl occur which vary slightly in appearance.

They are gregarious birds, gathering in flocks of up to 50 or so to feed on grain, grass shoots and crops, fruit, berries, insects and their larvae.

The breeding season is usually March to May. The female scrapes a hollow in the ground near a bush or bamboo clump and lines it with leaves. She incubates the clutch of 5 or 6 eggs for 19 to 21 days.

Gray Peacock-pheasant *Polyplectron bicalcaratum*

RANGE Himalayas to Hainan; S.E. Asia: Burma, Thailand, Indo-China

HABITAT Forest

SIZE 22–30 in (56–76 cm)

The gray peacock-pheasant is one of 6 species in the genus *Polyplectron*, all of which occur in India, Southeast Asia or Sumatra. The female is smaller than the decorative male and has fewer, smaller eye-spots, which are black with white borders. They are secretive, yet noisy, birds and feed on grain, fruit, berries and insects.

The male displays to his mate, calling as he spreads his tail and wing coverts. The female lays 2 to 6 eggs in a nest on the ground and incubates the clutch for about 21 days.

Golden Pheasant *Chrysolophus pictus* **LR:nt**

RANGE W. China; introduced in Britain

HABITAT Scrub on rocky hillsides; introduced in woodland

SIZE Male: 38½–42½ in (98–108 cm)
Female: 24–25½ in (63–65 cm)

The spectacularly beautiful male golden pheasant has brilliant plumage and a crest of golden feathers. The female bird is much plainer, with various shades of brown plumage, streaked with black. Wild golden pheasants move in pairs or alone and are shy birds, alert to any danger. They have short wings and are reluctant to fly, preferring to run from danger. Seeds, leaves, shoots and insects are their main foods.

Little is known of the breeding habits of this pheasant in its natural habitat, but in Britain, it makes a shallow scrape on the ground and lines it with plant material. The female lays 5 to 12 eggs, which she incubates for 22 days, apparently hardly ever, if at all, leaving the nest during this period.

Common Pheasant

Phasianus colchicus

RANGE Caspian area, east
across C. Asia to China,
Korea, Japan and
Myanmar; introduced in
Europe, N. America, New Zealand

HABITAT Woodland, forest edge, marshes, agricultural land

SIZE Male: 30–35 in (76–89 cm) Female: 20¾–25¼ in (53–64 cm)

Extremely successful as an introduced species, the pheasant is probably the best known of all gamebirds. So many subspecies have now been introduced and crossed that the plumage of the male is highly variable, but a typical bird has a dark-green head and coppery upperparts, with fine, dark markings; many have a white collar. The female is less variable and has brown plumage.

In the wild, pheasants feed on plant material, such as seeds, shoots and berries, and on insects and small invertebrates. They are ground-dwelling birds and spend much of their time scratching for food in undergrowth. They run fast, and their flight is strong over short distances, although low.

Male pheasants are polygamous and have harems of several females. The female scrapes a shallow hollow in the ground, usually in thick cover, which she lines with plant material. She lays 7 to 15 eggs on consecutive days and begins the 22 to 27-day incubation only when the clutch is complete. The young are tended and led to food by the female, rarely with any help from the male. Pheasants produce only one brood a season.

Indian/Blue Peafowl

Pavo cristatus

RANGE India, Sri Lanka

HABITAT Forest, woodland, cultivated land

SIZE Male: 3–4 ft (92 cm–1.2 m) without
train; 6½–7¼ ft (2–2.25 m) in full plumage;
Female: 33¾ in (86 cm)

The magnificent Indian peafowl is so widely kept in captivity and in parks and gardens outside its native range that it is a familiar bird in much of the world. The cock is unmistakable, with his iridescent plumage, wiry crest and glittering train, adorned with eyespots. The smaller female, or peahen, has

brown and some metallic green plumage and a small crest.

Outside the breeding season, peafowls live in small flocks of 1 male and 3 to 5 hens, but after breeding, they may split into groups made up of adult males or females and young. They feed in the open, early in the morning and at dusk, and spend much of the rest of the day in thick undergrowth. Seeds, grain, groundnuts, shoots, flowers, berries, insects and small invertebrates are all eaten by these omnivorous birds, and they may destroy crops where they occur near cultivated land.

In the breeding season, the male bird displays – fully spreading his erect train to spectacular effect by raising and spreading the tail beneath it. With his wings trailing, he prances and struts in front of the female, periodically shivering the spread train and presenting his back view. The female may respond by a faint imitation of his posture. In the wild, the nest scrape is made in thick undergrowth, and the female incubates her 4 to 6 eggs for about 28 days.

Congo Peafowl *Afropavo congensis* **VU**

RANGE Africa: Congo basin

HABITAT Dense rain forest

SIZE 23½–27½ in (60–70 cm)

First described in 1936, the Congo peafowl is the only gamebird larger than a francolin native to Africa. The male bird has dark, glossy plumage and a crest of black feathers on the head, behind a tuft of white bristles. The female has a crest, but no bristles, and is largely rufous brown and black, with some metallic green plumage on her upperparts. The habits of Congo peafowls in the wild have seldom been documented, but they are believed to live in pairs and to take refuge and roost in trees. They feed on grain and fruit.

Congo peafowls are monogamous in captivity and build a nest of sticks in a tree. The female incubates the 3 or 4 eggs for about 26 days.

GROUSE, TURKEYS, GUINEA FOWL AND NEW WORLD QUAIL

Black Grouse *Tetrao tetrix*

RANGE N. Europe, N. Asia

HABITAT Moor, forest

SIZE 16–20 in (41–51 cm)

Social display is a particularly well-developed activity in the black grouse. In spring males, or blackcocks, gather at a traditional display ground, known as a lek which is used year after year. Each day at about sunrise, males call, dance and posture – each in his own patch of the lek – in order to attract the females. The male black grouse has a distinctive lyre-shaped tail which he spreads and displays in courtship. Females, or grayhens, are smaller than males and have mottled brown plumage and forked tails.

Black grouse are polygamous birds and a successful dominant male may mate with many females. Each female lays a clutch of 6 to 11 eggs in a shallow leaf-lined hollow on the ground. She incubates the eggs for 24 to 29 days.

Prairie Chicken *Tympanuchus cupido*

RANGE C. North America

HABITAT Prairie

SIZE 16½–18 in (42–46 cm)

This increasingly rare bird was once common over a large area of North America. Male and female birds look similar, but females have barred tail feathers and smaller neck sacs. Prairie chickens feed on plant matter, such as leaves, fruit and grain. In the summer, they catch insects, particularly grasshoppers. Male birds perform spectacular courtship displays,

inflating their orange neck sacs and raising crests of neck feathers. They give booming calls and stamp their feet as they posture, to make the display even more impressive. Female birds lay 10 to 12 eggs and incubate them for 21 to 28 days.

Ptarmigan *Lagopus mutus*

RANGE Holarctic

HABITAT Forest, tundra

SIZE 13–15½ in (33–39 cm)

The ground-dwelling rock ptarmigans depend on camouflage for defence. In order to achieve this in the changing background of their northerly range, they adopt different plumages according to the season. The summer plumage is mottled to blend with the forest while, during the winter snows, ptarmigans have white plumage, only the tail feathers remaining dark. Rock ptarmigans feed on leaves, buds, fruits and seeds, and also eat some insects in the summer.

They are monogamous birds; the male defends a small territory at the breeding grounds. The female lays 6 to 9 eggs in a leaf-lined hollow on the ground and incubates them for 24 to 26 days.

Common Turkey *Meleagris gallopavo*

RANGE USA, Mexico

HABITAT Wooded country

SIZE 36–48 in (91–122 cm)

The common turkey is one of two turkey species. Both are large birds with bare skin on head and neck. Males and females look similar, but females have duller plumage and smaller leg spurs. The wild turkey has a lighter, slimmer body and longer legs than the domesticated version. Turkeys are strong fliers over short distances. They roost in trees, but find most of their food on the ground and eat plant food, such as seeds, nuts and berries, as well as some insects and small reptiles.

A breeding male has a harem of several females. Each female lays her eggs in a shallow leaf-lined nest on the ground; sometimes two or more females use the same nest. The female incubates the clutch of 8 to 15 eggs for about 28 days and cares for the young. The sexes segregate after breeding.

NUMIDIDAE: GUINEAFOWL FAMILY

The 6 species of guineafowl are heavybodied, rounded gamebirds with short wings and bare heads. Males and females look virtually the same. All species occur in Africa and Madagascar. The helmeted guineafowl is the ancestor of the domestic guineafowl.

Helmeted Guineafowl *Numida meleagris*

RANGE E. Africa

HABITAT Forest, dry brush

SIZE 25 in (63 cm)

The helmeted guineafowl, which is named for the bony protuberance on its crown, has the distinctive spotted plumage of most species of guineafowl. It feeds on insects and on plant material, such as seeds, leaves and bulbs.

The female lays a clutch of 10 to 20 eggs in a hollow scraped in the ground. She incubates the eggs and her mate helps her to care for the young.

ODONTOPHORIDAE: NEW WORLD QUAIL FAMILY

There are about 31 species of New World quail, distributed from Canada to northeast Argentina. Many are hunted for sport and food. They are larger, more diverse and more strikingly colored than the Old World quails and differ from them in certain anatomical features, the most important of which is the stronger, serrated bill, typical of the American birds.

Northern Bobwhite *Colinus virginianus*

RANGE E. USA to Guatemala; introduced in West Indies

HABITAT Brush, open woodland, farmland

SIZE 9–10½ in (23–27 cm)

The common name of this species is an imitation of its call. Bobwhites are gregarious birds for much of the year, moving in coveys of 30 or so. In spring the coveys break up, and the birds pair for mating.

Male and female birds look alike, but the male has striking face markings, while the female's face is buff-brown. The nest is a hollow in the ground. The average clutch is 14 to 16 eggs and both parents incubate the eggs.

California Quail *Callipepla californica*

RANGE W. USA

HABITAT Rangeland and agricultural land

SIZE 9½–11 in (24–28 cm)

The State bird of California, this quail is an attractive bird with a characteristic head plume. Females look similar to males and have head plumes, but they lack the black and white facial markings; they have buff-brown heads and chests.

California quails move in flocks, mostly on foot. They do not fly unless forced to do so. They feed on leaves, seeds and berries, and some insects.

The female lays her clutch of 12 to 16 eggs in a leaf-lined hollow on the ground and generally she incubates them for 18 days.

SCREAMERS, MAGPIE GOOSE, WHISTLING DUCKS AND DUCKS

ORDER ANSERIFORMES

A highly successful and diverse group of birds, this order contains 2 families – the Anatidae (ducks, geese and swans), and the Anhimidae (screamers).

ANHIMIDAE: SCREAMER FAMILY

The 3 species of screamer are similar to geese in body size but have longer legs and large feet with only partial webbing. The toes are long, enabling the birds to walk on floating vegetation. All species live in South America.

Northern Screamer *Chauna chavaria* **LR:nt**

RANGE	N. Colombia, Venezuela
HABITAT	Marshes, wet grassland
SIZE	28–36 in (71–91 cm)

The northern screamer has a typically noisy, trumpeting call (the origin of its common name) which it uses as an alarm signal. It feeds mostly on water plants. The female lays 4 to 6 eggs in a nest of aquatic vegetation and both parents incubate the eggs.

ANSERANATIDAE: MAGPIE GOOSE FAMILY

The single species in this family is a long-legged, long-necked goose that leads a semi-aquatic existence in swamps.

Magpie Goose *Anseranas semipalmata*

RANGE	N. Australia, S. New Guinea
HABITAT	Swamps, flood plains
SIZE	30–34 in (76–86 cm)

An interesting, apparently primitive species, the magpie goose is the only true waterfowl to have only partially webbed feet. Its bill is long and straight, and the head is featherless back to the eyes. Females resemble males but are smaller. Plant material is its major food source, and this goose forages by grazing and digging and by bending down tall grasses with its feet in order to reach the seeds. Magpie geese are gregarious and move in flocks of several thousands. Mates are usually kept for life, but a male may mate with two females. The female lays about 8 eggs in a nest of trampled vegetation; both partners incubate the clutch for 35 days and feed the chicks.

DENDROCYGNIDAE: WHISTLING DUCK FAMILY

The nine species of medium-sized ducks in this family are found from Asia to Australia, and from the Americas to tropical Africa. They have long legs, a long neck, and an upright stance. Whistling ducks are sociable and live and feed in large flocks.

White-faced Whistling Duck *Dendrocygna viduata*

RANGE	Tropical South America, Africa, Madagascar
HABITAT	Lakes, swamps, marshes
SIZE	17–19 in (43–48 cm)

The white-faced whistling duck eats aquatic insects, mollusks, crustaceans and plant matter such as seeds and rice. It will often dive for food. Much foraging activity takes place at night; during the day the birds roost near the water, often in flocks of several hundred. Mutual preening plays an important part in the formation of pairs and maintenance of bonds. Between 6 and 12 eggs are laid in a nest in a hole in a tree. Both partners incubate the eggs for 28 to 30 days.

ANATIDAE: TYPICAL WATERFOWL FAMILY

This family contains an assemblage of water birds, found in all areas of the world except continental Antarctica and a few islands. The 148 species include ducks, geese and swans.

All members of the family are aquatic to some degree and obtain plant and animal food from the surface of the water or beneath it by up-ending or diving. The majority are broad-bodied with shortish legs, and feet with front toes connected by webs. Beaks vary according to feeding methods, but are usually broad, flattened and blunt-tipped, with small terminal hooks. In many species males have brightly colored plumage and females plain, brownish feathers. Generally in such sexually dimorphic species, the female performs all parental duties.

Most ducks molt all the flight feathers simultaneously after the breeding season and undergo a flightless period of 3 or 4 weeks. During this period males of some species adopt "eclipse" plumage, similar to the female's muted plumage. After breeding, many species migrate to winter feeding grounds.

Tundra Swan *Cygnus columbianus*

RANGE Holarctic

HABITAT Tundra, swamps and marshes

SIZE 45–55 in (114–140 cm)

The whistling swan (above) and Bewick's swan (below) are sometimes treated as two separate species despite the fact that they interbreed freely. Both breed in the far north of their range and migrate to winter in Europe, China, Japan and the USA. Males and females look alike – the female is sometimes slightly smaller – and juveniles have mottled grayish plumage. The swans feed in shallow water on aquatic vegetation. Mating bonds are strong and permanent. They are formed and maintained by mutual displays. The female lays 3 to 5 eggs in a nest of sedge and moss lined with down, usually near water. She incubates the eggs for 35 to 40 days.

Graylag Goose *Anser anser*

RANGE Europe, Asia

HABITAT Hood plains, estuaries

SIZE 30–35 in (76–89 cm)

The graylag is the most numerous and widespread goose in Eurasia. Males of this sturdy, large-headed species are bigger than females, but otherwise the sexes look alike. The geese feed

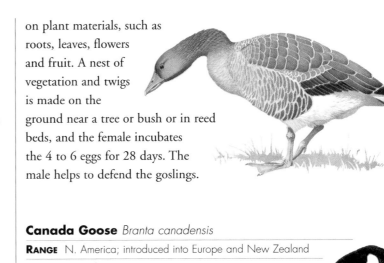

on plant materials, such as roots, leaves, flowers and fruit. A nest of vegetation and twigs is made on the ground near a tree or bush or in reed beds, and the female incubates the 4 to 6 eggs for 28 days. The male helps to defend the goslings.

Canada Goose *Branta canadensis*

RANGE N. America; introduced into Europe and New Zealand

HABITAT Varied

SIZE 22–43 in (56–110 cm)

Habitats of the 12 geographically distinct races of Canada goose vary from semidesert to temperate rainforest and arctic tundra. Races also vary greatly in size. Canada geese feed by day on grassland vegetation and aquatic plants. This migratory species uses the same routes from generation to generation and birds tend to return to their birthplace to breed. Pair and family bonds are strong and are maintained by displays. Females lay about 5 eggs in a shallow scrape on the ground, lined with down and plant material. Her mate stays nearby while she incubates the eggs for between 25 and 30 days.

Common Shelduck *Tadorna tadorna*

RANGE Europe, C. Asia

HABITAT Coasts and estuaries

SIZE 24 in (61 cm)

Shelducks are large gooselike ducks. They feed on mollusks, particularly on the estuarine snail *Hydrobia*, as well as on fish, fish eggs, insects and their larvae, and algae. Females are smaller than males and have white feathers between eyes and bill. Pair bonds are strong and thought to be permanent. At breeding grounds the pairs take up territories. The female lays about 9 eggs in a burrow or cavity nest or in the open. While she incubates the clutch for 28 to 30 days, the male defends her.

DUCKS CONTINUED

Falklands Steamer Duck *Tachyeres brachypterus*

RANGE Falkland Islands

HABITAT Coasts

SIZE 24–29 in (61–74 cm)

Steamer ducks are heavily built marine diving ducks and 2 of the 3 species are flightless. The female is smaller than the male and has a yellow-green bill and dark-brown head with white rings around the eyes.

These coastline foragers feed primarily on mollusks, bivalves, crabs and shrimps – there is a record of one bird found to have 450 mussel shells in its stomach and crop. The Falklands duck makes a nest on grass or dry seaweed, or even in an abandoned penguin burrow, and lines it with down. The female lays 5 to 8 eggs and the male guards her attentively while she incubates them.

Mallard *Anas platyrhynchos*

RANGE Throughout northern hemisphere

HABITAT Almost anywhere near water

SIZE 16–26 in (41–66 cm)

The mallard is a typical dabbling duck often feeding tail-up in shallow water. Female mallards have plain brownish plumage, with distinctive blue feathers on the wings. Pair bonds are renewed each year with a prolonged period of intricate social displays, including the ritualized preening of the bright wing patches.

The female lays her 8 to 10 eggs in a nest on the ground. Her mate deserts her early in the incubation period and flies off to undergo his annual molt with the other males.

The mallard duck is the ancestor of all domestic ducks except for muscovies.

Northern Shoveler *Anas clypeata*

RANGE Europe, Asia, N. America

HABITAT Inland marshes, coastal waters

SIZE 17–22 in (43–56 cm)

The shoveler's distinctive spatulate bill is an adaptation for feeding on plankton. As the bird swims, it sucks water into the bill; the water is strained out through hairlike lamellae lining the bill which retain the tiny planktonic creatures.

Female birds have much duller plumage than males; they are mostly brown, but have blue and green feathers on the wings. Northern shovelers usually move in small groups or pairs for most of the year.

The female makes a nest in a reed bed and lays 7 to 14 eggs which she incubates for 23 to 25 days. The ducklings are born with normal bills; the spatulate shape develops as they mature.

Common Eider *Somateria mollissima*

RANGE Circumpolar (north)

HABITAT Coasts, inland rivers and lakes

SIZE 22–28 in (56–71 cm)

Like most ducks, the female eider lines her nest with down plucked from her breast. The down of the eider is particularly soft and warm and has long been collected and used by man. The female duck has barred, brownish plumage, and both male and female have Y-shaped bill extensions of membrane reaching almost up to the eyes. During the breeding season, eiders frequent coasts and feed on mollusks, crustaceans and other small creatures. They nest in colonies but fight over nest sites, and each pair holds its own territory. The female incubates the clutch of about 5 eggs alone for 27 to 28 days while her mate goes off with the other males to undergo his annual molt.

Greater Scaup *Aythya marila*

RANGE Circumpolar (north)

HABITAT Coastal and inland waters

SIZE 16–20 in (41–51 cm)

One of the group of ducks known as pochards, the scaup breeds in tundra regions and winters to the south. It feeds on small invertebrates, such as mollusks and crustaceans. Like other pochards, such as the canvasback, *A. valisineria*, and the tufted duck, *A. fuligula*, it is an excellent diver and frequently dives as deep as 26 ft (8 m) in search

of food. Scaups gather in huge flocks, and at breeding grounds pairs overlap their ranges. The female lays 8 to 10 eggs which she incubates for 23 to 27 days.

Mandarin Duck *Aix galericulata* **LR:nt**

RANGE E. Asia, Korea, China, Japan; introduced in Britain and N. Europe

HABITAT Inland swamps, lakes and pools

SIZE 17–20 in (43–51 cm)

The mandarin has been celebrated in Japanese and Chinese art for centuries. Mandarins are most active at dawn and dusk; they feed on plant food, such as seeds, acorns and rice, and on insects, snails and small fish. They are social ducks, and the pair bond continues from year to year when possible. Courtship displays are particularly elaborate, including ritualized preening of the enlarged saillike feathers on the flanks and display drinking. The female lays 9 to 12 eggs, often in a tree-hole nest, and incubates them. The closely related wood/Carolina duck, *Aixsponsa* of North America is also brilliantly marked.

Red-breasted Merganser *Mergus serrator*

RANGE Holarctic

HABITAT Coastal and inland waters

SIZE 19–26 in (48–66 cm)

Mergansers are fish-eating, diving ducks with long, thin, serrated bills, well-adapted for catching fish under water. They also feed on crustaceans. Courtship rituals are complex. The male stretches his neck and sprints over the water; before copulating he performs a series of drinking, preening and wingflapping movements. The female lays her 9 or 10 eggs in a hole or cavity. The male deserts his mate early in the incubation period. Once the young have hatched, several females collect their young together into one brood which they tend together.

Muscovy Duck *Cairina moschata*

RANGE Central America, tropical South America

HABITAT Rivers and marshes in forest

SIZE 26–33 in (66–84 cm)

These birds, familiar in their domestic form, are rare in their pure form outside the native range. The male has warty skin around the eyes and an enlarged bill base; the female's head is entirely feathered and there is no bill enlargement. The wild form is attractive, but some of the domestic strains have grotesque warts and huge bill carbuncles. Muscovies eat plants, seeds, small fish and insects and termites, which are plentiful in their habitat. Muscovies have no real migratory pattern, but may move to coasts in dry seasons. They do not form large flocks, and pair and family bonds are weak. Courtship displays are simple and brief. The female lays 8 to 15 eggs in a hollow or among rushes. She incubates them alone. The male plays no part in the care of the young.

Ruddy Duck *Oxyura jamaicensis*

RANGE USA, Central America, Andes; introduced in Britain

HABITAT Inland lakes and rivers; estuaries

SIZE 14–19 in (35–48 cm)

The ruddy duck is one of a group of ducks known as stifftails. All are small, stocky, freshwater diving ducks with the habit of holding the tail up at an angle while swimming. Ruddy ducks are usually active at night and feed on aquatic plants, insects and small invertebrates. They are not highly developed socially and do not hold nesting territories. Females lay about 8 eggs in a ground nest, but may lay more eggs in other nests.

BUTTONQUAIL, HONEYGUIDE AND WOODPECKERS

ORDER TURNICIFORMES

TURNICIDAE: BUTTONQUAIL FAMILY

There is a single family in this order. The 17 species of buttonquail are dumpy, ground-living birds, which closely resemble quails, but have only three toes on each foot. Their wings are short and rounded and they seldom fly. Females are larger and more brightly plumaged than males. All species occur in tropical and subtropical regions of the Old World.

Little Buttonquail *Turnix sylvatica*

RANGE S. Spain, Africa; S. Asia to Indonesia, Philippines

HABITAT Grassland, scrub

SIZE 6 in (15 cm)

A shy, secretive bird, the little or small buttonquail spends much of its time in the undergrowth, although it is able to fly. It feeds on plants, seeds and insects. The female bird takes the dominant sexual role, displaying to the male and competing with other females. Both birds make the nest, which is usually a hollow in the ground, lined with grass.

From 3 to 8 oval eggs, usually 4, are laid, and the male incubates the clutch for an average of 13 days – one of the shortest incubation periods for any bird.

ORDER PICIFORMES

This order includes 5 families of mostly tree-dwelling, cavity-nesting birds – Indicatoridae (honeyguides), Picidae (woodpeckers), Megalaimidae (Asian barbets), Lybiidae (African barbets), and Ramphastidae (New World barbets and toucans). The 355 species in the order have in common a zygodactyl foot – a foot with two toes pointing forward and two pointing backward – which aids climbing up vertical tree trunks.

INDICATORIDAE: HONEYGUIDE FAMILY

There are 17 species of honeyguide. Most are found in Africa with one species in Southeast Asia and one in the Himalayas. Honeyguides feed on wax and larval bees, and some species have developed the habit, for which the family is named, of leading humans and other mammals to bees' nests in the hope that they will break the nests open. The birds are unique in being able to feed on wax, which they can digest by means of symbiotic bacteria in their intestines. They also feed on other insects, some of which they catch in the air.

As far as is known, all species are brood parasites and lay their eggs in the nests of barbets and woodpeckers. Male and female look slightly different in most species.

Greater/Black-throated Honeyguide *Indicator indicator*

RANGE Africa, south of the Sahara

HABITAT Varied, forest edge, arid bush, acacia woodland, cultivated land

SIZE 73 in (20 cm)

The greater honeyguide is one of the 2 species in the family that actively lead other creatures to bees' nests. Chattering loudly, the bird approaches a human being or another honey-eating mammal, such as the ratel, and having attracted the attention, leads the way to the nest, flying a short distance at a time. The honeyguide needs the help of another creature to break open the nest and, once this has been done, will feed on the remains of the honey, the wax and larval bees. The skin of this bird is particularly thick and must guard it against stings. Like all honeyguides, this bird also feeds on other insects.

The honeyguide lays its eggs in the nests of other birds and its young are reared by their foster parents.

PICIDAE: WOODPECKER FAMILY

Woodpeckers and their relatives the wrynecks and piculets must be among the best-known of all specialized tree-living birds. There are about 215 species, found almost worldwide except in Madagascar, Australia, the Papuan region and most oceanic islands. Males and females have slight plumage differences.

Woodpeckers are highly adapted for climbing in trees, extracting insect food items from bark and wood and making holes in tree trunks. The woodpecker clings tightly to the bark of the trunk with its sharply clawed feet, on which two toes face forward and two backward, giving it maximum grip. The stiff tail acts as an angled strut and gives the bird additional support as it bores into the wood with hammerlike movements of its strong, straight beak. A few woodpeckers are ground-living.

Ivory-billed Woodpecker

Campephilus principalis **EX**

RANGE	Formerly S.E. USA, Cuba
HABITAT	Swamps, forest
SIZE	20 in (51 cm)

The largest North American woodpecker, this species is characterized by its pointed crest and long, ivory-colored bill. The destruction of this woodpecker's habitat – mature forest – has led to a dramatic decline in its numbers. Although there may be a few birds left in remote parts of Cuba, it is listed as extinct by the IUCN.

It feeds on the larvae of insects, especially of the wood-boring beetles that live between the bark and wood of dying or newly dead trees, and also eats some fruit and nuts. Both members of a breeding pair help to excavate a nest cavity, and the female lays 1 to 3 eggs. The clutch is incubated for about 20 days, the male taking a turn at night, and both parents feed the young.

Northern/Eurasian Wryneck *Jynx torquilla*

RANGE	Europe, N. Africa, N. Asia; winters in Africa and S. Asia
HABITAT	Open deciduous forest, cultivated land
SIZE	6¼–8 in (16–20.5 cm)

A skulking, solitary bird, the wryneck is an unusual member of the woodpecker family, with a shorter, weaker bill than the true woodpeckers. Although it can cling to tree trunks, it does not have the stiff, supporting tail of the typical woodpecker and more often perches. It does not bore into trees for its food, but picks ants and other insects off leaves or from the ground, using its long, fast-moving tongue. The common name comes from its habit of twisting its head into strange positions while feeding and during the courtship display.

The wryneck breeds in summer in Europe, north Africa and central Asia. It does not excavate its own nest, but uses an existing cavity in a tree trunk, an abandoned woodpecker hole or a crevice in a wall or bank. The female lays 7 to 10 eggs, and both parents, but mainly the female, incubate the eggs for 13 days. Both parents feed insects and larvae to the young, which leave the nest about 3 weeks after hatching. After breeding, some populations of wrynecks migrate south to tropical Asia and Africa for the winter.

Great Spotted Woodpecker *Dendrocopos major*

RANGE	Europe, N. Africa, Asia
HABITAT	Mixed forest, woodland
SIZE	9 in (23 cm)

The most common European woodpecker, the great spotted woodpecker is an adaptable species, living in all types of woodland, including parks and gardens. As it bores into tree trunks to extract its food – wood-boring insects and their larvae – it makes a characteristic drumming noise, which it also makes in spring in place of a courtship song. It supplements its diet with nuts, seeds and berries and has a habit of wedging a pine cone into a crevice and chipping out the kernels with its bill. The male bird has a red band at the back of his head, which the female lacks, and the juvenile has a red crown.

In Europe, the breeding season begins in mid-May, and both partners help to excavate a hole in a tree, 10 ft (3 m) or more above ground. The female lays 3 to 8 eggs in this unlined nest and, with some assistance from the male, incubates them for 16 days. Both parents care for the young, bringing them insects in their bills. Most great spotted woodpeckers are resident birds, but some northern populations may migrate south in winter to find food.

WOODPECKERS CONTINUED

Eurasian Green Woodpecker *Picus viridis*

RANGE Europe, N. Africa, Turkey to Iran, W. Russia

HABITAT Open deciduous woodland, gardens, parks

SIZE 12½ in (32 cm)

A large, vividly plumaged woodpecker, this species has a short tail and a long, pointed bill. The male has a characteristic red mustachial stripe with a black border; in the female the stripe is all black. Like other woodpeckers, the green woodpecker feeds in trees on the larvae of wood-boring insects, but it also feeds on the ground, where it hops along ponderously, searching for ants. It will also eat fruit and seeds. The flight of this species is typical of the woodpecker family, being deeply undulating, with long wing closures between each upward sweep.

The breeding season starts in April in the south of the range and May in the north. Both partners of a breeding pair help to excavate a nest cavity, often in a rotten tree trunk and usually at least 3¼ ft (1 m) above ground. The female lays 4 to 7 eggs, sometimes as many as 11, which both parents incubate for 18 or 19 days. The chicks hatch naked and helpless and must be fed by their parents on regurgitated food for about 3 weeks, when they are able to fend for themselves.

In a hard winter, green woodpeckers, a non-migratory species, can suffer severe food shortages, which cause large drops in population.

Golden-tailed Woodpecker

Campethera abingoni

RANGE Africa, south of the Sahara

HABITAT Woodland, brush, mountain forest

SIZE 8 in (20.5 cm)

The golden-tailed woodpecker can be identified by the broad black streaks on the white plumage from its chin to its belly and by the yellow-tipped tail feathers. There are some dark-red and black markings on the nape and head and the rest of the plumage is largely green with white flecks. Usually seen in pairs,

these woodpeckers are noisy birds and utter calls like derisive laughter; they also give a screeching alarm signal. They are restless birds, continuously on the move, with swift deeply undulating flight, in search of the arboreal ants and the larvae of other insects, such as beetles, that form their main foods.

The nest hole is usually excavated in the soft wood of a dead tree, and the female lays 2 or 3 eggs.

Great Slaty Woodpecker *Mulleripicus pulverulentus*

RANGE Asia: N. India to S.W. China, Sumatra, Java, Borneo, Palawan

HABITAT Forest, swamp forest

SIZE 20 in (51 cm)

The great slaty woodpecker is a large species that associates in groups of about 6 birds, which follow one another from one tree-top to the next, calling noisily with loud cackles as they fly. Their flight is leisurely, without the normal woodpecker bounds and undulations. The larvae of wood-boring beetles and other insects are the main foods of this woodpecker, and it drills into trees with its powerful bill to find them. Both males and females of this species have some buffy-brown plumage on the chin and neck, but males also have mustachial streaks, which the females lack. Juvenile birds resemble the females but they are a darker and duller color, with more pale spots on the underparts.

In the breeding season, the groups break up into pairs, which then excavate their nests high up in tree trunks, often in dead or decaying wood. Both parents incubate the 3 or 4 eggs, which are laid in the unlined nest cavity, and share in the care and feeding of the nestlings.

Ground Woodpecker *Geocolaptes olivaceus* **LR:nt**

RANGE South Africa

HABITAT Dry, open hill country

SIZE 11 in (28 cm)

This woodpecker lives almost entirely on the ground and hops everywhere. On the rare occasions when it does take to the air, it flies heavily and only for short distances, its red rump feathers showing conspicuously. Male and female look alike, with gray plumage on the head, olive-brown upperparts flecked with white, and rose-pink chest and belly. Juvenile birds are duller, with mottled olive and off-white plumage on the belly.

Ground woodpeckers live in small groups of up to 6 or so and are usually found on high ground above 2,000 ft (600 m), where they perch on rocks or boulders or, very occasionally, on the low branches of trees and bushes. They feed on ants and other ground-living insects and their larvae, which they find by probing under rocks and stones. Their call is sharp and metallic, and they may also utter highpitched whistles.

This species nests on the ground in a long tunnel with a small chamber at the end, which both partners dig in a bank of clay or sand. The female lays 4 or 5 eggs.

Greater Flame-backed/Golden-backed Woodpecker

Chrysocolaptes lucidus

RANGE India, S.E. Asia to the Philippines

HABITAT Woodland, forest fringe, mangroves

SIZE 13 in (33 cm)

This medium-sized woodpecker is widespread in the wooded areas of India and Southeast Asia, where many races of the species inhabit a variety of forest types. Often found near flocks of other woodpeckers, drongos, bulbuls and babblers, these birds usually associate in pairs. After flying noisily from tree to tree, with characteristic bounds and undulations, they alight on a trunk and, working their way up in jerky spirals, bore into the wood with their beaks in order to feed on insect larvae. Flamebacked woodpeckers have also been observed catching winged termites in the air. They seldom feed on the ground. However they are known to occasionally drink the nectar of some flowers.

Although this is an extremely variable species, greater flamebacks can generally be identified by the two black mustachial streaks, separated by a patch of white plumage, on each side of the bill. The female bird lacks the male's distinctive red crest and has a flat black crown, spotted with white.

In the breeding season, the male flamebacked woodpecker drums particularly energetically as a courtship signal. The birds nest in a hole in a tree trunk, and the hole may be used many times, with a fresh entrance, which always leads to the same breeding chamber, being cut each season. It is not known whether the same birds return to the same hole every year.

The female lays a clutch of 4 or 5 eggs, which are incubated for 14 or 15 days, and the young woodpeckers remain in the nest being fed and cared for by the parents until they are able to fly at between 24 and 26 days old.

Blond-crested Woodpecker

Celeus flavescens

RANGE South America: Amazonian Brazil, Paraguay, N.E. Argentina

HABITAT Forest

SIZE 11 in (28 cm)

With its long, shaggy crest, the blond-crested woodpecker may appear to be rather larger than it actually is. The yellow feathers of the crest are narrow and soft so that when they are held erect they blow freely in the breeze.

This species is particularly widespread in southeastern Brazil, however, the blond-crested woodpecker is not confined to the lowlands, but has been observed at altitudes of up to 3,000 ft (900 m).

WOODPECKERS, ASIAN BARBETS AND AFRICAN BARBETS

Rufous/White-browed Piculet *Sasia ochracea*

RANGE N.E. India through S.E. Asia and S.E. China

HABITAT Woodland, especially bamboo

SIZE 9 cm (3½ in)

This tiny, dumpy, stub-tailed woodpecker is an active, restless bird. It is usually seen singly or in pairs. With jerky movements, it creeps over thin twigs of low trees and bushes or hops around the litter of the woodland floor, searching for its food – mainly ants and their larvae. The female bird looks similar to the male but lacks his golden forehead.

The piculet's nest is a tiny hole about 1 in (2.5 cm) across, drilled in a decaying, hollow bamboo or an old tree. The female lays a clutch of 3 or 4 eggs.

Yellow-bellied Sapsucker

Sphyrapicus varius

RANGE Canada, N. and E. USA; winters in Central America, West Indies

HABITAT Forest, woodland

SIZE 8 in (20.5 cm)

The sapsucker migrates northward in the spring from its wintering grounds in Central America and the West Indies. On reaching its breeding range, it drills rows of holes in the bark of trees and returns from time to time to drink the oozing sap and to eat the insects that are attracted to it. The bird also collects other insects in and around the trees using its brushlike tongue.

A breeding pair bores a nest hole, usually in the trunk of a dead tree, with the male doing most of the excavation work. The cavity takes 2 to 4 weeks to complete.

The female lays 5 to 7 eggs, which both birds then incubate for about 12 days.

Northern/Common Flicker *Colaptes auratus*

RANGE Alaska to Mexico, Cuba, Grand Cayman Island

HABITAT Woodland, open country

SIZE 10–14 in (25.5–35.5 cm)

The flicker is a ground-feeding bird, which lives on ants and other insects. It also eats fruit and berries. There are 2 forms, now considered to be subspecies of the same species – the eastern birds have yellow wing linings, and the western birds, red wing linings. The two subspecies are often called yellow-shafted and red-shafted flicker respectively. In the Midwest, the forms meet and interbreed.

During courtship, or to communicate possession of its territory, the flicker drums with its bill on a tree or the metal roofing of buildings.

The male flicker selects a site for the nest hole, usually a hole in a tree trunk, stump or telegraph pole, and does most of the excavation work. Both parents incubate the eggs for about 12 days, the male taking the night shift.

White-barred Piculet *Picumnus cirratus*

RANGE South America: Guyana to N. Argentina

HABITAT Forest, woodland, parks

SIZE 3½ in (9 cm)

A small, busy woodpecker, the white-barred piculet scrambles over trees, hanging upside down, moving over, under and around the branches in search of larvae to feed on.

Predators are deterred from attacking this piculet because of its curious and particularly offensive odor.

The nest is made in a bamboo stem, and to excavate it, the piculet clings to the bamboo in true woodpecker fashion, speedily chipping it away with its beak.

MEGALAIMIDAE: ASIAN BARBET FAMILY

Barbets are small to medium-sized chunky birds that are often brightly-colored and are found in tropical areas of Asia, Africa, and the Americas. They have large heads, and a stout, sometimes notched, beak often fringed with tufts of bristles. Males and females look alike in most species.

Most barbets are solitary, tree-dwelling birds that feed on insects and fruit. Once grouped together in a single family, barbets are now placed in three separate families – Megalaimidae (Asian barbets), Lybiidae (African barbets) and Ramphastidae – this family includes both the American barbets and the toucans. Asian barbets are generally larger than other barbet species. The 26 species are found in forest and woodland from south Tibet and south China to Indonesia and the Philippines. They nest in a hole bored into a tree.

Coppersmith/Crimson-breasted Barbet

Megalaima haemacephala

RANGE Pakistan east to China and Philippines, south to Sri Lanka, S.E. Asia, Sumatra, Java and Bali

HABITAT Woodland, gardens, urban areas

SIZE 6 in (15 cm)

A stocky bird, the coppersmith barbet is identified by the patches of bright red and yellow plumage on the throat and head, and the streaked belly. Alone, or sometimes in pairs or

small groups, the coppersmith hunts in the trees for fruit particularly figs, or may make clumsy aerial dashes after insects.

The breeding season lasts from January to June, and the barbets excavate a hole in a dead or rotting branch, which their beaks can penetrate easily. Both parents incubate the clutch of 2 to 4 eggs and tend the young birds.

LYBIIDAE: AFRICAN BARBET FAMILY

The 42 species of African barbets form the most diverse barbet family. They resemble the Asian barbets, but also include the tiny tinkerbirds, which are just 3 in (8 cm) long, and other species that live in open savanna or scrub.

While most species nest in tree holes, three more sociable species make nesting burrows in banks or termite mounds and feed mainly on insects.

Double-toothed Barbet *Lybius bidentatus*

RANGE Africa: S. Sudan, Ethiopia, south to Uganda, W. Kenya, Tanzania

HABITAT Light forest, wooded savanna, cultivated land

SIZE 9 in (23 cm)

Identified by its deep-red throat and breast, the double-toothed barbet feeds on fruit, particularly figs and bananas, and will often invade plantations.

The nest is excavated in a dead branch of a tree, and the female is thought to lay 3 or 4 eggs. Like all barbets, both partners of a pair share the nesting duties.

TOUCANS

RAMPHASTIDAE: NEW WORLD BARBET AND TOUCAN FAMILY

This family includes two subfamilies: the 14 species of American barbets which resemble the African and Asian barbets and live in similar habitats; and the 41 species of toucans. The toucans are among the most extraordinary birds in the world. All toucan species are found living in the canopy layers of the dense rain forests of the Amazon basin and in neighboring forested areas of South America. They are medium-sized birds, ranging in size from 12 to 24 in (30 to 61 cm), and have enormous, boldly colored beaks that account for almost half the total body length. These bills are constructed of a honeycomb of bony material and are consequently light but very strong. The gaudy coloration varies greatly, not only between species but within a species. The plumage is usually dark, often black, with patches of boldly contrasting color on head and neck, which accentuates the bill colors. Toucans' wings are short and rounded and their flight weak. The legs are strong, and the claws well adapted for grasping branches, with two toes pointing forward and two backward. Male and female look alike in most species.

The specific functions of the toucan's remarkable beak are poorly understood. It may act as an important visual signal in territorial or courtship behavior or, it has been suggested, it may help the bird to obtain food otherwise out of its reach. Many other birds, however, manage without such bills. The bill may even help to intimidate other birds when the toucan raids their nests for young. Toucans feed on fruit of many types and on large, tree-living insects; occasionally they take larger prey such as nestling birds, eggs and lizards. The toucan seizes food with the tip of its bill and then throws its head back to toss the morsel into its mouth. An extremely long, narrow tongue, with a bristlelike appendage at the tip, aids manipulation of the food.

Toucans nest in tree cavities, either in natural holes or abandoned woodpecker holes. A few species line their nests with leaves, but in others regurgitated seeds from food-fruit form a layer on the nest floor. The 2 to 4 eggs are incubated by both parents, who are able to flex their long tails forward over their backs so as to accommodate to the confines of the nesting cavity. Young toucans hatch naked and blind and develop slowly. At 3 weeks their eyes are only just opening, and they are not fully fledged for more than 6 weeks. They have specialized pads on their heels, on which they sit, which may be a form of protection against the rough floor of the nest. Both male and female feed and care for the young during this period.

Emerald Toucanet *Aulacorhynchus prasinus*

RANGE S. Mexico to Nicaragua, Venezuela, Colombia, Ecuador and Peru

HABITAT Humid mountain forest, open country with trees

SIZE 14 in (35.5 cm)

The shy emerald toucanet lives at altitudes of between 6,000 and 10,000 ft (1,800 and 3,000 m). The birds sit inconspicuously among the foliage or fly for short distances in pairs or small groups to forage for food, calling to one another as they do so with a variety of noisy sounds. Their diet is wide ranging and includes insects, small reptiles and amphibians, and the eggs and young of other bird species, as well as the more usual fruit and berries. Striking birds, emerald toucanets are unmistakable with their bright green plumage and bold yellow and black bills.

The nest is made in a hole in a tree, often an old woodpecker hole. Emerald toucanets have even been known to harass woodpeckers until they give up their nests. Both parents incubate the 3 or 4 eggs and bring food, mostly fruit, to the nestlings. The young of the emerald toucanet, like all toucans, hatch naked and develop their first feathers at about 2 weeks. Their beaks, however, grow faster than their bodies, and the young toucanet has a full-sized, 3 in (7.5 cm) bill before its body is even half the size of that of the adult.

Saffron Toucanet
Baillonius bailloni **LR:nt**

RANGE S.E. Brazil

HABITAT Forest

SIZE 14 in (35.5 cm)

The saffron toucanet has fine, gold-colored plumage, which is especially lustrous on the cheeks and breast. Shy, graceful birds, they live in small groups and feed mainly on berries, preferring to forage high in the tree-tops rather than in the lower levels of the forest.

Plate-billed Mountain Toucan *Andigena laminirostris* **LR:nt**

RANGE Andes in Colombia, W. Ecuador

HABITAT Forest

SIZE 20 in (50 cm)

Also known as the laminated toucan, this species lives at altitudes of between 1,000 and 10,000 ft (300 and 3,000 m). The bill is about 4 in (10 cm) long and extremely unusual in shape. On each side of the upper bill there is a horny yellow plate, which grows out from the base of the bill. The function of these plates is not clearly understood, since little is known of the habits of these toucans.

Spot-billed Toucanet *Selenidera maculirostris*

RANGE Tropical Brazil, south of the Amazon to N.E. Argentina

HABITAT Lowland rain forest

SIZE 13 in (33 cm)

An uncommon toucanet, this species has a patch of feathers, usually orange or yellow, behind each eye – a feature which is peculiar to the *Selenidera* genus and is thought to be important in the male's courtship display. The bill of the male is distinctive, with a yellowish tip and black markings on the upper mandible; the female's bill is less clearly marked.

The spot-billed toucanet feeds on berries and large fruit – swallowing them whole and then disgorging the skins, stones and seeds. All toucans aid the seed dispersal of a number of fruit-bearing plants in this way.

Once their eggs are hatched, spot-billed toucanets often visit citrus plantations in groups, in order to feed and find termites and other small insects to take to their young.

Toco Toucan *Ramphastos toco*

RANGE E. South America: the Guianas to N. Argentina

HABITAT Woodland, forest, plantations, palm groves

SIZE 24 in (61 cm)

A common toucan and one of the largest of its family, the toco toucan lives in small groups and frequents coconut and sugar plantations, as well as the normal toucan habitats. Its golden-yellow bill is about 7½ in (19 cm) long, and it feeds on a wide range of fruit but has a particular preference for capsicums. Toco toucans are not at all shy and will enter houses, steal food and tease domestic pets.

Curl-crested Aracari

Pteroglossus beauharnaesii

RANGE Amazonian Peru, W. Brazil, N. Bolivia

HABITAT Forest

SIZE 14 in (35.5 cm)

This toucan is normally shy and nervous, but can be aggressive and active. It has curious plumage quite unlike that of any other toucan. The feathers on its crown are like shiny, curly scales, and those on the cheeks and throat have black scaly tips. It has pronounced jagged notches in its beak.

Groups of 5 or 6 adult aracaris roost together in an abandoned woodpecker hole or in a hollow in a tree, folding their tails over their backs so as to fit into the confined space.

JACAMARS, PUFFBIRDS AND HORNBILLS

ORDER GALBULIFORMES

Jacamars and puffbirds are the two families that make up this order. Both are tree-dwelling insect eaters that are found in Central and South America. Jacamars and puffbirds have zygodactyl feet, with two toes in front and two behind.

GALBULIDAE: JACAMAR FAMILY

The 18 species of jacamar are graceful, long-billed birds. They look similar to bee-eaters and catch insects on the wing in a similar way, but they are unrelated. Males are often brightly colored, but females are a little duller. Jacamars dig tunnels in the ground to nest in. Jacamars occur from Mexico to Brazil.

Rufous-tailed Jacamar
Galbula ruficauda

RANGE Mexico, Central America, through tropical South America to N. Brazil; Trinidad and Tobago and from E. Brazil to N.E. Argentina

HABITAT Forest clearings, second growth forest, scrub

SIZE 9–11 in (23–28 cm)

The rufous-tailed jacamar is brightly plumaged, with glossy iridescent upperparts. The female has a buff throat. Young birds are duller. The jacamar sits on a branch, watching for insects. It darts after them with swooping flight, snapping them out of the air, then returns to its perch to eat its catch, and may beat large specimens against the branch to kill them.

The female jacamar digs a breeding tunnel in the ground. Both birds incubate the eggs for 19 to 23 days. The young are fed until they can fly, at about 3 weeks old.

BUCCONIDAE: PUFFBIRD FAMILY

The 33 species of puffbird and nunbird are insect-eating birds, found from Mexico south through Central and tropical South America. Puffbirds are stouter, more lethargic birds than the agile jacamars, although they do make aerial sallies after prey. Male and female look more or less alike, both with large heads for their size and sober plumage.

White-necked Puffbird
Notharchus macrorhynchos

RANGE Central and South America to N.E. Argentina

HABITAT Open forest, forest edge, savanna with trees

SIZE 10 in (25.5 cm)

This species has the typical puffbird habit of fluffing out its plumage as it perches watching for prey, thus creating a bulky appearance, which is the origin of the common name. Once an insect is sighted, the puffbird flies out to catch it in the air with its broad, hook-tipped bill.

Breeding white-necked puffbirds excavate a tunnel in the ground and then camouflage the entrance with leaves and twigs. The female lays 2 or 3 eggs in a leaf-lined chamber at the end of the tunnel, and both birds incubate the clutch.

Black-fronted Nunbird
Monasa nigrifrons

RANGE East of the Andes: Colombia to Peru, N.E. Bolivia, Brazil

HABITAT Forest

SIZE 11½ in (29 cm)

Puffbirds of the genus Monasa have black or black and white plumage, hence the common name – nunbirds. They are more gregarious than other puffbirds and often gather in flocks. Otherwise they are similar in their habits. They perch on branches to watch for insects and then fly out to seize the prey in the air.

Breeding pairs excavate tunnels in which to nest, and the female is thought to lay 2 or 3 eggs.

ORDER BUCEROTIFORMES

There are two families in this order of long-beaked birds – Bucerotidae (typical hornbills), the group to which most species belong; and Bucorvidae (ground-hornbills).

BUCEROTIDAE: HORNBILL FAMILY

The 54 species of hornbill occur in Africa, south of the Sahara, and in tropical Asia, south to Indonesia. Most have brown or black and white plumage, but are instantly recognizable by their huge bills, topped with horny projections, or casques. Despite its heavy appearance, the hornbill's beak is actually a light honeycomb of bony cellular tissue, encased in a shell of horn. Many hornbills live and feed in trees in forest and savanna. Most are omnivorous, eating fruit, insects, lizards and even small mammals. Male and female look similar in some species but differ in others.

Hornbills are probably best known for their extraordinary nesting habits. Once the female has laid her eggs in a suitable nest hole, the entrance is walled up with mud, leaving a small slitlike opening. The male may do this or the female may barricade herself in, using material that the male supplies. She remains there throughout the incubation and part of the fledgling period, totally dependent on her mate for food supplies, but perfectly protected from predators. The male brings food, which he passes to her through the slit.

While she is a captive, the female molts, but by the time the appetites of the young are too much for the male to cope with, her feathers have regrown. Using her beak, she hacks her way out of the nest, and the young repair the barricade. Both parents then bring food until the young hornbills can fly. Details vary slightly between species, but all hornbills keep their nests clean, throwing out food debris and excreting through the slit.

Red-billed Hornbill

Tockus erythrorhynchus

RANGE W., E. and S.E. Africa

HABITAT Dry savanna, open woodland

SIZE 18 in (46 cm)

Although brightly colored, the beak of the red-billed hornbill has little, if any casque. Male and female look similar with gray and brownish-black plumage and light markings on the wings. The female does not always have a black base to the lower bill. Usually in pairs or small family parties, red-billed hornbills feed on the ground and in trees on insects, such as grasshoppers, locusts and beetles, and on fruit.

The female lays her 3 to 6 eggs in a hole in a tree, which is barricaded with mud in the usual manner of hornbills.

Helmeted Hornbill

Buceros vigil **LR:nt**

RANGE Malaysian Peninsula, Sumatra, Borneo

HABITAT Forest

SIZE 4 ft (1.2 m)

The greatly elongated central tail feathers of this huge hornbill may add as much as 20 in (50 cm) to its length. The female is slightly smaller than the male.

This bird is unusual in that while all other hornbills have bills that are deceptively light, its casque is formed of solid ivory making its skull the heaviest of any bird's. This heavy head could cause problems for the bird when in flight, but the elongated central tail feathers help to counterbalance the skull. Unfortunately the attributes of the helmeted hornbill have created much demand for it, and it has long been hunted both for its ivory casque and its tail feathers.

Helmeted hornbills feed on fruit, lizards, birds and their eggs. The breeding procedure is believed to be similar to that of other hornbills.

Great Indian Hornbill

Buceros bicornis

RANGE India, S.E. Asia, Sumatra

HABITAT Forest

SIZE 5 ft (1.5 m)

Although a large bird, the great Indian hornbill has a top-heavy appearance, with its huge bill and casque. The female bird is much smaller, particularly her bill and casque, and has white instead of red eyes, but she is otherwise similar to the male.

These hornbills spend much of their time in trees, feeding on fruit, especially figs, as well as on insects, reptiles and other small animals.

The female bird lays 1 to 3 eggs in an unlined nest hole in a tree and walls up the entrance from within, using her own feces and material brought to her by the male. She incubates the eggs for about 31 days.

GROUND-HORNBILLS, HOOPOES, WOOD-HOOPOES AND TROGONS

BUCORVIDAE: GROUND-HORNBILL FAMILY

The two species of ground-hornbills are large birds that inhabit savanna, arid grasslands, and open woodlands in tropical Africa.

Southern Ground-Hornbill *Bucorvus cafer*

RANGE Parts of Africa south of the equator

HABITAT Open country

SIZE 42 in (107 cm)

The southern ground hornbill and the closely related Abyssinian ground hornbill, *B. abyssinicus*, are the largest African hornbills. These mainly ground-living, turkey-sized birds walk in pairs or small family groups, eating insects, reptiles and other animals.

Females lay 1 to 3 eggs in a hole in a tree or stump, lined with leaves. She is not walled up in the nest, but comes and goes freely, covering the eggs with leaves when she is not sitting.

ORDER UPUPIFORMES

The members of this order all have long, slightly downcurved beaks used for probing the ground and crevices for insects and other small animals. There are 3 families – Upupidae (the hoopoe), Phoeniculidae (woodhoopoes), and Rhinopomastidae (scimitar-bills). The hoopoe is found in Eurasia, Asia and Africa, while the woodhoopoes and 3 species of scimitar-bills are found in Africa south of the Sahara desert.

UPUPIDAE: HOOPOE FAMILY

The single hoopoes species is ground-living. The sexes look similar, but females may be smaller and duller.

Hoopoe *Upupa epops*

RANGE Europe (not Scandinavia or Britain), N. Africa, C. and S. Asia; tropical Africa, S. Asia

HABITAT Open country with trees, forest edge, parks, gardens, orchards

SIZE 11 in (28 cm)

The hoopoe has pinkish to cinnamon body plumage, boldly barred wings and tail and a huge crest, which is usually held flat. It walks and runs swiftly, probing the ground with its bill for worms, insects and invertebrates. The hoopoe perches and roosts in trees and flies efficiently, if slowly. It may occasionally hunt insects in the air.

The female lays 5 to 8 eggs (but up to 12) in a hole in a tree, wall or building. The male feeds his mate while she incubates the clutch for 16 to 19 days.

PHOENICULIDAE: WOODHOOPOE FAMILY

The 5 species of woodhoopoe live in wooded grassland, forest and forest edge in central and southern Africa. The sexes look similar, but the female is often smaller and sometimes browner.

Green Woodhoopoe *Phoeniculus purpureus*

RANGE Africa, south of the Sahara

HABITAT Woodland, often near rivers

SIZE 15 in (8 cm)

This woodhoopoe has glossy dark-green and purple plumage and a long, deep-purple tail. Its distinctive red bill is long and curves downwards. Male and female look alike, but young birds have brownish neck and breast plumage and black bills. These noisy, gregarious birds fly from tree to tree in small parties, searching for insects to eat and calling harshly.

Females lay 3 to 5 eggs in a hole in a tree. She incubates the clutch. Her mate helps to tend and feed the young.

ORDER TROGONIFORMES

TROGONIDAE: TROGON FAMILY

Trogons are a family placed in its own order. The 39 species are among the most colorful birds in the world. Males are more brilliantly marked than females. Trogons inhabit forests in the southern regions of Africa; India and Southeast Asia; and Central and South America.

Trogons are between 9 and 14 in (23 and 35.5 cm) long with short, rounded wings and long tails. Their feet are zygodactyl, (two toes point forward and two point back).The first and second digits point forward. (In other birds with such feet, the first and fourth digits do so.) Trogons are mainly arboreal. They eat insects, small invertebrates, berries and fruit.

Resplendent Quetzal *Pharomachrus mocinno* **LR:nt**

RANGE Mexico, Central America

HABITAT High-altitude rain forest

SIZE Body: 11¾ in (30 cm)
Tail feathers: 24 in (61 cm)

The quetzal has greatly extended feathers overlying the tail (coverts), which form a magnificent train but are shed and regrown after each breeding season. These feathers were highly prized for ceremonial use by the ancient Mayans and Aztecs. Females are plainer than males. Their upper tail coverts do not form a train.

Quetzals are quite solitary birds, which inhabit the lower layers of the tropical forest. They eat fruit, insects, frogs, lizards and snails. The nest is a hole in a tree and 2 or 3 eggs are laid. The male helps to incubate them, bending his tail forward over his head, so that it hangs out of the nest hole. His feathers become damaged from moving in and out of the nest.

Coppery-tailed/Elegant Trogon *Trogon elegans*

RANGE Extreme S.W. USA to Costa Rica

HABITAT Forest, woodland

SIZE 11–12 in (28–30.5 cm)

This trogon has a stout yellow bill and a broad, blunt tail which is coppery-red seen from above, but gray and white from below, with a black band at the base. The female is duller, with a brownish head. This is the only species of trogon in the USA.

These birds are solitary and generally quiet, but they do make monotonous, froglike calls. They perch in the trees for long periods then take to the air, to dart about the branches in search of insects, small animals and fruit. Most feeding is done in flight, and the birds sometimes hover in front of leaves to glean food from their surfaces. The trogon's legs and feet are weak and used almost entirely for perching.

Both partners of a breeding pair help to excavate a hole in a tree for use as a nest, or they take over an existing hollow or abandoned woodpecker hole. The 3 or 4 eggs are incubated by both the male and female, probably for 17 to 19 days. The young hatch naked and helpless and are cared for and fed by both parents and leave the nest at 15 to 17 days old.

Red-headed Trogon *Harpactes erythrocephalus*

RANGE Nepal: Himalayas, S. China; S.E. Asia, Sumatra

HABITAT Forest

SIZE 13¼ in (34 cm)

There are 11 species of trogon in Asia, all in the genus *Harpactes*. All are beautifully colored, with broad, squared-off tails. The male has distinctive dark-red plumage on its head, while the female has a brownish head, throat and breast. They are mainly solitary and perch on trees, darting out to catch insects. They also eat leaves, berries, frogs, and lizards. Both parents incubate the 3 or 4 eggs in an unlined hole for about 19 days.

Narina Trogon *Apaloderma narina*

RANGE S. Africa, S. and E. coastal regions

HABITAT Forest, scrub

SIZE 11½ in (29 cm)

This is one of 3 African trogon species. It lives in the lower levels of dense forest and perches for long periods on a branch or creeper in a hunched posture. It eats mainly insects, which it catches among the branches, and occasionally fruit. The 2 or 3 eggs (laid in a hollow tree trunk) are incubated for about 20 days.

ROLLERS, GROUND-ROLLERS, CUCKOO-ROLLERS, MOTMOTS AND BEE-EATERS

ORDER CORACIIFORMES

There are 9 families in this order – rollers, ground-rollers, cuckoo-roller, motmots, todies, bee-eaters, and three families of kingfisher. The birds generally have large bills in proportion to their body size and bright plumage.

CORACIIDAE: ROLLER FAMILY

Most of the 12 species of roller live in Africa, although they occur in warm temperate and tropical parts of the Old World, from Europe to Australia. They are brightly colored, stocky birds, with large heads, long, downward-curving bills and long wings. Their common name originates from their tumbling, aerobatic courtship displays. Males and females look alike.

European Roller
Coracias garrulus

RANGE Breeds in Europe, N. Africa, S.W. Asia. Winters in E. and S. Africa, Middle East

HABITAT Forest, woodland, open country

SIZE 11¾ in (30 cm)

Robust, gregarious birds, European rollers like to perch above the ground (telephone wires are particularly favored spots) in order to watch for prey such as insects, small lizards, frogs and birds. They dart out to seize the prey and return to the perch in order to feed. Fruit is also part of the rollers' diet.

The male roller courts his mate with extraordinary flight displays in which he dives to the earth from high in the air tumbling and rolling as he descends.

The nest is made in an existing hole in a tree, wall or bank. Alternatively, the abandoned nest of another bird species is used. Both parents incubate the clutch of between 4 and 7 eggs for a total of 18 or 19 days and also share the care of the young.

BRACHYPTERACIIDAE: GROUND ROLLER FAMILY

The 5 species of ground roller all live in Madagascar. They differ from the rollers in that they are ground-living rather than arboreal.

Short-legged Ground Roller
Brachypteracias leptosomus **VU**

RANGE E. Madagascar

HABITAT Dense forest to 6,000 ft (1,800 m)

SIZE 10–12 in (25.5–30.5 cm)

Typical of its family, the short-legged ground roller is a squat bird, with short wings, strong legs and a stout, downward curving bill. It lives on the forest floor, feeding on insects and reptiles, and flies up into trees only when alarmed.

LEPTOSOMATIDAE: CUCKOO-ROLLER FAMILY

The cuckoo-roller is related to true rollers and ground rollers. However the sexes look unalike.

Cuckoo-roller *Leptosomus discolor*

RANGE Madagascar, Comoro Islands

HABITAT Forest, savanna

SIZE 16–18 in (41–46 cm)

Cuckoo-rollers are noisy birds. They live in trees and feed on insects (especially hairy caterpillars) and lizards. Their short legs are weak, but they are strong, spectacular fliers. The female is plainer than the male, with rufous plumage and black markings.

MOMOTIDAE: MOTMOT FAMILY

Motmots are beautifully plumaged birds, with decorative, elongated tail feathers. There are 9 species of motmot, found from Mexico to northeastern Argentina. All have slightly downward-curving bills with serrated edges, which they use to seize prey from the dense vegetation among which they live. Male and female look alike, or nearly so.

Blue-crowned Motmot *Momotus momota*

RANGE Mexico, Central America, South America to N.W. Argentina; Trinidad and Tobago

HABITAT Rain forest, plantations

SIZE 15–16 in (38–41 cm)

The blue-crowned motmot has two greatly elongated central tail feathers with racket-shaped tips. Although the feathers are initially fully vaned, the vanes just above the ends of the feathers are loosely attached and fall away as the bird preens or brushes against vegetation, leaving the racket tips. The motmot perches to watch for prey, such as insects, spiders or lizards, often swinging its tail from side to side like a pendulum while it waits. It darts out from the perch to seize prey, then returns to consume the item, having briefly beaten it against a branch.

Motmots nest in a burrow, which is dug by both members of a breeding pair, in a bank or opening off the side of a mammal's burrow. The burrow may be up to 13 ft (4 m) long and have several sharp turns. In the enlarged chamber at the end of the tunnel, the female lays her 3 eggs on bare ground. Both parents incubate the eggs for about 21 days.

TODIDAE: TODY FAMILY

The 5 species of tody all live in the West Indies and are extremely similar in size and appearance, with mostly green and red plumage. Males and females look alike. They are insect-eating birds which catch their prey, flycatcher-fashion, in the air.

Jamaican Tody *Todus todus*

RANGE Jamaica

HABITAT Wooded hills and mountains

SIZE 4 in (10 cm)

The Jamaican tody is typical of its family, with its small, compact body, relatively large head and long, sharp bill. It hunts close to the ground, catching flying insects and, occasionally, baby lizards.

Todies live in pairs or singly and are strongly territorial. They nest in burrows, which they dig with their bills, usually in the sides of banks. The nest tunnel is about 11¾ in (30 cm) long, with a tiny entrance just big enough for the birds to squeeze through. It opens out at the end into a breeding chamber. Both parents incubate the 3 or 4 eggs and care for the young.

MEROPIDAE: BEE-EATER FAMILY

The 26 species of bee-eater are brightly plumaged birds, with streamlined bodies, long wings and small, weak legs. They occur in tropical and warm temperate areas of the Old World. As their name suggests, they are adept at the aerial capture of insects, such as bees and wasps, which they seize with their long, downward-curving bills. While they are considered a menace by beekeepers, these birds are much appreciated in the tropics, where they consume large numbers of locusts.

Bee-eaters are gregarious birds, feeding together and nesting in colonies of sometimes hundreds of pairs. Males and females look alike. Many species are migratory.

European Bee-eater *Merops apiaster*

RANGE Breeds in Europe, S. Russia, N. Africa, S.W. Asia; winters in tropical Africa and Middle East

HABITAT Open country, woodland

SIZE 11 in (28 cm)

One of the most tropical-looking European birds, the gaudy bee-eater makes swift darts from a perch to catch prey, mainly bees and wasps. It rubs its prey against a branch or the ground before swallowing it, presumably to destroy the sting. Bee-eaters nest in colonies. A pair makes a tunnel 3¼ to 9¾ ft (1 to 3 m) long, often in a river bank. The female lays 4 to 7 eggs at the end of the tunnel, and both parents incubate the clutch for about 20 days. Together, they care for and feed their young.

KINGFISHERS

ALCEDINIDAE ALCEDINID: KINGFISHER FAMILY

Kingfishers are found all over the world, but the majority of the 94 or so known species inhabit the hotter regions of the Old World. They range in length from 4 to 18 in (10 to 46 cm) and have stocky bodies, large heads and short necks. The beak is almost always straight with a pointed tip and is large in proportion to the body. Wings are short and rounded, and tail length is variable. Most kingfishers have multicolored plumage, with patches of iridescent blue, green, purple or red. Male and female differ slightly in appearance in some species.

Several species eat fish and aquatic invertebrates which they hunt by diving headlong from a perch just above the water, but they do not actually swim. Most species, however, feed on dry land on insects, lizards, snakes and even birds and rodents, catching prey by swooping down from a high vantage point.

Kingfishers nest in tunnels, often in river banks, or in cavities in trees or termite nests; there is little or no nesting material. Some northern populations migrate south in winter. There are 3 kingfisher families – the Alcedinid, Dacelonid, and Cerylid Kingfishers. The 24 species of Alcedinid Kingfishers live close to water from temperate Eurasia to Australia and in Africa.

Common Kingfisher *Alcedo atthis*
RANGE Europe, N. Africa to Asia, Indonesia, New Guinea and Solomon Islands
HABITAT Inland waterways, marshes, mangroves, sea shores
SIZE 6¼ in (16 cm)

The common kingfisher is the only European kingfisher. It has a wide range and is unmistakable with its brilliant plumage and long, daggerlike bill. A solitary bird, it lives in the vicinity of water. When hunting, it perches on branches overhanging the water, watching for fish and other small aquatic animals. Alternatively it flies low over the water, often hovering for a few seconds before diving.

A breeding pair excavates a slightly upward-sloping tunnel, up to 24 in (61 cm) long, in the bank of a stream, with a nesting chamber about 6 in (15 cm) across at the end of it. They start the tunnel by hurling themselves repeatedly against the riverbank so that their bills always strike the same spot.

The female lays a clutch of 4 to 8 eggs which both parents incubate in shifts for 19 to 21 days. Both the male and female share in the care and feeding of the young.

African Pygmy Kingfisher *Ispidina picta*
RANGE Africa, south of the Sahara to Zambia
HABITAT Bush, woodland
SIZE 5 in (12.5 cm)

One of the smallest kingfishers, this species has the curious habit of diving from its perch into grass, much as other kingfishers dive into water. Grasshoppers, caterpillars, beetles and other insects, as well as some lizards, make up its diet. The insects are caught in the air or on the ground. The pygmy kingfisher's nest is made at the end of a tunnel in a river bank or in a termite mound or anthill, and the female lays a clutch of 3 to 5 eggs.

DACELONIDAE: DACELONID KINGFISHER FAMILY

Dacelonid kingfishers are stocky, with long tails and blunt, thick beaks. The 61 species occur from southern Asia to Australia, the Philippines and Pacific islands, and in Africa. The family includes kookaburras, white-collared kingfishers, and bush kingfishers. Some species live by water, but others live in dry areas of scrub, forest or open country.

Laughing Kookaburra
Dacelo novaeguineae
RANGE Australia; introduced in Tasmania
HABITAT Dry forest fringe, savanna, any open country with trees
SIZE 18 in (46 cm)

The largest of the kingfishers, the kookaburra is renowned for its noisy, laughlike call. If one bird starts calling, others nearby will join in, particularly at dawn or at dusk. Kookaburras eat practically anything, including large insects, crabs, small reptiles, mammals and birds, as well as rodents and other harmful vermin.

Kookaburras nest in holes in trees or sometimes in arboreal termite nests, in cavities in banks or even on buildings. The female lays 3 or 4 eggs.

Shovel-billed Kingfisher *Clytoceyx rex* **DD**

RANGE New Guinea

HABITAT Forest

SIZE 12 in (30.5 cm)

The soberly colored shovel-billed kingfisher is a solitary bird which inhabits forest at altitudes of up to 7,700 ft (2,350 m). It perches for long periods on tree stumps and branches, swooping down suddenly to catch large insects, larvae and small mice. Using its short, heavy bill as a shovel, it also probes in the mud beside streams and rivers, searching for worms, crabs and reptiles. Little is known about its breeding habits, but it is thought to make its nest on the ground.

White-collared/Mangrove Kingfisher

Todirhamphus chloris

RANGE Ethiopia to India, S.E. China, Australia, S.W. Pacific islands

HABITAT Mangroves, estuaries, rivers, forest clearings

SIZE 10 in (25.5 cm)

This widely distributed kingfisher is found in a variety of habitats but most commonly in mangroves. Perching on branches, it watches for prey; then swoops down to the swamp mud or dives into the water in pursuit of crabs and small fish, its main foods. Before swallowing a crab, the kingfisher will dash it against a branch a few times in order to crush the shell.

These kingfishers nest in holes in trees, among the roots of an arboreal fern or in termite or ant nests. The female lays a clutch of 3 or 4 eggs.

Common Paradise Kingfisher *Tanysiptera galatea*

RANGE New Guinea to Molucca Islands

HABITAT Forest

SIZE 11 in (28 cm)

The common paradise kingfisher has greatly elongated tail feathers, thought to be used in courtship display. Deep in the forest understorey, it perches on branches to watch for its prey, mainly millipedes and lizards, but also insects and other invertebrates. It may dig in the forest litter for earthworms.

Paradise kingfishers are normally solitary birds, but in the breeding season both partners of a pair help to dig a hole in an arboreal termite nest in which to lay their eggs. Alternatively, the birds will nest in patches of vegetation at the forest edge. The female lays a clutch of between 3 and 5 eggs which are incubated by both parents.

CERYLIDAE: CERYLID KINGFISHER FAMILY

The 9 species of Cerylid kingfishers are larger with longer tails than the Alcedinid kingfishers. They live by lakes and rivers, or the sea, in the Americas, Africa and south and south-east Asia.

Belted Kingfisher

Megaceryle alcyon

RANGE Alaska, Canada, USA, south to Mexico and Panama; West Indies

HABITAT Fresh water, coasts

SIZE 11–14 in (28–35.5 cm)

The only American kingfisher occurring north of Texas and Arizona, this common bird inhabits any territory near water. The sexes look similar, but the female has a chestnut band across the breast and down her flanks. Solitary birds out of the breeding season, each holds its own territory. They eat small fish, crabs, crayfish, tadpoles, frogs, lizards and some insects, and generally hover above the water before diving for prey.

Both members of a breeding pair dig a nesting tunnel 4 to 8 ft (1.2 to 2.4 m) long in the river bank, at the end of which they make a nesting chamber. The female lays a clutch of 5 to 8 eggs which are incubated for about 23 days.

MOUSEBIRDS AND CUCKOOS

ORDER COLIIFORMES

COLIIDAE: MOUSEBIRD FAMILY

The 6 species of mousebird, or coly, are a distinctive family that modern taxonomists place in an order of its own. All the forms are similar in appearance, and the sexes look alike in all species. The body of the mousebird is about the same size as that of a house sparrow, but it has extremely long tail feathers of graduated lengths. The plumage is soft and loosely attached to the skin. All species have crests, and their bills are short, curved and quite strong. Mousebirds are distributed in the savanna regions of Africa, south of the Sahara. They are sociable, living in small groups and roosting together, huddled up for warmth.

Speckled Mousebird *Colius striatus*

RANGE Africa, south of the Sahara

HABITAT Savanna, dense forest

SIZE Body: 4¾ in (12 cm)
Tail: 7–7¾ in (18–20 cm)

The speckled mousebird's tail is almost twice the length of its body. It lives mainly in trees and climbs expertly among the branches, using its strong, adaptable feet – the hind toes can be turned forward – and long, sharp claws. This species is gregarious and feeds and roosts in small groups. Soft vegetable matter, particularly young shoots and fruit, is its normal diet, but it will eat insects.

The speckled mousebird makes a nest of twigs and rootlets, lined with leaves, in a tree or bush. Usually 3 eggs are laid, and they are incubated by both parents for 12 to 14 days. Chicks can leave the nest at a few days old and fly at 16 to 18 days old.

ORDER CUCULIFORMES

This order contains 143 species of cuckoos in 6 families – Cuculidae (Old World cuckoos), Centropodidae (coucals), Coccyzidae (American cuckoos), Opisthocomidae (hoatzin), Crotophagidae (anis and guira cuckoos), and Neomorphidae (roadrunners and ground-cuckoos). They range between 6 and 28 in (15 and 71 cm) long, and most are slender bodied, with long tails and short legs. Males and females look alike in most species. Fifty or so Old World cuckoos are nest parasites.

CUCULIDAE: OLD WORLD CUCKOO FAMILY

The 79 species in this family are found from Eurasia south to Africa and Australia. This diverse family includes both tree-dwelling and terrestrial species. Some build nests and rear their own young, but the females of many species in the family lay their eggs in the nests of another species which then incubates and rears her young. In some species this habit of nest parasitism is now highly developed, and the cuckoo's eggs resemble those of the host species. Since parasitic cuckoos generally lay their eggs in the nests of much smaller passerine birds, their eggs must be smaller and hatch more quickly than those of nonparasitic cuckoos.

Common Cuckoo *Cuculus canorus*

RANGE Europe, N. Africa, N. and S.E. Asia; winters south of range in Africa and S. Asia

HABITAT Forest, woodland, moors

SIZE 13 in (33 cm)

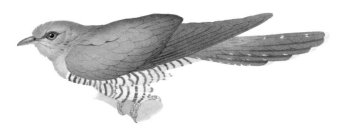

The male cuckoo's song, the origin of its common name, heralds the arrival of spring, when the bird flies north to breed in Europe and Asia. A slim, long-tailed bird, it leads a solitary life outside the breeding season and haunts trees, hedges and thickets, where it eats large insects, particularly hairy caterpillars.

Breeding starts in mid-May, and each female has a well-defined territory in which she searches for nests in which to lay her eggs. She uses the same host species, usually small passerine birds such as dunnocks, wagtails or redstarts, throughout her life. The species she chooses is probably that of her own foster parents. On alternate days, she lays a single egg, each in a different nest, at the same time removing one of the host's eggs, until she has laid a total of 8 to 12 eggs. She must lay her egg stealthily, for if the foster parents are alarmed, they may reject the whole clutch. The young cuckoo hatches in about 12 days. Since it is much the bigger, stronger and faster growing it is able to oust the hosts' own young from the nest. The hosts have to work extremely hard in order to satisfy the demands for food made by the young cuckoo, which is much larger than they are.

African Emerald Cuckoo

Chrysococcyx cupreus

RANGE Africa, south of the Sahara

HABITAT Forest edge and clearings

SIZE 7¾ in (20 cm)

A shy bird which haunts the dense foliage of tall forest trees, the emerald cuckoo is more often heard than seen, for it darts for cover at the slightest hint of danger.

Considered to be one of the most beautiful of African birds, the male has a golden-yellow belly and an emerald-green back. The female has moss green upperparts, a brown crown and a white belly, barred with mossgreen. Emerald cuckoos feed on a variety of insects, including caterpillars, ants and beetles.

The female lays her eggs in the nests of such birds as bulbuls, orioles, puff-back shrikes and black-headed weavers.

The emerald cuckoo is thought to be migratory. A smaller relative, the shining cuckoo, *C. lucidus*, migrates some 2,000 miles (3,200 km) across the southwest Pacific Ocean from New Zealand to the Solomon Islands.

Drongo Cuckoo

Surniculus lugubris

RANGE India, S.E. Asia, S. China, Indonesia

HABITAT Forest, scrub, cultivated land

SIZE 10 in (25.5 cm)

The drongo cuckoo resembles the drongo, *Dicrurus macrocercus*, in its plumage and forked tail, unique among cuckoos, and uses it as a foster-parent in some areas. A solitary, mainly nocturnal bird, it feeds on insects, particularly grasshoppers and caterpillars, and on fruit such as figs. It also catches winged insects by leaping up into the air after them in the manner of the drongo.

The female lays her eggs in the nests of various drongo species and in those of other birds. Juveniles have white flecks in their black plumage, which disappear as the birds mature.

Common/Asian Koel *Eudynamys scolopacea*

RANGE India, Pakistan, Sri Lanka, S. China, S.E. Asia, New Guinea, Australia

HABITAT Forest fringe, scrub, cultivated land, gardens

SIZE 17 in (43 cm)

The koel is a solitary bird, keeping to leafy trees and seldom descending to the ground. It feeds on fruit, particularly

figs, but also eats insects and small invertebrates such as snails. The male and female do not look alike – the male is black and glossy, while the female has brownish plumage, spotted and barred with white and buff.

The female koel lays her eggs in the nest of the house crow, *Corvus splendens*, or of a friarbird or honeyeater. Birds which use the crow as a foster-parent lay several eggs which resemble those of the host species, but are smaller. The young koels are black and look similar to young crows.

Channel-billed Cuckoo

Scythrops novaehollandiae

RANGE Australia to New Guinea, Indonesia

HABITAT Forest, woodland

SIZE 25 in (63.5 cm)

The channel-billed cuckoo is the largest cuckoo of the Australasian region. With its large, deep bill, it is reminiscent of a toucan or hornbill. It will devour almost anything, but insects, fruit and berries are its preferred foods.

Channel-billed cuckoos migrate north in March, returning south in September in order to breed. The female lays 2 or more eggs in the nest of a crow, magpie or currawong. The 2 blind, naked cuckoo chicks attempt to push one another out of the nest at first, but are usually unable to do so, and normally both are reared by the foster parents.

CUCKOOS CONTINUED

Small Green-billed Malkoha *Phaenicophaeus viridirostris*

RANGE S. India, Sri Lanka

HABITAT Forest, scrub, bamboo forest

SIZE 15 in (38 cm)

This distinctive cuckoo is a common Indian species. It has a green bill and sky-blue eye patch, which is the origin of its alternative common name – the blue-faced malkoha.

The small green-billed malkoha flies feebly and reluctantly and spends most of the time under cover of bushes and undergrowth. Large insects, such as grasshoppers, mantids and caterpillars, form the bulk of its diet, and it occasionally catches small lizards.

This nonparasitic species builds a shallow nest, made of sticks and lined with leaves. The female lays 2 eggs.

Running Coua *Coua cursor*

RANGE S.W. Madagascar

HABITAT Arid brush

SIZE 14¼ in (36 cm)

The running coua is a terrestrial bird and usually moves on foot, although it is able to fly reasonably well. Single birds or small groups walk about looking for insects, such as caterpillars; if alarmed, they run quickly away, interspersing their strides with hops. A nonparasitic cuckoo, the coua builds its own nest, but little is known about its breeding habits.

CENTROPODIDAE: COUCAL FAMILY

The 30 species of coucals are terrestrial cuckoos found in forests and grasslands from southern Asia to the Philippines, Australia and sub-Saharan Africa. They have strong legs and either walk or run along the ground, or skulk in dense vegetation.

Buff-headed Coucal

Centropus milo

RANGE Solomon Islands

HABITAT Forest

SIZE 26 in (66 cm)

One of the largest cuckoos, the buff-headed coucal has short wings, a long tail and a big, curved bill. It is a poor flier and spends most of its time on the ground, but even there moves awkwardly. It will sometimes flap up into a tree, moving from branch to branch and then gliding clumsily down. It feeds on large insects, frogs and reptiles.

The coucal's nest is a rounded, domed structure, made of grass and built in the undergrowth just above ground level. The female lays a clutch of 3 to 5 eggs.

COCCYZIDAE: AMERICAN CUCKOO FAMILY

These medium-sized tree dwellers resemble Old World cuckoos, but none of the 18 species is parasitic. They are found from southern Canada to northern Argentina.

Yellow-billed Cuckoo *Coccyzus americanus*

RANGE Breeds from Canada to Mexico and Caribbean islands; winters in Central and South America

HABITAT Woodland, orchards, thickets

SIZE 11–13 in (28–33 cm)

The yellow-billed cuckoo is secretive and shy. It frequents undergrowth and brush, searching for hairy caterpillars, beetles, grasshoppers, tree-crickets, army ants, wasps and flies. It also feeds on summer fruit and small frogs and lizards.

A nonparasitic cuckoo, it builds a nest of sticks in a tree or bush and lines it with dry leaves, grass or even pieces of rag. The female lays 3 or 4 eggs, one every 2 or 3 days, and both parents incubate the eggs, each of which hatches 14 days after laying. The nestlings are almost naked when they hatch, with only a sparse covering of down. Both parents feed and tend the young.

OPISTHOCOMIDAE: HOATZIN FAMILY

The hoatzin is the single species in this family.

Hoatzin *Opisthocomus hoazin*

RANGE South America: Amazon and Orinoco basins

HABITAT Wooded river banks

SIZE 24 in (61 cm)

The hoatzin has large wings and tail, a long neck and a small head, topped with a ragged crest. The sexes look alike. It is a poor flier and uses its wings more for support and balance when moving about in the trees. Hoatzins live in flocks of 10 to 20. They eat fruit and leaves, particularly mangrove and arum leaves.

The hoatzin builds its untidy stick nest in a tree overhanging water so that if threatened, the young birds, which can swim, can drop down into the water to escape. Both parents are believed to incubate the 2 or 3 eggs. The young hoatzin has a pair of hooked claws on each wing, which help it to clamber among the trees. The claws are lost as the bird matures.

CROTOPHAGIDAE: ANI AND GUIRA CUCKOO FAMILY

The 3 anis species and 1 species of guira cuckoo are all gregarious, and roost and breed communally. They occur from southern USA to northern Argentina.

Smooth-billed Ani *Crotophaga ani*

RANGE From C. Florida south to Central and South America, West Indies

HABITAT Forest edge, grassland, pasture

SIZE 13 in (33 cm)

Anis are nonparasitic cuckoos, with long square-ended tails, heavy bills and short wings. They fly weakly and feed mainly on the ground on insects, fruit and berries. Anis often follow grazing cattle which disturb ground insects.

Smooth-billed anis live in flocks of up to 25. They build a bulky communal nest from sticks, weeds and grass in a small tree or bush. Females each lay 3 or 4 eggs, and share the incubation. The whole flock feeds the chicks.

NEOMORPHIDAE: ROADRUNNER AND GROUND-CUCKOO FAMILY

These medium to large cuckoos occur from south-western USA to northern Argentina. They are mainly ground-dwellers that pursue their prey on foot. Of the 11 species, 3 are nest parasites.

Striped Cuckoo

Tapera naevia

RANGE S. Mexico, Central America, South America to N. Argentina

HABITAT Savanna, swamps

SIZE 12 in (30.5 cm)

The striped cuckoo is a shy bird that perches on a tree, calling for hours at a time, often during the hottest part of the day. Its call is a melancholy, carrying whistle, which sounds like "sa-ci". The striped cuckoo has parasitic breeding habits.

Greater Roadrunner *Geococcyx californianus*

RANGE S.W. USA: S. California, Utah, Kansas, south to Mexico

HABITAT Semi-arid open country

SIZE 19¾–23½ in (50–60 cm)

A slender, fowllike bird, with a small, shaggy crest, a long tail and long legs, the roadrunner is a fast-running ground-bird which can attain speeds of 15 mph (24 km/h) or more. Its short, rounded wings are functional and it can fly clumsily. Like its cousin, the lesser roadrunner, *G. velox*, of Mexico and Central America, it lives in dry, open places and eats ground-living insects, such as crickets and grasshoppers, and other small invertebrates, birds' eggs, lizards, snakes (even rattlesnakes) and fruits such as prickly pear. It usually kills with a sudden pounce.

Roadrunners form permanent pair bonds and live in their territory all year round. They build shallow nests of sticks, lined with leaves and feathers, in trees or cactus clumps. The female lays 2 to 6 eggs in April or May which are incubated for about 20 days. The eggs hatch over several days. Both parents care for the young, which hatch naked and helpless. Their eyes open at about 7 days, and they can feed themselves at about 16 days.

PARROTS

ORDER PSITTACIFORMES

PSITTACIDAE: PARROT FAMILY

The 358 species of parrot make up one of the most easily identified groups of birds. Despite a size range of between 4 and 40 in (10 and 101 cm), all types have a general similarity of appearance and structure. Species include lories, cockatoos, lovebirds, budgerigars and lorikeets.

Most parrots are brightly colored tree-living birds. Their beaks are short, powerful and strongly hooked, with a bulging base or cere. The upper part of the parrot's bill is hinged and moved by muscles, and the flexibility that this gives allows the bill to become almost like a third manipulative limb, which is used in climbing and feeding. Although many birds have hinged bills, this feature is more marked in the short-billed parrots. Males and females look alike in most species, but there are plumage differences in a few instances.

Parrots are distributed through the tropical and subtropical zones of both hemispheres. The largest number of species occur in Australasia and the Amazon in South America. In the forests of these regions, parrots feed largely on fruit, nuts, seeds, nectar and fungi. They manipulate food with their feet, beaks and strong, mobile tongues. Many parrots are gregarious and vocal, making screaming and discordant calls. Although they mimic sound in captivity, they are not known to do so in the wild.

Black-capped Lory *Lorius lory*

RANGE	New Guinea, Papuan Islands
HABITAT	Forest
SIZE	12 in (31 cm)

Several races of this lory, with slight plumage differences, occur on the various islands in its range. Shy birds, black-capped lories frequent the upper levels of the forest, usually moving in pairs or small groups of up to a dozen. They eat pollen, nectar, flowers, fruit, and insects and their larvae. Little is known of the breeding habits of this lory, but it appears that the female lays 2 eggs, which she incubates for about 24 days.

Rainbow Lorikeet *Trichoglossus haematodus*

RANGE	E. and N. Australia, Tasmania; Bali, east to New Hebrides
HABITAT	Forest, coconut plantations, gardens, parks
SIZE	10¼ in (26 cm)

One of the most attractively plumaged birds in the parrot order, the adaptable rainbow lorikeet inhabits almost any wooded land, even near human habitation. Usually seen in pairs or flocks of anything from 3 or 4 to 100 birds, rainbow lorikeets are active and noisy and continually fly about the trees searching for food and calling loudly. Pollen, nectar, fruit, berries, seeds, leaves, insects and larvae are all included in their diet, and they will feed on grain crops and invade orchards.

Rainbow lorikeets nest in holes in trees, high above the ground. The female lays 2 eggs, rarely 3, which she incubates for about 25 days. Both parents feed the chicks which stay in the nest until they are about 7 or 8 weeks old.

Cockatiel *Nymphicus hollandicus*

RANGE	Australia
HABITAT	Open country
SIZE	12½ in (32 cm)

The slender cockatiel has long wings and tail and a tapering crest on its head. Males and females differ slightly – males having brighter markings than females. In pairs or small flocks, cockatiels forage on the ground for seeds, and feed in the trees on fruit and berries.

Breeding usually takes place between August and December, but the exact timing depends on the conditions, particularly on rainfall. The 4 to 7 eggs are laid in a hole in a tree and are incubated by both parents for 21 to 23 days.

The young leave the nest at 4 or 5 weeks and males acquire their bright facial markings at about 6 months.

Sulfur-crested Cockatoo *Cacatua galerita*

RANGE New Guinea and offshore islands, Aru Islands, N. and E. Australia, Tasmania; introduced in New Zealand

HABITAT Forest, savanna, farmland

SIZE 19¾ in (50 cm)

Noisy, gregarious birds, sulfur-crested cockatoos move in pairs or family groups in the breeding season, but join in flocks for the rest of the year. In open country, these flocks may number hundreds of birds. Each flock has an habitual roosting site which the birds leave at sunrise, in order to fly to daytime feeding grounds where they forage for seeds, fruit, nuts, flowers leaves, insects and larvae.

After a brief courtship display, culminating in a spell of mutual preening, the sulfur-crested cockatoos nest in a hole in a tree. Both parents incubate the clutch of 2 or 3 eggs for about 30 days, and the young stay in the nest for 6 to 9 weeks.

Kea *Nestor notabilis* **LR:nt**

RANGE New Zealand: South Island

HABITAT Forest, open country

SIZE 18¾ in (48 cm)

The kea is a bold, stocky bird with a long, curving upper bill. The female's bill is shorter and less curved. Keas fly strongly, wheeling in wide arcs, even in stormy, windy weather. They feed in trees and on the ground on fruit, berries, leaves, insects and larvae. They will also scavenge on refuse dumps and eat carrion. The belief has long persisted that keas attack and kill sheep, and many birds have been destroyed by farmers for this reason. Although they may well attack sick, injured or trapped sheep, these activities are thought to have been exaggerated, and keas are now protected by law.

Nesting takes place at almost any time of year, but usually occurs between July and January. Males are polygamous. The nest is made in a crevice, under rocks among the roots of a tree or in a hollow log. The female lays 2 to 4 eggs which she incubates for 21 to 28 days.

Red-breasted Pygmy Parrot

Micropsitta bruijnii

RANGE Buru, Ceram, New Guinea, Bismarck Archipelago, Solomon Islands

HABITAT Mountain forest

SIZE 3½ in (9 cm)

In pairs or small groups, these tiny parrots clamber over branches of trees feeding on the lichens and fungus prevalent in high forest. The short tail has stiff shafts and can be used as a prop in the manner of a woodpecker. Pygmy parrots may also feed on other plant material and insects.

PARROTS CONTINUED

Eclectus Parrot *Eclectus roratus*
RANGE New Guinea, Solomon Islands, Lesser Sunda Islands; Australia: extreme N. Queensland

HABITAT Lowland forest

SIZE 13¾ in (35 cm)

Male and female eclectus parrots differ so radically in plumage that for years they were thought to be separate species. Both are glossy, brilliant birds, males with primarily green plumage and females with red. The body is stocky and the tail short and square. They are noisy, gregarious birds, roosting in groups of as many as 80 and flying off at sunrise in pairs or small groups to feed on fruit, nuts, seeds, berries, leaves, flowers and nectar.

The nest is made high up in a tree at the edge of the forest or in a clearing. The 2 eggs are laid in a hole in the tree trunk and the female incubates them for about 26 days.

Gray Parrot *Psittacus erithacus*
RANGE Central Africa: W. coast to Kenya and N.W. Tanzania

HABITAT Lowland forest, savanna, mangroves

SIZE 13 in (33 cm)

Flocks of gray parrots roost together in tall trees at the forest edge or on small islands in rivers and lakes. At sunrise they fly off swiftly in pairs or small groups to find food, following regular routes to and from the roosting area. Climbing from branch to branch, gray parrots feed in the trees on seeds, nuts, berries and fruit, particularly the fruit of the oil palm.

The timing of the breeding season varies according to area, and there may occasionally be two broods a year. There have been very few observations of nesting in the wild, but the female is believed to lay 3 or 4 eggs in a hole in a tree and to incubate them herself.

Peach-faced/Rosy-faced Lovebird *Agapornis roseicollis*
RANGE S.W. Africa: Angola, Namibia, S. Africa: N. Cape Province

HABITAT Dry open country

SIZE 6 in (15 cm)

Flocks of these noisy, abundant lovebirds maneuver skilfully and swiftly among the trees and bushes. They eat seeds and berries and never move far from some form of water supply. Lovebirds are so called because of their conspicuous mutual preening habits.

Colonies of lovebirds nest in crevices in cliffs or in buildings, or take over large parts of the communal, many-chambered nests of weaver birds. The female is thought to lay 3 to 6 eggs which she incubates for 23 days.

Kakapo/Owl Parrot *Strigops habroptilus* **EW**
RANGE New Zealand: parts of South and Stewart Islands

HABITAT Mountain forest all altitudes to 4,100 ft (1,250 m)

SIZE 25¼ in (64 cm)

Although the highest priority has been given to its protection, the kakapo is in serious danger of extinction. The population has declined steadily over the last 1,000 years, with the settlement of New Zealand, the resulting land clearance and the introduction of predators such as stoats and rats. Despite efforts made to establish kakapos on offshore islands which are free from predators, the kakapo is listed by the IUCN as being extinct in the wild.

The kakapo is a most unusual parrot. It is a ground-living and flightless, nocturnal bird. During the day it shelters among rocks or bushes or in a burrow and emerges at dusk in order to feed on fruit, berries, nuts, seeds, shoots, leaves, moss and fungi. The kakapo climbs well, using its beak and feet to haul itself up tree trunks and along branches, and can flap its wings to help balance itself as it climbs or jumps from trees.

Courtship habits, too, are different in the kakapo from those of other parrots, for the males display communally in traditional areas, or leks. Each male excavates several shallow, bowl-shaped areas in which he displays: the bowl helps to amplify the booming calls which accompany his show.

The nest is a burrow made among rocks or tree roots and 1 or 2, occasionally 3, eggs are laid. The female is thought to incubate the clutch and to care for the young alone. Kakapos do not appear to breed every year, and breeding may be linked to the availability of food.

Rose-ringed Parakeet
Psittacula krameri

RANGE Central Africa, India to Sri Lanka; introduced in Mauritius, Middle East, Singapore, Hong Kong, Hawaiian Islands
HABITAT Woodland, cultivated land
SIZE 15¾ in (40 cm)

The bold, noisy rose-ringed parakeets are usually seen in small flocks, although they may gather in hundreds at feeding or roosting sites. These parakeets fly well, but tend not to travel far afield. Seeds, berries, fruit, flowers and nectar are the main items of their diet and they are relentless in their search, invading orchards and plantations, decimating sunflower crops and rice paddies and even ripping open bags of stored grain.

Males and females differ slightly in plumage – the female lacks the pink collar and black facial markings and has shorter central tail feathers than the male.

At the onset of the breeding season, the pair perform their courtship ritual, the female rolling her eyes and head until the male approaches her. He then rubs bills with her and feeds her.

They nest in a hole in a tree, which they excavate or take over from woodpeckers or barbets, or under the roof of a building. The female lays a clutch of 3 to 5 eggs which she incubates for 22 days. The young leave the nest about 7 weeks after hatching.

Crimson Rosella *Platycercus elegans*

RANGE E. and S.E. Australia; introduced in New Zealand and Norfolk Island
HABITAT Coastal and mountain forest, gardens, parks
SIZE 14¼ in (36 cm)

Crimson rosellas are bold, colorful birds, abundant in most of their range. Adults live in pairs or groups of up to 5, while juveniles form large groups. Much of the day is spent feeding on the ground or in the trees, mainly on seeds but also fruit, blossoms, insects and larvae.

The breeding season starts in late August or early September. In his courtship display the male lets his wings droop while he fans his tail out, moving it from side to side. The female nests in a hole in a tree and lays 5 to 8 eggs which she incubates for 21 days, leaving the nest only briefly each morning to be fed by her partner. The young leave the nest at about 5 weeks, but remain with their parents for another 5 weeks before joining a flock of other young rosellas.

Budgerigar *Melopsittacus undulatus*

RANGE Australia (interior); introduced in USA: Florida
HABITAT Scrub, open country
SIZE 7 in (18 cm)

So popular as a cage bird, with its many color variations, the budgerigar is a small parrot with mainly green plumage in the wild. Its numbers vary with conditions, but it is generally common and in years of abundant food supplies is one of the most numerous Australian species. Active mainly in the early morning and late afternoon, flocks of budgerigars search on the ground for grass seeds, their main food. They are swift, agile birds in the air and flocks are nomadic, continually moving from one area to another in search of food and water.

Breeding takes place at any time of the year, usually after rains which ensure food supplies. A nest is made in a hollow in a tree stump or log, and 4 to 6, sometimes 8, eggs are laid and incubated by the female for 18 days. The young leave the nest after about 30 days.

PARROTS CONTINUED

Scarlet Macaw *Ara macao*

RANGE Mexico, Central America, N. South America to Brazil and Bolivia

HABITAT Forest, savanna, plantations

SIZE 33½ in (85 cm)

A spectacular, brilliantly plumaged bird, the scarlet macaw is one of the largest and most striking members of its family. A much-photographed and painted species and the most familiar of South American parrots, it is nevertheless declining in numbers because of the widespread destruction of its rain forest habitat and the collection of large numbers of young birds and nestlings for the lucrative cage-bird trade. It is already rare in some parts of its range.

Scarlet macaws maintain strong pair bonds and are generally seen in pairs, family groups or flocks of up to 20. As they make their daily journeys from roosting areas to feeding grounds, pairs will fly together, wings almost touching. They feed up in the trees on seeds, fruit, nuts, berries and other plant matter and, although they eat in silence, they fly off, squawking noisily, at any disturbance.

Surprisingly little is known of the breeding habits of these splendid birds. Nests have been observed in holes in tree trunks well above the ground, but there is little reliable data on clutch size or incubation.

Spectacled Parrotlet *Forpus conspicillatus*

RANGE Central and South America: E. Panama, Colombia (not S.E.), W. Venezuela

HABITAT Open forest, thorn bush

SIZE 4¾ in (12 cm)

About 3 races of this little parrotlet occur within the range, all with slight plumage differences. Generally, however, males have dull, greenish upperparts, with yellow markings on the forehead, cheeks and throat and some blue markings. Females have brighter green upperparts than males and lack the blue markings. Out of the breeding season, spectacled parrotlets move in small flocks of 5 to 20, making constant chattering calls. These busy, active birds, forage in trees and bushes for berries, fruit, buds and blossoms or they search on the ground for the seeds of grasses and herbaceous plants. Their flight is swift and erratic.

During the breeding season, the parrotlets associate in pairs. Little is known of their breeding habits, but it is probable that they make their nests in natural holes in trees or posts. The female is believed to lay a clutch of 2 to 4 eggs. There are several species of parrotlet in the genus *Forpus*, all with similar habits and appearance.

Sun Parakeet *Aratinga solstitialis*

RANGE South America: Guyana, Surinam, French Guiana, N.E. Brazil

HABITAT Open forest, savanna

SIZE 11¾ in (30 cm)

The sun conure is a beautiful bird, with vibrant yellow plumage. It is not a common species, and little is known of its habits. Generally seen in small flocks, conures are noisy birds, which make frequent screeching calls. They feed on seeds, fruit, nuts and berries, usually foraging up in the treetops.

From the few observations of breeding habits, the female lays 3 or 4 eggs which she incubates for 4 weeks. Both parents feed the chicks, which remain in the nest for about 8 weeks.

The golden-capped conure, *A. aurocapilla*, and the jendaya conure, *A. jendawa*, are both similar to the sun conure and may even be races of the same species.

Yellow-headed Parrot/
Yellow crowned Amazon

Amazona ochrocephala

RANGE Mexico, Central America,
south to E. Peru, N. Bolivia and
N. Brazil; Trinidad, Tobago

HABITAT Forest, wide
range of wooded
habitats

SIZE 13¾ in
(35 cm)

The yellow-headed parrot is one of the
29 or so species in the genus *Amazona*, all
sometimes referred to as "amazons". Most are
medium-sized parrots with predominantly green plumage and
some brilliant markings. Like many amazons, this species is
declining in numbers both because of the destruction of its
forest habitat in some areas and because of the collection of large
numbers of young for the cage-bird trade. Yellow-headed parrots
are particularly sought after because of their reputation as good
mimics and talkers.

During the day, small groups of these parrots feed in the
treetops on fruit, seeds, nuts, berries and blossoms and will also
come down to within 6½ ft (2 m) of the ground to find food.
Yellow-headed parrots are strong fliers and travel well above the
trees except when going only short distances. At dusk they
return to regular roosting areas.

A breeding pair finds a hollow in a tree trunk, which both
enlarge, and the female lays 3 or 4 eggs. She incubates them for
29 days, during which the male remains nearby. Twice a day, the
female leaves the eggs briefly in order to join her mate, who
feeds her by regurgitation.

Monk Parakeet *Myiopsitta monachus*

RANGE South America: C.Bolivia, S. Brazil to C. Argentina;
introduced in Puerto Rico and N.E. USA

HABITAT Open woodland, palm groves, cultivated land,
eucalyptus plantations

SIZE 11½ in (29 cm)

A popular cage bird and abundant in the wild, the monk
parakeet is a medium-sized parrot, with long tail feathers and a
heavy bill. It is an adaptable species and readily inhabits trees

planted by man in orchards or on ranchland, even when near to
human habitation. The highly gregarious monk parakeets occur
in flocks of 10 to 100 or more and build enormous communal
nests, unique in the parrot order. The nest is used for breeding
and for roosting and so is inhabited throughout the year and is
always the centre of much activity as the birds come and go,
shrieking noisily.

Monk parakeets leave the nest in small groups to find food,
and if they are feeding in open country or fields, a few birds will
sit up in nearby trees to act as sentinels. At the first sign of
danger, they call a warning, and the feeding birds quickly
disperse. Seeds, fruit, berries, nuts, blossoms, leaves, insects and
larvae are all eaten, and monk parakeets can cause much damage
by feeding on cereal crops and in orchards.

Although the nest is used all year round, at the start of the
breeding season in October, the birds add to it and repair any
damage. The nest is usually situated at the top of a tree and is
made of twigs, particularly thorny twigs, which hold together
well and deter predators. It may start with only a few
compartments, but it is gradually added to until it has anything
up to 20 compartments, each occupied by a pair of birds. Each
compartment has its own entrance at the bottom of the nest,
leading into the brood chamber. The whole structure is so strong
that other birds may nest on top of it.

The female parakeet lays 5 to 8 eggs, but because of the
obvious difficulties of observing behavior in such a structure,
little is known of the incubation of the clutch or the care of the
chicks. The young birds leave the nest at about 6 weeks old.

SWIFTS AND CRESTED SWIFTS

ORDER APODIFORMES

This order includes 2 families – swifts and crested swifts. All are birds with highly developed flight abilities.

APODIDAE: SWIFT FAMILY

Swifts are the most aerial of birds. The 99 species in this fast-flying family seem to be able to carry out every avian activity on the wing, other than nesting. They catch food, eat, drink, collect material for nest construction and even copulate while flying. Some species may also be able to sleep aloft. Although they can take off with difficulty from flat ground, swifts normally alight only on vertical surfaces, such as cliffs or buildings, and they cannot perch. They are usually active in the daytime and feed on insects.

Swifts range in length between 3½ and 10 in (9 and 25.5 cm), and male and female look alike. Owing to similarity of habits rather than close relationship, swifts have a superficial resemblance to swallows and martins, for they possess the same narrow, pointed, although longer, wings and short, normally forked tails. Their legs and feet are tiny since they seldom, if ever, walk, but they have strong, curved claws for gripping landing and nesting surfaces. In most species, all four toes point forward. The beak is typically short and slightly down-curving and has a wide gape.

All swifts glue their nests together with glutinous saliva from specialized salivary glands.

Brown-backed Needletail

Hirundapus giganteus

RANGE India through S.E. Asia to the Philippines

HABITAT Forest up to 6,000 ft (1,800 m)

SIZE 10 in (25.5 cm)

One of the fastest-flying bird species, the brown-backed needletail can reputedly attain speeds of 155 to 186 mph (250 to 300 km/h). It feeds on insects and will hover motionless, like a hawk, watching for prey. The female lays 3 to 5 eggs in a nest made on the ground.

White-throated Swift *Aeronautes saxatalis*

RANGE W. Canada and USA to Mexico and El Salvador

HABITAT Vicinity of mountain and coastal cliffs, canyons, rugged foothills

SIZE 6–7 in (15–18 cm)

The white-throated swift is able to attain speeds of up to 186 mph (300 km/h) and it is probably the fastest-flying bird in North America. The swift catches insects, such as flies, beetles, bees, wasps, flying ants and leaf-hoppers, on the wing.

The swifts court in flight and copulate either on the wing, with their bodies pressed together as they tumble downward through the air, or in a nesting site. The nest, made in a crack or crevice in a coastal cliff or mountainside, is cup shaped and constructed from feathers and grass, glued together with saliva. The 4 or 5 eggs are laid in May and June and incubation duties are shared by both parents.

African Palm Swift *Cypsiurus parvus*

RANGE Subsaharan Africa

HABITAT Open country

SIZE 7 in (18 cm)

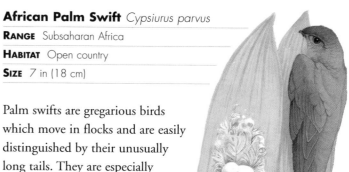

Palm swifts are gregarious birds which move in flocks and are easily distinguished by their unusually long tails. They are especially active at dusk, when many insects swarm.

The palm swift nests on the underside of a palm frond. The breeding pair constructs a pad of feathers, which are glued together and to the leaf with saliva. They then glue their clutch of 1 or 2 eggs to the nest, also with saliva. Assuming a vertical posture and gripping the sides of the nest with their claws, both partners take turns at incubating the eggs. When the chicks hatch, they must cling on to the nest with their claws and maintain their hold until they are fully fledged and ready to fly.

Edible-nest Swiftlet *Collocalia fuciphaga*

RANGE Andaman and Nicobar Islands, S.E. Asia, Philippines

HABITAT Coasts, islands; feeds over forest and scrub

SIZE 5 in (12.5 cm)

This swiftlet is one of 31 similar species in the genus *Collocalla*, all of which are found in Southeast Asia and the islands of the Pacific. The differentiation of the species is extremely difficult but has now been clarified by considering nest construction and sites and the ability to echolocate.

The swiftlets build their nests in caves, often in colonies of many thousands. They find their way in the darkness of the deeper caves by using echolocation, a rare ability among birds. As they fly, they make rapid clicking sounds and use the high-frequency echoes off the cave walls to navigate.

All swiftlets use saliva to make their nests and to glue them to cave walls, but the edible-nest swiftlet's nests are made almost entirely from hardened saliva with only a few feathers included – probably by accident. And it is these nests which give the bird its common name, for they are harvested in huge numbers to make the birds' nest soup which Chinese gourmets consider a delicacy. The female lays 2 or 3 eggs.

Common Swift *Apus apus*

RANGE Breeds in Europe, east to China; N.W. Africa; winters in Africa

HABITAT Over open country, fresh water, urban areas

SIZE 6¼ in (16 cm)

A common, gregarious bird, this swift is almost always seen in the air and only occasionally alights on walls, rocks or buildings. Uttering harsh, screaming cries, it flies in search of aerial insects, alternating rapid wing beats with long spells of gliding flight.

The breeding season starts in mid-May. The swifts select nest sites under the eaves of buildings or in rock crevices and make shallow cup-shaped nests of grass and feathers, glued together with saliva. There are usually 3 eggs in a clutch, laid at intervals of 2 or 3 days, and they are incubated for 14 to 20 days. Both parents feed the young, but may leave them for several days at a time. When this happens, the young burn up their fat stores and development slows down. If the fast is prolonged, the nestlings' body temperature may drop as much as 50°F (27.5°C) and they lapse into torpor, without any ill effects, until food is once again available.

HEMIPROCNIDAE: CRESTED SWIFT FAMILY

The 4 species of crested swift all have crests and long, deeply forked tails. Their plumage is softer and brighter than that of other swifts and they are less aerial in their habits. Unlike true swifts, they are able to perch. Males and females have some slight plumage differences. Crested swifts occur in India and Southeast Asia, south to New Guinea and the Solomon Islands.

Crested/Gray-rumped Tree Swift *Hemiprocne longipennis*

RANGE Malay Peninsula, Indonesia to Sulawesi

HABITAT Forest edge, open woodland

SIZE 8 in (20.5 cm)

The crested swift can perch on branches and telephone wires, from which it swoops down to feed on airborne insects.

Males and females of the species look similar, but the male has a chestnut patch behind the eye, while in the female this plumage is green.

The nest of the crested swift is a tiny cup-shaped structure, made from thin flakes of bark, glued together with saliva and attached with saliva to the branch of a tree. There is just enough room on it for the 1 egg, which both parents take it in turns to incubate by sitting on the branch and puffing up their breast feathers to cover the egg. Both parents care for the chick.

HUMMINGBIRDS

ORDER TROCHILIFORMES

TROCHILIDAE: HUMMINGBIRD FAMILY

This family is the only one in its order. Named for the drone produced by the extremely rapid beating of their wings, the spectacular hummingbirds occur all over the Americas, from Alaska to Tierra del Fuego and high in the Andes, but mainly in the tropics. The 319 or so species include the smallest, and some of the most striking, birds known.

Hummingbirds range in length from 2¼ to 8½ in (5.7 to 21.5 cm), but the tail often makes up as much as half of this length. Their wings are long and narrow relative to body size, and hummingbirds are quite unsurpassed in their aerial agility. They can hover motionless in front of a flower, their wings beating so fast that they are virtually invisible; fly upward, sideways, downward and, uniquely, even backward. The keel of the breastbone in a hummingbird is proportionately bigger than that of any other bird, to support the massive flying muscles needed to power their movements.

The hummingbird's main foods are insects and nectar, which it obtains by plunging its long, slender, often curved bill (which has become adapted for the task) deep inside the flower. It uses its tubular tongue to extract the nectar. The shapes of the bill and tongue are often closely related to the flower shape.

There is a great variety of tail shapes among male hummingbirds, and these decorative feathers are used in courtship display. Females have duller plumage than males and lack the ornamental tail feathers. Except in the breeding season, hummingbirds are solitary and defend their territory aggressively, even against much larger birds. The female builds a cup-shaped nest on a branch, palm frond or a rock, and normally lays 2 eggs. In all but 1 species, she alone incubates the eggs and cares for the young.

Sword-billed Hummingbird *Ensifera ensifera*

RANGE Andes: Venezuela, Colombia, Ecuador, Peru, Bolivia
HABITAT Shrubby slopes at 8,200–10,000 ft (2,500–3,000 m)
SIZE Bird: 3 in (7.5 cm) Bill: 5 in (12.5 cm)

The sword-billed hummingbird has the longest bill, relative to its size, of any bird. The bird probes deep into trumpet shaped flowers with its bill to feed on nectar and insects which feed on the nectar.

White-tipped Sicklebill

Eutoxeres aquila
RANGE Costa Rica, Panama, Colombia, Ecuador, N.E. Peru
HABITAT Forest
SIZE 5 in (12.5 cm)

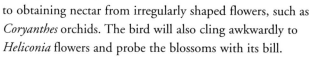

This little hummingbird's strongly downward curving bill is adapted to obtaining nectar from irregularly shaped flowers, such as *Coryanthes* orchids. The bird will also cling awkwardly to *Heliconia* flowers and probe the blossoms with its bill.

Ruby-throated Hummingbird

Archilochus colubris
RANGE Breeds in S.E. Canada, E. USA; winters in Mexico, Central America and West Indies
HABITAT Woodland, gardens
SIZE 3½ in (9 cm)

This tiny bird migrates 500 miles (800 km) or more across the Gulf of Mexico to its wintering grounds – an extraordinary feat for such a small bird. The male has a distinctive ruby red throat, and the female has white throat plumage and a rounded tail.

Bee Hummingbird

Calypte helenae
RANGE Cuba, Isle of Pines
HABITAT Forest
SIZE 20 in (5.7 cm)

The smallest bird in the world, the bee hummingbird's actual body measures only ½ in (1.25 cm), and its bill is a similar size. The tail makes up the remainder of its length. The bee hummingbird weighs only ¹⁄₁₄ oz (2 g). Its tiny wings beat between 50 and 80 times a second as it hovers in the air in order to feed from flowers.

Giant Hummingbird

Patagona gigas

RANGE Andes from Ecuador to Chile and Argentina

HABITAT Arid land

SIZE 8½ in (21.5 cm)

The largest hummingbird, this species weighs ¾ oz (20 g). It beats its wings only 8 or 10 times a second, and though it feeds at flowers, it also catches insects in flight.

Frilled Coquette

Lophornis magnifica

RANGE E. and C. Brazil

HABITAT Forest, scrub

SIZE 2¾ in (7 cm)

The brilliant frilled coquette can easily be mistaken for a butterfly, either as it hovers, feeding from a flower, or when pairs are courting, for the male chases the female until she slows down, and they then hover together, fluttering up and down. The female builds a cup-shaped nest among low vegetation and covers the outside with cobwebs, pieces of bark and plant fibers, which camouflage it.

Marvelous Spatule-tail

Loddigesia mirabilis **VU**

RANGE Andes in Peru

HABITAT Forest at 7,500–8,500 ft (2,300–2,600 m)

SIZE Body: 5 in (12.5 cm) Tail: 5½ in (14 cm)

The male of this little-known hummingbird species has an extraordinary long tail with only four feathers, two of which are greatly elongated and wirelike and expanded into racket shapes at the ends. During his courtship display, the male bird frames his iridescent throat plumage with his decorative tail feathers and flies back and forth in front of his prospective mate.

Ruby-topaz Hummingbird *Chrysolampis mosquitus*

RANGE Colombia, Venezuela, the Guianas, Brazil, N.E. Bolivia, Trinidad, Tobago

HABITAT Forest, scrub, savanna

SIZE 3½ in (9 cm)

The male of this species has glittering, colorful plumage, while the female's feathers are greenish and gray. It feeds on nectar and insects, both in low vegetation and tall trees.

Long-tailed Sylph

Hummingbird *Aglaiocercus kingi*

RANGE Venezuela to Bolivia, Peru and Ecuador

HABITAT Forest, scrub

SIZE Male: 7 in (18 cm)
Female: 3¾ in (9.5 cm)

The outer tail feathers of the male of this species are almost 5 in (12.5 cm) long and are used in courtship display. The female's tail feathers are not elongated, and she has a buff-white throat and cinnamon underparts.

Crimson Topaz *Topaza pella*

RANGE The Guianas, Venezuela, Brazil and east of the Andes in Ecuador

HABITAT Rain forest

SIZE 7¾ in (20 cm)

The glittering, colorful male crimson topaz has two elongated black tail feathers, which are 2¼ in (6 cm) longer than the rest of the tail. The female is less startling, but she also has gleaming green and red plumage and a bronze and violet tail.

Andean Hillstar *Oreotrochilus estella*

RANGE Andes: from Ecuador to Argentina, Chile and N. Peru

HABITAT Rocky slopes

SIZE 4¾ in (12 cm)

The neck and throat plumage of the male Andean hillstar varies, but usually includes glittering green or violet. The female has an olive-green back and head, a white throat and grayish underparts.

TURACOS, BARN OWLS AND OWLS

ORDER MUSOPHAGIFORMES

MUSOPHAGIDAE: TURACO FAMILY

The 23 species of turaco are fowllike, tree-dwelling birds of tropical Africa. Except for the go-away birds, which are gray and white, turacos are glossy and brightly colored, with long, broad tails and short, rounded wings. Many species have hairy crests and bare skin around the eye. The brilliant red of the head and wing feathers of some species is the result of a unique copper complex pigment which is soluble in alkalis. The green pigment is also unique. Turacos have short, stout bills and feed largely on insects and fruit. Males and females look alike.

Red-crested Turaco *Tauraco erythrolophus*

RANGE Africa: Angola, Zaire

HABITAT Woodland, savanna

SIZE 16 in (40.5 cm)

The red-crested turaco is a fruit-eating bird, which lives in trees and seldom descends to the ground. It is a poor flier but is agile and swift in the trees and can run, hop and climb among the branches. In addition to fruit, it eats seeds, insects and snails.

This turaco is almost identical to Bannerman's turaco, *T. bannerrnani,* and the most obvious distinguishing feature is the nostrils: rounded in the red-crested and slit-shaped in Bannerman's turaco. Nothing is known of their breeding habits.

Gray Go-away Bird, *Corythaixoides concolor*

RANGE Africa: Tanzania, Congo River basin to South Africa

HABITAT Open bush, acacia scrub

SIZE 20 in (51 cm)

Although wary, the common go-away bird is not timid. At the hint of danger, it alerts all the animals in the area with its penetrating call which sounds like "g'away, g'away". In pairs or small groups, the go-away birds perch on trees or fly clumsily from one tree to another; they eat berries, fruit and insects. The breeding season is from October to January. The birds display, one partner perches in a treetop and the other hovers

above. Both help to build a nest of sticks in dense creepers or an acacia tree. The female lays 2 or 3 large eggs, which both parents incubate for, it is thought, about 18 days.

ORDER STRIGIFORMES

This order contain 9 families and 291 species. Two families – Tytonidae (barn owls) and Strigidae (true owls) contain the owls. With their flattened faces, enormous eyes, taloned feet and predatory, usually nocturnal habits, owls are the nighttime equivalent of hawks, eagles and falcons. Owls kill with their talons – each toe is tipped with a sharp, hooked claw. They swallow prey whole and regurgitate the bones, fur and feathers in pellets. The sexes look alike in most species, although females are sometimes larger.

The remaining 7 families in the order are the Aegothelidae (owlet-nightjars), Podargidae (Australian frogmouths), Batrachostomidae (Asiatic frogmouths), Steatornithidae (oilbird), Nyctibiidae (potoos), Eurostopodidae (eared-nightjars), and Caprimulgidae (nightjars).

TYTONIDAE: BARN OWL FAMILY

The 12 species of barn and bay owl differ from typical owls in many minor details. They have a heart-shaped facial disc, relatively small eyes and long, slender legs. The long, hooked beak is mostly concealed by feathers. The toes are strong with sharp, curved claws. Barn owls are night hunters.

Oriental Bay Owl *Phodilus badius*

RANGE N. India, Sri Lanka, S.E. Asia, Greater Sunda Islands

HABITAT Forest

SIZE 11½ in (29 cm)

The oriental bay owl is similar in appearance to the barn owl. It is strictly nocturnal and is believed to feed mostly on insects, which it hunts in and around the trees. It lays 3 to 5 eggs, usually in a hole in a tree. An African species of bay owl has been discovered recently.

Barn Owl *Tyto alba*

RANGE Worldwide, except temperate Asia
and many Pacific islands

HABITAT Open country, woods, inhabited areas

SIZE 13¼ in (34 cm)

The barn owl is a long-legged, usually pale-
plumaged bird with a white face. There are over
30 subspecies, found over its wide range,
which differ mainly in intensity of plumage
coloration. Barn owls generally live alone or in
pairs and roost during the day in farm buildings,
hollow trees or caves. At night, they emerge to hunt,
feeding primarily on small rodents, which they catch and kill on
the ground, and also on small birds.

Breeding usually starts in April in the north. The female
nests in an old building, a hollow tree trunk or a rock crevice
and lays 4 to 7 eggs, which she incubates for about 33 days. The
male brings food to her during this period, and both parents
care for the young.

STRIGIDAE: OWL FAMILY

The 161 species of typical owl occur the world over, except on
some oceanic islands. They are soft-feathered, short-tailed birds,
with big heads and enormous eyes set in a circular facial disc. In
all species the beak is hooked and is partly hidden by feathers.

Most owls hunt at night and all feed entirely on animals,
from insects and invertebrates to birds and medium-sized
mammals such as rabbits. They have exceptionally keen eyesight
and excellent hearing.

Brown Fish Owl *Ketupa zeylonensis*

RANGE Middle East to S. China, Sri Lanka,
S.E. Asia

HABITAT Forested streams and lakes

SIZE 22 in (56 cm)

A specialized, semiaquatic owl, the brown fish
owl is always found near water and feeds on
fish, as well as on the more typical
prey of owls. Its feet and ankles

are unfeathered, an adaptation which allows it to wade in the
shallows to catch fish without the plumage getting wet.

The breeding season of this species begins in February or
March. It makes a nest platform in a tree by joining some
branches together, or nests on a ledge or rock. Only 1 or 2 eggs
are laid. They are then incubated by both parents for a total of
about 35 days.

Elf Owl *Micrathene whitneyi*

RANGE S.E. USA, Mexico

HABITAT Wooded canyons, desert
with saguaro cactus

SIZE 5–6 in (12.5–15 cm)

One of the smallest owls in the world the elf
owl is distinguished by its short tail from other
small owls in its range. During the day, it roosts in a tree or
bush and comes out at dusk to hunt. Insects are its main prey,
many being caught in the owl's feet while it is in flight. It will
also hover over foliage or dart out from a perch after prey like a
flycatcher. Beetles, moths, grasshoppers, crickets and scorpions
(the sting is removed or crushed) are frequent prey, and it
occasionally catches small snakes and lizards.

Elf owls nest in deserted woodpecker holes in cactus plants
or tree trunks. The male finds a suitable site and sings to attract
a female, who responds and enters the nest. In April or May, she
lays 1 to 5 eggs which she incubates for 24 days. The male feeds
the female while she incubates and also brings food for her to
give to the young when they have hatched.

Eastern Screech Owl
Otus asio

RANGE N. America: S. Canada,
E., C., and S. USA, N.E. Mexico

HABITAT Open woodland, cactus desert

SIZE 7–10 in (18–25.5 cm)

A small owl with conspicuous
ear tufts, the screech owl
roosts during the day in a
hollow tree or old building and starts to
hunt at dusk. It catches insects and mice,
shrews and other small mammals, as well as frogs, lizards and
some birds. Breeding starts from February to July, according to
area. Screech owls nest in a hole in a tree, such as an abandoned
woodpecker hole. Normally 4 or 5 eggs are laid, but there may
be as many as 8. The male brings food while the female
incubates, but once the eggs hatch, both parents feed the young.

OWLS CONTINUED

Snowy Owl *Nyctea scandiaca*

RANGE Circumpolar: Arctic Canada, Greenland, N. Eurasia

HABITAT Tundra, marshes, coasts

SIZE 20½–25½ in (52–65 cm)

The snowy owl is a large bird with distinctive, mainly white plumage. Females have more dark, barred markings than males. They usually hunt during the day. Prey includes mammals up to the size of arctic hares, smaller rodents, and birds. The snowy owl begins nesting in mid-May in a shallow scrape in the ground or on a rock, lined with moss and feathers. The female lays a clutch of between 4 and 15 eggs. The male feeds her while she incubates the eggs for 32 or 33 days.

Great Horned Owl *Bubo virginianus*

RANGE N., Central and South America

HABITAT Varied, woods, forest, city parks, suburbs

SIZE 18–25¼ in (46–64 cm)

Great horned owls are large, powerful birds. The ear tufts are feathers and are not connected with hearing. The owls roost in trees and hunt mainly at night for mammals, birds, insects and reptiles.

Breeding time depends on area, but it can be as early as January or February. The owl nests in an old nest of another bird, a cave, a hollow in a tree or on a cliff ledge. Usually 3 eggs are laid, but there can be as many as 6. The eggs are incubated for 30 to 35 days by both parents.

Morepork/Boobook *Ninox novaeseelandiae*

RANGE New Zealand, Australia, Tasmania, S. New Guinea, Lesser Sunda Islands

HABITAT Forest, scrub, open country with caves for roosting

SIZE 11½ in (29 cm)

The morepork is the most widely distributed owl in New Zealand and Australia. It is usually seen at dusk when it begins to hunt for its food, which consists largely of insects, particularly moths, as well as spiders, lizards, small birds, rats and mice. It occasionally hunts during the day. The common names are derived from one of its calls which sounds like "morepork" or "boobook". One subspecies, the Norfolk boobook, is now listed as rare.

The morepork nests in November and lays 3 or 4 eggs in a nest in a hollow tree or in a patch of thick vegetation. The female begins her incubation of 30 to 31 days after laying the first egg, but she lays the rest later, at 2-day intervals. After hatching, the young remain in the nest for about 5 weeks, guarded and fed by their parents.

Long-eared Owl *Asio otus*

RANGE N. America, Europe, N.W. Africa, Asia

HABITAT Coniferous forest, woodland, parks

SIZE 13–16 in (33–40.5 cm)

The long-eared owl is more slender than the tawny owl and has distinctive ear tufts which are simply feathers and have no connection with hearing. In flight, the ear tufts are kept flat against the owl's head. One of the most nocturnal owls, it preys on rats, mice, shrews, moles, bats, squirrels, rabbits and other small mammals, as well as on birds and insects. During the day it roosts in trees – camouflaged by its mottled brown plumage.

Long-eared owls nest from March to May, according to area; when food supplies are abundant they may produce two broods. The female lays 3 to 10 eggs, usually 4 or 5, in an abandoned nest of another bird species or even in a squirrel's nest. Alternatively, she lays her eggs on the ground under a tree or bush. She incubates the eggs for 26 to 28 days and her partner feeds her during this period and for the 3 to 4 weeks before the chicks leave the nest.

Some northern populations of long-eared owls migrate south in winter, to Mexico, northern Egypt and India, and northward again in spring.

Northern Hawk Owl

Surnia ulula

RANGE Canada, extreme N. USA, N. Asia, Scandinavia

HABITAT Open areas in coniferous forest

SIZE 14¼–17 in (36–43 cm)

The hawk owl's tail is longer than usual for an owl. Its has a pale facial disc, bordered with black. Its fairly short, pointed wings give it a hawklike appearance in flight. It hunts by day, swooping from a perch in the trees to catch small mammals, such as mice and voles, as well as birds and insects.

Nesting occurs from April to June, depending on the area. The clutch varies from 5 to 9 depending on food supply. The eggs are laid in the hollow top of a tree stump or an abandoned nest or woodpecker hole and are incubated for 25 to 30 days.

Eurasian Pygmy Owl *Glaucidium passerinum*

RANGE N. Europe, east through Russia and C. Asia to China

HABITAT Open forest

SIZE 6 in (16 cm)

The smallest European owl, the pygmy owl has a small head and a long tail. It hunts mainly at night and feeds on small rodents and birds. Pygmy owls breed from March to May. They often nest in disused woodpecker holes. The male feeds the female while she incubates the 2 to 7 eggs for about 28 days and feeds the young once they are hatched.

Little Owl

Atbene noctua

RANGE Europe, Africa, W. and C. Asia, east to China

HABITAT Forest, open country, urban land

SIZE 8¼ in (21 cm)

The little owl has a frowning expression. It is active in the day. Insects and small rodents are its main foods, but it occasionally eats small birds and carrion. In Europe, it nests from mid-April onward. The female lays 3 to 5 eggs and incubates them for about 29 days. The male feeds the young when they first hatch, but later the parents share the hunting.

Tawny Owl *Strix aluco*

RANGE Britain, Europe, N. Africa, W. and C. Asia to Korea

HABITAT Woods, gardens, parks, urban areas

SIZE 15 in (38 cm)

The tawny owl is a strongly built bird, with mottled plumage, a rounded head and black eyes. One of the most common European owls, it is distinguished from the long-eared and short-eared owls by its lack of ear tufts and its dark eyes. It is strictly nocturnal, roosting in a tree during the day and hunting small rodents, birds and some insects at night.

Breeding starts in late March. The tawny owl nests in a hole in a tree or occasionally on the ground or in an old nest of another species. Usually 2 to 4 eggs are laid, but there can be up to 8. The female incubates the clutch for 28 to 30 days. The male feeds the newly hatched young for the first few weeks, but then both parents hunt. The young leave the nest at about 5 weeks.

Burrowing Owl *Speotyto cunicularia*

RANGE S.W. Canada, W. USA and Florida; Central and South America

HABITAT Semidesert, grassland without trees

SIZE 9–11 in (23–28 cm)

The burrowing owl is a small ground-living owl with a short tail and long legs. It often lives in the abandoned burrows of prairie dogs and other mammals and usually adapts the burrow to its needs by digging with its feet to enlarge the hole and make a nesting chamber. In a complex of burrows, such as those left by prairie dogs, a number of owls may take over and form a colony. The owls do not share burrows with prairie dogs.

Burrowing owls usually hunt in the evening, but are often seen during the day standing at the burrow entrances. They eat small rodents, birds, frogs, reptiles and insects. They often follow animals, such as horses, perhaps to catch prey that they disturb.

Burrowing owls nest from March to July. The female lays 6 to 11 eggs in a chamber at the end of the burrow. Both parents incubate the eggs for about 28 days. Northern populations migrate south in winter.

OWLET-NIGHTJARS, FROGMOUTHS, OILBIRD AND POTOOS

AEGOTHELIDAE: OWLET-NIGHTJAR FAMILY

Owlet-nightjars are small, dumpy birds, which resemble their relatives the nightjars in many respects, but have the flat-faced look of owls. They hunt at dawn and dusk, catching insects in the air or, more often, on the ground, where they move easily. There are 8 species of owlet-nightjar, found in New Guinea, Australia and some nearby islands.

Australian Owlet-nightjar *Aegotheles cristatus*

RANGE Australia, Tasmania, S. New Guinea

HABITAT Forest, woodland, scrub

SIZE 7¾–9½ in (20–24 cm)

A shy, solitary bird, the Australian owlet-nightjar spends the day perched in an upright posture on a branch, disguised by its mottled and barred plumage. It starts to hunt for insects and invertebrates at dusk, taking much of its prey on the ground, but also chasing aerial insects. Its bill is small and flat, but with a large gape, and is almost obscured by erect bristles.

The clutch of 3 or 4 eggs is laid in a hole in a tree or bank, lined with green leaves. The lining is renewed as the leaves wither. There may be more than one brood in a year.

PODARGIDAE: AUSTRALIAN FROGMOUTH FAMILY

The frogmouths are tree-dwelling birds that occur from India through Southeast Asia to New Guinea and Australia. They have a flat, shaggy head and large eyes. Poor fliers, they have short, rounded wings and stumpy tails and a large beak, which is surrounded by tufts of bristles and can open into a wide gape. Poor fliers, they have short, rounded wings and stumpy tails. They are crepuscular and nocturnal feeders that watch for prey on branches or on the ground and then pounce on it. Males and females look more or less alike. There are two families of frogmouths. The 3 species of Australian frogmouths are found in Australia, New Guinea, and the Solomon Islands.

Tawny Frogmouth *Podargus strigoides*

RANGE Australia, Tasmania

HABITAT Forest, open woodland, trees in scrub, gardens, parks

SIZE 13–18½ in (33–47 cm)

The nocturnal tawny frogmouth spends the day resting in a tree, where its mottled, streaked plumage blends perfectly with the lichen-covered branches. At any hint of danger, the bird stretches out its body, with head and bill pointing upward, and in this posture it is almost indistinguishable from a broken branch or stump. Much of the frogmouth's hunting is done at dusk, when it watches for prey from a tree or post, then descends silently to seize it on the ground. Insects, snails, frogs and even small mammals and birds are all included in its diet. There are at least 7 subspecies of tawny frogmouth, all varying slightly in size and shade of plumage.

The nest is a flimsy platform of sticks and leaves, made on a forked branch, or an old nest of another species may be used. The female incubates the 2 eggs for about 30 days, and both parents feed the young.

BATRACHOSTOMIDAE: ASIATIC FROGMOUTH FAMILY

There are 11 species of Asiatic frogmouths. They are similar to the Australian family. They occur from the Himalayas to the Philippines.

Ceylon Frogmouth *Batrachostomus moniliger*

RANGE Sri Lanka, S.W. India

HABITAT Forest

SIZE 7½–9 in (19–23 cm)

The Ceylon frogmouth is a tree-dwelling bird, but it takes most of its food on the ground after short flights from a perch;

frogmouths of this genus seem to be more skilful in flight than those of the genus *Podargus*. Insects and small invertebrates are its main food. Like all frogmouths, this bird has mottled graybrown plumage, which provides excellent camouflage as it sits on branches.

A single egg is laid in a small padlike nest, made from the bird's own down with a covering of lichen and cobwebs.

STEATORNITHIDAE: OILBIRD FAMILY

The single species of oilbird is sufficiently unusual to merit its own family. A large-eyed nocturnal bird, it has a patchy distribution in northern South America. The male and female birds look alike.

Oilbird *Steatornis caripensis*

RANGE Locally in Peru, through Ecuador, Colombia and Venezuela to French Guiana; Trinidad

HABITAT Seaside and mountain caves

SIZE 17 in (43 cm)

A long-winged, long-tailed bird, the oilbird has small, almost useless legs and feet. It lives in deep, totally dark caves where even its large eyes, specialized for night-time vision, are ineffective. However, it can nest and fly about in these caves with ease by means of a system of echolocation similar to that used by bats. As it flies, the bird makes a series of high-pitched clicking sounds, which bounce off the walls of the cave and enable it to navigate.

After dark, the oilbird emerges to feed on fruit, particularly that of palms. It seizes the fruit in its strong bill, swallows it whole and digests the entire night's intake the following day, back in its roost. The oilbird has a well-developed sense of smell and probably uses this, as well as its good nighttime vision, to find ripe fruit.

Oilbirds live in colonies of up to 50 pairs. The nest is made on a ledge from droppings, mixed with regurgitated fruit, and the female lays 2 to 4 eggs. Both parents incubate the eggs for about 33 days and feed the young on palm fruit.

During their period on the nest, the young oilbirds become enormously fat, weighing at least half as much again as an adult, since they are not able to fly until they are about 4 months old. Local people used to capture these fledglings and render down their fat for use as cooking oil – hence the common name – but this practice is now prohibited by law in most areas.

NYCTIBIIDAE: POTOO FAMILY

The 7 species of potoo occur in the West Indies and adjacent areas of Central and South America. Although related to nightjars and similar to them in appearance, potoos feed like flycatchers, darting out from a perch to catch insects. Males and females look alike, or nearly so.

Common Potoo
Nyctibius griseus

RANGE Jamaica, Hispaniola, Trinidad and Tobago; Mexico, Central America, tropical South America

HABITAT Forest edge, open forest, cultivated land with trees

SIZE 16 in (41 cm)

The common potoo has a long tail, sometimes accounting for as much as half of the bird's total length, and very short legs. Its grayish-brown plumage is heavily mottled and streaked, rendering it almost invisible among the lichen-covered branches of its habitat.

During the day it sits in an extremely upright posture, often on a broken branch or stump, with its head and bill pointing upward so that it looks like part of the tree. At night, the potoo hunts for food, flying out from a perch to catch insects and returning to the same spot to consume them.

The single egg is laid on top of a tree stump and is incubated by both parents. If disturbed, the sitting bird adopts the upright posture and freezes or may retaliate by opening its eyes and bill wide and fluffing out its plumage in threat. Both parents feed the young, which sit in the upright posture in the nest. The young fly about 44 days after hatching.

NIGHTJARS

EUROSTOPODIDAE: EARED NIGHTJAR FAMILY

The 7 species in this family resemble the nightjars although they lack bristles around the bill. They are found in forest and scrub from southern Asia and south China to Australia.

Great Eared Nightjar *Eurostopodus macrotis*

RANGE India: Assam to S.E. Asia, Philippines, Sulawesi

HABITAT Forest, scrub

SIZE 16 in (41 cm)

Mainly solitary birds, these large nightjars occasionally gather in small groups. They feed on insects caught in the air. Flying high around the treetops at dawn or dusk, they perform skilful aerobatics in pursuit of their prey and call constantly, with a clear whistle. The female lays 1 egg on dead leaves, often in the shade at the foot of a tree.

CAPRIMULGIDAE: NIGHTJAR AND NIGHTHAWK FAMILY

The 76 species of this family of nocturnal birds are distributed almost worldwide: they are absent from only New Zealand and some Pacific islands. They do not occur at high latitudes. Many have evocative names, such as nightjar, goatsucker, poorwill and chuck-will's-widow, usually derived from their calls.

Nightjars have long, pointed wings, and large eyes for good night vision. The bill is short and weak, but it opens very wide and is fringed by sensory bristles. Most nightjars call for a period each evening at dusk, before they begin hunting. Flying silently and slowly, they make sudden darts after insects, which the bristles help to funnel into their wide, open mouths. They also occasionally eat young birds. Nightjars are masterly in flight, but have short, weak legs and avoid walking far on the ground.

During the daytime, nightjars roost in trees or on the ground, hidden from predators by their camouflaging plumage. In trees they perch with their bodies lengthways along the branch. All species have finely mottled gray, black and brown heads and backs, which blend with foliage and vegetation. The sexes do not look alike in most species.

Common Poorwill *Phalaenoptilus nuttallii*

RANGE Breeds S.W. Canada, W. USA; winters S. USA, Mexico

HABITAT Arid bush on hills and mountains, open woodland

SIZE 7–8½ in (18–21.5 cm)

A small, short-tailed nightjar, the common poorwill flits around at night, hunting moths, beetles and grasshoppers on or near the ground. By day, it roosts in shrubbery or tall woods. The poorwill is the only bird known to hibernate. Each October it finds a rock crevice in which to spend the winter. Its temperature falls from about 106°F (40°C) to about 64°F (18°C). Its heartbeat and breathing rates drop to almost undetectable levels in order to conserve energy.

In early summer, poorwills breed. The female lays 2 eggs on bare ground or gravel. The clutch is incubated by both parents.

Lyre-tailed Nightjar *Uropsalis lyra*

RANGE South America: Andes in Venezuela, Colombia, Ecuador, Peru

HABITAT Mountain forest, savanna, open woodland

SIZE Male: 31 in (79 cm); Female: 10 in (25.5 cm)

The male lyre-tailed nightjar has two long lyre-shaped outer tail feathers. They are thought to be used in the male's courtship display. This solitary, nocturnal bird perches on low branches, often near water, and calls at dusk. Little is known of its feeding or breeding habits, but they are probably similar to those of other nightjars.

Standard-winged Nightjar *Macrodipteryx longipennis*
RANGE Africa: Chad, Sudan, Ethiopia, N. Uganda, Kenya
HABITAT Wooded savanna, scrub
SIZE 9 in (23 cm)

The standard-winged nightjar feeds on insects, which it catches in the air. A migratory species, it breeds in the southern part of its range from January to March and then moves north to Chad and northern Sudan.

In the breeding season, the male nightjar develops one elongated flight feather on each wing that grows to about 9 in (23 cm) in length. These are used in courtship displays, when the male flies around the female raising his elongated feathers and arching and vibrating his wings. The male is believed to mate with more than one female, each of which lays 2 eggs on the ground. Several birds may lay in the same area. The male bird then migrates, leaving the females to incubate the eggs and to care for the young alone.

Pauraque *Nyctidromus albicollis*
RANGE S.W. USA; Mexico; Central and South America to N.E. Argentina
HABITAT Semiopen scrub, woodland clearings
SIZE 11 in (28 cm)

Perching in a tree at night, the pauraque watches for insects, such as moths, wasps, and beetles, then launches into the air and flies close to the ground to catch them in its wide, gaping bill.

During the day it roosts, hidden among the dead leaves on the woodland floor where it is virtually invisible. Males and females have some plumage differences – the female's outer wing and tail feathers are black, barred with rufous brown, while the male's tail feathers are brown, barred with white, and are conspicuous in flight.

Pauraques live alone or in pairs. The female lays 2 eggs on bare ground, under the cover of bushes, and both parents incubate the clutch. They feed the nestlings by inserting the tip of the bill into a gaping mouth and regurgitating insects from the throat. The young birds begin to hop out of the nest at 2 or 3 days old, although not yet able to fly.

Eurasian Nightjar *Caprimulgus europaeus*
RANGE Breeds in Europe, N. Africa, W. and C. Asia; winters in tropical Africa
HABITAT Open country, forest edge, moors, heaths, semidesert
SIZE 10¼ in (26 cm)

This long-winged, long-tailed bird is the only nightjar that is widespread in Europe, and it tolerates many different habitats.

The male bird has some white spots on the outer wing tips and his tail feathers are tipped with white, but the sexes are otherwise similar in plumage.

After spending an inactive day perching on a branch, or on the ground, the nightjar takes wing at sunset and can be seen wheeling and gliding in the air and making sudden darts after moths and other nocturnal insects. It makes a churring call – the "jar" of its name.

The breeding season starts in mid-May. The male courts the female by clapping his wings together, and both birds sway their tails from side to side before mating.

The female lays 2 eggs in a slight scrape on the ground or on top of vegetation. The parents share the incubation of the eggs – the female takes the day shift and the male the night shift. The eggs hatch after 18 days. Both parents then care for the young, which are able to fly at about 17 or 18 days old. Pairs produce 2 broods of chicks in a season.

PIGEONS

ORDER COLUMBIFORMES

This order includes 2 living families – the sandgrouse and the pigeons – and the now extinct dodo family.

COLUMBIDAE: PIGEON FAMILY

The only family in this order contains 310 species of pigeon and dove, found in most parts of the world except the Antarctic and some oceanic islands. The greatest variety occurs in Asia and Australasia, where there are many extremely beautiful species. The name "pigeon" is generally used to describe larger birds in the family, while "dove" is applied to smaller forms, but there are exceptions to this rule, such as the rock dove.

Pigeons and doves vary in size from birds about the size of a sparrow to a few almost as large as a turkey. Most have dense, soft plumage, rounded, compact bodies and relatively small heads. The sexes look alike in most species, but in a few birds the male has more striking plumage. Both share an unusual reproductive feature – the lining of the crop secretes "pigeon milk", with which they feed their young for the first few days. This nutritious fluid is high in protein and fats and smells like cheese. Pigeons and doves generally lay only 1 or 2 eggs in a flimsy, but effective, nest, made of sticks.

Many pigeons and doves spend much of their lives in and around trees, eating seeds, fruit, buds and other plant material. Others are ground-dwelling, but have much the same diet. Pigeons and doves are strong fliers, with good homing abilities.

Common Ground Dove *Columbina passerina*

RANGE S. USA; Mexico, south to central Ecuador, N. Brazil; West Indies
HABITAT Open scrub, cultivated land
SIZE 6–6¾ in (15–17 cm)

These tiny, ground-living doves walk about briskly in pairs or small groups with heads nodding, picking up seeds, waste grain,

insects and small berries and even scraps of human food. The scaly-breasted ground dove is a plump, compact bird with a short, broad tail and rounded wings. The female has much duller plumage than the male.

Mating occurs from February to October over the range. The male courts the female on the ground, puffing up his neck and bobbing his head and neck in time to his monotonous cooing while pursuing her. A flimsy nest is made in a low bush or tree or on the ground, and 2 eggs are laid and incubated by both parents for 13 or 14 days.

Rock Dove/Pigeon *Columba livia*

RANGE Islands and coasts of W. Britain, countries bordering Mediterranean; E. Europe, east to India and Sri Lanka
HABITAT Sea and inland cliffs; fields
SIZE 13–14 in (33–35.5 cm)

This species is the ancestor of all the domestic pigeons, including the homing pigeon, and of the feral pigeons (wild birds descended from birds bred in captivity) found in towns almost worldwide. Rock doves generally move in pairs or small groups, although large flocks are quite frequent. They feed on open ground, mainly on seeds, especially cultivated grains, but also on grasses, snails and other mollusks.

Mating takes place throughout the year, after much bowing, nodding, billing and cooing. The nest is flimsily made of twigs and grass on a sheltered cliff ledge or in a hole in a cliff, in a building or, occasionally, a tree. Two eggs are laid, which are incubated for 17 or 18 days.

Band-tailed Pigeon *Columba fasciata*

RANGE Western N. America, south to Mexico;
Central America, Colombia

HABITAT Coniferous forest, oak woodland in mountainous areas

SIZE 14¼–15¼ in (36–39 cm)

This is a heavily built pigeon. The tail, which is notable in flight and gives the bird its common name, is distinctly banded, with a pale end, a dark band across the middle and a blue-gray base.

The band-tailed pigeon flies strongly and swiftly and spends much time perching in trees, where it also seeks most of its food – nuts, berries, seeds, buds and blooms. It also eats insects and, in autumn, gorges on acorns.

Depending on area, the pigeons mate from March to September, and the female lays 1 egg, occasionally 2, which both parents incubate for 18 to 20 days.

Mourning Dove *Zenaida macroura*

RANGE Temperate areas in Canada; USA: all states;
Mexico, Bahamas, Cuba, Hispaniola

HABITAT Woodland, grain fields with trees,
semi-desert, suburbs

SIZE 11–13 in
(28–33 cm)

The mourning dove has short
legs, a rounded body, neat head and a
thin delicate-looking bill. The sexes look
similar, but the central tail feathers are very long in
the male and the wings are long and pointed. In flight
the white outer tail feathers are obvious. Juvenile birds are
heavily spotted on their wings.

The birds generally move in pairs or small groups, but large numbers may gather at feeding grounds. Ground-living birds, they eat mainly weed seeds or grain spilled in harvesting, but also take snails and other invertebrates.

The common name derives from the sweet, melancholy cooing of the male, which is followed by a courtship flight. Mating begins in January in the south of the range to April in the north. The nest is loosely constructed of twigs in a tree or bush, a roof gutter or chimney corner, or even on the ground. The female lays 2 eggs, which are incubated by both birds for 14 or 15 days. Each season 2 or 3 broods are produced.

Blue-headed Quail Dove *Starnoenas cyanocephala* **EN**

RANGE Cuba, formerly Jamaica

HABITAT Lowland forest and shrubbery; locally highland forest

SIZE 12–13 in (30.5–33 cm)

Numbers of this medium-sized dove are becoming fewer, owing to the destruction of its habitat, and little is known about it. It feeds on the ground in areas where it is able to walk freely, taking mainly seeds, snails and berries. The nest is made low in a tree or shrub or on the ground, and usually 2 eggs are laid.

PIGEONS CONTINUED

Collared Dove *Streptopelia decaocto*

RANGE Ireland, Britain, Europe (not Spain, Portugal); India, Sri Lanka, Burma; introduced in Middle East, China, Japan.

HABITAT Towns, villages, farmland; arid scrubland, palm groves (in India)

SIZE 12½ in (31.5 cm)

This species has enormously expanded its range over recent years by adapting to live in close association with man in both towns and countryside. It now breeds regularly in Great Britain and can be identified by its gray-brown coloration and by its proportionately long white-edged tail and dark primary feathers. Ground-feeding birds, collared doves feed chiefly on seeds, often spilled grain, but they also take human food, berries and other plant material. In Europe, to the dismay of fruit-growers, they raid cherry orchards.

In India, these birds breed throughout the year, whenever food supplies are plentiful. In Europe, from March to October. The male makes frequent and showy display flights, rising up with clapping wings then gliding down, often in a spiral, with its wings and tail spread out. The scanty twig nest is made in a tree or bush or on a ledge on a building, and the female lays 2 eggs which are incubated for 14 to 16 days.

Nicobar Pigeon *Caloenas nicobarica* **LR:nt**

RANGE Andaman and Nicobar Islands, east to Philippines, New Guinea and Solomon Islands

HABITAT Small, off-lying wooded islands

SIZE 15¾ in (40 cm)

The Nicobar pigeon is quite a large bird, with long legs, a short white tail and heavy bill. Its stance is rather like that of a vulture and,

unlike most pigeons, it has short, hard plumage, except on the neck, where the feathers are elongated to form hackles that cover most of the body. The female is slightly smaller than the male, with a smaller bill cere, and the juvenile looks like the female, but duller and without the white tail.

These birds are found throughout their range only on small islands and tiny islets off larger islands, but their flight is swift and strong and they wander freely between groups of islands. Little is known about their habits, but they appear to be ground-feeders, feeding on seeds, fruit and some invertebrates, mainly at dusk, or by day in the gloom of the forest. The white tail and large eyes seem to be adaptations for this way of life.

Nicobar pigeons may nest in large colonies, building their nests in trees or bushes. The female lays a single egg.

Yellow-footed Green Pigeon

Treron phoenicoptera

RANGE India, Sri Lanka, S.E. Asia to Vietnam (not Malaysia)

HABITAT Forest, scrubland, fruiting trees in open country, parks and gardens

SIZE 13 in (33 cm)

The yellow-legged green pigeons is about the size of a feral pigeon, but is more heavily built. Females look similar to males, but are not quite as bright, while juveniles have no mauve shoulder patches and are much duller and paler.

These pigeons are swift, strong fliers. They usually move in groups of up to 10 birds, although they will gather in trees in huge flocks to feed. They clamber about the branches, even hanging upside down to reach berries and fruit (especially wild figs), buds and shoots. They drink by clinging to branches which overhang water.

In India, green pigeons breed from March to June. The male courts the female by parading in front of her with feathers puffed out, making a tuneful call rather like a human whistle. The twiggy nest is built in a shrub or tree, often close to other green pigeons' nests. The 2 eggs are incubated for about 14 days.

Torresian Imperial/Nutmeg Pigeon

Ducula spilorrhoa

RANGE New Guinea, islands and archipelagos
to N.E. and E. Australia

HABITAT Woodland, mangroves, savanna, forest edge,
plantations, gardens

SIZE 15¼–17½ in (39–44.5 cm)

Nutmeg pigeons roost and breed in large numbers on small
off-lying islands, but parties of them daily fly long distances over
the sea to feed on larger islands or in coastal areas of the
mainland. They search among the branches of trees and shrubs
for fruit and berries and, as their name suggests, they eat wild
nutmegs, although these are not an important part of their diet.
Observations indicate that birds breeding on islands of the Great
Barrier Reef off Australia fly high in large flocks when going to
feed but return in the evening, just skimming the water, in a
stream of small parties.

Flying also plays a part in the mating behavior of these birds,
when males display to females by bowing and then shooting
swiftly up into the air to glide down, time and again. The
breeding season appears to be from September to January in
New Guinea and October and November in Australia. The birds
build a twiggy nest in a shrub or tree, and the female lays 1 egg,
which is incubated by both parents for 26 to 28 days.

Superb Fruit Dove *Ptilinopus superbus*

RANGE Sulawesi, Sulu Archipelago, islands and archipelagos of
W. Papua and New Guinea to N.E. Australia

HABITAT Forest, forest edge, river banks,
cultivated land with trees

SIZE 8½–9½ in (22–24 cm)

This compact, medium-sized
dove is truly superb, with its
green and coppery
plumage but, despite
this, is remarkably

inconspicuous when sitting in the treetops. The female is a more
uniform blue-green, while the feathers of the juvenile are yellow-
green. Superb fruit doves fly with a whirring flight from tree to
tree, usually singly or in pairs, but dozens may congregate to
feed on berries and small fruit as it ripens.

The nest is normally a small collection of twigs, set low in a
tree or shrub, and the female lays a single egg. Both parents
incubate the egg for about 14 days, the male during the day and
the female at night.

Diamond Dove *Geopelia cuneata*

RANGE N. and inland Australia; sometimes coastal areas of
S. Australia

HABITAT Open woodland, mulga (acacia) scrub,
open land with trees, near water

SIZE 7½–8½ in (19–21.5 cm)

A delicate-looking, rather plump little bird about the size of a
house sparrow, the diamond dove is the smallest pigeon. They
are gregarious and are only rarely seen alone. Normally they
move about in pairs, not always of opposite sexes, or in groups
of 20 or so. Although they usually roost and nest in trees, they
feed on the ground and walk around with a quick toddling
action, searching for tiny seeds of grasses and herbaceous plants.
They also eat the larger seeds of the acacia and probably leaves
and shoots of weeds and grasses. They are sun lovers and will
often rest in the sunshine, even in the heat of the day. Their
flight is fast and swooping, rather like that of parakeets.

Mating is accompanied by unusual behaviour by the male:
he displays to the female by lifting his wings, then mounts her
and immediately dismounts and strikes above her head with his
wing. He remounts and repeats the action on the other side of
the female, he then mounts her for the third time and copulates.
He appears to attack the female, but does not actually touch her.
The nest is a typical pigeon nest, although small, usually low
down in a bush or tree or a tangle of fallen branches and dry
grass, in which the female lays 2 eggs. The eggs hatch after 12 or
13 days and the young can fly 11 or 12 days later.

PIGEONS CONTINUED

Brown Cuckoo Dove/Brown Pigeon

Macropygia phasianella

RANGE E. Australia; Java and Sumatra and adjacent islands; N. Borneo to the Philippines

HABITAT Glades and clearings in forest

SIZE 15–17 in (38–43.5 cm)

The brown cuckoo dove has rich, reddish-brown plumage with faint gray barring and spotting on the neck, breast and underparts; the speckling is more marked in the female and the juvenile is even more noticeably barred. In eastern Australia, this is one of the commonest pigeons in the remaining pockets of rain forest, but populations are being reduced by forest clearance and by hunting. The long tail gives the bird an awkward appearance when it is flying among the trees but in fact it seems to be an adaptation to the bird's largely arboreal way of life, since the spread tail is often used as a balancing aid. Cuckoo doves eat fruit and berries, which they take from the ground as well as from trees and shrubs.

In Queensland, Australia, where breeding has been observed, mating takes place between July and January. The female lays 1 egg which is incubated for 16 to 18 days.

Crested Pigeon *Geophaps lophotes*

RANGE Australia

HABITAT Arid areas: lightly wooded grassland, open country and agricultural land with some trees and shrubs, near water

SIZE 12¼–13¾ in (31–35 cm)

This slimly built pigeon, with its longish tail, long dark crest like that of a lapwing and strikingly barred wing coverts, has a sprightly air. The impression of jauntiness is emphasized by its swift, distinctive flight, in which several rapid wing beats alternate with periods of gliding with the wings held still and almost horizontal. Since these birds live in arid country, reliable watering places, such as steady streams, dams or even cattle troughs, are essential to them. They normally come to drink before feeding, about an hour after sunrise, and in dry periods a flock of up to a thousand may gather. Generally, however, crested pigeons move about in pairs or in groups of from 4 to 30 individuals, feeding on the ground on seeds of herbaceous plants and Acacia trees, young green shoots and small bulbs.

They nest mainly in spring and summer, but breeding can take place almost year-round, usually after heavy rains. The female lays 2 eggs which are incubated for 18 days. There may be up to 7 successive broods.

Luzon Bleeding-heart

Gallicolumba luzonica **LR:nt**

RANGE Philippines: islands of Luzon and Polillo

HABITAT Forest

SIZE 12 in (30.5 cm)

The most striking characteristic of this pigeon is the patch of hairy, blood-red feathers in the middle of the breast that gives the bird its common name. The illusion that the breast of the bird is bleeding is enhanced by the fact that the red feathers of the "wound" form an indentation in the surrounding white feathers. Both male and female have this "bleeding heart". The bleeding-heart pigeon has a plump, compact body, short to medium-length wings and tail and long legs. When alarmed, it tends to fly only a short distance and then to land and run rapidly, or to crouch with its head lowered and tail raised. Although it roosts in trees, it is mainly a groundliving bird and feeds on seeds, fallen berries and probably many insects and other invertebrates (the pigeons in this genus appear to take more animal food than most other pigeons).

They are thought to nest fairly low down in bushes, trees or vines and to lay 2 eggs in a clutch.

Other closely related species of *Gallicolumba* are found on neighboring islands. There are 3 species of bleeding heart in New Guinea, but generally most islands and archipelagos support only one species.

Victoria Crowned Pigeon *Goura victoria* **VU**

RANGE N. New Guinea: Siriwo River to Astrolabe Bay; Yapen and Biak Islands

HABITAT Rain forest, muddy lowland flats

SIZE 23–29 in (58.5–73.5 cm)

The 3 species of crowned pigeon are remarkable chiefly for their size – about that of a large domestic fowl – and for their erect, laterally compressed, fan-shaped crests of feathers. These feathers are long, with slightly separated barbs at the ends, which gives them a beautiful lacelike appearance. Male and female look alike; juveniles are much duller.

Little is known of the habits of the Victoria crowned pigeon in the wild, but it probably behaves in much the same way as other closely related species in the same area, spending most of its time on the ground, feeding on fallen fruit, berries and possibly small invertebrates. In captivity, it will also eat lettuce, maize, carrots and peanuts and is particularly fond of wild figs. It perches on branches and flies up into trees when alarmed.

Courtship display seems to consist of bowing and "dancing" by the male bird. The female responds by spreading her wings and raising them up high. She also runs around the male with slightly bent legs, uttering short hissing cries. The proportionately large nest is built among the branches of a tree and is more compact and less makeshift than a typical pigeon nest. In captivity, the female has been observed to lay 1 egg, which was incubated by both parents for 30 days. The young bird left the nest at about 4 weeks, but it was fed by both parents until it was 13 weeks old.

Tooth-billed Pigeon *Didunculus strigirostris* **VU**

RANGE Samoa: Upolu and Savaii Islands

HABITAT Wooded mountainsides

SIZE 15 in (38 cm)

This species takes its name from its unique bill, which is strong and curved, with two notches anrd three projections – or teeth – on each side of the lower mandible. The scientific name, *strigirostris*, means "owl bill". The tooth-billed pigeon is a thickset bird about the size of a feral pigeon, with a short tail, rather long legs and tight plumage, which has a silvery sheen, on head and breast. In the female, the feathers have less sheen and the juvenile is much browner and the plumage is more barred.

These birds live on the ground, feeding on seeds, fruit, berries and the mountain plantain which grows in their habitat. When eating, they hold their food down with their feet and, with the bill, tear it apart or nibble it into pieces before swallowing it. It is thought that the shape of the bill may have evolved as a response to these specialized feeding habits. When numbers of these birds were still plentiful, they were usually found in groups of 10 to 20.

When flushed, tooth-billed pigeons will fly with loudly beating wings for about 100 ft (30 m), beneath the lowest branches of tall trees, and then glide for a comparable distance before settling in a tree. They fly with agility among undergrowth and perch in low trees, although they seem to roost in tall ones. It is said that formerly these birds nested on the ground, but they now nest in trees because of the destruction wrought by introduced pigs. No definite information about their nesting habits is available.

SUNBITTERN, BUSTARDS, CRANES AND TRUMPETERS

ORDER GRUIFORMES

A diverse group of wading and ground-living birds, this order contains 9 families, 2 of which contain a single species.

EURYPYGIDAE: SUNBITTERN FAMILY

The sunbittern, found in Central and South America, is the sole member of its family. Its exact affinities are uncertain. Males and females of the species look alike.

Sunbittern *Eurypyga helias*

RANGE Central America, South America to Brazil

HABITAT Forest streams and creeks

SIZE 18 in (46 cm)

The sunbittern is an elegant bird, with a long bill, a slender neck and long legs. It frequents the well-wooded banks of streams, where it is perfectly camouflaged in the dappled sunlight by its mottled plumage. Fish, insects and crustaceans are its main foods, which it hunts from the river bank or seizes with swift thrusts of its bill, while wading in the shallows.

In courtship display, the beautifully plumaged wings are fully spread, revealing patches of color. The wing tips are held forward, framing the head and neck. Pairs perform a courtship dance, with tail and wings spread. Both partners help to build a large domed nest in a tree and incubate 2 or 3 eggs for about 28 days.

OTIDIDAE: BUSTARD FAMILY

Bustards are heavily built, ground-dwelling birds, which tend to run or walk rather than fly, although they are capable of strong flight. The majority of the 25 species occur in Africa, but there are bustards in southern Europe, Asia and Australia. Male birds are more boldly plumaged than females.

Great Bustard *Otis tarda* **VU**

RANGE Scattered areas of S. and central Europe, east across Asia to Siberia and E. China

HABITAT Grassland, grain fields

SIZE 29½ in—3¼ ft (75 cm–1 m)

The male great bustard is a large, strong bird, with a thick neck and sturdy legs. The female is smaller and slimmer, lacking the male's bristly "whiskers" and chestnut breast plumage. Insects and seeds are their main foods, but they are omnivorous.

The male performs a courtship display, raising his wings and tail, puffing himself out. The 2 or 3 eggs are laid in an unlined scrape on the ground and incubated by the female for 25 to 28 days.

Black Bustard *Eupodotis afra*

RANGE South Africa

HABITAT Grassland, bush

SIZE 20¾ in (53 cm)

Male black bustards are showy birds, with distinctive markings on the head and neck. Females are quieter, with plumage mottled with black, tawny and rufous spots. Only the underparts are pure black. They live in pairs in a well-defined territory and eat mainly vegetable matter and some insects.

The female usually lays only 1 egg on the ground and incubates it herself.

GRUIDAE: CRANE FAMILY

The 15 species of crane are splendid, long-legged, long-necked birds, which often have brightly colored bare skin on the face and decorative plumes on the head. The larger crane species stand up to 5 ft (1.5 m) tall. They are found over most of the world, except in South America, Madagascar, Malaysia, Polynesia and New Zealand.

Except during the breeding season, when they consort only in pairs, they are gregarious birds and, after breeding, they migrate in large flocks, flying in V-formation or in line, with their necks extended and legs trailing. Males and females have similar plumage.

Whooping Crane

Grus americana **EN**

RANGE N. America

HABITAT Wetlands in prairies and other open habitats

SIZE 4–4½ ft (1.2–1.4 m) tall

Exceedingly rare birds in the wild, whooping cranes have been at the point of extinction, although vigorously protected, since the 1930s when they almost disappeared. They breed in Canada and winter on the Texas Gulf Coast, and their annual migrations are carefully monitored.

An omnivorous bird, the whooping crane feeds on grain, plants, insects, frogs and other small animals.

It lays 2 eggs on a flat nest of sticks on the ground. Both parents incubate the eggs and care for the young.

Black Crowned Crane

Balearica pavonina

RANGE Africa, south of the Sahara

HABITAT Swamps

SIZE 3¼ ft (1 m) tall

The common name of this bird is derived from the crest of yellow feathers on its head. Cranes perform courtship dances in the breeding season and, in a simpler form, through the year. The crowned crane postures with wings outstretched to display its feathers, struts about and jumps into the air. Both parents incubate the 2 or 3 eggs and care for the young.

PSOPHIIDAE: TRUMPETER FAMILY

The 3 species of trumpeter are soft-plumaged, predominantly black birds, with weak, rounded wings. They inhabit the lowland forests of South America. Trumpeters rarely fly, but run swiftly on long legs. The sexes look similar, but males make loud, trumpeting calls.

Gray-winged/Common Trumpeter *Psophia crepitans*

RANGE South America: Amazon basin

HABITAT Forest

SIZE 20¾ in (53 cm)

Common trumpeters are gregarious birds, which move in flocks around the forest floor, feeding on fruit, berries and insects. Trumpeters perform dancelike courtship movements and are believed to nest in holes in trees. The 6 to 10 eggs are incubated by the female.

LIMPKIN, FINFOOT, SUNGEESE, SERIEMAS, KAGU AND MESITES

HELIORNITHIDAE: LIMPKIN AND SUNGREBE FAMILY

This family contains four species. The limpkin is a marsh wading bird, similar to cranes, found from the southern USA to Argentina. It is now protected by law, having been hunted almost to extinction earlier in the 20th century. There are 3 species of sungrebe and finfoot, one in each of the world's major tropical areas: Central and South America, Africa, and Asia (India to Sumatra). They frequent wooded areas near to water and can swim well.

Limpkin *Aramus guarauna*

RANGE USA: S. Georgia, Florida; Mexico, Central and South America; Caribbean

HABITAT Swamps

SIZE 23¼–28 in (59–71 cm)

The limpkin is a long-legged bird, with long toes and sharp claws. It flies slowly and infrequently. The limpkin is most active at dusk and at night, when it uses its sensitive, slightly curved beak to probe the mud for water-snails.

Limpkins breed between January and August, depending on the area, but in the USA the nesting season is usually March or April. A shallow nest is built using sticks, usually on the ground near to water. Both of the parents share the incubation duties for their clutch of 4 to 8 eggs.

African Finfoot *Podica senegalensis*

RANGE Africa: south of the Sahara

HABITAT Wooded streams, pools, mangroves

SIZE 20¾–25 in (53–63.5 cm)

An aquatic bird, the finfoot skulks at the edges of well-wooded streams, among overhanging vegetation. It swims low in the water, sometimes with only its head and neck visible. It is also an accomplished diver.

Once aloft, it flies strongly and also leaves the water to clamber around in vegetation and to climb trees. Insects and small invertebrates, amphibians and fish make up the majority of its diet. Male and female birds of the species look similar, although the male is larger than the female and has buff gray plumage on the front of his neck, while the female's throat and neck are a whitish hue.

The nest is constructed from twigs and rushes on a branch overhanging water or else among flood debris. The female lays a clutch of 2 eggs.

Sungrebe *Heliornis fulica*

RANGE S. Mexico, through Central and South America to N. Argentina

HABITAT Stagnant streams, wooded rivers

SIZE 11 in (28 cm)

Although smaller than the African finfoot, the sungrebe has the same elongate body and lobed toes. Its common name is particularly unsuitable, since the bird frequents shady overgrown margins of streams and rivers and is rarely seen out in the open.

The sungrebe feeds on insects, especially larvae, found on leaves. It also eats small invertebrates, amphibians and fish. It flies strongly, but tends to take cover in undergrowth in order to escape danger, rather than to fly.

The 4 eggs are laid in a bush or tree overhanging water.

CARIAMIDAE: SERIEMA FAMILY

The 2 species of seriema are long-legged, ground-living birds, both of which occur through South America. They are believed to be the only surviving descendants of some long-extinct, carnivorous, ground-dwelling birds, which are known from fossils. Males and females of the species look alike or nearly so.

Red-legged Seriema *Cariama cristata*

RANGE E. Bolivia, Brazil, Paraguay, Uruguay, N. Argentina

HABITAT Grassland

SIZE 28 in (70 cm)

The graceful red-legged seriema runs fast, but rarely flies and tends to rely on its running speed to escape danger. The sharp, broad bill is used to kill reptiles and amphibians, as well as to feed on insects, leaves and seeds. The nest is built from sticks in a tree. Both parents incubate the 2 or 3 eggs for about 26 days.

RHYNOCHETIDAE: KAGU FAMILY

The classification and relationships of the kagu, the sole member of its family, have been the subject of much dispute.

Kagu *Rhynochetos jubatus* **EN**

RANGE New Caledonia

HABITAT Forest

SIZE 22 in (56 cm)

Once abundant, the nocturnal, virtually flightless kagu is now rare, largely due to the onslaught by introduced dogs, cats and

rats. The kagu feeds on insects, worms and snails, which it finds on or in the ground by probing with its long pointed bill. The male and female of the species look more or less alike.

In display, the two birds face each other, spreading their wings to show off the black, white and chestnut plumage. They may perform remarkable dances whirling round with the tip of the tail or wing held in the bill. A nest is made on the ground, and both parents incubate the single egg for about 36 days.

MESITORNITHIDAE: MESITE FAMILY

The 3 species of mesite all live in Madagascan forests. They run well but rarely fly, and 1 species, Bensch's mesite, *Monias benschi*, has yet to be seen in flight. Males and females look alike in 2 species, but unalike in Bensch's mesite.

White-breasted Mesite

Mesitornis variegata **VU**

RANGE N.W. Madagascar

HABITAT Dry forest

SIZE 10 in (25.5 cm)

The white breasted mesite is a ground-dwelling bird and spends much of its life searching the forest floor for the insects and seeds that make up its diet.

Mesites generally move about the forest floor in pairs, heads bobbing as they walk.

The nest is built in a bush or a low tree so that the birds can climb up to it. It consists of a platform of twigs, lined with leaves. A clutch of 1 to 3 eggs is laid. There is some doubt as to whether it is the male or female that incubates the eggs.

RAILS

RALLIDAE: RAIL FAMILY

There are 142 species of rail, crake, wood rail, gallinule and coot in this distinctive, cosmopolitan family. They are ground-living birds, often found in or around water and marshy areas, and are well adapted for life in dense vegetation. Typical species are small to medium sized birds – 5½ to 20 in (14 to 51 cm) long – with moderately long legs and toes and short rounded wings. Their bodies are laterally compressed, enabling them to squeeze through clumps of vegetation. Males and females look alike ,or nearly so, in most species, although males are sometimes larger. Most are solitary, secretive birds.

There are two groups within the family: first, the rails, crakes and woodrails, with their camouflaging mottled plumage; and second, the darker gallinules and coots, which are much more aquatic in their habits. Most species fly reasonably well but may ordinarily be reluctant to take to the air, although many make long migrations between winter and summer habitats. Island-dwelling rails have been particularly prone to becoming flightless, which has then led to their extinction.

Diet is varied in the rail family. Species with long, thin bills probe in soft soil and leaf litter for insects, spiders, mollusks, worms and other invertebrates, while species with shorter, thicker bills feed on vegetation. Coots are aquatic feeders and dive or up-end in search of a variety of underwater plant and animal food.

Takahe *Porphyrio mantelli* **EN**

RANGE New Zealand: now confined to Murchison Mountains, South Island

HABITAT High valleys at 2,500–4,000 ft (750–1,200 m)

SIZE 24¾ in (63 cm)

First discovered in 1849, the takahe was sighted only four times in the following 50 years and was assumed to be extinct until it was rediscovered in 1948. Despite careful conservation, however, there were thought to be only 100 pairs alive in 1977. Competition for its plant-food diet from introduced deer and predation by introduced stoats are major reasons for its decline.

A stout bird, the takahe runs well, but it is flightless. It may venture into shallow water, but it does not swim as a rule. It feeds on the coarse fibrous vegetation of its habitat, particularly on snow-grass (*Danthonia*), taking the seed heads and stems. Holding down the clump with one foot, it cuts out stems with its heavy beak and consumes their tender bases.

Pairs remain together for life when possible and usually breed in November. After several trial nests, a nest of grass stalks is made either between or under clumps of grass which provide some shelter. Both parents incubate the clutch of 2 eggs for up to 28 days, but many nests are destroyed by bad weather or predators and only 1 chick from each clutch is ever reared.

Common Moorhen *Gallinula chloropus*

RANGE Worldwide (not Australasia)

HABITAT Swamps, marshes, ponds, slow rivers with cover on banks

SIZE 13 in (33 cm)

A familiar water bird, the moorhen is one of the most adaptable and successful members of its family. It frequents almost any fresh water and adjacent land and readily adapts to man-made environments such as urban parks and farms. It is a lively, active bird, far less secretive than the rail or crake, and swims freely on open water. Plant foods, such as pond weeds, berries and fallen fruit, make up the bulk of the moorhen's diet, but it also eats a small amount of insects.

In the breeding season, the timing of which varies over its vast range, the moorhen pair defends a territory and performs intricate courtship displays on both land and water.

Both sexes help to build a nest of dead reeds and other aquatic plants among reeds or in a bush at the water's edge. The 5 to 11 eggs are laid on consecutive days and are incubated for between 19 and 22 days by both parents. Some pairs may produce a second brood during the season. Northernmost populations migrate south in winter.

Water Rail

Rallus aquaticus

RANGE Europe, N. Africa, N. Asia to Japan

HABITAT Marshes, reedbeds

SIZE 11 in (28 cm)

The slim-bodied water rail moves easily and skilfully through the tangled aquatic vegetation which it frequents. A shy bird, it runs for cover when alarmed, but is less retiring than the small rails and will come on to open land when the marshes freeze over in winter. It swims short distances near cover. Its varied diet includes plant material, such as roots, seeds and berries, as well as insects, crustaceans, small fish and worms.

April to July is the normal breeding season in most of the rail's range, and it sometimes produces two broods. The nest, which is made of dry reeds and other plants, is situated on the marsh. Both parents share the incubation of the 6 to 11 eggs for 19 to 21 days.

Giant Wood Rail *Aramides ypecaha*

RANGE South America: E. Brazil, Paraguay, Uraguay, E. Argentina

HABITAT Marshes, reedbeds, rivers

SIZE 20¾ in (53 cm)

A large, handsome bird, the giant wood rail is an abundant species in its range. These birds feed alone during the day on plant and animal material, but at night they gather in small groups in the marshes and call in chorus.

The nest is made of grass and plant stems in a low bush just above the marsh surface. About 5 eggs are laid.

American Coot *Fulica americana*

RANGE C. and S. Canada, USA, Central and South America along Andes; Hawaiian Islands, Caribbean, Bahamas

HABITAT Marshes, ponds, lakes, rivers

SIZE 13–15¾ in (33–40 cm)

A dark-plumaged, ducklike species with a white bill, the American coot is a conspicuous, noisy water bird. Its flight is strong and swift, although it seldom flies far unless migrating. It has lobed toes and is a strong swimmer and a good walker.

Water plants are its main food, but it also eats aquatic insects, mollusks and some land plants. Coots often feed in flocks, hundreds of birds swimming together.

In North America, the birds breed from April to May. After prolonged courtship rituals, a cup-shaped nest is made of dried marsh plants in a reedbed or on floating vegetation. The 8 to 12 eggs are incubated by both male and female for 21 or 22 days. Northernmost populations migrate south in winter.

Corncrake *Crex crex* **VU**

RANGE Europe, Asia, Africa

HABITAT Grassland, cultivated land

SIZE 10½ in (26.5 cm)

The small, slender corncrake seldom flies, although it migrates thousands of miles to winter in tropical Africa. It is a land-dweller and runs swiftly. It eats seeds, grain and insects. Dawn and dusk are the Corncrake's main periods of activity but in spring males make rasping calls day and night. Corncrakes are seen alone or in pairs except when migrating.

The female builds the nest on the ground from grass and weeds. She incubates the 8 to 12 eggs for 14 to 21 days. The young are fed for a few days by the female or by both parents.

SANDGROUSE, SEEDSNIPE, PLAINS-WANDERER, PAINTED SNIPE AND JACANAS

ORDER CICONIIFORMES

A large and diverse order, the Ciconiiformes contains 1,027 species in two suborders. Suborder Charadrii (shorebirds) has 10 families: Thinocoridae (seedsnipe), Pedionomidae (plains-wanderer), Scolopacidae (woodcock and sandpipers); Rostratulidae (paintedsnipe), Jacanidae (jacanas), Chionididae (sheathbills), Burhinidae (thick-knees), Charadriidae (oystercatchers, avocets, and plovers), Glareolidae (crab plover, pratincoles), and Laridae (Skuas, skimmers, gulls and auks). Suborder Ciconii (waders) consists of 18 families: Accipitridae (osprey, birds of prey), Sagittariidae (secretarybird), Falconidae (falcons), Podicipedidae (grebes), Phaethontidae (tropicbird), Sulidae (boobies), Anhingidae (anhingas), Phalacrocoracidae (cormorants), Ardeidae (herons), Scopidae (hammerhead), Phoenicopteridae (flamingos), Threskiornithidae (ibises), Pelecanidae (shoebill, pelicans), Ciconiidae (storks and New World vultures), Fregatidae (frigatebirds), Spheniscidae (penguins), Gaviidae (loons), and Procellariidae (petrels and albatrosses).

PTEROCLIDIDAE: SANDGROUSE FAMILY

The 16 species of sandgrouse are all terrestrial birds, found in the deserts and open plains of south Europe, Asia and Africa. They are not related to grouse. Sandgrouse are sturdy with short necks, small heads and long, pointed wings and short legs. They cannot run, but move fast with a waddling gait. Most are sandy colored, with spotted and barred feathers, which provide good camouflage. Females are usually smaller than males.

Pallas's Sandgrouse
Syrrhaptes paradoxus
RANGE C. Asia, S. Siberia, S. Mongolia
HABITAT High-altitude semidesert, steppe
SIZE 13¾–15¾ in (35–40 cm)

Pallas's sandgrouse is a rounded, short-legged bird about the size

of a small pigeon. It is a strong, fast flier with a long and pointed central tail and outer wing feathers. It is distinguished from other sandgrouse by the black patch on the belly. Adults eat hard seeds and shoots of desert plants and also take much hard grit.

These sandgrouse nest in large colonies from April to June, laying 3 or 4 eggs in a scrape on the ground. Both parents incubate the eggs for 22 to 27 days and feed the young by regurgitation. There are probably two or three clutches a year.

THINOCORIDAE: SEEDSNIPE FAMILY

The 4 species of seedsnipe all live in South America. The common name derives from the fact that all are seed-eating birds that have the rapid zigzagging flight of the snipes.

Seedsnipes are rounded, groundfeeding birds which range in size from 6¾ to 11 in (17 to 28 cm). The wings are long and pointed, the tail short and the bill strong and conical. The plumage is cryptic and partridgelike. The sexes show some differences in plumage.

Least Seedsnipe
Thinocorus rumicivorus
RANGE Andes: Ecuador to Tierra del Fuego; east to Patagonia and Uruguay; Falkland Islands
HABITAT Dry plains, coastal and inland
SIZE 6¾ in (17 cm)

The smallest of the seedsnipes, the least seedsnipe has typical mottled camouflaging plumage. The male bird's black markings give a "necktie" effect. Primarily a ground-living bird, the seedsnipe runs rapidly, despite its short legs. It blends well with its surroundings and, if threatened, it stays still and almost invisible, flying off at the last minute.

The nesting season varies according to latitude. The 4 eggs are laid on the ground in a shallow hollow and are incubated by the female. If she has to leave the eggs for a time she will half bury them in the sand. The young are able to run about soon after hatching.

PEDIONOMIDAE: PLAINS-WANDERER FAMILY

The single species in this family resembles the buttonquail, but it has four toes on each foot and lays pointed, not oval, eggs. The plains-wanderer is found in inland Australia.

Plains-wanderer *Pedionomus torquatus* **VU**

RANGE S.E. Australia

HABITAT Open grassland

SIZE 6–6¾ in (15–17 cm)

A small, compact bird with short, rounded wings, the female plains-wanderer has a chestnut-colored breast and a distinctive collar of black spots. Plains-wanderers seldom fly, but search for their food – which is insects, seeds and plants – on the ground.

The nest is a simple hollow in the ground, lined with grass. The female lays 3 or 4 eggs which are incubated by the male.

ROSTRATULIDAE: PAINTED SNIPE FAMILY

There are only 2 species in this family, one in the Old World and the other, the lesser painted snipe, *Rostratula semicollaris*, in South America. It is an unusual family in that the normal sexual roles are reversed.

Greater Painted Snipe *Rostratula benghalensis*

RANGE Africa, south of the Sahara; Madagascar, S. Asia, Australia

HABITAT Marshes

SIZE 9½ in (24 cm)

The greater painted snipe is a secretive crepuscular bird, which is

rarely seen in the open. It feeds on insects, snails and worms, (most of which it finds in muddy ground with its sensitive bill) and some plant food.

The female bird is the showily colored partner of breeding pairs, the male is smaller with brownish plumage. The female performs an impressive courtship display, spreading her wings forward and expanding her tail in order to show the spots on the feathers. Females will fight over males.

The male bird makes a pad of grass as a nest and, when the female has laid the 3 or 4 eggs, he incubates the clutch and cares for the chicks.

JACANIDAE: JACANA FAMILY

The 8 species of jacana, which are also known as lily-trotters, are all longlegged water birds found in tropical and subtropical areas worldwide. The jacanas have extraordinary feet, which are an adaptation for their habit of moving over floating vegetation. Their toes and claws are so exceedingly elongated that their weight is well distributed over a large surface area, and they are able actually to walk over precarious floating lily pads. Males and females look alike, with mainly brown plumage and black and white on the head. Females are slightly larger than males.

American/Northern Jacana *Jacana spinosa*

RANGE Central America, Greater Antilles, USA: S. Texas

HABITAT Lakes, ponds

SIZE 9¾ in (25 cm)

American jacanas feed on insects and other aquatic life and on the seeds of water plants, all of which they take from the water surface or vegetation. They swim and dive well, but fly slowly.

A nest is made of aquatic plants and the clutch of 3 to 5 (usually 4) eggs is incubated by both of the parents for a total of 22 to 24 days.

SANDPIPERS, WOODCOCK AND SNIPE

SCOLOPACIDAE: SANDPIPER FAMILY

There are 88 species which make up this diverse family of typical shorebirds. Under a wide range of common names, such as sandpiper, curlew, turnstone, snipe, woodcock and redshank, species are found worldwide, on every continent and on almost every island of any size. Most species are ground-living wading birds, which find much of their food in water. Males and females generally look alike, but some species develop special breeding plumage.

Whimbrel *Numenius phaeopus*

RANGE Breeds in Canada, Alaska, Asia, N. Europe;
winters in S. America, Africa, S.E. Asia, Australasia

HABITAT Breeds on moors, tundra; winters on muddy and sandy shores, estuaries, marshes

SIZE 15¾ in (40 cm)

One of the group known as curlews, the whimbrel has a distinctive striped crown and a long, curving bill. It eats small invertebrates, including crabs, which it often partially dismembers before swallowing. It also eats insects and berries.

Whimbrels breed in subarctic and subalpine tundra and arrive at breeding grounds in the spring, often returning to the same territory year after year. As the snows disperse, males begin their courtship displays. The nest is made on the ground, usually in the open, and the female bird lays 4 eggs, which are incubated for 27 or 28 days by both parents. Once the chicks are fully fledged, at 5 or 6 weeks, the adults leave almost immediately, starting the migration south to wintering areas. The young birds follow a few weeks later.

American Woodcock *Scolopax minor*

RANGE N. America: breeds from Manitoba to Louisiana and Florida; winters from southern part of breeding range to Gulf Coast

HABITAT Woodland, young forest

SIZE 11 in (28 cm)

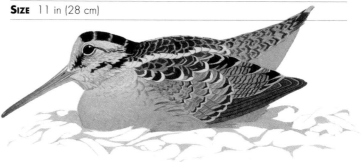

Woodcocks are inland wood and forest birds. The American woodcock is a shy, chunky bird with rounded wings. It probes the soil in search of worms and fly larvae with its long, slender bill, the tip of which is flexible and can open underground.

Males arrive at breeding grounds in March and April. They establish territories and make courtship flights. Females are attracted by the males' calls. A male will mate with several females. The female nests under a small tree or bush and lays 4 eggs which she incubates for 21 days. The female can fly the chicks to safety one at a time by carrying them between her legs.

Common Redshank *Tringa totanus*

RANGE Breeds in Europe, C. and E. Asia; winters in S. Europe, N. Africa, S. Asia

HABITAT Breeds on moorland, marshes; winters on mud flats, meadows, estuaries, shores

SIZE 11 in (28 cm)

An abundant and widespread sandpiper, the redshank adapts well to almost any habitat near water. It has red legs and dark stripes on its head and neck, which fade in winter. It eats mainly insects and also mollusks and crustaceans. Redshanks arrive at breeding grounds from March to May and pair off after courtship displays. The 4 eggs, laid in a nest on the ground, are incubated for 23 days.

Common Snipe *Gallinago gallinago*

RANGE Breeds in Canada, N. USA, Europe to N.E. Asia; winters in Central and South America, Africa, India, Indonesia

HABITAT Marshes, wet meadows, moors

SIZE 10 in (25.5 cm)

A shy bird, the common snipe has pointed wings, a long bill and striped, barred plumage, which provides effective camouflage among vegetation. Insects are the snipe's most important food items, but it also eats earthworms, small crustaceans, snails and plant material.

Males arrive at breeding grounds before females and establish territories for display. In the most common display the male dives through the air at great speed, causing a drumming sound as air rushes through his outer tail feathers. The nest is made on dry ground when possible and near clumps of grass, which the birds pull down over it. The 3 or 4 eggs are incubated for 17 to 19 days, usually by the female alone.

Ruff *Philomachus pugnax*

RANGE Breeds in N. Europe, Asia; winters in Europe, Africa, S. Asia, Australia

HABITAT Tundra, grassland, marshes

SIZE 9–12 in (23–30.5 cm)

Male ruffs perform complex communal displays to attract mates. In the breeding season, males develop large frills of feathers around their heads and necks and gather at a traditional display ground, called a lek. There is great individual variation in the color of frills. Each older, dominant male holds an area within the lek and may be attended by several males, who must display with him and pay court to him in the hope of a chance to mate with one of his females.

Once mated, the female bird, called a "reeve", leaves the display ground and makes a nest in long grass. She incubates her 4 eggs for 20 to 23 days.

Ruddy Turnstone *Arenaria interpres*

RANGE Circumpolar: breeds on Arctic coasts; winters south of breeding range

HABITAT Breeds on marshes, tundra; winters on rocky shores

SIZE 7–9 in (18–23 cm)

In the breeding season, the turnstone has bold black, white and reddish-brown markings, which dulls in winter. Insects, particularly midges, and some plant material are its main food in summer. In winter it forages on seashores, turning over stones and debris with its bill to find mollusks, crustaceans and carrion.

Breeding birds arrive from wintering areas in late May or early June. The 4 eggs are laid in a grass-lined hollow on the ground and incubated by both parents for 21 to 23 days.

Red Phalarope *Phalaropus fulicarius*

RANGE Breeds in N. America: Alaska to Hudson Bay and Arctic islands; winters off W. Africa and Chile

HABITAT Breeds in tundra and wet meadows; winters at sea

SIZE 7 in (18 cm)

The only swimming bird in its family, the toes of the phalarope are adapted for swimming, with flattened fringing scales. It comes ashore only to breed. In the breeding season the female is is brightly colored with a reddish throat and underparts. The male is smaller and duller. In winter both sexes have grayish plumage. Phalaropes eat beetles, flies, crustaceans and fish.

Normal sexual roles are reversed. Females take the initiative in courtship and mating and the male incubates the clutch of 4 eggs for about 19 days and cares for the young.

SHEATHBILLS, THICK-KNEES AND PRATINCOLES

CHIONIDIDAE: SHEATHBILL FAMILY

The 2 species of sheathbill are medium-sized – 14 to 17 in (35.5 to 43 cm) – white plumaged, shore-living birds, found on the islands of the far southern oceans. They are squat and heavy-bodied, resembling pigeons in build, and have a comblike covering over the upper beak, which gives them their common name. Their legs are short and stocky and their feet powerful. Male and female sheathbills look alike, but females are usually smaller.

Snowy Sheathbill *Chionis alba*

RANGE Subantarctic islands of the S. Atlantic Ocean, extending to Graham Land and S. South America when not breeding.

HABITAT Coasts

SIZE 15¼ in (39 cm)

Snowy sheathbills are gregarious and pugnacious birds and, except during the breeding season, they live in small flocks, feeding together and often fighting. Although they fly well and will make long journeys, even over sea, they spend most of their time on the ground. They swim well although their feet have only rudimentary webs. Sheathbills are avid scavengers and haunt seal and penguin colonies to seize afterbirths or weak young. They also search the shore for all kinds of fish, invertebrates, carcasses and almost any other debris that they can eat. They consume quantities of seaweed for the invertebrates that it harbors.

Sheathbills nest in isolated pairs in a crevice or among rocks. The 2 or 3 eggs are laid on feathers, seaweed and other soft material. Both parents incubate the eggs for 28 days, but it appears that only 1 chick is actually reared as a general rule.

In winter, sheathbills in the extreme south of the range migrate north, but those on subantarctic islands usually remain there. The other species in this family, the black-billed sheathbill, C. *minor*, is found in the subantarctic sector of the Indian Ocean.

BURHINIDAE: THICK-KNEE FAMILY

The 9 species in this family have a variety of common names, including thick-knee, stone curlew and dikkop. All have thickened joints between tarsus and shin and three partially webbed toes on each foot. Thick-knees are active at dusk and at night and their large yellow eyes are an adaptation for this. The sexes look alike. The family is widely distributed in the Old World and 2 species occur in Central and South America.

Beach Thick-knee
Burhinus giganteus

RANGE S.E. Asia and Australasia

HABITAT Coasts and rivers

SIZE 20 in (50 cm)

A sturdy, large headed bird, this thick-knee has a strong, slightly upturned bill and large yellow eyes. It feeds mostly at night on insects, worms, mollusks and crustaceans, and some small vertebrates. It runs fast, in short dashes, and is a reluctant but strong flier. To avoid danger, it may crouch or flatten itself on the ground.

The great shore plover lays 2, sometimes 3, eggs in a shallow hollow in the ground. They are incubated by the female, with some help from the male. Both parents care for the chicks which are able to fend for themselves almost immediately.

Stone Curlew *Burhinus oedicnemus*

RANGE S. England, Europe, N. Africa, S.W. Asia; winters to the south of its range

HABITAT Open country, heath, farmland

SIZE 16 in (41 cm)

Although some populations migrate, the stone curlew is the only migratory thick-knee, northern birds wintering in East Africa. Like all its family, the stone curlew's plumage camouflages it well. The two bold wing bars are conspicuous in flight. Its bill is short and straight, and it eats mainly invertebrates, snails and worms. The female lays her 2 eggs on the ground in a hollow and incubates them with some help from her mate.

GLAREOLIDAE: PRATINCOLE FAMILY

This family contains 18 species – pratincoles, coursers and the crab plover. All are fairly small ploverlike birds with sharply pointed bills. Pratincoles have short beaks, narrow, pointed wings, forked tails, short legs and feet with four toes. Coursers have longer bills, broader wings and tails and longer legs with three-toed feet. Birds of both groups eat insects, mollusks, leeches, small lizards and seeds. They inhabit warmer areas of the Old World, including Australia. Males and females have similar plumage but may differ in size.

Cream-colored Courser

Cursorius cursor

RANGE Africa, Canary and Cape Verde Islands; S.W. Asia, W. India

HABITAT Desert and semidesert

SIZE 9 in (23 cm)

A slender, pale bird with dark eye stripes, the cream-colored courser merges well with its desert surroundings. Its flight is rapid, but it tends to run rather than fly, often crouching on the ground between bursts of movement.

Cream-colored coursers do not make regular migrations, but do wander out of their range, often flying to Europe, although they do not breed there. The female lays 2 or 3 eggs on the ground. She incubates them at night, when the temperature falls, but may need to stand above them by day to shade them.

Egyptian Plover *Pluvianus aegyptius*

RANGE N.E., W. and W. C. Africa

HABITAT Shores and sandbanks of rivers and lakes

SIZE 7¾ in (20 cm)

The Egyptian plover has more striking plumage and rather shorter legs, than the related coursers. It is usually found near water, and has long been known as the crocodile bird because of the belief that it feeds on the food particles remaining in the mouths of basking crocodiles. Though this is unconfirmed, the bird often feeds near crocodiles and on their body parasites. Its main food is insects.

The female lays 2 or 3 eggs which she covers with sand while they incubate. She may cover chicks temporarily, to hide them from danger.

Collared/Common Pratincole *Glareola pratincola*

RANGE S. Europe, S.W. Asia, Africa

HABITAT Open land, sun-baked mud-flats, freshwater banks

SIZE 9¾ in (25 cm)

The collared pratincole, with its deeply forked tail, is ternlike in its swift, agile flight, but can run easily on the ground like a plover. It has a characteristic creamy, black-bordered throat, but the border is less distinct in winter.

Pratincoles are gregarious birds, and flocks gather at dusk to feed on insects, which they chase and catch in the air, often in the vicinity of water. They breed in colonies of anything from a few pairs to hundreds of birds and generally breed after the rainy or flood season in their area.

Their 2 to 4 eggs are laid on the ground and are well camouflaged by their blotched, neutral coloration, which blends with the background, whether soil, sand or rock. Both parents incubate the eggs for a total of 17 or 18 days. The young are able to run around immediately after hatching. After breeding, European collared pratincoles migrate to Africa, south of the Sahara.

Crab Plover *Dromas ardeola*

RANGE Breeds on islands from E. Africa to the Persian Gulf; winters on coasts and islands of the W. Indian Ocean

HABITAT Estuaries, reefs

SIZE 15 in (38 cm)

A stocky bird with a heavy, compressed bill, the crab plover flies strongly and runs swiftly. Its black and white markings are striking and distinct in flight. The legs are long and the toes are partially webbed. Crabs are, indeed, the main item of its diet, but it also feeds on other crustaceans and on mollusks, which it breaks open with its strong, pointed bill.

Crab plovers are noisy, gregarious birds and they nest in colonies. The female lays her single egg at the end of a burrow in a sandbank, often in a crab burrow. Although it is able to run about soon after hatching, the chick is cared for by both parents and is fed in the burrow.

OYSTERCATCHERS, AVOCETS AND PLOVERS

CHARADRIIDAE: PLOVER AND AVOCET FAMILY

The 89 species of wading birds in this family are placed in 2 subfamilies – Recurvirostrinae (Oystercatchers, Avocets, Stilts), and Charadriinae (Plovers and Lapwings).

RECURVIROSTRINAE: OYSTERCATCHER, AVOCET AND STILT SUBFAMILY

Oystercatchers are large, noisy, coastal birds found throughout the world, except on oceanic islands and in polar regions. The 11 species show only slight sexual and seasonal plumage differences. The 11 species of avocets and stilts are long-billed, long-legged wading birds found throughout much of the world, except in northernmost regions. These birds fly and sometimes swim well and generally live near water. Their feet are usually at least slightly webbed. Aquatic insects, mollusks, fish, frogs and some plant food are the main items of their diet. Many species have black and white plumage, and the sexes look more or less alike. The ibisbill differs from other avocets and stilts because of its downcurving beak and its high altitude habitat.

Common/Eurasian Oystercatcher *Haematopus ostralegus*

RANGE Breeds Eurasia; winters S. to Africa, India and South China

HABITAT Coasts, estuaries

SIZE 18 in (46 cm)

The common oystercatcher has a typical long, blunt, flattened bill which it uses to pry shellfish off rocks. Mollusks and crustaceans are its main food, but it also seeks insects and worms on farmland farther inland.

Oystercatchers are gregarious and live and move in large flocks. The nest is a hole in the ground, often lined with grass or decorated with moss. The female lays 2 to 4 eggs and both partners incubate them for 24 to 27 days.

Pied Avocet *Recurvirostra avosetta*

RANGE Europe, W. and C. Asia; northern populations winter in Africa, S. Asia, China

HABITAT Mud flats, estuaries, sandbanks

SIZE 16½ in (42 cm)

The avocet has striking black and white plumage and a long upward curving bill. In flight, the long legs usually project beyond the tail. Avocets eat insects, small aquatic animals and some plant matter, all of which they find by sweeping their bills from side to side at the surface of mud or shallow water. In deeper water, the avocet dips its head below the surface and will swim and "up-end" like a duck.

Avocets breed colonially; pairs mating after displays involving both partners. The nest is usually a scrape near water in which the female lays 3 to 5 eggs. Both parents incubate the eggs and later guard their chicks against predators. Juveniles have some brownish plumage but are similar to adults. The American avocet, *R. americana*, resembles this avocet, but has cinnamon plumage on head, neck and breast in the breeding season.

Black-winged Stilt *Himantopus himantopus*

RANGE Eurasia and Africa: tropical, subtropical and temperate latitudes

HABITAT Mainly freshwater swamps, marshes, lagoons

SIZE 15 in (38 cm)

The stilt has long pink legs, longer in proportion to its body than those of any bird except the flamingo. In flight, its legs project far beyond the tail. Stilts walk quickly, with long strides. They wade in water to pick insects and small aquatic animals off plants and the water surface with their long slender bills.

Stilts nest in colonies near water. Nests are large, built in shallow water from sticks and mud or small flimsy ground nests. Between April and June females lays 3 to 5 eggs which both parents incubate for 26 days.

Ibisbill *Ibidorhyncha struthersii*

RANGE High plateaux of C. Asia; Himalayas

HABITAT Shingle banks, shingle islands in mountain streams

SIZE 15 in (38 cm)

The ibisbill uses its down curving bill to probe for food under stones in the shingly river beds it frequents. It often wades into the water and submerges its head and neck. Small groups of ibisbills generally live and feed together. The female bird lays 4 large eggs in a ground nest, and the clutch is incubated by both parents.

CHARADRIINAE: PLOVER AND LAPWING SUBFAMILY

The members of this subfamily are found worldwide apart from Antarctica. The 67 species of plovers, lapwings, and dotterels are small to medium-sized, fairly plump wading birds. The typical plover has a short, straight bill, round head and short legs. Males and females are alike, or nearly so, but some species have seasonal differences in plumage. Plovers occur in sparsely vegetated areas, from sandy shores to semideserts, and eat insects and small invertebrates.

Ringed Plover *Charadrius hiaticula*

RANGE Breeds Arctic E. Canada and Eurasia; winters in Africa, S. Europe

HABITAT Seashore

SIZE 7½ in (19 cm)

A common northern shorebird, the ringed plover has distinctive head and breast markings in its summer plumage. It feeds on mollusks, insects, worms and some plants.

The female lays 3 to 5 eggs and will defend eggs or young with a distraction display technique used by many plover species. If a predator approaches the nest, the parent bird flaps awkwardly away as if injured and unable to fly, all the time leading the enemy away from the young. Once the predator is well away from the nest, the plover flies up suddenly and escapes, to return to the nest later.

Northern Lapwing *Vanellus vanellus*

RANGE Europe, W. and N. Africa, Asia

HABITAT Grassland, farmland, marshes

SIZE 12 in (30 cm)

A distinctive bird with a crested head and broad, rounded wings, the lapwing is also known as the peewit after the cry it makes in flight. Lapwings feed mostly on insects but also on worms, snails and some plant matter. The male makes a ceremonial nest scrape to initiate breeding behavior in the female. She completes the nest and lays 3 to 5 eggs. The clutch is incubated for 24 to 31 days.

American Golden Plover

Pluvialis dominica

RANGE Northern N. America, Asia; winters in South America

HABITAT Tundra, marshes, fields, open country

SIZE 9–11 in (23–28 cm)

This plover flies to wintering grounds 8,000 miles (12,800 km) south of its breeding grounds on the tundra of North America and Siberia.

American golden plovers eat insects and some mollusks and crustaceans. They lay 3 or 4 eggs in a shallow dip in the tundra, lined with moss and grass. Both parents incubate the eggs for 20 to 30 days. In winter this plover loses its distinctive facial markings, and its head and breast are a speckled golden color.

Wrybill *Anarhynchus frontalis* **VU**

RANGE New Zealand

HABITAT River beds, open country

SIZE 8 in (20 cm)

The wrybill is a small plover with a unique bill, the tip of which turns to the right. To find its insect food, it tilts its head to the left and sweeps the tip of its bill over the mud with a horizontal scissoring action. Wrybills winter in North Island and travel to South Island to breed. They nest in large estuaries on a particular type of shingle, the stones of which are a similar color to the wrybill and its eggs. The female lays 2 or 3 eggs among the shingle in October.

SKUAS, GULLS AND SKIMMERS

LARIDAE: GULL AND AUK FAMILY

Most of the 129 species in this family are seabirds. There are two subfamilies.

LARINAE: SKUA, SKIMMER, GULL, AND TERN SUBFAMILY

There are four groups, or tribes, in this subfamily. The 8 species of skuas, or jaegers as they are called in North America, are dark-plumaged seabirds characterised by their practical method of obtaining food – they chase other seabirds, such as gulls and terns, in the air and force them to disgorge their prey.

Skuas are widespread throughout tundra and polar regions, where they breed, and the open seas, where they range at other times. Males and females are outwardly alike, but the females are sometimes larger.

The 3 species of skimmers resemble large terns. Two are tropical freshwater birds, 1 in Africa and the other found from India to South China. The third, from the Americas, is coastal in its habits. Skimmers have eyes with slit-like pupils, unique among birds.

Gulls are solidly-built seabirds with long, broad wings and long legs with webbed feet. Most are white with black or gray markings. They are the classic shoreline birds; they seldom dive and few species catch fish. Most are opportunist feeders, scavenging, stealing food from others birds, or killing small prey. The 50 species of gulls are found along sea coasts worldwide, although they are more predominant in the cooler regions.

Terns are gulllike but smaller with long, narrow wings, a narrow bill, and forked tail. They dive for fish and most species also catch insects in the air or on water. The 45 tern species are found worldwide at sea, near coasts, and on inland waters.

Great Skua *Catharacta skua*
RANGE N. Atlantic Ocean: Iceland, Faeroes, Shetland and Orkney Islands; winters as far south as the Tropic of Cancer
HABITAT Oceanic, coastal waters
SIZE 20–22 in (51–56 cm)

A strongly built bird with a hooked bill and sharply curved claws, the great skua not only attacks other birds to steal their prey, but also kills and eats ducks and gulls and preys on eggs and young at breeding grounds. It also follows ships to feed on scraps thrown overboard and takes carrion.

An otherwise solitary bird, it nests in colonies. A shallow scrape is made on a rocky slope or at the foot of a cliff, and 1 to 3 eggs, usually 2, are laid. Both partners incubate the eggs for 26 to 29 days and care for the chicks.

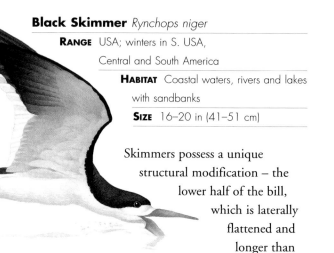

Black Skimmer *Rynchops niger*
RANGE USA; winters in S. USA, Central and South America
HABITAT Coastal waters, rivers and lakes with sandbanks
SIZE 16–20 in (41–51 cm)

Skimmers possess a unique structural modification – the lower half of the bill, which is laterally flattened and longer than the upper half, is an adaptation for a special method of fishing. The skimmer flies just above a smooth water surface, with its bladelike lower bill cleaving a furrow through the water. When the bill strikes a small fish or crustacean, the skimmer clamps down its upper bill and pulls its head back to swallow the prey, while flying.

Black skimmers breed in spring in colonies of up to 200 pairs. The female lays 2 to 4 eggs in a hollow scraped in the sand.

Ivory Gull *Pagophila eburnea*
RANGE Arctic coasts and islands; winters among ice floes, sometimes south of the Arctic Circle
HABITAT Coasts, pack-ice
SIZE 14–17 in (35.5–43 cm)

The only gull with all-white plumage, the ivory gull is a striking, plump-bodied bird with black legs. It seldom swims but can run over ice. It feeds on fish and invertebrates and scavenges on carrion and refuse. It breeds in colonies and lays 2 eggs on the ground or on a cliff ledge.

Herring Gull

Larus argentatus

RANGE Most of northern hemisphere

HABITAT Coasts, estuaries; inland water and fields

SIZE 21½–26 in (55–66 cm)

The commonest coastal gull in North America and Europe, the herring gull has a varied diet. It eats small surface-dwelling fish, scavenges on waste and sewage, steals eggs and preys on young birds and small mammals. It also flies inland to feed on worms and other invertebrates on farmland.

Herring gulls nest in colonies on cliff slopes, islands or beaches. The nest is usually made of weeds and grass in a hollow in the ground. It is sometimes built in a tree or on a building. The 2 or 3 eggs are incubated for 25 to 27 days by both parents. In their first year, the young have dark-brown plumage. They do not attain full adult plumage for 3 years. Male and female adult birds look alike, but males are often larger.

Black-headed Gull *Larus ridibundus*

RANGE Iceland, N. Europe and Asia; winters south of range to N. Africa, S. Asia and Philippines

HABITAT Coasts, inland marshes

SIZE 14–15 in (35.5–38 cm)

This small, active gull is often seen inland in winter (when it is not black-headed), and thrives in freshwater habitats, where it feeds on insects and invertebrates. It scavenges, especially on refuse tips, and feeds on the coast.

Black-headed gulls breed colonially on marshes, moors and coasts in the spring. A pair builds a nest, usually on the ground and made of plant material, and the female lays 3 eggs, which are incubated for 20 to 24 days.

Black-legged Kittiwake *Rissa tridactyla*

RANGE N. Pacific, N. Atlantic Oceans, parts of Arctic Ocean

HABITAT Oceanic

SIZE 16–18 in (41–46 cm)

The kittiwake is much more oceanic in its habits than the *Larus* gulls and normally comes ashore only to breed. It seldom walks, so its legs are much shorter than those of most gulls and it has only three toes on each foot. It feeds on fish, small mollusks and crustaceans and also scavenges on the waste dumped from fishing boats.

Kittiwakes nest in huge colonies of thousands of birds, normally on high cliffs. A pair builds a nest from plants, seaweed and guano, cementing it to the cliff ledge with mud. The usual clutch of 2 eggs is incubated for 23 to 32 days by both parents.

Common Tern *Sterna hirundo*

RANGE E. N. America, N. Europe, Asia; winters south of range to the tropics

HABITAT Coastal islands, coasts; inland rivers and lakes

SIZE 13–16 in (33–41 cm)

A common and widespread coastal bird, the common tern feeds on small fish and other marine creatures, which it catches by hovering over the water and then diving rapidly to seize the prey it with its bill.

Terns nest in colonies of hundreds of thousands on isolated beaches, islands or cliffs. A pair scrapes a hollow in the ground which is then lined with vegetation. Both parents take turns at incubating the 2 or 3 eggs for 21 to 26 days.

Brown Noddy *Anous stolidus*

RANGE Tropical oceans

HABITAT Offshore waters, islands

SIZE 16–17 in (41–43 cm)

The 5 species of noddy tern are all inhabitants of tropical seas. The noddy seldom dives, but it will float on the surface of the water or perch on buoys, driftwood or reefs, watching out for prey. It often flies just above the water and snatches small fish when they are driven to the surface by larger fish.

Brown noddies make their untidy twig nests in bushes or on the ground. Both parents incubate the single egg.

AUKS

ALCINAE: AUK SUBFAMILY

The auks are a small family of short-tailed, short-necked diving seabirds found in the North Pacific, North Atlantic and Arctic Oceans, and along their coasts. They are truly marine birds, only coming to land to breed. The 23 species include the guillemots, razorbills, auklets, puffins, murres and auks. All have dark-brown or black plumage, usually with white underparts. Auks swim well and dive from the surface to pursue prey underwater, propelling themselves with their short, narrow wings. They stand upright on land and this, combined with their general body shape and marine habits, makes them the northern equivalents of the penguins, found in the southern hemisphere.

Indeed, the name penguin was first applied by early mariners to the largest member of the family, the great auk; it was only later used for the similarly adapted birds that we know today as penguins. The great auk was flightless – its short, powerful wings were of use only for underwater propulsion. Because of this it could not easily escape from man, so great auks were constantly slaughtered for food and have now been extinct for more than a century.

Auks are not, however, closely related to penguins evolutionarily: the resemblance is an example of two groups of birds adapting in a similar way to fill the same niche in northern and southern hemispheres.

Auks nest in colonies of hundreds or thousands of birds on cliff tops and rocks. They fly fast, with rapid wing beats, but some of the small species are better adapted for swimming than flying. Some species migrate south in winter. Males and females look alike but there are some seasonal plumage changes. In their annual molt, most species lose all the flight feathers at once and are temporarily flightless.

Guillemot/Common Murre

Uria aalge

RANGE N. Atlantic, N. Pacific Oceans
HABITAT Offshore waters, oceanic
SIZE 16–17 in (41–43 cm)

One of the most common auks, the guillemot has a longer, narrower bill than is usual for auks and a less bulky body. In breeding plumage, the head, neck and upperparts are dark brown, but in winter, the throat and front and sides of face and neck are white, with dark stripes extending back from the eyes. Guillemots feed on fish, mollusks and worms which they catch underwater.

At the end of May, colonies of guillemots gather in breeding areas on top of rocks or on cliffs. Each female lays 1 egg on bare rock; the egg is pear-shaped and this led to the long-held belief that, if it moves, it rolls round in a circle, rather than off the ledge. However, this is probably not so and the reason why the egg is this shape may well be related to its large size and the narrow pelvis of the female guillemot. The eggs vary enormously in color and pattern and this may help the birds to recognize their own eggs in the crowded breeding colony. Both parents incubate the egg for 28 to 30 days. In winter guillemots migrate south of their normal breeding range.

Atlantic Puffin *Fratercula arctica*

RANGE N. Atlantic Ocean: Arctic coasts of E. N. America and W. Eurasia
HABITAT Open sea, rocky coasts
SIZE 11½–14¼ in (29–36 cm)

A small, round-bodied auk with a large head, the Atlantic puffin has a spectacular striped bill, which it uses to catch food and for display. In summer the puffin's bill is colorful, the upper parts of the body and collar are black and the underparts white. In winter, the face is grayish and the bill smaller and duller. Young birds resemble adults in winter plumage, but have smaller, darker bills. The puffin feeds on fish and shellfish and can carry several items at a time in its capacious bill as it flies back to its nest. Its flight is strong and fast but, like all auks, it has short legs set well back on the body and waddles along clumsily on land.

Atlantic puffins breed from late May in colonies on turfed cliff tops or on islands. The female lays 1 egg, rarely 2, in a burrow abandoned by a shearwater or rabbit, or in a hole which she digs herself with her feet. Both parents incubate the egg for 40 to 43 days. After breeding, most puffins spend the winter at sea, offshore from the breeding range, but some populations migrate southward.

Crested Auklet
Aethia cristatella

RANGE N. Pacific Ocean, Bering Sea

HABITAT Ocean, sea cliffs

SIZE 9½–10½ in (24–27 cm)

In the breeding season the crested auklet develops a dark crest of long plumes that fall forward over its bright bill, and white plumes behind the eyes. In winter, the crest and eye plumes are smaller, and the bill becomes a dull yellow. Young birds have no crests. These small auklets feed mainly on crustaceans.

Colonies of crested auklets gather on cliffs in order to breed, and the female lays a single egg in a rock crevice or among stones.

Razorbill *Alca torda*

RANGE N. Atlantic Ocean

HABITAT Coasts, open sea

SIZE 15¾–16½ in (40–42cm)

A well-built auk, with a heavy head and a thick neck, the razorbill has a stout, compressed bill with distinctive white markings. In summer, the razorbill's head, neck and upper parts are black, with prominent white lines running from bill to eyes. In winter, the auk's cheeks and forehead are white. Razorbills feed on fish, crustaceans and mollusks. Colonies of razorbills nest on sea cliffs and rocky shores on the Atlantic coasts of Europe and North America often near guillemot colonies. The breeding season starts about mid-May, and the female lays 1 egg, rarely 2, in a hole or crevice. Both parents incubate the egg for about 25 days, and the young leaves the nest after about 15 days.

Little Auk/Dovekie *Alle alle*

RANGE Arctic Ocean; winters in N. Atlantic Ocean

HABITAT Coasts, open sea

SIZE 7¾ in (20 cm)

The smallest auk, the little auk is a squat, rounded bird, with a short thick neck and a stout, strong bill. In winter the throat and breast, which are dark in summer plumage, become white. The little auk feeds on crustaceans, small fish and mollusks. An excellent swimmer, it dives rapidly if alarmed.

From mid-June, thousands of little auks gather in crowded colonies on Arctic coasts and cliffs. They do not make nests, and the female lays 1 egg, occasionally 2, in a crack in the rock. Both sexes take it in turns to incubate the egg for 24 to 30 days.

Little auks spend the winter at sea, moving as far south as Iceland and Norway. They may even appear inland in particularly bad weather. This species occurs in vast numbers in its Arctic habitat and is believed to be one of the most abundant birds in the world.

Marbled Murrelet *Brachyramphus marmoratus*

RANGE N. Pacific Ocean

HABITAT Coasts, islands

SIZE 9½–9¾ in (24–25 cm)

In the breeding season, the marbled murrelet has distinctly barred and speckled underparts, which become white in winter. It feeds, like the rest of the auks, on fish and other marine animals and, when on water it holds its slender bill and tail pointing upward.

Unusually for an auk, it flies inland to breed in mountains or forest areas and lays 1 egg on a twig platform, on moss, or in a nest abandoned by another species of bird.

HAWKS

ACCIPITRIDAE: HAWK FAMILY

This is the largest family in the Falconiformes order and contains about 239 species of diverse predatory and carrion-eating birds. Representatives occur in almost all regions of the world except Antarctica, northern parts of the Arctic and small oceanic islands.

The accipiter family contains many different types and sizes of bird. The family includes the 14 or so carrion-feeding Old World vultures, the "true hawks" (including buzzards and eagles), harrier eagles and serpent eagles, harriers, kites and fish eagles, honey-buzzards and a few other specialized types.

Females tend to be significantly larger than the males in almost every case, excluding the vultures. Characteristic physical features of this family are the down-curved pointed beak, the base of which is covered with a fleshy cere carrying the external nostrils, and large wings with rounded tips and often barred or streaked underparts. All the birds have widely spaced toes and long, sharp, curving claws. On the soles of the feet are roughened, bulging pads to facilitate the seizing of prey.

Most species nest in trees, while some of the larger eagles and buzzards use cliff ledges. These large species are long-lived birds which reach breeding maturity slowly. They have small clutches of only 1 or 2 eggs. There are 2 subfamilies – one contains the single osprey species, the other the remaining hawk species.

Osprey *Pandion haliaetus*
RANGE Almost worldwide
HABITAT Lakes, rivers, coasts
SIZE 21–24 in (53–62 cm)

The osprey, or fish hawk, feeds almost exclusively on fish, but it will take small mammals and wounded birds. When hunting, it flies over water and may hover briefly before plunging into the water, feet forward. Grasping the fish in both feet, the soles of which are studded with spikes to aid its grip, it returns to feed at its perch.

A breeding pair makes a large nest on the ground, using sticks, seaweed and other debris. The same nest may be repaired and used year after year. A clutch of 2 to 4 eggs, usually 3, is incubated mainly by the female. The male feeds her during incubation and for the first 4 weeks of the chicks' fledgling period. Northern populations migrate south for the winter.

Egyptian Vulture *Neophron percnopterus*
RANGE S. Europe, Africa, Middle East, India
HABITAT Open country
SIZE 23½–27½ in (60–70 cm)

The Egyptian vulture is a small species. It defers to larger vultures at a carcass and must often be content with scraps. It also eats insects and ostrich and flamingo eggs. It is one of the few creatures to use a tool. In order to break into an ostrich egg the vulture drops rocks on it to crack it open. This vulture scavenges on all kinds of refuse, including human excrement.

Display flights of swoops and dives precede mating, and the pair builds a nest on a crag or a building. The parents incubate 1 or 2 eggs for about 42 days.

Lammergeier/Bearded Vulture *Gypaetus barbatus*
RANGE S. Europe, Africa, Middle East to C. Asia
HABITAT Mountains
SIZE 37–41 in (95–105 cm)

An uncommon and magnificent bird, the lammergeier descends from the mountains only to forage for food. It spends most of its day on the wing, soaring with unequaled grace. It feeds on carrion of all sorts, including human, but defers to larger vultures at carcasses. As one of the last in line, the lammergeier is often left with the bones, and it has developed the knack of dropping them on rocks to split them and reveal the marrow.

Each breeding pair holds a large territory, and the birds perform spectacular diving and swooping flight displays. They nest in cliff niches or on ledges and lay 1 or 2 eggs which are incubated for 53 days. Normally only 1 chick is reared.

Lappet-faced Vulture

Torgos tracheliotus

RANGE Africa, Israel, parts of Arabian peninsula

HABITAT Bush, desert

SIZE 39–45 in (100–115 cm)

The lappet-faced vulture is a typical Old World vulture with perfect adaptations for scavenging. The powerful hooked bill cuts easily into the flesh of carrion. Its bare head and neck save lengthy feather-cleaning after plunging into a messy carcass. The immense broad wings, with widely spaced primary feathers, are ideal for soaring and gliding for long periods, using few wing beats. No real mating display has been observed. A huge stick nest is made at the top of a tree or on a crag, and the female lays 1 egg.

European Honey-buzzard *Pernis apivorus*

RANGE Eurasia; winters south to S. Africa

HABITAT Woodland

SIZE 20–24 in (52–61 cm)

The honey-buzzard has broad, barred wings, a long tail and specially adapted feathers to protect it from the stings of bees and wasps whose nests it attacks. Larvae and honey are a major food source and it also feeds on live wasps, nipping off the sting before swallowing them. Small vertebrates and flying termites also feature in the honey-buzzard's diet.

A mating pair holds a home territory and the male performs a distinctive display flight, striking his wings together above his head. They make a tree nest of sticks and leaves. Both parents incubate the clutch of 1 to 3 eggs for 30 to 35 days and feed the young. Northern Eurasian populations migrate south to Africa in winter.

Red Kite *Milvus milvus* **LR:lc**

RANGE Europe, Middle East, N. Africa

HABITAT Woodland, open country

SIZE 24–26 in (61–66 cm)

The red kite is a large bird with long wings and a distinctive, deeply forked tail. It

breeds in woodland but hunts in open country. As it flies low over fields, it searches for prey. It can hover briefly and pursues its quarry with great agility. Small mammals up to the size of a weasel, birds, reptiles, frogs, fish, insects and carrion are all eaten, and red kites also kill domestic poultry.

A breeding pair nests in a tree, often adding sticks and oddments to an old nest. Between 1 and 5 eggs, usually 3, are laid. It is mainly the female that incubates the eggs for 28 to 30 days. The male feeds her and takes over from time to time.

Brahminy Kite *Haliastur indus*

RANGE India, S. China, S.E. Asia, Australasia

HABITAT Near water, coasts

SIZE 18 in (46 cm)

The brahminy kite feeds on frogs, crabs, snakes, fish, insects and some carrion. It also scavenges around human habitation for all kinds of scraps and refuse. At the breeding site the birds perform display flights before starting to build a nest. The nest is made of sticks and lined with leaves and is sited in a tree or among mangroves. The female lays 1 to 4 eggs which she incubates for 26 or 27 days, while her mate keeps her supplied with food.

Everglade/Snail Kite *Rostrhamus sociabilis*

RANGE USA: Florida; Caribbean, Mexico, Central and South America

HABITAT Freshwater marshes

SIZE 15 in (8 cm)

The Everglade kite feeds solely on water snails of the genus *Pomacea*; the elongated upper bill is an adaptation for this diet. The kite flaps slowly over the water on its large broad wings. When it sees a snail, it swoops down, grasps it with one foot and takes it back to a perch. Standing on one foot, the kite holds the snail in such a way that it can emerge from the shell. The instant the snail appears, the kite strikes it with its sharp bill; the snail's impaled body goes limp and the kite shakes it free.

Breeding pairs build nests which are simple structures in marsh grass or bushes. The female lays 3 or 4 eggs, and both parents incubate the clutch and care for the young.

This unusual bird is now rare, particularly in Florida, and is protected by conservation laws.

HAWKS CONTINUED

Bald Eagle

Haliaeetus leucocephalus

RANGE N. America

HABITAT Coasts, rivers and lakes

SIZE 32–40 in (81–102 cm)

The national symbol of the USA, the bald eagle is one of 8 species of eagle in the genus *Haliaeetus*, all of which have a liking for fish. Most of the others are called "sea" or "fish" eagles and are coastal birds. Dead and dying fish are the staple diet of the bald eagle, but it also takes live fish from the water and catches some birds and mammals. Groups of these impressive birds gather together where food is available, particularly by rivers near the Alaskan coast, where they prey on exhausted salmon which are migrating upriver to their breeding grounds.

Bald eagles breed in northern North America on inland lakes, migrating south, if necessary, in the winter to find food. Pairs remain together and reestablish bonds each year with spectacular courtship displays, when the birds lock talons in mid-air and somersault through the air together. The nest is made of sticks and sited in a large tree or on rocks. It is added to, year after year, and can be as large as 8 ft (2.5 m) across and 11½ ft (3.5 m) deep, one of the largest of all birds' nests. Most of the time the female incubates the 1 to 3 eggs, but the male takes an occasional turn. The young remain in the nest for 10 or 11 weeks and are aggressive and competitive. Often the youngest of the brood is starved or killed.

All populations of this fine eagle have declined, seriously in some areas. It has suffered from the contamination of its habitat and prey by toxic chemicals and, with its slow breeding rate, it is hard for the species to recover.

Palm-nut Vulture

Gypohierax angolensis

RANGE Africa, south of the Sahara

HABITAT Forest, mangroves, savanna

SIZE 28 in (71 cm)

This curious bird resembles both vultures and sea eagles, and some authorities believe it to be a link between them. It feeds almost exclusively on the husk of the fruit of the oil palm *Elaeis guineensis*, and its distribution coincides with that of the plant. The diet is supplemented with fruit of the raphia palm, crabs, mollusks, snails and locusts, but all are rejected in favour of oil palm. A sedentary bird, the palm-nut vulture tends to stay around the same haunts and may remain near its breeding grounds all year. A pair builds a nest in a tree, using sticks and pieces of oil palm, or repairs an old nest. The female lays 1 egg which is incubated for about 44 days.

Bateleur *Terathopius ecaudatus*

RANGE Africa, south of the Sahara, S.W. Arabia

HABITAT Savanna and plains

SIZE 22–28 in (55–70 cm)
Wingspan: 67–71 in (170–180 cm)

The most interesting bird in a group of birds of prey known as snake eagles or snake hawks, the bateleur has an unmistakable flight silhouette, with its exceptionally long wings and very short tail; its feet project beyond the tail tip in flight. Unlike other snake eagles, the bateleur feeds mostly on carrion, but also kills for itself. It makes fierce attacks on other carrion-feeding birds, robbing them of their spoils. A spectacular bird in flight, it soars effortlessly for hours and probably travels about 200 miles (320 km) every day. Once it gets aloft by means of rapid flapping, the bateleur makes scarcely a wing beat, and it performs aerobatic feats such as complete rolls.

Breeding pairs nest in trees and make compact, cup-shaped nests of sticks. A third adult is often present throughout the whole breeding cycle – an unusual occurrence in the bird world that has not been fully explained. The third adult does not incubate or visit the actual nest, but roosts nearby with the male and appears at the nest if an intruder troubles the parents. This habit may be a development of the tendency of juvenile and sub-adult birds to stay near the parents' nest during breeding. The single egg is normally incubated by the female for about 42 days. The young bird is particularly weak at first but has a long fledgling period, during which it is fed by both parents.

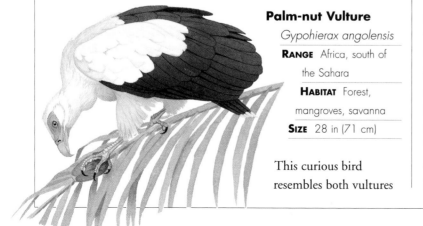

Crested Serpent Eagle
Spilornis cheela

RANGE India to S. China; S.E. Asia, Indonesia, Philippines
HABITAT Forest
SIZE 20–28 in (51–71 cm)

The crested serpent eagle is a variable species and the many races differ in size and plumage tones. The birds soar above the land, calling occasionally, but do not hunt in the air; they generally catch prey by dropping down on it from a perch. Like other snake eagles, the crested serpent eagle feeds mainly on reptiles, particularly tree snakes; its feet, with short, strong, roughsurfaced toes, are adapted for grasping its slippery prey.

A pair often remains together all year. In the breeding season, The birds perform flight displays, then build a small nest of sticks in a tree. The female incubates her 1 egg for about 35 days during which period the male supplies her with food.

African Harrier Hawk *Polyboroides typus*

RANGE Africa, south of the Sahara
HABITAT Forest, savanna, open grassland
SIZE 25 in (63 cm)

The African harrier hawk is a long-tailed, long-legged bird with a bare-skinned face. The young of other birds are its main source of food, although it also eats other creatures and the fruit of the oil palm. It clambers about on trees with great agility, searching for nests, and even hangs upside-down, with wings flapping, to attack pendulous weaverbird nests. The hawk's own nest is built in a tree, and both parents incubate the clutch of 1 to 5 eggs for about 40 days.

Hen/Northern Harrier *Circus cyaneus*

RANGE N. America, Eurasia
HABITAT Moors, marshes, plains
SIZE 17–20½ in (44–52 cm)

A widely distributed bird, the hen harrier breeds in North America, Europe and Asia, then migrates south of its breeding grounds in winter. There are 14 species of harrier, all in the genus *Circus*. All hunt by flying low over the ground, carefully searching the area for prey. Once a creature is spotted, the harrier drops down on it and kills it on the ground.

Hen harriers feed on small mammals, birds, including those wounded by hunters, and some reptiles, frogs and insects. A nest is made on the ground in marshy land or among low vegetation, and the average clutch contains 4 to 6 eggs. The female incubates the eggs and the male brings food, both during this period and after the chicks hatch.

Dark Chanting-goshawk *Melierax metabates*

RANGE W.C. and E. Africa; S. Arabia
HABITAT Bush, scrub
SIZE 15–19 in (38–48 cm)

The handsome dark chanting-goshawk perches on a vantage point in a tree or bush ready to glide swiftly down on a prey animal on the ground. The bird's long legs enable it to pursue quarry on the ground too, where it runs quickly, like a small secretary bird. Lizards, snakes and insects are the chief prey animals, but small mammals and ground birds are also caught.

At the onset of the breeding season, the male bird chants his melodious song in order to attract the female and the pair fly together over the breeding site. A small nest of sticks and mud is built in a tree, and the female lays 1 or 2 eggs.

The habits of the closely related pale chanting-goshawk, *M. canorus*, are almost identical.

HAWKS AND SECRETARY BIRD

Northern Goshawk

Accipiter gentilis

RANGE N. America, Europe,
N. Asia, Turkey, Iran, Tibet,
C.S. China, Japan

HABITAT Forest, woodland

SIZE 20–26 in (51–66 cm)
Wingspan: 47¼ in (120 cm)

These aggressive hawks are the largest birds in the genus *Accipiter* and are efficient killers. They fly through the forest, weaving skilfully in and out of trees, and sometimes soar over the treetops. They kill prey with a vicelike grip of the powerful talons, then pluck it (if a bird) and eat it on the ground. A goshawk is capable of killing birds as large as pheasant and grouse and mammals the size of rabbits and hares. The birds are often trained for falconry.

Goshawk pairs usually mate for life. They winter alone and in the spring meet at the breeding grounds where they perform flight displays. A new nest is made in a tree or an old nest is repaired. The pair roost together while nest-making and perform a screaming duet each day before sunrise. They mate about 10 times a day during the egg-laying period which lasts 6 to 8 weeks.

The clutch contains from 1 to 5 eggs, usually 3, but the number is affected by the availability of suitable prey. The female incubates the clutch for 36 to 38 days; the male brings her food and takes over occasionally. Some northern populations of goshawks migrate south after breeding.

Cooper's Hawk *Accipiter cooperii*

RANGE S. Canada, USA, N. Mexico

HABITAT Woodland

SIZE 14–20 in (36–51 cm)

Cooper's hawk is a medium-sized bird with rounded wings and tail. It is a typical *Accipiter* in its habits. It lives in the cover of woodland and ventures out to find prey. When hunting,

Cooper's hawk usually perches to watch for prey, which it quickly swoops down and seizes unawares. Bobwhite quail, starlings, blackbirds, chipmunks and squirrels are common prey. The hawk also pursues creatures on the ground, half running and half flying.

At the breeding site, the male defends a territory and, when a female appears he feeds her. Both then perform courtship flights. The clutch is usually 4 or 5 eggs, sometimes 6, and the female does most of the incubation. She helps the chicks to emerge from their shells and feeds and guards them closely in the first weeks of life. Some northern populations migrate south after breeding.

Black-collared Hawk *Busarellus nigricollis*

RANGE Tropical lowlands, Mexico to Paraguay and Argentina

HABITAT Open country near water

SIZE 18–20 in (46–51 cm)

A specialized hawk, the black-collared hawk has long, broad wings, a short, broad tail and a slightly hooked bill. The bottoms of its toes are covered with tiny prickly spines – an adaptation for catching and holding fish. In open areas the fishing buzzard can swoop down and catch its prey while scarcely wetting its plumage; elsewhere it will plunge into the water to fish, then sit drying its wings.

Common Buzzard *Buteo buteo*

RANGE Breeds in Europe, Asia to Japan; winters in E. Africa, India, Malaya and S. China

HABITAT Woodland, moorland

SIZE 20–22 in (51–56 cm)

The buzzard is not a bold hunter and spends more time perching than on the wing. Once aloft it soars well. It eats mainly small ground mammals, reptiles, insects, carrion and some ground birds. It kills most of its prey by dropping on it from its perch or from hovering flight and nearly always kills on the ground.

The size of the buzzard's breeding territory varies from year to year according to food supplies. The courtship flights are uncharacteristically energetic and the birds dive and swoop with great vigour. A nest is built on a tree or crag, and the female lays 2 to 6 eggs.

Red-tailed Hawk *Buteo jamaicensis*

RANGE North and Central America, West Indies

HABITAT Varied, deserts, forest, mountains

SIZE 18–24 in (46–61 cm)

A powerful, thickset, aggressive bird with a loud voice and a distinctive chestnut tail, the red-tailed hawk occupies a wide variety of habitats. It is an opportunistic hunter. Although its staple diet is rodents and rabbits, it also eats snakes, lizards, birds and insects. It hunts on the wing or from a perch, swooping down on prey.

Pairs display in the breeding territory. A nest is made of twigs high in a tree or cactus plant. The female stays on or near the nest for some weeks before laying 1 to 4 eggs. Her mate feeds her during this period. The pair share the incubation for 28 to 32 days.

Harpy Eagle *Harpia harpyja* **LR:nt**

RANGE S. Mexico to N. Argentina

HABITAT Lowland rain forest

SIZE 35½ in (90 cm)

The harpy is the world's largest eagle. It has huge feet (each the size of a man's hand), equipped with sharp talons. Its broad wings are relatively short. The harpy flies from tree to tree in search of prey, and can give chase through the branches with agility. Arboreal mammals, such as monkeys and opossums, are its main food. It may also catch large birds.

The harpy's nest is a platform of sticks high in the tallest trees, perhaps 150 ft (45 m) above the forest floor. The bird is believed to lay 2 eggs. The young birds stay with their parents for as long as a year, and pairs probably breed every other year. Now rare, harpy eagles have declined in numbers, largely due to destruction of their habitat and hunting by man.

Golden Eagle *Aquila chrysaetos*

RANGE Holarctic, as far south as N. Africa and Mexico

HABITAT Moor, mountain forest

SIZE 30–35 in (76–89 cm)

Golden eagles are probably the most numerous large eagles in the world. They have huge talons with long curved claws, a hooked bill and exceptionally sharp-sighted eyes. When hunting the golden eagle soars for long periods then dives to seize and kill the animal with its talons. Mammals such as hares and rabbits are the chief prey. Grouse and other birds are also caught, and carrion is an important food source.

Golden eagles perform spectacular flight displays over the nest site which is high on a ledge or tree. Some pairs have several nests, used in rotation. The 2 eggs are usually incubated by the female, but the male takes an occasional turn. In most cases, the first chick to hatch killed the younger one.

SAGITTARIIDAE: SECRETARY BIRD FAMILY

This family contains only 1 species, an eaglelike bird with a distinctive crest, long tail feathers and long legs.

Secretary Bird *Sagittarius serpentarius*

RANGE Africa, south of the Sahara

HABITAT Open, grassy country

SIZE 59 in (150 cm)

The secretary bird spends most of its time on the ground, walking with long strides, and may cover 30 km (20 miles) or so every day. It can run to catch prey which it takes with a swift thrust of its head; it kills larger animals by stamping on them. Small mammals, insects, some birds and eggs, reptiles, in fact almost anything crawling on the ground, are the secretary bird's prey.

In the breeding season, pairs are strongly territorial and chase intruders from their breeding range. The nest is usually on top of a tree and is made of sticks and turf, lined with grass and leaves. The female incubates the 2 or 3 eggs.

FALCONS

FALCONIDAE: FALCON FAMILY

The 63 species of falcon are all daytime-hunting birds of prey. They are found nearly all over the world. In appearance they are close to similar-sized accipiters, having sharp curved claws and powerful hooked beaks. Most species, however, have long pointed wings in contrast to the more rounded, slotted outlines of accipiters. There are also specific skeletal differences between the groups, such as details of skull structure and breastbones. Many falcons have so called "tomial" teeth – cutting edges on the upper bill with corresponding notches in the lower bill. Males and females look similar, but females are generally larger.

The family includes caracaras, laughing falcons, forest falcons, falconets, pygmy falcons and the typical falcons of the genus Falco, of which there are some 39 species. Falcons (except caracaras) do not build nests.

Crested Caracara
Polyborus plancus
RANGE S. USA; Central and South America
HABITAT Open country
SIZE 22–24 in (56–61 cm)

Caracaras are a group of neotropical birds quite unlike the rest of the falcons. They eat all kinds of animal food, from insects to mammals, and also scavenge on carrion. Both members of a pair build the nest, usually in a tree or on the ground. The female lays 2 to 4 eggs, and both parents incubate them for 28 days and care for the young. The young remain in the nest for two or three months, being fed by their parents.

Barred Forest Falcon *Micrastur ruficollis*
RANGE S. Mexico to N. Argentina
HABITAT Forest
SIZE 13–15 in (33–38 cm)

One of a group of 6 neotropical forest falcons, the barred forest falcon is adapted for life in dense jungle. A long-legged, short-winged bird, it flies deftly through the trees and waits in cover to attack prey. It feeds on small mammals, lizards and birds and often hunts the birds that follow army ants. Little is known of its breeding habits.

Collared Falconet
Microhierax caerulescens
RANGE Himalayas, N. India, S.E. Asia
HABITAT Forest
SIZE 7½ in (19 cm)

The 5 species of falconet are the smallest birds of prey. All species have similar habits. The collared falconet hunts for its food more in the manner of a flycatcher than that of a true falcon; it makes short flights from a perch to catch insects and, occasionally, small birds. The female lays a clutch of 4 to 5 eggs in a hole in a tree.

Common Kestrel *Falco tinnunculus*
RANGE Europe, Asia, Africa
HABITAT Open country, plains, cultivated land
SIZE 13¼–15 in (34–38 cm)

Kestrels hunt over open ground and are the hovering specialists in the hawk family. They fly some 30 to 50 ft (10 to 15 m) above ground in order to search for prey over an area. They hover and watch and, if something is sighted, drop gently down on it. The staple diet of kestrels consists of small mammals, but they will also catch small birds, reptiles and insects.

The clutch of 4 to 9 eggs is laid on a ledge, in a hole in a tree or in the abandoned nest of another bird. The female does the greater share of the incubation which lasts between 27 and 29 days. She remains with the chicks when they are first hatched and the male brings food to her and the brood, but later she leaves the nest in order to assist her mate with hunting and feeding duties.

Eurasian Hobby

Falco subbuteo

RANGE Britain to China; winters in Africa and the Far East

HABITAT Open country, bush, savanna

SIZE 12–14 in (30–36 cm)

Hobbies are small, long-winged falcons found all over the world. All are exceedingly swift in flight and catch almost all of their prey on the wing. They are specialists in taking flying prey (such as birds, insects and bats) from among a swarm or flock and can even catch the aerially acrobatic swallows and swifts.

In the breeding season, pairs perform mutual aerobatic displays with great speed and agility. The 2 or 3 eggs are laid in an old abandoned nest of another bird and while the female does most of the incubation, her mate feeds her.

Brown Falcon *Falco berigora*

RANGE Australia, New Guinea, Tasmania, Dampier Island

HABITAT Open country

SIZE 15¾–20 in (40–51cm)

The brown falcon is one of the commonest birds of prey in Australia. Its appearance and behavior are more like those of an Accipiter hawk than a falcon, hence its name. Less active than other falcons, it spends much time perching, but is capable of swift flight. It kills prey on the ground, mammals such as rabbits, young birds, reptiles, insects and some carrion making up its diet. The female lays 2 to 4 eggs in the abandoned nest of another bird and both parents incubate the eggs.

Gyrfalcon *Falco rusticolus*

RANGE Arctic Europe, Asia, N. America, Greenland, Iceland

HABITAT Mountains, tundra, sea cliffs

SIZE 20–25 in (51–63 cm)

This impressive bird is the largest of the falcons. The gyrfalcon has a stockier build than the peregrine falcon. Plumage can be dark, white or gray. Most breed north of the treeline and remain in the Arctic all year, but some populations migrate south for the winter.

When hunting, the gyrfalcon flies swiftly near to the ground. It can make rapid dives in order to catch its prey, like the peregrine, but this is less characteristic in this species. Birds make up the majority of its prey, although it also feeds on some mammals, particularly in winter. Ptarmigan and willow grouse account for the bulk of the gyrfalcon's diet and as a consequence their numbers can in turn affect its breeding rate. In years when these prey birds are abundant, gyrfalcons produce large clutches, but in years of scarcity the female will lay only a couple of eggs or pairs will not breed at all.

Gyrfalcons perform display flights when courting. The female lays 2 to 7 eggs on a ledge or in an old cliff nest. She incubates the clutch for 27 to 29 days during which her mate supplies her with food. When the young hatch, both parents bring food to them.

Peregrine Falcon

Falco peregrinus

RANGE Almost worldwide

HABITAT Varied, often mountains and sea cliffs

SIZE 15–20 in (38–51 cm)

The 17 races of this widespread bird vary greatly in plumage color. The peregrine's wings are tapered and pointed and its tail is slim and short. The peregrine falcon is virtually without equal in the speed and precision of its flight. Birds are its chief prey. The peregrine makes a dramatic, high-speed, near-vertical dive at its prey, then kills it outright with its talons, or seizes it and takes it to the ground in order to feed. The peregrine can also chase prey through the air, changing direction with supreme ease. Because of its skills it is the most highly prized bird for falconry.

At the onset of the breeding season, peregrines perform spectacular flight displays as part of their courtship ritual. The 2 to 6 eggs are laid on a ledge site, on the ground or even on a city building. The female does most of the incubation, but the male takes an occasional turn and brings food for his mate.

When the young are about 2 weeks old the female begins to leave them alone in the nest in order to help the male to hunt for food for them. The young chicks begin to fly at about 40 days old.

These birds are seriously declining in numbers, partly because of poisoning through the incidental ingestion of pesticides, which reach them via the insect-feeding birds on which they in turn feed.

GREBES, TROPIC-BIRDS AND GANNETS

PODICIPEDIDAE: GREBE FAMILY

Twenty one species of these satin plumaged water birds are found scattered around the world; some species are widespread. They all breed in fresh water, usually making a nest of floating decaying vegetation. Like penguins, grebes are built as fast swimmers, with legs set well back on the body. Large grebes are highly streamlined birds which chase and catch fish under water with their long pointed beaks. Other species feed on bottom-feeding mollusks and are smaller and more compact with stubby thick bills. Males and females look similar in most species, while juveniles have striped heads and necks.

Little Grebe *Tachybaptus ruficollis*

RANGE Europe, Africa and Madagascar, Asia, Indonesia, New Guinea

HABITAT Lakes, ponds, rivers

SIZE 10½ in (27 cm)

The little grebe is one of the smaller grebes and is rotund and ducklike in shape. It feeds on insects, crustaceans and mollusks. In winter its plumage is gray brown and white, but in the breeding season it has a reddish throat and foreneck. The female lays 2 to 10 eggs in a floating clump of vegetation in shallow water or among aquatic plants. Both parents incubate the clutch for a total of 23 to 25 days.

Great Crested Grebe *Podiceps cristatus*

RANGE Europe, Asia, Africa, south of the Sahara; Australia, New Zealand

HABITAT Lakes, ponds, rivers, coastal waters

SIZE 20 in (51 cm)

Easily recognized on water by its long slender neck and daggerlike bill, the great crested grebe is rarely seen on land (where it moves awkwardly) or in flight. It feeds mainly on fish, which it catches by diving from the surface of the water. The great crested is one of the largest grebes; adults are particularly striking in their breeding plumage, when they sport a double horned crest on the head and frills on the neck. In winter the crest is much reduced, the frills lost and the head largely white. The sexes look alike, but males generally have longer bills and larger crests and frills. Before mating, the grebes perform an elegant courtship dance. Both partners perform head-wagging and reed-holding displays and other ritualized movements. They mate on a reed platform near the nest, which is among the reeds. The female lays 2 to 7 eggs which are incubated by both parents for 27 to 29 days.

PHAETHONTIDAE: TROPICBIRD FAMILY

Tropicbirds are elegant seabirds easily distinguished by their two long central tail feathers. The 3 species in the family occur in tropical oceans, where they fly far out to sea and breed on islands. They are poor swimmers and tend to hunt by hovering above the water, then plunging down to seize the prey. Fish, squid and crustaceans are their main food. The sexes look alike.

Red-tailed Tropicbird
Phaethon rubricauda

RANGE Indian and Pacific Oceans

HABITAT Oceanic

SIZE Body: 16 in (41 cm) Tail: 20 in (51 cm)

The red-tailed tropicbird, with its dark red tail feathers, is a particularly striking species; in the breeding season, the bird's white plumage takes on a rosy tinge. Tropicbirds move awkwardly on land, so they tend to nest on ledges or cliffs where they are in a position for easy takeoff.

Although usually solitary at sea, they are numerous at breeding grounds and fight over nest sites and partners. No actual nest is made; the single egg is laid on the ground. Both parents incubate the egg for about 42 days and feed the downy chick until it leaves the nest at 12 to 15 weeks.

SULIDAE: GANNET FAMILY

The 9 birds in this family fall into two distinct groups – the 6 species of booby and the 3 species of gannet. They occur in all the oceans of the world: the boobies in tropical and subtropical areas, and the gannets generally in temperate zones. All are impressive marine birds that feed by plunge-diving for prey. Most have stout bodies, long pointed wings and short legs.

Male and female generally look alike, occasionally differing in bill and foot color. Juveniles have brownish feathers at first and develop the adult plumage over a few years.

Brown Booby *Sula leucogaster*

RANGE Tropical Atlantic and Pacific Oceans

HABITAT Mostly coastal

SIZE 29½–31½ in (75–80 cm)

Boobies were apparently given their common name because of their folly in allowing sailors to approach and kill them for food. Like gannets, boobies plunge-dive for fish and squid but specialize in feeding in shallow water and in the catching of flyingfish. The brown booby stays nearer to the coast than the gannet and breeds on cliffs and rocks or even on beaches and coral reefs. The female lays 1 or 2 eggs in a hollow on the ground or among rocks and both parents share the incubation and feeding duties.

Northern Gannet *Morus bassanus*

RANGE North Atlantic Ocean

HABITAT Coastal waters

SIZE 34–39¼ in (87–100 cm)

Gannets are streamlined, heavily built seabirds with thick necks, strong legs and webbed feet. Offshore rather than oceanic birds, they are magnificent in the air and fly or soar over the water searching for fish and squid. Once prey is sighted, the gannet will plummet 100 ft (30 m) or more down to the sea, grasp the catch and bring it to the surface.

The bird's stout bill and specially adapted skull, with resilient, air-filled spaces, take much of the initial impact of these expert dives. Other adaptations perfect gannets for marine life. First, there are no external nostrils. The nostril openings are covered by bony flaps so that water cannot be forced into them when the bird dives. The rear edge of the upper bill bows outward so that the gannet can breathe. Second, salt glands above the eye orbits produce a concentrated salt solution which enters the mouth by the internal nostrils and drips away from the beak, and this enables the gannet to feed on salty fish and to drink seawater without having to excrete vast quantities of urine in order to eliminate the salt.

Gannets are extremely gregarious birds, breeding in colonies of thousands of birds on rocks and islands. Attempts to breed gannets in small groups have failed, and it could be that the social stimulation of the colony is a crucial factor for breeding success. The birds display to establish and maintain pair bonds, and each pair occupies and defends a breeding territory. Nests are so closely packed that incubating birds can reach out and touch one another. The female lays 1 egg which both parents incubate for 43 to 45 days.

ANHINGAS AND CORMORANTS

ANHINGIDAE: DARTER FAMILY

These superb underwater fish-hunters look much like streamlined cormorants, but they have longer more slender necks and sharply pointed bills. Also known as anhingas, the 4 species of darter are found in a variety of freshwater habitats throughout the tropics.

There are some differences in the plumage of males and females, and males have light plumes on head and neck in the breeding season.

Anhinga *Anhinga anhinga*

RANGE S. USA to Argentina

HABITAT Lakes, rivers

SIZE 35 in (90 cm)

Anhingas dive deep in pursuit of fish, keeping their wings in at their sides and paddling with their feet. While under water, the bird keeps its long neck folded in, ready to dart out and impale prey on its sharp beak. The edges of the beak are serrated providing a firm grip on the fish. At the water surface, the anhinga often swims with all but its head and sinuous neck submerged – hence its other common name "snake bird". Crustaceans, amphibians and insects also form part of the anhinga's diet.

Anhingas are colonial breeders, often nesting near other large water birds. They build nests in a tree near or overhanging water. The female lays 3 to 6 eggs which both partners incubate.

PHALACROCORACIDAE: CORMORANT FAMILY

There are about 38 species of these mainly black, medium-sized water birds. Typically, cormorants have long necks and bodies, wings of moderate length, short legs and large webbed feet. Male and female resemble each other with small plumage differences in the breeding season. All cormorants are specialist fish-eaters and are found in marine and freshwater habitats. They are coastal birds, rarely seen over open sea. They swim well and dive from the surface to catch prey. In flight, their necks are fully extended, and they often fly in lines or V-formations.

Cormorants are gregarious birds. They nest colonially and defend small nest territories. After feeding excursions they rest on rocks, trees or cliffs, often with their wings, which quickly become waterlogged when diving, spread out to dry.

Great Cormorant *Phalacrocorax carbo*

RANGE E. North America, Europe, Africa, Asia, Australia

HABITAT Coasts, marshes, lakes

SIZE 31–39¼ in (80–100 cm)

Also sometimes known as the black cormorant, this bird is the largest species in its family and the most widely distributed. Habitats and nesting sites vary greatly over its enormous range. Male and female birds look alike, but the breeding male acquires some white feathers on his head and neck and a white patch on each flank. Immature birds have brownish plumage with pale underparts.

Cormorants feed primarily on fish, but they will also eat crustaceans and amphibians. Prey is caught underwater during dives which last between 20 and 30 seconds. This bird swims by using its webbed feet for propulsion and its long tail as a rudder. Most prey is brought back up to the surface and shaken before being swallowed.

Breeding pairs make their nests in trees or on the ground, inland or on the coast, depending on the situation in their particular range. The usual clutch is 3 or 4 eggs. Both parents incubate the eggs and feed the chicks. The chicks make their first flight about 50 days after hatching, but are not completely independent for another 12 to 13 weeks.

Long-tailed Cormorant *Phalacrocorax africanus*

RANGE Africa, Madagascar

HABITAT Rivers, lagoons

SIZE 23 in (58 cm)

One of four small, long-tailed, shorter necked cormorants, the reed cormorant is primarily an inland water bird but it is also found on the west coast of southern Africa. The male and female generally look alike, but in the breeding season the male's plumage darkens and he develops a tuft of feathers on the forehead and white plumes on face and neck. Young birds are brown and yellowish-white.

Reed cormorants feed on fish and some crustaceans, which they catch under water by diving from the surface. Like other cormorants, they return to the surface in order to consume their prey. During the breeding season, reed cormorants build their nests on the ground or in trees, and the female lays a clutch of 2 to 4 eggs.

Flightless Cormorant *Phalacrocorax harrisi* **VU**

RANGE Galápagos Islands

HABITAT Coastal waters

SIZE 36–39 in (91–99 cm)

This species occurs only on two islands in the Galápagos islands. It is a large bird and moves clumsily on land, but is superbly agile in the water. It has lost all power of flight and its wings have shrunk to tiny, useless appendages with only a few flight feathers remaining.

There are no mammalian predators in the Galápagos so, unlike its fellow cormorants, this species has no need to fly in order to escape from danger. The stable climate of their habitat also means that there is no need for these birds to move south in winter or to travel great distances in search of food. The flightless cormorant is able to catch all of the food that it needs in the nutrient-rich waters around the island coasts and octopus make up a large part of its diet.

The flightless cormorant breeds all year round with a peak between March and September. Both partners share the incubation duties, making a ritual presentation of a strand of seaweed as they swap over on the nest. Birds may produce several clutches of young each year. However, the population of the flightless cormorant is small and they are now rare.

HERONS

ARDEIDAE: HERON FAMILY

The 65 species of heron, bittern and egret in this family are all moderate to large birds with slim bodies, long necks and legs, and large, broad wings. Male and female look alike in most species. All herons have patches of powder-down feathers on the breast and rump – a feature probably associated with their mucus-laden diet of fish and amphibians. The powder produced by these specialized feathers is utilized in preening in order to remove slime from the plumage.

Herons hunt in water of varying depth, either while standing motionless or while wading. Prey is grasped (rather than impaled) with the powerful, dagger-shaped beak. Herons usually breed in colonies. During the breeding season, many species undergo changes of plumage color and develop long plumes on the head or back.

American Bittern *Botaurus lentiginosus*

RANGE C. North America; winters in S.USA, Central America

HABITAT Marshland

SIZE 26 in (66 cm)

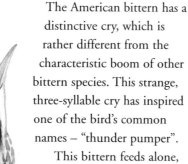

The American bittern has a distinctive cry, which is rather different from the characteristic boom of other bittern species. This strange, three-syllable cry has inspired one of the bird's common names – "thunder pumper".

This bittern feeds alone, moving slowly and deliberately with bill always at the ready to jab quickly at fish, crabs, snakes, frogs, insects or small mammals.

It is a migratory species; although birds in milder areas do not actually migrate, they do disperse after breeding.

The clutch of between 4 and 6 eggs is laid in a nest platform on land or in water, and the female bird seems to perform most of the parental duties.

Black-crowned Night Heron *Nycticorax nycticorax*

RANGE Europe, Asia, Africa, North and South America

HABITAT Varied, usually near marshes

SIZE 24 in (61 cm)

Probably the most numerous of all herons, the night heron is a stocky bird with white ribbonlike plumes extending from the back of its head; these are erected in courtship display. This bird feeds mainly at night and at dusk, it preys on fish, reptiles, frogs and insects and also raids the nests of other birds.

At the beginning of the breeding season, the male finds a nest site, usually among reeds or in a bush or a tree which he then uses as a base for his displays. His mate finishes the building of the nest and lays 3 to 5 eggs. Both parents feed and care for the chicks.

Gray Heron *Ardea cinerea*

RANGE Europe, Asia, Africa

HABITAT Varied, near shallow water

SIZE 36 in (92 cm)

A large, long-legged, long-billed bird, the gray heron is familiar throughout most of the Old World except Australia. Its New World equivalent, the great blue heron, *A. herodias*, is similar, but slightly larger, with reddish coloring on neck and thighs. The gray heron eats fish, eels, young birds, eggs, snakes and plants. It fishes from the land, with its head stretched forward, or wades in shallows. The bird grasps its prey with a swift, lethal thrust of the bill.

Gray herons breed in colonies, the female lays 3 to 5 eggs, and both parents feed the young.

Cattle Egret *Bubulcus ibis*

RANGE Iberia, Africa, Asia, Indonesia,
North and South America, Australia

HABITAT Open land,
drier than the habitat of most herons

SIZE 19½ in (50 cm)

The cattle egret is an extremely successful species and has expanded its range all over the world. Its success is partly due to its association with herbivorous animals. The birds follow large grazing animals, wild or domesticated, and catch the insects, particularly grasshoppers, disturbed by them. Cattle egrets feeding in this way gain about 50 per cent more food for less effort than birds feeding by other methods. The cattle do not really benefit from the association, since cattle egrets do not remove parasites; they may, however, be warned of approaching danger by the birds. Cattle egrets have now learned that the same results can be achieved by following farm machinery. In water the egrets feed on frogs and fish.

The male gathers material for the nest and the female builds it, usually in a small tree. The pair copulate on the nest and the female lays a clutch of between 2 and 5 eggs.

Black Heron *Egretta ardesiaca*

RANGE Africa, south of the Sahara,
Madagascar

HABITAT Swamps,
mangroves, mud-flats

SIZE 18¾–19½ in (48–50 cm)

Physically, the black heron is much like a black-plumaged version of an egret, but it is well known for its odd feeding method. The heron stands in shallow waters, bill pointing downward, and spreads its wings in a circle, forming a canopy over its head. Specialized broad flight feathers aid the effectiveness of the canopy. The exact purpose of this behavior is not known, but it has been suggested that fish are attracted to the apparent shelter of the patch of shade that is formed, thus making them easy prey for the heron. Fish must also be more easily visible within the canopy's shade. When young birds first begin to fish they make one-winged canopies. The canopy posture is also used in the courtship display. Black herons build a nest from twigs above the water in a tree or bush. The clutch usually contains 3 or 4 eggs.

Great Egret

Casmerodius alba

RANGE Almost worldwide;
absent from much of Europe

HABITAT Shallow water

SIZE 35–47 in (90–120 cm)

This egret, also sometimes known as the American egret, is one of the most widespread of its family. Non-breeding and immature birds have yellow bills, but as the breeding season approaches, the adult's bill becomes mostly black. It finds its food – fish, mollusks, insects, small mammals, birds and plants – either by standing and waiting in the water or by slowly stalking its prey. The nest is made in a tree or reed bed, and the female lays 2 to 5 eggs. Both parents incubate the clutch in shifts for a total of 25 or 26 days.

Boat-billed Heron *Cochlearius cochlearius*

RANGE Mexico to Bolivia, N. Argentina

HABITAT Swamps and wetlands

SIZE 17¾–19½ in (45–50 cm)

The only important distinction of the boat-billed heron from other herons is the broad, scooplike bill. Boat-billed herons generally feed at night on fish and shrimps. The bill seems to be extremely sensitive and opens at the merest touch, drawing in water and prey; it is also used with a scooping action.

These birds perform bill-clattering and preening displays, accompanied by vocal signals, at mating time. They nest alone or in groups in trees and bushes. The female lays a clutch of 2 to 4 eggs which both parents incubate.

HAMMERKOP, FLAMINGOS, IBISES AND PELICANS

SCOPIDAE: HAMMERKOP FAMILY

The single species in this family has been the subject of much dispute as to its classification.

Hammerkop *Scopus umbretta*

RANGE	Africa, Madagascar, Middle East
HABITAT	Tree-lined streams
SIZE	19½ in (50 cm)

The hammerkop gets its common name from the resemblance of its head in profile – with its long, heavy, slightly hooked bill and backward-pointing crest – to a hammer. In flight the hammerkop holds its neck slightly curved back. Male and female birds look alike.

Hammerkops are generally active at dusk and feed on amphibians, fish, insects and crustaceans. They live in pairs and build remarkable nests – elaborate roofed structures of sticks and mud, measuring up to 6 ft (1.8 m) across placed in the branches of trees. The female lays 3 to 6 eggs, and both parents care for the downy young.

PHOENICOPTERIDAE: FLAMINGO FAMILY

There are 5 species of flamingo. All are tall, pinkish-white birds with long necks, large wings and short tails. Their toes are short and webbed. All swim and fly well; the neck and legs are extended in flight. Males and females look alike. Huge numbers of flamingos live and breed in colonies: in Africa, a colony of lesser flamingos, *P. minor*, may number a million or more individuals. They are irregular breeders and may only breed successfully every two or three years.

Flamingos feed in the water, filtering out minute food particles with their highly specialized bills.

Greater Flamingo *Phoenicopterus ruber*

RANGE	Caribbean, Galápagos Islands, S. Europe, S.W. Asia, E., W., and N. Africa
HABITAT	Lagoons, lakes
SIZE	49–57 in (125–145 cm)

The greater flamingo has an air of frivolous fantasy, but in fact, it is perfectly adapted for its way of life. The long legs enable it to stand in shallow water while it filter-feeds with the strangely shaped bill. The flamingo holds its bill so that it lies horizontally beneath the water, the upper half below the lower. Water flows into the bill and, by movements of the large, fleshy tongue, is pushed through hairlike lamellae which sieve out food particles before the water is expelled again at the sides of the bill. Flamingos feed on mollusks, crustaceans, insects, fish and minute aquatic plants.

The nest is a mound of mud which the female scrapes together with her bill. She lays 1 or 2 eggs in a shallow depression at the top of the mound. The young birds are dependent on their parents for food until their filtering mechanism develops and they are able to fly – about 65 to 70 days.

THRESKIORNITHIDAE: IBIS FAMILY

Ibises and spoonbills are medium-sized wading birds. The typical family member has a moderately long neck, long wings, short tail and toes webbed at the base. Male and female look more or less alike. In some species the face or even the whole head and neck is unfeathered. All ibises fly well, with neck extended. There are about 28 species of ibis, all with long curved bills, and 6 species of spoonbill, with broad spatulate bills. Most are gregarious birds. Northern species are migratory.

in mongolia ↓ pelican threatened with extinction because of bill

Glossy Ibis *Plegadis falcinellu...*

RANGE Temperate and tropical ...
Indonesia, Australia, Afric...
Indies, Caribbean

HABITAT Marshes, lakes

SIZE 21½–25½ in
(55–65 cm)

The glossy ibis is the most widespread member of the family. It feeds on insects and small aquatic life. The female lays 3 or 4 eggs in a nest in a tree or reed bed. Both parents incubate the eggs and care for the young. The range and numbers of this species have been reduced by the drainage of marshland.

PELECANIDAE: PELICAN AND SHOEBILL FAMILY

The pelicans, which give this order its name, comprise 8 species found in large lakes and on sea coasts; there is a single species of shoebill in a separate subfamily. Pelicans are gregarious, strong-flying birds which feed on fish, caught while the birds are swimming in shallow water or, in one case, by diving from the air. The most dramatic anatomical feature is the huge gular pouch beneath the long broad bill. Males and females look alike.

Shoebill *Balaeniceps rex* **LR:nt**

RANGE E. C. Africa
HABITAT Marshes
SIZE 46 in (117 cm)

The shoebill was formerly placed in a family of its own, but is now included with pelicans. It is a large bird, its most obvious feature being a large shovellike bill with a hooked tip. The bird seems to use this bill for searching out food – fish, frogs, snakes, mollusks and carrion – in the mud of its marshland home.

A solitary, nocturnal bird, the shoebill can fly well and even soar, holding its neck drawn in, pelican-fashion. It lays 2 eggs on the ground in a nest made of rushes and grass.

The pelican is well adapted for aquatic life. The short strong legs and webbed feet propel it in water and aid takeoff from the water surface. Once aloft pelicans are powerful fliers and often travel in spectacular V-formation groups. The pelican's bill pouch is simply a scoop. As the pelican pushes its bill under water the lower bill bows out, creating a large pouch which fills with water and fish. As the bird lifts its head the pouch contracts, forcing out the water, but retaining the fish. A group of 6 to 8 pelicans will gather in a horseshoe formation in the water to feed together. They dip their bills in unison, creating a circle of open pouches, ready to trap every fish in the area.

Pelicans breed together in large colonies. The female lays 2 to 4 eggs in a nest of sticks in a tree or on the grass. The young are cared for by both parents.

Brown Pelican *Pelecanus occidentalis*

RANGE USA, Caribbean, S. America, Galápagos Islands
HABITAT Coasts
SIZE 50 in (127 cm)

The brown pelican is the smallest pelican and is rather different from the rest of its family. It is a seabird and catches fish by diving into the water from as high as 50 ft (15 m). When it dives, it holds the wings back and the neck curved into an S-shape, so that the front of the body, which is provided with cushioning air sacs, takes some of the impact of the plunge into the water. The bird generally returns to the surface to eat its catch.

The female brown pelican lays 2 or 3 eggs in a nest built in a tree or on the ground.

NEW WORLD VULTURES AND STORKS

CICONIIDAE: NEW WORLD VULTURE AND STORK FAMILY

This order contains two subfamilies – the New World vultures and the storks.

CATHARTINAE: NEW WORLD VULTURE SUBFAMILY

There are 7 species of New World vultures and condors, with a geographical range from Tierra del Fuego and the Falkland Islands to as far north as southern Canada. The cathartid vultures are superficially similar to Old World vultures, but are in fact, a quite distinct group with close affinity to the storks. None the less, like the Old World vultures, these birds feed on carrion and their unfeathered heads and necks enable them to plunge into messy carcasses without soiling their plumage. The feet, with long toes and weakly hooked claws, are adapted for perching rather than grasping. Vultures and condors are solitary birds, although some do roost in colonies. Nests are usually made in hollow trees. Males and females look alike.

King Vulture
Sarcoramphus papa

RANGE Mexico to Argentina

HABITAT Tropical forest, savanna

SIZE 31 in (79 cm)

The king is a medium-sized vulture with broad wings and tail. The featherless skin on its head is marked with extraordinary, garish patterns. The king vulture is reputed to kill live animals, but it feeds mainly on carrion. As its name suggests, this large, big-billed bird takes precedence over other vultures at carcasses. Carrion can be hard to spot in the dense tropical forest so the king vulture is one of the few birds that relies heavily on its sense of smell in order to detect food. Stranded fish on river banks are an important food item.

The breeding habits of this vulture are poorly known, but in one observation an egg was laid in a hollow tree stump and incubated by both parents. Young king vultures in their first full plumage have black feathers. The brilliant facial markings and creamy plumage develop over the first 2 years.

California Condor *Gymnogyps californianus* **CR**

RANGE USA: California

HABITAT Mountains

SIZE 45–55 in (114–140 cm)

One of the largest birds in the world this immense vulture is also one of the heaviest flying birds at over 25 lb (11 kg). The range of this bird was once much larger, but the population has declined drastically because of the destruction of its habitat and the onslaught of hunters, and the species is now probably on the verge of extinction. The condor is fully protected under the United States Endangered Species Act and by California law. There is a captive breeding program as a last attempt to save the species.

A spectacular bird in flight, with its extremely long, broad wings, the California condor soars at great heights and can glide as far as 10 miles (16 km) without wing movements. It must have the right air conditions for soaring and may stay at its roost in bad weather or on calm days. The California condor spends at least 15 hours a day at the roosting area, and out of the breeding season, roosting and foraging are its main activities. It feeds on carrion, mostly large animals, and is not known to attack living creatures.

At the start of the breeding season the male displays to his prospective mate. The female lays her egg on the ground in a cave or hole in a cliff. Both parents incubate in shifts. The young bird is fed and tended by the parents for over a year; thus California condors can breed only every other year.

Turkey Vulture *Cathartes aura*

RANGE Temperate and tropical North
and South America, Falkland Islands

HABITAT Plains, desert, forest

SIZE 26–52 in (66–132 cm)

Also known as the turkey
buzzard, this most widespread
New World vulture soars high
over open country in search
of carrion. It feeds on waste
of all sorts, including sea lion
excrement, rotten fruit and
vegetables and small carrion.
Turkey vultures have been trapped and
destroyed by man in many parts of their range
because they are mistakenly believed to carry anthrax and other
diseases of livestock. They are, however, pests on some Peruvian
guano islands where they take eggs and young birds.

At night groups of 30 or more birds roost together, but this
is really the only time that turkey vultures are social.

No real nest is made at breeding time; the female lays her
clutch of 2 eggs in a cave or in a hollow log on the ground. Both
parents incubate the eggs and care for the young.

CICONIINAE: STORK SUBFAMILY

Storks are large, long legged birds with elongated necks and long
broad wings. Although their feet are webbed at the base, a
feature which tends to denote aquatic habits, storks feed in drier
areas than most other members of their
order. They are strong fliers and look
particularly striking in the air, with
neck and legs stretched out, the
legs trailing down slightly. Males
and females look alike. There
are 19 species, all but 3 of
which are found in the Old World.
Northern populations are migratory.

White Stork *Ciconia ciconia*

RANGE E. Europe, W. and S. Asia;
winters in Africa, India and S. Asia

HABITAT Forest and near human habitation

SIZE 39–45 in (100–115 cm); 4 ft (1.2 m) tall

Legend has it that the white stork brings
babies, and for this reason these birds have always

been popular and protected to some degree. They are gregarious
birds and tolerant of human habitation. Storks feed mostly on
frogs, reptiles, insects and mollusks. The nest is a huge structure
of sticks which the stork builds up in a tree or on a building.
The female lays a clutch of between 1 and 7 eggs which both
parents incubate.

Although they are not vocal birds, white storks perform a
greeting ceremony, making bill-clattering sounds as they change
shifts at the nest. In doing so, they turn their heads round over
their backs thus turning away their bills – or weapons. This
action, in direct contrast to their bill-forward threat display,
appeases any aggression between the partners.

In winter white storks migrate south. Most go to Africa
by way of Gibraltar or Istanbul, so avoiding long journeys over
open sea for which their particular type of soaring flight is not
well-suited.

Asian Openbill *Anastomus oscitans*

RANGE India to S.E. Asia

HABITAT Inland waters

SIZE 32 in (81 cm); 24 in (61 cm) tall

The openbill, as its name suggests,
has a remarkably adapted bill. There is a gap
between the mandibles which meet only at the
tips. This feature, which develops gradually
and is not present in juvenile birds, seems
to be an adaptation for holding the large,
slippery water snails on which the birds
predominantly feed.

Openbills are more aquatic than most storks
but still make their nests in trees. The female
lays 3 to 6 eggs which are incubated by both
parents. The African openbill, *A. iamelligerus*,
has the same bill shape.

FRIGATEBIRDS, PENGUINS AND DIVERS

FREGATIDAE: FRIGATEBIRD FAMILY

Frigatebirds are the most aerial of all water birds and are graceful and spectacular in flight. They soar over huge oceanic distances. These large birds have long, pointed wings and long forked tails. All 5 species inhabit tropical and subtropical areas. Females are generally larger than males and have white breasts and sides. Males have bright-red throat pouches which they inflate in their courtship displays.

other birds. Having spotted a homecoming booby or other seabird, the frigatebird gives chase and forces its quarry to regurgitate its catch, which it then grabs in midair.

The nest of the magnificent frigatebird is a flimsy construction of sticks. The female lays a single egg which both parents incubate. Both feed and care for the chick for about 7 weeks. Both parents feed the chick until it can fly at 4 or 5 months old and feed it occasionally for some weeks more.

SPHENISCIDAE: PENGUIN FAMILY

Penguins are primitive and highly specialized marine birds. All 17 species are flightless and exquisitely adapted for marine existence. Their wings are modified into flat unfoldable paddles, which are used to propel them rapidly underwater in pursuit of fish and squid. Feathers are short and glossy and form a dense furlike mat which is waterproof, streamlined and a superb insulating layer. Their short legs, with webbed feet, are set far back to act as rudders, but this position means that the birds must stand upright on land or slide along on their bellies.

Penguins usually come ashore only to breed and molt; the rest of the year is spent entirely at sea. All forms, except the Galápagos penguin, breed on the Antarctic continent, subantarctic islands or the southern coasts of South America, southern Africa and Australia, often in extremely harsh conditions.

Little Penguin Eudyptula minor
RANGE New Zealand, Tasmania, S. Australia
HABITAT Coastal waters
SIZE 15¾ in (40 cm) tall

Magnificent Frigatebird Fregata magnificens
RANGE Central America; South America; Galápagos Islands
HABITAT Coastal waters, islands, bays, estuaries
SIZE 37–43 in (95–110 cm) Wingspan: 85–96 in (215–245 cm)

The frigatebird has a particularly large and splendid throat pouch and the greatest wing area, relative to body size, of any bird. It eats chiefly fish, squid, crustaceans and jellyfish, which it catches by swooping down to the water surface. It rarely alights on the sea. Frigatebirds supplement their diet by stealing fish from

The smallest penguin, the little blue penguin, lives around coasts and islands in its range, seeking food in shallow waters. Birds tend to return to the same nesting sites and to the same mates. A brief courtship re-establiscolore pair bond. This species nests in a crevice or a burrow. The females lays 2 eggs, which both parents incubate for between 33 and 40 days.

Emperor Penguin *Aptenodytes forsteri*

RANGE Antarctic coasts

HABITAT Ocean and pack ice

SIZE 4 ft (1.2 m) tall

Emperor penguins, largest of the penguin family, endure the worst breeding conditions of any bird. These penguins never come to land, but gather in huge colonies on the Antarctic pack ice in order to breed.

After pairing, the female lays 1 egg at the beginning of winter and returns to the sea. Her partner incubates the egg on his feet, where it is protected by a flap of skin and feathers. The males huddle together for warmth and protection during their vigil in the cold and dark. The male fasts for the 64-day incubation period.

When the chick is born, the male feeds it from secretions in his crop and the chick remains protected on his feet. By this time the ice is breaking up and the female returns in order to take over caring for the young while the male recovers and feeds.

Galápagos Penguin

Spheniscus mendiculus **VU**

RANGE Galápagos Islands

HABITAT Coastal waters

SIZE 20 in (51 cm) tall

This rare penguin is the only species to venture near the Equator. The cool waters of the Humboldt Current bathe the Galápagos islands, making them habitable for a cold-loving penguin. The current is rich in nutrients, supplying plenty of food. The birds breed from May to July, making nests of stones in caves or crevices on the coast. Two eggs are laid.

GAVIIDAE: DIVER FAMILY

Divers, or loons, are foot-propelled diving birds. All 5 species live in the high latitudes of the northern hemisphere and are the ecological counterparts of grebes in those areas. The birds feed primarily on fish, which they chase and seize under water. Males and females look alike.

Red-throated Diver/Loon *Gavia stellata*

RANGE Circumpolar: N. America, N. Europe, N. Asia

HABITAT Lakes, ponds, seas

SIZE 21–27 in (53–69 cm)

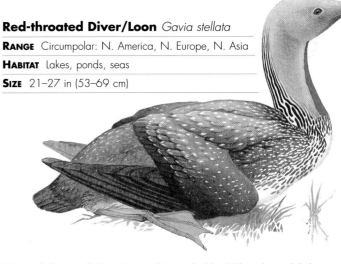

The red-throated diver has a thin grebelike bill and a reddish throat patch at breeding time; in winter its back is spotted with white and its head is gray and white. The red-throated diver flies strongly and, because it is smaller than other species, takes off relatively easily. After a courtship display of bill-dipping and diving, 1 to 3 eggs are laid in a heap of moss or other vegetation, or in a shallow dip in the ground. The parents share the incubation of the clutch for 24 to 29 days and feed the young.

PETRELS

PROCELLARIIDAE: PETREL ALBATROSS AND STORM PETREL FAMILY

This family contains three subfamilies – petrels, albatrosses and storm petrels. All are totally marine birds with webbed feet and hooked beaks surmounted by elongated tubular nostrils. About 115 species of these "tubenoses" are distributed around the oceans of the world.

Most species store stomach oil as a long-distance food reserve, this oil can also be discharged from the mouth or nostrils as a foul-smelling chemical defence mechanism. Typical species in this order have low reproductive rates, long periods of immaturity and tend to be long-lived.

PROCELLARIINAE: PETREL SUBFAMILY

This family, with about 80 species, is the largest group of tubenoses and contains birds such as petrels, shearwaters, fulmars, prions and diving petrels. Most species have long slender wings and short tails. Males and females of the species look alike. Representatives of the family occur in all oceans; most species are migratory. Except when breeding, these birds rarely come to land and spend most of their lives flying over the ocean. They are expert at flying through the most severe weather.

Within the family, species have become adapted to different feeding methods. Fulmars feed on plankton and scavenge around fishing fleets; prions filter planktonic animals from the water; the gadfly petrels (such as *Pterodroma* sp.) catch squid and octopus at night, and shearwaters are surface predators on fish.

Most species nest in burrows or rock crevices, although a few nest on cliff ledges or open ground. The female usually lays a single egg which both parents incubate in shifts of between 2 and 12 days. Petrels usually nest in colonies.

Diving petrels form a highly distinctive group of 4 tubenose birds within the petrel subfamily, all classified in a single genus: Pelecanoides. All species have a compact body form, with short neck, wings, legs and tail, and their overall appearance is similar to that of the auks (Alcinae). The similarities are linked to their shared basic feeding method – they dive from the air into the sea and use their short wings in order to swim under water in search of prey. Food items include crustaceans and small schooling fish such as anchovies.

Diving petrels fly with rapid wing beats. All species are found in the southern oceans and along the west coast of South America as far north as Peru.

Broad-billed Prion/Whale Bird
Pachyptila vittata

RANGE	Southern oceans
HABITAT	Oceanic
SIZE	12¼ in (31 cm)

The 6 species of prion, all in the genus *Pachyptila*, are similar in appearance and size and virtually indistinguishable at sea. The broad-billed prion is slightly larger than the others and can be identified by its markedly broader bill. It feeds on small planktonic animals, which it filters from the water through the hairlike fringes of lamellae at the sides of the bill. The birds often form huge feeding flocks in areas of plankton-rich water. Colonies of broad-billed prions breed in summer on islands in the South Atlantic, southern Indian Ocean and off New Zealand.

Manx Shearwater *Puffinus puffinus*

RANGE	Atlantic and Pacific Oceans, Mediterranean Sea
HABITAT	Oceanic and coastal
SIZE	11¾–15 in (30–38 cm)

There are several geographically distinct races of the Manx shearwater with slight plumage differences. Shearwaters feed by day, seizing fish, squid, crustaceans and debris at the water surface or diving in pursuit of prey. They have complex migration routes between feeding grounds and travel long distances. A shearwater, removed from its burrow in Britain and taken to the USA, returned home, a distance of about 2,800 miles (4,500 km) in 13 days. The birds nest in huge colonies on offshore islands. The female lays her egg in a burrow, and both parents care for the chick.

Northern Fulmar *Fulmarus glacialis*

RANGE	N. Atlantic, N. Pacific Oceans
HABITAT	Oceanic
SIZE	17¾–19½ in (45–50 cm)

Fulmars exploit the waste from commercial fishing and, with the spread of this industry, these large, robust petrels have dramatically increased their numbers. They swim but seldom dive, catching most of their food at the water surface. Male and female birds look alike, but the males have bigger bills. They nest on cliff ledges on coasts or islands; the female lays 1 egg, incubated by both parents. The adults feed the chick and defend it by spitting stomach oil at predators.

Mottled Petrel *Pterodroma inexpectata*

RANGE	South and North Pacific to 55°N
HABITAT	Oceanic
SIZE	14¼ in (36 cm)

The mottled petrel is a fairly small species with long narrow wings. Its flight is fast and it swoops and dives with great ease. Primarily a nocturnal bird, it feeds largely

on squid and octopus. It breeds on Stewart and Snares Islands near New Zealand and migrates north in winter to the western North Pacific. Like most petrels it lays only 1 egg.

Common Subantarctic Diving Petrel *Pelecanoides urinatrix*

RANGE	S. Atlantic, Indian and Pacific Oceans
HABITAT	Coastal waters
SIZE	7–8¼ in (18–21 cm)

This diving petrel, like its fellows, is a coastal rather than an oceanic seabird. It breeds, sometimes colonially, on South Atlantic islands, from the Falklands east to Australia and New Zealand. Breeding birds dig a burrow nest several feet long. The parents take turns incubating their 1 egg for a total of about 8 weeks, and they share the feeding of the chick. The chick leaves the nest when it is about 7 or 8 weeks old.

ALBATROSSES AND STORM PETRELS

DIOMEDEINAE: ALBATROSS SUBFAMILY

The 14 species of albatross are all large pelagic birds, noted for their spectacular gliding flight over vast ocean distances. Most occur in the southern hemisphere, but a few do live in the North Pacific. The birds have an unmistakable body form with extremely long narrow wings. The albatross bill is large and hooked. Male and female look alike in all species except the wandering albatross. Albatrosses feed on fish, squid and other marine animals which they catch at the surface of the water or just below it. Most species are migratory.

Wandering Albatross *Diomedea exulans* **VU**

RANGE Southern oceans, approximately 60°S to 250°S

HABITAT Oceanic

SIZE 43–54 in (110–135 cm) Wingspan: 114–127½ in (290–324 cm)

The wandering albatross has long wings and glides and soars for long periods. It feeds on fish and squid, and follows ships and scavenges on refuse. Females have brown flecks on the crown, juveniles have brown bodies and underwings, which turn white.

Wandering albatross land on subantarctic islands in the South Pacific, Indian and South Atlantic Oceans only to breed. The birds rattle their bills, touch bill-tips and spread their huge wings. The female lays 1 egg which is incubated for about 80 days by both parents then the chick is fed intermittently for about a year. This means that the birds can breed only every other year.

Light-mantled Sooty Albatross *Phoebetria palpebrata*

RANGE Southern oceans to about 330°S

HABITAT Oceanic

SIZE 28 in (72 cm)

The small, graceful light-mantled sooty albatross is able to maneuver well in the air. It breeds on Antarctic and subantarctic islands and makes a neat cup-shaped nest of plant material. The female lays 1 egg, and both parents care for the chick for a few months.

HYDROBATINAE: STORM PETREL SUBFAMILY

These small seabirds occur in most oceans, mainly south of the Arctic Circle. There are about 21 species which divide into 2 groups – those of the northern and southern hemispheres. Their ranges overlap in the tropics. Northern birds have short legs, long pointed wings and forked tails. They feed by swooping and skimming low over the water. Southern birds have long slender legs, short rounded wings and square tails. They feed by "stepping" over the surface of the water with wings spread to seize food items.

All have black, or black and brown, plumage with white rump feathers. Males and females look alike and all have a distinctive musky smell. Most storm petrels are deep-water birds and come to land on remote islands only to breed. Breeding usually takes place in colonies and long-term pair bonds are the rule. Pairs return to the same nest year after year. They nest in crevices and burrows. Most migrate after breeding.

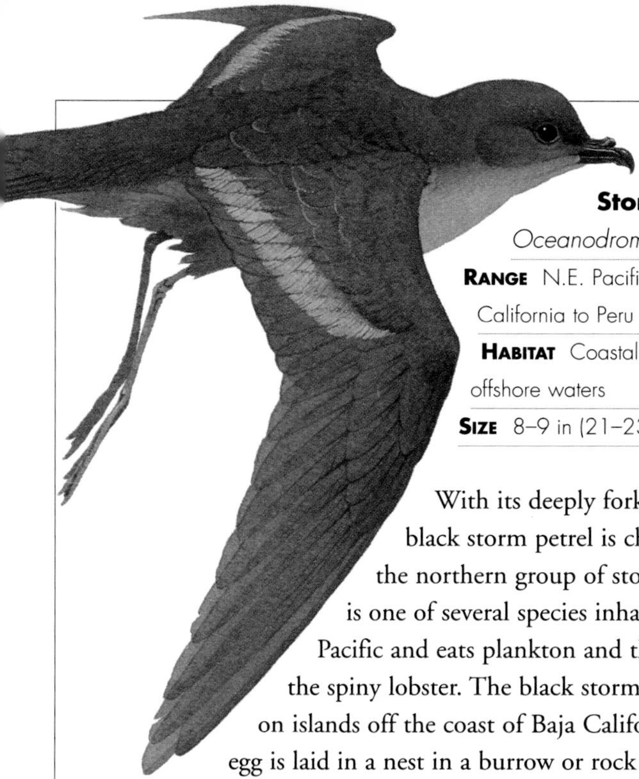

Black Storm Petrel

Oceanodroma melania

RANGE N.E. Pacific Ocean: California to Peru

HABITAT Coastal and offshore waters

SIZE 8–9 in (21–23 cm)

With its deeply forked tail, the black storm petrel is characteristic of the northern group of storm petrels, It is one of several species inhabiting the Pacific and eats plankton and the larvae of the spiny lobster. The black storm petrel breeds on islands off the coast of Baja California. A single egg is laid in a nest in a burrow or rock crevice.

European Storm Petrel

Hydrobates pelagicus

RANGE N.E. Atlantic Ocean, W. Mediterranean Sea

HABITAT Oceanic

SIZE 5½–7 in (14–18 cm)

This is the smallest European seabird and one of the 3 Atlantic species of storm petrel. It eats fish, squid and crustaceans and often follows ships to feed on their waste. It lands only in the breeding season, to nest in remote coastal areas. The female lays 1 egg in a burrow or in a hole on a cliff-face. Both parents incubate the egg. In winter storm petrels fly south to the Red Sea and the west coast of Africa.

Wilson's Storm Petrel *Oceanites oceanicus*

RANGE Antarctic, Atlantic and Indian Oceans

HABITAT Oceanic

SIZE 6–7½ in (15–19 cm)

Wilson's petrel is typical of the southern group of storm petrels. Its legs are long and toes short, and it hops and paddles over the surface to pick up prey. This species eats mostly plankton and the oil and fat debris at whaling stations. Breeding is usually on islands off the tip of South America. The single egg is incubated

by both birds. In winter the birds migrate north, to the tropics or north of the Equator, and can sometimes be seen off the Atlantic coast of North America. Some ornithologists believe this to be the most abundant bird species in the world.

Ringed Storm Petrel *Oceanodroma hornbyi* **DD**

RANGE Pacific coast of South America

HABITAT Oceanic

SIZE 7¾–8½ in (20–22 cm)

The ringed storm petrel has a white collar around the neck and a dark band across the chest. This species flies inland to breed in the Chilean Andes.

White-faced Storm Petrel

Pelagodroma marina

RANGE Atlantic, Indian and S. Pacific Oceans

HABITAT Oceanic

SIZE 8 in (20.5 cm)

This southern species has black and white plumage. It splashes down on the surface of the sea to feed on plankton and squid. Colonies breed on islands in the Atlantic and on the coasts of Australia and New Zealand. A single egg is laid in a burrow in the ground. This bird is vulnerable to attack by cats and birds during its breeding season.

NEW ZEALAND WRENS, PITTAS, BROADBILLS AND ASITIES

ORDER PASSERIFORMES

Usually known as the perching birds, or songbirds, this is the largest of all bird orders. It includes about half of the 9,000 or so bird species. There are about 47 families in the order and the most advanced 35 or so of these are grouped together in the suborder Passeri – the oscine perching birds or songbirds. The other families – the suborder Tyranni – are known as the suboscines; these birds have a simpler organ of song. Perching birds are usually small – the lyrebirds are the largest species – but they have adapted to almost all types of land-based habitat.

The group as a whole is identified by a number of structural and behavioural features. The foot is particularly characteristic and is excellently adapted for grasping any thin support, such as a twig or grass stem. There are always four toes all on the same level, with the hallux (big toe) pointing backward. The toes are not webbed. Male perching birds normally sing complex songs and give voice when courting or defending territory.

SUBORDER TYRANNI: PRIMITIVE PASSERINES

ACANTHISITTIDAE: NEW ZEALAND WREN FAMILY

This family of 4 species of small wrenlike birds is confined to forest and scrubland in New Zealand.

Rifleman *Acanthisitta chloris*

RANGE New Zealand and neighboring islands

HABITAT Forest and modified habitats with remnants of forest

SIZE 3–4 in (7.5–10 cm)

The tiny rifleman feeds mainly in the trees, searching trunks and branches for insects and spiders; occasionally it comes down to the forest floor. The female has dark and light-brown striped upperparts; the male is yellowish-green. Nests are made in a crevices in trees. Both parents incubate the clutch of 4 or 5 eggs and feed the young.

PITTIDAE: PITTA FAMILY

The 31 species of pitta occur in Africa, Asia and Southeast Asia to Australia. They are thrushlike, stout birds, with long legs and short tails and most species have brightly colored plumage. Male and female look alike in some species but differ in others. Nests are usually large domed or oval-shaped constructions in branches or bushes.

Indian Pitta *Pitta brachyura*

RANGE N. and C. India; winters in S. India and Sri Lanka

HABITAT Varied, including semi-cultivated land and forest

SIZE 7 in (18 cm)

This brightly plumaged little bird forages on or close to the forest floor, searching among fallen leaves and debris for food such as insects and spiders. It will also eat worms and maggots at excrement sites.

If alarmed the Indian pitta flies up into a tree with a whirring sound and then sits still, with only its tail moving slowly up and down.

The nest, built in a tree, is a domed, globular structure, made of moss and covered with twigs. It is lined with plant material and has a side entrance. Both parents incubate the clutch of 4 to 6 eggs and feed the helpless, naked young. Large flocks of Indian pittas migrate south in winter.

Garnet Pitta *Pitta granatina*

RANGE Malaysia, Sumatra, Borneo

HABITAT Lowland forest, swamps

SIZE 6 in (15 cm)

Both male and female garnet pittas have brilliant, jewellike plumage, while the juveniles are a dull brownish hue and acquire the bright adult coloration only gradually. The adults make a prolonged whistling call.

Much of the garnet pitta's life is spent running about on the ground, foraging for ants, beetles and other insects, as well as snails, seeds and fruit. It will fly short distances.

Its nest, typical of the pitta family, is made on the ground and is a domed structure of rotting leaves and fibers, roofed with twigs and leaves. There is a small entrance to the chamber in which the female lays her clutch of 2 eggs.

The numbers of this species are declining, due mainly to the destruction of its forest habitat.

EURYLAIMIDAE: BROADBILL FAMILY

There are about 14 known species in the broadbill family, all of which are found in Africa and south and Southeast Asia in forest and wooded land.

The broad-bills are rather rotund little birds, with bright plumage, heavy, flattened, wide bills, large eyes and short legs and tails. Male and female look unalike, with differences in size and coloration in most species.

Broadbills feed on insects, fruit, seeds and other plant material. Most build oval or pear-shaped nests, which are suspended from branches or twigs, often over water. Clutches of between 2 and 8 white or pinkish eggs are usually laid.

Green Broadbill *Calyptomena viridis*

RANGE Malaysia, Sumatra, Borneo

HABITAT Forest on lowland and hills

SIZE 7½ in (19 cm)

The green broadbill spends much of its life foraging for fruit, its main food, high in the forest trees, where it is hard to spot among the leaves. The male is bright and iridescent, but the female is a duller green and often larger than the male.

The nest is made of coarse, matted plant fibers and is suspended from thin twigs just above the ground. It is wider at the top than at the bottom and there is an entrance hole near the top. The female bird lays 2 eggs, which both parents are believed to incubate.

PHILEPITTIDAE: ASITY FAMILY

The 4 species in this family are divided into two distinct groups – the asities and the false sunbirds. They are plump, tree-dwelling birds, all found in Madagascar. Males and females of the species differ in plumage.

Wattled False Sunbird *Neodrepanis coruscans*

RANGE E. Madagascar

HABITAT Forest

SIZE 3½ in (9 cm)

The long, downward-curving bill of the wattled false sunbird gives it a strong superficial resemblance to the true sunbirds (*Nectariniidae*), hence the common name. The bill is used for the same purpose, that is, to drink nectar from flowers. The false sunbird also feeds on fruit, insects and spiders.

TYRANT FLYCATCHERS

TYRANNIDAE: TYRANT FAMILY

The 537 species in the large and diverse family are found only in the Americas. There are five subfamilies – Pipromorphinae (mionectine flycatchers), Tyranninae (tyrant flycatchers), Tityrinae (tityras and becards), Cotinginae (cotingas) and Piprinae (Manakins).

PIPROMORPHINAE MIONECTINE: FLYCATCHER SUBFAMILY

The 53 species of small, dull-colored birds are found in the forests and open woodlands of tropical Central and South America. Most, as their name suggests, are insect eaters although species belonging to the genus Mionectes also eat small fruits.

Ocher-bellied Flycatcher
Mionectus oleaginus
RANGE S. Mexico, through Central and South America to Peru and Brazil
HABITAT Forest, clearings
SIZE 4¾ in (12 cm)

The slender, long-tailed ocher-bellied flycatcher is mainly olive-green, with grayish plumage on the throat and ocher underparts. Its bill is long and slender, with a hooked tip.

This active little bird, constantly twitches its wings above its back, one at a time. Unlike other flycatchers, this species does not make aerial dashes after prey, but seizes insects and spiders from foliage as it flits from tree to tree. It also feeds on fruit and berries, particularly mistletoe berries. An extremely solitary bird, it never gathers in flocks or even pairs, except during the brief period of courtship and mating.

Normally silent, in the breeding season male ocher-bellied flycatchers take up territories in which they perch and sing tirelessly to attract mates. Several males may sing within hearing of each other. They do not assist females in nest-building or rearing of young.

A pear-shaped nest, covered with moss, is suspended from a slender branch or vine or from the aerial root of an airplant. It takes the female about 2 weeks to build this nest. She incubates the 2 or 3 eggs for 19 to 21 days and feeds the young for between 2 and 3 weeks.

Common Tody-flycatcher
Todirostrum cinereum
RANGE S. Mexico, Central and South America to Bolivia and Brazil
HABITAT Open country, plantations, parkland
SIZE 4 in (10 cm)

The long, straight bill and the narrow, graduated tail feathers make up over half of this bird's body length. Avoiding closed woodland, it feeds wherever there are scattered trees, making short darts from branch to branch and seizing insects and berries from foliage and bark. It hops sideways along branches, continuously wagging its tail as it goes. Male and female look alike and live in pairs throughout the year.

Both partners of a pair help to make the nest, which is suspended from a slender twig or vine. They mat together plant fibers and then excavate an entrance hole and central cavity in the resulting mass. The female lays 2 or 3 eggs, which she incubates for 17 or 18 days, and both parents feed the young.

TYRANNINAE: TYRANT FLYCATCHER SUBFAMILY

The 340 species of tyrant flycatchers constitute one of the largest subfamilies of perching birds. These small to medium-sized birds are found in most habitats through the Americas where they replace, and are in several respects similar to, the Old World Flycatchers, Muscicapinae. The rain forests of the Amazon hold the greatest density of species, but they have spread wherever food is available. Most species catch insects on the wing, but some eat fruit, small mammals, reptiles, amphibians and fish too. The insect-eaters' beaks are flattened and slightly hooked, with well-developed bristles at the base. The sexes look alike in most species.

Scissor-tailed Flycatcher *Tyrannus forficata*
RANGE Southcentral USA; winters S. Texas, Mexico to Panama
HABITAT Open grassland (prairie), ranchland
SIZE 11–15 in (28–38 cm) including tail of up to 9 in (23 cm)

When these elegant birds fly, the black feathers of their remarkably long tails open and close like the blades of a pair of scissors, but when they perch, the birds close up the blades. The female is smaller than the male, with a shorter tail. Scissor-tailed flycatchers spend much of their time perched on fences, telephone wires and trees. They catch insects in the air or on the ground. Grasshoppers and crickets are the main food, but bees, moths, caterpillars, spiders, berries and seeds are also eaten.

The bulky nest is made from weeds, rootlets and cotton. It is lined with hair and rootlets. The female lays 4 to 6 eggs, and incubates them for about 14 days.

White-headed Marsh Tyrant *Arundinicola leucocephala*

RANGE South America, east of the Andes, to N. Argentina; Trinidad

HABITAT River banks, marshes, wet grassland

SIZE 4½ in (11.5 cm)

Sociable birds, these marsh tyrants live in pairs or family groups and feed on insects, which they catch on the wing. They make their nests in low bushes or clumps of grass, using boll cotton in their construction. The female lays 2 or 3 eggs.

Eastern Phoebe *Sayornis phoebe*

RANGE Eastern N. America; winters in S. USA and Mexico

HABITAT Woodland near water, rocky ravines, wooded farmland

SIZE 6¼–7¼ in (16–18.5 cm)

This flycatcher has an erect posture and appears to wag its tail when it alights. Its name is derived from its two-note call. In summer phoebes can be seen on farmland and wooded country roads, searching for beetles, ants, bees, wasps and invertebrates. Their cup-shaped nests are made from mud and moss and sited on rocky ledges, or in farm buildings. The 3 to 8 eggs are laid and incubated for 16 days.

Great Kiskadee

Pitangus sulphuratus

RANGE S.E. Texas, Central and South America to C. Argentina

HABITAT Groves, orchards, wooded banks of streams

SIZE 9–10½ in (23–26.5 cm)

A large bird with a big head, the great kiskadee is active and noisy, with a loud "kis-ka-dee" call. It is conspicuous at dawn and dusk and behaves much like a kingfisher, perching quite still above water and then plunging into it after fish and tadpoles. Its plumage needs to dry out after three dives, so it turns to catching flying insects such as beetles and wasps. In winter, when these are scarce, it feeds on fruit and berries.

Kiskadees make their large, oval nests about 20 ft (6 m) up in trees. The female lays 2 to 5 eggs, usually 4.

Eastern Kingbird *Tyrannus tyrannus*

RANGE C. Canada, through USA to Gulf of Mexico. Winters in Central and South America to N. Argentina

HABITAT Open country with trees, orchards, gardens

SIZE 8–9 in (20.5–23 cm)

The eastern kingbird is a noisy and aggressive bird and will attack other birds, such as hawks, vultures and crows, sometimes landing on the other bird's back. It has even been known to occasionally attack low-flying aircraft.

The kingbird has been observed to eat more than 200 types of insect, which it takes in the air or from the ground or scoops up from water. It will also pick berries, while hovering.

Both male and female kingbirds incubate the clutch of 3 to 5 eggs for about 2 weeks and both help to feed the young.

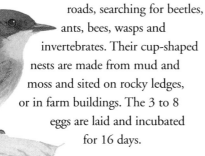

TYRANT FLYCATCHERS CONTINUED

Willow Flycatcher *Empidonax traillii*

RANGE S. Canada, USA: Maine to Virginia,
west to Arkansas and California

HABITAT Open country near water to 7,900 ft (2,400 m)

SIZE 5¼–6 in (13.5–15 cm)

True to its common name, this bird is most frequently
encountered where willow trees abound – on islands in rivers, in
shrubs along streams and in beaver meadows. In appearance it is
similar to the alder flycatcher (*E. alnorum*), but it has a slightly
longer bill and more rounded wings. It is a prodigious insect
eater, known to catch at least 65 species of beetle, as well as
aphids, bees, wasps, crane flies, caterpillars, spiders and millipedes,
all of which it takes in flight. It also eats some berries.

Traill's flycatchers usually build their nests about 8 ft
(2.5 m) above the ground in the upright fork of a bush or tree,
in an area where willows or plants of the rose family grow. The
shredded bark of milkweed, cat tail and the silky catkins of
aspen and willow are used in its construction, and it is softly
lined with grass and feathers. The female lays 3 or 4 eggs, which
are incubated for about 12 days. The young leave the nest when
they are about 2 weeks old.

Many-colored Rush-tyrant

Tachuris rubrigastra

RANGE South America: Peru, S.E. Brazil,
Paraguay, Uruguay, Argentina, Chile

HABITAT Fields, meadows near water,
swampy ground

SIZE 4¼ in (10.5 cm)

There are seven colors visible in the
plumage of these pretty little birds –

yellow, blue, white, bronze, black, carmine and green. They
are sprightly and flit about constantly among the stems of tall
grasses, particularly cat tails, searching for small insects to eat.
Although they are so active, many-colored tyrants are seldom
seen and often can be located only by their frequently repeated,
sharp, ringing calls.

The cone-shaped nest is attached to the stalk of a cat tail
or a reed, 20 to 30 in (50 to 80 cm) above the water. It is
intricately woven from small pieces of dry reed, with the point
of the cone at the bottom, and the reeds are cemented with a
sticky substance, which gives the nest a smooth, shiny surface.
The female lays her eggs in multiples of three – 3, 6 or 9.

Royal Flycatcher *Onychorhynchus coronatus*

RANGE C. and S. America: Mexico south to Guianas, Bolivia, Brazil

HABITAT Rain and cloud forest, forest edge

SIZE 6½ in (16.5 cm)

The royal flycatcher has a rather dull brown body, but a
spectacular large crest of crimson feathers on its head that end in
discs with a metallic blue lustre. In the female the crest is orange
or yellow. Normally the crest lies flat, but in display it is opened
and closed like a fan.

The bill is broad and flat and quite wide, a shape that is well
suited to the birds' diet of insects which are caught on the wing.

These flycatchers are usually found singly or in pairs in
secondary growth or at the forest edge where they perch
on low branches.

The long, loose, bag-shaped nest, which can be up
to 6 ft (1.8 m) long, is built in a tree, often near a
stream, and the female lays 2 eggs.

Eastern Wood Peewee

Contopus virens

RANGE Breeds S.E. Canada, E. USA; winters Central America, N. South America

HABITAT Deciduous or mixed woodland, tall shade trees in gardens

SIZE 6–6¾ in (15–17 cm)

The eastern peewee is so similar in appearance to the western species (*C. sordidulus*) that in western Manitoba and Nebraska, where their ranges overlap, it is possible to distinguish it only by its plaintive, whistling call. It perches in the deep shade of tall trees, darting out to catch flying insects, beetles and treehoppers.

Eastern peewees build thick-walled, cup-shaped nests high up on the horizontal branches of trees. The nest is made of weeds and fibers, lined with wool, grass and hair, and well covered with lichen, which makes it invisible from the ground. Normally 3 eggs are laid, which are incubated until they hatch after about 13 days.

Short-tailed Pygmy-tyrant *Myiornis ecaudatus*

RANGE N. South America, east of the Andes, Amazonian Brazil; Peru, Bolivia, Trinidad

HABITAT High open rain forest, clearings in forest, plantations

SIZE 2½ in (6.5 cm)

The smallest of the tyrants, this tiny bird has an exceptionally short tail, scarcely longer than the tail coverts. Male and female look alike. Alone or in pairs, the birds dart about in the forest trees, from the bottom branches to the canopy, looking for insects to feed on.

Pygmy-tyrants are not shy, but because they live in such dense vegetation, they are hardly ever seen, and no information is available about their breeding or nesting behavior.

White-crested Spadebill

Platyrinchus platyrhynchos

RANGE N. South America to Amazon basin

HABITAT Rain forest, forest edge

SIZE 3 in (7.5 cm)

A tiny, stout-bodied bird, with a round head and a wide, short bill, the white-crested spadebill is distinguished by the white feathers on its head. Pairs stay together throughout the year, flitting busily through the bushes and the lower branches of forests searching for insects and spiders to eat. Occasionally they are seen among the many birds that follow columns of army ants.

The female spadebill builds a bulky, cup-shaped nest, rather like a hummingbird's, using tree fern, plant fibers and cobwebs. The nest is usually in the vertical fork of a tree about 6½ ft (2 m) from the ground. Two eggs are laid, two days apart, and are incubated for about 17 days by the female. Both parents feed the young, which can fly at about 2 weeks old.

Yellow-bellied Elaenia *Elaenia flavogaster*

RANGE Central and South America: S. Mexico to N. Argentina; Trinidad, Tobago

HABITAT Shady pasture, savanna, parks, plantations, to 6,000 ft (1,800 m)

SIZE 6¼ in (16 cm)

The most remarkable characteristic of this flycatcher is the double crest of stiff gray feathers that stands up on each side of the head, revealing the white patch between. The bird's breast and belly are pale yellow, the tail is long and the bill short. Male and female look alike. Elaenias live in pairs all year round, always in open country with trees, where they eat insects taken on the wing and on many different types of berries.

Both birds help to build the nest in the fork of a tree, generally about 6½ to 15 ft (2 to 4.5 m) above the ground. It is a shallow, open structure, made from rootlets, plant fibers and cobwebs covered with lichen and moss and lined with feathers. The female lays 2 eggs, which she incubates for about 15 days. The chicks are fed by both parents and leave the nest at 17 or 18 days old. There are often two broods produced in a year.

TYRANT FLYCATCHERS, SHARPBILL AND PLANTCUTTERS

Cliff Flycatcher
Hirundinea ferruginea

RANGE N. South America to Brazil and N. Argentina

HABITAT Arid hillsides, ravines, cliffs, open woodland

SIZE 7¼ in (18.5 cm)

A mainly brown and black bird, this flycatcher has bright chestnut underparts and wing patches, which are conspicuous in flight. Its wings are long and swallowlike, and it catches much of its insect prey in skilful aerial dashes.

The nest is made in a crevice in a rock or cliff.

Great Shrike Tyrant
Agriornis livida

RANGE South America: S. Argentina, Chile

HABITAT Open scrub, fields

SIZE 11 in (28 cm) including Tail: 4¼ in (11 cm)

This silent bird avoids woodland and populated regions and frequents lonely, open areas. It has a powerful beak and eats insects, other birds' eggs and small animals, such as newts, and mice.

On the coast, the birds begin nesting in October, but farther inland, in the Andean foothills, breeding does not start until November. A bulky nest, made of grass and sticks and lined with sheeps' wool, is built in a thick bush. The female lays 2 to 4 eggs, usually 3.

Vermilion Flycatcher *Pyrocephalus rubinus*

RANGE S.W. USA, Mexico, Central and South America to Argentina; Galápagos Islands

HABITAT Scrub, savanna, riparian woodland

SIZE 5½–6¾ in (14–17 cm)

The male vermilion flycatcher has a bright red head and underparts. The female is brownish above, with a lighter, streaked belly and breast. These flycatchers eat flying insects, particularly bees, darting into the air from a high perch in pursuit of their prey. They also feed on the ground on grasshoppers and beetles, especially in areas of sparse vegetation.

The courting male flies up from a tree, singing ecstatically, his vermilion crest erect and his breast feathers puffed out. He hovers briefly, then flutters down to the female. A flattish, cup-shaped nest, made of twigs, grass and rootlets, is built on a horizontally forked branch. The female incubates the 2 to 4 eggs, and the male defends the nest. Chicks leave the nest at about 2 weeks old.

Piratic Flycatcher *Legatus leucophaius*

RANGE S. Mexico, Central and South America to N. Argentina

HABITAT Open woodland

SIZE 5¾ in (14.5 cm)

A dull bird, the piratic flycatcher makes itself conspicuous by being one of the noisiest flycatchers, with a wide range of calls. It eats insects, especially dragonflies, and berries.

Piratic flycatchers appear to be the only members of the tyrant flycatcher family to depart from normal nest-building habits, and this earns them their common name. They do not build their own nests but usurp the freshly built nests of other birds, often other species of flycatcher. Having chosen their victims, the pair of piratic flycatchers perches nearby to watch the building progressing. They chatter noisily and make their presence felt, but do not usually attack until the nest is complete. Then they harass the rightful owners until they abandon the nest. Any eggs are thrown out, and the female piratic flycatcher lays 2 or 3 eggs, which she incubates for about 16 days. Both parents feed the nestlings on berries and insects until they leave the nest almost 3 weeks after hatching. Central American and northern South American populations migrate south after breeding.

Torrent Tyranulet *Serpophaga cinerea*

RANGE Central and South America: mountains of Costa Rica and Panama, Andes from Venezuela to Bolivia

HABITAT Rocky streams

SIZE 4 in (10 cm)

The torrent tyranulet lives amid the fast flowing waters of mountain streams, and its gray and black plumage echoes its rocky habitat. It plucks insects, not only from the air, but also from slippery boulders surrounded by foaming water, often becoming drenched in the process. It also alights on wet rocks to search for tiny invertebrates. Male and female look alike and live together all year, holding a stretch of river as their territory.

A cup-shaped nest, covered with moss, is made in vegetation overhanging water, rarely over the bank. The 2 eggs are incubated by the female for 17 or 18 days, but the male stays nearby. Both parents feed the young on insects for 2 or 3 weeks, and even after leaving the nest, the young birds stay with their parents for a further 5 or 6 weeks before seeking their own territory.

COTINGINAE: COTINGA SUBFAMILY

This subfamily of 69 species, which includes the sharpbill, plantcutters, and the cotingas, is found from southern Mexico south to Brazil. The single species of small, conical-billed sharpbill is found in the upper layers of humid forests from Costa Rica south to

Paraguay. The plantcutters, of which there are three species, are found in the more open areas of western South America. Despite their close relationship with the cotingas, plantcutters, with their strong, conical beaks, bear more resemblance to the finches of the Old world. The edges of their bills are finely serrated and used for cropping the buds, fruit, and leaves that make up much of their diet. The 65 species of cotingas constitute a colorful and varied group of birds, some with common names such as bellbird, umbrellabird, fruiteater and cock-of-the-rock. This variety of nomenclature mirrors the diversity in body form and habit. Cotingas are non-migratory birds in forested areas and often spend most of their time in the canopy layers, feeding on fruit and insects.

Sharpbill *Oxyruncus cristatus*

RANGE Patchy distribution in Costa Rica, Panama to Paraguay, Amazonian Brazil

HABITAT Humid tropical forest from 1,300–6,000 ft (400–1,800 m)

SIZE 6½–7 in (16.5–18 cm)

The sharpbill has a straight, pointed beak, which gives it its common name. It is a strong flier, with rather rounded, long wings. Male and female look similar, but the male has a black and scarlet crest, bordered with black, while the female may have a pale crest. Sharpbills are secretive birds, which forage actively for fruit in the middle to canopy layers of the forest.

Rufous-tailed Plantcutter *Phytotoma rara*

RANGE Central Chile, W. Argentina

HABITAT Open scrub, orchards, gardens, mountain valleys

SIZE 8 in (20.5 cm)

These short-legged birds have bright reddish-orange eyes and stout, serrated beaks. The male has reddish-chestnut underparts and tail; the female is paler with a buff throat and underparts. Plantcutters usually occur singly or in small groups, flying sluggishly among fruit trees. They eat the buds, shoots and young leaves and often destroy fruit.

In spring plantcutters move to high mountain valleys, where they mate between October and December. A clutch of 2 to 4 eggs is laid in a cup-shaped nest, made of twigs and lined with fine twigs and rootlets.

COTINGAS AND MANAKINS

Andean Cock-of-the-Rock *Rupicola peruviana*

RANGE Andes, N. Venezuela to N. Bolivia

HABITAT Forest along river gorges 1,640–1,875 ft (500–2,400 m)

SIZE 15 in (38 cm)

The male of this species is one of the most brilliantly colored of all birds, with its flashing orange or red plumage and strong, golden-colored beak. On its head is a crest of feathers that almost conceals the beak. Both male and female have powerful legs and sharp claws.

The Andean cock-of-the-rock lives in the lower levels of the forest, where its swift, weaving flight and maneuverability enable it to move about easily as it searches for fruit to eat. Females also catch frogs and lizards to feed to their young.

Males roost alone at night, and forage in pairs and display in pairs at dawn and dusk at traditional leks, where each has his own place near to that of his paired male. Only the dominant male of the lek mates with females. The female builds the nest on a rocky cliff face. Often several nests are grouped together. The nest is a large truncated cone, made of mud, with a deep, 2½ in (6.5 cm), lined nest cup in which 2 eggs are laid.

Barred Fruiteater

Pipreola arcuata

RANGE Andes, N.W. Venezuela to C.W. Bolivia

HABITAT Cloud forest at 4,000–11,000 ft (1,200–3,350 m)

SIZE 8½ in (21.5 cm)

The heavy-bodied barred fruiteater is the largest fruiteater. It is found at higher altitudes than any other. Males have striking coloration, but females are mostly olive-green. Both sexes have rather weak, slightly hooked beaks and red legs and feet. They live in the middle and lower layers of the forest and eat mainly fruit and some insects. No breeding information is available.

Bearded Bellbird *Procnias averano*

RANGE Parts of Colombia, Guyana, Venezuela, N. Brazil; Trinidad

HABITAT Forest to 5,250 ft (1,600 m)

SIZE 10 in (25.5 cm)

The fringe of black wattles hanging from the throat of both male and female gives this species its common name. They are shy birds, feeding singly or in pairs on large, single-seeded berries, particularly laurel, which they take on the wing and then sit on a branch to eat.

In the breeding season, male bearded bellbirds display to other males and to females on special "visiting" perches in the lower forest layers. They jump as high as 4 ft (1.2 m) into the air and land crouched, on another perch, with tail spread. After mating, the female builds a light, thin, cup-shaped nest of twigs from specific trees, about 8 to 50 ft (2.4 to 15.25 m) up, in the horizontally forked outer branch of a tree. She lays 1 egg, which she incubates for about 23 days.

Spangled Cotinga

Cotinga cayana

RANGE S. America, E. of Andes from Colombia and Guianas south to Bolivia and Amazonian Brazil

HABITAT Forest, woodland, savanna

SIZE 8½ in (21.5 cm)

The blue plumage of the male spangled cotinga is iridescent, hence the name. These are gregarious birds, usually feeding in groups, sometimes with birds of other species, on large berries.

The female alone builds the flimsy, shallow nest, using twigs and rootlets and coating the whole structure in white fungal threads. She lays and then incubates 1 large egg, sometimes 2.

Amazonian Umbrellabird

Cephalopterus ornatus

RANGE N. South America to Amazonian Brazil, N. Bolivia

HABITAT Virgin forest to 4,600 ft (1,400 m), islands in larger rivers

SIZE 16–19 in (40.5–48 cm)

The largest of the cotingas, the ornate umbrellabird is distinguished by its erect crest of long, silky feathers and by the wattle at the base of the neck. The female is much duller than the male, with a smaller wattle and "umbrella". The wings are short. These strange birds live in the forest canopy and spring noisily through the branches, looking for fruit and insects.

Males have their preferred calling trees, where they perch, spread their umbrellas and, filling two specially modified sacs in the trachea with air, make loud booming noises. The shallow, open nest is built of twigs in the fork of a fairly low tree, and the female lays 1 egg, which she incubates alone.

PIPRINAE: MANAKIN SUBFAMILY

This intriguing and showy family contains 52 species, all of which are found in the tropical forests of Central and South America. They are small, colorful birds, rarely more than 5 to 6 in (12.5 to 15 cm) in length. Males and females are dramatically different in appearance. Males, typically, have a solid background plumage color, commonly black, brilliantly counterpointed with areas of contrasting primary colors. Females are generally olive-green. The decorative males utilize their plumage in intricate courtship dances.

Blue-backed Manakin

Chiroxiphia pareola

RANGE N. South America to S.E. Brazil, N. Bolivia; Tobago

HABITAT Rain forest, secondary growth

SIZE 4 in (10 cm)

These lively, agile little birds forage in pairs or small groups for insects and fruit in low bushes, often near wet ground or streams. They are square tailed, with the male showing dazzling patches of pale blue and red feathers on back and crown.

Male manakins have display perches or "bowers", which they keep clear by plucking at the surrounding leaves from flight and pecking at the bark while perching. They wear the perch smooth by continually moving around. Before display the dominant male summons a subordinate male by calling and then duets with him, the subordinate following a fraction of a second behind. The males dance together, but the dance only becomes fully developed if a female appears. The other bird drops out, leaving the dominant male to mate with the female after a quite different solo display. She lays 2 eggs in a nest, made of fine plant fibers, so cobwebby and transparent that eggs and young can be seen through it.

Wire-tailed Manakin *Pipra filicauda*

RANGE S. America E. of Andes from Columbia and Venezuela S. to N.E. Peru, W. Brazil

HABITAT Rain forest, plantations

SIZE 4½ in (11.5cm)

The male wire-tailed manakin has dramatic black, red and yellow patches typical of the family, and the tails of both male and female end in long wiry filaments, from which the common name is derived. These birds prefer humid areas and are found from the middle story to the forest canopy, as well as in clearings and cocoa plantations. Solitary birds, they forage alone for insects and fruit.

TYPICAL ANTBIRDS, AND GROUND ANTIBIRDS

THAMNOPHILIDAE: TYPICAL ANTBIRD FAMILY

Antbirds are found exclusively in Central and South America, mostly on the floor and in the lower vertical levels of the tropical rain forests of the Amazon basin, as well as in some drier and more open habitats. About 240 species of small to medium-sized birds are known in two families: Thamnophilidae (typical antbirds) and Formicaridae (ground antbirds). The 188 species of typical antbirds are found mainly in tropical forest and scrub. Many do actually feed on ants and other social insects; some eat the invertebrates disturbed by columns of army ants which they follow through the forest, while others, although insectivorous, have no particular predilection for ants.

The plumage is usually dull, and there are usually differences between that of male and female birds. Little is known of their breeding biology, but open, cup-shaped nests seem to be the rule.

Ocellated Antbird *Phaenostictus mcleannani*
RANGE Tropical Nicaragua to Panama; S. Colombia, N.W. Ecuador
HABITAT Undergrowth of humid, lowland forest
SIZE 7½–7¾ in (19–20 cm)

The dark markings in the plumage of the ocellated antbird give it a spotted appearance. It's tail is relatively long and the eyes are surrounded with an area of bright-hued bare skin, and it is these two colored circles, one within the other, that give the bird its common name. Males and females of the species look alike.

It is an uncommon, timid species and often found in association with bicolored antbirds. It is seldom seen away from the columns of army ants that march through the forests, for it feeds on the invertebrates, such as cockroaches and spiders, which are disturbed by the ants' progress. The call is a fast series of whistles.

Ocellated antbirds form lasting pair bonds, and before mating, the male feeds the female with titbits.

White-cheeked Antbird *Gymnopithys leucaspis*
RANGE S. E. Colombia, E. Ecuador, N. Peru, Amazonian Brazil
HABITAT Forest undergrowth up to 6,600 ft (2,000 m)
SIZE 5½ in (14 cm)

Although there is some disagreement, this bird is generally considered conspecific with the bicolored antbird, *G. bicolor*, of Central America, north Colombia and west Ecuador. The plumage of male and female are alike, and there are patches of bare skin around the eyes. It is a fairly common species and usually the most numerous and noisy of the birds that follow army ants. It spends much of the time on the ground but will perch just above the forest floor, watching for insects, spiders and other invertebrates which are driven out of the leaf litter as the ants advance.

The nest of the bicolored antbirds is usually a few feet from the ground in the stump of a decaying palm tree. It is made from small pieces of leaf, especially palm leaf, and lined with rootlets and plant fibers. The female lays 2 eggs, which both parents incubate for about 15 days.

Streaked Antwren *Myrmotherula surinamensis*
RANGE Amazonian Brazil, west to Pacific coast of South America
HABITAT Clearings in rain forest, forest edge, woodland, swampy areas
SIZE 4 in (10 cm)

The male of this species is largely black and white, while the female has a bright orange-red head and nape and pale orange-buff underparts. Both sexes have two white bars on the wings. Streaked antwrens are fairly common birds, often found near rivers and on wet ground, where they can generally be seen in pairs, busily searching for grasshoppers and spiders among the undergrowth, vines and leaves. They have a fast, rising, chipping call.

The nest is made in a tree, and the female lays 2 eggs.

Great Antshrike *Taraba major*

RANGE Tropical S. Mexico, Central and South America to N. Argentina

HABITAT Undergrowth in humid forest, brush and grassland up to 6,600 ft (2,000 m)

SIZE 7¾ in (20 cm)

The great antshrike is a fairly large bird with a thick, hooked bill and a crest; males and females have quite dissimilar coloration. These common but shy birds are usually found only in pairs or, occasionally, alone. They move stealthily through the bushes and low branches of small trees, searching for beetles, grasshoppers, bees and even small lizards to eat. When disturbed the male performs a threat display, pointing his bill straight upward and raising his crest so that the dorsal patch shows clearly.

The flimsy nest is cup shaped, made of dried grass and roots, sometimes lined with leaves, and is about 2½ in (6.5 cm) deep. The female lays 2 or 3 eggs, which both parents incubate for 2 to 3 weeks; they then feed the young until they are ready to leave the nest, about 2 weeks after hatching.

Barred Antshrike *Thamnophilus doliatus*

RANGE Tropical Mexico, Central and South America to N. Argentina; Trinidad and Tobago

HABITAT Varied, forest, brush, savanna, gardens; rarely above 6,600 ft (2,000 m)

SIZE 6 in (15 cm)

The plumage of this antshrike is conspicuously barred and streaked. The male is mainly black and white, while the female is chestnut, shading to buff, with black barring. Both birds have a crest, which the male always carries partially erect, and a toothed beak. Barred antshrikes are common birds, usually found in pairs. They are always on the move through bushes and branches in thickets and forest edge about 15 ft (4.5 m) up, they are usually heard calling to one another before they are seen. Insects, such as beetles and caterpillars, and berries make up their diet.

There seems to be no clearly defined mating season, but the male feeds the female during courtship and they may form a permanent pair bond. The female lays 2, rarely 3, eggs in a deep cup-shaped nest, made of grass and plant fibers and suspended by the rim in the fork of a low branch of a tree. Both parents incubate the eggs for about 14 days; only the female incubates at night. The young leave the nest 2 to 3 weeks after hatching.

FORMICARIIDAE: GROUND ANTBIRD FAMILY

This family of 56 species of mainly terrestrial antbirds are found from Mexico to northern Argentina, mainly on the forest floor of forests and bamboo thickets.

The family includes antthrushes and antpittas.

Chestnut-crowned Antpitta

Grallaria ruficapilla

RANGE Tropical and subtropical areas, Venezuela to N.W. Peru

HABITAT Dense cloud forest, damp woodland and open grassland

SIZE 7¾ in (20 cm)

The chestnut-crowned antpitta is a long-legged bird, with a short tail and a noticeably large head. The feathers on head and neck are reddish brown, hence its common name. It is a groundliving bird, usually found alone, looking for the insects that make up its diet. Even though difficult to see, it is not shy, and its three-note call is often heard. In fact, it will respond to imitations of its call and has a number of local names that suggest it, such as "Seco estoy".

OVENBIRDS

FURNARIIDAE: OVENBIRD AND WOODCREEPER FAMILY

The family of small to medium-sized birds, found in Central and South America, consist of two subfamilies – the ovenbirds and the woodcreepers.

FURNARIINAE: OVENBIRD SUBFAMILY

The 231 or so known species in this family occur from southern Mexico through Central and South America, in a wide variety of habitats. As well as the ovenbirds proper, the family includes birds such as spinetails and foliage-gleaners.

All the birds in the family have gray, brownish or russet plumage and are between 4¾ and 11 in (12 and 28 cm) long. They tend to be quick-moving, yet skulking, birds, which generally remain well hidden within vegetation.

The diversity of this family is best shown by their breeding behavior. The true ovenbirds, for which the family is named, construct ovenlike mud nests, which are baked hard by the sun. Others build domed nests of grass or sticks, while some make well-lined nests in holes in the ground or in trees. Females generally lay from 2 to 5 eggs, and both parents care for the young. In most species, male and female look more or less alike.

Rufous Hornero
Furnarius rufus
RANGE Brazil, Bolivia, Paraguay, Uruguay, Argentina
HABITAT Trees, often near habitation
SIZE 7½–8 in (19–20.5 cm)

There has been an increasing tendency to refer to the ovenbirds by their South American name (hornero), to avoid confusion with a North American wood warbler which is also called the ovenbird. The rufous hornero is a dignified bird, which walks with long, deliberate strides, holding one foot aloft as it hesitates between steps. It feeds on insect larvae and worms and is vocal throughout the year.

Pairs stay together all year round, often for life, and breed during the wettest months. Each year they build a domed, ovenlike nest on a branch, post or building, using clay, with a little plant material mixed into it, which is then baked hard by the hot sun. A small entrance leads to the interior chamber, lined with soft grass, where up to 5 eggs are laid. Both parents incubate the clutch, and, after leaving the nest, the young birds stay with their parents for a few months.

Plain Xenops *Xenops minutus*
RANGE S. Mexico, through Central and South America to N. Argentina
HABITAT Humid forest, forest edge
SIZE 5 in (12.5 cm)

One of several species of xenops, the plain xenops is distinguished by its unstreaked back. An active little bird, it forages in shrubs and thin branches of trees in search of insects to eat.

The nest is made by both partners of a breeding pair in a hole in an old, decaying tree and is lined with fine pieces of plant material. Alternatively, the birds may take over a hole abandoned by another bird. The 2 eggs are incubated by both parents for about 16 days.

Stripe-breasted Spinetail *Synallaxis cinnamomea*
RANGE Venezuela, Colombia; Trinidad and Tobago
HABITAT Forest, undergrowth, open woodland
SIZE 6½ in (16.5 cm)

Distinguished by its streaked cinnamon breast, this spinetail moves jerkily and makes low, short flights as it forages for small insects and spiders. It may also jump into the air in order to catch flying ants.

Both partners of a breeding pair help to build the nest, which is a round structure, made of twigs and placed in the fork of a branch in low scrub or on the ground. The nest is lined with soft plant material and has an entrance tunnel. The 2 or 3 eggs are incubated by both parents.

Red-faced Spinetail *Cranioleuca erythrops*

RANGE Costa Rica to Ecuador

HABITAT Humid mountain forest

SIZE 5½–6½ in (14–16.5cm)

Adult red-faced spinetails have reddish markings on the crown and sides of the head; juveniles have brownish crowns. They are active, acrobatic birds and much of their life is spent in the low levels of the forest, foraging in thickets and undergrowth for insects and other small invertebrates. They tend to move alone or in pairs but sometimes join in a flock of other highland birds.

The bulky, ball-shaped nest is made from vines and hangs from the end of a slender branch, well above ground. Both sexes incubate the 2 eggs and feed the young.

Larklike Bushrunner *Coryphistera alaudina*

RANGE S. Brazil, Bolivia, Paraguay, Uruguay, N. Argentina

HABITAT Dry scrub regions

SIZE 6 in (15 cm)

Identified by its prominent crest and streaked breast plumage, the larklike bushrunner generally moves in groups of 3 to 6, which are possibly family groups. Active both on the ground and in bushes and low trees, they stride along in the open but, if alarmed, take to the trees.

A rounded nest is made in a low tree from interwoven thorny twigs. A small entrance tunnel leads to the central chamber, where the eggs are laid.

Point-tailed Palmcreeper *Berlepschia rikeri*

RANGE Amazonian Brazil, also Venezuela, Guyana,

HABITAT Palm groves, often near water

SIZE 8½ in (21.5 cm)

An elegant little bird, the pintailed palmcreeper has distinctive black, white and chestnut plumage and pointed tail feathers. In pairs or small groups, it frequents palm trees of the genus Mauritia and forages for insects on the trunks and leaves of the trees. When it catches an insect, the palm creeper bangs it sharply against the trunk or branch before swallowing it.

Des Murs' Wiretail *Sylviorthorhynchus desmursii*

RANGE W. Argentina, adjacent Chile

HABITAT Humid forest with thick undergrowth

SIZE 9½ in (24 cm)

Over two-thirds of the length of this species is taken up by its long and decorative tail, which consists of only two pairs of feathers, plus a vestigial pair. Otherwise this spinetail is an inconspicuous little bird, revealed only by its persistent calls. The wiretail frequents the most dense parts of the forest and seems to be on the move ceaselessly in search of food.

A globular nest is made just off the ground amid twigs and grass. It is constructed from dry plant material, lined with soft feathers, and has a side entrance. Usually 3 eggs are laid. The bird holds up its tail when it is in the nest.

WOODCREEPERS, GNATEATERS, TAPACULOS AND AUSTRALIAN TREECREEPERS

DENDROCOLAPTINAE: WOODCREEPER SUBFAMILY

The 49 species of woodcreeper found in wooded areas of Central and South America, from Mexico to Argentina, are in many ways the New World equivalent of the treecreepers of the Old World. These birds also known as woodhewers, vary in length from 6 to 15 in (15 to 38 cm). Their laterally compressed beaks, range from short and straight to long and curved.

Woodcreepers are insectivorous and peck their food from crevices in the bark as they climb up the trunks of trees, with the aid of their sharp claws and the strong shafts of their tail feathers. They are usually solitary but may join mixed flocks.

Red-billed Scythebill
Campylorhamphus trochilirostris

RANGE E. Panama to N. Argentina

HABITAT Swampy and humid forest, woodland

SIZE 8–12 in (20.5–30.5 cm)
including Bill: 3 in (7.5 cm)

These shy, arboreal birds live in the middle to upper stories of forest trees. They are usually found alone, although they may feed among other types of insectivorous birds. Their strong legs and stiff tail feathers help them to climb quickly. They probe for insects with their long, thin, curved bills, under the bark of trees and inside bromeliads. The female lays 2 or 3 eggs in a hole in a tree or in a crevice, and incubates them for about 14 days.

Barred Woodcreeper *Dendrocolaptes certhia*

RANGE Tropical S. Mexico, through Central America to Bolivia, Amazonian Brazil

HABITAT Lowland rain forest to 4,600 ft (1,400 m), forest edge

SIZE 10½ in (26.5 cm)

Both male and female barred woodcreepers are strongly built and have light olive-brown, barred plumage. The medium-length beak is heavy and slightly curved. These birds live in the undergrowth and secondary growth of the rain forest. They are not timid and can be seen alone or in twos and threes often following army ants and feeding on the insects disturbed by their progress.

The female lays 2 eggs, in a hole or crevice in a tree, which are incubated for 14 or 15 days.

Long-billed Woodcreeper
Nasica longirostris

RANGE Tropical N. South America to Brazil and Bolivia

HABITAT Rain forest at 330–650 ft (100–200 m)

SIZE 14 in (35.5 cm)
including Bill: 2½ in (6.5 cm)

The solitary, agile long-billed woodcreeper climbs about in the trees, looking for insect food under the bark and in bromeliads. It has a long, slightly curved bill, and the sexes look similar. The female lays 2 eggs in a nest in a tree hole. They are incubated for about 2 weeks.

Olivaceous Woodcreeper
Sittasomus griseicapillus

RANGE Tropical and subtropical Mexico, through Central and South America to N. Argentina

HABITAT Deep forest, forest edge, open woodland, to 7,500 ft (2,300 m)

SIZE 6–6½ in (15–16.5 cm)

The buff bands on the wings of these active little birds are conspicuous in the air. The sexes look alike. They are more or less solitary, but may associate with other types of birds. They forage for insects on the trunks of trees with soft bark and may catch insects in the air. Only one nest has ever been found, in a hole in a tree.

CONOPOPHAGIDAE: GNATEATER FAMILY

The gnateaters, or antpipits, are a small group of forest-dwelling birds, quite closely related to the antbirds and ovenbirds. Eight species are recognized, all in Central and South America. Most are long-legged brown birds with round bodies and short tails. They live largely on the forest floor, capturing insect food on the ground with their flycatcherlike bills.

Black-cheeked Gnateater
Conopophaga melanops

RANGE	E. Brazil
HABITAT	Rain forest
SIZE	5 in (12.5 cm)

These neat little birds have long legs and appear almost neckless. Females are more olive-brown than males. They are quite tame, but are not often seen because they forage in the undergrowth.

Black-cheeked gnateaters make an open, cup-shaped nest on the ground, using big leaves, and line it with plant fibers. The female lays 2 eggs which both parents incubate. The nesting bird protects the eggs by feigning injury to lure predators away.

RHINOCRYPTIDAE: TAPACULO FAMILY

The approximately 28 described species of tapaculo are found among low-growing plants in habitats as varied as dense forest, grassland and semiopen arid country in Central and South America. They are ground-living birds, with poor powers of flight, but can run fast on their strong legs. Tapaculos vary in size from 5 to 10 in (12.5 to 25.5 cm) and have rounded bodies; they often cock their tails vertically. They have curious movable flaps covering the nostrils; the exact function of these is not known, but they presumably protect the openings against dust. Males and females look alike, or nearly so.

Elegant Crescentchest *Melanopareia elegans*

RANGE	W. Ecuador to N.W. Peru
HABITAT	Arid scrub, deciduous forest undergrowth
SIZE	5½ in (14 cm)

These small birds seldom fly, but they have long legs and large feet and run about rapidly, gathering up insects; when excited, they cock up their tails.

Elegant crescentchests are shy birds that are not often seen, although their calls can be heard. No information is available about the breeding biology of these birds.

Chestnut-throated Huet-huet *Pteroptochos castaneus*

RANGE	Chile
HABITAT	Forest
SIZE	10 in (25.5 cm)

This is a medium-sized bird with a rounded body, long legs and a relatively long tail – about 4 in (10 cm). The upperparts are mostly blackish-brown, but the throat and underparts are a dark reddish-brown, with some black and buff bars. Male and female look alike. These huet-huets are ground-dwellers which rarely fly, and they run, rather than hop, about looking for their insect food.

The nest is made from roots and soft grasses in a hole in the ground or in a tree stump, and the female lays 2 eggs.

CLIMACTERIDAE: AUSTRALIAN TREECREEPER FAMILY

The 7 species of Australian treecreeper resemble the treecreepers of the family Certhiidae. With the aid of their long curved bills, they eat mainly bark-dwelling insects. Some species also come to the ground to feed. They occur in New Guinea and Australia. The plumage of the sexes differ slightly.

Brown Treecreeper *Climacteris picumnus*

RANGE	Australia: Queensland to Victoria
HABITAT	Forest, woodland
SIZE	6 in (15 cm)

The brown treecreeper feeds largely on insects, which it picks from crevices in the bark of a tree trunk as it climbs upward in a spiral path; it makes short, fluttering flights from tree to tree. It also occasionally feeds on the ground. Male and female look more or less alike, but the female has a chestnut, not black, patch on the throat.

A cup-shaped nest is built in a hole, low down on a tree or in a rotting stump or post, and the female lays 3 or 4 eggs.

LYREBIRDS, BOWERBIRDS, FAIRY WRENS AND GRASS WRENS

SUBORDER PASSERI: ADVANCED PASSERINES

MENURIDAE FAMILY

This small family of Australian birds include 2 subfamilies – the lyrebirds and the scrub-birds.

MENURINAE: LYREBIRD SUBFAMILY

The 2 species of lyrebird live in the mountain forests of southeast Australia. Both sexes have brownish plumage, but males have long and elaborate tails.

Superb Lyrebird *Menura novaehollandiae*

RANGE Australia: S.E. Queensland to Victoria; introduced in Tasmania

HABITAT Mountain forest

SIZE Male: 31½–37½ in (80–95 cm) Female: 29–33 in (74–84 cm)

Although male and female lyrebirds are similar in body size and general appearance, the male's tail is up to 21½ in (55 cm) long and is a flamboyant mix of boldly patterned, lyre-shaped

feathers and fine, filamentous feathers. The lyrebirds are mainly ground-living and rarely fly but hop and flap up into trees to roost. They search on the ground for insects and larvae, scratching around with their large, strong legs and feet.

Prior to mating, the male makes several earth mounds and displays near them before the female, spreading his shimmering tail right over himself and dancing. The nest is a large, well camouflaged dome, made of grass and plant fiber and lined with rootlets. It is built on the ground near rocks or logs or sometimes in a tree. The female incubates her 1 egg for about 6 weeks and cares for the nestling.

PTILONORHYNCHIDAE: BOWERBIRD FAMILY

The 20 bowerbird species all occur in New Guinea and Australia and are closely related to the birds of paradise. Bowerbirds have stout bills, straight or curved, and strong legs and feet. Much of their life is spent on the ground, but they feed and nest in trees. Females have duller plumage than males, usually brownish and gray.

The family gets its common name from the "bower-building" activities of all but a few species – the males build ornate bowers on the ground, which they decorate with colorful objects in order to attract females.

MacGregor's Bowerbird

Amblyornis macgregoriae

RANGE Mountains of New Guinea (not N.W.)

HABITAT Forest

SIZE 10 in (25.5 cm)

The male MacGregor's bowerbird is distinguished by his spectacular crest, but otherwise has sober plumage. The female looks similar but lacks the crest. They are common, but shy, birds and feed on fruit. The male's bower consists of a saucer-shaped platform of moss with a central column of twigs. The column and the outer rim of the saucer are both decorated. The bird repairs and cleans his bower daily. Once he has attracted a mate, he displays and then chases her before mating. The female builds a cup-shaped nest in a tree and incubates her single egg herself.

Satin Bowerbird *Ptilonorhynchus violaceus*

RANGE Australia: Queensland to Victoria

HABITAT Forest

SIZE 10½–13 in (27–33 cm)

The male satin bowerbird has a violet sheen to his black plumage – hence the common name. The female is mainly olive-green, tinged with yellow. Noisy, gregarious birds outside the breeding season, they feed on fruit and insects and often raid orchards. They make a variety of calls and also mimic other sounds. The male's display bower is of the "avenue" kind, which sweeps upward at both ends and is decorated with berries, flowers and other bright objects. This bird is particularly attracted to blue items, such as bits of blue glass, paper or plastic. If a female shows interest, the male dances in his bower, alternately drooping and raising his wings and puffing up his feathers.

The female builds a nest of twigs and leaves in a tree and lays 2 eggs, which she alone incubates for 19 to 23 days.

MALURIDAE: FAIRY WREN AND GRASS WREN FAMILY

There are 26 species in this family of Australasian wrens. There are two subfamilies. The subfamily Malurinae includes the fairywrens, found in Australia and New Guinea, and the emu wrens, found in Australia. These small birds are mainly insect-eaters whose habitats range from tropical forests to semidesert. Male fairy wrens are brightly or boldly plumaged, with long, slender tails. Some have unusual social and reproductive habits, which may be their way of dealing with the often harsh conditions of their habitat. Groups of birds hold a territory together, which they defend from other birds, and each group builds

a single, spherical nest, in which one dominant female lays her eggs. All other adult members of the group then assist in the incubation and care of the young. Sometimes pairs nest alone, but they tend to have a high failure rate. The subfamily Amytornithinae consist of 8 species of grasswrens that live on rocky outcrops and in ground vegetation in the drier parts of Australia. Grasswrens rarely fly, and forage on the ground for seeds and insects.

Superb Fairywren

Malurus cyaneus

RANGE Australia: Victoria to Queensland; Tasmania

HABITAT Woodland, savanna, parks

SIZE 5 in (13 cm)

The breeding male has shiny blue plumage around the head and neck, contrasting with some bold black markings. Older, dominant males tend to keep this plumage all year. Nonbreeding males and females are mainly brownish and dull white. The birds live in groups, ruled by a dominant pair, and together defend a territory from intruders. Hopping about with tails cocked, they forage for insects on the ground and among the vegetation.

All members of the group combine to build the dome-shaped nest, which is situated near the ground in a bush or on a tussock and is made of grass, rootlets and bark, bound with spiders' webs. The dominant female lays 3 or 4 eggs, and again, all the group members assist with the 14-day incubation and the rearing of the young.

Eyrean Grasswren *Amytornis goyderi* **LR:lc**

RANGE Parts of C. Australia

HABITAT Canegrass on sandhills, spinifex grassland

SIZE 5½ in (14 cm)

The Eyrean grass wren is a rare bird. In 1976, it was recorded in some numbers in the sandhills of Simpson Desert, in South Australia, but by the following year, the habitat had deteriorated, and the birds had largely gone. Prior to 1976, it had been recorded only at its discovery in 1874, in 1931 and in 1961. This furtive bird stays hidden as it forages among vegetation. Little is known of its breeding habits, but the observed nests were partly domed, made of interwoven grass and stems.

SCRUB BIRDS AND HONEYEATERS

ATRICHORNITHINAE: SCRUB-BIRD SUBFAMILY

There are 2 species of scrub-bird, both found in Australia. They have small wings, long, broad tails and strong legs. Male and female differ slightly in coloration and females are smaller.

Noisy Scrub-Bird *Atrichornis clamosus* **VU**
RANGE Extreme S.W. of W. Australia
HABITAT Coastal scrub, vegetated gullies
SIZE 9 in (23 cm)

The noisy scrub bird is extremely rare and is protected by law. It was thought to be extinct for over 70 years until it was found again in 1961 at Two People's Bay. Noisy scrub birds live among dense vegetation on or near the ground and feed on insects and seeds. They usually live alone and rarely move far afield. The female builds a domed nest of dried rushes in which she lays 1 egg. She incubates the egg for 36 to 38 days.

MELIPHAGIDAE: HONEYEATER FAMILY

The 182 species of honeyeater occur in Australia and New Guinea and Southwestern Pacific islands from Samoa to Bali. The honeyeaters eat nectar from flowers in a similar manner to sunbirds. They are usually larger than sunbirds however, and most have duller, green or brownish plumage. They are diverse, having adapted to a variety of habitats. Honeyeaters have remarkable specializations for nectar feeding. Despite the variation in body size and beak shape all species have a highly modified, long, protrusible tongue. At its base, the tongue can be curled up to form two long, nectar-transporting grooves. At its tip, it splits into four parts, each of which is frilled, making the entire end of the tongue an absorbent brush for nectar collection. Honeyeaters also eat insects, for protein, and fruit.

Generally tree-dwelling, honeyeaters are gregarious birds, aggressive to other species. Male and female look alike in some species, unalike in others.

Kauai O-o *Moho braccatus* **CR**
RANGE Hawaiian Islands: Kauai
HABITAT Montane rain forest
SIZE 7½–8½ in (19–21.5 cm)

Thought to be extinct, like the 2 other species of Hawaiian O-o, the Kauai species was rediscovered, in 1960, in the Alaka'i Swamp. Its relatives were hunted to extinction for their yellow feathers, but this species' sober coloration saved it. It is, however, intolerant of any alteration in its rain forest habitat. The present population is protected but very small.

The Kauai O-o eats nectar berries, spiders, insects and snails. It makes its nest in a cavity in an ohia tree and lays 2 eggs on a bed of dead plant material. Both parents feed the young.

Brown Honeyeater *Lichmera indistincta*
RANGE Australia, New Guinea, Aru Islands
HABITAT Forest, woodland, mangroves, cultivated land, gardens
SIZE 4¾–6 in (12–15 cm)

A restless, active brown honeyeater feeds among flowering trees and bushes on nectar and insects. It is always found near water and has a beautiful voice. The nest is cup-shaped and made of tightly packed bark shreds and grass, bound with cobwebs. It is suspended from a twig or placed among the foliage of a bush or tree. The female lays a clutch of 2 eggs.

Strong-billed Honeyeater

Melithreptus validirostris

RANGE Tasmania,
islands in Bass Strait

HABITAT Open forest, woodland

SIZE 5½ in (14 cm)

Popularly known as the bark-bird, this honeyeater hops about on tree trunks, stripping off the bark in its search for insects. It is often seen on *Eucalyptus* trees. Nectar forms only a small part of this bird's diet. The sexes look alike. The nest, suspended from a branch is made of bark strips and grass. The female lays 2 or 3 eggs.

Cardinal Honeyeater

Myzomela cardinalis

RANGE Islands of Vanuatu, Samoa, Santa Cruz and Solomon

HABITAT Forest, open woodland, cultivated land

SIZE 5 in (13 cm)

This is one of the smallest honeyeaters. With its bright coloration, it resembles a sunbird. It forages for small insects and nectar and will often form large groups at favored feeding sites. Its flight is fast and direct. Male and female differ in appearance; the male has vivid red and black plumage, while the female is mainly olive gray, with some red on her rump and lower back.

A small, cup-shaped nest, made of grass stems, is built on a forked branch. The female lays 1 or 2 eggs.

Fuscous Honeyeater

Lichenostomus fusca

RANGE Australia from N.E. Queensland to S.E. south Australia

HABITAT Open forest

SIZE 6 in (15 cm)

The fuscous honeyeater forages busily among the foliage at various heights searching for nectar and insects. It also catches insects on the wing. It is a fairly common bird and generally lives alone or in small parties. The sexes look alike, with olive brown plumage with touches of yellow and dark markings on the cheeks. The female lays 2 or 3 eggs in a cup-shaped nest, made of plant fiber and grass and hung in a tree.

Little Friarbird *Philemon citreogularis*

RANGE E. and N. Australia, S. New Guinea, islands in Banda Sea

HABITAT Open forest, woodland

SIZE 9¾–11 in (25–28 cm)

Like all friarbirds, the little friarbird has an area of bare skin on its head, the origin of its common name. Male and female look similar and, despite the name, are not much smaller than other friarbirds. The little friarbird forages in all kinds of trees and bushes for fruit, insects and nectar. It makes a variety of harsh cries, particularly when feeding in a squabbling flock, but also has a more attractive musical song. In the south of Australia, these birds are thought to make regular seasonal movements.

The cup-shaped nest is made of bark strips and plant fiber and is built on a forked branch or suspended from a branch, often overhanging water. The female lays 2 to 4 eggs.

Long-bearded Melidectes *Melidectes princeps*

RANGE New Guinea

HABITAT Mountain forest, alpine grassland

SIZE 10½ in (26.5 cm)

Distinguished by the white "whiskers" on its throat, the long-bearded melidectes has largely black plumage, with some light-colored bare skin around the eyes. Less arboreal than other honeyeaters, this bird spends much of its time on the ground, probing the leaf litter with its long, curved bill to find insects and sedge seeds. It also flies jerkily from tree to tree and will climb trees occasionally in order to feed on berries and fruit. A bulky nest, made of moss and fungal threads, is built in a bush or tree a meter or so above the ground. The female lays 1 egg.

HONEYEATERS CONTINUED

Smoky Honeyeater *Melipotes fumigatus*

RANGE Mountains of C. New Guinea

HABITAT Forest at 4,300–9,000 ft (1,300–2,700 m)

SIZE 8½ in (21.5 cm)

A quiet, slow-moving bird, the smoky honeyeater moves about the trees in search of insects, particularly the sedentary, rather than the active, varieties. It may, however, chase any flying insects that it disturbs. The smoky honeyeater also feeds on fruit, but is rarely seen on a flowering tree; its tongue has no brushtip for nectar feeding.

It lives alone or in pairs or sometimes gathers in flocks. Male and female look alike, with short bills and some bare, orange-yellow skin on the face.

The nest is a deep cup, made of mosses and plant fibers and lined with dead leaves and ferns. It is attached by its rim to the end of a branch. Like many mountain-dwelling honeyeaters with sparse food supplies, this species lays only 1 egg. The young bird is fed with berries.

Tui *Prosthemadera novaeseelandiae*

RANGE New Zealand and coastal islands; Kermadec, Chatham and Auckland Islands

HABITAT Forest, suburban areas

SIZE 11½–12½ in (29–32 cm)

Also aptly known as the parson bird, the tui has a bib of white tufts at the throat and a ring of fine, lacy feathers which form a collar. The female tui has smaller throat tufts than the male and a paler belly. Juveniles develop throat tufts within a month of hatching and have full adult plumage by about 3 months.

Tuis are noisy, vigorous birds, which fly around in the trees at high speed, sometimes plummeting down from considerable heights. They feed on insects, fruit and, using their brushlike tongues, on nectar. Tuis are aggressive, defending their food and nests against intruders.

In the breeding season, male tuis make spectacular aerial dives, rolling and looping as they descend. The nest is usually made in the fork of a tree and is built with sticks and twigs and lined with fine plant material. The female incubates the 2 to 4 eggs for about 14 days. Throughout the incubation period, the male seems to sing almost continually from a nearby tree but helps the female to feed the young once they hatch. There are often two broods a season.

Red/Common Wattlebird *Anthochaera carunculata*

RANGE Australia: New South Wales to Western Australia

HABITAT Open forest, woodland, suburban parks and gardens

SIZE 12½–13¾ in (32–35 cm) including Tail:6¼ in (16 cm)

The aggressive, noisy red wattlebird is the largest honeyeater in mainland Australia. It is active in the trees, preferring *Banksia*

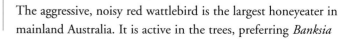

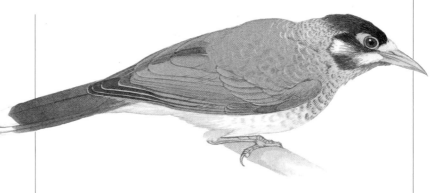

and *Eucalyptus*, and feeds on nectar, fruit and insects. It lives alone or wanders in small parties; in the west of its range it makes regular north-south movements. The sexes look alike, both with fleshy red wattles behind the eyes.

The nest is made of sticks and twigs on a horizontal branch of a bush or tree; it is sometimes lined with grass. The female lays 2 or 3 eggs.

Eastern Spinebill *Acanthorhynchus tenuirostris*

RANGE Australia: Queensland to Victoria and S. Australia; Tasmania, islands in Bass Strait

HABITAT Rain forest, scrub, cultivated land and gardens

SIZE 4¾–6 in (12–15 cm)

The eastern spinebill is a restless, swift-flying bird, which flits from tree to tree, in search of insects and nectar. It often hovers beside a flower while it probes the bloom with its spinelike bill and takes nectar. Primarily an arboreal bird, the eastern spinebill lives alone or in groups and seems to make regular seasonal movements. The female has duller plumage than the male.

The cup-shaped nest is built by the female, using grass, bark and moss. The nest is suspended from a thin forked twig in a bush or small tree. The female incubates the 2 or 3 eggs while the male guards the territory. Both parents feed the young, and they may produce two broods a season.

Noisy Miner *Manorina melanocephala*

RANGE Australia: Queensland to Victoria; Tasmania, islands in Bass Strait

HABITAT Woodland, suburban parks

SIZE 10¼–11 in (26–28 cm)

The noisy miner spends much of its life in trees and bushes, but will also forage on the ground; it feeds on insects, fruit and nectar. An active, inquisitive bird, it often harasses other birds

and, in groups, will mob an owl or hawk. Noisy miners nearly always live in colonies, which forage, feed and roost together.

A cup-shaped nest, made of grass, twigs and pieces of bark, is built on a forked branch of a tree or sapling and lined with soft plant material, on which the female lays her clutch of between 2 and 4 eggs.

Crimson Chat *Epthianura tricolor*

RANGE Inland and W. Australia

HABITAT Grassy plains with some bush cover

SIZE 4–4¼ in (10–11 cm)

The male crimson chat is a vividly plumaged little bird, with his red, white and brownish-black markings. The female bird is plainer, with more brown plumage, but she does have a bright crimson rump.

Crimson chats forage on or near the ground in grass or low trees and bushes and may poke their bills into flowers to find insects. If a large insect is caught, the chat wedges it in a forked twig and then tears it apart as it devours it.

Breeding takes place after heavy rainfall, when good food supplies are assured, and the birds usually breed in loose colonies. Courting males perform display flights, with their crimson crown feathers erect. The cup-shaped nest, which is made of grass and twigs, is situated in a bush or on a tussock, and the female lays 3 or 4 eggs. Both the male and female incubate the eggs and tend the young.

PARDALOTES, AUSTRALASIAN ROBINS AND LEAFBIRDS

PARDALOTIDAE: PARDALOTE FAMILY

The birds in this family occur in Australia, New Guinea, Indonesia, and the western Pacific islands. There are 68 species of these small birds, found in a range of habitats including forest, heathland, scrub, and semidesert. Most are insect eaters. There are three subfamilies – pardalotes; bristlebirds; and scrubwrens and thornbills (a group which also includes the gerygones).

Spotted Pardalote *Pardalotus punctatus*
RANGE Australia, Tasmania
HABITAT Forest, woodland
SIZE 3½ in (9 cm)

The colorful spotted pardalote has characteristic spots on its plumage that are mostly white in the male and yellow in the female. It feeds on insects, which it finds on the ground and in trees. An agile climber, it clings to twigs in almost any position as it makes a thorough search of the foliage. Outside the breeding season, these pardalotes live alone or in small flocks, sometimes including other species.

A breeding pair excavates a tunnel in a bank or slope and makes a globular nest of bark and grass in a chamber at the end of it. There are usually 4 eggs, incubated by both parents for 14 to 16 days.

White-browed Scrubwren *Sericornis frontalis*
RANGE E. and S.E.and S.W. Australia, islands in Bass Strait
HABITAT Dense forest undergrowth, bushy coastal vegetation
SIZE 40 in (11 cm)

The white-browed scrubwren lives on or near the ground, keeping hidden in the thick undergrowth while it hops about in search of insects and other small invertebrates. The domed nest is built in the undergrowth on or near the ground. It is made of leaves and fibers and has a side entrance. The female lays 3 eggs.

Yellow-rumped Thornbill *Acanthiza chrysorrhoa*
RANGE Australia, south of Tropic of Capricorn
HABITAT Open woodland, savanna
SIZE 4 in (10 cm)

The male and female of this species both have somewhat sober plumage but with deep-yellow rump feathers, the origin of their common name. They eat insects and plant matter, such as seeds, which they find on the ground and by foraging in bushes and trees.

The large, untidy nest is made of grass and plant fibers and has a hooded brood chamber with a low, overhung entrance. It is usually situated in a low bush or other foliage. The female lays 3 eggs, which she incubates for 18 to 20 days; both parents then tend the young. The birds produce up to four broods a season, and young from earlier broods assist in the care of subsequent nestlings. This unusual habit is common to many members of this subfamily.

White-throated Gerygone *Gerygone olivacea*
RANGE S.E. New Guinea, coastal N. and E. Australia
HABITAT Open forest, woodland
SIZE 4¼ in (11 cm)

An arboreal bird, the white-throated warbler forages for insects on bark and foliage and occasionally chases prey on the wing. It usually occurs alone or in scattered, loosely knit groups. Male and female look alike, both with grayish-brown upperparts and yellow underparts.

The long, oval shaped nest is suspended from twigs up to 50 ft (15 m) above the ground. It is constructed from plant fiber and strips of bark, interwoven with spiders' webs and lined with feathers or plant down. The nest has a hooded entrance near to the top. The female lays 2 or 3 eggs.

EOPSALTRIIDAE: AUSTRALASIAN ROBIN FAMILY

This family of small, arboreal birds is found mainly in Australia and New Guinea, but 1 species is found in Malaysia and another in the Himalayas and south China. Most of the 46 species occupy the lower vegetation in forests or woods and eat insects.

Flame Robin *Petroica phoenicea*

RANGE	Tasmania, S.E. Australia
HABITAT	Dry forest, woodland, open country
SIZE	5–5½ in (13–14 cm)

The male flame robin has a bright red throat and belly, reminiscent of those of the European robin. The female has pale buff underparts, with occasionally a touch of orange-red on the belly. It eats insects, taken on the ground and in trees. Normally solitary birds, they may form flocks outside the breeding season.

The nest is made of grass and bark strips, bound with spiders' webs. It may be in a tree fork or hollow on a bank or among tree roots. The female lays 3 eggs.

Citrine Canary Flycatcher *Culicicapa helianthea*

RANGE	Philippines, Greater Sunda Islands
HABITAT	Forest, woodland
SIZE	About 4 in (10 cm)

Also called the sunflower flycatcher, the plumage of this bird is largely yellow of various shades; the upperparts of juveniles tend to be darker and greener than those of adults. It perches on the outer branches of trees and makes short aerial dashes after insects in true flycatcher fashion. It sometimes feeds in mixed flocks.

IRENIDAE: LEAFBIRD FAMILY

The leafbird family consists of 10 species divided into 2 groups – leafbirds and fairy bluebirds. All occur in southern and Southeast Asia, generally in forest, but sometimes in orchards. Leafbirds are bright green and eat fruit and berries, as well as insects, pollen, and nectar. They are gregarious, moving in flocks. The 2 species of fairy bluebirds are brilliant blue, highly arboreal and gregarious birds. They gather in small flocks and feed on fruit. In all species females are usually duller than males.

Gold-fronted Leafbird *Chloropsis aurifrons*

RANGE	India, Sri Lanka, S.E. Asia, Sumatra
HABITAT	Forest fringe, open country, gardens, damp hill country to 3,000 ft (900 m)
SIZE	7 in (18 cm)

These brightly colored arboreal birds are seldom seen, except when they fly briefly from clump to clump of trees or attract attention by calling or imitating other birds. The male is brilliant green, with a blue throat patch and a bright orange crown. With this primarily green plumage, leafbirds blend well with foliage. They are agile and acrobatic in the trees even swinging from the branches as if on a trapeze. They live in pairs or small groups, feeding among the leaves on insects, particularly caterpillars, spiders, berries and the nectar of the flowers of the coral tree (*Erythrina*), loranthus and the silk cotton tree. As they search for nectar, they pollinate plants.

The small, cup-shaped nest is built among thick foliage at the outer end of a branch, high up in a tree. The female lays 2 or 3 eggs and is thought to incubate them alone.

Asian Fairy Bluebird *Irena puella*

RANGE	India to S.E. Asia, Greater Sunda and Andaman Islands, Philippines: Palawan
HABITAT	Hill forest to 5,600 ft (1,700 m)
SIZE	10 in (25.5 cm)

Fairy bluebirds are almost totally arboreal, preferring to spend their time high up in the branches of evergreen trees near running water. Males, particularly, are shy birds, not often clearly seen except when they come down to drink or bathe, when their striking coloration – bright ultramarine upperparts, with velvety black below and red eyes – make them conspicuous. Females are duller, with peacock-green and blackish-brown plumage. These birds feed mainly on the nectar of the flowers of the coral tree (*Erythrina*), and on fruit, especially ripe figs, often in the company of hornbills and pigeons.

The nest is built 10 to 21 ft (3 to 6.5 m) up in a small tree, in the darkest part of the forest, and is made of roots and twigs, covered with moss. Usually 2 eggs are laid.

SHRIKES AND VIREOS

LANIIDAE: SHRIKE FAMILY

The 30 species in this family are found in North America and Eurasia south to Indonesia, New guinea, and the Philippines. Shrikes are small to medium-sized songbirds that feed mainly on large insects, but will also take small reptiles, birds, and mammals. They have a large head, and a strong, hooked-tip beak used to pull prey apart. They inhabit savanna, scrub, bush, and open woodland, All habitats that have a mixture of tall vegetation and open spaces.

Typically shrikes keep watch from a high vantage point, swooping down to the ground to take prey or else catching it flycatcher fashion, on the wing, then returning to the perch. Some species impale prey on thorns before eating it.

Great Gray/Northern Shrike *Lanius excubitor*

RANGE Widespread in N. America, Asia, Europe, N. Africa; winters south of breeding range

HABITAT Varied, woodland, open country, marsh, tundra, savanna, desert

SIZE 9½ in (24 cm)

Great gray shrikes perch in a prominent position and from there fly out to capture their prey – mainly insects, although small birds, mammals, reptiles and frogs are also sometimes taken. Normally the birds return to the perch to eat, but they will sometimes store food in a kind of larder. Great gray shrikes defend their territory strongly against all intruders, even hawks, and like hawks, they hover when hunting. The female looks similar to the male, but she is duller, with crescent-shaped markings on the underparts; the juvenile is even more heavily marked.

The bulky nest is constructed by both birds from twigs, moss and grass and is usually placed about 40 ft (12 m) from the ground. In the north, the female lays 5 to 7 eggs, which she incubates for 14 to 16 days. Fewer eggs are laid at a time in the southern area of the range, but there may be two clutches in a year.

The great gray shrike is one of only 2 species found in North America; the other is the loggerhead shrike, *Lanius ludovicianus*, which is fairly similar to the great gray shrike both in its physical appearance and its habits.

Magpie Shrike *Corvinella melanoleuca*

RANGE Africa: Kenya, Tanzania, Mozambique across to S. Angola

HABITAT Open country with scattered trees and bush, neglected cultivation

SIZE 17½ in (45 cm)

The black and white plumage of this large bird resembles that of a magpie, and it is also known as the magpie shrike. Male and female look alike, the juvenile is duller. Despite its striking coloration and its habit of sitting conspicuously on the tops of trees, this shrike is a rather shy bird. It usually moves in pairs or small parties, often with other bird species, and feeds on insects, which it catches on the ground by dropping down on them from a high perch. Long-tailed shrikes often skewer their prey on a thorn before eating it.

The nest is a bulky, untidy structure, sited among thorny branches, and is usually made of thorny twigs. There are normally 3 or 4 eggs.

VIREONIDAE: VIREO FAMILY

There are about 51 species in this family, all found in the New World. The true vireos dominate the group – there are about 45 species. All feed on insects among the foliage in forested and wooded areas. Similar to the wood warblers in appearance, vireos are more stoutly built, have heavier bills and tend to be more deliberate in their movements.

The remaining birds in the family are divided into two groups – 2 species of peppershrikes and 4 shrike-vireos. All are slightly larger birds than vireos and have heavy, hooked bills; they feed in the trees, mainly on insects and fruit. In all species of this family, male and female look alike, or nearly so.

Red-eyed Vireo *Vireo olivaceus*

RANGE Canada, much of USA (not S.W.), Central and South America to Argentina; West Indies

HABITAT Deciduous forest and woodland, gardens, parks, orchards

SIZE 5½–6¾ in (14–17 cm)

This widespread vireo is distinguished by its ruby-red eyes; immature birds have brown eyes. It occurs almost anywhere that there are deciduous trees and moves slowly through the lower

levels and undergrowth, foraging for insects and berries. It sings more than any other bird on hot summer days.

The neat, cup-shaped nest is suspended between the twigs of a horizontal fork in a tree or bush. There are usually 4 eggs in a clutch, which the female incubates for between 11 and 14 days. The young leave the nest some 10 to 12 days after hatching.

Tawny-crowned Greenlet *Hylophilus ochraceiceps*

RANGE S. Mexico, Central and South America to Bolivia

HABITAT Rain forest, woodland

SIZE 4¼ in (11 cm)

This little vireo has predominantly yellowish and brown plumage, with a tawny forehead and crown. It forages among the leaves of bushes and saplings for insects and other small invertebrates. It usually moves in small groups, often in mixed flocks with other forest birds.

The female lays 2 eggs in a strongly built, cup-shaped nest, which is attached by its rim to a forked twig. Both parents feed their young with insects and larvae until they leave the nest at about 14 days old.

Rufous-browed Peppershrike *Cyclarhis gujanensis*

RANGE N.E. Mexico, through Central and South America to N. Argentina; Trinidad

HABITAT Forest, woodland, cultivated land

SIZE 6 in (15 cm)

A heavy-bodied bird, with a large head and strong legs and feet, this peppershrike is a good climber and forages in trees, but it is weak in flight. It is slow and deliberate in its movements as it

searches for insects and berries, particularly at the ends of branches and twigs. If a large insect is caught, the bird holds it down with its foot and tears it apart with its strong, hooked bill.

A secretive bird, this peppershrike rarely comes out into the open, but it can often be heard singing loudly and persistently from a perch. It usually lives alone or in pairs.

The nest is woven from bark and grasses and suspended in the fork of a branch in a bush or tree. Both parents incubate the clutch of 2 or 3 eggs and feed the young.

Chestnut-sided Shrike-vireo *Vireolanius melitophrys* **LR:nt**

RANGE Mexico to Guatemala

HABITAT Forest

SIZE 7 in (18 cm)

All 4 species of shrike-vireo are more brightly plumaged than typical vireos, and the chestnut-sided shrike-vireo is particularly attractive, with its green back, chestnut flanks and boldly striped head. It has a stout, hooked bill and strong legs and feet.

Seldom seen, this bird lives high up in the forest canopy and rarely flies in the open or perches in exposed spots. It feeds on insects, holding down large ones with its foot and tearing them apart with its bill, and it also eats some fruit.

The nest is suspended from a forked branch of a tree, but the breeding habits of this shrike-vireo are not known.

WHIPBIRDS, QUAILTHRUSH, APOSTLEBIRDS, SITELLAS, SHRIKE TITS AND WHISTLERS

CORVIDAE: CROW FAMILY

Members of this large and diverse family are found worldwide. There are 647 species in 7 subfamilies.

CINCLOSOMATINAE: QUAIL THRUSH AND WHIPBIRD SUBFAMILY

There are 15 species of quail thrush and whipbird. All but the 1 in Southeast Asia, occur in Australia and New Guinea.

Eastern Whipbird *Psophodes olivaceus*

RANGE Australia: Queensland to Victoria

HABITAT Thickets in or near forest

SIZE 9¾–11 in (25–28 cm)

The eastern whipbird has mainly dark plumage, with some white, and a long, broad tail. The sexes look alike.

It lives on or near the ground, but usually stays in dense undergrowth, searching for insects, larvae and spiders among the leaf litter. It hops and runs swiftly and climbs into bushes, but flies rarely and only for short distances.

The nest of twigs and rootlets is made near the ground in dense undergrowth. The female lays 2 eggs.

Cinnamon Quail Thrush

Cinclosoma cinnamomeum

RANGE Australia: drier areas, Western Australia to Queensland and Victoria

HABITAT Semidesert, scrub

SIZE 7¾ in (20 cm)

Alone or in small family groups, the cinnamon quail thrush skulks among bushes or hides in holes and burrows to escape predators and the heat of the day. It usually feeds at dawn and dusk, on seeds and insects. It also hunts for insects over open country, flying low with noisy, whirring wings. The female lacks the male's characteristic black markings.

The nest is sited in a shallow dip in the ground or under a bush or fallen branch and is made of grass and twigs, lined with bark and leaves. The female lays 2 or 3 eggs.

CORCORACINAE: AUSTRALIAN CHOUGH AND APOSTLEBIRD SUBFAMILY

The two species in this subfamily are gregarious birds that inhabit scrub and open woodlands of eastern Australia. Both forage on the ground for insects, invertebrates, and seeds. They rarely fly, but roost, and build communal nests, in trees.

Apostlebird *Struthidea cinerea*

RANGE Australia: Victoria, New South Wales, Queensland

HABITAT Open woodland, scrub, cultivated land

SIZE 13 in (33 cm)

The apostlebird usually lives in groups of about 12 birds – hence its common name – which stay together even in the breeding season. The group may be led by a dominant pair. The birds feed mainly on the ground on insects and seeds, but they also jump from branch to branch and fly for short distances.

The bowl-shaped mud nest is lined with grass and made in a tree, usually near other nests. The female lays 4 or 5 eggs which are incubated for 19 days. More than one female may lay in one nest. The chicks are fed by the group.

PACHYCEPHALINAE: SITELLA, MOHOUA, SHRIKE-TIT AND WHISTLER SUBFAMILY

A diverse group of 59 species, sitellas and their relatives are small, mainly arboreal birds found in New Zealand, Australasia and Southeast Asia. There are 4 groups within the subfamily – sitellas, mohouas, shrike-tits, and whistlers or thick-heads.

Varied Sitella *Daphoenositta chrysoptera*

RANGE Australia

HABITAT Open forest, woodland

SIZE 4–4¾ in (10–12 cm)

The agile varied sitella runs up or down tree trunks with ease. Most of its life is spent in the trees and it flits from place to place, probing crevices in the bark for insects. It is gregarious and usually moves in small groups. There are many forms, all included in this one species, which differ greatly in coloration.

The cup-shaped nest is made on a forked branch and camouflaged with pieces of bark. Both parents incubate the 3 or 4 eggs and feed the young.

Crested Shrike-tit

Falcunculus frontatus

RANGE Australia (patchy distribution)

HABITAT Dry forest, woodland

SIZE 6¾–7½ in (17–19 cm)

The crested shrike-tit has a rather unusual bill for an insect-eater – it is deep, laterally compressed and slightly hooked. The bird often clings to tree trunks and uses its bill to strip off bark in its search for insects and larvae. It also forages among foliage for insects and is beneficial to mankind in that it eats many larvae of the codlin moths that attack orchards.

The deep, cup-shaped nest is built in a fork of a tree, such as a eucalyptus sapling, and the male often clears the area around it by breaking twigs above the nest. The female lays 2 or 3 eggs.

Golden Whistler *Pachycephala pectoralis*

RANGE Indonesia: Java to the Moluccas; Bismarck Archipelago to Fiji and Tonga; E., S. and S.W. Australia, Tasmania

HABITAT Forest, woodland, mallee (eucalyptus) scrub

SIZE 7 in (18 cm)

Divided into 70 or 80 races distributed among the many islands in its range, the golden whistler may have more subspecies (some of which are as distinct as species) than any other bird. Races vary enormously, particularly the head plumage. The male bird is generally olive-green, yellow and black or gray. Females usually have olive-brown to olive-gray upperparts, with grayish throat and breast and whitish belly plumage.

A tree-dwelling bird, the golden whistler feeds in the trees on insects and sometimes on berries. It perches for long periods and is rather inactive compared to most flycatchers.

Both partners of a breeding pair help to build the nest, which is usually in a fork of a small tree or bush. It is made of grass, bark and leaves, lined with fine grass. Both birds incubate the 2 or 3 eggs and tend the young.

Gray Shrike-thrush *Colluricincla harmonica*

RANGE Australia, Tasmania, islands in Bass Strait, S.E. New Guinea

HABITAT Forest, woodland, grassland, suburban parks

SIZE 9 in (23 cm)

The gray shrike-thrush is a wide-spread species, common in Australia but found only in a restricted area of New Guinea. A solitary bird, it feeds in undergrowth, on the ground and among lower branches of trees. It sings with clear, musical notes. The female differs slightly from the male in plumage, having a touch of brown on the upperparts, less distinct white facial markings and streaks on the breast.

The bowl-shaped nest is built on the ground, in a tree or bush or on a rock ledge, from bark strips and grass. The birds may take over an old nest of another species. The female lays 2 or 3 eggs, and there may be more than one brood.

Rusty Pitohui

Pitobui ferrugineus

RANGE New Guinea area, Aru Islands

HABITAT Lowland forest

SIZE 10–11 in (25.5–28 cm)

One of the largest whistlers, the rusty pitohui is gregarious and lives in pairs or small parties. It moves slowly through the low levels of the forest, feeding on insects and fruit and often uttering soft calls. The sexes look alike, with mainly brown and rufous plumage.

The deep, cup-shaped nest is built on a multiple-forked branch, high in a tree. It is made of twigs, vine and fiber, lined with leaves and fine plant material. The female lays 1 egg.

CROWS

CORVINAE: CROW, BIRDS-OF-PARADISE, CURRAWONG AND ORIOLE SUBFAMILY

The 297 species of this subfamily make up 4 tribes.

The 117 species of crows, jays and magpies are successful, intelligent, and adaptable birds. They occur worldwide, apart from the polar regions. All species are large with powerful, often hooked bills. The jays are most brightly colored; nutcrackers are spotted, and crows are mainly black.

Birds-of-paradise are medium to large arboreal birds found in the rain forests of New Guinea, north east Australia, and the Moluccas. There are 45 species, and this group probably contains the most visually spectacular of all birds. Males have colorful plumage, often with long, decorative tail and head feathers, which is used to attract females. Females have dull, usually brown, plumage.

The third tribe in the subfamily contains 24 species in 2 groups – the currawongs, Australian butcherbirds and Australian magpies (which resemble crows) and the wood swallows (which resemble martins). Currawongs and their relatives include arboreal species and ground-feeders, and are found in Australia and New Guinea. Magpies have been introduced to New Zealand and Fiji. Most eat insects and other small invertebrates. Wood swallows are found from Australia and Fiji to South China and India. They have stocky bodies and long, pointed wings and are skilled fliers.

The oriole and cuckoo-shrike tribe consists of two groups. The 29 species of orioles are found from temperate Eurasia to Australia, and in tropical Africa. They are noted for their clear, melodious calls. Orioles are arboreal and feed in trees on insects and fruit. The 82 species of cuckoo-shrikes and minivets occur from northern India to Australia and the islands of the western Pacific, and in Africa. Most are arboreal, drab birds, with strong, notched beaks, long pointed wings, and bristles round the base of the bill. Minivets are colorful. Many cuckoo-shrikes and minivets have erectile feathers on the back and rump.

American Crow *Corvus brachyrhynchos*
RANGE S. Canada, USA
HABITAT Open country, farmland, open woodland, woodland edge, parks
SIZE 17–20¾ in (43–53 cm)

This stocky, black crow is abundant and widespread and adapts well to most habitats. Almost omnivorous, it feeds largely on the ground, but also in trees, on insects, spiders, frogs, reptiles, small mammals, birds and their eggs, and carrion. It also eats grain, fruit and nuts and scavenges on refuse. They usually forage in pairs, although lone males are seen in the breeding season. In winter, huge flocks gather to fly to communal roosts. A nest of sticks and twigs is made in a tree, bush or, on a telegraph pole. The 3 to 6 eggs are incubated for about 18 days, probably by the female. Northern populations migrate south in winter.

Rook *Corvus frugilegus*
RANGE Europe, Middle East, C. and E. Asia
HABITAT Open country and farmland with clumps of trees, small woods
SIZE 17¾ in (45 cm)

The glossy black rook is distinguished by the patch of bare skin on its face in front of the eyes and the shaggy, loose feathers on its thighs. It feeds largely on grain and earthworms, which it obtains by driving its bill into the earth and forcing it open to seize the worm. Insects and other invertebrates, small mammals, young birds, eggs, nuts and fruit are also included in its diet. Primarily a groundfeeder, the rook will fly up into trees to take nuts or other specific items. Rooks live in pairs but in autumn and winter gather in large, communal roosts.

Colonies nest at the tops of tall trees, each pair making a nest of sticks and twigs. The male feeds the female while she incubates the 3 to 5 eggs for 16 to 18 days. Both parents feed the young. Northern birds migrate south in winter.

Tibetan Ground Jay *Pseudopodoces humilis*
RANGE W. China, Tibet, N.E. India
HABITAT Open, sandy country
SIZE 7¾ in (20 cm)

One of a group of ground-living corvids, the Tibetan ground jay runs speedily on its long legs and has a heavy bill, with which it probes and digs in the ground for its insect food. It digs its own nest in the earth, and the female lays 4 to 6 eggs.

Black-billed/Common Magpie
Pica pica

RANGE Europe to N. Africa; Asia to Himalayas and just into S.E. Asia; Alaska, W. Canada and USA to Utah

HABITAT Open country with trees, woodland edge, grassland

SIZE 17¼–22½ in (44–57 cm)

This sprightly magpie has black and white plumage and a long tail; the many subspecies show slight variations in plumage, some having a pronounced green, purple or golden sheen. Insects, snails, slugs and spiders are the main foods, but grain, small mammals and carrion may also be taken. The magpie will fly up into a tree to take fruit, nuts and young birds. Some magpies remain in their breeding territory all year round usually in pairs or small groups, while others gather in communal roosts out of the breeding season.

The large, domed nest is made in a tree or bush by both members of a pair. The male feeds the female while she incubates the 5 to 8 eggs for 17 or 18 days.

Blue Jay *Cyanocitta cristata*

RANGE S.E. Canada, E. USA to Gulf of Mexico

HABITAT Woodland, city parks, gardens

SIZE 11¾ in (30 cm)

This noisy, colorful jay is mainly blue with black and white plumage on the wings and tail and black markings on the face. It feeds on the ground and in trees on nuts, seeds, grain, fruit, berries, insects and invertebrates, and the eggs and young of other birds. Seen in family parties in summer, blue jays gather in large groups in autumn, which often mob predators or intruders.

They nest in a tree or bush, and the female incubates the 2 to 6 eggs for 16 to 18 days. The male feeds her and the brood.

Eurasian Jay *Garrulus glandarius*

RANGE Europe to N. Africa; C. Asia to E. and S.E. Asia

HABITAT Forest, woodland, orchards, towns

SIZE 13¼ in (34 cm)

An extremely variable species over its range, the European jay generally has a pinkish-brown body, with brilliant wing patterns of blue and black bars. Alone or in pairs, it feeds in trees and on the ground on insects and small invertebrates and also on acorns, berries and grain.

The female lays 3 to 7 eggs in a nest made in a tree. The male feeds her while she incubates them for 16 to 19 days and feeds the brood until she can leave the nest to help him.

Green Jay *Cyanocorax yncas*

RANGE USA: S. Texas; through Mexico and Central and South America to Brazil and Bolivia

HABITAT Forest, woodland, thickets

SIZE 11¾ in (30 cm)

This bright green, yellow and blue bird has green tail feathers. The many subspecies show slight variations in plumage. Green jays live in pairs or small groups and eat mainly insects as well as acorns and seeds and the eggs and young of other birds.

The 3 to 5 eggs are laid in a nest in a tree or bush and are incubated by the female. Both parents tend the young.

Ceylon Magpie *Urocissa ornata*

RANGE Sri Lanka

HABITAT Forest, gardens

SIZE 18 in (46 cm)

The Ceylon magpie lives alone, in pairs or in small groups. It feeds in trees and on the ground on insects, invertebrates and fruit. The nest is made in a small tree. The female lays a clutch of between 3 and 5 eggs.

Piapiac *Ptilostomus afer*

RANGE Africa: Senegal to Nigeria, east to Ethiopia

HABITAT Open country, palm groves

SIZE 18 in (46 cm)

A slender, long-tailed bird, with a thick bill, the piapiac lives in flocks of 10 or more. It feeds mainly on the ground on insects and invertebrates, often following herds of large animals in order to pick up the insects they disturb; it also takes insects from the backs of large mammals and eats the fruit of the oil palm.

The nest is made in a palm or other tree, and the female lays a clutch of between 3 and 7 eggs.

BIRDS OF PARADISE, BUTCHERBIRDS, AUSTRALIAN MAGPIE AND CURRAWONGS

King of Saxony's Bird of Paradise

Pteridophora alberti

RANGE Mountains of New Guinea

HABITAT Rain forest up to 9,500 ft (2,850 m)

SIZE 9 in (23 cm)

The male King of Saxony's bird of paradise has two plumes, one extending from each side of its head, that are unique to it. These plumes are two or three times the body length and consist of wirelike shafts, bearing a series of horny plates The bird chooses a display site on a high branch, holds his head plumes up, and bounces up and down, while expanding and retracting his back feathers and hissing. The whole effect is quite spectacular. As the female approaches, the male sweeps the long head plumes in front of her and then follows her, and they mate.

The female bird is brownish-gray, with black-barred white underparts. The birds live in the middle and upper layers of the forest and feed on fruit.

Crinkle-collared Manucode *Manucodia chalybata*

RANGE New Guinea, Misoöl Island

HABITAT Rain forest

SIZE 14½ in (37 cm)

The crinkle-collared manucode is a glossy purplish-black bird, with curly green feathers adorning its head and neck. Male and female look alike and have none of the spectacular adornments which are associated with the other species of birds of paradise. They live in the middle to upper stories of the forest and feed on fruit.

These manucodes form monogamous pairs and nest on forked branches. The female is thought to lay 1 egg.

Blue Bird of Paradise *Paradisaea rudolphi* **VU**

RANGE Mountains of S.E. New Guinea

HABITAT Rain forest

SIZE 11 in (28 cm) excluding tail, which is 13½ in (34 cm) long

The male blue bird of paradise has a velvety black breast, long, lacy, flank plumes and distinctive tail feathers. These are narrow and straplike and play an important part in the display dance he performs to attract the much plainer female. The male hangs upside-down from a branch, with the flank plumes spread out and the tail straps held in curves. In this position, he swings to and fro making a grating call.

A nest is made by the female in a low tree, and she is thought to lay 1 egg.

King Bird of Paradise *Cicinnurus regius*

RANGE New Guinea; Yapen, Misoöl, Sulawati and Aru Islands

HABITAT Lowland rain forest

SIZE 12 in (30.5 cm) including tail (male)

A spectacular crimson bird, the king bird of paradise has two wirelike, lyre-shaped tail feathers, tipped with metallic green, and a fanlike plume at each shoulder. The female lacks the tail wires and has brown plumage, edged with chestnut and olive. These birds eat mainly on fruit at all levels of the forest. The male uses a horizontal branch as his display ground and spends much time there adopting display postures to attract a mate. He raises his tail wires, hangs upsidedown, and vibrates his wings.

The female makes her nest in a hole in a tree – the only bird of paradise to do so. She lays 2 eggs, which she is thought to incubate for about 12 days.

Ribbon-tailed Astrapia

Astrapia mayeri **VU**

RANGE Mountains of
C. New Guinea

HABITAT Rain forest

SIZE 4 ft (1.2 m) including tail of up
to 36 in (91.5 cm)

The spectacular ribbonlike central tail
feathers are the main identifying feature of
the male of this species, which is mainly black, with
patches of green iridescent plumage on the head and
throat. The tail feathers play a central role in the male's
courtship display, when they are twitched from side to side
to attract the attention of a female.

The female bird has a much shorter tail and glossy black,
green and brown plumage.

This species was one of the last birds of paradise to be
discovered, and was first described in 1939 and then only on
the basis of a pair of the tail feathers that were found in a
tribal headdress. It lives in a very restricted area of the
central highlands of New Guinea. It frequents the
branches of tall trees and feeds on fruit, insects, spiders
and small mammals and reptiles. The shallow, cup-
shaped nest is constructed on a base of leaves
from moss and vine tendrils.

Black Butcherbird

Cracticus quoyi

RANGE Australia:
Queensland, coast
of Northern Territory; New
Guinea, Yapen and Aru Islands

HABITAT Forest

SIZE 12½–14¼ in (32–36 cm)

A bold, often aggressive bird, the black
butcherbird feeds mostly on the ground, where
it hops along on its short legs. Using its sharp,
hooked bill, it tears up prey too large to be swallowed
whole, such as large insects (particularly grasshoppers)
and small vertebrates. Male and female look alike and
live alone or in small family groups.

A nest of twigs is made on a forked branch, and the
female lays 3 or 4 eggs.

Australian Magpie *Gymnorhina tibicen*

RANGE S. New Guinea, Australia, Tasmania;
introduced in New Zealand

HABITAT Open woodland, grassland, parks, gardens

SIZE 14¼–15¾ in (36–40 cm)

Although it roosts and nests in trees, the Australian magpie does
much of its feeding on the ground, searching for larvae, beetles
and grasshoppers. Fruit and vegetation also make up part of its
diet. Australian magpies are gregarious birds, and live in groups
consisting of two pairs of adults or a larger number of
birds, led by a dominant, polygamous male.
Males and females look more or less alike.

The nest is made in a tree,
and the female lays 3 eggs,
which she incubates for 20 to
21 days. She also does most of
the feeding of the young.

Pied Currawong *Strepera graculina*

RANGE Australia: Queensland to Victoria; Lord Howe Island

HABITAT Forest, clumps of trees in parks, suburban land

SIZE 17¾ in (45 cm)

Primarily an arboreal bird, the pied
currawong climbs trees
in search of insects,
larvae and fruit, it
will also eat the young and
eggs of other bird species. It
sometimes searches for insects on the
ground. These noisy, gregarious birds,
live in flocks. The name is derived from
their call. The female lays
3 or 4 eggs in a nest in a tree.

CUCKOO SHRIKES AND MINIVETS

Ground Cuckoo-shrike *Coracina maxima*

RANGE Australian interior

HABITAT Dry, open country

SIZE 13 in (33 cm)

The ground cuckoo-shrike is far more terrestrial than other cuckoo shrikes which only occasionally forage on the ground. A stout-legged bird, it walks and runs well as it searches for insects to eat. It usually lives in family groups.

The nest, usually placed in the fork of a tree, is made of grass, stems and rootlets, and spiders' webs may be used to bind the plant material together. It may sometimes be built on top of the old nest of another bird species. The female usually lays 2 or 3 eggs; more than one female may lay eggs in the same nest.

Slender-billed Cicadabird *Coracina tenuirostris*

RANGE Sulawesi to Solomon Islands, New Guinea, Australia

HABITAT Forest edge, grassland, mangroves

SIZE 10 in (25.5 cm)

Known as a cicadabird because of its high, shrill song, this bird is rather shy and is more often heard than seen; it is usually silent, however, outside the breeding season. Insects, such as

beetles, caterpillars and cicadas, are its main foods, and most are caught up in the trees.

The nest of the cicadabird is about 3 in (7.5 cm) across. It is made of twigs and spiders' webs, camouflaged with lichen and is usually placed on a horizontal, forked branch. The female lays 1 egg, and the male defends the nest and his territory against intruders. He feeds his mate while she incubates the egg.

Black-faced Cuckoo-Shrike *Coracina novaehollandiae*

RANGE India to S.E. Asia and Australia

HABITAT Light forest, gardens, suburbs, plantations

SIZE 13 in (33 cm)

A heavily built, largely gray bird, the male large cuckoo shrike has some black, shrikelike markings on its head. The female looks similar in most respects, but the markings on her head are dark gray.

Small groups of cuckoo shrikes forage for food, mainly fruit such as figs, insects and insect larvae high in the treetops. They sometimes dive to pick up food from the ground, or take insects in the air. Their flight is undulating and they land with a characteristic shuffling of wings. They maintain contact as they move with a rolling call and make a high-pitched, trilling call during displays.

Large cuckoo shrikes tend to return to the same breeding site, even the same branch, year after year. The nest is saucer-shaped and constructed from twigs and spiders' webs and is usually sited in the fork of a branch. The female lays a clutch of 2 or 3 eggs.

Bar-winged Flycatcher-Shrike *Hemipus picatus*

RANGE India, Sri Lanka, S.E. Asia, Sumatra, Borneo

HABITAT Woodland, forest, forest edge

SIZE 5 in (12.5 cm)

The bar-winged flycatcher shrike is a small cuckoo shrike, which pursues insects in the air as skilfully as a true flycatcher. It also finds food by hopping around the branches, gleaning insects from leaves, and may sometimes feed on the ground, although it is primarily a tree-living bird.

Small groups of about 6 birds usually live together out of the breeding season and may also join in mixed flocks. The male and female look similar, but the black plumage of the male is replaced by dark brown in the female in some races.

The shallow, saucer-shaped nest is built on a branch of a tree and is constructed from grass and rootlets, bound together with spiders' webs. Lichen is used to camouflage the outside of the nest, and the sitting bird appears to be on a clump of lichen rather than a nest. The female lays 2 or 3 eggs. Once hatched, the young birds sit still, with their eyes closed and their heads raised together, and can easily be mistaken by the casual observer for a spur of dead wood.

Red-shouldered Cuckoo-shrike

Campephaga phoenicea

RANGE Africa, south of the Sahara

HABITAT Forest, woodland

SIZE 8 in (20.5 cm)

Some races of this species have the distinctive red markings they are named for, but others have small yellow shoulder patches or none at all. Males have glossy black plumage, while females are predominantly olive-brown or gray with yellow-edged wings and tail. Restless, active birds, red-shouldered cuckoo shrike are always on the move in pairs or in parties of several species. They feed on caterpillars and insects, gleaned from foliage or found on the ground. Some insects may even be taken in the air.

A cup-shaped nest, constructed from moss and lichen bound together with spiders' webs, is built in the fork of a tree and the female lays a clutch of between 2 and 3 eggs. She incubates the eggs for about 20 days, and both parents then feed the newly hatched nestlings.

White-winged Triller

Lalage sueurii

RANGE Java, Lesser Sunda Islands, Sulawesi, Australia, New Guinea

HABITAT Open forest, woodland

SIZE 7 in (18 cm)

The white-winged triller makes its melodious calls as it flies from tree to tree taking insects from leaves and branches. Male and female differ in plumage, the female being largely brown, while the male is glossy black, gray and white.

Both partners of a breeding pair help to build a nest of plant material, usually situated in the fork of a branch. They both incubate the 1 to 3 eggs for about 14 days and feed the young.

Scarlet Minivet *Pericrocotus flammeus*

RANGE India, Sri Lanka, S. China, S.E. Asia to Philippines, Bali and Lombok

HABITAT Forest, woodland

SIZE 9 in (23 cm)

One of the 13 species of minivet, the scarlet minivet, with its bright plumage, is typical of the group. The male is red and black, while the female has dark gray and yellow plumage, distributed in the same manner. Both can be identified by the oval patch on each wing that is red in males and yellow in females. Strictly arboreal, scarlet minivets search among the treetops for large, soft-bodied insects to eat, often catching them in flight.

The shallow, cup-shaped nest is constructed on the branch of a tree from twigs, roots and grass stems, bound together with spiders' webs. A covering of lichen and fragments of bark camouflages the nest from predators. The female lays a clutch of 2 or 3 eggs and incubates them alone. Both parents feed and tend the young.

WOOD SWALLOWS, ORIOLES AND FANTAILS

White-breasted Wood Swallow

Artamus leucorynchus

RANGE Australia and New Guinea, Philippines, Andaman, Palau and Fijian Islands

HABITAT Woodland, mangroves

SIZE 6¾ in (17cm)

The white-breasted wood swallow lives in groups of 10 or more birds, which often huddle together on a branch, waiting for insect prey. They return to the perch to eat a catch. If there is a shortage of flying insects, these birds eat ground insects and larvae.

Both members of a pair help to build a cup-shaped nest in the fork of a tree, in a hole in a tree or in an old magpie-lark's nest. Both parents incubate the 3 or 4 eggs for about 19 days.

White-browed Wood Swallow

Artamus superciliosus

RANGE Australia: breeds Victoria, New South Wales to S.E. Queensland; winters throughout continent

HABITAT Arid scrub, savanna

SIZE 7–7¾ in (18–20 cm)

The nomadic white-browed wood swallow disperses over much of the continent out of the breeding season, often moving in mixed flocks with other species of wood swallow. They perch in groups on branches and fly out to catch insects in the air. Females have less distinct "eyebrow" streaks than males.

The nest is built from sticks and grass in a tree or on a tree stump. Both parents incubate the 2 or 3 eggs for about 16 days.

Bornean Bristlehead *Pityriasis gymnocephala* **LR:nt**

RANGE Borneo

HABITAT Lowland forest to 4,000 ft (1,200 m), peat swamp, forest

SIZE 10 in (25.5 cm)

This rare bird has a large, extremely heavy, hooked bill and relatively short tail feathers, which gives it a top-heavy look. These self-confident birds are ponderous fliers, which keep to the middle layers of the forest. They eat insects and their larvae, mainly beetles, grasshoppers and cockroaches, noisily snapping them up with their large bills.

Golden Oriole *Oriolus oriolus*

RANGE Breeds in Europe, as far north as S. Finland, Sweden and Britain, N. Africa, Asia; winters in Africa and N.W. India

HABITAT Forest, woodland, orchards

SIZE 9½ in (24 cm)

The golden oriole frequents the treetops, feeding on insects and fruit. Even the brightly plumaged male is seldom seen. Females and juveniles are duller with yellowish-green upperparts and lighter, grayish-white underparts. Golden orioles rarely descend to the ground, and their flight is swift and undulating. Although they may remain in family groups for a while after breeding, they usually live alone or in pairs.

The courting male chases the female at top speed through the branches. She does most of the work of building the hammocklike nest, which is suspended by its rim from a forked branch. It is mainly the female partner that incubate the 3 or 4 eggs for 14 to 15 days.

Figbird *Sphecotheres viridis*

RANGE Lesser Sunda Islands, S.E. New Guinea, Cai Islands, W., N., and E. Australia

HABITAT Forest, savanna, fruiting trees

SIZE 11 in (28 cm)

Although they differ strikingly in appearance, all forms of *Sphecotheres*, from Timor to southern New Guinea and New South Wales, are now regarded as conspecific under the name *S. viridis*. Females have duller plumage than males. An arboreal bird, the figbird moves in noisy flocks, eating figs and other fruit and insects caught in the air.

The saucer-shaped nest is built of twigs and plant tendrils on a high branch. Usually 3 eggs are laid.

DICRURINAE: FANTAIL, MONARCH AND DRONGO SUBFAMILY

This subfamily of insect-eating birds has three distinct groups or tribes. The 42 species of fantails are arboreal birds found mainly in Australasia but with some species in Asia. Their common name comes from their habit of continually spreading and wagging their tails as they move through low vegetation. They catch insects either on the wing or by flushing out prey using the fantail when moving through vegetation and holding it down using a foot.

Monarchs are boldly plumaged birds of forest areas that occur from central Asia and northern China, south to Australia and the western Pacific islands, and in Africa. The 98 species also include paradise flycatchers, Australian flycatchers, magpie-larks and the silktail. Most species are arboreal flycatchers, some species dart out from perches to catch insect prey, while others search the foliage of the trees.

Drongos occur in Africa and from south Asia to Australia. The 24 species are tree-dwellers with dark plumage, pointed wings and square or forked tails, often with long, decorative feathers. Drongos spend much of their time perched, on the look out for insect prey, which they catch in the air. They are skilful, but not sustained, fliers. Males and females look alike, but females are usually slightly smaller.

Yellow-bellied Fantail
Rhipidura hypoxantha

RANGE Himalayas to S.W. China; northern S.E. Asia: Myanmar, Thailand, Laos

HABITAT Forest, rhododendron thickets

SIZE 5 in (13 cm)

The yellow-bellied fantail has bright yellow underparts and distinctive white tips to some of the tail feathers. Male and female birds look similar, but the male has black, masklike markings on the face, which are dark olive-brown in the female.

A lively, restless little bird, this fantail frequents the undergrowth up to the lower levels of the forest canopy, where it prances around with its tail fanned out, foraging for insects. It also feeds on tiny insects, which it takes in the air during brief, aerobatic flights, and may flush insects out of vegetation with its spread wings.

The nest is made the same width as the horizontal branch on which it is sited, which provides a measure of camouflage. It is built from moss covered with lichen and spiders' webs and lined with hair and feathers. The female lays 3 eggs.

Willie Wagtail *Rhipidura leucophrys*

RANGE Australia, Tasmania, New Guinea, Solomon Islands, the Moluccas

HABITAT Forest edge to desert edge, parks, gardens, cultivated land

SIZE 7¾ in (20 cm)

A common, adaptable bird, the willie wagtail has learned to take advantage of man-made environments. Male and female birds look alike, and their black and white plumage gives them a resemblance to the European pied wagtail, hence the common name. The willie wagtail generally lives alone, outside the breeding season, and finds food on the ground as well as in flight. It also sometimes sits on the backs of cattle and feeds on the insects disturbed by their hoofs.

The nest is made of grass bark strips or plant fiber bound tightly with spiders' webs. It is usually built on a horizontal branch, but may be made almost anywhere above ground. The female lays 4 eggs.

Rufous Fantail *Rhipidura rufifrons*

RANGE Lesser Sunda and W. Papuan Islands, N. and E. Australia, coastal areas of New Guinea, Louisiade Archipelago, Solomon and Santa Cruz Islands, Micronesia

HABITAT Forest, mangroves

SIZE 6½ in (16.5 cm)

With its tail fanned out, this flycatcher flies with great speed and dexterity through the undergrowth, catching insects in flight and picking them off the foliage. Although it is mainly a tree-living bird, it also feeds on the ground.

A pear-shaped nest, made of coarse plant material bound together with spiders' webs, is built on a thin, forked branch as much as 30 ft (9 m) from the ground. Both parents incubate the clutch of 2 eggs for about 15 days and feed the young. The young fantails are able to fly about 15 days after hatching out. Breeding birds may produce two to five broods a year, depending on the abundance of food.

MONARCH, MAGPIE-LARK AND SILKTAIL

Black-naped Monarch
Hypothymis azurea

RANGE India, S. China, S.E. Asia to Lesser
Sunda Islands and Philippines

HABITAT Forest, scrub, bamboo, cultivated land

SIZE 6½ in (16.5cm)

The male black-naped monarch has bright blue
plumage, with a little patch of black feathers
on the nape of the neck that are erected when
the bird is excited. There is also a narrow black
band across his chest. The female looks similar to the male
but has grayish brown plumage on the upperparts and lacks
the black nape and chest markings.

This flycatcher tends to perch in higher trees than other
species and makes agile looping flights after insect prey; it also
forages in undergrowth and on the ground. When a large insect
is caught the bird holds it down with its foot and tears it apart
before eating it. Usually seen alone or in pairs, the black-naped
monarch is an active bird, constantly on the move.

The neat, cup-shaped nest is built on a forked branch, to
which it is bound with spiders' webs, or in a bush, sapling or
bamboo clump. The female bird does most of the work, using
grass and bark for the cup and covering the outside with moss,
spiders' webs and egg-cases; the male attends her closely
throughout the nest-building. She lays 3 or 4 eggs, which she
incubates for 15 or 16 days. Both parents tend the young.

White-tailed Crested
Flycatcher *Trochocercus albonotatus*

RANGE Africa: Uganda, W. Kenya
to Malawi, Zambia, Zimbabwe

HABITAT Highland forest

SIZE 4 in (10 cm)

The white-tailed crested flycatcher has black,
gray and white plumage. The sexes look
alike. The bird eats insects, making short,
jerky flights after prey or foraging over
foliage. The male displays to his mate,
hopping around her with his tail raised
and wings trailing. The nest is moss, bound with cobwebs,
woven around a fork of a low tree. The female lays 2 eggs.

Asian Paradise Flycatcher *Terpsiphone paradisi*

RANGE Turkestan to N.E. China; S.E. Asia, Indonesia

HABITAT Open forest, mangroves, gardens, cultivated land

SIZE 8¾ in (22.5 cm)

The male Asian
paradise flycatcher is a
beautiful bird, with
extremely long central
tail feathers, which
add 10 in (25.5 cm) or more to
his length. Males occur in two color
phases – white and rufous. The white
male has white body and tail plumage, with
a black head, crest and throat, the rufous
male is more variable, according to race, but
has rufous tail, back and wings. The female is
similar to the rufous male, but lacks the crest
and long tail feathers.

Alone, or sometimes in pairs or mixed hunting
parties, the paradise flycatcher frequents the higher
branches of trees, flitting from perch to perch. Its
flight is swift and it makes brief sallies from a perch to
catch insect prey, returning to the same tree or to
another to consume the item. It may also flush out
insects on the ground. Flies, dragonflies, beetles, moths
and butterflies are its main prey.

The courting male displays to his mate by arching his tail
streamers gracefully, while singing and beating his wings.
Both sexes help to build the nest, which is a deep, inverted
cone, made in a horizontal forked branch of a tree often near or
overhanging water. The 3 or 4 eggs are incubated mostly by the
female for 15 or 16 days; unusually for such a decorative bird,
the male may sometimes assist and sits with his long tail hanging
out behind him. The male bird also helps to tend the nestlings.

Yellow-breasted Boatbill

Machaerirhynchus flaviventer

RANGE Australia: N.E. Queensland;
New Guinea and adjacent islands

HABITAT Rain forest

SIZE 4¾ in (12 cm)

The broad, flat bill is the distinctive feature of this flycatcher and the reason for its common name. Male and female differ slightly in appearance – the female has yellowish-olive upperparts, with areas of brownish-black. She has fewer yellow and more white markings than the male.

A tree-living bird, the yellow-breasted boat-bill gleans insects from the foliage, moving busily from branch to branch, mainly keeping to the top of the tree canopy, and making soft trills to maintain contact. Short flights may be made in order to catch prey on the wing.

The shallow, cup-shaped nest is constructed from strips of bark, which are bound together with spiders' webs and decorated with lichen to provide camouflage. The interior of the nest is lined with vine tendrils. It is usually built fairly high up in the forest canopy on a slender, forked branch. The female lays a clutch of 2 eggs.

Spectacled Monarch

Monarcha trivirgatus

RANGE E. Australia,
New Guinea, the Moluccas,
Timor, Flores

HABITAT Wet forest,
mangroves, woodland

SIZE 6 in (15 cm)

Both the male and female spectacled monarchs have black, masklike markings on the face that are the origin of this bird's common name.

A solitary, arboreal species, the spectacled monarch frequents low, dense vegetation in wooded areas, where it moves swiftly yet quietly, hunting for its insect prey. It may sometimes feed on the ground.

The cup-shaped nest is constructed from bark strips, lined with spiders' webs, and is usually situated low in a bush or sapling. The female lays a clutch of 2 eggs.

Magpie-Lark

Grallina cyanoleuca

RANGE Australia,
S. New Guinea

HABITAT Open woodland,
parks

SIZE 9¾–11 in
(25–28 cm)

A distinctive black and white bird, the magpie-lark spends much of its time on the ground, feeding on insects. It is not shy and is common near human settlements and by roadsides. Many of the insects it consumes are considered pests by man, and it also feeds on the freshwater snails that harbor the liver fluke, so often transmitted to cattle and sheep.

The female differs from the male in having a white throat and forehead and lacks the male's patches of white plumage above or below her eyes.

Magpie-larks pair for life and tend to nest in the same tree year after year, several pairs nesting near one another. The bowl-shaped nest is made from mud lined with grass and is situated on a branch. The female lays 3 to 5 eggs, which are incubated by both parents. The young are also fed by both parents and are independent at 4 weeks.

Silktail *Lamprolia victoriae* **VU**

RANGE Fiji

HABITAT Mature mountain forest

SIZE 4¾ in (12 cm)

The silktail is a striking bird, with dark velvety plumage, scattered with metallic blue spangles, and a white rump. It forages for its insect prey on the foliage of the forest understory and also goes down to the ground in order to find food. This bird is swift and agile in flight, it darts between the trees and may also pursue slow-flying insects.

The nest is made in a tree, of fibers, rootlets, vines and slivers of bark and is lined with feathers. The female lays a single egg.

DRONGOS, IORAS AND BUSH-SHRIKES

Fork-tailed Drongo *Dicrurus adsimilis*
RANGE Africa, south of the Sahara
SIZE 9–10 in (23–25.5 cm)

A typical drongo, with its black plumage and deeply forked tail, this bird is a common inhabitant of almost any type of woodland, including coconut plantations. It darts out from a perch to catch insects and then returns to the same perch; a wide range of insects is eaten, including butterflies. This drongo is fast and highly maneuverable in flight.

The nest, woven from plant stems, is made on a forked branch of a tree, and there are usually 3 eggs. Like all drongos, this bird is extremely aggressive in defence of its nest and will chase away even much larger birds.

Greater Racquet-tailed Drongo
Dicrurus paradiseus
RANGE India, Sri Lanka, Andaman and Nicobar Islands, S.W. China, Hainan, S.E. Asia, Sumatra, Java, Borneo
HABITAT Forest, cultivated land
SIZE 13 in (33 cm)

The elongated, racquet-tipped, outer tail feathers may add another 12½ in (32 cm) or more to the total length of this bird. The female has slightly shorter tail streamers, but otherwise resembles the male. This drongo is also identified by its prominent crest which is smaller in young birds.

A bold, noisy bird, it hunts for its insect prey mainly at dusk, when it darts out from the treetops to seize creatures, such as moths termites and dragonflies. It also picks larvae off tree trunks and branches and sometimes eats lizards and even small birds. Nectar from flowers is another important item of diet.

The nest is a loosely constructed cup, made on a forked branch of a tree. There is usually a clutch of 3 eggs, and both parents are believed to incubate the clutch and feed the young. The parents are extremely pugnacious in their defence of the nest and their young.

Pygmy Drongo *Chaetorhynchus papuensis*
RANGE New Guinea
HABITAT Forest on mountain slopes
SIZE 8 in (20.5 cm)

Rather different from other drongos and the only species in its genus, the pygmy drongo has a heavier, more hooked bill than other species and twelve, instead of ten, tail feathers. It perches to watch for insect prey and then darts out to seize it in the air. This unusual drongo can be mistaken for a monarch flycatcher, which it resembles.

AEGITHININAE: IORA SUBFAMILY

The 4 species of ioras are small, arboreal birds. They are found from south Asia to Indonesia and the Philippines. Ioras feed mainly on insects but may also eat nectar.

Common Iora *Aegithina tiphia*
RANGE India, Sri Lanka to S.E. Asia, Java, Sumatra, Borneo
HABITAT Open country and gardens up to 5,600 ft (1,700 m)
SIZE 5 in (12.5 cm)

There are considerable variations in coloration in this species, according to sex and season. The male, in winter, tends to lose almost all of his black feathers, and the yellow ones become paler. The female is green above and yellow below throughout the year, merely becoming paler in winter. Both sexes have soft, abundant feathers on their rumps. Ioras are often found in gardens, hopping about among the branches of trees and shrubs. They eat insects (such as ants and beetles) and seeds.

In the breeding season, the male displays by fluffing out his feathers, particularly those on the rump, so he looks like a ball, then spiralling down to a perch making a croaking noise, rather like a frog. The nest is made from soft grass covered in spiders' webs, in which 2 to 4 eggs are laid.

MALACONTHINAE: BUSH-SHRIKE, HELMET-SHRIKE AND VANGA SUBFAMILY

There are two groups or tribes within this subfamily of insect-eaters – the first is the bush-shrikes and the second is helmet-shrikes and vangas.

Bush-shrikes are found in a wide range of habitats throughout Africa and the southern Arabian peninsula. They generally hunt for their insect prey among leaves and other vegetation. The 48 species in this tribe include puffbacks, gonoleks and tchagras.

The second tribe includes 58 species of helmet-shrikes and vangas. Helmet-shrikes are arboreal shrikes that occur in open forests, savanna and scrub in southern and Southeast Asia. They include batis and wattle-eyes. Some hunt in vegetation for insects, while others catch insects on the wing. Vangas are found in Madagascar and include the coral-billed nuthatch.

Black-backed Puffback *Dryoscopus cubla*

RANGE Africa: Kenya, west and south to Angola and South Africa

HABITAT Open woodland, gardens, scrub

SIZE 6 in (15 cm)

There are 4 races of black-backed puffback. The race that is illustrated here is found in South Africa, and the other 3 occur in the rest of the range. The female is duller and paler than the male, with pale yellow eyes.

When excited this bird puffs up the feathers on its back and rump until it looks like a ball. These sociable little birds are usually found in pairs or in small parties along with other bird species, hunting among the leaves of shrubs and trees for insect larvae. They often catch insects in flight and, during the breeding season, will also eat the eggs and young of small birds.

The cup-shaped nest is constructed from bark fiber and rootlets. It is well hidden and tightly bound to the fork of a tree with spiders' webs. The female lays a clutch of 2 or 3 eggs.

Crimson-breasted Gonolek *Laniarius atrococcineus*

RANGE Parts of southern Africa

HABITAT Thorn veld, acacia bush

SIZE 8 in (20.5 cm)

Surprisingly these strikingly marked birds are not easy to see in the dense cover of the thornbushes where they prefer to perch,

but they are not timid by nature and as soon as they come out into the open, they are conspicuous. Male and female look alike, but the juvenile is duller in appearance, with distinct crimson feathers found only under the tail.

Crimson-breasted shrikes usually travel in pairs, keeping in touch by calling, the male with a clear, deep whistle that the female answers with a throaty, growling sound. They feed mainly on insects.

The nest is a shallow cup, made from grass, plant fibers and dry bark, and is sited in the forked branch of a thorn tree. The female lays a clutch of 2 or 3 eggs.

Gray-headed Bush-shrike *Malaconotus blanchoti*

RANGE Africa, south of the Sahara (not extreme south)

HABITAT Woodland, acacia trees, often near water (East Africa)

SIZE 10 in (25.5 cm)

Despite their size and quite bright coloration, these birds are not easily seen in the thick foliage of the trees and bushes they frequent. Most often they can be located by their calls – either a brisk, chattering sound or a two- or three-note whistle. They have big hooked bills and, in South Africa, are known to take prey as large as mice and lizards, which they find among leaf litter on the ground. Male and female look alike.

The conspicuous nest is built close to the ground. It is either a rough heap of grass and leaves or a platform of twigs with an inner cup, in which 2 or 3, or, rarely 4, eggs are laid.

HELMET SHRIKES, VANGAS, AND NEW ZEALAND WATTLE BIRDS

White/Long-crested Helmet Shrike *Prionops plumata*

RANGE Africa: S. Ethiopia to Angola, Namibia, N. South Africa

HABITAT Open bush country, woodland

SIZE 8 in (20.5 cm)

The tame and gregarious white helmet shrikes live in small flocks of 8 to 12 birds. They move close together through the lower branches of trees and bushes, where they forage for insects often with birds of other species. The sexes look alike. A number of birds will share the brooding and feeding at a single nest and 3 or 4 eggs are laid.

Black-headed Batis *Batis minor*

RANGE Africa: Sudan to Somalia, south to Cameroon and Angola

HABITAT Open woodland, bush

SIZE 4 in (10 cm)

A small, rather stumpy flycatcher, the batis can erect the plumage on its back, making itself appear round and fluffy. The sexes look alike in most respects, but the female lacks the male's black head plumage and has a dark chestnut band on the chest. These birds move in pairs, searching foliage for insects or making brief hunting flights.

The nest is made of fibers and lichen, bound with spiders' webs, and is usually placed in a forked branch of a tree. The female lays 2 or 3 eggs.

Common/Brown-throated Wattle-eye *Platysteira cyanea*

RANGE W., C. and N.E. Africa

HABITAT Forest, woods, crops

SIZE 5 in (13 cm)

Distinctive red wattles over the eyes make the common wattle-eye easily recognizable. Wattle-eyes behave more like warblers than flycatchers, foraging in pairs over foliage for insect prey. In noisy, chattering flocks they make some seasonal migrations.

The cup-shaped nest is made of fine grass, plant fibers and lichen and is bound to a forked branch with spiders' webs. The female lays 2 eggs.

Maroon-breasted Philentoma

Philentoma velata

RANGE Malaysia, Sumatra, Java, Borneo

HABITAT Forest

SIZE 8 in (20.5 cm)

A noisy, active bird, the maroon-breasted philentoma frequents the lower to middle layers of the forest, often perching on low branches, vines and creepers. It catches all its prey on the wing and does not forage on foliage. It normally lives in pairs, and both sexes have loud, harsh calls. Male and female differ slightly in plumage: the female is a darker blue than the male and lacks his maroon chest patch. Nearly always found near water, these flycatchers love to bathe.

The nest is made on a forked branch of a tree.

Coral-billed Nuthatch

Hypositta corallirostris

RANGE E. Madagascar

HABITAT Humid forest

SIZE 5 in (13 cm)

The coral-billed nuthatch has been a taxonomical problem for ornithologists. It feeds like a treecreeper and looks somewhat like a nuthatch, but more recently it has been regarded as a close, but highly aberrant, relative of the vangas. A brightly colored little bird, it clings with its feet to the bark on the upper part of tree trunks, while it searches diligently in cracks and crevices for insects to eat. The female and young are blue above, with gray underparts.

American Robin *Turdus migratorius*

RANGE N. America, Mexico, Guatemala

HABITAT Open woodland, forest edge, gardens, city parks

SIZE 9–11 in (23–28 cm)

The American robin lives in urban areas. The coloration varies. In the breeding season, the male is gray above, with a black head and tail and reddish breast. The female is duller, with a gray head and tail. Robins feed on insects, earthworms, fruit and berries.

Some robins winter in the northern states, but generally they are migratory, breeding north of the Gulf Coast. The nest is a cup of mud, enclosed by twigs, and stems and lined with grass. The 3 to 6 eggs are incubated for 12 to 14 days.

Eurasian Blackbird *Turdus merula*

RANGE Europe, N. Africa, parts of Asia, introduced in New Zealand, Australia

HABITAT Forest, woodland, scrub, gardens, parks

SIZE 10 in (25.5 cm)

The blackbird finds the short grass of lawns and parks ideal for foraging for insects and worms. It also eats many kinds of fruit and berries. It spends a lot of time on the ground, but it finds a prominent perch from which to sing. The male is black, with a yellowish-orange bill and eye-ring. The female has dark brown plumage with paler underparts.

A variety of nest sites is used. The female builds the nest, which has an outer layer of plant stems, twigs and leaves covering the inner cup of mud and plant material and is lined with fine grass or dead leaves. She lays up to 9 eggs at daily intervals and incubates them for 12 to 15 days. Both parents feed the young in the nest and for a further 3 weeks.

Olive Thrush *Turdus olivaceus*

RANGE Africa, south of the Sahara

HABITAT Forest, cultivated land

SIZE 9½ in (24 cm)

Several races of olive thrush, which vary in coloration, occur over its range. Male and female look alike, but juveniles have streaked upperparts and dusky spots on underparts. This thrush has taken well to life in urban gardens. Much of its food is found by scratching around on the ground to uncover insects and invertebrates such as snails and worms. It also eats fruit.

The courting male puffs himself up, spreads his tail, then shuffles around the female with his wings trailing. The nest is made of grass, on a foundation of twigs, roots and earth, and is situated on a branch, tree stump or bush. The 2 or 3 eggs are incubated for about 14 days.

Austral Thrush *Turdus falcklandii*

RANGE S. America: S. Argentina, S. Chile; Falkland and Juan Fernandez Islands

HABITAT Open country with shrubs

SIZE 11–11½ in (28–29 cm)

The southern counterpart of the robin of North America, the austral thrush is common on both sides of the Andes up to about 6,600 ft (2,000 m). It digs for earthworms and other invertebrates on grassland and in damp places. It also eats fruit.

The cup-shaped nest is made of twigs, bound with grass and mud, and is usually concealed in dense vegetation. Females produce two or three clutches a season, each of 2 or 3 eggs.

Island Thrush *Turdus poliocephalus*

RANGE Islands from Christmas Island through Indonesia, New Guinea to New Caledonia, Fiji and Samoa

HABITAT Forest edge

SIZE 9–10 in (23–25.5 cm)

There may be 50 or more forms of island thrush, all varying slightly in appearance, some found on only one island or on a small group of islands. Most males have largely black plumage, and females look similar, but usually duller, in color. Generally a shy, solitary bird the island thrush takes refuge in trees but feeds on the ground in the open, on plant matter, such as seeds and fruit, and on a few insects.

The female normally lays 1 egg in a nest on a bush or rocky ledge.

THRUSHES, OLD WORLD FLYCATCHERS AND CHATS

Eastern Bluebird *Sialia sialis*

RANGE N. America: S. Canada, east of the Rockies to Gulf coast, USA;
Mexico, Central America

HABITAT Open country, farmland, gardens, parks

SIZE 6½–7½ in (16.5–19 cm)

A beautiful bird, the male eastern bluebird has distinctive, bright blue plumage on its upperparts and a chestnut breast and a melodious song. The female looks similar, but has paler, duller plumage. The juvenile is mainly brown with a mottled white and brown chest.

This bluebird often perches in a hunched posture on wires and fences, but takes most of its insect prey on the ground. Berries are also an important component of its diet, particularly in winter. Flocks often form in autumn and winter and several birds may roost together.

The male bluebird performs flight displays in order to court his mate and once a pair bond is made both partners build a nest from grass, twigs and other plant material, lined with hair, fine grass and feathers. The nest is situated in a natural hole in a tree or stump, in an abandoned woodpecker hole, or even in a bird box. Competition for nest sites has caused some decline in recent years and nest boxes are increasingly important for conservation of bluebird numbers.

The female lays between 3 tand 7 eggs, usually 4 or 5, which she incubates for 13 to 15 days, sometimes with assistance from her mate. The young chicks are fed by both of the parents and leave the nest about 15 to 20 days after they hatch. There are usually two broods produced in a season. Some northern populations of bluebirds migrate south for the winter.

Andean Solitaire
Myadestes ralloides

RANGE South America: Colombia
and Venezuela
south through the Andes to Ecuador,
Peru and Bolivia

HABITAT Mountain forest

SIZE 7 in (18 cm)

The shy, secretive Andean solitaire usually lives between altitudes of 3,000 and 15,000 ft (900 and 4,500 m). It is an excellent songster and sings more or less throughout the year in a pure, clear voice. True to its name, the solitaire tends to live alone for much of the time, but birds are also found in pairs. Its bill is rather short and wide, and it feeds on fruit and insects.

A nest is made on the ground or in a tree, and about 3 eggs are laid and incubated for 12 or 13 days.

White-browed/Blue Shortwing
Brachypteryx montana

RANGE E. Nepal to W. and S. China, south to S.E. Asia,
Indonesia and Philippines

HABITAT Forest undergrowth

SIZE 6 in (15 cm)

The male of this species is a distinctive little bird, with dark blue plumage and conspicuous, long white eyebrows; females have brownish plumage, with rusty-red markings on the forehead and indistinct eyebrows. In some areas, males are colored like females but with white eyebrows. Shy, retiring birds they skulk around in the densest undergrowth, searching for insects, especially beetles, and usually staying on or close to the ground.

The globular nest is made on a tree trunk or rock face, and the female lays 3 eggs.

Fire-crested Alethe *Alethe castanea*

RANGE Africa: Nigeria to Zaire and Uganda
HABITAT Lowland forest
SIZE 7 in (18 cm)

One of 6 species of alethe living in Africa, the fire-crested alethe is a bird of dense forest and shady undergrowth. Although it does not eat ants, it follows army ants as they march through the forest in order to catch the other insects that flee from their path.

Male and female birds look alike, both with dark-brown plumage and an orange streak of feathers along the crown. When the bird becomes excited, it erects this crest, while spreading out its tail.

The cup-shaped nest is made of moss and roots, lined with soft rootlets, and is situated in a tree stump or among heaps of debris on the forest floor. The female lays 2 or 3 eggs.

MUSCICAPINAE: OLD WORLD FLYCATCHER AND CHAT SUBFAMILY

This large subfamily of the family Muscicapidae includes 270 species of insect-eating songbirds. The 115 species of flycatchers all occur in the Old World, with the greatest diversity in Africa, Asia and Australasia. Some are brightly plumaged, others are dull, and flycatchers have diversified into a wide range of body forms and habits to fit different niches. Males and females look alike in some species and differ in others.

The "typical" flycatchers, which include some examples that occur in Europe, have a flat, wide beak, the base of which is surrounded by prominent bristles. Their method of insect capture is extremely characteristic – the feeding bird sits on a perch in a good vantage position for observing prey. If an insect passes, the bird launches itself into the air for a brief, agile, hunting flight and deftly captures the prey in its bill; it takes the prey back to its perch to eat. Some birds, of course, do use other methods of catching prey and feed on the ground or on foliage.

The 155 species of chats are found in Eurasia south to Indonesia, New Guinea, and the Philippines, and in Africa. One species, the Northern wheatear, also occurs in Alaska and Canada. Chats are thrushlike birds that live in a wide range of habitats from woodland to the sides of rivers to semidesert. Most feed on insects which are caught with their thin bills in flight or on the ground after swooping down from a perch. The chat subfamily includes redstarts, wheatears, robins, and nightingales.

Spotted Flycatcher

Muscicapa striata

RANGE Europe: Scandinavia southeast to S.W. Siberia and south to Mediterranean countries; N. Africa to C. Asia; winters tropical Africa and S.W. Asia
HABITAT Forest edge, woodland, scrub, gardens, parks
SIZE 5½ in (14 cm)

The spotted flycatcher feeds in the manner which is typical of its group, perching in exposed spots and making swift aerial sallies after insects. While perched, it constantly flicks its wings and tail. Male and female look alike, both have mainly grayish-brown plumage.

The female does most of the work of nest-building, making a neat structure of moss, bark and fibers, lined with rootlets and feathers. The nest may be in a variety of sites, such as on a ledge, in a cavity or tree fork or on a wall or rock. Both parents incubate the clutch of between 4 tand 6 eggs for 12 to 14 days and tend the young. Breeding pairs often produce two broods of chicks in a season.

Rufous-tailed Jungle Flycatcher

Rhinomyias ruficauda

RANGE Philippines, Borneo
HABITAT Forest
SIZE 5½ in (14 cm)

A rather rare bird, the rufous-tailed jungle flycatcher frequents dense undergrowth, where it feeds on insects and spiders. Much of its food is gleaned from foliage, but it also makes swift flights into the air to catch winged insects.

The subspecies of this bird vary slightly in coloration, but all have the distinctive chestnut tail. The female looks similar to the male in most respects.

The breeding habits of this species are not known.

OLD WORLD FLYCATCHERS AND CHATS CONTINUED

Blue-throated Flycatcher *Cyornis rubeculoides*

RANGE Himalayas through northern S.E. Asia to China; winters south of range

HABITAT Forest, gardens

SIZE 5½ in (14 cm)

The blue-throated flycatcher lives in well-wooded areas with plenty of undergrowth. It makes aerial dashes after insect prey, but hardly ever returns to the same perch, or even the same tree, to consume the catch. It may also drop down to the ground to find food and may flush out a concealed cricket or grasshopper with its open wings. Male and female differ in plumage, the female having mainly olive-brown and black feathers instead of the distinctive blue of the male.

The nest is made in a hollow in a mossy bank, in a rock crevice or in a hole in a tree or bamboo stem. The female lays 3 to 5 eggs, which both birds incubate for 11 or 12 days.

Pale Flycatcher *Bradornis pallidus*

RANGE Africa, south of the Sahara

HABITAT Woodland, coastal scrub, gardens, maize fields

SIZE 6–7 in (15–18 cm)

The pale flycatcher has largely grayish-brown plumage and is less conspicuous than many flycatchers. Juveniles have some streaked and spotted plumage. In pairs or small, loosely knit groups, they forage on the ground for much of their food, such as spiders and termites, but also catch flies and moths in the air. They are quiet, making only occasional twittering calls.

Breeding begins at the start of, or just before, the rainy season. The small neat, cup-shaped nest is made from rootlets and is sited on a forked branch of a tree or bush. The female lays a clutch of 2 or 3 eggs. Families remain together for a prolonged period, and there is some evidence that birds other than the parents help to rear broods.

Common Stonechat *Saxicola torquata*

RANGE Europe, Africa, W. and C. Asia

HABITAT Moors, fields, hill scrub, agricultural land

SIZE 5 in (13 cm)

The plump little stonechat is a lively, restless bird. It seldom moves on the ground, but flies fast and perches in exposed spots, such as on a post or on top of a bush, to watch for insect prey. It also eats plant matter and grain. The female has paler, browner plumage than the male and her white markings are less distinct.

The breeding season begins between late March and early June, depending on area. The male displays to the female by spreading his wings and tail to show off his markings. The nest is usually made by the female from coarse grass, moss and plant stems, lined with hair, fine grass or feathers. It is sited in an open area on the ground, under cover of a bush or actually in a bush. The female lays 5 or 6 eggs, which she incubates for about 14 days, sometimes assisted by the male. The young remain in the nest for 12 or 13 days, being fed on insects by both parents. Some northern populations may migrate south in winter.

Northern Wheatear *Oenanthe oenanthe*

RANGE Europe, N.W. Africa, W. and C. Asia, Arctic North America; winters mainly in Africa

HABITAT Open country, moors, tundra, heaths

SIZE 5½ in (14 cm)

A widely distributed species, this is the only wheatear to have become established in the New World. In summer breeding plumage, the male has a grayish crown, black marks on the cheeks and a white stripe above each eye. Both sexes have distinctive white rumps, but the female is brownish and buff. In winter the male resembles the female.

Primarily a ground dweller, the wheatear finds much of its food, such as insects, spiders, centipedes and small mollusks, on

the ground. It flits from one perch to another and may sometimes fly up to catch an insect on the wing.

In display, the male reveals his white rump to the female and dances with wings outspread. The nest is made in open country in a hole on the ground, in a rock or wall, or in debris such as a can or drainpipe. The female lays a clutch of 5 or 6 eggs, occasionally up to 8, which are incubated for about 14 days. She does most of the incubation, although the male may assist. Both of the parents feed the young, which remain in the nest for about 15 days.

Oriental Magpie Robin *Copsychus saularis*

RANGE India, S. China, S.E. Asia, much of Indonesia, east to the Philippines

HABITAT Brush, gardens, cultivated land

SIZE 8½ in (21.5 cm)

A widespread, common bird, the male magpie robin has distinctive black and white plumage. The female looks similar but she has dark-gray instead of black plumage. This species

often lives near human habitation and feeds in the open, usually near or on the ground. The magpie robin is a good mimic, and it imitates other birds, but it also has a loud and melodious song of its own, which it uses to announce its presence. Insects, such as crickets, beetles and ants, are its main foods.

The large, cup-shaped nest is constructed from fine roots and is situated among tree roots or branches or in any protected hole. The female lays a clutch of between 3 and 6 eggs, usually 5, which both parents incubate for 12 or 13 days.

White-crowned Forktail *Enicurus leschenaulti*

RANGE Sikkim to S. China and Hainan, S.E. Asia to Bali

HABITAT Rocky streams in forest

SIZE 8–11 in (20.5–28 cm)

Both male and female white-crowned forktails have similar, sharply contrasting black and white plumage and long tails. These long-legged birds frequent streams and feed on aquatic insects, which they take from the water surface or the stream bed. They wade from stone to stone, searching for food and occasionally dipping under the water in pursuit of prey.

Their cup-shaped nest is built from moss and rootlets. It is always built in a damp area, often near a stream, and is generally sited on a rock, in a crevice or among stones or tree roots. The female lays a clutch of 2 eggs.

OLD WORLD FLYCATCHERS AND CHATS CONTINUED

Black Redstart *Phoenicurus ochruros*

RANGE Europe, N. Africa, Asia, east to China and just into N. India

HABITAT Open rocky areas, near human habitation

SIZE 5½ in (14 cm)

The black redstart is an adaptable bird that has learned to live alongside man in some areas. Both sexes have rusty-red tails, although the male's is brighter, and the male has dull black upperparts while the female is brownish.

The black redstart spends much of its time on the ground and it also perches on rocks and buildings. Insects, which are caught on the ground and in flight, are its main food, but it will also eat some berries. Holes in rocks and buildings are used as night-time roosts.

The breeding season starts in early to late April, depending on the area. The female builds a loose, cup-shaped nest from dry grass moss and fibers lined with hair, wool and feathers. The nest is built on a cliff or building or in a hollow tree.

The female lays a clutch of between 4 and 6 eggs, which she incubates for 12 to 16 days. Both of the parents feed the young until they leave the nest, 12 to 19 days after hatching. There are usually two broods in a season, sometimes three.

Karroo Scrub-robin *Cercotrichas coryphaeus*

RANGE Africa: Namibia to South Africa: Cape Province

HABITAT Arid sandy regions

SIZE 6¼ in (16 cm)

An abundant, lively bird, the karroo scrub-robin spends much of its time on the ground, where it searches for insects, as well as for seeds and berries when they are available. It runs swiftly and darts for cover if it is alarmed, after dancing around and flicking its tail for a moment or two.

A cup-shaped nest, made of grass, is built in a hollow in the ground, in a bush or under vegetation. The female lays 2 or 3 eggs, which are incubated for 14 or 15 days.

Nightingale *Luscinia megarhynchos*

RANGE Europe: S.E. England to Mediterranean and N. Africa; east to S.W. Siberia, Afghanistan; winters in tropical Africa

HABITAT Woodland, thickets, hedgerows

SIZE 6¼ in (16 cm)

The nightingale sings from dawn to dusk or even to midnight, and its melodious song is its most characteristic feature. Male and female look alike, with brownish and creamy plumage. A sturdy, solitary bird, the nightingale skulks among dense vegetation, foraging for food, such as worms, insects and larvae and berries, on the ground. It moves around with long hops, rarely flying for other than short distances.

The breeding season begins in May and the female builds a nest of leaves on or close to the ground, amid vegetation. She lines the nest with grass or hair and lays 4 or 5 eggs, which she incubates for 13 or 14 days. Both parents feed the young, which are able to fly at about 11 or 12 days.

European Robin *Erithacus rubecula*

RANGE Europe, Mediterranean islands, N. Africa, east to W. Siberia and Iran

HABITAT Forest, woodland, gardens

SIZE 5½ in (14 cm)

The familiar robin is easily identified by its orange-red breast and face, separated from the olive-brown upperparts by a gray-blue border. Male and female of the species look alike.

Although it is a shy, forest bird over much of its range, the robin has learned to make use of man and his gardens in Britain and parts of western Europe, and has become a bold, easily tamed species. Robins usually feed on the ground on small insects, larvae, spiders, worms and snails. They also eat berries and small fruit in season.

Aggressive little birds, robins live alone in winter, each defending its own territory against any intruders by presenting the red breast, with feathers erected, and emphasizing the warning color by swaying from side to side.

In the breeding season, robins form pairs, and males court the females before mating, using a less aggressive form of the threat display. The female then builds the cup-shaped nest on an ivy-covered bank, in a bush or hedge, in a hole in a tree or stump or on a building or ledge. She lays a clutch of between 5 and 7 eggs, which she incubates for 12 to 14 days, and both parents feed the young. There may be two or even three broods produced by each pair a year.

Orange-flanked Bush-robin *Tarsiger cyanurus*

RANGE Lapland, across N. Asia; winters in S. Asia; separate population in Himalayas and W. China

HABITAT Swampy coniferous forest, open woodland

SIZE 5½ in (14 cm)

An attractive little bird, the orange-flanked bush-robin has characteristic reddish-orange patches on its sides. The male has

largely blue plumage, and this is replaced in the female, except on the tail, by olive-brown. It forages for food, mainly insects, on the ground and in low vegetation, quivering its tail as it moves. It may also catch insects in the air.

The nest is made of moss and situated in a hollow in the ground among moss or tree roots. The female lays a clutch of between 3 and 7 eggs which she alone incubates.

Cape Robin-chat *Cossypha caffra*

RANGE E. and S. Africa: S. Sudan to Cape of Good Hope

HABITAT Forest, bush, cultivated areas, town shrubberies

SIZE 7 in (18 cm)

Rather like the Eurasian robin, the robin chat is usually a shy, retiring bird, but it has become tame and accustomed to man in inhabited areas. The male and female of the species look alike, and both have distinctive white eye stripes. They feed mainly on the ground on insects, spiders, worms small frogs and lizards and berries, but dart for cover at any sign of danger.

The nest is made of moss and rootlets and is situated in an overgrown tree stump or on a well-vegetated bank. The female lays a clutch of 2 or 3 eggs, which she incubates for between 13 and 19 days. Both parents feed the nestlings for between 14 and 18 days.

STARLINGS

STURNIDAE: STARLING AND MOCKINGBIRD FAMILY

This family of 148 species divides into two tribes: the starlings and the mockingbirds. Apart from the species introduced into other locations by humans, all 114 species of starling occur in the Old World, with the greatest diversity in Asia. As well as starlings, the tribe includes the mynas and 2 species of oxpecker. Starlings are medium-sized songbirds with a sturdy appearance and active habits. Most have long bills and strong legs and feet; wings may be rounded and short or long and pointed. Typically the plumage is dark, often enlivened with a beautiful iridescent sheen of blue, green or purple, particularly in the breeding season. Male and female look alike in some species and differ slightly in others. Many starlings live in open country and feed on the ground, although some occur in more wooded areas and are arboreal. They feed on almost anything, but largely on insects, fruit, grain, birds' eggs and lizards. Starlings fly swiftly and run or walk on the ground. Generally gregarious birds, they roost communally, often making characteristic loud whistles while flying to roosting sites in huge flocks. Most starlings nest in holes in trees or buildings, but some dig nesting burrows in river banks or build domed nests in trees.

The 34 species belonging to the mockingbird tribe are all found in the Americas. As well as the mockingbirds, this group of thrushlike birds also includes thrashers, tremblers and catbirds. Most live in wooded country or scrub, and feed on or near ground level on insects and other invertebrates, as well as on fruit and seeds. Typically they are slim-bodied birds, with long legs and tails, that are well known for their ability to mimic the songs of other birds and sounds such as piano notes, barking dogs and sirens. Male and female look alike or nearly so.

plumage both male and female are blackish, with a green or purple iridescent sheen. In winter, the plumage is heavily spotted with white, particularly in the female. Juveniles are grayish-brown with pale throats. Starlings are adaptable birds and take to a wide variety of habitats, although deciduous woodland and built-up areas are preferred in the breeding season. They feed on the ground on insects, larvae, earthworms, slugs, snails and centipedes, among other invertebrates, constantly probing the surface with their bills. Fruit, grain, berries and seeds are also included in their widely varying diet. Starlings may sometimes feed in the trees, and they also pursue insect prey in the air, with swift, wheeling flight.

Starlings breed in colonies or in separate pairs. The nest is usually built in a hole in a tree or building or among rocks, and is made of stems, leaves and other plant material. The female lays 4 to 9 eggs, usually 5 to 7, which both parents incubate for 12 or 13 days. They feed their young for about 3 weeks, but even after leaving the nest, the young starlings follow their parents and solicit food. There may be one or two broods a season. Northernmost populations migrate south in winter.

Red-winged Starling
Onychognathus morio

RANGE Africa: Senegal to Sudan, south through E. Africa to South Africa: Cape Province

HABITAT Rocky hills and cliffs, cultivated and city areas, woodland

SIZE 12 in (30.5 cm)

Starling *Sturnus vulgaris*

RANGE Europe, Asia; introduced almost worldwide

HABITAT Near habitation, cultivated land

SIZE 8½ in (21.5 cm)

One of the most familiar birds in city areas, starlings roost in huge numbers on buildings, often performing spectacular massed flights over the site prior to settling. In breeding

A noisy, conspicuous bird, the red-winged starling moves in pairs or small flocks, searching for its main foods – fruit and insects. Its flight is fast and dipping, and it makes a constant whistling call while in the air. The male bird is mainly blue-black, with brown-tipped, rufous flight feathers; the female has a gray head and neck and a gray-streaked breast but otherwise looks similar to the male.

The nest is made of grass and mud and is built in a hole in a cliff, cave or building or in the roof of a hut. The female lays 3 to 5 eggs, which she incubates for 12 to 23 days.

Hill Myna Gracula religiosa

RANGE India, Sri Lanka, Andaman and Nicobar Islands, S. China, Hainan, S.E. Asia, Indonesia; introduced elsewhere

HABITAT Forest

SIZE 12 in (30.5 cm)

A stockily built bird, the hill myna has glossy black plumage, with bright golden-yellow wattles on the head and a conspicuous white patch on each wing. Male and female look similar. A noisy, sociable bird, it lives in small groups of up to 6 outside the breeding season, occasionally gathering in larger groups at feeding trees. It spends most of its life in trees or bushes and feeds on fruit, particularly figs, berries, buds, nectar, and some insects and lizards. It rarely descends to the ground. Hill mynas have a wide repertoire of calls, but although "myna-birds" are first-rate mimics in captivity, they do not mimic sounds in the wild.

The nest is made in a hole in a tree trunk, often an old woodpecker hole. Both parents incubate the 2 or 3 eggs and feed the young.

Superb Starling Lamprotornis superbus

RANGE Africa: Ethiopia, Sudan to Tanzania

HABITAT Scrub, near habitation

SIZE 7 in (18 cm)

One of the most brilliantly plumaged starlings, the superb starling has metallic green and blue plumage. Male and female look alike, but juveniles have dull black plumage on head, neck and breast. The superb starling is a gregarious bird and is quite fearless of man where it occurs near villages and towns. It feeds on the ground on insects and berries.

The ball-shaped nest is made of grass and thorny twigs and is usually situated on a branch of a thorn tree or in a bush. A hole in a tree may sometimes be used or the old nest of another bird. There are usually 4 eggs in a clutch.

Metallic/Shining Starling Aplonis metallica

RANGE The Moluccas, across New Guinea region to Bismarck Archipelago and Solomon Islands; migrates to N. coast of Australia

HABITAT Rain forest

SIZE 9¾ in (25 cm)

The black plumage of the metallic starling has a purple and green sheen and the bird is also characterized by its long, sharply graduated tail and its red eyes. A gregarious, noisy bird, it is mainly tree-dwelling but does sometimes feed on the ground. Fruit and insects are its main foods.

Metallic starlings nest in large colonies of as many as 300 pairs. The large, domed nests are made of plant tendrils and suspended from branches. The usual clutch is 2 to 4 eggs.

Yellow-billed Oxpecker Buphagus africanus

RANGE Africa, south of the Sahara (not extreme south)

HABITAT Dry open country

SIZE 9 in (23 cm)

Common sights in African game reserves, the yellow-billed oxpecker and the similar, red-billed oxpecker, *B. erythrorhynchus*, both specialize in feeding on ticks, which they pull off buffalo, zebra and other large mammals. Their heavy bills are well suited to this, and they have strong, sharp claws with which they cling to the animal's skin. They clamber nimbly all over the body in their search, even probing ears and nostrils. Flies are also eaten. Oxpeckers give a warning call when alarmed, often alerting the mammal to danger. Male and female birds look alike.

The nest is made in a hole in a tree or rock, or under the eaves of a building. The female lays a clutch of 2 to 5 eggs, which are incubated for about 12 days.

MOCKINGBIRDS, NUTHATCHES AND WALLCREEPERS

Charles/Galápagos Mockingbird *Nesomimus trifasciatus* **EN**

RANGE Galápagos Islands

HABITAT Varied

SIZE 10 in (25.5 cm)

There are 4 species of Galápagos mockingbird, of which this one is rare and found only on Champion and Gardner islets. The birds appear to use all available habitats on the islands and to feed on anything they can find, mainly insects, fruit and berries, but also carrion and seabirds' eggs. The twig nest is built in a cactus or low tree and 2 to 5 eggs are laid.

Northern Mockingbird *Mimus polyglottos*

RANGE S. Canada, USA, south to Mexico; West Indies; introduced in Hawaii

HABITAT Open woodland, gardens, orchards

SIZE 9–11 in (23–28 cm)

This is one of the best-known American songbirds and is the state bird of five USA states. The male mockingbird sings night and day, often mimicking other birds and other sounds. Mockingbirds are aggressive and hold territories, which they defend vigorously against all enemies; in winter, female birds hold their own separate territories. They feed on insects, particularly grasshoppers and beetles, and also on spiders, snails and small reptiles. Fruit, too, is an important part of the diet.

At the onset of the summer breeding season, males court mates, flashing the white markings on the wings as they make display flights. Both partners help to build the nest, from twigs, leaves and bits of debris such as paper and wool which is placed in a low tree or bush. The female incubates the clutch of 3 to 6 eggs for 12 days, and both parents help to feed the young. There may be two or three broods produced a year.

California Thrasher *Toxostoma redivivum*

RANGE USA: California; Mexico: Baja California

HABITAT Chaparral, mountain foothills, parks, gardens

SIZE 11–13 in (28–33 cm)

This large thrasher has a distinctive downward-curving, sickle-shaped bill, which it uses to rake through leaves and dig in the soil for insects and berries. Its wings are rather short, and it is an awkward bird in flight, so it lives mainly on the ground, where it runs around with its long tail raised. The male bird sings for prolonged periods from a perch on a bush and is an excellent mimic. Females also sing.

Both parents help to build a large, cup-shaped nest of plant material three feet or so off the ground, in a low tree or bush. They incubate their clutch of between 2 and 4 eggs for about 14 days. When the young leave the nest 12 to 14 days after hatching out, the male continues to feed them for a few days longer, even while the second brood is being incubated in the nest by the female.

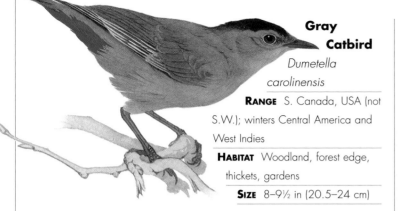

Gray Catbird

Dumetella carolinensis

RANGE S. Canada, USA (not S.W.); winters Central America and West Indies

HABITAT Woodland, forest edge, thickets, gardens

SIZE 8–9½ in (20.5–24 cm)

Named for its mewing, catlike call, the gray catbird usually lives in dense vegetation, where it forages for insects and berries, mainly on the ground. At the end of the winter, catbirds migrate north to breeding grounds in huge flocks, often at night.

The males arrive at breeding areas and sing to attract females. They display to, and chase, their mates. Both partners of a pair help to build a ragged nest of plant material in a low tree or bush. The 2 to 6 eggs, usually 4, are incubated for 12 to 15 days, mostly by the female, but the male helps to feed the newly hatched young. There are usually two broods a season.

Brown Trembler *Cinclocerthia ruficauda*

RANGE Lesser Antilles

HABITAT Rain forest, woodland

SIZE 9–10 in (23–25.5 cm)

Tremblers are identified by, and named after, their characteristic habit of violently shaking the wings and body. Their main foods are insects and invertebrates, most of which are found on the forest floor. A nest is made in a cavity in a tree or tree fern, and the female lays 2 or 3 eggs.

SITTIDAE: NUTHATCH FAMILY

There are 25 species in this family, found in North America, Europe and Asia. There are two subfamilies – the nuthatches and the single species of wallcreeper. They are all robust little birds, with strong legs and feet and sharp claws to help them climb. Nuthatches are the only birds to routinely look for food by walking down tree trunks head first. Their strong, pointed bills are ideal for probing crevices in bark or rocks for insects. The sexes look alike in many species, but differ slightly in others.

Red-breasted Nuthatch *Sitta canadensis*

RANGE Alaska, Canada, USA

HABITAT Coniferous or mixed woodland

SIZE 4¼–4¾ in (11–12 cm)

The male red-breasted nuthatch is identified by his white-edged black cap, black eye stripe and rusty-colored breast. The female has a dark-gray cap. The birds move rapidly over tree trunks and branches, searching for seeds and insects, and deftly investigate pine cones with their bills and extract any food items. Large insects may even be wedged into bark crevices so that the nuthatches can bite off pieces. They pursue insects in the air and collect seeds on the ground.

The breeding season begins in April or May. The nest is made in a tree hole, or a cavity is excavated in the stump or branch of a dead tree. Resin from coniferous trees is smeared around the entrance. Both parents incubate the 4 to 7 eggs for about 12 days.

Wallcreeper *Trichodroma muraria*

RANGE C. and S. Europe, across Asia to Mongolia and W. China

HABITAT Mountain cliffs

SIZE 6½ in (16.5 cm)

An unusual bird, with similiarities to both nuthatches and treecreepers, the wallcreeper is sometimes placed in its own monotypic family. It has a long curved bill and broad, rounded wings with distinctive red patches. In its search for insects to feed on, it climbs up cliff faces, investigating every crevice, and then flits down to the bottom and starts again on another section of rock. It also forages on the ground under stones but is rarely seen on trees.

The male courts the female with display flights, which show off his wing colors. He helps the female build a nest of moss, grass and rootlets in a rock crevice. The female incubates the 3 to 5 eggs, and both parents feed the young.

WRENS AND TREECREEPERS

CERTHIIDAE: WREN, TREECREEPER AND GNATCATCHER FAMILY

These small songbirds are found in the Americas and Eurasia, with one species in Africa. There are three subfamilies.

TROGLODYTINAE: WREN SUBFAMILY

There are 75 species of wren, all except one are confined to the Americas. The exceptional species is the bird known as the wren in Europe and the winter wren in North America. Most wrens are between 4 and 9 in (10 and 23 cm) long and are generally brown, with barred patterning. Wings are short and bodies plump. Some have stumpy tails. The sexes look alike or nearly so.

Wrens occur in a wide range of habitats, including rain forest, cooler wooded areas, marshes, deserts, moorland and mountains. They generally frequent dense, low vegetation, where they hunt for insects and other invertebrates with great agility and speed. They are excellent and varied songsters, often with loud voices for birds of their size. In many species the female also sings, and some tropical wrens perform "duets". Wrens generally produce two or more broods a season. Eggs are usually incubated by the female, but both parents care for the young.

Wren/Winter Wren *Troglodytes troglodytes*
RANGE Iceland, Europe, N.W. Africa, Middle East, east to E. China, Japan; S. Canada, E. USA and Pacific coast
HABITAT Undergrowth in coniferous forest, gardens, heaths and parks
SIZE 3¼ in (8 cm)

This is the only Old World wren. It is a plump bird with a short tail, (usually held cocked up), and a loud, vibrant song. The wren is extremely active and forages in undergrowth for insects, mainly larvae, and a few berries.

Breeding begins in April in most of the range. The male makes several nests, in which he installs various females. The bulky, domed nest is made of plant material and situated in a cavity in a bank, among tree roots or in a hollow stump. The male may also make "dummy" nests, which may help to divert potential predators.

Having lined her chosen nest with hair and feathers, the female lays 4 to 16 eggs, which she incubates for 14 to 16 days. The young are fed by the female and fly at 16 or 17 days. Some populations migrate south of the breeding range in winter.

House Wren *Troglodytes aedon*
RANGE S. Canada through USA and Central and South America; Trinidad and Tobago
HABITAT Woodland, gardens, parks
SIZE 4¼–5½ in (11–14 cm)

The common house wren is gray-brown with a faint stripe above each eye. It eats a variety of insects, such as crickets, flies and caterpillars, as well as spiders and snails. House wrens winter to the south of their range and migrate north in spring.

Males build nests of twigs, leaves and other plant material, usually in cavities in trees or rocks. When the females arrive, each selects a nest, which she lines with feathers, wool and hair. She lays up to 9 eggs, which she incubates for 13 to 15 days. The young leave the nest 12 to 18 days after hatching.

There are many subspecies of house wren; two Caribbean races are endangered and thought to be near extinction.

Cactus Wren *Campylorhynchus brunneicapillus*
RANGE S.W. USA to C. Mexico
HABITAT Desert, arid scrubland
SIZE 7–8½ in (18–22 cm)

The cactus wren has a distinctive white stripe over each eye and a long tail than many wrens, which it rarely cocks up. Cactus wrens frequent areas with thorny shrubs, cacti and trees and forage mostly on the ground for insects and occasionally lizards or frogs. Some cactus fruit and berries and seeds are also eaten. They run swiftly but usually fly over any distance. Nests are made for roosting at night and for shelter in bad weather.

The breeding season is March or April, and there may be two or three broods. The bulky, domed nest is made of plant material and lined with fur or feathers. It has a tubelike side entrance. It is sited on a prickly cactus or a yucca. The female lays 3 to 7 eggs and incubates them for about 16 days.

Long-billed Marsh Wren *Cistothorus palustris*

RANGE S. Canada, USA, Mexico

HABITAT Marshes

SIZE 4–5½ in (10–14 cm)

The marsh wren has a dark head, stripy marks on its back and a white streak over each eye. It inhabits dense vegetation in marshland and eats aquatic insects. The male wren builds several "dummy" nests before the females arrive in the breeding area. She completes the building of the nest that she uses. It is a large coconut-shaped structure, lashed to bulrushes or other upright vegetation, and made of water-soaked sedges and grasses, woven with rootlets and stems. There is a tubelike side opening. The interior is lined with feathers and shredded plant material. The 3 to 10 eggs are incubated by the female for 13 to 16 days.

Bewick's Wren *Thryomanes bewickii*

RANGE S.W. and central Canada, USA, Mexico

HABITAT Open woodland, thickets, gardens, pastures

SIZE 5½ in (14 cm)

Bewick's wren has a long, slim bill, which it uses to forage on the ground and on vegetation for insects, as well as for spiders. It also delves into crevices in buildings for food.

The nest is made by both partners in almost any available cavity in a tree, rock or building, or in any hollow object, natural or manmade. It is cup-shaped and constructed with plant material and lined with feathers. The female incubates her 4 to 11 eggs for 14 days.

Rock Wren *Salpinctes obsoletus*

RANGE S.W. Canada, W. USA, south to Costa Rica

HABITAT Dry rocky valleys, cliffs

SIZE 5–6 in (13–15 cm)

The rock wren blends well with its arid, bare habitat. It moves with great agility over rocks, in search of insects and spiders.

Both partners build the nest in a crevice in a rock, a pile of stones or a burrow. It is made of plant

material and lined with fur and feathers. Although the nest is carefully concealed, there may be a path of small pebbles leading to it, and the entrance may be lined with stones bones and other debris. The female usually lays 5 or 6 eggs which she incubates.

CERTHIINAE: TREECREEPER SUBFAMILY

The 6 species of treecreeper occur throughout the northern hemisphere in North and Central America, Europe, North Africa and Asia; and 1 species, the spotted creeper, lives in Africa south of the Sahara. Treecreepers are arboreal and clamber up tree trunks searching for insects. Their sharp claws enable them to cling to bark. Their long, thin bills are used for probing insect holes. All but the spotted creeper have stiff tails, which help to support them as they climb. The sexes look alike, or nearly so.

Eurasian/Common Treecreeper *Certhia familiaris*

RANGE Europe and Asia, from Britain to Japan, south to the Himalayas

HABITAT Forest, parks

SIZE 4¾ in (12 cm)

Using its stiff tail feathers as a prop, the treecreeper slowly makes its way up a tree trunk in a spiral path, searching crevices in the bark for insects. When it reaches the top of one tree, it flies off to another and begins again at the base of that trunk. It also eats nuts and seeds. The sexes look alike, and both have long claws and slender, curved bills.

The nest is usually made behind a piece of loose bark and lined with moss and feathers. The female incubates her 5 or 6 eggs for 14 or 15 days, sometimes assisted by the male.

Spotted creeper *Salpornis spilonotus*

RANGE Africa: irregular distribution south of the Sahara to Angola and Zimbabwe; N. India

HABITAT Forest, savanna, woodland

SIZE 5 in (13 cm)

The spotted creeper differs from other treecreepers – it has a soft tail, which it holds away from the tree trunk as it clambers up, searching for insects. With its long, curved bill, it probes every crevice in the bark for insects.

The cup-shaped nest is made in a vertically forked branch. Both parents incubate the 2 or 3 eggs.

GNATCATCHERS, PENDULINE TITS, TITMICE AND LONG-TAILED TITS

POLIOPTILINAE: GNATCATCHER SUBFAMILY

There are 15 species in this subfamily of the family Certhiidae, which are found in North, Central and South America. They are small, dainty birds, related to and resembling Old World warblers, but with more bluish-gray and white plumage. The sexes differ slightly.

Blue-gray Gnatcatcher *Polioptila caerulea*

RANGE USA, Mexico, Cuba and Bahamas

HABITAT Forest, woodland, swamps, inhabited areas

SIZE 4–5 in (10–13 cm)

The blue-gray gnatcatcher is a slender, lively little bird with a long tail often held cocked like a wren's. The male and female look similar, but the female tends to be less blue colored and lacks the black head markings of the breeding male. The birds search for insects, larvae and spiders in the trees, sometimes launching themselves into the air to catch prey.

The cup-shaped nest is usually sited on a horizontal branch of a tree and is made from plant fibers, lined with fine bark, grass and feathers. The parents incubate the clutch of 3 to 6 eggs in shifts for about 14 days and care for the young.

PARIDAE: TIT FAMILY

The birds in this family occur in Eurasia, Africa, and North and Central America. There are 65 species in two subfamilies.

REMIZINAE: PENDULINE-TIT SUBFAMILY

The 12 species of penduline-tit differ from other tits in possessing finely pointed beaks. Most live in Africa or Asia, but there is 1 species each in Europe and North America. They tend to inhabit more open country than other tits, which favour woodland. Male and female generally look alike.

Yellow Penduline-tit *Anthoscopus parvulus*

RANGE Africa: Senegal to Sudan, Zaire and Uganda

HABITAT Dry savanna and acacia woodland

SIZE 3 in (7.5 cm)

A rare, little-known species, the yellow penduline-tit is an active, but quiet, bird. It eats caterpillars and other insects and larvae, which it finds by foraging over foliage and large flowers.

The elaborate nest is suspended from a branch and takes some time to build. It is made of felted plant matter and has a short, tubelike opening near the top that is self-closing. The female usually lays 4 eggs.

Verdin *Auriparus flaviceps*

RANGE S.W. USA: S.E. California to S. Texas; C. Mexico

HABITAT Desert

SIZE 4–4¼ in (10–11 cm)

The verdin has a distinctive yellow head and throat and a chestnut patch at the bend of the wing, conspicuous only when the wings are open. The female's yellow plumage is slightly duller than the male's, and juveniles lack both yellow and chestnut plumage.

The verdin lives among the thorny bushes and cactus plants of its arid habitat and flits about in search of insects and their eggs and larvae. Berries and fruit are also eaten for moisture.

The globular nest is made of thorny twigs, lined with softer material, such as feathers and leaves, and has a tiny side-entrance. It is suspended from a prickly branch or a crotch of a tree or cactus and gains some protection both from its surroundings and the outward-facing thorns of the nest itself. The female lays 3 to 6 eggs, which are thought to be incubated for 10 days.

PARINAE: TITMOUSE SUBFAMILY

Titmice are small, stocky songbirds, found throughout the northern hemisphere and Africa, usually in wooded areas. There are 53 species. Many titmice live alongside humans. Their normal diet is insects and seeds. Active birds, tits are constantly on the move, flitting around the trees in search of food. Male and female may look alike or differ slightly in plumage.

Black-capped Chickadee

Parus atricapillus

RANGE Alaska, Canada,
S. to C. USA

HABITAT Coniferous forest,
woodland

SIZE 4¾–6 in (12–15 cm)

Identified by its "chickadee-dee-dee" call, the black-capped chickadee has a black throat and cap and a white face. It is always on the move, hopping over twigs and branches in search of insect larvae, spiders, snails, seeds and berries.

Both partners of a pair help to excavate the nest cavity in a soft, rotting stump or branch, and the female lines the nest with plant fibers, moss or feathers. Sometimes chickadees nest in an abandoned woodpecker hole or even in a nesting box. The 5 to 10 eggs are incubated for 11 to 13 days.

Sultan Tit *Melanochlora sultanea*

RANGE Himalayas, mountains of
S. China and S.E. Asia; Sumatra

HABITAT Forest on foothills,
trees near cultivated land

SIZE 7¾ in (20 cm)

The striking, showy sultan tit is large for its family and has a distinctive yellow crest. The sexes look similar, but the female has olive, not black, plumage on the throat and an olive tinge to her back plumage. Pairs or small parties search for insects, seeds and berries in foliage. Birds often hang upside down to peer into crevices or under leaves. The female lays 6 or 7 eggs on a thick pad of moss and plant material placed in a hole in a tree.

Red-throated Tit *Parus fringillinus*

RANGE Africa: S. Kenya, Tanzania

HABITAT Savanna with scattered trees

SIZE 4½ in (11.5 cm)

The agile, lively red-throated tit lives in pairs or small family groups, foraging on vegetation for insects and larvae. The female lays 3 eggs in a cavity in a tree, which is lined with down and plant fibers.

Great Tit *Parus major*

RANGE Europe, N.W. Africa, Asia (except N.), S.E. Asia, Indonesia

HABITAT Forest, woodland, cultivated land, parks, gardens

SIZE 5½ in (14 cm)

Many forms of great tit, with varying plumage, occur over its vast range. Typically, the plumage is blue and yellow with a black cap and a black stripe down the middle of the chest, which is broader on the belly of the male than of the female. A noisy, sometimes dominant and aggressive bird, the great tit lives in large family groups after the breeding season and may join mixed flocks. It feeds in trees and on the ground, eating insects, spiders, worms and small mollusks, as well as seeds, fruit, nuts and buds. It will use its strong bill to hammer at nuts.

The male courts and chases the female before mating. Both partners build the nest of moss and grass in a hole in a tree or wall, or in a nest box and line it with hair or down. The 5 to 11 eggs are incubated by the female for 13 to 14 days, and the male helps her to feed the young. There may be two broods in a season.

AEGITHALIDAE: LONG-TAILED TIT FAMILY

The 8 species of long-tailed tit are closely related to the true tits, Paridae, and occur in Europe, Asia and North and Central America. They are small, with tails often as long or longer than their bodies.

Long-tailed Tit *Aegithalos caudatus*

RANGE Europe (not N. Scandinavia or Iceland); Asia to Japan

HABITAT Woodland, scrub, bushy heaths, hedgerows, parks

SIZE 5½ in (14 cm)

The plumage of the tiny long-tailed tit varies over its range, but is usually a mixture of black, white and pink feathers. The sexes look alike. This restless, active bird feeds in trees and undergrowth on insects and their larvae, spiders, seeds and buds. Both parents construct a long, oval nest, with a side entrance near the top, from moss, bound with spiders' webs and covered with lichen. The 8 to 12 eggs are incubated mostly by the female, but the male may help and does take a share in feeding the young.

SWALLOWS

HIRUNDINIDAE: SWALLOW FAMILY

The 89 species of swallow and martin are all swift-flying birds, which display great agility in the air. They are found almost worldwide, and many make regular migrations between breeding and wintering areas, sometimes travelling as far as 8,000 miles (13,000 km).

There are two subfamilies – the river martins (of which there are 2 species) and the swallows and martins themselves. There is little consistent difference between the swallows and martins. All forms have smallish bodies, short necks and long, pointed wings. They are fast, agile fliers and catch their prey on the wing in their wide, gaping beaks. Swallows and martins are the passerine equivalents of swifts. The two families have become alike by adapting to a similar way of life in the air; swifts, however, do have longer wings and tend to fly higher than swallows.

On the ground, their short legs and weak feet allow "little more than a feeble shuffle," but they do perch. They frequently nest close to or in human dwellings, or use natural hollows in trees, caves or cliffs in which to construct a burrow. Clutches of 3 to 7 eggs are laid, which both parents incubate.

Swallows and martins are generally gregarious birds and feed, nest and migrate in large flocks. Males and females look more or less alike, but in some species there may be minor differences, such as the male having longer tail feathers.

White-eyed River Martin
Pseudochelidon sirintarae **CR**

RANGE Winters central Thailand

HABITAT Reedbeds in marshes

SIZE 9½ in (24 cm) including tail streamers of 3½ in (9 cm)

The white-eyed river martin is identified by its distinctive white spectacles and rump and by the long streamers flowing from its rounded tail. It also has a large swollen, yellow bill, unusual for a swallow. The juvenile has a darker head and only very short tail streamers.

This rare species was discovered only in 1968 and is believed to be a migrant from the north. Its nearest relative, and the only other member of its subfamily, is *P. eurystomina*, which lives in Africa, in Zambia. The white-eyed river martin winters in central Thailand, at Bung Boraphet, where it roosts at night in large lakeside reedbeds in flocks with other species of swallows. By day, it perches on trees and wires and catches insects in flight.

The summer migration and breeding habits of this species remain a mystery, although it may breed in holes in river banks in Thailand or China.

Barn Swallow *Hirundo rustica*

RANGE Almost worldwide; breeds between 30°N and 70°N; winters in Southern hemisphere

HABITAT Open cultivated country with buildings, near water

SIZE 7¾ in (19.5 cm)

The barn swallow is absent only from very high latitudes and some oceanic islands. The male is a metallic blue hue, with a deeply forked tail covered in white spots, and a white breast. Females and young birds have shorter tails and less vibrant plumage. They feed on insects, which are caught on the wing or plucked from the surface of water.

In summer, barn swallows are often seen in pairs and small groups, but in autumn they form huge flocks and roost in reedbeds before migrating south for the winter. The Old World races spend the winter months in Africa, south of the Sahara, on the Indian subcontinent and in northern Australia. The North American birds fly down to Panama, central Chile and northern Argentina.

Both sexes help to build the open nest, using mud and straw and lining it with feathers. They now seem to prefer to use ledges on buildings to the original cave or cliff sites. The female lays a clutch of 4 or 5 eggs and incubates them for about 15 days, with some help from the male. Both parents feed the nestlings, which can fly at about 3 weeks old. There are two, sometimes three, broods a year.

Sand Martin/Bank Swallow *Riparia riparia*

RANGE Temperate regions of Eurasia, N. America; winters in S. America, Africa, N. India, S.E. Asia

HABITAT Steep sand or gravel banks, near water

SIZE 4¾–5½ in (12–14 cm)

The tiny sand martin is the smallest swallow in North America, with a wingspan of only 10 to 11 in (25.5 to 28 cm). This energetic little bird darts, twists and zigzags in the air, snapping up a variety of winged insects, including termites, leafhoppers and mosquitoes.

Sand martins live in burrows, which they dig straight into sand or gravel banks, often by water, or alongside roads and railway tracks. The birds start the burrow with their bills, and both male and female take turns to kick out the soil until the burrow is about 3¼ ft (1 m) long.

Each spring, the sand martins flock north, often returning to the previous year's nesting hole, and fights over ownership are not unusual. The nest is built at the end of the burrow from soft grass, feathers, hair and rootlets. The female lays a clutch of up to 8 eggs, usually 4 or 5, which are incubated alternately by both parents for 16 days. The young fly at 3 weeks old.

Purple Martin *Progne subis*

RANGE Breeds Canada to Mexico; winters south to West Indies, Venezuela, Brazil

HABITAT Suburban gardens and farmland

SIZE 7 in (18 cm)

The purple martin is one of the tamest birds of the family. The male's metallic blue plumage gradually fades out to brown on the wings and tail; the female is mainly brown, and the juveniles are a grayish-brown. The purple martin supplements its diet of insects, which are taken on the wing, with snails, which are probably a source of calcium.

These birds build their nests in trees or cliff holes, using grass, feather and often green leaves, which may help to keep the nest cool and moist. The clutch of 3 to 5 eggs is incubated for 13 days, mainly by the female, and the young leave the nest within a month of hatching.

There are 2 races of purple martin; *P. s. subis* breeds in southern Canada down the west coast of the USA to central Mexico and east to the Gulf Coast and Florida. It winters in Venezuela and southeast Brazil. *P. s. hesperia* breeds in the lowlands of Arizona, Baja California and the Mexican coast, but it is not known where it winters.

Blue Saw-wing

Psalidoprocne pristoptera

RANGE Africa: Ethiopia

HABITAT High plateaux

SIZE 7 in (18 cm)

The blue saw-wing swallow has glossy blue-black plumage above, with an oily green look to its wings and tail. The tail is broad and not as deeply forked in the female as in the male. The juvenile is a dull, dark brown and blue.

These birds are often seen in pairs, making swooping flights over streams in search of insects, which they take on the wing.

The nesting hole is at the end of a tunnel, chiseled into a river bank or cliff face, and is padded with layers of soft grass. The female lays 3 eggs, which are glossy white and thin shelled.

Golden Swallow

Tachycineta euchrysea **LR:nt**

RANGE Jamaica, Hispaniola

HABITAT Dry, wooded, limestone hills

SIZE 5 in (12.5 cm)

This delicate, graceful bird earns its common name from the bright golden gloss over its olive-green plumage. The juvenile keeps its duller colors and gray chest band until maturity. The Jamaican race is now believed to be rare, although there is insufficient information available at present to classify it as such.

Golden swallows feed entirely on the wing and nest in tree holes or under the eaves of houses. The female lays 3 eggs.

BULBULS

PYCNONOTIDAE: BULBUL FAMILY

The bulbuls are a family of 137 species, found in forest, orchards and cultivated land in the tropical regions of Africa in particular, but also in Madagascar, southern and Southeast Asia.

With only a few exceptions, they are noisy, gregarious birds of medium size, with shortish wings and comparatively long tails. Beaks are long and notched, with stiff bristles at the base. Some forms possess a crest. Males and females look alike, although occasionally the male is larger.

Their food consists mainly of fruit, berries, buds, flower nectar and insects removed from vegetation.

Yellow-bellied/Yellow-breasted Greenbul

Chlorocichla flaviventris

RANGE Africa: Tanzania to Namibia

HABITAT Forest, woodland with heavy undergrowth, coastal scrub

SIZE 8½ in (22 cm)

Unexpectedly shy and skulking birds for their family, the greenbuls are generally found only in pairs or small parties, although they are widespread throughout their range. The male and female of the species look alike, with yellowish underparts and olive green plumage on the back, wings and head; in juveniles, the head and mantle are the same color.

These birds creep through undergrowth and dense vegetation in search of seeds and berries to eat and they will also cling to the trunks of trees like woodpeckers, looking for insects underneath the bark.

The flimsy nest is neatly constructed from tendrils, grass and some stems and it is well hidden in dense cover. The female lays a clutch of 2 eggs.

Leaflove *Phyllastrephus scandens*

RANGE Africa: Senegal to Sudan, Uganda, Tanzallia

HABITAT Forest

SIZE 8½ in (22 cm)

The charmingly named leaflove is a mostly dusky, gray-green bird, with creamy-white and yellow underparts. Male and female look alike; the juvenile is duller and paler. Completely arboreal, these birds frequent thickets, often near streams, climbing among the foliage, looking for insects to eat. They move about in small parties, chattering incessantly; when disturbed they become extremely noisy.

The cup-shaped nest is made from fine grass and leaves and is often slung between the stems of a vine or creeper. There are normally 2 eggs in a clutch.

Garden Bulbul

Pycnonotus barbatus

RANGE Africa

HABITAT Gardens, woodland, coastal scrub, open forest

SIZE 7 in (18 cm)

Both male and female garden bulbuls have grayish-white plumage on breast and belly and white under-tail coverts. In fact, albinism is not uncommon in this species. The head appears slightly crested when the feathers are raised on the nape. They are tame, lively birds and have a habit of warbling briefly and slightly raising their wings when they land. They seem to eat equal quantities of fruit and insects.

The nest is a neat cup shape, lightly made from grass and a few dead leaves, and is often suspended in the fork between two twigs. The female normally lays a clutch of 2 or 3 eggs.

Red-whiskered Bulbul

Pycnonotus jocosus

RANGE India, S.E. Asia, S. China, Andaman Islands; introduced in USA, Australia, Nicobar Islands, Mauritius

HABITAT Low scrub, cultivated land near villages, gardens, orchards

SIZE 8 in (20.5 cm)

This widespread bird is locally abundant throughout its range. It is named for the tufts of deep-red feathers that sprout, like a mustache, on each side of the head; it also has red undertail feathers. Male and female look alike, but the tufts are white in the juvenile. It is a sprightly, cheerful bird, with a musical call, and in the summer, dozens can be seen feasting together in fruit trees. They do a great deal of damage to the crop, since they eat both green and ripe fruit; they also eat the insects they come across when feeding.

The cup-shaped nest is made from grass, roots and stalks, lined with fine grass, and some dry leaves and pieces of fern are woven into the bottom of it. The female lays 2 to 4 eggs.

Crested Finchbill *Spizixos canifrons*

RANGE Assam to S.W. China, Myanmar, Laos, Tonkin

HABITAT Deciduous and evergreen forest

SIZE 8 in (20.5 cm)

This handsome bird has a black crest, which, when erected, hangs forward like Punch's cap, and a thick, finchlike beak: noticeable characteristics that give it its common name. Male and female look alike. Also known as the crested finchbilled bulbul, this bird is a typical bulbul in its habits, traveling in flocks of up to 100 through the trees and undergrowth and calling constantly with a typically chattering note. It feeds on seeds and fruit and on insects, which it often takes in the air, flycatcher-fashion. It is one of the few birds to profit by the slash-and-burn agricultural methods of the seminomadic tribes in its habitat, for it flourishes where scattered low trees grow through dense undergrowth.

The distinctive cup-shaped nest is always made from corkscrew tendrils of a vine, sometimes with a few twigs added, and is placed low in a tangle of bushes and brambles. There are 2 or 3, rarely 4, eggs.

Black/Madagascar Bulbul *Hypsipetes madagascarensis*

RANGE Madagascar, Aldaboa, Glorieuses and Comoro Islands

HABITAT Forest up to 6,560 ft (2,000 m)

SIZE 10 in (25.5 cm)

The bold, noisy black bulbul lives entirely in the trees. Its flight is swift and agile, but its legs and feet are weak, so it does not hop about in the branches but flies everywhere. It feeds on berries – preferring mulberries and bukain berries – and may catch flies or other insects, which it snaps up when they visit flowers for their nectar.

The nest is cup-shaped and made of coarse grass, dry leaves and moss, bound with spiders' webs and lined with fine grass, moss roots and pine needles. Partners seem to be very attached to each other – the male stays close to the female as she incubates their 2 to 4 eggs.

White-throated Bulbul *Alophoixus flaveolus*

RANGE Himalayas in India, China: Yunnan Province, Myanmar, Thailand

HABITAT Humid forest with thick undergrowth

SIZE 9 in (23 cm)

These large, crested bulbuls are usually found in rowdy parties of 6 to 15 birds. They chatter to each other as they climb about in the trees and bushes, or fly in a stream from one dense patch of undergrowth to another. They are seldom found more than about 10 ft (3 m) from the ground, where they forage for berries, wild figs and insects, which they sometimes take on the wing. Their flight is strong and direct, and when they perch they fan out their tails.

Both male and female help to build a substantial nest from fine roots, bamboo leaves and dead leaves, which is concealed in the cover of vines or brambles about 3¼ ft (1 m) from the ground. The 3 or 4 eggs are incubated by both parents for 13 days.

BULBULS, KINGLETS, HYPOCOLIUS AND AFRICAN WARBLERS

Common Bristlebill *Bleda syndactyla*

Range Africa: from Senegal to S. Sudan, Kenya, Uganda, Zaire

Habitat Dense forest

Size 8½ in (21.5 cm)

The bristlebill is a large heavily built bird, with olive-brown plumage on the upperparts and a yellow throat and belly. Like all bulbuls, it has tufts of bristles near the bill base. Male and female look alike; the juvenile is duller and more rusty colored. The bill of the male is larger and more hooked than that of the female. These uncommon birds are shy and alert and difficult to observe as they move around in small trees and forest undergrowth, consequently little is known of their habits.

They are known to build a shallow, cup-shaped nest from leaves, sticks and plant fibers and to lay 2 eggs.

Common/Yellow-spotted Nicator *Nicator chloris*

Range W. and C. Africa

Habitat Tropical forest, thick woodland, scrub

Size 8½ in (21.5 cm)

This shy forest bird is inconspicuous, often revealing itself only by a burst of clear, chattering song or by grunting, almost squirrellike calls. It lives among the lower branches of trees or in dense undergrowth, feeding on plant matter and insects. Male and female look alike, but the juvenile has paler plumage on the upperparts and narrower, more pointed tail feathers.

Normally 2 eggs are laid in a nest that is either a shallow grass cup or a flat platform of stalks and tendrils, sited in the cover of thick vegetation.

Hook-billed Bulbul

Setornis criniger **LR:nt**

Range Borneo, Sumatra, Bankga Island

Habitat Primary lowland forest

Size 7½ in (19 cm)

This bold and busy bird moves about among the branches, searching for beetles, dragonfly nymphs, and small, stoneless berries. Usually seen alone, sometimes in pairs, hook-billed bulbuls are silent, only occasionally making loud, harsh cries. Males, females and juveniles look alike, but the plumage of young birds is duller. No information is available on mating and nesting behavior.

REGULIDAE: KINGLET FAMILY

The 6 species in this family are very small, insect-eating arboreal birds. They include the firecrests and the goldcrests. Kinglets occur in the coniferous and mixed woodlands of Eurasia and North America.

Golden-crowned Kinglet *Regulus satrapa*

Range Alaska, S. Canada, USA; winters Mexico and Central America

Habitat Forest, usually coniferous

Size 3–4 in (8–10 cm)

This tiny bird's plumage is restrained for the most part, but there is a conspicuous black-bordered crown, which is orange in the male and yellow in the female, hence the common name. Juveniles develop the crown patch as they mature. Kinglets join mixed flocks to forage in the trees and bushes for insects and larvae.

The birds nest high in a conifer, usually spruce. The female builds a globular nest of moss, lichen, pine needles and grass, bound together with spiders' webs and lined with fine rootlets, fibers and feathers. This structure has an opening at the top and is suspended from twigs, to which it is bound with spiders' webs. The female alone is thought to incubate the 8 to 10 eggs for 14 to 17 days, but both parents tend the young.

HYPOCOLIIDAE: HYPOCOLIUS FAMILY

The gray hypocolius, the single member of this family, is a shrikelike bird found in Iraq, Iran and North India.

Gray Hypocolius *Hypocolius ampelinus*

RANGE S.W. Asia: Iran, Iraq to Arabian Peninsula and to India

HABITAT Semidesert

SIZE 9 in (23 cm)

The unique gray hypocolius is sociable, and outside the breeding season small parties are to be found foraging for fruit and berries. They also eat some insects. Females look like males, lacking only the black feathers on the head that can be erected into a crest. Juveniles are a buffy-brown, with no black on the tail. They are shy, slow-moving birds, like the waxwings, but their flight is strong and straight. Both sexes help to build the large, cup-shaped nest, which is usually well hidden among the leaves of a palm tree. It is roughly constructed from twigs and lined with soft plant matter and hair; the female lays 4 or 5 eggs. When disturbed, the pair desert the nest and reputedly return to destroy it, then build a new one a week or so later.

CISTICOLIDAE: AFRICAN WARBLER FAMILY

This family of warblers includes apalises, cameropterans, and cisticolas. Most of the 119 species of African warblers occur in Africa, although two species of cisticolas extend to Eurasia and Australia. The scrub-warbler also occurs in Afghanistan and Iraq.

Zitting Cisticola *Cisticola juncidis*

RANGE Africa, south of the Sahara; S. Europe; India, China, Japan; S.E. Asia to N. Australia

HABITAT Grassland, scrub, ricefields, cultivated land

SIZE 4 in (10 cm)

This bird skulks in grass, feeding on insects. It flies only when disturbed or during courtship. The sexes look similar, but breeding males have more strongly defined streaks on the head.

In the breeding season, males perform various courtship displays, including a jerky, dipping flight, accompanied by a particular song. The unique nest is built amid grass taller than itself, for camouflage. It is pear-shaped, with the entrance at the top, and is made of soft grass stems, bound together with spiders' webs and lined with plant down. Some blades of the surrounding grass are woven into the nest for support. The 3 to 6 eggs are incubated by both parents for about 10 days.

Graceful Prinia *Prinia gracilis*

RANGE E. Africa: Egypt to Somalia; east across S. Asia to N. India

HABITAT Scrub, bushy areas

SIZE 4 in (10 cm)

As much as half the length of this little warbler is accounted for by its tail of graduated feathers, the outer ones of which are tipped with white. The graceful prinia tends to frequent sandy ground near rivers, where there is some grass and bushy cover. It forages for insects in the vegetation and comes into the open only to fly clumsily from one patch of cover to the next.

The courting male sings a somewhat monotonous song from a perch on a tall grass stem. The tiny, domed nest is made of fine grass and is woven into a thick clump of grass stems, three feet or so above ground; there is an entrance at one side. Both parents incubate the 3 or 4 eggs for about 12 days. There are usually two broods a year.

Yellow-breasted Apalis *Apalis flavida*

RANGE Africa, south of the Sahara to South Africa: Transvaal

HABITAT Forest, bush

SIZE 4¼ in (11 cm)

The yellow-breasted apalis occurs in a variety of well-vegetated areas. It usually moves in pairs or small family groups, carefully searching through the foliage for insects.

The domed, pear-shaped nest is constructed from moss, lichen and spiders' webs and is bound to a twig of a low bush with spiders' webs; there is a side opening. Alternatively, this apalis may take over an old domed nest abandoned by another bird species. The female lays 2 or 3 eggs.

WHITE-EYES AND LEAF WARBLERS

ZOSTEROPIDAE: WHITE-EYE FAMILY

The 96 species of white-eye are a remarkably uniform group of birds. Most are small, with rounded wings and short legs, and have a greenish back, yellow underparts and characteristic rings of white feathers around the eyes. Some exceptions are larger in size with duller in plumage. The center of their distribution is Indonesia, but they also extend into Africa, New Zealand, Japan and the Pacific islands. They tend to live in wooded country and gardens, and eat insects, fruit and nectar. The sexes look alike.

Japanese White-eye *Zosterops japonicus*

RANGE Japan, E. and S. China, Taiwan, Hainan, Philippines, Korea

HABITAT Woodland, scrub

SIZE 4½ in (11.5 cm)

The Japanese white-eye has some gray plumage on the lower part of its belly; its beak is slender and pointed. A small, active bird, it forages in flocks over trees and bushes, searching for insects, particularly ants, and their eggs and larvae; it also feeds on buds, seeds and fruit. It flits from tree to tree, constantly making its faint, plaintive call, and never comes to the ground.

A cup-shaped nest is made of grass stems and fiber, lined with moss, and is placed in the fork of a thin branch. The female lays 3 or 4 eggs.

Gray-backed White-eye/Silver-eye *Zosterops lateralis*

RANGE E., S.E., S. and S.W. Australia, Tasmania, New Zealand, Vanuatu, Fiji

HABITAT Varied, with trees

SIZE 4¾ in (12 cm)

An adaptable bird, the gray-backed white-eye tolerates almost any habitat at any altitude, particularly on the islands in its range. It forages at any level of trees, on agricultural land or in gardens, feeding on fruit, insects and nectar from flowers. It occasionally comes to the ground to feed and even into open country. Male and female look alike both with sharply pointed and slightly curved bills.

The nest is made of plant fiber and grasses, bound together with cobwebs and is attached to twigs of a tree or bush by its rim. The female lays 2 to 4 eggs, which are incubated by both parents for about 11 days.

Príncipe Island Speirops *Speirops leucophoeus* **VU**

RANGE Príncipe Island (Gulf of Guinea)

HABITAT Forest

SIZE 5¼ in (13.5 cm)

One of the few African species of white-eye, this speirops has largely buff-gray plumage, with some white on throat and belly. In small parties, these restless, active little birds feed in the trees, searching the foliage for insects and also consuming seeds. Their movements are quick and agile, with much flicking of the wings. The nest is made of grass and bound to a branch with cobwebs or fine plant fiber. The female lays 2 eggs.

SYLVIIDAE: WARBLER FAMILY

This large family of songbirds has 552 species in 4 subfamilies – Acrocephalinae (Leaf-warblers), Megalurinae (Grass-warblers), Garrulacinae (Laughingthrushes), and Sylviinae (babblers, wrentit, and the typical warblers). Warblers are small, often dull-colored birds, some of which are noted for their melodious songs. Most species occur in Europe, Asia, and Africa but there are several in Australia and 1 species, the wrentit, in North America. Most warblers are active, quick-moving birds, found in woodland, moorland, marshes and reedbeds feeding on insects and fruit. Male and female generally look alike.

ACROCEPHALINAE: LEAF-WARBLER SUBFAMILY

This subfamily contains 221 species and includes the grasshopper warbler, reed-warblers, tailorbirds, and the willow warbler, as well as the leaf-warblers. Leaf-warblers are found from Eurasia south to New Guinea and the Solomon Islands, and in Africa.

Long-billed/Tahiti Reed-warbler *Acrocephalus caffer* **VU**

RANGE Society and Marquesas Islands

HABITAT Woodland bordering rivers, hillside forest

SIZE 8½ in (22 cm)

One of the largest warblers, the long-billed reed-warbler has a distinctive beak that can be 1½ in (4 cm) long. Subspecies on the different islands vary in coloration, and on Tahiti alone, there are some birds with olive upperparts and yellow underparts, and others that are blackish-brown all over.

Long-billed reed-warblers forage in trees and bushes for insects; they do not feed on the ground. They have a musical varied song, performed from a high perch. The nest is usually made in a bamboo thicket, 30 ft (9 m) or more above ground.

Chestnut-headed/Chestnut-crowned Warbler *Seicercus castaniceps*

RANGE Himalayas, S. China, S.E. Asia, Sumatra

HABITAT Forest

SIZE 4 in (10 cm)

An attractive little bird, the chestnut-headed warbler has a reddish-brown crown, with dark bands at the sides of the head, and yellow underparts. Male and female look alike. They live in dense forest and, outside the breeding season, move in mixed flocks, searching for insects in the middle to canopy layers of the forest. In the Himalayas, the warblers breed at between 6,000 and 7,900 ft (1,800 and 2,400 m), moving down the mountains during the winter months.

The compact, oval nest is situated on the ground. It is well hidden by moss or creepers in a hollow at the base of a tree or bush or in a bank or hillside. Both partners help to build the nest, which is constructed from densely woven moss. They both incubate the clutch of 4 or 5 eggs.

The emerald cuckoo, *Chrysococcyx maculatus*, often lays its eggs in the nests of this warbler.

Grasshopper Warbler *Locustella naevia*

RANGE Europe: Britain and S. Sweden, south to N. Spain and Italy, east to S. Siberia, W. China, S. Russia and C. Asia; winters in Africa and Asia

HABITAT Marsh edge, open woodland

SIZE 5 in (13 cm)

The grasshopper warbler is a retiring, secretive bird species, which quickly disappears into thick cover when it is disturbed. It feeds on insects and larvae. Male and female birds have similar streaked plumage.

The male warbler performs courtship displays to attract the female, spreading his tail and flapping his wings. The nest, which is built by both birds, is placed in thick cover on the ground or just above it in grasses or rushes and is made of plant stems and grass on a base of dead leaves.

The female lays a clutch of between 4 and 7 eggs, usually 6, which both parents incubate for 13 to 15 days. The young then spend 10 to 12 days in the nest, tended and fed by both parents. Birds in the south of the range produce two broods, and those in the north usually only one. In autumn, the birds migrate south for the winter.

LEAF WARBLERS, GRASS WARBLERS AND LAUGHING THRUSHES

Willow Warbler *Phylloscopus trochilus*

RANGE N. Europe and Asia: Britain and Scandinavia, south to
C. France, east to Russia; winters in Africa and S. Asia

HABITAT Open woodland, cultivated land with scattered trees and bushes

SIZE 4¼ in (11 cm)

Typical of the many species in the genus *Phylloscopus* in
appearance, the willow warbler is extremely hard to distinguish
from the chiffchaff, *P. collybita*, except by its song. It is said to
look "cleaner" than the chiffchaff, and its eyebrow streak is more
marked. Male and female birds look similar, but juveniles have
much more yellow on their underparts. Willow warblers search
in the vegetation for insects and also sometimes catch prey in
the air. In autumn, they feed on berries, before migrating south
for the winter. Some northern birds travel as far as 7,500 miles
(12,000 km) to winter in African forest and savanna.

Willow warblers nest on the ground, in vegetation under a
bush, tree or hedge, or sometimes a little above ground in a bush
or on a creeper-covered wall. The female builds the domed nest
from grass, moss, stems and roots, lined with finer stems and
feathers. She lays 6 or 7 eggs, which she incubates for 13 days.
Both parents tend the young, which spend 13 to 16 days in the
nest. Birds in the south of the range may produce two broods.

Ceylon Bush Warbler *Bradypterus palliseri* **LR:nt**

RANGE Sri Lanka

HABITAT Montane forest undergrowth, dwarf bamboo

SIZE 6¼ in (16 cm)

Ceylon bush warblers live at altitudes of over 3,000 ft (900 m).
In pairs, they skulk in dense undergrowth, searching under
leaves and among stems for insects and worms, and rarely climb
more than 6½ ft (2 m) above ground.

The male performs a sketchy courtship, climbing a little
farther than usual up a stem to sing a brief song and then flying

from one patch of vegetation to another. The nest is relatively
large for the size of the birds and is made of moss, grass and
bamboo leaves, lined with fine fibers. It is situated in a bush,
close to the ground. The female lays 2 eggs.

Brownish-flanked Bush Warbler *Cettia fortipes*

RANGE Himalayas, S. China and S.E. Asia

HABITAT Open forest, swamp-jungle, gardens

SIZE 4 in (10 cm)

A small, skulking warbler, the brownish-flanked bush warbler
has a distinctive whistling call, culminating in a loud, explosive
phrase, but it is rarely seen. It is a solitary bird and forages
for insects in the dense undergrowth which is found in its
habitat. It may hop up into bushes but rarely climbs trees.
Mountain birds make seasonal movements, descending to lower
altitudes in winter and breeding between 6,600 and 10,000 ft
(2,000 and 3,000 m).

The untidy nest is built in a bush usually less than a meter
or so above ground. It may be a cup-shaped or sometimes a
domed structure, with an entrance near the top. Both parents
incubate the 3 to 5, usually 4, eggs.

Longtailed/Common Tailorbird

Orthotomus sutorius

RANGE India, S. China,
S.E. Asia to Java

HABITAT Scrub,
bamboo, gardens

SIZE 4¾ in (12 cm)

Both sexes of this species have similar plumage, but in the breeding season, the male's two central tail feathers grow much longer than the others, adding about 1½ in (4 cm) to his length. The tailorbird is a common, widespread species. It spends much of its time hopping about in bushes and low trees, searching for insects, larvae and small spiders. It also eats nectar.

Pairs mate for life and nest on a bush or low branch. The nest is made in a cradle, formed by sewing together the edges of a large leaf or two smaller leaves. A series of small holes is made in the edges of the leaf with its beak and strands of wool, spiders' web or cocoon silk, are used to draw them together. The 2 or 3 eggs are laid inside the cradle, on a nest of soft fibers. Both parents incubate the eggs and tend the young.

MEGALURINAE: GRASS-WARBLER SUBFAMILY

The 21 species in this subfamily include songlarks and fernbirds. They occur in a variety of habitats ranging from forest to semidesert in south and Southeast Asia, the western Pacific islands, Africa and Madagascar. Most are slender birds with short wings that skulk in reeds, tall grass, or other vegetation.

Little Grassbird

Megalurus gramineus

RANGE Australia (except N.); Tasmania

HABITAT Swamps

SIZE 5½ in (14 cm)

The little grassbird lives amid the vegetation of coastal and inland swamps. This furtive bird stays in cover as it creeps about, foraging for insects and small aquatic animals. It seldom flies, but it occasionally makes long flights to find a new home, if its swamp dries out. The sexes look alike, with streaked brownish plumage and white eye

stripes. The tail accounts for almost half of the bird's length. The cup-shaped nest is made in thick vegetation, sometimes over water. It is made of grass, lined with feathers. The female lays 3 or 4 eggs.

GARRULACINAE: LAUGHINGTHRUSH SUBFAMILY

These sociable birds communicate with shrieking calls that give the group its name. The 54 species of laughingthrushes are found from Pakistan to Borneo, and most species live in forest or scrub.

White-crested Laughing thrush

Garrulax leucolophus

RANGE Himalayas, S.W. China,
S.E. Asia, W. Sumatra

HABITAT Forest

SIZE 12 in (30.5 cm)

The white-crested laughing thrush has an erectile crest on its white head, a white throat and breast and characteristic black masklike markings on its head. The several races within the range differ slightly in the shade of the darker areas of plumage. They are sociable and move in small flocks, foraging in dense undergrowth and on the ground and communicating by chattering calls often followed by wild, cackling sounds, which resemble laughter and are the origin of the common name. Insects, berries and seeds are their main foods, but they take nectar and small reptiles as well. Large items of prey are held down with the foot while being torn to pieces with the bill.

The cup-shaped nest is hidden in a low tree or bush. It is made of grass, bamboo leaves, roots and moss, bound with tendrils of vine and lined with rootlets. The female lays 3 to 6 eggs and both parents incubate the clutch for about 14 days. The chestnut-winged cuckoo, *Clamator coromandus*, is known to lay its eggs in the nest of this species.

BABBLERS

SYLVINAE BABBLER, WRENTIT AND TYPICAL WARBLER SUBFAMILY

This large and diverse subfamily contains 256 species in three tribes – babblers, the wrentit, and typical warblers.

The 233 species of babblers are all found in the warmer parts of the Old World, with the greatest diversity of species occuring in Africa and south Asia. As their name suggests, most are extremely vocal, noisy birds, and some are fine songsters.

Babblers are either warblerlike or thrushlike birds that tend to have short, rounded wings. They are poor fliers and spend much of their time on the ground or clambering around in trees and bushes. Their feathers are soft, and the plumage varies from dull browns to bright colors, often with bold markings on the head and neck. Most babblers have thickset bodies and fairly long tails. Their legs and feet are strong which enables them to probe and dig in thick vegetation and ground litter in search of invertebrate prey, such as slugs and snails. They also eat small berries and some fruit.

Feeding activity is generally accompanied by the loud and varied "babbling" calls that give the group its common name. Much of this calling behavior may be linked to keeping the small feeding flocks together as they move through the dense vegetation. The babbler tribe also includes parrotbills, yuhinas, fulvettas, and rhabdornis.

The single species of wrentit is a warblerlike North American babbler.

The 22 species of typical warblers, that include the blackcap and whitethroats, are found in Eurasia, Africa, the middle East and northern India. Most warblers are slender arboreal birds that inhabit areas of shrubs or woodland where they feed on insects and fruits. Many warblers are migratory and winter in the southern part of their range.

Brown-cheeked Fulvetta *Alcippe poioicephala*

RANGE	India to S.W. China, S.E. Asia
HABITAT	Forest, scrub, bamboo
SIZE	6 in (15 cm)

The brown-cheeked fulvetta is a rather plain little bird, with mainly buffy brown plumage. Both the male and female of the species have gray plumage on the top of the head.

In small groups of 4 to 20, these babblers forage among the forest undergrowth for insects. They rarely, if ever, descend to the ground but may climb farther up trees into the canopy layers. The birds keep in touch as they search for food by calling to one another and they are extremely wary of any possible danger that might arise.

The nest is constructed on a branch of a tree or bush a few meters above ground or it is suspended from a few twigs. It is cup-shaped and is built of moss and dead leaves, lined with fine moss and ferns. The female usually lays a clutch of 2 eggs, which are incubated by both parents.

Stripe-throated Yuhina *Yuhina gularis*

RANGE	Himalayas to northern S.E. Asia and W. China
HABITAT	Forest
SIZE	6 in (15 cm)

The stripe-throated yuhina is a distinctive little bird. It has a prominent head crest, dark streaks on its throat and an orange-rufous streak on the wings. The male and female of the species look alike.

Small parties of these active little birds forage in the trees for insects, such as beetles and wasps, calling to each other as they go. They will sometimes join in mixed flocks with other species of babbler. They also feed on seeds and nectar, and their crests become coated with pollen as they fly from flower to flower.

Little is known of the breeding habits of these birds, but nests made of roots and of moss have been described. The female is thought to lay a clutch of 4 eggs.

Brown Babbler *Turdoides plebejus*

RANGE Africa: Senegal, east to Sudan, Ethiopia and W. Kenya

HABITAT Bush, savanna

SIZE 9 in (23 cm)

Both male and female brown babblers have mainly grayish-brown plumage, with some white markings and light underparts. Typical babblers, they form noisy flocks flying from one bush to another while making chattering, babbling calls. They feed on insects and some fruit, which they find in the low levels of bushes or by scratching about on the ground.

The cup-shaped nest is made of rootlets, lined with fine plant material, and is situated in a dense bush. The female lays a clutch of 2 to 4 eggs.

Red-billed Leiothrix *Leiothrix lutea*

RANGE Himalayas, mountain areas of northern S.E. Asia and S. China; introduced in Hawaii

HABITAT Forest undergrowth, scrub, grass

SIZE 6 in (15 cm)

The male red-billed leiothrix is an attractive bird, with an orange-red bill and bright yellow and orange plumage on the throat, breast and wing feathers; his bill has a blackish base in winter. The female has duller plumage, with a paler throat and breast, and she lacks the bright wing feathers. The courting male perches on top of a bush and fluffs out his feathers to attract his mate, while delivering what has been described as "a delightful song."

These birds live in many different types of forest where they forage in the undergrowth for insects. They are lively, gregarious birds, usually seen in small groups, except in the breeding season when they form pairs.

The cup-shaped nest is made of leaves, moss and lichen, of moss only or of bamboo leaves, depending on what plant material is available, and it is lined with fine threads of fungal material. Usually rather conspicuous, the nest is placed on a horizontally forked branch or in an upright fork, or is bound to several twigs or stems. The female lays a clutch of 3 eggs and there is usually more than one brood. This leiothrix is a familiar cage bird, under the name of the Peking robin.

Fire-tailed Myzornis *Myzornis pyrrhoura*

RANGE Himalayas from Nepal to Myanmar; S.W. China

HABITAT Bush, forest

SIZE 5 in (12.5 cm)

An exquisite little bird, the fire-tailed myzornis has touches of black, white and red on its mainly green plumage. The female looks similar to the male, but her red plumage is duller, and the throat and belly tend toward buff brown.

Generally found in forest at altitudes above 6,000 ft (1,800 m), the myzornis lives either alone or in small groups of 3 or 4, which may sometimes join with mixed flocks of other babblers and warblers.

It is a most adaptable bird in its feeding techniques – it forages on foliage and flowers for insects and spiders, like other babblers, but can also run up mossy tree trunks to find prey or hover like a sunbird in front of flowers. Using its bristly tongue, it will probe the flowers of shrubs, such as rhododendrons, for nectar and also feeds on sap which it obtains from trees.

Little is known of the breeding habits of this bird, the only representative of its genus. The one nest that has ever been observed was in dense, mossy forest, and both parents appeared to be feeding the young.

BABBLERS CONTINUED

White-necked/White-eared Babbler

Stachyris leucotis

RANGE Malaysian Peninsula, Sumatra, Borneo

HABITAT Forest

SIZE 6 in (15 cm)

The white-necked
babbler is
identified
by its white
eyebrow streaks, linked to the row
of white spots on the sides of its
neck. Male and female look
similar. It is mainly a ground-living
bird, found in the undergrowth of forest, and does not fly well.
It feeds on insects such as black beetles and flies.

The neat, cup-shaped nest is made of grass, roots and plant
fibers, in a tree or dense undergrowth. The female is thought to
lay 3 eggs, but few nests have been observed.

Large Wren-babbler *Napothera macrodactyla* **LR:nt**

RANGE Malaysian Peninsula, Sumatra, Java

HABITAT Lowland forest

SIZE 7½ in (19 cm)

A big, plump, short-tailed babbler, the large wren-babbler has
white patches between the beak and eyes, a white throat and
characteristic scalelike markings on breast and upperparts. The

bill is stout and the feet large and strong. An uncommon bird,
this babbler lives in undergrowth and feeds near or on the
ground on insects. It perches on bushes to sing.

Little is known of this bird's nesting habits, but it is
thought that the female lays a clutch of 2 eggs.

Scaly-breasted Illadopsis *Illadopsis albipectus*

RANGE Africa: S. Sudan, Zaire, east to Kenya

HABITAT Forest, dense high bush

SIZE 5½ in (14 cm)

The scaly-breasted illadopsis lives on the floor or in the
undergrowth of thick forest, often side by side with the
pale-breasted illadopsis, *T. rufipennis*, which it closely resembles.
A rather quieter bird than most babblers, it moves around in
small groups, close to or on the ground, searching for ants,
beetles and other insects. The male and female of the species
look alike, both with pale chest feathers edged with gray – a
coloration which creates the scaly appearance from which the
bird's common name is derived.

The cup-shaped nest is constructed from dead leaves and is
hidden among leaves or on an overgrown tree stump. The
female lays a clutch of 2 eggs.

Rufous-crowned Babbler *Malacopteron magnum*

RANGE Malaysian Peninsula, Sumatra, Borneo

HABITAT Forest

SIZE 7 in (18 cm)

The rufous-crowned babbler is identified by its reddish-brown
crown and the black plumage at the back of the neck. Its wings
and tail are longer than those of many babblers. An arboreal

Stripe-sided Rhabdornis *Rhabdornis mysticalis*

RANGE Philippines

HABITAT Forest

SIZE 6 in (15 cm)

The stripe-sided rhabdornis, or creeper, has strong legs and feet, which are well suited to climbing tree trunks. It uses its long, slightly curved bill to probe the bark for insects and feeds in the same manner as the treecreepers, gradually working its way up a tree. It also licks up nectar from flowers with its brush-tipped tongue and feeds on fruit.

The female has lighter plumage than the male and she is brown where he is black.

Little is known of the breeding habits of this bird other than that it makes its nest in a hole in a tree.

Wrentit *Chamaea fasciata*

RANGE USA: Pacific coast, Oregon to California; coast of Baja California

HABITAT Scrub, chaparral

SIZE 6–6¾ in (15–17 cm)

The single species of wrentit is included within the main babbler subfamily, although its relationships and classification have been the subject of much dispute.

The wrentit is an elusive, inconspicuous little bird, which spends all of its life within its selected territory, and which it defends throughout the year. It flies weakly and seldom takes to the air across any distance of open country. Pairs mate for life and once they have bonded they forage and roost together. Insects, including spiders, ants, caterpillars, flies and beetles

make up the majority of its diet. It also eats berries and occasionally visits bird feeders.

The paired wrentits work together to construct a neat, cup-shaped nest from bark, plant fiber and grass, bound together with spiders' webs. The nest is usually above ground in a bush or small tree. The female lays a clutch of 3 to 5 eggs, generally 4, which are incubated for 15 or 16 days by the female, although the male may take a turn.

Blackcap *Sylvia atricapilla*

RANGE Breeds in Europe, Britain and Scandinavia to Mediterranean countries, east to Iran and Siberia; winters south of range and in Africa

HABITAT Woodland, gardens, orchards

SIZE 5½ in (14 cm)

The male blackcap is distinguished from other *Sylvia* (typical) warblers by his glossy black crown and gray neck. He has a rippling song and is also an accomplished mimic. Females and juveniles have rusty brown caps and are otherwise similar to males, but are browner. It is an active, lively bird and forages in trees and bushes for insects. This species eats more fruit than most other warblers.

The male courts his mate by raising his head and back feathers and drooping and flapping his wings. He builds several rough nests as part of his courtship ritual. She may reject them all and build her own or finish off one of his. The final nest is made in a low bush or other low cover and is constructed from dry stems, spiders' webs and is lined with wool. Both parents incubate the clutch of between 3 and 6 eggs for between 10 and 15 days. They both feed their newly-hatched young.

The species of blackcap *S.a. heineken* which is found on Madeira has darker plumage.

LARKS

ALAUDIDAE: LARK FAMILY

The larks, about 91 species in all, are concentrated in the Old World except for a single species, the shore lark, *Eremophila alpestris*, which also occurs in the Americas. Typically, the wings are fairly long and pointed and the beak rather long and slightly down-curved. Males and females look more or less alike, but the female is often smaller.

Most species favor an open habitat with low vegetation, such as tundra, meadowland or desert, where they are commonly seen walking or running along the ground. The diet consists of seeds, buds, insects and small underground invertebrates, obtained by bill-probing or digging.

Desert Lark *Ammomanes deserti*

RANGE	Africa: Sahara; Middle East, through Iran to N.W. India
HABITAT	Stony, hilly desert, dry wooded slopes
SIZE	6 in (15 cm)

The plumage of the desert lark matches the color of the desert soil. The dark subspecies, *A. d. annae*, blends with the black larval sand of central Arabia, while the pale race, *A. d. isabellina*, does not stray from areas of white sand.

The nest is usually built up against a rock or tuft of grass and is reinforced on the windward side by small decorative pebbles. In the harsh desert interior, 3 eggs are laid, while 4 or 5 may be produced at the desert edge.

Singing Lark *Mirafra cantillans*

RANGE	W., C. and E. Africa, Middle East, Pakistan, India
HABITAT	Open bush or scrub, rice fields
SIZE	6 in (15 cm)

The vibrant songs of the singing bush lark can often be heard issuing from bushes or the air, even on bright moonlit nights. Darker and more evenly colored than other larks, this plump

gregarious bird has a heavy, finchlike bill, which it uses to pick up grass seeds and insects. Its shape, strong rapid gait and weak flight suit the bush-lark to life on the ground.

The igloo-shaped grass nest is built in the shelter of a rock or a tuft of grass and has a side entrance and soft, grass lining. The female lays a clutch of 3 to 5 eggs.

Thick-billed/Clotbey Lark *Ramphocoris clotbey*

RANGE	N. Africa to Syria
HABITAT	Stony desert
SIZE	6¾ in (17 cm)

True to its name, this lark is distinguished by its large, powerful bill. The bird uses it to crush tough seed cases and hard-shelled desert insects, and carries its head very straight or thrown backward, to counteract the weight of the bill. The male is sandy colored, with black spots on the underparts, the female has a redder tinge and fewer spots.

Although this species is normally sedentary, some birds move away from the heat of the desert outside the breeding season.

The nest is sited up against a stone or grass tussock and starts out as a small hollow, filled with soft plant material. As it begins to overflow, the nesting material is supported by a collection of small pebbles. The female lays a clutch of between 2 and 5 eggs.

Greater Short-toed/Red-capped Lark

Calandrella cinerea

RANGE E. and S. Africa

HABITAT Sandy or stony plains

SIZE 5½ in (14 cm)

There are three other species of short-toed larks that range through southern Europe, the Middle East, Central and Eastern Asia and that are considered by some ornithologists to be conspecific with *C. cinerea*. The 14 or so races of short-toed larks vary in color throughout the range, from sandy to reddish – the South African race, for example, has a rufous cap on its head and reddish patches on the sides of its breast. This bird is a speedy runner and when alarmed it escapes by flying low, then landing abruptly and sprinting away. Short-toed larks feed on the ground on seeds and insects but perform long, undulating song flights at a height of about 50 ft (15 m).

Short-toed larks gather in large flocks out of the breeding season but disperse to mate, when they are seen singly or in pairs. The nest, deep and cup-shaped, holds two clutches of 3 to 5 eggs each in a year. Incubation lasts for 11 to 13 days.

Shore/Horned Lark *Eremophila alpestris*

RANGE N. America, Europe, N. Africa, Asia

HABITAT Varied, rocky alpine meadows up to 17,300 ft (5,275 m), stony steppe, tundra and desert, open grassland

SIZE 6¼ in (16 cm)

The only lark native to the Americas, the shore lark comprises 40 widespread races. The male has a black and yellow head with short black tufts of feathers. Females and juveniles are less black. In winter, northern groups migrate to southern breeding grounds. Most populations winter in lowland fields, and may form flocks with buntings. They eat seeds, buds and insects and their larvae, small crustaceans and mollusks.

The nest is a simple structure on the ground made from plant stems, lined with soft plant material. It is surrounded with sheep droppings, plant debris and pebbles. There are usually two broods of 4 eggs each, which are incubated for 10 to 14 days.

Eurasian/Common Skylark

Alauda arvensis

RANGE Europe, Asia, N. Africa; introduced in Australia, New Zealand, Canada, Hawaiian Islands

HABITAT Moorland, marshes, sand-dunes, arable and pasture land

SIZE 7 in (18 cm)

The skylark has dark wings and a long tail, both with a white fringe, a boldly streaked breast and a short, but prominent, crest. It is a terrestrial bird and roosts on the ground. It walks rather than hops and crouches when uneasy, emitting a liquid chirrup when flushed.

Skylarks enjoy dust baths and prefer to perch on low walls, fences or telephone wires. They usually sing early in the morning and have a characteristic song flight, fluttering high in the sky. Their diet consists of seeds and ground-living invertebrates.

The female builds a well-concealed grass nest in which she lays 3 to 5 eggs. She then incubates them for 11 days. Two or three broods are raised each year. Northern races migrate south of their range for the winter.

Greater Hoopoe Lark/Bifasciated Lark

Alaemon alaudipes

RANGE Cape Verde Archipelago, across the Sahara to Middle East, W. India

HABITAT Open sandy desert

SIZE 8 in (20.5 cm)

The greater hoopoe lark is long legged, long billed and distinguished by its white eyebrow tufts. It uses its down-curved bill to dig into the desert soil in search of grubs, locust pupae and seeds. This bold bird defends its territory. It has a long, melodious call, but its song is a series of pipes and whistles. It rarely flies except during its song flight. It nests on the ground, although in the hottest areas, the nest is placed a few inches off the ground in the shady lower

SUNBIRDS

NECTARINIIDAE: SUNBIRD, FLOWERPECKER, AND SUGARBIRD FAMILY

Some 169 species of nectar and insect feeders are found in this family. There are 2 subfamilies – Nectariniinae (sunbirds and flowerpeckers) and Promeropinae (sugarbirds).

Sunbirds are the Old World counterparts of the hummingbirds of the Americas, but they are less skilful fliers. There are 123 species of sunbird and more than half live in Africa, south of the Sahara. Others occur in southern Asia and Australasia. In all species (except for the spiderhunters, which are soberly colored) the males have more showy plumage than females. Typical sunbirds have short, rounded wings and a long, downward-curving bill. Most eat nectar and insects. The beak is inserted into the flower, and the nectar is sucked through the tubular, split-tipped tongue. Sunbirds can hover only briefly, but their sturdy legs and feet enable them to perch as they feed.

The 44 species of flowerpeckers live in Asia, from India to China, and south to Australasia. The greatest diversity is found in the New Guinea area and the Philippines. They are small birds with short legs and tails and their bills vary in shape but are partially serrated. The tongue is forked, with the edges rolled into almost complete tubes. Fruit and berries are the most important foods, but they do take some nectar and insects associated with the flowers. Some flowerpeckers have dull plumage, but in other species, however, the male is brightly colored.

The 2 species of sugarbirds resemble larger, drabber versions of the sunbirds and are found in South Africa, living on mountain slopes where Protea bushes grow.

Crimson/Yellow-backed Sunbird Aethopyga siparaja

RANGE India, S.E. Asia, Sumatra, Java, Borneo, Sulawesi, Philippines
HABITAT Forest, cultivated land
SIZE 4½ in (11.5 cm)

The metallic green tail of the male crimson sunbird has elongated central feathers. The female lacks his bright plumage and is olive-green, with yellowish underparts. Crimson sunbirds cling to stems and twigs as they suck nectar from flowers. Some insects and spiders are also eaten.

A pear-shaped nest, made of plant down, rootlets, moss and grass is hung from a branch or twig. The female lays 2 or 3 eggs.

Ruby-cheeked Sunbird Anthreptes singalensis

RANGE E. Himalayas to Myanmar, Thailand, Malaysia, Sumatra, Java, Borneo and adjacent islands
HABITAT Open forest, scrub
SIZE 4½ in (11.5 cm)

Both male and female ruby-cheeked sunbirds have pale orange throats and yellow bellies, but the female is otherwise less brilliantly colored than the male and has largely olive-green plumage. These sunbirds flit quickly around the foliage, searching for insects and probing blossoms for nectar.

The pear-shaped nest is suspended in a bush from twigs not far from the ground. It is made of fine plant fiber and stalks and has a side entrance, sheltered by an overhanging porch. The female lays a clutch of 2 eggs.

Long-billed Spiderhunter Arachnothera robusta

RANGE Thailand, Malaysia, Sumatra, Java, Borneo
HABITAT Forest
SIZE 7½–8½ in (19–21.5 cm)

The long-billed spiderhunter is a large sunbird, with an extremely long, thick bill. Like all spiderhunters, it has duller plumage than other sunbirds; male and female look similar, but the male has small orange-yellow tufts at each side of his breast. This spiderhunter usually forages at the tops of tall trees, darting from one to another in search of insects and spiders or perching on high branches. Its flight is strong and direct.

The nest is made under a large leaf such as banana, which forms the top of the nest. This structure of coarse plant fiber is neatly attached to the leaf by threads of fiber, which are passed through the leaf and twisted into knots on its upper surface. An entrance hole is left near the tip of the leaf. The female lays a clutch of 2 eggs.

Olive-backed Sunbird *Nectarinia jugularis*

Range S.E. China, S.E. Asia, Indonesia, New Guinea, Bismarck Archipelago, Solomon Islands; Australia: N.E. Queensland

Habitat Forest, scrub, mangroves, gardens

Size 4¾ in (12 cm)

The only sunbird found in Australia, this species is common throughout its range. Darting from tree to tree, it searches flowers for insects and nectar, sometimes also catching insects in the air. It will hover briefly before a flower, but normally clings to the foliage.

The male and female of the species differ in appearance, the female having a bright yellow throat and underparts but the same olive back as the male. Non-breeding males are sometimes similar to females but have a blue-black band down the center of the throat and an orange tinge to the throat and upper breast.

The nest is made of plant fibers and bark, bound with cobwebs and suspended from a twig of a bush or low tree. The female lays a clutch of 2 or 3 eggs.

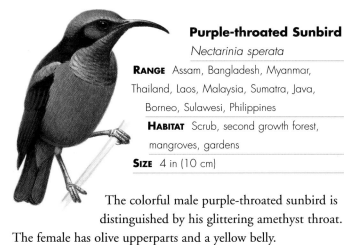

Purple-throated Sunbird
Nectarinia sperata

Range Assam, Bangladesh, Myanmar, Thailand, Laos, Malaysia, Sumatra, Java, Borneo, Sulawesi, Philippines

Habitat Scrub, second growth forest, mangroves, gardens

Size 4 in (10 cm)

The colorful male purple-throated sunbird is distinguished by his glittering amethyst throat. The female has olive upperparts and a yellow belly.

This sunbird does eat small insects, but its main food is nectar, which it extracts from flowers with its slender, curved bill. It hops and climbs with ease around trees and bushes, but its flight is rather weak.

An oval nest is constructed from plant fiber and rootlets bound with spiders' webs. It is suspended from a branch or palm frond up to 20 ft (6 m) above the ground. The female lays a clutch of 2 eggs.

Scarlet-tufted Malachite/
Red-tufted Sunbird

Nectarinia johnstoni

Range Africa: mountain ranges in E. Zaire, W. Uganda, Kenya, Tanzania, Malawi, Zambia

Habitat Alpine zone of mountains up to the limits of plant growth

Size Male: 10–12 in (25.5–30.5 cm)
Female: 5½–6 in (14–15 cm)

The elongate central tail feathers of the male of this species account for much of the difference in length between the sexes. In non-breeding plumage the male's gleaming, metallic feathers are dark brown, but the long tail feathers are retained. The female is dark brown but, like the male, she has red tufts at each side of the breast.

This sunbird is attracted to the flowers of the protea bushes and giant lobelias found in its alpine habitat. Its main food, however, is insects, particularly flies, which it often catches on the wing.

Its oval nest is built in a low shrub from plant down, dried stems and rootlets. The female lays 1 or 2 eggs.

Superb Sunbird *Nectarinia superba*

Range Africa: Sierra Leone to Angola, Uganda

Habitat Forest edge, clearings

Size 5½ in (14 cm)

The superb sunbird forages in the forest canopy for insects and also sucks nectar from flowers. It is partial to the flowers of *Erythrina* trees, which occur near forest, and also to the flowers of forest creepers. The male bird has multicolored plumage, some of it with a metallic sheen, while the female is olive-green with greenish-yellow underparts.

An untidy nest is made of grass, leaves and lichen and suspended from a branch. The female lays 1 or 2 eggs.

FLOWERPECKERS, SUGARBIRDS, BERRYPECKERS AND DUNNOCKS

Crimson-breasted Flowerpecker *Prionochilus percussus*

RANGE Malaysia, Borneo, Java, Sumatra and adjacent small islands

HABITAT Forest, secondary growth

SIZE 4 in (10 cm)

The male of this species has a red patch on the breast and one on the crown, a bright yellow belly and blue upperparts. The female is mainly olive-green, with some grayish plumage and an indistinct orange patch on the crown. An active little bird, the crimson-breasted flowerpecker flies with quick, darting movements and feeds high in the trees, mostly on berries.

The purse-shaped nest is suspended from a branch of a tree and is made of pieces of tree fern. Little is known of the laying habits of this species, but it is thought to produce 1 egg.

Mistletoebird *Dicaeum hirundinaceum*

RANGE Australia, Aru Islands

HABITAT Forest, scrub

SIZE 4 in (10 cm)

The handsome male mistletoebird has shiny, blue-black, red and white plumage, while the female is a duller, brownish-gray. A tree-dwelling species, the mistletoebird forages high in the trees for berries, particularly those of the mistletoe; the young also feed on insects. The soft part of the berry passes to the stomach while the hard seeds bypass the specialized digestive system and are quickly expelled. Thus the bird is of great aid to the plant in dispersing its seeds. A solitary bird, this flowerpecker wanders wherever it can find mistletoe in fruit.

The female makes a nest the shape of an inverted cone, which hangs from a branch of a tree. She lays 3 eggs and incubates them for about 12 days. Both parents feed the young.

Cape Sugarbird *Promerops cafer*

RANGE South Africa: Cape Province

HABITAT Mountain slopes where protea bushes grow

SIZE Male: 17 in (43 cm); Female: 9–11 in (23–28 cm)

The male Cape sugarbird's extremely long tail feathers account for the difference in size between the sexes. Male and female look otherwise similar in plumage. Cape sugarbirds are generally associated with protea bushes, where they forage for insects and take nectar from the flowers. They do, however, visit many other trees and bushes and take some insects in the air. Their flight is swift and direct, the tail held straight out behind. Outside the breeding season, sugarbirds are gregarious and live in small groups.

Breeding takes place in the winter months, particularly April to June. The male bird establishes a territory and perches on top of a protea bush to sing and warn off other males. He performs a courtship display for the female over the nesting site, twisting and turning the tail feathers, which are held curved over his back, and clapping his wings. The female bird builds a cup-shaped nest of twigs, grass and stems, lined with fine plant material and the down from protea leaves. The nest is positioned in the fork of a bush, usually protea. She incubates the 2 eggs for about 17 days and does most of the work of feeding the young on insects, spiders and nectar. The young are able to fly about 20 days after hatching but are tended by their parents for another 2 weeks. There are usually 2 broods a season.

MELANOCHARITIDAE: BERRYPECKER AND LONGBILL FAMILY

The forests of New Guinea and nearby islands are home to the 10 species of small birds that make up this family. Berrypeckers forage among the trees and shrubs within the forest, and at the forest edge, in search of spiders and fruit.

The 4 species of longbills have longer and more curved bills than the berrypeckers. They feed at all levels in the forest and, like the berrypeckers, can hover briefly in order to take insects and other invertebrates from leaves and branches. They also eat some nectar.

Black Berrypecker *Melanocharis nigra*

RANGE New Guinea, other associated islands, including Aru Islands

HABITAT Lowland forest

SIZE 4½ in (11.5 cm)

An agile, quick-moving bird, the black berrypecker usually feeds in the lower levels of the forest, eating mainly berries and fruits but also spiders and insects; it will occasionally drink nectar. It may fly to an isolated tree outside the forest to feed.

Although usually solitary, black berrypeckers do sometimes congregate at feeding trees. Male and female differ in appearance: the male is all black or black and green, while the female is dull green and gray.

Pygmy Longbill *Oedistoma pygmaeum*

RANGE New Guinea and adjacent islands

HABITAT Forest

SIZE 3 in (7.5 cm)

One of the smallest of New Guinea birds, the male pygmy longbill has olive plumage with lighter underparts and an off-white throat. The female of the species is slightly smaller and has duller plumage. Both sexes have short tails and curved bills.

The pygmy longbill frequents the lower levels of the forest but it also forages in the tallest flowering trees. It feeds on nectar and insects and spiders.

PASSERIDAE: DUNNOCK, WAGTAIL, SPARROW, WEAVER, AND GRASS FINCH FAMILY

The passeridae family of small birds contains 386 species, which are found throughout the Old World. Some species have also been introduced elsewhere.

There are 5 subfamilies – Prunellinae (dunnocks), Motacillinae (wagtails), Passerinae (sparrows), Ploceinae (weavers), and Estreldinae (grass finches).

PRUNELLINAE: DUNNOCK SUBFAMILY

These are small, sparrowlike birds with inconspicuous plumage. They are found in Europe and Asia. There are 13 species, all in the genus *Prunella*. Male and female birds look similar.

Dunnock/Hedge Accentor *Prunella modularis*

RANGE Europe, Asia, east to Urals, south to Middle East

HABITAT Woodland, scrub, gardens

SIZE 6 in (15 cm)

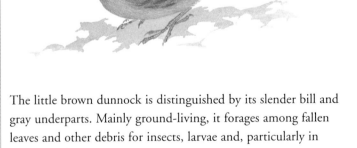

The little brown dunnock is distinguished by its slender bill and gray underparts. Mainly ground-living, it forages among fallen leaves and other debris for insects, larvae and, particularly in winter, seeds.

The neat, cup-shaped nest is made of twigs, grass and roots and is situated in a bush. The female lays a clutch of 3 to 6 eggs which she incubates for between 12 and 14 days. The male partner of the pair helps to feed the young. There may be two broods produced by a pair in a season.

PIPITS AND WAGTAILS

MOTACILLINAE: PIPIT AND WAGTAIL SUBFAMILY

The family of longclaws, pipits and wagtails is absent only from the extreme north and small oceanic islands. Most of the 65 species are characterized by a long tail, which they wag up and down, and some by a long hind claw. All forms are essentially ground-living birds, with strong feet, and have narrow, pointed beaks and slender bodies, which, among the wagtails, have an elongated appearance. Males and females look alike in some species, unalike in others.

Yellow-throated Longclaw *Macronyx croceus*

RANGE Africa, south of the Sahara

HABITAT Wet grassland, open woodland, swamps, cultivated land

SIZE 8 in (20.5 cm)

The hind claw of this widespread species is nearly 2 in (5 cm) long. Male and female look alike, but the juvenile lacks the black chest marking of the adults and has only black spots. These confident birds live in pairs and are often seen, perching in trees or on farmland. In flight they flap, rather like the larks, and occasionally dive into the grass to rummage for insects.

The male's courtship flight is more leisurely, and he fans out his tail and sings at the same time. The loosely constructed nest, made of grass and roots, is usually hidden among long grass or under a tussock. The female lays 3 or 4 eggs.

Golden Pipit *Tmetothylacus tenellus*

RANGE Africa: Ethiopia, Somalia, Sudan to Tanzania

HABITAT Dry scrub

SIZE 6 in (15 cm)

The shy golden pipit is bright yellow, but the darker bars and mottling help it to blend with its arid scrub habitat. The female and juvenile are browner and paler than the male. All have a long hind claw. These birds are usually seen alone or in small family groups, wagging their tails as they perch above the ground, watching for the insects that form their food.

In his courtship display, the male flies down from a tree, with wings raised in a V-shape over his back, whistling as he goes. The female makes a grass nest, lined with rootlets, just off the ground in a clump of grass and lays 2 to 4 eggs.

Forest Wagtail *Dendronanthus indicus*

RANGE E.Asia: breeds Siberia to N.China; winters south from India and China to the Philippines

HABITAT Glades and clearings in montane forest, near water

SIZE 8 in (20.5 cm)

The forest wagtail can be identified by the loud chirruping sound it makes as it flies, perches or runs about looking for the snails, slugs, worms and insects on which it feeds. When standing, by rotating its body, it wags its tail from side to side, rather than up and down as other wagtails do.

Bundles of plant material are bound together with spiders' webs to form a compact nest, which is usually built on a horizontal branch overhanging water. The female lays 4 eggs.

Meadow Pipit *Anthus pratensis*

RANGE Europe, Asia; winters in N. Africa, Middle East

HABITAT Tundra, grassland, heaths

SIZE 6 in (15 cm)

The meadow pipit has typical pipit plumage, with white outer tail feathers, although its body coloration is variable. In winter, meadow pipits gather in small, loose groups. In summer, individuals perch high – on telephone wires for instance – or on the ground in open grassland or alpine meadows. The diet is varied and generally includes flies, mosquitoes, spiders, worms and some seeds.

The male displays to court a mate by flying up and then, with wings stretched out and tail lifted, gliding down singing a simple song. The nest is made and lined with soft grasses and is often tucked into a tussock of heather or grass to hide it. The female lays two clutches of 4 or 5 eggs and incubates them for 2 weeks. The male helps to feed the young.

Water Pipit *Anthus spinoletta*

RANGE S. European mountains east to C. and E. Asia, winters in S. Asia

HABITAT Summers in marshy areas of tundra, mountain and coast; winters in plains and lowlands

SIZE 6–7 in (15–18 cm)

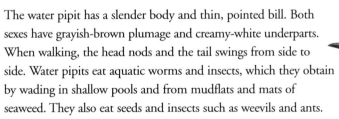

The water pipit has a slender body and thin, pointed bill. Both sexes have grayish-brown plumage and creamy-white underparts. When walking, the head nods and the tail swings from side to side. Water pipits eat aquatic worms and insects, which they obtain by wading in shallow pools and from mudflats and mats of seaweed. They also eat seeds and insects such as weevils and ants.

In spring, flocks of up to 500 birds feed together before flying to the breeding grounds. The female builds a nest of dried grass and twigs in the shelter of a rock, bank or grass tussock. The nest may be a scraped hollow on the ground. She incubates the 4 or 5 eggs for about 2 weeks.

Yellow Wagtail *Motacilla flava*

RANGE Europe, Asia to W. Alaska; winters in tropical Africa and Asia

HABITAT Marshy grassland, heaths, moors, steppe, tundra

SIZE 6½ in (16.5 cm)

All forms of yellow wagtail are greenish and black, with yellow underparts, but males display a variety of head colors. The female has a pale patch above the eye, and the juvenile has dark throat spots. Several races flock together to migrate to the tropics, where they winter by rivers and lakes. They eat insects on the ground or in the air.

During his courtship display flight, the male puffs up his feathers, fans out his tail, which he holds bowed, and vibrates his wings. The nest is made of plant fibers, lined with hair and wool, and is well hidden on the ground. The female lays 5 or 6 eggs, which she incubates for 13 days.

Pied/White Wagtail *Motacilla alba*

RANGE Europe, Asia, N. Africa; winters south to S. Africa, S. Asia

HABITAT River banks, steppe, tundra, alpine meadows, cultivated land, gardens, near water

SIZE 7 in (18 cm)

The two races of wagtail both have similar black and white markings and develop a white throat in winter. The mantle and rump of the white wagtail, *M. a. alba*, of continental Europe, are gray, while those of the pied wagtail, *M. a. yarrellii*, of the British Isles, are black, or dark gray in the female. These birds often roost in hundreds in trees and reedbeds and occasionally wade in shallow water. They take off from a fast run into undulating flight and catch insects in the air.

The cup-shaped, grassy nest is usually made in a hollow in a steep bank, on a building or on flat ground. The two, sometimes three, broods of 5 or 6 eggs, are incubated for 2 weeks.

SPARROWS AND WEAVERS

PASSERINAE: SPARROW SUBFAMILY

Sparrows and their relatives are found in Africa and Eurasia to Indonesia; some species have been introduced into other parts of the world. Sparrows are generally gregarious and roost, feed and breed together. Most of the 36 species are ground-feeders found in open habitats, though there are some woodland species.

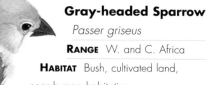

Gray-headed Sparrow
Passer griseus

RANGE W. and C. Africa

HABITAT Bush, cultivated land, near human habitation

SIZE 6 in (15 cm)

A bold little bird, the gray-headed sparrow is common in towns and villages and is similar to the house sparrow in its behavior. It feeds on almost any grain, plant matter and insects and does some damage to crops. The male is slightly larger than the female, but the two look alike, both with distinctive gray heads and mottled wings.

An untidy nest, made of grass, is built in a tree, a thatched roof or any other suitable site, or the birds may use an old nest of another species. There are usually 2 to 4 eggs in a clutch.

House Sparrow *Passer domesticus*

RANGE Temperate Europe and Asia, Africa, north of the Sahara; introduced worldwide

HABITAT Cultivated land, human habitation

SIZE 5¾ in (14.5 cm)

An extremely adaptable and successful bird, the house sparrow lives in close association with humans all over the world and is one of the most familiar of all birds. House sparrows were first introduced into North America in 1850, when a few birds were released into Central Park, New York City. Since then, house sparrows have spread all over North and South America, and the birds seem to be able to adapt remarkably quickly to new environments.

House sparrows often perch on trees and buildings but they feed mainly on the ground. They eat almost anything – grain, weed seeds, insects, refuse and food scraps put out by people.

Gregarious birds, they usually move in flocks and roost in closely packed groups. The male bird is identified by his gray crown, edged with chestnut, his black bib and brown and black-striped back and wings. The female is a brownish-gray color, with gray underparts.

Both members of a breeding pair help to build the nest, although the male does most of the work. The nest is built in any hole or crevice in a building or wall, such as under eaves or in pipes, or sometimes in a tree or creeper. It is constructed from straw, plant stems, paper, cloth or any other available material. The 3 to 5 eggs are incubated, mostly by the female, for between 11 and 14 days. Both parents feed the young, mainly on insects. There may be two or three broods a year.

Rock Sparrow *Petronia petronia*

RANGE N. Africa, Madeira and Canary Islands; S.W. Europe, east through Balkans and central Asia to N. China

HABITAT Stony mountain slopes, ruined buildings, semidesert

SIZE 5½ in (14 cm)

Although they are not as bold with humans as the house sparrow, the rock sparrow often lives near villages and dwellings. It is a gregarious bird and moves in flocks, searching for seeds, insects and berries to eat. Males and females look alike.

The nest is made in a crevice in a rock, wall or building or sometimes in a tree or a rodent's burrow. The female lays a clutch of 4 to 8 eggs, usually 5 or 6. Both parents tend and feed the young, and there may be a second brood.

White-billed Buffalo Weaver
Bubalornsis albirostris

RANGE Africa, from Senegal to Ethiopia
and S. to Uganda and Kenya

HABITAT Savanna, scrub, cultivated land

SIZE 9½ in (24 cm)

Usually seen in small flocks, the buffalo
weaver feeds mainly on the ground on a
variety of grass seeds and insects. The
male's plumage is black, but with
white bases to the feathers, and he has
a black and white or reddish bill. The
female has mottled brown plumage and a
blackish or red bill.

Up to 8 pairs of buffalo weavers make a
huge communal nest in a tree; it is maintained
all year round and used for years on end. The
framework is made of thorny sticks, and each
individual nest inside is lined with fine grass and
rootlets. Females usually lay clutches of 2 to
4 eggs and feed their young on insects.

White-winged Snowfinch *Montifringilla nivalis*

RANGE S. Europe, across central Asia to W. China

HABITAT Barren, stony ground on mountains at
6,000–7,000 ft (1,800–2,100 m)

SIZE 7 in (18 cm)

Although it seldom leaves its mountain habitat, the snowfinch
may descend to alpine valleys in bad winter weather. It perches on
rocks and buildings and hops and walks quickly on the ground as
it forages for insects and, in summer, the seeds of alpine plants. A
bold little bird, it is often seen by skiers in alpine resorts and
readily approaches to collect crumbs of food. The male is
identified by his gray head, black throat and black and white wing
and tail feathers. The female has a brownish head and less white
on the wings and tail. Adults have black bills in the breeding
season and orange-yellow bills in the autumn and winter.

The nest of feathers, dead grass and moss is made in a hole
in a rock or building, where these exist, or in a mammal's
burrow. The female lays 4 or 5 eggs on a warm lining of feathers
and hair. Both parents incubate the eggs for 13 to 14 days and
feed the young; a second brood may follow.

PLOCEINAE: WEAVER SUBFAMILY

This subfamily of 117 species includes the weavers, queleas,
bishops, and widowbirds. Weavers take their name from the
intricate, often colonial, nests "woven" by members of the group.
They are found in a range of habitats in
the tropical and
subtropical
regions of Africa,
Madagascar, and south and
south-east Asia. Some species live in
woodland and forest while others are
ground-dwellers, found in grassland or
scrub. Like the sparrow, they have short,
stubby beaks which are used to feed on seeds,
insects, flower parts, and nectar. During the breeding season,
males are often brightly colored.

Sociable Weaver *Philetarius socius*

RANGE Africa: Namibia, South Africa

HABITAT Dry scrub

SIZE 5½ in (14 cm)

Sociable weavers move in flocks of up to a few hundred birds.
They eat insects and seeds, all of which they take on the ground.
Male and female look alike and are identified by their
grayish-brown crowns, black bibs and the cream-edged dark
feathers on the back that give the plumage a scaly look.

These birds build an enormous communal nest, usually
made in a large *Acacia* tree, which may house up to a hundred
pairs. The birds breed, live and roost in the nest all year round.
Nests are constantly repaired and rebuilt and may be used for
years. Sociable weavers are
monogamous, and within
the communal nest,
each pair has its
own chamber
and entrance.
A clutch
contains
3 or 4 eggs.

WEAVERS CONTINUED

Red-headed Weaver *Malimbus rubriceps* ·

RANGE Africa, south of the Sahara

HABITAT Open woodland, bush country, savanna, cultivated land

SIZE 5½ in (14 cm)

In the breeding season, the male of this species has bright red plumage on the head, neck and breast. The female looks similar, but is yellow where the male is red. The non-breeding male resembles the female. A rather shy, quiet bird compared to most weavers, the red-headed weaver lives in pairs or small groups and forages in the branches of trees for insects; it also eats seeds.

The polygamous male builds a pendulous woven nest for each of his mates. The nests hang from the ends of high branches and have long entrance tubes. Females lay 2 or 3 eggs.

Grosbeak/Thick-billed Weaver *Amblyospiza albifrons*

RANGE Africa, south of the Sahara

HABITAT Bush country, marshes

SIZE 7½ in (19 cm)

Identified by its thick, heavy bill, the grosbeak weaver is a fairly common species, which lives in small parties or pairs. It eats mainly seeds and some berries when available. The male usually has a white forehead and white wing patches but is otherwise various shades of brown. The female is brown, with heavily streaked underparts.

The birds usually nest in small colonies of about 6 nests. Males may be polygamous. The male weaves a neat nest of fine grass, which is strung between two reed or grass stems. The 3 eggs are incubated by the female.

Cuckoo/Parasitic Weaver *Anomalospiza imberbis*

RANGE Africa: Sierre Leone to Ethiopia, south to South Africa: Transvaal

HABITAT Grassland, bush, cultivated land

SIZE 4½ in (11.5 cm)

A gregarious bird, the cuckoo weaver congregates in large flocks outside the breeding season. It feeds mainly on grass seeds. Male and female differ in plumage – the female lacking the male's bright yellow markings and having buff and brown plumage. Juvenile birds are quite different in plumage from the adults being dull olive-green streaked with black, with dusky edges to the feathers.

Cuckoo weavers are brood parasites – they lay their eggs in the nests of other birds and leave the foster-parents to incubate and rear their young. With plumage markedly different from that of their true parents, the young cuckoo weavers resemble the young of Cisticola warblers, birds which are often used as foster parents.

Baya Weaver *Ploceus philippinus*

RANGE India, Sri Lanka to S.W. China, parts of S.E. Asia, Sumatra, Java

HABITAT Cultivated land, grassland, secondary scrub

SIZE 6 in (15 cm)

A common, gregarious bird, the baya weaver lives in flocks all year round and nests in colonies. It hops around on the ground, feeding on grass and weed seeds and also raids grain crops; this damage is compensated for by its huge consumption of insects, some of them pest species. In breeding plumage, the male has a yellow cap and blackish face mask, but in winter he resembles the female, which has a buff-brown crown. The male builds a globular nest, with a long entrance tube at the bottom which is suspended from a branch. There may be up to 200 nests in a single tree. There are usually 3 eggs, which the female incubates for 14 or 15 days. Males are polygamous and may have several mates and nests.

Village Weaver *Ploceus cucullatus*

RANGE Africa, south of the Sahara (not extreme south), Principe Island

HABITAT Forest, bush, cultivated and inhabited areas

SIZE 7 in (18 cm)

Noisy, conspicuous birds, the village weavers live in flocks and breed in colonies. They generally frequent the lower levels of trees in areas near water. Although they damage grain crops, these weavers compensate to some degree by feeding on vast quantities of weed seeds, as well as on some insects. The brightly plumaged male bird is largely yellow, with a black throat and mask and characteristic mottling on the back. The female is duller, with olive-brown on the upperparts and yellowish white below.

Village weavers breed in colonies, with as many as 100 nests in the same tree. Males are polygamous and may mate several times. The nest is woven from long grass stems and hangs from an outer branch; it has an entrance low down. The female incubates the 1 to 3 eggs.

Red-billed Quelea *Quelea quelea*

RANGE Africa, south of the Sahara

HABITAT Savanna, cultivated land, almost anywhere with trees

SIZE 5 in (12.5 cm)

An extremely abundant and gregarious species, the red-billed quelea flies in cloudlike flocks of thousands of birds, which feed on grain crops. They also eat weed seeds. Because of the damage that they cause to crops in Africa they have been destroyed on a huge scale. Numbers have decreased, apparently due to natural causes, and controls have been relaxed. The male's breeding plumage has a reddish tinge on his crown and chest; his face, chin and throat may be white, buff or black. Out of the breeding season, the male's bill is red, but he resembles the female, with streaky brown and buff plumage and a brownish crown.

Red-billed queleas form monogamous pairs and breed in colonies. The male builds the kidney-shaped nest, which hangs from a branch and has a side entrance. The female incubates her 2 or 3 eggs for 12 days. Both parents feed the young.

Red Bishop *Euplectes orix*

RANGE Africa, south of the Sahara

HABITAT Open grassland, often near water

SIZE 5 in (12.5 cm)

Outside the breeding season, these abundant weavers form huge flocks, which can cause great damage to grain crops. They also eat grass seeds.

In breeding plumage the male is largely red and black, while the female is streaked buff and brown; the non-breeding male resembles the female but is darker.

Each male has 3 or 4 mates, which nest in his territory. He weaves an oval grass nest among bulrushes, reeds, sugarcane or maize. The female lines the nest and lays 3 eggs, which she incubates for 11 to 14 days. She feeds her young with insects until they fly, 13 to 16 days after hatching.

GRASS FINCHES AND PARASITIC WHYDAHS

ESTRILDINAE: GRASS FINCH SUBFAMILY

The 155 species of small, seed-eating birds in this subfamily occur in open habitats from Africa across southern Asia to Australasia and the western Pacific islands. Many species nest socially. Most are colorful, while some are drab with striking patches. The sexes look alike in some species, different in others. There are two tribes. One includes waxbills, firefinches, parrot-finches, the zebra finch, and the gouldian finch. The other contains 15 species of parasitic whydahs which lay their eggs in the nests of other grass finches.

Red-billed Firefinch

Lagonosticta senegala

RANGE Africa, south of the Sahara (not extreme south)

HABITAT Scrub, thickets, cultivated land

SIZE 3½ in (9 cm)

A widespread, common bird in Africa, the red-billed firefinch eats grass and seeds. The female is plainer than the male, with only a touch of red on the face and rump, her underparts are buff, with white spots on the breast.

Out of the breeding season, these birds gather in small flocks. The globular nest, usually made of dry grass, is built on a wall or in a bush or roof. Both parents incubate the 3 to 6 eggs.

Red-cheeked Cordon-bleu

Uraeginthus bengalus

RANGE Africa, Senegal to Ethiopia, south through E. Africa to Zambia

HABITAT Open country, cultivated land

SIZE 5 in (12.5 cm)

The male of this species has crimson cheek patches. Females and juveniles are duller and lack the red markings. These common birds eat grass seeds.

Cordon-bleus live in pairs or family groups. The globular or oval nest is made of dry grass with an entrance hole at the side. It is built in a bush, tree or roof. Females lay 4 or 5 eggs.

Red Avadavat *Amandava amandava*

RANGE India, Pakistan, S.W. China, Hainan, S.E. Asia (introduced in Malaysia), Java, Lesser Sunda Islands

HABITAT Scrub, grassland, reedbeds, cultivated land

SIZE 3½–4 in (9–10 cm)

The male red avadavat has bright crimson plumage, dotted with many white spots, his dark wings, too, are spotted with white. Outside the breeding season, he resembles the female, with a grayish-buff throat and breast. Both sexes have red bills and a patch of red at the base of the tail. Often found in swampy land, the red avadavat feeds on grass seeds. It lives in pairs or groups of up to 30, often with other waxbill species.

The ball-shaped grass nest has an entrance at the side, it is built low in a bush or among rushes or grass. The female incubates the 6 to 10 eggs.

Java Sparrow *Padda oryzivora* **VU**

RANGE Java, Bali; introduced in India, Sri Lanka, China, S.E. Asia, Malaysia, Sumatra, Sulawesi, Lesser Sunda Islands, Philippines, Moluccas, Hawaiian Islands, Fiji, Florida, Puerto Rico

HABITAT Ricefields, scrub, mangroves, urban areas

SIZE 6¼ in (16 cm)

The Java sparrow is widely established outside its native range, in some places by deliberate introduction, in others due to the escape of caged birds. The sexes look alike, both with pinkish-red bills and black and white heads. This sparrow largely eats rice and is considered a pest. It also eats fallen seeds of other plants. It climbs with great agility on stalks and trees. A gregarious bird, it moves in flocks.

The domed nest is made of grass and built on a wall, under a roof or in a tree. The female lays up to 7 or 8 eggs, which are incubated for 13 or 14 days. The young are fed on insects until they can digest rice and seeds.

Blue-faced Parrot-finch *Erythrura trichroa*

RANGE Sulawesi, the Moluccas, New Guinea, Bismarck Archipelago, Solomon Islands, Guadalcanal, N.E. Australia, Caroline Islands, Vanuatu, Loyalty Islands

HABITAT Rain forest, mangroves

SIZE 4¾ in (12 cm)

The blue faced parrot-finch lives alone or in small groups and feeds on seeds on bushes, low trees and vegetation. The sexes look alike, both with blue, green, scarlet and black plumage.

The domed or pear-shaped nest is made of moss and plant fiber and has a side entrance, it is built in a tree or bush. There are 3 to 6 eggs in a clutch.

Zebra Finch *Taeniopygia guttata*

RANGE Australia, Lesser Sunda Islands

HABITAT Woodland, dry open country with bushes and trees

SIZE 3½ in (9 cm)

A common bird in Australia, the zebra finch is gregarious and sometimes occurs in large flocks. It feeds in the trees and on the ground on seeds and insects. The sexes differ in appearance: the female lacks the male's facial markings and chestnut flanks and has a grayish-brown throat, with no gray barring. The timing and frequency of the breeding depend on rainfall. A domed nest is made of grass and twigs low in a tree or bush. A clutch usually contains 4 to 6 eggs.

Gouldian Finch *Chloebia gouldiae* **EN**

RANGE Tropical N. Australia

HABITAT Savanna

SIZE 5½ in (14 cm)

The 3 forms of gouldian finch vary in the color of the forehead and face, which may be black, scarlet or yellow. The sexes look similar, but females have duller plumage. The gouldian finch mainly eats seeds and some insects. It seldom comes to the ground, but clings to grass stems or low twigs on bushes and bushes and trees within reach of grass heads. Outside the breeding season it lives in flocks.

The gouldian finch lays its 4 to 8 eggs in a hole in a tree or in a termite mound sometimes on a sketchy, globular nest.

Paradise Whydah

Vidua paradisaea

RANGE E. and S. Africa: Sudan to Angola; South Africa: Natal

HABITAT Dry open country

SIZE Male: 15 in (38 cm)
Female: 6 in (15 cm)

The elongated central tail feathers of the male account for the great discrepancy in size between male and female paradise whydahs. The female of the species has mottled brown and buff plumage similar to, but duller than, that of the male in his nonbreeding plumage. Often gathering in small flocks, paradise whydahs usually feed on the ground on seeds.

In his courtship display, the male bird flies with his spectacular, long central tail feathers raised almost at a right angle to his body, and may also hover near the female, slowly beating his wings.

Like all whydahs, this species is a brood parasite. It lays its eggs in the nests of other bird species, most usually the melba finches that belong to the same subfamily. The young of the melba finch have complex patterns on the lining of their mouths which stimulate their parents to feed them, and the association between this brood parasite and its host, the melba finch has become so strong that the young whydahs have similar mouth patterns. The whydah chicks are also able to mimic the calls and postures of their foster siblings.

FINCHES, BUNTINGS AND TANAGERS

FRINGILLIDAE: FINCH, BUNTING, AND TANAGER FAMILY

This large and diverse family of small to medium-sized songbirds contains 993 species in 3 subfamilies – Peucedraminae (the olive warbler), Fringillinae (finches and Hawaiian honeycreepers), and Emberizinae (buntings, wood warblers, tanagers, cardinals, and icterids).

FRINGILLINAE: FINCH AND HAWAIIAN HONEYCREEPER SUBFAMILY

Finches are a successful, widely distributed group of small, tree-dwelling, seed-eating songbirds. They are most numerous in Europe and northern Asia, but species occur in other parts of the Old World and in the Americas. The 139 species include the chaffinches and the cardueline finches, such as crossbills, grosbeaks, redpoll, and goldfinch. There is a great diversity of bill shapes in the tribe. The sexes usually differ in appearance.

It is likely that the 22 extant species of Hawaiian honeycreepers, as well as the extinct forms, are derived from a one-off colonisation by one type of wood warbler. Existing forms divide into 2 groups. The nectar feeders, which also eat insects and have reddish and black plumage. The second group of finchlike birds, which eat seeds and have yellowish-green plumage. Bill shape differs according to feeding habits. Sexes differ in some species and look alike in others. Most species are threatened.

Chaffinch
Fringilla coelebs
RANGE Europe, across Asia to Afghanistan, Mediterranean region, N. Africa, Canary Islands, Azores
HABITAT Forest, woodland, gardens
SIZE 6 in (15 cm)

The abundant, widespread chaffinch varies in coloration over its range, and its attractive song exists in many different dialects. The female has duller plumage than the male, being mostly grayish and olive-brown. The chaffinch searches for food in the trees and on the ground, where it hops or moves with short, quick steps, it flies in the undulating manner typical of the finches. Three-quarters of

its food intake is plant material, mostly seeds, fruit and corn, but it also eats insects, spiders and earthworms.

A neat, well-constructed nest is made in a tree or bush, and the female lays 4 or 5 eggs, which she incubates for 11 to 13 days. Northern populations migrate south for the winter.

Purple Finch *Carpodacus purpureus*
RANGE N. America: British Columbia, south to Baja California, east to Quebec, Newfoundland, Minnesota and New Jersey; winters in S. USA and Mexico
HABITAT Woodland, coniferous forest
SIZE 5½–6¼ in (14–16 cm)

The male purple finch is distinguished by his rich, reddish coloration, while the female's plumage is mainly brown and gray. Outside the breeding season, these finches form large feeding flocks and search out seeds of weeds and trees. In spring and summer, they also feed on beetles and caterpillars.

The male displays to the female, dancing around her and beating his wings and singing a warbling song. A nest is made of twigs and grasses, usually in a conifer. The female lays 4 or 5 eggs, which she incubates for 13 days.

Island Canary *Serinus canaria*
RANGE Canary Islands, Madeira, Azores; introduced in Bermuda
HABITAT Wooded areas, gardens
SIZE 5 in (12.5 cm)

All races of domestic canaries are descended from this species, which was first made popular as a cage bird by the Spanish conquerors of the Canary Islands. The female is generally brown and duller than the bright yellow and brown male. Canaries feed on seeds and usually remain hidden in the trees, but their attractive song is often heard.

A cup-shaped nest is made in a tree or bush, and the female lays 4 or 5 eggs, which she incubates for 13 or 14 days.

Red Crossbill

Loxia curvirostra

RANGE N.W. Africa, Europe, Asia, south to Himalayas; Japan, Vietnam, Philippines, N. America, south to Nicaragua

HABITAT Coniferous forest

SIZE 5–6¼ in (13–16 cm)

The crossbill feeds almost entirely on conifer seeds, which it extracts from the cones by using its crossed mandibles. The bird may hang upside down to feed or tear off the cone and hold it in its foot. It rarely comes down to the ground. In summer, it also eats insects. Male and female differ in plumage, the female being greenish-gray.

A cup-shaped nest is made in a conifer. The female lays 3 or 4 eggs, which she incubates for 13 to 16 days; both parents feed the young, which hatch with symmetrical bills.

Eurasian Goldfinch

Carduelis carduelis

RANGE Europe, N. Africa, Azores, Canary Islands, Madeira; Asia, east to Lake Baikal, south to Himalayas

HABITAT Open woodland, gardens, orchards, cultivated land

SIZE 4¾ in (12 cm)

Both male and female goldfinches have red faces and black and white heads. The wings are long and pointed and their bills almost conical. Outside the breeding season, they often fly to open country and feed near the ground on thistles and other weed seeds; they also eat some insects.

The female builds a nest on a branch of a tree in a wooded area and lays 5 or 6 eggs. The male feeds her while she incubates the eggs for 12 or 13 days.

Pine Grosbeak

Pinicola enucleator

RANGE N. Scandinavia, Russia, N. Asia; Alaska, Canada, N. USA

HABITAT Coniferous and mixed forest

SIZE 7¾ in (20 cm)

A large, long-tailed finch, the pine grosbeak uses its stout, heavy bill to crush the stones of fruit such as cherries and plums. It also eats seeds, buds and insects in

summer. It finds its food in trees and on the ground and is a strong flier. The sexes differ in plumage, the female being largely a bronzy color.

The nest is usually made in a conifer or a birch tree, and the female lays 4 eggs, which she incubates for 13 or 14 days. The male feeds her during this period and helps to feed the young.

Common/Mealy Redpoll

Carduelis flammea

RANGE Breeds in Iceland, Ireland, Britain, Scandinavia, central European mountains, N. Asia to Bering Sea, northern N. America; winters south of breeding range

HABITAT Woodland, forest, tundra

SIZE 5–6 in (13–15 cm)

The redpoll can survive lower temperatures than any songbird except the Arctic, or hoary, redpoll, *C. hornemanni.* It eats seeds, particularly those of birch and alder, and will hang upside down to reach the catkins. It also scratches on the ground to find seeds and in summer feeds on insects.

At the start of the breeding season, males perform display flights. The female builds a nest on a forked branch and lays 4 or 5 eggs. She incubates the eggs for 10 or 11 days.

Eurasian Bullfinch

Pyrrhula pyrrhula

RANGE Scandinavia, Britain, south to Mediterranean regions (not S. Spain); Asia to Japan

HABITAT Coniferous forest, woodland, parks, gardens, cultivated land

SIZE 5½–6¼ in (14–16 cm)

The male bullfinch is identified by his black cap, rose-red underparts and black and white wings. The female looks similar but has pinkish-gray underparts. This shy bird usually perches in cover in a bush or tree and does not often come to the ground. In spring, it feeds largely on the buds of fruit trees and can cause considerable damage to crops; buds of other trees are also eaten, as well as berries and seeds.

A nest of twigs and moss is built by the female in a bush or hedge. She lays a clutch of 4 or 5 eggs, which she incubates for 12 to 14 days.

FINCHES, BUNTINGS AND TANAGERS CONTINUED

Palila *Loxioides bailleui* **EN**

RANGE Hawaii: Mauna Kea

HABITAT Forest

SIZE 6 in (15 cm)

The palila is now found only on the western slope of Mauna Kea and is a seriously endangered bird, largely due to the disturbance and destruction of its forest habitat. It feeds principally on the seeds and flowers of the mamane tree.

The female nests in a mamane tree. She lays 2 eggs, and incubates them for 21 to 27 days. Both parents feed the chicks.

Akepa *Loxops coccineus* **EN**

RANGE Hawaii, Maui, Kauai

HABITAT Forest

SIZE 4–5 in (10–12.5 cm)

Abundant in some areas of the Hawaiian Islands until the end of the 19th century, the akepa is in serious decline. The Oahu Island race is extinct. A sprightly bird, with a short, conical bill, it eats mainly caterpillars and spiders, which it finds on leaves and small twigs. It also drinks nectar. The female lays 3 eggs in a cavity in a tree.

Akiapolaau

Hemignathus wilsoni **EN**

RANGE Hawaii

HABITAT Forest

SIZE 5½ in (14 cm)

This bird is found only in small numbers in a few areas. It has declined due to the deterioration of its forest home and the introduction of predators, particularly arboreal rats. The akiapolaau forages on branches and tree trunks, which it creeps up and down with ease. Its unique bill – the upper mandible is long and curved and the lower short, straight and wedge-shaped is used to open out the burrows of woodboring insects. It uses its thin, brushlike tongue to extract its prey.

EMBERIZINAE: BUNTING, TANAGER, CARDINAL, WOOD WARBLER, AND ICTERID SUBFAMILY

This largest and most diverse subfamily of the finch family Fringillidae contains 823 species in 5 tribes.

The 156 species of bunting are small finchlike birds, usually with somber brown or black plumage, occasionally with patches of yellow and orange-brown. Their beaks are short and conical. Their diet includes seeds and insects. Buntings are found in a range of habitats in the Americas, Africa, and Eurasia.

The 413 species of tanagers occur through the Americas, apart from polar regions. They are vividly colored. In many species the sexes look alike, but in the 4 species in the temperate zones of North America they differ in appearance. Tanagers frequent the upper layers of forests and woods. The feet and legs are well developed. Their diet usually consists of fruit and insects.

Cardinals, which include the American grosbeaks, saltators, and dickcissels, are found in the New World, from Canada to Argentina. The 42 species are stocky with short, strong bills. Males are brightly colored and females are duller.

The 115 species of American wood warblers, or parulid warblers, are found from Alaska and northern Canada to the south of South America. Small, slender birds, with pointed bills, most are brightly colored, particularly in breeding plumage. The sexes look alike in some species and differ in others.

The 97 species of icterids are found throughout the Americas. Icterids include many groups such as oropendolas, caciques, and American blackbirds. The majority live in woodland or forest, but others occur in all types of habitat.

Reed Bunting

Emberiza schoeniclus

RANGE Europe, N. Africa, C. and N. and E. Asia

HABITAT Reedbeds, swamps; in winter, farmland and open country

SIZE 6 in (15 cm)

The male reed bunting has a black head and throat and white collar, while the female has a brown and buff head, with black and white mustachial streaks. The reed bunting forages on low vegetation and reed stems and on the ground for seeds. In spring and summer, it also eats insects and larvae.

The female nests on the ground or in low vegetation and lays 4 or 5 eggs. She incubates them for about 14 days. The male helps to feed the young.

Yellowhammer

Emberiza citrinella

RANGE Europe, W. Asia to Urals

HABITAT Grassland, farmland, open country with bush and scrub

SIZE 6¼ in (16 cm)

The yellowhammer feeds for the most part on the ground eating seeds, grains, berries, leaves and some insects and invertebrates.

The male has a mainly yellow head and chestnut rump, while the female of the species is duller and has less yellow plumage.

After a courtship chase and display, a nest is made on or near the ground often in a hedge or under a bush. The female lays 3 or 4 eggs, which she incubates, mostly on her own, for 12 to 14 days. There may be two or three broods.

Dark-eyed Junco *Junco hyemalis*

RANGE N. America: Alaska, east to Newfoundland, south through Canada and USA to Mexico

HABITAT Clearings, woodland edge, roadsides, parks, gardens

SIZE 5–6¼ in (13–16 cm)

There are 4 subspecies of this junco, with considerable variations in color. Females of all races are less colorful than males. This junco feeds largely on the ground, eating mainly seeds in the winter and seeds, berries, insects and spiders in summer.

The male establishes a breeding territory, and his mate builds a nest on the ground, near vegetation or tree roots or in the shelter of a bank or ledge. She lays 3 to 6 eggs and incubates them for 11 or 12 days. There are usually two broods. Northernmost populations migrate to southern USA in winter.

Savannah Sparrow *Passerculus sandwichensis*

RANGE Alaska, Canada, much of USA (does not breed in S.E.), Mexico, Guatemala

HABITAT Tundra, open grassland, marshes

SIZE 4¼–6 in (11–15 cm)

The many subspecies of savannah sparrow, differ slightly in coloration and song. This species hops about, while scratching and foraging, or runs, mouselike, through grass. Its main foods are seeds and insects, such as beetles, grasshoppers and ants.

The female makes a grassy nest on the ground, usually in a natural hollow, and lays 4 or 5 eggs. Both parents incubate the eggs for about 12 days. Northern populations migrate south to winter in southern USA and Central America.

Snow Bunting *Plectrophenax nivalis*

RANGE Breeds in Iceland, Scandinavia, N. Scotland, Arctic and subarctic Asia, N. America; winters south of breeding range

HABITAT Open stony country, tundra, mountains; winters also on coasts and open country

SIZE 6¼ in (16 cm)

In breeding plumage, the male snow bunting is almost pure white, except for his black back, central tail and primary wing feathers. In winter, his white plumage becomes mottled with rusty brown. The female has a gray-brown head and back in summer and is paler and duller in winter. The snow bunting feeds on seeds and insects on the ground.

The nest is made from dead grass, moss and lichen and is concealed among stones. The female lays 4 to 6 eggs, which she incubates for 10 to 15 days. The male bird feeds his mate during the incubation period and helps to feed the young.

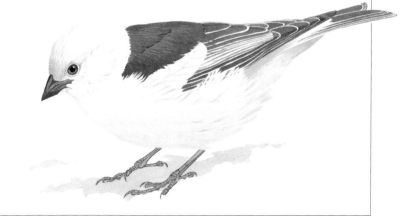

FINCHES, BUNTINGS AND TANAGERS CONTINUED

Chipping Sparrow *Spizella passerina*

RANGE Canada, USA, Mexico, Central America to Nicaragua

HABITAT Open woodland, clearings in forest, gardens, parks

SIZE 5–6 in (13–15 cm)

Both sexes of chipping sparrow have distinctive chestnut caps, edged by white eyebrow stripes. They are inconspicuous birds and often live in suburban and inhabited areas. Grass seeds are their main food, but they also eat weed seeds, insects and spiders.

The female bird makes a nest in a vine or on a branch of a bush or tree. She lays 3 to 5 eggs, and her mate feeds her while she incubates the eggs for 11 to 14 days. There may be two broods in a season.

White-naped Brush Finch *Atlapetes albinucha*

RANGE Mexico

HABITAT Forest edge, scrub

SIZE 7 in (18 cm)

Male and female of this species look alike, both with distinctive black and white heads. Basically terrestrial birds they flutter and hop about on the ground and up on to stems and low branches. They forage in the litter of the forest floor by flicking leaves aside with sweeps of the bill as they search for grass seeds and some insects.

A grassy nest is built by the female in a low bush. She usually lays 2 eggs.

Rufous-sided Towhee

Pipilo erythrophthalmus

RANGE S. Canada, USA, Mexico, Guatemala

HABITAT Forest edge, woodland, parks, gardens

SIZE ·7–8½ in (18–22 cm)

The male rufous-sided towhee is recognized by his mainly black and white plumage and the distinctive rufous patches on each side of the belly. The female has a similar plumage pattern but is brown where the male is black. Both sexes have red eyes. The birds scratch around on the ground and under vegetation for a wide variety of food, including insects, small lizards, snakes, salamanders, spiders, millipedes, seeds and berries.

The courting male chases the female and fans his tail to expose the white markings; he sings to her from a perch in a bush or tree. The female builds the nest on or close to the ground, using grass, rootlets, leaves, bark shreds and twigs. She incubates the 3 to 4 eggs for 12 or 13 days. The young leave the nest 10 to 12 days after hatching, and there may be a second brood. Birds from the north and mountainous areas migrate south in winter.

Scarlet Tanager *Piranga olivacea*

RANGE Extreme S.E. Canada, E. C. states of USA; winters in E. South America

HABITAT Woodland, parks and gardens

SIZE 7½ in (19 cm)

In his summer breeding plumage, the male scarlet tanager is unmistakable with his gleaming red head and body and black wings and tail; in winter, he is similar to the female, with mainly olivegreen plumage, but retains his black wings and tail. Despite

his brilliance, the scarlet tanager is hard to see when he moves slowly or perches high in the trees, eating berries and fruit. The scarlet tanager also eats insects, slugs, snails and spiders.

Male birds return from the wintering grounds a few days before females, and each establishes a territory in the trees. When the female birds arrive, they are courted by the singing males. The female builds a nest in a large tree, using twigs, rootlets, weed stems and grass. She lays 3 to 5 eggs, which she incubates for 13 or 14 days.

Magpie Tanager *Cissopis leveriana*
RANGE N. South America, south to Brazil and N.E. Argentina
HABITAT Rain forest, scrub, cultivated land, clearings
SIZE 11 in (28 cm)

As its common name suggests, this large tanager resembles a magpie and is certainly different from all other tanagers. It is a black and white bird, with long, graduated tail feathers, tipped with white. Male and female look alike, and both have black eyes. Little is known of this tanager, which inhabits areas up to 6,600 ft (2,000 m) in some parts of its range. In pairs or small groups of 4 or 5 birds, it frequents the middle layers of the forest, flying from tree to tree, feeding on insects and berries.

There is no information available about the breeding habits of this tanager.

Song Sparrow *Melospiza melodia*
RANGE N. America: Aleutian Islands, east to Newfoundland, south through Canada and USA to Mexico
HABITAT Forest edge, scrub with nearby water, cultivated and suburban areas
SIZE 5–7 in (13–18 cm)

The song sparrow has more than 30 subspecies, which vary in appearance from the small sandy-colored scrub and desert birds to the larger, dark-plumaged northern varieties. Song sparrows

eat insects, wild fruit and berries and seeds.

The male bird establishes a territory, and his mate builds a neat nest, concealed among vegetation on the ground or in a bush. She incubates her 3 to 6 eggs for 12 or 13 days. There may be two or three broods a season.

Black-capped Hemispingus *Hemispingus atropileus*
RANGE Andes, from N.W. Venezuela to Peru
HABITAT Forest at 7,500–10,000 ft (2,300–3,000 m)
SIZE 6½ in (16.5 cm)

The black-capped hemispingus inhabits the high-altitude cloud forests and the sparse, stunted woods above this zone. Alone or in small groups, it forages among the trees for fruit and insects. Male and female look similar, both with black crowns and largely olive plumage. The cup-shaped nest is made in a tree.

White-shouldered Tanager *Tachyphonus luctuosus*
RANGE Honduras to Panama, south to N. Bolivia, Amazonian Brazil
HABITAT Rain forest, open woodland, plantations, clearings
SIZE 5 in (13 cm)

The white-shouldered tanager varies slightly in coloration over its range – for example, males in western Panama have yellow or tawny crowns – but in most instances, males are bluish-black with the white shoulders of their common name, while females are gray, olive and yellow. These active, noisy birds live in pairs or small groups or may join in mixed flocks. They forage for fruit and insects from the treetops down to the undergrowth, calling to each other with harsh, loud calls.

The open, cup-shaped nest is made of leaves and grasses and is built in a tree not far from the ground. The female incubates the 2 eggs, and both parents feed the young.

FINCHES, BUNTINGS AND TANAGERS CONTINUED

Blue-gray Tanager

Thraupis episcopus

RANGE S.E. Mexico, Central and South America to Brazil and Bolivia; Trinidad and Tobago

HABITAT Open and cleared woodland, cultivated land, parks, gardens

SIZE 6½ in (16.5 cm)

An adaptable, widespread bird, the blue-gray tanager is at home in humid and dry areas, in coastal lowlands and up to 7,200 ft (2,200 m). Birds remain paired throughout the year, and together or in small flocks, they forage in the trees for berries, fruit and insects, which they take from foliage or catch on the wing.

The cup-shaped nest may be made in a variety of sites: high in a tree, in a low bush, even in an open shed or the abandoned nest of another bird. It is made of rootlets, plant fibers, moss and grass, matted together and bound with cobwebs. The blue-gray tanager may even take over the nest of another tanager and incubate the eggs with its own. Normally the female lays 2 or 3 eggs, which she incubates for 13 or 14 days. Both parents feed the young until they leave the nest at about 17 to 20 days old.

Common Bush-tanager *Chlorospingus ophthalmicus*

RANGE Mexico, Central and South America to N. Argentina

HABITAT Rain and cloud forest, woodland

SIZE 5¾ in (14.5 cm)

The common bush-tanager is a noisy, active bird, common in many areas. In small groups, these birds roam the forest, foraging for insects and fruit, mainly in low vegetation but also in the treetops. They may join mixed flocks of birds. Males and females are similar in appearance.

The female builds a nest on a branch under a bromeliad or fern, on a pad of moss on a tree trunk, or on the ground under a bush. She lays 2 eggs, which she incubates for 14 days.

Patagonian Sierra-finch *Phrygilus patagonicus*

RANGE South America: Chile, C. Argentina to Tierra del Fuego

HABITAT Heavily vegetated ravines

SIZE 6–6¼ in (15–16 cm)

This bunting prefers areas with plenty of seedbearing bushes, and rocky outcrops covered with vines. It eats mainly seeds, but also some insects. Females differ from males in having mainly dark-olive upperparts and yellowish-green underparts.

The nest is concealed by tangled roots and is made of grass and 2 to 4 eggs are laid.

Variable Seedeater *Sporophila americana*

RANGE Central and South America: Mexico to Peru and Brazil

HABITAT Forest, grassland, parks, gardens

SIZE 4½ in (11.5 cm)

Small flocks of variable seedeaters often associate with other seedeater species. These birds eat grass seeds and insects and the catkins of the *Cecropia* tree. Males may vary in plumage, but are generally black and white, while females are olive-brown, with some buffy-white on the lower belly.

The female makes a nest of rootlets and fibers, in a tree or bush and fastened to a branch with cobwebs. She usually lays 2 eggs, which she incubates for about 12 or 13 days. The male occasionally feeds her during this period, and helps to feed the young. There are at least two broods a year.

Grassland Yellow-finch *Sicalis luteola*

RANGE S. Mexico, through Central and South America to Brazil

HABITAT Grassland, open pasture, cliffs

SIZE 4½–5½ in (11.5–14 cm)

Primarily a ground-dweller, the grassland yellow-finch hops about, rather than runs. Sometimes it perches on low branches of shrubs and trees, and it will also fly in the open. It feeds on the seeds of a variety of plants. In Chile and Argentina, it is the most numerous small bird, and in winter and spring, large flocks will gather and sing. The female has duller plumage than the male; her upperparts are tinged with brown, and her underparts are pale gray, washed with yellow.

The male courts the female with a display flight and song. She lays 3 to 5 eggs in a cup-shaped nest, concealed among grass or small plants. There are two, sometimes three, broods. Birds in the south of the range migrate north in winter.

Large Ground Finch *Geospiza magnirostris*

RANGE Galápagos Islands

HABITAT Arid zones

SIZE 6½ in (16.5 cm)

The large ground finch is one of the 13 species known as Darwin's finches found only on the remote Galápagos islands; they were a key factor in the formation of Darwin's theories. It is almost certain that all species are derived from a single finchlike form that colonized the islands less than a million years ago. As there are few passerine species in the Galápagos, there were plenty of vacant ecological niches for the birds to adapt to hence the gradual separation into different species. Although most species are similar in plumage, they differ in their ways of life and feeding habits and this is reflected in their varying bill shapes. Some have huge bills for cracking hard seeds; others have parrotlike bills, used for tearing soft plants; another, a slender bill for seizing insects.

The massive, powerful bill of the large ground finch is ideally suited to coping with its diet of hard seeds; this bird only rarely eats insects. Male and female differ in appearance, the male being largely black and the female gray.

The breeding habits of the large ground finch are similar to those of all Darwin's finches. The male establishes a territory and builds several domeshaped nests. He displays to the female and she selects a nest or helps to build another one. The male feeds the female during the period before she lays her 2 to 5 eggs and for about 12 days while she incubates them. Both parents feed the young birds until they leave the nest 13 or 14 days after hatching. There may be several broods in a year, depending on the abundance of food supplies.

Warbler Finch *Certhidea olivacea*

RANGE Galápagos Islands

HABITAT Humid to dry zone

SIZE 4 in (10 cm)

The most agile and lively in flight of all the Darwin's finches, the warbler finch maneuvers well as it flits through the vegetation, searching for insects and spiders. Its bill is thin and pointed like that of a warbler, and its manner of picking its food from the foliage is distinctly warblerlike. Some males have orange throat patches, but otherwise males and females of this species look alike.

The male bird selects a territory and builds several nests in bushes or low trees for the female to choose from. She lays 2 to 5 eggs, which she incubates for about 12 days.

FINCHES, BUNTINGS AND TANAGERS CONTINUED

Blue-crowned Chlorophonia

Chlorophonia occipitalis

RANGE S.E. Mexico to W. Panama

HABITAT Forest, usually over 5,000 ft (1,500 m)

SIZE 5½ in (14 cm)

The male blue-crowned chlorophonia has bright green and blue plumage set off by touches of yellow. The female is largely green, with less blue and yellow. Young males resemble females until they acquire full adult plumage at about a year old. Arboreal birds, these chlorophonias frequent the treetops, where they eat fruit; when fruit is scarce in their high-altitude habitat, they may sometimes descend to lower levels. For a few months after the end of the breeding season in July, the birds move in flocks of up to 12, but for the rest of the year, they live in pairs.

The breeding season begins in March. Both partners of a pair build a domed nest high in a tree, usually among camouflaging moss and epiphytic plants – which are profuse in these high forests. The nest is made of moss, roots of epiphytes and spiders' webs. There are believed to be 3 or more eggs in a typical clutch, and these are incubated by the female alone. Whenever she leaves the nest to feed, she drops almost to the ground before flying off, in order to confuse predators. Once hatched, the young are fed by both parents on regurgitated food, and they remain in the nest for 24 to 25 days. A second brood may follow.

Blue Dacnis *Dacnis cayana*

RANGE E. Nicaragua to Panama, tropical South America to N. Argentina

HABITAT Open forest, secondary growth, orange groves

SIZE 4½ in (11.5 cm)

The blue dacnis is one of the honey-creeper group of tanagers but differs from them in having a short, conical bill. The male bird is bright blue and black, while the female is bright green, with some blue, gray and black plumage. These active little birds forage in the treetops, alone or in small groups sometimes joining mixed flocks of tanagers and other honeycreepers. They eat fruit, nectar and insects and are particularly partial to the flowerheads of mango trees and figs.

The female makes an open, cup-shaped nest in a tree, using fine plant material. She incubates the 2 or 3 eggs and does most of the work of feeding the young, although the male does help.

White-vented Euphonia *Euphonia minuta*

RANGE Mexico, Central and N. South America to Amazonian Brazil

HABITAT Rain forest, secondary growth, scrub, clearings

SIZE 3½ in (9 cm)

The white-vented euphonia lives in pairs or small groups and forages high in the trees, feeding primarily on mistletoe berries but also on insects and spiders. The birds may have to travel considerable distances to find the berries. The hard seeds of the mistletoe are excreted in due course, usually up in the trees, where they stick to the branches and germinate. All the euphonia species feed on mistletoe berries, and they are the birds most responsible for the spread of this parasitic plant. The male bird is a colorful mixture of yellow, white, black and gray-blue while the female is green, gray and yellowish. Both have short bills and tails.

Like the chlorophonias, the white-vented euphonia builds a rounded nest with a side entrance. The nest is made of moss or dry plant material and is placed in a cleft in bark or rock or in a hole in a tree trunk. The female incubates her 2 to 5 eggs for 14 to 18 days. Both parents feed the young.

Silver-beaked Tanager *Ramphocelus carbo*

RANGE N. South America east of Andes, south to Bolivia, Paraguay, Brazil

HABITAT Woodland, secondary growth, cultivated land

SIZE 7 in (18 cm)

The distinguishing feature of this tanager is the conspicuous silvery-white base to the lower mandible of its black beak. The plumage of male birds varies slightly from area to area, being either black or dark maroon on the upperparts, with a red throat and breast. Females seem always to be a dark maroon. Often found near water, silverbeaked tanagers tend to live on or near the edge of wooded areas, rather than inside them. Alone or in small groups they forage actively for insects and fruit from the lowest branches to the middle story of trees.

The female bird builds a large nest in a bush or thicket. Her mate brings food to her while she incubates the 2 eggs for about 12 days. The young birds are able to leave the nest about 11 to 13 days after hatching.

Paradise Tanager *Tangara chilensis*

RANGE N. South America east of the Andes, south to Bolivia and Amazonian Brazil

HABITAT Rain forest

SIZE 5½ in (14 cm)

An extremely beautiful bird, the paradise tanager has gleaming, multicolored plumage. Males and females of the species look alike. In groups that often include other species, paradise tanagers forage for berries, spiders and insects in the middle and upper layers of the forest.

The breeding habits of this species are probably similar to those of other tanagers.

Purple Honeycreeper *Cyanerpes caeruleus*

RANGE Trinidad; N. South America to Bolivia, Paraguay, Brazil

HABITAT Rain forest, forest edge, mangroves, plantations

SIZE 4 in (10 cm)

Groups of purple honeycreepers frequent flowering trees in many different types of wooded areas. Fruit, especially bananas, and insects are important foods, but these birds also perch by flowers and suck nectar from them with their long, curved bills. Male and female differ in plumage; the male is largely bluish-purple and black, with yellow legs, while the female is rich green, with buff and blue patches on the head and breast.

The female builds a cup-shaped nest in the fork of a tree or bush and lays 2 eggs, which she incubates for 12 to 14 days. The young leave the nest about 14 days after hatching.

Giant Conebill *Oreomanes fraseri* **LR:nt**

RANGE South America: Andes in S. Colombia to Bolivia

HABITAT Forested and scrub slopes

SIZE 6¾–7¼ in (17–18.5 cm)

Although not really a giant, this conebill is distinctly larger than other conebills. It has fairly sober, mainly gray and chestnut plumage and a straight, sharp bill about ½ in (1.25 cm) long. Little is known about this bird, which inhabits the Polylepis woods at high altitudes in the Andes – between 10,000 and 13,000 ft (3,000 and 4,000 m). These woods are cold and impoverished, with only the *Polylepis* trees and little other vegetation except for mosses and ferns. The giant conebill explores the trunks and branches of the trees for insects, its plumage providing good camouflage against the bark of the trees. It is usually found in chattering groups, sometimes along with mixed flocks of flycatchers and finches.

FINCHES, BUNTINGS AND TANAGERS CONTINUED

Swallow-tanager

Tersina viridis

RANGE E. Panama to Bolivia, Paraguay, N.E. Argentina, S.E. Brazil

HABITAT Open forest, clearings, parks

SIZE 5½ in (14 cm)

The swallow-tanager is a gregarious bird out of the breeding season and moves in pairs or small groups. It forages at all levels, from the ground to the highest branches of trees, eating fruit and catching insects on the wing. Both sexes are eye-catching birds, the male has mainly turquoise and black plumage, and the female bright green, with a brownish face and throat and touches of yellow on flanks and belly.

The male establishes and defends the breeding territory, and the female makes a cup-shaped nest at the end of a burrow, which she digs in a bank, or in a hole in a wall. She lays 3 eggs, which she incubates for 14 to 17 days. In some parts of their range, swallow-tanagers breed in highland regions.

Plush-capped Finch *Catamblyrhynchus diadema*

RANGE Andes, from Venezuela to N.W. Argentina

HABITAT Cloud forest, forest edge, clearings

SIZE 5½ in (14 cm)

This bird has a golden-yellow crest of short, erect feathers. Male and female have similar plumage. Little is known of this species, which occurs in inaccessible mountain forest, but it appears to live alone or in pairs, foraging in low vegetation and on the ground for its insect food.

Rose-breasted Grosbeak *Pheucticus ludovicianus*

RANGE S. Canada, central and E. USA, south to N. Georgia; winters from Mexico to N. South America

HABITAT Woodland, borders of swamps and streams, cultivated land

SIZE 8 in (20.5 cm)

The male rose-breasted grosbeak is easily identified by his black and white plumage and his red breast patch; the female has streaked brown and white plumage. This grosbeak forages in trees, for seeds, buds, blossoms and insects. It is a popular bird with farmers because it eats the harmful potato beetles and their larvae.

The nest is made on a low branch, usually by the female. The 3 or 4 eggs are incubated by both parents for 12 or 13 days.

Buff-throated Saltator *Saltator maximus*

RANGE Mexico; Central and South America: Panama to Brazil

HABITAT Forest edge, tangled secondary growth, plantations

SIZE 8 in (20.5 cm)

A long-tailed, thick-

berries and fruit such as the fruiting catkins of *Cecropia* trees.

The female builds a bulky nest in a tree or bush close to the ground. The male stays near her, singing and feeding her from time to time. She incubates the 2 eggs for 13 or 14 days, and both parents feed the young. There may be two or more broods.

Painted Bunting *Passerina ciris*
RANGE S. USA, Mexico; winters from Gulf states to Central America
HABITAT Woodland edge, thickets beside streams, gardens, roads
SIZE 5–5½ in (13–14 cm)

An extremely colorful bird, the male painted bunting would look quite at home in a tropical forest; the female is bright yellowish-green. Painted buntings feed on a variety of grass seeds, and also on spiders and insects such as grass hoppers, caterpillars and flies. The male is strongly territorial and will battle fiercely with intruders.

The cup-shaped nest, made of grasses, stalks and leaves, is built in a bush, low tree or vine a meter or so above ground. The female incubates her 3 or 4 eggs for 11 or 12 days.

Dickcissel
Spiza americana
RANGE USA: Great Lakes, south through Midwest to Gulf states; winters from Mexico to N. South America
HABITAT Grassland, grain and alfalfa fields
SIZE 6–7 in (15–18 cm)

The common name of this little bird is derived from its constantly repeated call, which sounds like "dick-dick cissel". The male is characterized by his heavy bill, yellow breast and black bib and chestnut wing patches. The

female is sparrowlike, with streaky plumage, but has a yellowish breast and small chestnut wing patches. Dickcissels feed mainly on the ground on weed seeds, grain, spiders and insects such as crickets and grasshoppers.

The male establishes the nesting territory by calling from a conspicuous perch. The cup-shaped nest, made of weed stems, grasses and leaves, is built on the ground, often in the shelter of alfalfa or grain crops, or in a tree or bush. The female usually lays 4 eggs, which she incubates for 12 or 13 days. There are generally two broods a year.

Northern Cardinal *Cardinalis cardinalis*
RANGE Canada: S. Ontario; E. USA: Great Lakes and New England, south to Gulf Coast, S. Texas and Arizona; Mexico, Guatemala
HABITAT Woodland edge, thickets, parks, gardens
SIZE 7¾–9 in (20–23 cm)

The male cardinal is an unmistakable, brilliant red bird, while the female is buffy-brown, with a reddish tinge on wings and crest and a red bill. Cardinals are strongly territorial and aggressive birds and have a rich and varied repertoire of songs; both sexes are heard singing at all times of year. They feed on the ground and in trees on seeds and berries and, in the breeding season, also take insects.

The female builds the nest on a branch of a small tree or bush, usually among tangled foliage and vines. She incubates the 3 or 4 eggs for 12 or 13 days. Two or more broods may follow.

FINCHES, BUNTINGS AND TANAGERS CONTINUED

Bananaquit *Coereba flaveola*
RANGE Mexico, Central and South America to N. Argentina; West Indies
HABITAT Forest, mangroves, gardens, parks, plantations
SIZE 3¾ in (9.5 cm)

An extremely adaptable, widespread bird, the bananaquit is equally at home in dense rain forest or dry coastal areas, but must have some cover. It lives alone or in pairs and never forms flocks. Bananaquits feed mainly on insects and fruit, but also on nectar, probing blossoms with their curved bills or piercing large blooms at the base to obtain the nectar.

A globular nest is built, usually suspended from a branch or vine. The female incubates the 2 or 3 eggs for 12 or 13 days, and both parents feed the nestlings with nectar or insects. There are at least two broods a year.

Black-and-White Warbler *Mniotilta varia*
RANGE Breeds S. Canada, USA, east of Rockies; winters S. USA to N.W. South America
HABITAT Deciduous and mixed forest, parks, gardens
SIZE 4½–5½ in (11.5–14 cm)

Both male and female of this species are boldly striped with black and white, but the male has a black throat while the female's is white. Insects are their main food, and these warblers creep over branches and tree trunks, searching for caterpillars, ants, flies and beetles and also spiders.

The cup-shaped nest is made on the ground at the foot of a tree or by a rock and the female incubates the clutch of 4 or 5 eggs for between 10 and 12 days. The young are tended by both parents until they leave the nest 8 to 12 days after hatching.

Golden-winged Warbler *Vermivora chrysoptera*
RANGE Breeds N.E. USA; winters south to Central America and Venezuela
HABITAT Woodland, thickets
SIZE 4¼–5½ in (11–14 cm)

Identified by their bright yellow wing patches and crowns, male and female golden-winged warblers look similar, but the female has a lighter throat and eye patch. They forage at all levels of trees and bushes, searching the foliage for insects and spiders.

The nest is made on the ground or just above it in vegetation, and the female incubates the 4 or 5 eggs sometimes 6 or 7, for about 10 days. Both parents feed the young, which leave the nest about 10 days after hatching. This warbler often interbreeds with the blue-winged warbler, *V. pinus*, where their ranges overlap.

Northern Parula *Parula americana*
RANGE Breeds S.E. Canada, eastern USA; winters S. Florida, west Indies, Mexico to Nicaragua
HABITAT Coniferous forest, swamps, mixed woodland in winter
SIZE 4¼ in (11 cm)

A sedate little warbler, the northern parula forages for insects, especially caterpillars, in the trees, creeping over the branches and hopping perch; it also feeds on spiders. Male and female look similar, but the female is slightly duller.

The nest is usually built in hanging tree lichen or Spanish moss. The female incubates the 4 or 5 eggs for 12 to 14 days. Both parents tend the young.

Yellow Warbler
Dendroica petechia

RANGE Alaska, much of
Canada, USA, Mexico, Central and South America to Peru; West Indies

HABITAT Damp thickets, swamps

SIZE 4¼–5 in (11–13 cm)

An extremely widespread species, the yellow warbler varies considerably over its range, but the male breeding plumage is, typically bright yellow with chestnut or orange streaks. Males are duller outside the breeding season, and females are generally more greenish. Yellow warblers forage in trees and shrubs for insects, mainly caterpillars but also beetles, moths and spiders.

The female builds a cup-shaped nest in a tree or bush and incubates the 4 or 5 eggs for about 11 days.

Ovenbird *Seiurus aurocapillus*

RANGE Breeds central and E. Canada and USA to N. Gulf states; winters Gulf of Mexico to N. South America

HABITAT Forest

SIZE 5½–6 in (14–15 cm)

The ovenbird has a brownish-orange crown, edged with black, and its white eye rings. It finds most of its food on the forest floor. It eats insects, spiders, slugs, snails and other small creatures; it also eats seeds and berries.

The female builds a domed, oven-shaped nest on the ground. She incubates her 4 or 5 eggs for 11 to 14 days.

Mourning Warbler *Oporornis philadelphia*

RANGE Breeds central and E. Canada, N.E. USA; winters from Nicaragua to Ecuador and Venezuela

HABITAT Thickets, wet woodland

SIZE 5–5¾ in (12.5–14.5 cm)

Male and female mourning warblers both have gray hoods, and the male has a black patch on the throat. This species forages among low vegetation for insects and spiders.

The bulky nest is made on the ground or in a low bush, and the female incubates the 3 to 5 eggs for 12 to 13 days.

Painted Redstart *Myioborus pictus*

RANGE S.W. USA, Mexico to Nicaragua

HABITAT Woodland, mountain canyons

SIZE 5–5¾ in (12.5–14.5 cm)

Both sexes of painted redstarts have distinctive bright red breasts and white bellies. They eat insects, most of which are caught in the air.

The nest is made in a small hollow in the ground near a boulder or clump of grass. The female incubates the 3 or 4 eggs for 13 or 14 days.

Golden-crowned Warbler *Basileuterus culicivorus*

RANGE Mexico, through Central and South America to N. Argentina; Trinidad

HABITAT Rain forest, plantations, scrub

SIZE 5 in (12.5 cm)

This warbler has a yellow or rufous-orange patch on the crown, bordered with black. Alone or in pairs, it forages in the lower levels of dense vegetation and rarely flies into the open. Insects are its main food – caught among the foliage or on the wing.

The female builds a domed nest on the ground and incubates her clutch of 3 eggs for 14 to 17 days.

FINCHES, BUNTINGS AND TANAGERS CONTINUED

Yellow-rumped Cacique *Cacicus cela*

RANGE Panama, south to N. Bolivia, E. Brazil; Trinidad

HABITAT Rain forest, secondary growth, open country with scattered trees

SIZE 9–11 in (23–28 cm)

The yellow-rumped cacique is gregarious. Much of its food, such as fruit and insects, is found in the trees but it may also catch flying termites.

The female cacique weaves a long, pouchlike nest, from grass and plant fibers, which is suspended from a branch, close to other nests of the colony. The 2 eggs are incubated for about 12 days.

Chestnut-headed/Wagler's Oropendola

Psarocolius wagleri

RANGE S. Mexico, through Central America to N.W. Ecuador

HABITAT Forest, clearings

SIZE 11–14 in (28–35.5 cm)

Wagler's oropendola has dark plumage, with a chestnut head and yellow tail feathers. The male is larger than the female and has a crest of hairlike feathers. It hops and flutters in the middle and upper layers, in search of fruit, seeds and insects.

Colonies of 50 to 100 pairs make their nests in the same tree or clump of trees. Females weave long, pouchlike nests, which hang from outer branches.

Common Grackle *Quiscalus quiscula*

RANGE S. Canada, USA, east of Rockies

HABITAT Open woodland, fields, parks, gardens, orchards

SIZE 11–13¼ in (28–34 cm)

The common grackle is glossy black, with a sheen of purple or other colors, depending on the race. Females are smaller than males. Common grackles gather in large noisy flocks and roost in groups. They forage in trees and bushes for nuts, fruit and the eggs and the young of small birds. On the ground, they probe for worms and chase insects, mice and lizards, and will wade into water to catch aquatic creatures such as frogs and crayfish.

A bulky nest of twigs, stalks and grass is made in a bush or tree or on a building. The birds usually nest in colonies. The female incubates the 5 or 6 eggs for 13 or 14 days, and both parents tend the young. Most populations winter just south of their breeding range, but some are resident.

Northern Oriole

Icterus galbula

RANGE S. Canada, much of USA except Gulf Coast and Florida, N. Mexico; winters from S. Mexico to Colombia

HABITAT Woodland, parks, gardens

SIZE 7–8¼ in (18–21 cm)

There are two forms of this species – the Baltimore oriole (left), found in the east, and Bullock's oriole, found in the west. The western race is similar, but the male has an orange head and white wing patch. Northern orioles eat insects, fruit and berries.

The female weaves a deep pouchlike nest from plant fiber hung from a forked twig. She lays 3 to 6 eggs.

Bobolink

Dolichonyx oryzivorus

RANGE S. Canada;
USA, south to Pennsylvania,
Colorado, California;
winters in South America

HABITAT Prairies, cultivated land

SIZE 6–7¾ in (15–20 cm)

In breeding plumage the male bobolink is
largely black, with a white rump, a white streak
on the back and a yellow nape. In winter, however, he looks
like a larger version of the female, with yellow-brown plumage.
Insects are the main food source of the bobolink in summer,
but in winter, as it migrates south, it feeds on grain crops – in
former times particularly on rice.

The bobolink performs the longest migration of any
member of its family, travelling at least 5,000 miles (8,000 km)
on its trek from Argentina to northern USA and Canada. Once
they arrive at the breeding grounds, males court females with
display flights and bubbling songs. Each male may have many
mates. The female builds a nest on the ground and lays a clutch
of 5 or 6 eggs, which she incubates for 13 days.

Brown-headed Cowbird *Molothrus ater*

RANGE S. Canada, USA; winters south of breeding range, from Maryland
to Texas and California; Mexico

HABITAT Woodland, farmland, fields, open country

SIZE 6–7¾ in (15–20 cm)

As the common name suggests, the male of this species is
distinguished by his shiny brown head; the female is uniformly
gray. They are gregarious birds, forming large flocks in winter
and gathering in small groups of up to 6 in the breeding season.
They feed largely on plant food, such as grain, seeds, berries and
fruit, and on some insects, spiders and snails.

These cowbirds are brood parasites: the female lays her eggs
in the nests of other birds. She lays up to 12 eggs a season, each

in a different nest. The eggs each need to be incubated for 11 or
12 days. This cowbird has been known to use over 185 different
species as hosts. Most of the host species have smaller eggs than
the cowbird. The young cowbirds hatch more quickly and are
bigger than the hosts' young, which usually perish.

Eastern Meadowlark *Sturnella magna*

RANGE S.E. Canada; USA: New England to Minnesota,
south to Florida, Texas and New Mexico; Mexico,
Central and South America to Brazil

HABITAT Open country: prairies, fields, grassland

SIZE 8½–11 in (21.5–28 cm)

The eastern meadowlark bears a close resemblance to the yellow-
throated longclaw, *Macronyx croceus*, of the Wagtail and Pipit
family. The two are not related but they have adapted to a
similar way of life in a similar habitat.

The eastern meadowlark often perches in a conspicuous spot,
such as wires and posts, but it finds much of its food on the
ground. It eats insects, such as grasshoppers, ants, beetles and
caterpillars, as well as grain and weed seeds. It will also consume
the remains of other birds which have been killed by traffic.

After wintering just south of their breeding range, eastern
meadowlarks return to it in the spring, the male birds arriving
before females in order to establish their territories. Each male
may have more than one mate. The grass nest is made in a dip
in open ground and is often dome-shaped. The female usually
lays a clutch of 5 eggs, which she incubates for 13 or 14 days.
Both parents feed the young.

REPTILES

Survivors from a prehistoric age.

THE REPTILES THAT STILL WALK, BURROW, CLIMB AND SWIM ON OUR PLANET REPRESENT THE SURVIVORS IN A DRAMATIC EVOLUTIONARY HISTORY OF REPTILIAN EXPERIMENTATION. FROM AMPHIBIAN BEGINNINGS SOME 300 MILLION YEARS AGO, A WIDE RANGE OF MORE THOROUGHLY TERRESTRIAL FORMS OF VERTEBRATE DEVELOPED. THESE REPTILE STARTING-POINTS HAVE HAD FAR-REACHING IMPLICATIONS FOR THE REST OF VERTEBRATE EVOLUTION. FROM THESE EARLY REPTILE STOCKS OUR MODERN REPTILES CAME. FROM THEM, TOO, HOWEVER, CAME A PLETHORA OF MAGNIFICENT DEAD ENDS, INCLUDING THE ONCE-MIGHTY DINOSAURS, THE WINGED PTEROSAURS AND THE SWIMMING ICHTHYOSAURS AND PLESIOSAURS. AND FROM THE MIDST OF THE COMPLEX EARLY FAMILY TREE OF REPTILE PROTOTYPES DEVELOPED THE ANCESTORS OF THE REMAINING TWO GROUPS OF TERRESTRIAL HIGHER VERTEBRATES: THE MAMMALS AND THE BIRDS. REPTILES THUS LINK THE BEGINNINGS OF LIFE ON LAND, THE AMPHIBIANS, WITH THE MOST ADVANCED AND SOPHISTICATED VERTEBRATES.

False Map Turtle

Different systems exist for classifying the class Reptilia. The most recent classification by cladistic methods does not recognize "Reptiles" as a taxonomic group at all, simply as a group in which animals with different ancestries are "lumped" together. The term "reptile" will continue to be used here, however, because it is such a familiar one. Most of the existing systems, however, recognize about 16 or 17 orders, known by fossils alone or from fossils and still existing animals. Only four orders persist today: first, the chelonians – turtles and tortoises; second, the crocodilians; third, the Squamata, which includes all lizards, snakes and the amphisbaenians; fourth, with only 2 living representatives, the Sphendontia or tuatara order. Even though these four orders represent only a small fraction of past reptilian diversity, they still show something of the interesting variation of which the reptile body form is capable.

The chelonians are a varied and successful assemblage of reptiles with about 250 known species. They have short, broad bodies, enclosed by a bony box into which, to a variable extent, head, tail and limbs can be retracted for protection. The protective box consists of internal bony plates upon which is superimposed tough, horny material, similar to the scales of other reptiles. Chelonians have no teeth but consume vegetation or prey items by grasping the foods with the sharp edges of a beak, developed from the upper and lower jaws.

Crocodiles and their allies are the only remaining representatives of the archosaurian reptiles. The archosaurs, in the form of dinosaurs and pterosaurs, were the dominant terrestrial animals on earth from about 200 million years ago to approximately 63 to 70 million years ago. The characteristic elongate, heavy-headed crocodilians have been effective amphibious predators on earth for around 200 million years and are the largest living reptiles today. They are all carnivores, equipped with rows of sharp, peglike teeth which are continually replaced as they become worn.

Lizards, snakes and the burrowing amphisbaenians make up the order Squamata, meaning the scaly ones. The elongate, long-tailed bodies of lizards have become modified to enable them to live in a wide range of habitats. Lizards can be expert burrowers, runners, swimmers and climbers, and a few can manage crude, short-distance gliding on rib-supported "wings".

Gavial

Mangrove Snake

Most are carnivores, feeding on invertebrate and small vertebrate prey, but others feed on vegetation. The elongate, limbless snakes have some of the most highly modified skulls to be found among vertebrates, with a high degree of flexibility to accommodate large prey and sometimes effective fang and venom systems. Other snakes use their long, powerful bodies to constrict and suffocate their prey in their embrace.

The final order of reptiles includes only the tuataras of New Zealand. They seem to have changed little in their essential details in 200 million years.

Each of the four orders of living reptiles shows different adaptations which mark a distinct advance from the amphibians. Perhaps the most crucial of these modifications relate to temperature control, skin structure and methods of reproduction.

Like the amphibians, reptiles seem not to have any significant ability to control their body temperature independently of external heat sources. They do, however, have a set of behavior patterns which enable them to regulate the effect of external heat sources (sun, hot rocks) on their own temperature. By the use of specific postures and activities in or on the heat sources, reptiles can attain high body temperatures and regulate them to some degree. But their ultimate reliance on the sun for body heat means that the main bulk of reptile species occurs in tropical and warm temperate climates.

The moist skin of the amphibians is important as a respiratory surface. Reptiles, in contrast, have waterproofed themselves with a scaly outer layer that is physically and chemically tough and relatively impermeable to water.

Compared with amphibian methods of reproduction, those of all reptiles show a great leap forward in solving the problem of sexual reproduction on land. Instead of having to return to water to breed and being dependent on the water to bring eggs and sperm together, male reptiles fertilize their mates internally by means of their one or two penises.

The great reproductive advance of the reptiles, however, is their eggs with their tough shells, sometimes doubly strengthened with mineral salts to protect them from abrasion, damage and water loss in the soil where they are normally laid. The egg contains enough yolky food reserves and enough liquid to allow the reptile to develop directly into a miniature adult, instead of passing through an intermediate larval phase as do the amphibians. Systems of blood vessels, running in special membranes enclosing the embryo, transfer the food reserves to it, exchange oxygen and carbon dioxide with the outside air via the shell, or transfer nitrogenous waste products, to be deposited in a special sac that is left behind in the shell when the reptile hatches out. The hatchling has an egg tooth which it uses to slit open the shell and which it sheds afterward.

In some reptiles, eggs are retained within the female's body and hatch within it or as they are laid, so that the female produces fully formed live young. In these species the shell is only a thin transparent membrane. A few reptiles and snakes have advanced still further, and their young develop inside the body with no shell membrane, having instead a primitive form of placenta. Young which develop inside the mother have many advantages in that they are protected from predators and physical dangers. By sunning herself, the mother can keep her body temperature as high as possible, in turn ensuring that the embryos develop rapidly. Live-bearing species occur even in predominantly egg-laying families and are often reptiles that live in particularly harsh climates or at high altitudes.

Reptiles in their evolution have produced all the basic adaptations necessary for efficient terrestrial life that the more advanced birds and mammals carry to higher levels of sophistication. Successful in their own right, they have provided the springboard for the even greater adaptive modifications of the body plans and abilities of the vertebrate animal.

Caiman Lizard

KEY TO REPTILE CLADOGRAM A

1 Chelonia (turtles)

2 Sphenodontia
(tuataras) and Squamata
(lizards and snakes)

3 Crocodilia (crocodiles
and alligators)

4 Aves (birds)

5 Mammalia (mammals)

CLADOGRAM A

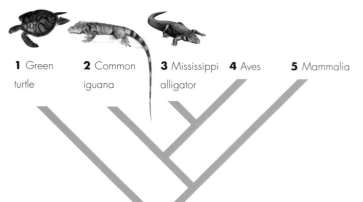

1 Green
turtle

2 Common
iguana

3 Mississippi
alligator

4 Aves

5 Mammalia

KEY TO REPTILE CLADOGRAM B

1 Chelidae (matamatas)

2 Pelomedusidae
(greaved turtles)

3 Chelydridae
(snapping turtles)

4 Dermochelyidae
(leatherback turtles)

5 Cheloniidae
(marine turtles)

6 Kinosternidae
(American mud and
musk turtles)

7 Dermatemyidae
(Central American
river turtle)

8 Carettocelyidae (plateless
river turtle)

9 Trionychidae
(softshell turtle)

10 Testudinidae (tortoises)

11 Emydidae
(emydid turtles)

***Cladogram showing possible phylogenetic relationships within
the "reptiles".*** *Traditional classification places turtles, crocodiles,
lizards, and snakes, within the class Reptilia, and places the birds
into a group of similar rank, the class Aves. Cladists regard the
group known as reptiles as an artificial assemblage which includes
members of more than one monophyletic group. This cladogram
shows the possible relationships between turtles, crocodiles, and
lizards and snakes. It reveals the separation of turtles, which have
distinctive skulls and shells, from the other groups, the relationships
between lizards, snakes and crocodiles, and the equal ranking of
birds with the "reptilian" taxa shown here. The other cladograms on
this page show the probable relationships within the turtles, lizards,
and snakes, respectively.*

CLADOGRAM B

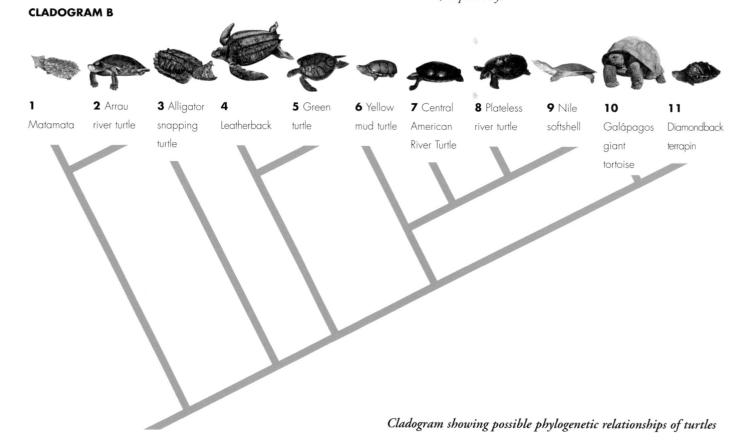

1
Matamata

2 Arrau
river turtle

3 Alligator
snapping
turtle

4
Leatherback

5 Green
turtle

6 Yellow
mud turtle

7 Central
American
River Turtle

8 Plateless
river turtle

9 Nile
softshell

10
Galápagos
giant
tortoise

11
Diamondback
terrapin

Cladogram showing possible phylogenetic relationships of turtles

CLADOGRAM C

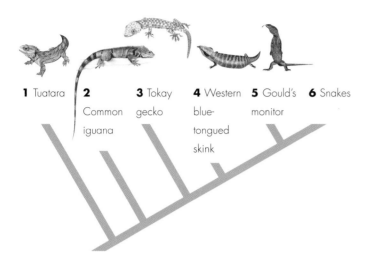

1 Tuatara **2** Common iguana **3** Tokay gecko **4** Western blue-tongued skink **5** Gould's monitor **6** Snakes

KEY TO REPTILE CLADOGRAM C

1 Sphenodontia (tuataras)
2 Iguanidae (iguanas, agamids, chameleons)
3 Gekkonidae (geckos, scaly-footed lizards)

4 Scincomorpha (teiid lizards, lacertid lizards, skinks)
5 Anguimorpha (slow worms, monitors, gila monsters)
6 Snakes

Cladogram showing possible phylogenetic relationships of tuataras and lizards. Iguanidae includes iguanas, agamids, and chameleons. Gekkonidae includes geckos and scaly-foot lizards. Scincomorpha includes dibamids, teiids, lacertids, skinks, and girdled and plated lizards. Anguimorpha includes crocodile lizards, legless and alligator lizards, monitors and Gila monster.

KEY TO REPTILE CLADOGRAM D

1 Leptotyphlopidae (thread snakes)
2 Typhlopidae (blind snakes)
3 Anomolepidae (dawn blind snakes)
4 Aniliidae
5 Uropeltidae (shieldtail snakes)
6 Xenopeltidae (sunbeam snake)
7 Boidae (boas and pythons)

8 Acrochordidae (wart snakes)
9 Atractaspidae (burrowing asps)
10 Colubridae (colubrid snakes)
11 Elapidae (cobras and sea snakes)
12 Viperidae (vipers and pit vipers)

CLADOGRAM D

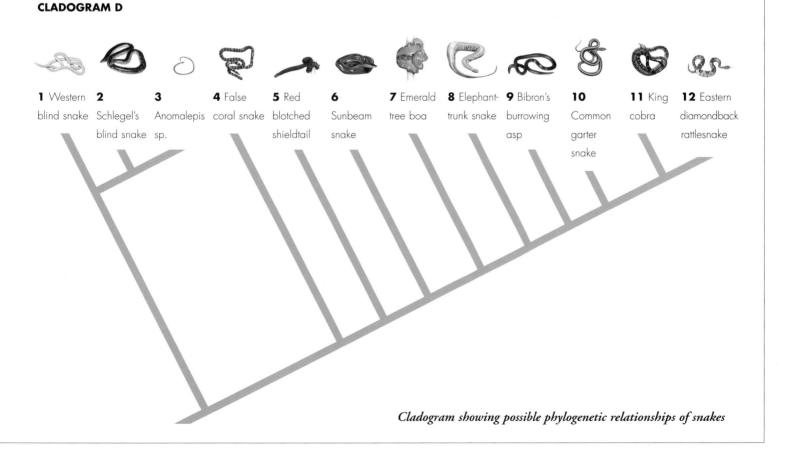

1 Western blind snake **2** Schlegel's blind snake **3** Anomalepis sp. **4** False coral snake **5** Red blotched shieldtail **6** Sunbeam snake **7** Emerald tree boa **8** Elephant-trunk snake **9** Bibron's burrowing asp **10** Common garter snake **11** King cobra **12** Eastern diamondback rattlesnake

Cladogram showing possible phylogenetic relationships of snakes

EMYDID TURTLES

ORDER CHELONIA

This order contains all turtles and tortoises. There are about 230 living species. A typical chelonid has its body enclosed in a shell made of modified horny scales and bone. The shell is in two parts – on the animal's back is the carapace, and the shell underneath the body is the plastron. The ribs and most of the vertebrae are attached to the shell. Both pelvic and pectoral girdles lie within the shell and the limbs emerge sideways. The neck is long and flexible and can usually be withdrawn into the shell. In most families (the hidden-neck turtles or cryptodires) the neck bends up and down to retract, but in the greaved turtles (Pelomedusidae), and the matamata and snakenecked turtles (Chelidae), (called the side-neck turtles or pleurodires) the neck bends sideways when being retracted.

Chelonids have no teeth, but their jaws have horny beaks of varying strength. All lay eggs, usually burying them in sand or earth. Hatchlings must dig their own way out to the surface.

EMYDIDAE: EMYDID TURTLE FAMILY

A varied group of freshwater and semi-terrestrial turtles, the emydid family is the largest group of living turtles with about 85 species. The family is closely related to land tortoises (Testudinidae). Some authorities group them as one family. The hind feet of emydids are adapted for swimming. Most species live in the northern hemisphere. Emydid turtles have a varied diet and eat both plants and animals. Some species start life as carnivores, but feed mainly on plants as adults.

Pond Slider *Trachemys scripta* **LR:nt**

RANGE USA: Virginia to N. Florida, west to New Mexico; Central America to Brazil

HABITAT Slow rivers, ponds, swamps

SIZE 5–11¾ in (13–30 cm)

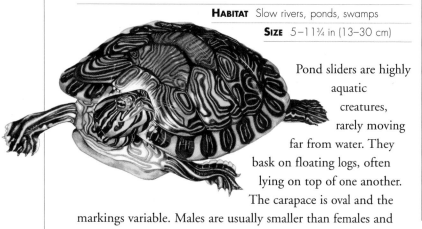

Pond sliders are highly aquatic creatures, rarely moving far from water. They bask on floating logs, often lying on top of one another. The carapace is oval and the markings variable. Males are usually smaller than females and

have elongated, curved claws. Young pond sliders feed on insects, crustaceans, mollusks and tadpoles, but as they mature they feed more on plants.

In June and July pond sliders lay up to three clutches of 4 to 23 eggs each. Millions of these turtles are raised on farms and sold as pets.

False Map Turtle *Graptemys pseudogeographica*

RANGE USA: Minnesota to Sabine River area of Louisiana and Texas

HABITAT Rivers, lakes ponds

SIZE 3–9¾ in (8–25 cm)

False map turtles have intricate shell patterns and clear markings on their small heads. Males are smaller than females and have enlarged foreclaws. These turtles prefer habitats with plenty of vegetation and feed on aquatic plants, crustaceans and mollusks.

After a courtship ritual, during which the male swims above the female then faces her and drums her snout with his claws, the pair mate. The nesting period is from May to July. The female turtle digs a pit in the soil of the river or lake bank with her hind feet and deposits her 6 to 15 eggs. Up to three clutches are laid in a season. The numbers of this once common species have been reduced by pollution of its habitats.

Diamondback Terrapin *Malaclemys terrapin* **LR:nt**

RANGE USA: Atlantic and Gulf coasts

HABITAT Salt marshes, estuaries, lagoons

SIZE 4–9 in (10–23 cm)

This terrapin is the only North American emydid species that is adapted for life in brackish and salt water. It is a strong, fast swimming turtle with large hind limbs. Females are bigger than males.

Diamondbacks spend their days on mudflats or tidal marshes, feeding on snails, clams and worms and on some plant shoots. At night they bury themselves in mud, and in the northern part of their range they hibernate throughout the winter, buried in mud. Diamondbacks mate in the spring and lay 5 to 18 eggs in cavities which they dig in the marshes or dunes.

Wood Turtle *Clemmys insculpta* **VU**

RANGE USA: Nova Scotia to N. Virginia; Great Lakes region
HABITAT Woods, marshy meadows, swamps
SIZE 5–9 in (12.5–23 cm)

The rough-shelled wood turtle spends most of its life on land but is usually in the vicinity of water. It is a good climber and feeds on fruit as well as on worms, slugs and insects. In May or June females lay 6 or 8 eggs, which usually hatch by October, but which may overwinter and hatch the following spring in the north. Adults hibernate in the north of the range. Wood turtles are popular pets, but they have been overhunted and are now rare and protected in some states of the USA.

Eastern Box Turtle *Terrapene carolina* **LR:nt**

RANGE USA: E. states west to Texas
HABITAT Moist forested areas
SIZE 4–8 in (10–20 cm)

A poor swimmer, the box turtle stays in shallow water and spends most of its life on land. Its carapace is nearly always domed in shape and it is variable in coloration and pattern. Box turtles eat almost anything, but slugs, earthworms and fruit are favored foods; they are able to eat mushrooms that are poisonous to humans, and anyone then eating the turtle is poisoned. Usually active early in the day or after rain, box turtles may take refuge in swampy areas in the heat of the summer.

In the spring, after hibernating throughout the winter, box turtles perform prolonged courtship rituals. The female lays 3 to 8 eggs in a flask-shaped pit which she digs. The hatchlings may remain in the nest over the following winter. Females can store sperm and lay fertile eggs several years after mating.

European Pond Turtle *Emys orbicularis* **LR:nt**

RANGE C. France, south to N. Africa, east to Iran
HABITAT Ponds, marshes, rivers
SIZE 5–6 in (13–15 cm)

An aquatic species, the European pond turtle prefers water with plenty of vegetation, but suns itself on river banks and hunts prey on land as well as in water. It is entirely carnivorous and feeds on prey such as fish, frogs, snails and worms.

In winter these turtles hibernate burying themselves in mud or in specially built chambers in the river bank. They mate in spring and, having dug an egg pit with her tail, the female lays 3 to 16 eggs. She generally uses the same nest site every year.

Batagur/River Terrapin *Batagur baska* **EN**

RANGE S.E. Asia from Bengal to Vietnam
HABITAT Tidal areas, estuaries
SIZE 23 in (58 cm)

A large herbivorous turtle with a smooth heavy shell, the batagur is often found in brackish or even salt water. It has only four claws on each foot.

Batagurs nest on sandbanks and usually lay three clutches in a season – a total of 50 to 60 eggs. Numbers have declined due to the excessive collection of eggs and killing of adults for food. The batagur has been eliminated from some parts of its range.

LAND TORTOISES

TESTUDINIDAE: LAND TORTOISE FAMILY

There are about 35 species of land tortoise, found in North America, Europe and Asia, and in Africa and Madagascar. All are strictly terrestrial and have stumpy, elephantine hind legs; on the front legs are thick, hard scales. The head and limbs can be retracted completely inside the shell, leaving only the soles of the hind feet, tail region and scaly fronts of the forelimbs exposed. Most depend on their armor for protection and do not usually show aggression or attempt to flee when disturbed. All species are predominantly herbivorous.

African Pancake Tortoise *Malocochersus tornieri* VU

RANGE Africa: Kenya, Tanzania

HABITAT Rocky outcrops in arid land

SIZE 6 in (15 cm)

The African pancake tortoise is an unusual species. Its shell is extremely flat and soft, and rather than retreating into its shell when disturbed, the tortoise runs to hide in a rock crevice. Once there, it inflates its lungs, thus increasing its size, so that it is wedged in and is almost impossible to remove. Females are slightly larger than males.

The pancake tortoise feeds on dry grass. It nests in July and August, laying 1 egg at a time, and it may lay two or more times in a season. The eggs hatch after about 6 months.

Gopher Tortoise *Gopherus polyphemus* VU

RANGE USA: South Carolina to Florida, west to Louisiana

HABITAT Sandy areas between grassland and forest

SIZE 9¼–14½ in (23.5–37 cm)

This tortoise has a domed shell and heavily scaled front legs, flattened for efficient digging. An excellent burrower, it makes a long tunnel, ending in a chamber which serves as a refuge where humidity and temperature remain relatively constant. One tunnel recorded was over 46 ft (14 m) long. Other small animals may share the tortoise's burrow.

Gopher tortoises emerge from their burrows during the day to bask in the sun and feed on grass and leaves. They mate in spring and nest from April to July. Several clutches of 2 to 7 eggs are laid in a shallow pit during the nesting period.

Bowsprit Tortoise *Chersine angulata*

RANGE South Africa

HABITAT Coastal areas

SIZE 6–7 in (15–18 cm)

The bowsprit tortoise has distinctive triangular markings on its carapace. The front opening of the carapace is particularly small, providing good protection against predators. Males are bigger than females and are aggressive toward one another. Bowsprits are believed to eat plant material. They nest in August and lay 1 or 2 eggs in a hole about 4 in (10 cm) deep. Eggs take about a year to hatch.

Galápagos Giant Tortoise *Geochelone nigra* VU

RANGE Galápagos Islands

HABITAT Varied, cool, moist forest to arid land

SIZE Up to 4 ft (1.2 m)

There are at least 13 subspecies of these giant tortoises, which may weigh over 500 lb (215 kg). Because the populations are isolated from one another on separate islands, over thousands of years subspecies have evolved. The discovery of these subspecies on the different islands was one of the observations that caused Darwin to start his speculations on the origin of species.

The tortoises vary in size, length and thickness of limbs and, most importantly, in the shape of the carapace. Some species have a "saddleback" shell which rises up above the head, allowing the tortoise to lift its head right up and enabling it to graze on a greater range of vegetation. These species occur only on those islands which have highgrowing vegetation.

Galápagos tortoises eat almost any vegetation, which they seek in the more fertile highlands.

Males are always markedly larger than females. They mate at any time of year. Nesting has been closely observed on Indefatigable Island where there is a tortoise

Schweigger's/Serrated Hingeback Tortoise

Kinixys erosa **DD**

RANGE	W. and C. Africa
HABITAT	Rain forest, marshes, river banks
SIZE	13 in (33 cm)

A unique hinge on the carapace of this tortoise, located in line with the junction of the second and third back plates, allows the rear of the carapace to be lowered, if the tortoise is attacked, to protect its hindquarters. This hinge is not present in young tortoises. By digging itself into plant debris, the hingeback remains hidden for much of its life. It feeds on plants and may also eat small animals. There are usually 4 eggs in a clutch.

reserve. After mating, the female descends to the lowland area where there is bare soil in full sun. She chooses a site for her nest then urinates in order to soften the earth and digs a pit up to 12 in (30.5 cm) deep with her hind feet. After laying a clutch of up to 17 eggs, she plasters the excavated soil over the cavity so that it is well closed and the soil dries again in the sun. As usual with tortoises, the young must dig themselves out of the cavity unaided after they hatch out.

Leopard Tortoise *Geochelone pardalis*

RANGE	Africa: Sudan and Ethiopia to South Africa
HABITAT	Savanna, woodland
SIZE	24 in (61 cm)

The leopard tortoise has a markedly domed, boldly patterned carapace. It feeds on a great variety of plant material, including fruit and beans.

Courting males compete for females, butting at each other until one is overturned. They nest in September and October in South Africa, but the season is longer in tropical Africa. The female prepares a nest cavity by urinating on the soil in order to soften it, then excavating a pit using her hind limbs. She lays batches of 5 to 30 eggs, and there may be several clutches in a season.

Spur-thighed Tortoise *Testudo graeca* **VU**

RANGE	N. Africa; extreme S.E. and S.W. Europe; Middle East
HABITAT	Meadows, cultivated land, woodland
SIZE	6 in (15 cm)

This tortoise has a moderately domed shell and a small spur in the thigh region of each front limb. Females are larger than males. The tortoises hibernate in winter but, in coastal areas, will emerge as early as February. They court in spring, the male butting and biting the female before mating with her. The eggs, usually 2 or 3 in a clutch, are laid in May and June and generally hatch in September and October, although this varies with the local climate. The young tortoises are similar to adults but they have more rounded shells and clearer markings. Thousands of these tortoises are collected and exported as pets, many of which die because of the unsuitable climate and conditions of their new homes.

SOFTSHELL TURTLES, RIVER TURTLES AND MUD TURTLES

TRIONYCHIDAE: SOFTSHELL TURTLE FAMILY

This family contains about 22 species of aquatic turtles which have only three claws on each foot. All species have rounded, flexible carapaces with no horny plates, hence their pancakelike appearance and their common name. Most species have long mobile necks. Softshells move fast in water and on land but spend most of their lives in water. Species are found in eastern North America and Southeast Asia, and there is a single species in the Middle East.

Softshells lay up to three clutches of hardshelled eggs each year. Females usually grow larger than males and, as they mature, their carapace patterns become obscured by blotches. Males tend to retain clear carapace patterns.

Spiny Softshell *Trionyx spiniferus*

RANGE N. America: Ontario and Quebec, south to Florida and Colorado

HABITAT Rivers, creeks, ponds

SIZE 6–18 in (15–46 cm)

Conical projections, known as tubercles, around the front edge of this turtle's shell are the origin of the species' common name. There are about six geographically distinct races found within the range and some have more pronounced spines than others. Females are notably larger than males.

Spiny softshells are highly aquatic. They feed on insects, crayfish, and some fish and plant food. They nest in summer and females lay clutches of about 20 eggs.

Narrow-headed/Indian Softshell *Chitra indica* **VU**

RANGE India, Pakistan, Thailand

HABITAT Rivers

SIZE 36 in (91 cm)

A fast-swimming, large turtle with flipperlike limbs, this softshell does indeed have an elongated narrow head, with eyes placed far forward near the snout. This species seems to prefer clear, sandy-bottomed water and is carnivorous, feeding in the main on fish and mollusks.

Nile Softshell *Trionyx triunguis*

RANGE Africa: Egypt to Senegal

HABITAT Ponds, lakes, rivers

SIZE 36 in (91 cm)

The Nile softshell can weigh up to 100 lb (45 kg) and is hunted for food by man in many parts of its range. Although it is a freshwater species, groups have been found living off the coast of Turkey. It is omnivorous and feeds on mollusks, fish, insects and fruit. In Egypt it breeds in April and lays 50 to 60 eggs; elsewhere clutches may be smaller.

Zambesi Softshell/Zambesi Flapshell Turtle *Cycloderma frenatum* **LR:nt**

RANGE Africa: Tanzania, Mozambique, Zambia, Malawi

HABITAT Ponds, lakes, rivers

SIZE 20 in (51 cm)

A carnivorous turtle, the Zambesi softshell feeds mainly on mollusks. It lays its clutch of 15 to 20 eggs between December and March and is most active in rainy weather. The hatchlings have pale green carapaces and dark lines on their heads. In adults these lines are outlined with white dots and become gradually fainter with age. The only other species within this genus is Aubry's softshell, *C. aubryi,* which is found in West Africa.

CARETTOCHELYIDAE: PLATELESS RIVER TURTLE FAMILY

Fossils found in Europe, Asia and North America show that this was once a widespread family. There is now only 1 species.

New Guinea Plateless River/Pig-Nose Turtle

Carettochelys insculpta **VU**

RANGE New Guinea: Fly River area

HABITAT Rivers

SIZE 18 in (46 cm)

This New Guinea species, now also found to be living in northern Australia, is better adapted for aquatic life than most freshwater turtles. Its limbs are modified into long paddles, but retain two claws and resemble the limbs of sea turtles. There are few known details about the nesting habits of this species, but it lays 17 to 27 eggs and hatchlings are about 2¼ in (6 cm) long.

DERMATEMYIDAE: CENTRAL AMERICAN RIVER TURTLE FAMILY

A single species survives from this family, that was formerly found in North and Central America, Europe and Africa.

Central American River Turtle *Dermatemys mawii* **En**

RANGE Mexico to Guatemala and Belize (not Yucatan)

HABITAT Clear rivers and lakes

SIZE 18 in (46 cm)

This turtle has long been hunted for its meat and is now scarce throughout much of its range. Although protected by conservation laws, there is still concern for its future.

A smooth-shelled turtle, it has a small head with a pointed, projecting snout and large nostrils. Males have a golden-yellow patch on the head, but the females and juveniles have grayish heads. It has large webbed feet and rarely leaves the water, but basks while floating. On land this turtle is awkward, but it swims

well and is able to stay submerged for long periods. Aquatic vegetation is its main food source. It nests in the flood season and lays its 6 to 16 eggs in mud near the water's edge.

KINOSTERNIDAE: MUD AND MUSK TURTLE FAMILY

The 20 species in this family are mainly aquatic turtles living in North and Central America and northern South America. They give off a musky odor from 2 pairs of glands, positioned on each side of the body where skin and shell meet. Their heads are retractile.

Yellow Mud Turtle *Kinosternon flavescens*

RANGE USA: Nebraska to Texas; Mexico

HABITAT Slow streams

SIZE 3½–6¼ in (9–16 cm)

The yellow mud turtle does indeed seem to prefer water with a mud bottom, but it may also be found in artificial habitats such as cattle drinking troughs and ditches. It feeds on both aquatic and terrestrial invertebrates. Breeding females lay 2 to 4 eggs.

Common Musk Turtle *Sternotherus odoratus*

RANGE USA: E. states, west to Texas

HABITAT Slow, shallow, muddy streams

SIZE 3–5 in (8–13 cm)

Also known as the stinkpot, this turtle exudes a strong-smelling fluid from its musk glands when molested. It is a highly aquatic species, rarely found far from water, but it does emerge to bask on branches overhanging water. It feeds on carrion, insects and mollusks as well as on small amounts of fish and plants. Nesting is from February to June, depending on the latitude; females lay 1 to 9 eggs under trees, logs or dead leaves.

LEATHERBACK AND MARINE TURTLES

DERMOCHELYIDAE: LEATHERBACK FAMILY

There is a single living species in this family. It has many distinctive features but resembles other sea turtles in many details of skull structure and has similar nesting habits.

Leatherback *Dermochelys coriacea* **EN**

RANGE Worldwide, usually in warm seas

HABITAT Oceanic

SIZE 61 in (155 cm)

The world's largest turtle, the leatherback has an average weight of 800 lb (360 kg) and a maximum of 1,300 lb (590 kg). Its foreflippers are extremely long, with a span of about 9 ft (2.7 m). It has no horny shields on its shell, no scales and no claws. The carapace resembles hard rubber and has three longitudinal ridges. Leatherbacks feed mainly on jellyfish, a diet in keeping with their weak, scissorlike jaws.

Leatherbacks apparently perform long migrations between nesting and feeding sites. Most breed every other year and lay clutches of about 80 to 100 eggs. The nesting procedure is much the same as that of the other sea turtles, but after laying, the leatherback always turns one or more circles before returning to the sea. Several clutches are laid in a season at roughly 10-day intervals. Hatchlings are 2¼ in (6 cm) long and have scales on shell and skin which disappear within the first 2 months of life.

CHELONIDAE: MARINE TURTLE FAMILY

The larger of the 2 families of marine turtles, Chelonidae contains 6 species, all generally found in tropical and subtropical waters. All have nonretractile heads and limbs. The forelimbs are modified into long, paddlelike flippers with one or two claws. The turtles swim by making winglike beats of the foreflippers. On land, the green turtle moves particularly awkwardly, heaving itself forward with both flippers simultaneously, but the others move with alternating limb movements, as most four-legged animals do.

The 6 species have become specialized for different niches and diets, to compensate for the overlap of their ranges.

Green Turtle *Chelonia mydas* **EN**

RANGE Worldwide in seas where temperature does not fall below 68°F (20°C)

HABITAT Coasts, open sea

SIZE 40–50 in (102–127 cm)

This large, thoroughly aquatic turtle rarely comes to land except to bask and sleep and to lay eggs.

Males have slightly longer, narrower carapaces than females and enlarged curved claws on the front flippers for gripping the female when mating.

Green turtles are primarily herbivorous animals and have serrated jaw surfaces, well suited to feeding on sea grasses and seaweed; some crustaceans and jellyfish may also be eaten. The best feeding grounds, where there are vast underwater pastures of plants, are often far away from the best nesting beaches, and green turtles have evolved astounding migratory habits. At nesting time they travel hundreds of miles to the beach of their birth to lay eggs and, as a result, there tend to be a limited number of important nesting sites, to which hundreds of turtles go. One such site is Ascension Island in the mid-Atlantic.

Every second or third year, green turtles travel to their nesting site and mate. The female heaves herself up the beach well away from the tidal area. With her foreflippers she sweeps away sand to create a hollow for her body in which she lies, her shell flush with the beach. She then uses her hind flippers to dig a hole about 16 in (40 cm) deep, immediately beneath her tail. She deposits her eggs into the hole, covers the area with sand and returns to the sea. The average clutch contains about 106 eggs. Sometimes a female lays several clutches in a season at 2-week intervals.

After an incubation period of 2 to 3 months, the young turtles hatch and dig their way through the sand to the surface. Having oriented themselves, they rush for the sea, past a horde of eager predators. Mortality is high, and those which do reach the sea will have to face yet more predators.

The green turtle is now an endangered species, and the population has been eliminated in some areas although it is still reasonable in others. The turtles have been overexploited for their meat, hides and eggs, and the predictability of their nesting habits has made them easy victims. Exploitation is now strictly controlled, and imports are banned in many countries.

The closely related flatback turtle, *C. depressa*, is slightly smaller and lives off the North Australian coast.

Loggerhead Turtle *Caretta caretta* **EN**

RANGE Temperate and tropical areas of the Pacific, Indian and Atlantic Oceans

HABITAT Coasts, open sea

SIZE 30–40 in (76–102 cm)

A large turtle with a long, slightly tapering carapace, the loggerhead has a wide chunky head housing powerful jaws. It can crush even hardshelled prey and feeds on crabs and mollusks as well as on sponges, jellyfish and aquatic plants.

Loggerheads usually breed every other year and lay three or four clutches of about 100 eggs each in a season.

The loggerhead population has been reduced by over collection of eggs and lack of hunting controls, but in southeast Africa, where the turtles have been protected for more than 10 years, their numbers have increased by over 50 per cent.

Pacific Ridley *Lepidochelys olivacea* **EN**

RANGE Tropical Pacific, Indian and S. Atlantic Oceans

HABITAT Coasts, open sea

SIZE 26 in (66 cm)

The Pacific ridley is small and lightly built for a sea turtle. It feeds on small shrimp, jellyfish, crabs, snails and fish, which it crushes with strong jaws. Like its close relative Kemp's ridley, *L. kempi*, the Pacific ridley breeds every year and always returns to the same nesting beaches. The female lays about 100 eggs in a pit in the sand and covers them. She then begins a strange movement peculiar to ridleys, rocking from side to side so that each edge of the shell thumps the sand in turn. Both ridleys are in grave danger due to over-exploitation by man.

Hawksbill *Eretmochelys imbricata* **CR**

RANGE Tropical Atlantic, Pacific and Indian Oceans; Caribbean

HABITAT Coral reefs, rocky coasts

SIZE 30–36 in (76–91 cm)

The hawksbill's beautiful carapace provides the best tortoiseshell and is the reason for the endangered status of the species. Conservation controls have been introduced after many years of hunting, and imports are now banned in some countries.

The carapace is serrated at the back and has particularly thick horny plates. The tapering head of the hawksbill is an adaptation for searching out food, such as mollusks and crustaceans, in rocky crevices and reefs.

In many areas hawksbills are opportunistic breeders, nesting on any beach convenient to feeding grounds. They lay more eggs at a time than any other turtle, usually a batch of about 150.

SNAPPING TURTLES, GREAVED TURTLES AND MATAMATAS

CHELYDRIDAE: SNAPPING TURTLE FAMILY

The 3 species in this family are predatory freshwater turtles. The 2 American species are large, while the Asian species is smaller. Their massive heads do not retract. The big-headed turtle is placed in a family of its own (Platisternidae) by some authorities.

Snapping Turtle *Chelydra serpentina*

RANGE	S. Canada to Ecuador
HABITAT	Marshes, ponds, rivers, lakes
SIZE	8–18½ in (20–47 cm)

The highly aggressive snapping turtle shoots its head forward with surprising speed while snapping its strong jaws. It eats all kinds of aquatic and bankside life, including fish, amphibians, mammals and birds, as well as aquatic plants. Usually found in water with plenty of aquatic vegetation, the snapping turtle lies at the bottom, concealed among plants and is an excellent swimmer. The sexes are alike, but males are slightly larger.

Snapping turtles hibernate in winter and begin nesting in early summer. The average clutch is 25 to 50 eggs, laid in a flask-shaped cavity, dug by the female. As the eggs are laid, she pushes each one into place with movements of her hind feet. The eggs incubate for 9 to 18 weeks, depending on the area and the weather; in cooler areas, the hatchlings may remain in the nest through the winter.

Alligator Snapping Turtle *Macroclemys temmincki* **VU**

RANGE	C. USA
HABITAT	Deep rivers, lakes
SIZE	13–26 in (36–66 cm)

The alligator snapping turtle has three strong ridges on the carapace and a rough-textured head and neck. The carapace is shaped, allowing the head to be raised. A resident of dark, slow-moving water, this turtle is so sedentary that algae grow on its shell, contributing to the existing camouflage of the lumpy irregular outline. It rests, practically invisible to passing fishes, with its huge mouth gaping open to reveal a pink, fleshy appendage. Unsuspecting fish come to investigate the "bait" and are swallowed whole or sliced in half by the turtle's strong jaws. It also eats crustaceans.

These turtles continue to grow after maturity and some old specimens, at over 30 in (76 cm) long and 200 lb (91 kg) in weight, are the largest freshwater turtles in the USA. They nest between April and June and lay from 15 to 50 eggs in a flask-shaped pit dug near water. The young are born with a rough-surfaced shell and the lure already in place.

Big-headed Turtle *Platysternon megacephalum* **DD**

RANGE	Burma, Thailand, S. China
HABITAT	Mountain streams, rivers
SIZE	6–7 in (15–18 cm)

Although a relatively small species in carapace length, this turtle has a huge head, almost half the width of the carapace. The head is not retractile and the carapace is slightly shaped to allow the head and the short, thick neck to be raised. The feet of this turtle are small and only partially webbed, and there are enlarged, flattened scales on the forelimbs.

The big-headed turtle is an unusually agile climber and, using its outstretched claws, it clambers over branches and rocks in search of food or a basking spot. It lays only 2 eggs at a time.

PELOMEDUSIDAE: GREAVED TURTLE FAMILY

This family of 19 species is one of the 2 families of side-neck turtles. A side-neck retracts its head by moving it sideways under the carapace. This leaves an undefended area of the head and neck exposed, and may have prevented the evolution of any terrestrial side-necks, since they would be too vulnerable to mammalian predators. All these turtles live in fresh water in Africa, Madagascar and South America, east of the Andes.

Arrau River Turtle *Podocnemis expansa* **LR:cd**

RANGE	Northern South America
HABITAT	Orinoco and Amazon river systems
SIZE	24–30 in (61–76 cm)

The largest of the side-necks, the Arrau turtle may weigh over 100 lb (45 kg). Females of the species have wide, flattened shells and are larger and more numerous than the males. Adults feed entirely on plant food.

The nesting habits of these turtles are similar to those of sea turtles in that they gather in large numbers in order to travel to certain suitable nesting areas. The females lay their eggs on sandbanks which are exposed only in the dry season, and there are relatively few such sites. The females come out on to the sandbanks at night and each lays as many as 90 or 100 soft-shelled eggs. They then return to their feeding grounds.

The hatchlings, which are about 2 in (5 cm) long, head straight for the sea, but they emerge to the attentions of many predators and even without man's activities, only about 5 per cent ever reach the adult feeding grounds.

Uncontrolled hunting of adults and excessive collecting of eggs have seriously reduced the population of this turtle. It is now an endangered species and is protected in most areas.

CHELIDAE: MATAMATA AND SNAKE-NECKED TURTLE FAMILY

The other family of side-neck turtles contains 30 species, found in South America, Australia and New Guinea. This family shows a number of structural advancements over the more primitive Pelomedusids. They are carnivorous animals and live in rivers and marshes.

Matamata

Chelus fimbriatus

RANGE	N. South America
HABITAT	Rivers
SIZE	16 in (41 cm)

The matamata is one of the most bizarre of all turtles. Its carapace is exceedingly rough and ridged and, from above, its head is flat and virtually triangular. Its eyes are tiny and positioned close to the thin, tubelike snout. Fleshy flaps at the sides of the head wave in the water, possibly attracting small fishes. The neck is thick and muscular and its mouth wide. Its limbs are small and weak.

Well camouflaged by its irregular outline, the matamata lies at the bottom of the water. It is so sedentary that algae grow on its shell. When a fish swims by, the turtle opens its huge mouth, sucking in water and fish. The mouth is then closed, leaving only a slit for the water to flow out.

Matamatas lay 12 to 28 eggs; the young have light-tan-colored carapaces.

Murray River Turtle *Emydura macquarri*

RANGE	S.E. Australia
HABITAT	Rivers
SIZE	11¾ in (30 cm)

The Murray River turtle is a well-known Australian side-neck. The shape of its carapace alters with age – hatchlings have almost circular carapaces; in juveniles, carapaces are widest at the back; and adults have virtually oval shells. The head of the Murray River turtle is quite small, with bright eyes and a light band extending back from the mouth. It is an active species and feeds on frogs, tadpoles and vegetation.

In summer it lays a clutch of between 10 and 15 eggs in a chamber dug in the river bank. These normally hatch in 10 or 11 weeks.

TUATARA AND IGUANAS

ORDER SPHENODONTIA

A part from 2 species of tuatara, living in New Zealand, this order of reptiles is known only from fossils.

SPHENODONTIDAE: TUATARA FAMILY

The sole family in the Rhynchocephalia order contains only 2 species, which are believed to be extremely similar to related species alive 130 million years ago. The scientific name means "the wedge-toothed ones" and refers to the sharp teeth, fused into both jawbones.

Cook Strait Tuatara

Sphenodon punctatus **LR:lc**

RANGE New Zealand

HABITAT Woods with little undergrowth

SIZE Up to 25½ in (65 cm)

A powerfully built reptile, the tuatara has a large head and a crest running from its head down its back. The male is generally larger than the female. Active at dusk and at night, the tuatara has the least need of warmth of any reptile – it is quite content at 53°F (12°C) whereas most reptiles prefer over 77°F (25°C). Its metabolism and growth rate are correspondingly slow.

Tuataras are ground-living and shelter in burrows which they dig in loose soil or take over from shearwaters. They feed on crickets, earthworms, snails, young birds and lizards.

The female tuatara lays up to 15 eggs in a hole she digs in the soil. They hatch 13 to 15 months later – the longest development time of any reptile. She probably does not breed every year. Tuataras are long-lived and probably do not attain sexual maturity until they are about 20 years old. Once in danger of extinction from introduced predators, healthy tuatara populations now live in special island sanctuaries and are protected by conservation laws.

ORDER SQUAMATA

T he largest reptilian order, the Squamata includes all the lizards, snakes and amphisbaenians – over 6,000 species.

IGUANIDAE: IGUANA FAMILY

There are more than 600 species in this family. The vast majority live in the Americas, though there are a few species in Madagascar and Fiji. They are the New World equivalents of the Old World agamid lizards. The two families never occur together.

Most iguanas are ground or tree-living and feed on insects and small invertebrates. Many are brightly colored and perform elaborate courtship displays.

Common Iguana *Iguana iguana*

RANGE Central and N. South America; introduced into USA: Florida

HABITAT Forest, trees near water

SIZE 3¼–6½ ft (1–2 m)

The common iguana has a crest of comblike spines running all the way down its body and tail. The bands across the shoulders and tail become darker as the iguana gets older – juveniles are bright green. Active by day, these iguanas are agile tree-dwelling lizards which also swim readily. They are herbivores, but defend themselves with their teeth and claws if attacked.

In autumn, the female lays 28 to 40 eggs in a hole she digs in the ground. The eggs hatch in about 3 months.

Eastern Fence Lizard *Sceloporus undulatus*

RANGE USA: Virginia to Florida, west to New Mexico; Mexico

HABITAT Open woodland, grassland

SIZE 3½–7¾ in (9–20 cm)

This iguana occurs in many subspecies, with varying coloration over its range, but it always has a characteristic roughened surface because of its keeled scales. Either arboreal or terrestrial, depending on its habitat, it is active during the day and feeds on most insects (particularly beetles) as well as spiders, centipedes and snails.

The courting male holds a territory which he vigorously defends against competitors while he attracts his mate. The female lays 3 to 12 eggs under a log or other debris and may produce up to four clutches a season.

Chuckwalla *Sauromalus obesus*

RANGE USA: S. California, Nevada, Utah, Arizona; Mexico

HABITAT Rocky desert

SIZE 11–16½ in (28–42 cm)

A dark-skinned, plump-bodied lizard, the chuckwalla has a thick, pale yellow tail with a blunt tip. The male tends to be darker than the female, with some red or yellow speckling on the body, while females and juveniles often have dark crossbands. The chuckwalla hides under a rock or in a crevice during the night and emerges in the morning to bask in the sun and warm its body. An herbivorous lizard, it then searches for leaves, buds and flowers to eat, often feeding on the creosote bush.

The chuckwalla is well adapted for desert life. In the folds of skin on its sides are accessory lymph glands in which it can store liquid, when it is available, for use in prolonged dry seasons. The female is thought to breed every other year and lays 5 to 10 eggs at a time.

Green Anole *Anolis carolinensis*

RANGE USA: Virginia to Florida, west to Texas

HABITAT Forest edge, roadsides

SIZE 4¾–7¾ in (12–20 cm)

The green anole has a slender body and long toe pads as an adaptation for its tree-dwelling habits. Although usually green, it can turn brown in seconds. It is active during the day and feeds on insects and spiders.

The remarkable pink, fanlike flap on the throat of the male is used in courtship display. His display triggers sexual receptivity and ovulation in the female. She lays her eggs, one at a time, at 2-week intervals throughout the breeding season, from April to September. The eggs hatch in 5 to 7 weeks.

Collared Lizard
Crotaphytus collaris

RANGE USA: Utah, Colorado, south to Texas; Mexico

HABITAT Rocky hillsides, forest

SIZE 7¾–14 in (20–35.5 cm)

The robust collared lizard has a large head and a distinctive collar of dark and light markings. Active in the daytime, this species particularly likes to bask in the sun around rocks where there are crevices where it can readily take refuge. It feeds on insects and small lizards.

The female collared lizard lays a clutch of up to 12 eggs in midsummer. The young, measuring about 3½ in (9 cm) long, hatch 2 to 3 months later.

Texas Horned Lizard *Phrynosoma cornutum*

RANGE USA: Kansas to Texas, Arizona; introduced in Florida

HABITAT Arid country

SIZE 2¼–7 in (6–18 cm)

The well-armored Texas horned lizard has a flattened body with pointed scales fringing each side. Behind its head are two enlarged horns, flanked by enlarged scales. In its arid habitat, it may bury itself under loose soil or seek refuge under bushes. It feeds largely on ants.

The female lizard digs a hole in which she lays her 14 to 36 eggs in midsummer; the eggs hatch in about 6 weeks.

Forest Iguana *Polychrus gutterosus*

RANGE Tropical South America

HABITAT Forest

SIZE Up to 19¾ in (50 cm) including tail of up to 14½ in (37 cm)

A tree-dwelling iguana, this long-legged lizard lies on a branch, its flattened body pressed inconspicuously to the surface, waiting for its insect prey. It is a good climber, and is able to hold on to a branch with its hind legs alone, but it is slow-moving.

The female forest iguana lays clutches of between 7 and 8 eggs.

IGUANAS CONTINUED

Marine Iguana

Amblyrhynchus cristatus **VU**

RANGE Galápagos Islands

HABITAT Lava rocks on coasts

SIZE 4–5 ft (1.2–1.5 m)

The only present-day lizard to use the sea as a major habitat, the marine iguana swims and dives readily as it forages for seaweed, its main food. Vital adaptations to marine life are the nasal glands that remove the excess salt the iguana takes in with its food; the salt is expelled in a thin shower of water vapor which the iguana blows out through its nose. When swimming, the iguana uses its powerful tail for propulsion; its feet are normally held against the body, but they are sometimes used to steer a course. The iguana cannot breathe under water, but when it dives, its heart rate slows down, reducing the blood flow through the body and thus conserving the limited supplies of oxygen.

Male marine iguanas are highly territorial and fight to defend their own small areas of breeding territory on the shore. The combat is ritualistic, each individual trying to overthrow the other by butting him with his head. In one race of marine iguanas, breeding males develop green crests and red flanks. After mating, the female finds a sandy area in which to bury her eggs. She digs a hole about 12 in (30.5 cm) deep, lays 2 or 3 eggs and covers them with sand. The eggs incubate for about 112 days.

Numbers of these once abundant creatures have been reduced by predators, introduced by settlers and sailors. Previously there were no native mammalian predators to threaten their existence.

Galápagos Land Iguana *Conolophus subcristatus* **VU**

RANGE Galápagos Islands

HABITAT Arid land coasts to volcanoes

SIZE Up to 4 ft (1.2 m)

Once common on all of the Galápagos islands, this iguana is now extinct in some and rare in others. Many have been shot for food or sport, and others have suffered from the ravages of introduced predators. Conservation measures have now been established in a bid to save this iguana.

A stout-bodied animal with a rounded tail, the land iguana is generally yellow or brown, sometimes with irregular spots on the body. It has a crest at the back of the neck, and older individuals have rolls of fat around the neck. It lives in arid land where there is some vegetation and where it can dig into the soil to make a burrow for shelter. Plants, including cacti, are its main food, it may also eat some small animals. Breeding females lay clutches of about 9 eggs.

Basilisk Lizard *Basiliscus plumifrons*

RANGE South America

HABITAT Forest

SIZE 31½ in (80 cm)

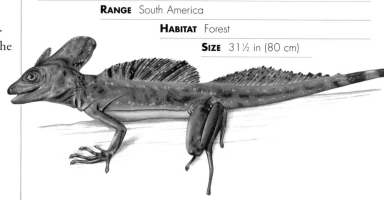

Male basilisk lizards sport prominent, impressive crests on back and tail and bony casques on the head. The 5 species in the genus are all extremely alike and can be distinguished only by the characteristic shapes of the head casques of the males; these casques are poorly developed in females and absent in juveniles.

The long-legged basilisks are among the few four-legged animals to run on two legs. They rear up on their hind legs and run in a semierect position, with the long tail held up to help balance. This counterweighting effect is vital and if too much of the tail is amputated the iguana is unable to rise up on its hind legs. Adults have achieved speeds of 6.8 mph (11 km/h) but only over short distances. Basilisks can even run a few yards over smooth water, held up by the surface film, and then swim when it is no longer possible for them to remain on the surface.

Active in the daytime, basilisks feed on fruit and small animals, often climbing into trees to find food.

In the breeding season, females lay 10 to 15 eggs which incubate for about 80 days.

Rhinoceros Iguana *Cyclura cornuta* **VU**

RANGE Haiti and other islands of the Lesser Antilles

HABITAT Arid scrub

SIZE Up to 4 ft (1.2 m)

The male rhinoceros iguana is easily identified by the characteristic protuberances on the tip of his snout that are formed from enlarged scales. The female has only small, inconspicuous protuberances.

A large, powerful species, this iguana has a strong tail and a somewhat compressed body. Some individuals, particularly old males, develop rolls of fat at the back of the head. There are many races of rhinoceros iguana with only minor physical variations. They are among the most primitive iguanas.

Rhinoceros iguanas live on land, among thorn bushes and cacti, and feed on plants, worms and mice. Breeding females lay clutches of about 12 eggs which incubate for 120 days or more. In some islands of the Lesser Antilles this iguana has been displaced by the common iguana which has recently become established there.

Spiny-tailed Iguana *Ctenosaura pectinata*

RANGE Mexico, Central America

HABITAT Forest

SIZE 3¼ ft (1 m)

A land-dwelling lizard, the spiny-tailed iguana is so called because its tail is ringed with spiny scales, making it an effective weapon. These iguanas feed mainly on plant material, particularly on beans, but also catch some small animals. Their diet is rich in potassium salts, and they are equipped with nasal glands in order to excrete excess salt, which then collects as encrustations round the nostrils.

Highly gregarious and territorial, these iguanas live in colonies, ruled by a strict pecking order. One male in the colony is dominant and, although the other males also hold territories, they will only defend them against one another although not against the leader.

In the breeding season, females dig burrows in which to lay their clutches of about 50 eggs.

Fijian Banded Iguana *Brachylophus fasciatus* **EN**

RANGE Islands of Fiji and Tonga

HABITAT Woodland, forest

SIZE 35½ in (90 cm)

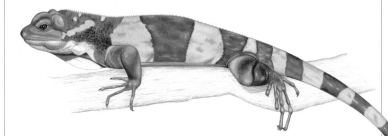

One of the few iguana species found outside the Americas, the Fijian iguana has an extremely long tail, often more than twice the length of its slender body. It sports a low crest along its back.

An arboreal iguana, its elongate fingers and toes are equipped with sharp claws for climbing. The female has a uniformly green body, while the male is banded with lighter green and has light spots on his neck. They feed on leaves and other plant material.

The Fijian iguana is a little-known species that may be nearing extinction because of the destruction of much of its forest habitat and the introduction into its range of mongooses, which prey on the iguana and its eggs.

Madagascan Iguana *Oplurus* sp.

RANGE Madagascar, small offshore islands

HABITAT Forest

SIZE Up to 15 in (38 cm)

There are 2 iguana genera in Madagascar – Oplurus and Chalarodon. The 6 species of Oplurus are all similar in appearance, with rings of spiny scales on their tapering tails. Chalarodon species are easily distinguished by their small crests, which Oplurus species lack and their smooth-scaled tails.

Although primarily land-dwelling, these iguanas can climb and often take refuge in bushes and trees when danger threatens.

AGAMID LIZARDS

AGAMIDAE: AGAMID LIZARD FAMILY

The agamid family contains more than 300 species of plump-bodied lizards, found throughout the warmer regions of the Old World except in Madagascar and New Zealand.

Most agamids have thin tails, long legs and triangular-shaped heads. They live on the ground, in trees or among rocks and feed mainly on insects and other small invertebrates, but also on some plant matter.

Common Agama *Agama agama*

RANGE	Central Africa
HABITAT	Tropical forest
SIZE	4¾ in (12 cm)

Agamas live in groups of 2 to 25 in a defined territory, ruled by one dominant male. They are active during the day, emerging at dawn to bask in the sun and feed, mainly on insects. If the dominant male is challenged by another male, he adopts a threat posture, bobbing his head, raising his body off the ground and spreading the folds of his neck skin as far as possible.

Mating usually coincides with the rainy season, when the earth is sufficiently moist for the female agamid to make her nest. She digs a small hole in damp soil in which she lays 4 to 6 eggs. She covers the eggs over and smooths the ground surface to conceal the nest. While they develop, the eggs absorb moisture from the soil. The young hatch in 2 or 3 months.

Flying Dragon *Draco volans*

RANGE	Philippines to Malaysia and Indonesia
HABITAT	Rain forest, rubber plantations
SIZE	7½–8½ in (19–22 cm)

An arboreal lizard, the so-called flying dragon actually glides from tree to tree on winglike skin flaps. At each side of its body, between front and hind limbs, there is a large flap of skin supported by extended movable ribs. Usually these flaps are held folded at the sides of the body, but they can be extended to carry the lizard in an almost horizontal glide for many meters. The flying dragon feeds on insects, particularly ants.

To breed, the flying dragon descends to the ground and buries its 1 to 4 eggs in the soil.

Frilled Lizard *Chlamydosaurus kingii*

RANGE	Australia: N. Western Australia, N. Northern Territory, E. Queensland; New Guinea
HABITAT	Dry forest, woodland
SIZE	26 in (66 cm) including tail of 17¼ in (44 cm)

This slender, long-tailed lizard has an extraordinary rufflike collar of skin around its neck which may be as much as 10 in (25.5 cm) in diameter. Normally this collar lies in folds around the neck and shoulders, but if alarmed, the lizard opens its mouth wide and at the same time the brightly colored frill erects, giving the animal a startling appearance and making it look larger than it really is in order to intimidate the enemy.

Active in the daytime, the frilled lizard forages in trees and on the ground for insects and other small animals.

Thorny Devil *Moloch horridus*

RANGE	Australia: W., N. and S., Queensland
HABITAT	Arid scrub, desert
SIZE	6¼ in (16 cm)

The grotesque thorny devil is the only species in its genus and one of the strangest of lizards. Its body bristles with large, conical spines. It also has spines above each eye and a spiny hump behind its head. The tail, too, is covered in spines. The thorny devil is a slow-moving creature which forages for its food, mainly ants and termites, on the ground.

The female thorny devil lays 3 to 10 eggs, usually 8, in November or December. The newly hatched young are tiny, spiny replicas of their parents.

Soa-soa Water Dragon

Hydrosaurus amboinensis

RANGE New Guinea, Moluccas, Sulawesi

HABITAT Rain forest

SIZE 43¼ in (110 cm), including tail of 29½ in (75 cm)

One of the largest agamids, the soa-soa is a powerfully built lizard with strong forefeet. The adult male has a showy crest on the base of the tail which can be erected, supported by bony extensions of the tail vertebrae. As its name suggests, this is an aquatic lizard, which is usually found close to rivers. It can swim well, propelling itself with its laterally compressed tail, and it will run on its hind legs on land.

Despite its formidable appearance, the soa-soa feeds largely on plants, particularly tender leaves, it also consumes insects and millipedes. It reproduces by laying eggs.

Eastern Water Dragon

Physignathus leseueri

RANGE E. Australia

HABITAT Coasts, forested slopes

SIZE 28¾ in (73 cm), including tail 19¾ in (50 cm)

The eastern water dragon varies in coloration over its wide range, but always has a long, powerful tail and a crest running along the length of its body and tail. A semiaquatic, tree-living lizard, it lies on a branch overhanging a river or stream and, if disturbed, will tumble down into the water. It also forages on rocky seashores. Its diet is varied, including insects, small aquatic animals (such as frogs) terrestrial animals and fruit and berries. The breeding female lays about 8 eggs under a rock or in a burrow she digs in the soil. The eggs hatch in 10 to 14 weeks.

Arabian Toad-headed Agamid *Phrynocephalus nejdensis*

RANGE S.W. Asia

HABITAT Desert, semidesert

SIZE Up to 5 in (12.5 cm)

The Arabian toad-headed agamid has a rounded head, long slender legs and a tapering tail. It is a burrowing lizard and digs short tunnels for shelter; it also buries itself in sand by wriggling from side to side. If alarmed it adopts a defence posture, with tail raised. It then rolls and unrolls its tail. It eats mainly insects and some flowers, fruit and leaves. Females lay several clutches of eggs during the year.

Bearded Dragon *Amphibolurus barbatus*

RANGE Australia: E. and S.E. (except Cape York Peninsula and Tasmania)

HABITAT Arid land to forest

SIZE 17½ in (44.5 cm) including tail of 7¾ in (19.5 cm)

This large, formidable-looking lizard is adorned with spiny scales above its ears, at the back of its head and behind its mouth. On its body are a mixture of small and enlarged keeled scales. Adults have throat pouches or beards which are bordered with spiny scales. Most bearded dragons are semiarboreal and feed on insects, flowers and soft plant growth in low vegetation.

The female bearded dragon lays 10 to 20 eggs in a nest which she digs in the soil. She covers the eggs with soil and, warmed by the sun, they incubate in the pit for about 3 months.

Princely Mastigure *Uromastyx princeps*

RANGE Africa: Somali Republic

HABITAT Rocky, stony land

SIZE About 9 in (23 cm)

A plump-bodied lizard, the princely mastigure has a short, thick tail, studded with large spines, and a small turtlelike head. It is active by day, sheltering at night in holes or crevices in the rocks. Grass, flowers, fruit and leaves are its main foods. If attacked, it defends itself against the enemy with its spiny tail, lashing it to and fro.

CHAMELEONS

CHAMAELEONIDAE: CHAMELEON FAMILY

The chameleons are probably the most specialized group of tree-living lizards, superbly adapted in both structural and behavioral ways. About 85 species are known; most live in Africa and Madagascar, but a few occur in Asia and there is one European species. Although primarily an arboreal group, a few species are ground-living.

Most chameleons are between 6 and 11¾ in (15 and 30 cm) long, but a few are smaller, and one species in Madagascar reaches 27½ to 31½ in (70 to 80 cm). Whatever their size, all chameleons are recognizable by certain characteristic attributes. The typical chameleon has a body which is flattened from side to side; the head often has prominent crests or horns, and the large eyes are protuberant and can be moved independently of one another to locate insect prey. The toes on hind and forefeet are arranged to provide a pincerlike grip on branches. Each foot divides clearly, with three toes on one side and two on the other. The muscular prehensile tail can be curled around a branch and helps the chameleon to stay immobile as it watches for prey.

Although several groups of lizards are able to change the color of their skins usually for camouflage purposes, the chameleon is the most accomplished. Camouflage helps the chameleon in its slow, stalking approach to prey animals and also helps to hide it from predators. The mechanism behind the chameleon's color change abilities is complex. The pattern of pigmentation in the skin cells is controlled by the nervous system, and pigment can be spread out or contracted, thus lightening or darkening the skin. The strength of the light seems to be the most important influence on the mechanism.

Perhaps, however, the most extraordinary adaptive feature of the chameleons is their protrusible tongue. It can be shot out, from its tongue-bone support, to capture insects a body-length away from the reptile; at the tip of the tongue is a sticky pad to which the insect adheres. The chameleon has superb eyesight, which enables it to take accurate aim at the prey.

Chameleons generally reproduce by laying eggs, which the mother buries in a hole in the ground. A few African species, however, give birth to live young. In these forms, completely developed young chameleons grow inside their egg membranes, but free themselves from these enclosures immediately after the eggs are laid.

Jackson's Chameleon *Chamaeleo jacksonii*

RANGE E. Africa: Uganda, Tanzania to N. Mozambique

HABITAT Savanna vegetation

SIZE 4¼–4¾ in (11–12 cm)

The three prominent horns on his head make the male Jackson's chameleon instantly recognizable. The female has only one small horn on the snout and rudimentary horns by each eye. Usually colored a drab green, this chameleon resembles lichen on the bark of a tree.

One of the live-bearing species in the chameleon family, the female Jackson's chameleon may carry 20 to 40 eggs, but only 10 or so young ever actually survive. At birth, the young are about 2¼ in (5.5 cm) long and have two tiny horns in front of the eyes and a conical scale in the position of the middle horn.

Meller's Chameleon *Chamaeleo melleri*

RANGE E. Africa: Tanzania, Malawi

HABITAT Savanna vegetation

SIZE 21¼–2¾ in (54–58 cm) including tail of 11–11½ in (28–29 cm)

The largest chameleon found outside Madagascar, the male Meller's chameleon has only a tiny snout horn which is also present in the female. Its body is distinctively marked with broad yellow stripes and black spots. As it sits on a branch, the chameleon often sways slightly, as a leaf might in a breeze, and this, combined with its camouflaging coloration and patterning, makes it extremely hard to detect in foliage, despite its large size. Meller's chameleons feed on small birds, as well as on insects.

Flap-necked Chameleon *Chamaeleo dilepis*

RANGE Tropical and S. Africa

HABITAT Forest, scrubland

SIZE 9¾–14¼ in (25–36.5 cm)

This aggressive chameleon has lobes of membranous skin at the back of its head which it erects in threat when it meets another member of its own species. It may raise only the lobe on the side of the opponent. A tree- and bush-dwelling species, it descends to the ground only to move from one tree to another or to lay eggs. Its coloration varies with the background, being green when among leaves and yellow or reddish-brown when on bark. When angry or alarmed, for example when confronting the boomslang (tree snake), its main enemy the chameleon turns dark blackish-green with yellow and white spots and makes hissing sounds.

The female lays 30 to 40 eggs in a hole she digs in the ground and then conceals the nest with grass and twigs. The eggs hatch in about 3 months.

European Chameleon *Chamaeleo chamaeleon*

RANGE S. Spain and Portugal, Crete, N. Africa, Canary Islands

HABITAT Bushes in dry country

SIZE 9¾–11 in (25–28 cm)

The only chameleon to occur in Europe, this species is usually yellowish-brown with dark bands on the body, but may turn green among grass or other green vegetation. When alarmed, it turns very dark and inflates its body with air so as to appear larger than its true size. In vegetated areas, this chameleon lives in bushes and descends to the ground only to lay eggs. In North Africa, however, in areas of sparse plant growth, it is a ground-dweller and lives in holes, which it digs itself, on the outskirts of oases. It feeds on insects, particularly locusts.

At mating time, males fight one another for females, and paired males and females may also fight. The female lays 20 to 30 eggs which she buries in the ground.

Brookesia spectrum

RANGE Cameroon, Gabon to E. Africa

HABITAT Forest floor

SIZE 3–3½ in (7.5–9 cm)

This tiny, dusty-brown chameleon closely resembles the dead leaves among which it lives on the forest floor. The effect is enhanced by the stumpy tail, little peaks on the head and body and the irregular lines on the body which mimic leaf veins. There are two tiny appendages on the snout. Its legs are extremely thin and bony and the tail is not prehensile – as a ground-living chameleon it has no need of the fifth limb. It rarely changes color; it has little need being so well camouflaged already. Like all chameleons, it moves slowly and deliberately and may remain still for hours. It feeds on insects.

Little is known of the breeding habits, but females are believed to lay 3 to 6 eggs in a clutch.

Rhampholeon marshalli

RANGE Africa: Zimbabwe, Mozambique

HABITAT Forest on mountain slopes

SIZE 1¼–3 in (3.5–7.5 cm)

The shape of this chameleon, with its flattened body and highly arched back, contributes to its leaflike appearance as it sits, swaying gently from side to side as if blowing in the wind. Rows of light-colored tubercles scattered over the body are particularly prominent in males. Females are usually twice the size of males. Much of this chameleon's life is spent among the leaf litter of the forest floor.

The female lays 12 to 18 eggs.

GECKOS

GEKKONIDAE: GECKO FAMILY

Throughout the tropical, subtropical and warm temperate zones of the world are distributed some 700 species of gecko. These lizards may inhabit forests, swamps, deserts or mountainous areas; in fact, any place with sufficient insect life for them to feed on and where nights do not become too cold. They range in size from 2 to 11¾ in (5 to 30 cm), although most are between 2¾ and 6 in (7 and 15 cm) long.

The typical gecko has a flattened head and a body with soft skin, containing many minute scales. Most are nocturnal and have enormous eyes, each with a permanently closed transparent eyelid. Many have "friction pads" of specialized scales under the toes which enable them to climb easily up vertical surfaces and even to walk upside down, on a ceiling for instance.

The males of many of the nocturnal species are among the most vocal lizards and make loud, repetitive calls. Females lay only 1 to 3 eggs at a time but may breed several times a year. The eggs of most geckos are harder shelled than those of other lizards; they are soft when laid and harden with exposure to air.

Tokay Gecko *Gekko gekko*

RANGE	Asia, Indonesia
HABITAT	In or near houses
SIZE	11 in (28 cm)

One of the largest and most common geckos, the tokay gecko is believed to bring good luck to the houses that it frequents. It eats insects, particularly cockroaches, and young lizards, mice and small birds, all of which it seizes in its powerful jaws. The male makes his loud barking call, "tokeh" or "gekoh", most frequently in the mating season; the female is mute.

The female tokay gecko lays 2 sticky-surfaced eggs, which are usually stuck fast to a perpendicular object and are almost impossible to remove without breaking. Eggs are laid in the same locations year after year, and it is common to find 8 to 10 sets of eggs together, all laid by different females and in various stages of incubation.

White-spotted Gecko *Tarentola annularis*

RANGE	Africa: Libya, Egypt, Sudan, Ethiopia, Somalia
HABITAT	Trees, rocks, ruins in semidesert
SIZE	8 in (20.5 cm)

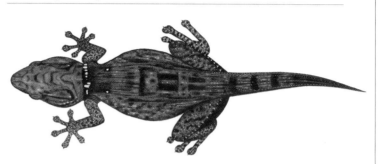

The body color of these geckos varies according to the surface that they are on. Geckos on the black rocks above the first Nile Cataract are black, however, those found on white-washed walls are almost white.

Aggressive, active creatures, they feed primarily on insects but also eat spiders and lizards. They are able to survive long periods without water, although they drink eagerly when the opportunity presents itself.

Mating is triggered by the arrival of the rains, and the female gecko lays her eggs in a crevice or hole in a rock or wall.

Leopard Gecko *Eublepharius macularius*

RANGE	Afghanistan, S. Turkestan, Pakistan, W. India
HABITAT	Dry, rocky regions
SIZE	Up to 11¾ in (30 cm)

Also known as the panther gecko, this chunky lizard has a spotted body and a large head. Unlike most geckos, which have fused transparent eyelids, this species is one of the few with movable eyelids – a primitive characteristic in the gecko family. Its legs are long and thin and it holds its body well off the ground when it runs. Leopard geckos feed on grasshoppers, scorpions, beetles and spiders. They are nocturnal and hide during the day under rocks or in burrows in the sand.

During the year, the female gecko usually lays several clutches, each of 2 eggs.

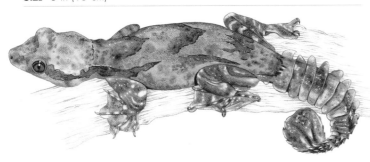

Web-footed Gecko
Palmatogecko rangei

RANGE S.W. Africa: Namib Desert

HABITAT Sand dunes, rocks

SIZE 5 in (12.5 cm)

This extremely rare species, which lives on the seaward slopes of the Namib Desert where rain is almost unknown, absorbs moisture from the sea breezes and from the mists that roll in from the sea. It laps dew from the stones and licks its own eyes for moisture.

Since this gecko lives on the ground, it has no need of friction pads on its feet for climbing vertical surfaces; instead its almost clawless toes are connected by webs which act like snowshoes in the soft sand. When running, the gecko holds its body well off the hot ground, and its feet leave little or no trace of its movements. The webbed feet are also used for burrowing into the sand to escape from predators or from the blistering sun. The gecko makes a chamber in which it lies with its head facing the entrance, waiting to pounce on the termites, beetles, flies and worms that are its main food. If a predator should try to pull it out, the gecko clings to the side of the chamber with its strong tail, engaging in a tug-of-war.

Kuhl's Gecko *Ptychozoon kuhli*

RANGE S.E. Asia, Indonesia, Borneo

HABITAT Forest

SIZE 6 in (15 cm)

Geckos of this genus, often known as the fringed or "flying" geckos, have fringes of skin along the sides of the head, limbs, body and tail, and webs between the toes. When jumping or falling from trees, the gecko extends its legs and tail to expand the flaps and uses them like a parachute. Perhaps even more important is the camouflage the fringes give as the gecko rests on the branch of a tree. It presses the skin flaps down against the bark, thus removing any shadows and breaking up its outline.

The female Kuhl's gecko lays her eggs in November. The eggs, coated with a sticky substance when laid, adhere to each other and to the branch of the tree and gradually develop a hard shell. The young geckos hatch the following May.

Marbled Gecko *Phyllodactylus porphyreus*

RANGE South Africa, Australia

HABITAT Arid mountain slopes

SIZE 4½ in (11.5 cm)

This active little gecko lives in cracks in rocks or beneath stones and varies in coloration according to its surroundings. It feeds on insects and is often parasitized by mites.

The female marbled gecko lays her eggs under a stone or on a tree, where they remain until they hatch out approximately 115 days later. The newly hatched young are about ¾ in (2 cm) long, with tails that are over half their body length.

Brook's Gecko *Hemidactylus brookii*

RANGE Asia, Africa, South America, East and West Indies

HABITAT Coastal plains to upland savanna to 7,000 ft (2,100 m)

SIZE 6 in (15 cm)

This unusually widespread gecko lives under stones, in cracks in rocks, in abandoned termite mounds, beneath fallen tree trunks and even under heaps of garden debris.

With its sharply curving claws, it climbs with great agility up even vertical surfaces. It feeds on insects and at night will enter houses to prey on those which are attracted to the light. It is difficult to ascertain the exact length of this species since adults rarely have their long tails intact, although the tail breaks off easily, muscles in the main tail artery contract speedily in order to prevent any undue loss of blood.

In the breeding season the female Brook's gecko lays 2 eggs.

GECKOS AND SCALY-FOOT LIZARDS

Leaf-tailed Gecko *Uroplatus fimbriatus*

RANGE Madagascar

HABITAT Forest

SIZE 8 in (20.5 cm)

A flat-bodied gecko with large bulging eyes, the leaf-tailed gecko's mottled body blends excellently with bark or lichen. It lies with its body pressed against a branch or trunk of a tree and the small scales bordering its legs and sides reduce any shadow. In addition to this camouflage, it can change the intensity of its coloration, becoming darker by night and lighter again in the morning. When alarmed, it turns dark brown or black. The broad, flat tail can be rolled up dorsally – toward the back – and is used as a fifth limb for holding on to branches.

Mainly active at night, this gecko feeds on insects. Each individual has a preferred resting place where, after a meal, it retires to clean itself, using its tongue to lick over its whole body, even the eyes.

Green Day Gecko *Heteropholis manukanus*

RANGE N. New Zealand
(Marlborough Sound, Stephens Island)

HABITAT Forest, scrub

SIZE 5–6½ in (12.5–16.5 cm)

Unlike most geckos, the green day gecko is active in the daytime when it forages in trees for insects and small invertebrates. It is found mainly on the manuka, or tea tree, (*Leptospermum scoparium*). Its bright green coloration has yellow undertones, and the female's belly is yellowish green, the male's bluish green. In both sexes the soles of the feet

are a yellowish shade. The head is large in size and the snout deep and blunt.

Most geckos lay eggs, but the female of this species gives birth to 2, occasionally only 1, live young. The young are similar in appearance to the adults.

Numbers of these geckos have fallen because large areas of their forest and scrub habitat have been cleared for development.

Phelsuma vinsoni

RANGE Mauritius and neighboring islands

HABITAT Forest

SIZE 6¾ in (17.5 cm)

An unusual gecko species with its vivid coloration, the male *Phelsuma vinsoni* has bright red spots on a blue and green back and brown lines on the head and neck region. The female has similar patterning but is less vivid and is tinged with brown or gray. This gecko is also unusual in that it is active during the day; most are nocturnal. A good climber, it is often found on screwpine trees, the fruit of which attracts the insects on which it feeds. Fruit such as bananas and the nectar of flowers sometimes supplement the gecko's diet.

The female gecko lays 2 sticky-surfaced eggs which are usually left attached to a branch; several females may lay their eggs together. They hatch after 9 to 12 weeks, depending on the temperature, and the young geckos measure about 4¾ in (12 cm).

PYGOPODIDAE: SCALY-FOOT LIZARD FAMILY

The scaly-foots, or snake lizards, are one of the groups of lizards which, although they are limbless and snakelike, are anatomically different from true snakes. There are 30 or so known species, all found in Australia or New Guinea.

Although externally so similar to snakes, the scaly-foots are, in fact, most closely related to geckos and share certain characteristics with them, such as fused eyelids and their ability to make sounds. Their hind limbs are present as vestigial scaly flaps, and the tail is extremely long. The flat, fleshy tongue is slightly forked and can be extended well out of the mouth.

Burton's Snake-lizard *Lialis burtonis*

RANGE Australia: central areas, Queensland; New Guinea

HABITAT Semidesert, rain forest

SIZE Up to 24 in (61 cm)

The most widespread species of its family, this snake-lizard is able to adapt to the contrasting habitats of rain forest and semidesert. A ground-dweller, it hides in clumps of grass or under plant debris. Its color and pattern vary but they are not related to geographical distribution, and it always has a distinctive brown stripe on each side of the head. The snout is long and pointed.

Active during both day and night, Burton's snake-lizard feeds on insects, skinks and other small lizards. Its long pointed, backward-curving teeth enable it to overcome quite large prey, which it seizes with a quick snap of its jaws and swallows whole.

Unlike other snake-lizards, which make geckolike barks or soft squeaks, this lizard emits a long drawn-out note. The female lays 2 or 3 large elongate eggs which have parchmentlike shells.

Hooded Scaly-foot *Pygopus nigriceps*

RANGE Western Australia

HABITAT Dry inland country, coastal forest

SIZE 18 in (46 cm)

Also known as the black-headed or western scaly-foot, this species has a tail that is slightly longer than its body and a rounded snout. The hind limbs are present as scaly flaps, each containing miniature leg bones and four toes. These flaps usually lie flat against the body, but when the animal is handled or injured, they are held out at right angles.

If threatened, the hooded scaly-foot mimics the poisonous elapid snake *Denisonia gouldii*, to try to deter its enemy. It draws back its head, bends its neck into an S-shape, puffs out its throat slightly and hisses. It feeds on insects and small lizards and is most active at dusk and at night. The female lays 2 eggs.

Delma nasuta

RANGE Australia: Western and Northern Territories, South Australia

HABITAT Sandy and stony desert, arid scrub

SIZE 11¾ in (30 cm) including tail of 8½ in (22 cm)

The 3 species of scaly-foot in the genus *Delma* are all slender bodied and move exactly like snakes. They resemble the smaller elapid snakes of Australia. These scaly-foot lizards feed on insects and small lizards both at night and during the day, but species living in the hot desert areas of central Australia are strictly nocturnal. The hind limbs are present as tiny but movable flaps which are held against the body.

The female lays 2 eggs.

Aprasia striolata

RANGE Australia: isolated populations in S. W. Western Australia, S. Australia to W. Victoria; Northern Territory

HABITAT Varied, sandy or loamy soils

SIZE 6 in (15 cm)

There are 4 species in the genus *Aprasia*, all of which are alike in habits and appearance. A small burrowing creature, this species has a rounded snout and inconspicuous flaps which are vestiges of its hind limbs. Its tail is short. This lizard feeds on insects and lizards and is mainly active in the daytime. The females of this genus of lizard generally lay clutches of 2 eggs at a time.

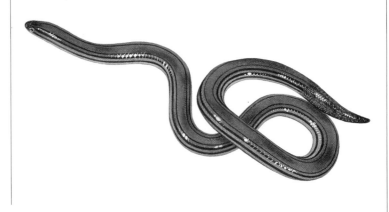

BURROWING LIZARDS AND TEIID LIZARDS

DIBAMIDAE: OLD WORLD BURROWING LIZARD FAMILY

This small family contains only 3 species of small, wormlike, limbless lizards, all in the genus *Dibamus*. They live in parts of Southeast Asia, the Philippines and New Guinea.

Dibamus novaeguineae

RANGE New Guinea

HABITAT Forest

SIZE Up to 11¾ in (30 cm)

All three *Dibamus* species are blind limbless lizards, specialized for a burrowing, underground life. The body is wormlike and the eyes and ears are covered by skin. The nostrils are positioned on an enlarged scale at the tip of the snout, and the teeth are small and backward curving. The male has stumplike vestiges of hind limbs that are used for clasping the female during mating. Dibamids will burrow into rotting logs as well as soil. Little is known of their habits. Eggs, which were probably dibamid eggs, have been discovered in rotting logs and forest floor humus.

TEIIDAE: TEIID LIZARD FAMILY

There are about 80 species in this exclusively American family, the majority of which live in South America. Teiids are slender lizards with thin, whiplike tails and characteristic long, deeply divided tongues, which they use to search for food. Most species have scales on the back and belly.

In many ways, teiids represent the New World equivalent of the lacertid lizards. Most species are ground-living, feeding on a variety of small animals, but some have become specialized for a particular way of life, for example the caiman lizard, which is semiaquatic and feeds on snails.

Teiids reproduce by laying eggs. Most must mate first in the normal way, but in a few unisexual species no mating is necessary. In these teiids, all individuals are female and can lay eggs, which do not need to be fertilized and which hatch into more females, so completely dispensing with the need for males.

Caiman Lizard *Dracaena guianensis*

RANGE N.E. South America

HABITAT Swampy flooded ground, often woodland bordering rivers

SIZE 4 ft (1.2 m)

The large, powerful caiman lizard has an oarlike, laterally flattened tail and rough, horny, platelike scales along its back. It inhabits areas which are flooded for much of the time, except when the rivers are at their lowest, and frequents the resulting pools and ponds. It spends much of the day in water and dives and swims well, using its tail. At night, it finds shelter above water level, often in trees or bushes. It feeds almost entirely on aquatic snails, taking the snail in its jaws, then raising its head so that the snail slides back into its mouth, where it is broken up by the huge, crushing back teeth. The pieces of shell are spat out and the soft body swallowed.

The female caiman lizard, having mated, lays eggs which she buries, often in a deserted arboreal termites' nest.

Common Tegu *Tupinambis teguixin*

RANGE Central America, N. South America

HABITAT Forest, woodland

SIZE 4–4½ ft (1.2–1.4 m), including tail of 27½–33½ in (70–85 cm)

A robust lizard with a long cylindrical tail, the tegu has prominent yellow markings on its dark body. It frequents dense undergrowth and is also found in cultivated areas where food is abundant. Chickens and their eggs are included in its diet, as well as small mammals, frogs, large insects, worms and some fruit and leaves. It hunts by day and hides in a burrow at night and in cool weather. A formidable opponent, the tegu will lash out at an enemy with its powerful tail before attacking with its jaws. However, it will run away from danger when possible, and juveniles are able to run on their hind legs. Local tribespeople catch the tegu and use the yellow body fat as a cure for inflammations.

The female tegu lays her eggs in an inhabited arboreal termites' nest, tearing the outer wall open to deposit her 6 to 8 eggs inside. The ever-vigilant termites then repair the wall of their nest, thus sealing the tegu eggs safely away from predators and changes in temperature or humidity while they develop. The newly hatched young must break out of the termites' nest by themselves.

Jungle Runner

Ameiva ameiva

RANGE Central America, South America, east of the Andes; introduced in USA: Florida

HABITAT Open grassland

SIZE 6–7½ in (15–20 cm)

A ground-living, extremely active lizard, the jungle runner emerges in the morning to forage for food, flicking out its long forked tongue to search for insects, spiders, snails and other small invertebrates and small lizards. The protrusible tongue is tactile and can also detect scents. In coastal regions, the jungle runner may be found in burrows, such as those made by crabs and, in Panama, it is reported to be extending its normal range by moving into areas recently cleared by man.

The male jungle runner is usually larger than the female and is marked with conspicuous light spots, whereas the female has distinctive stripes along her body. After mating, the female lays a clutch of 1 to 4 eggs.

Teyu *Teius teyou*

RANGE S.E. Brazil to Argentina

HABITAT Open, rocky land

SIZE 11¾ in (30 cm)

One of the most numerous and widespread of South American teiids, the adaptable teyu lives wherever there is open land with some rock cover. For shelter, it makes a tunnel under a large stone that leads down to a small chamber, measuring about 1 in by 1½ in (2.5 cm by 4 cm). Here it lies, curled in a U-shape, its body in the chamber and its head and long tail in the tunnel. It feeds on insects and, occasionally, on spiders.

Strand Racerunner *Cnemidophorus lemniscatus*

RANGE Central America to N. South America; Trinidad, Tobago

HABITAT Lowland plains, open regions of food-plain forest

SIZE 11¾ in (30 cm)

One of the fastest-moving of all the lizards, the strand racerunner is always on the move, continually darting off in different directions and sometimes running on its hind legs. Speeds of 15 to 17 mph (24 to 28 km/h) have been recorded over short distances. The racerunner is active during the day and, although mainly ground-dwelling, it also climbs low trees and bushes in search of food. A long-bodied lizard, it has an elongate, tapering, ridged tail; its snout may be blunt or pointed.

To mate, the male sits astride the female, holding the skin of her neck in his mouth. He curves his body around hers while copulating. The female lays 4 to 6 eggs which hatch some 8 to 10 weeks later.

LACERTID LIZARDS AND NIGHT LIZARDS

LACERTIDAE: LACERTID LIZARD FAMILY

About 180 species of lacertid lizard are distributed throughout Europe, Asia and Africa, excluding Madagascar. Within this range, they occur from the hottest tropical habitats to locations within the Arctic Circle. Most are ground-dwelling, but others live in trees or among rocks.

The elongate, longtailed lacertids are mostly small to medium-sized lizards between 4 and 29½ in (10 and 75 cm) in total length. All have large scales on head and belly. Externally, males can generally be distinguished from females by their larger heads and shorter bodies. Almost all species reproduce by laying eggs, depositing their clutches in earth or sand.

Lacertids are highly territorial in their behavior. Males in particular adopt characteristic threat postures to warn off intruders, with the head tilted upward and the throat expanded.

Lacertids feed on small, mainly invertebrate prey animals. A few species, particularly island-dwelling forms, also consume large amounts of plant material.

Green Lizard *Lacerta viridis*

RANGE Europe: Channel Islands, south to N. Spain, Sicily, Greece; E. to S.W. Russia

HABITAT Open woodland, field edges, river banks, roadsides

SIZE 11¾–17¾ in (30–45 cm) including tail of 7¼–11¾ in (20–30 cm)

Also known as the emerald lizard, this is the largest lizard found north of the Alps. Males are brilliant green, finely stippled with black. Females are variable, often duller green or brownish. The color of mature adults is most vivid in the spring and fades later in the year.

An adaptable lizard, the green lizard lives almost anywhere that there is dense vegetation but avoids arid areas. It is an agile climber and can move speedily up trees, bushes and walls to find a spot in which to bask in the sun. Insects and their larvae and small invertebrates, particularly spiders, are its main foods.

Solitary creatures for most of the year, green lizards mate in the spring, when males compete fiercely for females. When copulating, the male grasps the female with his jaws. She lays 4 to 21 eggs in a hole she digs in the soil. She covers the eggs with earth and they incubate for several months. In winter, green lizards hibernate in tree hollows or other crevices.

Viviparous Lizard

Lacerta vivipara

RANGE Europe: Arctic Scandinavia, Britain, south to N. Spain, N. Italy, former Yugoslavia; N. Asia

HABITAT Meadows, open woodland, marshes, any grassland

SIZE 5½–7 in (14–18 cm)

The viviparous lizard is the only lizard found within the Arctic Circle. Its coloration is variable over its wide range, but this lizard is commonly gray or yellowish-brown, with pale spots and dark stripes on the back. In the hotter parts of its range, it is rarely found below 1,650 ft (500 m) except in humid areas, but it basks in the sun for much of the day. Alert and agile, it is a fairly good climber and an excellent swimmer. Insects, spiders, earthworms, slugs and other small invertebrates make up its diet. It lives alone except in the hibernation and breeding seasons.

The breeding habits of this lizard are unique, hence its name meaning "live-bearing". The 5 to 8 young develop inside the mother, feeding on the yolks of their eggs, and break out of their thin membranous shells fully formed, as they are expelled from her body or shortly afterward.

Wall Lizard *Lacerta muralis*

RANGE Europe: N. France to N. Spain, S. Italy, Greece, east to Romania

HABITAT Dry, sunny areas; walls, rocks, tree trunks

SIZE Up to 9 in (23 cm)

A slender, flat-bodied reptile, the wall lizard has a tapering tail which may be up to twice its body length. The coloration and markings of this species are variable over its range, but many individuals are brownish-red or gray, with dark markings. A sun-loving lizard, it spends much of the day basking on any form of wall even near human habitation; in the midday heat, it shelters in the shade. It is extremely active and alert and an expert climber. It feeds on insects such as flies and beetles, and on invertebrates such as earthworms, spiders, snails and slugs. A gregarious species, it lives in small colonies.

Soon after their winter hibernation, the lizards mate, males competing for females. The female digs a hole and lays 2 to 10 eggs which she covers with soil. The eggs hatch in 2 to 3 months. When food supplies are abundant there may be several clutches.

Bosc's Fringe-toed Lizard

Acanthodactylus boskianus

RANGE Egypt, Saudi Arabia

HABITAT Desert

SIZE 5 in (12.5 cm)

A sand-colored, desert-living lizard, this species has long toes bordered with broad combs of scales. This arrangement enlarges the surface area of the feet and thus improves the grip on the sand. It can run quickly over sand and digs deep burrows for refuge. The female lays 2 to 4 eggs which she buries in a hole she digs in the sand.

Algerian Sand Racer *Psammodromus algirus*

RANGE Spain, Portugal, S.W. France, N. Africa

HABITAT Dense vegetation in sandy areas, woodland, gardens, parks

SIZE 11¾ in (30 cm)

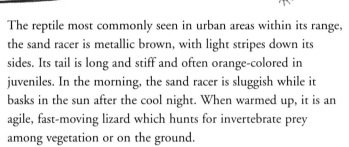

The reptile most commonly seen in urban areas within its range, the sand racer is metallic brown, with light stripes down its sides. Its tail is long and stiff and often orange-colored in juveniles. In the morning, the sand racer is sluggish while it basks in the sun after the cool night. When warmed up, it is an agile, fast-moving lizard which hunts for invertebrate prey among vegetation or on the ground.

The female sand racer lays 6 or more eggs which hatch in about 2 months.

Racerunner *Eremias* sp.

RANGE Europe, C. Asia to Mongolia; Africa

HABITAT Desert, semiarid scrub, grassland, rocky desert

SIZE 6–8½ in (15–22 cm)

There are many species of *Eremias* lizards, many not yet properly classified. Most have scaly bodies and well-developed legs and are marked with spots, arranged in rows along the body. They tend to live in dry areas, taking refuge among rocks and in crevices, and feed on invertebrates, mainly insects and spiders.

Some *Eremias* lizards reproduce by laying clutches of 2 to 12 eggs, but others give birth to living young.

Essex's Mountain Lizard *Tropidosaura essexi*

RANGE South Africa

HABITAT Mountains

SIZE 5½ in (14 cm)

A small lizard with a blunt, rounded snout, Essex's mountain lizard is marked with pale stripes, running from behind its head down its body and tail. A ground-dweller, it is active in the daytime and is quick and agile. It eats insects and small invertebrates.

XANTUSIIDAE: NIGHT LIZARD FAMILY

As their name suggests, night lizards are nocturnal, beginning their hunting activities at dusk and spending the daylight hours hidden among rocks and under stones. There are about 18 species in the family, found in the south-west of the USA, Central America and Cuba, mostly in rocky, arid habitats. They feed on nocturnal insects.

Night lizards have a superficial resemblance to geckos, with their immobile eyelids, the lower of which have transparent "windows". Unlike the geckos, they have scales on the back and belly and shields on the head. All night lizards give birth to live young which develop inside the mother's body, nourished by a form of placenta.

Desert Night Lizard *Xantusia vigilis*

RANGE S.W. USA: Nevada, Utah to California; Mexico

HABITAT Rocky, arid and semiarid land

SIZE 3¾–5 in (9.5–12.5 cm)

The desert night lizard varies in coloration over its range but is marked with many small dark spots. It frequents yucca plants and agaves and feeds on termites, ants, beetles and flies, which it finds among vegetation or rocks.

Night lizards give birth to live young. They mate in early summer, usually May or June, and 1 to 3 young are born, tail first, a few months later.

SKINKS

SCINCIDAE: SKINK FAMILY

One of the largest lizard families, with many hundreds of species, skinks occur on every continent except for Antarctica. They are most abundant in Southeast Asia and the Australasian region. Skinks live on or below the ground and are normally smooth-scaled, with elongate, rounded bodies and tapering tails. Their legs are short, and some burrowing skinks have tiny legs or none at all. Many families of lizards include species with reduced or no limbs, but this is particularly common in the skink family. The majority are between 3¼ and 13¾ in (8 and 35 cm) long, although there are a few giant forms.

Most skinks feed on insects and small invertebrates; the giant forms, however, are herbivorous. Their reproductive habits vary: most species lay eggs but some give birth to live young.

Legless Skink *Acontias* sp.

RANGE	South Africa, Madagascar
HABITAT	Sandy regions
SIZE	4½ in (10 cm)

Legless skinks spend most of their lives in their underground burrows. They are indeed limbless, with long cylindrical bodies and short tails. Their eyes and ears are protected by scales, and their lower eyelids are equipped with transparent "windows", to enable them to see when burrowing without getting soil in their eyes. Their bodies are covered with hard, smooth scales, enabling them to move easily through the earth. They also move quickly on the surface, using snakelike undulations of the body. Legless skinks are largely insectivorous, but may also eat small invertebrates and frogs.

Females bear live young, producing litters of 3 or 4 at a time.

Round-bodied Skink *Chalcides bedriagai*

RANGE	Spain, Portugal
HABITAT	Varied, arid, sandy land, hilly areas, grassland
SIZE	Up to 6¼ in (16 cm)

An elongate, short-legged species, this skink keeps out of sight in ground vegetation or burrows into loose sand. It is usually a buff or grayish-brown with dark-edged markings, and its scales are large, smooth and shiny. It varies somewhat in color and proportions over its range – southern individuals, for example, have shorter legs than the western populations, while those in the east have medium-length legs. Round-bodied skinks feed on a variety of small invertebrates.

Females give birth to 2 or 3 fully formed live young, which have developed inside the body, nourished during their growth by a form of placenta.

Sundeval's Skink *Riopa sundevalli*

RANGE	Africa: Zambia to South Africa
HABITAT	Open plains, sandy savanna
SIZE	Up to 7 in (18 cm)

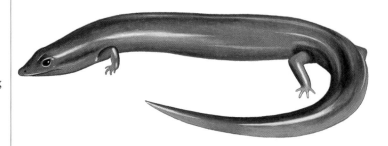

A burrowing species, Sundeval's skink has tiny limbs and smooth scales. It comes to the surface in search of food – insects and their larvae, spiders, wood lice and soft snails – and may hide under stones or leaf debris. Termite hills and manure heaps are also favorite spots for these skinks. On the ground, the skink moves in a snakelike fashion, its tiny limbs are of little use. The tail breaks away easily from the body, and adults are seldom seen with a complete tail.

Females lay a clutch of 2 to 6 eggs, usually 4, in a nest underground or in a termite mound. The newly hatched young skinks measure 2 in (5 cm).

Sandfish *Scincus philbyi*

RANGE Saudi Arabia

HABITAT Sandy desert

SIZE Up to 8¼ in (21 cm)

Unlike most burrowing skinks, this species retains well-developed legs and feet. Its digits are flattened and have fringes of scales in order to help it move easily over loose sand. The body of the sandfish is robust and cylindrical, and it has a broad, wedge-shaped snout. The sandfish is active through the heat of the day, for it spends most of its time under the surface of the sand, looking for prey such as beetles and millipedes. It pushes its way along, literally seeming to swim through the sand, hence its name.

The female sandfish gives birth to fully formed live young which have developed inside her body.

Feylinia cussori

RANGE Tropical Africa

HABITAT Forest

SIZE 13¾ in (35 cm)

A large burrowing skink, *Feylinia cussori* has a rather flattened head, which merges smoothly with its limbless cylindrical body. There are no external eardrums and its tiny eyes are protected by transparent scales. It is often found under decaying wood and feeds largely on termites, which it locates by the sounds they make in the wood.

The female bears litters of 2 or 3 live young which have developed inside her body. There is a local superstition that *Feylinia* can enter the human body whenever it desires and, when it leaves again, the person dies.

Great Plains Skink *Eumeces obsoletus*

RANGE S. C. USA: Wyoming and Nebraska to Arizona and Texas; Mexico

HABITAT Rocky grassland, usually near water

SIZE 6¼–13¼ in (16.5–35 cm)

The Great Plains skink has well-developed sturdy limbs. Its body is spotted with dark brown or black; these spots may merge to give the impression of lengthwise stripes. Active in the day, it eats insects, spiders and small lizards. It is aggressive and will bite if alarmed.

The Great Plains skink displays an unusual degree of maternal care. A few weeks after mating in April or May, the female lays 17 to 21 eggs in a nest which she makes beneath a rock. She guards the eggs while they incubate and turns them regularly to ensure even warming. When, a couple of months later, the eggs begin to hatch, the female rubs and presses them with her body, stimulating the young to move and then to wriggle free of the shell. For a further 10 days after hatching, she attends her young, cleaning them regularly. Juveniles are generally black with blue tails and some white spots. This coloration gradually fades.

Florida Sand Skink *Neoseps reynoldsi* **VU**

RANGE USA: C. Florida

HABITAT Sandhills

SIZE 4–5 in (10–13 cm)

This small skink is an expert digger and burrower. Using its chisel-shaped snout, it burrows speedily into the sand, undulating its body as it goes, as if swimming. Its limbs are tiny and it has only one digit on each forelimb and two on each hind limb. It eats termites and beetle larvae, which it finds by the sound vibrations they cause. Although it is active in the daytime and comes to the surface to shelter under logs and other debris, the sand skink is a secretive species and rarely seen. If alarmed, it quickly buries itself.

Sand skinks mate in spring and the female lays 2 eggs.

SKINKS CONTINUED

Mabuya *Mabuya wrightii*

RANGE Seychelles

HABITAT Granite islands with guano deposits

SIZE 12¼ in (31 cm) including tail of up to 7 in (18 cm)

The stocky-bodied mabuya has well-developed hind limbs with long digits. Its snout is slightly elongate and blunt. It is a fast-moving, ground-dwelling lizard. The mabuya is active in the daytime and has a great need of warmth.

Mabuyas are usually found on the smaller islands of the Seychelles, often in close association with the nesting colonies of seabirds. In the breeding season mabuyas feed on birds' eggs, especially those of terns, which they break by rolling them off rocks or branches. They then lap up the contents. Their diet is not known outside the birds' breeding season.

Most mabuya species give birth to live young, but the exact details of the breeding habits of this particular mabuya have not been observed. One South African mabuya species, *M. trivittata*, is one of the few reptiles to assist her newborn young. She helps the young to escape from the soft membranes in which they are born, by tearing the coverings open with her teeth.

Spiny-tailed Skink *Egernia stokesii*

RANGE Western Australia through arid interior to Queensland, New South Wales and South Australia

HABITAT Stony hills, mountains

SIZE Up to 10½ in (27 cm)

The spiny-tailed skink is a most unusual species, with a stout body covered with rough-edged, sometimes spiny scales. The tail is short and much flattened and particularly well endowed with spinous scales. All four limbs are strong and well developed. This skink frequents rocky areas, where it can shelter in deep crevices or underneath boulders; the spines on its tail make it virtually impossible to dislodge once it has wedged itself in such a hiding place.

The spiny-tailed skink is active during the day, when it basks in the sun and forages for insects within easy reach of its refuge. It is a gregarious species, and lives in colonies and the presence of spiny-tailed skinks in an area is signalled by their regular defecation sites, where small piles of feces accumulate.

Spiny-tailed skinks are live-bearers. The female gives birth to about 5 fully formed young, which develop inside her body, nourished during their growth by a form of placenta. The young measure about 2¼ in (6 cm) when they are born.

Emoia cyanogaster

RANGE Australia: extreme N. Queensland; Indonesia

HABITAT Forest, banana groves

SIZE Up to 10½ in (27 cm)

This slender, glossy skink has a slim tapering tail. The *Emoia cyanogaster* also has a pointed, somewhat flattened snout. Its limbs, particularly the hind limbs, are long and well formed, with elongate digits.

It is an agile, primarily tree-dwelling species and can jump easily from branch to branch. This skink spends much of the day basking in the sun on low vegetation or sheltering among the trailing leaves of banana trees, but it often descends to the ground in order to search for food.

These skinks breed throughout the year, although there are some seasonal fluctuations. The female usually lays a clutch of 2 eggs at a time.

Leiolopisma infrapunctatum

RANGE New Zealand

HABITAT Open country with some vegetation

SIZE 9½ in (24 cm)

This smooth-scaled skink has beautiful markings, which may vary slightly in coloration and intensity, but are usually constant in pattern. The most striking are the broad, broken bands of reddish-brown, which run from behind each eye, above the limbs, to the tail. The belly is usually yellow with scattered dark markings. The head and body are elongate and there is no distinct neck.

Active in the daytime, this skink often lives near petrel nesting sites. It basks in the sun, but is easily scared and swiftly takes refuge at the least sign of disturbance. It feeds on small land-living invertebrates and insects. Mating takes place in spring, and the female gives birth to a litter of live young about 4 months later.

Western Blue-tongued Skink *Tiliqua occipitalis*

RANGE S. Australia

HABITAT Arid areas

SIZE 17¾ in (45 cm)

The heavily built western blue-tongued skink has a stout body and large head but its limbs are relatively small. Bands of dark brown scales pattern its body and tail and there are characteristic dark streaks behind each eye. The blue-tongued skink is active in the daytime when it forages around on the ground for insects, snails and berries. An abandoned rabbit warren may sometimes be used for shelter.

The female gives birth to about 5 live young, each of which is distinctly banded with dark brown and yellow.

Prickly Forest Skink *Tropidophorus queenslandiae*

RANGE Australia: N. Queensland

HABITAT Rain forest

SIZE 5–7¾ in (13–20 cm)

The prickly forest skink is easily distinguished from other Australian skinks by its covering of strongly keeled small scales. Its rounded tail is also covered with keeled scales, and its limbs are well developed. A nocturnal skink, it lives beneath plant debris or rotting logs on the forest floor, where its dark body with irregular pale markings keeps it well camouflaged. It is a slow-moving, sluggish skink which does not like to bask in sunlight and is usually found in a rather torpid state. Worms and soft-bodied insects are its main foods.

Little is known of the breeding biology of this skink, but several of the 20 *Tropidophonts* species are known to produce litters of 6 to 9 live young. These develop inside the mother's body and break from their thin shells as the eggs are laid.

Brown Skink *Scincella lateralis*
(previously *Lygosoma lateralis*)

RANGE USA: New Jersey to Florida, west to Nebraska and Texas

HABITAT Humid forest, wooded grassland

SIZE 3¼–5 in (8–13 cm)

This smooth, shiny skink, also known as the ground skink, has dark stripes on the sides of its body and a pale, often yellowish or whitish belly. Its body is long and slender and its legs well developed, with elongate digits on the hind feet. The brown skink has movable eyelids with a transparent window in each lower lid; a feature which enables it to see clearly even when it must close its eyes to avoid dirt getting into them when it is burrowing into cover. It lives on the ground and prefers areas with plenty of leaf litter in which to shelter. Active in the day, particularly in warm, humid weather, it feeds mainly on insects and spiders. The closest relatives of this species live in Central America and Australia.

A prolific breeder, the female brown skink lays a clutch of 1 to 7 eggs every 4 or 5 weeks. There is a maximum of about 5 clutches during the breeding season, which lasts from April to August in most areas.

GIRDLED AND PLATED LIZARDS

CORDYLIDAE: GIRDLED AND PLATED LIZARD FAMILY

The cordylid lizards are an African family of about 40 species, found largely in rocky or arid habitats, south of the Sahara and in Madagascar. Names include plated, whip, girdled, crag, snake and flat lizards, which gives some idea of the range of adaptations within the family.

The typical cordylid lizard has a body covered with bony plates which underlie the external and visible scales. This undercoat of armor, however, is not continuous over the whole body: on each side there is a lateral groove, without a plate layer, which allows body expansion, when the belly is full of food for example, or, in egg-laying females, when distended with eggs. There are many variations of form within the family. The girdle-tailed lizards have short tails, armored with rings of spines, and often have spines on the head. Flat lizards of the genus *Platysaurus* have flattened bodies and skin covered with smooth granules. Snake lizards of the genus *Chamaesaura* are very elongate, with tails up to three-quarters of their body length. Some cordylids have well-developed limbs, while in others the limbs are much reduced or even absent.

Most lizards in the family feed on insects and small invertebrates such as millipedes. Some of the larger forms also consume smaller lizards, and others are almost entirely vegetarian in their habits. Their reproductive habits vary, some species laying eggs and others bearing live young.

Cordylosaurus subtessellatus

RANGE Africa: S. Angola, Namibia

HABITAT Dry, rocky areas

SIZE 6 in (15 cm)

The greatly compressed head and body of this lizard make it easy for it to hide in crevices and crannies in the rocks, to escape enemies and intense heat or night-time cold. It may also shelter under stones. In each lower eyelid there is a transparent "window", so that the lizard can close its eyes in windy weather, when sand and dust might blow into them, but is still able to see. Under its digits are keeled scales, perhaps to help it grip on rocks. Its tail is easily shed and regenerated.

This agile, ground-dwelling lizard, eats insects and other small invertebrates. The species reproduces by laying eggs.

Imperial Flat Lizard *Platysaurus imperator*

RANGE Africa: N.E. Zimbabwe, contiguous Mozambique

HABITAT Rocky knolls of granite and sandstone in grassland

SIZE 15¼ in (39 cm)

The head, body, limbs and tail of this lizard are all flattened laterally; in consequence it can take refuge in narrow cracks and crevices in the rocks among which it lives. As these rocky knolls weather, many crevices are formed, ideal as hiding places; once in a crevice, the lizard expands its body with air and braces itself against the rock, making it virtually impossible for any predator to remove it. This lizard tends to frequent the tops of the knolls, whereas the other platysaurans live at the base.

The biggest species in its genus, the imperial flat lizard has large scales on its neck and a smooth back. The male, with his yellow, red and black body, is larger and more brightly colored than the female, which is largely black, with three distinctive yellow stripes on her head that taper off toward the back. Males hold territories which they compete for and defend against intruders by adopting an aggressive posture, rearing up and displaying throat and chest colors.

Active in the daytime, flat lizards hunt insects, particularly locusts and beetles. They shelter from the midday heat and emerge again to hunt in the afternoon.

The female flat lizard lays 2 eggs, elongate in shape, in a crevice in the rocks.

Transvaal Snake Lizard *Chamaesaura aena*

RANGE South Africa

HABITAT Grassland

SIZE 15¾ in (40 cm)

This snakelike lizard has an elongate body and a tail which is about three-quarters of its total length. It has four small limbs, each with five clawed digits; the other 3 species in this genus

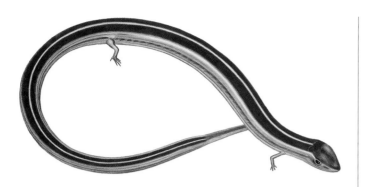

have at most two digits per limb, and one species, *C. macrolepsis*, has no front limbs at all. Active in the daytime, it moves quickly through the grass with serpentine undulations of its body, often with its head and forelimbs lifted off the ground. It feeds on insects, spiders, earthworms and other small invertebrates.

The female's 2 to 4 young develop inside her oviduct. The fully formed young break from their soft shells as they are expelled from her body.

Armadillo Lizard *Cordylus cataphractus* **VU**

RANGE	South Africa: W. Cape Province
HABITAT	Arid rocky areas
SIZE	8¼ in (21 cm)

The armadillo lizard is heavily armored, with strong spiny scales which extend from its head right along its back and tail. Its head, body and clublike tail are all flattened, enabling it to wriggle easily into rock crevices for shelter. The nostrils are elongated into little tubes.

A ground-dwelling lizard, it is active in the daytime and feeds on a wide variety of insects, as well as on spiders and other small invertebrates.

This species is fairly slow moving and, rather than darting for cover when it is threatened, it may adopt a curious defensive posture which earns it its common name. It rolls itself up like an armadillo, its tail tightly held in its jaws; thus presenting a spiny defensive ring to the predator and protecting its softer, vulnerable belly area.

The 1 to 3 young of the armadillo lizard develop inside the female's body. The tiny, fully formed lizards break from their soft membranous shells as they are expelled from her body.

Plated Lizard *Gerrhosaurus flavigularis*

RANGE	Africa: Sudan, Ethiopia, south through E. Africa to South Africa: Cape Province
HABITAT	Grassland, scrub
SIZE	18 in (45.5 cm)

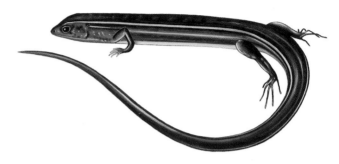

A ground-living and burrowing lizard, this species is usually greenish-gray or brownish, with a red or yellow throat and often a narrow stripe down each side. It is well armored, with hard body plates, and head shields fused to the skull. The tail is generally about two-thirds of the total length. Its limbs are well-developed and it has five toes on each foot. These are not specially adapted for digging, and the lizard probably does most of its tunnelling after rain when the ground is soft.

Active by day, it hunts insects and is rarely seen, despite its size. It moves rapidly through the grass and at any sign of danger darts into its burrow, usually positioned under a bush.

The female plated lizard lays clutches of 4 or 5 eggs in a shallow pit which she excavates.

Girdled Lizard *Zonosaurus* sp.

RANGE	Madagascar
HABITAT	Forest
SIZE	15–24 in (38–61 cm)

There are 3 *Zonosaurus* species, all of which are large, strong, ground-dwelling lizards. They have well-developed limbs and distinct grooves along their sides to allow for body expansion. Little is known of their habits or biology.

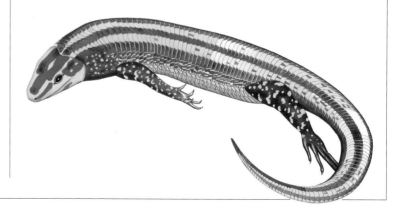

CROCODILE LIZARDS, ALLIGATOR LIZARDS AND LEGLESS LIZARDS

XENOSAURIDAE: CROCODILE LIZARD FAMILY

There are 4 species in this family, 3 in Central America and Mexico and 1 in south China. They are related to the anguid lizards and, under the body scales, have bony plates, which may be tiny or large but are not joined together. Unlike many anguids, however, their limbs are well developed.

Xenosaurus sp.

RANGE Mexico, Guatemala

HABITAT Rain forest

SIZE About 7¾ in (20 cm)

These powerful, strong-limbed lizards have flat heads and robust bodies. They are inconspicuous creatures and are not often seen, spending much of their time in refuges beneath tree roots or in rocky crevices. They will also lie in water for long periods. Active at night, they feed on insects, particularly winged termites and ants. If alarmed, *Xenosaurus* adopts a threat posture, with mouth agape, revealing a black membrane.

The females gives birth to litters of 3 fully formed live young which are about 1½ in (4 cm) long at birth.

ANGUIDAE: LEGLESS AND ALLIGATOR LIZARD FAMILY

There are about 80 species in this family of elongate, snakelike lizards, found in North, Central and South America, the West Indies, Europe, North Africa and Asia. Typically, they have smooth elongate bodies and tails, movable eyelids and external ear openings. Most are land-dwelling or burrowing animals and many, such as the slow worms and glass lizards and snakes, are limbless or have only vestigial limbs. The alligator lizards of North and Central America, however, have well-developed limbs.

Many of these lizards have stiff bodies, armored by bony plates under the surface skin. In order that their bodies can expand when breathing, or to accommodate food or eggs, there are grooves of soft scales along their sides. Their long tails easily become detached if seized by an attacker, usually along one of the series of fracture planes. The tail is regrown in a few weeks, but not always completely.

Most anguids feed on insects, small invertebrates and even small mammals and lizards. All but a few species reproduce by laying eggs. The others, mostly species found at high altitudes, give birth to live young.

Galliwasp *Diploglossus lessorae*

RANGE Central America, N. South America

HABITAT Forest

SIZE Up to 13¾ in (35 cm)

The smooth, shiny galliwasp resembles the alligator lizards but has a more elongate body and lacks the expandable grooves along the sides of the body that the heavily armored alligator lizards possess. It is a ground-dwelling species, active in the daytime, and feeds on insects, worms and mollusks. It is believed to reproduce by laying eggs.

Southern Alligator Lizard *Gerrhonotus multicarinatus*

RANGE W. USA: Washington; Baja California

HABITAT Grassland, open woodland

SIZE 10–17 in (25.5–43 cm)

The agile southern alligator lizard has a strong prehensile tail, which it can wrap around branches and use like a fifth limb when climbing in bushes. There are 5 subspecies of this lizard, which vary in coloration from reddish-brown to

yellowish-gray, usually with some dark markings, but all have distinct folds along their sides, where flexible scales allow the stiff, armored body to expand.

These lizards are active in the daytime, when they hunt for insects and any other small creatures that they are able to catch and swallow, including scorpions and black widow spiders.

Alligator lizards breed in the summer, females laying several clutches over the season. There are usually 12 eggs in a clutch, but there may be up to 40 on occasion.

Glass Snake *Ophisaurus apodus*

RANGE Europe: Former Yugoslavia, Greece to Black Sea region, east to S.W. and C. Asia

SIZE Up to 4 ft (1.2 m)

The largest species of
its family, the glass snake
is a heavy-bodied, snakelike animal
with vestiges of hind limbs. The
body is rather stiff, with a bony layer
under the smooth scales. Grooves of flexible
scales on each side allow the body to expand when necessary.
The glass snake is active in the daytime and at dawn and dusk,
feeding on lizards, mice and other small animals which it kills
with its powerful jaws.

Males become aggressive and competitive in the breeding season and there is fierce rivalry for mates. The female lays 5 to 7 eggs in a hollow under a rock or log, or in a pile of rotting vegetation. She curls around her eggs and guards them from predators while they incubate. The young hatch in about 4 weeks and are about 5 in (12.5 cm) long.

Slow Worm *Anguis fragilis*

RANGE Europe (not Ireland, S. Spain and Portugal or N. Scandinavia), east to central and S.W. Asia; N.W. Africa

HABITAT Fields, meadows, scrub, heath, up to 7,900 ft (2,400 m)

SIZE 13¾–21¼ in (35–54 cm)

The slow worm is a smooth, extremely snakelike creature with no visible limbs. It is reddish-brown, brown or gray above; females usually have a dark stripe on the back, while some males may have blue spots. It moves by serpentine undulations and can shed its long tail if seized by an enemy. The tail does not

fully regenerate, however, and is then stumplike. The night and heat of the day are spent under rocks or logs, and the slow worm emerges in the morning and evening in order to hunt for slugs and worms, as well as spiders, insects and larvae. It is slower-moving than most lizards but can disappear into cover with considerable speed.

In late spring, breeding males become aggressive and compete with one another for mates. As they copulate, the male holds the female's neck or head in his jaws. About 3 months later, the female gives birth to live young, usually 6 to 12, but sometimes as many as 20. The young develop in thin-shelled eggs inside her body and break out of the membranous shells as they are laid. The young slow-worms are about 2¼ to 3½ in (6 to 9 cm) long at birth.

California Legless Lizard *Anniella pulchra*

RANGE USA: California; Mexico, Baja California

HABITAT Beaches, sand dunes, banks of streams, soft loamy soil

SIZE 6–9 in (15–23 cm)

Specialized for burrowing, this legless lizard has a smooth body, which helps it to move easily through soil, and a shovel-shaped snout for digging. Its eyes are small and have movable lids. Most of this creature's life is spent underground or burrowing in leaf litter, searching for insects and insect larvae. It rarely moves in the open. One race of this species, *A. pulchra nigra*, is in danger of extinction.

These lizards are live-bearing; females produce litters of up to 4 fully formed young.

MONITORS AND GILA MONSTER

VARANIDAE: MONITOR LIZARD FAMILY

The monitor lizards of the Old World include within their number the largest of all lizards – the komodo dragon. This species may be as much as 10 ft (3 m) long and weigh 360 lb (163 kg); several other species within the family exceed 6½ ft (2 m) in length. There are about 30 species of monitor in a single genus and the single species of Lanthanotus (earless monitor). This species is sometimes placed in a family of its own, the Lanthanotidae. All are elongate lizards with long necks and tails and well-developed limbs. Their snakelike forked tongues can be retracted into the lizard's mouth.

Monitors occur in Africa (except Madagascar), the Middle East, southern Asia, Indonesia and Australasia. All are voracious carnivores. Male monitor lizards may perform spectacular ritualized fights to assert their dominance. They rear up on their hind legs and wrestle with their forelimbs until one contestant is pushed over and defeated. Monitors reproduce by laying eggs, and several species are known to dig pits in the ground in which the eggs are buried to incubate.

Komodo Dragon

Varanus komodensis **VU**

RANGE Islands of Komodo, Flores, Pintja and Padar, east of Java

HABITAT Grassland

SIZE 10 ft (3 m)

The awe-inspiring komodo dragon dwarfs most present-day lizards. It has a heavy body, a long, thick tail and well-developed limbs with talonlike claws. Its teeth are large and jagged and it has a forked tongue that can be flicked in and out of the mouth. Despite its size, it is a good climber, and moves surprisingly quickly. It also swims well; and tends to live near water. It is active during the day and preys on animals as large as hog deer and wild boar, as well as on small deer and pigs.

The female komodo lays about 15 eggs which she buries in the ground to incubate.

Nile Monitor *Varanus niloticus*

RANGE Africa: south and east of the Sahara to Cape Province

HABITAT Forest, open country

SIZE Over 6½ ft (2 m)

The versatile, yet unspecialized, Nile monitor is a robust, strong reptile, which is typical of the monitor group. Using its broad tail as a rudder, it swims and dives well and can climb trees with the aid of its huge claws and strong prehensile tail, which it uses to hold on to branches. It can also dig burrows.

Nile monitors tend to stay near water and do not venture into desert areas. They feed on frogs, fish and snails, as well as on crocodile eggs and young.

This is one of the most prolific egg-laying lizards. The female Nile monitor lays up to 60 eggs at a time in a termite mound. She tears a hole in the wall, lays her eggs inside and departs, leaving them to hatch unguarded. The termites then repair their nest, thus enclosing the eggs in the warm, safe termitarium. When they hatch, the young monitors must make their own way out of the nest.

Gould's Monitor *Varanus gouldi*

RANGE Australia

HABITAT Coastal forest to sandy desert

SIZE About 5 ft (1.5 m)

The widespread Gould's monitor, which is also known as the sand monitor, varies in size, coloration and pattern over its range. Like those of all monitors, its limbs are powerful, and its distinctly ridged tail is laterally compressed, except at the base.

Gould's monitor is a ground-dweller, sheltering in burrows, which it digs or takes over from other animals, or under logs and debris. To find food, it must roam over large areas of sparsely populated country, searching for birds, mammals, reptiles, insects, even carrion. Like all monitors, the female reproduces by laying eggs.

Earless Monitor *Lanthanotus borneensis*

RANGE Sarawak

HABITAT Forest

SIZE Up to 17 in (43 cm)

The earless monitor has an elongate, rather flattened body and short but strong limbs, each with five digits. On each body scale there is a small tubercle. Its eyes are tiny with movable lids, the lower of which have transparent "windows", and there are no external ear openings, which is the origin of its common name.

Much of the earless monitor's life is spent burrowing underground or swimming; it avoids bright light and does not need intense warmth. In captivity the earless monitor will eat fish, but its natural diet is not known.

HELODERMATIDAE: GILA MONSTER FAMILY

There are only 2 species in this family which are related to the monitor lizards and the rare, earless monitor. They are the gila monster, from western North America, and the Mexican beaded lizard.

Gila Monster *Heloderma suspectum* **VU**

RANGE S.W. USA: S. Utah, Arizona to New Mexico; Mexico

HABITAT Arid and semiarid areas with some vegetation

SIZE 17¾–24 in (45–61 cm)

This formidable looking, heavy-bodied lizard has a short, usually stout tail, in which it stores fat. It can then live off these fat reserves during periods of food shortage. It is a gaudily patterned lizard and has brightly colored beadlike scales on its back.

The gila lives on the ground and takes shelter under rocks or in a burrow which it either digs itself or takes over from another animal. It is primarily a nocturnal creature, but it may emerge into the open during the day in spring.

The two members of the gila monster family are the only venomous lizards. The venom is produced in glands in the lower jaw and enters the mouth via grooved teeth at the front of the lower jaw. The poison flows into the gila's victim as the lizard chews. The gila will also eat the eggs of birds and other reptiles.

Gila monsters mate during the summer, and the female lays her clutch of 3 to 5 eggs some time later, in the autumn or winter.

AMPHISBAENIANS

AMPHISBAENIDAE: AMPHISBAENID FAMILY

The 150 or so species of amphisbaenians are extraordinary, wormlike, burrowing reptiles. Known as worm lizards, they are not true lizards and are given their own suborder within the Squamata order, on a parallel with the much larger lizard and snake groups.

There are three families of amphisbaenians – amphisbaenidae, the bipedidae (3 species) and trogonophiidae (6 species). Most species occur in Central and South America and Africa, but there are a few species that inhabit the warmer parts of North America and Europe.

These strange creatures prefer moist habitats in which they can build semipermanent tunnel systems that will not collapse after the animal has passed through. They quickly dehydrate in dry soil. Water is taken into the mouth and swallowed, not absorbed through the skin as was once believed.

Most species are limbless. The skin is loosely attached over the simple cylindrical body, which is ringed with small scales. The tail is pointed in some species and rounded in others, but it is always covered with horny scales. Amphisbaenids have no external ear openings, and their tiny eyes are covered with scales.

Amphisbaenids and the other amphisbaenians live underground in burrows which they dig themselves, often near to ant or termite colonies. Bracing their long bodies against the walls of the tunnel, they excavate new lengths by repeated battering strokes of their hard, strong heads. Like worms, they can move backward or forward in a straight line with no body undulations, a form of locomotion ideally suited to life in tunnels. Indeed, the Greek word amphisbaena means "goes both ways". This ability, combined with the similar appearance of the head and tail, has caused many to see the amphisbaenid as a two-headed monster, and it is even mentioned as such in a Roman epic poem.

Amphisbaenids find all their prey – mostly insects and worms – below the ground. Larger species may also attack and eat small vertebrate animals. Despite the lack of external ears they are able to hear their prey crawling in the ground and move accurately in its direction. The sense of smell also seems to play a part in locating prey. Once it has found its quarry, the amphisbaenid grabs it and tears it apart with its strong, interlocking teeth, set in its powerful jaws.

Little is known of the breeding habits of amphisbaenids, but most species are believed to lay eggs which incubate and hatch in their underground burrows.

Florida Worm Lizard *Rhineura floridana*

RANGE USA: N. and C. Florida

HABITAT Sandy, wooded areas

SIZE 7–16 in (18–40.5 cm)

The only blind, limbless lizard in North America, the Florida worm lizard is just over 1/5 in (0.5 cm) in diameter and has a rather shovel shaped head. It lives underground, feeding on worms, spiders and termites, and rarely comes to the surface unless driven by rain or disturbed by cultivation. Unlike an earthworm, it leaves a tunnel behind it as it burrows, pushing through the earth with its spadelike snout and compacting the soil as it goes, to form the tunnel.

In summer, the Florida worm lizard lays up to 3 long, thin eggs in a burrow. The young hatch out in autumn, when they are about 4 in (10 cm) long.

Fossil research has shown that this amphisbaenid was at one time widely distributed in North America.

South African Shield Snout *Monopeltis capensis*

RANGE Africa: C. South Africa, Zimbabwe

HABITAT Sandy soil

SIZE 11¾ in (30 cm)

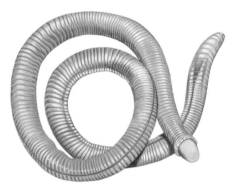

The thick horny plates on the shovellike head of this amphisbaenid enable it to burrow into harder soils than many other species. It tunnels down to depths of 7¾ in (20 cm) and only emerges above ground when driven by rains, or if attacked by ants. When they do emerge, shield snouts are preyed on by birds, such as ravens and kites. Shield snouts themselves feed on termites, beetles and other ground-living insects.

Worm Lizard *Blanus cinereus*

RANGE Spain, Portugal, N.W. Africa

HABITAT Sandy soil or humus, often in woodland

SIZE 8½–11¾ in (22–30 cm)

The only European amphisbaenid, this worm lizard has a small, pointed head and a tapering tail. It spends most of its life in underground burrows and is only rarely seen above ground except after heavy rain or when it is disturbed by cultivation. It feeds on small invertebrates, particularly ants.

White-bellied Worm Lizard *Amphisbaena alba*

RANGE Tropical South America; Trinidad

HABITAT Rain forest

SIZE 24 in (61 cm)

The body of this worm lizard, the most widespread in South America, is cylindrical over its entire length, the tail being almost as thick and blunt as the head. Tail and head look similar, and the species is known as the two-headed blind snake in some areas. It is over 1 in (2.5 cm) in diameter.

Although a burrowing, underground animal, this species often crawls over the forest floor, particularly after heavy rain. It eats earthworms and ants and is often found in ants' nests. Indeed some tribes call it "ant king" or "mother ant" and believe it to be reared by ants. If in danger, this worm lizard lifts its tail and moves it around as if it were a head. Presumably this tricks the enemy into attacking the tail, keeping the vulnerable head area safe and enabling the worm lizard to make a counterattack.

BIPEDIDAE: BIPED FAMILY

The 3 species in this family are found in Mexico. They are unique among amphisbaenians in retaining forelimbs to assist with digging. Underground, the head is used for burrowing.

Two-legged Worm Lizard
Bipes biporus

RANGE Mexico, Baja California

HABITAT Arid land

SIZE 7¾ in (20 cm)

The worm lizards of this genus are the only members of the family to possess limbs. They have two tiny front legs with five clawed toes on each limb. Despite their size, these limbs are powerful, and the digits are adapted for digging and climbing. The two-legged worm lizard spends most of its life underground in burrows and uses its limbs to start digging its tunnels. Once the burrow is begun, it pushes through with its head, compacting the soil as it goes. It may use its limbs as well as its head when digging a large tunnel.

These worm lizards eat worms and termites. Although little is known of their breeding habits, they are believed to lay eggs.

TROGONOPHIIDAE: TROGONOPHIID FAMILY

The 6 species in this family are found in North Africa and western Asia. They use an oscillating movement of the head when digging.

Somali Edge Snout *Agamodon anguliceps*

RANGE Africa: Somali Republic, S.E. Ethiopia

HABITAT Sandy soil

SIZE 4¼ in (11 cm)

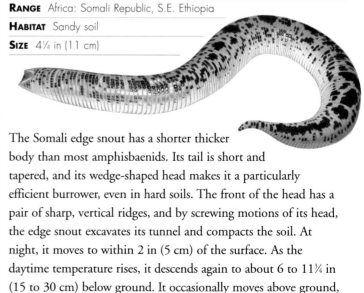

The Somali edge snout has a shorter thicker body than most amphisbaenids. Its tail is short and tapered, and its wedge-shaped head makes it a particularly efficient burrower, even in hard soils. The front of the head has a pair of sharp, vertical ridges, and by screwing motions of its head, the edge snout excavates its tunnel and compacts the soil. At night, it moves to within 2 in (5 cm) of the surface. As the daytime temperature rises, it descends again to about 6 to 11¾ in (15 to 30 cm) below ground. It occasionally moves above ground, swinging its head from side to side and pulling itself along.

THREAD, BLIND, PIPE, SHIELDTAIL AND SUNBEAM SNAKES

LEPTOTYPHLOPIDAE: THREAD SNAKE FAMILY

Thread snakes are small, worm-shaped, burrowing snakes that grow to about 15 in (38 cm) long. They possess minute vestiges of a pelvic girdle and hind limbs, and their tiny rudimentary eyes are hidden beneath scales. Like their relatives Typhlopidae and Anomalepidae, these snakes are specialized for a burrowing existence. The size of the mouth has become reduced, and it is only about half the length of the head, whereas in most snakes the mouth is as large as possible.

Thread snakes feed on termites and ants. The approximately 80 species live in Africa, tropical Asia and southern USA, through Central and South America to Argentina.

Western Blind Snake *Leptotyphlops humilis*

RANGE S.W. USA: S.W. Utah, south to N. Mexico and Baja California

HABITAT Desert, grassland, scrub, rocky canyons

SIZE 7–15 in (18–38 cm)

A smooth, round-bodied snake, the western blind snake has a blunt head and tail. It lives almost anywhere where there is sandy or gravelly soil, and spends much of its life below ground, emerging only occasionally. It eats ants and termites which it finds by smell. With its slender body, it can slide into their nests.

The snakes mate in spring. The female lays 2 to 6 eggs. She watches over the eggs, which may be laid in a communal nest.

TYPHLOPIDAE: BLIND SNAKE FAMILY

The 150 or so species in this family of burrowing snakes occur in tropical and warm temperate regions throughout the world. They rarely exceed 23½ in (60 cm) in length. Well adapted for burrowing, they have thin, cylindrical bodies, smooth, polished scales and narrow, streamlined heads. Their eyes are extremely small and each is covered with a translucent scale. They eat small invertebrates, particularly ants.

Schlegel's Blind Snake *Typhlops schlegelii*

RANGE Africa: Kenya to South Africa

HABITAT Sandy or loamy soil

SIZE 23½ in (60 cm)

Schlegel's blind snake has a spine on the end of its tail which helps to provide leverage when it is burrowing. Although most of its life is spent underground, it will come near the surface in damp or wet weather.

The female lays 12 to 60 eggs, which are already well advanced in their development when they are laid and take only 4 to 6 weeks to hatch.

ANOMALEPIDAE

Sometimes grouped in the Typhlopidae family, there are about 20 species in this family, all found in Central and South America. They closely resemble the blind and thread snakes.

Anomalepis sp.

RANGE Mexico, tropical Central and South America to Peru

HABITAT Forest

SIZE Up to 15¾ in (40 cm)

There are 4 species of *Anomalepis* snakes, all little-known wormlike burrowing snakes with cylindrical bodies. They spend much of their lives buried under leaf litter in damp humus and are rarely seen on the surface, except after rain. They feed on termites, ants and other small invertebrates.

ANILIIDAE: PIPE SNAKE FAMILY

There are 10 species in this family, all of which have a variety of primitive characteristics, including a pelvis and vestigial hind limbs, which appear as spurs, close to the vent. One species lives in northern South America and the other 9 are found in Southeast Asia. All are excellent burrowers and feed on vertebrates such as other snakes.

False Coral Snake *Anilius scytale*

RANGE N. South America, east of Andes

HABITAT Forest

SIZE 29½–33½ in (75–85 cm)

A burrowing species, the false coral snake has a cylindrical body, small head and smooth scales. Its tiny eyes lie beneath transparent scales. Its small mouth is not particularly flexible and it is restricted to slender prey animals such as other snakes, caecilians (limbless wormlike amphibians) and the snakelike amphisbaenids. The young develop inside the female's body and are born fully formed.

UROPELTIDAE: SHIELDTAIL SNAKE FAMILY

There are about 40 species in this family of burrowing snakes, all found in India and Sri Lanka.

Red-blotched Shieldtail *Uropeltis biomaculatus*

RANGE India, Sri Lanka

HABITAT Mountain forest

SIZE Up to 12 in (30.5 cm)

The red-blotched shieldtail has the typical cylindrical body of a burrowing snake. It tunnels by forming the body into a series of S-bends, which press against the sides of the tunnel, and then thrusting the head forward into the soil. It is a secretive, inoffensive snake and feeds mainly on earthworms and grubs.

The female gives birth to 3 to 8 fully formed live young, which have developed inside her body and hatch from their membranous shells as they are laid.

Blyth's Landau Shieldtail *Rhinophis blythis*

RANGE Sri Lanka

HABITAT Forest

SIZE Up to 14 in (35.5 cm)

This small shieldtail burrows through the soil. Most of its life is spent beneath the ground and it feeds on earthworms. Males tend to have longer tails than females. The female gives birth to litters of 3 to 6 fully formed live young which are about ⅓ in (1 cm) long at birth.

XENOPELTIDAE: SUNBEAM SNAKE FAMILY

Placed in a family of its own, the sunbeam snake of Southeast Asia has both primitive and advanced features. Although much of its skull structure is primitive and inflexible, its lower jaw is flexible, which permits a more varied diet. Like the more advanced snakes, it has no pelvic girdle.

Sunbeam Snake *Xenopeltis unicolor*

RANGE S.E. Asia: Myanmar to Indonesia

HABITAT Rice fields, cultivated land

SIZE Up to 3¼ ft (1 m)

The iridescence of its smooth, blue scales gives the sunbeam snake its name. It spends time both above and below ground and, using its head, can burrow rapidly in soft soil. With its flexible lower jaw, it is able to take a wide range of fair-sized prey, including frogs, small rodents and birds.

PYTHONS, BOAS AND WART SNAKES

BOIDAE: PYTHON AND BOA FAMILY

There are about 60 species of snake in this family, many of them well known. Most specialists regard the group as primitive, since its members retain characteristics which are found in lizards, but which have been lost by the more highly evolved snakes, such as vipers. For example, a pelvic girdle and diminutive hind limbs are discernible in some species. All species have two working lungs, while advanced snakes have lost the left lung.

Within the family are 2 groups – the pythons and the boas. These are sometimes placed in separate families, pythonidae and boidae. The 20 species of python inhabit the more tropical parts of the Old World. They are often found in or near water, but also spend much of their time in trees and may have prehensile tails. They lay eggs which develop and hatch outside the body. The boas are found mainly in the New World and live on the ground, in trees or in or near water. The young develop inside the body and hatch from thin-shelled eggs as the eggs are laid.

Boid snakes are predators, but they are nonvenomous, capturing their prey with their teeth or killing it by constriction – wrapping the prey in the body coils until it suffocates.

adapts to widely contrasting climatic conditions but seems to prefer swampy rain forest. Primarily a ground-living snake, it does, however, climb trees and has a slightly prehensile tail which allows it to grasp branches. It kills its prey, mostly birds and mammals, by encircling them in the muscular coils of its body until the prey is suffocated or crushed.

Rubber Boa *Charina bottae*

RANGE W. USA: Washington to S. California, east to Montana and Utah

HABITAT Woodland, coniferous forest, meadows, sandy banks of streams

SIZE 13¾–33 in (35–84 cm)

This small boa ranges farther into the temperate zone than any other. It varies in coloration from tan to olive-green, and the confusing appearance of its broad snout and blunt tail are the origin of its other common name of "two-headed snake".

Usually active in the evening and at night, it is a good burrower and swimmer and can climb, using its prehensile tail. During the day, it hides under rocks or logs, or burrows into sand or leaf litter. It feeds on small mammals, birds and lizards which it kills by constriction. In late summer, the female gives birth to 2 to 8 live young which measure 6 to 9 in (15 to 23 cm).

Emerald Tree Boa *Boa caninus*

RANGE South America: Guyana, south to Brazil and Bolivia

HABITAT Rain forest

SIZE 4 ft (1.2 m)

This boa spends much of its life in trees, where it rests with its body flattened and pressed to a branch, which it grasps with its prehensile tail. It watches for prey, often birds and bats which it catches and kills with its strong front teeth. It is the most fast-moving of all boas and is also a good swimmer.

Boa constrictor *Boa constrictor*

RANGE Mexico, Central and South America to N. Argentina; West Indies

HABITAT Desert to rain forest

SIZE Up to 18¼ ft (5.6 m)

The second-largest snake in the Americas, the boa constrictor

Anaconda

Eunectes murinus

RANGE South America, south to Argentina

HABITAT Swampy river valleys, stream banks

SIZE 29½ ft (9 m)

One of the world's longest snakes, the anaconda spends much of its life in sluggish fresh water but also climbs small trees and bushes with the aid of its slightly prehensile tail. It does not pursue its prey but lurks in murky water waiting for birds and animals to come to the edge to drink. It seizes its victim and then kills it by constriction. It can only remain submerged for about 10 minutes and usually glides along with the top of its head showing above the water.

In the breeding season, males court their mates by making loud booming sounds. Females produce litters of as many as 40 live young, each of which is about 26 in (66 cm) long at birth.

Carpet Python

Morelia argus

RANGE Australia, New Guinea

HABITAT Forest, scrub, bush

SIZE 11 ft (3.4 m)

A common, widely distributed snake, the carpet python is usually found inland, less often on the coast. The dark pattern on its body mimics dead leaves and provides camouflage as it lurks among plant debris. It moves well on the ground, in trees or in water. Usually active at night, it rests during the day in a tree or hollow stump and occasionally basks in the sun.

A nonvenomous snake, the carpet python kills small mammals such as mice and rabbits, and birds, such as domestic fowl, with its sharp teeth. The female lays up to 35 eggs.

Indian Python *Python molurus* **LR:nt**

RANGE India, S.E. Asia, Indonesia

HABITAT Estuarine mangroves, scrub jungle, cool rain forest

SIZE 16½–20 ft (5–6.1 m)

One of the largest species in the world, the Indian python has suffered a reduction in numbers in some areas where it is hunted for its fine skin. It is a thick-bodied, smooth snake with a head shaped like the head of a spear. Like others of its genus, it is believed to have heat sensors near the nostrils to help it find its warm-blooded prey. Coloration varies by locality, but the pale gray race found in west India is reputedly less irritable than others and is used by "snake-charmers".

By day, the Indian python basks in the sun or rests in a cave, abandoned burrow or other refuge. At night it prowls around, looking for prey, or lies in wait at a water hole or other spot where it is sure to encounter its prey – mice, civets, small deer, wild boar and birds. It stalks the animal, then grasps and encircles it with its body coils, restricting the breathing and heartbeat until they fail.

The female python lays up to 100 eggs in a hole, cave or tree hollow and, coiling herself around the eggs, incubates them for 60 to 80 days. She occasionally makes rhythmic contractions of her body muscles, and by this gradual shuffling she moves the eggs into the warmth of the sun or the protection of the shade.

ACROCHORDIDAE: WART SNAKE FAMILY

The 3 species in this family are both aquatic, nonvenomous snakes, found in India, Southeast Asia and Australia. They are most unusual, having loose, sagging skin and distinctly tapering bodies. Highly specialized for aquatic life, wart snakes have flaps in the roof of the mouth which close off the nasal passages when they are under water. In the same way, the notch on the upper lip, through which the sensory tongue is protruded, can be closed off by a pad on the chin.

Elephant-trunk Snake *Acrochordus javanicus*

RANGE India, S.E. Asia, New Guinea

HABITAT Rivers, streams, canals

SIZE 5 ft (1.5 m)

This stout, sluggish snake is almost helpless on land but an expert swimmer. It is generally more active at night and feeds exclusively on fish. The female gives birth to 25 to 30 live young which are active and able to feed immediately.

BURROWING ASPS AND COLUBRID SNAKES

ATRACTASPIDAE: BURROWING ASP FAMILY

These small to medium sized slender snakes have blunt heads and short tails. The 16 species of burrowing asps are found in Africa and the middle East. They are secretive snakes, living in leaf litter and burrowing into the soil.

Bibron's Burrowing Asp/Viper *Atractaspis bibroni*

RANGE	South Africa
HABITAT	Dry, sandy regions
SIZE	Up to 31½ in (80 cm)

Also known as the southern mole viper, this snake is a member of a group of burrowing snakes all of which are found in Africa and the Middle East. Like its relatives, it has a shovel-shaped head, with no distinct neck, a rounded, slender body and short tail. Its eyes are small.

A venomous snake, the burrowing asp has a sophisticated venom apparatus which is similar to that of the true vipers and, because of this, it was originally believed to be a viper. Its fangs are huge, relative to the small head, and can be folded or erected independently of each other. Once swung into the attack position, the fangs eject venom which is pumped into them from the connected poison glands.

The burrowing asp burrows into the soil with its strong snout. It usually emerges at the surface only at night after rain. If it finds itself on the surface in sunlight, it coils itself into a ball and hides its head inside the coils. The burrowing asp feeds on other reptiles, such as burrowing lizards and blind snakes which it kills with its venomous bite.

The female burrowing asps reproduce by laying eggs.

COLUBRIDAE: COLUBRID SNAKE FAMILY

The colubrid family is the largest of the three groups of advanced snakes and contains 1,600 species – two-thirds of all living snakes. Although a convenient assemblage of species, this large, diverse family may not be a natural one, and is often divided into subfamilies in order to clarify the relationships. Colubrids are found on all continents except Antarctica.

There is as much variation within the colubrid family as there is between the other two families of advanced snakes, the Vipers and Elapids, but there are a few shared characteristics. No colubrids have any vestiges of a pelvis or hind limbs, and all have the left lung reduced or even absent (for streamlining of the body). The lower jaw is flexible, but there are no hollow poison-injecting fangs. Instead there are solid teeth on both jaws and, in some cases, teeth on the upper jaw, with grooves which are connected to a poison gland (rear-fanged snakes).

Most colubrids are harmless; all those which are dangerous, such as the boomslang (*Dispholidus typus*) and the twig snake (*Thelotornis kirtlandii*), occur in Africa.

Colubrids occur in all habitats. There are ground-dwelling, arboreal, burrowing, even aquatic species. All are predators, and eat anything from insects to small mammals. Most colubrids lay eggs, but some give birth to fully formed live young.

Fimbrios klossi

RANGE	Vietnam, Kampuchea
HABITAT	Mountains with low vegetation
SIZE	15¾ in (40 cm)

This little-known snake is ground-dwelling and probably nocturnal. The scales around the mouth are curved, forming a fringe of soft projections the exact function of which is unknown, although they may be sensory. *Fimbrios* feeds mainly on earthworms. Like other members of its subfamily, Xenodermatinae, *Fimbrios klossi* probably lays 2 to 4 eggs.

Slug Snake *Pareas sp.*

RANGE	S.E. Asia
HABITAT	Forest
SIZE	12–30 in (30.5–76 cm)

The slug snakes, also known as bluntheads, are mostly nocturnal and have slender bodies and short, wide heads. They feed mainly on slugs and snails, and their lower jaws are adapted for removing the snails from their shells, for they are capable of being extended and retracted independently of the upper jaws. Having seized a snail, the slug snake inserts its lower jaw into the shell so that the curved teeth at the tip of the jaw sink into the snail's soft body. It then retracts its jaw, winkling out the snail from the shell.

These snakes lack the so-called dental groove on the chin possessed by most snakes that allows the jaw to be distended when taking in large prey. Thus their diet is restricted to the small items for which they are admirably specialized. As far as is known, these snakes reproduce by laying eggs.

Snail-eating Snake *Dipsas indica*

RANGE	Tropical South America
HABITAT	Forest
SIZE	About 26¾ in (68 cm)

The snail-eating snake is a nocturnal, ground-dwelling species with a strong body, large head and blunt, short snout. Its upper jaw is short with few teeth, and its lower jaw long with elongate, curved teeth. The structure of the jaws is such that the lower jaw can be swung backward and forward without movement of the upper jaw.

It feeds entirely on snails in a manner similar to the Pareas snakes, inserting its lower jaw into the snail's shell, twisting it to sink the teeth into the soft body and then pulling it out. As it attempts to defend itself, the struggling snail produces large quantities of slime which clogs up the snake's nasal openings; while extracting the snail, the snake relies, therefore, on air stored in its lungs to breathe.

Spotted Water Snake *Enhydris punctata*

RANGE	Australia: coast of Northern Territory
HABITAT	Creeks, swamps, rivers
SIZE	11¾–19¾ in (30–50 cm)

The spotted water snake is one of a subfamily of about 34 colubrids, all specialized for life in water. It is able to move on land as well as in water and comes ashore to bask on river banks and shores. Its small eyes are directed upward and its nostrils, too, are on the upper surface of the head. Pads of skin close off the nostrils completely when the snake is diving.

Mildly venomous, the water snake is rear-fanged – grooved teeth at the back of the upper jaw are connected to a poison gland. It preys on aquatic creatures such as fish and frogs. Females give birth to fully formed live young.

White-bellied Mangrove Snake *Fordonia leucobalia*

RANGE	Coast of N. Australia, S.E. Asia
HABITAT	Mangroves
SIZE	2½–3¼ ft (60 cm–1 m)

A member of the subfamily of aquatic colubrids, the white-bellied mangrove snake has similar adaptations to those of the rest of its group, such as nostrils near the top of its head and upward facing eyes. Large numbers of these snakes frequent the edges of swamps, where they forage among the roots for food. It is a rear-fanged snake and feeds mainly on crabs, which seem strongly affected by its venom, unlike frogs and mammals, which are not. Fish are also included in its diet. If alarmed, the snake will take refuge in a crab burrow.

COLUBRID SNAKES CONTINUED

Dark-green Whipsnake

Coluber viridiflavus

RANGE Europe: N.E. Spain, C. and S. France, Italy, S. Switzerland, former Yugoslavia, Corsica, Sardinia

HABITAT Dry, vegetated areas: hillsides, woodland edge, gardens

SIZE Up to 6¼ ft (1.9 m)

A slender, elongate snake, the dark-green whipsnake has a rounded snout, large eyes and a long tapering tail. Some individuals may, in fact, be almost all black, rather than dark green. Males are generally longer than females. Usually active in the daytime, it is a ground-dwelling snake but can climb well on rocks and bushes. It locates its prey by sight and usually feeds on lizards, frogs, mammals, birds and other snakes.

Males compete fiercely for mates in the breeding season. The female lays her 5 to 15 eggs among rocks or in cracks in the soil. The young hatch in 6 to 8 weeks.

Egg-eating Snake *Dasypeltis scabra*

RANGE Africa, south and east of the Sahara

HABITAT Woodland, scrub

SIZE 29½ in (75 cm)

This slender snake is one of the few snakes to exist entirely on hard shelled birds' eggs. It hunts for eggs on the ground and in trees, mainly at night, although it is sometimes active during the day. Most other snakes which eat eggs take only the softer-shelled lizard and snake eggs, since they are not able to cope with such tough, unwieldy food. The egg-eating snakes however have developed specialized equipment for dealing with hard-shelled eggs.

The egg-eating snake's mouth and jaws are extremely flexible and are hinged in such a way as to enable them to accommodate large eggs. It has only a few small teeth in each jaw, but special projections of the neck vertebrae form a serrated edge of "teeth" which pierce the wall of the snake's esophagus.

When the snake swallows an egg, which may be twice the size of its head, it pushes its mouth against the egg, gradually engulfing it in its jaws, while stretching the elastic ligament joining the two halves of the lower jaw to the utmost. The small neck scales stand apart in rows, exposing the skin beneath. The esophagus teeth slit the egg open and the contents pass into the stomach, while a specialized valve rejects the shell which is then regurgitated.

When the supply of eggs is plentiful, the snake eats as many as possible and stores up fat reserves in its body on which it is able to survive during those seasons when few eggs are available.

Females of this species lay between 8 and 14 eggs, which they deposit singly rather than in a clutch – an unusual habit for an egg-laying snake.

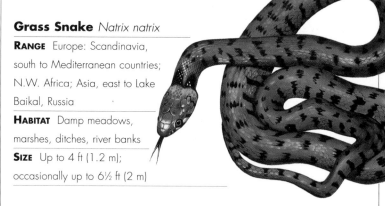

Grass Snake *Natrix natrix*

RANGE Europe: Scandinavia, south to Mediterranean countries; N.W. Africa; Asia, east to Lake Baikal, Russia

HABITAT Damp meadows, marshes, ditches, river banks

SIZE Up to 4 ft (1.2 m); occasionally up to 6½ ft (2 m)

The grass snake swims well and spends some time in water, although it is less aquatic than some other *Natrix* species. It is one of the most common and widespread European snakes and 3 subspecies, which differ in coloration and pattern, occur over its large range. Females are generally longer and thicker-bodied than males.

The grass snake is active during the day, hunting for food in water and on land. It eats mainly frogs, toads and newts, but also takes fish and occasionally small mammals and young birds. Much of its prey is swallowed alive. It has a venomous secretion that is toxic to small animals but harmless to man.

Depending on the latitude, grass snakes start to breed from April onward. The male courts the female, by rubbing his chin over her body. He works his way up to her neck and they intertwine and mate. Some 8 or more weeks later, the female lays 30 to 40 eggs, which are fairly advanced in embryonic development. She deposits the eggs in a warm spot, preferably in decaying organic matter such as a compost or manure heap. The young hatch out after 1 or 2 months, depending on the warmth of their surroundings.

Red-bellied Snake *Storeria occipitomaculata*

RANGE Extreme S. Canada; E. USA: Maine to Minnesota, south to Texas and Florida

HABITAT Woodland on hills and mountains, bogs

SIZE 7¾–16 in (20–40.5 cm)

There are 3 subspecies of this widely distributed snake which vary in coloration and the arrangement of the characteristic bright spots on the neck. In the Florida subspecies the spots may be fused, forming a collar. The red-bellied snake lives from sea level to 5,600 ft (1,700 m) and is active mostly at night, when it preys on insects and small invertebrates such as earthworms and slugs. When alarmed the snake may curl its upper lip in threat, while discharging a musky secretion from its cloacal opening.

The snakes mate in spring or autumn. Before copulation, the male throws his body into a series of waves from tail to head and rubs his chin, equipped with sensory tubercles, over the female's body. He also has sensory tubercles around the cloaca (genital opening) region which appear to help him position himself correctly. The young develop inside the female's body and are born fully formed and measuring 2¾ to 4 in (7 to 10 cm).

Common Garter Snake

Thamnophis sirtalis

RANGE S. Canada; USA, except desert regions

HABITAT Damp country, often near water: marshes, meadows, ditches, farmland, woodland

SIZE 17¾ in–4¼ ft (45 cm–1.3 m)

The most widely distributed snake in North America and one of the most familiar, the garter snake occurs in many subspecies over its huge range. The coloration is, therefore, extremely variable, but the garter snake nearly always has distinctive back and side stripes. It is active during the day and hunts for frogs, toads, salamanders and small invertebrates among damp vegetation on the ground.

One of the few snakes to occur in the far north, the garter snake is able to withstand cold weather well and is found as far as 67° North. In the southern part of its range, it may remain active all year round, but in the north it hibernates in communal dens.

Garter snakes usually mate in spring, sometimes communally as they emerge from hibernation. They may, however, mate in autumn, in which event the sperm spend most of the winter in the female's oviduct and do not move into position to fertilize the eggs until spring. Before copulation, the male snake throws his body into a series of waves and then rubs his chin over the female's body. The tubercles on his chin must receive the right sensory responses before he will mate. As many as 80 young develop inside the female's body, nourished by a form of placenta, and are born fully formed.

Rat Snake *Elaphe obsoleta*

RANGE S. Canada; USA: Vermont to Minnesota, south to Texas and Florida; N. Mexico

HABITAT Forest, swamps, farmland, wooded slopes

SIZE 33¾ in–8¼ ft (86 cm–2.5 m)

A large, powerful species, the rat snake tolerates a variety of habitats in wet and dry situations. There are 6 or more subspecies which occur in one of three main color patterns – plain, blotched or striped. It is an agile snake, good at climbing, and hunts rodents and other small mammals, birds and lizards in trees and in barns or ruined buildings. Usually active during the day, it may tend to be nocturnal in summer. In much of its range, it hibernates throughout the winter.

Rat snakes mate in spring and autumn. The female lays a clutch of between 5 and 30 eggs in leaf debris or under a rock or log. The eggs hatch in 2 to 4 months, depending on the temperature – the warmer the weather, the quicker they hatch.

COLUBRID SNAKES CONTINUED

Smooth Snake *Coronella austriaca*

RANGE Europe: S. Scandinavia, S. England, south to N. Spain,
Italy and Greece; east to Russia, N. Iran

HABITAT Dry rocky areas, heathland, open woodland

SIZE 19¾–31½ in (50–80 cm)

The slender, round-bodied smooth snake varies in coloration
over its wide range but nearly always has a dark streak on each
side of its head. The head is fairly small and pointed and there is
no clear neck. It is a secretive snake, although active in the
daytime, and adapts to a variety of dry habitats up to 5,900 ft
(1,800 m); it is even occasionally found in moist areas. Although
it rarely basks in full sun, the smooth snake likes to retreat to
warm, shady areas under rocks or stones. Lizards, particularly
lacertids, make up the bulk of its diet and it also eats small
snakes, young mammals and insects. It holds its prey in a few
coils of its body to subdue it while it starts to swallow.

In the breeding season, males fight one another for mates.
The female gives birth to 2 to 15 live young in autumn; they
emerge in transparent, membranous shells from which they free
themselves immediately. The newly born young measure 4¾ to
7¾ in (12 to 20 cm) in length. Males mature at 3 years and
females at 4.

Common Kingsnake *Lampropeltis getulus*

RANGE USA: New Jersey to Florida in east,
Oregon to California in west; Mexico

HABITAT Varied, forest, woodland, desert, prairie, swamps, marshes

SIZE 35½ in–6½ ft (90 cm–2 m)

A large snake with
smooth, shiny
scales, the common
kingsnake usually
has alternating dark
and light rings, but
some of the many

subspecies have more irregular speckled patterns. It is primarily a
ground-dwelling species, although it may sometimes climb into
small trees or bushes, and is active in the daytime, usually in the
early morning and at dusk. Found in almost every type of
habitat it will take refuge under rocks, in vegetation and under
logs. It feeds on snakes, including rattlesnakes and coral snakes,
lizards, mice and birds which it kills by constriction, holding the
prey in the powerful coils of its body until it suffocates. Indeed,
the description "king" seems to be applied only to those snakes
which feed on other snakes.

Kingsnakes mate in spring. The female lays 3 to 24 eggs
which usually hatch in 2 to 3 months, depending on the
warmth of the weather.

Gopher Snake *Pituophis melanoleucas*

RANGE S.W. Canada; USA: W. and C. states, Florida; Mexico

HABITAT Dry woodland, grassland, prairies, rocky desert

SIZE 4–8¼ ft (1.2—2.5 m)

The large, robust gopher snake is found in a
variety of habitats and is a good climber and
burrower. Its head is small and somewhat pointed and,
although the coloration varies in the many subspecies over its
wide range, most gopher snakes have pale bodies with black,
brown or reddish markings.

Usually active by day, the gopher snake may become nocturnal
in hot weather. It feeds largely on rodents, as well as on rabbits,
birds and lizards, all of which it kills by constriction – throwing
its powerful body coils around the victim until it suffocates. It
may burrow underground for shelter or take over mammal or
tortoise burrows. If alarmed, the gopher snake flattens
its head, hisses loudly and vibrates its tail
before attacking the enemy.

Gopher snakes mate in spring and the
female lays up to 24 eggs in a burrow or
beneath a rock or log. The young hatch in
9 to 11 weeks and are up to 17¾ in (45 cm)
long on hatching.

Paradise Tree Snake

Chrysopelea paradisi

RANGE S.E. Asia: Philippines to Indonesia

HABITAT Forest

SIZE Up to 4 ft (1.2 m)

Also known as the flying snake, this species glides from tree to tree, from one branch down to another. It launches itself into the air, its body stretched out and its belly pulled in to make a concave surface with maximum resistance to the air. It glides downward at an angle of 50 or 60 degrees to the ground for 65 ft (20 m) or more and lands safely. It seems to have little control over its "flight", however, and cannot glide upward or steer with any degree of efficiency.

A further adaptation for its tree-dwelling life are the ridged scales on the snake's belly which help it to climb almost vertically up tree trunks. The ridges are thrust against the bark and enable the snake to gain a hold on every tiny irregularity of surface. Thus, it can ascend right into the trees, where few other snakes can go, and feed on the abundant tree-dwelling lizards. The closely related oriental tree snake, *C. ornata*, can glide and climb in the same manner.

The female paradise tree snake lays up to 12 eggs.

Mangrove Snake *Boiga dendrophila*

RANGE S.E. Asia: Philippines to Indonesia

HABITAT Forest, mangroves

SIZE 8¼ ft (2.5 m)

The beautifully marked mangrove snake has a slender body with hexagonal scales on its back and sides. It is primarily an arboreal species, and hunts birds in the trees although it may also descend to the ground in order to prey on rodents. It is a venomous, rear-fanged snake – the grooved teeth toward the back of the jaw carry venom from the poison gland above the jaw into the prey. The female mangrove snake lays 4 to 7 eggs.

Boomslang *Dispholidus typus*

RANGE Africa: central to South Africa

HABITAT Savanna

SIZE Up to 6½ ft (2 m)

The boomslang is one of only two dangerously poisonous snakes in the colubrid family. It has three large grooved fangs, set farther forward than the usual two fangs of colubrids, and extremely toxic venom which causes respiratory failure and hemorrhaging and can even kill a human being. Normally, however, it uses its venomous bites on lizards, particularly chameleons and on frogs and birds.

The boomslang is a tree-dwelling snake, usually active in the daytime. It varies in coloration but is usually predominantly black, brown or green on the upper surface.

The female boomslang lays 10 to 14 eggs.

Vine Snake *Oxybelis fulgidus*

RANGE Central America to N. South America

HABITAT Rain forest, cultivated land

SIZE 5–6½ ft (1.5–2 m)

Barely the thickness of a man's finger, about ½ in (1.25 cm) in diameter at the most, the vine snake is a remarkably slender, elongate species. As it lies amid the branches of forest trees, its proportions and greeny-brown coloration make it almost indistinguishable from the abundant creepers and vines. Its head, too, is thin and elongate and equipped with rear fangs and mild venom.

A slow-moving predator, active in the daytime and at night, the vine snake feeds mainly on young birds (which it steals from nests) and on lizards. If threatened, it puffs up the front of its body, revealing vivid coloration usually hidden under scales, and opens its long mouth wide. A frightened snake may also sway from side to side, like a stem in the breeze.

COBRAS AND SEA SNAKES

ELAPIDAE: COBRA AND SEA SNAKE FAMILY

There are about 250 species of highly venomous snake in this family, found mainly in tropical and subtropical areas of Australia, Asia, Africa (except Madagascar) and America. Elapids are most abundant in Australia.

The family is often divided into two groups – the elapids proper, including cobras, kraits, mambas and coral snakes, all of which are land- or tree-dwelling; and the sea snakes. The 50 or so species of sea snake lead entirely aquatic lives; most are marine but a few live in lakes or enter rivers. All elapids have fangs, situated near the front of the upper jaw, which are either deeply grooved for the transport of venom or have grooves the edges of which have fused to form a venom canal.

Eastern Green Mamba *Dendroaspis angusticeps*

RANGE E. and S. Africa

HABITAT Savanna

SIZE 6½ ft (2 m)

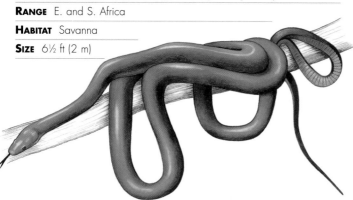

The slender, fast-moving mambas spend much of their lives in trees, where they feed on birds and lizards. Their venom is extremely toxic, but these snakes are not generally aggressive unless provoked and tend rather to flee from danger or threat.

In the breeding season, two or three males compete in ritualized fights for females. They wrap their bodies around one another and threaten with their raised heads. Mating may last for many hours. The female lays her 10 to 15 eggs in a hole in the ground or in a hollow tree stump. The young mambas hatch in 17 to 18 weeks.

De Vis's Banded Snake *Denisonia devisii*

RANGE Australia: N. New South Wales, S. Queensland

HABITAT Dry, wooded areas

SIZE 19¾ in (50 cm)

A nocturnal species, De Vis's banded snake shelters under leaf litter or a log during the day and emerges at night to hunt for food, mainly lizards, which it kills with its toxic venom. It has a distinctive defense posture which it often adopts when threatened – it flattens its body, which is thrown into a series of stiff curves – and lashes out and bites if approached.

The female gives birth to about 8 live young, which have developed inside her body, nourished by a form of placenta.

King Cobra *Ophiophagus hannah*

RANGE India, S. China, Malaysia to Philippines and Indonesia

HABITAT Forest, often near water

SIZE 13–18 ft (4–5.5 m)

The biggest poisonous snake in the world, the king cobra's head can be as big as a man's. It can make itself still more impressive by adopting the cobra threat posture, with the flexible neck ribs and loose skin spread out to form a wide hood. Despite its size, it is an agile, secretive snake and will flee into cover or even water if pursued. It feeds mainly on other snakes – its scientific name means "snake-eater" – but it will also eat monitor lizards.

The female king cobra constructs a nest of vegetation for her eggs, perhaps the only snake to do so. She gathers together twigs, branches and foliage with a coil of her forebody and then makes a chamber in the middle of the nest material by revolving her coiled body. She lays her clutch of between 18 and 40 eggs in this chamber, covers them and lies coiled on top of the nest to guard them while they incubate.

Indian Cobra *Naja naja*

RANGE India, C. Asia, S.E. Asia

HABITAT Rain forest, rice fields, cultivated land

SIZE 6–7 ¼ ft (1.8–2.2 m)

The large, highly venomous Indian cobra eats rodents, lizards and frogs. This cobra can attack or defend itself from a distance by "spitting" venom which, can cause severe pain and damage if it reaches the eyes. The snake forces venom through its fangs, by exerting muscular pressure on the venom glands, so that it sprays out in twin jets for 6½ ft (2 m) or more. In its threat posture, it raises the front of its body and spreads its neck ribs and loose skin to form a disclike hood, which has markings resembling eyes on the back.

The female lays her 8 to 45 eggs (usually 12 to 20) in a hollow tree, a termite mound or earth. She guards them through the incubation period, leaving them only to feed. The young hatch after about 50 or 60 days.

Eastern Brown Snake *Pseudonaja textilis*

RANGE E. Australia, E. New Guinea

HABITAT Wet forest, rocky hillsides

SIZE 5 ft (1.5 m)

This fast-moving, venomous snake is equally at home in dry or swampy land. It is active during the day and feeds on small mammals, frogs and lizards. Its coloration varies from yellow to dark brown with bands of varying intensity.

Bandy-bandy *Vermicella annulata*

RANGE Australia (not extreme S.E., S.W. or N.W.)

HABITAT Varied, damp forest to desert sandhills

SIZE 15¾ in (40 cm)

The bandy-bandy's distinctive black and white rings vary in width and number, between the sexes and geographically. It is a nocturnal snake and eats mainly, blind snakes (Typhlopidae). Although venomous, its fangs and venom supply are too small to cause harm to anything other than small animals. An egg-laying species, the female deposits her eggs under rocks or logs.

Eastern Coral Snake *Micrurus fulvius*

RANGE USA: North Carolina to Florida, west to Texas; Mexico

HABITAT Forest, often near water, rocky hillsides.

SIZE 22 in–4 ft (56 cm–1.2 m)

One of the only two elapids in North America the Eastern coral snake is a highly colorful species, with red, black and yellow or white bands ringing its body. The bright markings on the bodies of these highly poisonous snakes may serve as a warning to potential predators.

The coral snake is a secretive species, spending much of the time buried in leaf litter or sand. In the morning and late afternoon, it prowls on the surface in search of small lizards and snakes, which it kills with its highly toxic venom.

The female lays between 3 and 12 eggs which hatch out after about 3 months.

Banded Sea Snake *Hydrophis cyanocinctus*

RANGE Persian Gulf, Indian Ocean, Pacific Ocean to Japan

HABITAT Coastal waters

SIZE 6½ ft (2 m)

The banded sea snake is fully adapted to aquatic life and never goes on land. Its body is laterally flattened and its tail is paddle-shaped and is used to provide propulsion when swimming. It breathes air but it can remain submerged for up to 2 hours at a time. Its nostrils are directed upward and can be closed off by pads of tissue bordering the front of the nostrils. The sea snake's body muscles have degenerated so far due to its aquatic lifestyle that if washed ashore, it collapses helplessly. Like all sea snakes, this species feeds on fish and has extremely toxic venom. The venom of one species of sea snake, *Enhydrina schistosa*, has been shown in laboratory tests to be more powerful than that of any other snake.

All but one species of sea snake bear live young in the water. The banded sea snake gives birth to between 2 and 6 young.

VIPERS

VIPERIDAE: VIPER AND PIT VIPER FAMILY

This family has 2 subfamilies – viperinae (true vipers) and crotalinae (pit vipers).

There are about 50 species of viper, found all over the Old World except in Australia and Madagascar. Most species are short, sturdy snakes which live on the ground. A few species have become arboreal and have prehensile tails.

Vipers hide and ambush and strike their prey. The large hollow fangs fold back when the mouth is closed, then swing forward and become erect when the mouth is opened wide. Venom pumps into the fangs from venom glands at their base and the poison is injected as they pierce the prey.

The 120 species of pit vipers are highly venomous. They occur in eastern Europe and throughout mainland Asia and Japan. Although they are closely related to true vipers, they are considered by some experts to be a separate family. Unlike true vipers, pit vipers are absent from Africa and they possess some significant anatomical differences. The most important of these are the organs which give the snakes their common name – sensory pits on each side of the head in front of and just below the eyes which can detect heat and are used by these nocturnal snakes to locate warm-blooded prey. A pit viper strikes accurately at prey by moving its head from side to side and using the pit organs to discover its distance and direction. The viper kills with a rapid strike. The long, curved fangs of the upper jaw impale the target and inject venom. Small or weak creatures may be swallowed whole, but large prey is subdued with venom first.

One group of pit vipers, the rattlesnakes, has rattles on the tail which are a series of flattened, interlocking hollow segments. Each segment was once the tip of the tail, and a new one is added each time the snake sheds its skin. However, there are rarely more than 14 rattles at any time. The sound produced warns enemies to keep their distance.

Common Viper *Vipera berus*

RANGE Britain, Europe to Siberia

HABITAT Moors, meadows, chalk hills, forest edge

SIZE Up to 19¾ in (50 cm)

The widely distributed common viper, or adder, is active in the day in the north of its range where it basks in the sun at every opportunity. Farther south, it is active in the evening and at night. In winter it hibernates, often using the abandoned burrow of another creature, until the temperature rises to an average of about 46°F (8°C) – the length of hibernation, therefore, varies with latitude. This viper moves slowly and does not climb but is a good swimmer. Mice, voles, shrews, lizards and frogs, all of which it kills with its venom, are its main foods, and it may occasionally take birds' eggs.

In the mating season, which may occur only every other year in areas where the hibernation period is long, males perform ritualistic aggressive dances before mating. They rear up in front of one another, swaying and trying to push each other over. The female retains her 3 to 20 eggs in the body until they are on the point of hatching. The young are about 7 in (18 cm) long when they hatch and are already equipped with venom and fangs.

Desert Sidewinding Viper

Vipera peringueyi

RANGE Africa: Namibia

HABITAT Desert

SIZE 10 in (25.5 cm)

A small, rare viper, this species is found on the coastal sand dunes of the Namib Desert. It glides over the dunes with a sidewinding motion of lateral waves, leaving tracks like two parallel grooves where two parts of the body touch the sand and support the snake. During the day it half buries itself in the sand – a feat it can accomplish in about 20 seconds – to shelter from the sun or to lie in wait for prey such as rodents or lizards.

Horned Viper *Vipera ammodytes*

RANGE Europe: Austria, Hungary, Balkan peninsula

HABITAT Arid, sandy regions

SIZE 30 in (76 cm)

Identifiable by the small horn on its snout, this viper is also called the sand viper because of its preference for sandy areas. It avoids woodland but is found in clearings, paths and often in vineyards. Its movements generally are slow, but it can strike rapidly with its fangs to kill small mammals, lizards, snakes and small birds. Horned vipers hibernate throughout the winter.

Gaboon Viper
Vipera gabonica

RANGE W. Africa, south of the Sahara to South Africa

HABITAT Rain forest

SIZE 4–6½ ft (1.2–2 m)

One of the largest vipers, the Gaboon viper is well camouflaged, as it lies among the leaf litter on the forest floor, by the complex geometric patterns on its skin. It has a broad head, slender neck and stout body, tapering to a thin tail. Its fangs, the longest of any viper, are up to 2 in (5 cm) long and are supplied with a venom which causes hemorrhaging in the victim and inhibits breathing and heartbeat.

The Gaboon viper is nocturnal and, although it moves little, manages to find plenty of prey, such as rodents, frogs, toads and ground-living birds, on the forest floor. The female bears live young in litters of up to 30 at a time, each young snake is about 12 in (30.5 cm) long at birth.

Aspic Viper *Vipera aspis*

RANGE Europe: France, Germany, Switzerland, Italy, Sicily

HABITAT Warm dry areas up to 9,800 ft (3,000 m)

SIZE Up to 30 in (76 cm)

Also known as the European asp, this species varies in coloration from area to area. A sluggish snake except when alarmed, it spends much of its time basking in the sun on a tree stump or rock, particularly in the early morning or late afternoon. It feeds on small mammals, lizards and nestling birds.

Mating takes place in the spring, after males have performed ritualistic combat displays, and females lay 4 to 18 eggs. In winter, aspic vipers hibernate singly or in groups in underground burrows or in wall crevices.

Puff Adder *Bitis arietans*

RANGE Africa: Morocco, south of the Sahara to South Africa; Middle East

HABITAT Savanna up to 6,000 ft (1,800 m)

SIZE 4½–6½ ft (1.4–2 m)

Perhaps the most common and widespread African snake, the puff adder adapts to both moist and arid climates, but not to the extremes of desert or rain forest. It is one of the biggest vipers, with a girth of up to 9 in (23 cm), and can inflate its body even more when about to strike. Its fangs are about ½ in (1.25 cm) long, and the venom causes hemorrhaging in the victim.

Primarily a ground-living snake, the sluggish puff adder relies on its cryptic pattern and coloration to conceal it from both enemies and potential prey. It occasionally climbs into trees and is a good swimmer. Ground-living mammals, such as rats and mice, and birds, lizards, frogs and toads are its main prey.

The female puff adder lays 20 to 40 eggs which develop inside her body and hatch minutes after laying. The young are 6 to 7¾ in (15 to 20 cm) long when they hatch and can kill small mice.

Saw-scaled Adder *Echis carinatus*

RANGE N. Africa to Syria, Iran, east to India

HABITAT Arid, sandy regions

SIZE 20¾–28¼ in (53–72 cm)

An extremely dangerous snake, the saw-scaled adder causes the majority of human deaths from snake bite in North Africa. This adder uses serrated scales on its sides to make a threatening noise; it coils its body into a tight spiral and then moves the coils so that the scales rub against one another, making a loud rasping sound. It is these scales which give the snake its common name.

The saw-scaled adder often uses a sideways motion, known as sidewinding, when on sandy ground. It throws its body, only two short sections of which touch the ground, into lateral waves. All the adder's weight is, therefore, pushing against the ground at these points, so providing the leverage to push it sideways.

During the day, the saw-scaled adder lies sheltered from the heat under a fallen tree trunk or rock, or flattens its body and digs into the sand by means of the "keeled" lateral scales.

This snake feeds at night on small rodents, skinks, geckos, frogs and large invertebrates such as centipedes and scorpions. Breeding usually takes place in the rainy season, and the female lays about 5 eggs. The young adders are about 7¾ in (20 cm) long when they hatch.

PIT VIPERS

Massasauga *Sistrurus catenatus*

RANGE USA: N.W. Pennsylvania to Arizona; N. Mexico

HABITAT Varied, swamp, marshland, woodland, prairie

SIZE 17¾ in–3¼ ft (45 cm–1 m)

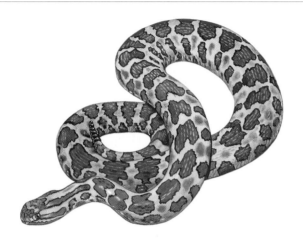

The massasauga tolerates a wide range of habitat and although it seems to prefer swampy land, it also occurs even in arid grassland in the west of its range. It has up to eight rattles on its tail and is distinguished from other rattlers by the nine enlarged scales on its head. It preys on lizards, frogs, insects, small mammals and birds.

In April or May, the massasaugas mate and a litter of between 2 and 19 live young is born in the summer.

Sidewinder *Crotalus cerastes*

RANGE S.W. USA: S. California, Nevada and Utah, south to Mexico

HABITAT Desert, rocky hillsides

SIZE 17–32¼ in (43–82 cm)

A small agile snake, the sidewinder has a distinctive hornlike projection over each eye. It is chiefly nocturnal and takes refuge in the burrow of another animal or under a bush during the day.

At night it emerges to hunt its prey, mainly small rodents, such as pocket mice and kangaroo rats, and lizards. A desert inhabitant, this snake moves with a sideways motion, known as sidewinding, thought to be the most efficient mode of movement for a snake on sand. It throws its body into lateral waves, only two short sections of it touching the ground. All the snake's weight, therefore, is pushing against the ground at these points, and this provides the leverage to move it sideways. As it travels, the snake leaves a trail of parallel J-shaped markings. An ideal form of movement in open, sparsely vegetated country, sidewinding has the advantage of reducing contact between the snake's body and the hot sand.

Sidewinders mate in April or May, and the female gives birth to 5 to 18 live young about 3 months later.

Fer-de-Lance *Bothrops atrox*

RANGE S. Mexico to South America; West Indies

HABITAT Low coastal areas

SIZE 8 ft (2.45 m)

A common pit viper, the fer-de-lance varies in color and pattern over its wide range. A sheath of membranous flesh covers its fangs, but when the snake bites the sheath is pushed back. The fer-de-lance feeds mainly on small mammals and its venom causes rapid and severe internal bleeding. The female is an unusually prolific breeder for a pit viper, giving birth to up to 50 live young in a yearly litter.

Eastern Diamondback Rattlesnake *Crotalus adamanteus*

RANGE E. USA: North Carolina to Florida Keys, west to Louisiana

HABITAT Woodland, farmland

SIZE 35¾ in–7¾ ft (91 cm–2.4 m)

The largest rattler, the eastern diamondback is the most dangerous snake in North America. Its potent venom attacks the

Manushi/Asiatic Pit Viper *Agkistrodon halys*

RANGE Caspian Sea area, S. Russia, China

HABITAT Steppe, semidesert, taiga (coniferous forest)

SIZE 18–30 in (46–76 cm)

blood cells of its victims. Its striking diamond patterned skin provides camouflage as it lies coiled in vegetation, watching for prey such as rabbits and birds which it then ambushes.

The female diamondback bears litters of between 8 and 12 live young – each of which measures between 11¾ to 14¼ in (30 and 36 cm) – in late summer. The female defends the young snakes aggressively.

One of the few pit vipers found in the Old World, the manushi is found as far as 51° North. It is a mainly nocturnal snake and emerges at sunset in order to hunt its prey, which consists mostly of small mammals. Its venom is fatal to small creatures such as mice, but is seldom dangerous to larger animals and causes only mild temporary paralysis in humans.

The manushi hibernates through the winter, awaking in March. The males usually wake a week or more before females. Mating takes place shortly after the end of hibernation and the female lays a clutch of between 3 and 10 eggs which hatch about 3 months later.

Cottonmouth *Agkistrodon piscivorus*

RANGE S. and S.E. USA

HABITAT Marshes, streams, lakes, swamps

SIZE 20 in–6¼ ft (51 cm–1.9 m)

Bushmaster *Lachesis muta*

RANGE S. Nicaragua to Amazon basin of South America

HABITAT Rain forest

SIZE 8–11½ ft (2.45–3.5 m)

A rare, deadly and formidable pit viper, the bushmaster is the largest of its family. It is a strictly nocturnal snake, hiding during the day in a cave or tree hollow and emerging at night in order to hunt. It preys on small rodents and other mammals up to the size of small deer.

Although its venom is not as poisonous as that of some pit vipers, the bushmaster produces such large quantities of poison, and has such huge fangs with which to inject it, that it is one of the world's most dangerous snakes. The female bushmaster is the only New World viper to lay eggs.

The heavy-bodied cottonmouth spends much of its life either in or near water. It swims well, holding its head up out of the water. This snake is most active at night, when it preys on amphibians, fish, snakes and birds, and it is one of the few snakes to eat carrion. The cottonmouth is an extremely dangerous species. Its venom is hemolytic – it destroys the red blood cells and coagulates the blood around the bite. The venom is actually extracted and used medically for its coagulating properties in the treatment of hemorrhagic conditions.

Female cottonmouths breed every other year and produce litters of up to 15 young which measure between 7 and 13 in (18 and 33 cm) at birth.

CROCODILES, ALLIGATORS, CAIMANS AND GAVIAL

ORDER CROCODILIA

The crocodiles, alligators and caimans and the single species of gavial are the 3 families which together make up this order. All are powerful amphibious carnivores, preying on a range of vertebrate animals, although juvenile crocodiles also eat insects and other small invertebrates. Crocodilia are the most direct evolutionary descendants of the archosaurs, the dominant animal life forms from 190 to 65 million years ago. There are about 21 species alive today – 13 in the crocodile family, 7 alligators and caimans, and 1 gavial. All inhabit tropical and subtropical regions. Males and females look alike in all species, though males tend to grow larger than females.

All members of the order have elongate short-limbed bodies, covered with horny skin scales. Thickened bony plates on the back give added protection. The crocodilians have long snouts with many conical teeth anchored in deep sockets in the jaw bones. Breathing organs are highly modified for underwater predation – the external nostrils, on a projection at the snout-tip, have valves to close them off. A pair of flaps in the throat forms another valve which enables the animal to hold prey in its open jaws beneath the surface, without inhaling water.

Both crocodiles and alligators possess a pair of large teeth near the front of the lower jaw for grasping prey. In the crocodiles, these teeth fit into notches in the upper jaw and are visible when the jaws are closed, while in the alligators, the large teeth are accommodated in bony pits in the upper jaw.

Gavial *Gavialis gangeticus* **EN**

RANGE	N. India
HABITAT	Large rivers
SIZE	23 ft (7 m)

The Indian gavial has an extremely long narrow snout, studded with about 100 small teeth – ideal equipment for seizing fish and frogs underwater.

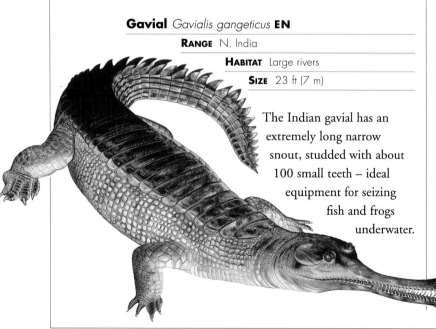

Like all crocodilians, the gavial has been hunted for its skin and it is now one of the rarest in Asia. Its hind limbs are paddlelike, and the gavial seems rarely to leave the water except to nest. The female lays her eggs at night in a pit dug in the river bank.

American Alligator

Alligator mississipiensis (sic)

RANGE	S.E. USA
HABITAT	Marshes, rivers, swamps
SIZE	Up to 18 ft (5.5 m)

The American alligator, once struggling for survival against hunters and habitat destruction, has been so effectively protected by conservation laws that the population is now on the increase.

These alligators usually mate in shallow water in April, and courtship is slow and quiet. The male stays with the female for several days before mating, occasionally stroking her body with his forelimbs. As she nears acquiescence, he rubs her throat with his head and blows bubbles past her cheeks. The female finds a nest site near water and scrapes up whatever plant debris is available with sweeping movements of her body and tail. She packs the vegetation together to form a mound, with a cavity for the eggs. She lays 28 to 52 eggs and crawls over the mound to close the cavity with more vegetation. She guards the nest while the eggs incubate for about 65 days. The hatching young call to their mother, prompting her to open the nest and free them. They remain with her for up to 3 years.

Spectacled Caiman *Caiman crocodilus*

RANGE	Venezuela to S. Amazon basin
HABITAT	Slow still waters, lakes, swamps
SIZE	5–6½ ft (1.5–2 m)

There are several species and subspecies of this caiman and its name has been the subject of much dispute, it is often known as *C. sclerops*. Its common name derives from the ridge on the head between the eyes which resembles the bridge of a pair of spectacles. The population of wild caimans has declined drastically since they are not only hunted for skins, but the young are also collected and sold as pets or stuffed as curios. The female caiman makes a nest of plant debris scraped together into a pile and lays an average of 30 eggs.

West African Dwarf Crocodile *Osteolaemus tetraspis* **VU**

RANGE W. Africa, south of the Sahara

HABITAT Streams and lakes

SIZE 5 ft (1.5 m)

Also known as the short-nosed crocodile, this animal is indeed characterized by its unusually short snout. It is now extremely rare owing to over exploitation for skins and to the destruction of its habitat. It resembles the New World alligators in appearance and size, although it is a member of the crocodile family. Little is known of its biology and breeding habits.

Estuarine Crocodile *Crocodylus porosus* **LR:lc**

RANGE S. India through Indonesia; S. Australia

HABITAT Estuaries, coasts, mangroves

SIZE Up to 19½ ft (6 m)

The estuarine crocodile is one of the largest and most dangerous species and has been known to attack man. It is rapidly being exterminated since its hide is considered the most valuable of all crocodiles for leather. It is now illegal to catch the estuarine crocodile in many areas, but the population is still low. Where hunting is allowed, it is restricted, and skin exports are controlled.

The most aquatic and most marine of all crocodile species, the estuarine crocodile spends little time on land and swims great distances. The female lays 25 to 90 eggs in a mound of plant debris which she scrapes together near water. She guards the eggs for about 3 months while they incubate.

Nile Crocodile *Crocodylus niloticus*

RANGE Africa (not Sahara or N.W.)

HABITAT Large rivers, lakes, marshes

SIZE 15–16½ ft (4.5–5 m)

The population and range of the once widespread Nile crocodile is now seriously reduced, by both the demand for skins and the destruction of natural habitats. The Nile crocodile preys on large mammals and birds which come to the water's edge to drink. After seizing its catch, the crocodile drowns it by holding it under water, and then twists off chunks of flesh by spinning its own body in the water while holding on to the prey. Adult crocodiles swallow stones, which remain in the stomach and act as stabilizing ballast when the crocodiles are in water.

The Nile crocodile spends its nights in water and comes out on to the river banks just before sunrise in order to bask in the sun during the day. It leads a rather leisurely existence and does not need to feed every day.

The male defends a territory and enacts a courtship display at breeding time. The mated female lays 25 to 75 eggs in a pit near the water. She covers her eggs well and guards them during the 3-month incubation period. When ready to hatch, the young are sensitive to the footfalls of their mother overhead. They call to her from the nest; she uncovers them and carries them inside her mouth to a safe nursery area, where she cares for them assiduously for another 3 to 6 months. The young feed on insects, then progress to crabs, birds and fish before adopting the adult diet.

AMPHIBIANS

The first land vertebrates.

Spotted Salamander

COMPARED WITH THE HUGE NUMBERS OF EXISTING FISHES, REPTILES, BIRDS AND MAMMALS, THE TOTAL GLOBAL COUNT OF LIVING AMPHIBIAN SPECIES IS RATHER MEAGER. ONLY ABOUT 4,350 FORMS ARE AUTHORITATIVELY RECOGNIZED AT PRESENT.

All modern forms can be accommodated in three major subgroupings, of which two are commonly recognizable animal types: first the Caudata or Urodela (newts and salamanders), and second, the Anura (frogs and toads). The third group is the Gymnophonia, which contains several families of limbless, elongate burrowing amphibians known as caecilians.

The amphibians were the first group of vertebrates to colonize the land. The distant evolutionary origins of amphibianlike animals from fish ancestors are a key phase in vertebrate evolution, heralding as they do all the subsequent developments of land-living vertebrates. Probably between 375 and 350 million years ago, lobe-fin fishes (crossopterygians) which already possessed lungs and four solidly constructed, downward-directed fins, began, more and more, to move out of freshwater habitats into adjacent terrestrial ones. The development of amphibians had begun.

Almost all the early amphibians must have retained fishlike habits. They were entirely or largely aquatic and were fish-eating animals like their lobe-finned fish ancestors. Only a few of these early amphibians were truly terrestrial forms.

Of the modern amphibians, it is the newts and salamanders that have kept the most fishlike appearance, with elongate bodies, sinuous swimming movements in water and dorsal and ventral fins on the body. Larval and adult newts and salamanders are relatively similar to one another in these respects, and adults frequently possess some larval characteristics.

The anuran frogs and toads all have a characteristic shortened body with no true tail. This dramatic alteration of the primitive, long-bodied amphibian has opened up a wide range of opportunities for new ways of living. In general, the limbs have become more powerful. Jumping and climbing have

been developed to a considerable degree in many species and others have become efficient burrowers. The caecilians are extraordinary earthwormlike amphibians which are highly adapted for a burrowing life: the skull of the caecilian is solid and bony, the limbs have completely disappeared.

Amphibians as a group demonstrate an interesting range of methods of locomotion, some very fishlike, others more suitable for life on land. Newts and salamanders have two basic forms of movement on land: when in haste, they move much as they do in water, by a sinuous wriggling of the body with little motion of the limbs; when moving more slowly, the body is lifted off the ground and supported on the four limbs, which move in the typical manner of four-legged vertebrates.

Frogs and toads, having lost their swimming tail, possess a completely different means of progression. Double, synchronized kicks of the long back legs are used for swimming

Bullfrog

in water and hopping and jumping on land. Both frogs and toads can also walk. Several groups of frogs and toads have independently developed rather similar specializations for moving in trees: they have adhesive pads on

Fire Bellied Toad

elongate toes enabling them to climb in vegetation. The limbless caecilians move by sinuous undulations similar to those of snakes.

Just as locomotion in amphibians is a fascinating amalgam of fishlike and terrestrial attributes, respiration shows a similar intriguing mix of "technologies". Amphibians may possess gills which are externally visible or tucked away inside a flap of skin. In both instances, the gills are developed from the outer skin and are not equivalent to the more internally placed gills of fishes. The gills are used by larval or adult amphibians for gaseous exchange (oxygen in, carbon dioxide out) in water. Amphibians on land use a mixture of two different mechanisms for the same function. Most possess lungs – paired sacs which open ultimately into the mouth cavity. This buccal cavity is used as a pump chamber to pull air in through the nostrils, before pushing it alternately a few times between lungs and mouth, then expelling it through the nostrils. The skin of the buccal cavity is itself well supplied with blood vessels and acts as a minor extension of the respiratory surface of the lungs.

In a similar way, the moist scaleless skin of the amphibians is also important for gaseous exchange. Indeed, the vital need of amphibians to keep their bodies moist for respiration is a major constraint on their utilization of habitats. Only rarely are they able to be active in potentially drying conditions. It also limits their size because, as an animal increases in size, its surface area becomes smaller in proportion to its body volume. A large

amphibian, therefore, has a correspondingly less adequate area of respiratory skin to provide for its larger body.

Like the reptiles, amphibians operate on a quite different basis of energy balance from that of birds and mammals. The latter two groups maintain a constant high temperature, somewhere between 96.8°F and 107.6°F (36°C and 42°C). Amphibians and reptiles, on the other hand, have body temperatures close to that of the air or water in which they live and gain heat by basking in the sun. They are dependent on external temperature or sunlight for full activity. They can, however, exist on smaller amounts of food than birds and mammals because of the low energy requirements of the cold-blooded condition.

Although two species of newt are known to be parthenogenetic (capable of virgin birth), all other amphibian species include both male and female forms. The females either lay eggs or produce live young. Almost all amphibians must return to water to breed, even those which are otherwise highly adapted to terrestrial conditions. A few species have sidestepped this constraint in extraordinary ways: for example, by providing a sac on the back in which egg development occurs.

In many amphibians, males and females have different appearances. In many frogs and toads, the males move to the water before the females and attract the latter with loud, species-specific calls. Males cling to the backs of the females, when mating, by means of roughened pads which develop on the hands, and fertilize the eggs externally as they are expelled.

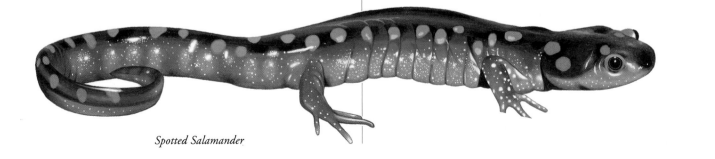

Spotted Salamander

Newts have complex courtship rituals. The males expel their sperm in packets, called spermatophores, which the females pick up in their genital openings (cloacas); the sperm then fertilizes the eggs internally.

Most amphibians pass through a distinctive tadpole larval stage or series of stages, after the hatching of the jelly-covered eggs. During this tadpole phase, the larvae are fully aquatic and possess prominent fins; they progressively acquire adult characteristics such as limbs and lungs. In some species of tailed amphibians, sexual maturity is reached at a stage which in other species would be regarded as larval. This process of neoteny or paedogenesis (breeding as a larva) is partly connected with effects of the hormone thyroxine, which is involved in larva-adult metamorphosis.

Although less adaptable and complex than the reptiles, birds and mammals, the amphibians in appropriate habitat conditions are clearly able to hold their own against other vertebrates. Due to their extremely low nutrient requirements, they are successful in conditions where food is sparse, seasonal or intermittent in availability.

Cladogram showing possible phylogenetic relationships in amphibians. The three lineages of amphibians – frogs, salamanders, and caecilians – despite their differences in appearance share a number of derived characters, including a moist, permeable skin, that indicate that as a group they share a single common ancestor.

CLADOGRAM A

1 Golden arrow poison frog **2** Fire salamander **3** South American caecilian **4** Amniota

KEY TO AMPHIBIANS CLADOGRAM A

1 Anura (frogs and toads)
2 Caudata or Urodela (salamanders)
3 Gymnophonia (caecilians)

4 Amniota (turtles, lizards and snakes, crocodilians, birds, mammals)

Cladogram showing possible phylogenetic relationships of frogs. Bufonidae is a collection of families which includes glass frogs, ghost frogs, toads, gold frogs, treefrogs, mouth-brooding frogs, leptodactylid frogs, myobatrachid frogs, and sooglossid frogs. Ranidae is a collection of families which includes poison dart frogs, hyperoliid frogs, narrow-mouthed frogs, true frogs, and rhacophorid treefrogs.

KEY TO AMPHIBIANS CLADOGRAM B

1 Ascaphidae (tailed frogs)
2 Leiopalmatidae (New Zealand frogs)
3 Discoglossidae (discoglossid frogs)
4 Pipidae (pipid frogs)
5 Rhinophrynidae (Mexican burrowing toads)

6 Pelodytidae (parsley frogs)
7 Pelobatidae (spadefoot toads)
8 Bufonidae (toads and treefrogs)
9 Ranidae (narrow-mouthed frogs and true frogs)

Cladogram showing possible phylogenetic relationships in salamanders

KEY TO AMPHIBIANS CLADOGRAM C

1 Sirenidae (sirens)
2 Cryptobranchidea (giant salamanders)
3 Hynobiidae (Asiatic land salamanders)
4 Amphiumidae (Congo eels)
5 Proteidae (olms and mudpuppies)

6 Plethodontidae (lungless salamanders)
7 Ambystomatidae (mole salamanders)
8 Dicamptodontidae (dicamptodontid salamanders)
9 Salamandridae (newts and salamanders)

CLADOGRAM B

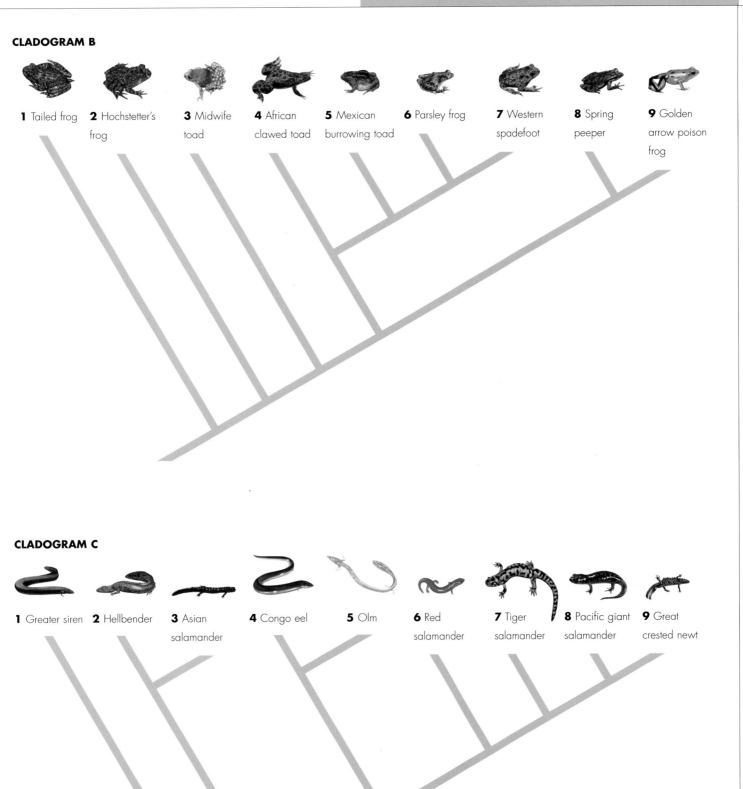

1 Tailed frog **2** Hochstetter's frog **3** Midwife toad **4** African clawed toad **5** Mexican burrowing toad **6** Parsley frog **7** Western spadefoot **8** Spring peeper **9** Golden arrow poison frog

CLADOGRAM C

1 Greater siren **2** Hellbender **3** Asian salamander **4** Congo eel **5** Olm **6** Red salamander **7** Tiger salamander **8** Pacific giant salamander **9** Great crested newt

TAILED, NEW ZEALAND, DISCOGLOSSID AND PIPID FROGS

ORDER ANURA

There are over 3,500 species of frog and toad, but all are similar in appearance whatever their habits. As adults they are tailless and have well-developed limbs. Most breed in water, laying eggs which hatch into tailed tadpoles. The tadpoles live in water, feeding on vegetation, and later change to adult form.

The word "frog" was originally used only for members of the family Ranidae, and the word "toad" for members of the family Bufonidae. However the two words are also used indiscriminately for members of other families, so there is now no taxonomic implication in their use.

ASCAPHIDAE: TAILED FROG FAMILY

This family of primitive frogs contains just one species. It shares many characteristics with members of Leiopalmatidae but is sufficiently distinct to be placed in a family of its own.

LEIOPALMATIDAE: NEW ZEALAND FROG FAMILY

The three species found in this family are primitive frogs.

Hochstetter's Frog *Leiopelma hochstetteri* **LR:lc**

RANGE New Zealand

HABITAT Mountains, mountain streams

SIZE 1¾ in (4.5 cm)

The 3 species in the genus Leiopelma are the only native frogs in New Zealand, and all are now rare and rigorously protected. Other frogs on the islands are introduced species.

First discovered in 1852, Hochstetter's frog is a robust species with partially webbed hind feet. Although it usually lives in or near water, it has also been found in mountain country some distance from streams. Like its relatives it is nocturnal and feeds on beetles, ants, earthworms, spiders and slugs.

The breeding habits of this frog are probably an adaptation to its habitat. Groups of 2 to 8 eggs are laid on moist earth under logs or stones, or in tunnels left by dragonfly nymphs. Each egg is surrounded by a water-filled gelatinous capsule and, within this capsule, the embryo passes through all the tadpole stages until it hatches out as a tiny tailed froglet, about 40 days after laying. The tail is resorbed about a month later.

DISCOGLOSSIDAE: DISCOGLOSSID FROG FAMILY

The 14 species in this family include the fire-bellied toads, painted frogs and midwife toads, all of which live in the Old World – in Europe, North Africa and parts of Asia.

They are characterized by their disk-shaped tongues which are entirely joined to the floor of the mouth and cannot be flipped forward to capture prey. Most frogs have tongues which are fixed only at the front, leaving the back free to be swiftly flipped over and protruded.

Midwife Toad *Alytes obstetricans*

RANGE W. Europe, south to Alps, Spain and Portugal

HABITAT Woodland, cultivated land

SIZE Up to 2 in (5 cm)

The small, plump midwife toad varies in coloration from gray to olivegreen or brown, often with darker markings. It is a nocturnal, land-dwelling animal, and hides by day in crevices in walls or quarries or under logs. Some individuals live in burrows, which they dig with their strong forelimbs. Midwife toads feed on insects and small invertebrates.

The midwife toad is best known for its unusual breeding habits, which are the origin of its common name. The toads mate on land at night, the male clasping the female as she lays strings of up to

60 eggs. Once he has fertilized the eggs, he then inserts his hind legs among them and twists the strings of eggs around his legs. He carries the eggs in this way while they develop, taking care that they do not dry out and moistening them at intervals in pools. After 18 to 49 days, depending on the temperature, the male deposits his eggs in shallow water, where they hatch out into tadpoles.

Oriental Fire-bellied Toad

Bombina orientalis

RANGE	Siberia, N.E. China, Korea
HABITAT	Mountain streams, rice fields
SIZE	2 in (5 cm)

A brilliantly colored species, the oriental fire-bellied toad's rough skin exudes a milky secretion which is extremely irritating to the mouths and eyes of potential predators.

The female fire-bellied toad lays her eggs on the underside of submerged stones in small clumps, each containing 2 to 8 eggs.

PIPIDAE: PIPID FROG FAMILY

There are 20 or more species of highly aquatic frogs in this family, found in Central and South America and in Africa, south of the Sahara. All have powerful hind limbs and large webbed hind feet but only small forelimbs and feet. As they swim, these forelimbs are held out in front of the head with the fingers spread as sensory probes, to search for food items.

African Clawed Toad

Xenopus laevis

RANGE	South Africa
HABITAT	Ponds, lakes
SIZE	2½–5 in (6.5–12.5 cm)

This streamlined toad is as fast and agile in water as any fish and is even able to move backward. It can change its coloration from black to gray to mottled in order to match

its background. The four digits on its forelimbs are tipped with claws, which it uses to forage in the mud around pools and streams for food, and it consumes any animal matter, even its own tadpoles.

The toads mate in water, the male making a soft buzzing sound underwater in order to attract the female. The eggs each of which is enclosed in jelly, attach to submerged plants and hatch out after 7 days.

Surinam Toad *Pipa pipa*

RANGE	N. South America
HABITAT	Streams, rivers
SIZE	4¾–7¾ in (12–20 cm)

This active, strong-swimming toad is a voracious predator and will eat almost anything it can find even carrion. It uses its slender, tactile fingers to forage for food items.

At the beginning of the Surinam toads' extraordinary mating ritual, the male clasps the female from the back, round her hind legs; this stimulates the skin on her back to swell. The clasped pair then somersault through the water and as they flip over, the female lays between 3 and 10 eggs on the male's belly. He then fertilizes the eggs and, still somersaulting, pushes them on to the female's back. This procedure is repeated until between 40 and 100 eggs have been laid. The eggs are then enveloped in the swollen skin of the female's back, each in its own separate cell. Some 2 to 4 months later, the eggs hatch out into fully formed miniature toads.

MEXICAN BURROWING AND SPADEFOOT TOADS, PARSLEY, GLASS AND GHOST FROGS

RHINOPHRYNIDAE: MEXICAN BURROWING TOAD FAMILY

The single species in this family, the Mexican burrowing toad is highly specialized for a burrowing existence. It enters water only in order to breed.

Mexican Burrowing Toad *Rhinophrynus dorsalis*

RANGE	Mexico, Guatemala
HABITAT	Woodland
SIZE	2½ in (6.5 cm)

This unusual frog has horny, shovellike appendages on its feet and is an expert burrower. At night, it emerges from its burrow to hunt for termites which it licks up with its tongue.

Males court the females with guttural calls. They mate in water; he clings to her back and as she lays her eggs, he fertilizes them as they are laid. The tadpoles have sensory barbels around their mouths and lack the true lips possessed by most other tadpoles.

PELODYTIDAE: PARSLEY FROGS

This Eurasian family contains two species of small terrestrial frogs which have aquatic larvae.

Parsley Frog *Pelodytes punctatus*

RANGE	Europe: Spain, Portugal, France, W. Belgium, N. Italy
HABITAT	Various damp areas
SIZE	Up to 2 in (5 cm)

A nocturnal, mainly terrestrial creature outside the breeding

season, the parsley frog is often found among vegetation near streams or by walls. It is a small, active frog with warty skin and virtually unwebbed hind feet.

Parsley frogs climb, swim and jump well and can dig shallow burrows, despite the fact that they lack the spadelike hind foot appendages that are characteristic of the rest of the family.

Parsley frogs mate in spring and may breed more than once in a season. Bands of eggs, which are held together by a thick gelatinous substance, twine round submerged vegetation, where they remain until they hatch into tadpoles.

PELOBATIDAE: SPADEFOOT TOAD FAMILY

The 80 or so species of spadefoot toad are found in North America, Europe, North Africa and southern Asia. Many are highly terrestrial and nocturnal, spending their days in underground burrows. They are known as spadefoots because of the horny tubercle found on the inner edge of each hind foot, which is used as a digging tool.

Spadefoots breed rapidly after rains, in temporary rainpools. Because the pools will soon dry up, development must be accelerated and eggs may hatch, pass though the tadpole stage and metamorphose into frogs in only 2 weeks.

European Spadefoot *Pelobates fuscus*

RANGE	W., central and E. Europe to W. Asia
HABITAT	Sandy soil, cultivated land
SIZE	Up to 3¼ in (8 cm)

The plump, European spadefoot has a large, pale-colored spade on each virtually fully webbed hind foot. Males are usually smaller than females and have raised oval glands on their upper forelimbs. Like most spadefoots, this species is nocturnal outside the breeding season.

In the breeding season, however spadefoots may be active during the day. They breed once a year in spring, usually in deep pools or in ditches. Although spadefoots do not develop the rough nuptial pads which males of many other families have to help them grasp their mates, they clasp the females and fertilize the eggs as they are laid.

Western Spadefoot *Scaphiopus hammondi*

RANGE	W. USA: California, Arizona, New Mexico; Mexico
HABITAT	Varied, plains, sandy areas
SIZE	1¼–2½ in (3.5–6.5 cm)

An expert burrower, the western spadefoot has a wedge-shaped spade on each hind foot. It is a nocturnal toad and spends the day in its burrow in conditions of moderate temperature and humidity, despite the arid heat typical of much of its range.

Temporary rainpools are used for breeding, any time between January and August, depending on rainfall. The eggs are laid in round clumps which attach to vegetation and hatch only 2 days later. Since development must be completed before the temporary pool dries up, metamorphosis from tadpole to adult form takes place in under 6 weeks.

CENTROLENIDAE: GLASS FROG FAMILY

Glass frogs are so called because of their lightly pigmented skin that allows the internal organs to be seen through the body wall. The 70 or so species of these treefrogs are found in tropical Central and South America.

Glass Frog *Centrolenella albomaculata*

RANGE	N. South America
HABITAT	Forest
SIZE	Up to 1¼ in (3 cm)

The delicate glass frog behaves much like the hylid treefrogs and lives in small trees and bushes, usually near to running water. Its

digits are expanded into adhesive disks which give a good grip when it is climbing. Its eggs are laid in clusters on the underside of leaves overhanging running water and are guarded by the male. When the tadpoles hatch out they tumble down into the water below, where they complete their development and metamorphose into frogs.

HELEOPHRYNIDAE: GHOST FROG FAMILY

Ghost frogs are so called not because of any spectral appearance, but because a species was discovered in Skeleton Gorge in South Africa. About 3 or 4 species are known, all found in southern Africa in fast-flowing mountain streams. They are long-limbed frogs with flattened bodies, enabling them to squeeze into narrow rock crevices, and expanded digits with which to grip on to slippery surfaces.

Natal Ghost Frog *Heleophryne natalensis*

RANGE	N.E. South Africa
HABITAT	Forested streams
SIZE	Up to 2 in (5 cm)

A nocturnal species, the ghost frog takes refuge by day among rocks and pebbles or in crevices, concealed by its mottled and speckled coloration.

In the breeding season, male frogs develop nuptial pads on the forelimbs and small spines on the fingers and armpits for grasping their mates.

The eggs are laid in a pool or even out of the water on wet gravel. Once hatched, tadpoles move to fast-flowing streams. They are able to withstand being swept away by the currents by holding on to stones in the riverbed with their suckerlike mouths.

BUFONID TOADS AND GOLD FROG

BUFONIDAE: TOAD FAMILY

The common name "toad" was originally applied only to the approximately 330 species in the bufonidae family, although many other anurans with warty skins and terrestrial habits tend to be called toads.

Bufonid toads are found over most of the world, except in the far north, Madagascar and Polynesia. A species has now been introduced into Australia, where previously there were no bufonid toads.

The typical bufonid toad has a compact body and short legs. The skin is not moist and is covered with characteristic wartlike tubercles. These contain the openings of poison glands, the distasteful secretions of which protect the toads to some extent, particularly from mammalian predators.

With their short legs, toads tend to walk rather than hop and are, in general, slower-moving than frogs. Breeding males develop rough nuptial pads on their three inner fingers for clasping females when mating.

Boulenger's Arrow Poison Toad *Atelopus boulengeri*

RANGE South America: Ecuador, Peru

HABITAT Forested slopes of the Andes, near fast-flowing streams

SIZE About 1 in (2.5 cm)

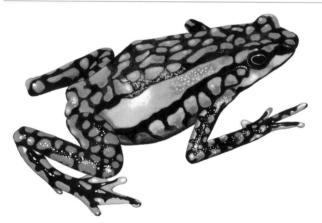

The contrasting black and orange markings of Boulenger's arrow poison toad warn of the poisonous skin secretions that defend it from predators. An uncommon, slow-moving species, this toad is active during the day and may climb up into bushes at night.

Little is known of its breeding habits, but it is believed to lay its eggs under stones in streams. The tadpoles probably have sucking mouths in order to anchor themselves to rocks on the riverbed to prevent them being swept away in the fast-flowing water.

American Toad

Bufo americanus

RANGE S.E. Canada: Manitoba to Labrador, south to Great Lakes; USA: south to Georgia, east to Kansas

HABITAT Grassland, forest, gardens

SIZE 2–4¼ in (5–11 cm)

A stout, broad-headed toad, the American toad is liberally covered with warts. Females are usually larger than males.

Mainly nocturnal, the American toad takes refuge during the day under stones, logs or other debris or burrows into the soil. It feeds on insects, but also eats small invertebrates such as spiders, snails and earthworms.

American toads usually breed between March and July in ponds or streams. The female lays two strings of spawn, each containing up to 8,000 eggs, which hatch into tadpoles between 3 and 12 days later. The tadpoles metamorphose into adults about 2 months after hatching.

Giant Toad *Bufo marinus*

RANGE USA: extreme S. Texas; Mexico to Central and South America; introduced in many areas, including Australia

HABITAT Varied, near pools, swamps

SIZE 4–9½ in (10–24 cm)

One of the largest toads in the world, the giant toad has been widely introduced by man outside its range, often in order to feed on, and thus control, the insects which destroy crops such as sugar. It adapts well to many habitats and feeds on almost anything, including small rodents and birds and many insects, particularly beetles.

Toxic secretions from the glands at each side of its body are highly irritating to mucous membranes and in some cases may be fatal to mammalian predators.

Giant toads breed at any time of year, given sufficient rainfall and warmth. They lay strings of eggs in permanent water, where they usually hatch into tadpoles in 3 days. One female may lay up to 35,000 eggs a year.

Green Toad *Bufo viridis*

RANGE Europe: S. Sweden through Germany to Italy and Mediterranean islands; N. Africa, C. Asia

HABITAT Varied, often lowland sandy areas, not forest

SIZE 3¼–4 in (8–10 cm)

A thickset species but less plump than the common toad, the green toad has warty skin and distinctive green markings. The female is larger than the male, with brighter markings, and the male has an external vocal sac. Green toads are mainly nocturnal, but they may occasionally emerge during the day to forage for their insect food. Although primarily a land-living toad, the green toad has partially webbed toes and can survive in even brackish water.

Green toads breed from April to June, males courting females with their trilling, musical calls. The mating male clasps the female under her armpits while she lays two long strings of gelatinous spawn, each containing 10,000 to 20,000 eggs.

Natterjack Toad *Bufo calamita*

RANGE W. and C. Europe (including Britain), east to Russia

HABITAT Varied, often sandy areas

SIZE 2¾–4 in (7–10 cm)

The male natterjack has the loudest call of any European toad: his croak will carry 2 km (1¼ miles) or more. The female is usually larger than the male, but both are robust and relatively short-limbed. Although mainly terrestrial, natterjacks are often found near the sea and may even breed in brackish water. On land they run in short spurts and are most active at night.

The breeding season lasts from March to August. Natterjacks mate at night and the female lays several strings of gelatinous spawn, each containing up to 4,000 eggs, in shallow water. The eggs hatch in 10 days into tadpoles which metamorphose to adult form in 4 to 8 weeks. The young toads are not fully grown and mature until they are 4 or 5 years old.

Common Toad
Bufo bufo

RANGE Europe (including Britain and Scandinavia); N. Africa, N. Asia to Japan

HABITAT Varied, often fairly dry

SIZE Up to 6 in (15 cm)

The largest European toad, the common toad varies in size over its wide range, but females are generally larger than males. It is a heavily built toad with extremely warty skin; males do not have external vocal sacs. A nocturnal species, it hides during the day, often using the same spot time after time, and emerges at dusk to feed on a variety of invertebrate prey. It usually moves by walking but, if distressed, may hop.

In much of their range, common toads hibernate in winter and then congregate in large numbers to breed at about the end of March, frequently returning to the same pond every year. Thousands of eggs are laid in gelatinous strings up to 10 ft (3 m) long. The eggs hatch in about 10 days and, if the weather is warm, the tadpoles metamorphose in about 2 months. In cold weather they take longer.

BRACHYCEPHALIDAE: GOLD FROG FAMILY

Closely related to the bufonid toads are the 3 species of frog in this family, the gold frog.

Gold Frog *Brachycephalus ephippium*

RANGE South America: S.E. Brazil

HABITAT Mountain forest

SIZE Up to ¾ in (2 cm)

This tiny, but exquisite, frog is common among the leaf litter of the forest floor, although it may hide in crevices in trees or rocks in dry weather. On its back is a bony shield, made of hard plates fused to the spines of the vertebrae. The frog may use this shield to block the entrance of its hiding place, so maintaining its humidity.

Its breeding habits are unknown but, since the tadpoles are aquatic, it is presumed that the frog lays its eggs in or near water.

TREEFROGS AND MOUTH-BROODING FROGS

HYLIDAE: TREEFROG FAMILY

There are approximately 600 species of treefrog, found on all continents except the Antarctic. The greatest diversity occurs in tropical areas of the New World. The majority live in trees and have a range of adaptations which make them extremely efficient insect-eating, tree-dwellers. The most important of these adaptations are on the feet. Each digit is tipped with a sticky adhesive pad to aid climbing, and inside the digit is a disk-shaped zone of cartilage before the end bone which allows the digit great mobility, while keeping the adhesive pad flat on the surface when the frog is climbing.

European Green Treefrog *Hyla arborea* **LR:nt**

RANGE	Most of Europe except N. Turkey, S. Russia to Caspian Sea
HABITAT	Bushes, trees, reeds near ponds and lakes
SIZE	Up to 2 in (5 cm)

This smooth-skinned treefrog spends most of its life in trees where it catches flying insects. It can change color rapidly, from bright green in sunlight to a dark gray in shade. In early summer, frogs congregate at night in ponds. The male grasps the female just behind the forelegs and fertilizes her eggs as they are shed into the water. Clumps of up to 1,000 eggs float on the water until they hatch into tadpoles.

Common Gray Treefrog *Hyla versicolor*

RANGE	S.E. Canada; USA: North Dakota, east to Maine, south to Texas and Florida
HABITAT	Bushes, trees near water
SIZE	1¼–2¼ in (3–6 cm)

This treefrog's color camouflages it in trees. The orange areas on its thighs can be flashed to confuse predators. It lives high up in vegetation and is mainly active at night, when it preys on insects. It descends only to call and breed. It mates in water and the eggs are shed in small clusters of 10 to 40. The tadpoles hatch 4 or 5 days later.

Spring Peeper *Hyla crucifer*

RANGE	S.E. Canada; USA, south to C. Florida, west to Texas
HABITAT	Woodland, near ponds, swamps
SIZE	¾–1¼ in (2–3 cm)

One of the most abundant frogs in eastern North America, the spring peeper's song does indeed herald the arrival of spring in the north of its range. This agile little frog can climb into trees and bushes, using its well-developed adhesive toe pads, and jump over 17 times its body length. It feeds mainly on small spiders and insects, including flying insects which it leaps into the air to catch.

Courting males call from trees overhanging water, making a belllike chorus. The male frog climbs on to a female who enters water and lays her 800 to 1,000 eggs, one at a time, on to stems of aquatic vegetation. He fertilizes the eggs which hatch within a few days. The tadpoles metamorphose about 3 months later and leave the pond.

Northern Cricket Frog *Acris crepitans*

RANGE	USA: New York, south to N. Florida, west to Minnesota and Texas
HABITAT	Shallow ponds, slow streams
SIZE	½–1½ in (1.5–4 cm)

This tiny rough-skinned frog is a poor climber and spends its life on land and in water. Unlike the arboreal treefrogs which do not jump readily, the cricket frog can jump as much as 36 times its own length. Breeding starts in April in the north of its range or as early as February in the south. Thousands of frogs congregate to call and mate. The male's call is a shrill, metallic clicking sound. The eggs are shed on submerged vegetation or into the water in small clusters or singly. In warm weather, they hatch in 4 days but may take longer if the temperature is below 72°F (22°C).

Green and Gold Bell Frog *Litoria cydorhynchus*

RANGE	W. Australia: south coast
HABITAT	Large ponds
SIZE	Up to 3¼ in (8 cm)

This bell frog climbs only rarely and lives mostly in water or on reeds. It moves on land only in heavy rainfall. Active during the day, it is a voracious predator, feeding on any small animals, including its own tadpoles.

In the breeding season, males call from the water to attract mates, making a sound rather like wood being sawn. The female lays her eggs among vegetation in the pond.

Lutz's Phyllomedusa *Phyllomedusa appendiculata*

RANGE	South America: S.E. Brazil
HABITAT	Forest, near moving water
SIZE	1½ in (4 cm)

A tree-dwelling frog, Lutz's phyllomedusa has triangular flaps of skin on each heel, which may help to camouflage its outline. Areas of red skin inside thighs and flanks can be flashed to confuse predators. It eats mainly insects.

The breeding pair selects a leaf overhanging water. They fold the leaf over, making a nest which is open at both sides, and about 50 eggs are laid in a ball of mucus in the nest. The tadpoles hatch 2 or 3 days later and drop into the water.

Marsupial Frog *Gastrotheca marsupiata*

RANGE	South America: Ecuador, Peru
HABITAT	Forest
SIZE	Up to 1½ in (4 cm)

The female frog is larger than the male and has a special skin pouch on her back. While she lays about 200 eggs, one at a time, the male sits on her back. As each egg is laid, she bends forward so that it rolls down her back; the male then fertilizes the egg before it settles into the skin pouch. When all the eggs are laid, the male helps to pack them into the skin pouch

and the edges of the pouch seal over to protect them.

A few weeks later the female frog finds some shallow water – a pond or puddle – in which to release her brood. By this time her back is very swollen. She raises one hind leg and, with her fourth and longest toe, slits open the pouch and frees the young tadpoles which then complete their metamorphosis in water.

RHINODERMATIDAE: MOUTH-BROODING FROG FAMILY

This South American family contains these 2 species of unusual mouth-brooding frogs of the genus Rhinoderma. Males of these species carry the developing eggs, and then the tadpoles, in their vocal sacs until they transform into small frogs. The species was discovered by Charles Darwin.

Darwin's Frog *Rhinoderma darwinii* **DD**

RANGE	S. Chile, S. Argentina
HABITAT	Shallow, cold streams in forest
SIZE	1¼ in (3 cm)

The small, slender Darwin's frog has a pointed extension of skin on its head. Its digits are long and webbed on the hind feet but free on the forefeet.

Its breeding habits are unique among amphibians. The female lays 20 to 45 eggs on land. They are guarded by several males for 10 to 20 days until the embryos, which are visible from the outside, begin to move around inside the capsules. Each male then gathers up to 15 eggs and lets them slide into his large vocal sac. The tadpoles develop inside the sac, feeding on their own yolks. Once they are small adults about ½ in (1.25 cm) long, the male expels them into water and his vocal sac shrinks back to its normal size.

LEPTODACTYLID, MYOBATRACHID, SOOGLOSSID, POISON DART AND REED FROGS

LEPTODACTYLIDAE: LEPTODACTYLID FROG FAMILY

This is a large and varied family with several hundred species, found mainly in Central and South America, Africa and Australia. Their anatomy is similar to that of true treefrogs, but although Leptodactylid frogs may have adhesive disks on the digits, the digits are not as flexible.

Horned Frog

Cetatophrys cornuta

RANGE N. and C. South America

HABITAT Litter on forest floor

SIZE 7 ¾ in (20 cm)

The horned frog is almost as broad as it is long and has a wide, powerful head and large mouth. Its eyes are small, with a small protuberance on each upper eyelid. The toes are partially webbed, although the frog spends much of its life half-buried in the ground. Snails, small frogs and rodents are all eaten, and it is also believed to eat the young of its own species.

South American Bullfrog *Leptodactylus pentadactylus*

RANGE Central and South America: Costa Rica to Brazil

HABITAT Forest, close to water

SIZE Up to 8 in (20.5 cm)

The South American bullfrog has powerful hind legs, which are eaten by man in some areas. The male has powerful arm muscles and hard protuberances on each thumb which fit into horny structures on the female to help him grip on to her when mating.

In the winter spawning season, the sides of the bullfrog's legs turn deep orange or red. The male clasps the female in the water. She secretes a jellylike substance which he whips into foam to form a floating nest in which the eggs are laid and fertilized. Tadpoles stay in the nest until they become froglets.

MYOBATRACHIDAE: MYOBATRACHID FROG FAMILY

This small family of frogs appears to have affinities with the bufonid toads and was previously classified with them. Members of the family tend to walk on the tips of their toes.

Corroboree Frog

Pseudophryne corroboree

RANGE Australia: New South Wales

HABITAT Mountain, marshland

SIZE 1 ¼ in (3 cm)

The corroboree frog lives on land but near water, often at altitudes of over 5,000 ft (1,500 m), and shelters under logs or in a burrow, which it digs itself.

In summer, the frogs seek out sphagnum bogs, where they dig nesting burrows. Up to 12 large eggs are laid and one parent usually stays with the eggs while they develop. The tadpoles remain in the eggs until there is sufficient rainfall to wash them into a creek, where they hatch at once.

Cyclorana cultripes

RANGE Australia: N. coasts, W. Australia to Queensland

HABITAT Underground

SIZE 2 in (5 cm)

This burrowing frog comes above ground only to breed and to find food. It breeds after heavy summer rains, often in temporary ponds. Eggs are laid in the water, where they attach to plants until they hatch into fat tadpoles with pointed snouts and deep tail fins.

SOOGLOSSIDAE: SOOGLOSSID FROG FAMILY

The origins and relationships of the frogs of this family, all found in the Seychelles, have been a matter of some contention.

Seychelles Frog *Sooglossus sechellensis* **VU**

RANGE Seychelles: Mahe and Silhouette Islands

HABITAT Moss forest on mountains

SIZE Up to 1 in (2.5 cm)

The tiny Seychelles frog has thin, weak front limbs but more powerful hind limbs, with long digits on its feet. It is mainly ground-dwelling and lives in rotting plant matter on the forest floor, needing water for a short phase of tadpole development only. It eats small invertebrates.

The frogs breed in the rainy season. The female lays eggs in small clumps of gelatinous substance on moist ground. The male guards the eggs and after 2 weeks incubation, they hatch. The tadpoles wriggle on to his back. They respire through their skin and do not have gills. Most of their development takes place on the male's back, but they are carried to water, where they complete their metamorphosis before returning to land.

DENDROBATIDAE: POISON DART FROG FAMILY

Found in the forests of Central and South America, most of the 120 or so species in this family are small, brightly colored frogs. Their bright color advertises a warning to potential predators that their skin contains highly toxic alkaloids.

Golden Arrow-poison Frog *Dendrobates auratus*

RANGE Central and South America: Nicaragua to Panama and Colombia

HABITAT Forest

SIZE 1½ in (4 cm)

The brilliant colors of this ground-dwelling frog warn potential enemies of its poisonous glandular secretions. This poison is extracted by local tribesmen and used on the tips of arrows.

Before mating, these frogs contest with each other until they have paired. The female lays up to 6 eggs in a gelatinous substance, on land. The male visits the clutch until, after about 2 weeks, the tadpoles hatch. They wriggle on to the male frog's back and he carries them to a hole in a tree where a little water has collected. The tadpoles complete their development in about 6 weeks.

HYPEROLIIDAE: HYPEROLIID FROG FAMILY

The hyperoliids are climbing frogs, closely related to the ranid frogs. They differ in that they possess adaptations for climbing similar to those of the hylid frogs – each digit on the frogs' feet has a zone of cartilage which allows greater flexibility in the use of the adhesive disk at the tip when climbing. Most of the 220 species in this family live in Africa, often near fresh water.

Arum Lily Frog

Hyperolius horstockii

RANGE South Africa: S. and W. Cape Province

HABITAT Swamps, dams, streams, rivers, with vegetation

SIZE Up to 2¼ in (6 cm)

The long-limbed arum lily frog has bands running from its snout along each side. A good climber, its feet are equipped with expanded, adhesive disks and are only partially webbed. The under-surfaces of the limbs are orange. The rest of the body changes color according to conditions, becoming a light cream in bright sun and dark brown in shade. This helps the frog control its body heat.

Courting males often climb up on to arum lilies to call to females. They then mate in water, where the small clusters of eggs are laid on submerged water plants.

Gold Spiny Reed Frog *Afrixales brachycnemis*

RANGE South Africa: E., S.E. and S. coastal regions

HABITAT Pools, swamps

SIZE ¾ in (2 cm)

Also known as the golden leaf-folding frog, this tiny, slim amphibian, equipped with adhesive disks on each digit, is a good climber. Its back may be covered with tiny dark spines, hence one of its common names. This feature is common in frogs in the south of the range but rare in the north.

Breeding males take up position among reeds or on waterlily leaves in pools or vleis (temporary, rain-filled hollows) and call to females. The female lays a batch of eggs on a leaf above or below water level. Once fertilized, the leaf is folded and the edges are glued together with secretions from the female's oviduct. Tadpoles complete their development in the water.

NARROW-MOUTHED AND TRUE FROGS

MICROHYLIDAE: NARROW-MOUTHED FROG FAMILY

There are 300 or more species of burrowing, terrestrial and tree-living frogs in this family, found in tropical regions all over the world and extending into temperate areas in North and South America. Tree-living forms are equipped with adhesive pads on finger and toe tips to aid climbing.

Sheep Frog *Hypopachus cuneus*

RANGE	USA: S.E. Texas; Mexico
HABITAT	Margins of damp areas in arid country
SIZE	1–1¾ in (2.5–4.5 cm)

A small, stout frog with a pointed snout, the sheep frog is a nocturnal species which hides during the day under rocks or debris or in a rodent burrow; at night it emerges in order to feed on ants and termites.

Sheep frogs mate at any time of year when stimulated by sufficient rainfall. The male attracts the female to the breeding pond by making his bleating call – the origin of the common name. He clasps the female's body, and her sticky body secretions help the pair to stay together while they lay and fertilize about 700 eggs.

South African Rain Frog *Breviceps adspersus*

RANGE	South Africa, Namibia, Botswana, Zimbabwe
HABITAT	Savanna
SIZE	1¼ in (3 cm)

An extremely rotund frog, the South African rain frog has a short snout and small, sturdy limbs. Its back is covered with warty protuberances, and coloration and pattern are variable.

It burrows well, using its hind feet, and seldom emerges above ground except during rain. It feeds on insects and small invertebrates.

The courting male makes a repeated croaking chirp to attract his mate. They mate in a burrow, held together by sticky body

secretions. The few eggs are enclosed in thick jelly and lie in a compact mass in the burrow while they develop. There is no tadpole stage; metamorphosis takes place within the egg capsules and the young hatch as miniature, land-living frogs.

Eastern Narrow-mouthed Frog
Gastrophryne carolinensis

RANGE	S.E. USA: Missouri and Maryland, south to Florida, Gulf coast and Texas
HABITAT	By ponds and ditches; under moist vegetation
SIZE	¾–1½ in (2–4 cm)

An excellent burrower, this small smooth-skinned frog can disappear into the soil in a moment. It rests in a burrow during the day and comes out at night to hunt for its insect food, mainly ants.

Breeding is stimulated by rainfall, sometime between April and October. The dark-throated male calls to the female, usually from water, and continues to call as they mate. The eggs float on the water surface for 3 days and then hatch into tadpoles.

Termite Frog *Phrynomerus bifasciatus*

RANGE	Africa, south of the Sahara
HABITAT	Savanna
SIZE	2 in (5 cm)

The termite frog has a more elongate body than most members of its family and an unusually mobile head. Its distinctive markings warn of its toxic skin which contains substances which irritate the skin and mucous membranes of predators. A land-dwelling frog, it may climb up tree stumps and rocks or burrow in search of prey or to shelter from dry weather. Termites and ants are its main foods.

Breeding takes place in shallow pools. The small, jelly-coated eggs are laid in masses and attach to submerged plants or lie at the bottom of the water. They hatch into aquatic tadpoles.

RANIDAE: TRUE FROG FAMILY

There are over 600 species in this family, found almost worldwide on every continent except Antarctica, but sparsely represented in Australasia and the southern parts of South America. Typically, these frogs have slim, streamlined bodies and pointed heads. Their hind legs are long and hind feet extensively webbed. They are usually smooth-skinned and often brown or green in color.

Most ranid frogs live near fresh water and enter it readily to find prey or escape danger. A few species, however, can thrive in brackish waters or warm sulfur springs and others have become adapted to a ground-living existence and can burrow like spadefoot toads. Some live in trees and have adhesive pads on their toes for grip when climbing, similar to those of the treefrogs (Hylidae). All are carnivorous as adults, feeding mainly on insects, spiders and small crustaceans.

Large numbers of ranid frogs congregate at the start of the breeding season and males chorus to attract females to the breeding site. The breeding male develops swollen pads on forelimbs and thumbs with which he grasps his mate's body. As she lays her eggs, he fertilizes them by spraying them with sperm. The eggs are usually surrounded by a jellylike substance which protects them to some degree and prevents dehydration. Although females lay thousands of eggs, many of these are destroyed by adverse conditions or eaten by predators, and relatively few survive to adulthood.

Common Frog *Rana temporaria*

RANGE Europe (including Britain and Scandinavia, but excluding much of Spain and Italy), east to Asia

HABITAT Varied, any moist area near ponds, marshes, swamps

SIZE Up to 4 in (10 cm)

European frogs are divided into two groups – green and brown frogs. The brown frogs, of which the common frog is an example, tend to be more terrestrial and have quieter voices than

the green frogs. The robust common frog varies in coloration over its wide range, from brown or gray to yellow. It is tolerant of cold and is found up to the snowline in some areas. Much of its life is spent on land, and it rarely enters water except to mate or hibernate.

Breeding occurs from February to April, and males attract females to the breeding sites with their deep, rasping croaks. They mate in water and females lay 3,000 to 4,000 eggs in large clusters.

Bullfrog *Rana catesbeiana*

RANGE E. and C. USA; introduced in western areas and in Mexico, Cuba and N. Italy

HABITAT Lakes, ponds, slow streams

SIZE 3½–8 in (9–20.5 cm)

The largest North American frog, the bullfrog makes a deep, vibrant call, amplified by the internal vocal sac. Although an aquatic species, it also spends time on land and is often seen at the water's edge. It is most active by night, when it preys on insects, fish, smaller frogs and, occasionally, small birds and snakes. Like all American ranid frogs, it is a good jumper and can leap nine times its own length.

In the north of their range, bullfrogs breed from May to July, but farther south the season is longer. The female lays 10,000 to 20,000 eggs in water which may float on the surface or attach to vegetation. The eggs hatch in 5 or 6 days, but the tadpoles take 2 to 5 years to transform into adults.

TRUE FROGS AND RHACOPHORID TREEFROGS

Northern Leopard Frog *Rana pipiens*

RANGE Most of northern North America except Pacific coast

HABITAT Varied, fresh water to brackish marshes in arid to mountain land

SIZE 2–5 in (5–12.5 cm)

The slim northern leopard frog is a distinctive species, with large spots on its body and prominent back ridges. It is the most widely distributed North American amphibian and the pattern and intensity of its spots vary over its large range. It adapts to almost any habitat near a permanent body of water and is equally accommodating in its diet; insects, spiders and crustaceans are its main food, but this voracious frog will eat almost anything it can find. Primarily a nocturnal species, the leopard frog may sometimes search for food during the day. If disturbed on land, it leaps away in a series of zigzagging jumps to seek refuge in water.

In the north of its range, the breeding season usually extends from March to June, but in southern, arid areas, leopard frogs are ready to breed at almost any time of year whenever there has been sufficient rainfall. Males gather at breeding sites and make low grunting calls to attract females.

Each female lays about 20,000 eggs which her mate fertilizes. The eggs then lie at the bottom of the water on submerged vegetation until they hatch about 4 weeks later. The tadpoles metamorphose into adult form in 6 months to 2 years, depending on the temperature and conditions.

Marsh Frog *Rana ridibunda*

RANGE S.W. Europe: S.W. France, Spain and Portugal; E. Europe: Germany, east to Russia and Balkans

HABITAT Ponds, ditches, streams, lakes, rivers

SIZE Up to 6 in (15 cm)

The marsh frog is one of the several noisy, aquatic, gregarious green frogs found in Europe. Apart from its color, this long-legged frog is easily distinguished from the brown frogs by the external vocal sacs at the sides of its mouth. Most

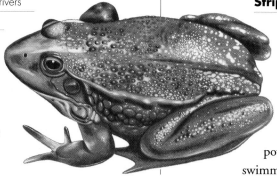

of its life is spent in water, but it will come out on to banks or float on lily pads. As well as catching invertebrate prey, these large frogs feed on small birds and mammals.

Marsh frogs sing night and day and are particularly vocal in the breeding season, when they make a variety of sounds. They mate in April or May, and females lay thousands of eggs in several large clusters.

South African Bullfrog *Pyxicephalus adspersus*

RANGE E. South Africa

HABITAT Open grassland (veld); in temporary puddles when available

SIZE Up to 7¾ in (20 cm)

The largest South African frog, this bullfrog has a stout body and broad head. The male usually has a yellow throat while the female's is cream. On its lower jaw are toothlike projections which it uses to restrain struggling prey such as mice, lizards and other frogs. Its hind toes are webbed, but the front toes are not.

A powerful burrower, it spends much of the year underground but comes to the surface after heavy rain to breed. Males call from a breeding site in shallow water, where females then lay their many eggs, one at a time.

Striped Grass Frog *Ptychadena porosissima*

RANGE Africa: central tropical areas to E. South Africa

HABITAT Marshy areas

SIZE 1½ in (4 cm)

This small, streamlined frog has a pointed snout and a ridged back. Its hind limbs are powerful, making it a good jumper and strong swimmer. Secretive in its habits, it often makes its

home among dense vegetation. Breeding males sit among aquatic vegetation and call to females with a rasping sound, which is amplified by their paired external vocal sacs. Their mates lay their eggs, one at a time, in the water. The eggs float at first and then sink to the bottom; the tadpoles swim and feed near the bottom.

Mottled Burrowing Frog *Hemisus marmoratum*

RANGE N.E. South Africa

HABITAT Open country near pools

SIZE Up to 1¼ in (3 cm)

A stout, squat-bodied frog, this species has a small pointed head with a hardened snout used for burrowing. It burrows head first, pushing into the soil with its snout and clawing its way forward with its strong forelimbs. It is rarely seen above ground, although it can move rapidly on land.

Breeding males establish themselves in small holes, preferably in a mudbank, and call to attract mates. The female excavates an underground nest and lays her large eggs, each surrounded by a thick jellylike substance. When her young hatch some 10 to 12 days later, she tunnels to the nearest water, providing a canal for the tadpoles, which complete their development in water.

Bush Squeaker *Arthroleptis wahlbergi*

RANGE S.E. South Africa

HABITAT Coastal and inland bush among leaf litter and low vegetation

SIZE Up to 1¼ in (3 cm)

This small, rounded frog is a land-dweller. Its legs are short but its digits, particularly the third on each foot, are elongate, well-suited to searching through vegetation for prey.

The bush squeaker's breeding habits, too, are adapted to its terrestrial existence. The eggs, each enclosed in a stiff jelly capsule, are laid among decaying vegetation. There is no tadpole stage; metamorphosis takes place within the capsule and tiny froglets emerge about 4 weeks after laying.

RHACOPHORIDAE: RHACOPHORID TREEFROG FAMILY

The 200 or so species in this family of treefrogs are found in Africa, Madagascar, and Asia.

Wallace's Flying Frog *Rhacophorus nigropalmatus*

RANGE S.E. Asia

HABITAT Rain forest

SIZE 4 in (10 cm)

This specialized frog glides from tree to tree in the forest. It has a distinctive broad head and a long slim body with elongate limbs. The feet are greatly enlarged and fully webbed, and the tips of the digits expand into large disks. Flaps of skin fringe the forelimbs and heels. All of these modifications add little to the frog's weight, but extend its surface area. It can launch itself into the air, webs with skin flaps outstretched, and glide gently down to another branch or to the ground.

The breeding habits of this extraordinary frog are little known, but are believed to be similar to those of others of its genus. Rhacophorid frogs lay their eggs in a mass of foam which makes a kind of nest to protect them from excessive heat while they incubate. The male frog grasps the female and fertilizes her eggs as they are laid. The eggs are accompanied by a thick fluid which the frogs then beat with their hind legs to form a dense light foam. Surrounded with this substance, the eggs are left on a leaf or branch overhanging water. At hatching time the bubble nest begins to liquefy, forming a miniature pool for the emerging tadpoles. In some species, the tadpoles complete their development in this custom made pool, but in others they drop down into the water beneath.

SIRENS, CONGO EELS, OLMS AND MUDPUPPIES

ORDER CAUDATA

There are 10 families of salamanders, newts and relatives in this order. All have elongate bodies and long tails.

SIRENIDAE: SIREN FAMILY

The 3 species of sirens are aquatic salamanders which retain feathery external gills throughout life. Their bodies are long and eellike and they have tiny forelimbs and no hind limbs. All species occur in the USA and northern Mexico.

Sirens swim by powerful undulations of the body. They forage among water weeds for food and they are active at night. They breathe with external gills at each side of the neck.

Dwarf Siren *Pseudobranchus striatus*

RANGE USA: coastal plain of South Carolina, Georgia, Florida

HABITAT Ponds, swamps, ditches

SIZE 4–9¾ in (10–25 cm)

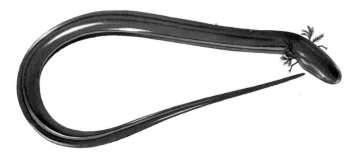

The smallest of its family, the dwarf siren is a slender, eellike creature which lives among dense submerged vegetation. It has no hind limbs and only tiny forelimbs with three toes on each foot. The external gills are retained throughout life. A nocturnal creature, the siren feeds on tiny invertebrate animals it finds among the plant debris near the bottom of the water. If its habitat is in danger of drying up, in a drought for example, the siren can burrow into the mud and remain there, dormant, for up to 2 months. Mucus produced by skin glands prevents the body drying out during such a period.

The female siren lays her eggs, one at a time, on aquatic plants and the larvae hatch out about 4 weeks later. There are about 5 races of dwarf siren over the range, which vary in coloration and in the shade and distribution of the stripes along the sides of the body.

Greater Siren *Siren lacertina*

RANGE USA: coastal plain from Virginia to Florida, S. Alabama

HABITAT Shallow, muddy fresh water with plenty of vegetation

SIZE 19¾–38¼ in (50–97.5 cm)

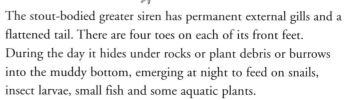

The stout-bodied greater siren has permanent external gills and a flattened tail. There are four toes on each of its front feet. During the day it hides under rocks or plant debris or burrows into the muddy bottom, emerging at night to feed on snails, insect larvae, small fish and some aquatic plants.

In drought conditions, the siren undergoes a period of dormancy; it seals itself in a cocoon made from secretions from the skin glands and buries itself in the muddy bottom until danger is past.

Sirens breed in February or March, laying eggs which hatch 2 or 3 months later into larvae, about ½ in (1.25 cm) long.

AMPHIUMIDAE: CONGO EEL FAMILY

The 3 species of elongate, eellike creatures in this family are among the world's largest aquatic salamanders; they are all found in the southeastern USA. They have cylindrical bodies and tiny hind and forelimbs, each with one, two or three toes. These limbs are so small that they are probably of no use for moving. The skin of these amphibians is smooth and slippery.

Until 1950 there were thought to be only 2 species in this family, but a third species, the one-toed amphiuma, *Amphiuma pholeter*, was then discovered.

Two-toed Congo Eel *Amphiuma means*

RANGE USA: S.E. Virginia to Florida, E. Louisiana

HABITAT Swamps, bayous, drainage ditches

SIZE 17¾–45½ in (45–116 cm)

This aquatic salamander has tiny, virtually useless limbs, each with two toes. Mainly active at night, it hunts in water for crayfish, frogs, small snakes and fish and may occasionally come on to land in extremely wet weather. It takes refuge during the

its eyes hidden beneath the skin. It feeds on small aquatic worms and crustaceans.

The female olm lays 12 to 70 eggs at a time. The eggs are deposited under a stone and guarded by both parents. They hatch in about 90 days. Some females may reproduce in a different manner, retaining a small number of eggs inside the body and giving birth to 2 fully developed young. The young are miniature versions of the parents but have rudimentary eyes.

Once a common species, the olm is now becoming rare because of water pollution in its restricted habitat and the taking of large numbers for the pet trade.

Mudpuppy *Necturus maculosus*

RANGE S. Canada: Manitoba to Quebec; USA: Great Lakes, south to Georgia and Louisiana

HABITAT Lakes, rivers, streams

SIZE 7¾–17 in (20–43 cm)

An aquatic salamander, the mudpuppy inhabits a variety of freshwater habitats, from muddy, sluggish shallows to cold, clear water. It has four toes on each limb and a flattened tail. Its feathery gills vary in size according to the water the individual inhabits: mudpuppies in cold, well-oxygenated water have shorter gills than those in warm, muddy, poorly oxygenated water, which need large, bushy gills in order to collect all the available oxygen. It hunts worms, crayfish, insects and small fish, mainly at night, but may sometimes catch fish during the day.

The breeding season is from April to June. The female lays between 30 and 190 eggs, each of which is stuck separately to a log or rock. The male guards the eggs until they hatch out about 5 to 9 weeks later. The larvae do not mature until they are 4 to 6 years old.

day in a burrow that it digs in the mud or takes over the burrow of another creature.

Congo eels mate in water, and the female lays about 200 eggs in a beadlike string. The female coils around the eggs as they lie on the bottom and protects them until they hatch about 5 months after being laid. When the larvae hatch, they are about 2 in (5 cm) long; their tiny limbs are of more use to them at this stage than when they metamorphose to adult form, at about 3 in (7.5 cm) long. The three-toed amphiuma, *Amphiuma trixlactylum*, also found in the southern United States, is similar in appearance and habits but has three toes on each of its tiny limbs.

PROTEIDAE: OLM AND MUDPUPPY FAMILY

There are 5 species of stream- and lake-dwelling mudpuppies in North America and 1 species of cave-dwelling olm in Europe. Because these amphibians live permanently in the water, they retain the external feathery gills throughout their lives, even into the adult breeding shape. They, therefore, resemble the larvae of other amphibians that do lose their gills when they become adult and leave water for at least part of the time.

Olm *Proteus anguinus* **VU**

RANGE Former Yugoslavia: E. Adriatic coast; N. E. Italy

HABITAT Streams and lakes in underground limestone caves

SIZE 7¾–11¾ in (20–30 cm)

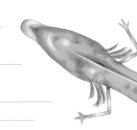

The olm is a large aquatic salamander with a pale cylindrical body and red feathery gills. Its tail is flattened and its limbs weak and poorly developed. It has three toes on the forelimbs and two on the hind limbs. It lives in total darkness in its cave home and is virtually blind,

LUNGLESS SALAMANDERS

PLETHODONTIDAE: LUNGLESS SALAMANDER FAMILY

This, the most successful group of living salamanders, includes over 200 of the 350 or so known tailed amphibians. As their name suggests, these salamanders are primarily characterized by their total absence of lungs. The pulmonary artery, which would normally take blood to the lungs, is reduced to minute proportions in a lungless salamander and runs in the body wall. The animal obtains oxygen instead across its moist skin or through the internal surface of the mouth cavity, both of which are well supplied with blood vessels.

Nearly all lungless salamanders live in North or South America. Two species occur in Europe – the cave salamanders which are found in Sardinia and mainland Italy. These forms can be distinguished from all other European salamanders by their partially webbed toes.

Texas Blind Salamander *Typhlomolge rathbuni* **VU**

RANGE USA: extreme S. Texas

HABITAT Underground waters of the creek system

SIZE 3½–5¼ in (9–13.5 cm)

This rare species has an extremely restricted distribution. The Texas blind salamander is a typical cave-dweller, with its ghostly pale body and much reduced eyes. Its external gills are red and feathery and it has long thin legs.

Many bats roost in the caves which are the only entrance to the salamanders' habitat. Nutrients in the droppings (guano) of these bats provide food for the invertebrate animals which inhabit the caves, and these creatures, many of which are themselves unique, are in turn eaten by the salamanders.

Nothing is known about the breeding habits of this species.

Red-backed Salamander *Plethodon cinereus*

RANGE S.E. Canada, N.E. USA, south to North Carolina, S. Indiana

HABITAT Cool, moist forest

SIZE 2½–5 in (6.5—12.5 cm)

This abundant, widespread salamander lives its whole life on land. The "red back" of its common name is, in fact, a stripe which may vary greatly from red to gray or yellow; some forms have gray bodies and lack the stripe altogether. It is nocturnal, hiding by day under stones or forest litter and emerging at night to search for insects and small invertebrates.

Breeding takes place every other year. The salamanders court and mate during the winter, and in June or July the female lays 6 to 12 eggs, which hang in a cluster in a crevice under a rock or in a rotten log. She coils herself around the eggs and protects them until they hatch 8 or 9 weeks later. The larvae do not have an aquatic stage and take 2 years to reach maturity.

Slimy Salamander *Plethodon glutinosus*

RANGE E. and S.E. USA: New York to Florida, Missouri, Oklahoma

HABITAT Floodplains, cave entrances

SIZE 4½–8 in (11.5–20.5 cm)

The slimy salamander's skin exudes a sticky substance that may be protective. By day, it hides under rocks or logs or in a burrow. At night it searches the forest floor for invertebrate prey.

Southern females breed every year and northern females only every other year, laying 6 to 36 eggs in a burrow or a rotten log and guarding them while they develop.

Spring Salamander *Gyrinophilus porphyriticus*

RANGE S. Canada: Quebec; USA: Maine, to Georgia, Mississippi

HABITAT Wet caves, cool, clear mountain springs

SIZE 4–8¾ in (10–22 cm)

The spring salamander occurs in several races, with variations of color and pattern. It spends most of its life in water but on rainy nights may come on to land to search for food. Large insects, worms and other salamanders are its main prey.

In July or August, the female lays 20 to 60 eggs, which are attached singly to the under-surfaces of submerged rocks. She guards the eggs until they hatch. Larvae do not attain adult form for about 3 years.

Red Salamander *Pseudotriton ruber*

RANGE E. USA: S. New York, west to Indiana, south to Louisiana

HABITAT Springs, surrounding woodland, swamps, meadows

SIZE 3¾–7 in (9.5–18 cm)

A brilliantly colored species, the red salamander has a stout body and short tail and legs. It spends much of its life on land but is usually in the vicinity of water. Earthworms, insects and small salamanders are its main foods.

After courting and mating in summer, the female red salamander lays a clutch of between 50 and 100 eggs in autumn. The larvae hatch about 2 months later and do not transform into the adult form until some 2 years later. Females first breed when they are 5 years old.

Yellow-blotched Salamander

Ensatina eschscholtzi croceator

RANGE USA: California

HABITAT Moist forest, canyons

SIZE 3–6 in (7.5–15 cm)

The yellow-blotched salamander is one of several subspecies of Ensatina with a wide variety of colors and patterns. All have the distinguishing feature of a tail which is constricted at its base. The male usually has a longer tail than the female.

A land-dwelling species, it shelters under rocks and logs, making forays in search of spiders and large insects such as beetles and crickets.

The female lays a clutch of between 7 and 25 eggs in spring or early summer in a burrow or rotting log. She guards the eggs while they develop. The larvae live on land and do not have an aquatic phase. They become mature at between 2 and 3 years old.

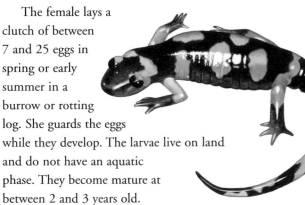

Dusky Salamander

Desmognathus fuscus

RANGE S. Canada; N.E. USA, south to Louisiana

HABITAT Springs, woodland creeks, floodplains

SIZE 2½–5½ in (6.5–14 cm)

Young dusky salamanders have pairs of yellow or red spots on the back but, as they mature, these fade or become obscured. The dusky salamander can jump well when alarmed, leaping several times its own length to escape an enemy. It feeds mainly on insect larvae and earthworms.

In summer, the female lays 12 to 36 eggs in a cluster near water, usually under a rock or log. The larvae hatch in 2 to 3 months and reach maturity in 3 to 4 years.

California Slender Salamander *Batrachoseps attenuatus*

RANGE USA: S.W. Oregon, California, western slopes of Sierra Nevada

HABITAT Redwood forest, grassland, mountains and foothills

SIZE 3–5½ in (7.5–14 cm)

True to its name, this salamander has a slim, elongate body and tail. Its legs and feet are tiny and narrow, with four toes on each foot. Coloration varies with area. The most common Californian salamander, it lives on land and moves with undulating movements of its body rather than by using its limbs. During the day, it hides in damp vegetation or among tree roots, and emerges at night to hunt for worms and spiders and other invertebrate prey. It is particularly active in rainy periods.

In late autumn or winter, stimulated by rainfall, the female lays 4 to 21 eggs under a rock or log. The eggs hatch in spring and the larvae do not undergo an aquatic phase.

MOLE SALAMANDERS AND DICAMPTODONTID SALAMANDERS

AMBYSTOMATIDAE: MOLE SALAMANDER FAMILY

There are about 32 species of mole salamander, all found in North America from Canada to Mexico. Typically, these salamanders have broad heads and a thick-bodied, sturdy appearance. Many species are ground-living, burrowing animals, rarely seen except in the breeding season when they migrate to ponds or streams to mate and lay eggs. Others have developed more aquatic habits and live in or near water most of the year. Larvae are aquatic and have feathery external gills and well-developed tail fins.

In most salamanders, the larvae remain permanently in the water while the adults spend at least part of the time on land. When the larva transforms into a mature, breeding adult, therefore, it loses such features as feathery external gills and the flattened tail, which are only useful in water. The mole salamander family is notable because some species can breed while still living in the water and still retaining these normally larval characteristics. This is known as neotenous breeding. Some geographical races of otherwise normal species are neotenous, for example, western forms of the North American tiger salamander, *Ambystoma tigrinum*, are neotenous, while the eastern relatives are normal.

Insects and small invertebrates are the main foods of all members of the family. Male and female mole salamanders look alike, but males usually have longer tails than females.

Spotted Salamander *Ambystoma maculatum*

RANGE S.E. Canada, E. USA to Georgia and E. Texas
HABITAT Hardwood forest, hillsides near pools
SIZE 6–9½ in (15–24 cm)

This stout-bodied salamander is identified by the irregular spots on its back, which run from head to tail. Rarely seen, it spends most of its life underground and feeds on slugs and worms.

In early spring, heavy rains stimulate the salamanders to migrate to breeding pools. The female lays about 100 eggs at a time, in a compact mass which adheres to submerged vegetation in the pond; she may lay more than one such mass. Some 4 to 8 weeks later, the eggs hatch into larvae ½ in (1.25 cm) long, which develop into adult form at 2 to 4 months. Spotted salamanders may live for 20 years.

In some areas these salamanders are becoming rare because acid rain is polluting their breeding ponds and preventing the successful development of eggs. Acid rain contains dilute sulfur and nitric acids from the gases released into the atmosphere by the burning of fossil fuels and is a source of increasing anxiety to biologists. In the temporary rain and snow pools used by salamanders for breeding, acidity is often extremely high, causing a high failure rate of eggs and severe deformities in those young that do survive.

Marbled Salamander *Ambystoma opacum*

RANGE E. USA: New Hampshire to Florida, west to Texas
HABITAT Woodland: swamp areas and drier, high ground
SIZE 3½–5 in (9–12.5 cm)

A dark-colored, stout species, the marbled salamander has some light markings that are the origin of its common name. The male's markings are brighter than the female's; juveniles are dark gray to brown with light flecks. The salamander emerges at night to hunt for slugs and worms but before morning hides under a log or stone where it remains for the day. Marbled salamanders breed from September to December, depending on latitude, and mate and nest on land. The female lays 50 to 200 eggs, one at a time in a dip on the ground that will later fill with rain. Until the rains come, the salamander curls itself round the eggs to protect them. The larvae hatch a few days after being covered by rain. If there is insufficient rainfall to fill the nest, the eggs may not hatch until the spring. Once hatched, the larvae develop adult form at between 4 and 6 months.

Tiger Salamander *Ambystoma tigrinum*

RANGE S. C. Canada, C. USA, south to N. Florida and Mexico

HABITAT Arid plains, damp meadows, mountain forest

SIZE 6–15¾ in (15–40 cm)

The world's largest land-dwelling salamander, the tiger salamander has a stout body, broad head and small eyes. Its coloration varies greatly, and it adapts to a variety of habitats, from sea level to 11,000 ft (3,350 m). Tiger salamanders live near water among plant debris or use crayfish or mammal burrows for refuge. They are often active at night and feed on earthworms, insects, mice and some small amphibians.

The timing of the breeding season varies according to area but it is usually prompted by rainfall. The salamanders mate in water and the female lays her eggs in masses which then adhere to submerged vegetation or debris.

Axolotl *Ambystoma mexicanum* **VU**

RANGE Mexico: Lake Xochimilco

HABITAT Permanent water at high altitude

SIZE Up to 11½ in (29 cm)

Now rare, the axolotl is threatened by the destruction of its habitat, the introduction of predatory fishes, such as carp, and the collection of specimens for the pet trade. It has a dorsal fin, which extends from the back of its head to the tip and round the underside of its long tail, and three pairs of feathery external gills. Its legs and feet are small and weak. The name "axolotl" is an Aztec word meaning water monster.

Axolotls breed in water. The female is attracted to the male by secretions of his abdominal glands which he fans in her direction with his tail. The female approaches and noses the male's glands. He then sheds his sperm in a small packet, known as a spermatophore, which sinks to the bottom of the water. The female settles over it and picks up the sperm packet with her cloaca (the external reproductive chamber) and is thus fertilized internally. In the wild, the axolotl lays about 400 eggs but may lay thousands in captivity.

Axolotls normally breed neotenously (in the larval state), retaining the gills and remaining in water. However, some individuals metamorphose into land-dwelling, gill-less adults.

DICAMPTODONTIDAE: DICAMPTODONTID SALAMANDERS

The four species in this family of semiaquatic salamanders are found in the coastal forests of western North America. Like the mole salamanders, members of this family also show some neoteny, although only one species, *Dicamptodon copei*, is permanently neotenous.

Pacific Giant Salamander *Dicamptodon ensatus*

RANGE Pacific coast of N. America: British Columbia to California; Idaho, Montana

HABITAT Cool, humid forest, rivers, streams and lakes

SIZE 2¾–11¾ in (7–30 cm)

This smooth-skinned salamander is unusual in that it can make a low-pitched cry – most salamanders are silent. Adults live on land under logs, rocks and forest debris and may even climb into trees and bushes. Mainly active at night, they feed on snails, slugs, insects, mice and small snakes, and other salamanders.

In spring, adults breed in water, usually in the headwaters of a spring, and the female lays about 100 eggs on a submerged branch. The larvae live in cold clear lakes or streams; they are predatory and eat smaller larvae, as well as tadpoles and insects.

They mature into adults in their second year or become sexually mature (neotenic) larvae when about 7¾ in (20 cm) long.

NEWTS AND SALAMANDERS

SALAMANDRIDAE: NEWT FAMILY

There are about 49 species of salamander and newt in this family, found in temperate regions of northwest Africa, Europe, Asia and North America. All have well-developed limbs with four or five digits and movable eyelids, adults have fully functional lungs and no external gills. There are both aquatic and terrestrial forms, but most are found in or near water, at least in the breeding season.

Sharp-ribbed Salamander *Pleurodeles waltl*

RANGE Portugal and Spain (except N. and N.E.), Morocco

HABITAT Slow rivers, ponds, ditches

SIZE 6–11¾ in (15–30 cm)

One of the largest European amphibians, the sharp-ribbed salamander has a stout body and a broad, flat head. Its skin is rough and there is a row of small protuberances along each side which lie at the tips of the ribs; the ribs are often distinct and may even protrude through the skin. A powerful swimmer, it is usually active at night when it searches for small invertebrate animals to eat.

A courting male carries his mate on his back in the water before depositing his package of sperm on the bottom. He then lowers the female on to the sperm and she collects it with her reproductive organ and is fertilized internally. She lays her eggs on a submerged stone.

Fire Salamander
Salamandra salamandra

RANGE Central, W. and S. Europe; N.W. Africa, parts of S.W. Asia

HABITAT Forest on hills and mountains

SIZE 7¾–11 in (20–28 cm)

A heavily built species with a rather short tail, the fire salamander has bright markings, which may be in the form of spots or stripes. These markings provide warning to potential predators of the salamander's unpleasant body secretions, which irritate the mouth and eyes of enemies and may even be fatal to small mammals. Although a land-dweller, it prefers moist areas and is seldom far from water. It emerges from daytime refuges to hunt for its invertebrate prey at night.

Fire salamanders mate on land. The male carries the female around on his back, then deposits his sperm package on the ground and lowers her on to it. She collects the sperm with her reproductive organ and is fertilized internally. The eggs develop inside the female's body and about 10 months after fertilization she gives birth to 10 to 50 live young in the water.

Warty/Great crested Newt *Triturus cristatus* **LR:cd**

RANGE Europe (not S. and S.W. France, Iberia, Ireland or S. Greece)

HABITAT Still or slow water, woodland

SIZE 5½–7 in (14–18 cm)

A large, rough-skinned newt, the male warty newt develops a jagged crest on his back in the breeding season. Females are often larger than males, but do not develop crests. Warty newts eat invertebrates. They will also take some small fish and other amphibians and their eggs.

The courting male performs an energetic display for his mate then deposits his sperm, over which the female either walks or is led, and which she collects with her reproductive organ. She lays between 200 and 300 eggs, one at a time, which hatch out after 4 or 5 months.

Eastern Newt
Notophthalmus viridescens

RANGE S.E. Canada, E. USA: Great Lakes area to Florida and Texas

HABITAT Ponds and lakes with vegetation, ditches, swamps

SIZE 2½–5½ in (6.5–14 cm)

The eastern newt occurs in several different patterns and colors over its wide range. Adults are aquatic and are eager predators, searching in shallow water for worms, insects, crustaceans and the eggs and young of other amphibians.

The breeding season begins in late winter or early spring. The female lays from 200 to 400 eggs, one at a time, on submerged plants and, after an incubation of up to 2 months, the eggs hatch into larvae. In later summer, these larvae transform into subadults, known as efts, and leave the water to spend up to 3 years living on land and feeding primarily on insects. They then return to the water and become mature, fully developed adults.

Rough-skinned Newt

Taricha granulosa

RANGE W. North America: Alaska to California

HABITAT Ponds, lakes, slow streams and surrounding grassland or woodland

SIZE 2½–5 in (6.5–12.5 cm)

The most aquatic of Pacific newts, the rough-skinned newt is identified by its warty skin and its small eyes with dark lower lids. It searches for its invertebrate prey both on land and in the water, and its toxic skin secretions repel most of its enemies.

In the breeding season, the male's skin temporarily becomes smooth and his vent swells. Unlike other western newts, the female rough-skinned lays her eggs one at a time, rather than in masses, on submerged plants or debris. The eggs hatch into aquatic larvae.

CRYPTOBRANCHIDAE: GIANT SALAMANDER FAMILY

This family contains the largest amphibians alive in the world today. Only 3 species are known – the Chinese and Japanese giant salamanders and the hellbender of the eastern USA. The Asiatic giant salamanders can reach lengths of over 5 ft (1.5 m).

Hellbender *Cryptobranchus alleganiensis*

RANGE E. USA: S. New York to N. Alabama, Missouri

HABITAT Rocky-bottomed streams

SIZE 12–29 in (30.5–74 cm)

Despite the implications of its common name, this giant salamander is a harmless creature which feeds on crayfish, snails and worms. It has the flattened head characteristic of its family and loose flaps of skin along the lower sides of its body.

A nocturnal salamander, the hellbender hides under rocks in the water during the day. It depends on its senses of smell and touch, rather than on sight, to find its prey, since its eyes are set so far down the sides of its head that it cannot focus on an object with both eyes at once.

Hellbenders breed in autumn – the male makes a hollow beneath a rock or log on the stream bed and the female lays strings of 200 to 500 eggs. As she lays the eggs, the male fertilizes them and then guards the nest until the eggs hatch 2 or 3 months later.

HYNOBIIDAE: ASIATIC LAND SALAMANDER FAMILY

The 35 species in this family are considered the most primitive of living salamanders. All occur in central and eastern Asia.

Asian/Amber-colored Salamander

Hynobius stejnegeri **DD**

RANGE Japan

HABITAT Mountain streams

SIZE 5½ in (14 cm)

Like all members of its family, the Asian salamander's methods of breeding are primitive, involving external fertilization. The female lays her eggs in water in paired sacs, each sac containing 35 to 70 eggs. The male then takes the sacs and fertilizes the eggs but shows no interest in the female.

CAECILIANS

ORDER GYMNOPHONIA

This order contains 6 families of caecilians, over 170 species in all. Caecilians are limbless amphibians with cylindrical, ringed bodies and resemble giant earthworms. One family is aquatic, but the others are blind, burrowing creatures, rarely seen above ground. They burrow into the rich, soft soil of tropical or warm temperate forests in search of their prey, usually earthworms, insects and other invertebrates. Adults have a sensory tentacle beneath each eye which is probably used for finding prey. Many species have small scales embedded in the surface of the skin. This is probably a primitive feature which all other amphibian groups have since lost.

ICHTHYOPHIDAE

There are 43 species in this family of terrestrial caecilians, found in Southeast Asia, Central America and tropical South America. They have short tails and scales on the body.

Sticky Caecilian *Ichthyophis sp.*

RANGE	S.E. Asia
HABITAT	Forest
SIZE	Up to 15 in (38 cm)

Adult caecilians of this Southeast Asian genus live in burrows and feed on earthworms and small burrowing snakes. They breed in the spring. The female lays 20 or more eggs in a burrow she makes in moist ground near to water. She coils around her eggs while they develop, in order to protect them from predators. As they incubate, the eggs absorb moisture and gradually swell until they are double their original size. On hatching, the larva is four times the weight of a newly laid egg and has a pair of breathing pores on its head. The larvae undergo a prolonged aquatic phase before becoming land-based adults.

SCOLECOMORPHIDAE

The 6 species of caecilian in this family are all of the same genus and occur only in central Africa. They are tailless and have no primitive body scales. All species live on land in burrows.

Scolecomorphus kirkii

RANGE	Africa: Tanzania, Malawi, Zambia
HABITAT	Mountain forest
SIZE	Up to 16½ in (41 cm)

This caecilian lives in burrows it digs under the leaf mold on the forest floor. Unlike other caecilians, it does not even come to the surface after rain. Termites and worms are its main foods.

Little is known of the breeding habits of this family. The male has a protrusible copulatory organ, and the female probably retains her eggs, which then develop inside her body like those of the Typhlonectes species, and hatch in an advanced state of development.

CAECILIAIDAE: CAECILIAN FAMILY

There are 90 species in this family, all of which are land-dwelling burrowers. Many species have scales on the body. Females reproduce either by laying eggs, which develop and hatch outside the body, or by producing eggs, which are retained to develop and hatch inside the body, and are then born as live young. The young have external gills and may spend some time as free-swimming larvae. Species occur in Old and New World tropics.

Panamanian Caecilian *Caecilia ochrocephala*

RANGE	Central and South America: E. Panama, N. Colombia
HABITAT	Forest
SIZE	Up to 24 in (61 cm)

The Panamanian caecilian has a small slender head and a wedge-shaped snout. It burrows into soft, usually moist earth and seldom appears above ground except when heavy rains flush

it from its burrow. It eats mainly insects and earthworms. Snakes often enter the burrows of these caecilians and devour them.

Little is known of the breeding habits of this rarely seen creature, but females are thought to lay eggs which then develop and hatch outside the body.

South American Caecilian *Siphonops annulatus*

RANGE South America, east of Andes to Argentina

HABITAT Varied, often forest

SIZE 13¾ in (35 cm)

This widespread caecilian has a short thick body and no scales. It spends most of its life underground and feeds largely on earthworms. The female lays eggs, but it is not known whether the young pass through a larval stage.

São Tomé Caecilian

Schistometopum thomensis

RANGE São Tomé Island in Gulf of Guinea, off W. Africa

HABITAT Forest

SIZE Up to 12 in (30.5 cm)

The body of this brightly colored caecilian is usually about ½ in (1.25 cm) in diameter. Its snout is rounded and it has no tail. It lives underground, feeding on whatever invertebrate prey it can find, mainly on insects and worms. The female retains her eggs in her body where they develop and hatch; the young are then born in an advanced state of development.

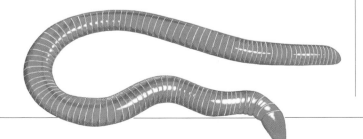

Seychelles Caecilian *Hgpogeophis rostratus*

RANGE Seychelles

HABITAT Swampy coastal regions

SIZE 7½ in (20 cm)

The Seychelles caecilian has a slightly flattened body which tapers at both ends. The body darkens as the caecilian matures. It burrows wherever the soil is moist. It often lives beneath rocks or logs or digs into rotting trees. It eats small invertebrates and frogs.

Mating takes place at any time of year when there is plenty of rain. The female lays 6 to 30 eggs and coils her body around them to guard them. The young do not have a larval stage, but hatch as miniature adults.

TYPHLONECTIDAE

There are 18 species of aquatic caecilian in this family, all found in tropical South America. They live in freshwater. Although they have no tails, the end of the body is laterally flattened for propulsion in water. This family lacks the primitive body scales, present in other families.

Typhlonectes compressicauda

RANGE Guianas, Brazil

HABITAT Rivers, streams, pools

SIZE 20½ in (52 cm)

This aquatic caecilian swims with eellike movements of its compressed tail. The sexes look similar, but the male has a protrusible copulatory organ with which he fertilizes his mate internally. The female retains her eggs inside her body while the young develop. Having eaten all the yolk that surrounds them in their eggs, the young hatch and distribute themselves along the mother's oviduct. They feed on cells and drops of oil from the uterine wall which they obtain with the rasping plates in their mouths. More nutrients are obtained through the thin delicate skin which the young possess; they also have broad, baglike, external gills which disappear before they hatch. When the young are born; their thin skin is replaced by firmer, stronger skin, and the rasping plates by teeth.

FISHES

The first vertebrates.

Imperial Angelfish

MORE THAN 45,000 OR SO KNOWN SPECIES OF VERTEBRATE ANIMALS ARE FISHES, WHICH IN THEIR AQUATIC ENVIRONMENT HAVE EVOLVED INTO A HUGE RANGE OF SPECIALIZED FORMS, AT LEAST AS DIVERSE AS THAT OF FOUR-LEGGED ANIMALS. THE FIRST MAJOR DIVISION IN THIS GROUP IS BETWEEN JAWLESS AND JAWED FISHES, WITH THE FORMER GROUP TODAY CONSISTING OF ONLY LAMPREYS AND HAGFISHES, REMNANTS OF AN EARLY STAGE OF VERTEBRATE EVOLUTION. THE JAWED FISHES, WHICH AROSE JUST UNDER 400 MILLION YEARS AGO, ARE THEMSELVES DIVIDED INTO VASTLY DIFFERING GROUPS. FIRST ARE THE CARTILAGE-SKELETONED FISH (CHONDRICHTHYES) SUCH AS SHARKS, SKATES AND RAYS, RATFISH, RABBITFISH AND ELEPHANTFISH. SECOND, THERE ARE THREE MAIN TYPES OF BONY-SKELETONED FISHES: THE RAY-FINNED FISHES, WITH NARROW-BASED FINS AND FIN RAYS WHICH SUPPORT THEM (ACTINOPTERYGIAN FISHES); AND TWO TYPES OF FLESHY- OR LOBE-FINNED FISHES, NAMELY, THE LUNGFISHES AND THE COELACANTHIMORPHS, REPRESENTED TODAY ONLY BY THE COELACANTH (LATIMERIA).

Lampreys and hagfishes, like the earliest vertebrates before them, have no jaws. They have only the most rudimentary vertebrae and cylindrical bodies, with small unpaired fins at the rear end. Only about 30 species of lamprey and 32 of hagfish survive today. The former are found in the cool areas of the world both in the sea and in fresh water; the latter are marine fishes of worldwide distribution. Lampreys live parasitically on other fishes, hanging on to their outer surfaces with a sharply toothed sucker that bears a small mouth and a rasping tongue at its center. The lamprey uses its tongue to make a wound in the host's body and then feeds on its blood. Larval lampreys are bottom-dwelling filter-feeders, and lamprey life cycles sometimes involve both marine and freshwater stages. Hagfishes are an entirely marine group, and although well known as scavengers which suck out the body contents of dead or dying fishes, they feed mainly on crustaceans and worms.

Both lampreys and hagfishes swim by lateral undulations of the body, produced by the contractions of repeating blocks of muscles along the flanks. These simplest living vertebrates possess what is basically a prototype of the water-breathing gill apparatus used by all higher fishes. The side walls of the pharynx are perforated to provide gill openings from the gut cavity to the outside world; there are seven such openings on each side in lampreys. Because of the lamprey's sucker, respiratory water cannot usually pass through the mouth. Instead, when the sucker is in action, water passes both in and out through the gill openings and oxygenates the blood, which is pumped from the heart to the gills through 8 pairs of

Conger Eel

Piranha

branchial arteries.

Despite their superficial similarities, lampreys and hagfishes are very different. Some biologists even exclude hagfishes from the vertebrates altogether and place them within a separate group within the chordates.

The cartilaginous fishes, of which about 850 species are known, are marine fishes, which vary in size between the huge sharks of more than 49 ft (15 m) in length and tiny forms about 11¾ in (30 cm) long. Most are active predators on other fish and are equipped with sharp-edged teeth in both jaws. Although their skeletons are made of cartilage, not bone, these fishes conform to the orthodox body plan of jawed fishes, with paired fins and proper vertebrae. The body is beautifully streamlined, with the greatest width some way down it, a pointed anterior end and a tapering rear part, terminating in a two-vaned propulsive tail. This is moved from side to side, using muscles similar to those which produce undulations of the body in the jawless fishes.

In many cartilaginous fishes the upper vane of the tail is larger than the lower one, and the front pair of paired fins, the pectorals, act as winglike control surfaces for changing directions. Like the large, unpaired dorsal fins, they also provide directional stability against rolling, pitching and yawing when the fish is swimming. Cartilaginous fishes have between 5 and 7 pairs of gill slits, opening to the outside world, on each side of the head. Typically the respiratory current passes in through the mouth and out through the gill slits.

There are 24,000 or so species of bony fish – about half the known total of living vertebrate species – and, unlike the cartilaginous fishes, they thrive in fresh as well as salt water. The body plan of these successful animals is similar to that of the cartilaginous fishes, but with some crucial changes. The skeleton, including the fin rays, is made of bone; the tail vanes are characteristically, but not always, equal in size, and there is often a gas-filled swim-bladder in the body for buoyancy control. This can be adjusted to make the fish weightless in the water so that it can rest or stay motionless – a great advance over the cartilaginous fishes, which must keep moving or sink. There is also a difference in the gill system. In bony fishes there are usually four respiratory gills on each side of the pharynx, but the openings associated with them are enclosed by a large flap, the operculum, which effectively produces a single, ultimate opening on each side of the fish. The bodies of most bony fishes are covered with overlapping scales, set in the skin, which form a protective armor.

Bony fishes feed in a wide variety of ways and fill every underwater feeding niche. Some are herbivorous, living on aquatic vegetation and microscopic plant plankton. Others catch small invertebrate animals or strain them from the water by means of gill rakers, comblike structures attached to the gill bars. Still others are active, fast-moving predators, equipped with sharp teeth; while species such as flatfishes and angler fishes rely on their camouflage to keep them hidden while they lie in wait for prey.

Many fishes reproduce by simply shedding vast numbers of eggs into the water, where they are fertilized by the male depositing sperm on to them. There is rarely any parental care, and although most eggs hatch, few survive to maturity. Some

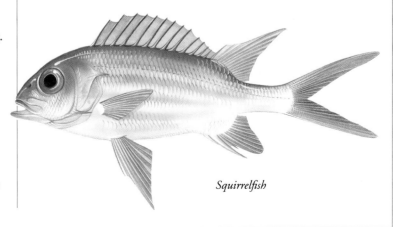

Squirrelfish

male fishes, notably sharks, fertilize their mates internally and have clasping organs, developed from modified pelvic fins, which help them hold the female while depositing sperm in her genital opening. These internally-fertilized females may retain their eggs and developing young inside the body and give birth to fully formed young.

Most bony fishes are marine and freshwater forms of actinopterygians (ray-finned fishes), but there is also the single marine genus of lobe-finned coelacanth and the 3 surviving genera of lungfishes that all live in fresh water. Lungfishes

Sheepshead

Cladogram showing possible phylogenetic relationships in fishes. Although we use the term "fish" to refer to any fish-shaped aquatic vertebrate, the term in fact covers a diverse assortment of vertebrates that have arisen along different evolutionary pathways.

KEY TO FISH CLADOGRAM A

1 Myxini (hagfishes)
2 Cephalaspidomorphi (lampreys)
3 Chondrichthyes (cartilaginous fish)
4 Actinopterygii (ray-finned fishes)
5 Coelacanthiformes (coelacanth)
6 Dipnoi (lungfishes)
7 Tetrapoda (land vertebrates)

CLADOGRAM A

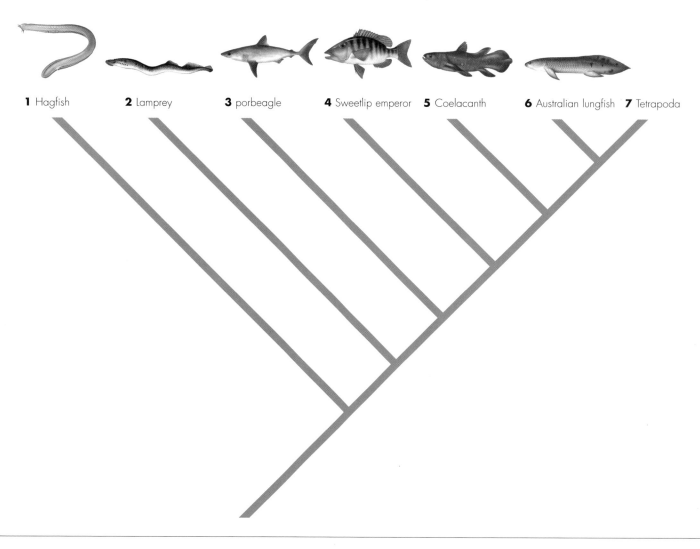

1 Hagfish   **2** Lamprey   **3** porbeagle   **4** Sweetlip emperor   **5** Coelacanth   **6** Australian lungfish   **7** Tetrapoda

breathe air, and most make burrows, in which they live when the rivers and lakes of their tropical habitats seasonally dry up. In these fishes the swimbladder is connected to the gut cavity via a tube and operates as an air-breathing lung.

The huge number of fish species and the proportionately large number of fish families have made it impossible to treat them in the family-focused format of the rest of this book. Consequently the section on fishes is completely comprehensive at order level, but with mention of families only in the largest orders.

Clown Triggerfish

Cladogram showing possible phylogenetic relationships in the Actinopterygii (ray-finned fishes). Bony fishes form the largest of all fish groups, and most bony fishes are ray-finned. There are two evolutionary groups within the Actinopterygii: the Chondrostei, which include the bichirs and sturgeons and the Neopterygii, the more advanced group that includes most modern bony fishes. Apart from the gars and bowfins, most fish in this group belong to the Teleostei, the group that contains the dominant bony fishes.

CLADOGRAM B

KEY TO FISH CLADOGRAM B

1 Polypteriformes (bichirs)
2 Acipenseriformes (sturgeons)
3 Lepisosteiformes (gars)
4 Amiiformes (bowfin)
5 Osteoglossiformes (bony-tongues)
6 Elopomorpha (eels)
7 Clupeimorpha (herrings)

8 Ostariophysi (carps, catfish)
9 Protacanthopterygii (pikes, salmon)
10 Stenopterygii (cods, anglerfishes)
11 Atheriniformes (flying fishes, silversides)
12 Percomorpha (perch, mullets)

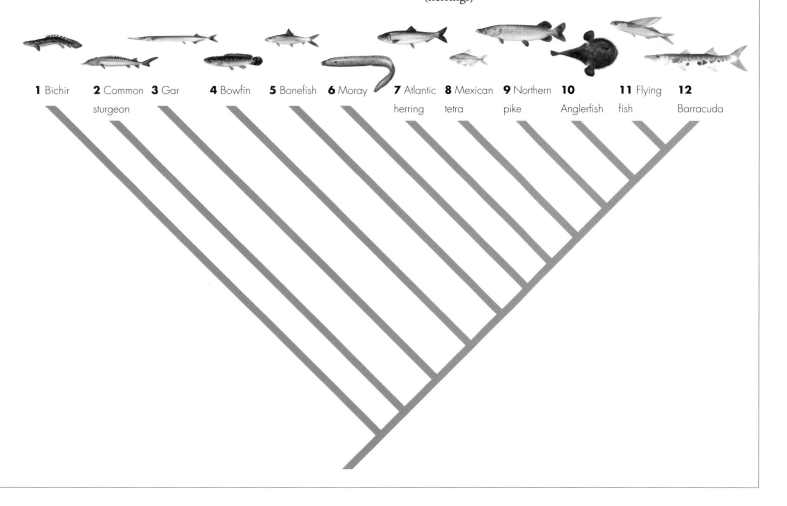

1 Bichir 2 Common sturgeon 3 Gar 4 Bowfin 5 Bonefish 6 Moray 7 Atlantic herring 8 Mexican tetra 9 Northern pike 10 Anglerfish 11 Flying fish 12 Barracuda

HAGFISH, LAMPREYS AND SHARKS

MYXINIFORMES: HAGFISH ORDER

The 43 species of hagfishes make up the only living family in this order. They are all marine and occur in temperate and subtropical waters of the Atlantic, Indian and Pacific Oceans. They are jawless fishes and have slitlike mouths surrounded with fleshy filaments. Some zoologists do not regard hagfish as vertebrates because they lack vertebrae, placing them instead in their own chordate subphyllum.

Hagfish *Myxine glutinosa*

RANGE	N. Atlantic, Arctic Oceans
HABITAT	Ocean bed
SIZE	24 in (61 cm)

Hagfishes live in fairly deep water where there is a soft muddy bottom into which they can burrow. They have no paired fins nor scales; their eyes are hidden under skin and they are almost blind. The surface of the skin is particularly slimy since it is copiously supplied with mucus-secreting glands.

Hagfishes feed on some marine worms and crustaceans, but they are best known for attacking dead and dying fish, or fish that are trapped in nets. Using the toothlike plates on the tongue and the single tooth in the mouth, the hagfish bores into the prey's body and eats away all its flesh and intestines, leaving only skin and bone.

PETROMYZONIFORMES: LAMPREY ORDER

This order includes only 1 family, the lampreys, with about 41 species. All are primitive fishes which have no true jaws, but only sucking, funnellike mouths lined with small teeth. Many are parasitic and live on the blood of other fishes. Some are freshwater species, others are anadromous – they live in salt water but travel to fresh water in order to spawn. Most lampreys occur in the northern hemisphere, but there are some species which occur in and around southern South America, south Australia and New Zealand.

River Lamprey/Lampern *Lampetra fluviatilis* **LR:nt**

RANGE	Britain, N.W. Europe
HABITAT	Rivers, coastal waters
SIZE	11¾–20 in (30–50 cm)

The parasitic lampern feeds on the blood of other fishes. It attaches itself to the host's body by its round suckerlike mouth and rasps away the skin and scales with its sharp teeth.

At spawning time, lamperns leave the coast and migrate upriver. They lay their eggs in spring in shallow pits excavated in the river bed. The larvae hatch then move downstream and bury themselves in mud. They stay her for up to 5 years, filter-feeding on microorganisms until they reach maturity.

Sea Lamprey *Petromyzon marinus*

RANGE	Atlantic coasts of Europe and N. America; W. Mediterranean Sea
HABITAT	Coastal waters, rivers
SIZE	35½ in (90 cm)

Adult sea lampreys are blood-feeding parasites. The lamprey attaches itself to its victim so firmly that it is almost impossible to remove. A secretion in the lamprey's mouth prevents the host's blood from clotting, allowing the lamprey to feed. Victims often die from blood loss or from infection of the wound.

Adults leave the sea and travel up into rivers to spawn. They make a shallow pit in a stony-bottomed area by moving stones with their mouths, the eggs are deposited in this nest. The blind, toothless larvae live buried in mud, filter-feeding for 4 to 6 years, until as juveniles, they migrate to the sea. Lampreys also occur in inland lakes where they prey on commercial fish, but efforts are made to control their numbers in such waters.

HETERODONTIFORMES: BULLHEAD SHARK ORDER

This is a small order containing one family of 8 primitive species of shark, found in the tropical Indian and Pacific Oceans. All have two dorsal fins preceded by a thick spine.

Port Jackson Shark

Heterodontus portusjacksoni

RANGE S. Pacific Ocean, Southern Ocean: coasts of Australia
from S. Queensland to S.W. Western Australia

HABITAT Coastal waters to depths of 600 ft (180 m)

SIZE Up to 5 ft (1.5 m)

The Port Jackson shark has the large, heavy head, prominent forehead and ridge over each eye that are typical of all bullhead sharks. Other characteristic features are the dark-brown markings encircling its grayish-brown body and the stout spines in front of each dorsal fin. The shark's small mouth has sharp, pointed teeth at the front and broader, crushing teeth farther back, suggesting that it eats hardshelled items such as mollusks and crustaceans. Most feeding takes place at night.

Year after year, these sharks are believed to migrate to the same shallow, reef areas to breed. Like all bullheads they are egg-laying, producing eggs protected by strong, horny cases with spirally twisted edges. This formation helps the egg-case to lodge in a rock crevice, where it remains until the young shark hatches out.

LAMNIFORMES: LAMNIFORM SHARK ORDER

This order contains 7 families of sharks, 16 species in all. Lamniformes have skeletons made of cartilage. Almost all these species have two dorsal fins, one anal fin and five gill slits.

Sand Tiger *Odontaspis taurus*

RANGE Atlantic Ocean: N. American and African coasts

HABITAT Coastal waters

SIZE 10½ ft (3.2 m)

The sand tiger is a predatory shark which tends to live at the bottom of shallow water, feeding on fish. It has characteristic yellow spots on its body, and dorsal, pelvic and anal fins are much the same size. Its long pointed teeth project forward noticeably. The female gives birth to 2 young which develop inside her body for 12 months while feeding on the yolks of unfertilized eggs. The young are about 39 in (1 m) long at birth.

A similar species, the raggedtooth shark, *O. ferox*, is found in the Mediterranean and off European Atlantic coasts, as well as the Pacific coast of the USA.

Thresher Shark *Alopias vulpinus*

RANGE Temperate and tropical oceans

HABITAT Surface waters in open sea

SIZE 19½ ft (6 m)

The distinctive thresher shark has a tail as long as the rest of its body which it uses to advantage when hunting. The sharks feed mainly on schooling fish and, working in pairs or alone, they lash their tails to herd the fish into a compact mass where they make easy prey. A thresher may also strike and stun an individual fish with its tail. Threshers sometimes hunt in coastal waters, particularly in summer, when they are seen along the American Atlantic coast.

Females give birth to litters of 2 to 4 fully formed young, which may be as long as 5 ft (1.5 m) at birth.

In Australian waters, the thresher shark is known by different scientific names – *A. caudatus* and *A. grayi*.

Basking Shark *Cetorhinus maximus* **VU**

RANGE Worldwide, outside the tropics

HABITAT Oceanic

SIZE 34 ft (10.4 m)

The basking shark is the second-largest living species of fish. It shares the streamlined body shape of other sharks but is distinguished by its extra large gill slits. It feeds entirely on plankton which it sieves from the water by means of comblike bristles on its gill arches. The shark simply swims with its mouth agape, taking in a vast quantity of water and plankton and filtering it through the gill slits. As the name implies, basking sharks often float sluggishly at the surface of the water.

Little is known of the basking shark's breeding habits, but its eggs are believed to develop inside its body, hatching as they are expelled. The young sharks are about 5 ft (1.5 m) long at birth.

SHARKS CONTINUED

Porbeagle *Lamna nasus* **VU**

RANGE N. Atlantic Ocean: Newfoundland, south to South Carolina, Iceland, south to N. Africa; Mediterranean Sea

HABITAT Open sea; coastal waters

SIZE 6–9¾ ft (1.8–3 m)

The porbeagle is a swift-swimming, heavy-bodied shark with five gill slits. It feeds on surface-dwelling fish, such as mackerel and herring, and on squid and some bottom-dwelling fish. Identifying characteristics are the position of the dorsal fin (above the base of the pectoral fin) and of the second dorsal fin (directly above the anal fin). This species and the related sharks (mako and great white) have body temperatures higher than the surrounding water, an adaptation linked with great muscular activity that improves their swimming efficiency.

The eggs hatch inside the mother and remain there for a short time before she gives birth to fully formed live young. Litters usually contain 1 to 5 young, which are sustained for a few weeks by the yolks of unfertilized eggs that they eat before birth.

The closely related salmon shark, *L. ditropis*, which lives in the Pacific, is similar to the porbeagle both in its appearance and habits.

Mako *Isurus oxyrinchus*

RANGE Atlantic, Pacific and Indian Oceans: temperate and tropical areas

HABITAT Open sea

SIZE 9¾–13 ft (3–4 m)

A powerful, streamlined shark, with a slender body and a pointed snout, the mako is a fast-swimming predator. Distinguishing features are the slightly rounded tip to the first dorsal fin, which is positioned in line with the rear edge of the base of the pectoral fin, and the small second dorsal fin, positioned just in front of the anal fin. The mako is usually deep blue above and white below.

An active surface-dweller itself, the mako usually feeds on surface-living fish, such as tuna, mackerel, herrings and sardines, and on squid.

It is renowned for its habit of leaping clear of the water, and, although known to be dangerous and aggressive, the mako is a popular sporting fish with shark fishermen because of the spectacular struggle that it puts up and the leaps it performs when it is hooked.

The female mako gives birth to live young, which develop and hatch inside her body.

White Shark *Carcharodon carcharias* **VU**

RANGE Atlantic, Pacific and Indian Oceans: warm temperate and tropical coastal areas

HABITAT Open sea; seasonally enters coastal waters

SIZE 19¾ ft (6 m)

The white shark, also known as the great white shark, is not actually white, but ranges in color from gray to brown with white underparts. Its long snout is pointed, and its large, powerful teeth are triangular and serrated. The top lobe of its tail is slightly longer than the lower lobe.

It feeds on a variety of aquatic animals, such as fish (including other sharks), seals and dolphins, and it also scavenges on dead animals and refuse. This is an extremely large and aggressive fish, and it has acquired the formidable reputation of a maneater and has, indeed, been involved in many attacks on humans.

Little is known of its breeding habits other than that it bears litters of up to 9 live young.

CARCHARINIFORMES: REQUIEM SHARK ORDER

With 210 species in 8 families, the requiem or ground sharks make up more than half of the 350 shark species. Many of the order have the "typical" shark shape.

Bull Shark *Carcharhinus leucas*

RANGE W. Atlantic Ocean: North Carolina to S. Brazil

HABITAT Inshore waters, rivers and connecting lakes

SIZE 8¼–11½ ft (2.5–3.5 m)

The bull shark has a chunky body, with the first dorsal fin placed well forward. Normally quite slow-moving, it is usually found in shallow water and regularly swims into rivers. Bull sharks eat a wide range of fish, including rays and small sharks, and they also eat shrimps, crabs, sea-urchins and refuse.

The female produces live young, generally born from May to July in brackish, inshore waters.

Smooth Hammerhead *Sphyrna zygaena*

RANGE Atlantic, Pacific and Indian Oceans: tropical and warm temperate areas

HABITAT Coastal and inshore waters

SIZE 14 ft (4.3 m)

This is one of 10 species of hammerhead shark, all of which have flattened projections at the sides of the head. The eyes are on the outer edges of these lobes, and the nostrils also are spread far apart. The advantages of this head shape are not clear, but it may be that the shark gains some improvement of its sensory abilities by the spacing out of eyes and nostrils, or that the head shape improves manoeuvrability or simply increases lift.

The smooth hammerhead feeds on fish, particularly rays, and also scavenges on occasion. In summer, it makes regular migrations to cooler waters. Hammerheads have been known to attack man, and are thought to be aggressive sharks.

Sandy Dogfish *Scyliorhinus canicula*

RANGE N. Atlantic Ocean: coasts of Norway, Britain, Europe, N. Africa; Mediterranean Sea

HABITAT Sandy or gravel bottoms

SIZE 23½ in–3¼ ft (60 cm–1 m)

A common fish, the sandy dogfish is one of a family of 60 species of small, shallow-water sharks. Its dorsal fins are placed well back toward the tail, which is long, with the lower lobe barely developed. Usually light sandy-brown in color, this dogfish is boldly marked with dark-brown spots and has a creamy or white belly. Primarily a bottom-dweller, it occurs in shallow water to depths of 330 ft (100 m), but may sometimes be found in deeper water, down to 1,300 ft (400 m). Its diet consists of many types of bottom-living invertebrates as well as fish.

Reproduction may take place throughout the year, but in the northern hemisphere most eggs are laid between November and July. The female deposits her eggs, each of which is encased in a horny capsule with tendrils at each corner, among seaweed in shallow water. The tendrils anchor the eggcase to weeds or other objects, where it remains for 5 to 11 months. The newly hatched young are 4 in (10 cm) long; they are sexually mature when about 19¾ in (50 cm) long.

Blue Shark *Prionace glauca*

RANGE Atlantic, Pacific and Indian Oceans: temperate and tropical areas

HABITAT Open sea, surface waters

SIZE 9–12½ ft (2.7–3.8 m)

A slender, elongate fish, the blue shark is easily distinguished by its long pectoral fins, pointed snout and bright coloration. It feeds on a range of surface-dwelling fish, such as mackerel, herring and pilchard, and on squid. It will also eat waste thrown from fishing boats.

Females give birth to live young, and litters of as many as 50 to 60 at a time have been reported. Blue sharks make regular migrations to warmer waters in the winter months.

SHARKS CONTINUED

ORECTOLOBIFORMES: CARPET SHARK ORDER

This diverse order of sharks contains 31 species in 7 families including the bottom-dwelling wobbegongs and the whale shark, the largest of all fishes.

Whale Shark *Rhincodon typus* **DD**

RANGE All tropical seas

HABITAT Surface waters

SIZE 50 ft (15.2 m)

The huge whale shark is the largest living fish, growing up to 60 ft (18 m) long. It eats small fish and plankton which it filters from the water. The shark opens its mouth to take in a rush of water. The water is filtered out through the gills and plankton is retained. Little is known of this species' breeding habits.

SQUATINIFORMES: ANGEL SHARK ORDER

The 13 species of angel sharks look more like rays because they are flattened. Unlike rays, the large pectoral fins are not attached to the head.

Monkfish *Squatina squatina*

RANGE North Sea; E. Atlantic Ocean: Scotland to N. Africa and Canary Islands; Mediterranean Sea

HABITAT Coastal waters, seabed

SIZE 6 ft (1.8 m)

The monkfish appears to be almost a cross between a shark and a ray, but the gills, positioned at the sides, the mouth at the end of its head and well-developed dorsal fins all reveal it to be a true shark (rays have mouth and gill slits positioned on their undersides). Its broad pectoral fins strongly resemble those of rays. Female monkfishes are larger than males.

The monkfish lies almost buried in sand or mud much of the time, but it can swim well. It feeds on bottom-living fish, such as dab plaice, sole and rays, and on crabs and mollusks. It bears live young, in litters of 9 to 20, from eggs which develop and hatch inside the mother.

HEXANCHIFORMES: COW AND FRILL SHARK ORDER

The 5 species in this order are all primitive sharks, with long bodies and only one dorsal fin. All have six or seven pairs of gill slits – sharks generally have only five pairs. Most are deep-sea species, and relatively little is known of their habits.

Bluntnose Six-gilled Shark *Hexanchus griseus* **VU**

RANGE Atlantic, Pacific and Indian Oceans: temperate and warm temperate areas

HABITAT Open sea, inshore waters

SIZE 6–16½ ft (1.8–5 m)

An elongate shark, with a long tail fin and one dorsal fin positioned near the tail, this species has six pairs of gills.

Although apparently fairly sedentary and sluggish, it is a powerful shark and feeds on a wide range of bottom-living fish, such as rays, as well as on crustaceans. It is thought to mate in spring; the eggs develop and hatch inside the mother, and the young are 18 to 24 in (46 to 61 cm) long when they are born. There are often 40 or more in a litter, depending on the size of the female.

SQUALIFORMES: SQUALIFORM SHARK ORDER

This order includes 74 species of shark in 3 families – dogfish sharks, bramble sharks and sleeper sharks. All have two dorsal fins, no anal fin and five or six pairs of gill slits. The species occur worldwide, and the order contains the world's smallest sharks.

Spurdog/Spiny dogfish *Squalus acanthias*

RANGE N. Atlantic Ocean: coasts of Norway, Britain to N. Africa, W. Greenland to Florida; Mediterranean Sea; N. Pacific Ocean

HABITAT Inshore waters, near seabed

SIZE 3¼–4 ft (1–1.2 m)

A common shark, which is easily identified by the large spine in front of each dorsal fin, the spurdog has a long, slender body, a pointed snout and large eyes. Females are longer and heavier than males and do not become sexually mature until they reach 19 or 20 years of age. Males mature at 11 years.

Spurdogs feed on schooling fish, such as herrings and whiting, and on bottom-living fish and invertebrates. They themselves move in schools sometimes numbering thousands of individuals and often of only one sex. These schools may be migrating to warmer or cooler waters or, if females, to shallow water in order to give birth.

The spurdog bears live young, which develop for 18 to 22 months. From 3 to 11 young are born at a time, but the exact number and development time depend on the size of the mother. The combination of a small litter, long gestation and late maturity make this species particularly vulnerable to fishing pressure, and at one time it was fished in considerable quantities.

Greenland Shark *Somniosus microcephalus*

RANGE N. Atlantic Ocean: inside Arctic Circle, south to Gulf of Maine and Britain

HABITAT Seabed at depths of 600–1,800 ft (180–550 m)

SIZE 21 ft (6.4 m)

The Greenland shark is the giant of its group, but unlike other Atlantic squalid sharks, it has small dorsal

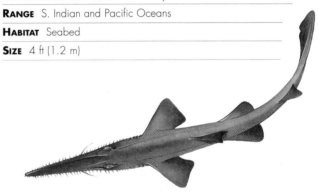

fins with no spines in front of them. It appears to be a sluggish bottom-dweller, but will come to the surface in search of food, particularly during the winter. It preys on many kinds of fish, both surface and bottom-living, and also feeds on mollusks, crustaceans and squid and, reputedly, on seals, porpoises and seabirds. In Arctic whaling stations, it was well known as a scavenger.

Female Greenland sharks bear live young, from eggs which develop and hatch inside the mother's body. The usual litter is believed to be about 10 young.

PRISTIPHORIFORMES: SAW SHARKS FAMILY

The single family in this order contains 5 species of saw sharks. The extended snout of the saw shark has teeth attached to it, forming a long blade. This is used by some species for slashing at fish, cutting them into pieces which are then eaten.

Common Saw Shark *Pristiophorus cirratus*

RANGE S. Indian and Pacific Oceans

HABITAT Seabed

SIZE 4 ft (1.2 m)

The common saw shark, one of 5 species of saw shark, has a distinctive, bladelike snout with sharp teeth, which are alternately large and small, along each side. The fish's slender body and fin shapes show its relationship to the sharks, despite its strangely adapted snout.

This sedentary shark probes in the mud of the seabed with its saw, searching for invertebrates and bottom-living fish, which it detects with the aid of sensitive barbels on its snout.

The young are born well developed, but their teeth are enveloped within the skin and do not erupt until after birth.

SKATES, RAYS AND CHIMAERAS

RAJIFORMES: SKATES AND RAY ORDER

There are 12 families of cartilaginous fishes in this order, about 456 species in all. Most are marine fishes of temperate and tropical waters. All, except for the sawfish, have broad, flattened bodies and greatly expanded pectoral fins which extend along the head and trunk, giving the fishes a diamond shape. Tails are small and whiplike and dorsal fins tiny. Gill openings and the slit mouth are on the underside of the body, but there are small openings, or spiracles, on the upper surface through which they breathe when on the seabed. Most skates live on or near the seabed and eat mollusks and crustaceans.

Eggs are either deposited in egg cases, or develop and hatch inside the mother, who gives birth to fully formed live young.

Smalltooth/Greater Sawfish *Pristis pectinata* **EN**

RANGE	Temperate and tropical oceans
HABITAT	Shallow coastal waters
SIZE	25 ft (7.7 m)

The smalltooth is the largest of the 6 sawfish species and is well known off the Atlantic coast of the USA and the East African coast. It has a bladelike snout, each side studded with 24 to 32 large teeth of equal size. Its body is more sharklike than raylike, apart from the enlarged pectoral fins and the gill openings on its underside.

Sawfishes live on the seabed in shallow water and use their saws to probe the sand and mud for small invertebrate prey. It is claimed that sawfishes also lash out with their snouts at schools of fish to obtain food. This is unconfirmed, but they can seriously wound other fish, and fishermen, if caught.

Atlantic Guitarfish *Rhinobatus lentiginosus*

RANGE	W. Atlantic Ocean
HABITAT	Shallow waters, bays, estuaries
SIZE	30 in (76 cm)

A common fish along the American Atlantic coast from North Carolina to Yucatan, the guitarfish is halfway between sharks and rays in body shape. Its body is long and rounded with well-developed dorsal fins, but the pectoral fins are enlarged and the gill slits are on the underside of the body. It is a bottom-dweller and feeds mainly on crustaceans and mollusks. There are about 45 species of guitarfish.

Skate *Raja batis*

RANGE	E. Atlantic Ocean: Arctic Ocean to Madeira; Mediterranean Sea
HABITAT	Deep waters
SIZE	8 ft (2.4 m)

Large numbers of skate are caught for food. Skates live in waters 98 to 2,000 ft (30 to 600 m) deep; only young fishes are found in the shallower part of this range. The skate has a flat body, broad pectoral fins and a tiny tail. There are small spines on the tail and on the underside of the body; adult females also have spines on the front edge of the body, while males have spines on their backs.

Skates are bottom-dwellers; they eat fish, crabs, lobsters and octopuses. Their eggs, deposited on the seabed, are encased in horny capsules which have long tips at each corner. Hatchlings are about 80 in (21 cm) long.

Southern Stingray *Dasyatis americana*

RANGE	Atlantic coast: New Jersey to Brazil; Gulf of Mexico; Caribbean
HABITAT	Shallow coastal waters
SIZE	5 ft (1.5 m) wide

Stingrays are almost rectangular and have long thin tails; they have no dorsal or anal fins. The stingray has a sharp spine near the base of the tail which has venom-secreting tissue in its underside and can inflict a serious wound that may be fatal, even to humans. The stingray wields its tail with great speed and force to drive the spine into its victim.

Stingrays usually live buried in sand on the seabed; they feed on fish, crustaceans and mollusks which they crush with their strong, flattened teeth. The 3 to 5 young of the stingray develop inside the mother and are about 7 in (18 cm) wide at birth. All stingray species have much the same habits.

Eagle Ray *Myliobatis aquila*

RANGE E. Atlantic Ocean: Britain to Senegal; Mediterranean and Adriatic Seas

HABITAT Coastal waters

SIZE 6 ft (1.8 m)

Eagle rays are large, graceful fishes, with pointed, winglike pectoral fins and long thin tails. They feed on the seabed on crustaceans and mollusks, but are more active than stingrays.

In the north of its range, the eagle ray is seen only in summer; in winter it moves south to breed. The female produces up to 7 live young which are nourished before birth by secretions of her uterine membrane.

Atlantic Manta *Manta birostris*

RANGE Atlantic Ocean: North Carolina to Brazil, Madeira to W. Africa

HABITAT Coastal waters, open sea

SIZE 17 ft (5.2 m); 22 ft (6.7 m) wide

The gigantic manta, also known as the giant devil ray, is the largest ray. It has huge pointed pectoral fins, a fairly short tail and a short dorsal fin. Two fleshy appendages at each side of the mouth act as scoops for food. Mantas feed on tiny planktonic creatures which they filter from the water on to their gill arches. They also swallow fish and large crustaceans. The young hatch inside their mother and are born well developed.

Atlantic Torpedo/Electric Ray *Torpedo nobiliana*

RANGE Atlantic Ocean: Scotland to South Africa, Nova Scotia to North Carolina; Mediterranean Sea

HABITAT Seabed

SIZE 6 ft (1.8 m)

Torpedo rays can give electric shocks of 70 to 220 volts, sufficient power to kill or stun a prey fish or to throw a man to the ground. The electric discharges of these fishes are produced by modified muscle cells. Torpedos eat fish, which they trap and envelop in their pectoral fins while delivering the shock. Females produce live young which are about 94 in (25 cm) long when they are born.

CHIMAERIFORMES: CHIMAERA ORDER

This is the third major group of cartilaginous fishes. It includes 31 species of marine fishes distributed throughout the world. Chimaeroids are long-bodied fishes with long thin tails. Their gills open into a single external opening on each side, covered by a flap. Male chimaeroids have pelvic claspers for internal fertilization of females at spawning time.

Ratfish *Chimaera monstrosa*

RANGE E.N. Atlantic Ocean: Iceland to Azores; Mediterranean Sea

HABITAT Deep water

SIZE 5 ft (1.5 m)

The ratfish has a prominent dorsal fin, large pectoral fins and large eyes. The spine on the dorsal fin is linked to a venom gland. Males have a clublike appendage on the head and are often slightly smaller than females. Ratfishes often occur in one-sex schools. Ratfish are generally found close to the seabed and eat starfish, mollusks and crustaceans. In summer the ratfish breeds and lays eggs in shallow water.

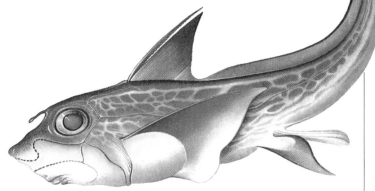

BICHIRS, STURGEONS, GARS AND BOWFIN

POLYPTERIFORMES: BICHIR ORDER

This order contains a single family of 11 species, all found in African freshwater habitats. The fishes strongly resemble the earliest fossil fishes and have primitive features, such as a swimbladder which can be used as a means of breathing air.

Bichir *Polypterus weeksi*

RANGE	C. Africa: upper Congo
HABITAT	Lakes, rivers
SIZE	15¾ in (40 cm)

A long-bodied fish covered with hard diamond-shaped scales, this bichir, like the rest of its family, inhabits overgrown water margins. Its distinctive dorsal fin is made up of small flaglike fins, each supported by a bony ray. The fan shaped pectoral fins are mounted on fleshy lobes. Bichirs feed on fish and amphibians.

ACIPENSERIFORMES: STURGEON ORDER

There are 2 families in this order. First there are the 24 species of sturgeon which are mainly freshwater and coastal fishes of temperate regions, the marine species of which migrate into rivers to spawn. All have five rows of bony plates along the sides of the body. Second there is the paddlefish family, in which there are 2 species of sturgeonlike freshwater fishes with long paddlelike snouts and no bony plates.

Beluga *Huso huso* **EN**

RANGE	Basins of Caspian and Black Seas; Adriatic Sea, Sea of Azov
HABITAT	Sea, rivers
SIZE	16½ ft (5 m)

Huge heavy fishes, belugas certainly weigh up to 2,645 lb (1,200 kg), sometimes more. They are now relatively uncommon, partly because of river pollution interfering with their migrations, and partly because of pressure of fishing. The taking of eggs for caviare from mature females is damaging to stocks, particularly because these fishes mature late – males at 14 years and females at 18 years. A single ripe female may contain up to 7 million eggs.

Belugas migrate into rivers in winter or spring and spawn on rocky river beds. The newly hatched young immediately start moving towards the sea, feeding on small bottom-living invertebrates. At sea, the adult belugas feed on fish, particularly herringlike species and members of the carp family.

Paddlefish *Polyodon spathula* **VU**

RANGE	USA: Mississippi river system
HABITAT	Large rivers and lakes
SIZE	6½ ft (2 m)

The paddlefish has a long flattened snout and a large head. It swims with its large mouth agape and lower jaw dropped, filtering any planktonic creatures from the water on to the comblike gill rakers; it closes its mouth periodically to swallow. Its skeleton is mostly cartilage and there are only a few small scales on the skin.

Paddlefish spawn in April and May in gravel or sandy-bottomed areas. As the female deposits the eggs, the male fertilizes them. The eggs then develop an adhesive coating which makes them sink and attach to the first object they touch. The newly hatched larva lacks a long snout, but it starts to develop in 2 to 3 weeks. The only other species *Psephurus gladius*, lives in China, where it is critically endangered.

Common Sturgeon *Acipenser sturio* **CR**

RANGE European coastline: Norway and Baltic Sea
to Mediterranean and Black Seas

HABITAT Shallow sea, rivers

SIZE 10 ft (3 m)

Sturgeons are increasingly rare fishes and are in need of
protection in Europe. They have been used by man for centuries
as food fish, and the female's unshed eggs are collected, salted
and eaten as caviare. Overfishing, combined with pollution and
man-made obstructions in spawning rivers, has led to the
sturgeon's decline.

   A bottom-dwelling species, the sturgeon feeds on invertebrates,
such as worms, mollusks and crustaceans, and on some fish. In
spring, breeding sturgeons migrate into rivers to spawn. A large
female may contain from 800,000 to 2,400,000 sticky black
eggs which she sheds on to the gravel of the river bed. The eggs
hatch in about a week. The young fishes remain in the river for
up to 3 years, feeding on insect larvae and crustaceans. A closely
related, if not identical species, *A. oxyrhynchus*, occurs along the
Atlantic coast of North America.

LEPISOSTEIFORMES: GAR ORDER

The single surviving family in this previously abundant and
widely spread order occurs in North and Central America.
It contains 7 species of gars or garpikes, all with some primitive
characteristics. They are mostly freshwater fishes, although
sometimes found in brackish or salt water. All have long bodies
and jaws, and anal and dorsal fins which are placed well back.
Their bodies are covered with hard scales.

Longnose Gar *Lepisosteus osseus*

RANGE N. America: Quebec and the Great Lakes
to Florida and New Mexico

HABITAT Rivers, lakes

SIZE 5 ft (1.5 m)

The most abundant and
widely distributed of the gars, the
longnose has particularly long jaws, studded with
sharp teeth. It is a predatory fish, waiting concealed among
vegetation for fishes and crustaceans to come
near; it then thrusts forward and seizes its prey.

   In spring gars congregate in shallow water in order
to spawn. The eggs are adhesive and stick to weeds or
stones. The newly hatched young have adhesive suckers under
their mouths and they attach themselves to floating objects
until their yolk sacs have been absorbed and they must start to
hunt for food.

AMIIFORMES: BOWFIN ORDER

Only 1 family with a single species remains in this order that
once contained at least 7 other families, all now extinct.
The modern bowfin possesses many of the features of its fossil
relatives, which have been found in Europe and Asia as well as
in North America.

Bowfin *Amia calva*

RANGE N.E. America

HABITAT Quiet streams and ponds

SIZE 3 ft (91 cm)

A stout-bodied fish with a long dorsal fin and a rounded tail, the
bowfin has the primitive feature of two bony plates under the
throat. Males are usually smaller than females and have an
orange bordered dark spot at the base of the tail.

   The bowfin generally lives in densely vegetated sluggish
waters which are poor in oxygen, but by using its swim bladder
as a lung and breathing oxygen from the air, it can withstand
such conditions. Bowfins feed on fish and some crayfish.

   In spring, the male bowfin clears a hollow in the riverbed,
making a nest from small roots and gravel. The eggs are then
laid in the nest and the male guards them for 8 to 10 days until
they hatch out. Each larva attaches itself to the
nest by the cement gland on its head and is
nourished by its yolk sac. After
about 9 days, the larvae are able to
swim and feed themselves, but
they are still guarded and herded
by their male parent until they are
about 4 in (10 cm) long.

OSTEOGLOSSIFORMS, ELOPIFORM FISHES, BONEFISH AND SPINY EELS

OSTEOGLOSSIFORMES

This group of freshwater fish includes bonytongues, butterflyfishes, mooneyes, knifefishes and elephantfishes. They are distributed in South America, Africa, Southeast Asia, and Australasia, with 2 species of mooneye in North America. They eat fish and insects and have well-developed bony tongues. Of the 220 or so species in the order, about 200 belong to one African family, the Mormyridae (elephant fish), so called because of the trunklike appendage on the snout. Many species of elephantfish have muscles at the base of the neck that are modified into electric organs that set up an electric field in the water. The fish can detect any disturbances in this field, such as an obstruction or prey, and can navigate and hunt even at night. *Gymnarchus niloticus* uses electricity in a similar way.

Pirarucu *Arapaima gigas* **DD**

RANGE Tropical South America

HABITAT Rivers, swamps

SIZE Up to 13 ft (4 m)

Said to be the largest freshwater fish in the world, this bonytongue may weigh up to 441 lb (200 kg) and reach 16½ ft (5 m) long. It has large body scales, but a scaleless head, and long, low dorsal and anal fins, set back near the tail. The pirarucu has a large swim bladder which can be used as a lung. Pirarucus breed in sandy-bottomed water and make a small hollow in the river bed, where the eggs are laid and guarded.

Aruana *Osteoglossum bicirrhosum*

RANGE Tropical South America

HABITAT Freshwater lakes, quiet rivers

SIZE 3¼ ft (1 m)

The aruana has prominent chin barbels and an upward-slanting mouth. Its back forms a virtually straight line with the head, and the dorsal and anal fins are long and low.

Thought to incubate its eggs in its mouth, the aruana has a pouchlike structure on its lower jaw.

Goldeye *Hiodon alosoides*

RANGE N. America: S. Canada to Mississippi basin

HABITAT Rivers, lakes

SIZE 12–16 in (30.5–41 cm)

The goldeye is one of the small family of mooneyes, characterized by their large golden eyes, adapted for night vision, and the many small teeth. This silvery fish is herringlike in appearance, with a long anal fin. Insects and their larvae, as well as small fish, are its main foods. It is generally active at night.

Elephant-snout Fish *Mormyrus kannume*

RANGE Africa: Nile river system

HABITAT Rivers, lakes

SIZE 31½ in (80 cm)

The elephant-snout fish has an elongated snout. All these mormyrid fishes appear to have good learning abilities and well-developed brains; relative to their body size, the brain is comparable in size to that of humans. This species can produce weak electric impulses, which set up an electric field around the body. Via specialized pores in the head region, it can detect any disturbances caused to this field. It feeds mainly on insect larvae.

Gymnarchus niloticus

RANGE Africa: upper Nile, W. Africa

HABITAT Swamps, lakes, still water

SIZE 35½ in–5 ft (90 cm–1.5 m)

An elongate, slender fish, *Gymnarchus* has no anal, pelvic or tail fins, the dorsal fin is long and low, and the body tapers to a point. The fish swims by undulations of its dorsal fin and can swim backward by reversing the direction of the undulations. Capable of generating an electric field around its body, *Gymnarchus* is sensitive to any disturbance within it, so is able to navigate and hunt for prey fish in turbid waters.

Breeding fishes build a nest of plant fibers, in which about 1,000 eggs are laid. The parents guard the eggs for a few days just before they hatch. The young fishes feed on insects and other small invertebrates.

ELOPIFORMES

There are 8 species in this order, grouped in 2 families – tenpounders and tarpons. All are marine fishes, but some may enter fresh or brackish water. Related to eels and herrings, they are slender-bodied fishes, with deeply forked tails. The order includes several important game fishes.

TARPON Tarpon atlanticus

RANGE W. Atlantic Ocean: Nova Scotia to Gulf of Mexico and Brazil; E. Atlantic: off W. Africa

HABITAT Coastal and oceanic waters

SIZE 4–8 ft (1.2–2.4 m)

The tarpon is a huge, silvery fish, its body covered with large scales. It is characterized by its compressed body and flattened sides, protruding lower jaw and pointed dorsal fin, with an elongate last ray. Tarpons feed on many types of fish and on crabs.

One of the most prolific breeders of all fishes, a large female may contain more than 12 million eggs. These are shed out at sea, but the larvae drift to inshore waters and live in estuaries, swamps and river mouths while they grow. Tarpons are not sexually mature until about 6 or 7 years of age.

Ladyfish Elops saurus

RANGE Tropical Atlantic, Indian and W. Pacific Oceans

HABITAT Shallow inshore waters, estuaries

SIZE 4 ft (1.2 m)

A slender, silvery-blue fish, with fine scales, the ladyfish has dark, fairly small fins and a deeply forked tail. Fishes and crustaceans are its main foods. The ladyfish is a popular game fish because of its habit of leaping and struggling fiercely when it is hooked.

Ladyfishes spawn offshore, but the larvae then drift inshore and live in bays and salt marshes while they develop; they may also enter fresh water.

ALBULIFORMES

The 29 species in this group divide into 2 groups. Bonefishes (*Albulidae*) are predators that resemble tarpons, and are found in shallow seas in the tropics. The 25 species of spiny eels (*Notacanthidae*) and halosaurs (*Halosauridae*) have an eellike body shape, and are mostly deep-sea fishes that live on the bottom eating small invertebrates extracted from the seabed.

Bonefish Albula vulpes

RANGE Worldwide in tropical seas

HABITAT Inshore waters, especially over sand flats

SIZE 35½ in (90 cm)

The bonefish has a slender, body, with dark, silvery scales and a deeply forked tail. Its snout projects slightly beyond its mouth. Shoals of bonefishes feed together, foraging over the seabed, with heads down and tails near or above the surface, for bottom-living invertebrates such as clams, crabs and shrimps.

The thin, eellike larvae drift to inshore waters, where they metamorphose to adult form.

Spiny-eel Notacanthus chemnitzii

RANGE N. Atlantic Ocean: temperate areas; possibly temperate areas of all other oceans

HABITAT Deep sea

SIZE 4 ft (1.2 m)

The spiny-eel has a slender, elongate body and a rounded snout that projects beyond the ventrally placed mouth. On its back are a series of short, sharp spines, and there are similar spines preceding the anal fin. The fish is usually brown to grayish-brown in color. Spiny-eels are thought to eat bottom-living invertebrates, especially sea anemones, and they probably feed in a head-down position on the seabed. Few details are known of the biology of this rarely seen fish.

EELS, SNIPE-EELS AND GULPER EELS

ANGUILLIFORMES: EEL ORDER

There are more than 730 species of eel, grouped into about 15 families. They occur worldwide, except in polar regions. Most are marine, but there are some freshwater eels. All have long slender bodies and long dorsal and anal fins; pelvic fins are absent. All species produce eggs which hatch into thin, transparent larvae.

Chain Moray *Echidna catenata*
RANGE W. Atlantic Ocean: Bermuda to Brazil, including Caribbean
HABITAT Coastal waters
SIZE 35½ in (90 cm)

Moray eels of this genus are most abundant in the Indian and Pacific Oceans, but some occur in the tropical Atlantic. The chain moray is common in the Caribbean, where it leads a retiring life among rocks or rocks and sand, usually in shallow water. A striking fish, it is distinctively patterned with brownish-black and yellow or white; young fishes have more light than dark areas.

Unlike most morays, which have sharp, pointed teeth, the chain moray has blunt teeth resembling molars. It feeds mainly on crustaceans and, on occasion, can be seen chasing crabs at the water's edge and even out of water.

Moray *Muraena helena*
RANGE Mediterranean Sea; E. Atlantic Ocean: Azores and Cape Verde Islands, north to Bay of Biscay
HABITAT Rocky shores
SIZE 4¼ ft (1.3 m)

The most abundant eels, the 100 species of moray are widely distributed in tropical and warm temperate oceans. This moray is typical of the group, with its scaleless, boldly patterned body, which is somewhat laterally compressed. It has no pectoral fins but it does have well-developed dorsal and anal fins, and its large mouth is equipped with strong, sharp teeth.

A voracious predator, the moray habitually lurks in underwater rock crevices with only its head showing, watching for prey – largely fish, squid and cuttlefish. When it is disturbed, it is a vicious fish and can deliver savage bites.

Morays breed between July and September, and their eggs float at the surface of the sea until they hatch.

European Eel *Anguilla anguilla*
RANGE N. Atlantic Ocean: coasts from Iceland to N. Africa; Mediterranean and Black Seas; fresh water in Europe and N. Africa
HABITAT Coastal waters, estuaries; fresh water: rivers, streams
SIZE 19¾ in–3¼ ft (50 cm–1 m)

The European eel is easily identified in fresh water, where it is the only eellike fish, but elsewhere it is characterized by its rounded pectoral fins, the dorsal fin that starts well back from the head, and its small teeth. Its body is covered with tiny scales.

As they approach sexual maturity, European eels migrate from their fresh water homes to the mid-Atlantic, where they spawn and then die.

The eggs hatch, and the larvae drift in surface waters for some 3 years, gradually being brought back to coastal waters by ocean currents. Here they metamorphose into elvers and then enter estuaries and rivers, where they grow and mature, feeding on insects, crustaceans and fish. During the freshwater stage, the eels are yellowish-brown in color, but as they mature, they become darker, until they are almost black, with silvery bellies.

The European eel is a valuable traditional food fish and is caught by man in large quantities.

The American eel, *A. rostrata*, found along the Atlantic coasts of North America, closely resembles the European species. It spawns in the west-central Atlantic and the larvae take only 1 year to drift back to coastal waters.

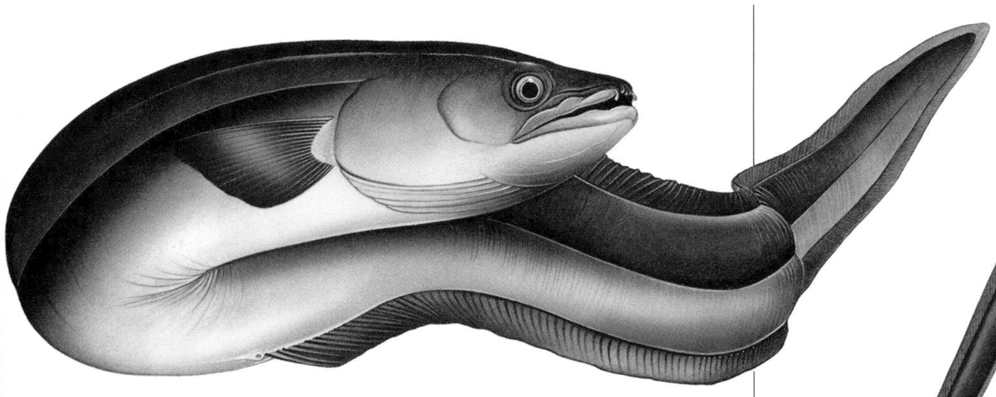

Conger Eel *Conger conger*

RANGE N. Atlantic Ocean: coasts from Iceland to
N. Africa; Mediterranean Sea

HABITAT Shallow waters, often close to rocks

SIZE 9 ft (2.7 m)

This large fish is fairly common on rocky shores, the conger eel
has a large scale-less cylindrical body, with prominent pectoral
fins and a long-based dorsal fin, which originates well forward
near to the eel's head. The conger-eel's upper jaw overlaps the
lower one, giving its face a brutish appearance.

The conger feeds on fish and crustaceans, particularly
crabs, and octopus.

Though they are usually found hiding in rock crevices in
shallow water, adult congers migrate into deeper water in order
to mate and spawn. The eggs hatch out into transparent larvae,
which then drift in the ocean's surface waters for between 1 and
2 years before they develop into small eels.

SACCOPHARYNGIFORMES

This order of deep sea eels includes among its 26 species the
bobtail snipe eels, swallowers, gulpers, and pelican eels.
Many species in the order have a large mouth and pharynx,
probably an adaptation to catching prey larger than themselves.

It is thought that saccopharyngiformes may attract prey in
the darkness of the deep ocean by using a light-producing organ
located on the tip of the tail to lure them within striking range.

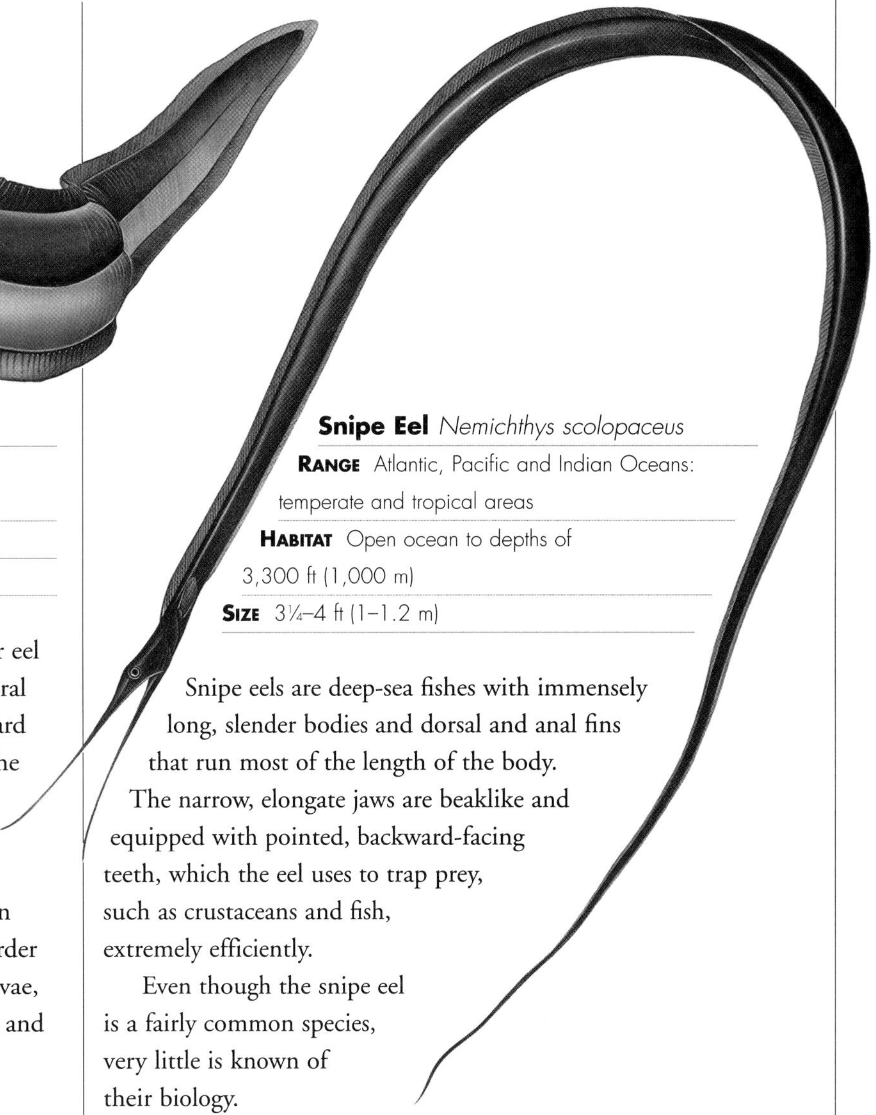

Snipe Eel *Nemichthys scolopaceus*

RANGE Atlantic, Pacific and Indian Oceans:
temperate and tropical areas

HABITAT Open ocean to depths of
3,300 ft (1,000 m)

SIZE 3¼–4 ft (1–1.2 m)

Snipe eels are deep-sea fishes with immensely
long, slender bodies and dorsal and anal fins
that run most of the length of the body.
The narrow, elongate jaws are beaklike and
equipped with pointed, backward-facing
teeth, which the eel uses to trap prey,
such as crustaceans and fish,
extremely efficiently.

Even though the snipe eel
is a fairly common species,
very little is known of
their biology.

Gulper Eel *Eurypharynx pelecanoides*

RANGE All oceans (particularly Atlantic):
warm temperate and tropical areas

HABITAT Deep sea at 4,500 ft (1,400 m) or more

SIZE 24 in (61 cm)

The gulper eel has a highly unusual appearance, with its long,
delicate body and its relatively huge, gaping jaws. Clearly too
thin and fragile to be a very powerful swimmer, the gulper eels
nevertheless does manage to feed on quite large fish. It is
thought that the gulper may swim with its large jaws held wide
open, thus engulfing any fish or crustaceans that swim
unwittingly into its gaping mouth.

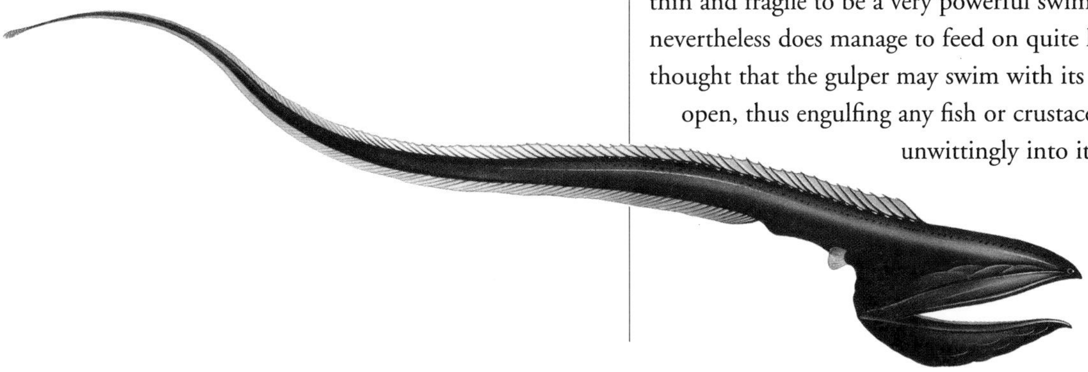

HERRINGS

CLUPEIFORMES: HERRING ORDER

The herring order contains 5 families – one, the denticle herring has only a single species, while another, the wolf herrings, contains 2 species. The two major families are the anchovies, and the largest family of about 180 species that includes all the true herrings, shads, sardines and menhadens. Over 350 species are known. It is one of the most important groups of food fish – the herring, sardine and anchovy alone account for a large proportion of the total world fish tonnage. Indeed some populations, such as that of the North Sea herring, provide the clearest examples of commercial fish stocks that have been overfished to the point of declining catches.

Most clupeoid fishes are marine and live in schools near the surface of the open sea or in inshore waters. Local populations of some species return to traditional spawning grounds, and the partial genetic isolation thus produced leads to recognizable races. Typically, clupeoids eat plankton which they filter from the water through long gill rakers. Their bodies are considerably flattened laterally, and covered with large, reflective, silvery scales. One set of specialized scales found in most clupeoids is the group of enlarged scales (scutes) that form a jagged series of backward-pointing teeth along the middle line of the belly.

Twaite Shad *Alosa fallax* **DD**

RANGE Europe, Icelandic coasts, Baltic to Mediterranean Seas

HABITAT Open sea, coastal waters, estuaries

SIZE 22 in (55 cm)

The twaite shad is a heavy-bodied fish with large fragile scales. It is similar to the allis shad, *A. alosa,* but can be easily distinguished by the number of gill rakers on the first gill arch – 40 to 60 in the twaite, and 80 to 130 in the allis. Crustaceans and small fish are its main diet. To spawn, the fishes migrate from coastal waters to the tidal reaches of rivers, but river pollution and man-made obstructions have affected these journeys badly in some areas. The shads spawn at night, spreading their eggs over the gravel of the river bed. The young fishes move slowly downriver to the sea.

Alewife *Alosa pseudoharengus*

RANGE N. American Atlantic coast, Great Lakes

HABITAT Coastal waters, rivers

SIZE 15 in (38 cm)

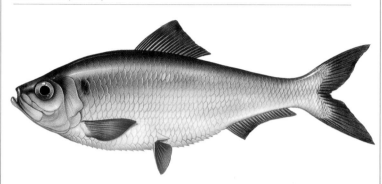

Although primarily a marine fish, the alewife, like all shads, enters rivers to spawn, so is often found in fresh water. The fishes start their journey in February and most have returned to the sea by May.

There are some landlocked, freshwater populations which spend their whole lives in lakes, including the Great Lakes. The freshwater alewife is only about half the size of the marine form. Alewife feed mainly on plankton and also take small fish.

Sardine/Pilchard *Sardina pilchardus*

RANGE European coasts; Mediterranean and Black Seas

HABITAT Open sea, coastal waters

SIZE 10 in (25 cm)

The sardine is a herringlike fish but has a more rounded body and larger scales. Its gill covers are marked with distinct radiating ridges. Shoals of sardines move in surface waters and make seasonal migrations northward in summer, south in winter. They spawn in spring and summer and after spawning generally move farther inshore.

Young sardines feed mainly on plant plankton, adults on larger types of animal plankton.

Sardines are extremely valuable food fish. Species of sardine in the closely related genus *Sardinops* are found off the coasts of Chile and Peru, South Africa, Japan, Australia and along the Pacific coast of the USA.

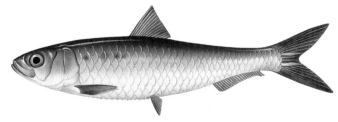

Atlantic Herring *Clupea harengus*

RANGE N. Atlantic Ocean

HABITAT Open sea, coastal waters

SIZE 16 in (41 cm)

The Atlantic herring can be divided into a number of races, each with its own characteristics and breeding season. Some races spawn in shallow inshore bays, others offshore on ocean banks and the eggs form a layer over the seabed. The larvae swim in surface waters in large schools and are generally found inshore during the first year of life. Adults, too, swim in surface waters.

Herrings select different items of planktonic food as they grow and also eat other small crustaceans and small fish. The herrings are preyed on by birds, other fish, dolphins and seals and are an important link in many marine food chains. Atlantic herring has long been an important food fish, and it is one of the top commercial species. The Pacific herring, *C. pallasi*, is closely related to the Atlantic species and has similar habits.

Wolf Herring *Chirocentrus dorab*

RANGE Indo-Pacific Oceans: Red Sea to Australia

HABITAT Surface waters, shallow sea

SIZE 12 ft (3.7 m)

A herringlike fish of dramatic size, the wolf herring has a long cylindrical body and fanglike teeth. Unlike other members of the order, it does not filter-feed but hunts for its food. Its flesh is of little commercial value.

Atlantic Menhaden *Brevoortia tyrannus*

RANGE N. American Atlantic coast

HABITAT Surface waters

SIZE 18 in (46 cm)

Menhaden are abundant fishes and travel in huge schools of hundreds of thousands, moving north in spring and summer, and south to warmer waters in winter. Also known as the mossbunker, the adult has a large head and straight-edged body scales with comblike teeth at their free edge. There is always a definite black spot behind the menhaden's head and a number of smaller spots on its upper sides.

The menhaden does not select particular items of plankton, but eats whatever planktonic creatures it filters from the water.

It has extremely oily flesh and is used to produce fishmeal, oil and fertilizer rather than as food for humans. Many other creatures, such as birds, whales, porpoises, sharks, cod and bluefishes eat the menhaden and it is often used as a baitfish.

European Anchovy *Engraulis encrasicolus*

RANGE European seas

HABITAT Surface waters

SIZE 8 in (20 cm)

The 110 species of anchovy are found all around the world in temperate to tropical seas. The shape of the anchovy head is distinctive and characteristic, with the snout overhanging the huge mouth. The body is rounded. Anchovies are important food items for many creatures including tuna, and many species are valuable commercial fish, which are caught in large quantities, especially in the seas off the coast of Peru.

The European anchovy is a slender fish with large, fragile scales. It moves in schools of many thousands of individuals and feeds on plankton, particularly small crustaceans, and the larvae of fish and invertebrates. Found in offshore waters in winter, anchovies move farther inshore in summer to spawn. Eggs and larvae float in surface waters.

The northern anchovy, *E. mordax*, is a common Pacific form, similar to the European species in appearance.

GONORYNCHIFORM FISHES AND CYPRINIFORM FISHES

ORDER GONORYNCHIFORMES

This order contains only about 35 species of mostly freshwater fish, which occur in tropical Africa and the Indian and Pacific oceans.

The milkfish, the single species in the family Chanidae, is the largest and most important member of the order, but it also includes the family Kneriidae, with 27 species of small, loachlike fish. These fishes live in tropical areas of Africa in swift-flowing water and feed on plant matter. Male kneriids develop horny protuberances on their gill covers, which they rub over the females to stimulate them sexually.

Milkfish *Chanos chanos*

RANGE Indian and tropical Pacific Oceans

HABITAT Open sea, coasts, estuaries; occasionally fresh water

SIZE 6 ft (1.8 m)

A large, silvery fish, with a pointed tail and a prominent dorsal fin, the milkfish is a fast-swimming species. It is toothless and feeds on planktonic plant material.

Normally a fish of the open sea, it enters coastal waters to breed and may venture into fresh water. One female may shed as many as 6 million eggs in a season.

Milkfishes are important food fish in Southeast Asia and are the centre of a considerable industry in some areas of Indonesia and the Philippines, where newly hatched young are caught and reared in coastal ponds.

ORDER CYPRINIFORMES

An enormously successful group of freshwater fish, this order contains nearly 2,700 species and includes the carps, minnows, barbs, algae eaters, suckers, and loaches. Cypriniform fish dominate the streams, rivers, and lakes of Eurasia and North America, and are also found in Africa. They have scaled bodies and scaleless heads, a single dorsal fin, and their swim bladders are connected to the inner ear, which gives them acute hearing abilities. Of the 5 families in the group, the carp family (Cyprinidae) is the largest with over 2,000 species.

Dace *Leuciscus leuciscus*

RANGE N. Europe and Asia: Ireland to Siberia, north to Sweden, south to S. France

HABITAT Rivers, streams

SIZE 6–11¾ in (15–30 cm)

A slim-bodied fish, the dace has characteristic concave edges to both dorsal and anal fins. It moves in large schools and eats insects and their larvae, some plants, spiders and other terrestrial invertebrates which fall into the water.

Although normally a river fish, some dace occur in lakes. Dace spawn in spring, often in gravel-bottomed shallow streams, and shoals gather in the breeding areas a few days before spawning. The eggs lodge among the gravel where they remain until they hatch about 25 days later.

Carp *Cyprinus carpio*

RANGE Originally S. Europe and Black Sea area; introduced in N. Europe, N. and South America, Australia, New Zealand, parts of Asia and Africa

HABITAT Lowland lakes, and rivers

SIZE 20 in–3¼ ft (51 cm–1 m)

Now an extremely widely distributed fish, the carp belongs to the large, freshwater family, Cyprinidae. Carp are robust, fairly deep-bodied fishes; some are fully scaled, but there are other varieties, such as leather carp, which are scaleless, and mirror carp (illustrated here), which have some exceptionally large scales on the sides and at the base of the dorsal fin.

Inhabitants of slow-moving waters with much vegetation, carp are able to tolerate low oxygen levels, which would be fatal for many other fish species.

They feed mostly on crustaceans, insect larvae, mollusks and some vegetation. Breeding occurs in spring and summer. The eggs are laid in shallow water, where they adhere to aquatic plants until they hatch.

Goldfish *Carassius auratus*

RANGE Native from E. Europe across to China; introduced in temperate areas worldwide

HABITAT Well-vegetated pools, lakes

SIZE Up to 12 in (30.5 cm)

An extremely familiar species, the goldfish is bred in a variety of forms as an ornamental fish. It is typical of the family Cyprinidae, to which it belongs, in its body shape and its teeth on the pharyngeal bones, but it has strong spines at the front of both dorsal and anal fins.

Goldfishes spawn in summer over aquatic vegetation. The eggs adhere to the plants and hatch in about a week.

Barbel *Barbus barbus*

RANGE Europe: Britain, south to Alps and Pyrenees, east to Hungary

HABITAT Lowland rivers, streams

SIZE 19¾–35¾ in (50–91 cm)

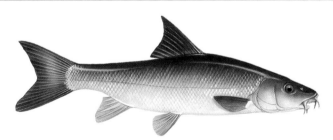

A slender, long-bodied fish, the barbel has a characteristic high dorsal fin and two pairs of sensory barbels around its fleshy lips. It is a bottom-living fish, which is most active at night and at dusk. It feeds on insect larvae, mollusks and crustaceans. It is a member of the family Cyprinidae.

Barbels breed in late spring, often migrating upstream before spawning. They shed their eggs in shallow, gravel-bottomed water, where they lodge among the stones until they hatch from 10 to 15 days later.

Mahseer *Barbus tor*

RANGE N. India

HABITAT Varied, sluggish rivers, fast hill streams

SIZE 4 ft (1.2 m)

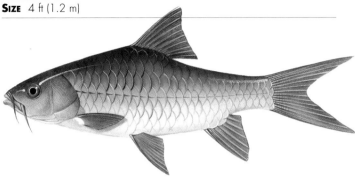

A heavily built fish, with large body scales, the mahseer is a member of the family Cyprinidae and is a common species in its range. It feeds on invertebrates, particularly mollusks, as well as on algae and other aquatic plants.

Tiger Barb *Barbus tetrazona*

RANGE Sumatra, Borneo

HABITAT Rivers, streams

SIZE 2¾ in (7 cm)

This tiny fish, with four black bands ringing its body, is a distinctive member of the family Cyprinidae. Although it is rather aggressive, the tiger barb is a popular aquarium species.

Tench *Tinca tinca*

RANGE Europe: Britain, S. Sweden and Denmark to Mediterranean, east to C. Asia; introduced in New Zealand, Australia, North America

HABITAT Lakes, ponds; sometimes in slow, lowland rivers

SIZE Up to 27½ in (70 cm)

The tench, a member of the family Cyprinidae, is identified by its thickset body, rounded fins and extremely small scales; these scales are plentifully covered with mucus. In males, the second ray in the pelvic fin is swollen and the fin may be longer than that of a female, but otherwise the sexes look alike. Tench feed mostly on the bottom on insect larvae, mollusks and crustaceans and are able to thrive in poorly oxygenated water.

Tench breed in shallow water in spring and summer. Eggs are often shed onto aquatic vegetation, and hatch in 6 to 8 days.

CYPRINIFORM FISHES

Bream *Abramis brama*

RANGE N. Europe: Britain, France, E. to C. Russia

HABITAT Slow rivers, lakes, ponds

SIZE 16–24 in (40.5–62 cm)

The bream has a deep body, flattened at the sides, and a curving, high back. Its anal fin has a distinctly concave edge. The bream's head is rather small for its size and its mouth protrudes into a tubelike structure with which it gathers insect larvae, mollusks and worms from the river bottom. It lives in shoals and usually feeds at night.

Bream breed in late spring or in summer, usually in shallow water where there is plenty of vegetation. The eggs adhere to submerged plants and take up to 12 days to hatch, depending on the temperature.

Roach *Rutilus rutilus*

RANGE Europe, W. Asia: England to C. Russia; N. Sweden to Black and Caspian Sea areas

HABITAT Lowland rivers, lakes

SIZE 13¾–18 in (35–46 cm)

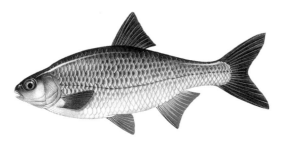

An abundant, adaptable fish, the roach can survive in poorly oxygenated and even slightly polluted water and has an extremely wide distribution; it can also tolerate brackish water. Its abundance and presence in otherwise sparsely populated waters make it an important prey for fish-eating birds and mammals, as well as for other fishes.

An attractively colored fish, the roach has a fairly deep body and small head. Its diet is varied, insects, larvae, crustaceans and other small invertebrates, as well as plants, being consumed. It breeds in well-vegetated shallow water, where its eggs stick to plants while they develop. The eggs hatch in under 2 weeks but, from then on, growth rates of the young vary enormously, according to conditions.

Gudgeon *Gobio gobio*

RANGE Europe: Britain to S. Sweden, south to France, east to Russia

HABITAT Rivers, streams, lakes, ponds, marshes

SIZE 4–7¾ in (10–20 cm)

A round-bodied fish, the gudgeon has a large head for its size and a sensory barbel at each side of its thick-lipped mouth. Found in a wide variety of habitats, it is always a bottom-dweller and feeds on insect larvae, mollusks and crustaceans.

Gudgeons spawn at night in early summer. The sticky eggs adhere to plants or rocks and take up to 4 weeks to hatch. Young gudgeons feed largely on planktonic crustaceans.

Bitterling *Rhodeus sericeus*

RANGE N. and E. Europe: N. France, Germany, east to Black and Caspian Sea basins; introduced in N. America

HABITAT Lakes, ponds, slow rivers

SIZE 2¼–3½ in (6–9 cm)

The bitterling is a small, rather deep-bodied fish. It lives in densely vegetated areas and can tolerate poorly oxygenated water. It feeds on plants and small invertebrate animals.

The breeding habits of the bitterling are most unusual. The female develops a long egg-depositing tube that extends from her genital opening. Using this tube, she lays her eggs inside the gill chamber of a freshwater mussel. The male, who develops brilliant, iridescent coloration in the breeding season, sheds his sperm by the mussel's gills so that it is inhaled by the mussel and fertilizes the eggs. Safe from predators, the eggs develop inside the mussel for 2 or 3 weeks, and the young leave it about 2 days after hatching. The mussel is unharmed by this invasion.

Minnow *Phoxinus phoxinus*

RANGE Europe, N. Asia: British Isles, east to Siberia, south to the Pyrenees, north to Sweden

HABITAT Streams, rivers, lakes

SIZE 3½ in (9 cm); rarely 4¾ in (12 cm)

A small, slender fish, the minnow has a characteristic line of dark blotches along each side. It is an abundant fish, found in schools near the surface of shallow water in summer; it moves to deeper waters in winter. Insect larvae and crustaceans are its main foods and it will also feed on plants. It forms an important prey item itself for many fish-eating birds and larger fishes.

Breeding takes place in late spring, when courting males develop brilliant red bellies. Minnows spawn in gravel-bottomed water and the eggs lodge among the stones. They hatch within 5 to 10 days.

Grass Carp *Ctenopharyngodon idella*

RANGE China; introduced in S.E. Asia, Russia, parts of Europe and USA

HABITAT Rivers

SIZE 3¼–4 ft (1–1.25 m)

A native of China, the grass carp has been introduced into many other areas for two reasons. In China and Southeast Asia it is a valuable commercial species, and in Europe and Russia, this plant-eating fish is used to control vegetation in canals and reservoirs. Although, as an adult, the grass carp is entirely herbivorous, young fishes feed on insect larvae and crustaceans once their egg sacs have been absorbed.

Grass carp spawn in rivers in summer. The eggs float at the surface and must have warm water to grow well.

Stoneroller *Campostoma anomalum*

RANGE E. USA, west to Minnesota and Texas

HABITAT Clear creeks, streams, rivers

SIZE 4–7 in (10–18 cm)

Typically, the stoneroller lives in small streams in riffle areas (shallow areas of water where the flow is broken by the stones

and gravel on the stream bed). It feeds at the bottom on tiny plants, insect larvae and mollusks.

In spring, the dorsal and anal fins of breeding males turn bright orange and black, and tubercles develop on the upper half of the body. The male makes a shallow nest in the gravel of the stream bed in which the female lays her eggs.

Pearl Dace *Semotilus margarita*

RANGE Canada; N. USA, south to Virginia, Wisconsin, Montana

HABITAT Streams, lakes

SIZE 6 in (15 cm)

The pearl dace is a small fish which, with its blunt, rounded snout, resembles the European minnow. It feeds on insects, planktonic invertebrates and even other tiny fish.

During the breeding season, males establish territories on the stream bed which they defend against other males. Females are attracted to the territories, where spawning takes place.

Northern Squawfish *Ptychocheilus oregonensis*

RANGE N. America: Columbia river system, coastal streams of Oregon and Washington

HABITAT Lakes, slow streams and rivers

SIZE 35½ in–4 ft (90 cm–1.2 m)

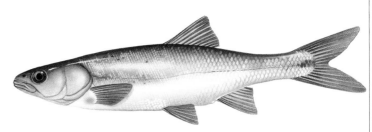

Squawfishes are the largest North American minnows. A long, slender fish, the northern squawfish lives close to the bottom of streams, lakes and rivers. It is a voracious predator, feeding largely on fish, including young trout and salmon.

CYPRINIFORM FISHES CONTINUED

Common Shiner *Notropis cornutus*

RANGE S. Canada; N. USA, south to Colorado and Virginia

HABITAT Clear streams

SIZE 2¼–4 in (6–10 cm)

Shiners are the largest group of American minnows. The common shiner is a round-bodied fish, usually found in fast-flowing water, but sometimes in lakes with tributary streams. It eats aquatic and terrestrial insects and some algae.

Common shiners spawn in spring or early summer in streams. Schools of breeding adults congregate in the breeding areas; male fishes develop bright blue coloration with pinkish fins at this time. Females shed their eggs into shallow nests, excavated in the gravel of the stream bed, where they are fertilized by the males.

Fallfish *Semotilus corporalis*

RANGE S.E. Canada; USA: Atlantic coast, south to Virginia

HABITAT Clear streams, lakes

SIZE 4–12 in (10–30.5 cm)

The fallfish is similar in appearance to another American minnow, the creek chub, *S. atromaculatus*, but can be distinguished by the lack of a dark spot on the base of the dorsal fin. Aquatic insects are the main diet of the fallfish, but some small invertebrates are also eaten. Young fallfishes move in schools in shallow waters, while adults inhabit deeper waters.

In spring, breeding males develop some pinkish coloration on their sides and small wartlike projections on the head. In a quiet shallow area, each pair makes a nest of stones which they carry in their mouths. Once the eggs are laid, more stones are added to the nest by the male. The nest protects the eggs while they develop and hatch.

Harlequin Fish *Rasbora heteromorpha*

RANGE Thailand, Malaysia, E. Sumatra

HABITAT Streams, lakes

SIZE 1¾ in (4.5 cm)

A tiny but attractive fish, the harlequin fish is a popular aquarium species. In its natural habitat, it moves in shoals and feeds on insect larvae.

Having been courted by her mate, the breeding female searches out a broadleaved water plant and lays her sticky-surfaced eggs on the underside of a leaf where they remain until they hatch.

White Sucker *Catostomus commersoni*

RANGE Canada: Labrador to Nova Scotia; N. USA, south to Georgia and New Mexico, west to Montana

HABITAT Large streams, lakes

SIZE 12–20½ in (30.5–52 cm)

The most common of the suckers, the white sucker is typical of its family, with its mouth positioned behind the point of the snout and its thick, suckerlike lips. Found in a variety of conditions, the white sucker tolerates some pollution and poorly oxygenated waters. It is a bottom-living fish and feeds on insect larvae, crustaceans and mollusks, as well as plant material.

Breeding takes place in spring. White suckers spawn at night, depositing their eggs in rocky or gravel-bottomed streams. The eggs, which are slightly sticky, sink to the bottom and are lightly covered by gravel which is stirred up by the vigorous spawning movements.

Northern Redhorse *Moxostoma macrolepidotum*

RANGE E. and C. Canada; USA: Great Lakes to New York, south to Arkansas and Kansas

HABITAT Rivers, streams, lakes

SIZE Up to 24 in (61 cm)

The northern redhorse is one of 18 or more in this genus of sucker. All are silvery to reddish-brown fishes, with round

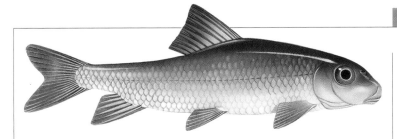

bodies, large heads and suckerlike mouths. They feed mainly on insect larvae and mollusks. Northern redhorses have a preference for clear, swift-flowing water and cannot tolerate muddy or polluted rivers – a characteristic which has led to a decline in their population.

In April or May, northern redhorses migrate up small streams or into shallow areas of lakes to spawn. Each breeding female lays from 10,000 to 50,000 eggs, which she leaves at the spawning site to develop. The eggs hatch in about 2 weeks. Young redhorses feed on tiny planktonic creatures until they are big enough to take the adult diet.

Bigmouth Buffalo *Ictiobus cyprinellus*

RANGE S. Canada; USA: North Dakota, east to Pennsylvania, south to Gulf Coast

HABITAT Large rivers, lakes

SIZE 3¼ ft (1 m)

The powerful, deep-bodied bigmouth buffalo is the largest of the American suckers and, in suitable conditions, may become extremely abundant at the expense of other fishes. Distinguishing characteristics are its long-based dorsal fin and its large, slanting mouth, the upper lip of which is almost level with the eyes. It feeds on crustaceans and plant material as well as on small quantities of insect larvae.

Bigmouth buffalo spawn in April or May. Groups of breeding adults gather in shallow well-vegetated water where females shed as many as 500,000 eggs randomly into the water. The eggs adhere to plants or other debris and take up to 2 weeks to hatch. The young fishes remain in the shallow breeding areas for some months, feeding on plankton. They are mature at about 3 years old.

Stone Loach *Noemacheilus barbatulus*

RANGE England, south to S. France, across Europe and N. Asia to Siberia and Korea

HABITAT Small fast-flowing rivers, lakes

SIZE 4–6 in (10–15 cm)

The sluggish stone loach is a bottom-living fish. It spends the day hidden among stones, where it is well camouflaged by its irregular markings and is active at night or in dull daylight. It eats bottom-living creatures such as crustaceans, insect larvae and worms.

In April or May, the stone loach breeds, shedding its sticky-surfaced eggs over stones or plants. The eggs usually hatch in just over 2 weeks.

Coolie Loach *Acanthopthalmus kuhlii*

RANGE Thailand, Singapore, Sumatra, Java

HABITAT Streams

SIZE 3¼ in (8 cm)

A tiny, elongate fish, the coolie loach has striking dark markings which vary in number. Its eyes are covered with transparent skin. It lives near the bottom, often lurking in dense vegetation, and is a shy, rarely seen fish in the wild. It is a popular aquarium species.

Spined Loach *Cobitis taenia*

RANGE E. England across Europe (including Mediterranean countries and S. Sweden) and C. Asia to China and Japan

HABITAT Lakes, canals, slow rivers

SIZE 4½ in (11.5 cm)

The spined loach has a long, laterally compressed body and a small head, with a few sensory barbels around the mouth. Beneath each eye is a tiny spine which is usually buried in the skin. A slow-moving fish, the spined loach spends much of its time buried in mud or weed and feeds on small bottom-living crustaceans. It is thought to be most active at night or at dusk.

The breeding season begins in April. The eggs are shed over aquatic plants and algae but few details of the spawning behavior are known.

CYPRINIFORM FISHES CONTINUED

ORDER CHARACIFORMES

The 1,400 or so species of characins and their relatives are found in freshwater habitats in Central and South America, and Africa. Most are predators with large eyes and numerous teeth, and many have an adipose fin, a small fleshy fin between the dorsal fin and the tail. The 10 families in the order show considerable diversity. The largest family (Characidae) includes the characins and tetras, as well as the South American piranhas. Although several piranhas are notorious for their carnivorous habits and have formidable teeth, their close relatives eat fruit and seeds fallen from the trees into the streams.

Jaraqui *Semaprochilodus insignis*

RANGE N. South America: Amazon basin

HABITAT Rivers, tributaries

SIZE Up to 14 in (35.5 cm)

The jaraqui belongs to the South American family Corimatidae. The fishes in this family are similar to the related characins but lack their complex dentition. The jaraqui feeds on the bottom on detritus and other fine material.

Around the time of the annual floods, the adults descend from tributaries to spawn in the muddy waters of the main river, where the poorer visibility may give the eggs and young a better chance of escaping predatory fishes. They then move back into the tributary, and the flooded forest, to feed. Later in the year the adults migrate again, this time moving down to the main river and upstream to yet another tributary. The vacated tributary is restocked by the arrival of young fishes, which are swept downstream by strong currents at spawning time.

Curimbata *Prochilodus platensis*

RANGE Central South America

HABITAT Rivers

SIZE 20 in (51 cm)

A member of the family Curimatidae, the curimbata is an abundant fish, which lives in huge schools. It feeds on bottom detritus and

fine plant matter and has a small mouth with fine teeth well suited to this diet.

Curimbatas make regular migrations upstream to spawn. When the males reach the spawning areas, they emit sounds, which may attract the females, though this is not confirmed. The eggs drift downstream, where young fishes find suitable shallow, nursery areas, in which they remain while they grow.

Red Piranha

Serrasalmus nattereri

RANGE N. South America: Amazon basin

HABITAT Rivers

SIZE Up to 12 in (30.5 cm)

The red piranha is not a large fish but swims in such large shoals that, together, the fishes form a formidable hunting group. They are armed with strong jaws and razor-sharp triangular teeth, which can chop pieces of flesh from a victim with alarming efficiency. Despite their very bloodthirsty reputation, carnivorous piranhas feed largely on fish and on seeds and fruit but will attack larger, usually wounded animals, which they quickly devour by their combined efforts.

Giant Tigerfish *Hydrocynus goliath*

RANGE Africa: Congo basin, Lake Tanganyika

HABITAT Streams, rivers, lakes

SIZE 5–6 ft (1.5–1.8 m)

One of the largest characins, the giant tigerfish has an elongate, fully scaled body and a well-developed, forked tail fin. It has a small number of large, sharp teeth, with half-grown replacement teeth behind them, and is a voracious predator, taking a wide variety of smaller fish.

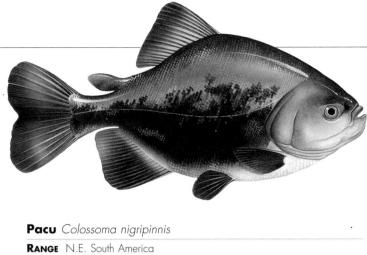

Pacu *Colossoma nigripinnis*

RANGE N.E. South America

HABITAT Rivers

SIZE 27½ in (70 cm)

The pacu is a plant-eater but is similar in appearance to the carnivorous piranhas. It has become adapted to feeding on the many fruits and seeds that fall into the forest bordered water and is equipped with strong jaws and teeth for crushing them.

Flame Tetra *Hyphessobrycon Flammeus*

RANGE South America: Rio de Janeiro area of Brazil

HABITAT Swampy areas

SIZE 1¾ in (4.5 cm)

The flame tetra has brilliant red fins and some red coloration on the body. Males and females differ slightly. The male has a black edge to the anal fin that is reduced or absent on the female's fin.

Mexican Tetra *Astyanax mexicanus*

RANGE USA: Texas, New Mexico; Mexico, Central America, south to Panama

HABITAT Coastal streams

SIZE 3–4 in (8–10 cm)

The only characin to occur in the USA, the Mexican tetra is plain compared to the brilliantly colored tetras from South America. It is sometimes considered to be a subspecies of *A. fasciatus*, some races of which are eyeless and found in caves.

Neon Tetra *Pracheirodon innesi*

RANGE N. South America: upper Amazon river system

HABITAT Rivers, streams

SIZE 1¾ in (4 cm)

The striking neon tetra has a bright blue or bluish-green stripe along its body and a band of red toward the tail. Like all tetras, it is a member of the characin family.

Sardinha *Triportheus elongatus*

RANGE N. South America: Amazon basin

HABITAT Rivers, streams, flooded forest

SIZE 7¾–11 in (20–28 cm)

Popularly known as sardinhas because of their resemblance to marine sardines, the fishes of this genus have long, compressed bodies and extended pectoral fins. This species is an adaptable surface-dwelling fish, able to eat fruit and seeds and invertebrate animals. Its small mouth, equipped with many fine teeth, fits it well for taking invertebrates from the surface, but means that it is unable to crush hard nuts and seeds and must take softer items. When fruit is scarce, it also eats leaves and flowers. When the forest is flooded and the fish has access to plenty of vegetation sardinhas lay down body fat, which sustains them in times of shorter supplies.

Boulengerella lucius

RANGE N. South America: Amazon basin

HABITAT Rivers

SIZE 24 in (61 cm)

Related to the characins, *Boulengerella* is a member of the family Ctenoluciidae, a small group of South American freshwater fishes. It is a predatory fish, with a pointed snout, long jaws, the upper of which has an extended tip, and many sharp teeth.

Hatchetfish *Gasteropelecus sternicla*

RANGE N. South America

HABITAT Rivers

SIZE 2½ in (6.5 cm)

The highly distinctive hatchetfish is a small fish, with an almost straight back but a dramatically curved belly. This body shape makes room for greatly enlarged shoulder muscles, which power the long pectoral fins and enable the fish to fly above the water surface for a short distance, beating its "wings" noisily. These hatchetfishes of the South American family Gasteropelecidae are the only fishes actually to use propulsive force while in the air.

Hatchetfishes feed at the surface of the water. They mainly feed on insects and crustaceans.

SILURIFORM FISHES

ORDER SILURIFORMES

The bottom-living catfishes, with clusters of sensory barbels around their mouths, have been remarkably successful in their "mud-grubbing" way of life. They have spread into many freshwater habitats throughout the world, being absent only from western Europe, Arctic regions of the northern hemisphere, the tip of South America, New Zealand and parts of Australia. Over 2,400 species have been described, ranging from tiny forms, only a few centimeters in length, to some giant forms, which can reach 5 ft (1.5 m) or more and weigh as much as 100 lb (45 kg).

Catfishes do not have ordinary scales, but some have bony plates, which cover them like jointed armor. Food is sought by a combination of touch and taste, by probing the bottom sediment until the sensory barbels locate small prey items.

Tadpole Madtom *Noturus gyrinus*

RANGE S. Canada, USA: North and South Dakota to Texas, New York to Florida

HABITAT Lakes, quiet streams, ponds, marshes

SIZE 4 in (10 cm)

Madtoms are small catfishes which have poison glands at the base of the pectoral spines. The tadpole madtom, like other species, has a characteristic, long fleshy fin on its back that virtually merges with the upper lobe of the tail. A species which favors muddy-bottomed, well-vegetated water, the tadpole madtom often hunts under stones or logs. It feeds on small fish, crustaceans and insect larvae. In early summer, it spawns, laying its eggs in a shallow hollow, which it excavates in the stream bed.

Bagrus docmac

RANGE W. and C. Africa

HABITAT Slow-running rivers, backwaters, lakes

SIZE 3¼ ft (1 m)

This species is one of a family of African and Asian freshwater

catfishes, most of which are slender bodied, with well-developed barbels and strong dorsal and pectoral spines. *Bagrus docmac* has a long, fleshy fin on its back, a flattened head and a narrow extension of the upper lobe of its tail.

A bottom-living predator, the adult feeds mainly on other fish, but the young eats insect larvae and crustaceans. It is a valuable commercial species in its range.

Blue Catfish *Ictalurus furcatus*

RANGE USA: Minnesota and Ohio, south through Mississippi river system and Gulf states; Mexico

HABITAT Rivers, lakes

SIZE 5 ft (1.5 m)

One of the largest catfishes in North America, the blue catfish can grow to over 100 lb (45 kg) in weight and is an important commercial species. It is a slender-bodied fish, generally a dull silvery-blue in color with a whitish belly, and has a deeply forked tail, long anal fin and small, fleshy adipose fin. There are several pairs of sensory barbels around its mouth. Often found in swifter, clearer waters than is usual for other catfish species, the blue catfish will even frequent rapids and waterfalls; it feeds largely on fish and crayfish.

Blue catfishes shed their eggs in a nest made in the shelter of a rock or submerged log on the river or lake bed. Both parents guard the nest and the young once they hatch.

Brown Catfish *Ictalurus nebulosus*

RANGE S. Canada, E. USA to Florida; introduced in W. USA, New Zealand, Europe

HABITAT Muddy-bottomed ponds and rivers

SIZE 11¾–18 in (30–46 cm)

The brown catfish is one of a group of North American catfishes known as bullheads,

although they are most easily distinguished from other catfishes by their rounded tails. A slender, medium sized catfish, the brown bullhead has a mottled, mainly brownish body, lighter on the underparts. It has a long-based anal fin, a small adipose fin and several sensory barbels around the mouth.

Generally a bottom-dwelling fish, it is usually found in well-vegetated waters, where it feeds mainly on invertebrates, such as insect larvae and mollusks, although it will consume anything from plant material to fish. It feeds at night, feeling for prey with its sensitive chin barbels.

In the spring, these catfishes scrape a shallow hollow in the mud, where they spawn, and the male then stands guard over the clusters of sticky-surfaced eggs. Once hatched, the young swim in schools, defended by one or both parents until they are about 2.5 cm (1 in) long.

Although it is not fished for commercially, the brown catfish has been widely introduced outside its native range.

Wels *Silurus glanis*

Range Central and E. Europe to S. Russia; introduced in Britain

Habitat Rivers, lakes, marshes; brackish water in Baltic and Black Seas

Size 3¼–9¾ ft (1–3 m)

A large, long-bodied catfish, with a broad head and a long anal fin, the wels lives in slow-moving or still waters. It is chiefly nocturnal, remaining close to the bottom during the day, concealed among vegetation or in a hollow.

Fish are its main food, but it also eats frogs, birds and small mammals such as water voles. It spawns in early summer. The male makes a hollow in the river bottom in which the female lays her eggs, and he then guards the eggs until they hatch. Young wels feed on plankton.

Glass Catfish *Kryptopterus bicirrhis*

Range Malaysia, Indonesia

Habitat Rivers, streams

Size 4 in (10 cm)

Unlike most catfishes, the glass catfish moves in small schools in surface and mid-waters during daylight hours. As its common name suggests, its body is virtually transparent, with some iridescent coloration on the sides. It has a long anal fin, a tiny dorsal fin and an apparently lop-sided tail fin.

Glass catfishes have been observed to balance themselves on the lower lobe of the tail fin, standing either obliquely or vertically in the water. These attractive fishes are a popular aquarium species.

Butterfish *Schilbe mystus*

Range W. and C. Africa

Habitat Lakes, rivers

Size 14¼ in (36 cm)

One of a family of catfishes found in Africa and Asia, the butterfish has a scaleless body and four pairs of barbels around its mouth. Its anal fin is long and its dorsal fin tiny. It usually lives in shallow water and feeds on small fish and insect larvae. Spawning takes place during the rainy season.

This species is caught as a food fish, and small specimens are kept in aquariums.

African Glass Catfish *Physailia pellucida*

Range Africa: upper Nile basin

Habitat Fresh water

Size 4 in (10 cm)

The body of the African glass catfish is so transparent that much of its internal structure, such as its organs, blood vessels and spine, are clearly visible. Its anal fin is long, and there is a tiny, fleshy fin on the back but it has no true dorsal fin. This catfish is a popular aquarium species.

SILURIFORM FISHES CONTINUED

Mekong Catfish *Pangasianodon gigas* **EN**

RANGE	China, S.E. Asia
HABITAT	Lakes, rivers
SIZE	Up to 8 ft (2.4 m)

The huge Mekong catfish is one of about 25 species in the family Pangasiidae, a group of Asian freshwater fishes. It is a distinctive fish, with its flattened back and deeply curving belly, and differs from the rest of its family in having extremely low-set eyes, which give it a rather upside-down look. It has no teeth. These catfishes migrate upstream to breed, spawning in lakes and tributaries.

Pungas Catfish *Pangasius pangasius*

RANGE	India, Burma, Thailand, Java
HABITAT	Rivers, estuaries
SIZE	4 ft (1.2 m)

The pungas catfish, a member of the catfish family Pangasiidae, is fairly slender, with a rather flattened back and curving belly. Its dorsal fin is high but short based, and its tail is deeply forked. It has one pair of sensory barbels near its mouth. Believed to be active mainly at night, the pungas catfish feeds on the bottom, on detritus and invertebrate animals.

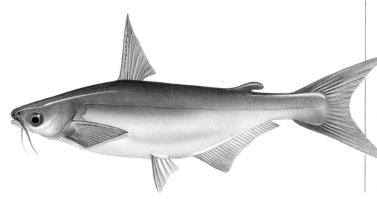

Walking Catfish *Clarias batrachus*

RANGE	India, Sri Lanka, S.E. Asia; introduced in USA: Florida
HABITAT	Slow-moving, often stagnant waters
SIZE	12 in (30.5 cm)

The walking catfish is, indeed, capable of moving on land and, when it does so is able to breathe air. It belongs to the family Clariidae, whose members have additional, specialized breathing organs opening off the gill arches. These are saclike structures, containing many-branched extensions, well supplied with blood vessels for respiration.

An elongate fish, this catfish has longbased dorsal and anal fins and several pairs of sensory barbels; its skin is scaleless but liberally supplied with mucus which protects the fish when it is out of water. These catfishes live in ponds or temporary pools, some of which may disappear in prolonged dry spells. When this happens, the catfish can move overland to another body of water, making snakelike movements and using its pectoral fins as "legs". If necessary, the walking catfish can bury itself in mud at the bottom of a pond and remain dormant throughout a dry season until the rains return. It feeds on aquatic invertebrates and fish.

Electric Catfish *Malapterurus electricus*

RANGE	Tropical Africa
HABITAT	Swamps, reedbeds in rivers
SIZE	8 in–4 ft (20.5 cm–1.2 m)

The electric catfish is a plump, scaleless fish, with no dorsal fin; it does, however, have a fleshy adipose fin near the tail. Its body is mottled with irregular black blotches, and its mouth bristles with several pairs of sensory barbels. Young fishes have a conspicuous black band near the tail fin. This catfish belongs to the family Malapteruridae, which is thought to contain only 1 other species, *M. microstoma*, also found in Africa. Capable of producing charges of several hundred volts, the electric catfish has well-developed electrical organs under its skin, which occupy much of the length of the body. This catfish uses its electrical powers to defend itself and can render even a human being unconscious. It is also thought to catch its prey by stunning it, and is certainly a sluggish fish that would probably find it hard to catch prey any other way.

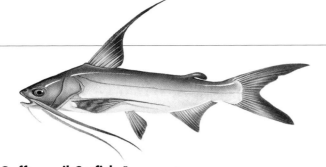

Gafftopsail Catfish *Bagre marinus*

RANGE W. Atlantic Ocean: Cape Cod to Panama,
including Gulf of Mexico

HABITAT Coastal waters, bays, estuaries

SIZE 24 in (61 cm)

One of the large family of sea catfishes, Ariidae, the gafftopsail
catfish is distinguished by its high dorsal fin, the first ray of
which is extended into a long, thin filament. The first rays of the
pectoral fins are also extended into spines, which can inflict
painful wounds. There are two pairs of barbels, one short and
one elongate and ribbonlike.

Although a more active fish than many of its freshwater
relatives, the gafftopsail catfish still does much of its feeding on
the bottom, taking crabs, shrimps and fish.

The breeding habits of this catfish are remarkable. It spawns
in summer, and as the eggs are laid, the male fertilizes them and
takes them into his mouth where they remain until they hatch.
There may be between 10 and 30 eggs, and the male is not able
to eat during the incubation period. Even after hatching, the
young use their parent's mouth as a refuge for several weeks.

Sea Catfish *Arius felis*

RANGE W. Atlantic Ocean: Cape Cod to Panama (rare north of Virginia)

HABITAT Coastal waters, estuaries

SIZE 12 in (30.5 cm)

The sea catfish, one of the Ariidae family of marine catfishes, is
slender and elongate, with a high, but not extended, dorsal fin
and a deeply forked tail. It is most active at night, feeding on
crabs, as well as on some shrimps and fish.

Large shoals swim together and the fishes are capable of
making quite loud sounds by vibrating their swim-bladders with
specialized muscles.

Spawning takes place in summer, and as the eggs are laid, the
male takes them into his mouth, where they incubate. He must
fast during the incubation period. The young fishes also use the
male's mouth as a refuge after they hatch.

Upside-down Catfish *Synodontis nigriventris*

RANGE Africa: Congo basin

HABITAT Streams

SIZE 2¼ in (6 cm)

The upside-down catfish belongs to the family Mochokidae, a
group of scaleless catfishes that are found in fresh waters in
Africa. There are about 150 species. Most species in the
Mochokidae family have long fins, forked tails and several pairs
of sensory barbels.

As its name suggests, this fish swims on its back, belly
upward, for long periods. Although many others in the family
swim upside down for part of the time, it is the usual method of
movement for this species. It is thought to adopt the posture in
order to feed on the algae that grow on the underside of leaves.
Young fishes swim the right way up at first, gradually spending
more and more time in the upside-down position.

The interesting habits of this little catfish have made it a
popular aquarium species.

Cuiu-cuiu *Oxydoras niger*

RANGE South America: Amazon basin

HABITAT Rivers, lakes, flooded forest

SIZE 4 ft (1.2 m)

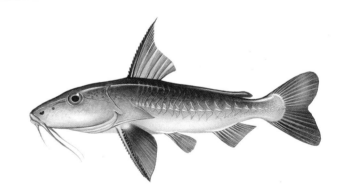

The cuiu-cuiu is one of about 130 species in the South
American family of catfishes, Doradidae. Known as thorny
catfishes, these fishes have rows of bony plates, most bearing
spines, along the sides of the body and toothed spines at the
front of both dorsal and pectoral fins.

A slow-moving, bottom-living fish, the cuiu-cuiu is toothless
and feeds on detritus, extracting insect larvae from the mud and
rotted leaves.

SILURIFORM FISHES CONTINUED

Barber-eel *Plotosus lineatus*

RANGE Indian and Pacific Oceans: E. Africa to Sri Lanka and S.E. Asia

HABITAT Coastal waters, estuaries, reefs

SIZE 11¾ in (30 cm)

The barber-eel is one of a family of eeltail catfishes, all found in Indo-Pacific areas. Its body is elongate and eellike, and there are two dorsal fins, one just behind the head, the other continuous with the tail and anal fins. As in many other catfishes, spines on the dorsal and pectoral fins can inflict painful wounds. There are several pairs of sensory barbels around the mouth.

Young barber-eels are particularly distinctive fishes, with light bands running the length of the body from snout to tail. Older fishes have brown backs, shading to light brown or white on the belly.

Australian Freshwater Catfish *Tandanus tandanus*

RANGE S. and E. Australia

HABITAT Rivers

SIZE 24 in (61 cm)

The Australian freshwater catfish is a member of the same family (Plotosidae) as the barber-eel and has a similar fin pattern; its first dorsal fin is high and short based and the second is continuous with the tail and anal fins. Spines on the dorsal and pectoral fins can cause painful wounds. Its body may be brownish or dull green in color but is always mottled with dark markings.

Several pairs of sensory barbels around the mouth help the catfish find food, mainly invertebrates such as mussels, prawns and worms. In the breeding season, the eggs are laid in a circular nest, made in sand or gravel and tended by one of the parents, usually the male.

Mandi *Pimelodus blodii*

RANGE South America: Amazon basin

HABITAT Rivers, streams, flooded forest

SIZE 7¾ in (20 cm)

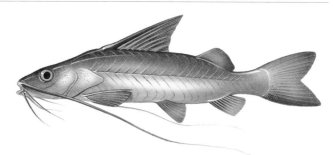

The mandi is a member of a family of South American catfish, known as the fat, or longwhiskered, catfishes (Pimelodidae). Typical of its family, it has a scaleless body and three pairs of sensory barbels, one pair of which is almost as long as the fish itself. Mostly active at night or at dusk, the fish uses these barbels to search for food. Although catfishes are generally bottom-dwellers, the mandi feeds both at the surface, on fruit and seeds, which drop into the water, and on detritus and old leaves at the bottom; it also eats invertebrate animals at both levels.

Surubim *Pseudoplatystoma fasciatum*

RANGE South America: Amazon basin

HABITAT Rivers, lakes, flooded forest

SIZE 19¾–35½ in (50–90 cm)

A distinctive fish, the surubim belongs to the Pimelodidae family of South American catfishes. It has an elongate snout, a slender body, marked with irregular dark stripes, and dark blotches on the fins and nose. There is considerable variation in the exact distribution of these markings.

Like most catfishes, the surubim is a bottom-dweller and is thought to feed mostly on invertebrate animals. It has several pairs of sensory barbels around its mouth which help it find food. Unlike many of the Amazonian fishes, the surubim does not appear to have adapted to feeding on the plant material that falls into the water.

Vieja *Plecostomus commersonii*

RANGE South America: S. Brazil, Uruguay, Paraguay, N. Argentina

HABITAT Rivers

SIZE 20¾ in (53 cm)

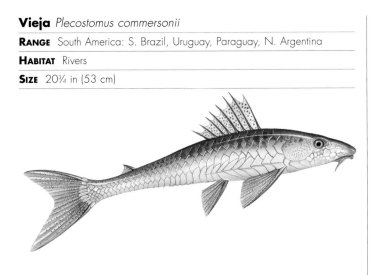

The vieja is one of a large South American family of heavily armored catfishes (Loricariidae). Its long, slender body is covered with overlapping bony plates, but unlike other members of its family, it has no such plates on the belly.

The fins of this species are well developed, with some dark spots on the high dorsal fin; the tail is large, and the lower lobe longer than the upper one. The rounded mouth is on the underside of the snout.

Viejas spawn in spring. The adults feed on worms and crustaceans, as well as aquatic plants, while the young fishes feed on algae.

Cascarudo *Callichthys callichthys*

RANGE Tropical South America: Guyana, south to Paraguay and Uruguay

HABITAT Rivers

SIZE 7 in (18 cm)

This widely distributed fish belongs to a South American family of armored catfishes (Callichthyidae). As the name suggests, their bodies are heavily armored with overlapping bony plates. The cascarudo has a more slender body than is usual in its family, a neat, pointed head, and two pairs of barbels around the mouth. It lives on the river bottom and is most active at dawn and dusk.

When the cascarudos spawn the male makes a nest, usually placed among floating plants, by blowing bubbles of air and mucus, which form a foamy mass. The eggs are then deposited in these protective bubbles.

Cascadura *Hoplosternum littorale*

RANGE South America: Venezuela, Guyana, south to Peru and Argentina; Trinidad

HABITAT Rivers, marshes, swamps

SIZE 7¾ in (20 cm)

The cascadura belongs to the armored catfish family (Callichthyidae), and its body is covered with neatly overlapping bony plates. It is a heavily built fish, greeny-gray in coloration and with several pairs of long barbels. Like many of its family, it lives on the bottom, often in oxygen-poor, swampy water. In such conditions, it is able to utilize atmospheric oxygen by gulping in air at the water surface that is then taken into its hind-gut. It is even believed to be able to travel short distances on land while using the air in its vascular gut. Cascaduras feed on aquatic plants.

Spawning cascaduras blow a bubble nest from air and mucus, which is placed among floating vegetation. The eggs are laid in this protective nest, and the male guards the nest and then the young fishes when they hatch.

Candirú *Vandellia cirrhosa*

RANGE South America: Amazon basin

HABITAT Rivers, streams

SIZE 1 in (2.5 cm)

The tiny, delicate candirú belongs to a family of parasitic catfishes, Trichomycteridae, all found in South America. Its scaleless body is slender, elongate and virtually transparent, and its dorsal fin is placed well back near the tail. It has two pairs of rather short sensory barbels.

Like other members of its family, the candirú is a parasite, living on the blood of other fishes. With small fishes, it simply pierces the skin with its sharp teeth to obtain blood, but it may penetrate the gill system of large fishes and live there, sucking blood. Its tiny body can swell considerably when gorged with food. It is generally active at night or at dawn and dusk and, when not feeding, may bury itself in the sand at the bottom of the river.

The candirú is notorious for its habit of entering the urethra of human bathers or of other mammals, which urinate in the water. It is thought that the fish mistakes the urine for the respiratory water flow of a large fish. Once in the urethra, it becomes lodged by the barbs on its gill covers that normally help it stay in the gill chambers of large fishes, and it is extremely difficult and painful to remove.

GYMNOTIFORM FISHES, PIKES, OSMERIFORM FISHES AND SALMON

ORDER GYMNOTIFORMES

The 62 species of freshwater fish in this order are all found in the South American tropics. There are six families including one, the Electrophoridae, whose sole member is the electric eel. Like the elephantfish of Africa, the gymnotiforms, or knifefishes, have evolved, albeit independently, electric organs that can generate an electric field for use in navigation, and the detection and capture of prey, in turbid waters.

Electric Eel *Electrophorus electricus*

RANGE	N.E. South America, including Amazon basin
HABITAT	Muddy streams and pools
SIZE	8 ft (2.4 m)

The electric eel is the only species in its family, Electrophoridae. It is not a true eel, but has a similar long and cylindrical body. Its anal fin runs much of the length of its body, to the tip of its tail, and it has no dorsal, tail or pelvic fins. An inhabitant of turbid, oxygen-poor water, the fish is able to gulp extra air at the surface, from which it absorbs some oxygen via specialized areas of blood vessels inside its mouth.

Much of its bulky body is occupied by its electric organs – modified muscles, which can release high-voltage charges, used for killing prey or for defence. Each organ is made up of many electroplates, each of which produces only a tiny charge but which together may amount to a charge of 500 volts. Such charges kill smaller fish easily and can give a human being a severe shock. The fish can produce slow pulses of low voltage to help it navigate in murky water, where vision is of little use. Young electric eels feed on bottom-living invertebrates, but adults eat mostly fish, many of which they stun before eating.

Banded Knifefish *Gymnotus carapo*

RANGE	Central and South America: Guatemala to N. Argentina
HABITAT	Creeks, slow murky water
SIZE	24 in (61 cm)

The banded knifefish is an elongate, eellike fish, which has an anal fin running the length of its body and small pectorals, but no other fins. It moves backward or forward by wavelike motions of the anal fin but is generally fairly sluggish. Usually active at dawn and dusk, in rather cloudy water, it relies on weak electrical pulses for navigation. Adults eat fish and crustaceans.

ORDER ESOCIFORMES

This small order of Eurasian and North American freshwater fish has just two families – Esocidae contains 5 species of pikes, while Umbridae has 5 species of mudminnows. All are predators that lie in wait for their prey. Pikes are large fish with long snouts. They hide in weeds then dart out to capture their prey. Mudminnows are smaller and feed on invertebrates.

Northern Pike *Esox lucius*

RANGE	Circumpolar: Britain, N. Europe, Russia, Alaska, Canada, N. USA
HABITAT	Lakes, quiet rivers
SIZE	5 ft (1.5 m)

The long-bodied northern pike has large jaws with sharp teeth and a pointed snout. The dorsal and anal fins are positioned near the tail and opposite one another. Females are larger than males and individuals may weigh 50 lb (23 kg) or more. The pike lurks among vegetation at the water's edge, then shoots out to trap prey. It feeds mainly on invertebrates when young, and then on fish, but also birds and even mammals.

In early spring, as soon as any ice has melted, northern pikes spawn at the water's edge or even in meadows flooded by melted snow. Females shed thousands of eggs over the vegetation.

ORDER OSMERIFORMES

This is a diverse order of 13 families and nearly 240 species of smelts and their relatives. These silvery, elongate fish include marine and freshwater species as well as anadromous forms (fish that migrate between the sea and freshwater). Most smelts are predators that feed on plankton and small fish.

Smelt *Osmerus eperlanus* **DD**

RANGE N. Atlantic Ocean: northern coasts of France, Britain, Holland, Germany, Scandinavia

HABITAT Coastal waters, estuaries, rivers, fresh water

SIZE 11¾ in (30 cm)

Smelts are marine fishes which breed in fresh water. This species is similar to the trout in shape and has a small, fleshy fin on its back, behind the dorsal fin that is itself set well back. Its mouth is large with powerful teeth. It eats small crustaceans and large smelts may eat young fish.

In winter, mature smelts leave the sea to travel up rivers to breed. In spring, they spawn, shedding the eggs on gravel on the river bed or on aquatic plants. Eventually the young fish descend to the sea to grow and mature.

There are isolated populations of smelts in freshwater lakes in Scandinavia which do not migrate. These are slow-growing fishes, smaller than the migratory race.

Jollytail *Galaxias maculatus*

RANGE New Zealand, Tasmania, Australia, S. America

HABITAT Rivers, estuaries, coastal waters

SIZE 7¾ in (20 cm)

The jollytail has a slender-body, a small head and dorsal and anal fins set close to the tail. Mature fish migrate downstream to spawn among estuarine vegetation, which is flooded by high spring tides at the time of the new moon. The eggs remain stranded among the vegetation, above the reach of the tides, until the next high spring tides two weeks later. If that tide does not reach them, the young are able to survive inside the eggs for a further 2 weeks. When immersed in water they hatch, and the larvae are swept out to sea. After spending some months at sea, the young fish travel up rivers, where they grow and mature.

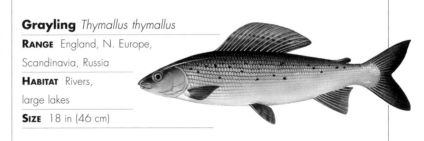

SALMONIFORMES SALMON ORDER

This order contains 1 family, the salmonidae, with approximately 76 species, including salmon, trout, whitefishes, graylings and charrs. Members of the order occur in freshwater and marine environments, mainly in the northern hemisphere. Some migrate from the sea into rivers to spawn. Most species are predatory.

Powan *Coregonus lavaretus* **DD**

RANGE Baltic and North Sea basins; Britain, N. Europe, N. Russia, Swiss Alps

HABITAT Marine, brackish water, lakes

SIZE 8–27½ in (20–70 cm)

The powan is a member of the whitefish family, all of which have large scales, no teeth and forked tails. Whitefishes tend to vary enormously in size and appearance according to habitat, for example, lake-dwellers are generally much smaller than ocean-dwellers because their food supply is often poor. Many lake populations have been isolated since the last ice age and have evolved their own characteristics.

Powan feed on planktonic crustaceans. They spawn in winter, ocean-dwellers migrating into rivers to spawn.

Grayling *Thymallus thymallus*

RANGE England, N. Europe, Scandinavia, Russia

HABITAT Rivers, large lakes

SIZE 18 in (46 cm)

The 4 species of grayling have high, saillike dorsal fins, forked tails, and small fleshy adipose fins near the base of the tail. Graylings have small teeth in both jaws, and they feed on insects and their larvae, crustaceans and mollusks.

In spring the male oftens displays before breeding; the female makes a hollow in shallow, gravel-bottomed water for her eggs. The eggs hatch 3 to 4 weeks after laying.

The American grayling, *T. arcticus*, is similar in appearance and habits.

SALMON AND STOMIIFORM FISHES

Arctic Charr *Salvelinus alpinus*

RANGE Circumpolar: Arctic and N. Atlantic Oceans,

Britain, Europe, Russia, N. America

HABITAT Open sea, rivers, lakes

SIZE 10–38 in (25–96 cm)

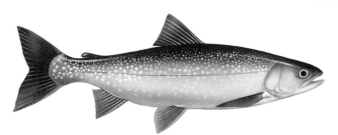

The Arctic charr is a highly variable species, according to its environment. In the north of its range, it lives in the sea, growing large on the rich supplies of fish, mollusks and crustaceans, and enters rivers to spawn. Farther south, Arctic charr live in mountain lakes, and because of their long isolation, populations have become quite unlike one another and the migratory form. The lake fishes are much smaller and feed on planktonic crustaceans, insects and larvae, and mollusks.

Migratory charr breed in gravel-bottomed rivers. The female makes a nest in the male's territory and lays her eggs; he then fertilizes them in the nest. Lake populations spawn in a similar manner on the lake bed or in streams. Growth is slow, although the rate varies from population to population. Migratory fish do not attain full size until they are about 20 years old.

Charr is a good food fish of particular importance to the people of arctic Canada.

Lake Trout *Salvelinus namaycush*

RANGE Canada, N. USA

HABITAT Lakes, rivers

SIZE 4 ft (1.2 m)

A popular sport-fishing species in North America, the lake trout is a charr, not a true trout. It has been introduced into lakes out of its natural range. It has pale spots on head, back and sides. Lake trout eat fish, insects, crustaceans and plankton.

From late summer to December, lake trout spawn in shallow gravel-bottomed water. There is no nest, but males clear the spawning ground of debris. Eggs are laid on the

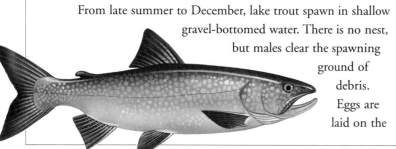

gravel and settle among the stones; they remain there for the winter and hatch in early spring.

Trout *Salmo trutta*

RANGE Europe; introduced worldwide

HABITAT Marine; lakes, rivers

SIZE 9 in–4½ ft (23 cm–1.4 m)

There are two forms of this well-known food- and angling-fish: the sea trout, which migrates from river to sea and back to river to breed, and the smaller brown trout, which spends all its life in fresh water. They are alike physically, but sea trout have silvery scales with scattered black markings, and brown trout have numerous dark spots. Both forms feed on fish and crustaceans.

Trout spawn in winter in gravel-bottomed fresh water; the female makes a shallow nest for her eggs. The young hatch in spring and remain in the gravel for a few weeks.

Rainbow Trout *Salmo gairdneri*

RANGE N.W. America, E. Pacific; introduced worldwide

HABITAT Marine; rivers

SIZE Up to 3¼ ft (1 m)

Now farmed in large quantities, rainbow trout are extremely popular with anglers and are an important food fish. There is a large migratory form, known as the steelhead, which bears the same relationship to the rainbow as the sea trout does to the brown trout. Both forms feed mainly on insect larvae, mollusks and crustaceans.

In their natural range, rainbow trout spawn in spring in shallow, gravel-bottomed streams. The female makes a shallow nest in the gravel and deposits her eggs which are then fertilized by the male and covered over.

Atlantic Salmon *Salmo salar*

RANGE N. Atlantic Ocean: Greenland to Cape Cod;
Arctic coast of Russia, south to N. Spain

HABITAT Open sea; rivers

SIZE Up to 5 ft (1.5 m)

The Atlantic salmon is a long-bodied, rounded fish with a
slightly forked tail. There are some salmon in inland lakes, but
most are migratory, moving from their natal river out to sea and
then back to the river to spawn. The salmon enter the river at
different times but all spawn in the winter. Breeding males
develop hooked protuberances on their lower jaws. Having
excavated a shallow nest in the gravel of the river bed, the female
lays her eggs while the male lies next to her fertilizing them.
The eggs overwinter and hatch the following spring. After 2 to 6
years in the river, the young salmon go out to sea, returning to
spawn from 1 to 4 years later. Unlike Pacific salmon, Atlantic
salmon can spawn more than once in their lifetime.

Sockeye Salmon *Oncorhynchus nerka*

RANGE N. Pacific Ocean: N. American coast: Alaska to California;
coast of Russia to Japan: Hokkaido

HABITAT Open sea, coastal waters, rivers and lakes

SIZE 33 in (84 cm)

The sockeye salmon lives in the ocean, eating small shrimplike
creatures, until it is 4 to 6 years old. In late spring, mature
adults enter rivers to ascend to their breeding areas, sometimes
1, 500 miles (2 ,400 km) inland. They breed in lakes or small
adjacent streams. Breeding males develop bright red skin on
back and sides, and the back becomes humped and jaws
hooked. Females show some red color.

At their breeding grounds the female digs a shallow pit in
the stream bed with her tail and body, and lays her eggs. They
are then fertilized by the male. After spawning the adults die.
The eggs hatch after 6 to 9 weeks, and the young spend 1 to
3 years in the lake before   migrating to the sea.

ORDER STOMIIFORMES

The 320 or so species of stomiiforms are
deep sea fishes and include bristlemouths,
marine hatchetfishes, lightfishes, dragonfishes, and
viperfishes. Bristlemouths are some of the most abundant fishes
in the oceans. Most stomiiforms have large mouths, long teeth,
and light organ used to attract prey in the dark, deep ocean.

Hatchetfish *Argyropelecus aculeatus*

RANGE Atlantic, Pacific and Indian Oceans:
tropical and subtropical areas

HABITAT Open sea at 330–2,000 ft
(100–600 m)

SIZE 2¾ in (7 cm)

The hatchetfish is a common species
which forms a major item of diet for many larger
fishes. Its silvery body is deep and laterally compressed, with a
sharp-edged belly. Its eyes are large, and its capacious mouth is
nearly vertical. On the fish's belly there are rows of
light-producing organs, which are arranged in a characteristic
pattern in each species, enabling the hatchetfishes to recognize
their own kind from below.

Hatchetfishes normally live at depths of 1,300 to 2,000 ft
(400 to 600 m) by day, but migrate nearer to the surface each
night in search of food.

Sloane's Viperfish *Chauliodus sloani*

RANGE Atlantic, Pacific and Indian Oceans:
temperate and tropical areas

HABITAT Deep sea

SIZE 11¾ in (30 cm)

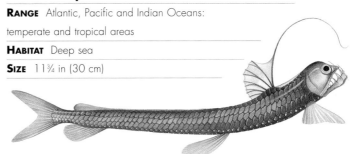

Sloane's viperfish is one of 6 species of deep-sea viperfishes all
with long, fanglike teeth. The skull is adapted to increase the
gape of the mouth, and the jaws open wide to maximize the
efficiency of the predatory teeth. The dorsal fin of the viperfish
is positioned close behind the head, and the first ray is greatly
elongated and bears a light-producing organ to attract
prey in the darkness of the deep sea. Viperfishes feed
on smaller fish, such as lanternfishes, which they
follow when they make their nightly migrations to
waters nearer the surface, where they feed on plankton.

AULOPIFORM FISHES, LANTERNFISHES AND TROUT-PERCHES

ORDER AULOPIFORMES

Most of the 219 species in this order are deep sea fishes, although one family, the lizardfishes, live in shallower waters. The aulopiforms form a diverse group. The deep sea members are mostly small predators, and include the 55 or so species of barracudinas, that resemble miniature barracudas, as well as bizarre-looking forms such as the telescopefishes and spiderfishes.

Lizardfishes are found in the shallow tropical and subtropical seas and are common inhabitants of coral reefs where they conceal themselves in order to ambush passing prey.

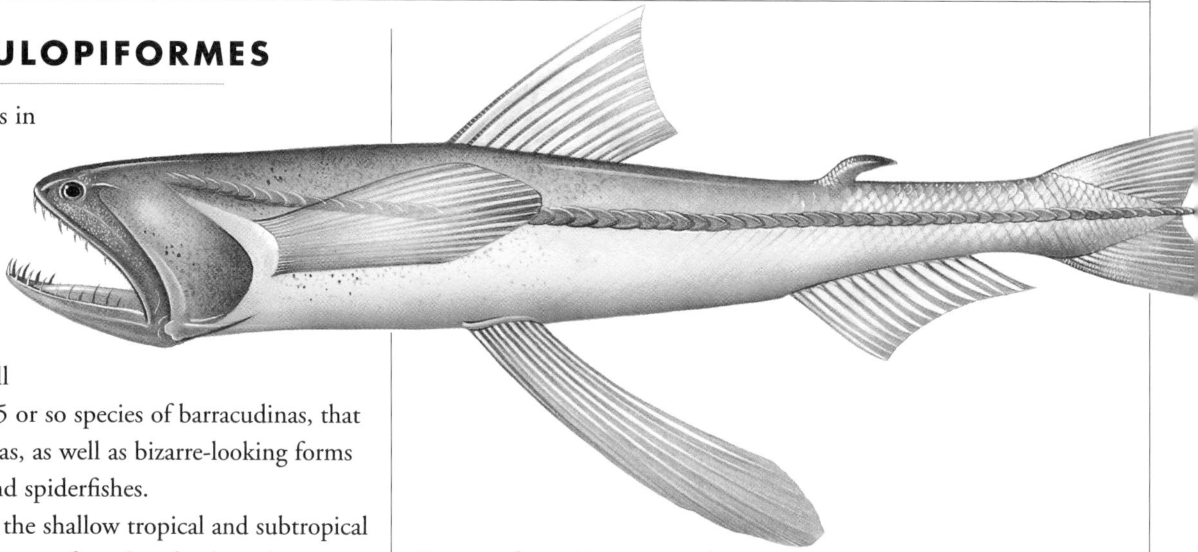

Red Lizardfish *Synodus synodus*

RANGE Atlantic Ocean: Florida, through Gulf of Mexico to Uruguay

HABITAT Coastal waters

SIZE 12½ in (32 cm)

The red lizardfish is one of a family of about 34 lizardfishes, all found in shallow areas of tropical and warm temperate seas. It has a large head and wide jaws, set with long sharp teeth. With its heavy, shiny scales, it is thought to have a reptilian appearance – hence its common name – and it has some reddish coloration on its tail.

The pelvic fins are unusually long, and the fish has the habit of lying on the seabed, supported on these fins. It is also able to partly bury itself. A voracious carnivore, it catches its prey by ambushing – suddenly darting upward from where it is concealed on the seabed.

Bummalow *Harpadon nehereus*

RANGE N. Indian Ocean

HABITAT Estuaries, shallow coastal waters

SIZE 16 in (41 cm)

The bummalow is one of a small family of 4 or 5 species, all of which are found in the Indian Ocean. It has an elongate body and large jaws with sharp curving teeth, It also has long pelvic and pectoral fins. This species is often found near the mouths of large rivers such as the Ganges, where it eats small fish and crustaceans, though it breeds farther out to sea.

This fish is better known as Bombay Duck, its name when it has been split, dried in the sun and served with curry. It is a valuable commercial species.

ORDER MYCTOPHIFORMES

Most of the 240 species in this family are found in one of the two families – the lanternfishes. They are small fish with blunt heads, large eyes, and photophores (light-producing organs) which are arranged in rows on the body and head. The photophores are arranged in patterns characteristic to each different species and are an important means of distinguishing between species in the darkness of the deep ocean.

Myctiforms are deep sea fishes that are found in all oceans from the Arctic to the Antarctic. They are important prey species for many other fish and also for some marine mammals.

Lanternfish *Myctophum punctatum*

RANGE N. Atlantic Ocean; Mediterranean Sea

HABITAT Deep sea

SIZE 4 in (10 cm)

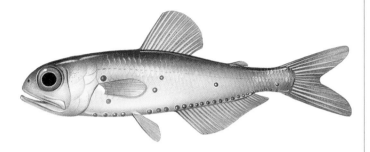

This species is typical of its family; with its blunt, rounded head and very large eyes, the lanternfish also has many light-producing organs, known as photophores, which are arranged in short rows and groups on its body.

Young fish start to develop their light-producing organs when they are about 4 in (2 cm) long, and the arrangement differs between males and females of the species.

The function and value of these photophores are not yet fully understood. They may help the fish to illuminate the dark depths and find prey, or they may be used to confuse predators; the lanternfish has photophores on its tail and it is said to lash its tail to and fro in order to dazzle an enemy.

Lantern-fishes feed on tiny planktonic animals, making vertical migrations from the ocean depths of as much as 1,300 ft (400 m) or more, in order to follow the nightly movements of the plankton to the ocean's surface waters.

Lanternfish move in large schools and, in the Mediterranean area, they are known to breed betweeen April and July.

PERCOPSIFORMES TROUT-PERCH ORDER

There are 9 species, grouped in 3 families, that are known to belong to this order. All percopsiformes are freshwater fishes, and are found in North America in larger streams, deep clear lakes and cave water, and have common names such as sand-roller, pirate-perch and the cavefish.

Trout-perches, as their name suggests, show some structural similarities to both the trout and perch, but they are never more than 6 in (15 cm) long. They are not actually related to either the trout or the perch.

Most species in the order feed on aquatic insects and crustaceans, but the pirate-perch preys on small fish.

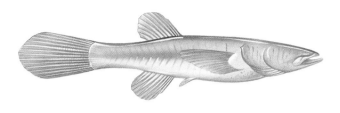

Northern Cavefish *Amblyopsis spelaea*

RANGE USA: Kentucky, Indiana

HABITAT Fresh water in limestone caves

SIZE 4 in (10 cm)

One of a small family of 10 species, many of which live in limestone caves, the northern cavefish was first discovered in 1842. It is a slender-bodied fish, with no scales on its head but small irregular scales on its body. Its eyes are rudimentary and covered with skin, since it has no need of vision in its dark cave habitat and has adapted accordingly. To compensate for its virtual blindness, its body is covered with tiny sensory protuberances with which it can detect even slight movements in water and thus find its prey and avoid obstacles.

The male cavefish fertilizes the female internally with a specially adapted genital organ. She has an unusual way of guarding her eggs – once they are fertilized and shed, she carries them in her gill chamber until they hatch.

Trout-perch *Percopsis omiscomaycus*

RANGE N. America: Alaska to Quebec; Great Lakes to Kentucky, Missouri, Kansas

HABITAT Lakes, muddy rivers

SIZE 7¾ in (20 cm)

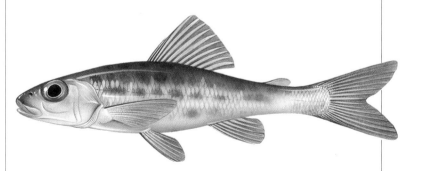

One of the 2 species of trout-perch, this fish has a silvery body, translucent in parts. Its head is scaleless, but the rest of its body is covered with rough, sawtoothed scales. The nocturnal trout-perch eats aquatic insects, crustaceans and mollusks. It spawns in spring or early summer in streams or shallow lakes. The eggs sink to the bottom, where they stay until they hatch.

The other trout-perch, the sandroller, *P. transmontana*, lives only in the Columbia River system in northwest USA. It is similar to *P. omiscomaycus*, but is usually greenish-yellow.

OPHIDIIFORM FISHES AND CODFISHES

ORDER OPHIDIIFORMES

The 355 species of ophidiiforms are mainly eellike fish with long tapering tails. The 6 families include cusk-eels and brotulas that live in a wide range of habitats from the brackish water of caves to the depths of the ocean. The 27 species of pearlfish are inquilines ("tenants") living inside the body cavities of marine invertebrates including starfish, clams, sea squirts, and sea cucumbers.

Pearlfish *Carapus acus*

RANGE Mediterranean and Adriatic Seas

HABITAT Seabed

SIZE 7¾ in (20 cm)

Pearlfishes are small, slender fishes with translucent, spotted skin, found in tropical and warm temperate waters. Many of them spend much of their lives inside other marine animals such as clams, sea urchins, starfish, sea cucumbers and even pearl oysters – hence the common name.

This species is a typical pearlfish, with its elongate tapering body and long, low dorsal and anal fins which form a continuous border to the body. The adult fish lives inside a sea cucumber. It enters the animal through its anus, inserting its tail first and then wriggling backward until it is inside the body cavity. Several pearlfishes may occupy one host, feeding on its internal organs until the host is destroyed.

Young pearlfishes pass through two larval stages before taking up residence in this way; in the first phase, the young fishes float in surface waters, in the second, they live near the seabed. Adult pearlfishes can live outside a host, feeding on small crustaceans.

New Providence Cusk-eel *Lucifuga spelaeotes* **VU**

RANGE Bahamas: near Nassau

HABITAT Freshwater pools in limestone

SIZE 4¼ in (11 cm)

This species was first discovered in 1967 and is known only

from this one location, although it is believed to be related to 3 species in the same genus, found in cave pools in Cuba.

A small but distinctive fish, the body of the new providence cusk-eel curves upward sharply behind the broad, flattened head and its long-based dorsal and anal fins are continuous with the tail fin. Much of its head is scaleless, but the body is covered with small scales. The Cuban species are blind, but *L. spelaeotes* has small yet well-developed eyes.

In view of its apparently extremely restricted distribution, it seems that this species may be in danger of disappearing only years after its discovery.

New Zealand Ling *Genypterus blacodes*

RANGE Seas off S. Australia, New Zealand

HABITAT Coastal waters

SIZE 35½ in (90 cm)

Not to be confused with the North Atlantic lings (*Molva*), this ling is one of a group known as cusk-eels, which belong to the cod order. A long, tapering fish, its dorsal, tail and anal fins are joined to form one continuous strip around the body. The head is flattened, and there are two thin pelvic fins under the lower jaw. The anus is positioned behind the head.

GADIFORMES COD ORDER

This order contains about 480 species only 5 of which are freshwater fishes. They are grouped into 12 families, and some of the most familiar forms, such as cod, haddock, whiting, hake, saithe and ling, are extremely valuable food fish.

The majority of the cod species lives in the northern

hemisphere in the relatively shallow waters of the continental shelves. Some species in the order, however, notably the grenadiers, which are also known as rat-tails, live in deep oceanic water. All species are carnivorous, feeding on fish, crustaceans and other forms of marine life.

The body of the codfish is covered with small scales, and the fins contain soft rays. Many members of the order have a sensory barbel on the chin. The barbel is equipped with additional taste buds.

Most cod spawn simply by coming together into large shoals. Then both sexes discharge their eggs and sperm into the water. The eggs are then abandoned by the parents and, although many millions of eggs are produced in each spawning, so many are destroyed by the elements or are eaten by other fishes that relatively few survive. In the case of the cod, for example, it is estimated that only about one egg in a million survives to adulthood.

Rough-head Grenadier *Macrourus berglax*

RANGE N. Atlantic Ocean: Nova Scotia to Greenland, Iceland, Norway

HABITAT Deep water, 650–3,300 ft (200–1,000 m)

SIZE 35½ in–3¼ ft (90 cm–1 m)

The rough-head grenadier is one of a family of about 15 species belonging to the cod order which are found in deep water; all are known as grenadiers or rat-tails. The males of many of these species can make surprisingly loud sounds by vibrating their swim-bladders with specialized muscles. Such sounds may be used for communication, particularly during the breeding season.

The rough-head grenadier has the characteristic appearance of its family, with its large, heavy head and tapering, pointed tail. It has a high first dorsal fin, but its second dorsal fin and anal fin are continuous with the tail. The head is ridged beneath the eyes and the body scales are rough and toothed.

The grenadier feeds on crustaceans, mollusks and brittle stars. It is believed to breed in winter to early spring.

Three-barbed Rockling *Gaidropsarus mediterraneus*

RANGE European coasts: S. Norway, W. British Isles to Mediterranean and Black Seas

HABITAT Rocky shores

SIZE 6–13¾ in (15–35 cm)

One of several species of rockling, the three-barbed is typical of the group, with its long slender body and two dorsal fins. The first of these fins has short, fine rays and the second fin is long based. The anal fin is also long based and, as the common name implies, there are three barbels, one on the chin and two on the fish's snout.

This is an abundant fish on many shores. The rockling nearly always occurs on rocky bottoms where it feeds on crustaceans, worms and small fish.

It spawns offshore, and eggs and larvae float on surface waters. When the young fishes measure about 1½ in (4 cm) long, they adopt the bottom-living habits of the adult rocklings.

Burbot *Lota lota*

RANGE Canada, N. USA, N. Europe, Asia

HABITAT Rivers, lakes

SIZE 20–39 in (51–99 cm)

One of the few fishes in the cod order that lives in fresh water, the burbot is similar to many marine codfishes, with its long body, chin barbel and long-based dorsal and anal fins.

It is a fairly sluggish fish, hiding among aquatic vegetation by day and emerging at dawn and dusk to feed. Adults eat fish, crustaceans and insects, while the young burbot feed on insect larvae and small crustaceans.

Burbot spawn at night in shallow water during the winter. They are prolific egg-layers – one female may shed up to 3 million eggs which then sink to the bottom, where they remain while development takes place.

CODFISHES CONTINUED

Ling *Molva molva*

RANGE N.E. Atlantic Ocean: Iceland, Norway to Bay of Biscay

HABITAT Deep water: 980–1,300 ft (300–400 m)

SIZE 5–6½ ft (1.5–2 m)

Ling are valuable commercial fish in some European waters. A long slim fish, the ling has two dorsal fins, the second of which is long based, and one long anal fin. It has a barbel on its chin. It is most common in rocky-bottomed areas and eats fish and large crustaceans. Although mainly a deepwater species, the ling may be found in shallower areas, where the bottom is suitable. It breeds from March to July, and a female may shed up to 60 million eggs which float in surface waters while they develop.

European Hake *Merluccius merluccius*

RANGE N. Atlantic Ocean: Iceland, Norway to N. Africa; Mediterranean

HABITAT Deep water, 550–1,800 ft (165–550 m)

SIZE 3¼–6 ft (1–1.8 m)

True hakes are a small family of codlike fish, all in the genus *Merluccius*. The European hake is typical with its slender body, large head and two dorsal fins, the first of which is triangular and the second long based and curving. It lives near the seabed migrating upward nightly to feed nearer the surface.

Hakes spawn in spring or summer. The eggs and larvae drift in surface waters, gradually being carried inshore, where young fish remain for the first year, eating mainly crustaceans.

The Pacific hake, *M. productus*, is similar to the European species in appearance and habits.

Cod *Gadus morhua* **VU**

RANGE N. Atlantic Ocean: Greenland and Hudson strait to North Carolina; Baltic sea to Bay of Biscay

HABITAT Coastal waters

SIZE 4 ft (1.2 m)

White Hake *Urophycis tenuis*

RANGE N.W. Atlantic Ocean: Gulf of St. Lawrence to North Carolina

HABITAT Inshore and offshore waters to depths of 3,300 ft (1,000 m)

SIZE 4 ft (1.2 m)

An elongate fish, the white hake has only two dorsal fins, the second of which is long based, a small, rounded tail and one long anal fin. It is commonly found near soft muddy bottoms where it feeds on crustaceans, squid and small fish. Spawning begins in late winter and eggs and larvae float at the surface.

Large quantities of white hake and the closely related red hake, *U. chuss*, are taken by commercial fisheries. Even though, confusingly, their common names are the same, these hakes are a quite separate group from the true hakes (*Merluccius* species).

A stout-bodied fish, the cod is identified by its three dorsal and two anal fins and the single long chin barbel. Its mouth is large, containing many small teeth, and its mottled coloration is variable. Cod usually swim in schools in surface waters but will search for food – crustaceans, worms and fish – at mid-depths or on the seabed.

Breeding takes place between February and April, and some cod populations make long migrations to specific spawning areas. Eggs drift in surface waters, at the mercy of currents and predators, while they develop and hatch into larvae. The young cod feed on small crustaceans.

The cod is an extremely valuable food fish which has been exploited by humans for centuries.

Haddock *Melanogrammus aeglefinus* **VU**

RANGE N. Atlantic Ocean: Barents Sea and Iceland to Bay of Biscay; Newfoundland to Cape Cod

HABITAT Coastal waters, near seabed

SIZE 30 in (76 cm)

The haddock resembles the cod, with its three dorsal and two anal fins, but the first dorsal fin is triangular and pointed and there is a distinct black mark on each dusky side. Haddock live near the seabed and feed on bottom-living animals such as brittle stars, worms, mollusks and some small fish.

Spawning takes place between January and June and eggs are left to float in surface waters while they hatch into larvae. Young haddock often shelter among the tentacles of large jellyfishes. Some haddock populations migrate south in winter or move from shallow inshore waters to deeper waters.

Blue Whiting *Micromesistius poutassou*

RANGE N. Atlantic Ocean: Barents Sea to Mediterranean and Adriatic Seas

HABITAT Oceanic

SIZE 13¾–16 in (35–41 cm)

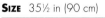

Shoals of blue whiting move in surface and mid-waters to depths of about 980 ft (300 m). They have three well spaced dorsal fins and two anal fins, the first of which is long based. They eat mainly crustaceans and some small fish. They are an important item of diet for many larger fishes.

Whiting *Merlangius merlangus*

RANGE European coasts, Iceland to Spain, Mediterranean and Black Seas

HABITAT Shallow inshore waters to 330 ft (100 m)

SIZE 11¾–15¾ in (30–40 cm)

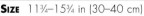

The whiting has three dorsal and two anal fins, the first of which is long based. The upper jaw is longer than the lower and there is a characteristic black mark at the base of each pectoral fin. Adult whiting eat fish and crustaceans, while young feed mainly on

small crustaceans. They spawn in spring in shallow water.

A common species, it is a valuable commercial food fish for humans and is also hunted and eaten by many larger fishes and also birds.

Walleye Pollock *Theragra chalcogramma*

RANGE N. Pacific Ocean: N.W. Alaska to California; Sea of Japan

HABITAT Surface to mid-waters, 1,200 ft (360 m)

SIZE 35½ in (90 cm)

The widely distributed walleye pollock has a tapering body, three well-spaced dorsal fins and two anal fins. Its head and mouth are large, and its eyes bigger than those of most codfishes. Unlike most codfishes, it spends little time near the seabed and feeds mainly in mid-depths on crustaceans and other marine invertebrates and some small fish.

Saithe *Pollachius virens*

RANGE N. Atlantic Ocean: Iceland, Greenland and Barents Sea to Bay of Biscay; Labrador to North Carolina

HABITAT Surface waters: coastal and offshore

SIZE 27½–31½ in (70–80 cm)

Although it has the typical cod fin pattern, the saithe is characterized by its slightly forked tail, the lower jaw, which protrudes slightly beyond the upper, and the lack of a chin barbel. Saithe usually move in small schools and feed on fish, particularly other cod species and herring; young saithe feed on crustaceans and small fish.

Saithe migrate to offshore breeding grounds to spawn in deep water between January and April. The eggs and then the larvae drift at the surface gradually being carried to shallower inshore waters, where the young fishes are found the following summer. Large numbers are caught commercially, and it is a popular species with sea anglers.

TOADFISHES AND ANGLER FISHES

BATRACHOIDIFORMES TOADFISH ORDER

There are about 69 species of bottom-dwelling toadfish, found in many of the oceans of the world, mostly in tropical or warm temperate areas. The common name comes from the resemblance of the broad, flattened head, with its wide mouth and slightly protuberant eyes, to that of a toad.

Atlantic Midshipman *Porichthys porosissimus*

RANGE	W. Atlantic Ocean: coasts of Brazil to Argentina
HABITAT	Inshore waters
SIZE	11¾ in (30 cm)

The bottom-dwelling Atlantic midshipman has a large, flattened head and eyes near the top of the head. The body is scaleless, and on each side there are rows of hundreds of light-producing organs, which are arranged in a regular pattern. Midshipmen are among the few shallow-water fishes to possess such organs.

Also known as the singing fish, this species can make a variety of sounds. Specialized muscles in the walls of the fish's swim bladder contract producing grunts and whistles.

LOPHIIFORMES ANGLER FISH ORDER

There are about 300 species of angler fish known. They are found at all depths in tropical and temperate seas. All have large heads, wide mouths filled with many rows of sharp teeth and small gills. The body is rounded in deep-water forms and flattened in shallow-water forms.

Most anglers have a fishing lure, which is a modified dorsal fin spine, tipped with a flap of skin. It can be positioned in front of the mouth. The shallow-water angler lies camouflaged on the seabed, gently moving its lure. Prey, mistaking the lure for food, approaches to investigate and is engulfed in the fishes' huge jaws.

In a number of deep-sea angler species, males, which are relatively tiny, attach themselves to females so intimately that their tissues fuse.

Angler *Lophius piscatorius*

RANGE	European coasts from Scandinavia and Iceland to N. Africa; Black and Mediterranean Seas
HABITAT	Coastal waters
SIZE	3¼–6½ ft (1–2 m)

A large, highly distinctive fish, the angler has a flattened body, dominated by its broad, flattened head. The mouth is extremely wide with well developed teeth. The head and mouth are fringed with small skin flaps that help conceal the fish's outline as it lies on the seabed. The pectoral fins are placed on the small fleshy limbs, and on the first elongated dorsal spine is a flap of skin, used as a fishing lure. The angler is a bottom-living fish found from shallow water down to 1,650 ft (500 m) or more. Half-buried in the sand or shingle of the seabed, it watches for prey and moves its lure to attract fish within easy reach of its capacious mouth. Once the angler opens its mouth, powerful water currents are created, sucking in the unfortunate prey.

Anglers move farther out to sea in spring and early summer to spawn over deep water. The eggs are shed enclosed in ribbonlike trails of gelatinous mucus which keeps them together as they float near the surface. The larvae, too, float near the surface, aided by their enlarged dorsal fins. The closely related goosefish, *L. americanus*, of the Atlantic coast of North America is similar in appearance and habits.

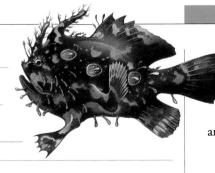

Sargassumfish *Histrio histrio*

RANGE Atlantic, Indian, Pacific Oceans, tropical areas

HABITAT Surface waters among sargassum weed

SIZE 7½ in (19 cm)

The sargassumfish is one of the family of anglers known as frogfishes which, typically, have a balloon-shaped body covered with bumps and flaps of skin. It is perfectly camouflaged to blend with the sargassum weed in which it lives and, while its coloration is variable, it always matches its own particular weed patch. Frondlike rays on the snout mimic the weed itself, and white dots on the body resemble the white encrustations of tiny animals that live on sargassum plants. The fish's pectoral fins are flexible and can be used actually to grasp the weed as it clambers around.

Small invertebrates are the main food of the sargassumfish, and it attracts prey with the small lure on its snout. If it is attacked by a predator, the sargassumfish may rapidly take in water, pumping itself into a ball too big to swallow.

Longlure Frogfish

Antennarius multiocellatus

RANGE Tropical W. Atlantic Ocean, Caribbean

HABITAT Seabed

SIZE 6 in (15 cm)

The longlure frogfish has a stout body typical of its family and a pronounced "fishing line" on its snout. Its coloration is variable but always merges well with its surroundings, whether rock, coral or seaweed. A bottom-living, slow-moving fish, it crawls around the seabed with the aid of its limblike pectoral fins, feeding on small fish and crustaceans.

Shortnose Batfish *Ogcocephalus nasutus*

RANGE Caribbean

HABITAT Seabed

SIZE 11 in (28 cm)

The shortnose batfish is typical of the 55 or so species of batfish, with its almost triangular body, dramatically flattened from top to bottom. Its pectoral fins are large and flexible and positioned on armlike stalks. Its snout is pointed and mouth small, and the upper surface of its body is studded with hard tubercles – rounded projections.

A slow-moving, awkward swimmer, the batfish crawls over the seabed on its pectoral and pelvic fins, using its tail as support. It eats fish, mollusks, crustaceans and worms.

Football-fish

Himantolophus groenlandicus

RANGE Worldwide (but uncommon)

HABITAT Deep sea: 330–980 ft (100–300 m)

SIZE 24 in (61 cm)

The football-fish is a deep-sea angler. Its extremely rotund body is studded with bony plates, each bearing a central spine, and the modified ray on the head makes a thick "fishing rod", tipped with a many-branched lure and with a central luminous bulb. It preys on fish attracted to the lure in the sparsely inhabited dark depths. Males are smaller than females but are not parasitic.

Linophryne arborifera

RANGE Atlantic, Pacific, Indian Oceans

HABITAT Deep sea

SIZE 2¾ in (7 cm)

One of a family of deep-sea anglers, *Linophryne* has a rounded body and a branched chin barbel, resembling a piece of seaweed. The prominent "fishing rod" on its snout is branched and bears a luminous lure. The tiny adult males are believed to live parasitically on the females, losing their own powers of vision and smell.

BELONIFORM FISHES

ORDER BELONIFORMES

This diverse order of about 190 species of mostly marine fishes includes 5 families – flyingfishes, halfbeaks, needlefishes, sauries, and medakas. Most are active near or above the surface of the water. Flyingfishes are tail-powered gliders, different species gaining lift from enlarged, winglike pectoral fins, but all propelling themselves forward with their rapidly beating tails to glide short distances over the water. Halfbeaks skip along the surface of the sea but do not become fully airborne like the flyingfishes. Flyingfishes usually "fly" to escape from predators such as the dolphin fish. Needlefish and sauries are fast-moving fish that swim near the surface and prey on small fishes. Medakas, or ricefishes, are common inhabitants of brackish and freshwater in tropical Asia.

Atlantic Flyingfish *Cypselurus heterurus*

RANGE W. Atlantic Ocean: S. Canada to Brazil; E. Atlantic: Denmark to N. Africa; Mediterranean Sea

HABITAT Surface waters: open sea and coastal

SIZE 11¾–17 in (30–43 cm)

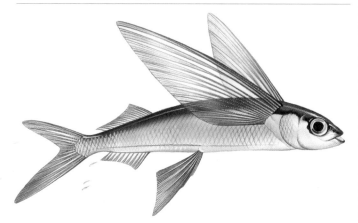

The Atlantic flyingfish is a four-winged flyingfish, with enlarged pectoral and pelvic fins to propel it on its "flights". When swimming underwater, its pectoral fins are kept folded against the body. The dorsal and anal fins are small and positioned near the tail, which has a long lower lobe. The body is fully scaled. Before a flight, the fish builds up speed in the water and then rises into the air, both pairs of fins expanded, and glides up to 300 ft (90 m) at 5 ft (1.5 m) above the surface. Most flights last about 10 seconds.

Flyingfishes breed in the spring and lay their eggs among seaweed or other debris. The eggs bear many fine threads which attach them to one another and anchor them to floating objects. Newly hatched flyingfishes have short barbels on the chin.

Flyingfish *Exocetus volitans*

RANGE All oceans: tropical and subtropical areas

HABITAT Open sea

SIZE 11¾ in (30 cm)

This species of flyingfish has only one pair of wings: the enlarged pectoral fins. Flights of two-winged flyingfishes are shorter and less controlled than those of four-winged species. Otherwise this species is similar to the Atlantic flyingfish in its habits. Like all flyingfishes it is carnivorous, feeding mostly on other fish.

Wrestling Halfbeak *Dermogenys pusillus*

RANGE Thailand, Malaysia, Singapore, Sunda Islands

HABITAT Fresh water

SIZE 2¾ in (7 cm)

A small slender fish, with dorsal and anal fins positioned near the broad rounded tail, the wrestling halfbeak has the elongated lower jaw typical of its group. It is one of the few freshwater halfbeaks. Mosquito larvae are its main food source, and it is an important controller of these pests.

Males are aggressive and fight one another by wrestling with their jaws. The anal fin of the male is modified to form a copulatory organ for internal fertilization of the female. About 8 weeks after her eggs have been fertilized, the female gives birth to 12 to 20 live young, each of which is about ½ in (1 cm) long.

Ballyhoo *Hemiramphus brasiliensis*

RANGE Atlantic Ocean: New England, USA to Brazil; Gulf of Mexico, Caribbean; off W. Africa

HABITAT Coastal waters

SIZE 17¾ in (45 cm)

The ballyhoo is a slender-bodied fish, with a greatly elongated lower jaw and small dorsal and anal fins set back on the body near the tail. It is a typical halfbeak with small pectoral fins which, although it cannot glide over the water like its relatives the flyingfishes, can skim over the surface. It is surface-living and moves in schools, feeding on sea grass and small fish. The form of its jaws may help it to scoop up food from the water surface.

Garfish *Belone belone*

RANGE N. Atlantic Ocean: Iceland to Spain and Scandinavia; Mediterranean and Black Seas

HABITAT Surface waters, mainly offshore

SIZE 37 in (94 cm)

The garfish is a long, slim fish with elongate jaws, which are studded with numerous needlelike teeth. Both dorsal and anal fins are long based and set well back near the tail. An active predator, the garfish feeds on many species of small fish and crustaceans. It spawns in late spring or early summer, in coastal waters. The small, round eggs bear many fine threads which attach to floating debris or seaweed.

Freshwater Needlefish *Belonion apodion*

RANGE South America

HABITAT Lakes, rivers

SIZE 2 in (5 cm)

A tiny, fragile fish, first discovered in 1966, the freshwater needlefish is one of a family of about 30 needlefishes and garfishes, most of which are marine. It is typical of its family, with its slender body and small anal and dorsal fins placed near the tail, but unlike most other species, which have elongate upper and lower jaws, only its lower jaw is long.

Houndfish *Tylosaurus crocodilus*

RANGE All oceans

HABITAT Inshore surface waters

SIZE 5 ft (1.5 m)

The largest, heaviest needlefish, the houndfish has a shorter, thicker beak than most species. Houndfishes sometimes leap out of the water and skip over the surface and, because of their size

and strong, pointed jaws, can be quite dangerous to man. The houndfish feeds on fish, which it seizes crosswise in its jaws and skilfully turns to swallow headfirst.

Saury *Scomberesox saurus*

RANGE N. Atlantic Ocean: N. American to European coasts; Mediterranean Sea; temperate waters in S. hemisphere, around the globe

HABITAT Open ocean, coastal waters

SIZE 15¾–19¾ in (40–50 cm)

The saury, or skipper, is a long, slim fish with elongate beaklike jaws, the lower of which is longer than the upper. Behind the saury's dorsal and anal fins are further rows of small fins. Sauries swim in shoals in surface waters, feeding on small crustaceans and small fish.

Sauries spawn in open sea. Their eggs, which are small and round and covered with many threads, float at the water surface while they develop. The young fishes hatch with short jaws of equal length; the elongate jaws develop as the fishes grow and mature.

Ricefish/Japanese Medaka *Oryzias latipes*

RANGE Japan

HABITAT Coastal marshes, rice fields

SIZE 1½ in (4 cm)

The ricefish is one of a family of 8 species of fish, known as medakas, and found in Southeast Asia and Japan. It is a small, slender fish, with a flattened head and an almost straight back. The underside of the body is distinctly curved, and there is a long-based anal fin. In the male the dorsal fin is pointed, but in the female it is rounded. Medakas are useful to mankind in that they feed on mosquito larvae and other small invertebrates.

Medakas breed by laying eggs. At first, the female carries her eggs around in a mucous sheath attached to her belly, but then she deposits them among submerged plants, where they complete their development and hatch out up to 12 days after they were laid.

CYPRINIDONTIFORM FISHES

ORDER CYPRINODONTIFORMES

This major group of freshwater fish includes 807 species in 8 families that include rivulines, killifishes, foureye fishes, livebearers, splitfins, guppies, and pupfishes. Most are small omnivorous fish although there are also some predatory and some herbivorous species.

Cyprinodontiforms are noted for their ability to live in habitats in both temperate and tropical regions that are unsuitable for most other fish. This includes stagnant, saline or even hypersaline conditions.

Most are surface swimmers that feed on insects and vegetation that has fallen onto the water. Because of their living near the surface cyprinodontiforms are sometimes referred to as top-minnows, although they are not related to true minnows (Cyprinidae). They are also referred to as toothcarps because of the presence of small teeth in the jaws and their superficial resemblance to carp.

Sheepshead Minnow *Cyprinidon variegatus*

RANGE USA coasts: Cape Cod to Texas, south to Mexico

HABITAT Bays, harbors, salt marshes

SIZE 3 in (7.5 cm)

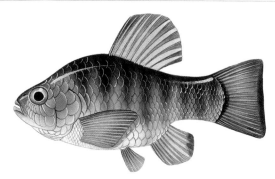

The sheepshead minnow has a short, stubby body and a high back and a prominent dorsal fin. Outside the breeding season, both males and females appear similar, but females have darker markings. Breeding males develop much brighter coloration, turning steely-blue and green, with orange or red bellies.

Sheepshead minnows feed on a wide range of tiny invertebrates and aquatic plants.

Breeding takes place between April and September and males compete for mates. The female lays her eggs a few at a time while the male clasps her round the tail and fertilizes the eggs as they are shed. The eggs have sticky threads on their surface which attach them to each other and to plants or objects on the bottom.

Mummichog/Common Killifish

Fundulus heteroclitus

RANGE N. American coasts: Labrador to Mexico

HABITAT Bays, marshes, river mouths

SIZE 4–6 in (10–15 cm)

The stout-bodied mummichog is an adaptable and hardy little fish which is able to tolerate brackish, salt and fresh water.

It is a voracious feeder and will eat almost any available plants and animals.

Mummichogs breed between April and August in shallow water. The male chases his mate in an extensive courtship ritual and then clasps her with his fins in order to fertilize the eggs as they are laid. The sticky-surfaced eggs then sink to the bottom in a cluster.

Aphanius dispar

RANGE Indian Ocean: coasts of E. Africa and Middle East; Red Sea

HABITAT Coastal waters

SIZE 3¼ in (8 cm)

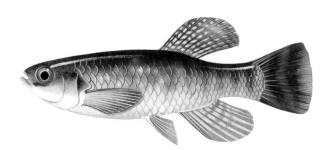

This adaptable toothcarp occurs in fresh- and saltwater pools in its range, as well as in the sea. Males and females of the species differ slightly in coloration. The males are brownish blue with dark markings near and on the tail, while females are a grayish blue with markings on their sides. This toothcarp feeds on small invertebrates and algae.

The female sheds her eggs on to submerged aquatic plants. The eggs hatch out in under 2 weeks, and the young fishes feed on plant plankton and algae.

Four-eyed Fish

Anableps anableps

RANGE S. Mexico, Central America and N. South America

HABITAT Coasts, estuaries, lakes

SIZE 11¾ in (30 cm)

The four-eyed fish has, in fact, only two eyes, which project well above the head and are divided into two parts. The top section of each eye is adapted for vision in the air and the lower for vision in water; the sections are separated by a dark band. The fish swims at the surface, the water reaching the level of the dividing bands on the eyes, and is able to watch for insect prey at the surface or in the air and any prey swimming just under water, at the same time.

Four-eyed fish bear live young and females are fertilized internally. The male's anal fin is modified into a copulatory organ which can be moved either to the left or the right, and the female's genital opening is covered by a specialized scale which opens to the left or right. It is believed that a "left-handed" male must copulate with a "right-handed" female and vice versa; fortunately it seems that the proportion of right and left mating types is more or less equal in both sexes. The eggs develop inside the mother's body, and 4 or 5 live young are born.

Guppy *Poecilia reticulata*

RANGE N. South America to Brazil; Barbados, Trinidad; introduced in many tropical areas

HABITAT Streams, pools

SIZE 2¼ in (6 cm)

The guppy occurs naturally over a wide range and has been spread by humans as a pest controller, since it feeds on the aquatic larvae of mosquitos. It is an extremely abundant fish, occurring in huge numbers in brackish as well as fresh water. Females are generally larger than males and less attractively colored, with dull, brownish bodies. As well as feeding on mosquito larvae, guppies eat other insect larvae, small crustaceans and the eggs and young of other fishes.

Guppies breed throughout the year bearing litters of live young. The male's anal fin is modified as a copulatory organ for internal fertilization of the female. The young develop inside the

mother and their egg membranes burst as they are born. Up to 24 young are born at a time and they achieve sexual maturity in between 4 and 10 weeks, depending on the temperature of their surroundings. This ability to mature fast and to breed many times a year leads to such large populations of guppies that they are called millions fish in some areas. Many different brilliantly colored forms are bred as aquarium fish.

Cape Lopez Lyretail *Aphyosemion australe*

RANGE Africa: Gabon, Cape Lopez area

HABITAT Swamps, ditches

SIZE 2¼ in (6 cm)

The male Cape Lopez lyretail is an attractive, brightly colored fish, with large, pointed dorsal and anal fins and a tail with extended lobes. The female is plainer, and her fins lack the decorative points and extensions.

The lyretail deposits its eggs among the mud and detritus at the bottom of its habitat. If there is then a prolonged dry season, the embryos cease their development and lie dormant in the mud, protected by their drought-resistant egg membrane. Although the parent fishes die in the drought, the eggs resume development with the arrival of rain and hatch shortly afterwards.

Least Killifish/Dwarf Top-minnow *Heterandria formosa*

RANGE Streams, ponds, ditches, swamps

HABITAT USA, South Carolina, Florida

SIZE ¾–1¼ in (2–3.5 cm)

One of the smallest vertebrates at only ¾ in (2 cm) long, adult males of this species are smaller than females. The fishes live among dense aquatic vegetation and feed on mosquitoes and minute crustaceans.

Least killifish have unusual breeding habits. After mating, the eggs develop a few at a time and are fertilized inside the female by sperm that were deposited by the male at mating.

The young are born over a period of a week or more at the rate of 2 or 3 a day. This is a popular aquarium species.

CYPRINODONTIFORM FISHES AND ATHERINIFORM FISHES

Pike Top-minnow *Belonesox belizanus*

RANGE Mexico, Central America to Honduras

HABITAT Muddy backwaters, marshes, lakes

SIZE 4 7 in (10–20 cm)

A long-bodied fish, the pike top-minnow has a pointed snout and a large mouth. It resembles a tiny pike and hunts in the same way, lurking among vegetation then dashing out quickly from its hiding place in order to seize passing prey.

Females are larger than males, sometimes reaching twice their size. These fishes are thought to have considerably reduced in number due to insecticides which have been sprayed on to the waters of their habitats in order to destroy mosquito larvae.

Female pike top-minnows produce 20 to 80 live young at a time. Although rather predatory, top-minnows are used as aquarium fish.

Swordtail *Xiphophorus helleri*

RANGE Mexico, Guatemala

HABITAT Springs, streams, rivers, lagoons, swamps

SIZE 5 in (12.5 cm)

In male swordtails the lower lobe of the tail is greatly extended into a slim, bladelike projection from which the common name is derived. Females lack this tail extension and are less brightly colored.

The range of habitats of this species is reflected in the number of forms, differing in coloration, shape and tail development, which have arisen to fit them. Swordtails feed on small aquatic invertebrates.

Like all members of the family Poeciliidae, the swordtail produces live young. The male fertilizes the female internally, and the young fish develop inside her ovarian cavity.

The female swordtail is known to change sex, but the reasons for this are not clear. She stops producing young, develops the tail extension and male coloration and gradually becomes a totally functional male. Males do not change into females.

These little fishes have become popular aquarium fish and have been bred in a variety of colors.

ORDER ATHERINIFORMES

These are mostly small, silvery fishes with large eyes and two dorsal fins. The 285 or so species include silversides, rainbowfishes, blueeyes, and grunions. About half of the species in the order are silversides. These plankton feeders are found in large shoals in lakes, estuaries, and shallow marine habitats.

Hardhead Silverside *Atherinomorus stipes*

RANGE N. Atlantic Ocean: Florida to Brazil, including Caribbean

HABITAT Inshore waters

SIZE 5 in (12.5 cm)

The hardhead silverside has an elongated, cylindrical body and two dorsal fins. The first dorsal fins consists of spines. The hardhead silverside's eyes are large relative to its body size. The coloration of this species is variable. During the day it is almost transparent, with a narrow silvery stripe running down its body. Then when night falls the color darkens.

These silversides are abundant, and they occur in large shoals. They lay eggs bearing threads, which anchor them to aquatic plants while they develop.

Phenacostethus smithi

RANGE Thailand

HABITAT Fresh water: muddy pools, ditches, canals

SIZE 1 in (2 cm)

One of the tiniest of fishes, this abundant species occurs in small schools and feeds on microscopic planktonic organisms. It has minute scales and two dorsal fins (one of which is just a spine) and a disproportionately long anal fin. Since the body is virtually transparent, the internal organs are visible.

These fishes have no pelvic fins, but the male has a complex copulatory organ, positioned just behind the chin, that involves some of the pelvic structure. The female's urogenital opening is in the same position and is covered by a specialized scale. The fishes spawn from May to December, the male clasping the female and fertilizing the eggs as they are laid.

California Grunion *Leuresthes tenuis*

RANGE Pacific Ocean: coasts of California and Baja California

HABITAT Inshore waters

SIZE 7 in (18 cm)

The California grunion is in tune with tidal and lunar rhythms and uses them in order to synchronize its spawning activities. These slender little fishes await the extremes of the spring or neap tides to bury their eggs on the sandy shore at the high-water mark.

They spawn at night between March and August, but the spawning peaks between May and June. Once the high-water mark is reached by the waves, the grunion swim ashore in huge numbers, mate and lay their eggs in shallow scrapes which they dig in the sand. The next wave covers the eggs with sand and carries the fish from the beach back into the sea. Two weeks later, at the extreme high of the next high tides, the eggs are exposed, which triggers hatching. The spawning cycle is thus entirely predictable and is associated with the tidal rhythms.

The vast numbers of California grunion that gather in order to take part in the fortnightly spawning runs attract many predators, including man. Fishermen are allowed to take only a limited quantity of the fishes.

Sandsmelt *Atherina presbyter*

RANGE E. Atlantic Ocean: coasts of Britain, Ireland, France, Spain, Portugal and N. Africa

HABITAT Inshore waters, estuaries

SIZE 6–8 in (15–2 cm)

Sandsmelts are small schooling fishes which are found worldwide, mostly in tropical and warm temperate seas. This species is one of the few found in northern waters and is fairly typical of its family with its long, slender body and two widely spaced dorsal fins; the first dorsal fin has seven or eight spines. Schools of sandsmelts are most common on sandy or muddy bottoms, and young fishes may sometimes be found in coastal rock pools.

The jaws of sandsmelts are highly protrusible, and small crustaceans form their main food, although they occasionally eat tiny fish. Sandsmelts are themselves preyed upon by larger fishes and by seabirds such as terns.

Breeding starts between late spring and midsummer. Sandsmelts often spawn in shore pools, laying eggs that bear long threads, which anchor them to seaweed. The newly hatched young are about ⅓ in (7 mm) long.

Crimson-spotted Rainbowfish *Melanotaenia fluviatilis*

RANGE Australia: South Australia, New South Wales, Queensland

HABITAT Rivers, streams

SIZE 3 in (9 cm)

The colorful crimson-spotted rainbowfish occurs over a vast area and is one of about 53 species of rainbowfish all found in Australia or New Guinea. In early summer it lays its eggs, which become safely anchored to aquatic plants by means of fine threads and hatch in about 9 days. This rainbowfish is a popular aquarium species.

LAMPRIDIFORM FISHES, WHALE FISHES AND BERYCIFORM FISHES

LAMPRIDIFORMES

There are about 19 species of marine fish in this little-studied, relatively little-known order. The lampridiformes include the opahs, crestfishes, oarfishes and ribbonfishes. Many of these fish are extremely large. The oarfish (*Regalecus*), for example, may sometimes exceed 20 ft (6 m) in length.

Most are without scales, and have laterally flattened bodies, but some species have fragile, modified scales. The opah is deep-bodied, but most other species are elongate, resembling flattened eels. They have no true spines in their fins.

Opah *Lampris guttatus*

RANGE Worldwide except Antarctic; most common in temperate and tropical seas

HABITAT Open sea, mid-waters at 330–1,300 ft (100–400 m)

SIZE 5 ft (1.5 m)

A striking, colorful fish, the opah is predominantly bright blue, dotted with white on the upper part of its body. It has well-developed red fins. An adult opah may weigh as much as 161 lb (73 kg) .

The opah has a protrusible mouth and it is toothless, but despite its lack of armory and its apparently awkward shape, it is a successful predator, feeding mainly on squid and fish such as hake and blue whiting.

Little is known of the biology and habits of this fish, and it is rarely seen.

Oarfish *Regalecus glesne*

RANGE Atlantic, Pacific and Indian Oceans: temperate and tropical areas

HABITAT Open sea at 980–2,000 ft (300–600 m)

SIZE Up to 23 ft (7 m)

The oarfish has a long, ribbonlike body, which is extremely compressed at the sides. The dorsal fin originates just behind the snout and runs the length of the body; its first few rays are elongate and form a crest. There is no anal fin, but the pelvic fins, tipped with flaps of skin, are long and slender. The oarfish swims with rippling movements and is thought to have given rise to many tales about sea serpents.

The oarfish has a small, protrusible mouth and no teeth and feeds on shrimplike crustaceans. There are thought to be only 1 or 2 species of these strange-looking fishes.

Dealfish *Trachipterus arcticus*

RANGE N.E. Atlantic Ocean: Greenland and Iceland to Madeira and N. Africa

HABITAT Open sea, mid-depths

SIZE 8¼ ft (2.5 m)

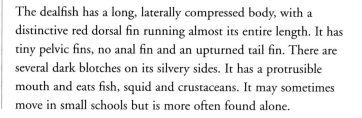

The dealfish has a long, laterally compressed body, with a distinctive red dorsal fin running almost its entire length. It has tiny pelvic fins, no anal fin and an upturned tail fin. There are several dark blotches on its silvery sides. It has a protrusible mouth and eats fish, squid and crustaceans. It may sometimes move in small schools but is more often found alone.

Atelopus japonicus

RANGE Indian and Pacific Oceans:
E. African coast to Japan

HABITAT Deep sea, 600–1,800 ft (180–550 m)

SIZE 24 in (61 cm)

This fish has a long, tapering body and a relatively large head. It has threadlike pelvic fins, a high, shortbased dorsal fin and a long anal fin, which unites with the reduced tail fin. The body is soft and fragile, and the few specimens found have been damaged. There are teeth only in the upper jaw; the lower jaw is set back under the protruding snout.

This little-known fish is thought to feed on the seabed on bottom-dwelling invertebrates.

ORDER STEPHANOBERYCIFORMES

The 86 species in this order are mainly nocturnal, predatory deep sea fish with light organs and weak or absent fin spines. Species include whalefish, gibberfish, and pricklefish.

Whalefish *Cetomimus indagator*

RANGE Indian Ocean

HABITAT Deep sea

SIZE 5½ in (14 cm)

This species belongs to a small family of 10 or more types of deep-sea whalefish. Whalefishes are generally rather stout, with large heads and jaws, and they lack scales and pelvic fins. *C. indagator* has a smaller, more pointed head than normal. It has the characteristic whalefish jaws, lined with many tiny teeth and rudimentary eyes. Its lateral line – the sensory organs along its sides – is a broad tube with twelve large openings.

At the bases of the dorsal and anal fins, whalefishes have soft luminous tissue that is believed to glow in the dark. These fishes have soft, fragile bodies and have rarely been caught undamaged. Only one specimen of *C. indagator* has been found.

BERYCIFORMES

This order includes about 123 species of marine fishes, grouped in 7 families. Forms include whalefish, squirrelfish, lanterneyes, pinecone fish, slimeheads and beardfish. Most are deep-bodied, large-eyed fishes with spiny fins. Most families contain fewer than a dozen species. The family of squirrelfishes, Holocentridae, is the largest with more than 60 species.

Pinecone Fish *Monocentris japonicus*

RANGE Indian and Pacific Oceans: South Africa to Japan

HABITAT Open sea at 100–600 ft (30–180 m)

SIZE 5 in (12.5 cm)

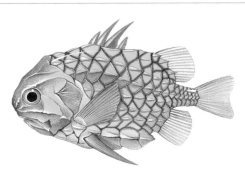

The body of the pinecone fish is encased in an armor of heavy, platelike scales. Its dorsal fin consists of stout spines, directed alternately to left and right, and it has large pelvic spines. Under the lower jaw it has two light-producing organs. Their luminescence is not generated by luminous cells in the fish – as in the case of photophores, possessed by some other fishes – but by luminous bacteria, living symbiotically with the fish.

Pinecone fish move in schools near to the bottom of the sea. There is only 1 other species in the family, also found in the Indian and Pacific oceans.

Squirrelfish *Holocentrus ascensionis*

RANGE Atlantic Ocean: Bermuda, Gulf of Mexico to Brazil; vicinity of Ascension Island

HABITAT Coastal waters in tropical and warm temperate areas

SIZE 24 in (61 cm)

This brightly colored squirrelfish is common on coral reefs or in rocky-bottomed areas. Its scales are large and rough, and it has a strong spine on the gill cover. It hides in crannies and rock crevices during the day and emerges at night to feed, mainly on small crustaceans.

Squirrelfishes make a variety of sounds by vibrating the swim bladder with the aid of specialized muscles. The sounds are believed to be part of territorial and breeding behavior.

BERYCIFORM FISHES

Adioryx xantherythrus

RANGE Pacific Ocean: Hawaiian Islands

HABITAT Coral reefs

SIZE 7 in (18 cm)

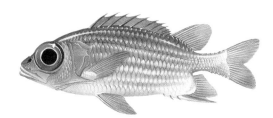

This Hawaiian squirrelfish resembles the other members of its family, with its reddish and pink body and stout dorsal spines. It is a nocturnal fish, remaining hidden in the reef during the day and emerging at night to feed on small invertebrates.

Like the rest of the squirrelfishes, this species is able to produce sounds with its swim bladder which are believed to form part of courtship behavior.

Anomalops kaptoptron

RANGE S. Pacific Ocean: Indonesian coasts

HABITAT Shallow offshore waters

SIZE 11¾ in (30 cm)

One of a small family of 3 species known as lanterneyes, this is a heavy, deep-bodied fish with stout dorsal spines. Its head is broad and strong, and it has the large eyes characteristic of the order. Active at night, it swims in small shoals.

Lanterneyes are among the few shallow-water fishes to possess luminous organs. Beneath each eye there is an oval bar, which appears white in daylight but shines brightly at night. Inside the bar-shaped organ are many tubes containing luminous bacteria, which live symbiotically with the fish and give off light. If the fish needs to dispense with its light for a while, the organs can be rotated so that the luminous sides are turned downward and masked. The fish blinks its lights as it swims, but it is not known whether this is to communicate with other fishes, to attract prey, or to help it navigate.

Roughie *Hoplostethus atlanticus*

RANGE N. Atlantic Ocean

HABITAT Deep sea at 1,650–3,300 ft (500–1,000 m)

SIZE 11¾ in (30 cm)

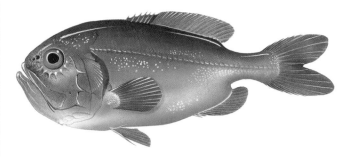

The brightly colored roughie has a large head and deep body, compressed at the sides, and there are strong spines on its belly and preceding its dorsal fin. Its mouth is large and upturned, and the jaws are equipped with many tiny, closeset teeth. Although little is known of its habits, the roughie is thought to feed mainly on crustaceans.

Fishes, such as the roughie, that belong to the family trachichthyidae are also known as slimeheads because of the many mucus-secreting cavities on their heads.

Photoblepharon palpebratus

RANGE Indian and Pacific Oceans

HABITAT Shallow offshore waters

SIZE 3¼ in (8 cm)

A stout fish, with prominent fins and a forked tail, *P. palpebratus* is active only at night. It is a member of the lanterneye family and, like its relatives, has a light organ beneath each eye which appears white in daylight but shines at night. Inside the organ are tubes containing luminous bacteria, which live on the fish and in return produce light. To turn the light off, the fish raises a fold of dark skin across the organ.

Local fishermen remove the lanterneye's light organs, which remain luminous for many hours, and use them as fishing lures.

Stout Beardfish *Polymixia nobilis*

RANGE	All oceans, tropical areas
HABITAT	Deep water
SIZE	9¾ in (25 cm)

Beardfishes are found in tropical and subtropical regions of the Atlantic, Indian and Pacific oceans, usually at depths of 600 to 2,000 ft (180 to 640 m). A deep-bodied fish, the stout beardfish has a pair of long barbels dangling from its lower jaw which may help it to find food on the seabed. The coloration of its fully scaled body is variable, but its tail fin and the tip of the dorsal fin are usually dark, almost black. The almost identical species, *P. japonicus*, is found in the Sea of Japan.

ZEIFORMES

There are about 39 species in this order, which includes the dories, the boarfishes and some lesser-known deep-sea species. All are marine fishes. Typically zeiformes have laterally compressed, deep bodies and large, prominent eyes. There are usually heavy spines in the anterior parts of the dorsal and anal fins. Most have jaws that open very wide.

American John Dory *Zenopsis ocellata*

RANGE	W. Atlantic Ocean: Nova Scotia to Chesapeake Bay
HABITAT	Offshore waters
SIZE	24 in (61 cm)

The American John dory, like its European relative, has a deep, greatly compressed body. Its protruding lower jaw is steeply angled, the tip being almost on a line with the eyes. There are nine or ten stout spines in the first dorsal fin. The anal fin bears three or four short, stout spines. Adults are silvery in color, but the young fish has several irregular dark spots on each side. These gradually disappear as the fish matures, most adults having only a single spot on each side near the gill opening. Like all dories, this species catches its

prey by slowly stalking it until it can engulf the victim within its vast jaws.

John Dory *Zeus faber*

RANGE	E. Atlantic Ocean: N. Scotland to South Africa; Mediterranean Sea
HABITAT	Inshore waters at 33–164 ft (10–50 m)
SIZE	15¾–26 in (40–66 cm)

The John dory is identified by its deep body and large head with protrusible, steeply sloping jaws. There are nine or ten stout spines in the front portion of the dorsal fin, and three or four preceding the anal fin. On each side, above the pectoral fin, there is a characteristic, light bordered black patch.

Usually a solitary fish, the John dory may occasionally move in small schools. It is not a fast swimmer and catches prey by stealth rather than speed. Keeping its flattened body head on and, therefore, harder to spot, it approaches prey slowly until close enough to engulf it in its huge mouth. Small fish and crustaceans make up the bulk of the fish's diet.

Although rarely caught in large numbers, the John dory is highly thought of as a food fish in Europe. An almost identical species of dory, *Z. japonicus*, occurs in the Indian and Pacific oceans.

Boarfish *Capros aper*

RANGE	E. Atlantic Ocean: Ireland to Senegal; Mediterranean Sea
HABITAT	Rocky-bottomed open sea at 330–1,300 ft (100–400 m)
SIZE	4–6¼ in (10–16 cm)

This small relative of the dories also has a deep, laterally compressed body. The head is pointed, with a small mouth, but the jaws are protrusible and lined with fine teeth. Each pelvic fin bears a strong spine, and there are long, stout spines in the first dorsal fin. Small, finely toothed scales cover the body, making it rough to the touch. Like all members of its family, the boarfish is reddish in coloration.

Boarfishes feed on crustaceans, worms and mollusks. They spawn in the summer, and the eggs float freely in surface waters until they hatch.

GASTEROSTEIFORM FISHES

ORDER GASTEROSTEIFORMES

The 260 or so species in this order include some of the most unusual and well-known of the bony fish, including sticklebacks, seahorses, and pipefish.

The sticklebacks and their relatives the tubesnouts are spiny-finned fishes found in both the sea and freshwater in the northern hemisphere. Sticklebacks are territorial nest-builders that are easily recognised by the presence of between 3 and 16 spines along the back. Within 2 of the 8 species of sticklebacks – the threespine stickleback, *Gasterosteus aculeatus*, and the ninespine stickleback, *Pungitius pungitius* – there is enormous diversity over their ranges.

The 225 species of unusually-shaped pipefishes and seahorses cannot move quickly and depend on armor and secretive behavior to camouflage them from predators. Most inhabit shallow marine waters.

Threespine Stickleback *Gasterosteus aculeatus*

RANGE N. America: Pacific and Atlantic coasts and fresh water; Europe: coasts and fresh water, north to Arctic Circle; N. Asia; N. Pacific Ocean: Bering Strait to Korea

HABITAT Coastal waters, lakes, rivers

SIZE 2–4 in (5–10 cm)

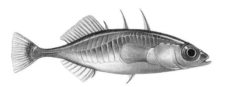

A small fish, with three characteristic spines on its back, this stickleback is scaleless but it is armored with bony plates. It feeds on almost any available small creatures, such as crustaceans, worms, mollusks, fish eggs and larvae, and even on some plant material.

In the breeding season – spring and early summer in North America and Europe – the male stickleback develops a bright red belly. He makes a nest on the bottom from plant fragments, glued together with mucous secretions. He then displays, to attract several females to his nest, where they lay eggs, which he immediately fertilizes. The male then guards the eggs carefully, driving away any predators and fanning water into the nest in order to aerate the eggs, which hatch in about 3 weeks.

Fifteenspine Stickleback *Spinachia spinachia*

RANGE Coasts of Scandinavia, Britain, N. Europe

HABITAT Shallow, coastal waters

SIZE 6–7½ in (15–19 cm)

A slender, long-bodied fish, with a pointed snout, this stickleback is identified by the 14 to 17 (usually 15) spines on its back. It lives only in the sea, generally in areas where there is abundant seaweed, and feeds on small crustaceans.

The male makes a nest from scraps of marine plants, stuck together with his mucous secretions, and then attracts a series of females into his nest to lay their eggs. He fertilizes and then guards the eggs until they hatch 18 to 21 days later.

Fourspine Stickleback *Apeltes quadracus*

RANGE W. Atlantic Ocean: E. coast of N. America, Nova Scotia to Virginia

HABITAT Coastal waters, brackish and fresh water

SIZE 2¼ in (6 cm)

Found in salt and fresh water, the fourspine stickleback prefers areas with plenty of seaweed. Its body is naked, lacking the plates of the threespine stickleback, but there are bony ridges on each side of the belly. Small crustaceans are its main food.

Like other sticklebacks, these fishes spawn in spring and early summer, and the male builds a nest in which females lay eggs. The male guards the eggs until they hatch.

Tubesnout *Aulorhynchus flavidus*

RANGE Pacific Ocean: coast of N. America from Alaska to Baja California

HABITAT Inshore waters

SIZE 6¼ in (16 cm)

The tubesnout has a long, cylindrical body which tapers toward the tail. The small mouth is at the tip of the long, rigid snout. There is one normal dorsal fin, placed opposite the anal fin, but in front of this are 24 to 26 isolated spines, which make up the first dorsal fin. Tubesnouts move in large shoals of hundreds, or even thousands, of individuals and feed on small crustaceans, as well as on other items of plankton.

The female deposits her eggs in a nest of algae, which is stuck together with threads of mucus, extruded by the male.

Winged Dragon *Pegasus volitans* DD

RANGE Indian and Pacific Oceans, E. Africa to N. Australia

HABITAT Sandy-bottomed shallow waters

SIZE 5½ in (14 cm)

A curious fish, the winged dragon has a broad, flattened body, surrounded with bony rings, and a tapering tail. The snout is long and flattened, with a small mouth on the underside. The pectoral fins are broad and winglike, while the other fins are all relatively small.

Shrimpfish *Aeoliscus strigatus*

RANGE Indian and Pacific Oceans to N. Australia

HABITAT Coastal waters, open sea

SIZE 6 in (15 cm)

The shrimpfish has a flat, compressed body with a sharp-edged belly. At the end of its body is a long spine, formed by part of the tail fin. The fish frequently swims in a vertical position, with its elongate snout held downward, propelling itself with its tail and anal fins. It is often found among the spines of sea urchins, where dark stripes along the sides of its body, which mimic the spines, provide camouflage. They also conceal the fish's eyes, which might otherwise reveal its presence.

Greater Pipefish *Syngnathus acus*

RANGE E. Atlantic Ocean: coasts of Norway to N. Africa; Mediterranean and Adriatic Seas

HABITAT Shallow waters with sandy or muddy bottoms

SIZE 11¾–18½ in (30–47 cm)

The body of the greater pipefish is encased in bony armor, which forms distinct segments. Its snout is long and tubular,

with a small mouth at the tip, and the main means of propulsion is the pronounced dorsal fin. It feeds on small crustaceans and other tiny planktonic creatures, as well as on young fish.

Breeding occurs from May to August. Like all pipefishes, the male incubates the eggs in a brood pouch, which in this species is a double fold of skin positioned under the tail. The eggs are incubated for about 5 weeks, and on hatching, the perfectly formed young are released through a slit, where the folds of the pouch meet.

Dwarf Seahorse

Hippocampus zosterae **VU**

RANGE W. Atlantic Ocean: Florida through Gulf of Mexico to Caribbean

HABITAT Shallow waters

SIZE 1½ in (4 cm)

Instantly recognizable, with its head set at an angle to the body and its curling prehensile tail, the dwarf seahorse is the smallest seahorse species. It moves slowly, using gentle movements of its tiny dorsal fin for propulsion, and can attach itself to vegetation by means of its tail. Small crustaceans and larvae are its main foods.

The breeding season extends from February to October, and the female lays 50 or more eggs, which she places in the male's brood pouch.

Weedy Seadragon *Phyllopteryx taeniolatus* **DD**

RANGE Coasts of S. Australia

HABITAT Shallow waters

SIZE 18 in (46 cm)

Although little is known of the habits of this strange seahorse, the many leaflike flaps of skin on its body are presumed to give it a protective resemblance to fronds of seaweed.

Like all seahorses, the male incubates the eggs on a flap of skin beneath his tail.

SWAMP EELS, FLYING GURNARDS AND SCORPAENIFORM FISHES

SYNBRANCHIFORMES ORDER

There are about 87 species in this order, 7 of which are marine. They are grouped in 3 families – swamp eels, spiny eels and chaudiriid eels. Swamp eels are not, however, true eels but have an eellike body shape and extremely reduced fins. Their gill system is minute and is linked with a variety of organs for breathing air and techniques of doing so.

Rice Eel *Monopterus alba*

RANGE Japan, N. China to Thailand and Burma

HABITAT Rivers, ponds, rice fields

SIZE 35¾ in (91 cm)

The rice eel has an elongate, scaleless body and lacks pectoral and pelvic fins. The dorsal and anal fins are low and join with the tail fin. There are one or two gill openings on the throat, but the fish, commonly lives in stagnant, oxygen-poor water, and often breathes air at the surface. In dry seasons, rice eels burrow into the mud and stay alive until rains arrive, provided their skin remains moist.

The male rice eel makes a nest by blowing a cluster of bubbles of air and mucus. The eggs are shed among these bubbles, and the whole structure floats freely, guarded by the male.

Spiny Eel *Mastacembelus armatus*

RANGE India, Sri Lanka, S.E. Asia, China, Sumatra, Java, Borneo

HABITAT Swamps, rivers, lakes

SIZE 29½ in (75 cm)

A slender, eellike fish, the spiny eel has a row of sharp, spines preceding its dorsal fin. It has no pelvic fins, and the dorsal and anal fins are near the tail. The head is narrow and pointed, and the upper part of the snout extends into a fleshy appendage. This eel eats insects and crustaceans; adults eat fish.

DACTYLOPTERIFORMES FLYING GURNARD ORDER

This order contains 1 family of 7 species of marine fishes, found in tropical and warm temperate areas of the Atlantic and Indo-Pacific Oceans. They have large pectoral fins, but there is no evidence that these fish fly above the water.

Flying Gurnard *Dactylopterus volitans*

RANGE W. Atlantic Ocean: Bermuda through Caribbean to Argentina; E. Atlantic: Portugal to W. Africa; Mediterranean Sea

HABITAT Bottom of shallow waters

SIZE 11¾–16 in (30–40.5 cm)

A bottom-dwelling fish, the flying gurnard uses its long winglike pelvic fins to "walk" over the seabed searching for crustaceans. If alarmed, the gurnard may spread its fins, revealing the blue spots on their surfaces.

SCORPAENIFORMES SCORPIONFISH ORDER

This large, widely distributed order contains 24 families and nearly 1,300 species of fish, most of which are marine. Body form is variable, but most species are thick-set and spiny.

Rascasse *Scorpaena porcus*

RANGE Mediterranean and Black Seas; N. Atlantic Ocean: Biscay to Madeira

HABITAT Shallow waters

SIZE 9¾ in (25 cm)

The rascasse lurks amid seaweed-covered rocks, where its camouflaging coloration and the weedlike flaps of skin on its head make it almost invisible. Its dorsal fin is spiny, with venom glands at the sides of the spines. The fish breed in spring or early summer. Eggs are shed in a mass of gelatinous mucus. Rascasse are an essential ingredient of the French fish-stew *bouillabaisse*.

Redfish/Ocean Perch *Sebastes marinus*

RANGE N. Atlantic Ocean: Arctic to Scotland and Sweden; USA: New Jersey

HABITAT Deep water: 330–1,300 ft (100–400 m)

SIZE 31¾ in–3¼ ft (81 cm–1 m)

A heavy-bodied fish, with a large head and a protuberant lower jaw, the redfish has a strongly spined dorsal fin and three spines on the anal fin. By day it stays close to the bottom, rising to surface waters at night to feed on fish such as herring and cod.

Redfishes bear live young. In the north of their range the male fertilizes the female internally in late summer. Females then migrate south during winter and give birth to up to 40,000 larval young the next May or June. The young are about ³⁄₁₀ in (8 mm) long at birth and eat plankton at first, then crustaceans.

Lionfish *Pterois volitans*

RANGE Indian and Pacific Oceans

HABITAT Shallow waters, reefs

SIZE 15 in (38 cm)

The lionfish has long, fanlike pectoral fins, branched dorsal fin and brightly striped body. This eye-catching coloration warns potential enemies that the lionfish's grooved spines are equipped with potent venom, which can have serious, perhaps fatal, effects, even in humans.

Stonefish *Synanceia verrucosa*

RANGE Indian and Pacific Oceans: Africa and Red Sea to N. Australia

HABITAT Shallow water, coral reefs

SIZE 11¾ in (30 cm)

About 20 species of stonefish occur in the Indo-Pacific. All have needlelike dorsal-fin spines, equipped with venom glands that produce the most deadly of all fish venoms. Wounds from a stonefish can kill any human unlucky enough to tread on the spines. This species is typical of its family, with its rough, scaleless body, large, upward-turning head and protuberant eyes. As its name suggests, the stonefish's coloring and shape camouflage it perfectly as it lies half-buried among stones or in rock crevices.

Tub Gurnard *Trigla lucerna*

RANGE E. Atlantic Ocean: Norway, British Isles to N. Africa; coasts of Black, Adriatic and Mediterranean Seas

HABITAT Inshore waters, sandy and muddy bottoms

SIZE 19¾–29½ in (50–75 cm)

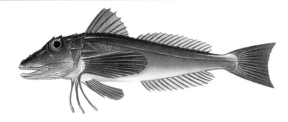

A member of the sea robin family, the tub gurnard has a bony head, pointed snout and well-formed fins. Several rays of the pectoral fins are elongate and free, and they are used by the fish to search for food on the bottom and as props on which to rest. It normally eats bottom-living crustaceans, mollusks and fish.

Tub gurnards are fished commercially in many areas.

Northern Sea Robin *Prionotus carolinus*

RANGE W. Atlantic Ocean: Bay of Fundy to Venezuela

HABITAT Seabed, coastal waters

SIZE 16 in (41 cm)

The northern sea robin is typical of its family, with its large head covered with bony plates and its fanlike pectoral fins. The lowest three rays of the pectoral fins are free, and they are used to feel for prey, such as fish and crustaceans, on the seabed. Coloration varies from grayish to brown, but the sea robin always has dark, saddlelike markings across its back.

Much of the sea robin's life is spent on the bottom, often supported on its pectoral fins. It quickly buries itself if threatened, leaving the top of its head and eyes exposed. Sea robins can make loud sounds by vibrating their swim-bladders with specialized muscles. They are particularly noisy in the breeding season, which lasts from June to September. The eggs are shed and float at the surface until they hatch.

SCORPAENIFORM FISHES CONTINUED

Bullrout/Shorthorn Sculpin *Myoxocephalus scorpius*

RANGE N. Atlantic Ocean: Labrador to Cape Cod; N. European coasts: Britain, Scandinavia, Iceland

HABITAT Shallow inshore waters to 200 ft (60 m)

SIZE 9¾–23½ in (25–60 cm)

Known as the shorthorn sculpin in the USA and the bullrout in Britain, this fish is one of the larger sculpins. It has a broad head, large fins and small spines near its gills and along each side. Females are usually larger than males and have creamy-yellow markings on the belly, where males have orange spots. A bottom-dwelling fish, it feeds mainly on bottom-living crustaceans, as well as on worms and small fish.

It breeds in winter, depositing its sticky-surfaced eggs in clusters among seaweed or in rock crevices. The male guards the eggs until they hatch some 4 to 12 weeks later, depending on the temperature of the water.

Sablefish *Anoplopoma fimbria*

RANGE Pacific Ocean: Japan to Bering Sea, south to Baja California

HABITAT Inshore waters, open sea

SIZE Up to 3¼ ft (1 m)

The sablefish is a long, slender fish with two well-separated dorsal fins. The head is smooth, lacking the spines and ridges of the related scorpionfishes. Adult sablefishes usually live near the bottom in areas of continental shelf, but young fishes swim in surface waters, often in the open ocean. Sablefishes spawn in winter and early spring.

Kelp Greenling *Hexagrammos decagrammus*

RANGE Pacific coast of N. America: Alaska to California

HABITAT Shallow, rocky-bottomed water, kelp beds

SIZE 20¾ in (53 cm)

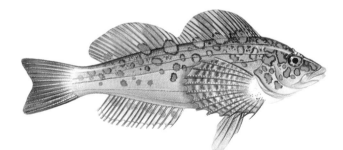

The kelp greenling is one of 11 species of greenling, all found in the North Pacific. Its head is smooth with no spines or ridges, and it has large pectoral fins and a long based dorsal fin which is notched halfway along its length. Males and females differ slightly in appearance, males having blue spots on the foreparts and females reddish-brown spots. Kelp greenlings are unusual in that they have five lateral lines (series of sensory organs) on each side of the body; most fishes have only one.

Kelp greenlings eat worms, crustaceans and small fish, and they themselves are preyed on by larger fishes and fish-eating birds. They spawn in autumn, laying clusters of eggs among the rocks. The young fishes swim in the surface waters of open sea.

Bullhead *Cottus gobio*

RANGE Europe: Sweden and Finland to England and Wales, south to the Pyrenees, Alps, former Yugoslavia

HABITAT Streams, small rivers, lakes

SIZE 4 in (10 cm)

A small, freshwater member of the sculpin family, the bullhead has a broad, flattened head with a small spine at each side. It is most at home in stony-bottomed water and takes refuge during the day under rocks and stones. At night, it emerges to forage for crustaceans and insect larvae.

Bullheads spawn in spring, from March to May. The male makes a shallow cavity under a rock so that the female can shed her eggs on the underside of the rock. The eggs are guarded by the male until they hatch 3 to 4 weeks later. On hatching, the tiny fishes disperse to find shelter among stones.

Cabezon *Scorpaenichthys marmoratus*

RANGE N. Pacific Ocean: Alaska to Baja California

HABITAT Shallow inshore waters to 200 ft (60 m)

SIZE 30 in (76 cm)

One of the largest sculpins, the cabezon has a heavy body, smooth, scaleless skin and a deeply notched dorsal fin. Its head and mouth are broad and there is a prominent flap on the snout. Coloration is very variable, but the skin is generally mottled with pale patches. Although most common in rocky bottomed waters, it also lives over sandy bottoms and in kelp beds. Crabs are its main food. It also eats crustaceans and small fish.

Cabezons spawn during the winter from November to March, often using communal sites. A breeding female carries as many as 100,000 eggs which she deposits in masses on rocks. Males guard the eggs until they hatch.

Oilfish/Baikal Cod *Comephorus baicalensis*

RANGE Russia: Lake Baikal

HABITAT Deep water

SIZE 7½ in (19 cm)

This strange freshwater sculpin is one of a family of only 2 species. It is a long-bodied fish, with no pelvic fins but with long-based dorsal and anal fins. Its head is covered with transparent, delicate skin and it has a large mouth. Although it lives in deep water, it migrates upward at night to feed near the surface on small crustaceans.

Female baikal cod bear live young in the summer in the surface waters of the lake. The other species, *C. dybotwski*, also lives in Lake Baikal.

Sturgeon Poacher *Agonus acipenserinus*

RANGE N. Pacific Ocean: N. American coast, Bering Sea to California

HABITAT Coastal muddy-bottomed water at depths of 60–180 ft (18–55 m)

SIZE Up to 11¾ in (30 cm)

An elongate, extremely slender fish, the sturgeon poacher has a body armor of non-overlapping bony plates. It has several spines on its large sturgeonlike head and clusters of slender barbels

around its mouth. It lives near or on the seabed and feeds mainly on crustaceans and marine worms. Although a common, abundant species, it has no commercial value.

Lumpsucker *Cyclopterus lumpus*

RANGE N. Atlantic Ocean: Arctic to Scandinavia, Iceland, British Isles; Newfoundland to New Jersey, USA

HABITAT Shallow waters to 650 ft (200 m), usually on seabed

SIZE 11¾–23½ in (30–60 cm)

The lumpsucker has a round, deep body, studded with rows of spined plates along the sides. Its skin is scaleless. The ventral fins are modified to form the powerful suction disk on its belly with which the lumpsucker attaches itself to the seabed or to rocks and other debris. It feeds on small crustaceans, jellyfishes and other invertebrates, as well as some small fish. Females are usually larger than males.

In late winter or spring, lumpsuckers gather in pairs in shallow coastal waters in order to spawn around the low-tide mark. The female lays as many as 200,000 sticky-surfaced eggs which sink to the bottom in a spongy mass. The male then guards the egg clusters and keeps water flowing through them until they hatch.

The young fishes remain in the coastal shallows during the summer and move out to deeper waters in their first winter.

Seasnail/Snailfish *Liparis liparis*

RANGE N. Atlantic Ocean: Arctic to coasts of Scandinavia, Iceland, British Isles; Greenland to Virginia, USA

HABITAT Inshore waters at 16½–490 ft (5–150 m)

SIZE 4–7 in (10–18 cm)

A relative of the lumpsuckers, the seasnail or snailfish, is a round-bodied fish with long dorsal and anal fins, both connected with the tail fin. The skin is slimy and scaleless, and on the belly is a strong suction disk with which the seasnail attaches itself to the seabed or to seaweed. It feeds mainly on small crustaceans and worms.

Seasnails spawn in winter or spring. The eggs settle in clusters on seaweed or other objects on the seabed and hatch in 6 to 8 weeks.

PERCHLIKE FISHES

PERCIFORMES PERCHLIKE FISH ORDER

This is the largest and most varied of all fish orders and contains more species than any other vertebrate order. There are 148 families and at least 9,300 species known. The five largest families are the sea basses (Serranidae) with 450 species; cichlids (Cichlidae) with 1,300 species; gobies (Gobiidae) with 1,875 species; wrasses (Labridae) with 500 species and combtooth blennies (Blenniidae) with 345 species.

Perciform fishes have found niches for themselves in almost every conceivable aquatic habitat and in so doing have evolved a diverse range of body forms and habits. They include species as different as the barracuda, the angelfish, the swordfish and the Siamese fightingfish. It is difficult to generalize about such a widely divergent order, but there are a few broad similarities. All forms have one or two dorsal fins. In forms with one dorsal fin, it is elongate and spiny at the front, while in fishes with two dorsal fins, the first is generally spiny and the second soft rayed. Most perciform fishes have pelvic fins, which are placed in close proximity to the head. Each pelvic fin usually has a spine and five rays. The body scales are generally of the type known as ctenoid – they have a rounded front edge and a serrated trailing edge.

Perhaps as many as three-quarters of the species live in waters close to the shore. There are 18 suborders of perchlike fish.

PERCOIDEI PERCOID SUBORDER

This is the largest perciform suborder with over 2,850 species in 71 families. Many have an elongate body, large mouth and eyes, and two dorsal fins. Mostly inshore predatory fish, the group includes sea bass, bluefish, perch, sunfish, and snappers.

Snook *Centropomus undecimalis*
RANGE Caribbean, north to Florida and South Carolina; south to Brazil
HABITAT Coastal waters, estuaries, bays, brackish water
SIZE 4½ ft (1.4 m)

One of the largest and most common of the 30 species in the snook family (Centropomidae), this fish has a long, tapering body, a slightly flattened snout and a protruding lower jaw. It eats mainly crustaceans and fish, and adults can tolerate a wide variety of habitats including almost fresh water.

Snooks spawn from June to November; young fishes, less than a year old, usually live in coastal lagoons and streams. They are mature in their third year. The snook is a popular species with marine fishermen.

Nile Perch *Lates niloticus*
RANGE Africa: Congo, Volta and Niger river systems, Lake Chad
HABITAT Rivers, lakes
SIZE 6½ ft (2 m)

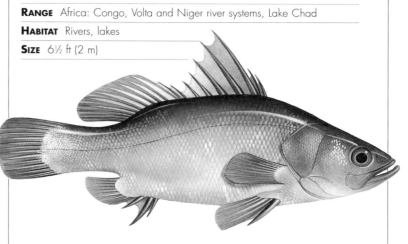

This widely distributed member of the snook family has been introduced into many man-made lakes and is fished commercially and for sport. It is one of the most important food fish in some areas of Africa. A large, heavy-bodied fish, the Nile perch has the spiny first dorsal fin characteristic of the perchlike fishes and three spines on the anal fin. It eats mainly fish. Introduction of the Nile perch into Lake Victoria in the 1960s caused the elimination of many cichlid species.

Striped Bass *Roccus saxatilis*
RANGE N. America: Atlantic coast from Gulf of St. Lawrence to N. Florida; Gulf of Mexico; Pacific coast from Washington to California
HABITAT Inshore waters, estuaries, bays, deltas
SIZE Up to 4 ft (1.2 m)

A distinctive fish, the striped bass may vary in coloration but always has seven or eight dark stripes along its sides. It has a long head and body, a pointed snout and projecting lower jaw. The female is usually larger and heavier than the male, and large specimens may weigh up to 66 lb (30 kg). They feed on fish and crustaceans. Originally a native of the Atlantic coast, the striped bass was first introduced to the Pacific coast in 1886 and is now well established. It is a member of the temperate perch family Percichthyidae.

In the breeding season, April to July, striped bass enter estuaries and ascend rivers to spawn. The female is courted by a number of males and sheds her eggs into the water, where they drift until they hatch about 3 days later. A mature female may produce several million eggs in a season.

Murray/Trout Cod *Maccullochella macquariensis* **EN**

RANGE Australia: New South Wales, Queensland
HABITAT Rivers, lakes; introduced in reservoirs
SIZE 6 ft (1.8 m)

The Murray cod has a long powerful body, usually with mottled markings on its back and sides, and an elongate snout. It eats mainly crustaceans and fish and is itself an important commercial food fish. It is a member of Percichthyidae, the temperate perch family.

Murray cod often spawn over trees and branches, which have fallen into the water. The eggs adhere to the surface of the bark and branches.

Giant Sea Bass *Stereolepis gigas*

RANGE Pacific Ocean: off coasts of California and Mexico
HABITAT Inshore waters
SIZE 7 ft (2.1 m)

The giant sea bass is a huge fish. Some specimens weigh over 550 lb (250 kg). It is known to live for about 70 to 75 years and eats fish and crustaceans. It is fished commercially and for sport.

Giant sea bass mature at about 11 to 13 years old, at a weight of about 50 lb (23 kg). They spawn in summer, and the young fishes are reddish in color and deeper bodied than adults. They gradually take on the adult appearance and coloration as they mature.

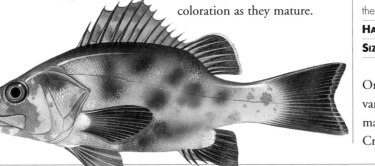

Jewfish *Epinephelus itajara*

RANGE W. Atlantic Ocean: coasts of Florida, Bermuda, Bahamas, West Indies; Pacific Ocean
HABITAT Coastal waters, around ledges, caves and wrecks
SIZE 8 ft (2.4 m)

One of the largest of the fishes known as groupers (all members of the sea bass family, Serranidae), the jewfish weighs as much as 700 lb (318 kg). It has a robust body and broad head and is usually dark brown, with irregular dark spots and bars on the body. It lurks around underwater crevices and feeds on crustaceans, fish and even turtles. Jewfishes are sought-after food fish and are popular with sporting fishermen.

Black Grouper *Mycteroperca bonaci*

RANGE W. Atlantic Ocean: New England, USA, south through Gulf of Mexico and Caribbean to Brazil
HABITAT Coastal waters, deeper waters over rocky bottoms
SIZE 4 ft (1.2 m)

The black grouper is a fairly common grouper, which may weigh up to 50 lb (23 kg). Its appearance is typical of the Serranidae family to which it belongs. There are irregular dark markings on the sides of its body. It is a good food fish and is caught commercially.

Coney *Cephalopholis fulvus*

RANGE W. Atlantic Ocean: Florida, USA, south through the Caribbean and Gulf of Mexico to Brazil
HABITAT Coastal waters, coral reefs
SIZE 11¾ in (30 cm)

One of the smallest but most abundant groupers, the coney varies from red to yellow or brown in coloration but is usually marked with blue spots. It has two black spots on its tail. Crustaceans are its main diet. It is a highly valued food species.

PERCHLIKE FISHES CONTINUED

Soapfish *Rypticus saponaceus*

RANGE E. Atlantic Ocean: off tropical W. Africa and Ascension Island; W. Atlantic: Florida to Brazil

HABITAT Shallow, coastal waters

SIZE 11¾ in (30 cm)

Soapfishes belong to the family Seranidae. The skin of the soapfish is slimy with body mucus, which creates a frothy effect, like soapsuds, in the water. This mucus is toxic and its presence deters predators. The soapfish is usually brownish, with some gray blotches on the body. There are several spines preceding the dorsal fin. Active at night, it feeds on fish and crustaceans and shelters in rock crevices during the day.

Pumpkinseed *Lepomis gibbosus*

RANGE S. Canada; USA: North Dakota and Great Lakes, east to Atlantic coast, south to Texas and Florida; introduced on the west coast of the USA and in Europe

HABITAT Brooks, clear ponds with plenty of vegetation

SIZE 6–9 in (15–23 cm)

The attractive pumpkinseed is a sunfish, belonging to the Centrarchidae family of about 29 species of sunfish. Aids to its identification are the black gill cover, surrounded with orange or red, the blue lines radiating from the snout and eye region and the three anal spines. It feeds on snails and aquatic insects, as well as small and larval fish.

Breeding takes place between May and July in sandy-bottomed water. The male fish hollows out a shallow nest with his tail and then attracts one or more females to lay eggs in his nest. He guards the eggs while they incubate for between 5 and 10 days, depending on the temperature of the water, and continues to look after the young fishes until they are able to disperse and fend for themselves. Pumpkinseeds may breed near one another in small colonies.

Rock Bass *Ambloplites rupestris*

RANGE S. Canada: Lake Winnipeg, east to coast; USA: Great Lakes, east to Vermont, south to Gulf Coast; introduced in other areas of USA

HABITAT Rocky-bottomed streams, lake shallows

SIZE 6–10 in (15–25.5 cm)

This sunfish lives among rocks and stones, where it feeds on insects, crayfish and fish. It is a sturdy, deep-bodied fish, with a large mouth and a protruding lower jaw.

The male rock bass excavates a nest at the bottom, often amid the roots of aquatic plants. The female lays about 5,000 eggs in the nest, which is then guarded by the male. He defends the young fishes when they first hatch.

Largemouth Bass *Micropterus salmoides*

RANGE S.E. Canada; USA: Great Lakes area, south to Gulf of Mexico; introduced in other areas of USA and in Europe and Africa

HABITAT Shallow lakes, ponds, rivers

SIZE 10–18 in (25.5–46 cm)

A member of the sunfish family, the largemouth bass is usually greenish and silvery in coloration, with a dark band along each side; its dorsal fin is divided almost in two by a notch. A predatory fish, it feeds on crustaceans and other invertebrates when young, gradually progressing to fish, frogs and larger invertebrates when mature.

Spawning takes place in spring or early summer, depending on temperature and latitude. The male excavates a nest in sand or gravel in shallow water and attracts a female to his nest to lay her eggs, usually a few hundred. The male fertilizes the eggs and may then attract more females to his nest. The sticky-surfaced eggs attach themselves to the bottom of the nest and are guarded by the male until they hatch, 7 to 10 days after laying.

Perch *Perca fluviatilis*

RANGE Europe: Britain, east across Scandinavia and Russia to Siberia; south to N. Italy, Black and Caspian Seas; introduced in Ireland, Australia, New Zealand and South Africa

HABITAT Lakes, ponds, slow rivers

SIZE 13¾–20 in (35–51 cm)

This fish is a member of the perch family (Percidae), which contains 162 fresh water species. It is a deep-bodied fish with two dorsal fins, the first joined to the second only by a membrane at the base. There is a characteristic black mark at the end of the spiny fin. The perch lives among aquatic vegetation, submerged tree roots or other debris, where its barred markings help to camouflage it. It feeds on fish.

Perch spawn in shallow water during April and May. The eggs are shed in long strings, which wind around plants or other objects, and they hatch in about 8 days. Young perch feed on plankton and then on insects and larger crustaceans until they are old enough to adopt the adult diet.

Orangethroat Darter

Etheostoma spectabile

RANGE Central USA: Mississippi and Missouri river systems

HABITAT Streams

SIZE 3¼ in (8 cm)

The orangethroat darter is one of the many species of darter found in the USA, all of which are members of the perch family (Percidae). It feeds on insects and planktonic crustaceans.

Breeding males develop some orange coloration on throat and breast, while females and non-breeding males have pale throats. The male of a pair selects a nesting site, and the female excavates a shallow nest and deposits several hundred eggs, which are fertilized and guarded by the male.

Conchfish *Astrapogon stellatus*

RANGE Tropical W. Atlantic Ocean, from Bahamas south through Caribbean

HABITAT Shallow waters

SIZE 2 in (5 cm)

The conchfish is one of approximately 320 species of cardinalfish (Apogonidae) found in tropical and subtropical seas. It is a tiny fish, with some dark and some silvery coloration and dark spots along its sides.

Some cardinalfish live in rock crevices or empty shells, but the conchfish lives inside the shell of a live conch, *Strombus gigas*, a large mollusk. The conch is unaffected by the association, but the fish gains the benefit of shelter.

Zander *Stizostedion lucioperca*

RANGE C. and E. Europe: Sweden and Finland, south to Black and Caspian Seas, east to Russia; introduced in England and W. Europe

HABITAT Large lakes, slow rivers

SIZE 23½ in–4¼ ft (60 cm–1.3 m)

A member of the perch family, the zander has the characteristic two dorsal fins of that group; the first spiny fin is just separated from the second. The zander prefers to inhabit cloudy water and does most of its hunting at dawn and dusk, remaining near the bottom at other times. It feeds on almost any species of fish.

Zanders spawn between April and June in either sandy or stony-bottomed water. The eggs are laid in a shallow nest, where they are guarded by the male.

PERCHLIKE FISHES CONTINUED

Bluefish *Pomatomus saltatrix*

RANGE Atlantic, Indian and N. Pacific Oceans:
tropical and warm temperate areas

HABITAT Coastal waters, open ocean

SIZE Up to 4 ft (1.2 m)

The bluefish has the reputation of being one of the most predatory of fish, killing more prey than it can eat and feeding voraciously on almost any fish, including smaller individuals of its own species.

It is a sturdy fish, with a forked tail, fully scaled body and large jaws equipped with formidable teeth.

Schools of bluefishes of a similar size travel together, often following shoals of prey fish. Young bluefishes, which are known as snappers, also form their own shoals, and, in general, the smaller the fish, the bigger the shoal.

Cobia *Rachycentron canadum*

RANGE Atlantic, Indian and W. Pacific Oceans:
tropical areas

HABITAT Open sea, occasionally inshore waters and estuaries

SIZE 6 ft (1.8 m)

The elongate, streamlined cobia is the only species in its family. It is easily recognized by its distinctive coloration; dark-brown bands on a light background. A line of dorsal spines runs down its back before the dorsal fin.

The cobia is an active predator, feeding mainly on fish but it will also consume crabs, squid and shrimps.

Remora *Remora remora*

RANGE Atlantic, Indian and N. Pacific Oceans:
tropical and warm temperate areas

HABITAT Wherever taken by, generally, offshore hosts

SIZE 6–18 in (15–46 cm)

The remora is one of the 7 or 8 species of sharksucker in the family Echeneidae. By means of a specialized sucking disk on the top of the head, sharksuckers attach themselves to sharks or other large fishes, whales or turtles and travel with them wherever they go. The disk is formed from a modified spiny dorsal fin and contains two rows of slatlike ridges divided by a central bar. The remora presses the disk flat against the host fish and creates a partial vacuum by moving the ridges, thus making it virtually impossible to remove it.

While some sharksuckers use many different types of host, others, including the remora, are adapted to only a few specific hosts. The remora seems nearly always to be associated with the blue shark. It feeds mainly on the parasites that live on the shark but may leave its host briefly to catch small fish or crustaceans.

Sharksucker *Echenis naucrates*

RANGE Atlantic, Indian and W. Pacific Oceans: tropical areas

HABITAT Wherever taken by host

SIZE Up to 36¼ in (92 cm)

The largest member of the Echeneidae family, the sharksucker is a long-bodied fish, with distinctive white-bordered black stripes down each side of the body, from snout to tail. On top of its rather flattened head is the powerful sucking disk, with which it attaches itself to a host so firmly that it is almost impossible to remove. Attached in this way, the sharksucker rides around effortlessly and presumably gains some protection from the larger animal; this species uses a wide range of hosts, including sharks, large rays and turtles. Sharksuckers were once used for catching sea turtles. The fish, with a line tied to its tail, was released near the turtle and would generally make straight for it and fasten itself to the tail. The fishermen could then gradually pull in the turtle, the sharksucker holding firm.

Greater Amberjack *Seriola dumerili*

RANGE W. Atlantic Ocean: New England to Brazil; E. Atlantic: Mediterranean Sea to coast of W. Africa

HABITAT Surface inshore waters

SIZE Up to 6 ft (1.8 m)

The greater amberjack is one of the large family, Carangidae, which includes about 140 species of fish, such as jacks and pompanos. It is a fairly deep-bodied fish, with a dark-blue or green back and lighter, golden or whitish sides. There is a distinctive dark line running from the snout through the eye to the top of the head. It feeds on many species of fish.

Crevalle Jack *Caranx hippos*

RANGE Probably worldwide in tropical and subtropical waters

HABITAT Juveniles in inshore waters, adults offshore, especially around reefs

SIZE 31½ in–3¼ ft (80 cm–1 m)

The exact distribution of this species is unknown because of confusion between similar species in the Carangidae family. However, it is certainly abundant on both sides of the Atlantic. The crevalle jack has a high, rounded forehead and a prominent dark spot on each gill cover; there are also dark spots on each pectoral fin. Its body is dark blue or metallic green on the back, with silvery or yellowish underparts. Fish are its main food, but crustaceans and some other invertebrates are also eaten.

Rainbow Runner *Elagatis bipinnulata*

RANGE Atlantic, Indian and N. Pacific Oceans: tropical and subtropical waters

HABITAT Open sea

SIZE Up to 4 ft (1.2 m)

Identified by its beautiful coloration, the rainbow runner has a blue back and yellow and blue stripes along the sides shading to a whitish belly. Its body is slender, tapering sharply toward the

deeply forked tail. It is a member of the pompano and jack family, Carangidae, and like so many of that family is a game fish, popular with sport fishermen.

Florida Pompano *Trachinotus carolinus*

RANGE W. Atlantic Ocean: Cape Cod to Brazil

HABITAT Shallow waters close to shore

SIZE 18–25 in (46–63.5 cm)

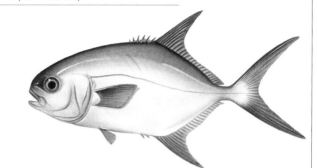

The Florida pompano closely resembles the permit, *T. falcatus*, but has a less strongly arched profile and lacks the elongate dorsal-fin spine of the permit. It has a rounded snout and a fairly deep body, which tapers sharply before the forked tail. Mollusks and crustaceans are its main foods, for which it roots around in the sand and mud of the seabed. It is itself considered an excellent food fish and is caught commercially.

Spawning is believed to take place offshore between March and September, depending on latitude. The young fishes then move inshore, where they feed on bottom-living invertebrates and small fish. The Florida pompano and the permit both belong to the Carangidae family.

Lookdown *Selene vomer*

RANGE W. Atlantic Ocean: New England, south to Bermuda and to Uruguay; E. Atlantic: off W. Africa

HABITAT Shallow sandy- or muddy-bottomed waters

SIZE 11¾ in (30 cm)

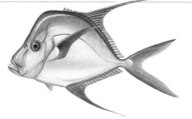

The lookdown is an extremely unusual-looking fish, which has a large head and a small, dramatically tapering body. The head arches up steeply above the snout and is almost one and a half times as deep as it is long. Both dorsal and anal fins have long extensions, which point back toward the sharply forked tail.

PERCHLIKE FISHES CONTINUED

Dolphinfish

Coryphaena hippurus

RANGE Atlantic, Pacific, Indian Oceans:
tropical and warm temperate areas

HABITAT Open sea

SIZE Up to 5 ft (1.5 m)

Immediately identifiable by the long dorsal fin that originates over its head, the dolphinfish is extremely beautiful, with its vivid blue, green and yellow coloration. As males grow older, their foreheads become increasingly steep, almost vertical, and they may grow larger than females; otherwise males and females look alike. Dolphinfishes move in small schools and feed on a variety of fish, squid and crustaceans. They often frequent the waters around patches of floating seaweed or other debris, which may harbor potential prey.

Dolphinfishes are popular game fish and excellent to eat. They belong to the family Coryphaenidae, which contains only 1 other species, the pompano dolphinfish, *C. equisetis*; this fish is similar in appearance but smaller than *C. hippurus*. They are also known simply as dolphins, but the name dolphinfish is preferable in order to distinguish them from mammalian dolphins.

Ray's Bream *Brama brama*

RANGE N. Atlantic Ocean: Iceland and Scandinavia to
N. Africa; Mediterranean Sea; off coasts of Chile, South Africa,
Australia, New Zealand

HABITAT Open sea

SIZE 15¾–27½ in (40–70 cm)

Ray's bream, a member of the Bramidae (Pomfret) family, which contains 18 species, has a deep body that tapers sharply toward the long, deeply forked tail. It migrates into the northern part of its range in summer, but such migrations are irregular and appear to be dependent on suitable water temperatures.

An unselective predator, it feeds on almost any fish or crustaceans available.

Mutton Snapper *Lutjanus analis*

RANGE W. Atlantic Ocean: Florida and Bahamas, south to Caribbean,
Gulf of Mexico and Brazil

HABITAT Coastal waters, bays

SIZE Up to 30 in (76 cm)

Common off American coasts, the mutton snapper is one of the approximately 125 species in the snapper family, Lutjanidae. It is a brightly colored fish, with a green and reddish or pink body and some blue markings; there is a black spot below the dorsal fin on both sides of the body. Like most snappers, it has large, caninelike teeth. Mutton snappers often frequent shallow waters, where there are mangroves or turtle grass, and feed on the fish and crustaceans found among the vegetation.

Some snappers are among the fishes that are known to cause the ciguatera type of fish poisoning, which can be fatal to humans who eat the flesh of affected fish. The poison originates in certain algae. Herbivorous fishes may feed on this algae and they are in turn eaten by carnivorous fishes, with no apparent ill effects to the predators. The flesh of the predator fish becomes toxic, however, and the poison can then affect any human consumer.

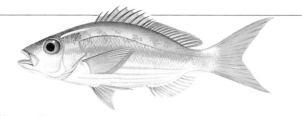

Yellowtail Snapper *Ocyurus chrysurus*

RANGE W. Atlantic Ocean: New England to Brazil,
including Gulf of Mexico and Caribbean

HABITAT Offshore waters, near coral reefs

SIZE 30 in (76 cm)

One of the snapper family (Lutjanidae), the yellowtail snapper is an attractive fish, with a bright yellow tail and a yellow stripe along each side. Its body is slender and its dorsal fin long and low. Yellowtail snappers feed near the bottom on crustaceans and fish but also occur offshore above reefs. They are popular with anglers and are excellent food fish.

Tripletail *Lobotes surinamensis*

RANGE Atlantic, Indian and W. Pacific Oceans:
tropical and warm temperate areas

HABITAT Coastal surface waters

SIZE 3¼ ft (1 m)

Although never common, the tripletail is a widely distributed fish, which occurs on both sides of the Atlantic. It belongs to the tripletail family (Lobotidae) which includes only about 4 species. It has a deep, heavy body and is usually dark brown in color, although some individuals may be yellow and brown. The large, rounded lobes of the dorsal and anal fins, which project back toward the tail, give the fish the appearance of having three tails, hence the name.

Young tripletails often live close to the shore in bays and estuaries, where they float on their sides among dead mangrove and other leaves. Their curving posture and brownish-yellow coloration imitate the movement and appearance of the leaves and are an excellent example of protective mimicry.

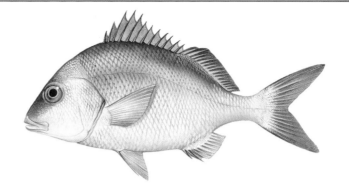

Margate *Haemulon album*

RANGE W. Atlantic Ocean: Bahamas and Florida,
south through Caribbean to Brazil

HABITAT Shallow inshore waters, often near reefs

SIZE 24¾ in (63 cm)

The margate is one of about 150 species in the grunt family, Haemulidae. These marine fishes occur in tropical waters and are related to the snappers but lack their large teeth. They are known as grunts because of the noise that they make by grinding their pharyngeal teeth together; the resulting sounds are amplified by the swim bladder. The margate is fairly typical of its family, with its high, spiny dorsal fin, which is continuous with the rayed dorsal fin. It is usually grayish in color, with darker dorsal and tail fins, but coloration does vary.

Small groups of margates often frequent reefs and wrecks, where they feed on small fish and also forage on the seabed for bottom-living invertebrates. This is the largest of the Atlantic grunts and is caught commercially.

Black Margate *Anisotremus surinamensis*

RANGE W. Atlantic Ocean: Florida and the Bahamas,
south through Gulf of Mexico and Caribbean

HABITAT Inshore waters, near rocks and reefs

SIZE Up to 24 in (61 cm)

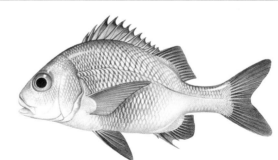

The black margate, a member of the grunt family, Haemulidae, is typical of its group in its body shape and continuous dorsal fin. It is grayish in color, with a dark spot on each scale on the back; the fins are dark gray. Most active at night, it feeds on crustaceans sea urchins and fish, often foraging in small groups. By day it shelters in caves or crevices.

PERCHLIKE FISHES CONTINUED

Scup *Stenotomus chrysops*

RANGE Atlantic coast of N. America: Cape Cod
(sometimes Nova Scotia) to Florida

HABITAT Sandy-bottomed inshore and offshore waters

SIZE 18 in (46 cm)

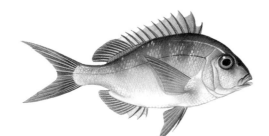

An abundant fish in the Atlantic, the scup, also called the
northern porgy, is one of the 100 species in the porgy family,
Sparidae. It has a deep, laterally compressed body, a deeply
forked tail and spines on both dorsal and anal fins. Its scales are
silvery, with indistinct dark bars on the sides of the body. Most
of its feeding is done on the bottom, and the scup takes
crustaceans, worms and some bottom-living fish.

In spring, adults spawn in waters close to the shore, often in
bays; the eggs float freely until they hatch. In winter, scups move
farther offshore and toward the south of their range.

Jolthead Porgy *Calamus bajonado*

RANGE Caribbean, Gulf of Mexico; W. Atlantic Ocean:
coasts of North and South America from New England to Brazil

HABITAT Coastal waters, near reefs

SIZE 24 in (61 cm)

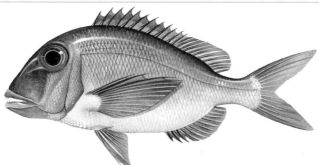

One of the larger members of the family Sparidae, the jolthead
porgy is a distinctive fish, with a high, rounded forehead. Its
scales have a silvery sheen, and there are some blue markings
around the eyes, which are placed characteristically high. Small
schools of jolthead porgies feed near the shore on invertebrates
such as sea urchins, mollusks and crustaceans. They are good
food fish, which are fished for by anglers and commercial
fishermen.

Sheepshead *Archosargus probatocephalus*

RANGE W. Atlantic Ocean: Nova Scotia, south to Gulf of Mexico
(now rare in north of range)

HABITAT Tidal streams, bays, seabed near jetties

SIZE 11¾–30 in (30–76 cm)

Sometimes called the
convict fish, the
sheepshead is
identified by the
broad black bars down
each of its silvery sides. These
bars vary in shape and number and are
most prominent in younger fishes. Otherwise the sheepshead is
typical in appearance of the porgy family, to which it belongs,
with its large head, thick lips and spiny dorsal and anal fins. It
feeds on crustaceans and mollusks, which it crushes with its
broad, flat teeth. It is itself an excellent food fish and is caught
in large quantities.

Spawning takes place in spring, and the eggs float freely until
they hatch only 3 or 4 days later, provided the temperature is
sufficiently high.

Snapper *Chrysophrys auratus*

RANGE Pacific Ocean: coasts of New Zealand,
Australia, Lord Howe Island

HABITAT Seabed, rocky reefs

SIZE 4¼ ft (1.3 m)

The snapper, a member of the porgy family, Sparidae, undergoes
slight changes of appearance and behavior as it matures. Young
snappers are pale pink in color, with dark bands, and live in
large schools in shallow water close to the shore, often in bays.
Adults are redder, with bright blue spots dotting the fins, back
and sides. They frequent the seabed and rocky reefs in deeper
waters but may come into shallow coastal waters in summer. In
the oldest specimens, the forehead becomes rather humped, and
the lips particularly fleshy; these older fishes
tend to be solitary. The snapper is a
valuable food fish.

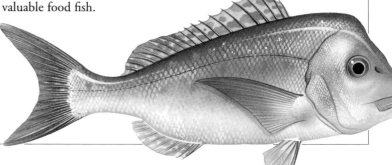

Red Sea Bream

Pagellus bogaraveo

RANGE Atlantic Ocean: coasts of S. Norway, Britain, Europe, N. Africa, Canary Islands; Mediterranean Sea

HABITAT Inshore waters, deeper waters at 330–650 ft (100–200 m)

SIZE 13¾–20 in (35–51 cm)

Quite common in the south of their range, red sea bream are rare in the north, and those fishes which do occur are mostly summer migrants. A member of the porgy family, Sparidae, the fish is distinguished by the reddish flush to its body and fins, the dark spot above its pectoral fin and its short, rounded head. Young fishes are paler in color than adults and may lack the dark spot. The young red sea breams form large schools and frequent shallow inshore waters, feeding on small crustaceans. Adults live farther offshore in deeper waters and form smaller groups; they feed on fish, and also on crustaceans.

Little is known of the breeding habits of the red sea bream, but it is thought to spawn in summer or autumn, depending on the area: the farther south, the earlier it spawns. Red sea bream are good-quality food fish and are caught commercially.

Gilthead Bream *Sparus aurata*

RANGE Atlantic Ocean: coasts of Ireland, S. England, Europe, N. Africa, Canary Islands; Mediterranean and Black Seas

HABITAT Shallow sandy-bottomed or muddy-bottomed waters at about 100 ft (30 m)

SIZE Up to 27½ in (70 cm)

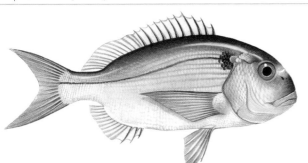

A golden stripe, which runs between the eyes of this fish, is the origin of its common name; the stripe fades on death. The gilthead is a fairly deep-bodied fish, with a markedly rounded snout and high-set eyes; there is a dark spot on each side, well above the pectoral fin. It feeds largely on mollusks and crustaceans, and its teeth are adapted to deal with this hard-shelled prey – those in the front of the jaws are pointed and curved for breaking into the shells, while those at the sides are broad and flattened for crushing and grinding down food. Because of their diet, giltheads can prove a menace on commercial oyster and mussel beds.

Like all sea breams, the gilthead is a member of the porgy family, Sparidae. Breeding takes place in winter in offshore waters, deeper than the giltheads normally frequent. They are not believed to breed in the north of their range.

Sweetlip Emperor *Lethrinus chrysostomus*

RANGE Off N. coast of Australia, Great Barrier Reef

HABITAT Inshore waters, reef areas

SIZE 36 in (91 cm)

The sweetlip emperor belongs to the family Lethrinidae, known as scavengers and emperors. The sweetlip has a rather large head for its body, a long snout and scaleless cheeks. Its coloration is striking, with deep-red fins, dark barring on the sides and vivid red patches around the eyes. It can attain a weight of 20 lb (9 kg) and is a valuable food fish.

Spangled Emperor *Lethrinus nebulosus*

RANGE Indian and Pacific Oceans: Red Sea and E. Africa to N. Australia and W. Pacific islands

HABITAT Coral reefs, open ocean

SIZE 30 in (76 cm)

The name of the attractively colored spangled emperor is well deserved. Identifying characteristics are the scattering of blue spots on its dorsal and anal fins, the blue on many of the scales on its sides and the blue lines on each side of the face, running from the eye toward the snout. A member of the family Lethrinidae, the fish has the long snout, thick lips and dorsal and anal spines typical of the group. Like several of the larger members of this family, it is a valuable food fish.

PERCHLIKE FISHES CONTINUED

White Seabass *Cynoscion nobilis*

RANGE Pacific Ocean: Alaska to Mexico

HABITAT Near kelp beds, shallow to deep waters

SIZE 24 in–6 ft (61 cm–1.8 m)

The white seabass is not a true sea bass, but a member of the drum family Sciaenidae. There are about 270 species of drum, so called because many of them can make sounds by vibrating their swim bladders with specialized muscles; in some species only the male makes sounds, and in others, both male and female can "drum". Most species of drum have a deeply, often almost completely, divided dorsal fin.

A large, elongate fish, the white seabass has a rather pointed head and large mouth, with the lower jaw projecting slightly beyond the upper. The two parts of its dorsal fin just touch. It moves in large schools and feeds on many kinds of fish and on crustaceans and squid. Spawning takes place in spring and summer, and young fishes generally live in quiet, inshore waters.

White seabass are important to sport and commercial fishermen along the Pacific coast of America. An almost identical but much larger fish, the totoaba, (*Totoaba macdonaldii*), occurs farther south, off the coast of Mexico. It is critically endangered.

Spotted Seatrout *Cynoscion nebulosus*

RANGE Atlantic Ocean: coast of USA from New York to Florida; Gulf of Mexico

HABITAT Coastal bays, estuaries; deeper waters in winter

SIZE 17¾–24 in (45–61 cm)

Although called "seatrout" because of its troutlike spots, the spotted seatrout belongs to the drum family, Sciaenidae. It has an elongate body and pointed head, with a slightly protruding lower jaw; its dorsal fin is deeply notched. Like many drums, the spotted seatrout can make sounds by vibrating its swim bladder. It feeds on crustaceans and fish.

Spawning takes place in sheltered coastal bays, from March to November. Once hatched, larval and juvenile fishes stay in the protection of marine vegetation, where they find plentiful supplies of food. In winter, they move into deeper waters. Spotted seatrout are caught for sport and commercially.

Black Drum *Pogonias cromis*

RANGE W. Atlantic Ocean: coasts from New England to Argentina

HABITAT Bays, coastal lagoons

SIZE 4–6 ft (1.2–1.8 m)

Identified by its short, deep body, somewhat flattened belly and arched back, the black drum is one of the largest members of the drum family and is known to weigh as much as 146 lb (66 kg). Several short barbels hang from its lower jaw. A bottom-feeding fish, the black drum eats crustaceans and mollusks, which it is able to crush with the large, flat teeth in its throat. Oysters are a particularly favored food, and black drums can do much harm to commercial oyster beds.

Jackknife-fish *Equetus lanceolatus*

RANGE W. Atlantic Ocean: coasts of North and South Carolina, Bermuda to Brazil; Gulf of Mexico, Caribbean

HABITAT Rocky- or coral-bottomed waters more than 50 ft (15 m) deep

SIZE 9 in (23 cm)

An unusual member of the drum family, the jackknife-fish is an extremely distinctive species, strikingly marked with three black stripes, bordered with white. One of these stripes curves down from the high dorsal fin to the tail fin disrupting the normal outline of the fish. Such markings are a form of camouflage, intended to confuse and distract the observer and to delay recognition.

A solitary species, the jackknife-fish hides among rocks or in crevices in the coral reef during the day and feeds at night.

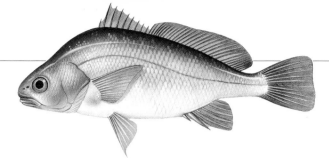

Freshwater Drum *Aplodinotus grunniens*

RANGE N. America: S. Canada through the Great Lakes and Mississippi river system to Gulf of Mexico; south to Mexico and Guatemala

HABITAT Large rivers, lakes

SIZE Up to 4 ft (1.2 m)

One of the few freshwater species in the drum family, this fish has a humped back and a long-based dorsal fin. As befits a bottom-feeder, its mouth is low slung; its main foods are mollusks, crustaceans and some insect larvae, all of which it crushes with the large, flattened teeth in its throat, spitting out the shells and swallowing the soft bodies. It produces sounds by vibrating its swim bladder and is one of the few freshwater fishes to do so.

Spawning takes place in April, May or June in shallow gravel-bottomed or sandy-bottomed water. Females may shed from 10,000 to 100,000 eggs, which hatch in about 2 weeks.

Meagre *Argyrosomus regius*

RANGE Indian Ocean; E. Atlantic Ocean: Britain to Senegal; Mediterranean Sea

HABITAT Shore line to deeper waters to 1,150 ft (350 m), estuaries

SIZE 5–6½ ft (1.5–2 m)

One of the giants of the drum family, the meagre is an elongate fish, with a rounded snout and large mouth. It is a common fish in southern waters and occasionally strays to northern European seas. It moves in shoals, eating fish, and usually occurs in sandy-bottomed water.

Spotted Goatfish *Pseudupeneus maculatus*

RANGE W. Atlantic Ocean: New Jersey to Brazil; Gulf of Mexico, Caribbean

HABITAT Shallow waters, reefs, turtle grass beds

SIZE 11 in (28 cm)

There are 55 species of goatfish, or red mullet, which occur worldwide in tropical and warm temperate seas. These fishes have elongate bodies and two widely spaced dorsal fins.

The spotted goatfish is typical of the family and has the characteristic feature of two long, sensory chin barbels, used for finding food on the seabed. With these barbels, the goatfish forages over the substrate for the small invertebrate animals on which it feeds.

Red Mullet *Mullus surmuletus*

RANGE Mediterranean Sea, E. Atlantic Ocean: Britain, south to Canary Islands and N. Africa

HABITAT Sandy-, muddy-, sometimes rocky-bottomed waters to 300 ft (90 m)

SIZE 15¾ in (40 cm)

The red mullet is a Mediterranean species, which sometimes occurs farther north, presumably as a summer migrant. It has a steeply rounded forehead and, like the other members of the family Mullidae, two sensory barbels on its chin, which it uses to search the seabed for food, mostly bottom-living invertebrates. Once prey is found, the red mullet will dig to uncover it. Red mullets usually travel in small schools of fewer than 50. They can change color quite dramatically, varying between reddish-brown, red and yellowish-brown. In the daytime, they are usually brownish, with several yellow stripes along the sides; at night, these lines break up into a marbled pattern. In deeper water, red mullets are a deep red, but color variations also occur when the fishes are alarmed.

Spawning takes place between July and September. The female sheds her eggs on the seabed, but once they hatch, the young live at the surface.

Archerfish *Toxotes jaculator*

RANGE India, S.E. Asia, Philippines, Indonesia, N. Australia

HABITAT Inshore waters, estuaries, lower reaches of rivers

SIZE 9 in (23 cm)

The archerfish in the family Toxotidae are so called because of their habit of shooting down insects by spitting water at them. The archerfish holds water in its throat and, with its tongue, makes the mouth opening into a narrow tube. By then using its tongue as a valve and compressing the gill covers to propel the water, the drops are ejected with some force and great accuracy. The fish has excellent vision, and its large mobile eyes allow it to look upward above the water surface. It shoots at insects on plants overhanging the water and also feeds on aquatic insects and small invertebrates.

PERCHLIKE FISHES CONTINUED

Foureye Butterflyfish *Chaetodon capistratus*

RANGE W. Atlantic Ocean: Cape Cod, south to
Caribbean and Gulf of Mexico

HABITAT Coral reefs, rocky-bottomed and
sandy-bottomed waters

SIZE 6 in (15 cm)

The approximately 114 species in
the family Chaetodontidae – the
butterflyfishes – are among the most
colorful inhabitants of coral reefs.

The foureye butterflyfish is typical of the family, with its
deep, laterally compressed body, so thin that it resembles a disk.
This body shape is ideal for twisting and turning among the
coral "forests" and utilizing the many crevices for shelter.

The black spots, on each side near the tail, presumably
mislead predators into thinking that these are the vulnerable eye
areas, while the actual eyes have additional protection from the
dark bands that run through and help to conceal them. The
butterflyfishes feed by grazing on the coral reef, eating polyps or
pieces of seaweed.

Copperband Butterflyfish *Chelmon rostratus*

RANGE Indian and Pacific Oceans: E. Africa to India, Indonesia,
Australia, Japan and Philippines

HABITAT Coral reefs, rocky areas

SIZE 7¾ in (20 cm)

Also known as the beaked butterflyfish, this fish has an
elongated, beaklike snout, with which it is able to reach into
crevices in the coral to find food. The beak is equipped with
tiny, sharp teeth. It is an attractive fish, with coppery bands
running down each side of the body, presumably as a
camouflaging device. There is a black spot near the dorsal fin,
which confuses predators into thinking that this is the
vulnerable head area.

Forceps Butterflyfish *Forcipiger longirostris*

RANGE Indian and Pacific Oceans: tropical areas from Hawaii to
Indonesia and Comoro Islands

HABITAT Coral reefs, rocky areas

SIZE 7 in (18 cm)

The forceps butterflyfish has a
long, beaklike snout, with a
small mouth at the tip,
which it pokes into crevices and
crannies in the coral to find food. With
its jaws like forceps, it picks out tiny invertebrates and polyps
from the densely packed coral heads.

Queen Angelfish *Holacanthus ciliaris*

RANGE Tropical W. Atlantic Ocean: Florida and Bahamas,
south to Brazil including Gulf of Mexico

HABITAT Coral reefs

SIZE Up to 18 in (46 cm)

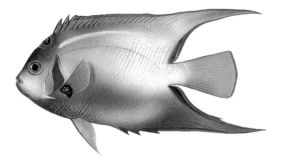

The brilliantly colored queen angelfish belongs to the family
Pomacanthidae. Angelfish are very similar to butterflyfish but
have a characteristic spine near each gill cover. It has a deep, slim
body, a blunt snout and greatly elongated lobes to dorsal and
anal fins that extend past the tail fin.

Imperial Angelfish *Pomacanthus imperator*

RANGE Tropical Indian and Pacific Oceans: Red Sea, E. Africa to
Indonesia, Philippines, Australia and Polynesia

HABITAT Coral reefs, rocky areas

SIZE Up to 15 in (38 cm)

The adult imperial angelfish is a striking fish, with attractive
yellow and blue markings and a dark, masklike area over the
eyes. Young fishes, however, are much darker, with blue and
white stripes on the body and a whitish spot near the tail. The

stripes are believed to lead a predator's eye toward the light spot and away from the vulnerable head area. The fish's slightly protuberant mouth enables it to graze over the coral.

Schomburgk's Leaffish *Polycentrus schomburgkii*

RANGE N.E. South America, Trinidad

HABITAT Freshwater streams, pools

SIZE 4 in (10 cm)

The leaffish is a member of the family Nandidae, a group of about 10 species of freshwater fish. Typical of its family, it has a laterally compressed body and many dorsal and anal spines, its mouth is large and protrusible. Although small, it is a voracious predator, lurking among vegetation, where it is well camouflaged by its leaflike appearance, to watch for prey and then dashing out to attack.

Bermuda Chub *Kyphosus sectatrix*

RANGE W. Atlantic Ocean: Cape Cod, south to Bermuda, Caribbean and Brazil; E. Atlantic: off coast of W. Africa; Mediterranean Sea

HABITAT Rocky-bottomed waters, reefs

SIZE Up to 30 in (76 cm)

The sea chubs of the family Kyphosidae are found worldwide in tropical and warm temperate waters. Most of the 42 or so species live in shallow water and feed on algae. The Bermuda chub is typical of its family, with its deep body and small head and mouth. Its coloration varies, but it is generally gray, with narrow dark bands running the length of the body and yellow markings on the head. Plants are its main food, but it also eats small invertebrates.

Although the range extends to Cape Cod, adult Bermuda chub are rarely found north of Florida. Young fishes are probably carried farther north by the Gulf Stream.

Australian Salmon *Arripis trutta*

RANGE S. Pacific Ocean: waters around S. and W. Australia, Tasmania, New Zealand

HABITAT Shallow inshore waters, often near river mouths

SIZE 36in (91 cm)

The Australian salmon is one of a family (Arripidae) of only 2 species, both confined to Australian waters. It is not related to the salmons of the northern hemisphere. It has a tapering, cylindrical body, a long dorsal fin and distinctive yellow pectoral fins, its sides are spotted with dark markings which are particularly plentiful on young fishes. Shrimplike crustaceans and small fish are its main foods.

Tigerfish *Therapon jarbua*

RANGE Indian and Pacific Oceans: Red Sea, E. African coast to S. China, Philippines, N. Australia

HABITAT Inshore waters, estuaries

SIZE 11¾ in (30 cm)

The tigerfish belongs to a family of about 45 species or more of grunters (Traponidae). A distinctive fish, it is identified by the dark, curving stripes on its sides. Like all grunters, it has many small teeth and is predatory, feeding on small fish. Although generally a marine species, it will enter fresh water on occasion. Tigerfishes can produce sounds by vibrating the swim bladder using specialized muscles.

PERCHLIKE FISHES CONTINUED

LABROIDEI LABROID SUBORDER

There are over 2,200 species of labroids in 6 families including the Cichlidae (cichlids), Embiotocidae (surfperches), Pomacentridae (damselfishes), Labridae (wrasses), and Scaridae (parrotfishes). The latter 3 families contain many species that are present in large numbers in coral reefs. The cichlids form a highly diverse family of lake-dwelling species, and also include many popular aquarium species.

Discus Fish *Symphysodon discus*

RANGE Tropical South America: Amazon and other large river systems

HABITAT Heavily vegetated backwaters and pools

SIZE 7¾ in (20 cm)

One of the most handsome members of the family Cichlidae, the discus fish has a laterally compressed body, marked with irregular red stripes. These stripes, and the dark vertical bars that cross them, help to camouflage the fish among the vegetation and dappled light of its forested habitat.

The discus fish lays its eggs on gravel bottoms and then moves the newly hatched young to submerged vegetation. About 3 days after hatching, the young swim to one of their parents, attach themselves to its body or fins and feed on slime secreted by the adult's skin. They feed in this way for 5 weeks or more.

Angelfish *Pterophyllum scalare*

RANGE South America: Amazon basin

HABITAT Densely vegetated, slow flowing rivers

SIZE 6 in (15 cm)

Its popularity with aquarium keepers makes this one of the most familiar cichlids. In its natural habitat, its compressed body, marked with dark vertical stripes, and extended, threadlike fins keep it well concealed in cloudy plant-filled water.

Nile Mouthbrooder *Oreochromis niloticus*

RANGE N. Africa, south to Congo basin and E. Africa

HABITAT Rivers, dammed-up pools

SIZE 19¾ in (50 cm)

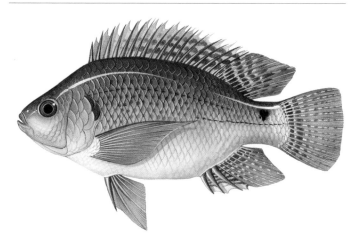

A large cichlid, the Nile mouthbrooder is a sturdy fish, with a long-based dorsal fin. It has a small mouth and tiny teeth and feeds mainly on plankton, although insects and crustaceans are also part of its diet.

Like many cichlids, this fish carries its developing eggs inside its mouth, thus keeping them safe and aerated at the same time. The female of this species broods the eggs, and even after the young fish are hatched, they will return to her mouth when danger threatens.

Ring-tailed Pike Cichlid *Crenicichla saxatilis*

RANGE South America: Venezuela, Amazon basin to Paraguay and Uruguay

HABITAT Rivers, pools

SIZE 14¼ in (36 cm)

A large, elongate fish, the ring-tailed pike cichlid has a distinctive black stripe running the length of its body. Its tail and dorsal fins are black-edged, and there is a black spot on the tail fin. Male and female fishes have the same markings, but males have pointed dorsal and anal fins and females have more rounded fins. An active predator, it snaps up prey in its large mouth as a pike does.

Barred Surfperch *Amphistichus argenteus*

RANGE USA: California, south to Baja California, Mexico

HABITAT Coastal waters

SIZE Up to 16 in (41 cm)

The barred surfperch belongs to the family Embiotocidae, which contains about 24 species, all but one are found in the North Pacific. Most members of the family do frequent the surf area of coasts, hence the common name. A deep-bodied fish, its sides are marked with gold or bronze vertical bars and spots. It feeds on small crabs and other crustaceans and mollusks.

Surfperches bear live young. The male fertilizes the female internally by means of the modified front portion of the anal fin, and the young develop inside her body, protected and nourished by ovarian fluid. The brood size varies from 4 to 113, depending on the size of the mother, but the average is about 33. Most young are born from March to July and are mature at about 2 years old, when they are just over 5 in (12.5 cm) long.

Kelp Perch *Brachyistius frenatus*

RANGE Pacific coast of N. America: Vancouver to California

HABITAT Shallow waters along rocky coasts, kelp beds

SIZE 7¾ in (20 cm)

A member of the surfperch family, Embiotocidae, the kelp perch has handsome coppery coloration on its sides, each scale having a dark spot. It feeds on crustaceans. It bears live young – the male fertilizes the female internally, and the young develop inside her body.

Sergeant Major *Abudefduf saxatilis*

RANGE Worldwide, warm temperate and tropical seas

HABITAT Inshore waters, coral reefs

SIZE 9 in (23 cm)

The sergeant major belongs to the damselfish family, Pomacentridae, which contains over 315 species of marine fish, found all over the world in warm temperate and tropical areas. A deep-bodied fish, its coloration changes according to the depth of water it is in; in shallow water, it is yellow with dark barring, but in deeper water or caves, it turns blue with darker blue vertical bars.

The eggs are laid on a rock or in a rock crevice, on a surface cleared of any algal plant growth. The male fish guards the eggs until they hatch.

Clown Anemonefish *Amphiprion percula*

RANGE W. and central Pacific Ocean

HABITAT Coral reefs

SIZE 2¼ in (6 cm)

Unmistakable with its broad bands of white and orange and its dark-rimmed fins, the clown anemonefish belongs to the damselfish family, Pomacentridae. Like the others in its genus, it has developed a relationship with large sea anemones, living among their stinging tentacles and even remaining inside when the anemone draws in its tentacles. Thus the fish shelters from predators, and, at the same time, it is protected from the anemone's poison by its own body mucus. It feeds on tiny crustaceans and other organisms, which are taken during brief dashes from its refuge.

The eggs are laid on rock or coral near the anemone and are guarded by both parents.

Beaugregory *Pomacentrus leucostictus*

RANGE W. Atlantic Ocean: coasts of Florida and Bermuda; Caribbean; Pacific coast of Mexico

HABITAT Inshore waters, coral reefs

SIZE 6 in (15 cm)

A member of the family Pomacentridae, the beaugregory is a handsome, rich orange-brown and blue fish, dotted with yellow spots. Like most members of its family, it is an active little fish, which darts around coral and rock crevices, feeding on algae, tiny crustaceans, worms and other small invertebrates.

PERCHLIKE FISHES CONTINUED

Ballan Wrasse *Labrus bergylta*

RANGE E. Atlantic Ocean: Norway and Britain, south to N. Africa; Mediterranean Sea

HABITAT Rocky coasts

SIZE 19¾–23½ in (50–60 cm)

There are several hundred species of wrasse. Like many wrasses, this species has interesting breeding behavior. After displays, the pair builds a nest of weeds, bound together with mucus and lodged in a rock crevice. Once the eggs are laid, the male fertilizes them and guards them until they hatch.

Tautog *Tautoga onitis*

RANGE W. Atlantic Ocean: Nova Scotia to South Carolina

HABITAT Coastal waters, around rocky shores and mussel beds

SIZE Up to 36 in (91.5 cm)

The tautog is a rather dull-colored fish, with a blunt snout and a well-rounded body. Adults eat various invertebrates, mostly barnacles, mussels, crabs and snails, which they crush with their strong jaws and teeth. Young fishes eat worms and small crustaceans.

Spawning occurs in the spring and summer, in deep water. The eggs float at the surface and gradually drift inshore as they develop and hatch. The young spend their first few months in shallow waters, where there is plenty of seaweed for protection.

Hogfish *Lachnolaimus maximus* **VU**

RANGE W. Atlantic Ocean: Bermuda and North Carolina to Brazil; Gulf of Mexico, Caribbean

HABITAT Coastal waters, coral reefs

SIZE 35¾ in (91 cm)

The first three spines of the hogfishes' dorsal fins are greatly elongated and thickened. The tips of the dorsal and anal fins are pointed. The hogfish's thick lips protrude slightly, and its forehead curves steeply above the mouth. Coloration is variable in this species, but males tend to be more intensely colored than females. Hogfishes eat mollusks, crabs and sea urchins.

California Sheepshead

Pimelometopon pulchrum

RANGE Pacific Ocean: Monterey Bay, California to Gulf of California

HABITAT Rocky coasts, around kelp and mussel beds

SIZE Up to 36 in (91.5 cm)

This distinctive wrasse has a deep body and a heavy, bulbous head. In the breeding season, the male develops a prominent bump on the forehead. The dorsal fin spines are shorter than the rayed portion of the fin, and the lobes of the dorsal, anal and tail fins are pointed. The middle of the male's body is red and the front and back black or purple. The female is reddish all over, sometimes with black markings.

The California sheepshead eats crustaceans and mollusks and is believed to spawn in summer.

Slippery Dick

Halichoeres bivittatus

RANGE W. Atlantic Ocean: Bermuda and North Carolina to Brazil; Caribbean

HABITAT Coastal waters, coral reefs

SIZE Up to 9 in (23 cm)

The slippery dick is a common inhabitant of coral reefs. It eats crustaceans, sea urchins worms and mollusks. The species is characterized by two black lines running along the body.

Rainbow Parrotfish

Scarus guacamaia **VU**

RANGE W. Atlantic Ocean: Bermuda and Florida through Caribbean to Argentina

HABITAT Coastal waters, coral reefs

SIZE 4 ft (1.2 m)

The rainbow parrotfish is one of approximately 83 species in the family Scaridae. It has a robust, heavy body and a large head. It has strong, beaklike jaws, formed from fused teeth, with which it scrapes algae and coral off reefs to eat. Farther back in the throat, the fish has large grinding teeth.

In common with some other parrotfish species, the rainbow parrotfish sometimes secretes a cocoon of mucus around its body at night. This natural "sleeping-bag" protects the fish from predators while it sleeps.

Blue Parrotfish *Scarus coeruleus*

RANGE W. Atlantic Ocean: North Carolina
to Brazil, including Gulf of Mexico and Caribbean

HABITAT Coral reefs

SIZE 4 ft (1.2 m)

The lower jaw of the blue parrotfish is far shorter than the upper; older males develop a prominent bump on the snout. The blue parrotfish feeds in the same manner as the rest of the family Scaridae, scraping algae and coral off reefs with its beaklike jaws; the food is then broken down for digestion by the grinding teeth, farther back in the throat.

Stoplight Parrotfish *Sparisoma viride*

RANGE Caribbean

HABITAT Coral reefs

SIZE 9¾–19¾ in (25–50 cm)

Males of this common parrotfish species are larger than females and differ in coloration. Males are bluish-green, while females are red and reddish-brown. These parrotfishes feed on algae and other plant material which they scrape from rocks and coral with their teeth.

ZOARCOIDEI: ZOARCOID SUBORDER

A group of marine fishes found primarily in the North Pacific but also in the North Atlantic and the tropical regions of both oceans. Most of the 320 species of zoarcoids are offshore or deep sea dwellers although some species are found in tidal pools. The 9 families in the suborder include the eelpouts, pricklebacks, wrymouths, gunnels, and wolf-fishes.

Ocean Pout *Macrozoarces americanus*

RANGE N. Atlantic Ocean: Labrador to Delaware

HABITAT Seabed, 50–600 ft (15–183 m)

SIZE 36½ in (93 cm)

The ocean pout is one of a small family collectively known as eelpouts. Their classification has been the subject of dispute, and some authorities have placed them with the blennies rather than the codfishes. Typical of the eelpouts, the elongate ocean pout has long anal and dorsal fins joined to the tail fin. Its head is broad and flattened and it has thick, protuberant lips. It is a bottom-living species and eats crustaceans, sea urchins, brittle stars and other small invertebrates. In autumn, ocean pouts migrate into deeper, offshore waters to spawn. A female may shed 4,000 or more eggs, massed together in a gelatinous substance, which lie on the bottom and hatch after 2 or 3 months. Some eelpouts, such as the European species *Zoarces viviparus*, give birth to live young.

Wrymouth *Cryptacanthodes maculatus*

RANGE W. Atlantic Ocean: Labrador to New Jersey

HABITAT Muddy seabed

SIZE 35½ in (90 cm)

A bottom-living fish, the wrymouth lives buried in mud, sometimes making a complex system of tunnels. It eats fish, crustaceans and mollusks. Rather eellike in appearance, the wrymouth has an elongate, scaleless body, with dorsal and anal fins continuous with the tail fin but no pelvic fins. Its head is flattopped, with the eyes set high, and its mouth slants obliquely, the lower jaw extending beyond the upper. Also known as the ghostfish, the wrymouth belongs to the family Cryptacanthodidae.

Butterfish *Pholis gunnellus*

RANGE W. Atlantic Ocean: Labrador to Massachusetts; E. Atlantic: N. coast of France, north to Barents Sea; coasts of Iceland and S. Greenland

HABITAT Rocky shores, intertidal pools, sometimes in deeper waters

SIZE 9¾ in (25 cm)

This widely distributed fish has a slender, elongate body, brownish in color, and a distinctive row of white-edged black spots along the bottom of its longbased dorsal fin. It is a member of the family Pholididae (Gunnels), which contains fish found in the cooler waters of the North Pacific and Atlantic. Small crustaceans, worms and mollusks are its main foods, and since the butterfish is so abundant near the shore, it is itself an important item of diet for many seabirds.

Spawning takes place in winter when eggs are laid in clusters among stones near the shore and the parents guard the eggs until they hatch.

PERCHLIKE FISHES CONTINUED

Atlantic Wolffish *Anarhichas lupus*

RANGE W. Atlantic Ocean: Labrador to Cape Cod, sometimes New Jersey; across to E. Atlantic: Iceland and Spitsbergen to N. France

HABITAT From shallow waters down to 980 ft (300 m)

SIZE 3¼–4 ft (1–1.2 m)

One of about 6 species in the family Anarhichadidae, the Atlantic wolffish has a huge head, fanglike teeth and long dorsal and anal fins. It eats mollusks, such as clams, and crustaceans, which it breaks open with its sharp fangs and crushes with the broad teeth farther back in its mouth.

Spawning takes place in winter. The sticky eggs are shed in clumps on the seabed, where they may adhere to stones.

NOTOTHENIOIDEI: ICEFISH SUBORDER

Commonly referred to as icefishes, the 120 notothenioid species are the dominant fish group of the Antarctic. They show many adaptations to their cold water habitat.

Antarctic Cod *Notothenia coriiceps*

RANGE Antarctic coasts

HABITAT Coastal waters

SIZE 24 in (61 cm)

Almost three-quarters of fishes in the arctic belong to the notothenioidae family. Some have a special protein in their blood, which lowers its freezing point, and so they are able to survive temperatures as low as 28°F (–1.9°C).

Young antarctic cod are blue and silver at first, turning reddish as juveniles. This cod is a bottom-dweller and eats algae, mollusks, small crustaceans and worms.

Icefish *Chaenocephalus aceratus*

RANGE Antarctic area off South Georgia, South Orkneys, South Shetlands

HABITAT Shallow waters to 1,100 ft (340 m)

SIZE 23½ in (60 cm)

The icefish is one of about 16 species in the family Channichthyidae, all found in the Antarctic. These fishes lack the oxygen-carrying pigment hemoglobin, which is common to all other vertebrates. Their blood appears whitish, almost clear. Oxygen is taken through the gills in the normal way for fishes but is carried within the body dissolved in the blood plasma. These fishes are sluggish, and need relatively little oxygen, so they are able to obtain sufficient oxygen from the cold, well-oxygenated waters that they inhabit.

An elongate, slender fish, the icefish has a large head, with beaklike jaws. It spends much of its time close to the bottom, eating fish and crustaceans.

TRACHINOIDEI: TRACHINOID SUBORDER

Most of the 210 or so species in this suborder are bottom dwellers that bury themselves in sand to ambush passing prey. They include weeverfish, stargazers, and sand eels.

Sand Eel/Sand Lance *Ammodytes tobianus*

RANGE E. Atlantic Ocean: Iceland and Norway to S. Portugal and Spain

HABITAT Inshore waters to depths of about 100 ft (30 m)

SIZE 7¾ in (20 cm)

Sand eels are so called because of their habit of burrowing extremely rapidly into clean, sandy bottoms, but they also swim in shoals near the surface. There are about 12 species in the sand eel family, Ammodytidae, all of which are thin, elongate fishes, with long dorsal and anal fins. Typically, the head is pointed, with a protruding lower jaw. The sand eel feeds on plankton and is itself an important food fish for many larger fishes.

Some sand eels spawn in autumn, others in spring, but all shed their eggs on the seabed, where they adhere to the sand.

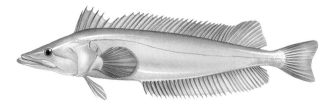

Lesser Weever *Echiichthys vipera*

RANGE European Atlantic coasts, Britain to N. Africa; Mediterranean sea

HABITAT Shallow, sandy-bottomed waters

SIZE 5½ in (14 cm)

A bottom-living fish, the lesser weever lies half-buried in the sand with only its head visible. If disturbed, it erects its dorsal-fin spines, which contain tissue that produces highly toxic venom; there are more venom-producing spines on the gill covers. These spines can cause extremely painful wounds, but are used only in defence and as a warning signal. The lesser weever eats small bottom living crustaceans and fish. It is one of about 6 species in the family Trachinidae, all of which have venomous spines.

Northern Stargazer *Astroscopus guttatus*

RANGE Atlantic coast of N. America: New York to North Carolina

HABITAT Shallow, sandy-bottomed waters

SIZE Up to 12 in (30.5 cm)

The northern stargazer has a large head, with the mouth directed upward; its eyes are on top of the head, facing upward. This structure allows the stargazer to lie partially buried on the seabed with only its eyes and mouth exposed, waiting for prey such as fish and crustaceans. Behind the eyes is a specialized area of electric organs, capable of producing charges of over 50 volts.

Spawning is believed to take place in spring or early summer, offshore. The young fishes gradually drift inshore to shallower waters, where they settle to the bottom-dwelling life of adults.

BLENNIOIDEI: BLENNIOID SUBORDER

The 730 fish in this suborder, which include the blennies, are small marine fishes of tropical and subtropical regions.

Giant Kelpfish *Heterostichus rostratus*

RANGE Pacific coast of N. America: British Columbia to Baja California

HABITAT Inshore shallow waters, near kelp beds

SIZE Up to 24 in (61 cm)

The giant kelpfish is the largest of the family Clinidae, which contains about 75 species of primarily tropical marine fish. It is distinguished by its elongate body, sharp, pointed head and longbased dorsal and anal fins, but its coloration is extremely variable, according to its surroundings. Fishes living in eel grass are bright green, others are dark green, brown, orange, yellow or reddish; their coloration always blends with the aquatic vegetation or other background of their habitat.

Shanny *Lipophrys pholis*

RANGE N. European coasts: S. Norway and Scotland, south to Portugal and Madeira

HABITAT Rocky shores, rock pools

SIZE Up to 7 in (18 cm)

The combtooth blenny family, Blenniidae, to which the shanny belongs, contains about 345 species of mostly marine, shore-living fish. The shanny is typical of the family, with its scaleless skin, rounded head and rows of fine sharp teeth – these teeth are the origin of the family's common name. The shanny's diet includes algae, barnacles, crustaceans and fish.

The eggs are laid in clusters under a rock or in a crevice and are guarded by the male until they hatch.

Redlip Blenny *Ophioblennius atlanticus*

RANGE W. Atlantic Ocean: North Carolina to Bermuda and south to coast of Brazil; Gulf of Mexico, Caribbean

HABITAT Rocky- or coral-bottomed waters

SIZE 4¾ in (12 cm)

Characterized by its steep, rounded snout bearing tufts and tentacles, red lips and red-edged dorsal fin, the redlip blenny is a common fish in its range. It is a member of the combtooth blenny family, Blenniidae, and is typical of the family in its bottom-living, secretive habits. It feeds on small invertebrates.

The eggs are laid amid coral or under rocks and are guarded by the male. The young fishes live in surface waters, farther offshore than adults.

GOBIESOCIFORM FISHES AND FLATFISHES

GOBIESOCOIDEI: CLINGFISH SUBORDER

The 120 species of fish in this suborder are – as their name suggests – adapted for life in the intertidal zone where pounding waves will wash marine organisms off rocks and seaweed unless they have a means of clinging on to them.

Shore Clingfish *Lepadogaster lepadogaster*

RANGE N. Atlantic Ocean: Scotland to N. Africa; W. Mediterranean coasts

HABITAT Rocky shores, between tide marks

SIZE 2½ in (6.5 cm)

A small, scaleless fish, with low fins lacking spiny rays, the shore clingfish is fairly typical of its family. On its underside is a strong sucking disk, formed partly from its pelvic fins, with which it can cling to rocks or other surfaces. Its snout is elongate and beaklike and topped with a fringed flap.

Shore clingfishes spawn in summer. The eggs are attached to the underside of a rock, and are guarded by one of the parents.

Diademichthys lineatus

RANGE Indian and Pacific Oceans: Mauritius to New Caledonia, north to Philippines

HABITAT Among sea urchin spines

SIZE 2 in (5 cm)

This extremely slender, long-snouted clingfish lives in association with the sea urchin *Diadema savignyi.* Its body shape is a perfect adaptation for its habit of hanging, head downward, among the urchin's spines. It gains protection from predators in its refuge, and feeds on the tiny tube feet of the urchin.

Northern Clingfish *Gobiesox maeandricus*

RANGE Pacific Ocean: British Columbia to S. California

HABITAT Coastal waters between tide marks

SIZE 6 in (15 cm)

One of the most common of the Pacific Coast clingfishes, the northern clingfish is

identified by its smooth body and broad head. Its dorsal and anal fins are low and set back near the tail. Like all clingfishes, its pelvic fins are modified to form part of a sucking disk on its belly, with which it clings to rocks or other surfaces in the turbulent intertidal zone. It feeds on mollusks and crustaceans.

CALLIONYMOIDEI: DRAGONET SUBORDER

The 137 species of dragonets are gobylike fish that are found mainly in the reef areas of the Indian and western Pacific Oceans. Many species spend most of their time half-buried on the seabed.

Dragonet *Callionymus lyra*

RANGE E. Atlantic Ocean: Iceland, Norway, south to N. Africa and Mediterranean Sea

HABITAT Shallow coastal waters and to depths of 650 ft (200 m)

SIZE 11¾ in (30 cm)

The male dragonet is particularly striking, with his blue and yellow dorsal fin and extended rays. Females are smaller, lack the fin extensions and are brownish in color. Like all dragonets, this fish has a rather flattened body and large head, with small gill apertures near the top of the head, in keeping with its habit of lying, often half-buried, in sand on the seabed. Bottom-dwelling crustaceans and worms are its main foods.

Dragonets spawn in the spring or summer, depending on the area and males perform complex courtship displays, posturing with their fins. The eggs are shed in surface waters where they float until they hatch.

Mandarinfish *Synchiropus splendidus*

RANGE Coasts of Philippines, Queensland and N. Australia

HABITAT Inshore waters, coral reefs

SIZE 3 in (7.5 cm)

An extremely striking little fish, the mandarinfish has irregular red markings on its greenish-blue body and on its fins; its pectoral fins are bright blue. Its body is rather stouter than that of other dragonets, and it has a bulbous head. The first spine of the dorsal fin is greatly extended. Although it is a popular aquarium fish, little is known of its life in the wild other than that it lives on the seabed among rocks or coral.

GOBIOIDEI: GOBIOID SUBORDER

The 2,100 species in this large suborder are typically small, mostly marine, sand-burrowing species with a short, spiny dorsal fin, and pelvic fins that are close to each other or are linked to form a sucking disk. The vast majority of species belong to 2 families: Eleotridae (sleepers) and Gobiidae (gobies), the latter being the largest family of marine fishes.

Fat Sleeper *Dormitator maculatus*

RANGE W. Atlantic Ocean: Bahamas and North Carolina to Gulf of Mexico and Brazil

HABITAT Muddy-bottomed shores, brackish pools, river mouths

SIZE 18 in (46 cm)

The fat sleeper and the other species of sleeper are sometimes included in the goby family; otherwise they are placed in a separate family, Eleotridae. The main difference between the two groups is that sleepers have separate pelvic fins, while gobies generally have united pelvics, which form a suckerlike disk.

A small but thickset, little fish, with a large, rounded head, the fat sleeper has the habit of resting motionless on the seabed for long periods, hence its common name.

Dwarf Goby *Pandaka pygmaea* **CR**

RANGE Philippines

HABITAT Lakes, streams

SIZE ⁴⁄₁₀ in (11 mm)

The dwarf goby is one of the smallest fishes in the world and is perhaps the smallest vertebrate animal, mature adults as tiny as ⁷⁄₁₀ in (6 mm) long have been found.

The dwarf goby's head is scaleless, but its slender body is scaled and marked with dark spots.

Rock Goby *Gobius paganellus*

RANGE N. Atlantic Ocean: Britain to N. Africa; Mediterranean coasts

HABITAT Rocky shores, coastal pools

SIZE 4¾ in (12 cm)

The goby family, Gobiidae, is one of the largest marine families, with many species also entering fresh water. The rock goby is one of the larger species, but is typical, with its big, blunt head, slender body and rounded tail fin. Its pelvic fins are fused to form a sucking disk, with which it attaches itself to rocks or other surfaces. The goby feeds on crustaceans and other small invertebrates and young fish.

Spawning occurs in spring and summer. The eggs are shed on to the roof of a hole in the rocks, where they are guarded by the male until they hatch.

ACANTHUROIDEI: ACANTHUROID SUBORDER

A small suborder with just 125 species, the acanthuroids include some of the most conspicuous fish, such as the spadefishes, rabbitfish, surgeonfish, and moorish idols, that are found in coral reef habitats.

Atlantic Spadefish *Chaetodipterus faber*

RANGE W. Atlantic Ocean: New England, Bermuda, south to Gulf of Mexico, Caribbean to Brazil

HABITAT Rocky-bottomed waters

SIZE 18–35½ in (6–90 cm)

The Atlantic spadefish has a deep body, much compressed from side to side, and extended dorsal and anal fins. Its coloration changes as it grows: small, young fishes are black, becoming silvery gray as they mature, with dark vertical bars down the sides which become indistinct in large adults. It is a member of the Ephippidae family, which contains about 14 species.

Spadefishes feed primarily on small invertebrate animals.

PERCHLIKE FISHES CONTINUED

Batfish *Platax pinnatus*

RANGE Indian and Pacific Oceans: Red
Sea, E. Africa to Philippines,
Indonesia, Australia

HABITAT Coastal waters;
lagoons when young, reefs
as adults

SIZE 30 in (76 cm)

A member of the
spadefish family,
Ephippidae, the batfish
has a deep, laterally
compressed body and high
dorsal and anal fins. Juvenile
batfish are black, with fins
outlined in orange. The fins look
similar to some aquatic flatworms
and mollusks, which fishes find unpleasant to eat. Batfish swim
on their sides, with undulatory movements, heightening this
similarity. They probably gain protection from this.

Scat *Scatophagus argus*

RANGE Indian and Pacific Oceans: E. Africa to
India, Indonesia and W. Pacific Islands

HABITAT Coastal waters; fresh and brackish water

SIZE 11¾ in (30 cm)

The scat is one of the 3 or so species in the Scatophagidae family
which means, literally, "dung-eaters". The scat is often found
near sewer outputs and is believed to feed on feces, but it
normally eats plant material. Adults are spotted with brownish
blotches. Young fishes have dark, barred markings on their sides.

Blue-lined Spinefoot *Siganus virgatus*

RANGE Indian and Pacific Oceans: India and Sri Lanka to Indonesia and
N. Australia, north to Philippines, China and Japan

HABITAT Inshore waters, edges of coral reefs

SIZE 10 in (25.5 cm)

This is one of 27 or so species in the
rabbitfish, or spinefoot, family, Siganidae.
Spinefoots have many strong, sharp venomous
spines, capable of inflicting serious wounds. This species has a
typically blunt, rounded head and strong jaws. It grazes on algae.

Blue Tang *Acanthurus coeruleus*

RANGE W. Atlantic Ocean: New York and
Bermuda, south to Caribbean and Brazil

HABITAT Coastal waters, coral reefs

SIZE 12 in (30.5 cm)

The brilliantly colored blue tang is one
of the 72 or so species in the surgeonfish
family, Acanthuridae. The fishes have extremely
sharp, movable spines on each side of the tail that are thought to
resemble a surgeon's scalpels. Normally the spines lie flat in a
groove, but if the fish is disturbed or alarmed, they are erected
and can inflict serious wounds on an enemy as the tail is lashed
to and fro. The blue tang uses these spines only for defensive
purposes, since it feeds entirely on algae, which it removes from
rocks with its sharp-edged teeth.

Although fairly typical of its family, the blue tang has a
particularly deep body and steep profile. Its coloration changes
as it matures. Young fishes are bright yellow, with blue spots
near the eyes; they then become blue over much of the front of
the body, with a yellow tail. Fully grown adults are a deep rich
blue all over, with narrow, dark blue lines running the
length of the body.

Moorish Idol *Zanclus cornutus*

RANGE Indian and Pacific Oceans: E. Africa to Hawaiian
Islands

HABITAT Shallow waters, coral reefs

SIZE 7 in (18 cm)

The spectacular moorish idol is an unmistakable fish, with its
extremely bold coloration and projecting snout. Its body is deep
and compressed, and its dorsal and anal fins are pointed and
swept back, making the fish appear deeper than it is long. The
dorsal fin has a long, filamentous extension. Adults develop
protuberances over the eyes that enlarge with age.

Although it is a member of the surgeonfish
family, Acanthuridae, the moorish idol lacks
the formidable tail spines of its relatives.
The young fish, however, does have a
sharp spine at each corner of the
mouth. These spines drop off as
the fish matures. Indeed, young
and adults appear so different that
they were originally thought to be
separate species.

Striped-face Unicornfish *Naso lituratus*

RANGE Indian and Pacific Oceans: E. Africa to Australia and Hawaiian Islands

HABITAT Coastal waters, coral reefs

SIZE 16 in (41 cm)

The unicornfish is a member of the surgeonfish family, but it has fixed, forward-pointing spines, not erectile spines, on each side of its tail. This species does not develop a horn on its forehead as it matures. Males do, however, have long, distinctive streamers on the lobes of the tail fin. Unicornfishes swim in small schools and graze on algae and coral.

MUGILOIDEI: MULLET SUBORDER

The 80 or so mullet species form the only family in this suborder. Mullets are inshore fish that have thick, streamlined bodies and two dorsal fins, the anterior being spiny and the posterior soft. They live in large shoals.

Striped Mullet *Mugil cephalus*

RANGE Worldwide, tropical and warm temperate seas

HABITAT Open sea, inshore waters, estuaries

SIZE Up to 35¾ in (91 cm)

The striped mullet is one of the gray mullet family, Mugilidae, which contains species that live in salt, brackish and fresh water. It has a typically rounded, heavily scaled body and widely spaced dorsal fins. It eats the minute algae and planktonic animals contained in the bottom detritus, by sucking up the detritus, filtering it through its gills and crushing the remaining material in its muscular stomach. A good deal of sand and mud is also taken into the gut.

SCOMBROIDEI: SCOMBROID SUBORDER

There are 1,365 species of scombroids in 6 families – barracudas, snake mackerel, cutlassfishes, mackerel and tunas, sailfishes and marlins, and swordfish. Most are voracious predators that move at fast speed, and are prized by anglers.

Great Barracuda *Sphyraena barracuda*

RANGE Worldwide, tropical seas except E. Pacific Ocean; best known in Caribbean and W. Atlantic Ocean

HABITAT Coastal lagoons, coral reefs; adults farther offshore

SIZE Up to 6 ft (1.8 m)

There are about 18 species of barracuda found in tropical and subtropical areas of the Atlantic, Indian and Pacific oceans. The great barracuda is characteristic of the family, with its long, slender body, pointed head and jutting jaw studded with formidable teeth. An aggressive predator, it eats fish but has been known to attack humans if disturbed or provoked. Barracudas are generally solitary, but may gather in groups before spawning.

Atlantic Cutlassfish *Trichiurus lepturus*

RANGE Atlantic Ocean: tropical and temperate waters, including Gulf of Mexico and Caribbean; Mediterranean Sea

HABITAT Surface waters of open sea

SIZE 5 ft (1.5 m)

The Atlantic cutlassfish has an elongate, ribbonlike body, with a pointed head and large jaws, armed with formidable teeth. Its dorsal fin runs the length of its silvery body to the end of the tail. A voracious predator, it eats fish and squid. It is a member of the Trichiuridae family.

Atlantic Mackerel *Scomber scombrus*

RANGE W. Atlantic Ocean: Gulf of St. Lawrence to North Carolina; E. Atlantic: Iceland, Scandinavia, south to N. Africa; Mediterranean Sea

HABITAT Offshore surface waters

SIZE 16–26 in (41–66 cm)

The abundant mackerel has a slender, well-rounded, body, marked with irregular black lines. Adults eat crustaceans and small fish. Young fishes eat planktonic crustaceans and fish larvae. Mackerel move north in spring and summer and south in winter. In winter, they group in deep, relatively warm waters along the edge of the continental shelf. Mackerel are one of about 50 species in the Scombridae family.

In summer a medium-sized female may produce as many as 450,000 eggs, shed in no particular place, which float until they hatch about 4 days later.

PERCHLIKE FISHES CONTINUED

Yellowfin Tuna *Thunnus albacares*

RANGE Worldwide, tropical and warm temperate seas

HABITAT Offshore surface waters, inshore waters

SIZE Up to 6½ ft (2 m)

The yellowfin tuna has long pectoral fins, small, yellow finlets behind the dorsal and anal fins and yellow markings along its sides. Its body is typically, spindle-shaped. Yellowfin tuna eat fish, crustaceans and squid. Like most Scombridae, they make seasonal migrations. Spawning takes place at any time of year in the tropics and in late spring and summer elsewhere. Each year females are believed to produce at least two batches of over a million eggs.

Wahoo *Acanthocybium solanderi*

RANGE Worldwide in tropical seas

HABITAT Open sea

SIZE Up to 6½ ft (2 m)

Unlike most of the family Scombridae, the wahoo is not a schooling fish. It usually occurs alone or in small groups. Its body is longer and more slender than most tunas, and it has a long, narrow snout, equipped with many strong teeth. It eats a range of fish and squid and it can reach extremely high speeds when in pursuit of prey – reputedly up to 41 mph (66 km/h).

The wahoo is not abundant and is not fished commercially, but it is popular with anglers.

Skipjack Tuna *Euthynnus pelamis*

RANGE Worldwide in tropical seas, seasonally in temperate areas

HABITAT Offshore surface waters

SIZE 3¼ ft (1 m)

A member of the family Scombridae the skipjack has the streamlined body typical of the fast swimming tunas. It has dark stripes on the lower half of its body. An extremely abundant fish, it swims in huge schools, containing up to 50,000 fishes, and is an important commercial fish. Skipjacks eat fish, squid and crustaceans.

Sailfish *Istiophorus platypterus*

RANGE Worldwide, tropical and warm temperate seas

HABITAT Surface waters, open sea and sometimes closer to shore

SIZE 12 ft (3.6 m)

The high, saillike dorsal fin is the outstanding characteristic of the sailfish but it also has elongate jaws, which are rounded, not flattened like those of the swordfish. It is one of the 10 species in the family Istiophoridae, all of which are spectacular, fast-swimming fishes. The sailfish has a varied diet and seems to eat almost any available type of fish and squid. It makes regular seasonal migrations, moving from cooler to more tropical waters in winter.

Sailfishes spawn in open sea, each female shedding several million eggs, which float in surface waters until they hatch. Those few that survive grow extremely quickly.

Blue Marlin *Makaira nigricans*

RANGE Worldwide, tropical and warm temperate seas

HABITAT Offshore waters, open sea

SIZE 10–15 ft (3–4.6 m)

An extremely impressive fish, the blue marlin weighs at least 400 lb (180 kg) on average and can be more than twice as heavy. It has the elongate, rounded snout common to all members of the family Istiophoridae, with which it is thought to stun prey such as schooling fishes and squid.

Blue marlins are among the fastest of all fishes and have perfectly streamlined bodies and the high, crescent-shaped tails characteristic of the high-speed species. They make regular seasonal migrations, moving toward the Equator in winter and away again in summer.

Striped Marlin *Tetrapturus audax*

RANGE Indian and Pacific Oceans: warm temperate waters, less common in tropical waters

HABITAT Open sea, inshore waters

SIZE 10 ft (3 m)

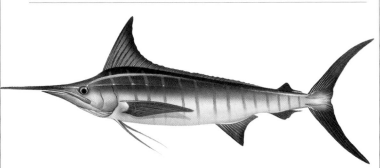

A steely-blue fish, marked with blue or white vertical bars, the striped marlin is distinguished from the blue marlin by its higher dorsal fin. Otherwise it is similar in appearance, with its elongate, beaklike snout and streamlined body. It feeds on fish and occasionally squid, both surface and deepwater species. Like all marlins, it is a member of the family Istiophoridae.

Swordfish *Xiphias gladius* **DD**

RANGE Worldwide, temperate and tropical seas

HABITAT Open sea, surface and deep waters

SIZE 6½–16 ft (2–4.9 m)

The huge and spectacular swordfish is the only member of the family Xiphiidae. It has a greatly elongated, flattened snout, and its dorsal fin is sickle-shaped and placed farther back from the head than that of the similar sailfish. Swordfishes can also be distinguished from marlins and sailfishes by their flattened bills and lack of pelvic fins. Adult swordfishes are generally solitary and do not form schools, except in the spawning season. They are fast, active predators and feed on a variety of small fish, as well as squid. The exact function of the sword is not clear; it may be used to strike at schooling fishes, or it may be simply a result of body streamlining.

In the northern hemisphere swordfishes make seasonal migrations, in winter moving south and into deeper waters. The elongated snout is not present in young fishes but develops gradually, as they mature.

STROMATEOIDEI: STROMATEOID SUBORDER

The 65 species in this suborder are found in tropical and warm temperate seas and include driftfishes, medusafishes, squaretails, and butterfishes. Juvenile fishes of these species are commonly associated with jellyfish or floating objects which provide protection as well as food.

Man-o'-war Fish *Nomeus gronovii*

RANGE Tropical areas of Indian and Pacific Oceans; tropical W. Atlantic Ocean and Caribbean

HABITAT Lives in association with the Portuguese man-o'-war jellyfish

SIZE 8½ in (22 cm)

Best known for its habit of living among the long, stinging tentacles of the Portuguese man-o'-war, *Physalia physalis*, this little fish seems to be immune to the Physulia's stinging cells or may even inhibit their operation. The jellyfish is usually thought to be unaffected by the fish's presence, but the details of the relationship are poorly known, and it is possible that the fish removes debris from its host's body.

The small man-o'-war fish is one of about 15 species in the family Nomeidae.

Butterfish *Peprilus triacanthus*

RANGE W. Atlantic Ocean: Gulf of St. Lawrence to S. Florida

HABITAT Coastal waters, bays, estuaries

SIZE 12 in (30.5 cm)

The attractively colored butterfish has a deep, but laterally compressed, body, a deeply forked tail and long dorsal and anal fins; adults have no pelvic fins. It feeds on crustaceans, squid and small fish. Butterfishes swim in small schools, and some appear to move northward in summer, returning south, but farther offshore, in winter. They belong to the family Stromateidae, which contains about 13 species of marine fish.

PERCHLIKE FISHES AND FLATFISHES

ANABANTOIDEI: GOURAMI SUBORDER

The 80 species of gouramis are freshwater fish that include several species that are well-known aquarium fish.

Climbing Perch *Anabas testudineus*

RANGE India, Sri Lanka, S.E. Asia, Indonesia, Philippines, S. China

HABITAT Rivers, canals, ditches, ponds

SIZE 10 in (25.5 cm)

The climbing perch often inhabits stagnant, poorly oxygenated water. This, combined with its small gills, means that it must obtain some of its oxygen from the air. In each gill chamber is a labyrinthine organ, well supplied with blood vessels. Air taken in through the mouth passes through this auxiliary breathing organ, where oxygen is absorbed. This fish has an astonishing capacity for movement on land, made feasible by its capacity for breathing air. Using its tail for leverage and its pectoral fins and spiny gill covers as props, it hauls itself considerable distances between bodies of water, usually because its previous home has dried up. It is thought to feed on insects and small crustaceans.

The climbing perch is one of about 40 members of the family Anabantidae. It is an important food fish in much of its range.

Paradisefish
Macropodus opercularis

RANGE China, S.E. Asia

HABITAT Ditches, rice fields

SIZE 3½ in (9 cm)

The paradisefish normally lives in poorly oxygenated water but, like the other members of the family Belontiidae, has auxiliary breathing organs in each gill chamber for extracting oxygen from the air. These operate in a similar manner to those of the climbing perch. A colorful little fish, it has greatly extended fins, those of the male being particularly long.

Its breeding habits are common to many of its family. The male makes a floating nest by blowing bubbles of air and mucus. The female sheds her eggs, which he fertilizes and transfers to the nest by spitting them into the bubbles.

Siamese Fightingfish *Betta splendens*

RANGE Thailand

HABITAT Ponds, ditches, slow rivers

SIZE 2¼ in (6 cm)

The Siamese fightingfish has long been bred in captivity to take part in staged fights. Many forms with extremely long fins have been developed. Male fishes may be green, blue or red, but females are usually yellowish-brown. In the wild, males are brown or green. Wild fishes fight for dominance or to maintain territory, but much of the contest takes the form of ritualized threat displays, rather than actual combat.

The Siamese fightingfish often lives in oxygen-poor water. It takes in air at the surface using auxiliary breathing organs in its gill chambers. Mosquito larvae are a major food and they are extremely important as controllers of these insect pests.

In the breeding season, the male fish selects a suitable nest site and blows a bubble nest from air and mucus, which both protects the eggs and keeps them at the well-oxygenated water surface. As the eggs are shed, they are fertilized by the male, who spits them into the nest. The male guards and maintains the nest.

Gourami *Osphronemus goramy*

RANGE Probably Indonesia; introduced in China, S.E. Asia, India, Sri Lanka, Philippines

HABITAT Ponds, swamps, streams

SIZE 24 in (61 cm)

A large, heavy-bodied fish, with a greatly extended pelvic fin ray, the gourami is the only species in its family, Osphronemidae. It is related to the Siamese fightingfish family and has auxiliary breathing organs in its gill chambers, to allow it to take in air at the surface. It often lives in oxygen-poor waters. The male makes a bubble nest and guards the eggs and larvae.

CHANNOIDEI: SNAKEHEAD SUBORDER

Snakeheads are voracious predators. The 21 species form a single family found in freshwater habitats in tropical Africa and Asia.

Snakehead *Ophicephalus striatus*

RANGE India, Sri Lanka, S.E. Asia, China, Philippines, Indonesia

HABITAT Lakes, rivers, canals, ditches, swamps

SIZE 3¼ ft (1 m)

An elongate fish, with long dorsal and anal fins, the snakehead is one of about 10 species in the family Channidae. It generally lives in oxygen-poor waters and has accessory organs in its gill chambers with which it can utilize oxygen from the air. It can live for prolonged periods out of water as long as its skin stays moist, and can survive dry spells by burrowing into mud.

Before spawning, parents clear a surface area of vegetation, and the eggs float there for 3 days, guarded by the male until they hatch.

PLEURONECTIFORMES: FLATFISH ORDER

This group contains 11 families and about 570 species, all but 3 of which are marine. The typical flatfish has a compressed body, and spends much of its life on the seabed. Young flatfishes swim normally, but as they develop, the eye on one side migrates so that both eyes are on the upper surface. The fishes lie and swim with the eyed side uppermost. Bone structure, nerves and muscles undergo complex modifications to achieve this change. All flatfishes are bottom-feeding predators.

Adalah *Psettodes erumei*

RANGE Red Sea, Indian Ocean from E. Africa to N. Australia, into W. Pacific Ocean

HABITAT Shallow waters down to 300 ft (90 m)

SIZE Up to 24 in (61 cm)

The adalah is one of the 2 species in the most primitive flatfish family, Psettodidae. It is thicker bodied and less dramatically compressed than other flatfishes, and the migrated eye is on the edge of the head, rather than on the top side. Some individuals have eyes on the left, some on the right. The adalah and its fellow species, *P. belcheri*, also differ in that they have spiny rays in front of the dorsal fins. These fish live on the seabed but also swim in midwaters.

Turbot *Scophthalmus maximus*

RANGE E. Atlantic Ocean: Scandinavia and Britain, south to N. Africa; Mediterranean Sea

HABITAT Shallow inshore waters to depths of 260 ft (80 m)

SIZE 3¼ ft (1 m)

The turbot is an extremely broad flatfish, with a large head and mouth; the female is bigger than the male. Its scaleless body varies in coloration but is usually brownish, with dark speckles that camouflage it on the seabed. The right eye is generally the one to migrate, so turbots have both eyes on the left side. Adults are active predators, feeding largely on fish. Young turbots feed also on crustaceans.

Spawning takes place in spring or summer, and females produce as many as 10 million eggs, comparatively few of which reach adulthood. Eggs and larvae float in surface waters while they develop, but by the time the young fish is 1 in (2.5 cm) long, it has adopted the adult body form and started its bottom-dwelling life. Turbot is one of the finest and most commercially valuable of all marine food fish.

Windowpane
Scophthalmus aquosus

RANGE W. Atlantic Ocean: Gulf of St. Lawrence to South Carolina

HABITAT Coastal waters to depths of about 230 ft (70 m)

SIZE 18 in (46 cm)

The windowpane is an extremely thin-bodied flatfish, white on the underside and brown with dark spots on the upper. The right eye is generally the one to migrate, so most individuals have both eyes on the left side. Young fishes feed on crustaceans, but adults normally eat fish. Although edible, this species is too thin-bodied to be of commercial value.

FLATFISHES CONTINUED

Peacock Flounder
Bothus lunatus

RANGE W. Atlantic Ocean: Bermuda and Florida through Gulf of Mexico and Caribbean to Brazil

HABITAT Shallow coastal waters

SIZE 18 in (46 cm)

An attractive fish, with scattered blue markings, the peacock flounder is one of the family of lefteye flounders, so called because both eyes are generally on the left side of the head. The eyes of males are more widely separated than those of females. Another characteristic feature is the dorsal fin, which begins well forward in front of the eyes. Even though it is a fairly common fish, the peacock flounder is rarely seen, spending much of its life partially buried in sand on the seabed.

Summer Flounder *Paralichthys dentatus*

RANGE W. Atlantic Ocean: Maine to South Carolina

HABITAT Coastal waters, bays, harbours; farther offshore in winter

SIZE Up to 3¼ ft (1 m)

The summer flounder is a slender, active flatfish, with both eyes normally on the left side of its head. It feeds on crustaceans, mollusks and fish and will pursue prey in mid-waters and even to the surface. However, despite the fact that it is a relatively fast swimmer, much of its life is spent lying half-buried on the seabed. Its coloration varies according to the type of bottom it is lying on, but it is generally grayish-brown, with dark spots. In summer, it lives in shallow waters close to the shore, moving farther offshore to deeper waters in the winter.

Spawning takes place between late autumn and early spring, depending on the latitude. The eggs are thought to float in surface waters, and the young fishes drift inshore, where they live in shallow water while they develop.

California Halibut *Paralichthys californicus*

RANGE Pacific Ocean: coast of California, sometimes as far north as Oregon

HABITAT Sandy-bottomed coastal waters

SIZE 5 ft (1.5 m)

The California halibut is a member of the lefteye flounder family, but perhaps as much as half the population have both eyes on the right side. It feeds on fish, particularly anchovies, and has a large mouth and strong teeth. The halibut, in turn, is eaten by rays, sea lions and porpoises and is also an important commercial food fish for man.

Spawning occurs in spring and early summer, and the growth rate of the young is fairly slow.

Atlantic Halibut *Hippoglossus hippoglossus* **EN**

RANGE N. Atlantic Ocean: New Jersey, north to Greenland, Iceland and Barents Sea, south to English Channel

HABITAT Sandy-bottomed, gravel-bottomed and rocky-bottomed waters at 330–5,000 ft (100–1,500 m)

SIZE 6½–8 ft (2–2.4 m)

One of the largest of all flatfishes, the Atlantic halibut is identified by its size, its slender, yet thickset, body and its slightly concave tail. It may attain a top weight of 700 lb (316 kg), although fishes of such size are probably rare today. Its mouth and teeth are large, and both eyes are on the right side in almost all individuals. Females are generally larger than males and tend to live longer. Despite its size, the halibut is an active and voracious predator and pursues prey in mid-water, rather than remaining confined to the seabed. Fish are the main food of adults, but young halibuts also feed on crustaceans.

Spawning occurs in winter and spring, each female shedding as many as 2 million eggs. The eggs drift near the surface of deep water until they hatch after 9 to 16 days. Their growth rate is slow, and

halibut are not sexually mature until they are 10 to 14 years of age. Adults migrate northward after spawning.

The Atlantic halibut has long been an important commercial species, but its slow growth rate and late maturity make the population extremely vulnerable to overfishing. Its numbers are now greatly reduced.

Starry Flounder *Platichthys stellatus*

RANGE N. Pacific Ocean: California to Alaska and Bering Sea, south to Japan and Korea

HABITAT Coastal waters, bays, estuaries; also deeper waters down to 900 ft (275 m)

SIZE 36 in (91.5 cm)

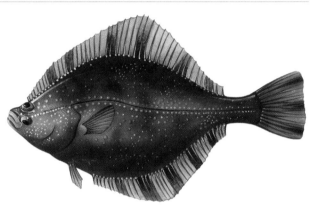

Identified by the distinctive pattern of dark and light bars on the fins, the starry flounder has a dark-brown body on the eyed side, scattered with sharp spines. Although a member of the righteye flatfish family, Pleuronectidae, more than half of the population has both eyes on the left side. This flounder feeds on worms, crustaceans, mollusks and fish.

Spawning takes place in late winter and spring, usually in shallow waters. Young fishes may enter brackish water or river mouths. Females are mature in their third year, males in their second. Starry flounders are caught commercially, particularly off the coasts of Japan and Korea.

Plaice *Pleuronectes platessa*

RANGE E. Atlantic Ocean: Scandinavia, south to N. Africa and Mediterranean Sea; coasts of Iceland and S. Greenland

HABITAT Shallow waters down to 165 ft (50 m), sometimes to 650 ft (200 m)

SIZE 19¾–35¾ in (50–91 cm)

The plaice is characterized by the rich brown color, dotted with prominent orange spots, of its eyed side; the underside is white. A member of the righteye flatfish family, Pleuronectidae, the plaice has both eyes on the right side of the body; reversed

specimens (those with eyes on the left) are rare. A bottom-dweller, it lives on mud, sand or gravel on the seabed and feeds on mollusks, worms and crustaceans. Even adults often come right inshore to the tidal zone to find food.

Spawning usually takes place from January to March. Eggs hatch in 10 to 20 days, depending on water temperature. The larvae live at the surface for up to 6 weeks before adopting the bottom-dwelling life, when they are about ½ in (1.25 cm) long. By this time, the structural adjustments and the migration of the eye have been completed. Males are mature at 2 to 6 years, females at 3 to 7 years. Plaice may live for up to 30 years.

Plaice is an important commercial fish in northern Europe.

Dab *Limanda limanda*

RANGE E. Atlantic Ocean: White Sea, coasts of Scandinavia and Britain to Biscay; coasts of Iceland

HABITAT Shallow sandy-bottomed waters

SIZE 9¾–16½ in (25–42 cm)

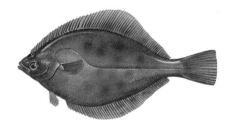

A small flatfish, the dab has toothed scales on its eyed side, which give its body a rough texture. The blind side is white and has toothed scales only at the edges of the body. Both eyes are on the right side and exceptions are rare. The dab feeds on the seabed on almost any bottom-living invertebrates, especially crustaceans, worms and mollusks. It makes seasonal migrations, moving inshore in spring and offshore in autumn.

The dab spawns in spring and early summer, and the eggs and larvae float in surface waters until they adopt the adult form and bottom-dwelling habits, when about ¾ in (2 cm) long. By this time, the structural modifications and migration of the eye to the right side are complete.

This extremely abundant fish is an important commercial species in Europe, despite its small size.

FLATFISHES CONTINUED

Greenland Halibut *Reinhardtius hippoglossoides*

RANGE N. Atlantic Ocean: Arctic Ocean, Norwegian Sea, Iceland, Greenland, coasts of N. America as far south as New Jersey; N. Pacific Ocean: Bering and Okhotsk Seas, south to California and Japan

HABITAT Deep waters at 650–6,600 ft (200–2,000 m)

SIZE 31½ in–4 ft (80 cm–1.2 m)

An active predator, the Greenland halibut hunts in mid-water rather than on the seabed, feeding on fish, crustaceans and squid. In keeping with its habits, it is more symmetrical in body form than most flatfishes and has a blind side almost as dark as its eyed side. Although both eyes are on the right side, the upper eye is at the edge of the head, giving a larger field of vision than is usual for flatfishes. The large jaws are equipped with strong, fanglike teeth.

Spawning occurs in deep water in summertime; eggs and larvae float freely until the metamorphosis to adult form is complete.

Winter Flounder *Pseudopleuronectes americanus*

RANGE W. Atlantic Ocean: Labrador to Georgia

HABITAT Shallow coastal waters, bays, estuaries, down to 300 ft (90 m)

SIZE 11¾–24 in (30–61 cm)

The winter flounder is most common in shallow waters over muddy sand, but the fish is also found over gravel or hard bottoms. In normal specimens, both eyes are on the right side, which is usually reddish-brown in color. The underside is white, but there are a few fishes with darker undersides. Winter flounders feed on the sea bottom on worms, crustaceans and mollusks and are thought to damage valuable soft-shelled clams by feeding on their breathing siphons.

In autumn, the flounders migrate to inshore waters, moving offshore again in spring.

Spawning takes place in winter and early spring, each female shedding up to half a million eggs. Unlike the eggs of most flatfishes, which float, these eggs sink to the bottom, where they stick to each other and to other objects. They hatch in about 2 weeks.

Winter flounders are important food fish, and are caught both commercially and by anglers.

American Plaice *Hippoglossoides platessoides*

RANGE W. Atlantic Ocean: Greenland, Labrador, south to Rhode Island; E. Atlantic: Iceland, Barents Sea, south to English Channel

HABITAT Depths of 130–600 ft (40–180 m)

SIZE 11¾–24 in (30–61 cm)

Also known as the long rough dab, this plaice has toothed scales on its eyed side, which give the skin a rough texture. Both of the eyes are on the right side, which is brown or reddish-brown. The underside is white.

American plaice live on sand or mud bottoms, feeding on bottom-living invertebrates, such as sea urchins, brittle stars, crustaceans, mollusks and worms.

Spawning takes place in summer in the north of the range and in spring in the south. Each female produces up to 60,000 eggs, which are buoyant and float near the surface until they hatch.

Sole *Solea solea*

RANGE E. Atlantic Ocean: Norway and Britain,
south to N. Africa and Mediterranean Sea

HABITAT Shallow coastal waters; winters farther offshore in deeper waters

SIZE 11¾–23½ in (30–60 cm)

The sole is the most abundant member of the family Soleidae in Europe and it is an important commercial food fish. Like other flatfishes, soles pass through a symmetrical larval stage, but as they develop, one eye migrates around to the other side of the head – the left eye usually moves to the right side. This, and other structural adaptations, fit the sole for an adult life spent partially buried on the seabed, eyed side uppermost.

The sole is a fairly slender-bodied flatfish. It is medium-brown on its upper side and white on its blind side. Its dorsal and anal fins extend as far as the tail fin.

Normally a night time feeder, the sole eats crustaceans, worms, mollusks and sometimes fish, often coming near to the water surface in search of prey. It may be active during the day in dull weather, but it usually spends daylight hours buried in sand or mud.

Soles make seasonal migrations, moving into shallow waters in spring and offshore again in winter. They spawn in spring and early summer, the eggs floating at the surface of the water until they hatch. Larvae live at the surface at first but by the time they are about ½ in (1.25 cm) long, they have metamorphosed into adult form and have drifted into shallow coastal waters, where they begin life on the seabed.

Naked Sole *Gymnachirus melas*

RANGE W. Atlantic Ocean: coasts of
Massachusetts, south to Florida, Bahamas
and Gulf of Mexico

HABITAT Coastal waters,
most common in depths of
100–150 ft (30–45 m)

SIZE 9 in (23 cm)

The naked sole is a thickset flatfish, with scaleless skin marked with dark stripes on the eyed side. Both eyes are on the right in most individuals. Much of their life is spent on the sandy seabed, but they can swim well if necessary.

Long Tongue-sole *Cynoglossus lingua*

RANGE Indian Ocean: E. Africa to India and Sri Lanka; W. Pacific Ocean

HABITAT Coastal waters, estuaries

SIZE 17 in (43 cm)

The long tongue-sole has an extremely narrow body for a flatfish but it is well adapted to life on the seabed, where it lives virtually buried in sand or mud with only its eyes showing. Both eyes are on the left side of the body, and the mouth, too, is situated on the left, low down, just below the eyes. The fish has no pectoral fins, and only the left pelvic fin is developed, the dorsal and anal fins join with the small, pointed tail fin. On the eyed side, the scales have toothed edges, giving a rough texture to the body.

There are about 86 species in the tongue-sole family, Cynoglossidae; most species are marine and are found in tropical and subtropical seas.

Blackcheek Tonguefish *Symphurus plagusia*

RANGE W. Atlantic Ocean: New York, south to Florida,
Bahamas and Gulf of Mexico

HABITAT Sandy bays, estuaries

SIZE 8 in (20.5 cm)

A member of the tongue-sole family of flatfishes, this fish is typical of the group, with a body that is broadest at the front and tapers to a pointed tail. Its dorsal and anal fins unite with the tail, but it has no pectoral fins, and only the left pelvic fin is developed. Both of the eyes are on the left of the head, and the small mouth is set low and is contorted to the left. The eyed side is pale brown, with some dark markings and a dark spot near the eyes. The blind side is creamy white. Like all flatfishes, the tonguefish passes through a larval stage when its eyes are symmetrical – one on each side of the head – before the metamorphosis to adult form occurs and the eye migrates.

TETRAODONTIFORM FISHES

TETRAODONTIFORMES ORDER

This order of spiny-finned fishes contains about 340 species, only about 8 of which live in fresh water. Common names, such as pufferfish, porcupinefish, boxfish, trunkfish and triggerfish, give an idea of the strange body forms of the fishes contained in the order; most of them are rotund, deep or boxlike in shape. Some accentuate this plumpness by inflating the body with water as a defensive mechanism, and in species such as the porcupinefish, this swelling erects an array of sharp body spines. Others, such as the triggerfishes, enlarge the body by expanding a flap on the belly.

Many tetraodontiformes produce sounds, either by grinding their teeth or by vibrating the swim bladder with specialized muscles.

Gray Triggerfish *Balistes carolinensis*

RANGE Atlantic Ocean: from W. Africa to Portugal in E. (seasonally north to Britain), across to Argentina and north to Nova Scotia in W.

HABITAT Open sea

SIZE 16 in (41 cm)

The gray triggerfish, a member of the family Balistidae, has a compressed, but deep, body and a slightly protruding snout, armed with sharp, incisorlike teeth. Its anal and second dorsal fins are prominent, and the first dorsal fin consists of three spines, the first of which is strong and thick and, when erect, is locked into place by the second spine. This "trigger" must be released before the spine can be flattened again. If the triggerfish is alarmed or pursued, it can take refuge in a crevice and wedge itself in by means of this "locking" spine, which makes it extremely hard to remove. It lacks pelvic fins but does possess a pelvic spine. It is thought to feed on crustaceans.

Young gray triggerfishes float among Sargassum weed in the open sea and hence become widely distributed.

Queen Triggerfish *Balistes vetula*

RANGE W. Atlantic Ocean: Florida, (sometimes New England) to Brazil, including Gulf of Mexico and Caribbean

HABITAT Inshore waters, coral reefs

SIZE 22 in (56 cm)

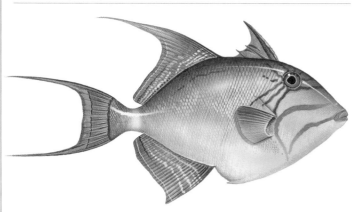

The attractive queen triggerfish is easily distinguished from other species by the slender extensions on its dorsal and tail fins and by its striking blue and yellow coloration. Like other triggerfishes, it has three dorsal spines, the first of which can be locked into an erect position by the second spine. It feeds on a variety of invertebrates, particularly sea urchins.

Clown Triggerfish *Balistoides conspicillum*

RANGE Indian and Pacific Oceans: E. Africa to India, S.E. Asia, N. Australia and Japan

HABITAT Rocky coasts, coral reefs

SIZE 13 in (33 cm)

A dramatically patterned fish, the clown triggerfish has large, light spots on the lower half of its body, contrasting with the dark coloration on its back. Its mouth is circled with bright orange, and there are green markings on its back and on its tail fin. Its second dorsal and anal fins are smaller than those of many triggerfishes, but the first of the dorsal spines is robust and can be locked into an erect position by the second spine, in the manner common to all members of the family Balistidae.

Black-barred Triggerfish *Rhinecanthus aculeatus*

RANGE Indian and Pacific Oceans: E. Africa through S.E. Asia to Hawaiian Islands

HABITAT Shallow waters on the outer edges of reefs

SIZE 12 in (30.5 cm)

The black-barred triggerfish, a member of the family Balistidae, has a strongly compressed body and a rather elongate snout. Its coloration is distinctive but variable, although there are always dark and light bands running down to the anal fin. In addition to the three dorsal spines, typical of the triggerfish family, there is a patch of spines on each side of its tail, surrounded by an area of black. This triggerfish is capable of making quite loud sounds by rubbing together bones supporting the pectoral fin. The sounds are amplified by the fish's swim bladder.

Sargassum Triggerfish *Xanichthys ringens*

RANGE W. Atlantic Ocean: North Carolina through Caribbean to Brazil; probably also occurs in tropical areas of Indian and W. Pacific Oceans

HABITAT Open sea

SIZE 10 in (25.5 cm)

A small, fairly soberly colored member of the family Balistidae, the sargassum triggerfish is marked with dark, broken stripes along the length of its body. Like other triggerfishes, it has no pelvic fins, but it does have a pelvic spine. The young of this species tend to live under patches of floating Sargassum weed at the water surface.

Scrawled Filefish *Aluterus scriptus*

RANGE Atlantic, Pacific and Indian Oceans: tropical seas

HABITAT Inshore waters, seabed

SIZE 35¾ in (91 cm)

The scrawled filefish is one of a group of about 95 species of filefish, which make up a subfamily of the triggerfish family. This filefish is long and

much more slender than most other members of its family, and its snout is long and sharppointed. It has one dorsal spine, and its dorsal and anal fins are small and soft. There are small spines on its scales giving the body a prickly texture, which is the origin of the fish's common name.

Bottom-living invertebrates and algae are the scrawled filefish's main foods. and it forages on the seabed with its nose down. It often feeds in clumps of eelgrass, where, with its head-down posture, undulating fins and mottled greenish coloration, it is perfectly camouflaged.

Planehead Filefish *Monacanthus hispidus*

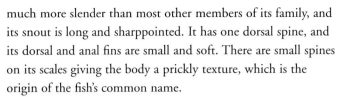

RANGE W. Atlantic Ocean: Cape Cod (sometimes as far north as Nova Scotia) to Florida and Caribbean, south to Brazil

HABITAT Inshore waters

SIZE 6–10 in (15–25.5 cm)

The planehead filefish has a compressed, deep body, covered with small, spiny scales, which give it a rough texture. A distinguishing feature is the fish's single dorsal spine, which has a toothed rear edge. There is also a large pelvic spine.

Scrawled Cowfish *Lactophrys quadricornis*

RANGE W. Atlantic Ocean: New England to Brazil, including Gulf of Mexico and Caribbean

HABITAT Coastal waters, among beds of eel grass

SIZE 18 in (46 cm)

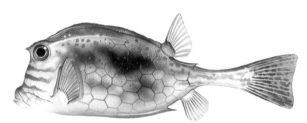

A member of the boxfish family, the scrawled cowfish has a bony shell, which is composed of fused plates, encasing most of its body. Only the mouth, eyes, gill and ventral openings, and fins are free of this rigid shell. On its head is a pair of forward-pointing spines, and there is another, backward-pointing pair at the rear of the shell near the tail – hence the scientific name meaning "four-horned".

Well protected by its body armor, the scrawled cowfish swims slowly, by means of paddlelike movements of the fins, but spends much of its life hidden amid eelgrass or close to the seabed. Bottom-living invertebrates and aquatic plants are the main part of its diet.

TETRAODONTIFORM FISHES CONTINUED

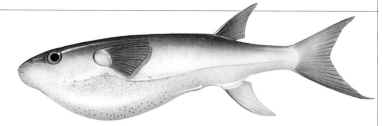

Blue-spotted Boxfish *Ostracion tuberculatus*

RANGE Indian and Pacific Oceans: E. Africa to S.E. Asia,
Australia, Philippines and W. Pacific Islands

HABITAT Coastal waters, coral reefs

SIZE 18 in (46 cm)

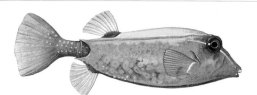

Like all members of the boxfish family Ostraciidae, the
blue-spotted boxfish has a body encased in a bony shell,
composed of fused plates. Mouth, eyes, fins, and gill and ventral
openings are the only breaks in this armor, which effectively
protects the fish from predators. This boxfish feeds on a variety
of bottom-living invertebrates, and although it normally swims
quite slowly, it can make a rapid spurt by moving its strong,
flexible tail.

Sharpnose Puffer *Canthigaster rostrata*

RANGE W. Atlantic Ocean: Bermuda and Bahamas,
south to Brazil, including Gulf of Mexico and
Caribbean; E. Atlantic: St. Helena, W. Africa,
Canary Islands, Madeira

HABITAT Coastal waters, coral reefs,
tidal pools, eelgrass beds

SIZE 4¼ in (11 cm)

A member of the pufferfish family, Tetraodontidae, the
sharpnose puffer, like most of its relatives, is a stout
round-bodied little fish. A characteristic dark ridge runs along
the middle of its back, and its head and body are scattered with
blue markings. Its varied diet includes worms, crustaceans
sea urchins crustaceans and aquatic plants.

Pufferfish *Lagocephalus lagocephalus*

RANGE Tropical and subtropical Atlantic Ocean, occasionally as far north
as Britain; Indian and Pacific Oceans

HABITAT Surface waters in open sea

SIZE 24 in (61 cm)

This pufferfish, a member of the family Tetraodontidae,
has a body that is stout behind the head and tapers
sharply toward the forked tail. Like most puffers, it is

capable of inflating its body with water, and when it does this,
the small spines embedded in its belly stand erect as a defensive
device. The skin on its back is smooth. Again, like all puffers, it
has beaklike jaws, formed by one pair of partially fused teeth in
each jaw. It is believed to feed on fish, crustaceans and squid,
although little is known about its habits.

Bandtail Puffer *Sphoeroides spengleri*

RANGE W. Atlantic Ocean: New England to Brazil; E. Atlantic:
Azores, Madeira, Canary and Cape Verde Islands

HABITAT Shallow inshore waters, sea grass beds, tidal inlets

SIZE 12 in (30.5 cm)

An elongate puffer, the bandtail has a long, blunt snout and large
eyes for its size. It is identified by the row of dark spots running
from head to tail; there are also barred markings on its tail. Like
all puffers, it has the ability to inflate its body enormously with
water until it is like a balloon, in order to deter its predators.
Any enemy would find it extremely difficult to swallow or even
bite the blown-up body. The skin is covered with tiny spines,
which stick out when the body is inflated. Once the danger is
past, the puffer quickly deflates.

Common Pufferfish *Tetraodon cutcutia*

RANGE India, Burma, Malaysia

HABITAT Rivers

SIZE 6 in (15 cm)

One of the few freshwater puffers, the common pufferfish has a
rotund body attractively colored with green and patches of
yellow. When threatened, it inflates its body with
water until it is virtually globular, but it
does not have skin spines. With its
plump, rather rigid, body the puffer
moves slowly, using undulations of its

small dorsal and anal fins, but it compensates for this lack of speed by its defensive techniques. It feeds on bottom-dwelling invertebrates and on fish. Common puffers are very popular aquarium fishes and have been bred in captivity. The female sheds her eggs on the bottom, where they are guarded by the male, who lies over them until they hatch.

Many members of the puffer family are considered to be good food fish, despite the fact that their internal organs – and occasionally even the flesh – are extremely toxic and can cause fatal poisoning. In Japan, chefs are specially trained in the cooking of puffers, known as *fugu*, but there are still cases of poisoning.

Porcupinefish *Diodon hystrix*

RANGE Pacific, Indian and Atlantic Oceans: tropical areas

HABITAT Most common in shallow waters, turtle grass beds

SIZE 35¾ in (91 cm)

Similar to its relatives the pufferfishes in that it can inflate its body, the porcupinefish is covered with long, sharp spines; these spines normally lie flat but stand out when the body is inflated. It is clearly almost impossible for any predator to tackle this globular pin cushion, and this method of defence compensates the fish for its lack of speed and mobility. It swims slowly, with undulations of its small dorsal and anal fins; it lacks pelvic fins.

The porcupinefish has two fused teeth in each jaw, making a sharp, birdlike beak with which it crushes hardshelled prey such as crabs, mollusks and sea urchins.

Striped Burrfish *Chilomycterus schoepfi*

RANGE W. Atlantic Ocean: Cape Cod to Florida, south through Gulf of Mexico and Caribbean to Brazil

HABITAT Shallow inshore waters

SIZE Up to 10 in (25.5 cm)

One of the approximately 15 species in the porcupinefish family, Diodontidae, the striped burrfish has an oval body, studded with stout, thornlike spines. The body can be inflated with water, but the spines are fixed in an erect position. The upper part of the body is marked with dark, irregular stripes, and there are a couple of dark patches on the sides.

Crustaceans and mollusks are the main foods of the striped burrfish which has fused, beaklike teeth, strong enough to crush their hard shells.

Ocean Sunfish *Mola mola*

RANGE Atlantic, Pacific and Indian Oceans: temperate and tropical areas

HABITAT Open sea

SIZE Up to 13 ft (4 m)

The extraordinary ocean sunfish is a member of the small, largely unstudied family Molidae, which contains 3 species. Quite unlike any other fish, it has an almost circular body, which ends rather abruptly in a curious frill, consisting of a series of lobes that form a modified tail. Both dorsal and anal fins are short based and high and placed near the end of the body. The ocean sunfish's pectoral fins are rounded, and it lacks pelvic fins. Its mouth is small for so large a fish and contains two fused teeth in each jaw, making a strong beak.

The fish feeds largely on small planktonic organisms, such as tiny jellyfishes and comb jellies, but also eats crustaceans and fish.

Although they are so huge and so widely distributed, ocean sunfishes are little known. They are so called because of the belief that they bask in the sun in surface waters, but fishes observed basking in this way may, in fact, be sick or disabled.

LUNGFISHES AND COELACANTH

COELACANTHIFORMES COELACANTH ORDER

The lobe-finned fishes (Class Sarcopterygii) are the fishes that are most closely related to the amphibians, reptiles, and other tetrapods. Their lobed fins, like tetrapod limbs, are supported by an internal skeleton attached to the pelvic or pectoral girdle. The few extant members of the class include the coelacanth and the lungfishes. There is a single living species of coelacanth in the order Coelacanthiformes, an order which was once widespread and abundant. Coelacanths were only known as 90-million-year-old fossils until one was caught by a fisherman off the coast of South Africa in 1938. This living species was so like its fossil relatives as to be unmistakably a coelacanth and has enabled scientists to learn about the bodies of animals hitherto known only from skeletons.

Coelacanth *Latimeria chalumnae* **EN**

RANGE Indian Ocean, off Comoro Islands

HABITAT Rocky or coral slopes

SIZE 6¼ ft (1.9 m)

Coelacanths are heavy-bodied fishes, with fleshy lobes at the base of all fins except the first dorsal fin; the pectoral fins can be turned through 180 degrees. Such fishes, known as the crossopterygians, were once widespread.

The internal structure of the coelacanth has many features which throw light on the evolution of fishes; for example, the heart is extremely simple compared with that of other fishes and is similar to the early fish heart which theorists had predicated. The kidneys, unlike those of any other vertebrate, are positioned on the underside of the body.

Modern coelacanths are carnivores, believed to feed mainly on fish. There has been much disagreement about their breeding methods, but now, since the discovery of a female with 5 almost fully developed young in her oviduct, they are known to be ovoviviparous: they bear fully formed young by means of eggs that hatch inside the mother.

CERATODIFORMES AUSTRALIAN LUNGFISH ORDER

There is only a single living species in this order, which has some relationship with the other lungfish order. All lungfishes have lunglike breathing organs which they can use to take breaths of air at the surface, when under water, they inhale water as other fishes do. Lungfishes are related to early air-breathing fishes and are the only remaining representatives of formerly abundant orders. How closely the lungfishes are related to terrestrial vertebrates is the subject of considerable debate.

Australian Lungfish *Neoceratodus forsteri*

RANGE Australia: Queensland

HABITAT Rivers

SIZE 5 ft (1.5 m)

First discovered in 1870, the Australian lungfish differs from other lungfishes in that it has only one lung. It lives in permanent waters, so does not generally undergo estivation, the period of dormancy in a mud burrow to withstand drought that is characteristic of African and South American lungfishes. In captivity it is mainly carnivorous and feeds on almost any animal food. The fishes spawn from August to October in shallow water.

The lungfish occurs naturally only in the Burnett and Mary rivers, but is being introduced into other rivers, including the Upper Brisbane, the Albert and the Coomera rivers in an attempt to protect the species.

LEPIDOSIRENIFORMES AFRICAN AND SOUTH AMERICAN LUNGFISH ORDER

This order contains 2 related families one with only a single species, the South American lungfish, and the other with 4 species of African lungfishes. The close relationship of these 2 families is one of the pieces of evidence suggesting that Africa and South America were once joined. While the Australian lungfish, with its flipperlike fins, single lung, and flattened body, most resembles fossil forms of lungfish, the South American and African lungfishes have eellike bodies, fins reduced to filaments, and paired lungs. Both families live in swampy areas where summer droughts are likely to occur. If swamps dry up, these fish dig burrows in the mud in which they survive in a dormant state until the waters return. During this dormant period, known as estivation, the lungfish's metabolism is reduced to a very low level. Estivating lungfishes survive by metabolising their own muscles. Muscle tissue is restored once the rains fall, and the lungfish emerges from its burrow and starts feeding.

South American Lungfish *Lepidosiren paradoxa*

RANGE	Central South America
HABITAT	Swamps, weeded river margins
SIZE	50 in (1.25 m)

The South American lungfish has a pair of lunglike organs connected with its oesophagus. This fish usually lives in oxygen-poor, swampy areas of the Amazon and Paraná river systems and the large swamps of the Chaco region. Because of its lungs it is able to supplement the oxygen obtained from the water by breathing air at the surface.

The swamps this lungfish inhabits are periodically flooded and then undergo a dry season. The fish survives the dry period by digging itself a burrow in which it lives,

breathing air, while the swamp dries out. Once the surroundings become really arid, the fish closes the burrow entrance with mud, curls up and covers itself with a protective covering of mucus secretion to conserve moisture. Its body slows down to a state of dormancy, but it continues to breathe air. When the rains return, the lungfish emerges from its burrow. This form of inactivity in a hot climate is known as estivation.

During the rainy season, lungfish pairs spawn in burrows made by the male. He guards the eggs and then the young. During this time his pelvic fins develop branched, well-vascularised projections that may supply additional oxygen to the incubating male and, by diffusion, to the developing young. The newly hatched South American lungfish have adhesive glands by which they hang from vegetation, and external gills that make them resemble salamander tadpoles. Both these larval features are lost after 6 to 8 weeks, by which time the 1.5 in (4 cm) long fins can breathe air.

African Lungfish *Protopterus aethiopicus*

RANGE	E. and C. Africa
HABITAT	Rivers, lakes
SIZE	6½ ft (2 m)

The African lungfish has a pair of lungs connected to its esophagus and can breathe air at the water surface. It has normal, but poorly developed, gills. Like other lungfish species, the air breathing apparatus of African lungfishes is equivalent to the lungs of terrestrial vertebrates. They come to the surface to breathe about every 30 minutes.

This species lives mostly in permanent waters, but if there is a long dry period and the water level drops, it can burrow and estivate in much the same way as the South American lungfish. The other 3 African species live in swamps ancl must estivate during the regular dry seasons.

In the breeding season the male makes a hole in which one or more females lay eggs. He then guards the eggs and the young when they hatch and will chase away and attack any predators.

P. aethiopicus is a predatory fish that feeds mainly in the inshore parts of the lakes in which it lives on crabs, mollusks and fishes, including catfishes and cichlids.

CLASSIFICATION

CLASS MAMMALIA: MAMMALS
Subclass Prototheria: Egg-laying Mammals

Order Monotremata: Monotremes
Family Tachyglossidae: Echidnas
Family Ornithorhynchidae: Platypus

Subclass Theria: Live-bearing Mammals
Infraclass Metatheria: Marsupials

Order Didelphimorpha
Family Didelphidae: Opossums

Order Paucituberculata
Family Caenolestidae: Shrew Opossums

Order Microbiotheria
Family Microbiotheriidae: Colocolo

Order Dasyuromorpha
Family Myrmecobiidae: Numbat
Family Dasyuridae: Marsupial Carnivores and Insectivores

Order Peramelemorpha
Family Peramelidae: Bandicoots and Bilbies
Family Peroryctidae: New Guinean Bandicoots

Order Notoryctemorpha
Family Notoryctidae: Marsupial Moles

Order Diprotodonta
Family Phascolarctidae: Koala
Family Vombatidae: Wombats
Family Phalangeridae: Phalangers
Family Potoroidae: Rat Kangaroos
Family Macropodidae: Kangaroos, Wallabies
Family Burramyidae: Pygmy Possums
Family Pseudocheiridae: Ring-tailed and Greater Gliding Possums
Family Petauridae: Striped and Lesser Gliding Possums
Family Tarsipedidae: Honey Possums
Family Acrobatidae: Pygmy Gliding Possum, Feather-tailed Possum

Infraclass Eutheria: Placental Mammals

Order Xenarthra: Edentates
Family Myrmecophagidae: Anteaters
Family Bradypodidae: Three-toed Sloths
Family Megalonychidae: Two-toed Sloths
Family Dasypodidae: Armadillos

Order Pholidota
Family Manidae: Pangolins

Order Lagomorpha
Family Ochotonidae: Pikas
Family Leporidae: Rabbits

Order Rodentia
Family Sciuridae: Squirrels
Family Geomyidae: Pocket Gophers
Family Heteromyidae: Pocket mice
Family Aplodontidae: Mountain Beaver
Family Castoridae: Beavers
Family Anomaluridae: Scaly-Tailed Squirrels
Family Pedetidae: Spring Hare
Family Muridae:
  Subfamily Sigmodontinae: New World Rats and Mice
  Subfamily Cricetinae: Hamsters
  Subfamily Calomyscinae: Mouse-like Hamster
  Subfamily Mystromyscinae: White-tailed Rat
  Subfamily Spalacinae: Blind Mole-rats
  Subfamily Myospalacinae: Eastern Asiatic Mole-rats
  Subfamily Rhizomyinae: Mole- and Bamboo Rats
  Subfamily Lophiomyinae: Crested Rats
  Subfamily Platacanthomyinae: Spiny Dormice
  Subfamily Nesomyinae: Madagascan Rats
  Subfamily Otomyinae: African Swamp Rats
  Subfamily Arvicolinae: Voles and Lemmings
  Subfamily Gerbillinae: Gerbils
  Subfamily Petromyscinae: Rock Mice, Swamp Mouse
  Subfamily Dendromurinae: African Climbing Mice
  Subfamily: Cricetomyinae: African Pouched Rats
  Subfamily Murinae: Old World Rats and Mice
Family Dipodidae: Jerboas and Jumping Mice
Family Myoxidae: Dormice
Family Ctenodactylidae: Gundis
Family Hystricidae: Old World Porcupines
Family Erethizontidae: New World Porcupines
Family Caviidae: Guinea Pigs
Family Hydrochaeridae: Capybara
Family Dinomyidae: Pacarana
Family Dasyproctidae: Agoutis
Family Agoutidae: Pacas
Family Chinchillidae: Chinchillas and Viscachas
Family Capromyidae: Hutias
Family Myocastoridae: Coypu
Family Octodontidae: Octodonts
Family Ctenomyidae: Tuco-tucos
Family Abrocomidae: Chinchilla-rats
Family Echimyidae: Spiny Rats
Family Thryonomyidae: Cane Rats
Family Petromuridae: Dassie Rat
Family Bathyergidae: African Mole-Rats

Order Macroscelidea
Family Macroscelididae: Elephant Shrews

Order Insectivora: Insectivores
Family Solenodontidae: Solenodons
Family Tenrecidae: Tenrecs
Family Chysochloridae: Golden Moles
Family Erinaceidae: Hedgehogs, Moonrats
Family Soricidae: Shrews
Family Talpidae: Moles, Desmans

Order Scandentia
Family Tupaiidae: Tree Shrews

Order Primates: Primates
Family Cheirogaleidae: Mouse Lemurs, Dwarf Lemurs
Family Lemuridae: Lemurs
Family Megaladapidae: Sportive Lemurs
Family Indridae: Indri, Sifakas, Avahi
Family Daubentoniidae: Aye-aye
Family Loridae: Lorises, Pottos
Family Galagonidae: Galagos
Family Tarsiidae: Tarsiers
Family Callitrichidae: Marmosets and Tamarins
Family Cebidae: New World Monkeys
Family Cercopithecidae: Old World Monkeys
Family Hylobatidae: Gibbons
Family Hominidae: Apes and Humans

Order Dermoptera
Family Cynocephalidae: Flying Lemurs or Colugos

Order Chiroptera: Bats
Family Pteropodidae: Fruit Bats
Family Rhinopomatidae: Mouse-tailed Bats
Family Emballonuridae: Sheath-tailed Bats
Family Craseonycteridae: Hog-nosed Bat
Family Nycteridae: Slit-faced Bats
Family Megadermatidae: False Vampire Bats
Family Rhinolophidae: Horseshoe Bats
Family Noctilionidae: Fisherman Bats
Family Mormoopidae: Moustached Bats
Family Molossidae: Free-tailed Bats
Family Phyllostomidae: New World Leaf-nosed Bats
Family Vespertilionidae: Evening Bats
Family Natalidae: Funnel-eared Bats
Family Furipteridae: Smoky Bats
Family Thyropteridae: Disc-winged Bats
Family Myzopodidae: Old World Sucker-footed Bat
Family Mystacinidae: New Zealand Short-tailed Bats

Order Carnivora: Carnivores
Family Canidae: Dogs, Foxes
Family Ursidae: Bears, Pandas
Family Procyonidae: Raccoons
Family Mustelidae: Mustelids
Family Viverridae: Civets
Family Herpestidae: Mongooses
Family Hyaenidae: Hyenas
Family Felidae: Cats

Family Otariidae: Sea Lions, Fur Seals
Family Odobenidae: Walrus
Family Phocidae: True Seals

Order Tubulidentata
Family Orycteropodidae: Aardvark

Order Artiodactyla: Even-toed Ungulates
Family Suidae: Pigs
Family Tayassuidae: Peccaries
Family Hippopotamidae: Hippopotamuses
Family Camelidae: Camels
Family Tragulidae: Mouse Deer
Family Moschidae: Musk Deer
Family Cervidae: Deer
Family Giraffidae: Giraffes
Family Antilocapridae: Pronghorn
Family Bovidae: Bovids

Order Cetacea: Whales
Family Platanistidae: River Dolphins
Family Phocoenidae: Porpoises
Family Delphinidae: Dolphins
Family Monodontidae: Narwhal, White Whale
Family Physeteridae: Sperm Whales
Family Ziphiidae: Beaked Whales
Family Eschrichtiidae: Grey Whale
Family Balaenopteridae: Rorquals
Family Balaenidae: Right Whales

Order Perissodactyla: Odd-toed Ungulates
Family Equidae: Horses
Family Tapiridae: Tapirs
Family Rhinocerotidae: Rhinoceroses

Order Hyracoidea
Family Hyracoidea: Hyraxes

Order Proboscidea
Family Elephantidae: Elephants

Order Sirenia: Sea Cows
Family Dugongidae: Dugong
Family Trichechidae: Manatees

CLASS AVES: BIRDS
Order Struthioniformes: Ratites
Family Struthionidae: Ostrich
Family Rheidae: Rheas
Family Casuariidae: Cassowaries, Emu
Family Apterygidae: Kiwis

Order Tinamiformes: Tinamous
Family Tinamidae: Tinamous

Order Craciformes: Curassows, Guans, Megapodes
Family Cracidae: Curassows, Guans, Chachalacas

Family Megapodiidae: Megapodes

Order Galliformes: Gamebirds
Family Phasianidae: Quails, partridge, francolins, pheasants, grouse, turkey
Family Numididae: Guineafowl
Family Odontophoridae: New World Quail

Order Anseriformes: Waterfowl
Family Anhimidae: Screamers
Family Anseranatidae: Magpie goose
Family Dendrocygnidae: Whistling ducks
Family Anatidae: Geese, swans, ducks

Order Turniciformes: Buttonquail
Family Turnicidae: Buttonquail

Order Piciformes: Barbets and woodpeckers
Family Indicatoridae: Honeyguides
Family Picidae: Woodpeckers
Family Megalaimidae: Asian barbets
Family Lybiidae: African barbets
Family Ramphastidae: New World barbets and toucans

Order Galbuliformes: Jacamars and Puffbirds
Family Galbulidae: Jacamars
Family Bucconidae: Puffbirds

Order Bucerotiformes: Hornbills
Family Bucerotidae: Hornbills
Family Bucorvidae: Ground-hornbills

Order Upupiformes: Hoopoes
Family Upupidae: Hoopoe
Family Phoeniculidae: Wood-hoopoes
Family Rhinopomastidae: Scimitar-bills

Order Trogoniformes: Trogons
Family Trogonidae: Trogons

Order Coraciiformes: Kingfishers, Rollers, Bee-eaters
Family Coraciidae: Rollers
Family Brachypteraciidae: Ground-rollers
Family Leptosomidae: Cuckoo-roller
Family Momotidae: Motmots
Family Todidae: Todies
Family Alcedinidae: Alcedinid kingfishers
Family Dacelonidae: Dacelonid kingfishers
Family Cerylidae: Cerylid kingfishers
Family Meropidae: Bee-eaters

Order Coliiformes: Mousebirds
Family Coliidae: Mousebirds

Order Cuculiformes: Cuckoos
Family Cuculidae: Old World cuckoos
Family Centropodidae: Coucals

Family Coccyzidae: American cuckoos
Family Opisthocomidae: Hoatzin
Family Crotophagidae: Anis and guira cuckoos
Family Neomorphidae: Roadrunners and ground-cuckoos

Order Psittaciformes: Parrots
Family Psittacidae: Parrots

Order Apodiformes: Swifts
Family Apodidae: Swifts
Family Hemiprocnidae: Crested-swifts

Order Trochiliformes: Hummingbirds
Family Trochilidae: Hummingbirds

Order Musophagiformes: Turacos
Family Musophagidae: Turacos

Order Strigiformes: Owls and Nightjars
Family Tytonidae: Barn owls
Family Strigidae: True owls
Family Aegothelidae: Owlet nightjars
Family Podargidae: Australian frogmouths
Family Batrachostomidae: Asiatic frogmouths
Family Steatornithidae: Oilbird
Family Nyctibiidae: Potoos
Family Eurostopodidae: Eared-nightjars
Family Caprimulgidae: Nightjars

Order Columbiformes: Pigeons
Family Columbidae: Pigeons

Order Gruiformes: Cranes and Rails
Family Eurypygidae: Sunbittern
Family Otididae: Bustards
Family Gruidae: Cranes
Family Heliornithidae: Limpkins and sungrebes
Family Psophiidae: Trumpeters
Family Cariamidae: Seriemas
Family Rhyncochetidae: Kagu
Family Rallidae: Rails
Family Mesitornithidae: Mesites

Order Ciconiiformes: Waterbirds and Birds of Prey
Family Pteroclidae: Sandgrouse
Family Thinocoridae: Seedsnipes
Family Pedionomidae: Plains wanderer
Family Scolopacidae: Woodcock, snipe, sandpipers
Family Rostratulidae: Painted snipe
Family Jacanidae: Jacanas
Family Chionididae: Sheathbills
Family Burhinidae: Stone curlews
Family Charadriidae: Oystercatchers, avocets, plovers
    Subfamily Recurvirostrinae: Oystercatchers, avocets, stilts, ibisbill
    Subfamily Charadriinae: Plovers, lapwings
Family Glareolidae: Coursers, pratincoles, crab plover

Family Laridae: Skuas, skimmers, gulls, terns, auks
    Subfamily Larinae: Skuas, skimmers, gulls, terns
    Subfamily Alcinae: Auks
Family Accipitridae: Osprey, birds of prey (eagles, kites, hawks, buzzards, harriers, Old World vultures)
Family Sagittariidae: Secretarybird
Family Falconidae: Falcons
Family Podicipedidae: Grebes
Family Phaethontidae: Tropicbirds
Family Sulidae: Gannets, boobies
Family Anhingidae: Anhingas
Family Phalacrocoracidae: Cormorants
Family Ardeidae: Herons, egrets, bitterns
Family Scopidae: Hammerkop
Family Phoenicopteridae: Flamingos
Family Threskiornithidae: Ibises, spoonbills
Family Pelecanidae: Pelicans, shoebills
Family Ciconiidae: New World vultures, storks
    Subfamily Cathartinae: New World Vultures
    Subfamily Ciconiinae: Storks
Family Fregatidae: Frigatebirds
Family Spheniscidae: Penguins
Family Gaviidae: Divers or loons
Family Procellariidae: Shearwaters, petrels, albatrosses, storm petrels
    Subfamily Procellariinae: Petrels, shearwaters, diving petrels
    Subfamily Diomedeinae: Albatrosses
    Subfamily Hydrobatinae: Storm petrels

Order Passeriformes: Songbirds
Suborder Tyranni: Primitive passerines
Family Acanthisittidae: New Zealand wrens
Family Pittidae: Pittas
Family Eurylaimidae: Broadbills
Family Philepittidae: Asities
Family Sapayoidae: Sapayoa
Family Tyrannidae: Tyrant flycatcher, cotinga, and manakin family
    Subfamily Pipromorphinae: MionectIne flycatchers
    Subfamily Tyranninae: Tyrant flycatchers
    Subfamily Tityrinae: Tityras, becards
    Subfamily Cotinginae: Cotingas, plantcutters, sharpbill
    Subfamily Piprinae: Manakins
Family Thamnophilidae: Antbirds
Family Furnariidae: Ovenbirds, woodcreepers
    Subfamily Furnariinae: Ovenbirds
    Subfamily Dendrocolaptinae: Woodcreepers
Family Formicariidae: Ground antbirds
Family Conopophagidae: Gnateaters
Family Rhinocryptidae: Tapaculos
Family Climacteridae: Australian treecreepers
Suborder Passeri: Advanced passerines
Family Menuridae: Lyrebirds, scrub-birds
Family Ptilonorhynchidae: Bowerbirds
Family Maluridae: Fairywrens, emuwrens, grasswrens
Family Meliphagidae: Honey-eaters
Family Pardalotidae: Pardalotes, bristlebirds, scrubwrens, thornbills
Family Eopsaltriidae: Australian robins
Family Irenidae: Leafbirds, fairy-bluebirds
Family Orthonychidae: Logrunners
Family Pomatostomidae: Australasian babblers
Family Laniidae: Shrikes
Family Vireonidae: Vireos
Family Corvidae: Crow family
    Subfamily Cinclosomatinae: Quail thrushes, whipbirds
    Subfamily Corcoracinae: Australian chough, apostlebird
    Subfamily Pachycephalinae: Sittellas, mohouas, shrike tits, whistlers
    Subfamily Corvinae: Crows, magpies, birds-of paradise, currawongs, wood-swallows, orioles, cuckoo-shrikes
    Subfamily Dicrurinae: Fantails, drongos, monarchs
    Subfamily Aegithiniae: Ioras
    Subfamily Malacotinae: Bush-shrikes, helmet-shrikes, vangas
Family Callaetidae: New Zealand wattlebirds
Family Picathartidae: Rock-jumpers, rockfowl
Family Bombycillidae: Palmchat, silky-flycatchers, waxwings
Family Cinclidae: Dippers
Family Muscicapidae: Thrushes, Old World flycatchers, chats
    Subfamily Turdinae: Thrushes
    Subfamily Muscicapinae: Old World flycatchers, chats
Family Sturnidae: Starlings, mockingbirds
Family Sittidae: Nuthatches, wallcreeper
Family Certhiidae: Wrens, treecreepers, gnatcatchers
    Subfamily Troglodytinae: Wrens
    Subfamily Certhiinae: Treecreepers
    Subfamily Polioptilinae: Gnatcatchers
Family Paridae: Penduline-tits, titmice
    Subfamily Remizinae: Penduline tit
    Subfamily Parinae: Titmice
Family Aegithalidae: Long-tailed tits
Family Hirundinidae: River martins, swallows, martins
Family Regulidae: Kinglets
Family Pycnonotidae: Bulbuls
Family Hypocoliidae: Hypocolius
Family Cisticolidae: African warblers
Family Zosteropidae: White-eyes
Family Sylviidae: Warblers
    Subfamily Acrocephalinae: Leaf-warblers
    Subfamily Megalurinae: Grass-warblers
    Subfamily Garrulacinae: Laughingthrushes
    Subfamily Sylviinae: Babblers, parrotbills, typical warblers
Family Alaudidae: Larks
Family Nectariniidae: Sugarbirds, flowerpeckers, sunbirds
Family Melanocharitidae: Berrypeckers, longbills
Family Paramythiidae: Paramythias
Family Passeridae
    Subfamily Passerinae: Sparrows
    Subfamily Motacillinae: Wagtails, pipits
    Subfamily Prunellinae: Dunnocks
    Subfamily Ploceinae: Weavers
    Subfamily Estrildinae: Grass finches, parasitic whydahs
Family Fringillidae
    Subfamily Peucedraminae: Olive warbler

Subfamily Fringillinae: Chaffinches, cardueline finches, Hawaiian honeycreepers
Subfamily Emberizinae: Buntings, wood warblers, tanagers, cardinals, icterids

CLASS REPTILIA: REPTILES
Order Chelonia: Turtles and Tortoises
Family Emydidae: Emydid Turtles
Family Testudinae: Tortoises
Family Trionychidae: Softshell Turtles
Family Carettochylidae: Plateless River Turtle
Family Dermatemydidae: Central American River Turtle
Family Kinosternidae: American Mud and Musk Turtles
Family Cheloniidae: Marine Turtles
Family Dermochelydidae: Leatherback Turtle
Family Chelydridae: Snapping Turtles
Family Pelomedusidae: Greaved Turtles
Family Chelidae: Matamatas

Order Sphenodontia
Family Sphenodontidae: Tuataras

Order Squamata: Lizards and Snakes

Lizards
Family Iguanidae: Iguanas
Family Agamidae: Agamid Lizards
Family Chamaeleonidae: Chameleons
Family Gekkonidae: Geckos
Family Pygopodidae: Scaly-footed Lizards
Family Dibamidae: Old World Burrowing Lizards
Family Gymnophthalmidae: Microteiid Lizards
Family Teiidae: Teiid Lizards
Family Lacertidae: Lacertid Lizards
Family Xantusiidae: Night Lizards
Family Scincidae: Skinks
Family Cordylidae: Girdled and Plated Lizards
Family Xenosauridae: Crocodile Lizards
Family Anguidae: Slow Worms and Alligator Lizards
Family Varanidae: Monitors
Family Helodermatidae: Gila Monsters

Amphisbaenians (Worm Lizards)
Family Bipedidae: Bipeds
Family Trogonophiidae: Trogonophiids
Family Amphisbaenidae: Amphisbaenids

Snakes
Family Leptotyphlopidae: Thread Snakes
Family Typhlopidae: Blind Snakes
Family Anomolepididae: Dawn Blind Snakes
Family Uropeltidae
Family Aniliidae: Pipe Snakes
Family Xenopeltidae: Sunbeam Snake
Family Loxocemidae: Loxocemid Snake
Family Boidae: Boas and Pythons
Family Boyleriidae: Round Island Snakes

Family Tropidophiidae: Neotropical Ground Boas
Family Acrochordidae: Wart Snakes
Family Atractaspidae: Burrowing Asps
Family Colubridae: Colubrid Snakes
Family Elapidae: Cobras and Sea Snakes
Family Viperidae: Vipers and Pit Vipers

Order Crocodilia: Crocodiles, Alligators and Gavial
Family Crocodylidae: Crocodiles
Family Alligatoridae: Alligators
Family Gavialidae: Gavial

CLASS AMPHIBIA: AMPHIBIANS
Order Anura: Frogs and Toads
Family Ascaphidae: Tailed Frogs
Family Leiopelmatidae: New Zealand Frogs
Family Discoglossidae: Discoglossid Frogs
Family Pipidae: Pipid Frogs
Family Rhinophrynidae: Mexican Burrowing Frog
Family Pelodytidae: Parsley Frogs
Family Pelobatidae: Spadefoot Toads
Family Centrolenidae: Glass Frogs
Family Heleophrynidae: Ghost Frogs
Family Bufonidae: Bufonid Toads
Family Brachycephalidae: Gold Frogs
Family Hylidae: Treefrogs
Family Pseudidae: Pseudid Frogs
Family Rhinodermatidae: Mouth-brooding Frogs
Family Leptodactylidae: Leptodactylid Frogs
Family Myobatrachidae: Myobatrachid Frogs
Family Sooglossidae: Sooglossid Frogs
Family Dendrobatidae: Poison-dart Frogs
Family Hyperoliidae: Reed Frogs
Family Microhylidae: Narrow-mouthed Frogs
Family Ranidae: True Frogs
Family Rhacophoridae: Rhacophorid Treefrogs

Order Caudata: Salamanders and Newts
Family Sirenidae: Sirens
Family Amphiumidae: Congo Eels
Family Plethodontidae: Lungless Salamanders
Family Rhyacotritonidae: Rhyacotritonid Salamanders
Family Proteidae: Olms and Mudpuppies
Family Salamandridae: Newts and Salamanders
Family Ambyostomatidae: Mole Salamanders
Family Dicamptodontidae: Dicamptodontid Salamanders
Family Cryptobranchidae: Giant Salamanders
Family Hynobiidae: Asiatic Land Salamanders

Order Gymnophonia: Caecilians
Family Rhinatrematidae: Rhinatrematid Caecilians
Family Ichthyophidae: Ichthyophid Caecilians
Family Uraeotyphlidae: Uraeotyphlid Caecilians
Family Scolecomorphidae: Scolecomorphid Caecilians
Family Caeciliaidae: Caeciliaid Caecilians
Family Typhlonectidae: Typhlonectid Caecilians

FISH
Class Myxini
Order Myxiniformes: Hagfishes

Class Cephalaspidomorphi
Order Petromyzontiformes: Lampreys

Class Chondrichthyes: Cartilaginous Fish
Order Heterodontiformes: Bullhead, Horn Sharks
Order Lamniformes: Sand Tigers, Goblin Sharks, Megamouth Sharks
Order Carchariniformes: Cat Sharks, Hound Sharks, Requiem Sharks
Order Orectolobiformes: Wobbegons, Nurse Sharks, Whale Sharks
Order Squatiniformes: Angel Sharks
Order Hexanchiformes: Frilled Sharks, Cow Sharks
Order Squaliformes: Bramble Sharks, Sleeper Sharks, Dogfish Sharks
Order Pristiphoriformes: Saw Sharks
Order Rajiformes: Rays, Skates, Sawfishes
Order Chimaeriformes: Chimaeras

Class Osteichthyes: Bony Fish
Subclass Actinopterygii: Ray-finned Fishes
Order Polypteriformes: Bichirs
Order Acipenseriformes: Sturgeons, Paddlefishes
Order Lepisosteiformes: Gars
Order Amiiformes: Bowfin
Order Osteoglossiformes: Bonytongues, Butterflyfish, Mooneyes
Order Elopiformes: Tarpons, Tenpounders
Order Albuliformes: Bonefishes, Halosaurs, Spiny Eels
Order Anguilliformes: Freshwater Eels, Moray Eels, Conger Eels
Order Saccopharyngiformes: Bobtail Snipe Eels, Swallowers, Gulpers
Order Clupeiformes: Herrings, Anchovies
Order Gonorynchiformes: Milkfish, Beaked Sandfishes, Snake Mudhead
Order Cypriniformes: Carps, Minnows, Loaches
Order Characiformes: Characins, Trahiras, Headstanders
Order Siluriformes: Catfishes
Order Gymnotiformes: Knifefishes, Electric Eel
Order Esociformes: Pikes, Mudminnows
Order Osmeriformes: Smelts, Slickheads, Noodlefishes
Order Salmoniformes: Salmon, Trout, Chars
Order Stomiiformes: Bristlemouths, Marine Hatchetfishes, Lightfishes
Order Atelopodiiformes: Jellynose Fishes
Order Aulopiformes: Telescope fishes, Greeneyes, Barracudinas
Order Myctophiformes: Lanternfishes
Order Percopsiformes: Trout-perches, Cavefishes
Order Ophidiiformes: Carapids, Cuskeels, Brotulas
Order Gadiformes: Cods, Hakes
Order Batrachoidiformes: Toadfishes
Order Lophiiformes: Anglerfishes
Order Beloniformes: Flying fishes, Needlefishes, Halfbeaks
Order Cyprinodontiformes: Killifishes, Rivulines, Splitfins, Pupfishes
Order Atheriniformes: Rainbow Fishes, Blueeyes, Silversides
Order Lampridiformes: Crestfishes, Oarfishes, Ribbonfishes
Order Stephanoberyciformes: Whalefishes, Gibberfishes
Order Beryciformes: Beardfishes, Lanterneyes, Squirrelfishes
Order Zeiformes: Dories, Oreos
Order Gasterosteiformes: Sticklebacks, Sand Eels, Tubesnouts
Order Synbranchiformes: Swamp Eels, Spiny Eels
Order Dactylopteriformes: Flying Gurnards
Order Scorpaeniformes: Scorpionfishes, Velvetfishes, Sculpins
Order Perciformes: Perchlike Fishes
  Suborder Percoidei: Percoid Fishes
  Suborder Elassomatoidei: Pygmy Sunfishes
  Suborder Labroidei: Cichlids, Damselfishes, Wrasses, Parrotfish
  Suborder Zoarcoidei: Eelpouts, Wrymouths, Gunnels, Wolffishes
  Suborder Notothenioidei: Icefishes
  Suborder Trachinoidei: Sand Lances, Weeverfishes, Stargazers
  Suborder Blennioidei: Blennies
  Suborder Icosteodei: Ragfish
  Suborder Gobiesocoidei: Clingfishes
  Suborder Callionymoidei: Dragonets
  Suborder Gobioidei: Gobies
  Suborder Kurtoidei: Nurseryfishes
  Suborder Acanthuroidei: Spadefishes, Scats, Rabbitfishes, Surgeonfishes
  Suborder Mugiloidei: Mullets
  Suborder Scombrolabracoidei: Scombrolabracoid Fishes
  Suborder Scombroidei: Barracudas, Mackerel, Tunas, Marlin
  Suborder Stromateoidei: Medusafishes, Squaretails, Butterfishes
  Suborder Anabantoidei: Gouramis
  Suborder Channoidei: Snakeheads
Order Pleuronectiformes: Flounders, Soles
Order Tetraodontiformes: Puffers, Triggerfishes, Porcupinefishes

Subclass Sarcopterygii: Lobe-finned Fishes
Order Ceratodontiformes: Australian Lungfishes
Order Lepidosireniformes: African and South American Lungfishes
Order Coelacanthiformes: Coelacanth

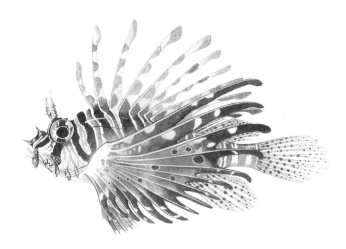

INDEX

ACKNOWLEDGEMENTS

The Publishers received invaluable help during the preparation of theAnimal Encyclopedia from: Heather Angel, who lent us reference slides, Angus Bellairs, who gave advice, Dr H. G. Cogger, who lent us reference slides; Rosanne Hooper and Zilda Tandy who assisted with research, Dr Pat Morris of Royal Holloway College, London, and Dr Robert Stebbings of the Institute of Terrestrial Ecology, Huntingdonshire, who both helped with reference on the Mammal section, Ed Wade, who helped with reference on the Fish section, the staff of the Herpetology Department of the British Museum (Natural History), London, particularly Colin McCarthy and Barry Clarke, who allowed us access to specimens and reference, the staff of the Ornithology Department of the British Museum (Natural History) outstation at Tring, particularly Peter Colston, who gave assistance with the specimen collection, the staff of the Science Reference Library, London, and the IUCN Conservation Monitoring Centre, Cambridge, England, for data on threatened species.

We acknowledge the contribution of Professor Carl Gans in his book Reptiles of the World (Bantam 1975).